THE

PARAMOUNT

PRETTIES

by

JAMES ROBERT PARISH

EDITOR:

T. Allan Taylor

RESEARCH ASSOCIATES:

John Robert Cocchi   Florence Solomon

PHOTO ASSOCIATE:

Gene Andrewski

ARLINGTON HOUSE   *New Rochelle, N.Y.*

PN
1998
.A2
P395
1972
June 1998

Library of Congress Catalog Card Number 72-78482

ISBN 0–87000–180–9

MANUFACTURED IN THE UNITED STATES OF AMERICA

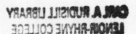

DEDICATED TO

IRENE ERICKSON FAGAN
(1884–1970)
WHO DEVOTED MORE THAN FIFTY YEARS OF
HER LIFE TO SHOW BUSINESS AS A
COSTUMIERE EXTRAORDINAIRE

ACKNOWLEDGMENTS

Rudy Behlmer
DeWitt Bodeen
Ronald L. Bowers
Richard Braff
Bruco Enterprises
Mrs. Loraine Burdick
Ben Carbonetto
Cinemabilia Book Shop (Ernest Burns)
Classic Film Collector (Samuel Rubin)
Film Collectors' Registry (Ted Riggs)
Filmfacts (Ernest Parmentier)
Film Fan Monthly (Leonard Maltin)
Films and Filming
Films In Review
Ray Gain
Stanley Green
Pierre Guinle
Mrs. R. F. Hasting
Charles Hoyt
Richard Hudson
Ken D. Jones
Kenneth G. Lawrence Movie Memorabilia (Arthur Peterson)
Albert Leonard
Doug McClelland
Albert B. Manski
Alvin H. Marill
Jim Meyer
Mrs. Earl Meisinger
Peter Miglierini
Norman Miller
Movie Poster Service (Bob Smith)
Arthur Nicholson
Michael R. Pitts
Screen Facts (Alan G. Barbour)
Mrs. Peter Smith
Roger Smith
Robert A. Smith
John Springer
Don Stanke
Charles K. Stumpf
Views and Reviews (Jon Tuska)
    And especial thanks to Paul Myers, curator of the Theater Collection at the Lincoln Center Library for the Performing Arts, and his staff: Monty Arnold, Rod Bladel, Donald Fowle, Dorothy Swerdlove, Maxwell Silverman, and page Anne Marie O'Farrell.

CONTENTS

ACKNOWLEDGMENTS   7

GLORIA SWANSON   13

CLARA BOW   57

CLAUDETTE COLBERT   92

CAROLE LOMBARD   142

MARLENE DIETRICH   180

MIRIAM HOPKINS   227

SYLVIA SIDNEY   261

MAE WEST   295

DOROTHY LAMOUR   332

PAULETTE GODDARD   372

VERONICA LAKE   408

DIANA LYNN   440

BETTY HUTTON   468

JOAN CAULFIELD   499

LIZABETH SCOTT   517

SHIRLEY MACLAINE   541

APPENDIX   577

Key to the Film Studios

AA ...... Allied Artists Picture Corporation

COL .... Columbia Pictures Industries, Inc.

FN ...... First National Pictures, Inc. (later part of Warner Brothers)

FOX .... Fox Film Corporation

MGM .. Metro-Goldwyn-Mayer, Inc.

MON .. Monogram Pictures Corporation

PAR ..... Paramount Pictures Corporation

RKO .... RKO Radio Pictures, Inc.

REP .... Republic Pictures Corporation

20th .... Twentieth Century-Fox Film Corporation

UA ...... United Artists Corporation

UNIV .. Universal Pictures, Inc.

WB ...... Warner Bros. Inc.

THE PARAMOUNT PRETTIES

GLORIA SWANSON

4'11"
95 pounds
Reddish-brown hair
Blue-gray eyes
Aries

GLORIA SWANSON made her screen debut in 1915, well after both Lillian Gish and Mary Pickford. Although the latter two women ranked for some time as the leading silent screen actresses, it is Gloria, still active in her seventh decade as a performer, who is the longevity queen (emeritus) of American motion pictures. Gloria's last important picture, *Sunset Boulevard*, was released in 1950, yet she has retained a magical aura of stardom that makes her name and profile known almost everywhere. This in itself is an achievement equal to her success in the 1920s, when she was every shopgirl's symbol of the glamorous cinema artiste. Throughout those halcyon days on screen and in her private and public life, no one could duplicate—though Joan Crawford would continually try—Gloria's extravagant posturing as an imitation grand sophisticate. Gorgeously gowned in high style, gesturing with jewel-bedecked hands, her nostrils flaring, her upper lip quivering to reveal big white teeth, she would widen her large eyes to express every emotion. Far better than her dramatic displays on the screen were her effervescent moments of movie comedy and mimicry, demonstrating her gifts as a supremely gifted comedienne and pantomimist.

Gloria began her film career at the Essanay Studios in Chicago in 1915; shortly thereafter she came to Hollywood, where she signed with Mack Sennett to play antic heroines in his two-reel Keystone comedies. By 1918 she had moved to Triangle Films and given up comedy for the much-preferred (in her mind) world of sophisticated drama, hoping to emulate the leading ladies of this genre, Clara Kimball Young and Norma Talmadge. She quickly gained a small but impressive reputation as an actress who could wear eccentric but modish clothes well and convince the public of her noble screen suffering. In those days, plump figures were chic and Gloria's was no exception.

The turning point of Gloria's career occurred with *Don't Change Your Husband* (1919), the first of six features for Cecil B. DeMille. Because De-Mille had a big public following, and since his Artcraft productions were released by the influential Famous Players-Lasky organization, Gloria's screen work under his guidance dramatically solidified her standing with filmgoers. To no one's surprise she rose above being a glorious clothes mannequin and became synonymous with all that was allegedly daring, advanced, and frank in the boudoir confections favored by DeMille. In 1920 she moved to the Paramount banner, and she remained there until 1926, performing in an average of four films a year. In these production-line major features, she attempted to vary her rags-to-riches or wronged-socialite-to-contented-woman vehicles with as many offbeat dramatic assignments as possible, often to her disadvantage.

In the unreality of the silent cinema during the unrestrained Roaring Twenties, tiny Gloria literally had the world on a string, capped by her 1925 marriage to a French marquis which legitimized her proclaimed royalty. Even when she was negotiating for million-dollar contracts she never had an agent, but shrewdly handled the bargaining herself. The profligacy of her private life merely demonstrated the capriciousness of a many-faceted, impulsive woman with a flamboyant personality. There were many domestic competitors for Gloria's Paramount and Hollywood crown, from Bebe Daniels to Leatrice Joy, but only Polish-import Pola Negri possessed the same heady chemistry of charisma and pomp needed to bowl over moviegoers and the general public.

Deciding that producing her own features would be artistically and financially more advantageous, Gloria left Paramount in 1926 and moved to United Artists, where her initial venture was the theatrical but popular *The Loves of Sunya* (1927). More important to strengthening her status as an actress was her dramatic performance in *Rain* (1928). After the debacle of the uncompleted *Queen Kelly* (1928–29) Gloria made a remarkable sound film debut in *The Trespasser* (1929), winning the first of her two Academy Award best-actress nominations. She still continued as a box-office success (if no longer as the imperious ruler of Hollywood) until the lame British-lensed *Perfect Understanding* (1933).

As a free-lance player without her own production-distribution outlet, Gloria floundered in the 1930s, unable to find or accept the proper comeback vehicle. Her dalliances with potential screen properties in this decade had more anticlimaxes than a 13-chapter serial. Much to her credit as an increasingly responsible citizen, few scavengers took the opportunity to pounce on Gloria, once her fame and fortune had badly dwindled. After the flat *Music in the Air* (1934), Gloria seemed to lose a tangible hold on changing Hollywood conditions and drifted back and forth across America and to Europe.

At one end of the 1940s, she made a perfunctory comeback appearance in RKO's *Father Takes a Wife* (1941), followed by several attempts at launching a successful Broadway stage, radio, and television career; the decade was capped by her perceptive portrayal of an aging silent screen queen in *Sunset Boulevard*. (1950).

Since then Gloria has adorned assorted film, television, and stage productions, returning to Broadway in 1971 as the take-over star in *Butterflies are Free*. Her greatest success by far has been in retaining her youthful vitality as the "glorious Gloria" best known to present-day viewers as a chronic matron with a rose in one hand, whose nostalgic theme song is "Love, Your Magic Spell Is Everywhere." Americans love longevity record-breakers, and while claiming the double standard, greatly admire gutsy females who spectacularly break through creative and business barriers. That she is human, humble, and capriciously feminine, makes her a more appealing living legend than Joan Crawford, Marlene Dietrich, the Great Garbo, or Mae West. Her inability to be happy in obscurity is touching. Her greed for fame is amazing.

Gloria Swanson (née Gloria Josephine May Swenson) was born March 27, 1898, near Wrigley Field in Chicago, the only child of Joseph Thomas and Adelaide (Klanowski) Swenson. Her mother was of Polish-French-German descent, and her father was of Swedish-Italian extraction. Mr. Swenson was a civilian transport agent for the United States Army who later enlisted in the service, and the family moved from Army post to Army post. Gloria later recollected: "My childhood on Army posts gave me an appreciation of rank that is the basis of good manners."

When Gloria was eight years old, Mr. Swenson was transferred to Key West, Florida, and the family went along. While in Key West Gloria participated in a charity show supervised by a vacationing Broadway actor, Frank Hayes. In this, her first public appearance, she sang a song.

The family moved to San Juan, Puerto Rico, when Gloria was 11. She appeared in a school production of *The American Girl* there and would later recall: "My father nailed a star on the door of my dressing room but it gave me no thrill, because I had no interest in acting. We saw no professional troupes in Puerto Rico and the only movies were bad Swedish imports. Like all the other girls, my daydreams were wrapped up in following the operatic career of Mary Garden, the big idol of the time. I thought I had a voice, and there was just enough money in the family to consider cultivating it.

"We managed to get by comfortably on my father's Army pay, equivalent to a captain's, by shopping in the commissary and living in low-rent houses on military bases. Mother had a small income and she lavished all of it on me, an only child. I suppose my mother made me clothes conscious. Other mothers always were lifting up my dress to look at my fancy lace panties. I never wore anything if the other kids had something like it. I must've been an insufferable brat."

Each summer, Mrs. Swenson and Gloria visited relatives in Chicago to escape the heat of Puerto Rico. When Gloria was 15 her mother and father separated. Mrs. Swenson returned to Chicago on a permanent basis and took Gloria with her. Although Gloria had only completed her first year of high school, she was enrolled at the Chicago Art Institute and also was given voice lessons.

One day in 1913, Gloria's aunt, Mrs. Ingrid Johnson, took her on a sightseeing trip to the local Essanay Film Studios. Gloria later recalled: "I had never been screen-struck, but I was fascinated by what I saw." As she sat enthralled on the sidelines, an assistant director asked Gloria to hand a bridal bouquet to Gerda Holmes, who was then appearing in George Ada's film *At the End of a Perfect Day* (1915).

Since it was difficult at that time to find extras who photographed well, Gloria was asked by Essanay to return a week later to handle a more elaborate assignment in a Francis X. Bushman-Beverly Bayne film, possibly *The Ambition of the Baron* (1915).

Soon after Gloria went to New York with her mother to visit Mr. Swenson, who was stationed at Governor's Island. While she was there, a letter arrived from Essanay with a contract for Gloria to be a guaranteed extra. It provided that she would have at least four days' work each week, at $3.25 per day. Gloria remembers: "I was far more excited about a bigger event in my life. I had just been kissed by a boy wearing an orange tie, and I was sure I was going to have a baby."

When Gloria returned to Chicago, she was cast (instead of Agnes Ayres) for a bit in a new Bushman-Bayne society comedy. But that movie team did not wish to portray yet another married couple, and the project was dropped for the moment. Gloria never forgave Bushman for one day giving her a playful love tap on the derriere.

At the time, Essanay's big new star was comedian Charlie Chaplin. Gloria was cast for a small part in *His New Job* (1915), his first two-reeler for that studio. Gloria remembers: "Someone had a brainstorm and put me in comedy. I know there's a lot of competition for the prize, but that was the worst piece of casting in the annals of the movies. I had absolutely no sense of humor. It was only years later that I developed it to keep my sanity in the business."

Gloria's role in *His New Job* required her to drop her purse in a doctor's office. While she was bending over to retrieve it, Chaplin was to kick her in the caboose. He practiced the routine a dozen times, and then, according to Gloria, gave up in disgust. Gloria allegedly replied: "I think it's vulgar anyway."

In his biography *Charlie Chaplin*, scholar Theodore Huff states: "Gloria Swanson, then an extra in the Chicago studio, very nearly became his [Chaplin's] leading lady. However, she resembled Chaplin too much in stature, coloring, and certain aspects of personality to be a perfect foil. She may be glimpsed in the bit role of a stenographer in *His New Job*, though she receives no billing and though she denies she ever played with Chaplin!"

Chaplin in his later autobiography (1969) reminisces that he did test Gloria for his leading lady but she failed to respond adequately to any of his instructions. She was later to tell him—after she became a top Hollywood star—that she had deliberately muffed the test because she preferred to work in drama rather than slapdash comedy.

Among the known guaranteed extra assignments Gloria had at Essanay were: *The Fable of Elvira and Farina and the Meal Ticket* (1915), in which she portrayed the pert, socially conscious daughter of a family crashing big town society; *Sweenie Goes to College* (1915), starring Wallace Beery, in which he played the Swedish maid Sweenie: *The Romance of an American Duchess* (1915), featuring Ruth Stonehouse, which offered Gloria her first sophisticated role as an adventuress; and *The Broken Pledge* (1915), in which Gloria was billed as Gloria Mae.

While at Essanay, Gloria and 26-year-old Beery fell in love. Louella Parsons, who was then a script writer at Essanay, recalled: "I remember the romance of my old diamond-in-the-rough friend, Wallace Beery, and shining little Gloria Swanson, who had enormous ice-water blue eyes and a head that seemed too big for her small body. She gave little indication of the queenly figure she is today."

By February, 1916, Mrs. Swenson and her husband had decided to divorce. (Mr. Swenson's funeral in the 1920s was the first and last funeral Gloria attended for years thereafter.) Gloria and her mother headed for Hollywood, where the following month she married Beery, already on the Coast and employed at Mack Sennett's Keystone Comedy studio. Gloria and Beery separated a month later but were not divorced for three years. She would say years later: "I don't blame people for thinking that I did [chase him]. He was considered a great catch. You won't believe that because you remember Wally as a fat gross character actor, but in those days he looked just like Melvyn Douglas. He was a handsome devil who had played the romantic leads in a couple of Broadway musicals. Yes, we lived together as man and wife for about three weeks. Wally is dead now, and it serves no purpose to talk about our breakup. There were many reasons, but the chief one was that I wanted to have a baby and Wally didn't want that responsibility."

Gloria made the rounds of studios seeking work although she was still considering a concert career. At Mack Sennett's fun factory, she met Frank Hayes (the actor from her Key West childhood days) and he introduced her to Sennett. At first she rejected Sennett's job offer, because ". . . [he] looked at me as though he was putting me in a bathing suit. I told him I was an actress, no cheap publicity bait." When he agreed to make her a featured comedienne, she accepted the Keystone offer. Soon she was costarring in slapstick comedies, usually teamed with impish Bobby Vernon.* She was then receiving $85 a week. Charles Parrott (Charley Chase) and Clarence Badger directed many of these shorts. Unlike Phyllis Haver, Marie Prevost, and others at the Sennett studios, Gloria only appeared in a bathing suit for occasional publicity poses, and "in one comedy [*A Pullman Bride*] there was an entire sequence at the beach, but I was the leading lady, *not one* of the bathing beauties. Not that I'd be ashamed of having been a Sennett bathing beauty, but the truth is I never was."

In early 1917 Gloria asked Sennett for a salary raise, and went on strike for three months when he balked. She used her spare time to make *Baseball Madness* (1917) at Universal. When he gave in, Gloria returned—Sennett bribed her with a $100 green suit trimmed in squirrel fur, along with the demanded raise.

On September 19, 1917, when Gloria's contract with Sennett expired, she refused to re-sign with him. He had transferred most of his players' contracts and assets to the relatively new Triangle Company but had refused to sell Gloria's agreement, partly because, according to Gloria, he insisted he was going to make her another Mabel Normand. Gloria supposedly informed him: "You aren't going to make a second anything out of me!"

Gloria would later concede about her Sennett years: "Comedy makes you think faster and after Keystone I was a human lightning-conductor. . . . I hated comedy because I thought it was ruining my chance for dramatic parts. I didn't realize that comedy is the highest expression of the theatrical art and the best training in the world for other roles. Emotional characterizations are easy, practically play themselves. The mark of an accomplished actor is timing, and it can be acquired only in comedy."

She then signed a contract with Triangle, which had acquired the producing-directing services of D. W. Griffith, Thomas Ince, and Mack Sennett. Gloria's agreement specifically called for her to appear in nonslapstick productions. Reporter-writer Adela Rogers St. Johns remembers meeting Gloria at the old Triangle studio in 1917: "She was awful. Short and inclined to be dumpy. A strange face dominated by sullen gray eyes, with a long nose tilted upward, and a defiant mouth, whose upper lip seemed too short to cover her big strong white teeth. Her sweater caught in bewildering scallops over her hips, and the heels of her slightly worn white pumps were badly run down. Her sailor hat kept a precarious perch upon her heavy, red-brown hair. When she spoke, which was seldom, her voice had a harsh and uncultivated note."

*1916: *A Dash of Courage* (with Wallace Beery); *Hearts and Sparks; A Social Club; The Danger Girl; Love on Skates; Haystacks and Steeples; The Nick of Time Baby;* 1917: *Teddy at the Throttle; Dangers of a Bride; The Sultan's Wife; A Pullman Bride* (with Chester Conklin).

Society for Sale (1918) was her first Triangle release. A society drama, it set the tone for her subsequent features at this studio. In it she plays mannequin Phyllis Clyne, who bankrolls impoverished nobleman William Desmond to pass her off in blue-blood society. They fall in love, and when it is revealed that her late father was a lord, they decide to marry since it will now be perfectly proper. *Moving Picture World* noted: "Gloria Swanson, who used to be a Keystone comedy queen, plays Phyllis surprisingly well. She is comely to look at and knows how to act, and indicates an unexpected depth of real feeling." Gloria was successfully invading the territory where once only Clara Kimball Young and Norma Talmadge held sway.

Her seven other Triangle releases of 1918 were run-of-the-mill features, usually presenting Gloria as a poor working girl who rises in the social world or as the bored society damsel whose moral fiber needs strengthening. Peggy Hamilton, fashion editor of the *Los Angeles Times*, designed most of Gloria's Triangle wardrobe, starting the actress on the path to being the screen's leading clothes-horse. It was the era when pictures were meant to entertain and sparkle, not to stimulate the intellect. In *Her Decision* (1918), Gloria discovers that she really loves her employer, whom she had married merely to aid her shamed sister. As queen of the summer colony in *You Can't Believe Everything* (1918), she is thought flirtatious and finds it difficult to stand by the playboy she comes to cherish. It was in this film that director Jack Conway required Gloria to dive off a pier to save the man she loves. *Moving Picture World* cited Gloria as "likeable and lovable," and possessed of a "fetching figure."

Everywoman's Husband (1918) presented married Gloria acquiring a lover, only to realize her husband's worth when her henpecked father commits suicide. *Shifting Sands* (1918) concerned wronged-girl Gloria sent to prison on the phony evidence of a German; years later, during World War I, he attempts to blackmail the now powerfully married Gloria into helping the cause of the Central Powers. *Station Content* (1918) traces Gloria's success as a songstress. She had left her railroad employee husband and became the inamorata of a railroad president. Later she rides through a storm to prevent a train wreck (proving she now has compassion and courage) and is able to patch up her marriage. *Secret Code* (1918) had the most improbable plot of the lot. An elderly senator marries young Gloria and their marriage soon falters. When World War I begins and secrets are leaking out, Gloria is suspected; but she manages to prove that her mysterious knitting is merely for a baby sweater. *Photoplay* complimented Gloria and costar J. Barney Sherry because they ". . . make [the movie] decidedly better." Her last Triangle feature was *Wife Or Country* (1918), focusing on a young woman who rehabilitates an alcoholic attorney and marries him. When World War I breaks out, she is persuaded to help the German cause and later commits suicide rather than compromise her husband's career and his new-found love for his secretary.

During Gloria's Triangle tenure, Cecil B. DeMille* had wanted her for the female lead in his Artcraft production for Paramount release, *Till I Come Back to You* (1918), a World War I tale which starred Bryant Washburn and Florence Vidor. At the time Triangle would not release Gloria. Later in 1918, when Triangle was nearing insolvency, Gloria was able to terminate her agreement with that company.

*See Appendix.

DeMille by then had already begun production of *Don't Change Your Husband* (1919). He shut down filming when Gloria was signed and started all over again. Said DeMille about his new star, whom he would always call "young fellow": "The way she leaned against a door. She showed complete poise, repose and grace. I saw all her comedy shorts and I knew she had the epitome of technique I was seeking."

Don't Change Your Husband (1919) has Gloria horrified by the bad habits of her wealthy spouse Elliott Dexter. She divorces him, and quickly marries playboy Lew Cody. When he proves to be a two-timing wolf, she sheds him and returns to repentant Dexter. Most contemporary reviews of *Don't Change Your Husband* were lavish in their praise: "She reads into the characterization of the wife a gentle personality which reaches the heart of everyone. She earns the sympathy of her audience, but not by any attempt at 'wishy-washy' heroics' (*Variety*). *Photoplay* magazine was the rare exception: "Gloria Swanson, delicious always, suggests a married chicken more than a serious-minded wife."

This six-reel feature established the archetypical format for Gloria throughout her silent film career. Usually she would be sumptuously gowned in lavish settings, enacting her role in a slightly unconventional tale which contained ample avant-garde morality. As Richard Griffith pointed out in *The Movie Stars*, "Cecil B. DeMille discovered and developed her . . . not as the standard virginal heroine of those days, but as a smart young married woman, lavishly gowned and jeweled, with a look about her of someone to whom things happen. This new kind of heroine did things, went places, and met men who would have been unthinkable for the previous standard breed. The difference excited the public of the budding Jazz Age, and she exploited it to the hilt." From the shopgirl to the housewife, Gloria soon came to represent the full-blown modern American female, who attained all her tangible desires with the minimum of moral sacrifice.

In retrospect, most of Gloria's DeMille features and the other silent pictures she made for Paramount seem rather vulgar in many unintentional ways, even taking into consideration the styles, techniques, and mores of the day. There was a slight but undeniable coarseness of personality and mannerism pervading her screen work till the end of the 1920s, by which time she had polished her own veneer of class, culture, and intellect. If she were portraying a working girl, she would come across just a wee bit cruder than necessary or intended. And when she was essaying a ritzy member of the upper crust, her lack of aristocratic breeding was all too evident. None of this seemed to matter to the majority of her fans, as her enormous popularity and box-office record prove.

For Better, For Worse (1919), directed by DeMille, cast Gloria as society lady Sylvia Norcross, infatuated with both a doctor, played by Elliott Dexter, and his friend, played by Tom Forman. Through a misunderstanding, Gloria renounces Dexter and weds Forman. She later learns that Dexter has not been unpatriotic, as she had believed, by staying home while others went to fight in World War I, and she gives vent to her passion. Believing her husband dead, she agrees to marry Dexter. But then Forman does return home, now a war-scarred veteran. He eventually divorces her so that she and Dexter can marry.

Next came the feature which projected Gloria into the ranks of a major silent cinema star, *Male and Female* (1919). DeMille reworked James M. Barrie's *The Admirable Crichton* into a contemporary account of Lady Gloria and her swank friends being shipwrecked on a desert island. The pampered creatures are soon reformed by resourceful butler Thomas Meighan. Gloria is smitten by Meighan and they consider the possibility of marriage, but the group is rescued and returns to England, where class reasserts itself. Gloria weds her lord, and the butler marries the maid.

In what had become typical DeMille fashion, he embroidered the story with a gaudy biblical flashback; this allowed him to indulge his fancy to its full extent because anything within reason was acceptable on the screen if tied in with the supposed promulgation of a religious moral. Thus there is a sequence of Gloria as a willful Christian slave who refuses to submit to the Babylonian king and is cast into the lion's den. DeMille demanded an authentic touch; he persuaded Gloria not to use a double, and to let the (hopefully) well-trained and well-fed lion rest his paw on her bejeweled shoulder. As a precaution, DeMille had a sharpshooter on the set ready to fire in case of difficulty, although he did not advise Gloria of the safety measure. Said DeMille: "That's what's wonderful about Gloria. She never even asked." After the scene was filmed, Gloria appeared in DeMille's office, still shaking from the ordeal. He unlocked a drawer and pulled out a tray of ultra-expensive jewelry, from which she was to select a piece. Gloria recalls: "I picked out a gold-mesh evening purse with an emerald clasp and immediately felt much better. . . . I acquired my expensive tastes from Mr. DeMille."

It was also in *Male and Female* that Gloria was shown disrobing (discreetly protected from the camera's eye) and dipping into an ornate bath. This byplay was repeated as standard fare in subsequent DeMille features, and was equated with wealth by the public, who seemed to believe that the possession of an elaborate bathroom complete with sunken baths, gold water faucets, and resplendent decorations was de rigeur for the truly rich.

Male and Female premiered at the Rivoli Theatre on November 23, 1919, and all the reviewers agreed that while Gloria's characterization could still improve, ". . . at all times she is assuredly an eyeful." The film was a solid hit and established Gloria as potentially big box office, more so than any of DeMille's prior leading ladies, from Geraldine Farrar up to, and including, Mary Pickford. He would always say, "The public, not I, made Gloria Swanson a star."

On December 20, 1919, Gloria, then 21 years old, married Herbert K. Somborn, age 36, at the Hotel Alexandria in Los Angeles. A Pasadena, California, millionaire, he was the former president of Equity Pictures (producer of Clara Kimball Young movies) and owner of the Brown Derby restaurants.

Why Change Your Wife? (1920) continued the lucrative Swanson-DeMille association. In this pseudosensual concoction, she and husband Thomas Meighan divorce only to discover their need for each other has not died. The plot switch has Gloria being high-minded but not high-fashioned till after Meighan unchivalrously leaves. Then she becomes a glorious clotheshorse. The swank production had the advantage of a charming Bebe Daniels as the other woman. *Variety* objected to Gloria "lacking the finesse expected of her."

Something to Think About (1920) eschewed the chic ambiance for melodrama. Blacksmith's daughter Gloria has her education financed by a wealthy cripple, Elliott Dexter. He proposes marriage, but she elopes with city dweller Monte Blue. Blue is killed in a subway accident, and the now-pregnant Gloria returns home. Her recently blinded father denounces her, but Dexter states that he will marry her in name only for the child's sake.

The couple learn to love one another, which, in turn, restores him to physical normalcy. A minor miracle not uncommon to silent cinema fare.

Gloria and DeMille agreed it would be advantageous for both to work apart, and she moved directly over to Artcraft's parent company Famous Players-Lasky where president Adolph Zukor* and first vice-president Jesse L. Lasky* controlled the creative and business facets of Paramount's product. Fashionable Madame Elinor Glyn was employed to devise a tale for Gloria that was known as *The Great Moment* (1920), in which for the first time Gloria's name would appear above the film's title. At one point, scenarist Glyn informed the press about Gloria: "I feel she has an old soul struggling to remember its former lives—not young, young, like this great America!" In *The Great Moment*, Gloria played the daughter of a Russian gypsy and a British nobleman, which accounted for her tempestuous personality. On a jaunt to the American West, she is bitten on the breast by a rattlesnake. Strong, silent mining engineer Milton Sills sucks out the venom, saving her life, not to mention creating great titillation for the film audience. Her father misconstrues the rescue scene, and forces Gloria and Sills to marry. Their marriage soon disintegrates, with her traipsing off to Washington to flirt with wealthy Arthur Hull. Eventually, Gloria and Sills are reconciled.

As a top-ranking Hollywood star, now only second to Mary Pickford in popularity and salary, Gloria earned $3,500 a week and enjoyed living on an unbelievably lavish scale. She purchased a 24-room estate that had belonged to razor tycoon King Gillette. The 11-servant home was one of the six great showplaces of Beverly Hills. Gloria later reminisced: "Oh, the parties we used to have! It was not uncommon to have seventy-five or one hundred people for a formal sit down dinner. But they weren't stuffy affairs. Everyone knew each other and we had fun. I remember once I had a ju-jitsu exhibition. After dinner, Ronald Colman and Dick Barthelmess insisted on trying it, and they threw each other all around the living room. Mary Pickford and Doug Fairbanks gave smaller parties at 'Pickfair,' and they were more formal."

Gloria was adamant in living up to her credo: "I have decided that when I am a star, I will be every inch and every moment the star! Everybody from the studio gateman to the highest executive will know it." As Adolph Zukor would write in his autobiography *The Public is Never Wrong*: "On the set Queen Gloria could be temperamental, refusing to make scenes over, criticizing her wardrobe, the scenery, or her dressing quarters. But finally someone would say, 'Look, Gloria, we've got to get the work done,' and she would come down to earth. The little Chicago west side girl was never far below the glamorous surface." Gloria, on the other hand, would attest differently years later: "I'm *not* temperamental. The only time I walked off a set was when Adolph Zukor promised me a letter (about going to France and the making of *Madame Sans-Gene*) and didn't give it to me. I stayed away for three days. But that was the only time. I'm not temperamental. Ask the people I worked with." According to screen historian DeWitt Bodeen: "The lowliest set-worker will testify that Gloria Swanson is (and has been) cooperative, hardworking, and a strict observer of the professional's code."

Gloria gave birth to a daughter, Gloria,** in 1920, and she took pains not

*See Appendix.
**Young Gloria would marry Robert Anderson, have two sons and a daughter, and reside in Bel-Air, California. From her father, she would inherit the exclusive owner-

to hide the fact, at a time when it was considered disastrous for a movie actress to admit being a mother.

Back with DeMille, Gloria performed in *The Affairs of Anatol* (1921), very loosely based on Arthur Schnitzler's play. Disenchanted with his new bride, played by Gloria, Manhattan social leader Wallace Reid finds excitement elsewhere. His dalliances with gold diggers Bebe Daniels, Wanda Hawley, and Agnes Ayres (three leading Paramount players of the time) discourage him, and he reconciles with his wife, who has meanwhile been courted by his friend Elliott Dexter. In a moment of total ennui, he mumbles: "Truth is dead. Long live illusion." With such a repertory of leading ladies, bedroom scenes, and fashion parades, *The Affairs of Anatol* (at one time titled *Five Kisses*) opened at the Rivoli and Rialto Theaters on September 11, 1921, to an enthusiastic audience reception. The *New York Times* noted Gloria as "decorative" and cited Daniels for her fine "mock vamp." *Variety* disapproved of the film: "It lacks spontaneity, suspense and comprehensive appeal, with the telling inferior." This was Gloria's sixth and final feature with DeMille.

Under the Lash (1921), the first of nine consecutive Gloria features directed by Sam Wood, presented a distinct change of milieu. Gloria essayed the young second wife of an elderly Boer farmer, Russell Simpson, who rules his farm and her life with a stern hand. She is attracted to British foreman Mahlon Hamilton, who reveals to her the beauty of culture and romantic love. Hamilton kills Simpson, to save her from her irrational husband. After Hamilton returns to England he discovers that his wife had died, so he and Gloria plan to wed. *Moving Picture World* decided: "She isn't exactly the type to be found on a Boer farm and she wears a frock in the last scene that is entirely out of character."

Don't Tell Everything (1921) was largely padded-out footage from an excised episode from *The Affairs of Anatol*. Wallace Reid and Elliott Dexter vie for Gloria's affection. She secretly marries Reid and must compete with her husband's old flame Dorothy Cummings, who has appeared on the domestic scene.

Gloria separated from her husband Somborn on May 5, 1921. They would sue for divorce on March 29, 1923, in Los Angeles, with the decree being granted in September, 1923. Gloria said: "I not only believe in divorce, I sometimes think I don't believe in marriage at all."

Her Husband's Trademark (1922) found Gloria as the well-groomed wife of unscrupulous businessman Stuart Holmes. Wealthy Westerner Richard Wayne, Gloria's former lover, arrives in New York, Holmes forces Gloria to be the bait to woo Wayne into a dubious business venture. Later, at Wayne's Mexican ranch, Holmes is killed by bandits, paving the way for Gloria and Wayne to rekindle their romance. Even the usually generous *Moving Picture World* advised its exhibitor readers to sell this weak film on the elegance of Gloria's costumes. But like all the movies Gloria appeared in at the time, it made money, regardless of its dubious artistic or entertainment qualities. There was an aura of success around all her picture-making ventures, and it permeated the public's viewing habits.

Paramount commissioned its Madame Elinor Glyn to concoct *Beyond the Rocks* (1922) as a vehicle to team Gloria with the studio's popular new

ship of the Wilshire Boulevard Brown Derby restaurant which her husband managed. After he died, she remarried a man in the aviation insurance field, and they moved to New York.

male lead, Rudolph Valentino. The tailor-made scenario cast Gloria as an impoverished British aristocrat who weds elderly millionaire Alec B. Francis; on her honeymoon trip to Switzerland, however, she encounters real love in the person of nobleman Valentino. *Beyond the Rocks* allowed for several protracted flashbacks so that Gloria and Valentino might enact their love scenes among the more romantic settings of past idyllic ages. The husband eventually dies on an African hunting exhibition, freeing Gloria to be with Valentino. The feature opened at the 2,210-seat Rivoli Theatre on May 7, 1922, and grossed $28,750 during its first week. Paramount's predictions for equally big grosses around the country were dampened when the film did only fair business in less cosmopolitan situations. The ads for *Beyond the Rocks* proclaimed: "Supremacy of the love that is youth's—with fitting exponents."

Her Gilded Cage (1922) offered Gloria as a French cabaret performer who agrees to an American tour billed as "Fleur d' Amour," the favorite of King Fernando. She needs money for her crippled sister and to refinance her bankrupt uncle. Because she has been linked for publicity purposes only with the playboy prince, her American artist lover misunderstands. They are later reconciled and her sister cured.

Gloria had a most sympathetic role in her fourth and final 1922 release, *The Impossible Mrs. Bellew*. As the self-sacrificing wife of an alcoholic scoundrel, she agrees to an unfavorable divorce to prevent her son from learning about his father's true character. Having lost her good name and being ostracized in America, she becomes the bon vivant of Deauville's fast set. (Herein Gloria wears assorted bathing attire with none of the qualms she had in her Sennett Keystone days.) In Europe she is introduced to novelist Conrad Nagel and neatly begins life anew. The *New York Times* claimed: "It seems designed for the special exploitation of Miss Gloria Swanson, who can wear clothes, look injured and be smart."

In July, 1922, Gloria's stepfather Matthew P. Burns died and his will was contested in the courts by his relatives. He had left $100,000 to Gloria and her mother. The plaintiffs claimed that the deceased had been of unsound mind at the time of making the will, and the court affirmed this hypothesis.

My American Wife (1923) cast Gloria as a wealthy girl from Dixie who attracts Spanish-American Antonio Moreno at the big Argentinian horse race. After villains Josef Swickard and Walter Long are disposed of, the couple can marry. *Photoplay* reported the feature was "lifted to some interest by the bizarre Gloria Swanson."

Gloria ill-advisedly attempted a flapper portrayal in *Prodigal Daughters* (1923), a new stereotype of the silent cinema, best exemplified by First National's star Colleen Moore. Gloria is a Jazz Age disciple who leaves her staid Fifth Avenue family mansion to make whoopee in Greenwich Village. She works in a department store for a spell, but is fired when she refuses to date the store manager. Eventually she repents of her carefree ways, and returns home on Christmas Eve. To emphasize the supposed decadence of the Roaring Twenties, a telling flashback to primitive jungle days is included, with the comparison intended to be a blatant contrast to twentieth-century jazz babies.

Variety frankly discussed the miscasting: "The picture presents an unfortunate mishandling of Gloria Swanson which injures it in many ways. The fan public has been long accustomed to see Miss Swanson as a certain type of heroine, a woman of sophistication and the wearer of the last word in mode. This time they have made her a giddy flapper, and the result is a disappointment.

"The fatal thing about the effort is that the star loses the interest of the startling dresses. In trying to make her a butterfly young thing they have adapted her frocks to the character and generally the whole affair is off key. Miss Swanson doesn't look herself, and from the way she plays she must have felt out of her element."

Gloria's last feature under Sam Wood's direction was the farce comedy *Bluebeard's Eighth Wife* (1923), an Ina Claire Broadway show of 1921. As impoverished French aristocrat Mona de Briac, Gloria discovers on her wedding eve that her husband-to-be (Huntley Gordon) had previously married and divorced seven other women. As newlyweds, Gloria makes his life intolerable, until he realizes she adores him and is only seeking to reform him. *Bluebeard's Eighth Wife* premiered at the 1,960-seat Rialto Theatre and grossed a hefty $18,000 in its first week, based on an 30–55–85¢ admission scale. It would be remade in 1938 with Claudette Colbert in the lead.

Despite the success of *Bluebeard's Eighth Wife,* there were persistent trade rumors that Gloria was slipping at the box office. She was now 25 years old, and had been a star for nearly five years, which in the usual run of events was just about the limit at the top of the heap. *Variety,* in its review of *Bluebeard's Eighth Wife,* referred to the "fading pep and beauty of Gloria Swanson. After witnessing her go through the role of Mona one cannot help to remark how much she has progressed as an actress and likewise what she would have done to that role from an alluring standpoint had she played it in the same manner in the full flesh of her beauty." The backwash from small-town theatres re Gloria's features also reflected diminishing enchantment with the queen of sophisticated comedy. *Moving Picture World* in its exhibitors' comment column contained such sallies as: "Exhibitors who pay fancy prices for this picture [*Bluebeard's Eighth Wife*] are going to be stung. Don't let salesmen try to kid you on prices. Too many good pictures made this year for any man to be held up. Quincy, Ill.—Orpheum Theatre."

Not too long after her divorce from Somborn in September, 1923, Gloria adopted a baby boy, whom she named Joseph * after her father. At the time, it was rumored that the four-month-old child might be her illegitimate offspring. Gloria was so enraged that she obtained affidavits from the Paramount studio crew, to prove that she had been at work making a film when the baby was born.

In September, 1922, Polish-born actress Pola Negri, age 25, arrived in Hollywood to start her Famous Players-Lasky contract. She had a built-in European star reputation, and proved from her first Paramount vehicle, *Bella Donna* (1923), onward to be a serious artistic, if not box-office threat to Gloria.

The Famous Players-Lasky publicity department invented a tremendous, instantaneous feud between Gloria as queen of the studio and Negri as newcoming royalty. At one point, someone knowing Gloria's passionate dislike of cats and Negri's love of the animals (as long as no black cat crossed her path), loosed a swarm of felines on Gloria's set. Although shaken, Gloria informed the press: *"Me* afraid of cats? Didn't I let the King of Beasts rest a paw on my bare back in *Male and Female*? Really, they'll have to do better!" Both Gloria and Negri (repeatedly in her *Memoirs of a*

*He is currently an electronics engineer, physicist, and inventor, the father of two, and resides near Palo Alto, California.

Star [1970]) have insisted throughout the years that any misunderstandings between them were strictly studio-manufactured. Since they were rarely allowed the opportunity to talk civilly to one another, they neither liked nor disliked each other. However, it would have been unnatural had they not possessed strong professional feelings regarding each other.

Realizing it was time for a change, Gloria renegotiated her Famous Players-Lasky contract in 1923 (the new agreement escalated her weekly salary to $6,500 and required her to appear in four films per year for three years). She demanded in addition that the majority of her future films be lensed in New York, where she claimed the cultural stimulus would be beneficial to her productions. The studio acquiesced.

Gloria's move to the East was featured in the fan magazines as a fabulous exodus, climaxed by her leasing of a penthouse apartment at the Park Chambers Hotel, and the purchase of a 25-acre estate in Croton-on-Hudson. Gloria kept insisting in interviews that her allegedly fabulous Manhattan abode was really the remodeled servants' quarters of a once-lush penthouse expanse at the Park Chambers Hotel, but no one paid much heed to her penchant for the truth. The press and the public seemingly could not be satiated with accounts of Gloria's glorious life, and they termed her "the second woman in Hollywood to make a million, and the first to spend it." (Mary Pickford may have been the first cinema actress millionaire, but she was an astute businesswoman from the start.) Gloria would state years later: "The public didn't want the truth and I shouldn't have bothered giving it to them. In those days they wanted us to live like kings and queens. So we did—and why not? We were in love with life. We were making more money than we ever dreamed existed, and there was no reason to believe that it would ever stop."

The first of Gloria's eight New York-made features was the Allan Dwan-directed *Zaza* (1923). In this and her subsequent Dwan-helmed pictures, Gloria steadily refined her acting technique and was seemingly encouraged to expand her remarkable ability for improvisations. The spontaneous bits of business which crop up consistently in this batch of Swanson movies demonstrate how instinctively she related to the medium. That her overtheatrical gesturing and mannerisms (quivering nostrils and her persistent habit of upturning her upper lip to reveal her two big front teeth) were ever present did not detract from the superiority of her pantomime skills.

Zaza had been a Broadway success years before with Mrs. Leslie Carter and was picturized in 1915 with Pauline Frederick. In this new version, provincial music hall star Gloria is kept by diplomat H. B. Warner. When she discovers he has a wife and child in Paris, she terminates their relationship. Years later, she has become an infamous Parisian entertainer. She reencounters Warner, now widowed, and they reaffirm their undying love. *Zaza* premiered at the Rivoli Theatre on September 16, 1923. Despite critical disapproval, it grossed $28,000 in its first week there, and was a strong commercial success. The *New York Times*'s rap stated: "It cannot be truthfully said that Miss Swanson makes a good, or even credible, Zaza. She seems real neither in her sin nor in her expiation—nor, one imagines, in the eventual happiness and benefit of clergy that the finish promises but does not reveal." But the public responded to the new Gloria. Whether in the raucous music hall scenes where she is temperamental and fighting with competing soubrette Mary Thurman, or in the country idyl sequences in which she feigns illness to keep Warner a bit longer at her side, Gloria radiated entertaining exuberance, if not excellent dramatic characterization. That the scenario transformed the fiery singing mistress into a coy carefree miss, was not Gloria's doing. *Zaza* would be remade in 1939 starring Claudette Colbert, to far less successful results.

In her last few years on the Coast before coming East, Gloria's screen outfits had been created by inspired studio designer Travis Banton. Once in New York, Gloria not only called upon local talent but began taking a hand in wardrobing herself. This experience would prove useful years later when she began merchandizing her own line of clothing. That she was barely 4 feet 11 inches tall with high heels, wore a small size hat, and squeezed into size 2½ shoes, were physical features Gloria manipulated to good advantage in creating her screen appearance.

Sidney Olcott directed Gloria in *The Humming Bird* (1924), which followed the star's dictate that each of her features should reveal her in a new type of role. She did not want to become typecast like Mary Pickford. In this 1924 film, Gloria eschewed the glamorous in order to portray Toinette, the gamin idol of the Paris apaches. Disguised as a man (in corduroy suit, trousers down to the ankles, and a cap over a pulled-up hairdo), she leads her gang on a series of successful burglaries. American reporter Edward Burns assists the French police track down the mysterious Humming Bird, the name with which they have tagged Gloria. Not realizing her true identity, Burns meets Gloria and is smitten with her. When he enlists during World War I, his patriotic example inspires Gloria to convince her gang to join up. While donating her spoils to the Church, she is apprehended and sent to prison. She escapes to visit the dangerously wounded Burns. He recovers, and she makes a full confession of her past to him. The police later pardon Gloria for her meritorious conduct, and she returns to her new love. This time the *New York Times* approved: "Miss Swanson is quick as a fly, and her facial expressions are quite fitting to the type she plays."

A Society Scandal (1924) was more typical of Gloria's past work. When she recklessly flirts with Ricardo Cortez at a house party, she finds herself in a compromising situation and her husband sues for divorce. Her unfriendly mother-in-law advises prosecuting attorney Rod La Rocque to ruin Gloria's reputation at the hearing. Gloria later has her revenge on La Rocque, only to realize that she loves him. The picture opened at the Rivoli Theatre on March 9, 1924, and did extremely well. It was refilmed as *Laughing Lady* in 1929 with Ruth Chatterton.

Manhandled (1924) proved to be one of Gloria's most successful characterizations, and it is a film constantly revived by cinema groups over the years. The plot was conceived by Sidney R. Kent, general sales manager of Famous Players-Lasky. Gum-chewing Gloria is a department store salesgirl in Manhattan. She adores mechanic Tom Moore, who lives at the same boarding house. While he is away merchandising the rights to his new invention, she attends a fashionable party hosted by a sculptor. The sculptor invites her to model for him. When he becomes fresh, she quits and is hired by a modish clothing shop to pose as a Russian countess and give the establishment an air of class. Moore returns and notices Gloria's elevated standard of living. Convinced she has been compromised, he will not marry her. Meanwhile, she has tired of high society and wants the simple life again. Moore slowly realizes that she truly loves him and has been essentially faithful. To make their wedding plans joyfully complete, he is advised that his invention has been sold and he is now a millionaire. Gloria's most memorable moments in the movie are the lengthy crowded subway scene in which she squirms and pushes to find an empty spot in the mobbed car, her calm and imaginative handling of the herd of customers at the store's bargain-day sale, and her expert mimicking of Charles Chaplin and Beatrice Lillie at the sculptor's party. The *New York Times* reported: "Miss Swanson proves her versatility as a film actress, this time as a clever comedienne." The feature opened at the Rivoli Theatre on July 28, 1924, grossing $29,771 in its first week. In her seventh year as a star player, her marquee magic had yet to reach its peak!

Years later, *Mannequin* director Allan Dwan recalled this production as one of his favorite films. He said about Gloria: "She was always just perfect—a pleasure on, off and everywhere—just great. She was a wonderful worker to star with, and very jolly—a clown if there ever was one. A little bit of a woman, yet she was the prize clothes-horse of the day. Astonishing. She was quite short, but perfectly put together I guess, carried herself like a queen and for that reason looked well in anything she did. . . . Gloria was always full of hell, always pulling things. It was always fun with her—a game—it wasn't just a studio because we'd be playing tricks on each other all the time—terrible things."

Gloria stumbled creatively in the Ruritanian romance *Her Love Story* (1924). Princess Gloria secretly weds soldier Ian Keith in a gypsy camp, but her father will not recognize the union, forcing her to marry a neighboring kingdom's ruler. She has a child by her new husband, and is then committed by him to a nunnery for being an unloving wife. Keith arranges her escape, but she insists upon returning to the palace to visit her ill son. She struggles with the king and he is accidentally killed. She then abdicates, preferring a commoner's life with Keith and her child. Paramount must have lavished much of its production budget on the costuming (Gloria's wedding gown reputedly cost $100,000) and the sets. The offbeat publicity campaign promised much: "Gone is Gloria the vamp, vanished is the jazzy flapper, forgotten the modeste's model. Now unsophisticated wide eyed innocent mother love." *Her Love Story* debuted at the Rivoli Theatre on October 6, 1924, and continued Gloria's string of successes. Mordaunt Hall *(New York Times)* quipped: "She seems not a little puzzled in handling the role of the Princess, not being certain about the Voltarian characteristics any more than millions of other people."

Wages of Virtue (1925), based on a Percival Wren novel and set in Algiers, showcased Gloria as Carmelita, the effervescent delight of the French Foreign Legion. She eventually settles on American legionnaire Ben Lyon in preference to her Italian protector.

Gloria had long wanted to star in a version of the Emile Moreau-Victorien Sardou play *Madame Sans-Gene* (1925). She finally convinced Zukor of the potential popular appeal of the story and the wisdom of the huge financial investment. In November, 1924, she sailed for France to begin production. She played the hoydenish laundress who befriends a penniless young artillery lieutenant named Napoleon Bonaparte—she steals stockings and other garments from her customers to give to him. Years later she weds a marshal of Napoleon's army but still remains as unpolished and basic as when she was a lowly working girl. Napoleon is about to force his marshal to divorce her, but she demands an audience, and undaunted by the emperor's enormous power, rekindles their past camaraderie and saves the day.

Famous Players-Lasky made the most of publicizing its lavish $700,000-production budget. Special permission had been granted for the movie unit to film at the Fontainebleau Palace, and even to utilize Napoleon's actual bed. Since the director, Leonce Perret, was French (permission to employ an American director had been denied) and spoke little English, a translator-liaison was assigned to the picture, Henri, the Marquis de la Falaise de la Coudraye (known as Hank). A romance soon developed between Gloria and the marquis. After completing *Madame Sans-Gene* and recovering from a bout of blood poisoning, Gloria was married to the marquis on February 5, 1925. (She had previously been dating director Marshal "Micky" Neilsen, in what was one of the zaniest romances in Hollywood.)

Gloria now added another distinction to her long list of American movie star firsts. She was the first to marry someone with a legitimate foreign title. After France bestowed the Legion of Honor on her, she returned to America and was accorded press coverage and public acclaim seemingly out of all proportion. Gloria and her husband arrived in New York and remained there to attend the $5 per ticket premiere of *Madame Sans-Gene* at the Rivoli Theatre on April 17, 1925. Famous Players-Lasky outdid itself to make sure the occasion would be noteworthy by anyone's standards. Gloria's name was emblazoned in the biggest lights on Broadway, above the Rivoli Theatre which had been decorated in an abundance of tricolor and stars and stripes bunting. There were literally thousands of fans and curiosity seekers blocking Broadway to catch a glimpse of the famous Gloria that evening. Mordaunt Hall *(New York Times)* was a little less enthusiastic about the film itself: "Miss Swanson gives a lively portrayal in this episode, but she is occasionally a little too demonstrative and her linen frocks are cut so low that one would think that the saucy Catherine was impervious to colds. Miss Swanson also has a little too much make-up on her eyelids, which one can forgive after she becomes the unceremonious Duchess of Dantzig. In the comedy sequences she is alert and clever, making the most of her effective eyes, shooting glances to right and left in telling fashion." Other critics cited the spectacle's lack of emotional wallop, blaming it on the French director and the predominantly European cast. *Variety* added: "But without Gloria Swanson, it would stand mighty little chance as a picture to attain box-office popularity." In its first week at the Rivoli Theatre, *Madame Sans-Gene* broke the house record, grossing $41,300, with an extra show being run every day.

Before proceeding to the Coast by train for the Hollywood premiere, Gloria supposedly wired Zukor: "Am arriving with the Marquis tomorrow. Please arrange ovation." According to cinema historian DeWitt Bodeen: "A brass band met her at the station and she drove in an open car with the marquis and Louella Parsons, who had hurried to meet them at the depot. From station to studio the streets were lined, and Gloria stood in the tonneau throwing kisses to her subjects. The marquis modestly kept his hat on, and his head lowered."

When Gloria entered Grauman's Million Dollar Theatre that night for *Madame Sans-Gene*'s Los Angeles premiere, the audience rose and sang "Home Sweet Home." She was wearing a cloth of silver gown and her diamonds, and tears in her eyes. When her mother asked if she didn't think it the greatest ovation Hollywood had ever accorded a star, Miss Swanson assented, and added: "But it should be happening when I'm fifty. I'm only twenty-six. What's left? How can I top it?"

Madame Sans-Gene would be remade in Argentina in 1945 with Nini Marshall and in 1963 as *Madame* with Sophia Loren.

Gloria's follow-up film, *Coast of Follies* (1925), was poor fare, although it offered her the challenge of essaying three different roles. It was filmed largely in Florida and New York. The plot has Gloria departing for Europe, unable to abide her priggish husband any more, nor caring very much about her little daughter Joyce, who remains behind. After a spectacular social career, Gloria drops out of sight, a worn-out Riviera countess. She later learns that her grown-up daughter is about to make the same mistake in life that she did, and she rushes to her rescue in America. Gloria attempts to persuade Joyce's paramour to obtain a divorce and marry the girl, particularly since any scandal will forfeit the girl's huge inheritance. Instead, Joyce is reconciled with her understanding husband, with Gloria and Joyce finding new respect for one another.

Despite the virtuosity of Gloria's triple performance in *Coast of Follies,* including an imitation of Mary Pickford's *Pollyanna,* the feature badly strained the credulity of the simplest mind. The photoplay was severely criticized for its too-strong reliance on title captions to carry the story line, and its excessive number of close-ups of Gloria, particularly as the elderly, vain Nadine. *Variety* opined: "It belongs in the daily change houses, with or without Gloria Swanson." However, Gloria's marquee lure was still potent and *Coast of Follies* grossed a huge $32,298.41 in its first week at the Rivoli Theatre, and almost as well in subsequent distribution. Glora later admitted she had based her telling characterization of the flapper (grandmother) on actress Fannie Ward and authoress Elinor Glyn. "I was scared to death they'd sue me."

The remaining three pictures under Gloria's Famous Players-Lasky contract were also filmed in New York. The infectious *Stage Struck* (1925) opens with a technicolor sequence of Gloria as Salome holding the head of John the Baptist in her hand. Then the scene fades to everyday reality. She is a stagestruck dumb waitress spilling an order of beans. The film is filled with comedy high jinks, particularly after she joins an Ohio showboat, the *Water Queen.* Memorable moments include her attempted suicide leap with her bloomers catching on the showboat's hull, or the episode of her participation in a vaudeville amateur night by boxing with an oversized female while prancing about with a stocking pulled over her face, and the moment when fleas from a flea circus break loose and repose on Gloria. Ford Sterling as the showboat's manager and Gertrude Astor as the leading lady provided fine backup performances. Most of the riverboat sequences were filmed on the Columbia River, near New Martinville, West Virginia. Mordaunt Hall *(New York Times)* criticized: "Miss Swanson is active and amusing, but this is hardly a worthy subject for her capabilities. . . . The captions in this film are most tedious and at times they are not even grammatical." It was Gloria's last film under Allan Dwan's direction for five years.

Untamed Lady (1926) was a too-slapstick variation of *The Taming of the Shrew,* based on a story by Fannie Hurst. It featured Gloria as a reckless society miss who marries conservative Lawrence Gray. When she slips aboard his Cuba-bound yacht and creates havoc, he sets about taming her. Mordaunt Hall *(New York Times)* noted: "Miss Swanson in her blazes of fury looks as if she were really sorry to have to appear angry. It is not a role suited to her, for few persons wish to see beauty marred by a frown."

Her second and final 1926 release was *Fine Manners.* Gloria is Orchid Murphy, a chorus girl in a cheap East Side New York burlesque company, transformed à la *Pygmalion* into a sophisticated darling by wealthy Eugene O'Brien and his aunt. The job completed, O'Brien fears that the qualities he once loved in Gloria do not exist any more, but is relieved to discover her transformation is only skin deep. *Fine Manners* opened at the Rivoli Theatre on August 29, 1926, and grossed a hearty $35,000 in its first week, demonstrating again that Gloria could still do no wrong, even in a weak vehicle. *Variety* commented: "The star has shed several pounds since her last picture appearance and has successfully regained the girlish figure she usually sports [There are closeups of Gloria in underwear—another first for her]. Her eyes work overtime in this one, and her comedy training stands her in good stead . . ."

Gloria's Famous Players-Lasky contract expired in 1926, and, since her return from France the previous year, the studio had been making every sort of attempt to induce her to stay on. For the past few years, she had been the key link in the company's block-booking system, which forced exhibitors to accept up to six run-of-the-mill Paramount pictures in order to get one of Gloria's money-making productions. The studio had not had much success in exploiting Pola Negri's elusive European fame into top American dollars—her features stubbornly refused to attract the expected wide audiences—and was forced to admit that Gloria was still its chief moneymaker. Adolph Zukor in New York and Jesse L. Lasky from the Coast bargained with Gloria, first offering her $13,000 a week for four films yearly for two years, and then raising the ante to $18,000. Gloria still rejected the offer. Finally Zukor put forth a staggering $1 million per year bid, and was as aghast as all of Hollywood and the country when Gloria had the bad manners to refuse it. In actuality, Gloria's decision was not a petulant whim. Having matured as a box-office attraction at Famous Players-Lasky, she well understood that her transfer from the DeMille stable to a Paramount product was part of the Zukor-Lasky-DeMille system of building stars from general nonentities (such as Bebe Daniels, Richard Dix, Leatrice Joy, Thomas Meighan, and Wallace Reid) and exploiting them for as long as they held profitable lure for the public. She was fully aware that if her magnetism ever faltered, Zukor would soon dispense with her services.

Meanwhile, Gloria had been courted by Joseph M. Schenck, chairman of the board of United Artists, and by Douglas Fairbanks, one of the company's three movie-star founders. She was finally persuaded to accept their offer to join the United Artists independent producers' group with the promise that she could become a full partner in the company and eventually share in the distribution earnings, as well as bank the profits from her own productions. The idea appealed to Gloria, flattered at the possibility of joining the legendary ranks of Fairbanks, Pickford, and Charlie Chaplin. The once extravagant Gloria was still careless about how she spent her money, but she was developing sharp insights into how to earn it.

By the time her Famous Players-Lasky contract expired in 1926, Gloria had formed Gloria Swanson, Inc. Its product was to be released through United Artists. Backing for her enterprise was supplied by entrepreneur Joseph P. Kennedy and his Eastern syndicate. She had met Kennedy shortly after returning from the European filming of *Madame Sans-Gene,* He was then 41 years old and the titular head of FBO Pictures, Keith Albee Orpheum, and Pathé. He raised the $12 million capital for Gloria's enterprise and would finance each of her upcoming films, maintaining control of the negative until the loans were repaid.

At United Artists, other notables who had recently been won over were: John Barrymore, Corinne Griffith, Norma Talmadge, and producer Samuel Goldwyn. Famous Players-Lasky would soon discover, under B. P. Schulberg's creative control of the West Coast studio, that its new contractee Clara Bow could well fill the gap left by Gloria's exit.

For her initial United Artists vehicle, Gloria selected *The Loves of Sunya* (1927), which Marjorie Rambeau had done on Broadway and Clara Kimball Young had filmed as *The Eyes of Youth*. The new edition proved to be expensively mounted, leisurely paced claptrap. (Evidently Gloria recognized the story's vapidness from the start of production, but reasoned that the melodrama offered her a showcase of five roles to portray for her adoring public. In 1952, when she donated a print of *The Loves of Sunya* to the Museum of Modern Art's film library, she told cinema historian Richard Griffith: "It was a turkey then and it's still a turkey, but if you want it, be my guest.") In the film, on the eve of flying off to South America with honest but poor John Boles, Gloria wonders if perhaps she should either jaunt to Paris with her impresario friend and embark on a singing career, or maybe marry the millionaire her money-troubled father has been promoting so earnestly. Suddenly a gypsy clairvoyant appears and allows Gloria to gaze into his crystal ball. She learns the dire fate that will be hers if she chooses either of the other men. The finale discloses Gloria marrying Boles and discovering a simple solution to her father's financial woes. Included in the extravaganza are flashbacks to ancient Egypt, with a ravishing young woman under the sway of a demanding prince, and scenes of imperial Rome and pre-revolutionary France, all to allow Gloria to look exotic in fabulous settings, and to dose the audience with morality via the comparison of ancient and contemporary standards.

Gloria was wise enough to know that as an independent producer, she had to manufacture tremendous publicity for her product. She made an agreement to have *The Loves Of Sunya* open at the new 6,200-seat Roxy Theatre. On February 2, 1927, she swept majestically into the just-completed theatrical showplace and signed the exhibition contract with S. L. Rothafel, creator of "the cathedral of the motion picture," giving the showplace her full blessing. *The Loves of Sunya* had its impressively gaudy premiere on March 11, 1927, and was tolerated by the rather indulgent critics. Said the *New York Times:* "Miss Swanson herein gives a far better performance than in any other of her films in the last two years. . . . Miss Swanson's impersonation of the intoxicated Sunya in this chapter is excellent—She expresses sarcasm, anger, and gives a clever portrayal of the luxury-loving prima donna." The lure of Gloria's name and the fanfare surrounding the new movie palace dragged the fans in by thousands. *The Loves of Sunya* took in $125,927.40 the first week, with a total of 157,602 viewers. Due to sharp promotion, the film did well in general release, with Gloria's company netting $630,370.

Realizing she needed a strong dramatic property for her next film to woo back the critics and keep her hold on her audience, Gloria boldly announced she would film *Rain* which had been a big hit on Broadway with Jeanne Eagels. Gloria purchased the rights to W. Somerset Maugham's short story, "Miss Sadie Thompson," the basis of *Rain,* and then ran into a headlong battle with the Hays Office. To appease their demands, the character of Reverend Davidson, the proselytizer who craves the whore Sadie, was altered to Oliver Hamilton, a moral reformer sanctioned by no particular religious denomination.

Sadie Thompson (1928) was filmed on Catalina Island under the direction of Raoul Walsh, whom Gloria also browbeat into playing the hero-sergeant. It premiered at the Rivoli Theatre on February 4, 1928, and proved to be a gutsy rendition of the play with Gloria giving a virtuoso performance as the harlot who ensnares the hypocritical, lusty moralizer, Lionel Barrymore. Within the bounds of the day's conventions, *Sadie Thompson* conveyed the sensuous nature of the tough gum-chewing broad forced to leave San Francisco and finding herself in Pago Pago ("It was too hot in Pago Pago to need bedclothes yet the rain came down in sheets"), outcast from even that port's crummy society ("I guess they think I'm Mrs. Halitosis"). The tumultuous seduction scene in which reformer Barrymore, who had wanted Gloria deported, is about to submit to her, ends abruptly with Barrymore standing poised at her bedroom door. Later, she goes away with her Marine lover (Walsh) and the transmuted Barrymore shoots himself.

Gloria received excellent critical notices—her best until *Sunset Boulevard* (1950). Mordaunt Hall *(New York Times)* stated: "While this actress may have given clever performances in some of her pictures, she displays more genuine ability and imagination in this present production." Yet there were some dissenting opinions: "Particularly, during the first two reels, her hard-boiled walk, gestures and facial expression seem out of proportion. She's let her hair grow too." *(Variety)*

Sadie Thompson grossed over $1 million, with Gloria's production company netting $776,539. In the first Academy Award competitions, she was nominated for the best actress award, but lost out to Janet Gaynor, who won for her performances in *Seventh Heaven, Street Angel,* and *Sunrise. Sadie Thompson* was remade as *Rain* (1932) with Joan Crawford, and as *Miss Sadie Thompson* (1953) with Rita Hayworth. Gloria recently said: "I had better luck with *Sadie* than any other movie star because I had the advantage of making a good silent of it. If you have to censor Sadie's language, how can you really portray her?"

For some unknown reasons that seem more preposterous in retrospect —and against everyone's advice—Gloria decided, again with Joseph Kennedy's full financial support, to film *Queen Kelly,* an original story by Eric Von Stroheim, who was also engaged to direct the venture. With two such strong personalities, each having opposing artistic viewpoints, there was bound to be chaos, and there was. After one-third of Von Stroheim's envisioned feature was completed in four months' time, Gloria excused herself from the set one day in March, 1929, to "make a phone call" and never returned. She called Kennedy and reportedly said: "There's a madman in charge here. The scenes he's shooting will never get past Will Hays." Kennedy immediately shut down production.

Originally the scenario concerned degenerate queen Seena Owen of Kronberg (she foams at the mouth, indulges in every variation of debauchery, etc.) who intends that scoundrel prince Walter Byron shall marry her. However, while out riding one day, he spies Irish girl Gloria among a group of orphan girls (her panties at that moment had fallen down), and immediately is smitten with her. He kidnaps the miss and takes her to the palace. That night, after an orgy banquet, the queen beats Gloria unmercifully for being in Byron's private chambers. The projected Von Stroheim finale had Gloria going to South Africa to receive an inheritance from a dying aunt. Years later the prince discovers her there as the veldt's most flourishing and corrupt madame, whose haughty manners have earned her the title of "Queen Kelly." Gloria had married her rich but degenerate Uncle, Tully Marshall, but had always refused to live with him. When he dies, the prince and she marry. The queen is assassinated and Byron ascends the throne and Gloria becomes a real Queen Kelly.

When production shut down, only a few of the African scenes, with Tully Marshall as the lecherous uncle, had been filmed. Approximately $800,000 had been spent. With Gloria refusing to deal any further with Von Stroheim, and the success of talking pictures already making the silent drama dated, Gloria's production company was financially out in the cold. In 1931 Gloria abandoned the Von Stroheim script, and under Edmund Goulding's and her own direction shot a new reel to climax *Queen Kelly*. It had the girl drown herself after being beaten, and the prince following her in death. Adolf Tandler was hired to add a musical sound track to the film. Because Von Stroheim owned part of the property and refused to grant releasing rights in the United States and elsewhere, the abortive *Queen Kelly* only had a few South American and European bookings. Gloria donated a print of the picture to the Museum of Modern Art in 1945. After her *Sunset Boulevard* "comeback," *Queen Kelly* had minor theatrical distribution. At that time *Variety* finally reviewed the 21-year-old film and termed Gloria's performance "coy." New York's educational television Channel 13 televised *Queen Kelly* March 28, 1966, and it was later screened at the special evening with Gloria Swanson at the Beacon Theatre in New York City on May 8, 1957, with excerpts from the African scenes that had been filmed.*

Gloria's producer-mentor Kennedy then signed Edmund Goulding to direct Gloria in her first talking film, *The Trespasser* (1929), an original story by Goulding. Laura Hope Crews was assigned to coach Gloria in her diction. The film presented Gloria as a stenographer to a Chicago lawyer. She weds wealthy Robert Ames. After his family causes the marriage to be annulled, she gives birth to a child, and accepts favors from her old boss to insure the child's welfare. Ames marries another woman, but she still loves him, and after several well-spaced anticlimaxes they are reunited. In the course of the melodrama, Gloria sang "Love, Your Magic Spell is Everywhere" (written especially for her by Goulding), dueted "I Love You Truly" with Ames, and sang "Toselli Serenade."

The Trespasser opened at the Rialto Theatre on November 11, 1929—the first new Gloria movie to premiere in 19 months. The critics and the public were amazed at Gloria's easy transition to sound films and delighted by her fine singing voice. Mordaunt Hall *(New York Times)* wrote: "Here she is more of an actress than ever, speaking lines naturally and without unnecessary pantomime gestures. Her work is restrained, particularly in the emotional scenes. She has also seen to it that time and a nerve-wracking ordeal show in her face." In its six-week, six-day engagement at the Rialto, *The Trespasser* grossed a big $272,600, and the subsequent release netted Gloria's company $1,241,091. She was nominated for her second Academy Award but lost out to Norma Shearer, who won for *The Divorcee*. *The Trespasser* would be remade as *That Certain Woman* (1937) with Bette Davis.

Gossip columnists had increasingly been linking Gloria and Kennedy on a nonbusiness level, but no comments were forthcoming from the star. Her husband the marquis had been packed off to Europe by Kennedy, where

*In October, 1971, Gloria told *New York Times* reporter Judy Klemesrud: *Queen Kelly* was Little Bo Peep compared to what we're seeing today. I was the one who put up the money, and I was the one who stopped it, because I knew it wouldn't get past the censor. What was censorable in those days and what is censorable now are two different things. Kindergarten kids will probably be reading *Queen Kelly* one of these days."

he ostensibly was employed by FBO and Pathé. Despite Gloria's lucrative income, she was still having difficulty making ends meet, not having learned yet to curb her penchant for unwise spending. Every time she attempted to reduce her debts, she would emerge even poorer. For example, there was the time in 1927 when she came to New York to borrow $25,000 and then indulged herself by returning to California in a private railroad car (which cost more than the loan).

Allan Dwan was signed to direct Gloria in *What a Widow!* (1930), on the prompting of Kennedy and United Artists that she try to recoup the losses sustained on *Queen Kelly* that had not been eradicated by the proceeds of *The Trespasser.* The new film, an ordinary farce, brought about the final transition from Gloria the legendary screen goddess to Gloria the most human actress. The end of the silent cinema and the beginning of the Depression ushered in a new awareness that decried the standards of America's age of innocence. Once motion pictures learned to talk, Gloria, like other silent movie queens, was forced to become mortal and to mouth pedestrian dialogue like any ordinary actress. The mystery disappeared from her personality, and she had to compete on entirely different terms than before. At age 32, that was no mean feat. *The Trespasser* had maintained Gloria's strong box-office position, not merely for its effective story line and her exceptionally taut performance, but because of the novelty of Gloria finally talking so her legion of fans could hear her as she was—at least on the screen. But now that novelty was gone.

In *What a Widow!* Gloria is bequeathed $5 million by her elderly husband. She travels from New York to Paris, and as part of the Continental fun set, becomes enamored of drifting rich guy Lew Cody. Owen Moore, a lawyer in her employ, reappears and Gloria decides to wed him. To keep the frou-frou rolling, Gloria sang several Vincent Youmans songs. The *New York Times* penned: "Sometimes the violent attempts to draw laughter cause one to think that Miss Swanson wishes to emulate her early efforts in pictures under Mack Sennett, but the antics of the players, including Miss Swanson, invariably misfire." Others noticed she was "vivacious and energetic" but deplored the poor synchronization of the sound track and the thin stretches in the plot not sufficiently disguised by the cumbersome slapstick.

This was Gloria's last Kennedy-financed film. Said Gloria: "I questioned his judgment. He did not like to be questioned." Their business partnership was abruptly terminated.

Meanwhile, Gloria's marriage to the marquis had reached its nadir (he had publicly complained on several occasions, "I married a businesswoman") and on November 5, 1930, they filed for divorce, which was finalized on November 5, 1931. He subsequently married Constance Bennett. Meanwhile, Gloria had been dating actor Joel McCrea and producer Gene Markey.

On August 16, 1931, she secretly wed Irish sportsman Michael Farmer in Elmsford, England. Because the divorce from the marquis was technically not final, she remarried Farmer again on November 9, 1931 in Yuma, Arizona, to avoid problems with the law. Her public was not appreciative of the fact that Gloria was still setting her own rules and seemed to show a shocking lack of respect for standards, particularly in the Farmer marriage business. On screen and off Gloria was still playing to the hilt the role of the luxury-bent queen surrounded by wealth and money. This posture was finding increasing disfavor with 1930s audiences and onetime fans.

Indiscreet opened on May 6, 1931. It was another lightweight farce in which Gloria almost sacrifices her relationship to author Ben Lyon when she rekindles a romance with scamp Monroe Owsley, who has threatened to marry her younger sister. Gloria sang "Come to Me" and "If You Haven't Got Love." To titillate the viewers, there was a shower bath scene in which a quite revealing silhouette of Gloria was coyly illuminated. This time around there were raps from many critical quarters. "Too free play has been given the famed Swansonian mannerisms, goo-goo-eyeing and curling her upper lip to show off her teeth" *(New York Times):* "Pretty narrow margin left for Miss Swanson in this role on looks. The extreme youthfulness of Barbara Kent as the sister helped or hurt, according to the way you see the Swanson role."

Tonight or Never (1931) featured Gloria as a youthful Viennese prima donna, tired of her elderly, rich suitors and the rigors of her loveless career. Mysterious stranger Melvyn Douglas (he had starred in the successful Broadway version of the play) enters the scene and woos Gloria. It develops he is an opera impresario out to get her signature on a new contract. Gloria sang no songs in *Tonight or Never.* Despite her sumptuous Chanel wardrobe, many thought Douglas's "bright interpretation" put Gloria "in the shade." And in several scenes it was quite evident that she was several months pregnant. The feature did only a modest $84,000 in its three-week engagement at the Rialto Theatre, a barometer indicator of the falling stock of Gloria with her once-ardent public.

Gloria was then off the screen for two years due to the birth of her daughter Michael Bridget,* born April 5, 1932, in London.

In June, 1932, Gloria incorporated Gloria Swanson British Productions, Ltd. to produce *Perfect Understanding* (1933). It was a disaster from beginning to end, with assorted production problems during the on-location shooting in London and on the Riviera, right up to the processing of the negative when the film laboratory burned down and *Perfect Understanding* was almost destroyed. Gloria and Laurence Olivier play carefree lovers who decide to marry on condition (via a written agreement) that they agree never to disagree. A slight infidelity on his part tears their marriage apart, and their lack of understanding of one another snowballs events. Finally they reconcile their differences in the divorce court and are reunited. Gloria sang a bit and scampered about but she was poorly photographed. The reviews were bad. "Miss Swanson is undeniably good-looking, but she does not show any particular talent for acting in this film. She speaks her lines in a nervous manner, and this often destroys what value there might to the episode" *(New York Times).* "She doesn't offer that appealing sensual quality that she used to have in the old days" *(New York Sun).* It grossed a mild $23,000 in its first week at the Rivoli Theatre (February 22, 1933) and was held on for an additional three weeks awaiting the replacement picture, *Secrets* (a Mary Pickford vehicle that also bombed out). Gloria's attempt to make husband Farmer a screen actor—he played the spouse of Genevieve Tobin—proved fruitless.

With *Perfect Understanding,* Gloria's United Artists agreement was terminated. It was later estimated that she personally lost some $2,651,000 in her United Artists contract by waiving profit interest in favor of straight salary: *The Loves of Sunya* and *Sadie Thompson* ($150,000 each); *The Trespasser* and *What a Widow!* ($100,000 each); *Indiscreet* and *Tonight or Never* ($250,000 each); and *Perfect Understanding* (approximately $150,-000).

*She is now Mrs. Robert Amon, has two children, and resides in Paris.

Gloria stated in 1933: "Sometimes I get tired of the pictures and think of giving them up. But then somebody comes along talking about a new studio or a new play and my ears go up like an old circus horse smelling the sawdust."

Nevertheless, she had been having financial problems. In September, 1932, her furniture was seized for $14,000 debts owed a New York importer. In February, 1933, the U.S. government claimed she owed $49,426 on her 1931 taxes, and Maurice Cleary, theatrical booking agent and husband of May McAvoy, sued her for unpaid commissions on six of her United Artists features. A weary Gloria told the press: "I know all about being poor. I was terribly poor while I was struggling for a place in filmdom. I know all about doing without things and wanting them terribly. But now I have tasted the sweets of life, literally have enjoyed everything money can buy. I know now that there is a relative value to both states. That's why if I were to go broke tomorrow, I could fill the gap of money artificiality with the real things of life which are free."

Gloria's ego was hurt though, and the once-busy film star hated to be professionally idle. She foolishly agreed to a contract of three films over two years, offered by Screen Plays, Inc., headed by J. Schnitzer and Sam Zierler. They intended loaning her to other production companies at a nifty percentage profit. No projects materialized, although Gloria was considered as a replacement for ailing Claudette Colbert in Cecil B. DeMille's *Four Frightened People* (1934).

Having withdrawn from her Screen Plays, Inc. agreement, she was more than happy to accept Irving Thalberg's MGM contract offer in early 1934. Gloria announced in April that year: "It's like an insurance, working for Irving. He's getting something ready for me, and I'm not worrying about it at all. Whatever it is, if Irving does it it'll be all right. I've gotten to the point where I'm glad to let someone else do the deciding." Thalberg planned a remake of Elinor Glyn's *Three Weeks,* but it never came about, nor did a scheduled original Frances Marion story, *Full Bloom.* Warner Brothers wanted Gloria to costar with Edward G. Robinson in a Napoleonic tale, but that fell through, as well as plans for Gloria to appear in Paramount's *Miss Fane's Baby Is Stolen* (1934), Columbia's *Twentieth Century* (1934), and a *Ziegfeld Follies* Broadway show.

In the interim, Gloria's marriage to Farmer had faltered and they separated in December, 1933. Gloria stated: " . . . [he] belongs in Europe, I belong in America. I have my work, and I like to do what I am doing." They were divorced on November 7, 1934, with Gloria receiving a default decree. ("Hardly a day of our married life passed without a quarrel," Gloria told the judge.) Gloria had begun dating actor Herbert Marshall, age 44, who was still married to Edna Best. Fan magazines described their strong romance as something "beautiful and brave with dialogue by Noel Coward."

Fox Films borrowed Gloria to play the prima donna lead in *Music in the Air* (1934), based on the Jerome Kern-Oscar Hammerstein II stage operetta. Gloria is the diva who cannot decide if she loves or loathes lyricist John Boles. Common folk Douglas P. Montgomery and June Lang (he is a schoolteacher and she is the daughter of composer Al Shean) come to Munich and soon find themselves paired off with Gloria and Boles, with much to-do before the right couples are reunited. *Music in the Air* premiered at Radio City Music Hall on December 13, 1934. Gloria looked lovely, but noted *Variety:* "Miss Swanson, who can sing but mildly, is wisely not permitted to strain her larynx." The overblown filmization did a disappointing $60,000 weekly gross at the Music Hall. It certainly was not the "right" or "proper" vehicle that Gloria had hoped would restore her former screen prestige in one fell swoop. It would be her last film for seven years.

When Thalberg died (September 14, 1936), Gloria's MGM hopes were gone, particularly after she had rejected *Maizie Kenyon* (about a cabaret singer with a child), switching her interest to *The Emperor's Candlesticks,* and then dropping out of that. The latter picture became a Luise Rainer vehicle in 1937. Republic Pictures offered her $50,000 to star in *Manhattan Merry-Go-Round* but she declined. She then agreed to do *The Second Mrs. Draper* at Columbia. Gloria announced: "I made up my mind that I wasn't to do another picture until I found something about which I could really get excited. I had done too many comedies, and all the new parts offered me were the same line. I wanted something different—something strongly dramatic." *The Second Mrs. Draper,* scripted by Frances Marion, concerned a newly married young matron who finds her husband's son (by his first marriage) is falling in love with her. Some test footage on the project was lensed in July, 1937, but then Gloria had disagreements with studio boss Harry Cohn and the film was abandoned.

In the following years, Gloria became a world traveler. "It was the old story of the reformed sinner turning into the loudest psalm singer in the congregation. After I was through with the movies—or vice versa—I was so sore at my stupidity that I could've cut my throat. I woke up and discovered I was the all-time Hollywood dumb-cluck who'd thrown away literally million of dollars to put up a big front that fooled nobody but me." Gloria formed Multiprises, Inc. at a cost of $200,000, to discover and exploit new patents. Its biggest commercial success was a plastic button patent which brought in a $3,000 yearly royalty. Because of her business venture, she had become involved in a plan to help four industrial engineers escape from Nazi-controlled Austria. Her successful efforts earned her new respect with the press and public. Gloria also took an interest in politics, and in 1940 campaigned for Wendell L. Willkie against Franklin D. Roosevelt.

Gloria was earning an average of $25,000 a year in the late 1930s from her enterprises, and finding it difficult to keep herself and her children in a suitable style. While she was in Hollywood visiting her mother, then married to Charles E. Woodruff of Glendale, RKO offered her $35,000 to costar with Adolphe Menjou in *Father Takes a Wife* (1941). Gloria completed her role within two weeks. It presented Gloria as the first lady of the theatre who weds shipping magnate Menjou. On their honeymoon they begin bickering, but forget their problems when Gloria takes a professional interest in stowaway Latin American singer Desi Arnaz. The middle-aged couple resolve their domestic problems (including the interfering habits of Menjou's two busybody children) and grow young together from love. RKO was undergoing an executive shakeup at the time and tossed away *Father Takes A Wife.* It opened at the Palace Theatre, with Gloria taking second billing to Menjou! *Variety* commented: "Miss Swanson shows her age to some extent in the face, but can only be tabled semi-matronly in that respect. Her figure is alluringly svelte, and she still carries that magnetic screen personality." The *New York Post* observed that her acting technique was "nothing to treasure." It was another big letdown for Gloria in her "comeback" bid.

Gloria had long considered appearing in a legitimate show. In 1940 she almost accepted the lead in the Edward Chodorov-H. S. Kraft drama, *Cue For Passion.* On June 30, 1942, in Poughkeepsie, New York, she made her official stage debut in a summer tour of George Kelly's *Reflected Glory.*

George Freedley (*New York Morning Telegraph*) reported: "Her range as an actress is something less than complete or truly satisfactory. She is inclined to kid the part and to mug it dreadfully at times. She sings the lines and the gamut of her expression is scarcely extended. Her voice is intended for drama rather than comedy." Her gowns by Valentina received fine notices. The following March (1943) she toured in the Harold J. Kennedy-directed *Three Curtains* (one-act plays—she was the Lady in G. B. Shaw's *Man of Destiny,* Mrs. Dowey in J. M. Barrie's *The Old Lady Shows Her Medals,* and the mistress in Arthur Pinero's *Playgoers*). Francis Lederer and Kennedy costarred. The tour played Boston, Philadelphia, Washington, and elsewhere. Some thought she "underplayed" too much, but, everyone agreed, "La Swanson looks tip-top, and wears millinery that had ladies gasping and still has plenty of symmetry to fill gowns neatly." In the summer of 1943 she toured in *Let Us Be Gay*.

On January 29, 1945, Gloria married William N. Davey, a 52-year-old investment broker. It was his third marriage; his second wife had been 1920s Paramount starlet Alyce Mills. Gloria and he lived together for 44 days and then separated.

A few days before her marriage, Gloria made her official Broadway stage debut in Harold J. Kennedy's *A Goose For the Gander* (Playhouse Theatre, January 23, 1945). (She had appeared on the Paramount Theatre stage in a comedy vignette in April, 1934, on the same bill with *Wharf Angel.*) This farce about a bored married couple featured Conrad Nagel as the dallying husband and Gloria as the modish wife who retaliated in kind. *Variety* said: "Attractive, youthful and charmingly garbed, Miss Swanson brings a strained quality to her acting that doesn't help carry off the farce." The show lasted 15 performances.

In December, 1948, Gloria and her husband Davey were divorced. She received a $300 weekly alimony settlement. (He died the following September in Los Angeles.) Gloria would philosophize: "The mess I made of marriage was all my fault. I can smell the character of a woman the instant she enters a room, but I have the world's worst judgment of men. Maybe the odds were against me. When I was young, no man my age made enough money to support me in the style expected of me. There's no sense kidding myself—I loved all the pomp and luxury of that style. When I die, my epitaph should read: 'She Paid the Bills.' That's the story of my private life."

In 1948 Gloria, who became a fabulous grandmother shortly before Marlene Dietrich, began her five-times-weekly one-hour video show, televised by New York's WPIX, for which she was paid $350 a week. The 4–5 P.M. program had segments devoted to fashions, travel, cooking, beauty care, and so forth. The set was modeled on the living room of Gloria's Fifth Avenue apartment. There were no scripts, and Gloria utilized the impromptu hostessing style that would bring Faye Emerson and Wendy Barrie equal popularity in the early days of live television.

Then, in 1949, scripter-director Billy Wilder asked Gloria to appear as Norma Desmond in Paramount's *Sunset Boulevard* (1950)—both Mary Pickford and Pola Negri had been considered first. That Gloria accepted the unusual role of a sophisticated silent movie queen who had gone bizarrely mad over the years amazed everyone as much as did her actually completing the assignment without problems. (Years before, Josef von Sternberg had offered her the part of Mother Gin-Sling in *The Shanghai Gesture* [1941] but had broken off negotiations when Gloria presented him with a revised version of the screenplay which built up her role extensively.)

The cynical melodrama opens with the scene of a dead man floating in a swimming pool. Then his voice begins relating the macabre story: unemployed screen writer William Holden, hiding out from creditors, takes refuge in the oversized mansion of ex-movie star Gloria. For years she has been elaborately planning a sensational movie comeback that never materializes. She takes a possessive fancy to Holden and insists that he formulate the screenplay that will showcase her eternally young talents. The situation reaches crisis proportions when she discovers he is still attached to his young girlfriend Nancy Olsen and plans to leave the 1920s sanctuary, and she shoots and kills him. In an equally bravura performance, Eric Von Stroheim is reunited with Gloria. He portrayed her former husband and director, now her ever-present butler. Originally Montgomery Clift had been considered for the male lead.

Sunset Boulevard is filled with moments of greatness: Gloria doing her Charlie Chaplin imitation; a moment of deluded glory in which she shows Holden one of her big silent films *(Queen Kelly)*, telling him: "We didn't need dialogue. We had faces! . . . I'm still big—it's pictures that have grown small." Later, she visits Cecil B. DeMille at work on a Paramount sound stage, convinced he intends discussing her movie return, but dismayed to learn that he only wishes to borrow her vintage limousine for a film prop. At the finale, when the police arrive to cart away the demented murderess, she sweeps majestically down the grand staircase, enunciating her words at her melodramatic best. Von Stroheim gallantly allows her a final bit of delusion—thinking that the crowd has assembled to witness her enact the big scene from her comeback picture: "I just want to tell you all how happy I am to be back in the studio, making a picture again! You don't know how much I've missed all of you. And I promise you, I'll never desert you again! Because after *Salome,* we'll make another picture, and another picture. You see, this is my life. It always will be. There's nothing else . . . just us . . . and the camera . . . and those wonderful people out there in the dark. All right, Mr. DeMille, I'm ready for my close-up."

Sunset Boulevard premiered at the Radio City Music Hall on August 10, 1950 and proved a big hit. Second-billed Gloria received glowing accolades, with most critics suggesting that only now had she matured as an actress. Otis L. Guernsey, Jr. *(New York Herald Tribune)* observed: "At first, her performance requires a bit of readjusting on the audience's part—it is bravura, mannered and out of proportion to the requirements of most sound pictures. One may easily fall into step with it, however, and it becomes strangely and vividly appropriate." The *New York Times* said: "It is inconceivable that anyone else might have been considered for the role as the wealthy, egotistical relic desperately yearning to hear again the plaudits of the crowd. Miss Swanson dominates the picture." Gloria was nominated for the third time for an Academy Award, but lost to Judy Holliday, who won for *Born Yesterday.*

More than annoyed that critics were *just* discovering her, Gloria snapped: "Go back through my career from Keystone to Triangle to DeMille to pseudo-DeMille. I played everything, and never the same thing twice. I was a French actress in *Zaza,* a gum-chewing clerk in *Manhandled.* I wore boy's clothes in *The Humming Bird.* Every part—*Stage Struck, Manhandled, Society Scandal, Madame Sans-Gene,* and later *Sadie Thompson, Music in the Air, Indiscretion,* and *Father Takes a Wife*—every role was different. I don't know anyone who's played more varied roles than I have. I was a good actress before *Sunset Boulevard.* People forget I played character roles for DeMille. I've played character roles all through my movie career. On the stage, too."

Gloria hoped *Sunset Boulevard* would lead to a renewal of her film career. Paramount vaguely suggested her starring in *Alice-Sit-By-The-Fire* (which became *Darling How Could You* [1951] with Joan Fontaine) and Hal Wallis mentioned a *December Bride* film project. William Dieterle was to produce-direct *The Besieged Heart* by Robert Hill in Turkey, with Gloria starred as a woman dying of a mysterious disease and her young lover seeking a cure. She was offered *Another Man's Poison* (1951) but she rejected it and Bette Davis accepted. Many people on the Hollywood scene at the time report that Gloria, once a big star, still considered herself a top celebrity, and refused to concede that times or she had changed in the intervening years. She may have been 52 years old chronologically but she would not dream of playing the mother of a grown child on the screen. Her delusions would be short-lived as time passed and fewer offers were made.

Gloria returned to New York, where she accepted an offer from Puritan Dress Company to head her own line of designer clothes, and she has been under contract to them ever since. She began hostessing her own WOR radio talk show, commencing September 30, 1950, with Ginger Rogers as her initial guest. Rumors that she would write her own glamour book never panned out.

On the stage, Gloria starred opposite Jose Ferrer in the revival of *Twentieth Century* (Anta Playhouse, December 24, 1950). She received excellent notices as the temperamental film star coaxed by her ex-husband, Ferrer, into starring in his new Broadway show. The show ran for 218 performances.

The following year Gloria starred in the French marital farce *Nina* costarring David Niven and Alan Webb. When the show was trying out in Philadelphia, she requested her release ("My lines are not good") but the producers refused. *Nina* (Royale Theatre, December 5, 1951) came and went in 45 showings.

Also in 1951, Gloria was heard on the *"Theatre Guild of the Air"* (ABC) broadcast of *Theatre,* opposite Melvyn Douglas. On September 1, 1951, she joined with William Holden and Nancy Olsen in recreating *Sunset Boulevard* for "Lux Radio Theatre."

Unlike other living legends such as Marlene Dietrich, who preferred to disguise facets of their past careers, Gloria was always bringing up references to her early years, candid, insofar as she remembered the bygone times: "I've always been on my own, been my own business manager, agent. My mother has never been a theatre person. Mary Pickford had her mother, Chaplin had his brother, Harold Lloyd had his uncle, the Talmadges had Schenck, the Gishes Griffith. I was always alone. Once I intended to take a course in corporation law at the University of California. Never got around to it. Business intervened."

Advance for Romance, a tentative film project in 1951, with Gloria as a businesswoman romantically involved with a tax expert, never developed. Instead, she accepted the lead in a flat comedy, *Three for Bedroom C* (1952). The film tells the story of a movie star and her very young daughter on their way to California who find that biochemistry professor James Warren has legitimate claim to the same drawing room compartment. It opened at the Astor Theatre on June 26, 1952, and soon was dismissed by the critics and the public as "Wretchedly insane flapdoodle." Gloria shrugged off the failure: "It was light, fluffy comedy, but damned if the critics didn't compare it with *Sunset Boulevard*. It's like comparing a steak with a soufflé. Anyway I wanted to do one picture in color before I died."

Throughout the 1950s, Gloria continued to travel with her line of dresses "Gowns By Gloria," and to crusade for projects that intrigued her (particularly health foods). She maintained her Manhattan apartment and a home at Eze, France, on the Côte d'Azur.

On television she hostessed 26 half-hour episodes of "Crown Theatre" (syndicated during the 1953–54 video season), acting in some of the segments. Previously, she had torn up a $800,000 TV series contract "because I didn't want to be driven crazy as the result of them." She was a guest on Milton Berle's variety show (1956, NBC), the subject of "This Is Your Life" (November 10, 1957, NBC), and star attraction of a Mike Wallace interview (1957, ABC). While she guested on "Ben Casey," "Burke's Law," "Straightaway," "My Three Sons," "Dr. Kildare," "Alfred Hitchcock," and "What's My Line" (mystery guest), Gloria's most famous television appearance was on "The Beverly Hillbillies" (November 20, 1966, CBS). In this episode, the group think she has lost all her money and set about producing a movie, *Passion's Plaything,* to star Gloria. About her television acting Gloria has said: "I prepare myself thoroughly for a role and I expect everybody else including the man who makes the coffee, to be equally well prepared."

In 1955 Gloria went to Rome to star in a movie farce, *Nero's Mistress,* which featured Vittorio De Sica and a brief appearance by starlet Brigitte Bardot. The film was released in Europe in 1957 and got to America in 1962 as *Nero's Big Weekend.* As Nero's glamorous mother, Gloria was cited for her "good performance." While in Italy, Gloria became a United Press guest columnist, writing on the international scene. Her first by-lined article dealt with American males, citing them as lousy lovers. Stated Gloria: "Nobody can say I'm too young to know what I'm talking about."

In October, 1960, Gloria was on hand for the demolition of the Roxy Theatre, and her extravagantly posed photo in the shambles of the former movie palace was widely reproduced. As always, she had words for the press: "You know my life is a constant surprise. I'm like a child waiting for what's going to happen tomorrow." Re Hollywood: "I didn't have a chance to become so set in my little kingdom out there that it was the beginning and the end of all life. My friends in New York are so varied—brain surgeons, painters, sculptors." On life: "I'm a gypsy fool. I don't think I could live in Paradise more than eleven months. I'd probably want to go to Hades for the twelfth month." Her youthfulness: "Curiosity about the world and about myself. There are so many things to look into, to learn to do. There's always a new beginning. Most women know so little about themselves and even less about what's around them. I feel I've lived 2,000 lives in my own way, and I'm not finished." Wherever she went, Gloria would espouse the virtues of her special diet of seaweed, bread, herb tea, and organically grown vegetables cooked in her own pressure cooker.

Gloria continued appearing in stock: *Red Letter Day* (1959) with Charles "Buddy" Rogers; *Between Seasons* (1961) ("The piquant Swanson profile is used to advantage"); and *The Inkwell* (1962) in which she portrayed a movie star, did the Charleston, and sang several songs.

In 1966 she attended the special George Eastman House (Rochester, New York) tribute to silent film stars and received an award for her "outstanding contribution to the art of the motion picture." After the retrospective, which included showings of clips from many of her films, she told newsmen: "I must say I got fed up looking at that face of mine. First it was a pudding then it was an old dumpling. Talk about the face that launched a thousand ships—this was a thousand faces that launched I don't know what—a career, I guess."

In the fall of 1967 she toured in Harold J. Kennedy's *Reprise,* which played Denver and Chicago and then opened at the Huntington Hartford Theatre in Los Angeles on October 3, 1967. The show concerned a onetime movie star who visits a Midwestern college town. The brightest moment in the play occurs when the lights go down, and the movie star (Gloria) runs a 15-minute recap of her film career. The play itself was very slight and indifferently written and produced. Said Gloria: "At my age it can't be anything but a lark." About returning to the cinema capital: "I've really known ten different Hollywoods. Everytime I come back here it has changed."

In January, 1969, Gloria turned up in Moscow, searching for prints of one of her silent movies and espousing the cause of health foods. She met with the head of the Soviet Nutrition Institute. On the way back to the United States, she stopped in London. She was quoted there as saying: "I have my nose in everything trying to find out how this or that works. Women keep saying they're bored, I don't know how that can be. There's so much to learn . . . I don't have enough time. Women have time-saving devices . . . for what? To sit under a dryer and bake their brains? I couldn't stand that. I wash and set my own hair when I get the time—three in the morning sometimes." She told a *Guardian* reporter: "Many directors enjoyed working with me because I was so much of a professional. I tell all actresses that failure is easy to deal with. Success is impossible unless you've had the experience."

In March, 1970, Gloria auditioned to replace Katharine Hepburn in the Broadway musical *Coco,* but her salary demands and terms were too stringent for producer Frederick Brisson. Instead, on October 12, 1970, she replaced Eve Arden in the national touring company of Leonard Gershe's comedy *Butterflies Are Free.* It had starred Eileen Heckart on Broadway as the Scarsdale, New York, matron who releases the apron strings so her blind son can lead his own life in his Greenwich Village apartment. Kevin Kelly *(Boston Globe)* reported during the Boston run: "She acts with decided limitation, in a voice sometimes not audible, with heavy posing (usually knees akimbo) but she gets better as the plot moves on. . . . she commands a tireless glamour. The role doesn't require it, but well, it's there." The road tour continued through the spring of 1971, and proved quite successful, grossing an average $38,000 weekly.

After this Gloria closed her New York apartment ("New York is so dirty, it's getting to be a slum") and purchased a Palm Springs home. But then, in August, 1971, the producers of *Butterflies Are Free* announced that Gloria had been wooed back to Broadway and would take over the lead in their show from Rosemary Murphy on September 7. Gloria told the press she had done the road show to "see America." "I knew that Americana was not on the East Coast or on the West Coast, but maybe in the middle. I fell in love with Arkansas, I almost wanted to buy a farm there.

"I always chose a dressing room on the second floor so that I could run up and down the steps during the performance. I guess I'm old ironsides, the iron butterfly."

When asked how she regarded commercial Broadway, 1971 style, Gloria replied: "I go along with change, and this too shall pass, no matter whether it's good or bad. Thank God for change."

Gloria's name proved viable marquee bait, and *Butterflies Are Free,* already on cut-rate tickets, experienced a resurgence in audience interest. The publicity surrounding Gloria's Broadway return, like the reviews, spurred on ticket buyers who wanted to catch up with the latest phase of La Swanson's long, long professional career. Walter Kerr, writing in the *New York Times,* reported about the show and Gloria:

"She is strong and freshly winning. She stylizes a few of her earlier comic responses a shade more than is necessary, freezing into stunned postures as though a playful animated-cartoon artist had pinned her to the drawing board. This does not seem so much a hangover from films—after all, she has made very few in the last 25 years—as from the road-company tour she has just completed; away from Broadway, things do get broader.

"The grace is there always: Miss Swanson is something to see as she crosses her lithe legs in her tailored beige trousers, locks her hands over one knee, gets her chin to full mast and defies anyone to make her more of a villain than she actually is. But the intelligence is there, too. As she stands in a corner matter-of-factly folding a dish towel, grimly but quite coolly assaying the qualities of the rattle-brained girl who is making her son so happy, she does as much for the part and the play as when she is speaking her determined piece. It is excellent, non-nostalgic work."

In all areas, Gloria shows no signs of letting up professionally. Ready to appear on a national television talk show or whatever at a moment's notice, she is currently crusading for revisions in the tax laws for singles. She is ruffled that most people believe her image "is straight out of *Sunset Boulevard.* When I meet people they expect me to bite them," and annoyed that several books on her career have appeared to enhance the authors' bank accounts rather than her own.

She admits: "I like making movies better than anything else, but in these days, when there are no real studios as there used to be, I don't know how you get a picture going. In the old days I found a script I liked, got a director who was right, and went to the Bank of America for financing if I didn't have enough money of my own to start the ball rolling."

Gloria has seven grandchildren, two of them married, but none of them have any children yet. She is most anxious to be a great-grandmother, she explains, because she remembers the example of her own great-grandmother, who died when she was 19 years old.

About life Gloria says: "I used to tell people what I thought they ought to do. Now I do what I know is right for me, and if they want to kill themselves with improper diet, breathe smog-laden air, exist in hypochondria and self-centered living, that's their business. They'll go to their rewards, poor things, long before I do, and I wish them, resignedly, farewell. Meanwhile, I'm going to make the 24 hours of every day count for something. The way of life may have changed, and it's not comfortable living in the atomic age, but I've still got a zest for living, thank God!"

The most exciting moment in her life: "The first time I held my first child in my arms. I wanted children more than a career, I tell you. I wanted children more than anything else. Oh, I could say it was coming back from Paris with a new husband the marquis and taking a private train across the country, or I could mention the film festival in Belgium, where every theatre was playing a Swanson picture. But when you come right down to it and you get old and they put you out to pasture, who's around? Your family and your dear ones, that's who."

Thus, for the seemingly eternal Gloria, the key of her vibrant life is: "I never look back, I always look ahead. I never regret. I have excitement every waking minute."

SOCIETY FOR SALE (Triangle, 1918) 5,000'

Director, Frank Borzage; story, Ruby M. Aipis; screenplay, Charles J. Wilson; camera, Pliny Horne.

William Desmond (Honorably Billy); Gloria Swanson (Phyllis Clyne); Herbert Pryor (Lord Sheldon); Lillian Langdon (Lady Mary); Lillian West (Vi Challloner); Charles Dorian (Furnival).

HER DECISION (Triangle, 1918) 5,000'

Director, Jack Conway; story, Laura Gannet; screenplay, Charles Jurlson; camera, Elgin Leslie.

Gloria Swanson (Phyllis Dunbar); J. Barney Sherry (Martin Rankin); Darrell Foss (Bobbie Warner); Ann Kroman (Inah Dunbar).

YOU CAN'T BELIEVE EVERYTHING (Triangle, 1918) 5,000'

Director, Jack Conway; screenplay, Norman Sherbrook; camera, Elgin Leslie.

Gloria Swanson (Patricia Reynolds); Darrell Foss (Arthur Kirby); James Cope (Club Danforth); Jack Richardson (Hasty Carson); Edward Peil (Jim Wheeler); Iris Ashton (Amy Powellson); Grover Franke (Ferdinand Thatcher); George Hernandez (Henry Pettet); Itty Brandburg (Mrs. Powellson); Bliss Chevalier (Mrs. Morton Danforth); Claire McDowell (Grace Dardley).

EVERYWOMAN'S HUSBAND (Triangle, 1918) 5,000'

Director, Gilbert P. Hamilton; screenplay, John Clymer, G. Logue; camera, Tom Buckingham.

Gloria Swanson (Edith Emerson); Joe King (Frank Emerson); Lilliam Langdon (Mrs. Rhodes); George Pearce (Johnathan Rhodes); Lillian West (Delia Marshall); Jack Livingston (Reginald Dunstan).

SHIFTING SANDS (Triangle, 1918) 5,000'

Director, Albert Parker; story, Charles T.D. Dazey; camera, Pliny Horne.

Gloria Swanson (Marcia Grey); Joe King (John Stanford); Harvey Clark (Von Holtz); Leone Carton (Minnie Grey); Lillian Langdon (Mrs. Stanford); Arthur Millett (Willis).

STATION CONTENT (Triangle, 1918) 5,000'

Director, Arthur Hoyt; story, Catherine Carr.

Gloria Swanson (Kitty Manning); Lee Hill (Jim Manning); Arthur Millett (Stephen Morton); Nellis Allen (Mrs. Morton); Ward Caulfield (Theatrical Manager); May Walters (Mrs. Rothfield); Diana Carrillo (Squaw).

THE SECRET CODE (Triangle, 1918) 5.000'

Director, Albert Parker; story, Adela Rogers St. John; camera, Pliny Horne.

J. Barney Sherry (Senator John Calhoun Rand); Gloria Swanson (Sally Carter Rand); Rhy Alexander (Lola Walling); Leslie Stewart (Baron de Vorjeck); Joe King (Jefferson Harrow); Dorothy Wallace (Mrs. Walker); Lee Phelps (Towen Rage).

WIFE OR COUNTRY (Triangle, 1918)

Director, E. Mason Hopper.

Harry Mestayer (Dale Barker); Jack Richardson (Dr. Meyer Stahl); Gretchen Lederer (Gretchen Barker); Gloria Swanson (Sylvia Hamilton); Charles West (Jack Holiday).

DON'T CHANGE YOUR HUSBAND (Artcraft-PAR, 1919)

Director, Cecil B. DeMille; screenplay, Jeanie Macpherson; camera, Alvin Wyckoff; editor, Anne Bauchens.

Elliott Dexter (James Denby Porter); Gloria Swanson (Leila Porter); Lew Cody (Schuyler Van Sutphen); Sylvia Ashton (Mrs. Huckney); Theodore Roberts (The Bishop); Julia Faye (Nanette); James Neill (Butler); Ted Shawn (Faun).

FOR BETTER, FOR WORSE (Artcraft-PAR, 1919)

Producer-director, Cecil B. DeMille; based on the play by Edgar Selwyn; adaptation, William C. deMille; screenplay, Jeanie MacPherson; camera, Alvin Wyckoff; editor, Anne Bauchens.

Elliott Dexter (Dr. Edward Meade); Tom Forman (Richard Burton); Gloria Swanson (Sylvia Norcross); Sylvia Ashton (Sylvia's Aunt); Raymond Hatton (Bud); Theodore Roberts (Hospital Head); Wanda Hawley (Betty Hoyt); Winter Hall (Doctor); Jack Holt (Crusader); Fred Huntley (Colonial Soldier).

MALE AND FEMALE (Artcraft-PAR, 1919)

Producer-director, Cecil B. DeMille; based on the play *The Admirable Crichton* by James M. Barrie; screenplay, Jeanie Macpherson; camera, Alvin Wyckoff; editor, Anne Bauchens.

Gloria Swanson (Lady Mary Lasenby); Thomas Meighan (Crichton, A Butler); Lila Lee (Tweeny); Theodore Roberts (Lord Loam); Raymond Hatton (Honest Ernest Wolley); Mildred Reardon (Agatha Lasenby); Bebe Daniels (The King's Favorite); Robert Cain (Lord Brockelhurst); Julia Faye (Susan); Rhy Darby (Lady Eileen Dun Craigie); Maym Kelso (Lady Brockelhurst); Edward Burns (Treherne); Henry Woodward (McGuire); Sydney Deane (Thomas); Wesley Barry ("Buttons"); Lillian Leighton (Mrs. Perkins); Guy Oliver (Pilot of Yacht); Clarence Burton (Yacht Captain).

WHY CHANGE YOUR WIFE (Artcraft-PAR, 1920)

Producer-director, Cecil B. DeMille; based on a story by William C. DeMille; adaptation by Olga Printzlau, Sada Cowan; camera, Alvin Wyckoff; editor, Anne Bauchens.

Gloria Swanson (Beth Gordon); Thomas Meighan (Robert Gordon); Bebe Daniels (Sally Clark); Theodore Kosloff (Radinoff); Sylvia Ashton (Aunt Kate); Clarence Geldart (The Doctor); Maym Kelso (Harriette); Lucien Littlefield (Butler); Edna Mae Cooper (Maid); Jane Wolfe (Woman Client).

SOMETHING TO THINK ABOUT (Artcraft-PAR, 1920)

Producer-director, Cecil B. DeMille; screenplay, Jeanie Macpherson; camera, Alvin Wyckoff, Karl Struss; editor, Anne Bauchens.

Elliott Dexter (David Markley); Gloria Swanson (Ruth Anderson); Monte Blue (Jim Dirk); Theodore Roberts (Luke Anderson); Claire McDowell (Housekeeper); Mickey Moore (Bobby); Julia Faye (Banker's Daughter); James Mason (Country Masher); Togo Yammamoto (Servant); Theodore Kosloff (Clown).

HER GILDED CAGE (PAR, 1922) 6,249'

Director, Sam Wood; based on the play *The Love Dreams* by Anne Nichols; screenplay, Elmer Harris, Percy Heath; camera Alfred Gilks.

Gloria Swanson (Suzanne Ornoff); David Powell (Arnold Pell); Harrison Ford (Lawrence Pell); Anne Cornwall (Jacqueline Ornoff); Walter Hiers (Bud Walton); Charles A. Stevenson (Gaston Petitfils).

THE IMPOSSIBLE MRS. BELLEW (PAR, 1922) 7,155'

Director, Sam Wood; based on the novel by David Lesle; screenplay, Percy Heath; Monte Katterjohn; camera, Alfred Gilks.

Gloria Swanson (Betty Bellew); Robert Cain (Lance Bellew); Conrad Nagel (John Helstan); Richard Wayne (Jerry Woodruff); Frank Elliott (Count Radistoff); Gertrude Astor (Alice Granville); June Elvidge (Naomi Templeton); Herbert Standing (Rev. Dr. Helstan); Mickey Moore (Lance Bellew, Jr.—Age 4); Pat Moore (Lance Bellew, Jr.—Age 6); Helen Dunbar (Aunt Agatha); Arthur Hill (Attorney Potter); Clarence Burton (Detective).

MY AMERICAN WIFE (PAR, 1923) 6,061'

Director, Sam Wood; story, Hector Turnbull; screenplay, Monte M. Katterjohn; camera, Alfred Gilks.

Gloria Swanson (Natalie Chester); Antonio Moreno (Manuel LaTassa); Josef Swickard (Don Fernando DeContas); Eric Mayne (Carlos DeGrossa); Gino Corrado (Pedro DeGrossa); Edythe Chapman (Donna Isabella LaTassa); Eileen Pringle (Hortensia de Vareta); Walter Long (Gomez); F. R. Butler (Horace Peresford); Jacques D'Auray (Gaston Navarre); Loyal Underwood (Danny O'Hare); Mary Land (Maid).

PRODIGAL DAUGHTERS (PAR, 1923) 6,216'

Director, Sam Wood; based on the novel by Joseph Hocking; screenplay, Monte M. Katterjohn; camera, Alfred Gilks.

Gloria Swanson (Swiftie Forbes); Ralph Graves (Roger Corbin); Vera Reynolds (Marjory Forbes); Theodore Roberts (J. D. Forbes); Louise Dresser (Mrs. Forbes); Charles Clary (Stanley Garside); Robert Agnew (Lester Hodge); Maude Wayne (Connie); Jiquel Lanoe (Juda Botanya); Eric Mayne (Dr. Marco Strong).

BLUEBEARD'S EIGHTH WIFE (PAR, 1923) 5,960'

Director, Sam Wood; based on the play by Alfred Savoir; adaptation by Charlton Andrews; screenplay, Sada Cowan; camera, Alfred Gilks.

Gloria Swanson (Mona deBriac); Huntley Gordon (John Brandon); Charles Greene (Robert); Lianne Salvor (Lucienne); Paul Weigel (Marquis deBriac); Frank R. Butler (Lord Henry Seville); Robert Agnew (Albert de Marceau); Irene Dalton (Alice George); and Majel Coleman, Thais Valdemar.

ZAZA (PAR, 1923) 7,076'

Producer-director, Allan Dwan; based on the play by Pierre Berton, Charles Simon; screenplay, Albert Shelby Le Vino; camera, Hal Rosson.

Gloria Swanson (Zaza); H. B. Warner (Bernard Dufresne); Ferdinand Gottschalk (Duke deBrissac); Lucille LaVerne (Aunt Rose); Mary Thurman (Florianne); Yvonne Hughes (Nathalie, Zaza's Maid); Riley Hatch (Regault); Roger Lytton (Stage Manager); Ivan Linow (Apache Dancer); Helen Mack (daughter).

THE GREAT MOMENT (PAR, 1920) 6,372'

Director, Sam Wood; story, Elinor Glyn; screenplay, Monte M. Katterjohn; camera Alfred Gilks.

Gloria Swanson (Nadine Pelham); Alec B. Francis (Sir Edward Pelham); Milton Sills (Bayard Delavel); F. R. Butler (Eustace); Arthur Hull (Hopper); Raymond Brathwayt (Lord Crombie); Helen Dunbar (Lady Crombie); Clarence Geldert (Bronson); Julia Faye (Sadie Bronson); Ann Grigg (Blenkensop).

THE AFFAIRS OF ANATOL (PAR, 1921) 8,806'

Producer-director, Cecil B. DeMille; based on the play *Anatol* by Arthur Schnitzler and the paraphrase by Granville Barker; screenplay, Jeanie Macpherson, Beulah Marie Dix, Lorna Moon, Elmer Harris; camera, Alvin Wyckoff, Karl Struss; editor, Anne Bauchens.

Wallace Reid (Anatol DeWitt Spencer); Gloria Swanson (Vivian Spencer); Elliot Dexter (Max Runyon); Bebe Daniels (Satan Synne); Monte Blue (Abner Elliott); Wanda Hawley (Emilie Dixon); Theodore Roberts (Gordon Bronson); Agnes Ayres (Annie Elliott); Theodore Kosloff (Nazzer Singh); Polly Moran (Orchestra Leader); Raymond Hatton (Hoffmeier); Julia Faye (Tibra); Charles Ogle (Dr. Bowles); Winter Hall (Dr. Johnson); Guy Oliver (Spencer Butler); Ruth Miller (Spencer Maid); Lucien Littlefield (Spencer Valet); Shannon Day (Chorus Girl); Elinor Glyn, Lady Parker (Bridge Players).

UNDER THE LASH (PAR, 1921) 5,675'

Director, Sam Wood; based on the novel *The Shulamite* by Alice and Claude Askew and the play by Claude Askew, Edward Knoblock; screenplay, J. E. Nash, assistant director, A. R. Hamm; camera, Alfred Gilks.

Gloria Swanson (Deborah Krillet); Mahlon Hamilton (Robert Waring); Russell Simpson (Simeon Krillet); Lillian Leighton (Tant Anna Vanderberg); Lincoln Steadman (Jan Vanderberg); Thena Jasper (Memke); Clarence Ford (Kaffir Boy).

DON'T TELL EVERYTHING (PAR, 1921) 4,939'

Director Sam Wood; story Loran Moon: secreenplay, Albert Shelby LeVino; camera, Alfred Gilks; assistant director, A.K. Hamm; supervision, Thompson Buchanan.

Wallace Reid (Cullen Dale); Gloria Swanson (Marian Westover); Elliot Dexter (Harvey Gilroy); Dorothy Cumming (Jessica Ramsey); Genevieve Blinn (Mrs. Morgan); Baby Gloria Wood (Cullen's Niece); de Briac Twins (Morgan Twins).

HER HUSBAND'S TRADEMARK (PAR, 1922) 5,101'

Director, Sam Wood; story, Clara Beranger; screenplay, Lorna Moon; camera, Alfred Gilks.

Gloria Swanson (Lois Miller); Richard Wayne (Allan Franklin); Stuart Holmes (James Berkeley); Lucien Littlefield (Slithy Winters); Charles Ogle (Father Berkeley); Edythe Chapman (Mother Berkeley); Clarence Burton (Mexican Bandit); James Neill (Henry Strom).

BEYOND THE ROCKS (PAR, 1922) 6,740'

Director, Sam Wood; based on the novel by Elinor Glyn; screenplay, Jack Cunningham; camera, Alfred Gilks.

Gloria Swanson (Theodora Fitzgerald); Rudolph Valentino (Lord Bracondale); Edythe Chapman (Lady Bracondale); Alec B. Francis (Captain Fitzgerald); Robert Bolder (Josiah Brown); Gertrude Astor (Morella Winmarleigh); Mabel Van Buren (Mrs. McBride); Helen Dunbar (Lady Ada Fitzgerald) Raymond Balthwayt (Sir Patrick Fitzgerald); F. R. Butler (Lord Wensleydon), June Elvidge (Lady Anningford).

THE HUMMING BIRD (PAR, 1924) 7,577'

Director, Sidney Olcott; based on the play by Maude Fulton; screenplay Forrest Halsey. camera, Harry Fischbeck; editor, Patricia Rooney.

Gloria Swanson (Toinette); Edward Burns (Randall Carey); William Ricciardi (Papa Jacques); Cesare Gravina (Charlot); Mario Majeroni (La Roche); Adrienne d'Ambricourt (The Owl); Helen Lindroth (Henrietta Rutherford); Rafael Bongini (Bouchet); Regina Quinn (Beatrice); Jacques D'Auray (Zi-Zi); Aurelio Coccia (Bosque).

A SOCIETY SCANDAL (PAR, 1924) 6,433'

Producer-director, Allan Dwan; based on the play *The Laughing Lady* by Alfred Sutro; screenplay, Forrest Halsey; camera, Hal Rosson.

Gloria Swanson (Marjorie Colbert); Rod LaRocque (Harrison Peters); Allan Simpson (Hector Colbert); Ida Waterman (Mrs. Maturin Colbert); Thelma Converse (Mrs. Hamilton Pennfield); Fraser Coalter (Mr. Schuyler Burr); Catherine Proctor (Mrs. Burr); Wilfred Donovan (Mr. Hamilton Pennfield); Yvonne Hughes (Patricia DeVoe); Catherine Coleburn, Marie Shelton, Dorothy Stokes, Cornelius Keefe (Friends of Marjorie).

MANHANDLED (Paramount, 1924) 6,998'

Producer-director, Allan Dwan; based on the story by Arthur Stringer; screenplay, Frank W. Tuttle; camera, Hal Rosson; editor, William LeBaron.

Gloria Swanson (Tessie McGuire); Tom Moore (Jim Hogan); Frank Morgan (Arno Riccardi); Lilyan Tashman (Pinkie Doran); Paul McAlister (Paul Garretson); Ian Keith (Robert Brandt); Frank Allworth (Salesman); Arthur Housman (Chip Thorndyke); Ann Pennington (Herself); Mrs. Carrie Scott (Boarding House Keeper); Marie Shelton (Model); Brooke Johns (Himself); M. Colosse (Bippo).

HER LOVE STORY (PAR, 1924) 6,750'

Producer-director, Allan Dwan; based on the story "Her Majesty, the Queen" by Mary Roberts Rinehart; screenplay, Frank W. Tuttle; camera, George Webber.

Gloria Swanson (Princess Marie); Ian Keith (Captain Kavor); George Fawcett (Archduke); Echlen Goyer (King); Mario Majeroni (Prime Minister); Donald Hall (Court Physician); Baroness de Hedeman (Lady in Waiting) Jane Auburn (Clothilde); Bert Wales (Boy); General Lodijensky (Minister of War).

WAGES OF VIRTUE (PAR, 1924) 7,093'

Director, Allan Dwan; based on the novel by Percival Christopher Wren; screenplay, Forrest Halsey; camera, George Webber.

Gloria Swanson (Carmelita); Ben Lyon (Marvin); Norman Trevor (John Boule); Ivan Linow (Luigi); Armand Cortez (Guiseppe); Andrienne d'Ambricourt (Madame Cantiniere); Paul Panzer (Sgt Le Gros); Joe Moore (Le Bro-way).

MADAME SANS-GENE (PAR, 1925) 9,994'

Director, Leonce Perret; based on the play by Victorien Sardou, Emile Moreau; screenplay, Forrest Halsey; camera George Webber.

Gloria Swanson (Catherine Hubscher); Emile Drain (Napoleon); Charles DeRoche (Lefebvre); Madeleine Guitty (La Rousette); Warwick Ward (Neipperg) Henry Favieres (Fouche); Arlette Marchal (Queen of Naples); Renee Heribell (Eliza, Princess of Bacciocni); Suzanne Bianchett (Empress); Denise Lorys (Madame De Bulow); Jacques Marney (Savary).

THE COAST OF FOLLY (PAR, 1925) 7,000'

Producer-director, Allan Dwan; based on the novel by Coningsby Dawson; adaptation, James A. Creelman; screenplay, Forrest Halsey.

Gloria Swanson (Nadine Gathway/Joyce Gathway); Anthony Jowitt (Larry Fay); Alec B. Francis (Count de Tauro); Dorothy Cumming (Constance Fay); Jed Prouty (Cholly Knickerbocker); Eugene Besserer (Nanny); Arthur Housman (Reporter); Lawrence Gray (Bather); and: Charles Clary, Richard Arlen.

STAGE STRUCK (PAR, 1925) 6,691'

Producer-director, Allan Dwan; based on the story by Frank R. Adams; adaptation, Sylvia La Varre; screenplay, Forrest Halsey; camera, George Webber.

Gloria Swanson (Jennie Hagen); Lawrence Gray (Orme Wilson); Gertrude Astor (Lillian Lyons); Marguerite Evans (Hilda Wagner); Ford Sterling (Buck); Carrie Scott (Mrs. Wagner); Emil Hock (Mr. Wagner); Margery Whittington (Soubrette).

UNTAMED LADY (PAR, 1926) 6,132'

Director, Frank Tuttle; story, Fanny Hurst; screenplay, James A. Creelman, camera George Webber.

Gloria Swanson (St. Clair Van Tassel); Lawrence Gray (Larry Gastlen); Joseph Smiley (Uncle George); Charles Graham (Shorty).

FINE MANNERS (PAR, 1926) 6,435'

Director, Richard Rosson, story, James A. Creelman, Frank Vreiland; screenplay, Creelman; camera, George Webber.

Gloria Swanson (Orchid Murphy); Eugene O'Brien (Brian Alden); Helen Dunbar (Aunt Agatha); Walter Goss (Buddy Murphy); John Miltern (Courtney Adams).

THE LOVES OF SUNYA (UA, 1927) 7,311'

Director, Albert Parker; based on the play *The Eyes of Youth* by Max Marcin, Charles Guernon; screenplay, Earle Brown; titles, Cosmo Hamilton; art director, Hugo Ballin; special camera, Dudley Murphy.

Hugh Miller (The Outcast); Gloria Swanson (Sunya Ashling); John Boles (Paul Judson); Florbelle Fairbanks (Rita Ashling); Raymond Hackett (Kenneth Ashling); John Miltern (Asa Ashling); Anders Randolf (Robert Goring); Andres de Segurola (Paolo de Salvo); Robert Schable (Henri Picard); Pauline Garou (Anne Hagan); Ivan B. Lebedeff (Ted Morgan).

SADIE THOMPSON (UA, 1928) 8,600'

Director, Raoul Walsh; based on the story "Rain" by W. Somerset Maugham; tales C. Gardner Sullivan, art director, William Cameron Merzela; assistant director, William Tummel; camera George Barnes, Robert Kurrle, editor, Gardener Sullivan.

Lionel Barrymore (Alfred Atkinson); Blanche Frederici (Mrs. Atkinson); Charles Lane (Dr. McPhail); Florence Midgley (Mrs. McPhail); James A. Marcus (Joe Horn); Sophie Arlega (Amiena); Will Stanton (Quartermaster Batas); Raoul Walsh (Sgt. Tim O'Hara); Gloria Swanson (Sadie Thompson).

QUEEN KELLY (UA, 1929) 90 M.

Director-screenplay, Erich von Stroheim; titles, Marion Ainslee; assistant director, Eddy Sowders; Louis Germonprer; camera, Gordon Pollock, Paul Ivano; editor, Viola Lawrence; music, Franz Lehar.

Gloria Swanson (Patricia Kelly); Walter Byron (Prince Wild Wolfram); Seena Owen (The Queen); Sidney Bracey (The Prince's Butler); William von Brincken (Wolfram's Lieutenant); Wilson Benge (Valet); Tully Marshall (Jan Vryheid); Sylvia Ashton (Kelly's Aunt); Gordon Westcott (Lackey).

THE TRESPASSER (UA, 1929) 90 M.

Executive Producer, Joseph P. Kennedy; producer-director-screenplay, Edmund Goulding; editorial associates, Cyril Gardner, Laura Hope Crews; music, Josiah Zuro; songs, Elsie Janis and Goulding, Enrico Toselli and Sig Spaeth; camera, George Barnes, Gregg Toland.

Gloria Swanson (Marion Donnell); Robert Ames (Jack Merrick); Purnell Pratt (Hector Ferguson); Kay Hammond (Catherine "Flip" Merrick); William Holden (John Merrick, Sr.); Henry B. Walthall (Fuller); Wally Albright (Jack Merrick); Blanche Frederici (Miss Potter); Marcelle Corday (Blanche); Mary Forbes (Mrs. Ferguson); Bill O'Brien (Butler); Lloyd Whitlock (Member of Board of Directors) Allan

Cavan (Doctor); Ed Brady (Moving Man); Henry Armetta (Barber); Stuart Erwin, Dick Cramer, Billy Bevan, Brooks Benedict (Reporters).

WHAT A WIDOW! (UA, 1930) 88 M.

Executive producer, Joseph P. Kennedy; producer-director, Allan Dwan; screenplay, Josephine Lovett; dialogue, James Gleason, James Seymour; songs, Vincent Youmans; music, Josiah Zuro; art director, Paul Nelson; orchestrations, Dr. Hugo Felix; camera, George Barnes; editor, Viola Lawrence.

Gloria Swanson (Tamarind Brook); Owen Moore (Gerry Morgan); Lew Cody (Victor); Margaret Livingston (Valli); William Holden (Mr. Lodge); Herbert Braggiotti (Jose Alvarado); Gregory Gaye (Baslikoff); Adrienne d'Ambricourt (Paulette); Nella Walker (Marquise); Daphne Pollard (Masseuse).

INDISCREET (UA, 1931) 92 M.

Director, Leo McCarey; based on "Obey that Impulse" by Lew Brown, B. G. DeSylva, and Ray Henderson; screenplay-songs, Brown, DeSylva, and Henderson; camera, Ray June, Gregg Toland; editor, Hal C. Kern.

Gloria Swanson (Geraldine Trent); Ben Lyon (Tony Blake); Monroe Owsley (Jim Woodward); Barbara Kent (Joan Trent); Arthur Lake (Buster Collins); Maude Eburne (Aunt Kate); Henry Kolker (Mr. Woodward); Nella Walker (Mrs. Woodward).

TONIGHT OR NEVER (UA, 1931) 80 M.

Director, Mervyn LeRoy; based on the play by Lily Hatvany; screenplay, Ernest Vadja; camera, Gregg Toland; editor, Grant Whytock.

Gloria Swanson (Nella Vago); Ferdinand Gottschalk (Rudig); Robert Grieg (Butler); Greta Meyer (Maid); Warburton Gamble (Count Albert Von Gronac; Melvyn Douglas (Unknown Gentleman); Alison Skipworth (Marchesa); Boris Karloff (Waiter).

A PERFECT UNDERSTANDING (UA, 1933) 80 M.

Director, Cyril Gardner; story, Miles Malleson; adaptation, Michael Powell; dialoguer, Malleson; camera, Curt Courant; editor, T. Dickinson.

Gloria Swanson (Judy); Laurence Olivier (Nicholas); John Halliday (Ronnson); Sir Nigel Playfair (Lord Portleigh); Michael Farmer (George); Genevieve Tobin (Kitty); Nora Swinburne (Stephanie); Charles Cullum (Sir John); Peter Gawthrone (Butler); Raslinde Fuller (Cook); Evelyn Bostock (Maid); O. B. Clarence (Dr. Graham); Mary Jerrold (Mrs. Graham).

MUSIC IN THE AIR (FOX, 1934) 85 M.

Director, Joe May; based on the play by Oscar Hammerstein II and Jerome Kern; screenplay, Howard Young, Billy Wilder; choreography, Jack Donahue; songs, Hammerstein and Kern; camera, Ernest Palmer.

Gloria Swanson (Frieda); John Boles (Bruno); Douglass Montgomery (Karl); June Lang (Sieglinde); Al Shean (Dr. Lessing); Reginald Owen (Weber); Joseph Cawthorn (Uppman); Hobart Bosworth (Cornelius); Sara Haden (Martha); Marjorie Main (Anna); Roger Imhof (Burgomaster); Jed Prouty (Kirschner); Christian Rub (Zipfelhuber); Fuzzy Knight (Nick).

FATHER TAKES A WIFE (RKO, 1941) 80 M.

Producer, Lee. S. Marcus; director, Jack Hively; screenplay, Dorothy and Herbert Fields; music, Roy Webb; camera, Robert de Grasse; editor, George Hively.

Adolphe Menjou (Senior); Gloria Swanson (Leslie Collier); John Howard (Junior); Desi Arnaz (Carlos); Helen Broderick (Aunt Julie); Florence Rice (Enid); Neil Hamilton (Vincent); George Meader (Henderson); Mary Treen (Secretary); Ruth Dietrich (Miss Patterson); Grady Sutton (Fitter); Frank Reicher (Captain); Grant Withers (Judge Waters); Pierre Watkin (Mr. Fowler); Georgie Choper (Agnes, The Maid); Teddy Peterson, Lorna Dunn, Mary Arden (Secretaries); George Murray (Tailor); Frank Jaquet (Inn Keeper); Netta Packer (Inn Keeper's Wife); Edythe Elliott (Mrs. Plant); William Dudley (Mr. Porter); Lois Austin (Mrs. Sturgis); Jerry Storm (Stage Manager); Cliff Bragdon (Taxi Driver); Dorothy Vernon (Sewing Woman); William Gould (Ship Captain); Sally Cairns (Cigarette girl); Broderick O'Farrell (Junior's Butler); Ruth Dwyer (Nurse).

SUNSET BOULEVARD (PAR, 1950) 110 M.

Producer, Charles Brackett; director, Billy Wilder; based on the story "A Can of Beans" by Brackett, Wilder; screenplay, Brackett, Wilder, D. M. Marshman, Jr.; art director, Hans Dreier, John Meehan; music, Franz Waxman; camera, John F. Seitz; editor, Doane Harrison, Arthur Schmidt.

William Holden (Joe Gillis); Gloria Swanson (Norma Desmond); Erich von Stroheim (Max Von Mayerling); Nancy Olson (Betty Schaefer); Fred Clark (Sheldrake); Jack Webb (Artie Green); Lloyd Gough (Mornio); Buster Keaton, Hedda Hopper, Cecil B. DeMille, Anna Q. Nilsson; H. B. Warner, Ray Evans, Jay Livinston, Sidney Skolsky (Themselves); Franklyn Farnum (Undertaker); Larry Blake, Charles Dayton (Finance Men); Eddie Dew (Assistant Coroner); Archie Twitchell (Salesman); Ruth Clifford (Sheldrake's Secretary); Bert Moorhouse (Gordon Cole); E. Mason Hopper (Doctor/Courtier); Stan Johnson, William Sheehan (Assistant Directors); Virginia Randolph, Gertrude Astor, Frank O'Connor, Eva Novak (Courtiers); Gertie Messinger (Hairdresser); John "Skins" Miller (Electrician); Robert E. O'Connor (Policeman); Gerry Ganzer (Connie); Tommy Ivo (Boy); Emmett Smith (Man); Julia Faye (Hisham); Ken Christy (Captain of Homicide); Howard Negley (Captain of Police); Len Hendry (Police Sergeant).

THREE FOR BEDROOM C (WB, 1952) 74 M.

Associate producer, Edward L. Alperson, Jr.; director, Milton H. Bren; based on the novel by Goddard Lieberson; screenplay, Bren; music, Heinz Roemheld; camera, Ernest Laszlo; editor, Arthur Hilton.

Gloria Swanson (Ann Haven); James Warren (Oli J. Thrumm); Fred Clark (Johnny Pizer); Hans Conried (Jack Bleck); Steve Brodie (Conde Marlow); Janine Porreau (Barbara); Ernest Anderson (Fred Johnson); Margaret Dumont (Mrs. Hawthorne).

MIO FIGLIO NERONE (NERO'S MISTRESS) (Titanus, 1958) 104 M.

Director, Steno; story, Rodolfo Sonego; camera, Mario Bava.

Alberto Sordi (Nero); Gloria Swanson (Agrippina); Vittorio DeSica (Seneca); Brigitte Bardot (Poppea).

CHAPLINESQUE, MY LIFE AND HARD TIMES (Xanadu, 1972) 60 M.

Producer-director-screenplay, Harry Hurwitz; music, Stuart Oderman.

Gloria Swanson (Narrator).

Keystone Comedy publicity pose, about 1916

A more exotic Gloria, about 1919–20

Gloria Swanson in 1934

In DON'T CHANGE YOUR HUSBAND (Artcraft-Par '19)

With Thomas Meighan in MALE AND FEMALE (Artcraft-Par '19)

With Wallace Reid in THE AFFAIRS OF ANATOL (Par '21)

In HER GILDED CAGE (Par '22)

In ZAZA (Par '23)

With Ford Sterling (left) in STAGE STRUCK (Par '25)

With Anthony Jowitt in THE COAST OF FOLLIES (Par '25)

With Lionel Barrymore in SADIE THOMPSON (UA '28)

With Seena Owen in QUEEN KELLY (UA '29)

With Owen Moore in WHAT A WIDOW! (UA '30)

In INDISCREET (UA '31)

With Melvyn Douglas in TONIGHT OR NEVER (UA '31)

With John Halliday in A PERFECT UNDERSTANDING (UA '33)

With Al Sheen, Reginald Owen, Douglass
Montgomery, John Boles, and June Lang
in MUSIC IN THE AIR (Fox '34)

With Florence Rice, John Howard, and
Adolph Menjou in FATHER TAKES A
WIFE (RKO '41)

With William Holden in SUNSET BOULE-
VARD (Par '50)

In SUNSET BOULEVARD

With Fred Clark, Hans Conried, and Steve
Brodie in THREE FOR BEDROOM C (WB
'52)

CLARA BOW

5′3 ½″
110 pounds
Fiery red hair
Brown eyes
Leo

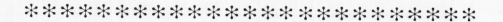

FEW OF today's generation have seen any of Clara Bow's 56 feature films, but the mention of her name immediately connotes America's age of innocence, the Roaring Twenties, and the wild flaming youth who epitomized the decade. Ever since she starred in Paramount's *It* (1927), Clara was branded as the exuberant symbol of the period, touted as the prize living exponent of all its liberated excesses. Actually, Clara portrayed the jazz age baby in only a dozen or so of her screen appearances, but it was this characterization that earned her star status as Paramount's top moneymaker in 1927 and 1928. She was never much of an actress, but in all her vehicles she displayed unbounded energy (more so than the later Lupe Velez or Betty Hutton) and a *joie de vivre* that instantly communicated itself to audiences. The mixture of her vibrant personality and cute good looks—bobbed hair, cupid's bow lips, wide, sparkling eyes, and ripe figure—made her the screen sensation of that self-enclosed era.

In the early 1920s, every American girl dreamed of winning a fan magazine beauty contest as a stepping stone into a screen career. Clara was one of the few winners who made good via this approach. After performing bits in assorted low-budget features in 1922–23, the best of which was *Down to the Sea in Ships,* Clara was signed to a film contract by independent producer B. P. Schulberg, head of the almost poverty-row production unit, Preferred Pictures. Schulberg effectively exploited Clara's vivacious screen personality by loaning her out to other producers at an increasingly lucrative profit. She was one of the Wampas Baby Stars of 1924 and in that year and the next, she appeared in 24 features, ranging from the superior Ernst Lubitsch *Kiss Me Again* (1925) to the best of her Preferred vehicles, the role of the flapper in *The Plastic Age* (1925) and to the dismal Fox feature, *Ancient Mariner* (1926).

When Schulberg returned to Paramount in 1926 in an executive capacity, Clara's contract was sold to the studio. Her initial vehicle, *Dancing Mothers* (1926), established her forte for emancipated flapper roles, and proved what the critics had been saying all along, that she should forget aspiring to high dramatic status and be the irrepressible doll she portrayed so well. She did just that to truly phenomenal success. She might do box-office duty as the pert Red Cross ambulance driver in *Wings* (1927), or adequately convey the reformed racketeer gal in *Rough House Rosie* (1927) and *Ladies of the Mob* (1928), but it was always her film appearances as the uninhibited, man-trapping sweetheart that brought the customers in droves to her pictures.

Of all the stars spawned by the movies, Clara was perhaps the least aware of her tremendous box-office power and Paramount took full advantage of this, paying her far less than her marquee lure was worth. Being uneducated and a child of whim who suffered from mental instability, Clara drifted along with the tide, easily satisfied as long as she had a surplus of social activity in her hectic private life.

When Paramount joined the industry in converting to talking pictures in 1928, the jazz age was fast dying and the Depression was about to set in. Clara's speaking voice proved to be adequate, although it lacked polished diction. Since she was not accustomed to following the script or staying put, it was difficult to record her voice with the primitive equipment then available, and her early sound films suffered accordingly. These obstacles could have been overcome, but Clara was stereotyped by both the studio and the public as a jazz baby, and no one seemed anxious to let her escape the mold.

Just as Clara was adjusting to the demands of 1930s cinema styles, personal crises occurred, further impairing her none too stable health. Paramount was happy to drop her in favor of its new crop of screen recruits.

Clara made a fine comeback in Fox's *Call Her Savage* (1932), proving she had matured as a personality actress and was rather effective in the confession story genre handed to her. After *Hoopla* (1933), an indifferent remake of *The Barker,* Clara retired from the screen at age 26. Thereafter she was plagued by poor health, mental instability, and continual sieges of overweight, which prevented any possible screen comeback, let alone trying to lead a normal life as the wife of cowboy actor Rex Bell and the mother of two sons.

Clara died in 1965, forgotten by the industry. But the public still remembered her as a flamboyant example of a bygone era. Unlike many contemporary and later movie stars, she never became a camp figure. She remains a rambunctious sex symbol of coy femininity.

✳✳✳✳✳✳✳✳✳✳✳✳✳✳✳✳✳✳✳✳✳✳

Clara Gordon Bow was born July 29, 1907, the only child of Robert and Sarah (Gordon) Bow. The family lived in a small apartment over a Baptist church on Bergen Street in Bay Ridge, Brooklyn, New York. Both her parents were Brooklyn-born, of English-French and Scottish descent. Her father had left school at the age of 12 to earn his keep, working as a Coney Island waiter and later as a part-time handyman.

Mrs. Bow had given birth twice before having Clara. Both infant girls had died—one survived only two hours, the other two days. These ordeals ruined Mrs. Bow's physical and mental health. When Clara was born, both mother and daughter almost died. Thereafter, Mrs. Bow was a nervous semi-invalid.

Clara later recalled her impoverished childhood: "No one wanted me in the first place. My mother never knew a moment free from illness. I've never forgotten how she suffered." She later amplified: "They weren't regular fainting spells, she just seemed to go into a trance, I wouldn't know what to do and I'd cry. Our doctor told us Mother had a nervous disease. I worried about her, but we didn't have enough money to do for her."

The Bows lived in various sections of Brooklyn, always in extreme poverty. Clara remembered: "Often I was lonesome, frightened and miserable. . . . I never had a doll in my life. . . . I never had any clothes, and lots of times didn't have anything to eat. We just lived, and that's about all. Girls shunned me because I was so poorly dressed—the worst looking kid on the street. I decided that girls weren't any good, and being lonely and needing child friends, cast my lot with the neighborhood boys. I became a regular tomboy—played baseball, football and learned to box." Whenever she had the chance and the money, Clara would attend the movies and dream about becoming a movie star.

As a child, Clara experienced traumatic reactions to the death of two persons close to her. Her maternal grandfather, who lived with them, died when Clara was five years old. "The first night as he lay in his coffin in the dining room," Clara recalled years later; "I crept out of my bed and lay down on the floor beside him, because I had a feeling that he might be lonely. My father found me there in the morning, almost frozen. I said, 'Hush, you mustn't wake grandfather. He's sleeping.' " A few years later, Clara's downstairs neighbors' young son Johnny—one of her best friends—accidentally set his clothes on fire and burned to death. "The little fellow died in my arms. He was just—just all burned up, that's all."

Clara was never much of a student, preferring roller skating and sports to studying. She attended P.S. 98 in Sheepshead Bay; after completing the eighth grade, she worked as a telephone receptionist in a Brooklyn doctor's office.

Then in 1921 she borrowed $1 from her father to have a photograph of herself taken so she could enter the "Fame and Fortune" contest sponsored by *Motion Picture, Motion Picture Classic,* and *Shadowland* magazines. She eventually became a finalist in the contest and was asked to appear before the judges, who included Howard Chandler Christy, Harrison Fisher, and Neysa McMein. Sufficiently impressing them with her natural pantomime skills, she won a screen test, and in November, 1921, she was selected as the contest's national winner. The prizes consisted of an evening gown, a silver trophy, and a part in one motion picture.

Mrs. Bow was unnaturally displeased about Clara's potential film career. One night, Clara awoke to find her mother standing over her with a long knife at her throat. Clara would never forget the frightening incident:

"She stood there, pressing the cold knife at my throat, and saying I'd be better off dead.

"I tried to reason with mother. Finally I managed to knock the knife from her hand and run from the room.

"I locked myself in another room and cried and cried. I cried for mother as much as for myself. I knew she couldn't help it.

"My mother went back to bed and never mentioned the incident to me again."

Mrs. Bow was subsequently committed to a state mental hospital and died in 1923.

Clara's screen debut occurred in *Beyond the Rainbow* (1922). Her cousin David Decker loaned her $40 to purchase two dresses for the film. She played a flirtatious sub-deb who stirs up trouble at a fashionable New York ball by sending all the guests there the message "Consult your conscience. Your secret is common gossip." Billie Dove was the star of the programmer. Clara's sequences were cut out of the initial release prints because her performance was thought too amateurish and her movements much too jerky. Later, when she became a movie personality, the feature was reissued with her scenes reinstated. She was paid $50 a week for her initial movie work.

Clara's budding cinema career might have ended there—making the rounds of the Manhattan film studios for jobs proved fruitless—had not director Elmer Clifton come across her contest photo in a past issue of *Motion Picture* magazine. Clifton was shooting a low-budget whaling yarn, *Down to the Sea in Ships* (1922), on location in New Bedford, Massachusetts, and required additional players for his inexpensive cast of general unknowns. Clara was hired at $35 a week to play Dot Morgan, a young New England girl who stows away aboard the whaler. The picture was lensed in the New Bedford area over a 13-week period.

Down to the Sea in Ships (previously premiered in Providence, Rhode Island, in November, 1922) opened at the Cameo Theatre on February 18, 1923, and amassed word-of-mouth audience approval, though there were few critical accolades at first. Largely because of her comedy scenes in which she masquerades as a boy aboard ship, Clara received highly positive mention by the reviewers. *Variety* reported: ". . . [she] lingers in the eye after the picture has gone." Reviewer Robert E. Sherwood included Clara in his top performances of the year, as detailed in his book *Best Motion Pictures of 1922–23.*

Back in New York, Clara landed an unbilled bit in the independent production *Enemies of Women* (1923) set in Monte Carlo. She plays a flapper who does a tabletop dance. While she was filming this movie, her mother died.

Clara's father astutely arranged for his daughter to meet New York playwright-agent Maxine Alton, who in turn, induced J. G. Bachman, partner of B. P. Schulberg* in Preferred Pictures, to give Clara a three-month film contract at $50 a week. Train fare to Hollywood was included.

Schulberg was far from impressed when he first met the new talent find Maxine Alton had chaperoned to Hollywood, but on the agent's insistence, he gave her a hasty screen test. As Miss Alton would recall in 1929: "It was the most brutal experience a girl could have had. An ordinary person would have been petrified with fear. She would have known that her future hung

*See Appendix.

in the balance, and an unjust balance at that. Not simple, direct Clara! She took the test as calmly as she'd take one now. Without make-up, still in a sweater and skirt, she ran the gamut of emotions. Schulberg told her to laugh. She did. Suddenly he said, 'Stop laughing. Cry!' Immediately, in the snap of a finger, a flood of tears drenched her cheeks. She was an emotional machine! Schulberg turned to me, threw up his hands, and said, 'You win.' "

Much of Schulberg's accumulated revenue from Preferred Pictures lay in loaning out his contract players to other producers when they were not being used in the B-product he slapped together. Clara was part of the set dressing in Preferred's *Maytime* (1923), an inelastic rendition of the Sigmund Romberg generation-chronicle operetta, and she took a back seat to cabaret girl Mildred Harris who attempted to steal her beau in Equity's *The Daring Years* (1923).

In *Grit* (1924), based on an original F. Scott Fitzgerald screenplay about Manhattan's underworld, Clara was Orchid McGonigle, a refugee from the state reformatory, in love with boxer Glenn Hunter and pursued by gangland leader Osgood Perkins. *Moving Picture World* reported: "Clara Bow as the orchid of the alley is exceptionally pretty and blessed with a vivid expressiveness."

Black Oxen (1924), directed by Frank Lloyd, featured Corinne Griffith as a 58-year-old matron who loses 28 years via a rejuvenating glandular treatment and X-ray surgery. She attracts playwright Conway Tearle, only to leave him when her Austrian prince lover Alan Hale beckons. Clara was fifth-billed as the ever-present flapper who later consoles Tearle.

In Preferred's *Poisoned Paradise* (1924), Clara was an amateur gambler who loses her Monte Carlo stake and finds romance with artist Kenneth Harlan, whom she had attempted to pickpocket. In saving a professor acquaintance who has developed a surefire gambling system, they are almost the victims of gangland reprisal.

Clara's fourth of eight 1924 releases was *Daughters of Pleasure* (1924), in which she is a French miss having a rendezvous with the nouveau riche father (Wilfred Lucas) of her classmate Marie Prevost.

In Universal's modestly produced *Wine* (1924), Clara portrayed a demure socialite who flies loose as a wild flapper when her bankrupt father enters a partnership with bootleggers and her mother goes temporarily blind from bad booze. *Variety* noted: "Miss Bow is an acceptable giddy young thing going to the extreme of three different coiffures to make it more realistic."

Clara had brief roles in *Empty Hearts* (1924) as an ill-fated spouse, and in Warner Brothers' *This Woman* (1924), an untidy melodrama, most of the story centered on Irene Rich as a young singer falsely sent to prison.

Black Lightning (1924) starred the canine tricks of Thunder, the police dog; Clara suffers the rigor of rural life and bad types, with Roy Chambers as the recuperating World War I veteran whom she adores. *Moving Picture World* decided: "In a serious role that is as different from her flapper types as possible . . . she shows unusual versatility and scores heavily."

Although the quality of Clara's features was still unexceptional, she was gaining a small foothold in the industry. She was among the 13 players chosen by the Western Association of Motion Picture Advertisers for its 1924 crop of Wampas Baby Stars. Others that year included Elinor Fair, Carmelita Geraghty, Dorothy Mackaill, Blanche Mehaffey, Marian Nixon, and Alberta Vaughn. In actuality the award meant little beyond singling Clara out from the crowd and providing her with some short-term publicity.

Clara's 14 film appearances in 1925 provided her with maximum screen exposure. Schulberg was still too busy with his own financial manipulations and assorted power plays within the film industry to be terribly concerned about the shape of Clara's active but stagnating film career to date. In Preferred's *Capital Punishment* (1925), based on Schulberg's own story idea, Clara is the fiancee of George Hackathorne. He has agreed to be a guinea pig in Elliott Dexter's plan to prove that any innocent man can easily be convicted of murder on circumstantial evidence. When Dexter actually kills the hypothetical victim, it takes much doing to establish Hackathorne's innocence. *Capital Punishment* has a strong similarity to the much later *Beyond a Reasonable Doubt*, which starred Joan Fontaine and Dana Andrews.

Clara was barely noticed in *Helen's Babies* (1925), a domestic comedy, in which bachelor novelist Edward Everett Horton takes care of his two nieces, one of whom is professional antic toddler Baby Peggy. *The Adventurous Sex* (1925) again displayed Clara as a flapper. This time she almost ends her plight by a melodramatic fall over Niagara Falls.

Although Clara had top billing in Preferred's *My Lady's Lips* (1925) as the daughter of a newspaper publisher framed in a gambling raid, the story line focused more on star reporter William Powell and his doomed infatuation for gang leader Alyce Mills.

Parisian Lovers (1925) presented Clara as a jealous apache who seeks revenge on Donald Keith, her criminal partner and lover, by marrying wealthy Lou Tellegen, whom her gang intends to rob.

For Warner Brothers' *Eve's Lover* (1925), Clara essayed a flapper entranced by playboy Bert Lytell, but he has married businesswoman Irene Rich and wants to prove he is worthy. In reviewing this programmer, *Moving Picture World* said: "Clara Bow is a flash of temper as the aggrieved flapper." The *New York Times* described her as "pretty and vivacious and a little more."

Clara jumped into a more prestigious picture when cast in Ernst Lubitsch's *Kiss Me Again* (1925), made at Warner Brothers. She was fourth-billed in this sophisticated marital farce dealing with Parisian newspaper owner Monte Blue, whose bored wife, Marie Prevost, ensnares impecunious musician John Roche. Clara bounded through her role as the man-hungry legal stenographer whom Blue dates to arouse Prevost's ire. *Kiss Me Again* would be remade by Lubitsch as *That Uncertain Feeling* in 1941.

Scarlet West (1925) was an assembly-line independent Western, purchased for distribution by First National Pictures. Alternating with the main story of Custer's last stand was the melodrama of Clara, daughter of the post commander, who is idolized by Indian Robert Fraser. She naturally prefers her white suitor, a lieutenant played by Johnny Walker.

Clara was top-cast in Arrow's *The Primrose Path* (1925), offering her interpretation of a successful cabaret dancer who dotes on weak-willed playboy Wallace MacDonald in spite of the fact that he is a diamond smuggler. He kills his smuggler partner, Stuart Holmes, in self-defense, but is sent to prison and pardoned only at the last moment.

Finally perking up to the potential of Clara's screen image, Schulberg paid out much more than usual to acquire Percy Marks' best-selling novel *The Plastic Age*, a romanticized account of the jazz age morality prevalent in colleges. While the script was episodic and the production values typical of Schulberg's stringency, it proved an excellent showcase for Clara's vivacious personality, which needed no soundtrack to convey her zest for life.

In *The Plastic Age* (1925) Clara appeared as carefree coed Cynthia Day. She was part of the collegiate fast set in which rolled stockings, cigarettes, bootleg booze, Charleston dancing, snappy talk, and petting was everything. She has to reassess her flighty values when swain Donald Keith makes a poor showing in the big crew race because he has blindly accepted her wild ways. Having learned her lesson, she tones down. At graduation she and Keith reach an understanding. The *New York Times* said: "She has all the lissomeness of Lya de Putti, and eyes that would drag any youngster away from his books, and she knows how to use lips, shoulders and all the rest of her tiny self in the most effective manner. She radiates an elfin sensuousness."

In promoting *The Plastic Age*, Schulberg touted Clara as "the hottest jazz baby in films." Clara was fast catching up with Colleen Moore, the silent screen's leading progenitor of the flapper, much to the financial pleasure of Schulberg.

The Keepers Of The Bees (1925) was a quickie tearjerker in which a philosophical beekeeper bequeaths his hives to tomboyish Clara and a distraught World War I veteran. Only after the soldier has been married to Clara's cousin and then widowed, do Clara and he find the path to happiness. *Variety* emphasized the unbridled nature of Clara's screen acting, even at this stage of her experience: "Clara Bow acts all over the lot and aside from weeping and swirling around, does little."

Free To Love (1925) finds Clara unjustly sent to jail and later adopted by the judge in the case. The criminal system, as depicted in this Preferred picture, was a favorite subject of Schulberg's, and he would harp on it continually through his later stay at Paramount (1926–32). It also provided Clara with one of her three major film types, that of the jailbird, a characterization she would play equally as often as the flapper or the hoydenish miss capering with the boys.

In Fox's *The Best Bad Man* (1925), a Tom Mix vehicle based on a Max Brand novel, Clara was the steel-nerved leader of the ranchers who require Mix to fulfill his late father's promise to build an irrigation dam. Cyril Chadwick, as Mix's crooked agent, dynamites the dam, providing the Western with some fine action shots. Clara was miscast as the ever-resourceful heroine.

Lawful Cheaters (1925) again used the gambit of having Clara masquerading as a boy; this time to prompt a gang of crooks into reformation. *Variety* complimented her: "There is one very nice feature to this picture. That's the work of Clara Bow as Molly Burns. She was in there acting all the time, keeping the film tempo up pronto."

The Ancient Mariner (1926) was the first of Clara's eight 1926 features, and the most cheaply produced on all accounts. In the modern sequence, Clara nurses a worldly man through a siege of temporary blindness. The skipper on their boat relates the parable of the ancient mariner, roughly hewing to the same account utilized by Samuel Taylor Coleridge in his epic poem. This Fox film was so poor in quality that *Motion Picture Herald* reported in its exhibitors' column: "The best thing for you to do if you have this bought will be to pay for it if you have to and let it stay at the exchange. Dixie Theatre, Russellville, Ky."

My Lady of Whims (1926) returned Clara to a bouncy contemporary setting. She exits from her stuffy home to share a Greenwich Village apartment with Carmelita Geraghty and immensely enjoys her bohemian emancipation.

When Schulberg was brought back to Paramount in November, 1925, as an associate producer—and later as general manager of the Hollywood studio—Paramount's first-vice-president, Jessie L. Lasky,* purchased several of Schulberg's actor contracts (for example, Ethel Clayton's) as a bonus to the former head of Preferred Pictures. Clara's contract was acquired by Paramount for $25,000.

At the time, Gloria Swanson ruled the artist roost at Paramount, followed by her imported rival Pola Negri, and such lesser star attractions as Bebe Daniels, Betty Bronson, Florence Vidor, Esther Ralston, Alice Joyce, and Dorothy Gish, and further on down the popularity ladder, Greta Nissen and Jobyna Ralston, and such newcomers as Louise Brooks, Mary Brian, and Fay Wray.

Clara's first Paramount feature was *Dancing Mothers* (1926) starring Alice Joyce. In well-turned fashion, it presented a new twist on the jazz age scene by having Joyce regain her zest for life by flirting with playboy Conway Tearle to save her spunky daughter (Clara) from his worthless clutches. Having accomplished her mission all too well, Joyce goes abroad to seek forgetfulness with the blessing of her none-too-pure husband, Norman Trevor. Clara was third-billed as the neglectful, fun-loving daughter. *Variety* reported: "Somebody has told her [Clara] to quit trying to make everybody believe she's a great actress and just be herself, for the dark makeup on the eyes is out—the artificial emotion stuff is canned and her performance generally is the excellent result of an excellent director" (Herbert Brenon). It was a good start for Clara at one of Hollywood's biggest film factories.

Shadow of the Law (1926) was an independent feature Clara made before joining Paramount, but was released after *Dancing Mothers*. It was another crime melodrama with Clara railroaded into prison and seeking appropriate revenge upon release. *Two Can Play* (1926) had also been made at Associated Exhibitors at the same time. It presented George Fawcett tricking his daughter Clara into staying on a desert island with Allan Forrest and Wallace McDonald to see if either is worth marrying.

Paramount's second Clara Bow feature, *The Runaway* (1926) directed by William DeMille, cast Clara as a movie player on the run, thinking she has accidentally killed her movie associate, William Powell. She is sheltered by a Kentucky mountain family, and decides that the sincere clan leader, Warner Baxter, is worth more than a movie career. *Moving Picture World* decided: "As hysterical flapper she's off, better as mountain girl showing a commendable reserve where not long ago she might have overplayed."

In April, 1926, Paramount's trade advertisements listed Clara number 38 in its galaxy of stars. The top ten were: Harold Lloyd, Gloria Swanson, Thomas Meighan, Pola Negri, Richard Dix, Raymond Griffith, Bebe Daniels, Marjorie Douglas MacLean, W. C. Fields, and Esther Ralston.

Mantrap (1926), directed by Victor Fleming and based on the Sinclair Lewis novel, presented Clara as Alverna, a hep Minneapolis manicurist who is living in Canada as the wife of a sincere but uncouth, older backwoodsman (Ernest Torrence). She finds herself attracted to Percy Marmont, a famous divorce lawyer on a country vacation. Marmont eventually leaves out of respect for Torrence, but no sooner have Clara and her husband been reconciled with each other than another stranger appears on the scene and

*See Appendix.

•64•

flirtatious Clara is at work again. *Mantrap* did well at the box office. The *New York Times* championed Clara: "She could flirt with a grizzly bear." It remained one of her favorite films.

In *Kid Boots* (1926), Eddie Cantor made his screen debut as a salesman bailed out of difficulty with an infuriated client by playboy Lawrence Gray. As a return favor, Cantor agrees to help Gray obtain a divorce from his estranged wife, Billie Dove; at the same time falling for Clara, the sweetheart of the irate customer. The finale finds Cantor and Clara rushing to the court to assist Gray in winning his divorce decree, but before they arrive, the duo encounters a host of slapstick plights, including falling off horses, dangling from mountain ledges on ropes, and so forth. They persuade the same judge who grants Gray's divorce, to marry them.

By the end of 1926, Clara was receiving 40,000 fan letters a week, a new high. Although she lived—to all appearances—rather quietly at her Beverly Hills bungalow or at her Malibu beach cottage, she was always flamboyant in public. She became a familiar sight on Wilshire Boulevard (thanks to the studio publicity department), driving her flaming red Kessel car and accompanied by her seven chow dogs with their coats dyed to match her hair. Her father ("the best friend I ever had") lived with her when he first moved to California, and Clara set him up in a dry cleaning business. She was not above roller skating to the studio lot to pick up bundles of laundry for the family business. Mr. Bow, who spent much of his time writing to the various film fan magazines berating their editors for the unsuitable publicity she was given in their publications, later remarried and moved elsewhere.

Screen historian Richard Griffith has said that Clara Bow "was probably the most undereducated aspirant to stardom ever to make the grade, Marilyn Monroe not excepted. What she had that cancelled out all her minuses was a blazing vitality which brooked no control. . . . She threw the script aside; she bounded all over the set; she did, not what she was told, but whatever came into her head, and you had to be fast with the footwork even to keep her in camera range." Paramount was not sure how to solidify her image to peak advantage, but it had the resources to keep trying all possible avenues.

Madame Elinor Glyn, the showy British author of several pseudosophisticated romantic novels, and assorted daring screenplays like *Three Weeks,* had been under Paramount contract since 1925. In 1926 she wrote a novelette, *It,* in which she elucidated the magical qualities required:

"To have 'It,' the fortunate possessor must have that strange magnetism which attracts both sexes. 'It' is a purely virile quality, belonging to a strong character. He or she must be entirely unself-conscious and full of self-confidence, indifferent to the effect he or she is producing, and uninfluenced by others. There must be physical attraction, but beauty is unnecessary. Conceit or self-consciousness destroys 'It' immediately."

Schulberg agreed with Glyn that her book could be exploited as a film, and it was agreed that Clara would be promulgated as the very essence of "It" in the lead role. *It* (1927) showcased Clara as a saucy department store worker out to land store-owner Antonio Moreno. She almost loses his interest, but she intrudes on his yachting trip and through assorted wiles and a strong dose of "It" wins her man. The finale finds the duo hanging onto the yacht's hoisted anchor, revealing their love for one another. Glynn made a cameo appearance as herself in the film, explaining the qualities of "It" to Moreno in a restaurant sequence. *It* was actually not one of Clara's better vehicles, but it was enormously successful at the box office, establishing

Clara as a top Hollywood star and the idol of countless shopgirls who adopted her hair and makeup styles. Clara's success in this role as the ultimate flapper spawned a succession of other flapper movies in the Hollywood copycat system, starring such actresses as Joan Crawford, Sue Carol, Madge Bellamy, and Louise Brooks. (As if to ward off these imitation flappers, Madame Glyn carefully stated that the only other creatures in Hollywood who possessed "It" were Rex the wild stallion and the doorman at the Ambassador Hotel.)

It was Adolph Zukor, boss of the Paramount studio, who best described Clara, the essential "It" girl. In his autobiography *The Public Is Never Wrong*, he recalls that Clara "was exactly the same off the screen as on. She danced even when her feet were not moving. Some part of her was in motion in all her waking moments—if only her great rolling eyes. Though not beautiful, Clara was a striking girl, with red hair, a soft heart-shaped face, and a plump figure. Yet it was an elemental magnetism—sometimes described as animal vitality—that made her the center of attraction in any company. Clara truly did not care what people thought about her—didn't notice. But her warm personality and spontaneous generosity made her popular with those about her."

After *It*, Clara made a feature that was atypical for her, *Children of Divorce* (1927), which offered the studio's hotcha girl a straight dramatic role. Through trickery, she weds her childhood love, Gary Cooper. He prefers Esther Ralston, whom he had not married for fear it would end in divorce like their wealthy, spoiled parents' assorted marital forays. Clara eventually repents of her selfish maneuvering and commits suicide, leaving Cooper free to marry Ralston once she divorces her own errant husband. Bow at this time was dating Gary Cooper as well as director Victor Fleming. (She had dated Gilbert Roland in 1925. Clara said of him: "I'd never been in love in all my life. Funny, because I suppose people think I was born being in love with somebody. But Gilbert was the first man I ever cared about.") Cooper was given the lead in *Children of Divorce* at Clara's request, but he was not up to the assignment and gave an awkward screen performance. Director Frank Lloyd was not able to blend the material of *Children of Divorce* into a consistent whole, and Schulberg called in director Joseph von Sternberg to spice up the film, which he did. The still sluggish drama opened at the Rialto Theatre on April 25, 1927, to unimpressive notices. The *New York Times* found Clara "pretty and active"; *Film Daily* rather extravagantly declared: "In her every gesture [she] stamps herself a great actress." Officially Clara was still known to one and all as the "It" girl, replacing her former movie tag of the "Brooklyn Bonfire."

Rough House Rosie (1927) followed one of the star's special formulas. She plays a poor girl from Tenth Avenue who attempts to crash into society. Finding out how society leaders put down their inferiors, she returns to her prize fight beau (Reed Howes) just in time to inspire him for the big match. In her nightclub scenes, she had an act called "Rough House Rosie and Her Snootin' Little Leathernecks." Clara projected herself in this film as saucy and persistent, which pleased the fans. Mordaunt Hall (*New York Times*) observed: "Miss Bow cavorts charmingly through this stream of clever nonsense, making the most of her big, long-lashed brown eyes."

Wings (1927) had its big $2 per ticket premiere at the Criterion Theatre on August 12, 1927, and lived up to all expectations as the biggest and longest (139 minutes) air war film of the silent screen to that date. It even boasted the use of Magnascope widescreen to highlight the aerial combat scenes. Although for box-office lure Clara was top-starred as the small-town girl who goes to the French front during World War I as a nurse, her role was relatively small, and some of her scenes had been deleted to speed up the action. Charles "Buddy" Rogers and Richard Arlen play the two Air Service recruits who vie for honors in training camp, in the air, and for the affection of Jobyna Ralston. As the rather sedate girl next door who loves Rogers, Clara is quite subdued in *Wings*, albeit grand in her pert Red Cross uniform. Her one sequence of typical red hot exuberance occurred when Rogers becomes drunk. To save him from the MPs and court-martial, Clara poses as a Parisian trollop, low cut gown and all. For her noble efforts, her reputation is ruined and she is sent home in disgrace. Thereafter, Rogers and Arlen become seasoned fighter pilots. One day, Rogers accidentally shoots Arlen down in combat (the latter had stolen a German plane and was flying back to the base). After the Armistice, Rogers returns to America and announces he loves Clara after all. Clara was complimented for being "bright-eyed and attractive" (*New York Times*) and for giving "an all around corking performance." (*Variety*), but the bulk of the film's honors were bestowed on the aerial photography of the dogfights, all actually staged in the sky. The $2 million *Wings* won Oscars in the picture and engineering effects categories. Gary Cooper had a memorable scene early on in *Wings*, as the seasoned pilot at the training camp who eats half a chocolate bar while advising trainees Rogers and Arlen on their new professions, before he takes off on a fatal test run.

Wings grossed $16,376 during its first week at the 873-seat Criterion Theatre. It lasted a long 63 weeks at the theatre, before being transferred to the Rialto Theatre for a subsequent run.

Hula (1927), directed by Victor Fleming, opened a few weeks after *Wings* on August 28, 1927, and was an an all-out Clara vehicle. As Hula Calhoun, the neglected but pampered daughter of a Hawaiian planter, she sets her sights on British engineer Clive Brook. Widow Arlette Marschal competes for Brook, only to discover he has a wife, Maude Truax. Clara properly sizes up Truax as a gold digger, and blows up Brook's excavation project to make the wife believe her husband is now a pauper. The gambit works and Clara wins Brook. To vividly demonstrate Clara's unbridled screen nature, *Hula* includes scenes of her riding a horse into a sitting room, taking her terrier to the dinner table, swimming (seemingly) au naturel in a mountain lake, and vibrating in a grass skirt to a hula dance. The hotsy-totsy theme song for the film was "The Love Nest." Due to censorship problems, the release version of *Hula* was more episodic and choppy than intended.

Get Your Man (1927) was Clara's final release of 1927. She plays a pert American who meets future duke, Charles "Buddy" Rogers, in Paris. At infancy, he had been promised in marriage to Josephine Dunn, but he is only too willing to throw Dunn over for Clara after the proper persuasion. Director Dorothy Arzner began *Get Your Man* as a French farce and let it evolve into American slapstick, with Clara vamping and compromising Rogers into freedom and into her arms. The best moments occur when the two are locked overnight in the Eden Musée waxworks and Rogers's initial anger thaws to Clara's charms. One fan magazine reviewer cautioned: "Clara Bow doesn't bother much about a good story any more, or about good acting. She evidently imagines that just being herself is enough. And I guess it is for most of her audiences. Almost too much, it seemed, in this last effusion."

In 1927 Clara's salary rose to $2,700 a week, still not very much for someone who had taken Gloria Swanson's post as queen of the Paramount lot and whose features were bait enough to get exhibitors to accept a lot of junk under the block booking system. Unlike many movie star contemporaries, Clara had not yet learned—and never would—to deal successfully with her tremendous (for her) income, or to appreciate the extent of her power as a top-ranking Hollywood and international celebrity. She much preferred staying at home to play poker with her servants to trotting out to the bright spots of Hollywood where her lack of social graces caused continued embarrassments. Sooner than become a pseudo-fashion plate, she would bound around town in slacks and blouse. Clara did prove to have an insatiable appetite for romance and attention. There were headlines when Yale ex-freshman football player Robert S. Salvage slashed his wrists because, he claimed, Clara had jilted him. He stated that her kisses had made his lips ache for two days. Gambling and short-term romances were her pet avocations. Typical of Clara's impromptu flings was the night she invited the entire University of Southern California football squad over for a midnight practice session on her lawn.

While Clara may have been oblivious to her professional status, with its rights and obligations, she was extremely vulnerable as a simple, highly emotional woman. Her simultaneous powerhouse courtships with director Victor Fleming (born in 1883) and Gary Cooper (born 1901) brought her up short. She was unable to choose between these two suitors, particularly Cooper ("He's so jealous—he always believes the worst about me"), and this indecision allegedly led to the first of her several nervous breakdowns, which occurred during the filming of *Rough House Rosie.*

The first of Clara's four 1928 releases was *Red Hair,* directed by Clarence Badger from an Elinor Glyn original screenplay. It was a frivolous tale of a barbershop manicurist, Clara, who has three middle-aged admirers. She will not take money from them, but gifts are acceptable. Each of the men views her as an entirely different creature: a temperamental young lady, a quiet miss, and a vamp. The trio happen to be the guardians of wealthy Lane Chandler, whom Clara is drawn to and for whom she acts herself. *Red Hair* is memorable for its opening scene, filmed in technicolor and displaying Clara in a white bathing suit, with her fiery red hair silhouetted against the blue sky. Late in the story, Clara becomes indignant at a fancy party, and righteously returns her gifts to the admirers. In the process she disrobes down to a parlor robe and ermine wrap and scampers outside, only to have the coat snatched back by its giver—she then plunges into a nearby pool. All this script action was designed to reveal, in Glyn's outrageous and dated style, what a free soul Clara really was.

Ladies of the Mob (1928) was another entry in Schulberg's gangster cycle. Based on a rugged, realistic story of Folsom Prison, the movie emerged as an unconvincing underworld melodrama. Clara, the daughter of a deceased criminal, brought up by her mother to revenge herself on the law, falls in love with crook Richard Arlen and induces him to reform. *Variety* lambasted: "It is not typical or good Clara Bow material neither is it typical or good modern crook melodrama."

The snappy *The Fleet's In* (1928) returned Clara to expected and profitable form. It revealed her as the siren of San Francisco's Roseland Dance Hall. Wholesome gob James Hall, a signalman on the U.S.S. *Vermont,* is attracted to Clara. She falls for him in a big way, only to discover that he thinks the worst of her just because she kids around a little. (She may accept gifts from the boys, but the scenario is careful to point out that she is doing it only in fun, that she walks home alone at night, and that her old mother is always waiting up for her. When Hall becomes embroiled in a free-for-all and lands in court, devoted Clara willingly takes the witness stand and vouches for his good character and innocence. Said *Variety*: "The way this modern type of lass can take 'em, fake 'em and shake 'em and still retain her standing is quite nifty." The more conservative Mordaunt Hall (*New York Times*) penned: "She is perfectly natural during the happy stages of this production, but when tears well from her long-lashed eyes one is apt to think of the onion or the crocodile." *The Fleet's In* was remade as *Lady Be Careful* (1936), then, in 1942, as a Dorothy Lamour outing, and in 1951 it was revamped for the comedy talents of Dean Martin and Jerry Lewis in *Sailor Beware.*

Clara's final 1928 release was *Three Weekends,* directed by Clarence Badger and written by Elinor Glyn. This time she was a cabaret singer who snares Neil Hamilton, who she thinks is a millionaire though he is only an ordinary insurance agent. The comedy scenes were more strained than usual, relying on the mild humor of such episodes as Clara's embarrassment when her dad appears in the living room wearing his nightshirt, while she is entertaining Hamilton. To show Clara's figure to the fullest, the script called for her to be photographed changing in and out of cabaret scanties and step-ins, and later sporting a snug bathing suit.

New York film critic Richard Watts, Jr., once described the basic characteristics, evident in all Clara's movies, which created the walloping charisma of her screen image: "All of Miss Bow's vehicles must over-run with youthful gaiety, and because she has had the misfortune to be labeled the 'It Girl!,' she must be a sort of Northwest Mounted Policeman of sex, who gets her man even if she has to bludgeon him. The result is a series of films in which a particularly engaging star gets coy and elfin all over the landscape, battering down the resistance of some man who, for an unaccountable reason, is cold to her loveliness, and, with all the force of her go-getting instincts, overthrowing the unfortunate and helpless rival who opposes her. The formula is particularly annoying when applied to one of the most pleasing stars of the cinema." Movie historian Rudy Behlmer adds: "An additional requirement of the scriptwriters and directors was to get Clara into as many situations as possible requiring her to appear in bathing suits, lingerie and other stages of undress."

In late 1928 and early 1929, Clara was still a free soul constantly on the loose in Hollywood. An untutored girl, she was amazingly perspicacious about herself: "I think wildly gay people are usually hiding from something in themselves. . . . The best life has taught them is to snatch at every moment of fun and excitement, because they feel sure fate is going to hit them over the head with a club at the first opportunity." A persistent insomniac, Clara was constantly clambering about town. Her every encounter was grist for the press. Hounded by the standard bearers of morality, she once asked journalist-writer Adela Rogers St. Johns: "Why do they [married women] think I want their husbands? Most of them are no bargains that I can see." One of the unknown sidelights to Clara's personality was her addiction to poetry and her subsequent memorization of random stanzas. Costar Neil Hamilton later recalled that she could rattle off lines at will.

Clara was earning $2,800 a week in 1929, a fraction of the salary Gloria Swanson or even Pola Negri commanded. But Clara never seemed to know the difference or to mind, let alone have a sharp enough business agent to arrive at a more equitable adjustment with her employer, Paramount. The studio had long refrained from putting Clara into sound features, reasoning that her box-office appeal was so strong it did not require the added lure of talking dialogue. After all, why tamper with a successful image?

Finally; she did make her talking film debut in *The Wild Party,* which opened at the Rialto Theatre on April 1, 1929. The plot was simple enough: Clara, the champ flame of Winston College, is enthralled with anthropology professor Fredric March. She takes the blame for her roommate's indiscretion and is expelled. On the train home, March is there to declare his devotion to his "little savage" and to suggest that they immediately marry and leave on a jungle expedition he has been planning. Most important to Clara's career and to Paramount's financial well-being, was how well her voice recorded and projected in sound pictures. *Variety* judged: "Laughing, crying or condemning, that Bow voice won't command as much attention as the Bow this and that, yet it's a voice. Enough of a voice to insure a general belief that Clara can speak, as well as look—not as well, but enough." The *New York Times* reported: "Sometimes it is distinct and during some passages it isn't. It may fail on account of technical deficiencies of the recording device." (There were problems involved in recording Clara's voice, since she was used to hopping about the set at random, and the sound engineers were never sure where to place the microphones to capture her dialogue.) Fans in general were rather disappointed to discover that their favorite flapper had unrefined diction, projected in flat, nasal tones. But her voice was certainly not the liability described by some as the cause of her screen downfall. The fact that many cinemas, particularly overseas, continued to prefer booking silent versions of Clara's early talking films, was more a case of economics than a preference to protect their patrons from the harsh speaking voice of the It girl.

The Saturday Night Kid (1929) was a reworking of the stage play *Love 'Em and Leave 'Em* which had been turned into a Louise Brooks movie in 1926. Clara was cast as demonstrator of gym appliances at Ginsberg's Department Store. She takes a shine to an up-and-coming company worker, James Hall, but her sister, Jean Arthur, another salesgirl there, gambles with the employees' welfare club funds on the horse races and lays the blame on Clara, who has meanwhile shot craps with Arthur's bookie and won back the money. Realizing what kind of a girl Arthur is, Hall is more than happy to plan marriage with Clara. Most of the critical and audience attention went to Arthur, one of the studio's newer contract players, who would make her mark as a light comedienne once away from Paramount. Billed eleventh as Hazel, a salesgirl, was Jean Harlow, then still playing bit parts. Mordaunt Hall *(New York Times)* penned: "Miss Bow opens her usual bag of tricks. She utters wisecracks. She goes into the customary tantrums of rage and reaches an emotion pitch that might stamp her an actress."

Dangerous Curves (1929) was a crude behind-the-scenes look at circus life, featuring Clara as the bareback rider in love with high-wire artist Richard Arlen. Arlen is besotten with vamp Kay Francis, paying more attention to her than to his work. At one show he performs while drunk, falls, and is dismissed from the circus. Loyal Clara aids him in regaining his job, only to have the now married Francis return to the big top and lure Arlen back to his careless ways. When he is too inebriated to go on, Clara dresses in a clown outfit and takes his spot on the high wire. Working with such cloying dialogue as "Ya ain't worth savin', Larry Lee, ya ain't worth savin'!", Clara managed to be extremely convincing in her characterization of the "female Grimaldi who plays while her heart is breaking." *Dangerous Curves* was lost in the shuffle of product (68 features in 1929) being churned out by Paramount and other studios to woo back filmgoers hit by the Depression, but it was one of her most efficient characterizations.

Paramount belatedly followed the major studio trend of an all-star talking musical revue with *Paramount on Parade,* featuring more than 20 stars. It premiered at the Rialto Theatre on April 20, 1930. There were more than 20 personalities from the studio's ever-increasing roster. Clara was featured in a lively song number, "I'm True to the Navy Now," backed by a chorus of dancing gobs. Her full-throated contralto voice recorded well and there was definitely nothing unpleasing about her guest spot. It was just not spectacular, buried between so many other variety numbers. And if anything, Clara had always been a standout in her screen appearances.

Continuing with her Navy motif, Clara next starred in *True to the Navy* (1930). As a soda jerk in a San Diego drugstore, she has a sweetheart on most every warship in the Pacific, but settles for ace gunner Fredric March (never convincing as a free soul). Her light comedy moments were the best. She sang "There is Only One Who Matters to Me."

Her third 1930 release was *Love Among the Millionaires* (1930), a prefabricated musical comedy too much in the mold of the time. As hashhouse waitress Pepper Green, Clara takes a liking to Stanley Smith, who is learning his father's railroad business from the bottom up. When he invites her to hobnob about among the Palm Springs swells, her lower-class manners show, but her genuineness wins out in the end. Clara, looking thinner than in some time, crooned two numbers. In addition, child comedienne Mitzi Green mimics Clara's singing of "Rarin' to Go."

Clara confided to one reporter in mid-1930: "People used to say that I had a feeling of closeness, a great warmth of loving everybody, that they could tell me their troubles." This utilization of the past tense, referred to the growing alienation of Clara from her few friends and the increasingly bad publicity surrounding her personal life. A Dallas, Texas, wife had named her the defendant in an alienation of affection suit, which was reportedly settled out of court for $30,000. While gambling at Cal-Neva, she lost $13,900 and refused to pay. Clara years later told writer Rudy Behlmer: "Gambling I loved, and I always paid off at Caliente, but when cards are marked—no dice. I never paid any woman $30,000 or 30,000 cents. Also, no blackmailer received one cent from me. In retrospect, perhaps I should have paid and saved myself many heartaches. I took it on the chin and my health suffered."

All through this troublesome period, Clara had been dating a 35-year-old womanizer and nightclub crooner, Harry Richman. Cynics suggested it was merely a publicity stunt to help along his movie debut. Their engagement was announced, publicized to the saturation point, and then suddenly called off. In his autobiography, *A Hell of a Life,* Richman described Clara as "one of the most luscious, sexiest women I ever saw in my life. Off screen she was even more beautiful. 'Ripe' was the only word for that figure of hers. And those eyes—well, I had never seen anything to equal them." He went on to say that whenever he and Clara went out on the town, she invariably preferred visiting low-life places, and that her manners and vocabulary were none too refined, she having a most facile way with expletives.

At the time, Al Jolson made a tasteless quip on the radio about Clara "sleeping cater-cornered in bed." Listeners were shocked, but everyone was prepared to believe the worst about Clara's unformulated moral code. That her past mentor Schulberg was now too busy with other interests was all too clear. Claudette Colbert, Miriam Hopkins, Marlene Dietrich, and soon Sylvia Sidney (Schulberg's own special protégée) were now at Paramount making healthy inroads in the free-for-all grab for the title of studio queen. Since early 1928, pert, red-headed Nancy Carroll had been a Paramount player, appearing to good advantage in *Abie's Irish Rose, The Dance of Life, Sweetie,* and other films. By 1930 she had established her own track record as a cute Irish colleen with her own special blend of charm and audience appeal. According to the *New York Daily News* popularity poll of mid-1930, she was the most popular actress on the screen. Carroll had an advantage over Clara in her delivery, for she did not come across like a vulgar, gum-chewing babe.

In the midst of all her problems, Clara's fourth and final 1930 release, *Her Wedding Night,* opened at the Paramount Theatre on September 28, 1930. This bedroom farce was a remake of the silent *Miss Bluebeard* which had starred Bebe Daniels. Clara was Norma Martin, an American movie star on vacation in the south of France (the scene of every high jinks in the early 1930s). She encounters Ralph Forbes, a composer of popular songs, and his sidekick Skeets Gallagher (the two men have swapped identities so Forbes will not be pestered by fans). Clara and Gallagher are later mistaken for two lovebirds and are promptly married by the mayor of the town. At a subsequent houseparty confusion is emphasized for laughs and Clara and her real husband (Forbes) are finally reunited. *Her Wedding Night* proved to be a watershed in Clara's screen career. In this film she displayed a new permanent wave style and a different mode of outfits, in order to complete the break from her old It girl image. The Depression had closed the flapper era completely, leaving Clara without a new silver screen identity to recaptivate the public.

On January 13, 1931, Clara brought Daisy De Voe (originally De Boe) to court on a $125,000 blackmail charge and a $16,000 embezzlement suit. De Voe had been a hairdresser in Paramount's beauty salon and later became Clara's secretary. Clara stated that the blackmail attempt occurred after De Voe was fired for allegedly dipping into Clara's special bank account. Unable to disprove her assorted wrongdoings, De Voe attempted to blacken Clara's character in order to show her prevailing bad influence as a mitigating circumstance. In the much-publicized trial, De Voe detailed all manner of facts concerning Clara's private life, her numerous suitors, affairs, gifts to men, huge liquor bills, gambling debts, rubber checks, and so forth. After the second day of the trial, Clara pathetically asked the presiding judge: "My best friend, Daisy was. Why did she have to do me like that?"

On January 17, 1931, Clara told the press from her bedside (she was home with an attack of bronchitis): "I don't think all this will hurt me. I've faith that the public will believe that Daisy is trying to make a reputation for herself and punish me for the dishonesty in which she was trapped."

The jury convicted De Voe on only one of the 37 larceny charges, and the defendant eventually served one year of her 18-month jail sentence. The Hollywood political weekly, *The Coast Reporter,* published a narrative account of Clara's peccadillos allegedly dictated by the convicted De Voe. The publisher, Fredric H. Birnau, was criminally charged with allowing obscene material to be sent through the mail and was brought to trial. It rehashed all of Clara's indiscretions once more for public consumption. In the 1971 sexploitation documentary-feature *Hollywood Babylon,* ever so loosely based on the titillating "factual" book of bedroom life in the movie colony, one of the dramatized segments dealt in graphic terms with Clara's lusty sexual penchants.

Clara had been scheduled to star in Rouben Mamoulian's *City Streets,* which was to start shooting on January 17, 1931. Paramount replaced her with Sylvia Sidney, and in Clara's next vehicle, *The Secret Call* (1931), Peggy Shannon was substituted.

As a result of the De Voe and Birnau trials, Clara suffered another nervous breakdown and was sent to a sanitarium to rest.

Meanwhile, two previously filmed Clara films were released by Paramount. *No Limit* opened January 16, 1931 at the Paramount Theatre. As a movie usherette in Manhattan, Clara wavers between wealthy Park Avenue suitor Stuart Erwin and mysterious Norman Foster. She marries Foster only to learn that he is a jewel thief and manager of a floating gambling club. He is eventually sent to prison, but Clara agrees to await the release of her reformed spouse. The *New York Times* noted Clara was less boisterous "and all the more effective for her sobriety." *Variety* pointed out, "Miss Bow seems more improved physically than histrionically this time." *No Limit* had only mild success at the box office. Despite the notoriety attached to Clara's name at the time, the film only did a poor $54,000 during its Paramount engagement, almost setting a new weekly low for the theatre.

Kick In (1931), a reworking of the John Barrymore stage play of 1914, debuted at the Paramount Theatre on May 24, 1931 and did even less business. After a week at $46,200, it was yanked out of the theatre. The lopsidedly heavy drama cast Clara as the loyal wife of ex-convict Regis Toomey, who has vowed to go straight. The young couple are hounded by the police and too easily enticed by their crook friends. Paramount had had second thoughts about this picture midway through production, and hired Richard Wallace as the new director. In the release print, most of the footage went to Toomey, and the few livelier moments were supplied by tough-as-nails Wynne Gibson. Clara received unfavorable notices for her melodramatic efforts: "[She] reveals her limitations. She is the least effective member of the cast" *(New York Times);* "Her vocal calisthenics are down off the flying ring and in tow, it's a pretty quiet session for the Bow" *(Variety).*

On May 30, 1931, while passing through Denver, Colorado, on business, Schulberg told the press about Clara: "There is no question that the girl, for two years, in my opinion, the greatest actress on the screen, is in poor physical condition, and there is a big chance she will never make another picture."

On June 8, 1931, production was halted on *Manhandled* (1931) and Clara was replaced by Claudette Colbert. Schulberg announced that Clara's Paramount contract—which had two more pictures to go before it expired at the end of 1931—had been terminated at her own request.

In the early 1960s, Clara told writer Rudy Behlmer: "When I decided to leave the screen, I told Ben Schulberg I would not finish my contract or ever work again for any one. He yelled and threatened to sue me and I said, 'Go ahead, Ben, sue me. I've fought a thief and a blackmailer and if after such heartaches I am forced to fight both you and the studio, so be it.' The thing that burned me up was that studio did nothing but scold me and threaten me all through the De Voe trial and the blackmailers, too. I felt the studio, or at least Ben, would help me with encouragement, or a little lift in morale, but no. All they were interested in was my box office appeal! I had made them millions with what I and many critics thought were lousy pictures, but I received nothing but a salary, untrained leading men, and any old story they fished out of wastebaskets. Schulberg finally told me I could never make another picture as long as I refused to finish out the year left of my Paramount contract. It was then I told Ben, 'Look, all I want is peace of mind and a long rest. I'll even give you and the studio my trust fund—I want out.' It was all the money I had, but I was so tired and discouraged I felt I could no longer give my fans the best of me they deserved. A sex symbol is always a heavy load to carry, especially when one is very tired, hurt and bewildered."

After departing Paramount, she spent some weeks in a sanitorium. Then a blond Clara (her change of appearance an attempt to avoid public annoyance) went to actor Rex Bell's ranch in Nipton, California, for further recuperation. She had met the film player (born George F. Beldam in Chicago in 1903) when he was in the cast of her *True to the Navy,* and they had been close friends throughout her trial difficulties.

On October 8, 1931, small-time film producer Sam E. Rork announced that he now held a contract for a new movie to star Clara and that *Get the Woman* by Nell Shipman would start production in December. However, nothing transpired on the film project. Clara and Bell were secretly married in Las Vegas on December 4, 1931. Clara was then 24 years old. Bell's pal, Deputy Sheriff R. G. McCubay, was one of the few attendees at the ceremony.

Although she had made a clean break from Hollywood by living with Bell on his Nevada ranch, there were recurrent rumors about Clara's pending return to the movies. She was mentioned for the lead in MGM's *Red Headed Woman* (1932), but Jean Harlow received the assignment. Prim Mary Pickford shocked a good many when she announced she would like Clara to play her sister in *Secrets* (1933) and stated: "She is a very great actress and her only trouble has been that she hasn't known enough about life to live it the way she wanted to live it." Clara appreciated Pickford's diplomatic offer, but negotiations were never completed.

Clara had little to say about her screen plans, being more concerned with pontificating on her new role as wife. After her honeymoon, she had a few tidbits of marital advice to offer the press like: ". . . never going to sleep with a kick in your mind. Just lean over and say, I'm sorry, dear."

On April 27, 1932, Fox Films, with appropriate hoopla announced it had completed negotiations with Rork to star Clara in a forthcoming feature, with options for future projects. Clara was to receive a reported $125,000 salary. Sidney R. Kent, former general manager at Paramount, had just been made president of Fox in early 1932, after the ouster of its founder William Fox. He was well aware of Clara's still vital potency at the box office. In its trade ads for 1932, Fox listed Clara tenth in prominence, following contract stars Janet Gaynor, Will Rogers, Warner Baxter, James Dunn, Sally Eilers, Spencer Tracy, Henry Garat, Lilian Harvey, and John Boles.

Clara officially returned to Hollywood in early July, 1932, with a few announcements of her own. She was planning to direct films herself and to produce pictures starring her husband. "Directing won't be anything new to me. In all the pictures I have made I helped in the direction. The deal for the Rex Bell picture is now being made with the producers." Whoever was putting such grandiose ideas into Clara's mind obviously did not have the ability to carry them through, for neither of these two avenues of creative endeavors panned out.

Instead, it was announced Clara had selected Tiffany Thayer's novel

Call Her Savage for her Fox film debut. She went on a special diet and lost 18 pounds before reporting to work.

The hastily packaged *Call Her Savage* premiered at the Roxy Theatre on November 24, 1932, and did a very respectable $34,000 for its week's run. The Radio City Music Hall had turned the production down as unsuitable. *Call Her Savage* presented Clara as impulsive Nasa, the temperamental and reckless daughter of a white woman's indiscretion with an Indian chief in the 1900s West. The riches-to-rags-to-respectability melodrama had her marrying cad Monroe Owsley to spite her wealthy, nominal father. After Owsley walks out on her, Clara has a child, becomes destitute, and takes to the street. While she is out one day, her child dies in a tenement fire. Ironically, she then learns that her father has died and left her his fortune. She returns to the West, discovers her actual parentage, and plans to marry her half-breed suitor, Gilbert Roland. The often crude story line was as unsubtle as the performances, but it did offer Clara an ample showcase to display a respectable range of emotions, from whipping Roland, rebuking Owsley, playing the bored socialite, vying with vixen Thelma Todd, shyly hustling escorts, displaying mother love, to finally romancing Roland. Clara looked extremely healthy and pretty and displayed vitality. If her diction was still a bit rough, she had learned more restraint in her enunciation and phrasing.

Richard Watts, Jr. *(New York Herald Tribune)* approved: "Despite certain definite weaknesses in her manner of dramatized emotions, she is, as always, a vivid and arresting screen personage, who plays with so much amiable vitality that she remains an invariably interesting performer to watch."

Call Her Savage made out quite nicely at the box office and promised a bright new future for Clara. Clara's three favorite films were *Mantrap, It,* and *Call Her Savage.*

Clara was in a rush to make another film, but it was a year later (November 31, 1933) before *Hoopla* was released. The film was a remake of Kenyon Nicholson's *The Barker,* which had starred Claudette Colbert on Broadway and Dorothy Mackail in the 1928 film version. Frank Lloyd, who had fumbled with Clara's *Children Of Divorce* at Paramount, but was now a successful director at Fox, was assigned to this revamped project. *Hoopla* shifted the narrative's focus to Clara, a hard-boiled hula dancer in Colonel Gowdy's carnival, who agrees to seduce Richard Cromwell, the son of the show's manager, Preston Foster. Clara ends up by marrying the hickish but callow Cromwell. The Chicago World's Fair was used for the finale.

Fox's advertisement for *Hoopla* read: "Clara Bow . . . red-headed, warm-blooded dynamite . . . again releases the torrent of her emotional genius . . . in the most colorful performance of her life." The critics did not all agree. The *New York Times* said "She's no Mae West as story would suggest. There is vitality in Miss Bow's acting but she requires a more shrewd and tactful supervision than she receives here."

Clara was dissatisfied with *Hoopla* and again left Hollywood. She later said: "I was glad to go. I'd had enough. It wasn't ever like I thought it was going to be. It was always a disappointment to me." She was the first to admit that whenever producers suggested film projects for her, the first thing they thought of was, "Well, how do we get Clara undressed?" There was talk of Clara going to England to star in a film, but nothing developed. She seemingly no longer cared enough to follow through on job offers.

Most of her time was spent with Bell on their 150,000-acre ranch near Searchlight, Nevada, 75 miles south of Las Vegas. (Bell would continue sporadically in films until 1944, mostly making low-budget Westerns for Fox and Monogram. He would come out of retirement to make a brief appearance with Clark Gable in *Lone Star* (1952) and with him again in *The Misfits* (1961). On December 16, 1934, Clara gave birth to Rex Anthony Bell in a Santa Monica hospital.

It was rumored that Clara had been asked to replace Simone Simon in *Under Two Flags* (1936) at Twentieth Century-Fox but could not reduce in time (she was having weight problems again). The role went to Claudette Colbert. In 1937 the Bells returned to Hollywood to open the "It" Cafe on North Vine. The venture soon folded, and they returned to Nevada.

Their second child, George Robert Bell, was born June 14, 1938 in a Caesarean birth. She reportedly told Bell: "Oh Rex. I'm so sorry it's a boy because I know you wanted a little girl." In the late 1930s Clara would say: "I don't want my two boys to become Hollywood kids. I wouldn't want them to go through what I did."*

In 1944, after Bell retired from moviemaking, they sold the Nevada ranch and moved to Las Vegas where he opened a Western haberdashery store.

Clara's last show business appearance was in 1947, when she agreed to be the mystery voice on pal Ralph Edwards' *"Truth Or Consequences"* radio program. The contest winner received $17,590 in prizes. In June, 1949, it was announced that Clara would star in *Personal Appearance* at the small El Teatro in Sante Fe, New Mexico. The project was abandoned.

In 1954 Bell ran for lieutenant governor of Nevada on the Republican ticket and won. He was reelected in 1958. After 1954 Clara resided in the Los Angeles area, first in a Culver City sanitarium and later in a modest Culver City bungalow, with swimming pool, two dogs, and three television sets. Her nurse-companion was Mrs. Estella Smith, who had been with the Bells for 16 years. Clara continued to receive treatment for her insomnia and other disorders from neuro-psychiatrist Dr. Karl von Hagen. In her spare time she would oil paint and she read a great deal. She always slept with a little radio turned on under her pillow.

Because of his political duties, Bell only visited Clara every four to six weeks. On May 28, 1956, he told Associated Press reporter Bob Thomas: "Mostly she is fine and dandy. But she has had emotional disturbances that have knocked out her health. She has trouble with sleeping and has been high strung.

"She has had to live an entirely different life since the trouble began. She needs the constant care of a doctor and must go to a sanitarium when her condition gets worse. That's why she must stay in Los Angeles; we don't have the facilities here. . . .

"Unfortunately, she doesn't have a bit of social life. That's one of the things she can't take in her condition.

"If she had been Minnie Zilch instead of Clara Bow, perhaps this never would have happened to her. But the emotional strain of her early years was just too much for her nervous system. It's like training horses. Sometimes

*At last report, the older son, a graduate of Nevada University, was supervising the Reno and Las Vegas Rex Bell Haberdashery Shops. In the early 1940s and the mid 1960s he acted in small roles in a few Western movies. The younger son is a floor man in a Las Vegas casino.

when you're starting thoroughbreds, you break 'em in too early, while you take a saddlehorse and bring him along easy."

Later that year, he told another reporter: "We've never discussed divorce. No, it is not painful to talk about it. It's an open book. Myself and Mrs. Bell are always interested in the fact that people will ask about her, I think she would probably be hurt if she thought that she was absolutely forgotten.

"She might not say so to anyone but I believe that it means something to her that after this many years people still ask about her."

Clara was in the news again in 1960 when she informed gossip columnist Hedda Hopper: "I slip my old crown of 'It' Girl not to Taylor or Bardot but to Monroe."

Reports on Clara's condition became scarce. Then in January, 1961, her onetime actor friend Richard Arlen (he was one of the few people she would see; other past acquaintances would receive handwritten messages from her at Christmastime) told *Hollywood Reporter* writer James Bacon: "I've visited her. She still looks as beautiful as ever. We talk of the old days, just like it was still 1927. She's as sharp as she ever was. And still has that great sense of humor. She knows everything that is going on in the business."

Rex Bell died July 4, 1962, of a heart attack while campaigning for the governorship of Nevada. Clara came out of seclusion to attend the funeral at Forest Lawn Memorial Park. She was accompanied by her nurse, Mrs. Smith, and waved to a few of the reporters there. Bell left the bulk of his $10,000 estate to his two sons, and an interest in the Reno clothing store to a longtime friend, Mrs. Katie Jenkins of Las Vegas. Regarding Clara, his will (dated November 17, 1961) stated: "I am married to Clara Bow Bell, but. . . . we have lived separate and apart for many years."

In her final years, Clara reportedly was unable to speak coherently most of the time, and rarely was able to recognize the few old friends who still visited her. But in 1965, during a period of lucidity, she expounded to a newsman about the good old days: "We had individuality. We did as we pleased. We stayed up late. We dressed the way we wanted. Today, stars are sensible and end up with better health. But *we* had more fun."

Clara died shortly before midnight on September 26, 1965, at her Culver City bungalow. She had been watching television. She was buried at Forest Lawn cemetery in the private family area. Among those attending the funeral were Jack Oakie, Richard Arlen, Maxie Rosenbloom, and Harry Richman. Clara had planned her own service: Reverend Kermit Kastellanos of All Saints Episcopal Church presided, reading the twenty-third Psalm from the Episcopal Book of Common Prayer, and Ralph Edwards read from Kahlil Gibran's *The Prophet.*

Clara had long planned to write her memoirs ("a sort of helpful story to girls who want to try for pictures and who are very poor") but she never did, largely for fear of the potential repercussions on her family. A long-projected film biography of Clara by producer Jerry Wald never materialized either.

Perhaps the most perceptive tribute to Clara was paid her by reviewer Whitney Bolton in the *New York Morning Telegraph* (September 30, 1965): "She had fright in her, this girl. She had defiance that was a flower of fright. She had a kind of jaunty air of telling you that she didn't care what happened, she could handle it." Bolton went on to recall that once in the late 1920s he had encountered superstar Clara on the Paramount lot and asked her: "Miss Bow when you add it all up, what is 'It'?"

Clara replied: "I ain't real sure."

BEYOND THE RAINBOW (Robertson-Cole, 1922) 6,000′

Director, William Christy Cabanne; based on the story "The Price of Feathers" by Solita Solano; screenplay, Cabanne, Loila Brooks; art director, Frank Campury; camera, William Tirers, Philip Armand.

Harry Morey (Edward Mallory); Lillian "Billie" Dove (Marion Taylor); Virginia Lee (Henrietta Greeley); Diana Allen (Frances Gardener); James Harrison (Louis Wade); Macey Harlam (Count Julien de Brisac); Rose Coghlan (Mrs. Burns); William Tooker (Dr. Ramsey); Helen Ware (Mrs. Gardener); George Fawcett (Mr. Gardener); Marguerite Courtot (Esther); Edmund Breese (Inspector Richardson); Walter Miller (Robert Judson); Charles Craig (Col. Henry Gartwright); Clara Bow (Virginia Gardener); Huntley Gordon (Bruce Forbes).

DOWN TO THE SEA IN SHIPS (Hodkinson, 1922) 12 reels

Presenter-director, Elmer Clifton; story-screenplay, John L. E. Pell; music score designed by Henry F. Gilbert; camera, Alexander G. Penrod.

William Walcott (William W. Morgan); William Cavanaugh (Henry Morgan); Ada Laycock (Henny Clark); Leigh R. Smith ("Scuff" Smith); Marguerite Courtot (Patience Morgan); Raymond McKee (Thomas Allen Dexter); Juliette Courtot (Judy Peggs); Clarice Vance (Nahoma); Curtis Pierce (Town Crier); Clara Bow ("Dot" Morgan); Patrick Hartigan (Jake Finner); J. Thornton Baston (Samuel Siggs); James Turfler (Cabin Boy), Captain James A. Tilton (Captain of the "Morgan"); Elizabeth Fuley (Patience as a child); Thomas White (Tommy as a child).

ENEMIES OF WOMEN (Cosmopolitan, 1923) 10,501′

Director, Alan Crosland; based on the novel by Vicente Blasco Ibañez; screenplay, John Lynch; camera, Ira Morgan.

Lionel Barrymore (Prince Lubimoff); Alma Rubens (Alicia); Pedro De Cordoba (Atilio Castro); Gareth Hughes (Spadoni); Gladys Hulette (Vittoria); William H. Thompson (Colonel Marcos); William Collier, Jr. (Gaston); Mario Majeroni (Duke De Delille); Clara Bow (Girl Dancing on Table); Betty Boyton (Alicia's Maid); Madame Jean (Madame Spadoni); Ivan Linow (Terrorist); Paul Panzer (Cossack).

MAYTIME (Preferred, 1923) 7,500′

Producer, B. P. Schulberg; director, Louis A. Gasnier; based on the operetta by Rida Johnson Young, Cyrud Wood, Sigmund Romberg; adaptation, Olga Printzlau; camera, Karl Struss.

Ethel Shannon (Ottilie Van Zandt); Harrison Ford (Richard Wayne); William Norris (Matthew); Clara Bow (Alice Tremaine); Wallace MacDonald (Claude Van Zandt); Josef Swickard (Col. Van Zandt); Martha Mattox (Mathilda); Betty Francisco (Ermintrude); Robert McKim (Monte Mitchell).

THE DARING YEARS (Equity, 1923) 6,702′

Producer, Daniel Carson Goodman; director, Kenneth Webb; story-screenplay, Goodman.

Mildred Harris (Susie La Motte); Charles Emmett Mack (John Browning); Clara Bow (John's Sweetheart, Mary); Mary Carr (Mrs. Browning); Joe King (Jim Moran, a Pugilist); Tyrone Power (James La Motte); Skeets Gallagher (The College Boy); Jack Richardson (Flaglier, Cabaret Owner); Sherman Sisters (Moran Girls); Joseph Depew, Helen Rowland (La Motte's Kids); Sam Sidman (Curly, Moran's Manager).

GRIT (Hodkinson, 1924) 5,800'

Director, Frank Tuttle; story, F. Scott Fitzgerald; screenplay, Ashmore Creelman; camera, Fred Waller, Jr.

Glenn Hunter ("Kid" Hart); Helenka Adamowska (Annie Hart); Roland Young (Houdini Hart); Osgood Perkins (Boris Giovanni Smith); Townsend Martin (Flashy Joe); Clara Bow (Orchid McGonigle); Dore Davidson (Pop Finkel); Martin Borden (Bennie Finkel); Joseph Depew (Tony O'Cohen).

BLACK OXEN (FN, 1924) 7, 937'

Director, Frank Lloyd; based on the novel by Gertrude Atherton; camera, Norbert Brodine.

Corinne Griffith (Madame Zatianny/Mary Ogden); Conway Tearle (Lee Clavering); Thomas Ricketts (Charles Dinwiddie); Thomas S. Gruise (Judge Trent); Clara Bow (Janet Oglethorpe); Kate Lester (Jane Oglethorpe); Harry Mestayer (James Oglethorpe); Claire MacDowell (Agnes Trevor); Alan Hale (Prince Rohenhauer); Clarissa Selwynne (Gora Dwight), Fred Gambold (Oglethorpe's Butler); Percy Williams (Ogden's Butler); Otto Nelson (Dr. Steinach); Eric Mayne (Chancellor); Otto Lederer (Austrian Advisor); Carmelita Geraghty (Anna Goodrich); Ione Atkinson, Mila Constantin, Hortense O'Brien (Flappers).

POISONED PARADISE (Preferred, 1924) 6,800'

Producer, B. P. Schulberg; director, Louis Gasnier; based on the novel *Poisoned Paradise: A Romance of Monte Carlo* by Robert W. Service; screenplay Waldemar Young; camera, Karl Struss.

Kenneth Harlan (Hugh Kildair); Clara Bow (Margot Le Blanc); Barbara Tennant (Mrs. Kildair); Andre de Beranger (Krantz); Carmel Myers (Mrs. Belmire); Raymond Griffith (Martel); Josef Swickard (Professor Durand); Evelyn Selbie (Mde. Tranquille).

DAUGHTERS OF PLEASURE (Principal, 1924) 6 reels

Director, William Beaudine; based on the story by Caleb Proctor; screenplay, Eve Unsell; titles, Harvey Thew; art director, Joseph Wright; camera, Charles van Enger; editor, Edward McDermott.

Marie Prevost (Marjory Hadley); Monte Blue (Kent Merrill); Clara Bow (Lila Millas); Edythe Chapman (Mrs. Hadley); Wilfred Lucas (Mark Hadley).

WINE (UNIV, 1924) 6,220'

Director, Louis Gasnier; based on the story by William MacHarg; adaptation, Raymond L. Schrock; screenplay, Philip Lonergan, Eve Unsil.

Clara Bow (Angela Warriner); Forrest Stanley (Carl Graham); Huntley Gordon (John Warriner); Myrtle Steadman (Mrs. Warriner); Robert Agnew (Harry Van Alstyne); Walter Long (Benedict, Count Montebello); Grace Carlyle (Mrs. Bruce Corwin); Leo White (The Duke); Walter Shumway (Revenue Officer); Arthur Thalasso (Amoti).

EMPTY HEARTS (Banner, 1924) 6 reels

Producer, Ben Verschleiser; director, Al Santell; story, Evelyn Campbell; screenplay, Adele Buffinton; camera, Ernest Hallen.

John Bowers (Milt Kimberlin); Charles Murrey (Joe Delane); John Miljan (Frank Gorman); Clara Bow (Rosalie); Lilian Rich (Madeline); Joan Standing (Hilda, The Maid); Buck Black (Val Kimberlin).

THIS WOMAN (WB, 1924) 6,842'

Director, Phil Rosen; based on the novel by Howard Rockey; adaptation, Hope Loring, Louis Leighton; camera, Lyman Broening.

Irene Rich (Carol Drayton); Ricardo Cortez (Whitney Duane); Louise Fazenda (Rose); Frank Elliott (Gordon Duane); Creighton Hale (Bobby Bleedon); Marc McDermott (Stratini); Helen Dunbar (Mrs. Sturdevant); Clara Bow (Aline Sturdevant); Otto Hoffman (Judson).

BLACK LIGHTNING (Gotham, 1924) 5,500'

Presenter, Samuel Sax; Director, James P. Hogan; story, Harry Davis; screenplay, Dorothy Howell; camera, James P. Hogan.

Clara Bow (Martha Larned); Harold Austin (Roy Chambers); Eddie Phillips (Ez Howard); James Mason (Jim Howard); Joe Butterworth (Larned); Mark Fenton (Doctor); John Prince (City Doctor); J. P. Hogan (Frank Larned); Thunder The Dog (Himself); Joe Butterworth (Dick).

CAPITAL PUNISHMENT (Preferred, 1925) 5,950'

Producer, B. P. Schulberg; art director, James P. Hogan; story, Schulberg; adaptation, John Goodrich; titles, Florence L. Gilbert; technical director, Frank Ormston; camera, Goodrich.

Clara Bow (Delia Tate); George Hackathorne (Dan O'Connor); Elliott Dexter (Gordon Harrington); Margaret Livingston (Mona Caldwell); Alec B. Francis (Chaplain); Mary Carr (Mrs. O'Connor); Robert Ellis (Harry Phillip); Joseph Kilgour (Governor); George Nichols (Warden); Eddie Phillips (Condemned Boy); Edith Yorke (Boy's Mother); John Prince (Doctor); Wade Boteler (Officer Dugan); Fred Warren (Pawnbroker); Sailor Sharkey (Convict); Harry Tenbrook (Executioner).

HELEN'S BABIES (Principal, 1925) 5,620'

Director, William A. Seiter; based on the story by John Habberton; adaptation, Hope Loring, Louis Leighton; camera, William Daniels; editor, Owen Marks.

Baby Peggy (Toddie); Jean Carpenter (Budge); Clara Bow (Alice Mayton); Edward Everett Horton (Uncle Harry); Claire Adams (Helen Lawrence); Richard Tucker (Tom Lawrence); George Reed (Rastus, The Coachman); Mattie Peters (Mandy, The Housekeeper).

THE ADVENTUROUS SEX (Associated Exhibitors, 1925) 5,039'

Director, Charles Giblyn; story, Hamilton Mannen; screenplay, Carl Stearns Clancy; camera, George Peters.

Clara Bow (The Girl); Herbert Rawlinson (Her Sweetheart); Earle Williams (The Adventurer); Harry T. Morey (Her Father); Mabel Beck (Her Mother); Flora Finch (The Grandmother); and: Joseph Burke.

MY LADY'S LIPS (Preferred, 1925) 6,609'

Producer, B. P. Schulberg; director, James P. Hogan; story-continuity, John Goodrich; camera, Allen Siegler.

Clara Bow (Lola Lombard); Frank Keenan (Forbes Lombard); Alyce Mills (Dora Blake); William Powell (Scott Seddon); Ford Sterling (Smike); Gertrude Short (Crook Girl); John Sainpolis (Inspector); Matthew Betz (Eddie Gault); and: Sojin.

PARISIAN LOVE (Preferred, 1925) 6,324'

Producer, B. P. Schulberg; director, Louis Gasnier; story, F. Oakley Crawford; adaptation, Lois Hutchinson; camera, Allen Siegler.

Clara Bow (Marie); Donald Keith (Armand); Lillian Leighton (Frouchard); James Russell (D'Avril); Hazel Keener (Margot); Lou Tellegen (Pierre Marcel); Jean de Briac (Knifer); Otto Matieson (Apache Leader).

EVE'S LOVER (WB, 1925) 7,237'

Director, Roy Del Ruth; story, Mrs. W. K. Clifford; adaptation, Darryl F. Zanuck; camera, George Winkler.

Irene Rich (Eva Burnside); Bert Lytell (Baron Geraldo Maddox); Clara Bow (Rena D'Arcy); Willard Louis (Austin Starfield); John Steppling (Burton Gregg); Arthur Hoyt (Amos Potts); Lew Harvey (The Agitator).

KISS ME AGAIN (WB, 1925) 6,722'

Director, Ernst Lubitsch; based on the play *Nous Divorcons;* screenplay, Hans Kraly; camera, Charles Van Enger.

Marie Prevost (Loulou Fleury); Monte Blue (Gaston Fleury); John Roche (Maurice); Clara Bow (Grizette); Willard Louis (Dr. Dubois).

THE SCARLET WEST (FN, 1925) 8,390'

Producer, Frank J. Carroll; director, John G. Adolfi; based on the story by A. B. Heath; screenplay, Anthony Paul Kelly; camera, George Benoit, Benjamin Kline, Victor Shuler; F. L. Hoefler.

Robert Edeson (General Kinnard); Martha Francis (Harriet Kinnard); Clara Bow (Miriam); Johnnie Walker (Lt. Parkman); Walter McGrail (Lt. Harper); Florence Crawford (Mrs. Harper); Robert Frazer (Cardelanche); Helen Ferguson (Nestina); Ruth Stonehouse (Mrs. Custer); Gaston Glass (Captain Howard).

THE PRIMROSE PATH (Arrow, 1925) 6,800'

Producer, Hunt Stromberg; Director, Harry O. Hoyt; based on the novel by E. Lanning Masters; screenplay, Leah Baird, Andre Barlatier.

Clara Bow (Marilyn Merrill); Wallace MacDonald (Bruce Armstrong); Stuart Holmes (Tom Canfield); Templar Saxe (Dude Talbot); Lydia Knott (Mrs. Armstrong); Pat Moore (Jimmie Armstrong); Tom Santschi (Big Joe Snead); Arline Pretty (Helen); Mike Donlin (Parker, Federal Officer); George Irving (John Morton, Prosecutor); Henry Hall (Court Officer).

THE PLASTIC AGE (Preferred, 1925), 6,488'

Producer, B. P. Schulberg; director, Wesley Ruggles; based on the novel by Percy Marks; adaptation, Eve Unsell, Frederica Sagor; camera, Gilbert Warrenton, Allen Siegler.

Clara Bow (Cynthia Day); Donald Keith (Hugh Carver); Mary Alden (Mrs. Carver); Henry B. Walthall (Henry Carver); Gilbert Roland (Carl Peters); J. Gordon Edwards, Jr. (Norrie Parks); David Butler (Coach Henley); Felix Valle (Merton Billings); Clark Gable (Athlete); Gordon "William" Elliott (Dancer); Churchill Ross (Boy with Glasses); Gwen Lee (Carl's Girl).

THE KEEPER OF THE BEES (FBO, 1925) 6,712'

Director, J. Leo Meeham; based on the novel by Gene Stratton Porter; continuity, Meehan; assistant director, William Fisher; camera, John Boyle.

Robert Frazer (James McFarlane); Josef Swickard (The Bee Master); Martha Maddox (Mrs. Cameron); Clara Bow (Lolly Cameron); Alyce Mills (Molly Cameron); Gene Stratton (Little Scout);Joe Coppa ("Angel Face"); Billy Osborn ("Nice Child"); Ainse Charland ("Fat Ole Bill").

FREE TO LOVE (Preferred, 1925), 4,825′

Producer, B. P. Schulberg; director, Frank O'Connor.

Clara Bow (Marie Anthony); Donald Keith (Reverend James Crawford); Raymond McKee (Tony); Hallam Cooley (Jack Garner); Charles Mailes (Kenton Crawford); Winter Hall (Judge Orr).

THE BEST BAD MAN (FOX, 1925) 4,893′

Presenter, William Fox; director, J. G. Blystone; based on the story "Senor Jingle Bells" by Max Brand; screenplay, Lillie Hayward; assistant director, Jasper Blystone; camera, Dan Clark.

Tom Mix (Hugh Nichols); Buster Gardener (Hank Smith); Cyril Chadwick (Frank Dunlap); Clara Bow (Peggy Swain); Tom Kennedy (Dan Ellis); Frank Beal (Mr. Swain); Judy King (Molly Jones); Tom Wilson (Sam); Tony The Wonder Horse (Himself); Paul Panzer (Sheriff); Tom Wilson (Sam The Butler).

LAWFUL CHEATERS (Commonwealth, 1925) 4,898′

Producer, B. P. Schulberg; director, Frank O'Connor; adaptation Adele Buffington; screenplay, O'Connor.

Clara Bow (Molly Burns); David Kirby (Rooney) Raymond McKee (Richard Steele); Edward Hearn (Roy Burns); George Cooper (Johnny Burns); Fred Kelsey (Tom Horan); Gertrude Pedlar (Mrs. Perry Steele); Jack Wise (Graveyard Lazardi); John T. Prince (Silent Sam Riley).

TWO CAN PLAY (Associated Exhibitors, 1926) 5,465′

Director, Nat Ross; story, Gerald Mygatt; screenplay, Reginald G. Fogwell; camera, Andre Barlatier; editor, Gene Milford.

George Fawcett (John Hammis); Allan Forrest (James Radley); Clara Bow (Dorothy Hammis); Wallace McDonald (Robert MacForth); Vola Vale (Mimi).

THE RUNAWAY (PAR, 1926) 6,218′

Director, William DeMille; based on the story "The Flight to the Hills" by Charles Neville Buck; screenplay, Albert Shilby LeVino; camera, Charles Boyle.

Clara Bow (Cynthia Meade); Warner Baxter (Wade Murrell); William Powell (Jack Harrison); George Bancroft (Lesher Skidmore); Edythe Chapman (Mrs. Murrell).

MANTRAP (PAR, 1926) 6,077′

Associate producer, Hector Turnbull, B. P. Schulberg; director, Victor Fleming; based on the novel by Sinclair Lewis; screenplay, Adelaide Heilbron; titles, George Marion, Jr.; camera, James Wong Howe.

Ernest Torrence (Joe Aster); Clara Bow (Alvena Easter); Percy Marmont (Ralph Prescott); Eugene Pallette (Woodbury); Tom Kennedy (Curly Evans); Josephine Crowell (Mrs. McGavvity); Charles Stevens (Jackfish); William Orlamond (McGarity); Miss DuPont (Mrs. Barker); Charlot Bird (Stenographer).

KID BOOTS (PAR, 1926) 5,650′

Associate producer, B. P. Schulberg; Director, Frank Tuttle; based on the play by William Anthony McGuire, Otto Harbach; screenplay Luther Reed, Tom Gibson; titles, George Marion, Jr.; camera, Victor Milner.

Eddie Cantor (Kid Boots); Clara Bow (Jane Martin); Billie Dove (Polly Pendleton); Lawrence Gray (Tom Sterling); Natalie Kingston (Carmen Mendoza); Malcolm Waite (George Fitch); W. J. Worthington (Polly's Father); Harry von Meter (Polly's Lawyer); Fred Esmelton (Tom's Lawyer).

THE ANCIENT MARINER (FOX, 1926) 5,548'

Director, Henry Bennett; based on the poem *The Rime of the Ancient Mariner* by Samuel Taylor Coleridge; story, Chester Barnett; adaptation, Eve Unsell; assistant director, James Tinling; titles, Tom Miranda; camera, Joseph August.

Clara Bow (Doris); Matthews Earle Williams (Victor Brandt); Leslie Fenton (Joe Barlowe); Nigel de Brulier (Skipper); Paul Panzer (Mariner); Gladys Brockwell (Life In Death); Robert Klein (Death).

MY LADY OF WHIM (Arrow, 1926) 6,089'

Director, Dallas M. Fitzgerald; based on the story "Protecting Prue" by Edgar Franklin; screenplay, Doris Schroeder; camera, Jack Young.

Clara Bow (Prudence Severn); Donald Keith (Bartley Greer); Carmelita Geraghty (Wayne Leigh); Lee Moran (Dick Flynn); Francis McDonald (Rolf); John Cossar (Severn); Robert Rose (Sneath); Lux MacBride (Yacht Captain); Betty Baker (Mary Severn).

DANCING MOTHERS (PAR, 1926) 7,169'

Producer, Herbert Brenon; associate producer, William LeBaron; director, Brenon; based on the play by Edgar Selwyn, Edmund Goulding; screenplay, Forrest Halsey; art director Julian Boone Fleming; camera, J. Roy Hunt.

Alice Joyce (Ethel "Buddy" Westcourt); Conway Tearle (Jerry Naughton); Clara Bow (Catherine "Kittens" Westcourt); Donald Keith (Kenneth Cobb); Dorothy Cumming (Mrs. Mazzarene); Elsie Lawson (Irma Raymond); Norman Trevon (Hugh Westcourt); Leila Hyams (Birdie Courtney); Spencer Charters (Butter And Egg Man).

THE SHADOW OF THE LAW (Associated Exhibitors, 1926) 4,526'

Producer, Arthur Beck, Leah Baird; director, Wallace Worsley; based on the novel *Two Gates* by Henry Chapman Ford; screenplay, Baird, Grover Jones; camera, Ray June.

Clara Bow (Mary Brophy); Forrest Stanley (James Reynolds); Stuart Holmes (Linyard); Ralph Lewis (Brophy); William V. Mong (Egan); J. Emmett Beck (Martin); Adele Farrington (Aunt); Eddie Lyons (Crook); George Cooper (Chauffeur);

IT (PAR, 1927) 6,542'

Producers, Clarence Badger, Elinor Glyn; associate producer, B. P. Schulberg; director, Badger; based on the novel by Glyn; adaptation, Glyn; screenplay, Hope Loring, Louis D. Lighton; titler, George Marion, Jr.; camera, H. Kinley Martin; editor, E. Lloyd Sheldon.

Clara Bow (Betty Lou); Antonio Moreno (Cyrus Waltham); William Austin (Monty); Jacqueline Gadsdon (Jane Daly) (Adela Van Norman); Julia Swayne Gordon (Mrs. Van Norman); Priscilla Bonner (Molly); Eleanor Lawson, Rose Tapley (Welfare Workers) Elinor Glyn (Herself); Lloyd Corrigan (Cabin Boy On Yacht); Gary Cooper (Reporter).

CHILDREN OF DIVORCE (PAR, 1927) 6,871'

Associate producer, B. P. Schulberg; producer, E. Lloyd Sheldon; director, Frank Lloyd; based on the novel by Owen Lloyd Johnson; screenplay, Hope Loring, Louis D. Lighton; camera, Victor Milner; editor, E. Sheldon.

Clara Bow (Kitty Flanders); Esther Ralston (Jean Waddington); Gary Cooper (Ted Larrabee); Einar Hanson (Prince Ludovico de Sfax); Norman Trevor (Duke de Gondreville); Hedda Hopper (Katherine Flanders); Edward Martindel (Tom Larrabee); Julia Swayne Gordon (Princess de Sfax); Albert Gran (Mr. Seymour); Iris Stuart (Mousie); Margaret Campbell (Mother Superior); Percy Williams (Manning); Joyce Marie Coad (Little Kitty); Yvonne Pelletier (Little Jean); Don Marion (Little Ted).

ROUGH HOUSE ROSIE (PAR, 1927) 5,952'

Associate producer, B. P. Schulberg; director, Frank Strayer; based on the story by Nunnally Johnson; adaptation, Max Marcin; screenplay, Louise Long, Ethel Doherty; assistant director, George Crook; titles, George Marion, Jr.; camera, James Murray, Hal Rosson.

Clara Bow (Rosie O'Reilly); Reed Howes (Joe Hennessey); Arthur Housman (Kid Farrell); Doris Hill (Ruth); Douglas Gilmore (Arthur Russell); John Miljan (Lew McKay); Henry Kolker (W. S. Davids).

WINGS (PAR, 1927) 12,682'

Associate producer, B. P. Schulberg; producer, Lucien Hubbard; director, William A. Wellman; story, John Monks Saunders; screenplay, Hope Loring, Louis D. Lighton; music score, John S. Zamecnik; assistant director, Richard Johnson; aerial camera, E. Burton Steene, Sgt. Ward, Al Williams; titler, Julian Johnson; Engineering; effects, Roy Pomeroy; camera, Harry Perry; editor, E. Lloyd Sheldon.

Clara Bow (Mary Preston); Charles "Buddy" Rogers (Jack Powell); Richard Arlen (David Armstrong); El Brendel (Herman Schwimpf); Jobyna Ralston (Sylvia Lewis); Richard Tucker (Air Commander); Gary Cooper (Cadet White), Gunboat Smith (Sergeant); Henry B. Walthall (Mr. Armstrong); Julia Swayne Gordon, (Mrs. Armstrong); Arlette Marchal (Celeste); George Irving (Mr. Powell); Hedda Hopper (Mrs. Powell); Nigel de Brulier (French Peasant); Roscoe Karns (Lt. Cameron); James Pierce (MP); Carl Von Haartman (German Officer).

HULA (PAR, 1927) 5,862'

Associate producer, B. P. Schulberg; director, Victor Fleming; based on the novel by Armene Von Tempski; adaptation, Doris Anderson; screenplay, Ethel Doherty; titles, George Marion, Jr.; assistant director, Henry Hathaway; camera, William Marshall; editor; Eda Warren.

Clara Bow ("Hula" Calhoun); Clive Brook (Anthony Haldane); Arlett Marchal (Mrs. Bane); Arnold Kent (Harry Dehan); Maude Truax (Margaret Haldane); Albert Gran (Old Bill Calhoun); Agostino Borgato (Uncle Edwin).

GET YOUR MAN (PAR, 1927) 5,718'

Associate producer, B. P. Schulberg; director, Dorothy Arzner; based on the play *Tu M'Epouseras* by Louis Verneuil; continuity, Agnes Brand Leahy; screenplay, Hope Loring; titles, George Marion, Jr.; camera, Alfred Gilks; editor, Louis D. Lighton.

Clara Bow (Nancy Worthington); Charles "Buddy" Rogers (Robert de Bellecontre); Josef Swickard (Duc de Bellecontre); Harvey Clark (Marquis de Villeneuve); Josephine Dunn (Simon de Villeneuve); Frances Raymond (Mrs. Worthington).

RED HAIR (PAR, 1928) 6,331'

Associate producer, B. P. Schulberg; director, Clarence Badger; based on the novel *The Vicissitudes of Evangeline* by Elinor Glyn; adaptation, Percy Heath, Lloyd Corrigan; assistant director, Archie Hill; titles, George Marion, Jr.; camera, Alfred Gilks; editor, Doris Drought.

Clara Bow ("Bubbles" McCoy); Lane Chandler (Robert Lennon); Lawrence Grant (Judge Rufus Lennon); Claude King (Thomas L. Burke); William Austin (Dr. Eustace Gill); Jacqueline Gadson (Minnie Luther).

LADIES OF THE MOB (PAR,1928) 6,792'

Director, William A. Wellman; story, Ernest Booth; adaptation, Oliver Garrett, John Farrow; titles, George Marion,Jr.; camera, Henry Gerrard; editor, Lloyd Sheldon.

Clara Bow (Yvonne); Richard Arlen (Red); Helen Lynch (Marie); Mary Alden ("Soft Annie"); Carl Gerard (Joe); Bodil Rosing (Mother); Lorraine Rivero (Little Yvonne); James Pierce (The Officer).

THE FLEET'S IN (PAR, 1928) 6,918'

Director, Malcolm St. Clair; story-screenplay, Monte Brice, J. Walter Ruben; titles, George Marion, Jr.; camera, Harry Fischbeck; editor; B. F. Zeidman.

Clara Bow (Trixie Deane); James Hall (Eddie Briggs); Jack Oakie (Searchlight Doyle); Eddie Dunn (Al Pearce); Jean Laverty (Betty); Dan Wolheim (Double Duty Duffy); Bodil Rosing (Mrs. Deane); Richard Carle (Judge Hartley); Joseph Gerard (Commandant).

THREE WEEKENDS (PAR, 1928) 5,962'

Director, Clarence Badger; story, Elinor Glyn; adaptation, John Farrow; screenplay, Percy Heath, Louise Lang, Sam Mintz; titles, Paul Perez, Herman Mankiewicz; choreographer, Fanchon and Marco; camera, Harold Rosson; editor, Tay Malarkay.

Clara Bow (Gladys O'Brien); Neil Hamilton (James Gordon); Harrison Ford (Turner); Lucille Powers (Miss Witherspoon); Julia Swayne Gordon (Mrs. Witherspoon); Edythe Chapman (Ma O'Brien); Guy Oliver (Pa Oliver); William Holden (Carter); Jack Raymond (Turner's Secretary).

THE WILD PARTY (PAR, 1929) 7,167'

Director, Dorothy Arzner; story, Warner Fabian; titles, E. Lloyd Sheldon, George Marion, Jr.; dialogue, Sheldon, John V. A. Weaver; costumes, Travis Banton; song, Leo Robin and Richard Whiting; camera, Victor Milner; editor, Otho Lovering.

Clara Bow (Stella Ames); Fredric March (Gil Gilmore); Shirley O'Hara (Helen Owens); Marceline Day (Faith Morgan); Joyce Compton (Eva Tutt); Adrienne Dore (Babs); Virginia Thomas (Tess); Kay Bryant (Maisie); Alice Adair (Thelma); Jean Lorraine (Ann); Renee Whitney (Janice); Amo Ingram (Jean); Jack Oakie (Al); Marguerite Cramer (Gwen); Phillips Holmes (Phil); Ben Hendricks, Jr. (Ed); Jack Luden (George); Jack Raymond (Baloam).

THE SATURDAY NIGHT KID (PAR, 1929) 63 M.

Director, A. Edward Sutherland; based on the play *Love 'Em and Leave 'Em* by George Abbott, John V. A. Weaver; screenplay, Lloyd Corrigan, Ethel Doherty; dialogue, Corrigan, Edward Paramore, Jr.; titles, Joseph L. Mankiewicz; camera, Harry Fishbeck; editor, Jane Loring.

Clara Bow (Mayme); James Hall (Bill); Jean Arthur (Janie); Charles Sellon (Lem Woodruff); Ethel Wales (Lily Woodruff); Edna May Oliver (Miss Streeter); Hyman Meyer (Ginsberg); Getty Bird (Riche); Frank Ross (Ken); Eddie Dunn (Jim); Leone Lane (Pearl); Jean Harlow (Hazel Carroll); Irving Bacon (McGonigle); Mary Gordon (Reducing Customer); Ernie Adams (Gambler); Alice Adair (Girl).

DANGEROUS CURVES (PAR, 1929) 75 M.

Director, Lothar Mendes; story, Lester Cohen; screenplay Donald Davis, Florence Ryerson; dialogue, Viola Brothers Shore; titles, George Marion, Jr.; camera, Harry Fischbeck; editor, Eda Warren.

Clara Bow (Pat Delaney); Richard Arlen (Larry Lee); Kay Francis (Zara Flynn); David Newell (Tony Barretti); Anders Randolf (G. P. Brock); May Boley (Ma Spinelli); T. Roy Barnes (Pa Spinelli); Joyce Compton (Jennie Silver); Charles D. Brown (Spider); Stuart Erwin (Rotarian); Oscar Smith (Bartender); Ethan Laidlaw (Roustabout); Russ Powll (Counterman), Jack Luden (Rotarian).

PARAMOUNT ON PARADE (PAR, 1930) 102 M.

Producer, Albert A. Kaufman; directors, Dorothy Arzner, Otto Brower, Edmund Goulding, Victor Heerman, Edwin H. Knopf, Rowland V. Lee, Ernst Lubitsch, Lothar Mendes, Victor Schertzinger, Edward Sutherland, Frank Tuttle; choreographer, David Bennett; production designer, John Wenger; songs, Elsie Janis and Jack King; Sam Coslow; L. Wolfe Gilbert and Abel Baer; Richard A. Whiting and Raymond Eagen;

Whiting and Leo Robin; Ballard McDonald and Dave Dreyer; Mana-Zucca; Robin and Ernesto De Curtis; David Franklin; camera, Harry Fischbeck, Victor Milner; editor, Merrill White.

With: Richard Arlen, Jean Arthur, William Austin, George Bancroft, Clara Bow, Evelyn Brent, Mary Brian, Clive Brook, Virginia Bruce, Nancy Carroll, Ruth Chatterton, Maurice Chevalier, Gary Cooper, Leon Errol, Stuart Erwin, Kay Francis, Skeets Gallagher, Harry Green, Mitzi Green, James Hall, Phillips Holmes, Helen Kane, Dennis King, Abe Lyman & Band, Fredric March, Nino Martini, David Newell, Jack Oakie, Warner Oland, Zelma O'Neal, Eugene Pallette, Joan Peers, William Powell, Charles "Buddy" Rogers, Lillian Roth, Stanley Smith, Fay Wray, and: Iris Adrian, Mischa Auer, Cecil Cunningham, Robert Greig, Henry Fink, Jack Luden, Jack Pennick, Jackie Searle, Rolfe Sedan.

TRUE TO THE NAVY (PAR, 1930) 71 M.

Director, Frank Tuttle; story, Keene Thompson, Doris Anderson; dialogue, Herman J. Mankiewicz; songs, L. Wolfe Gilbert, Abel Baer; camera, Victor Milner; editor, Doris Drought.

Clara Bow (Ruby Nolan); Fredric March (Bull's Eye McCoy); Harry Green (Solomon Bimberg); Rex Bell (Eddie); Eddie Fetherstone (Michael); Eddie Dunn (Albert); Ray Cooke (Peewee); Harry Sweet (Artie); Adele Windsor (Maizie); Sam Hardy (Brady); Jed Prouty (Dancehall Manager); Charles Sullivan (Shore Patrol); Louise Beavers (The Maid); Frances Dee (Girl At Table); Maurice Black (Sharpie).

LOVE AMONG THE MILLIONAIRES (PAR, 1930) 74 M.

Director, Frank Tuttle, story, Keene Thompson; screenplay, Grover Jones, William Conselman; dialogue, Herman J. Mankiewicz; songs, L. Wolfe Gilbert, Abel Baer; camera, Allen Siegler.

Clara Bow (Pepper Green); Stanley Smith (Jerry Hamilton); Skeets Gallagher (Boots McGee); Stuart Erwin (Clicker Watson); Mitzi Green (Penelope Green); Charles Sellon (Pop Green); Theodor von Eltz (Jordan); Claude King (Mr. Hamilton); Barbara Bennett (Virginia Hamilton).

HER WEDDING NIGHT (PAR, 1930) 75 M.

Associate producer, E. Lloyd Sheldon; Director, Frank Tuttle; based on the play by Avery Hopwood; screenplay, Henry Myers; camera, Harry Fischbeck; editor, Doris Drought.

Clara Bow (Norma Martin); Ralph Forbes (Larry Charters); Charlie Ruggles (Bertie Bird); Skeets Gallagher (Bob Talmadge); Geneva Mitchell (Marshall); Rosita Moreno (Lulu); Natalie Kingston (Eva); Wilson Bege (Smithers); Lillian Elliott (Mrs. Marshall).

NO LIMIT (PAR, 1931) 72 M.

Director, Frank Tuttle; story, George Marion, Jr.; screenplay, Vila Brothers Shore, Salisbury Field; camera, Victor Milner, editor, Tay Malarkey.

Clara Bow (Helen "Bunny" O'Day); Stuart Erwin (Ole Olsen); Norman Foster (Douglas Thayer); Harry Green (Maxie Mindil); Dixie Lee (Dotty "Dodo" Potter); Mischa Auer (Romeo); Keene Duncan (Curley Andrews); G. Pat Collins (Charlie); Maurice Black (Happy); Frank Hagney (Battling Hannon); Paul Nicholson (Chief of Detectives Armstrong); William B. Davidson (Wilkie, Building Superintendent); Lee Phelps (Ticket Taker); Robert Greig (Doorman); Allan Cavan (Board Member); Bill O'Brien (George The Butler); Perry Ivins (Butterfly Man); Sid Saylor (Reporter).

KICK IN (PAR, 1931) 75 M.

Director, Richard Wallace; based on the play by Willard Mack; screenplay, Bartlett Cormack; camera, Victor Milner.

Clara Bow (Molly Hewes); Regis Toomey (Chick Hewes); Wynne Gibson (Myrtle Sylvester); Juliette Compton (Piccadilly Bessie); Leslie Fenton (Charles James Murray (Benny LaMarr); Donald Crisp (Harvey); Paul Hurst (Whip Fogarty); Wade Boteler (Diggs).

CALL HER SAVAGE (FOX, 1932) 92 M.

Associate producer, Sam E. Rork; director, John Francis Dillon; based on the novel by Tiffany Thayer; screenplay, Edwin Burke; art director, Max Parker; assistant director, Jack Boland; camera, Lee Garmes.

Clara Bow (Nasa "Dynamite" Springer); Gilbert Roland (Moonglow); Monroe Owsley (Lawrence Crosby); Thelma Todd (Sunny De Lan); Estelle Taylor (Ruth Springer); Willard Robertson (Peter Springer); Weldon Heyburn (Ronasa); Arthur Hoyt (Attorney); Katherine Perry (Maid); John Elliott (Hank); Anthony Jowitt (Jay Randall); Hale Hamilton (Cyrus Randall); Mischa Auer (Agitator in Restaurant); Mary Gordon (Tenement Lady).

HOOPLA (FOX, 1933) 85 M.

Director, Frank Lloyd; based on the play *The Barker* by Kenyon Nicholson; adaptation, Bradley King, J. M. March; music score, Louis De Francesco; camera, Ernest Palmer.

Clara Bow (Lou); Preston Foster (Nifty); Richard Cromwell (Chris); Herbert Mundin (Hap); James Gleason (Jerry); Minna Gombell (Carrie); Florence Roberts (Ma Benson); Robert Imhof (Colonel Gowdy).

Winner of the Fame and Fortune Contest, 1921

On the set of IT (Par '27) with scenarist Elinor Glyn

Advertisement for HOOPLA (Fox '33)

With Harold Austin and Thunder The Dog in BLACK LIGHTNING (Gotham '24)

With Leila Hyams in DANCING MOTHERS (Par '26)

With William Powell in THE RUNAWAY (Par '26)

With Ernest Torrence in MANTRAP (Par
'26)

With Antonio Moreno in IT (Par '27)

With Gary Cooper in CHILDREN OF DI-
VORCE (Par '27)

With Charles "Buddy" Rogers and Richard Arlen in WINGS (Par '27)

With Frances Raymond and Charles
"Buddy" Rogers in GET YOUR MAN (Par
'27)

With Lane Chandler in RED HAIR (Par '28)

With Richard Arlen in LADIES OF THE MOB (Par '28)

With Neil Hamilton in THREE WEEKENDS (Par '28)

With Fredric March in THE WILD PARTY (Par '29)

In DANGEROUS CURVES (Par '29)

With Fredric March in TRUE TO THE NAVY (Par '30)

With Jean Arthur and James Hall in THE SATURDAY NIGHT KID (Par '29)

With Skeets Gallagher and Ralph Forbes
in HER WEDDING NIGHT (Par '30)

With Stuart Erwin and Dixie Lee in NO
LIMIT (Par '31)

With Regis Toomey in KICK IN (Par '31)

With Richard Cromwell in HOOPLA (Fox
'33)

With Estelle Taylor and Willard Robertson
in CALL HER SAVAGE (Fox '32)

CLAUDETTE COLBERT

5'4 ½"
108 pounds
Brown hair
Hazel eyes
Virgo

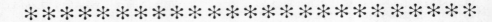

CLAUDETTE COLBERT brought a new kind of tongue-in-cheek vivacity to the sound cinema which sustained her as a major movie star for two decades. Her unique combination of physical assets—sleek appearance, trim figure, sparkling heart-shaped face, and throaty, vibrant voice—boosted her to the top ranks of cinema popularity. No matter what the role, she was always a lady. With her innate reticence, charm, and pose, she was unsuitable to portray anyone common or vulgar. Her mystique was as alluring as Marlene Dietrich's, but because she best fitted the stereotype of the practical-minded modern woman, she never attained to the living legend status reserved for those who play, and seem to be, aloof goddesses of physical and intellectual perfection.

Other new stage performers may have been as professionally industrious as Claudette during the 1920s, but few attained the degree of popularity she did on Broadway. When Claudette joined Paramount in 1929, she already had a solid background in a variety of major theatre roles. For three years Paramount wasted her talents in a succession of nice-heroine parts which, however insipid, still revealed what an engaging a personality she was and the viable extent of her potential. Her luck changed with Cecil B. DeMille's *The Sign of the Cross* (1932), in which she demonstrated her own brand of sexy screen magic.

In the next 12 years, Claudette proved how versatile a performer she was, winning an Academy Award for the comedy role in *It Happened One Night* (1934), and being Oscar-nominated for her dramatic portrayals in *Private Worlds* (1935) and *Since You Went Away* (1944).

At age 39, Claudette left Paramount to free-lance. She was still near the top of the screen heap, and had no difficulty throughout the rest of the 1940s in obtaining her salary demands. Finding suitable roles in well-produced features was something else.

Throughout the 1950s she made many distinguished television appearances, but failed to take advantage of lucrative video series offers made when TV executives still considered her name to be vital marquee bait. In the late 1950s she returned to the stage, revealing again how persuasive a performer she could be, as in the deft comedy *Marriage-Go-Round.*

Her last feature film to date, *Parrish* (1961), indicated that while she is now very matronly, she has lost none of her knack for pushing across a characterization. Few could so convincingly make a good deal out of so little.

When Claudette drifted into retirement in the mid-1960s, ignoring the perpetuation of her professional reputation, her admirers expressed dumbfounded amazement, indicating how little most people know of the real Claudette Colbert.

Claudette Colbert (née Lily Chaunchoin) was born in Paris, France, on September 13, 1905, the daughter of George and Jeanne (Loew) Chaunchoin. In 1912, when Mr. Chaunchoin suffered financial reverses in the banking business, the family, including the son Charles, came to the United States and settled in New York City. Claudette grew up near 53rd Street and Lexington Avenue, attending P.S. 15 and Washington Irving High School.

Of her home life Claudette once reminisced: "My mother spoke only French to my brother and me when we were children. Mother believes that many foreign-born parents err in speaking English to their youngsters when the adults themselves know little about it. The children should be taught the new tongue in schools, she says."

Claudette studied commercial art in school, planning to become a fashion designer upon graduation. She also continued her special interest in dramatics. As a youngster she had a slight lisp and studied speech to cure herself of the impediment. One of her teachers, Alice Rossetter, wrote a play, *The Widow's Veil,* and suggested that Claudette audition for a small role. The show opened at the Provincetown Playhouse in February, 1919, for a few weeks' run. Claudette, sporting a red wig and an Irish brogue, played a new bride.

After graduating from Washington Irving in 1923, Claudette enrolled at the Art Institute for a short period, earning her living by working in a dress shop and giving French lessons. One evening she was invited to a cocktail party and met playwright Anne Nichols, author of *Abie's Irish Rose.* Nichols invited Claudette to try out for her play *The Wild Westcotts.* Claudette agreed, since money was scarce and she reasoned that a stage career might offer a more lucrative income.

The Max Gordon-produced comedy of family life opened at Broadway's Frazee Theatre on December 24, 1923. Its cast included Cornelia Otis Skinner, Elliott Nugent, and Helen Broderick. Claudette's brief part called for her to mouth such one-liners as "It was so lovely," "The garden is very beautiful," "I am so hungry." After 25 performances, the show closed. By this time, Claudette had changed her name ("I hated the name Lily"), and adopted the maiden surname of her paternal grandmother with whom she had spent many of her early years on the isle of Jersey.

Claudette later said: "My father stormed, and was sure that actresses couldn't possibly be nice. He didn't want a stagestruck daughter. But I went ahead anyway. It seemed to me I must try this thing. . . . I was sure of one thing, and that was that I wanted to be an actress more than anything else in the world, that I could act, and could, if given proper opportunities, act well. I knew this in the back of my mind as clearly as I knew my own name. I didn't even have to convince myself, it was a fact that had always been there."

In the still active touring theatrical field of the mid-1920s, Claudette obtained a role in *We've Got to Have Money,* which played Chicago in February–March, 1924, *The Marionette Man* (Washington, D.C., April, 1925), and *Leah Kleschna* (Boston, Chicago, May–June, 1925).

There were no acting jobs available in the summer of 1925, but that fall she won the lead in Frederick Lonsdale's *The Fake,* being produced by Al Woods. After several weeks of rehearsal, the author insisted Claudette be replaced, offering her the humiliating alternatives of leaving the show or staying on as the understudy. She chose the latter and accompanied the production to Washington, D.C. where it folded in short order.

Then she won the role of Ginette, a wanton Montmarte habitué, in *The

Kiss in the Taxi (Ritz Theatre, August 25, 1925), produced by Woods, who thought she had talent and spunk. The show lasted 103 performances, and Claudette was termed "dark, agile, alive." Stereotyped French parts like this one bothered her: "In the very beginning, they wanted to give me French roles. You know—cute little maids with dark bangs and an accent. That was why I used to pronounce my name Col-bert just as it is spelt instead of Col-baire. I did not want to be typed as 'that French girl.'"

In her next production for Woods, Claudette had the lead in Avery Hopwood's *The Cat Came Back,* which played Pittsburgh and Chicago in January, 1926, and then she went immediately into *High Stakes*—as Anne Cornwall—which made the circuit of Chicago and other Midwestern cities that spring and early summer. It was at this time that her father died, which meant that Claudette now had to support her mother.

Claudette managed a Parisian trip in the summer of 1926, and returned to New York to comply with her recently signed five-year agreement with producer Woods. Employer and employee would have many fierce and well-publicized arguments re "that fatal contract," gaining Claudette the reputation of a battling dynamo. At least it assured her of steady employment under the prolific Woods banner.

She had a featured role in *The Ghost Train* (Ettinge Theatre, August 25, 1926) which costarred Eric Blore and Isobel Elsom. This mystery melodrama concerns six travelers forced to spend a night at a railroad station. It ran a short 62 performances.

Next she had an impressive assignment in *The Pearl of Great Price* (Century Theatre, November 1, 1926) in which she portrayed the Pilgrim in this allegorical spectacle by Robert McLaughlin. Roaring Twenties audiences were unmoved by the moralistic study of chastity and it folded after 33 showings. But Claudette received fine notices: "Makes a lovely and intensely living Pilgrim . . ."

At the time, she told the *New York American* about her theatrical success: "I'm lucky—it's half of stage success, you know. And I do work hard, sacrifice everything to get ahead. No beaux, for instance. Why I honestly think if the Prince of Wales should suddenly propose to me, I'd say after the first faint 'What! And give up my career?' I'm that earnest."

Woods lent her to producer Edgar Selwyn for the role of Lou, the side-show snake charmer in Kenyon Nicholson's *The Barker* (Biltmore Theatre, January 19, 1927). As the midway slut, she is asked to seduce Norman Foster, the son of carnival man Walter Huston. The two youths fall madly in love and depart for Chicago. About her trend-changing *Barker* role, Claudette exclaimed: "I'm mad about the part. She's a wicked, live baby, and I love her. I've got a flat, night-after-the-opening feeling, and the toothache. 'It hurts,' as Lou would say, 'like hell.' But nothing really matters, except Lou. The toothache won't last, and neither will the dumps. Lou will. And lady, lady, how good it feels to be human after wearing the pearl of virtue around my neck."

The daring realism of *The Barker* made it a long-running Broadway success (225 performances) and garnered extremely favorable notices for Claudette: "She is possessed of what vulgarians would call a come-hither too strong for criticism. She was delectable last night."

At this stage of her career Claudette was the darling of Broadway—not in the same league with Helen Hayes, Eva Le Gallienne, or Tallulah Bankhead, but a most popular marquee name. Her shapely figure impressed the journalists, who described her as possessing "the most Mistinguette-ish legs on Broadway" (Walter Winchell referred to her as "Legs" Colbert in his column).

One night during the run of *The Barker,* Claudette and coperformer Norman Foster, then 27 years old, eloped to a small Massachusetts town and were married. It was not until May of 1928 that a New York columnist broke the news of the marriage. Claudette later claimed she had kept the marriage a secret because she was afraid it would break her mother's heart.

With her stage career in full bloom, it was not long before film producers began making offers. Producer Robert Kane offered her a movie contract with First National Pictures. Her initial screen vehicle—filmed in New York—was *For the Love of Mike* (1927), directed by Frank Capra. The film script concerned Ben Lyon, the ward of three New York businessmen, George Sidney, Ford Sterling, Hugh Cameron—each of a different background so that ethnic humor could be rung in. Claudette, the cashier in their store, has a crush on Lyon, now a collegiate. The programmer opened in August, 1927, with Richard Watts, Jr. *(New York Herald Tribune)* reporting: "The only possible interest in *For the Love of Mike,* at the Hippodrome this week, lies in the fact that Claudette Colbert makes her screen debut in it. . . . She looks lovely, of course. She seems at ease before the camera and she does everything expected of her well enough, but the part itself is too characterless for one to judge her screen potentialities."

Claudette was depressed by the whole experience. She regarded her performance as "lousy" and had bad memories of the several arguments she and director Capra engaged in. Ten years later, she was still regaling the press with accounts of her tribulation in *For the Love of Mike.* She told Ed Sullivan: "On a cold, chilly morning, Frank [Capra] assembled us on the banks of the Harlem River for the rowing race sequence. I'll never forget it. I had on a light pink dress, 1927 collegiate model, and I stood on that damn river bank and waved my handkerchief to the hero, Ben Lyon, who was dying for Dear Old Yale out on the Harlem. Ford Sterling and George Sidney saved all of us by going to a restaurant half a mile distant for hot coffee."

At the finish of lensing *For the Love of Mike,* Claudette told one and all: "I shall never make another film." Her First National film contract was abrogated. The feature itself was a flop.

Claudette left *The Barker* to star in *The Mulberry Bush* (Republic Theatre, October 25, 1927). She was cast as Sylvia Bainbridge, the fiancee of aristocratic James Rennie, vying with widow Isobel Elsom for his love. The show collapsed after 29 showings, but Claudette won plaudits. The *New York World* reported: "Miss Colbert in the sort of role through which a woman of the world is usually indicated by the most elegant lifting of teacups, conceived the surprising idea of playing it as a human being—and incidentally as one of the most decorative human beings that ever trailed a negligee through a French villa."

Next came the undistinguished *La Gringo* (Little Theatre, February 1, 1928) which survived for 21 performances. Claudette was the half-breed Carlotta D'Astradente, brought home to New Bedford by sea captain George Nash. Alexander Woollcott *(New York World)* noted: "The role of Carlotta gives Miss Colbert a chance to remind us how slim and how comely she is and how excellent a newcomer among the actresses." It was later filmed as *South Sea Rose* with Lenore Ulric.

In May, 1928, Claudette and her husband Foster, along with James Kirkwood, went to London to appear in the West End production of *The*

Barker. When her marriage became known, Claudette stated that she and Foster would continue to maintain separate residences so that "love would never die."

Back in New York, Claudette made a striking appearance as Patricia Mason in *The Fast Life* (Ambassador Theatre, September 26, 1928), which featured Chester Morris and Crane Wilbur. A study of flaming youth and murder in a moment of passion, it died after 20 showings. Then came *Tin Pan Alley* (Biltmore Theatre, November 1, 1928). Although it folded in two and a half months, Claudette again pleased the critics. Robert Littell *(New York Evening Post)* wrote: "I am always afraid that Miss Colbert's roles, unfortunately, as a rule very feeble, will come apart, so naturally and violently does she tear into them."

Rarely without work, Claudette next accepted the female lead in the Theatre Guild's prestigious production of Eugene O'Neill's *Dynamo* (Martin Beck Theatre, February 1, 1929). Glenn Anders was cast as the minister's son who abandons God in favor of the new electronic age, represented by a dynamo machine. The allegory had Anders embracing the machine and being electrocuted, and concluded with Claudette staring intensely at the dynamo and stating in a most solemn voice, "Dynamo, I love you." (Claudette was teased for years about this preposterous bit of bad theatrics.) *Dynamo* was one of the few O'Neill productions to fail—it shut down after 66 performances. Once again the critics gave Claudette her due. Brooks Atkinson in the *New York Times* said she had given "the best performance of her career, vivid and descriptive without a trace of self-consciousness."

That fall Claudette appeared in Elmer Rice's comedy *See Naples and Die* (Vanderbilt Theatre, September 24, 1929). Audiences found it wearisome going: Claudette marrying a blackmailing Russian prince on condition he return passionate love letters her sister wrote to him years before. The prince is eventually killed, leaving Claudette free to marry her boyfriend, Roger Pryor. One reviewer remarked: ". . . [she] plays the glib girl in that confidentially hang-dog manner of hers without shading and looks swell, as always." The show faded before Christmas. It was Claudette's last Broadway stage appearance for 27 years.

The spate of bad plays, and the advent of talking films on a permanent basis, made Claudette reconsider her prior decision about the cinema. The production head of Paramount, B. P. Schulberg*, was then raiding Broadway for major talent to bolster his roster of performing stars. Whatever his faults, he was astute and, with the backing of Paramount's president Adolph Zukor,* charming enough to woo the bulk of the younger Broadway notables to the Paramount stable, a feat unparalleled by classy MGM or the other established film companies. Among the stars signed in 1928–30 by Paramount were Ruth Chatterton, Kay Francis, Phillips Holmes, Walter Huston, Fredric March, Helen Morgan, Jack Oakie, and Sylvia Sidney. While appearing in *Tin Pan Alley,* Claudette signed with Paramount. Her five-year contract gave her a healthy beginning salary, plus the option to continue starring on Broadway while filming at Paramount's Astoria, Long Island, studio. In buying up her stage contract from Woods, Jesse Lasky,* first vice-president of Paramount, stated in the official release: "We are convinced that Claudette Colbert is destined to be one of the outstanding figures on the audible screen of the near future. She combines rare native dramatic ability with unusual beauty and a thorough knowledge of the

*See Appendix.

technique of acting. Our plans for her include a number of important featured roles in the immediate future with stardom as her ultimate goal."

Claudette's initial sound feature was *The Hole in the Wall* (1929) which top-cast her over another stage star, Edward G. Robinson. Claudette appeared as a girl wrongly sent to prison who determines to have revenge on her accuser; Robinson was the Fox, an arch-criminal with whom she is involved. *Variety* observed: "Miss Colbert experiences the same difficulty which has confronted her in her stage career, lack of a sufficiently sturdy vehicle ... here she is but passably satisfying doing her average assignment quite well." Her deep throaty voice was well suited to the new medium and recorded well.

The Lady Lies (1929) reunited her with Walter Huston. He is a wealthy widowed attorney with two modern children who disapprove of his affair with lower-class Claudette. It was a deft handling of a delicate subject. *Variety* championed: "It is Miss Colbert who steals the picture with one of the most winning personalities the talkies now possesses." This film was completed during her *See Naples and Die* stage outing.

Needing an ingenue to play opposite its Gallic singing star Maurice Chevalier, Paramount selected Claudette. Her bilingual knowledge would allow her to work in both the English and the French versions of *The Big Pond* (1930). Besides, Chevalier had seen her on the stage and thought her "lovely, brunette, talented and a delicious comedienne, and her English was perfect." Filmed in Astoria, *The Big Pond*—partly scripted by Preston Sturges—had Venetian guide Chevalier romancing American tourist Claudette. She persuades her father, head of Billings Pepsin Chewing Gum, to import Chevalier to the States to work at his plant. The scheme nearly backfires, until the jovial boulevardier devises whiskey-flavored gum to whet the taste of Prohibition-bound Americans. The tune "You Brought a New Kind of Love to Me" was sung four times by Chevalier, with Claudette dueting in one of the encores. Claudette was pert but unremarkable in her portrayal—she was badly photographed and her voice this time was stridently reproduced. She and Chevalier also filmed a French version entitled *La Grande Mere*.

Claudette was next teamed with her husband Norman Foster in *Young Man of Manhattan* (1930), a domestic drama of a sportswriter and his too smug wife, a motion picture feature writer. Comedy relief was supplied by Charles Ruggles and Ginger Rogers. *Variety* felt that Claudette suggested "some of the qualities that distinguish Lois Wilson in her best roles." For performers that were married in real life, Claudette and Foster were not very convincing in their love scenes. (She had insisted he be cast in the feature.)

Next Claudette made *L'Enigmatique M. Parkes* (1930), the French-language version of *Slightly Scarlet* (1930), which had starred Evelyn Brent and Clive Brook in Paramount's original English-language version.

Due to Clara Bow's growing personal problems, Paramount replaced her with Claudette in *Manslaughter* (1930). This film was a remake of the Cecil B. DeMille silent drama of a careless young rich woman sent to prison for accidentally running down a pedestrian. After her release, she realizes she loves the former district attorney (Fredric March) whom she had spurned, and who had almost ruined his career due to feelings of guilt about prosecuting her case. Although *Manslaughter* was outdated melodrama, reviewers agreed that "given an even chance—[she] is capable of excellent acting."

It was Claudette's next assignment that really made filmgoing audiences aware of her screen personality and potential. In the well-mounted Ernst Lubitsch production, *The Smiling Lieutenant* (1931), she costarred with Maurice Chevalier and her old stage rival Miriam Hopkins. This light-hearted Ruritanian romance had Claudette as the saucy violinist Franzi, the apple of girl-chasing soldier Chevalier's heart. By accident he is forced to marry the dowdy princess, played by Hopkins, and he calls upon his mistress Claudette to instruct her in the art of charm and dress. The film premiered at the Criterion Theatre on May 22, 1931, and became a popular hit, with Claudette cited for her "splendid performance." It did much to elevate her position in the cinema industry.

Claudette then moved to the West Coast to continue her moviemaking. With typical abandon, Paramount casually cast her in a run of outdated dramas. Her picture lineup would be juggled with that of Sylvia Sidney, Miriam Hopkins, Carole Lombard, and others. The studio seemed unmindful at this point that these actresses were of very distinct and different acting styles and appeals.

In *Honor Among Lovers* (1931), Claudette was the worldly secretary of Fredric March. When he suggests that she accompany him on a global yacht trip, she hastily marries stockbroker Monroe Owsley to avoid temptation. She later discovers that Owsley is a cad, and decides that the seemingly reckless March is really her best bet. Claudette was a working girl again in *Secrets of a Secretary* (1931), which portrays her as a rich debutante who marries gigolo George Metaxa. When her family goes broke, he walks out, and Claudette finds employment as the secretary of a lord played by Herbert Marshall. He proves to be the perfect mate. Claudette was cited for her "talented work" in this drivel, in which she wore a blonde wig.

His Woman (1931), her fifth release of the year, teamed her with the studio's rising male lead, Gary Cooper. This tepid melodrama had been filmed before as *Sal of Singapore* with Phyllis Haver. Needing a "mother" to care for the orphaned baby he has found, skipper Cooper goes ashore at a Caribbean port. He hires Claudette for the post, not knowing she is a runaway witness in a criminal case and has been working as a dancehall girl plus in the hellhole city. Learning that the court case against her has been dropped, she accepts Cooper's offer in order to get free passage home. A mate on the ship recognizes her and makes advances. In the ensuing fight, Cooper knocks him overboard (he is picked up by another ship). Later, at the inquest, Claudette's evidence clears Cooper, but her shady past comes to light. In typical 1930s scriptwriting fashion, the sudden and dangerous illness of the baby reunites the lovers. Both stars were competent but miscast in *His Woman.*

Claudette's 1932 features got off to a dull start. *The Wiser Sex* (1932) found her posing as a swinger to uncover evidence to free her attorney boyfriend Melvyn Douglas, framed on a murder charge. Paramount's resident "other woman," Lilyan Tashman, offered diverting moments as the mistress of the lead crook. *The Misleading Lady* (1932) required Claudette to be a bored socialite again. This time she hankers to be the heroine in a forthcoming play. To win the role she must trap misogynist Edmund Lowe into proposing to her within three days. Stuart Erwin supplied the comedy relief as a crackpot who fancies himself to be Napoleon.

The Man from Yesterday (1932) was the first of three movies Claudette would make with Charles Boyer. She was cast as the wife of Clive Brook, reported missing in action during World War I. Now in love with the doctor, played by Boyer, she goes to Switzerland with him. There they meet Brook, slowly dying from a dose of poison gas. Richard Watts, Jr. *(New York Herald Tribune)* observed: "For the first time in a number of photoplays, the handsome Miss Colbert is properly photographed and one is permitted to see her again as the striking and alluring actress she really always has been. Her performance, too, is honest, sensible and believable."

In *Make Me a Star* (1932), a reworking of *Merton of the Movies,* with Stuart Erwin in the lead role, Claudette was a guest star seen on the Paramount lot along with Maurice Chevalier, Sylvia Sidney, Tallulah Bankhead, Jack Oakie, Fredric March, and others.

Phantom President (1932) found Claudette playing second fiddle to two George M. Cohans. The vaudeville star, in his talking film debut, portrayed a lackluster presidential candidate as well as a fast-talking quack doctor who is asked to double for the candidate. Both men love vivacious Claudette. Although she never looked lovelier, it was Jimmy Durante as Cohan's eccentric man Friday who caught the public's fancy.

At this point Claudette was disgusted with Paramount and her Hollywood career. Even with the changeover in executive control at the studio —Schulberg had been reduced to independent producer and Emanuel Cohen* was the creative head—there seemed nothing but a succession of dreary assembly-line roles and films ahead for her. She later said: "There was a time when I felt that one more sweet society girl would finish me. So when I was handed another colorless part and told I'd have to do it or go off salary, I went off salary."

It was at this juncture that Claudette attracted the attention of veteran producer-director Cecil B. DeMille* who was then staging his own comeback at Paramount, having directed a series of box-office disappointments at MGM. The showman thought Claudette had been badly mishandled by Paramount, which kept using her in "fluffy, light-headed roles which, I felt, did not give scope enough to her talent."

In his autobiography, DeMille recalls the situation in which he offered Claudette the secondary role of Nero's wife Poppaea in his pending spectacle *The Sign of the Cross* (1932). "I stopped her one day on the Paramount lot and without any warning or explanation asked her, 'How would you like to play the wickedest woman in the world?' Claudette Colbert's beautiful big eyes opened wider and she said: 'I'd love it.' Still, the part of Poppaea would be such a change for her I thought she had better be tested in it before being definitely cast. I gave her a page of the script containing a scene between Marcus and Poppaea, asked her to prepare it, and scheduled a screen test in costume.

"When she appeared in the costume of a Roman empress there was no doubt she fitted the part visually. But how would she handle the acting and the lines? I asked the empress and the noble Roman soldier to run through the lines once before we turned the camera for Claudette's test. It was the shortest dialogue test on record. Between them they spoke only five words of the script before I called a halt. It ran like this: March 'You harlot!' Colbert: 'I love you!' DeMille: 'That's enough. There's no need for a test. You have the part, Claudette.' "

The Sign of the Cross (1932) emerged as a typically elaborate DeMille pageant resplendent with crowd scenes, massacres, vulgarity, ludicrous dialogue, and below-par acting by most. It was set in ancient Rome with

*See Appendix.

mad Nero (Charles Laughton) on the throne and Claudette as his corrupt wife, capable of her own brand of outrageous behavior. March is introduced as the stalwart non-hero prefect of Rome, whose love for Christian martyr Elissa Landi brings out his humanity. Among the extravagant moments, Claudette's lengthy dip in the pool of asses' milk dramatically demonstrated that she possessed a fine anatomy—a fact overlooked by Paramount executives and most moviegoers till then. Bedecked in finery and wearing extreme makeup, Claudette provided a vivid contrast to her many previous nondescript movie assignments. *The Sign of the Cross* was not the box-office bonanza anticipated—movie musicals were doing better that season. There were some critics who agreed with Richard Watts, Jr. *(New York Herald Tribune)* when he pointed out: "She still gives the impression of being the nicest person in Rome, rather than its most evil citizen, as the story bills her."

After *The Sign of the Cross,* Paramount could no longer regard Claudette as a star by quantity (of film appearances) rather than quality. She still might be occasionally sluffed off into minor vehicles, but it was obvious from moviegoers' reactions to her Poppaea that her name meant something on the marquee.

Claudette was reteamed with Fredric March in *Tonight Is Ours* (1933) based on Noel Coward's play *The Queen Was in the Parlour.* This Ruritanian comedy of manners—the genre was then in vogue again—presented Claudette as a princess who almost renounces her love for Frenchman March in order to fulfill her royal obligations. Everything in this boudoir tale was sacrificed to emphasize the less gamey parts of Coward's dialogue which survived the transition to the screen. Claudette emerged second best or less to some: "... [she] carries off the Parisian revelries prettily enough, but her emotional range is too limited for her to realize even as much of the sadness of the Queen's light as the film tries to suggest" *(London Times).* Paramount came to the conclusion that Claudette and March were not sparkling box office, and did not pair them together again.

With her renegotiated Paramount contract, Claudette was allowed to make outside films. Her first loanout assignment was at United Artists in *I Cover the Waterfront* (1933). It aimed at rugged realism in its tale of reporter Ben Lyon using innocent Claudette to uncover the system her fisherman father (Ernest Torrence) uses for smuggling in rum and Chinese immigrants. The imaginative seaman sneaks the foreigners into San Diego sewn into the bellies of huge dead sharks. In the course of his racket being exposed, Torrence is killed; Claudette later forgives Lyon and weds him. In its time, *I Cover the Waterfront* was considered quite daring for its graphic presentation and rough dialogue. Claudette was disapproved of for not being convincing as a low-class fisherman's daughter.

Paramount's *Three Cornered Moon* (1933) was an early forerunner of the *My Man Godfrey* type of screwball comedy that Carole Lombard would essay so expertly. Daffy Mary Boland loses the family wealth in a bogus mine investment and her three unskilled children must seek employment in the Depression-glutted work world. Claudette is hired as a secretary in a shoe factory, but is more concerned with deciding between tempermental novelist Hardie Albright and sensible doctor Richard Arlen. Had the cast been less self-conscious or Elliot Nugent's direction more penetrating, their nutty behavior on screen would have produced a more contagious charm. Claudette was complimented for being "alert and able."

Her fifth 1933 release was grandiose soap opera, typical of the fallen woman genre then so popular. *The Torch Singer* (1933) offered Claudette as an unwed mother who supports her infant by working as a nightclub singer and subsequently as the accidental star of Aunt Jennie's radio hour. She was required in *The Torch Singer* to put across several songs—her theme song was "Give Me Liberty or Give Me Love"—and demonstrated that she had a modest contralto voice. The actress in her was able to project the desired husky yearning and the sob notes expected of a torch singer. During the feature's 72 minutes she ran the gamut of emotions, including a wild drunken scene. In her brittle, self-sufficient moments, Claudette's character fondly quotes her motto: "I'm like glass. Nothing will cut me but diamonds." Paramount at least provided Claudette with a lavish wardrobe.

By now Claudette had amassed a huge following, particularly among middle-class women who saw in her the prototype of the chic, superconfident female they had always hoped to be. She attacked her serious or comedy parts with energy and a tongue-in-cheek approach that made even the most improbable of her characterizations and pictures entertaining, and, more importantly, made her performance treasurable.

Cecil B. DeMille next utilized Claudette in *Four Frightened People* (1934), filmed on location in Hawaii. Claudette almost did not make the feature, for she underwent an emergency appendectomy just as filming was about to commence. DeMille offered Gloria Swanson the role, but the ex-Paramount star rejected the bid.

Four Frightened People had a very small cast for a DeMille production. Its principal characters were a prim Chicago schoolteacher (Claudette); a dedicated rubber chemist (Herbert Marshall); a bombastic newspaper correspondent (William Gargan); and the arrogant wife of a British official (Mary Boland). When a bubonic plague epidemic breaks out aboard a Dutch coastal steamer, this group commandeers a lifeboat and reaches the jungle coast. After tramping through the interior and surviving a pygmy attack and assorted jungle dangers, they reach safety, with those that survive becoming quite different people. The lumbering yarn was reminiscent of James M. Barrie's *The Admirable Crichton,* which DeMille had previously filmed as the silent *Male and Female* with Gloria Swanson. Claudette underwent the conventional movie transformation of a bespectacled girl who suddenly becomes beautiful once she removes her glasses and lets down her hair. Then Marshall and Gargan begin fighting over her. DeMille worked in a bathing scene, requiring Claudette to don palm leaves and later a leopard skin. *Four Frightened People* debuted at the Paramount Theatre on January 26, 1934, to a unanimously poor reception. It did not make back its costs. Also on the bill at the Paramount that week was a stage show featuring Miriam Hopkins in a condensed version of the drama *The Affairs of Anatol.*

Claudette was particularly unhappy about her next assignment on loanout to Columbia Pictures, for it required her to be directed by her past nemesis, Frank Capra. In retrospect, it seems outrageous folly that *It Happened One Night,* a hugely popular feature that won so many Oscars, should have had such a tenuous beginning. Originally MGM owned the rights to the basic story, Samuel Hopkins Adams's *Night Bus,* and Robert Montgomery and Myrna Loy were set for the leads. When studio boss Louis B. Mayer lost interest in the minor project, Columbia acquired it, planning to cast Robert Young and Arline Judge in the story. Time passed; Columbia was offered the services of Clark Gable—on punishment loanout—and it was decided that Judge was too young in contrast to Gable. Thus Claudette was eventually requested from Paramount to boost the production into a better-quality feature. She was on a four-week vacation at the time and agreed to the part after Columbia studio chief Harry Cohn accepted her $50,000 salary demand. (Margaret Sullavan, Constance Bennett, and Miriam Hopkins had also rejected the script. Hopkins reportedly said: "Not if I *never* play another part.")

Filming on *It Happened One Night* began in late November, 1933. Director Capra vividly recalls: "Colbert fretted, pouted, and argued about her part; challenged my slap-happy way of shooting scenes; fussed constantly about making her date [December 23, per her contract] at Sun Valley. She was a tartar, but a cute one."

The well-known plot of *It Happened One Night* finds snob Claudette arguing with her millionaire father Walter Connolly because he has annulled her marriage to a gigolo aviator. When the family yacht anchors near Miami, she swims ashore and boards a Greyhound bus bound for New York. Her seat partner on the bus is hard-boiled reporter Gable, who has just drunk his way out of a job. He discovers her real identity and threatens to expose her for the $10,000 reward unless she agrees to let him tag along to write a scoop story. Later, they are forced to leave the bus and hitch their way northward. What began as a hate relationship turns to love. Misunderstandings ensue, and only at the last moment does Claudette bolt away from a remarriage ceremony to the aviator and join Gable for a belated happy finale.

The highlight of this trend-setting comedy included the famous Wall of Jericho scene—in which a rope with a blanket tossed over it separates Claudette and Gable when they are forced to share the same auto camp room. Claudette had refused to partially disrobe before the cameras, so the set-up displayed her draping her undergarments on the blanket wall, one by one. Also famous was the subsequent hitchhiking sequence in which resourceful Claudette proved that a woman's shapely limb was more effective than cocky Gable's waving thumb. Claudette had rebelled at lifting her skirts for this interplay, until Capra brought a double on the set and threatened to use her legs for the close-ups.

It Happened One Night premiered at Radio City Music Hall on February 24, 1934, without much ballyhoo. The critics were pleased but in general not too impressed by the film, noting Claudette's "engaging and lively performance" and her "customary charm and skill." The feature caught filmgoers off guard and it was yanked from the Music Hall after the first week. But in subsequent release around the country, word of mouth quickly spread about this longer-than-usual comedy which had many memorable funny moments. The film, which cost under $300,000 to make, earned a sizable profit. It was remade as *Eve Knew Her Apples* and *You Can't Run Away From It*.

At the Academy Award ceremonies (February 27, 1935), *It Happened One Night* claimed five Oscars: best picture, best director, best screenplay (Robert Riskin), best actor, and best actress. Claudette remembers: "I was surprised when I got the prize. I really had no idea I would get it. In fact, I was ready to leave for New York the night they called to tell me about it. . . . Dressed in a mousy brown suit, I was escorted into the banquet hall full of diamonds and tail coats. It was especially embarrassing because I imagined they thought I was putting on an act, making an entrance. But it proved to be very nice, and I really am pleased about it all."

Claudette followed up her prize-winning comedy performance by appearing in the title role of Cecil B. DeMille's handsome epic *Cleopatra* (1934). She plays the resplendent queen of Egypt whom Julius Caesar (Warren William) craves. When the emperor is assassinated and she flees to Egypt, Marc Antony (Henry Wilcoxon) is dispatched to bring her back in chains. He succumbs to her worldly charms and is branded a traitor to Rome. After the Roman fleet defeats the Egyptian force at the battle of Actium, he commits suicide and she dies of a bite from the poisonous asp rather than be taken to Rome as a prisoner.

The sumptuous mounting of *Cleopatra* held the eye, but the trite colloquial dialogue often turned the drama into unwitting comedy. Claudette rose above the script to rivet viewers' attention as the devastating, long-haired temptress. Perhaps her most memorable moments occurred in her film entrance when she was unceremoniously dumped out of a rolled carpet before the amazed Caesar, and later on when she utilizes reverse psychology to make Antony capitulate to her will. In this particular sequence, she greets the reluctant emissary aboard her magnificent yacht and proceeds to describe in actuality the various ploys she intended using to ensnare him. As the camera pans back in a mighty sweep, the two would-be lovers are seen encased beneath a huge tent, surrounded by attendants, while the galley chieftain urges on the slave-oarsmen to the beat of drums and whips. *Variety* thought: "Miss Colbert's best moment is the death of Cleopatra. The rest of the time she's a cross between a lady of the evening and a rough soubrette in a country melodrama. It is not so much her fault as the shortcomings of the scenarists." Her pervading sense of *joie de vivre* carried the picture.

Claudette signed a new two-year contract with Paramount in 1934 and was now earning $5,000 a week. Her profile was considered the epitome of box-office beauty, capable of carrying a weak film on its own. Claudette would tell the press: "First of all, nobody can kid me about my beauty. I've looked at this 'pan' too many times. I'll admit that I can get by as an attractive girl, but mainly because I spend a lot of time on my appearance. Besides we're born with looks, but we have to acquire ability. Consequently, it is a far greater honor to have our ability recognized."

Claudette failed to mention that with her strong box-office value she could command, in all films in which she appeared, that she be photographed only from her left side or from the front. She firmly believed that her right profile was unflattering. This caused many a heartache to a producer-director who forgot her dictate and suddenly found himself with production suspended while a costly set was rebuilt or a camera replaced in new angles to abide by Claudette's decree.

For some time, Claudette and husband Norman Foster had been estranged in actuality as well as in spirit. Whenever one was on the East Coast on Broadway, the other was working in Hollywood, and so it went. Had it been someone other than Claudette, the fan magazines and gossip columnists would have had a field day elaborating on the ramifications of the Claudette-Foster separate residence policy. As it was, she had so enchanted the press and was so discreet at the proper time about all her behavior, that the press stories on her were blah pap, extolling her wonderful industry as an actress and her deportment as an avant-garde wife.

By mid-1934 the Claudette-Foster marriage was scarcely existent and Claudette had become a full-time active member of the Hollywood social scene. She had engineered a post as assistant director for her brother Charles at Paramount—he used the alias Charles Wendling—and he gradually drifted into becoming his sister's business agent.

Unlike most stars, Claudette was very shrewd in selecting vehicles for her outside assignments, usually picking a story far removed from the typical Paramount product. Sometimes she overstepped her own limitations and sank in the effort. In 1934 it was considered quite brave for Claudette to accept the lead in Fannie Hurst's tearjerker *Imitation of Life* (1934). Lensed at Universal, this chronicle story required her to enact a mother throughout the entire plot and also to have a grown-up daughter in the last half—a stigma no love goddess of the day would inflict on herself for her art. The contrived plot of *Imitation of Life* found widow Claudette and her black maid Louise Beavers, also widowed, creating the huge Aunt Delilah pancake business. Success brings financial happiness and emotional problems to each. Both Claudette and her daughter Rochelle Hudson are enamored of marine scientist Warren William, and after much trauma Claudette sends him away in a burst of self-denial. Beavers' daughter, Fredi Washington, is not satisfied with her material comforts but hopes to cross the color barrier. The death of Beavers, in a prolonged schmaltzy sequence, brings Washington to her senses. *Imitation of Life* was one of the first major Hollywood films to treat the taboo subject of racism.

The convenient solutions to the characters' problems, the plush and varied setting, and Claudette's earnest portrayal and elegant costumes made *Imitation of Life* exceedingly successful. Claudette was lauded because she "hits the harder sequences in easy strides" and projected her "usual charm and intelligence."

The Gilded Lily, the first of her four 1935 releases, showcased Claudette at her graceful best. Directed by Wesley Ruggles, the film teamed her with a new leading man, Fred MacMurray. He would be her most effective screen vis-à-vis. For many fans *The Gilded Lily* is the definitive Claudette performance. As stenographer Marilyn David, she is quite fond of newspaper reporter MacMurray. They meet each Thursday evening on a Fifth Avenue park bench in front of Manhattan's 42nd Street Library. There they discuss life and wage a continuing battle about which is the better snack, peanuts or popcorn. One day Claudette bumps into stuffy British peer Ray Milland in a subway. He is immediately infatuated with her, and soon asks her to marry him. When she refuses the lucrative offer, MacMurray and the newspapers tout her as the "no girl." She cashes in on her new celebrity status by becoming a swank club singer. After traveling to England to reconsider Milland's proposal, she realizes MacMurray is the only man for her. The *New York Times* review emphasized: "Claudette Colbert reminds us once more that her talents include a fine gift for comedy." One of Claudette's own very favorite scenes occurs in *The Gilded Lily:* She is performing her club act and in a moment of stage fright forgets her song and dance. She confides her confusion to the audience, who think it a fine bit of prearranged comedy. Claudette and MacMurray recreated their *Gilded Lily* roles on "Lux Radio Theatre," January 11, 1937.

In Walter Wanger's Paramount release *Private Worlds* (1935), Claudette switched to heavy dramatics. The movie was about the then taboo screen subject of mental illness. She played a hard working psychiatrist who comes into conflict with new staff supervisor, conservative doctor Charles Boyer. He disapproves of female physicians, but she wins his respect and love. Once she overcomes her haunting love for a boyfriend who was killed in World War I, she reciprocates his affectionate advances. Doctor Joel McCrea, who also admires Claudette, is almost undone by Boyer's vicious sister (Helen Vinson), who desires him, and by the horror of watching his own sister (Joan Bennett) go mad. The film's theme that everyone has his own private world of problems seems obvious nowadays, but the interaction between Claudette and Boyer holds up beautifully. Richard Watts, Jr. *(New York Herald Tribune)* wrote: "With remarkable skill, Miss Colbert succeeds in the hazardous feat of making the heroine both an attractive young woman and a credible scientist and I can assure you that in the cinema such an amalgamation is by no means simple."

Claudette was nominated for a best actress Academy Award, but lost out to Bette Davis for her performance in *Dangerous*.

Claudette was among the many celebrities attending Carole Lombard's Venice Amusement Park party on June 16, 1935. She and Marlene Dietrich, both wearing rather masculine garb, were photographed sliding down a long slide together. This in-tandem photograph was widely circulated and caused much scandalous speculation. The following month Claudette was in the news again with a $150,000 lawsuit filed against her by Mrs. Beatrice Manocci-Roncidelli of San Francisco, who claimed she had been injured in a car driven by Claudette. (The previous year, Claudette had to enjoin a Detroit distillery from an unauthorized use of her likeness in their Scotch whiskey advertising.)

In August, 1935, Claudette and Norman Foster ended their "adolescent attempt at wedlock" with a Mexican divorce. He would later marry Sally Blane, Loretta Young's actress sister, and would become a competent director of B-films.

She Married Her Boss (1935) was whipped up by Columbia, reteaming Claudette with the now adept farceur Melvyn Douglas. As Douglas's ultra-efficient private secretary-assistant, she forces the widower to admit he loves her. They marry, and she quickly adjusts to being an upper-crust matron. Taming his spoiled brat daughter (Edith Fellows) and nasty sister-in-law (Katherine Alexander) takes a bit of doing. In contrast, Douglas finds it near impossible to function at the office without his trusty helper. He almost loses Claudette before rediscovering that she is both a woman and a wife. Claudette made this comedy under an old Columbia agreement for $50,000, although her asking fee since the Oscar win had jumped to $100,000 per film.

The opening scenes of *She Married Her Boss* reveal a good deal about Claudette's acting technique. In the fast-paced sequences within the executive suite of Douglas's department store, Claudette is shown barking out orders (ever so ladylike), making snap decisions, and solving interoffice problems. With deft, subtle touches, she establishes the total credibility of her character's proficiency, making all (re)actions that follow consistent and believable. By a mere shrug of the shoulders, a hunching of the back, a quick turn away and look back, or a relaxed slouching with hands in pockets, Claudette projected the essence of the person she was depicting, both the woman's profession and her attitudes on life.

The Bride Came Home (1935) offered Claudette as a sharp-tempered, penniless socialite hired by wealthy Robert Young and his bodyguard Fred MacMurray to assist in their magazine venture. In a see-saw triangular love affair Claudette agrees to marry Young, but when MacMurray chases after the eloping couple on a motorcycle, she changes her mind and weds him instead. Edgar Kennedy provided laughs as the exasperated justice of the peace. The three leads did much to inject effervescent frivolity into this frail plot directed by Wesley Ruggles. *Variety* noted: "It's a made-to-measure framework for Miss Colbert, presenting her in the always attractive position of a young lady beset by two lovers, both fascinating and both collapsible at her slightest whim."

The year 1935 was another successful turning point in Claudette's career. She was named one of the ten top money–making stars of the year by the *Motion Picture Herald* (a position she would hold again in 1936 and 1947), and the press voted her the best dressed actress in Hollywood. She usurped the post from Warner Brothers' star Kay Francis. Claudette was always quick to tell the press that it was Paramount dress designer Travis Banton who deserved the credit for her modish outfits. Her famous bangs hair style, which softened her unusual heart-shaped face, was being worn by thousands of women everywhere.

At Paramount Claudette was known as the "frantic Frog" because of her seemingly nonstop work schedule. Each day she would appear on the lot with maid in tow, bringing her own lunch. In her dressing room she would apply her own makeup and start the business of the day.

When visiting New York in early 1935, Claudette informed the newsmen: "When I first started out there [Hollywood] I felt a little bit uneasy, but now I don't. Pictures were not nearly so good then as they are now. They were chiefly a mechanical device, limited by producers who belittled their audiences. This attitude has been changed to a large extent. Pictures are getting nearer an artistic goal all the time, and are demanding the best performance you are capable of."

Claudette met Philadelphia-born Dr. Joel Pressman, age 34, in mid-1935, when she had a checkup at his medical clinic. He was co-chief of head and neck surgery at the Cancer Division of City of Hope Medical Center in Los Angeles. They dated constantly, but even after her divorce from Norman Foster they refused to divulge to the press anything about marriage plans. On November 29, 1935, they arrived in San Francisco and registered at a local hotel as Mr. and Mrs. J. J. Pressman. When the press uncovered the pretext, they questioned the doctor. He soon engaged in a fist fight with one of the journalists, while the more calm Claudette insisted: "No, no, no! We're not married now. We're engaged. We're going to be married shortly after New Year's." A week earlier than planned, they were wed December 24, 1935 in Yuma, Arizona.

In 1936 Claudette was quoted as saying: "I have to like a role before I can play it at all. Mostly I prefer to do pictures that have new kinds of roles for me, and in any event I try not to do the same type of part in consecutive pictures." This proved true when she accepted Darryl F. Zanuck's offer to substitute for Simone Simon—who was not up to the role—in *Under Two Flags* (1936) at Twentieth Century-Fox. The story of Cigarette, a café girl in love with French Foreign Legionnaire Ronald Colman, had been filmed twice before: in 1916 with Theda Bara and in 1922 with Priscilla Dean. Spliced in between the conflict of Arabs versus Legion were the romantic chases of Claudette and swanky Rosalind Russell after Colman and Victor McLaglen after Claudette. The preposterous finale found Claudette rushing to Colman's aid at the cost of her own life. The $1.5 million actioner was roasted by the critics, who harped on the fact that Claudette's imposed French accent continually came and went, and that she was "more petulant than passionate" as the crude child of nature.

Under Two Flags was her only release of the year. Plans for her to star as Joan of Arc at Warner Brothers under Anatole Litvak's direction never jelled. She later claimed it was one of her greatest professional disappointments. On "Lux Radio Theatre" (July 20, 1936) she played with Walter

Huston and ex-husband Norman Foster in repeats of their roles in *The Barker.*

Her first costume film was *Maid of Salem* (1937), dealing with much the same subject as Arthur Miller's drama *The Crucible*. Both Claudette, as the demure Salem maid accused of demonry, and Fred MacMurray, as her refugee lover from Virginia, were too contemporary in bearing to convey the proper 1692 Colonial mood. Much more effective were Gale Sondergaard as a jealous woman of Salem and Madame Sul-te-wan as black Tituba, who inspired imaginative Bonita Granville with tales of witchcraft. The studio spent a good deal of money on the elaborate period sets, but the public did not buy the product.

Claudette returned to her specialty in *I Met Him In Paris* (1937). She is fashion designer Kay Denham, who has saved for five years to splurge on a three-week Parisian fling. Although her motto is: "I want peace, contentment, and security," she obviously finds suitor Lee Bowman too conservative. In France she attracts the attention of philanderers Robert Young and Melvyn Douglas. After a breezy stay in the capital, Young suggests going to Switzerland for skiing. Claudette agrees, but only if Douglas comes along as chaperone. Even when it is revealed that Young is already married, he does not give up the chase. In fact, at the fade-out, when Claudette and Douglas have already gotten married, Young is still pursuing her. It was all inconsequential, preposterous, but delightful escapism, and it also provided Claudette with an opportunity to demonstrate her skiing versatility in lengthy scenes filmed at Ketchum, Idaho. (She would later win trophies at Sun Valley, Idaho, for her athletic prowess on snow.)

Now at the height of her box-office popularity, Warner Brothers handed Claudette the choice assignment of *Tovarich* (1937), the film version of S. N. Behrman's play. The property had been originally promised to Warner star Kay Francis. Claudette costarred with Charles Boyer as royal Russian refugees who arrive in post-1917 Paris with 40 billion francs credit at the Bank of France. Loyal to the lost White Russian cause, they refuse to spend the royal funds on themselves or to turn it over to the Bolshevik government. When they can no longer steal enough to survive, they nonchalantly accept posts as maid and valet to banker Melville Cooper's bizarre family. Their reactions to the reversal of master-servant positions provided much of the comic sparkle. Eventually commissar Basil Rathbone appears, and they reluctantly agree it would be best for the new Russia if they release the funds. The two stars handled their roles with finesse, although some reviewers mentioned that Claudette lacked the high regal bearing projected by Marta Abba in the Broadway version. The $1.2 million *Tovarich* is one of Claudette's best remembered features; although during production she and director Anatole Litvak feuded so much, largely over his choice of a cameraman, that the film's scheduled completion was long in doubt. In the early 1960s, Vivien Leigh starred in an unsuccessful musical adaptation of *Tovarich*.

On "Lux Radio Theatre" (May 3, 1937) Claudette and Joel McCrea starred in *Hands Across the Table,* which had featured Carole Lombard and Fred MacMurray in the Paramount movie.

During 1937 Claudette earned a hefty $350,833, most of it deriving from her new (July, 1936) Paramount contract, which called for seven films at $150,000 per picture.

Her only 1938 release was Ernst Lubitsch's* remake of *Bluebeard's*

*See Appendix.

Eighth Wife, which had starred Gloria Swanson in 1923. Gary Cooper made do as the multimillionaire American who has divorced his first seven wives. In a Riviera department store, he meets Claudette (he wants to purchase pajama tops, she wants the bottoms—not for herself, it turns out). Sparked by her originality, he determines to marry the independent miss. But impoverished French aristocrat Claudette is not interested, at least not until her father Edward Everett Horton insists. She reluctantly weds Cooper, but leads him on a merry chase about Europe, determined to housebreak the roving playboy. He becomes browbeaten but divorces her, which whets her appetite. Now she chases him and matches his determination for dominance. All ends happily. Moviegoers were not impressed by the Charles Brackett-Billy Wilder script, nor by Cooper appearing out of his screen element. The film was not financially successful, and it was Lubitsch's last Paramount movie.

In 1938 Claudette was the sixth top money making career woman in America, with an income of $301,944, a decrease of some $50,000 from the previous year when she was fourteenth.

Claudette replaced Paramount's faltering import Isa Miranda in the studio's remake of *Zaza* (1939), which had been a Gloria Swanson silent film of 1923. Despite George Cukor's swank direction, the resulting study of a music hall tart in love with married aristocrat Herbert Marshall was embarrassingly flat. To appease the Hays Office, Claudette's wild soubrette characterization was tamed to just a coy songstress of the 1904 French stage, which was the prime fault of this reworked evergreen. Even her mild can-can dance was largely excised to please the censors. Her revenge on Marshall, by becoming the (bedroom) toast of the Folies Bergere, is merely hinted at in an oblique manner. The few sparks in the production, which barely focused on cabaret numbers or even backstage life, were provided by Bert Lahr as Claudette's stage partner and adviser, Helen Westley as her mercenary foster mother, and Constance Collier as her maid. Claudette was attired most attractively and her singing voice had improved, but the *New York Sun*'s Eileen Creelman said, "Miss Colbert seems more Hollywood and Broadway than of the French music halls." When *Zaza* opened at the Paramount Theatre, on January 4, 1939, the accompanying stage show starring Benny Goodman and his orchestra fared much better.

Claudette was back in her bubbling element in Mitchell Leisen's *Midnight* (1939). As a stranded American showgirl in Paris, she is hired by extravagant John Barrymore to lure gigolo Francis Lederer away from Barrymore's straying wife, Mary Astor. Don Ameche provides Claudette's love interest as the proletarian taxi driver who earns her respect and love. The Charles Brackett-Billy Wilder screenplay gave her one of her best comic situations. Posing as a Hungarian baroness, she is a winning mixture of naivete and sophistication, carrying off her guise among the social set while constantly overwhelmed by the luxuriant life around her. Frank S. Nugent *(New York Times)* wrote: "She has superb command of the comic style, can turn a line or toss a vase—with equal precision." Director Mitchell Leisen also helmed the remake of *Midnight, Masquerade in Mexico,* (1946), starring Dorothy Lamour.

At MGM Claudette appeared in *It's a Wonderful World* (1939), as an eccentric poetess mixed up with would-be detective James Stewart. On the way to prison for a crime he did not commit, he escapes and kidnaps Claudette when he steals her car. While he hunts the real criminal, she is on hand to bail him out of one jam after another. Even in this daffy role,

Claudette managed to be plausible and vibrant. *It's a Wonderful World* was greeted as just another glossily made entry in the waning madcap comedy genre.

Drums Along the Mohawk (1939), based on the Walter D. Edmonds novel, is one of the few American feature films about America in the era before the Revolutionary War. With a lavish Twentieth Century-Fox production budget and hearty direction by John Ford, the technicolor feature blended historical rightness with an action-filled story of a pioneer New York farming couple (Claudette and Henry Fonda) fighting to survive against nature and the Indians. Claudette emoted too earnestly to properly convey the rugged tribulations of frontier life. She overlayed her performance as a well-bred woman with a browbeaten look. Edna May Oliver offered a lusty sidelight performance as a self-sufficient pioneer woman, and Arthur Shields was properly humane as the fighting parson. Claudette and Fonda recreated their *Drums Along the Mohawk* roles on the "Kate Smith" radio program (November 3, 1939).

Claudette was among the numerous stars suggested for the Scarlet O'Hara role in *Gone with the Wind.* Plans for her to team with Cary Grant in *Passport to Life* at RKO in 1939 did not work out. One of her artistic off moments was her radio performance opposite Grant on the "Lux Radio Theatre" version of *The Awful Truth* (September 11, 1939). *Variety* reported: "Miss Colbert, ordinarily a deft comedienne, was surprisingly heavy. She pulled all the stops, and, except in the broad scene in which she breaks up her hubby's scheduled remarriage, played the piece as slapstick. Even her voice didn't sound natural."

Claudette took third billing in MGM's $2 million chronicle of wildcat oil drilling, *Boom Town* (1940). As the schoolteacher fiancee of Spencer Tracy, she decides to marry his friend Clark Gable instead. She remains on the sidelines while the two men make and lose their fortunes and camaraderie. As the loyal wife, her character was rather colorless, yet at 35 Claudette more than held her own against 26-year-old Hedy Lamarr, who portrayed the decorative other woman. The Gallup poll rated *Boom Town* the most popular picture of 1940.

In the early 1940s, with Carole Lombard gone. Claudette and relative newcomer Paulette Goddard were Paramount's top actresses of light comedy roles; each would continue to blossom under ace director Mitchell Leisen's supervision. In *Arise, My Love* (1940), director Leisen deftly blended comedy and drama in a tale about the aftermath of the Spanish Civil War. With a character name of Augusta Nash and a nickname of Gusto, Claudette was an enterprising reporter for Associated News, with Walter Abel as her boss. The film opens in a brittle vein as Claudette poses as the wife of condemned soldier of fortune, aviator Ray Milland, to free him from a Spanish prison so she can write a big scoop feature. After Claudette and Milland marry, the feature film is transformed into a serious propaganda study for the free world and concludes on a high-note of flag waving. Claudette and Milland have just been rescued from a torpedoed ship. They are so angered that they become determined to return to America and tell everyone what they have witnessed in Europe. With utter conviction, Claudette says to Milland and the audience: "Arise my love and make yourself strong. Is it going to be their way of life, or ours?" The film garnered excellent reviews. In a four-star critique, Kate Cameron of the *New York Daily News* said: " . . . [they] play their roles lightly but with a sensitive appreciation of the potential tragedy of their situation." *Arise, My Love* is Claudette's favorite film.

Even after turning down the lead in Columbia's remake of *The Front Page,* retitled *His Girl Friday* (1940), Claudette earned a whopping $426,944 in 1940.

Skylark (1941) again teamed her with Ray Milland in a screen version of a Samson Raphaelson play that had starred Gertrude Lawrence on Broadway. The frothy plot hinges on Claudette's fifth wedding anniversary decision that she is tired of being secondary to husband Milland's advertising business. Soon attorney Brian Aherne is flirting with Claudette, and agrees to marry her once she obtains a Reno divorce. But in time she concludes that Milland is not so bad after all. The film's best scenes include a lengthy squabble on a crowded subway and an emotional tossup while on a stormy sailboat jaunt in Long Island Sound. Binnie Barnes was at her arch best as the amorous wife of Milland's most important client, and Walter Abel drolly interpreted his stock assignment as Milland's indulgent friend. Claudette was praised for offering "one of the spunkiest and most body-bruising performances in her career." Claudette, Milland, and Aherne were heard in their *Skylark* roles on "Lux Radio Theatre" on February 2, 1942.

In 1941 Claudette joined with Ronald Colman, Charles Boyer, Irene Dunne, Lewis Milestone, and Anatole Litvak to form a producing unit at Twentieth Century-Fox to turn out meaningful films. This agreement was in addition to Claudette's three-films-per-year Paramount pact. Fox's *Remember the Day* opened at the Roxy Theatre on Christmas Day, 1941. This intimate drama opens with Claudette as an elderly schoolteacher visiting presidental candidate and former student Shepperd Strudwick. While waiting to talk with him, she recollects her past life. The extended flashback traces her courtship and marriage to fellow teacher John Payne, who is killed in World War I. Director Henry King largely avoided the mawkish aspects of the script by gliding over possible clichés and bathos. Claudette's decision that newcomer John Payne be given the male lead greatly boosted his film career.

Claudette dropped out of Paramount's *Take a Letter, Darling* (1942)—Rosalind Russell accepted—but did appear in *The Palm Beach Story* that year. Of all the Paramount actresses to be utilized by writer-director Preston Sturges in his comedies, Claudette was one of the few who did not have to rise to the occasion. She was already vastly adept at his mixture of light-hearted seriousness and mild slapstick. Herein, she is a flighty wife who calls it quits after five years of marriage to penurious civil engineer Joel McCrea, and takes off for Florida, planning to find a rich mate to finance McCrea's airport project. On the luxury train she becomes entangled with the mad Ale and Quail Club which adopts the bewildered miss as their mascot and provides her with a free trip. She encounters stuffy millionaire Rudy Vallee in the Pullman car and sets her sights on him. Once in Florida she plays footloose with pursuing McCrea to teach him a lesson. Then she has to compete with Vallee's much-married sister, Mary Astor, who hankers after McCrea. The finale reunites Claudette and McCrea, and reveals that they each have twin siblings, which nicely takes care of Astor and Vallee. The film concludes with the line: "They lived happily ever after—or did they?"

Claudette rejected the role of Loxi in Cecil B. DeMille's *Reap the Wild Wind* (Paulette Goddard was substituted), and *The Palm Beach Story* was her only 1942 release.

During World War II, Claudette's husband, Dr. Pressman, was a Navy lieutenant. She devoted much of her spare time to the various servicemen's canteens functioning in Hollywood and to selling war bonds.

No Time for Love (1943) was polished if mindless comedy, devoted to the proposition that fashionable women often prefer brawny, uncultured men. Photographer Claudette meets rough sandhog Fred MacMurray. They fight. He becomes her assistant and they make up. She discards her fey suitor Paul McGrath to land MacMurray, who really is a college graduate testing his new invention to keep tunnels free of mud. Claudette's big moments are the scene in which she socks vamp June Havoc, who insists she has stolen MacMurray back, and the finale, with Claudette and MacMurray scrambling for safety in the middle of a muddy tunnel. Ilka Chase plays Claudette's acid-tongued sister, and Richard Haydn is an effete member of their social set.

So Proudly We Hail (1943) was a 126-minute supersalute to the wartime nurses stationed in Bataan. Claudette plays the understanding mother hen, Paulette Goddard the glamorous nurse, and Veronica Lake the bitter soul. The few romantic scenes are played down—when Claudette finally marries soldier George Reeves, she falls asleep on their honeymoon. She voices with conviction all the hate dialogue so essential to World War II propaganda pictures, such as her exclamation "the slimy beasts" when the Japs begin bombing the Yank stronghold. As Bosley Crowther (*New York Times*) summed it up: "She does manage to strike occasional sparks and a measured note of sincerity, although she has a lot of trash to wade through." Claudette and her studio rival Paulette feuded during production, but they made up sufficiently to repeat their roles in *So Proudly We Hail,* along with Veronica Lake, on "Lux Radio Theatre," November 1, 1943.

For United Artists, Claudette portrayed the mother of Jennifer Jones and Shirley Temple in David O. Selznick's *Since You Went Away* (1944). Wags made much of the fact that Claudette was finally playing a role closer to her own age (39). However, she proved them wrong. In this idealized drama devoted to the "American fortress, the American home," she represented the typical, albeit glamorized, American mother. When husband Neil Hamilton enlists during World War II, she takes in crusty boarder Monty Woolley, and later does her patriotic bit by working as a defense plant welder (no factory worker ever looked so stunning). Jones endures the death of boyfriend Robert Walker, and Temple muddles through adolescence and a crush on Claudette's good friend, Navy lieutenant Joseph Cotten. The 172-minute feature abounds in maudlin moments but is constantly saved by rich performances: Hattie McDaniel as the loyal maid, Agnes Moorehead as the bitchy friend, Nazimova portraying the dedicated naturalized American, and Guy Madison as the wholesome young soldier. *Since You Went Away* has a very stylish upbeat ending with Claudette on Christmas eve receiving a phone call from her husband, previously listed as missing in action. As she jubilantly rushes upstairs to inform her daughters, the camera draws back for a grand exit of tearjerking splendor. Claudette received her third Oscar nomination for this film but lost out to Ingrid Bergman who won for *Gaslight.*

Claudette returned to Paramount for *Practically Yours* (1945), her fourth feature directed by Mitchell Leisen. The script, with its sloppy combination of pathos and humor, found aviator hero Fred MacMurray forced to court and marry Claudette when, on a suicide wartime mission, he is mistakenly quoted as bidding her (really his dog) farewell. Since the author of *Practically Yours,* Norman Krasna, had concocted the stage play *Dear Ruth,* there was much similarity of style and content.

This was her last Paramount film, for Claudette refused to renew her

Paramount contract. She stated: "Yes, I am free. I have been 15 years at that studio. My agent [her brother] is rather angry with me because I want to free-lance, but I am going to do it. I believe that I have reached a stage where nothing is gained by a long-term contract. I get a certain price ($150,-000) for my pictures and have worked hard to attain some economic freedom. Now I am going to do what I wish."

United Artists' *Guest Wife* (1945), directed by Sam Wood, was decidedly minor fare, suffering from very modest production values. As Dick Foran's wife, Claudette poses as Don Ameche's wife to solve a business dilemma. Otis L. Guernsey, Jr. *(New York Herald Tribune)* reported: "Claudette Colbert twists her features into an aching variation of moods as she is asked to become coy, angry, bewildered and scheming without sufficient material to back up her posing."

Much better was RKO's *Without Reservations* (1946) directed by Mervyn LeRoy, which successfully teamed Claudette with John Wayne. She is a famous authoress (her book showed how to solve postwar problems) heading to Hollywood where her book is being made into a film. She thinks Marine Wayne would be ideal for the male lead. Before the conclusion of this light comedy, they have been booted off the train for drunkenness and proceed to the West Coast via foot and car. Claudette and Robert Cummings were heard in the "Lux Radio Theatre" version on August 26, 1946.

The dramatic *Tomorrow Is Forever* (1946) found Orson Welles and Natalie Wood stealing all the plaudits. Claudette is Welles's wife. When he is reported missing during World War I, she marries loyal friend George Brent. A much physically altered Welles returns to America accompanied by German war orphan Wood. He refuses to reveal himself, and instead helps her to adjust to her son's enlistment during World War II. In this 1918–39 chronicle, Claudette had 18 Jean Louis-designed wardrobe changes. While *Newsweek* would state, "Miss Colbert plays with her customary sincerity and appreciation of what she is about," it was evident that Claudette's performance relied too much on her well-established bag of emoting tricks instead of digging deep for new avenues of approach. Her once effective use of playing with the catch in her voice, widening and blinking her saucer-big eyes, and the abrupt twisting of her upper torso to register strong emotion, were becoming repetitious habits.

MGM required an American Greer Garson to carry *The Secret Heart* (1946) and hired Claudette to portray the young widowed mother of emotionally disturbed June Allyson (she has a father fixation) and Robert Sterling (he is just out of the Navy). Hollywood's answer to *The Seventh Veil* proved to be a vehicle for Allyson, leaving Claudette and pipe-smoking suitor-neighbor Walter Pidgeon in the background. Claudette and Pidgeon repeated their *Secret Heart* roles on radio's "Screen Guild Players" (November 17, 1947, CBS).

Because of the high domestic rentals of *Tomorrow Is Forever* ($3.25 million) and the earlier *Without Reservations* ($3 million), Claudette finished twenty-fifth in *Variety*'s poll of top-grossing stars of 1946, with Bing Crosby in number-one position.

Claudette's career was definitely on the wane when Universal adroitly teamed her and Fred MacMurray in a filmization of Betty MacDonald's *The Egg and I* (1947), a top box-office winner of the year. It pandered to all the slapstick situations supposedly befalling city folk who attempt to run a farm. The surprise stars of *The Egg and I* were the winning combination of Marjorie Main and Percy Kilbride as the shiftless hicks, Ma and Pa

Kettle. So enormous was the response to these rural wonders that it spawned a long running series of "Ma and Pa Kettle" features at Universal. *The Egg and I* was Claudette's last major box-office hit.

In the spring of 1947, Claudette was signed for $200,000 to play opposite Spenscer Tracy in MGM's *State of the Union* (1948). At the last minute Claudette insisted director Frank Capra comply with her usual policy of quitting work at 5 P.M. daily. He refused, scrapped her $15,000 wardrobe, and substituted Katharine Hepburn who had been anxious to do the movie.

Sleep, My Love (1948) was an unconvincing spine-chiller produced by Mary Pickford. Don Ameche plots to murder wife Claudette so he can cavort with Hazel Brooks, but do-gooder Robert Cummings intervenes. It did nothing for anyone's film career.

Universal attempted to cash in on *The Egg and I*'s success by yet again teaming Claudette and Fred MacMurray in *Family Honeymoon* (1949). College professor MacMurray marries widow Claudette, and her three children join them on their Grand Canyon honeymoon. Rita Johnson was on hand as MacMurray's old flame. Filled with the expected, the movie lacked the needed zest and pacing. It was given a Radio City Music Hall premiere (February 24, 1949) and did only moderately well. Claudette and MacMurray recreated their roles on "Lux Radio Theatre" (April 4, 1949, repeated April 23, 1951).

Bride for Sale (RKO, 1949) was Claudette's last screen comedy, In a triangular love situation, she portrays a practical-minded businesswoman who attracts both Robert Young and George Brent. Her efforts to bring life to the film were wasted. She, Young, and Gene Raymond were heard on the "Lux Radio Theatre" version on May 5, 1950.

Claudette had been signed to star in *All About Eve* (1950) at Twentieth Century-Fox, but she suffered a back injury just as location filming at San Francisco's Curran Theatre was getting underway. She was hastily replaced by Bette Davis.

Instead, Claudette made *Three Came Home* (1950) for Fox, based on the true account of American authoress Agnes Newton Keith, who was captured in the 1941 Japanese invasion of Borneo. Her husband, Patric Knowles, is separated from Claudette and their son. Prison compound commander Sessue Hayakawa proves to be civilized and cultured, and an admirer of Claudette's writing. Their polite relationship is realistically contrasted with the barbaric conditions in the camp. Conforming to 1950s screen morality, director Jean Negulesco suggests rather than shows Claudette's rape by a Japanese soldier: a swirling sandstorm darkens most of the screen, with only Claudette's widening terrified eyes indicating what is happening. *Three Came Home* is her last major motion picture to date.

RKO's *The Secret Fury* opened February 21, 1950, at the Paramount Theatre, one day after *Three Came Home* premiered at the Astor Theatre. Its overwrought melodramatics were directed by sometime actor Mel Ferrer. Pianist Claudette is being driven insane by her architect fiance, Robert Ryan. She was quite unsubtle in delineating her mental unhinging.

RKO had offered Claudette the option of directing some features, but she declined when they later insisted that she also star in the productions (such as *All Women Are Human,* dealing with a female biochemist). "Very few people have managed both successfully, so I stuck to emoting," explained Claudette.

Thunder on the Hill (1951), set in Norfolk County, England, offered Claudette as a detective nun who saves wrongly convicted Ann Blyth from hanging. Claudette's nervous posturing in her nun's habit was not engaging.

Let's Make It Legal (1951) was assembly-line Twentieth Century-Fox domestic comedy, and a misfire. Trim grandmother Claudette wearies of husband MacDonald Carey's fondness for gambling, so she institutes divorce proceedings. He must compete against her old beau Zachary Scott to woo her back.

Claudette continued starring in radio drama, such as *The Age of Innocence* (November 11, 1951) with MacDonald Carey; and *Twentieth Century* (November 20, 1951) with Gregory Ratoff; both on ABC's "Theatre Guild of the Air." She made her television debut on the "Jack Benny Show" in April, 1951, with Basil Rathbone and Robert Montgomery as additional guests. In the fall of 1951, it was announced that she would star in a CBS teleseries "Leave It To Lizabeth" and she filmed a pilot episode as the young widow with a teenaged daughter. Despite the very lucrative terms offered ($1 million), she backed out. "My husband kept telling me that no matter how much money I could make on television, there isn't enough of it around to get involved with something that might impair my health. I went along with him at the time." It proved a big mistake in her mature acting career, and she later regretted the decision, filming another pilot about a glamorous congresswoman. Both pilot shows were eventually telecast as part of a summer-replacement anthology series. Her successful playing of the lead role in *The Royal Family of Broadway* ("Best of Broadway," September 15, 1954, CBS) convinced CBS to place her under a special five-appearance pact. She subsequently graced productions of *Magic Formula* (1955), *The Guardsman* (1955), *Private Worlds* (1955), and *Blithe Spirit* (1956). She walked out of one "Climax" (CBS) episode, but did appear in *After All These Years* on "Robert Montgomery Presents" (1956, NBC) guested on the "Steve Allen Show" (1956, NBC), was one of the celebrities on the "General Motors 50th Anniversary Special" (1957, NBC) and headlined *One Coat of White* for "Playhouse 90" (1957, CBS). She portrayed Mary Roberts Rinehart on "Telephone Time" (1957, ABC) and was in *Blood in the Dust* on "Zane Grey Theatre" (1957, CBS). She also did a two-part "G.E. Theatre" fantasy melodrama (1959, CBS) and starred in *The Bells of St. Mary* (October 27, 1959, CBS). *The Bells* was her last major acting vehicle on television. During the 1959–60 video season, she hostessed CBS's monthly afternoon-special-information series, "The Women." In 1963 she and Edward G. Robinson were among the veteran stars appearing in Maxwell House Coffee television and billboard advertisements.

Claudette had intended returning to the stage in 1949 in *Lily Henry* by Grace Klein and Mae Cooper. Two years later, producer Max Gordon presented her in a summer tour of Noel Coward's *Island Fling* (also known as *South Sea Bubble*). It had originally been written for Gertrude Lawrence, who was then too busy with *The King And I*. Claudette portrayed the daughter of a duke, married to the governor (Leon Janney) of a British island colony. Since he is a former greengrocer, there is a clash of traditions. George Freedley *(New York Morning Telegram)* reviewed the comedy at the Westport Playhouse: "She projects as delightfully now as then (1928). Her handling of the drunk scene was deft and delicious, taking the sting out of it but never losing characterization."

With no realistic film offers from Hollywood, Claudette went abroad where her cinema reputation still counted. *Outpost in Malaya* (1952) was an unevenly directed J. Arthur Rank feature, helmed by Ken Annakin. The domestic woes of rubber planter Jack Hawkins and his bored socialite wife Claudette are interrupted by a native uprising. Otis. L. Guernsey *(New York Herald Tribune)* quipped: "Miss Colbert runs around like a hostess at a busy party, lending a hand at the guns wherever needed."

The French-made *Daughters of Destiny* had a very limited United States release in 1954. In the first of the three episodes, "Elizabeth," Claudette plays an American widow visiting the site of her husband's World War II grave in Italy. She is understanding to farm girl Eleanora Rossi-Drago, who bore his child.

Back in Hollywood for RKO, Claudette graced *Texas Lady* (1955), her first Western feature. She travels from New Orleans to Ft. Ralston, Texas, to run the local newspaper, and is supported in her anticorruption campaign by gambler Barry Sullivan and the Texas Rangers. Although filmed in Superscope and color, the yarn was too genteel to arouse audience interest. The matronly Claudette seemed "somewhat out of her element."

During the summer of 1955, Claudette toured in *A Mighty Man Is He* by Arthur Kober and George Oppenheimer. She plays a former Follies girl married to a theatrical producer, and even sang snatches of "Rag Me That Mendelssohn March." It was decided not to bring the venture to Broadway.

Claudette rejected a featured role in Cecil B. DeMille's *The Ten Commandments* (1956) at Paramount, but accepted a two-month Broadway assignment. On April 2, 1956, she replaced Margaret Sullavan at the Plymouth Theatre in the mature social comedy *Janus,* costarring with Claude Dauphin and Robert Preston. Claudette said: "When you replace another actress you have to follow all her stage business so as not to throw the cast off. And my personality is very different from Maggie's. She has a fey quality in her comedy. But the more ridiculous the situation, the more serious I play it." *Variety* decided that Claudette was "obviously an excellent choice to hold the hit show together . . ." She left the cast on June 9, 1956, and was replaced by Imogene Coca.

The French-produced feature *Royal Affairs in Versailles* finally reached America in an aborted form in 1957. The mammoth Sacha Guitry chronicle covered the reigns of Louis XIV, Louis XV, and Louis XVI, portraying their most famous personages. Claudette was appropriately charming as the wily mistress of Louis XV (Guitry). The lengthy 152-minute talkfest was so ponderous that after its brief art house showing in Manhattan, it was chopped down for television sale.

Claudette was mentioned as a top contender for the London company of *Auntie Mame,* but the role did not materialize. She returned to Broadway in Leslie Stevens's *The Marriage-Go-Round* (Plymouth Theatre, October 29, 1958), costarring with Charles Boyer. The lively compendium of sex jokes focused on a mature married couple whose household is upset by a statuesque Scandinavian visitor (Julie Newmar) who intends having a baby by professor Boyer. Whether making her stage entrance through a window, showing off her still shapely legs and figure, knowingly lighting a match on the rump of a figurine, or delivering a lecture to the audience on marital knowhow, Claudette proved that at age 53 she was still a top-ranking theatre star. Brooks Atkinson *(New York Times)* praised her: "As the learned wife, Miss Colbert makes the perfect counterpart in the opposite sex, for she has charm and intelligence. Also, since the play touches on sensitive areas, the acting might easily become maudlin. But Miss Colbert skips briskly through the crises with a dry sense of humor, a mocking undertone and adroit transitions from academic assurance to womanly vexation. The comdey hit lasted 431 performances. Claudette was nominated for a Tony award, but lost to Helen Hayes in *Time Remembered.* When Twentieth Century-Fox produced the film version of *The Mariage-Go-Round* (1960), Susan Hayward had the lead.

After *The Marriage-Go-Round* closed, Claudette remained based in New York as a celebrity in residence. She was often quoted: "Some women think if you don't expect too much you won't be let down. I always expect miracles. Sure, I'm let down, But they're near miracles."

When Claudette was asked to play Troy Donahue's mother in *Parrish* (1951) she told the press: "But what are you going to do when just the right kind of part comes along. Refuse it? Not me." Joshua Logan dropped out as the film's director, and writer-producer Delmer Daves assumed the helm. Much of the picture was lensed along Connecticut's million-dollar tobacco strip. The Warner Brothers feature emerged as a lushly photographed, musically scored soap opera, devoted to promoting teenage hearthrob Troy Donahue. Claudette was fashionable in her Sophie of Saks Fifth Avenue wardrobe, but on screen as in the billing, she took a back seat to Donahue. Claudette was mentioned by reviewers as being "all charm and cupcake," while Karl Malden as her crude, power-crazed husband was panned along with the inept picture. However, it did make a bundle at the box office.

Oriana Atkinson had written *Over at Uncle Joe's,* reminiscing about her 1945 Russian sojourn with her newspaper correspondent husband, Brooks Atkinson. It was developed into the play *Julia, Jake and Uncle Joe,* and Claudette signed for the lead in the fall of 1961. During the Wilmington, Delaware, tryouts, Claudette demanded extensive rewrites which were not forthcoming. Her request to be released from her contract was denied. It opened (Booth Theatre, November 28, 1961) and closed the same night. Robert Colman *(New York Mirror)* summed it up: "Colbert a gem, But Play isn't." Whitney Bolton *(New York Morning Telegraph)* expounded: "She frowns, laughs, giggles, comforts, embraces, joshes, uses all the skills of an expert timer, does everything at an actress' command to pump reality, fun, and magic into the play. Seldom has a distinguished actesss worked harder to achieve not much." Claudette candidly admitted: "It taught me a lesson. Now I'll wait for the rewrites. It's always sad when this much effort is put into something. People ask, 'How do intelligent people get mixed up in something like this?' It's never that simple. Anyway, in the entertainment field, everyone falls on his face regularly."

Claudette was next paired with Cyril Ritchard in *The Irregular Verb to Love* (Ethel Barrymore Theatre, September 18, 1963). She portrayed a flighty British mother who bombs fur shops to protest cruelty to animals. Her actions are embarrassing to her aristocratic husband, who is curator of the mammals section of the London Zoo. Adding to the complications are a pregnant unwed daughter and an idealistic son who arrives home with a Greek girl in tow. Ritchard directed this British drawing room comedy with élan, but it was only a moderate success, with a run of 115 performances. Walter Kerr *(New York Herald Tribune)* described Claudette's stage manner: "Miss Colbert could not undo an evening, not even if she tried, any more than a pair of blue spectacles can take the animation out of her permanently startled eyes. With her lower lip curling magically as her face flowers into a smile, and with her habit of throwing nuisance lines over her shoulder as though she were cleaning out a drawer, she is the Miss Colbert we know. But she is quite thanklessly cast."

During the show's run, Claudette talked to the press on a variety of subjects: "I've given up films now, you know. There seems nothing for me to do in them anymore—just playing dull mother-roles. And I don't have to prove I can do those any more. After all I played my first mother role in 1935 [sic]. . . ."

Re marriage: "This I know for sure. Of all the marriages I've seen where the husband has love for his wife after fifteen years, the wife has the ability to make him laugh. She is gay when he comes home. She doesn't bore him with her petty ills."

On glamor: "I don't need that awful, unreal artificial 'glamor' that Hollywood devises for people who don't have any personalities. I'm a very happy person."

Concerning her figure: "Being French, I adore food. Yet, I never gain a pound. I think Hollywood did that for me. I always worked my tail off in pictures! I never was still a moment. There always was a broom or a vacuum cleaner in my fist, or I was at the sink, scrubbing away for dear life. Now, you take Garbo. She always was sulking on a sofa in her movies. Or Marlene Dietrich, languishing in the shadows somewhere. I was never idle."

About plastic surgery: "I would if I could, I think. Though it rarely works—because the eyes of a woman of fifty can't look like the eyes of a girl of twenty and that's all there is to it. Anyway, one can look as good as one chooses—look at Cary Grant. The thing that really hits you in later years is booze, I'm sure. Not sex, thank heavens."

In 1963 Claudette and her husband Dr. Pressman sold their home in Holmsby Hills, California. He remained on the West Coast as chief of neck surgery at the University of California Hospital. In California Claudette and Pressman had been part of the Frank Sinatra crowd, although she was never officially a rat pack member. In New York she joined the party-going circle of Bennett Cerf. She began devoting more time to her painting: "I like to paint portraits of people that look like them."

In 1965 Claudette made her last professional stage appearance to date, in the tryout of *Diplomatic Relations*. Brian Aherne was costarred in this Morton da Costa-directed drawing room comedy, which had engagements in Palm Beach and Miami in February, 1965. Claudette was ruffled by the constant rewriting of the play, and blew her lines on more than one occasion. When producer Elliot Martin put it on the touring circuit that summer, Anne Baxter assumed the role of Lady Alexander Shotter.

On February 26, 1968, Dr. Pressman died of cancer in Los Angeles at the age of 67. Claudette's mother and brother died shortly thereafter. Then Claudette moved on a more-or-less permanent basis to her estate in St. James, Barbados, where she and her husband had spent much of the preceding decade. There, when not traveling around the world, she is one of the ranking celebrities in residence. She still maintains apartments in Manhattan and Paris.

Rumors abounded throughout the late 1960s that Claudette would make her show business comeback in this or that project. In March, 1969, it was announced that she was going to write *How to Run a House* for her pal Bennett Cerf's Random House press. She was signed to record a French language LP album in Paris for Rod McKuen's Stanyan Company, but nothing came of it. Ross Hunter wanted her for a role in *Airport* (1970). Columnists were full of stories that she would star as Katharine Hepburn's replacement on Broadway in *Coco* or head the London company of that play.

Like many long-lived celebrities, Claudette has repeatedly been asked to write her memoirs. But she is adamant: "Books written by actresses are for the birds. Besides, what would I write? That I was in a high school play? That I never thought of being an actress but wanted to be a costume designer or a painter? That somebody was looking for an Italian type to play the ingenue in a film and they thought I might do?

"I write all this and then I tell how I got married and was happy. Of course a lot of funny things happened to me, like the time I was playing Cleopatra. I was sitting on a high throne and four Nubian slaves were carrying me through the street. One of them dropped the handles and I went head over heels. Years later on the Chief going to California, I looked up and the head waiter was the Nubian.

"People don't want to read books like that. They want to read about how poor and miserable you were. The trouble is I've been too happy, and that's no story."

To the *New York Times,* she recently said: "It's very lazy-making here [Barbados]. I have no desire to work anymore. . . . I worked 40 years and that's enough." But more recently, when she was in New York, she advised the *New York Post*'s Eugenia Sheppard that she would like to make another film: "You can't just play somebody's mother. They keep sending scripts about a mature woman in love with a young man. I find them revolting." Those in the know realize how much Claudette would like to be an active part of show business again, particularly after she made one of her rare public appearances at the "Fabulous Forties" nostalgia night at Manhattan's Roseland in June, 1972.

FOR THE LOVE OF MIKE (FN, 1927) 6,588'

Director, Frank Capra; based on the story "Hell's Kitchen" by John Morosco; screenplay, J. Clarkson Miller; camera, Ernest Haller.

Claudette Colbert (Mary); Ben Lyon (Mike); George Sidney (Abraham Katz); Ford Sterling (Herman Schultz); Hugh Cameron (Patrick O'Malley); Richard Skeets Gallagher ("Coxey" Pendleton); Rudolph Cameron (Henry Sharp); Mable Swor (Evelyn Joyce).

THE HOLE IN THE WALL (PAR, 1919) 73 M.

Supervisor, Monta Bell; director, Robert Florey; based on the play by Fred Jackson; screenplay, Pierre Collings; camera, George Folsey; editor, Morton Blumenstock.

Claudette Colbert (Jean Oliver); Edward G. Robinson ("The Fox"); David Newell (Gordon Grant); Nellie Savage (Madame Mystera); Donald Meek (Goofy); Alan Brooks (Jim); Louise Closser Hale (Mrs. Ramsy); Katherine Emmet (Mrs. Carslake); Marcia Kango (Marcia); Barry Macollum (Dogface); George McQuarrie (Inspector); Helen Crane (Mrs. Lyons); Gamby-Hall Girls (Dancers).

THE LADY LIES (PAR, 1929) 75 M.

Director, Hobart Henley; story, John Meehan; adaptation, Garrett Ford; dialoguer, Meehan; titles, Mort Blumenstock; camera, William Steiner; editor, Helene Turner.

Walter Huston (Robert Rossiter); Claudette Colbert (Joyce Roamer); Charles Ruggles (Charlie Tyler); Patricia Deering (Jo Rossiter); Tom Brown (Bob Rossiter); Betty Gadde (Hilda Pearson); Jean Dixon (Ann Gardner); Duncan Penwarden (Henry Tuttle); Virginia True Boardman (Amelia Tuttle); Verna Deane (Bernice Tuttle).

THE BIG POND (PAR, 1930) 78 M.

Director, Hobart Henley; story, George Middleton, A. E. Thomas; screenplay, Robert Presnell, Garrett Fort; dialoguer, Presnell, Preston Sturges; songs, Al Lewis and Al Sherman; Lew Brown, B. G. DeSylva and Ray Henderson; Irving Kahal, Pierre Norman, and Sammy Fain; camera, George Folsey; editor, Emma Hill.

Maurice Chevalier (Pierre Mirande); Claudette Colbert (Barbara Billings); George Barbier (Henry Billings); Marion Ballou (Emily Billings); Andree Corday (Toinette); Frank Lyon (Ronnie); Nat Pendleton (Pat O'Day); Elaine Koch (Jennie)'

LA GRANDE MARE (PAR, 1930) 78 M. (French Version of THE BIG POND)

Producer, Monta Bell; director, Hobart Henley; I.B.M.; songs, Al Lewis and Al Sherman; Lew Brown, B. G. DeSylva and Ray Henderson; Irving Kahal, Pierre Norman, and Sammy Fain; French lyrics, Jacques Bataille-Henri.

Maruice Chevalier (Pierre de Mirande); Claudette Colbert (Barbara Billings); Andree Corday (Toinette); Lorraine Jaillet (Jennie); Maude Allen (Mrs. Billings); Henry Mortimer (Mr. Billings); William Williams (Ronnie); Nat Pendleton (Pat O'-Day).

YOUNG MAN OF MANHATTAN (PAR, 1930) 75 M.

Director, Monte Bell; Catherine Brush; screenplay, Robert Presnell; dialoguer, Daniel Reed; camera, Larry Williams; editor, Emma Hill; songs, Irving Kahal, Pierre Nerman, Sammy Fain; sound, Ernest F. Zatorsky.

Claudette Colbert (Ann Vaughn); Norman Foster (Toby McLean); Ginger Rogers (Puff Randolph); Charles Ruggles (Shorty Ross); H. Dudley Hawley (Doctor); Four Aalbu Sisters (Sherman Sisters); Leslie Austin (Dwight Knowles).

L'ENIGMATIQUE MONSIEUR PARKES (PAR, 1930) 75 M. (French version of SLIGHTLY SCARLET)

Director, Louis Gasnier; based on the play *Slightly Scarlet* by Percy Heath; French adaptation, Jacques Battaille-Henri; camera, Allen Siegler; editor, Battaille-Henri.

Adolphe Menjou (Courtenay Parkes) Claudette Colbert (Lucy Stavrin); Emile Chautard (Sylvester Corbett); Sandra Revel (Edith Corbett); Armand Kaliz (Malatroff); Adrienne d'Ambricourt (Mrs. Corbett); Frank O'Neill (Jimmy Weyman); Andre Cheron (Police Captain); and: Jacques Jerville.

MANSLAUGHTER (PAR, 1930) 85 M.

Director, George Abbott; based on the story by Alice Duer Miller; screenplay, Abbott; camera, A. J. Stout; editor, Otho Lovering.

Claudette Colbert (Lydia Thorne); Fredric March (Dan O'Bannon); Emma Dunn (Miss Bennett); Natalie Moorhead (Eleanor); Richard Tucker (Albee); Hilda Vaughn (Evans); G. Pat Collins (Drummond); Gaylord Pendleton (Bobby); Arnold Lucy (Piers); Ivan Simpson (Morson); Irving Mitchel (Foster); George Chandler (Roadside observer); Bess Flowers (Party Guest); Louise Beavers (Inmate at Prison).

THE SMILING LIEUTENANT (PAR, 1931) 89 M.

Producer-director, Ernst Lubitsch; based on the play *The Waltz Dream* by Leopold Jacobson, Felix Dormann, and the novel *Nux der Prinzgemahl* by Hans Muller; adaptation-screenplay, Ernest Vajda, Samson Raphaelson, Lubitsch; songs, Oscar Strauss, Clifford Grey; camera, George Folsey.

Maurice Chevalier (Lt. Niki); Claudette Colbert (Franzi); Miram Hopkins (Princess Anna); Charles Ruggles (Max); Georege Barbier (King Adolf); Hugh O'Connell (Orderly); Robert Strange (Adjutant von Rockoff); Janet Reade (Lily); Con MacSunday (Emperor); Elizabeth Patterson (Baroness Von Schwedel); Harry Bradley (Count Von Halden); Karl Stall (Master of Cermonies); Werner Saxtorph (Joseph); Granville Bates (Bill Collector); Maude Allen (Woman); Charles Wasenheim (Arresting Officer).

(The French version, LE LIEUTENANT SOURIANT (PAR, 1931), also starred Chevalier, Colbert, and Hopkins.)

HIS WOMAN (PAR, 1931) 75 M.

Director, Edward Sloman; based on the novel *The Sentimentalist* by Dale Collins; screenplay, Adelaide Heilbron; Melville Baker; camera, William Steiner; editor, Arthur Ellis.

Gary Cooper (Captain Sam Whalan); Claudette Colbert (Sally Clark); Richard Spiro (Sammy); Averill Harris (Mate Gatson); Douglass Dumbrille (Alisandree); Raquel Davida (Estella); Hamtree Harrington (Aloysius); Sidney Easton (Mark); Joan Blair (Gertrude); Charlotte Wynters (Flo); Herschell Mayall (Mr. Morrisey); Joe Spurin Calleia (Agent); Lon Hascal (Captain); Harry Davenport (Customs Inspector); John T. Doyle (Doctor); Edward Keane (Boatswain); Preston Foster (Officer); Barton MacLane, Donald MacBride (Crewmen).

SECRETS OF A SECRETARY (PAR, 1931) 71 M.

Director, George Abbott; story, Charles Brackett; adaptation, Abbott; screenplay, Dwight Taylor; camera, George Folsey; editor, Helene Turner.

Claudette Colbert (Helen Blake); Herbert Marshall (Lord Danforth); Georges Metaxa (Frank D'Agnoli); Betty Lawford (Sylvia Merritt); Mary Boland (Mrs. Merritt); Berton Churchill (Mr. Merritt); Averell Harris (Don Marlow); Betty Garde (Dorothy White); Hugh O'Connell (Charlie Rickenbacker); H. Dudley Hawley (Mr. Blake); Joseph Crehan (Reporter); Charles Wilson (Police Captain); Edward Keane (Albany Hotel Manager); Porter Hall (Drunk); Millard Mitchell (Drunk).

HONOR AMONG LOVERS (PAR, 1931) 75 M.

Director, Dorothy Arzner; story-screenplay, Austin Parker; dialoguer, Parker, Gertrude Purcell; camera, George Folsey; editor, Helene Turner.

Claudette Colbert (Julia Traynor); Fredric March (Jerry Stafford); Monroe Owsley (Philip Craig); Charlie Ruggles (Monty Dunn); Ginger Rogers (Doris Blake); Avonne Taylor (Maybelle); Pat O'Brien (Conroy); Janet McLeary (Margaret); John Kearney (Inspector); Ralph Morgan (Riggs); Jules Epailly (Louis); Leonard Carey (Butler).

THE WISER SEX (PAR, 1932) 76 M.

Director, Berthold Viertel; based on the play by Clyde Fitch; screenplay, Harry Hervey, Caroline Francke; camera, George Folsey.

Claudette Colbert (Margaret Hughes); Melvyn Douglas (David Rolfe); Lilyan Tashman (Claire Foster); William Boyd (Harry Evans); Ross Alexander (Jimmie O'Neill); Franchot Tone (Phil Long); Effie Shannon (Mrs. Hughes); Granville Bates (City Editor); Paul Harvey (Blaney); Victor Kilian (Ed); Robert Fischer (Fritz); Douglass Dumbrille (Chauffeur).

THE MISLEADING LADY (Paramount, 1932) 70 M.

Director, Stuart Walker; based on the play by Charles W. Goddard, Paul Dickey; screenplay, Adelaide Heilbron, Caroline Francke; camera, George Folsey.

Claudette Colbert (Helen Steele); Edmund Lowe (Jack Craigen); Stuart Erwin (Boney); Robert Strange (Sydney Parker); George Meeker (Tracy) Selena Royle (Alice Connell); Curtis Cooksey (Bob Connell); William Gargan (Fitzpatrick); Nina Walker (Jane Neatherby) Edgar Nelson (Steve); Fred Stewart (Babs); Harry Ellerbe (Spider); Will Geer (McMahon); Donald McBride (Bill).

THE MAN FROM YESTERDAY (PAR, 1932) 71 M.

Director, Berthold Viertel; story, Nell Blackwell, Roland Edwards; screenplay, Oliver H. P. Garret; camera, Karl Struss.

Claudette Colbert (Sylvia Suffolk); Clive Brook (Captain Tony Clyde); Charles Boyer (Rene Goudin); Andy Devine (Steve Hand); Alan Mowbray (Dr. Waite); Ronald Cosbey (Baby Tony); Emil Chautard (Priest); George Davis (Taxi Driver); Reginald Pasch (Hotel Clerk); Christian Rub (Terrace Waiter); Boyd Irwin (British Colonel); Donald Stuart (Private Atkins); Barry Winton (Corporal Simpkins); Yola d'Avril (Tony's girl); Barbara Leonard (Steve's girl).

MAKE ME A STAR (PAR, 1932) 68 M.

Director, William Beaudine, based on the novel *Merton of the Movies* by Harry Leon Wilson and the play by George S. Kaufman, Moss Hart; adaptation, Sam Wintz, Walter Deleon, Arthur Kober; camera, Allen Siegler; editor LeRoy Stone.

Stuart Erwin (Merton Gill); Joan Blondell (Flips Montague); Zazu Pitts (Mrs. Scudder); Ben Turpin (Ben); Charles Sellon (Mr. Gashwiler); Florence Roberts (Mrs. Gashwiler); Helen Jerome Eddy (Tessie Kearns); Arthur Hoyt (Hardy Powell); Dink Templeton (Buck Benson); Ruth Donnelly (The Countess); Sam Hardy (Jeff Baird); Oscar Apfel (Henshaw); Frank Mills (Chuck Collins); Polly Walters (Doris Randall); Victor Potel, Bobby Vernon, Snub Pollard, Billy Bletcher, Bud Jamison, Nick Thompson (Fellow Actors); Tallulah Bankhead, Clive Brook, Maurice Chevalier, Claudette Colbert, Gary Cooper, Phillips Holmes, Fredric March, Jack Oakie, Charlie Ruggles, Sylvia Sidney (Themselves).

THE PHANTOM PRESIDENT (PAR, 1932) 78 M.

Director, Norman Taurog; story, George F. Worts; screenplay, Walter DeLeon, Harlan Thompson; songs, Richard Rodgers and Lorenz Hart; camera, David Abel.

George M. Cohan (Theodore K. Blair, Doc Peter Varney); Claudette Colbert (Felicia Hammond); Jimmy Durante (Curly Cooney); George Barbier (Boss Jim Ronkton); Sidney Toler (Professor Aikenhead); Louise Mackintosh (Senator Sarah Scranton); Jameson Thomas (Jerrido); Julius McVicker (Senator Melrose); Paul Hurst (Sailor); Hooper Atchley (Announcer); Charles Middleton (Lincoln); Alan Mowbray (Washington).

THE SIGN OF THE CROSS (PAR, 1932) 115 M.

Producer-director, Cecil B. DeMille; based on the play by Wilson Barret; screenplay, Waldemar Young, Sidney Buchman; music, Rudolph Kopp; camera, Karl Struss; editro, Anne Bauchens.

Fredric March (Marcus Superbus); Elissa Landi (Mercia); Claudette Colbert (Poppaea); Charles Laughton (Nero); Ian Keith (Tigellinus); Vivian Tobin (Dacia); Harry Beresford (Flavius); Ferdinand Gottschalk (Glabrio); Arthur Hohl (Titus); Joyzelle Joyner (Ancaria); Tommy Conlon (Stephan); Nat Pendleton (Strabo); Clarence Burton (Servillus); William V. Mong (Licinius); Harold Healy (Tibul); Richard Alexander (Viturius); Robert Manning (Philodemus); Charles Middleton (Tyros); Joe Bonomo (Mute Giant); Kent Taylor (A Lover); John Carradine (Leader of Gladiators/Christian); Lane Chandler (Christian In Chains); Ethel Wales (Complaining Wife); Lionel Belmore (Betto); Angelo Rossitto (Pygmy).

TONIGHT IS OURS (PAR, 1933) 75 M.

Director, Stuart Walker; based on the play *The Queen Was in the Parlor* by Noel Coward; screenplay, Edwin Justus Mayer; camera, Karl Struss.

Claudette Colbert (Princess Nadya); Fredric March (Sabien Pastal); Alison Skipworth (Grand Duchess Emilie); Paul Cavanagh (Prince Keri); Arthur Byron (General Krish); Ethel Griffies (Zana); Clay Gement (Seminoff); Warburton Gamble (Alex); Edwin Maxwell (Mob Leader).

I COVER THE WATERFRONT (1933) 75 M.

Director, James Cruze; story, Max Miller; adaptation, Wells Root; dialoguer, Jack Jevne; camera, Ray June; editor, Grant Whytock. song, Edward Heyman and Johnny Green.

Claudette Colbert (Julie Kirk); Ben Lyon (Joseph Miller); Ernest Torrence (Kirk); Hobart Cavanaugh (McCoy); Maurice Black (Ortegus) Harry Beresford (Old Chris); Purnell Pratt (John Phelps); George Humbert (Silva); Rosita Marstina (Mrs. Silva); Claudia Coleman (Mother Morgan); Wilfred Lucas (Randall); Lee Phelps (Reporter); Al Hill (Sailor).

THREE CORNERED MOON (PAR, 1933) 72 M.

Director, Elliott Nugent; story, Gertrude Tonkongy; screenplay, S. K. Lauren, Ray Harris; song, Leo Robin and Ralph Rainger; camera, Leon Shamroy.

Claudette Colbert (Elizabeth Rimplegar); Richard Arlen (Dr. Alan Stevens); Mary Boland (Nellie Rimplegar); Wallace Ford (Kenneth Rimplegar); Lyda Roberti (Jenny); Tom Brown (Eddie Rimplegar); Joan Marsh (Kitty); Hardie Albright (Ronald); William Bakewell (Douglas Rimplegar); Sam Hardy (Hawkins); Nick Thompson (Apple Peddler); John M. Sullivan (Briggs); Fred Santley (Clerk); Margaret Armstrong (Mrs. Johnson); Charlotte Merriam (Gracie); Joseph Sawyer (Swimming Pool Director); Leonid Kinsky (Interpreter); George LeGuere (Call Boy); Jack Clark (Stage Director); Jack Clark (Joe Willis); Elliott Nugent (Broker); Clara Blandick (Landlady); Edward Gargan (Mike); Sam Godfrey (Albert).

TORCH SINGER (PAR, 1933) 72 M.

Director, Alexander Hall, George Somnes; based on the play *Mike* by Grace Perkins; screenplay, Lenore Coffee, Lynn Starling; songs, Leo Robin and Ralph Rainger; camera, Karl Struss.

Claudette Colbert (Sally Trent alias Mimi Benton); Ricardo Cortez (Tony Cummings); David Manners (Michael Gardner); Lyda Roberti (Dora); Baby LeRoy (Bobbie); Florence Roberts (Mother Angelica) Shirley Ann Christensen (Baby Sally); Cora Sue Collins (Little Sally); Ethel Griffies (Martha Alden); Helen Jerome Eddy (Miss Spaulding); Mildred Washington (Carry); Charles Grapewin (Mr. Jusdon); Albert Conti (Carlotti); Virginia Hammond (Mrs. Judson); Kathleen Burke (Sobbing Girl); Davidson Clark (Detective); Edward J. LeSaint (Doctor); Bobby Arnst (The Blonde); William B. Davidson (Jarrett).

FOUR FRIGHTENED PEOPLE (PAR, 1934) 95 M.

Producer-director, Cecil B. DeMille; based on the novel by E. Arnot Robertson; screenplay, Bartlett Cormack, Lenore J. Coffee; music, Karl Hajos, Milton Roder, H. Rohenheld, Jonn Leipold; camera, Karl Struss; editor, Anne Bauchens.

Claudette Colbert (Judy Cavendish); Herbert Marshall (Arnold Ainger); Mary Boland (Mrs. Mardick); William Gargan (Stewart Corder) Leo Carrillo (Montague); Nella Walker (Mrs. Ainger); Tetsu Komai (Native Chief); Chris Pin Martin (Native Boatman); Joe De La Cruz (Native); Minoru Nisheda, Toru Shimada, E. R. Jinedas, Delmar Costello (Sakais); Ethel Griffles (Mrs. Ainger's Mother).

IT HAPPENED ONE NIGHT (COL, 1934) 105 M.

Producer, Harry Cohn; director, Frank Capra, based on the story "Night Bus" by Samuel Hopkins Adams; screenplay, Robert Riskin; art director, Stephen Goosson; assistant director, C. C. Coleman; music director, Louis Silver; camera, Joseph Walker; editor, Gene Havlick.

Claudette Colbert (Ellie Andrews); Clark Gable (Peter Warne); Roscoe Karns (Oscar Shapeley); Henry Wadsworth (Drunk Boy); Claire McDowell (Mother); Walter Connolly (Alexander Andrews); Alan Hale (Danker); Arthur Hoyt (Zeke); Blanche Frederici (Zeke's wife); Jameson Thomas (King Westley); Wallis Clark (Lovington); Hal Price (Reporter); Ward Bond, Eddy Chandler (Bus Drivers); Ky Robinson, Frank Holliday, James Burke, Joseph Crehan (Detectives); Milton Kibbee (Drunk); Matty Roubpert (Newsboy); Sherry Hall (Reporter); Mickey Daniels (Vender); Charles C. Wilson (Joe Gordon); George Breakston (Boy); Earl M. Pingree, Harry Hume (Policemen); Oliver Eckhardt (Dykes); Bess Flowers (Secretary); Fred Walton (Butler); Ethel Sykes (Maid Of Honor); Edmund Burns (Best Man); Father Dodds (Minister); Eva Dennison (Society Woman); Eddie Kane (Radio Announcer); Harry Holman (Manager Auto Camp); Tom Ricketts (Prissy Old Man); Maidel Turner (Manager's Wife); Irving Bacon (Station Attendant); Frank Yaconelli (Tony); Harry C. Bradley (Henderson); Harry Todd (Flag Man); Kate Morgan, Rose May, Margaret Reid, Sam Josephson, Bert Starkey, Ray Creighton, Rita Ross, Ernie Adams, John Wallace, Billy Engle, Allen Fox, Marvin Loback, Mimi Lindell, Blanche Rose, Dave Wengren, Jane Tallent, Charles Wilroy, Patsy O'Byrne, Kit Guard, Harry Schultz, Bert Scott, Emma Tansey, Marvin Shector, William McCall, S. S. Simon (Bus Passengers).

CLEOPATRA (PAR, 1934) 101 M.

Producer-director, Cecil B. DeMille; adaptation, Bartlett Cormack; screenplay, Waldemar Young, Vincent Lawrence; music, Rudolph Kopp; camera, Victor Milne; editor, Anne Bauchens.

Claudette Colbert (Cleopatra); Warren William (Julius Caesar); Henry Wilcoxon (Marc Antony); Gertrude Michael (Calpurnia); Joseph Schildkraut (Herod); Ian Keith (Octavian); C. Aubrey Smith (Enobarbus); Ian Maclaren (Cassius); Arthur Hohl (Brutus); Leonard Mudie (Pothinos); Irving Pichel (Apollodorus); Claudia Dell (Octavia); Eleanor Phelps (Charmian); John Rutherford (Drussus); Grace Durkin (Iras); Robert Warwick (Achillas); Edwin Maxwell (Casca); Charles Morris (Cicero); Harry Beresford (Soothsayer); Olga Celeste (Slave Girl); Ecki (Leopard); Ferdinand Gottschalk (Glabrio); William Farnum (Senator); Florence Roberts (Flora); Kenneth Gibson, Wedgwood Nowell (Scribes); John Carradine, Jane Regan, Celia Rylan, Robert Manning (Romans); Lionel Belmore (Party Guest); Dick Alexander (Egyptian Messenger); Jack Mulhall, Wilfred Lucas (Romans Greeting Antony); Hal Price (Onlooker At Procession); Edgar Dearing (Murderer).

IMITATION OF LIFE (UNIV, 1934) 106 M.

Director, John Stahl, based on the novel by Fannie Hurst; screenplay, William Hurlbut; camera, Merritt Gerstad; editor, Phil Cahn.

Claudette Colbert (Beatrice "Bes" Pullman); Warren William (Stephen Archer); Ned Sparks (Elmer); Louise Beavers (Delilah Johnson); Juanita Quigley (Jessie Pullman—Age 3); Marilyn Knowlden (Jessie—Age 4); Rochelle Hudson (Jessie—Age 18); Sebie Hendricks (Peola Johnson—Age 4); Dorothy Black (Peola—Age 5); Fredi Washington (Peola—Age 19); Alan Hale (Furniture Man); Clarence Hummel Wilson (Landlord); Henry Armetta (Painter); Henry Kolker (Dr. Preston); Wyndham Standing (Butler); Alice Ardell (French Maid); Paul Porcasi (Restaurant Manager); William B. Davidson (Man); G. P. Huntley, Jr. (Man at Party); Noel Francis (Mrs. Eden); Walter Walker (Hugh); Franklin Pangborn (Mr. Carven); Tyler Brooke (Tipsy Man); William Austin (Englishman); Alma Tell (Mrs. Carven); Hazel Washington (Black Maid); Lenita Lane (Mrs. Dale); Barry Norton (Young Man); Joyce Compton (Woman); Reverend Gregg (Minister); Curry Lee (Chauffeur); Claire McDowell (Teacher); Madame Sul-Te-Wan (Cook); Stuart Johnston (Undertaker); Fred "Snowflake" Toone, Hattie McDaniel (Bits At Funeral); Dennis O'Keefe (Dance Extra).

THE GILDED LILY (PAR, 1935) 80 M.

Producer, Albert Lewis, director, Wesley Ruggles; screenplay, Claude Binyon; story, Melville Baker, Jack Kirkland; song, Sam Coslow and Arthur Johnston; camera, Victor Milner; editor, Otto Lovering.

Claudette Colbert (Lillian David); Fred MacMurray (Peter Dawes); Raymond Milland (Charles Gray/Granville); C. Aubrey Smith (Lloyd Granville); Eddie Craven (Eddie); Luis Alberni (Nate); Donald Meek (Hankerson); Michelette Burani (Lily's Maid); Claude King (Captain of Boat); Charles Irwin (Oscar); Ferdinand Munier (Otto Bushe); Rita Carlyle (Proprietor's Wife); Forrester Harvey (Proprietor of English Inn); Edward Gargan (Guard); Leonid Kinskey (Vocal Teacher); Jimmie Aubrey (Purser); Charles Wilson (Pete's Editor); Walter Shumway (Assistant Editor); Rollo Lloyd (City Editor); Reginald Barkow (Managing Editor); Esther Muir (Divorcee); Grace Bradley (Daisy) Pat Somerset (Man In London Club); Eddie Dunn (Reporter); Tom Dugan (Bum); Warren Hymer (Taxi Driver); Rudy Cameron, Jack Egan, Jack Norton (Photographers); Albert Pollet, Cyril Ring (Head Waiters); Bob Thom (Customs Inspector).

PRIVATE WORLDS (PAR, 1935) 84 M.

Producer, Walter Wanger; director, Gregory LaCava; story, Phyllis Bottome; screenplay, Lynn Starling; camera, Leon Shamroy; editor, Aubrey Scotto.

Claudette Colbert (Dr. Jane Everest); Charles Boyer (Dr. Charles Monet); Joan Bennett (Sally MacGregor); Joel McCrea (Dr. Alex MacGregor); Helen Vinson (Claire Monet); Esther Dale (Matron); Samuel Hinds (Dr. Arnold); Jean Rouverol (Carrie); Sam Godfrey (Tom Hirst); Dora Clement (Bertha Hirst); Theodore von Eltz (Dr. Harding); Stanley Andrews (Dr. Barnes); Big Boy Williams (Jerry); Maurice Murphy (Boy In Car); Irving Bacon (Male Nurse); Nick Shaid (Arab Patient); Monte Vandergrift (Dawson); Arnold Gray (Clarkson); Julian Madison (Johnson); Harry Bradley (Johnson's Father); Eleanore King (Carrie's Nurse).

SHE MARRIED HER BOSS (COL, 1935) 85 M.

Producer, Everett Riskin; director, Gregory LaCava; story, Thyra Samter Winslow; screenplay, Sidney Buchman; camera, Leon Shamroy; editor, Richard Cahoon.

Claudette Colbert (Julie Scott); Michael Bartlett (Rogers); Melvyn Douglas (Richard Barclay); Raymond Walburn (Franklin); Jean Dixon (Martha); Katherine Alexander (Gertrude); Edith Fellows (Annabel); Clara Kimball Young (Parsons); Grace Hayle (Agnes); Charles E. Arnt (Manager—Department Store); Schuyler Shaw (Chauffeur); Selmer Jackson (Andrews); John Hyams (Hoyt); Robert E. Homans (Detective); Lillian Rich (Telephone Operator); Arthur S. Byron (Store Watchman); David O'Brien (Man); Buddy Roosevelt (Chauffeur); Ruth Cherrington (Old Maid Saleswoman); Lillian Moore (Department Head).

THE BRIDE COMES HOME (PAR, 1935) 83 M.

Producer-director, Wesley Ruggles; story, Elizabeth Sanxay Holding; screenplay, Calude Binyon; camera, Leo Tover.

Claudette Colbert (Jeannette Desmereau); Fred MacMurray (Cyrus Anderson); Robert Young (Jack Bristow); William Collier, Sr. (Alfred Desmereau); Donald Meek (The Judge); Richard Carle (Frank, The Butler); Edgar Kennedy (Henry); Johnny Arthur (Otto); Kate MacKenna (Emma); James Conlin (Len Noble); William R. "Billy" Arnold (Elevator Starter); Belle Mitchell (Helene, The Maid); Edward Gargan (Cab Driver); Tom Kennedy (Husky); Tom Dugan (Conductor); Eddie Dunn (Elevator Operator); A. S. Byron (Cop in Chicago Park); Tom Hanlon (Man in Nightclub); Charles West (Bystander); Art Rowland, Alice Keating, Mabelle Moore, Alex Woloshin, Jack Raymond, Gertrude Simpson, Howard Bruce (Passengers).

UNDER TWO FLAGS (20th, 1936) 111 M.

Producer, Darryl F. Zanuck; associate producer, Raymond Griffith; director, Frank Lloyd; based on the novel by Ouida; screenplay, W. P. Lipscomb, Walter Ferris; music director, Louis Silvers; assistant director, Ad Schaumer, A. F. Erickson; camera, Ernest Palmer; editor, Ralph Dietrich.

Ronald Colman (Corporal Victor); Claudette Colbert (Cigarette); Victor McLaglen (Major Doyle); Rosalind Russell (Lady Venetia); J. Edward Bromberg (Colonel Ferol); Nigel Bruce (Captain Menzies); Herbert Mundin (Rake); Gregory Ratoff (Ivan); C. Henry Gordon (Lt. Petaine); John Carradine (Cafard); William Ricciardi (Cigarette's Father); Lumsden Hare (Lord Seraph); Fritz Leiber (French Governor); Onslow Stevens (Sidi Ben Youssiff); Louis Mercier (Barron); Francis McDonald (Husson); Thomas Beck (Pierre); Harry Semels (Sgt.Malines); Frank Lackteen (Ben Hamidon); Jamiel Hasson (Arab Liaison Officer); Frank Reicher (French General); Gwendolyn Logan (Lady Cairn); Hans Von Morhart (Hans); Tor Johnson (Bidou); Marc Lawrence (Grivon); George Regas (Keskerdit); Douglas Gerrard (Colonel Farley); Ronald J. Pennick (Corp. Veux); Rolfe Sedan (Mouche); Eugene Borden (Villon); Harry Worth (Dinant); Tony Merl (Catouche); Alex Palasthy (Hotel Manager); Gaston Glass (Adjutant); Nicholas Soussanin (Levine); Rosita Earlan (Ivan's Girl); Fred Malatesta (Chasseur Lt.).

MAID OF SALEM (PAR, 1937) 85 M.

Producer-director, Frank Lloyd; story, Bradley King; adaptation, Walter Ferris, King, Durward Grinstead; music, Victor Young; camera, Leo Tover; editor, Hugh Bennett.

Claudette Colbert (Barbara Clarke); Fred MacMurray (Roger Coverman); Harvey Stephens (Dr. John Harding); Gale Sondergaard (Martha Harding); Louise Dresser (Ellen Clarke); Bennie Bartlett (Timothy Clarke); Edward Ellis (Elder Goode); Beulah Bondi (Abigail Goode); Bonita Granville (Ann Goode); Virginia Weidler (Nabby Goode); Donald Meek (Ezra Cheeves); E. E. Clive (Bilge); Halliwell Hobbes (Jeremiah); Pedro de Cordoba (Mr. Morse); Madame Sul-te-wan (Tituba); Lucy Beaumont (Rebecca); Henry Kolker (Crown Chief Justice Laughton); William Farnum (Crown Justice Sewall); Ivan F. Simpson (Reverend Parris); Brandon Hurst (Tithing Man); Sterling Holloway (Miles Corbin); Zeffie Tilbury (Goody Hodgers); Babs Nelson (Baby Mercy Cheeves); Mary Treen (Suzy Abbott); J. Farrell MacDonald (Captain of Ship);

Stanley Fields (First Mate); Lionel Belmore (Tavern Keeper); Rosita Butler (Mary Watkins); Kathryn Sheldon (Mrs. Deborah Cheeves); Clarence Dolb (Town Crier); Amelia Falleur (Sarah); Agnes Ayres, Ricca K. Allen, Wison Benge, Sidney Bracy, Carol Halloway, Ward Lane, Vera Lewis, Anne O'Neal, Walter Soderling, William Wagner (One Picture Stock Players); Chief Big-Tree (Indian); Colin Kenny, Sidney D'Albrook (Hunters); Harry Cording (Guard); Grace Kern (Convict); Wally Albright (Jasper).

I MET HIM IN PARIS (PAR, 1937) 86 M.

Producer-director, Wesley Ruggles; story, Helen Meinardi; screenplay, Claude Binyon; art director, Hans Dreier, Ernst Fegte; music director, Boris Morros; song, Helen Meinardi and Hoagy Carmichael; special effects, Farciot Edouart; camera, Leo Tover; editor, Otho Lovering.

Claudette Colbert (Kay Denham); Melvyn Douglas (George Potter); Robert Young (Gene Anders); Lee Bowman (Berk Sutter); Mona Barrie (Helen Anders); George Davis (Cutter Driver); Fritz Feld (Swiss Hotel Clerk); Rudolph Amant (Romantic Waiter); Alexander Cross (John Hailey); George Sorel (Hotel Clerk); Louis La Bey (Bartender); Egon Brecher (Emile, Upper Tower Man); Hans Joby (Lower Tower Man); Jacques Venaire (Frenchman—Flirt); Eugene Borden (Headwaiter); Captain Fernando Garcia (Elevator Operator); Albert Pollet (Conductor); Francesco Maran, Yola D'Avril (French Couple in Apartment); Alexander Schoenberg (Porter); Joe Thoben (Assistant Bartender); Gennaro Curci (Double Talk Waiter); Jean De Briac (Steward).

TOVARICH (WB 1937) 94 M.

Producer, Robert Lord; director, Anatole Litvak; based on the play by Jacques Deval; adaptation, Robert E. Sherwood; screenplay, Casey Robinson; assistant director, Chuck Hansen; music, Max Steiner; music director, Leo F. Forbstein; camera, Charles Lang; editor, Henri Rust.

Claudette Colbert (Grand Duchess Tatiana Petrovna); Charles Boyer (Prince Mikail Alexandrovitch Ouratieff); Basil Rathbone (Gorotchenko); Anita Louise (Helen Dupont); Melville Cooper (Charles Dupont); Isabel Jeans (Fernande Dupont). Maruice Murphy (Georges Dupont); Morris Carnovsky (Chauffourier-Dufieff); Gregory Gaye (General Count Brekenski); Montagu Love (Monsieur Courtois); Renie Riano (Madame Courtois); Fritz Feld (Martelleau); May Boley (Louise, The Cook); Victor Kilian (Gendarme); Clifford Soubier (Grocer); Heather Thatcher (Lady Corrigan); Curt Bois (Alphonso); Ferdinand Munier (Monsieur Van Hemart); Doris Lloyd (Mme. Chauffourier-Dufieff); Grace Hayle (Madame Van Hemert); Christian Rub (Trombone Player); Tommy Bupp, Jerry Tucker, Delmer Watson (Urchins); Torben Meyer (Servant); Alphonse Martel (Hairdresser); Leo White (Assistant Hairdresser).

BLUEBEARD'S EIGHTH WIFE (PAR, 1938) 80 M.

Producer-director, Ernst Lubitsch; story, Alfred Savoir; screenplay, Charles Brackett, Billy Wilder; camera, Leo Tover; editor, William Shea.

Claudette Colbert (Nicole De Loiselle); Gary Cooper (Michael Branden); Edward Everett Horton (Marquis De Loiselle); David Niven (Albert De Ragnier); Elizabeth Patterson (Aunt Hedwige); Herman Bing (Monsieur Pepinard); Warren Hymer (Kid Mulligan); Franklin Pangborn, Armand Certes (Assistant Hotel Managers); Rolfe Sedan (Floorwalker); Lawrence Grant (Prof. Urganzeff); Lionel Pape (Monsieur Potin); Tyler Brooke (Clerk); Tom Ricketts (Uncle Andre); Barlowe Borland (Uncle Fernandel); Charles Halton (Monsieur de la Coste-President); Pauline Garon (Woman Customer); Blanche Franke (Cashier); Albert D'Arno (Newsboy); Hooper Atchley (Excited Passenger); John Picorri (Conductor); Ellen Drew (Secretary); Joseph Crehan (American Tourist); Leon Ames (Ex-Chauffeur); Olaf Hytten (Valet); Grace Goodall (Nurse); Jimmie Dime (Prizefighter); Paul Bryar (Radio Announcer); Barbara Jackson, Marie Burton, Joyce Mathews, Paula de Cardo, Gwen Kenyon, Suzanne Ridgway, Lola Jenson, Carol Parker, Dorothy Dayton, Norah Gale, Harriette Haddon, Ruth Rogers, Dorothy White, Gloria Willians (Girls).

ZAZA (PAR, 1939) 83 M.

Producer, Albert Lewin; director, George Cukor; based on the play by Pierre Berton, Charles Simon; screenplay, Zoe Akins; songs, Frank Loesser and Frederick Hollander; camera, Charles Lang; editor, Edward Dmytryk.

Claudette Colbert (Zaza); Herbert Marshall (Dufresne); Bert Lahr (Cascart); Helen Westley (Anais); Constance Collier (Nathalie); Genevieve Tobin (Florianne); Walter Catlett (Marlardot); Ann Todd (Toto); Rex O'Malley (Bussy); Ernest Cossart (Marchand); Rex Evans (Michelin); Robert C. Fischer (Pierre); Janet Waldo (Simone); Dorothy Tree (Madame Dufresne); Duncan Renaldo (Animal Trainer); Olive Tell (Jeanne Liseron); John Sutton, Michael Brooke, Philip Warren (Dandies); Alexander Leftwich (Larou); Frederika Brown (Pierre's Wife); Clarence Harvey, John Power (Conductors); Maude Hume (Woman); Olaf Hytten (Waiter); Tom Ricketts (Old Gentleman); Frank Puglia (Rug Merchant); Monty Woolley (Fouget-Interviewer); Dorothy Dayton (Dancer); Billie Beurne, Darlyn Heckley, Virginia Larsen, Grace Richey, Virginia Rooney, Lillian Ross, Peggy Russell (Tiller Girls); Harriette Haddon, Helaine Moler, Dorothy White, Louise Seidel (Dancers); Dorothy Hamburg, Emily La Rue, Mae Packer, Colleen Ward, Jeanne Blanche, Penny Gill, Jacqueline Dax (French Girls).

MIDNIGHT (PAR, 1939) 94 M.

Producer, Arthur Hornblow, Jr; director, Mitchell Leisen; story, Edwin Justus Mayer, Franz Shulz; screenplay, Charles Brackett, Billy Wilder; song, Ralph Freed and Frederick Hollander; camera, Charles Lang; editor, Doane Harrison.

Claudette Colbert (Eve Peabody); Don Ameche (Tibor Czerny); John Barrymore (George Flammaion); Francis Lederer (Jacques Picot); Mary Astor (Helene Flammion); Elaine Barrie (Simone); Hedda Hopper (Stephanie); Rex O'Malley (Marcel); Monty Woolley (Judge); Armand Kaliz (Lebon); Lionel Pape (Edouart); Ferdinand Munier, Gennaro Curci (Major Domos); Leander de Cordova, William Eddritt, Michael Visaroff, Joseph Romantini (Footmen); Carlos de Valdez (Butler); Joseph De Stefani (Head Porter); Arno Frey (Room Clerk); Eugene Borden, Paul Bryar (Porters); Leonard Sues (Bellboy); Eddy Conrad (Prince Potopienko); Billy Daniels (Roger); Bryant Washburn (Guest); Nestor Paiva (Woman's Escort); Judith King, Joyce Mathews (Girls); Harry Semels (Policeman).

IT'S A WONDERFUL WORLD (MGM, 1939) 86 M.

Producer, Frank Davis; director, W. S. Van Dyke II; story, Ben Hecht, Herman J. Mankiewicz; screenplay, Hecht; camera, Oliver Marsh; editor, Harold F. Kress.

Claudette Colbert (Edwina Corday); James Stewart (Guy Johnson); Guy Kibbee (Cap. Streeter); Nat Pendleton (Sgt. Koretz); Frances Drake (Vivian Tarbel); Edgar Kennedy (Lt. Meller); Ernest Truex (Willie Heyward); Richard Carle (Major Willoughby); Cecilia Callejo (Dolores Gonzales); Sidney Blackmer (Al Mallon); Andy Clyde (Gimpy); Cliff Clark (Capt. Haggerty); Cecil Cunningham (Madame Chambers); Leonard Kibrick (Herman Plotka); Hans Conried (Stage Manager); Grady Sutton (Bupton Peabody).

DRUMS ALONG THE MOHAWK (20th, 1939) 103 M.

Executive producer, Darryl F. Zanuck; associate producer, Raymond Griffith; director, John Ford; based on the novel by Walter D. Edmonds; screenplay, Lamar Trotti, Sonya Levien; art director, Richard Day, Mark-Lee Kirk; music, Alfred Newman; camera, Bert Glennon, Ray Rennahan; editor, Robert Simpson.

Claudette Colbert (Lana Martin); Henry Fonda (Gil Martin); Edna Mae Oliver (Mrs. Sarah McKlennar); Eddie Collins (Christian Reall); John Carradine (Caldwell); Doris Bowden (Mary Reall); Jessie Ralph (Mrs. Weaver); Arthur Shields (Rev. Rosenkrantz); Robert Lowery (John Weaver); Roger Imhof (General Nicholas Herkimer); Francis Ford (Joe Boleo); Ward Bond (Adam Helmef); Kay Linaker (Mrs. DeMooth); Russell Simpson (Dr. Petry); Spencer Charters; (Landord); Si Jenks (Jacob Small); J. Ronald (Jack) Pennick (Amos Hartman); Arthur Aylsworth (George Weaver); Chief Big Tree (Blue Back); Charles Tannen (Dr. Robert Johnson); Paul McVey (Captain Mark DeMooth); Elizabeth "Tiny" Jones (Mrs. Reall); Beulah Hall Jones (Daisy); Edwin Maxwell (Reverend Daniel Gros); Robert Greig (Mr. Borst); Clara Blandick (Mrs. Borst); Tom Tyler (Morgan); Lionel Pape (General); Noble Johnson (Indian); Mae Marsh (Pioneer Woman); Clarence H. Wilson (Paymaster).

BOOM TOWN (MGM, 1940) 120 M.

Producer, Sam Zimbalist; director, Jack Conway; based on the story "A Lady Comes To Burknurnet" by James Edward Grant; screenplay, John Lee Mahim; music, Franz Waxman; art director, Cedric Gibbons; special effects, Arnold Gillespie; camera, Harold Rosson; editor, Blanche Sewell.

Clark Gable (Big John McMasters); Spencer Tracy (Square John Sand); Claudette Colbert (Betsy Bartlett); Hedy Lamarr (Karen Vanmeer); Frank Morgan (Luther Aldrich); Lionel Atwill (Harry Compton); Chill Wills (Harmony Jones); Marion Martin (Whitey); Minna Gombell (Spanish Eva); Joe Yule (Ed Murphy); Horace Murphy (Tom Murphy); Roy Gordon (McCreery); Richard Lane (Assistant District Attorney); Casey Johnson (Little Jack); Baby Quintanilla (Baby Jack); George Lessey (Jedge); Sara Haden (Miss Barnes); Frank Orth (Barber); Frank McGlynn, Jr. (Deacon); Curt Bois (Ferdie); Dick Curtis (Hiring Boss).

ARISE, MY LOVE (PAR, 1940) 113 M.

Producer, Arthur Hornblow, Jr; director, Mitchell Leisen; story, Benjamin Glaser, John S. Toldy; adaptation, Jacques Thery; screenplay, Charles Brackett, Billy Wilder; camera, Charles Lang; editor, Doane Harrison.

Claudette Colbert (Augusta Nash); Ray Milland (Tom Martin); Dennis O'Keefe (Shep); Walter Abel (Phillips); Dick Purcell (Pink); George Zucco (Prison Governor); Frank Puglia (Father Jacinto); Esther Dale (Susie); Paul Leyssac (Bresson); Ann Codee (Mme. Bresson); Stanley Logan (Col. Tubbs Brown); Lionel Pape (Lord Kettlebrook); Aubrey Mather (Achille); Cliff Nazarro (Botzelberg); Michael Mark (Botzelberg's Assistant); Nestor Paiva (Uniformed Clerk); Fred Malatesta (Mechanic); Juan Duval (Spanish Driver); George Davis (Porter); Alan Davis (Cameraman); Jean Del Val (Conductor); Sarah Edwards, Fern Emmett (Spinsters); Jacques Vanaire, Olaf Hytton, Louis Mercier, Guy Ropp (Employees); Paul Everton (Husband) Mrs. Wilfrid North (Wife); Blanca Vischer (Brunette At Maxim's); Poppy Wilde (Hungarian Girl); Major Fred Farrell (Cab Driver); George Bunny (Fiacre Driver); Tempe Pigott (Woman in Irish Pub); Alphonse Martel (Uniformed French Correspondent); Jack Luden, Sherry Hall (American Correspondents); Hans Fuerberg (German Sentry).

SKYLARK (PAR, 1941) 92 M.

Producer-director, Mark Sandrich; based on the novel and play by Samson Raphaelson; adaptation, Z. Myers; screenplay, Allan Scott; assistant director, Mel Epstein; art director, Hans Dreier, Roland Anderson; camera, Charles Lang; editor, LeRoy Stone.

Claudette Colbert (Lydia Kenyon); Ray Milland (Tony Kenyon); Brian Aherne (Jim Blake); Binnie Barnes (Myrtle Vantine); Walter Abel (George Gore); Grant Mitchell (Frederick Vantine); Mona Barrie (Charlotte Gorell); Ernest Cossart (Theodore); James Rennie (Ned Franklin); Fritz Feld (Maitre d'Hotel); Warren Hymer (Beefy Individual—Subway Car); Hobart Cavanaugh (Little Individual—Subway Car); Leon Belasco (Long-Haired Individual—Subway Car); Edward Fielding (Scholarly Individual—Subway Car); Irving Bacon (Ferryman); Leonard Mudie (Jewelry Clerk); Armand Kaliz (Jeweler); Patricia Farr (Lil—Waitress at Hamburger Stand); William Newell (Counterman At Hamburger Stand); Margaret Hayes (Receptionist); Robert Dudley (Pedestrian); James Flavin (Subway Guard); Howard Mitchell (Man in Front of Tony); Edward Peil, Sr. (Man behind Tony); Frank Orth (Subway Cashier); May Boley (Fat Woman—Subway Car); Minerva Ureca, Virginia Sale (Middle-Aged Women—Subway Car); Ella Neal (Usherette); Henry Roquemore (Bartender); Keith Richards (Counterman at Second Hamburger Stand) Francisco Maran (Mr. Harrison —Travel Agency Man).

REMEMBER THE DAY (20TH, 1941) 86 M.

Producer, William Perlberg; director, Henry King; based on the play by Philo Higley; screenplay, Tess Slesinger, Frank Davis, Allan Scott; camera, George Barnes; editor, Barbara McLean.

Claudette Colbert (Nora); John Payne (Dan Hopkins); Shepperd Strudwick (Dewey Roberts); Ann Todd (Kate—As A Child); Douglas Croft (Dewey—As A Boy); Jane Seymour (Mrs. Roberts); Anne Revere (Miss Price); Frieda Inescort (Mrs. Dewey Roberts); Harry Hayden (Mr. Roberts); Francis Pierlot (Mr. Steele); William Henderson (Peter); Chick Chandler (Mason); George Ernest (Bill); Harry Tyler (Mr. Avery); Jody Gilbert (Mrs. Avery); Paul Harvey (Mr. Phillips); Billy Dawson (Steve); Geraldine Wall (Beulah); Marie Blake (Miss Cartwright); John Hiestand (Announcer); Selmer Jackson (Graham); William Halligan (Tom Hanlon); Irving Bacon (Cecil); Kay Linaker (Society Reporter); Thurston Hall (Governor Teller); George Chandler (Telegraph Operator); Mae Marsh, Lillian West, Cecil Weston, Vera Lewis, Maxine Tucker (Teachers); Paul Stanton, William Davidson (Committee Men); Ed Dearing (Detective); Harry Harvey, Jr. (Third Baseman); David Holt (Pitcher); Virginia Brissac (Mrs. Hill); Byron Foulger (Photographer); Ruth Robinson (Mrs. Pettit); Paul McVey (Jeweler); James Blaine (Doorman); Allen Wood (Bell Boy); Mel Ruick (Hotel Clerk); Roseanne Murray (Flower Girl); Charles Tannen (Slicker).

THE PALM BEACH STORY (PAR, 1942) 88 M.

Producer, Paul Jones; direcor-screenplay, Preston Sturges; art director, Hans Dreier, Ernst Fegte; camera, Victor Milner; editor, Stuart Gilmore.

Claudette Colbert (Gerry Jeffers); Joel McCrea (Tom Jeffers); Mary Astor (Princess Centimillia); Rudy Vallee (J. D. Hackensacker III); Sig Arno (Toto); Robert Warwick (Mr. Hinch); Arthur Stuart Hull (Mr. Osmond); Torben Meyer (Dr. Kluck); Jimmy Conlin (Mr. Asweld); Victor Potel (Mr. McKeewie); William Demarest, Jack Norton, Robert Greig, Roscoe Ates, Dewey Robinson, Chester Conklin, Sheldon Jett (Members Of Ale And Quail Club); Robert Dudley (Weenie King); Franklin Pangborn (Manager); Arthur Hoyt (Pullman Conductor); Alan Bridge (Conductor); Snowflake (Colored Bartender); Charles B. Moore (Colored Porter); Frank Moran (Brakeman); Harry Rosenthal (Orchestra Leader); Esther Howard (Wife of Weinie King); Howard Mitchell (Man In Apartment); Harry Hayden (Prospect); Monte Blue (Doorman); Esther Michelson (Near-sighted Woman); Edward McNamara (Officer In Penn Station); Harry Tyler (Gateman At Penn Station); Mantan Moreland (Waiter In Diner); Keith Richards (Shoe Salesman); Frank Faylen (Taxi Driver); Byron Foulger (Jewelry Salesman); MaxWagner (Rough-Looking Comic); Wilson Benge (Steward), John Holland (Best Man).

NO TIME FOR LOVE (PAR, 1943) 83 M.

Producer, Mitchell Leisen; associate producer, Fred Kohlmar; director, Leisen; story, Robert Lees, Fred Renaldo; adaptation, Warren Duff; screenplay, Claude Binyon; music, Victor Young; special effects, Gordon Jennings; camera, Charles Lang, Jr.; editor, Alma Macrorie.

Claudette Colbert (Katherine Grant); Fred MacMurray (Jim Ryan); Ilka Chase (Happy Grant); Richard Haydn (Roger); Paul McGrath (Henry Fulton); June Havoc

(Darlene); Marjorie Gateson (Sophie); Bill Goodwin (Christley); Robert Herrick (Kent); Morton Lowry (Dunbar); Rhys Williams (Clancy); Murray Alper (Moran); John Kelly (Morrisey); Jerome De Nuccio (Leon Brice); Grant Withers (Pete Hanagan); Rod Cameron (Taylor); Willard Robertson (President of Construction Company); Arthur Loft (Vice-President); Fred Kohler, Jr., Tom Neal, Max Laur, Oscar G. Hendrian, Tex Harris, Ted E. Jacques, Art Potter, Sammy Stein, Jack Roper (Sand Hogs); Frank Moron (Erector Tender); Alan Hale, Jr. (Union Checker); Mickey Simpson (Doctor); Ben Taggart (City General Manager); Lillian Randolph (Hilda); Keith Richards (Reporter).

SO PROUDLY WE HAIL (PAR, 1943) 126 M.

Producer-director, Mark Sandrich; screenplay, Allan Scott; art director, Hans Dreier, Earl Hedrick; music, Miklos Rozsa; song, Edward Heyman and Rozsa; special effects, Gordon Jennings, Farciot Edouart; camera, Charles Lang; editor, Ellsworth Hoagland.

Claudette Colbert (Lt. Janet Davidson); Paulette Goddard (Lt. Jean O'Doul); Veronica Lake (Lt. Olivia D'Arcy); George Reeves (Lt. John Sumners); Barbara Britton (Lt. Rosemary Larson); Walter Abel (Chaplain); Sonny Tufts (Kansas); Mary Servoss (Capt. "Ma" McGregory); Ted Hecht (Dr. Jose Hardin); John Litel (Dr. Harrison); Dr. Hugh Ho Chang (Ling Chee); Mary Treen (Lt. Sadie Schwartz); Kitty Kelly (Lt. Ethel Armstrong); Helen Lynd (Lt. Elsie Bollenbacker); Lorna Gray (Lt. Toni Bacelli); Dorothy Adams (Lt. Irma Emerson); Ann Doran (Lt. Betty Paterson); Jean Willes (Lt. Carol Johnson); Lynn Walker (Lt. Fay Leonard); Joan Tours (Lt. Margaret Stevenson); Jan Wiley (Lt. Lynne Hopkins); James Bell (Colonel White); Dick Hogan (Flight Lt. Archie McGregor); Bill Goodwin (Captain O'Rourke); James Flavin (Captain O'Brien); Byron Foulger (Mr. Larson); Elsa Janssen (Mrs. Larson); Richard Crane (Georgie Larson); Boyd Davis (Colonel Mason); Will Wright (Colonel Clark); William Forrest (Major—San Francisco Dock); Isabel Cooper, Amparo Antenercrut, Linda Brent (Filipino Nurses); James Millican (Young Ensign); Damian O'Flynn (Young Doctor); Victor Kilian, Jr. (Corporal); Edward Earle, Byron Shores(Doctors); Harry Strung (Major Arthur); Edward Dew (Captain Lawrence); Yvonne DeCarlo (Girl); Hugh Prosser (Captain); Charles Lester (Soldier); Julia Faye, Hazel Keener, Frances Morris, Mimi Doyle (Nurses).

SINCE YOU WENT AWAY (UA, 1944) 172 M.

Producer, David O. Selznick; director, John Cromwell; based on the book *Together* by Margaret Buell Wilder; screenplay, Selznick; music, Max Steiner; production design, William L. Pereira; technical advisor, Lt. Col. J. G. Taylor; choreography, Charles Walters; assistant director, Lowell J. Farrell, Edward F. Mull; songs, B. G. DeSylva, Lew Brown and Ray Henderson; Kermit Goell and Ted Grouya; Larry Clinton; camera, Stanley Cortez, Lee Garmes; special effects, Jack Cosgrove, Clarence Slifer; editor, Hal C. Kern.

Claudette Colbert (Anne Hilton); Jennifer Jones (Jane Hilton); Joseph Cotten (Anthony Willett); Shirley Temple (Bridget "Brig" Hilton); Monty Woolley (Colonel Smollett); Lionel Barrymore (The Clergyman); Robert Walker (William G. Smollett II); Hattie McDaniel (Fidelia); Agnes Moorehead (Emily Hawkins); Guy Madison (Harold Smith); Keenan Wynn (Lt. Solomon); Lloyd Corrigan (Mr. Mahoney); Gordon Oliver (Marine Officer); Jane Devlin (Gladys Brown); Ann Gillis (Becky Anderson); Nazimova (Zosia Koslowska); Dorothy Garner ("Sugar"); Andrew McLaglen (Former Plowboy); Jill Warren (Waitress); Terry Moore (Refugee Child); Warren Hymer (Patient at Finger Ladder); Robert Johnson (Colored officer); Dorothy Dandridge (His Wife); Johnny Bond (AWOL); Irving Bacon (Bartender); George Chandler (Cabby); Jackie Moran (Johnny Mahoney); Addison Richards (Major Atkins); Barbara Pepper (Pin Girl); Byron Foulger (Principal); Harry Hayden (Conductor); Edwin Maxwell (Businessman); Florence Bates (Dowager); Theodore Von Eltz (Desk Clerk); Adeline de Walt Reynolds (Elderly Woman); Doodles Weaver (Convalescent); Eilene Janssen (Little Girl); Jonathan Hale (Conductor); Albert Basserman (Dr. Sigmund Gottlieb);

Craig Stevens (Danny Williams); Ruth Roman (Envious Girl); William B. Davidson (Taxpayer); Jimmy Clemons, Jr. (Boy Caroler) Neil Hamilton (Tim Hilton-Photograph).

PRACTICALLY YOURS (PAR, 1945) 90 M.

Producer-director, Mitchell Leisen; screenplay, Norman Krasna; music Victor Young; song, Sam Coslow; art director, Hans Dreier, Robert Usher; special effects, Gordon Jennings, J. Devereaux Jennings, Farciot Edouart; camera, Charles Lang, Jr.; editor, Doane Harrison.

Claudette Colbert (Peggy Martin); Fred MacMurray (Lt. [S. G.] Daniel Bellamy); Gil Lamb (Albert Beagell); Cecil Kellaway (Marvin F. Meglin); Robert Benchley (Judge Oscar Stimson); Tom Powers (Commander Harpe); Jane Frazee (Musical Comedy Star); Rosemary DeCamp (Ellen Macy); Isabel Randolph (Mrs. Meglin); Mikhail Rasumny (La Crosse); Arthur Loft (Uncle Ben Bellamy); Edgar Norton (Harvey, The Butler); Donald MacBride (Sam); Donald Kerr (Meglin's Chauffeur); Clara Reid (Meglin's Maid); Don Barclay (Himself); Rommie (Piggy, The Dog); Charles Irwin (Patterson); Will Wright (Senator Cowling); Isabel Withers (Grace Mahoney); Federic Nay (Michael); Stan Johnson (Pilot); Byron Barr (Navigator); Allen Fox, George Turner, Reggie Simpson (Reporters); Ralph Lynn, Jerry James, William Meader (Cameramen); John Whitney (Pilot With Bellamy); Gary Bruce (Camera Operator); John James (Young Man); Mike Lally (Asst. Cameraman); Ottola Nesmith (Hysterical Woman—Senate); Len Hendry (Naval Lt.—Senate); Charles Hamilton (Prudential Guard); Nell Craig (Meglin's Secretary); Jack Rice (Courturier); Yvonne De Carlo, Julie Gibson (Girl Employees); Allen Pinson (Stimson's Chauffeur); Edward Earle (Asst. Mgr—Hadley's Store); Mimi Doyle (Red Cross Worker); Jack Clifford (Subway Conductor); Earle Hodgins (Man With Pen Knife); Stanley Andrews (Shipyard Official); Charles A. Hughes (Radio Announcer); Kitty Kelly (Wife—Newsreel Theatre); Tom Kennedy (Burl Citizen—Newsreel Theatre); Hugh Binyon, Sonny Boy Williams, Michael Miller (Boys in Park); Anthony Marsh (Plane Captain).

GUEST WIFE (UA, 1945) 90 M.

Producer, John H. Skirball; director, Sam Wood; screeplay, Bruce Manning, John Klorer; art director, Lionel Banks; music director, Daniele Amfitheatrof; camera, Joseph Valentine; editor, William M. Morgan.

Claudette Colbert (Mary); Don Ameche (Joe); Richard Foran (Chris); Charles Dingle (Worth); Grant Mitchell (Detective); Wilma Francis (Susy); Chester Clute (Urban Nichols); Irving Bacon (Nosey Character); Hal K. Dawson (Dennis); Ed Fielding (Arnold).

WITHOUT RESERVATIONS (RKO, 1946) 107 M.

Producer, Jesse L. Lasky; director, Mervyn LeRoy; based on the novel by Jane Allen, Mae Livingston; screenplay, Andrew Solt; art director, Albert S. D'Agostino, Ralph Berger; assistant director, Lloyd Richards; music, Roy Webb; special effects, Vernon L. Walker, Russell A. Cully, Clifford Stine; camera, Milton Krasner; editor, Jack Ruggiero, Harold Stine.

Claudette Colbert (Kit); John Wayne (Rusty); Don DeFore (Dink); Anne Trioln (Connie); Phil Brown (Soldier); Frank Puglia (Ortega); Thurston Hall (Baldwin); Dona Drake (Dolores); Fernando Alvarado (Mexican Boy); Charles Arnt (Salesman); Louella Parson (Herself); Jack Benny (Guest Performer); Charles Evans (Jerome); Harry Haydon (Mr. Randall); Lela Bliss (Mrs. Randall); Griff Barnett (Train Conductor); Thelma Gyrath (WAC); Ian Wolfe (Charlie Gibbs); Grace Hampton (Lois); Minerva Urecal (Sue); Esther Howard (Sarah); Rosemary Lopez (Mexican Girl); Oscar O'Shea (Conductor); Ruth Roman (Girl In Negligee); Sam McDaniels (Freddy); Henry Hastings (Waiter); Ralph Hubbard (Sailor); Tom Hubbard (Marine); Erskine Sanford (Tim); Jane Wiley (Manicurist); Dudley Dickerson (Red Cap); Harry Holman (Gas Station Attendant); Lois Austin (Congresswoman); Eric Alden (Chauffeur);

Harry Strang (Policeman); Cy Kendall (Bond's Man); Fred Coby (French Officer); Raymond Burr (Paul Gill).

TOMORROW IS FOREVER (RKO, 1946) 105 M.

Producer, David Lewis; director, Irving Pichel; story, Gwen Bristol; screenplay, Lenore Coffee; art director, Wiard B. Ihnen; music, Max Steiner; camera, Joseph Valentine; editor, Ernest Nims.

Claudette Colbert (Elizabeth [MacDonald] Hamilton); Orson Welles (John [Mac-Donald] Kessler); George Brent (Larry Hamilton); Lucile Watson (Aunt Jessie); Richard Long (Drew); Natalie Wood (Margaret); Sonny Howe (Brian); John Wengraf (Dr. Ludwig); Ian Wolfe (Norton); Douglas Wood (Charles Hamilton); Joyce MacKenzie (Cherry); Tom Wirick (Pudge); Henry Hastings (Butler); Lane Watson (Hamilton's Secretary); Michael Ward (Baby Drew); Jesse Graves (Colored Servant); Irving Pichel (Commentator's Voice); Thomas Louden (Englishman On Ship); Evan Thomas (Ship Doctor); Milton Kibbee (Postman); Buster Phelps, Frank Wyrick, Bill Dyer (Fraternity Boys); Marguerite Campbell, Helen Gerald, Nena Ruth, Betty Greco (Girl Friends); Libby Taylor (Maid); Lane Chandler (Technician); Boyd Irwin (Dr. Callan); Jessie Grayson (Servant).

THE SECRET HEART (MGM, 1946) 97 M.

Producer, Edwin H. Knopf; director, Robert Z. Leonard; story, Rose Franken, William Brown Meloney; music, Bronislau Kaper; art director, Cedric Gibbons; camera, George Folsey; editor, Adrienne Fazan.

Claudette Colbert (Lee Addams); Walter Pidgeon (Chris Matthews); June Allyson (Penny Addams) Robert Sterling (Chase Addams, Jr.); Marshall Thompson (Brandon Reynolds); Elizabeth Patterson (Mrs. Stover); Richard Derr (Larry Addams, Sr.); Patricia Medina (Kay Burns); Eily Malyon (Miss Hunter); Ann Lace (Penny—As A Child); Dwayne Hickman (Chase—As A Child); Nicholas Joy (Dr. Rossiger); Anna Q. Nilsson (Miss Fox); Frank Darien (Mr. Wiggins); Donald Dewar (Page Boy); Chester Clute (Old Man); Harry Hayden (Minister); Wyndham Standing, Alex Pollard (Butlers); Audrey Totter (Brittle Woman's Voice); Hume Cronyn (Man's Voice); Hall Hankett (Young Man's Voice); Boyd Davis (Sheriff); Ruth Brady, Barbara Billingsley (Saleswomen); Virginia Randolph (Salesgirl); Joan Beeks (Woman Customer); John Webb Dillon (Conductor).

THE EGG AND I (UNIV, 1947) 108 M.

Producer-director, Chester Erskine; based on the novel by Betty MacDonald; screenplay, Erskine, Fred Finklehoffe; art director, Bernard Herzbrun; music, Frank Skinner; camera, Milton Krasner; editor, Russell Schoengarth.

Claudette Colbert (Betty); Fred MacMurray (Bob); Marjorie Main (Ma Kettle); Louise Allbritton (Harriet Putnam); Percy Kilbride (Pa Kettle); Richard Long (Tom Kettle); Billy House (Billy Reed); Ida Moore (Old Lady); Donald MacBride (Mr. Henty); Samuel S. Hinds (Sheriff); Esther Dale (Mrs. Hicks); Elizabeth Risdon (Betty's Mother); John Berkes (Golduck); Vic Potel (Crowbar); Fuzzy Knight (Cab Driver); Isabel O'Madigan (Mrs. Hicks' Mother); Dorothy Vaughan (Maid).

SLEEP, MY LOVE (UA, 1948) 97 M.

Executive producer, Mary Pickford; producer, Charles "Buddy" Rogers, Ralph Cohn; director, Douglas Sirk; based on the novel by Leo Rosten; screenplay, St. Clair McKelway; music, Rudy Schrager; art director, William Ferrari; camera, Joseph Valentine; editor, Lynn Harrison.

Claudette Colbert (Alison Courtland); Robert Cummings (Bruce Elcott); Don Ameche (Richard Courtland); Rita Johnson (Barby); George Coulouris (Charles Vernay); Hazel Brooks (Daphne); Anne Triola (Waitress); Queenie Smith (Mrs. Vernay); Keye Luke (Jimmie); Fred Nurney (Haskins); Maria San Marco (Jeannie); Raymond

Burr (Strake); Lillian Bronson (Helen); Ralph Morgan (Dr. Rhinehart); Jimmy Dodd (Elevator Boy); Ralph Peters (Mac); Syd Saylor (Milkman); Murray Alper (Drunk); Eddie Dun (Bartender); Lillian Randolph (Maid).

FAMILY HONEYMOON (UNIV, 1948) 80 M.

Producer, John Beck, Z. Wayne Griffin; director, Claude Binyon; story, Homer Croy; screenplay, Dane Lussier; art director, Bernard Herzbrun, Richard H. Riedel; Music director, Milton Schwarzwald; camera, William Daniels; editor, Milton Carruth.

Claudette Colbert (Katie Armstrong Jordan); Fred MacMurray (Grant Jordan); Rita Johnson (Minna Fenster); Gigi Perreau (Zoe); Peter Miles (Abner); Jimmy Hunt (Charlie); Lillian Bronson (Aunt Jo); Hattie McDaniel (Phyllis); Chill Wills (Fred); Catherine Doucet (Mrs. Abercrombie); Paul Harvey (Richard Fenster); Irving Bacon (Mr. Webb); Chick Chandler (Taxi Driver); Frank Jenks (Gas Station Attendant); Wally Brown (Tom Roscoe); Holmes Herbert (Reverend Miller); John Gallaudet (Prof. Pickering); Wilton Graff (Dr. Wilson); Fay Baker (Fran Wilson); O. Z. Whitehead (Jess); Lorin Raker (Hotel Clerk); Sarah Edwards (Mrs. Carp); Anne Nagel (Irene Barlett); Nancy Evans (Madge Saunders); Louise Austin (Louise Pickering; Frank Orth (Candy Butcher); Harry Hayden (Railroad Conductor); Almira Sessions (Maid); Minerva Urecal (Mrs. Webb); Jay Silverheels (Elevator Boy); Smoki Whitfield (Porter); Harold Goodwin (Guide); Edmund Cobb (Stage Driver); Snub Pollard (Man Passenger).

BRIDE FOR SALE (RKO, 1949) 87 M.

Producer, Jack H. Skirball; director, William D. Russell; story, Joseph Fields, Frederick Kohner; screenplay, Bruce Manning, Islin Auster; art director, Albert S. D'Agostino, Carroll Clark; music director, C. Bakaleinikof, camera, Joseph Valentine; editor, William Knudtson.

Claudette Colbert (Nora Shelly); Robert Young (Steve Adams); George Brent (Paul Martin); Max Baer (Litka); Gus Schilling (Timothy); Charles Arnt (Dobbs); Mary Bear (Miss Stone); Ann Tyrrell (Miss Swanson); Paul Maxey (Gentry); Burk Symon (Sitley); Stephen Chase (Drake); Anne O'Neal (Miss Jennings); Eula Guy (Miss Clarendon); John Michaels (Terry); William Vedder (Brooks); Thurston Hall (Mr. Trisby); Michael Branden (Archie Twitchell) (Officer White); Patsy Moran (Sarah); Harry Cheshire (Haskins); Robert Cautiero (Mgr. of Jewelry Store); Harry Wilson (Bruiser); Hans Conried (Jewelry Salesman); Frank Orth (Police Sgt.); Stan Johnson (Johnson).

THREE CAME HOME (20, 1950) 106 M.

Producer, Nunnally Johnson; director, Jean Negulesco; based on the book by Agnes Newton Keith; screenplay, Johnson; art director, Lyle Wheeler, Leland Fuller; music director, Lionel Newman; camera, Milton Krasner; editor, Dorothy Spencer.

Claudette Colbert (Agnes Keith); Patric Knowles (Harry Keith); Florence Desmond (Betty Sommers); Sessue Hayakawa (Colonel Suga); Sylvia Andrew (Henrietta); Mark Keuning (George); Phyllis Morris (Sister Rose); Howard Chuman (Lt. Nekata); Drue Mallory, Virginia Keley, Mimi Heyworth, Helen Westcott (Women Prisoners); Taka Iwashaiki (Japanese Captain); Devi Dja (Ah Yin); Leslie Thomas (Wet Man); John Burton (Elderly Resident); James Yanari (1st Lt.); George Leigh (Australian Prisoner of War); Li Sun (Wilfred); Duncan Richardson (English Boy); Melinda Plowman (English Girl); Lee MacGregor (Sailor); Masaji "Butch" Yamamota (Japanese Sgt.); Pat Whyte (Englishman); David Matsushama (Evil Guard); Alex Fraser (Dr. Bandy); Frank Kobata (Japanese Non-Com); Al Saijo (Japanese Boat Pilot); Jim Hagimori (Japanese Sea Captain); Patricia O'Callaghan (English Woman); Ken Kurosa, Giro Murashami (Orderlies); Leonard Willey (Governor General); Harry Martin, Pat O'Moore, Clarke Gordon, Douglas Walton, Robin Hughes, John Mantley, James Logan (Australian P.O.W.S.); Campbell Copelin, Leslie Denison (English Radio Announcers).

THE SECRET FURY (RKO, 1950) 85 M.

Producer, Jack H. Skirball, Bruce Manning; director, Mel Ferrer; story, Jack R. Leonard, James O'Hanlon; screenplay, Lionel House; music, Roy Webb; art director, Albert S. D'Agostino, Carroll Clark; music director, C. Bakaleinikoff; camera, Leo Tover; editor, Harry Marker.

Claudette Colbert (Ellen); Robert Ryan (David); Jane Cowl (Aunt Clara) Paul Kelly (Eric Lowell); Philip Ober (Kent); Elisabeth Risdon (Dr. Twining); Doris Dudley (Pearl); Dave Barbour (Lucian Randall); Vivian Vance (Leah); Percy Helton (Justice of Peace); Dick Ryan (Postman); Ann Godee (Tessa); Joseph Forte (Martin); Edith Angold (Flora); Adele Rowland (Mrs. Palmer); Howard Quinn (Bellhop); John Mantley (Hotel Clerk); Marjorie Babe Kane (Maid); Ralph Dunn (McCafferty); Ruth Robinson (Mrs Updyke); Pat Barton (Louise); Charmienne Harker (Ethel); Eddie Dunn (Mike); Willard Parker (Smith); Vivien Oakland (Mrs. Brownley); Abe Dinovitch (Man); Margaret Wells (Mrs. May); Burk Symon (Judge); Gene Brown (Hospital Nurse); Paul Picerni (Dr. Roth); Wheaton Chambers (District Attorney); Bert Moorhouse (Deputy Assistant Attorney); Vangie Beilby, June Benbow, Sonny Boyne, Connie Van (Patients); Gail Bonney (Nurse); Frank Scannel (Wilson).

THUNDER ON THE HILL (UNIV,1951) 84 M.

Producer, Michael Kraike; director, Douglas Sirk; based on the play *Bonaventure* by Charlotte Hastings; screenplay, Oscar Saul, Andre Solt; art director, Bernard Herzbrun, Nathan Juran; music Hans J. Salter; camera, William Daniels; editor, Ted J. Kent.

Claudette Colbert (Sister Mary); Ann Blyth (Valerie Carns); Robert Douglas (Dr. Jeffreys); Anne Crawford (Isabel Jeffreys); Philip Friend (Sidney Kingham); Gladys Cooper (Mother Superior); John Abbott (Abel Harmer); Connie Gilchrist (Sister Josephine); Gavin Muir (Melling); Phyllis Stanley (Nurse Phillips); Norma Varden (Pierce); Valerie Cardew (Nurse Colby); Queenie Leonard (Mrs. Smithson); Patrick O'Moore (Mr. Smithson).

LET'S MAKE IT LEGAL (20th, 1951) 77 M.

Producer, Robert Bassler; director, Richard Sale; story, Mortimer Braus; screenplay, F. Hugh Herbert, I.A.L. Diamond; music, Cyril Mockridge; art director, Lyle Wheeler, Albert Hogsett; music director, Lionel Newman; camera, Lucien Ballard; editor, Robert Fritsch.

Claudette Colbert (Miriam); Macdonald Carey (Hugh); Zachary Scott (Victor); Barbara Bates (Barbara Denham); Robert Wagner (Jerry Denham); Marilyn Monroe (Joyce); Frank Cady (Ferguson); Jim Hayward (Gardener); Carol Savage (Miss Jessup); Paul Gerrits (Milkman); Betty Jane Brown (Secretary); Vici Raaf (Hugh's Secretary); Joan Fisher (Baby Annabella); Kathleen Freeman, Rennie McEvoy, Wilson Wood, James Magill, Roger Moore, Beverly Thompson (Reporters); Abe Dinvitch, Frank Sully (Laborers); Jack Mather, Michael Ross (Policemen).

OUTPOST IN MALAYA (UA, 1952) 88 M.

Producer, John Stafford; director, Kenn Annakin; based on the novel *The Planter's Wife* by S. C. George; screenplay, Peter Proud, Guy Elmes; art director, Ralph Brinton; music, Allan Gray; music director, Ludo Philippa; camera, Geoffrey Unsworth; editor, Alfred Roome.

Claudette Colbert (Liz Frazer); Jack Hawkins (Jim Frazer); Anthony Steele (Insp. Hugh Dobson); Ram Gopal (Nair); Jeremy Spencer (Mat); Tom Macauley (Jack Bushell); Helen Goss (Eleanor Bushell); Sonya Hana (Ah Moy); Andy Ho (Wan Li); Peter Asher (Mike Frazer); Shaym Bahadur (Putra); Bryan Coleman (Capt. Dell); Don Sharp (Lt. Summers); Maria Baillie (Arminah); Bill Travers (Planter); John Stamp (Len Carter); John Martin (Harry Saunders); Myrette Mowen (Mildred Saunders); Patrick Westwood, Alfie Bass (Soldiers); Ny Cheuk Kwong (Ho Tang); Yah Ming (Ah Siong); Victor Maddern (Radio Operator).

DAUGHTERS OF DESTINY (French, 1954) 94 M.

Episode; ELIZABETH; director, Marcel Paglieo; screenplay, Vladimir Pozner.

Claudette Colbert (Elizabeth); Eleanore Rossi-Drago (Farm Girl); and: Mirko Ellis

Episode: JEANNE; director, Jean Delannoy; screenplay, Jean Aurenche Pierre Bost.

Michele Morgan (Joan of Arc); and: Andre Clement

Episode: LYSISTRATA; director, Christian Jacque; screenplay, Jean Ferry, Henry Jeanson.

Martine Carol (Lysistrata); and: Raf Vallone, Paolo Stoppa, Daniel Ivernel.

TEXAS LADY (RKO, 1955) 85 M.

Producer, Nat Holt; director, Tim Whelan; story-screenplay, Horace McCoy; song, Paul Sawtell and Johnnie Mann; music, Sawtell; art director, William Ross; camera, Ray Rennahan; editor, Richard Farrell.

Claudette Colbert (Prudence Webb); Barry Sullivan (Chris Mooney); Greg Walcott (Jess Foley); James Bell (Cass Gower); Horace McMahon (Stringy Winfield); Ray Collins (Ralston); Walter Sande (Sturdy); Don Haggerty (Sheriff Herndon); Douglas Fowley (Clay Ballard); Harry Tyler (Choate); John Litel (Mead Moore); Alexander Campbell (Judge Herzog); Celia Lovsky (Mrs. Gantz); LeRoy Johnson (Rancher); Florenz Ames (Wilson); Kathleen Mulgreen (Nameg Winfield); Robert Lynn (Reverend Callander); and: Grandon Rhodes, Bruce Payne, George Brand, Raymond Greenleaf.

ROYAL AFFAIRS IN VERSAILLES (Times, 1957) 152 M.

Producer-director-screenplay, Sacha Guitry; music, Jean Francaix; camera, Peirre Montazel.

Sacha Guitry (Louis XIV); Claudette Colbert (Mme. de Montespan); Orson Welles (Benjamin Franklin); Jean-Pierre Aumont (Cardinal de Rohan); Edith Piaf (Woman of the People); Gerard Philipe (D'Artagnan); Micheline Presle (Mme. du Pompadour); Jean Marais (Louis XV); Daniel Gelin (Jean Collinet); Daniele Delorme (Louison Chabray); George Marchal (Louis XIV Young Man); Gaby Morlay (Comtesse de la Motte); Gilbert Boka (Louis XVI); Lana Marconi (Marie Antoinette); Fernand Gravet (Moliere); Marie Margquet (Mme. de Maintenon).

PARRISH (1961) 140 M.

Producer-director-screenplay, Delmer Daves; based on the novel by Mildred Savage; assistant director, Chuck Hansen, Russel Llewllyn; art director, Leo K. Kuter; music, Max Steiner; camera, Harry Stradling, Sr.; editor, Owen Marks.

Troy Donahue (Parrish McLean); Claudette Colbert (Ellen McLean); Karl Malden (Judd Raike); Dean Jagger (Salla Post); Diane McBain (Alison Post); Connie Stevens (Lucy); Sharon Hugueny (Paige Raike); Dub Taylor (Teet); Hampton Fancher (Edgar Raike); Saundra Edwards (Evaline); Hope Summers (Mary); Bibi Osterwald (Rosie); Madeleine Sherwood (Addie); Sylvia Miles (Eileen); Alfonso Marshall (Gladstone); John Barracudo (Willie); Terry Carter (Cartwright); Ford Rainey (John Donati); Sara Taft (Gramma); Edgar Stehli (Tully); Wade Dumas (Maples); John McGovern (Skipper); Hayden Rorke (Tom Weldon); Irene Windust (Maizie Weldon); Don Dillaway (Max Maine); Gertrude Flynn (Miss Daly); House Jameson (Oermeyer) Ken Allen (Lemmie); Karen Norris (Operator); Frank Campanella (Foreman); Carroll O'Connor (Firechief); Michael Sean (Bellhop); Fred Marlow (Butler—Post Home); Martin Eric (Mr. Gilliam).

In THE GHOST TRAIN (1926)

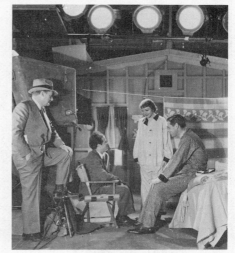

On the set of IT HAPPENED ONE NIGHT (Col '34), with director Frank Capra (seated) and Clark Gable

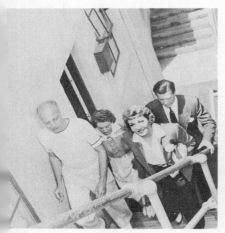

ith director Mitchell Leisen (left) and y Milland on the Paramount lot, 1940

With Don Ameche, director Sam Wood, and Dick Foran in GUEST WIFE (UA '45)

th Claude Dauphin and Robert Preston Janus (1956)

With her husband, Dr. Joe Pressman, at the Friars Club in New York City, about 1963

With Edward G. Robinson in THE HOLE IN THE WALL (Par '29)

With Miriam Hopkins in THE SMILING LIEUTENANT (Par '31)

With Richard Spiro and Gary Cooper in HIS WOMAN (Par '31)

With Charles Boyer in THE MAN FROM YESTERDAY (Par '32)

In THE SIGN OF THE CROSS (Par '33)

With Mary Boland, Herbert Marshall, and William Gargan in FOUR FRIGHTENED PEOPLE (Par '34)

With Clark Gable in IT HAPPENED ONE NIGHT (Col '34)

With Henry Wilcoxon in CLEOPATRA (Par '34)

With Jean Rouverol, Dora Clement, and Joan Bennett in PRIVATE WORLDS (Par '35)

With Katharine Alexander and Melvyn Douglas in SHE MARRIED HER BOSS (Col '35)

With Ronald Colman in UNDER TWO FLAGS (20th '36)

With Fred MacMurray in MAID OF SALEM (Par '37)

With Heather Thatcher, Isabel Jeans, and Melville Cooper in TOVARICH (WB '37)

With Gary Cooper in BLUEBEARD'S EIGHTH WIFE (Par '38)

With Henry Fonda and Chief John Big Tree in DRUMS ALONG THE MOHAWK (20th '39)

With Spencer Tracy, Hedy Lamarr, and Clark Gable in BOOM TOWN (MGM '40)

With Joel McCrea, Mary Astor, and Rudy Vallee in THE PALM BEACH STORY (Par '42)

In SINCE YOU WENT AWAY (UA '44)

With Orson Welles, Natalie Wood, and George Brent in TOMORROW IS FOREVER (RKO '46)

With Walter Pidgeon, June Allyson, and Marshall Thompson in THE SECRET HEART (MGM '46)

With Troy Donahue in PARRISH (WB '61)

In THE EGG AND I (Univ '47)

With Fred MacMurray in FAMILY HONEYMOON (Univ '48)

With Patrick O'Moore and Queenie Leonard in THUNDER ON THE HILL (Univ '51)

With Macdonald Carey and Zachary Scott in LET'S MAKE IT LEGAL (20th '51)

CAROLE LOMBARD

5'2"
112 Pounds
Blonde hair
Blue eyes
Libra

CAROLE LOMBARD has long been cherished as one of Hollywood's deftest comediennes and a strong dramatic actress. Her natural good-gal qualities on the screen usually confounded viewers into ignoring her striking good looks, though her appearance was a distinct asset to the projection of her role as a prankish miss who would just as soon deliver a solid left to the hero's jaw as bestow a kiss in order to win her way. Her serious characterizations were blessed with a sincerity that made her unmannered portrayals very real. Had she not died in 1942 at age 32, she would doubtlessly have endeared herself to further generations of moviegoers as a most delectable performer.

Unlike many of her contemporaries who joined Paramount after 1929, Carole did not have a theatre background. Rather, she had spent much of the 1920s as a second lead in minor Westerns, as a heroine of Mack Sennett comedy shorts, and later as a conventional female lead in Pathé pictures.

Up to 1934, Paramount used Carole as a sophisticated clothes-horse fill-in. Despite the severe handicap of a misguided studio-imposed image and inferior films, Carole managed not only to win a large following, but also to refine her acting talents in a remarkable manner.

With her zany appearance in *Twentieth Century* (1934), Carole found her own unique genre in which she could showcase her madcap comedy talent. She would be the screen's most successful practitioner of the art of screwball comedy throughout the 1930s, topping herself in *My Man Godfrey* and *Nothing Sacred.*

- When Carole left Paramount in 1937, she was one of Hollywood's highest paid stars, able to command any contract terms she desired. She ventured into straight dramatics under David O. Selznick's aegis and emerged successfully to follow up the new career in several RKO dramas.

Although there has been no official cult to champion her posthumous reputation, Carole remains unchallenged as an unquestionably unique screen immortal.

* *

Carole Lombard was born Jane Alice Peters on October 6, 1908, in Fort Wayne, Indiana, the daughter of Frederick G. and Elizabeth (Knight) Peters. She was of English and Scottish ancestry. One of her grandfathers was a bank director of the company which laid the initial trans-Atlantic cable.

Carole's parents were divorced when she was eight years old. That year (1916) Mrs. Peters took a trip to the San Francisco World's Fair accompanied by her three children, Carole (Jane), Frederick (born 1902), and Stuart (born 1907). Their sightseeing jaunt led them eventually to Los Angeles, where they settled.

As a child, Carole was "long-legged, tow-headed, bright-eyed, and imaginative." She was the most athletic tomboy in her neighborhood and was constantly involved in assorted scrapes. One of her neighbors, Paramount executive Albert A. Kaufman, had his pal, ex-lightweight boxing champ Benny Leonard, teach the Peters children the art of boxing. Carole made her first public appearance while attending Cahuenga Grammar School. She was Queen of the May in a school pageant.

One day, film director Allan Dwan was visiting the Kaufmans and spotted Carole playing baseball in the street. He later recalled, "She was a cute-looking little tomboy—about twelve—a hoyden, out there knocking hell out of the other kids, playing better baseball than they were. And I needed someone of her type for this picture. She'd never acted, so we talked to her parents [sic] and they let her do it and she was very good."

The feature was *A Perfect Crime* (1921), a Fox melodrama starring Monte Blue as a seemingly timid young man who commits a bank robbery, writes a best-selling book about his other imaginary adventures, and later returns the stolen money. Carole played Blue's sister. Dwan assessed the fledgling player: "She ate it up. Of course, it was silent. If we'd given her lines to remember, she'd probably have been terrified, but we always made kids feel they were playing and not working. When you give them words to learn, it becomes an ordeal."

Carole enjoyed her movie-making experience and made the rounds of the studios, hoping for another actress job, while continuing her education at Virgil Intermediate School and then Los Angeles High School. She was almost signed to a film contract by Mary Pickford's manager, but Miss Pickford felt Carole looked too much like her, and was too young besides. Finally, Carole was hired by Charles Chaplin for a projected film, but he and his then wife, Lita Grey, were spatting and the production was suspended.

At Los Angeles High School Carole continued to demonstrate her prowess in athletics, winning medals for sprinting and high jumping. When she was 15 Carole decided she had had enough of academics and quit, although she agreed to attend the Marian Nolks Dramatic School, an idea prompted by her mother Bessie. Carole enjoyed the acting lark and joined a little theatre organization called "The Potboilers," playing small roles in the group's amateur productions.

As the result of meeting a Fox executive at a dinner party, Carole was offered a studio screen test. She was given the female lead in a Buck Jones Western, *Hearts and Spurs* (1925), in which the cowboy hero had to endure, among other tribulations, the blame for robberies committed by Carole's brother. *Variety* reported about this formula Western: ". . .[Carole] is attractive looking, particularly in the fashionable eastern clothes she is permitted to wear, but as for expressiveness she might just as well have been labeled 'For decorative purposes only.' "Carole was paid $75 a week. She had selected her new screen name Carol Lombard because she "didn't feel like a 'Jane.'" Her surname was borrowed from her mother's close friend, Harry Lombard.

She then played a supporting role in *Durand of the Badlands* (1925), another Fox Western starring Buck Jones. Jones gallops through a Western town as the alleged badman Durand. He saves Marian Nixon from marrying Oro Grande's crooked sheriff. Carole is used as a human shield when the outlaws battle the law.

When option renewal time came at Fox, Carole was put on suspension for requesting a raise. A compromise was reached and the studio cast her in a rather sophisticated comedy, *Marriage in Transit*, (1925). It had Edmund Lowe playing opposite-sides-of-the-law look-a-likes—a scoundrel and a secret service agent. Carole marries the secret service agent by error, but discovers she is glad for the mistake. The feature was reasonably well received and Carole was awarded a five-year contract by Fox.

Shortly thereafter, Carole was returning from a hockey game on a foggy night with Harry Brand Cooper, the son of a Los Angeles banker. The car in front of theirs slid backwards down a hill, and the sudden impact thrust Carole against the windshield. Her face was cut from the corner of her nose to her left cheekbone. The attending medical interne sewed up the wound with 14 stitches, not utilizing any anesthesia for fear her facial muscles would relax. While Carole was recuperating in the hospital, she began studying motion picture photography. She realized she would have a facial scar, but that proper lighting and camera angles could minimize it. Even during this period of stress Carole retained her exuberant spirits, and she was noted as the hospital prankster.

By early 1927, when Carole had fully recuperated from plastic surgery, the scar was barely noticeable. However, due to the accident, Fox had canceled her contract, and Carole's projected loanout role in United Artists' *The Tempest* (1928), starring John Barrymore, went to Dorothy Sebastian, who herself was replaced by Camilla Horn.

Carole was advised by film industry friends to try her luck at Mack Sennett's comedy factory, where the focus was on shapely figures in bathing suits and the ability to take a pie in the face and execute a good pratfall. Carole was hired as a bathing beauty at $50 a week, and soon inherited the lucky dressing room once used by Sennett leading ladies Gloria Swanson and Phyllis Haver. One of her close friends on the lot was burly actress Madelayne Fields, who would become Fieldsie, Carole's private secretary, in the 1930s. In 1937, Fields married director Walter Lang.

During the next 18 months Carole made 13 two-reelers* at Sennett, most often costarring with Daphne Pollard, Irving Bacon, Vernon Dent, and Sally Eilers. Recalling this madcap period of her career, Carole once said "Little touches like having a lobster tied on behind and a nose painted as red as a neon light. Didn't get that paint off for two weeks. Lost a perfectly good boy friend over it. Said he didn't like girls who weren't dainty."

By 1928, with the onslaught of talking pictures and changing tastes,

---

*1927: Smith's Pony (director: Raymond McKee); *The Girl from Everywhere* (dr: Eddie Cline); *Hold that Pose* (dr: Eddie Cline); 1928: *Run Girl Run* (dr: Alf Goulding); *The Beach Club* (dr: Harry Edwards); *The Best Man* (dr: Harry Edwards); *The Swim Princess* (dr: Alf Goulding); *The Bicycle Flirt* (dr: Harry Edwards); *The Girl from Nowhere* (dr: Harry Edwards); *His Unlucky Night* (dr: Harry Edwards); *The Campus Carmen* (dr: Alf Goulding); *The Campus Vamp* (dr: Harry Edwards); 1929: *Matchmaking Mamas* (dr: Harry Edwards).

Mack Sennett was suffering financial reversals and was curtailing production. When Carole left the Sennett fold she was being paid $400 a week. While there she had acquired an excellent sense of comic timing which would prove helpful in her later film career.

Turning to free lance assignments, Carole had a minor supporting role in Fox's *Me, Gangster* (1928), a stark chronicle of a hoodlum in the making, starring Don Terry. Carole was a member of the confidence gang involved in Terry's underworld doings. In the same year, she was part of the French scenery in the low-budget *Divine Sinner* (1928). This romantic drama concerned impoverished Austrian aristocrat Vera Reynolds, who is hired by Paris police minister Nigel De Brulier to flirt with a prince for diplomatic reasons.

After this film Carole was hired as a contract player by the production division of Pathé Pictures, which had been releasing Mack Sennett's comedy shorts. In *Power* (1928), construction workers William Boyd and Alan Hale cavort in the nearby town, and vie for pretty Jacqueline Logan. Carole was just one of the available "dames." *Show Folks* (1928) was a backstage yarn that offered Carole a substantial role for a change, as the successful dance partner of a mediocre hoofer.

Her first 1929 Pathé release was the film of Sidney Howard's stage success *Ned McCobb's Daughter*. As a concession to the growing demand for talking pictures, Pathé added sound effects to this production as they had to *Show Folks*. Irene Rich had the title role as the restaurateur wife of a worthless rat; Carole was the waitress for whom Rich's husband steals.

Carole's first talking film was *High Voltage* (1929), a melodrama set in a Nevada mountain cabin, where a busload of people are stranded during a snowstorm. Carole was the blonde prisoner of detective Owen Moore. Escaped convict William Boyd arrives on the scene and he and Carole discover one another. Although Moore gallantly offers them a chance to escape, they agree to serve out their sentences and start life anew.

In the all-talking comedy drama *Big News* (1929), ace reporter Robert Armstrong nearly loses his position because of drinking, alienates his wife Carole (she is a sob sister writer on a rival paper), and has to prove his innocence of a framed-up murder charge. *Variey* noted: "[she] steps before the camera just often enough to provide the necessary touch and not spoil a good job."

The Racketeer (1929) cast Carole as New York society girl Rhoda Philbrooke, who becomes enamored of ailing violinist Roland Drew. Top gangster Robert Armstrong agrees to assist Drew if Carole will marry him. Armstrong is conveniently gunned down before the happy finale. *Film Daily* reported: "Carol Lombard proves a real surprise and does her best work to date. In fact this is the first opportunity she has had to prove that she has the stuff to go over. With looks and a good trouping sense, she also has the personality." This feature was the start of Carole being typecast as a vapid society heroine.

Since there was no likely future for Carole at Pathé—they were too involved in maneuvering the careers of studio stars Ann Harding and Constance Bennett—Carole did not renew her contract there. A proposed role for her in Cecil B. DeMille's first talking film, *Dynamite* (1929), did not materialize. He had moved from Pathé to a new contract at MGM.

On free-lance, Carole appeared in Fox's Western, *Arizona Kid* (1930). It was a followup to the studio's successful *In Old Arizona* (1929), and was filmed on location in Utah at Zion National Park. Warner Baxter repeated his Academy Award portrayal of the Cisco Kid (herein the Arizona Kid) as the good-bad horseman who realizes just in time that blonde siren Carole and her husband Theodore von Eltz—masquerading as her brother—are merely cheating gamblers out to milk the folk of Rockville, Arizona. The *New York Times* judged: "Carol Lombard is a beautiful girl but it is doubtful whether she is suited to the role of Virginia."

Carole's initial motion picture for prestigious Paramount was the programmer *Safety in Numbers*, which debuted at the Paramount Theatre on May 30, 1930. Its premise had song-writing hero Charles "Buddy" Rogers hiring three chorus girls to show him the less obvious but evil ways of big city life. Josephine Dunn hooks the eligible millionaire, while Carole and Kathryn Crawford must be content just to mother him and find rich pastures elsewhere.

On the cast credits of *Safety in Numbers*, Paramount accidentally spelled Carole's first name with a final "e," and it was decided that this would be the official spelling. And so it has remained. Later the studio would grind out much publicity copy claiming that the decision had been a deliberate one by executives and Carole, claiming that the new 13-letter name tied in more favorably with her astrological chart, and so forth. Forthright Carole would set the record straight: "That's a lot of bunk. But since they're paying me so well, I don't care how they spell my name." (As of November 6, 1936, she legally changed her name to Carole Lombard, making it "official and permanent.")

Paramount was sufficiently pleased with Carole's performance to sign her to a seven-year contract, starting at $350 a week. Unlike most of its new future star performers (Ruth Chatterton, Claudette Colbert, Kay Francis, Miriam Hopkins, Sylvia Sidney), Carole had not had any Broadway stage experience. Rather, she had to rely on whatever knowledge she had gained from appearing in 13 minor features and an equal number of quickly churned out short subjects. For the present, Paramount considered Carole just another spunky ingenue like its other contractees Jean Arthur, Mary Brian, and Fay Wray, Much later she would have the opportunity to demonstrate her natural bent for handling comedy action and witty repartee.

Fast and Loose (1930) was primarily a vehicle to introduce Miriam Hopkins to the screen. Hopkins appeared as a wealthy Long Island socialite attracted to chauffeur Charles Starrett. Henry Wadsworth, her playboy brother, is reformed by chorus girl Carole. Despite the Preston Sturges dialogue, *Fast and Loose* was not a memorable social comedy, merely a hasty A-feature tossed out as one of Paramount's 64 1930 releases. Carole had the role Esther Ralston had played in Paramount's first filming of the picture as *The Best People* in 1925.

Carole appeared in five Paramount releases in 1931, proving that at least in the early 1930's, Paramount could match prolific Warner Brothers in putting its contract players to top quantitative use. *It Pays to Advertise* (1931) was cocky trivia, dedicated to the proposition that in America, any product (even a nonexistent one) could be merchandised if properly publicized. Enterprising Skeets Gallagher (a mainstay in Paramount products of the 1930–31 period) has the assistance of his father's knowledgeable secretary (Carole) in launching a campaign to make "Thirteen Soap" ("unlucky to dirt") the leading product in the industry. Before he is through, Gallagher's empty corporation has surpassed that of his dad's (Eugene Pallette), and he has proven his worth as a businessman. Carole was again described by the press as "attractive and capable."

Man of the World (1931) was Carole's introduction to Paramount's special film genre of the period: high-society drama in which world-weary upper-crust people cannot compete with the optimistic lower classes for integrity, ambition, and happiness. Carole was cast opposite the studio's suave gentleman star in residence, William Powell (whom she would later marry). Powell plays a former novelist turned professional blackmailer, and Carole a sweet American innocent on her first visit to Paris. She is accompanied by wealthy uncle Guy Kibbee and her Pittsburgh fiancé Lawrence Gray (32-year-old actor and onetime Paramount production superintendent). Soon Carole is enchanted with worldly Powell, and romance blossoms, until she learns he is blackmailing her uncle. He almost repents of his criminal ways but decides his past is too black for any real happiness. Using his accomplice Wynne Gibson to point up what a blackguard he really is, Powell nobly embarks for Africa, tearing up Kibbee's check once aboard ship.

Ladies' Man (1931) featured William Powell as a dapper ne'er-do-well whose glib talk and fancy clothes can wilt any woman's pose of ennui. Carole was cast in the secondary role of a banker's daughter, who, like her mother, succumbs to Powell's engaging savoir faire. However, it is out-of-towner Kay Francis (Paramount's leading practitioner of the cosmopolitan lady about the social circuit) who wins Powell's love. Before he can marry Francis, Powell falls to his death in a terrace ledge struggle wih Carole's father. Save for the rich appointments and the snappy dialogue, *Ladies' Man* was dull going. Carole's brief highlight was a short drunk scene in which she gave indications of a blossoming comic talent.

Powell had taken quite an interest in Carole during their filming together. It was said that she regarded him as a sophisticated father substitute. They were married on June 26, 1931, in her mother's Beverly Hills home. He was 39, she 21; it was his second marriage. After their Hawaiian honeymoon, they purchased a Hollywood mansion, which Carole decorated in her own eccentric style. She informed movie fan magazines that she wanted to start raising a family in a few years and retire from film-making. Carole continued to be the active party-goer she had always been, while the reclusive Powell rarely attended any social functions.

Up Pops the Devil (1931) was a trite production-line domestic comedy. Norman Foster leaves the comfort of Greenwich Village life—he is an advertising worker and writes stories on the side—to marry Carole. A year later they are deep in the social swim which leaves him little time for his creative work. With the chance to sell his big novel, Foster stays home to concentrate on writing, and Carole accepts a dancing job in Skeets Gallagher's new Broadway revue. The marriage disintegrates further, but they come together again at the end when she learns she is pregnant. Lilyan Tashman added some wisecracking humor as a newspaper critic, with Joyce Compton as a gooey Southern belle who flirts with Foster. Mordaunt Hall (*New York Times*) noted: "But it must not be forgotten that the shining light of this film is Miss Lombard, whose sincerity in her portrayal is surpassed only by her exquisite beauty." *Up Pops the Devil* was remade as the more effective *Thanks for the Memory* (1939) with Bob Hope and Shirley Ross.

I Take This Woman (1931) was Carole's final release of the year. It was an out-of-date melodrama, given better handling by the cast than it deserved. Gary Cooper was top-billed as the cowhand with whom spoiled Easterner Carole flirts, and finally agrees to marry. Her father disinherits her, and Carole is determined to make a go of the paltry lot husband Cooper offers her. After a year of trying her best, she returns to the social life of New York. When Cooper discovers the chi chi type of existence to which she has been accustomed, he readily agrees to a divorce. She then changes her mind, follows him to the circus where he is performing, and is on hand to comfort him when he is thrown from a horse. This heiress role had originally been slated for past Cooper costar Fay Wray. Carole was cited again for her "capable performance" by the critics.

By now, Carole was considered one of Paramount's top people, on par with Claudette Colbert, Miriam Hopkins, and Sylvia Sidney, and only a rung below Nancy Carroll, Ruth Chatterton, and Kay Francis, and the studio's imported superstar Marlene Dietrich. Unlike these other luminaries, Carole had not been given a diversity of roles at Paramount. Rather, she had appeared in a succession of sophisticated dramas, usually dressed to the nines in slinky gowns which effectively offset her curvaceous figure and attractive legs. That her exuberant nice girl personality shone through this stock characterization made her screen image unique and winning. Her histrionic talents had become so refined that even the casual critic or viewer realized that Carole had untapped acting potential. Meanwhile, Paramount was content to boost her as their new orchid lady of drama, taking over where Kay Francis would leave off when Warner Brothers filched her, Chatterton, and William Powell in 1932. Carole had sufficient power at Paramount to decline a loanout assignment to Warner Brothers to costar with James Cagney in *Blonde Crazy* (1932).

Carole also made five undistinguished features in 1932, the only difference being that two were performed on loanout to Columbia. Paramount still refused to take special care about promoting her career, allowing her to muddle along like Claudette Colbert in a series of nondescript programmers. Seemingly, the studio felt that if she retained her growing following, everything was fine.

Carole was top-featured in *No One Man*, which opened at the Paramount Theatre on January 22, 1932. She was a divorcee member of the idle rich Palm Beach set. After her polo-playing pal Ricardo Cortez dies of a weak heart, she takes up with Viennese doctor Paul Lukas, a decided freak in her social group—he works! Before long, Lukas has redeemed her meandering nature, and converted her to worthwhile causes: nursing and marrying him. Unlike her usual well-coiffed and gowned production, *Variety* this time reported: "The lens has been none too kind to her here. Gorgeous in 'stills', the reproduction on the screen for her is such as to cause audible unfavorable comment from women in the audience."

Sinners in the Sun (1932) sported Carole as a Fifth Avenue model who passes up honest mechanic Chester Morris for philanderer Walter Byron. Not until Carole has wearied of being passed around the Long Island sleek set, and irked Morris wearies of being a gigolo husband, do they reunite. Along the way, Carole encounters playboy Cary Grant who seeks her momentary affection. Adrienne Ames, a promising Paramount starlet who never got the right break in filmdom, has some effective moments as Morris's wealthy employer-spouse. Marguerite Tazelaar (*New York Herald Tribune*) analyzed Carole's part in this rags-to-unhappy-riches tale: "[she] takes herself and her obligations in the role of Doris Blake quite seriously, squeezing all the honest emotion possible out of the part, which leaves her little time for a casual, light moment, and none for a momentary gleam of humor."

At Columbia in *Virtue* (1932), Carole was starred as ex-streetwalker Mae, now a waitress, who marries prudish taxi driver Pat O'Brien. A fast talker and quick to misunderstand, O'Brien denounces Carole when he discovers her in a compromising situation. Carole was praised for her "alabaster beauty and her talent for looking cruel and tender at the same time." In the mid–1930s, Carole would be romantically linked with Robert Riskin, who wrote the screenplay for *Virtue*.

Also at Columbia, Carole was tossed into *No More Orchids* (1932), in which she balks at grandfather C. Aubrey Smith's decision that she wed prince Jameson Thomas. She prefers impoverished lawyer Lyle Talbot. In her three-star *New York Daily News* review, Kate Cameron commented on Carole's "poise and skill."

When Miriam Hopkins refused the role of the fast-talking heroine in Paramount's *No Man of Her Own* (1932), Carole was substituted to star with MGM's rising young star, Clark Gable. Con man Gable lands in a small Midwestern town and on a bet marries the local beauty, librarian Carole. She is rather naive about his real occupation, even when they return to New York. He makes sporadic endeavors at reform. His ex-mistress Dorothy Mackaill spills the beans about Gable's true status—he is away in jail serving a 90-day sentence. When Carole determines that she still loves Gable, she puts him through a brief stretch of hell before admitting to him that she really cares. This was the only time Carole and her future husband would costar in a motion picture. They had good screen chemistry and the film was a popular success. The *London Film Weekly* decided: "Carole Lombard, cool, sincere and intelligent, makes the perfect heroine."

Plans to include Carole in an episode of the multisegment *If I Had a Million* (1932) never jelled.

It was no secret in Hollywood that Carole and William Powell were not making a go of their marriage. On August 18, 1933, they were divorced in the district court of Carson City, Nevada. The standard charge of mental cruelty was used, with Carole stating that Powell was "a very emotional man, cruel and cross in manner of language." Besides Robert Riskin, Carole's most constant escort after her divorce was singer-bandleader-movie personality, Russ Columbo. Carole once said: "His love for me was the kind that rarely comes to any woman." It was rumored that they were to be married. When the 26-year-old Columbo was killed in a freak shooting accident (September 14, 1934), it was Carole's idea to keep the news from his ailing mother by maintaining the pretense that he was away on tour in Europe.

From Hell to Heaven (1933) was *Grand Hotel* at the race track, even to track radio announcer Jack Oakie opening and closing the melodrama with the cliché: "People come and people go, but nothing ever happens at the Luray Springs Hotel." The multiple vignettes of *From Hell to Heaven* sprang from the effect of a big horserace on hotel guests: Carole, mistress of bookmaker Sidney Blackmer, who eventually returns to her old love; newlyweds Adrienne Ames and David Manners, who must win a jackpot or face embezzlement charges; prostitute Shirley Grey, maid Verna Hillie, in love with a jockey, and detective Thomas Jackson round off the leading players.

Supernatural was a complete change of pace. Heroine Carole stumbles into mad doctor H.B. Warner's laboratory and is subjected to having the soul of executed killer Vivienne Osborne instilled within her. Before she is released from the "transplant," Carole finds herself seeking revenge on the spiritualist, who was implicated in her twin brother's death. John S. Cohen, Jr. (*New York Sun*) reported: "When the spirit of the murderess enters her, she plays quite trickily effectively. She actually manages to look sinister—something that has seemed quite foreign to her histrionic nature." Smiling, ineffectual Randolph Scott was no help to Carole in her dual characterization. She always regarded this film claptrap as the low point of her cinema career.

In the quite remarkable World War I aviation drama, *The Eagle and the Hawk*, (1933), Carole was fourth-billed in the extraneous role of the "beautiful lady." Stalwart hero Fredric March and chipper Jack Oakie belong to the Royal Flying Squadron. On leave in London, March chances upon Carole and they enjoy a brief romance. The idyl served as a short respite from the focus of the realistic drama: the mental and physical pressure wartime pilots undergo. *The Eagle and the Hawk* climaxed believably with March shooting himself while out on a mission—on the last day of the war—and comrade Cary Grant making it appear as if he had died in action.

Carole was topbilled in Columbia's *Brief Moment*, which premiered at the Roxy Theatre on September 29, 1933. In this undistinguished filming of S. N. Behrman's bright play, Carole portrayed a lovely nightclub chanteuse who marries social aristocrat Gene Raymond. Under her influence, he substitutes hard work for liquor and frivolity. *Variety* was critical: "Occasionally, she strikes a spark, but in general her work is tame, almost colorless. She does not invest the character with a charm which might pull audience interest along with her." More outstanding in the film was Monroe Owsley as a "fumigated gigolo," the role that Alexander Woollcott had played on Broadway.

White Woman (1933) was a ludicrous jungle drama. Cockney Charles Laughton reigns as virtual king over whites and natives in the Malaysian jungle. On a trip to the settlement he is enchanted by cabaret singer Carole, and he takes her back as his bride. She is soon attracted to overseer Kent Taylor. Laughton is in the process of subjecting the lovebirds to grueling mental torture when blustering Charles Bickford turns up. He in turn fancies Carole, but is sport enough to help her and Taylor to escape. Laughton and Bickford are left behind to face the natives. Carole was far from her best in aping the world-weary woman à la Marlene Dietrich. She seemed rightfully embarrassed by the trashy dialogue (such as Taylor asking Carole, as they paddle along in a canoe, "Have you ever been incredibly, inexcusably happy?" She sighs: "Yes, once. Long ago"). In her nightclub sequences, dressed in a filmy black evening dress, Carole crooned: "Yes, My Dear" and "He's A Cute Brute"—it was her screen singing debut. In this example of the wonder-wonderland of potboiler films, there were such examples of dramatic license as Carole slinking around the jungle in garden party outfits. Although everyone else is wilted from the heat, she remains cool and crisp.

After Sylvia Sidney walked out of Paramount's musical *The Way to Love* (1933), starring Maurice Chevalier, Carole refused to replace her (a wise decision) and Ann Dvorak was utilized. Carole also turned down a loanout to Warner Brothers for *Hard to Handle* (1933), in which Mary Brian was finally employed to play James Cagney's vis-á-vis.

Starting off 1934, Carole replaced Miriam Hopkins in the improbable *Bolero* (1934). Her leading man was Paramount's finicky male star George Raft. The simplistic plot was loosely based on the career of pre-World War I café dancer Maurice Mouvet. Raft appeared as Raoul DeBaere, a honky-tonk performer from Hoboken, New Jersey, who is determined to crash the upper-crust Continental nightclub scene as a top dancer. It is his one hope to perform a new dance—the bolero—and he allows nothing to stand in his way, not even a woman's love. With dispatch he jettisons coperformers Sally Rand, Frances Drake, and even self-sufficient Carole. When he enlists in the Army as a joke, he finds himself caught up in the prolonged war. Later he is released due to a weakened heart, but insists on returning to his act. Carole, by now attached to nobleman Ray Milland, arrives for Raft's opening night at the Parisian club. She willingly substitutes for his missing partner in doing the much-awaited bolero (which, like Ravel's composition, was an endless pastiche of anticlimaxes). Afterwards, he collapses and dies. The fan dance performed by its originator, Sally Rand, proved far more impressive than Raft's intense but robot-like time-stepping or Carole's ballroom dipping and turning. Despite its faults, *Bolero* was a financial winner, and Carole was praised for her "effective directness."

By now Carole was a top Hollywood celebrity, much given to party-going and party-giving. She employed an ex-actor turned interior decorator, William Haines, to restyle her Hollywood home "to match her personality." A 1934 issue of *Motion Picture* magazine quoted her philosophy on marriage: "Hollywood. . .does not openly court the censure of the public. We respect human relationships—the fine loyalties, the thing called love, but the worn-out traditions that impede human progress have no place in this industry. My present philosophy, that marriage as it stands is all wrong for picture players, may be a delusion. Someday, I suppose, I shall marry again, because no woman can determine her emotions."

Paramount's scripters reworked James M. Barrie's *The Admirable Crichton* into a Bing Crosby musical, *We're Not Dressing* (1934). To distract from the old-fashioned whimsy, Carole was offered as the spoiled heiress who is civilized by sailor Crosby once they are shipwrecked on a Pacific island. Ethel Merman returned to the screen as a man-hungry hotshot, belting out "It's a New Spanish Custom." Leon Errol and Ray Milland were yachtside stuffed shirts and on shore the group encounters daffy naturalists George Burns and Gracie Allen (who along with W. C. Fields and later Martha Raye and Bob Hope spanned the 1930s as Paramount's musical comedy specialists). Carole was extremely fetching in her undemanding role, but generally all she had to do as the reformed socialite was to look moon-eyed when Crosby crooned such tunes as "Love Thy Neighbors," and allow the wind to blow sensually through her long blonde hair. *We're Not Dressing* made a profit for the studio.

Even staid Bing Crosby was captivated by Carole's irrepressible mirthmaking. In his autobiography, *Call Me Lucky* (1953), he reminisced about her "delicious sense of humor." While filming *We're Not Dressing* on Catalina Island, he recalls, Carole bounced into the dining room of the conservative Catherine Hotel one morning and yelled across the room to Crosby: "By the way, Bing, did I forget my nightie in your bedroom?"

The turning point for Carole's screen stardom was winning the female lead in Columbia's *Twentieth Century*, which opened at Radio City Music Hall on May 3, 1934. Ben Hecht and Charles MacArthur turned out a brilliant fast-paced entertainment based on their (and Charles Milholland's) hit Broadway farce which had starred Eugenie Leontovich. Eccentric stage producer John Barrymore has transformed lingerie salesgirl Mildred Plotka (Carole) into legitimate star Lily Garland. A success as his mistress and leading lady, she endured pompous outrages and selfishness for three years before storming off to Hollywood. Now on the New York-bound luxury train, he is inveigling her into signing a play contract. To make the situation spicier, Barrymore is hiding from creditors and disguises himself as a Southern planter. Carole's fiance is aboard, as well as a lunatic on the prowl; assorted bearded players wanting roles in Barrymore's play are included, and, rounding out the cast, cagey public relations man Roscoe Karns, theatre manager Walter Connolly, and an overwrought train staff. The critical consensus was that Carole was "admirably cast" and presented an "able portrayal" as the wacky celebrity who could match her egocentric mentor in any quirk or tantrum. Fights, histrionics, and a fake suicide are also tossed in for good measure, while Carole and Barrymore proved a dynamite combination, even if there was none of the old-fashioned romantic passion he used to engender with his leading ladies. Barrymore, who had requested Carole for the role, would later admit: "She is perhaps the greatest actress I ever worked with."

Long before *Twentieth Century* was released, Paramount stuck Carole with a second-fiddle assignment in the Shirley Temple picture *Now and Forever* (1934). Carole was reteamed with Gary Cooper as his moral-minded mistress. When Cooper plans to trade his long-unseen daughter (Temple) to his pompous brother-in-law for $75,000, Carole runs off to Paris. After Cooper gets to know the tyke, he becomes very attached to her, and soon Carole has returned to the fold. He plans to go straight, but circumstances and conniving Sir Guy Standing lead him back into a criminal life. Later, he induces wealthy, elderly Charlotte Granville to adopt Temple since he has been injured in a gun fight with Standing (who was killed) and is uncertain about his future. The Pollyanna story had been coauthored by Jack Kirkland, ex-husband of former Paramount star Nancy Carroll. The triple-star box-office lure brought in the customers in droves.

Columbia's *Lady by Choice* provided Carole with a juicy role. In this followup to the popular *Lady for a Day*, Carole plays a with-it dancer, Alabama Georgia Lee, who adopts an old rummy (May Robson) as a Mother's Day publicity stunt. Before long the odd couple have reformed one another through mutual affection, each making sacrifices to bring out the other's best qualities. A much publicized facet of *Lady by Choice* was to be Carole's explicit fan dance. What emerged on the screen was brief, effective, but distinctly not erotic. Carole garnered excellent reviews. Said *Variety*, "She is forceful, vibrant, and once or twice she shows far greater power than in her previous work." However, it was veteran performer May Robson, as the onetime stage queen turned quaint lush, who stole the show.

During 1934 Carole had proven troublesome to Paramount, who expected, if not demanded, that their contract stars appear in whatever assignments were handed out. She refused a loanout to Columbia for *Sisters Under the Skin* (1934), which Elissa Landi did, and on the home lot ixnayed *Miss Fane's Baby Is Stolen* (1934) (Dorothea Wiecks was used), *Kiss and Make Up* (1934) (Helen Mack accepted instead), and *The Notorious Sophie Lang* (1934) (eventually featuring Gertrude Michael). Other actresses on the rise at the studio now supervised by Emanuel Cohen* were Mary Carlisle, Patricia Ellis, Ida Lupino, Gertrude Michael, Ann Sheridan, and Toby Wing.

On her only loanout to MGM—*The Gay Bride* (1934)—Carole did not fare well. This gangster yarn spotted her as a gold-digging showgirl who

*See Appendix.

drives racketeer Nat Pendleton sappy. He marries her, but is later bumped off, leaving her broke. She takes up with his former bodyguard, Chester Morris. The attempted satire on the rackets and get-rich-quick girls never solidified, even with a cast that included Zasu Pitts as Carole's nervous accomplice. As for Carole's dizzy chorine role, Richard Watts, Jr. (*New York Herald Tribune*) lambasted: "Miss Lombard achieves the feat of being almost as bad as her picture and plays her part with neither humor nor conviction."

Despite her refusals, 1934 was Carole's busiest screen year, with six films in release.

Paramount reteamed deadpan George Raft with Carole in *Rumba* (1935), believing there was more box-office gravy left over from their *Bolero* film. With Manhattan and Havana as backdrops, Carole was showcased as a bored, thrill-seeking society girl with a yen for Broadway hoofer Raft. Once she snubs him, he nonchalantly takes up with his dance partners, Iris Adrian and then Margo. At the crucial moment (Margo has fainted), Carole appears on the scene and gamely substitutes as his partner for the big show (despite gangsters' threats that Raft and company were to be rubbed out). Both Carole and Margo performed the bouncy rumba with not-so-fleet-footed Raft. Marguerite Tazelaar (*New York Herald Tribune*) said: "Miss Lombard is growing more suave, svelt and sophisticated all the time. If she does not let stylization squeeze her work too thin, she should become a first-rate actress." Evidently Paramount ran out of popular dances around which to build flimsy movies, and as a result the Carole-Raft screen teaming came to an end.

Carole was receiving $3,000 a week from Paramount by the time she filmed *Rumba* in mid–1934. (In November, 1936, she would renegotiate her studio agreement: the new terms called for three films per year at $150,000 per film, the right to make one outside picture per year, and at Paramount to have approval rights of story, photographer, casting supervision, and directorial decision. This comprehensive contract gave her great power and made her one of Hollywood's highest paid stars.) After *Rumba* Carole had a nine-month layoff while the studio went through an executive reorganization, with producer-director Ernst Lubitsch* emerging as production head on the lot. Carole used the free time to enhance her reputation as one of the cinema capital's kookiest partygivers. Perhaps the height of her hostessing was an offbeat celebration given on May 16, 1935, at Venice Amusement Park near Hollywood. Guests (who ranged from stars Claudette Colbert, Marlene Dietrich, Cary Grant, and Randolph Scott, to grips, extras, and back-lot workers) were advised to come in old clothes, and invited to run the concessions. Those "stars" who felt mingling with lowly workers was beneath them got a fair sampling of Carole's directness put forth in the saltiest of language. It was not uncommon for her to break into a yell, guffaw, or string of expletives—whatever she felt the occasion called for.

Carole's only other 1935 release was the bubbly *Hands Across the Table*. Mitchell Leisen worked directorial wonders with her, transforming previously imposed mannered comic acting into nonchalant breeziness. As manicurist Regi Allen, Carole has mercenary matrimonial plans which go flooey after she meets good-natured but broke playboy Fred MacMurray. For a while they con one another, each believing the other to be a gold mine. Filling out the cast were Ralph Bellamy, a crippled aviator and confidant-

*See Appendix.

suitor of Carole's, Marie Prevost—in a comeback role—as a fellow nail surgeon, and Astrid Allwyn as the wealthy heiress MacMurray finally rejects. The critics outdid themselves in applauding the new-style Carole: "well-defined penchant for sophisticated foolery," "divertingly flippant," "has shed some of the sophistication that was a heavy burden," "tart humor that is perfectly suited to her role." More importantly, audiences went for the revamped Carole in a big way, identifying with her natural breeziness, which had finally revealed itself 14 years after her first screen appearance.

Carole was loaned to Universal—in exchange for Margaret Sullavan's services—for the diverting *Love Before Breakfast* (1936). Both Park Avenue gorilla Preston Foster and super-suave Cesar Romero hanker for upper-cruster Carole. It seems obvious to them that she must be rich to be so swaddled in silver fox furs. Foster offers Romero a tempting job in the Far East which knocks him out of the running, leaving the arena free for Foster and Carole to battle in and out of love. When not bickering on the bridle path, they argue while sailing on Long Island Sound—their boat turns over and they are both drenched. Kate Cameron in her three-star *New York Daily News* review summed up: "Delightful to look at and amusing to hear." Carole continued to enthrall the "little people"—the crews of her movies—who loved her for being such a genuine person. At the completion of *Love Before Breakfast*, they gave her a plaque with an enormous egg on it, inscribed: "To a good egg, from the boys."

At Paramount, Lubitsch had a brainstorm—he would mold Carole into a satirical Greta Garbo in *The Princess Comes Across* (1936). Ambitious Brooklyn girl Wanda Nash (Carole) hopes to crash the movies. To gain publicity, she travels to Europe and books passage on the S.S. *Mammoth* from London to the United States, under the alias of the aloof Swedish Princess Olga. Ensconced in the royal suite with conniving Alison Skipworth as her confidant, Carole fools everyone with her throaty accent, taut facial expressions, and furs and veils. She chances upon bandleader Fred MacMurray and finds herself assisting in the solution of a shipboard mystery. Conveniently for plot purposes there is a group of international detectives aboard (including Sig Rumann, Douglass Dumbrille, Mischa Auer, and Tetsu Komai). Sorting out the red herring in this group of weirdos offers diverting moments. At the time, many thought *The Princess Comes Across* was an entertainment misfire, but the feature has gained its own reputation thanks to constant television showings in recent years.

Carole's ex-husband William Powell advised Universal that Carole was the perfect choice for the female lead opposite him in *My Man Godfrey*, which premiered at the Radio City Music Hall on September 17, 1936. Cast as a somewhat demented aristocrat, Carole meets lofty, vagabond Powell while on a scavenger hunt at the city dump. He is hired as butler to her eccentric family, and soon converts them to near normalcy. The family consists of the harassed dad (Eugene Pallette), the birdbrained mother (Alice Brady); the snotty sister (Gail Patrick), and, thrown in for good measure, Mischa Auer as a mad gigolo Russian musician, Alan Mowbray as a bumbling millionaire pal, and Jean Dixon as the sentimentally hardboiled maid. Throughout, Carole proved she could outdo Gracie Allen in zaniness, pulling out all stops in her mock heroics and parodies of grief. Butler Powell finds it difficult to tame the wild heiress Carole, even when exerting all his savoir faire. *Variety* commented: "Miss Lombard's role is the more difficult of the two [i.e., hers and Powell's] since it calls for pressure acting all the way, and it was no simple trick to refrain from overworking the insanity plea in a many sided assignment." Film historian Lewis Jacobs would describe Carole as the most outstanding of the screwball comediennes because "Beautiful, frustrated, she asserts intense dissatisfaction with existing conventions and deep bewilderment in seeking justification of her desires." Carole won her only Academy Award nomination for her performance as Irene Bullock in *My Man Godfrey*, but lost out to Luise Rainer who won for *The Great Ziegfeld*. Carole and Powell recreated their roles for "Lux Radio Theatre" in a dramatization of the comedy on May 9, 1938. Two decades later, Universal threw together a pallid remake of *My Man Godfrey* starring June Allyson and David Niven.

By now, Carole could advise the press re Powell: "I must like the man or I wouldn't have married him the first place! Now that we're divorced, we're still the best of friends. We're both civilized people." (When they were married, she had nicknamed him Junior.)

Swing High, Swing Low was the first of Carole's three 1937 releases, and the least important. It had originally been slated for the team of Gary Cooper and Irene Dunne. Director Mitchell Leisen and costar Fred MacMurray joined Carole in this reworking of the stage play *Burlesque*, which had been previously filmed as *The Dance of Life* with Nancy Carroll. When trumpeter MacMurray is mustered out of the Army in Panama, he is attracted to ex-manicurist Carole, now a honky tonk dancer. They soon wed, and he heads northward, where drink and a tempting dancer, Dorothy Lamour, soon drive him to distraction. Carole divorces her negligent husband, but eventually returns to assist him in making a new life. To improve her singing abilities for this picture, Carole took voice lessons from coach Al Siegel. Her two numbers—"I Hear a Call to Arms" and "Then It Isn't Love"—were half-sung, half-talked. Howard Barnes (*New York Herald Tribune*) decided: "She falters at times in keeping the part of Maggie in focus, but for the most part does a really skillful piece of acting. Her voice is extremely pleasant." The studio over-ballyhooed *Swing High, Swing Low* and the film could not match the inflated expectations of the front office executives.

Carole, Cary Grant, and Randolph Scott had been slated to appear in the outdoor drama *Spawn of the North* (1938), which went into production in late 1936 and early 1937 with location shooting in Alaska. However, Carole became ill with flu and was unavailable in 1937 when director Henry Hathaway and crew returned to the studio for sound-stage filming. Dorothy Lamour was substituted. When Carole turned down *Exclusive* (1937) as programmer fodder, Frances Farmer replaced her. There was talk of her being paired with Fred Astaire in *Shall We Dance?* (1937), but Ginger Rogers was used instead.

On loanout to David O. Selznick (at $18,750 a week for eight weeks), Carole performed in her first technicolor feature, *Nothing Sacred* (1937), another screwball comedy gem. The Ben Hecht script targeted its satire at small-town bigotry and big-city exploitation. Carole is supposedly dying of radium poisoning and Manhattan reporter Fredric March sets out to make her a seven-day wonder celebrity and give her a send-off spree. March charges off to her small Vermont town and talks Carole into going along with his plan. When it develops that her illness is non-existent (there was a medical diagnostic mix-up), Carole and March must convince his bombastic newspaper editor, Walter Connolly, that she really is dying. In one shot, she even jumps into the river. She and March marry and carry on the battle of the century, with their marital spats outdoing championship matches. Finally she can tolerate the deception no more and confesses the truth to the "memorial committee." Put on the spot, the group agrees to announce that Carole has disappeared. Wisely, both Carole and March refrained from stressing the serious nature of their roles and played for non-stop broad laughs. Others adding to the hilarity were Charles Winninger as the country doctor, Frank Fay, as the master of ceremonies, and boxer Maxie Rosenbloom (sports fan Carole insisted on having him written into the script). *Nothing Sacred* premiered at Radio City Music Hall on November 25, 1937, and was a smash hit. Gagster Carole presented director William Wellman with a straitjacket. *Nothing Sacred* would be turned into the popular musical *Hazel Flagg* in the early 1950s and was also converted into the Dean Martin-Jerry Lewis movie *Living It Up.*

True Confession (1937) was Carole's last Paramount picture. In this courtroom farce, Carole plays beguiling Helen Bartlett, who just cannot tell the truth (every time she catches herself lying, her tongue rolls in her mouth). Her bad habit makes her the chief suspect in a murder trial, with her earnest husband, Fred MacMurray (with moustache), the defense attorney, Porter Hall as the determined district attorney, and eccentric John Barrymore as a drunken would-be criminologist. Carole had insisted that the professionally declining Barrymore be cast in this comedy as a return favor for *Twentieth Century.* Carole photographed much better in black and white than she had in the color *Nothing Sacred.* Howard Barnes (*New York Herald Tribune*) said Carole was "funny without forcing her preposterous role." The story was remade to far less successful results in 1946's *Cross My Heart,* starring Betty Hutton.

Carole was the highest paid actress in 1937, earning $465,000, which included her $5,000 per performance guest radio appearances. With part of her income, Carole bought 200 acres in the San Fernando Valley. She received many write-ups when she demonstrated her patriotic feeling for America by gladly paying $397,575 of her 1937 revenue for state and federal taxes, stating: "I enjoy this country. I like the parks and the highways and the good schools and everything that this government does. After all, every cent anybody pays in taxes is spent to benefit him. I don't need $465,000 a year for myself, so why not give what I don't need to the government for improvements of the country? There's no better place to spend it."

Carole was just as enthusiastic about helping on a more personal level. She engineered screen tests for movie hopefuls Cheryl Walker and Margaret Tallichet. Socially, Carole was dating Clark Gable. She had met him at a swank party tossed by Countess di Frasso in early 1936. He was still married to Rhea Langham, 17 years his senior, but they were separated. It would take some time for a satisfactory property settlement to be worked out. Partly to pay off the sum she demanded, Gable accepted the lead role in *Gone with the Wind.* While dating Gable, Carole continued to pull absurd practical jokes which made her the queen prankster in Hollywood, such as sending Gable a Ford ambulance painted red as a Valentine gift, signing a new contract with agent Myron Selznick which required him to pay her 10 percent of his earnings, and so forth.

When asked by the press if she had any retirement plans, Carole stated: "I don't want to spend the rest of my life acting in pictures. All I want to do is to put away enough money on which to live comfortably. But that's more difficult than it sounds. In spite of my large salaries, I figured out it would take me nearly twenty years to be able to save $500,000. I'm quitting when I get enough annuities laid aside."

Carole's only 1938 release was at Warner Brothers in the disappointing soufflé *Fools for Scandal*. Marquis Ferdinand Gravet accepts a post at American movie star Carole's London apartment, and promptly is smitten with her. Ralph Bellamy is the rival suitor for nutty Carole's matrimonial hand. This forced farce peters out long before the ending, with Carole ending up "in ridiculous rather than ludicrous grimacing." Carole did not have a high opinion of the Mervyn LeRoy production: "I knew it wasn't a sensation when my friends confined their comments to how beautifully I had been photographed."

Deciding she could do just as well free-lancing, Carole cut her ties with Paramount and signed a two-picture agreement with David O. Selznick in May of 1938, to be fulfilled prior to December 31, 1939. According to film scholar Rudy Behlmer, the deal was for $150,000 a film ($15,000 weekly for ten consecutive weeks). The zany actress obtained a large share of news coverage when she jokingly took over Selznick's publicity department one day in mid-1938, aided by writer Gene Fowler. They issued wilder edicts and dreamed up crazier stunts than her employer or his top publicity director, Russell Birdwell, could ever imagine. When she was appointed mayoress of Culver City, she declared her first day in office a public holiday. Boss Selznick was not amused by this bit of whimsy.

As her first Selznick film, she starred in *Made for Each Other*, which opened at Radio City Music Hall on February 16, 1939. Selznick thought it a bright piece of casting to have the queen of madcap comedy (a genre already dead at the box office) try her hand at heavy dramatics. In this excellent tearjerker, smoothly directed by John Cromwell, Carole portrays the earnest wife of lackadaisical James Stewart, a fledgling lawyer. His career at Charles Coburn's stuffy law firm is stagnating, especially since he has passed up a chance to marry the boss's daughter (Ruth Weston) and instead married Carole on the spur of the moment. Determined to give her husband the incentive and support he requires to succeed, Carole copes with an overbearing mother-in-law (Lucile Watson), the vicissitudes of married life and household management, and the near death of their infant. By the fadeout, Stewart realizes his wife's true worth and has marched himself onto the path of perseverance and success. *Made for Each Other* may not have been what the public expected from their fun-giving Carole, but the critics were firmly convinced that "she can handle a serious characterization as well as antic pranks." It was named one of the ten best films of the year by the *New York Times*. Carole recreated her role opposite Fred MacMurray in the "Lux Radio Theatre" adaptation of *Made for Each Other* on February 19, 1940.

On March 29, 1939, after completing his filming in *Gone with the Wind*, Gable wed Carole. He was 38, and it was his second marriage. Gable drove Carole the 350 miles to Kingman, Arizona, where they were married. Even cynical gossip columnist Louella Parsons hailed this wedding as "a match made in Heaven." Carole and Gable built a house at her San Fernando Valley ranch, where they soon took to raising cattle and horses, and growing fruit. To please her outdoors-loving husband, Carole took up hunting and soon became an expert shot. She was content to have him be the man in the family (even when she was earning twice his salary), and made drastic efforts to curtail her salty language and independent behavior to conform to his ideas of a good wife. On his part, he learned the carefree joys of naturalness and tomfoolery from her. They were one of the most popular couples on the Hollywood social scene when they occasionally stepped out.

Before they wed, there had been several attempts to team Carole and Gable on the screen again; one such suggestion was MGM's *Saratoga* (1937), but Paramount refused, and Jean Harlow took over in what was to be her last film—she died during production. Carole had been considered for Scarlett O'Hara in *Gone with the Wind,* but lost out to Vivien Leigh, which was probably a good thing for both actresses. In 1939 MGM wanted Carole to play with Gable in *Idiot's Delight,* but their studio queen, Norma Shearer, decided the project required her acting presence.

Selznick tossed around the idea of casting Carole in *The Flashing Stream,* with either Alfred Hitchcock or Robert Stevenson directing, but Carole did not care for it. Another title which Selznick touted for her in 1939 was a comedy, *American Sleeping Beauty.* Since they could not agree on a project, Carole and Selznick called off the agreement for a second film together.

Carole then signed on with RKO at $150,000 per feature plus a percentage of the profits. She was one of the first Hollywood stars to obtain such a profit-sharing deal. RKO in 1939 was in need of fresh star talent to supplement its star roster, which had dwindled down to Irene Dunne and Joan Fontaine (who would leave by late 1939), Ginger Rogers, and the lesser lights, Lucille Ball and Anne Shirley. Katharine Hepburn had already left RKO and the movies, hoping to erase the onerous box-office poison tag by appearing in Philip Barry's *The Philadelphia Story* on Broadway.

For RKO, Carole appeared in another drama, *In Name Only* (1939). To fill out the romantic triangle, RKO utilized its contract male lead, Cary Grant, and Carole insisted that her friend Kay Francis, now at liberty from Warner Brothers, be employed to portray the "other woman." John Cromwell did a most professional job in translating Bessie Breuer's novel *Memory of Love* to the screen. Carole is widow Julie Eden, a commercial artist, who lives with her young daughter, Peggy Ann Garner. She and Grant are mutually attracted, but he is harnessed by wealthy, selfish Francis, who will not divorce him, finding it too convenient to have a spouse around when playing her bedroom games among the upper-class set. Without the sincere playing of all concerned, the overwrought finale (in which the critically ill Grant is given faith to live by Carole) might well have been cloying soap opera. The *New York Times,* full of praise, said: "Miss Lombard plays her poignant role with all the fragile intensity and contained passion that have lifted her to dramatic eminence." Carole, Grant, and Francis repeated their *In Name Only* roles on "Lux Radio Theatre" on December 11, 1939.

Carole was mentioned as a possibility for *The Light That Failed* (1939) at Paramount, but in the revised script the leading female role proved to be the Cockney part and was assigned to Ida Lupino. When Orson Welles contracted to direct and star in films at RKO in 1939, he selected Joseph Conrad's *Heart of Darkness.* That project was shelved, however, and Welles chose Nicholas Blake's *The Smiler With a Knife.* Welles wanted to use an actress who was not a star. The studio insisted that either Carole or Rosalind Russell would be more suitable. Both ladies declined, Carole stated: "I can't win working with Welles. If the film is a hit *he* will get the credit. If it's a flop, *I'll* be blamed."

Instead, Carole agreed to *Vigil in the Night* (1940), a film which experienced difficulties during production and at the box office. While filming the A. J. Cronin story about dedicated nurses in England, Carole, in August,

1939, was stricken with acute appendicitis and was operated on, delaying the film's completion. *Vigil in the Night* premiered at the Roxy Theatre on March 8, 1940, and was a box-office dud. Audiences were not enthralled by the grim settings and the somber tale of two nursing sisters (Carole and Anne Shirley), Carole being very competent, and Shirley the careless one. Both are attracted to crusading doctor Brian Aherne. After several bouts of Shirley's medical negligence, for which Carole takes the blame, Shirley dies during a fever epidemic. The finale is badly downbeat, with no indication that Carole and Aherne will do anything but carry on their worthwhile work. George Stevens's direction displayed a smooth consistency, but Carole was criticized for the "somnambulistic quality to [her] too-subdued performance."

RKO purchased Grace Perkins's *Unbreakable Mrs. Doll* in February, 1940, as a future vehicle for Carole, but nothing developed. Carole continued with her radio guesting, appearing on the "Gulf Screen Guild Playhouse" in *The Awful Truth* (March 17, 1940) with Robert Young and Ralph Bellamy.

During 1940 Carole the businesswoman found she could do better financially by shifting for herself. When Myron Selznick, her agent, sued her for allegedly overdue back commissions, she discharged him in July, 1940. About her future, she told the press: "As soon as I get a couple of bad pictures out of my system, they can unroll the red carpet and gild up a halo for me. I'm going to become a producer, if I can stand the smell. They're the only ones that get red carpets and haloes this season. Actors are going at about two bucks a saloonful, with no takers but Monogram."

As her second RKO release of 1940, Carole appeared to excellent advantage in the third screen version of Sidney Howard's Pulitzer Prize-winning play *They Knew What They Wanted*. As Amy, the San Francisco hashhouse waitress, she agrees to become the mail order bride of Italian vineyard owner Charles Laughton. She is more interested in the security of his $15,000 bank account than in his physical appearance, even though he has sent her a photograph of his farm boss, William Gargan. Carole arrives in the Napoli Valley and is aghast to learn that the crude, physically unattractive Laughton is to be her husband. But in despair she goes through with the wedding. As she grows to love Laughton for his inner goodness, she succumbs to the surface charms of Gargan (Laughton is in bed recuperating from broken legs, gotten while showing off for his new bride and the neighbors). After a turbulent spell, Gargan quits the ranch, leaving Carole and Laughton safe in their love and respect for one another. Carole carried off this unglamorous dramatic role expertly, proving "extraordinarily fine" and gaining "enormous sympathy" from audiences when the film debuted at Radio City Music Hall on October 19, 1940. Adding atmosphere to young Garson Kanin's direction was Frank Fay as the local priest and Harry Carey as the wise country doctor.

Off screen Carole continued to be the same delightfully sassy gal she had always been. When columnist Hy Gardner asked Carole a series of nonsensical questions for his column, she parried in fine form:

Gardner: "Do you ever expect to retire?"
Carole: "Don't call me after midnight."
Gardner: "What do you worry about most?"
Carole: "I devote the same amount of worry to all problems. I don't play favorites."

Carole returned to domestic comedy for her next RKO vehicle, *Mr. and Mrs. Smith* (1941). It was to be director Alfred Hitchcock's only American-made pure comedy, with no murders involved whatsoever. Hitchcock later admitted: "That picture was done as a friendly gesture to Carole . . . she asked whether I'd do a picture with her. In a weak moment I accepted, and I more or less followed Norman Krasna's screenplay. Since I really didn't understand the type of people who were portrayed in the film, all I did was to photograph the scenes as written."

Mr. and Mrs. Smith energetically revolved around the question perpetually asked of one another by married people: "If you had it to do all over again, would you marry me." Carole and her wealthy lawyer husband Robert Montgomery are emerging from their latest three-day feud when they learn that their marriage was illegal. Carole is not convinced she wants Montgomery back, but is sufficiently interested to make him jealous by dating his law partner, stodgy Gene Raymond. This leads to bright domestic chaos on the homefront, and a rather slapstick wrap-up at a Lake Placid ski lodge, with Montgomery substituting physical force for wit and wiles in order to win Carole back. This marital romp was commercially successful and Carole was applauded for her "verve and dash." She and Bob Hope performed in a dramatization of *Mr. and Mrs. Smith* for the "Lux Radio Theatre" on June 9, 1941.

Carole was not one to be cajoled by working with the great Hitchcock. He had once made the oft-repeated statement that he considered most actors just cattle to be herded through a role. On the opening day of production of *Mr. and Mrs. Smith*, Hitchcock walked onto the RKO set to find three cows in corrals, each tagged with the name of one of the three stars. Hitchcock allowed Carole to direct him in his customary walk-on cameo in the film. At the time this incident received immense press coverage, with Carole advising "Alfie" to "Stop your mumbling!" because "I'd like it a little clearer, this is for an American audience." This lark was filmed for use in RKO's theatrical short-subject release, *Picture People #4* (1940).

Veteran cameraman Harry Stradling, who photographed Carole in both *They Knew What They Wanted* and *Mr. and Mrs. Smith*, would later exclaim: "She knows as much about the tricks of the trade as I do! In close-up work, I wanted to cover her scar simply by focusing the lights on her face so that it would seem to blend with her cheek. She told me a diffusing glass in my lens would do the same job better. And she was right!"

For United Artists, Carole was paired with Jack Benny in a brilliant black comedy *To Be or Not to Be* (1942), an Ernst Lubitsch satire aimed at Nazi Germany just as his *Ninotchka* had dealt with Soviet Russia. Carole and Benny were the leading players in a Warsaw acting troupe (as well as wife and husband). They attempt to carry on their professional work despite the chaos of the German invasion. Vain Benny is more concerned with the elegance of his *Hamlet* performance, until he gets involved in a spiraling underground deception against the Nazis. Meanwhile, fun-loving, glamorous Carole finds time to flirt with Robert Stack, who is an Allied flier. The supporting cast was superb: Sig Rumann, as a blustering Nazi colonel, Stanley Ridges as a sinister Gestapo agent, and Tom Dugan as the burlesque Hitler.

To Be or Not to Be was completed in December, 1941. The United States had entered World War II after Pearl Harbor, and Hollywood Victory Committee chairman Clark Gable scheduled his wife Carole to lead a bond drive at Indianapolis, Indiana, near her hometown of Fort Wayne.

Shortly before she left Hollywood, Carole told writer Adela Rogers St. Johns: "I don't seem to get solemn about it [i.e., God and religion] and some people might not understand. That's why I never talk about it. I think it's all here—in the mountain and the desert. I don't think God is a softie, either. In the end it's better if people are forced back into—well—into being right, before they're too far gone. I think your temple is your everyday living.

"I never can see into the future at all. I guess I'm too busy living every day, or something. Look—I'm not afraid of growing old. I think it's wonderful. Look at Bessie—my mother. She's nine times the woman I am. It sounds sort of nice. When you're out of all the tailspins of youth, when you're content, like Clark and I are, and have learned not to let emotional high blood pressure hit a boiling point and knock you all silly, then you begin to enjoy everything. So much you missed when you were skittering around when you were a kid."

On January 15, 1942, Carole sold more than $2.5 million in war bonds in Indianapolis. Her parting words to the crowd were: "Before I say goodbye to you all—come on—join me in a big cheer—V for Victory!" She gave a Victory sign, grinned, and disappeared into her waiting car. She had wavered between taking a plane or a train back to the Coast, but tossed a coin and decided on an air trip. Shortly after 7:30 P.M. on Friday, January 16, 1942, the TWA airliner she was on slammed into Table Rock Mountain, 30 miles southwest of Las Vegas, killing Carole, her mother, and 20 other passengers aboard. It was two days before rescue crews could remove her body from the site of the tragedy. She was then just 33 years old.

The President of the United States, Franklin D. Roosevelt, sent Clark Gable the following telegram: "Mrs. Roosevelt and I are deeply distressed. Carole was our friend, our guest in happier days. She brought great joy to all who knew her, and to millions who knew her only as a great artist. She gave unselfishly of time and talent to serve her government in peace and in war. She loved her country. She is and always will be a star, one we shall never forget, nor cease to be grateful to."

Private funeral services for Carole were held at Forest Lawn Cemetery on January 21, 1942. The honorary casket bearers were Walter Lang, Zeppo Marx, Danny Winkler (brother of publicity man Otto Winkler who died in the crash), Matt Wolff, Fred MacMurray, William Collier, Jr., and Al Menasco.

Carole had been scheduled to start work on *He Kissed the Bride* at Columbia Pictures on January 21, 1942, with Melvyn Douglas costarred. Joan Crawford, a close friend of Gable, substituted, and the film was released as *They All Kissed the Bride* (1942).

At the time of her death, Carole's film and radio commitments (through December 31, 1943) had netted her about half of the estimated $2 million income.

In respect for Carole's passing, United Artists revamped its publicity campaign for *To Be Or Not To Be*, which was released at the Rivoli Theatre on March 6, 1942. It met the same fate as Chaplin's *The Great Dictator*. Audiences were not prepared for a bubbly yet perceptive look at a frightening subject: dictatorship and the utter havoc it causes. Reviewers and audiences objected to its "callous" treatment of a sensitive subject. Carole was respectfully praised as being "very beautiful and comically adroit." In later years, *To Be Or Not To Be* was recognized for the sharp satire it really was, and has been quite popular in college film history courses and on television.

In July, 1942, Governor Henry Schricker of Indiana named the state's

Naval air squadron "The Lombardians," and in 1943 a liberty ship was named and christened in memory of Carole.

Clark Gable was in shock for a long time after Carole's death. Hollywood writer Adela Rogers St. Johns observed: "For months after her death, Clark was almost out of his mind with grief. I'd go to his house and he'd be having dinner alone in the dining room with Carole's dog and Siamese cats at the table. He refused to touch her room and left it just the way it was when she left. I asked, 'Why don't you go out? Why don't you call your old friends like Vic Fleming?' and he'd say, 'Carole used to make the calls when we wanted to go out.' "

Gable would later marry Lady Sylvia Ashley (December 20, 1949); they were divorced in 1951. On July 7, 1955 he wed Kay Williams Spreckels. Gable died of a heart attack on November 16, 1960, not living to see the birth of his only child, John Clark. Gable's body was entombed in a crypt next to Carole's at Forest Lawn Memorial Park.

As Jane Peters:

A PERFECT CRIME (FOX, 1921) 5 Reels

Producer-director-screenplay, Allan Dwan; story, Carl Clausen; assistant director, Wilfred Buckland; camera, Lyman Broening.

Monte Blue (Wally Griggs); Jacqueline Logan (Mary Oliver); Stanton Heck ("Big Bill" Thaine); Hardee Kirkland (Halliday); Jane Peters (Griggs' Daughter).

As Carol Lombard:

HEARTS AND SPURS (FOX, 1925) 4,600'

Director, W. S. Van Dyke; based on the story "The Outlaw" by Jackson Gregory; screenplay, John Stone.

Buck Jones (Hal Emory); Carol Lombard (Sybil Estabrook); William Davidson (Victor Dufresne); Freeman Wood (Oscar Estabrook); Jean Lamont (Celeste); J. Gordon Russell (Sid Thomas); Walt Robbins (Jerry Clark); Charles Eldridge (Sheriff).

DURAND OF THE BADLANDS (FOX, 1925) 5,844'

Director, Lynn Reynolds; based on the novel by Maebelle Heikes Justice; adaptation-screenplay, Reynolds; assistant director, Leslie Selander; Harry Welfar; camera, Allan Davey.

Buck Jones (Dick Durand); Marion Nixon (Molly Gore); Malcolm Waite (Clem Allison); Fred DeSilva (Peter Garson); Luke Cosgrove (Kingdom Come Knapp); George Lessley (John Boyd); Buck Black (Jimmie); Ann Johnson (Clara Belle Seesel); James Corrigan (Joe Gore); Carol Lombard (Ellen Boyd).

MARRIAGE IN TRANSIT (FOX, 1925) 4,800'

Director, R. William Neill; story, Grace Lutz; screenplay, Dorothy Yost; camera, G. O. Post.

Edmund Lowe (Cyril Gordon); Carol Lombard (Cecilia Hathaway); Frand Beal (Burnham); Adolph Milar (Haynes); Marvey Clark (Aide); Fred Walton (Valet); Byron Douglas, Wade Boteler, Fred Butler, Fred Becker, Edward Chandler (Conspirators).

ME, GANGSTER (FOX, 1928) 6,042'

Director, Raoul Walsh; story-adaptation, Charles Francis Coe; assistant director, Archibald Buchanan; titles, William Kernell; camera, Arthur Edelson; editor, Louis Loeffler.

June Collyer (Mary Regan); Don Terry (Jimmy Williams); Anders Randolf (Russ Williams); Stella Adams (Lizzie Williams); Al Hill (Danny); Burr McIntosh (Bill Kane); Walter James (Police Captain Dodd); Gustav Von Seyffertitz (Factory Owner); Herbert Ashton (Slicker); Harry Castle (Philly Kid); Joe Brown (Himself); Arthur Stone (Dan The Dude); Nigel DeBrulier (Danish Louie); Carol Lombard (Blonde Rosie); Bob Perry (Tuxedo George).

THE DIVINE SINNER (Rayart, 1928) 5,683'

Producer, Tremm Carr; director, Scott Pembroke; story-screenplay, Robert Anthony Dillon; camera, Hap Depew; editor, J. S. Harrington.

Vera Reynolds (Lillia Ludwig); Nigel DeBrulier (Minister of Police); Bernard Seigel (Johann Ludwig); Ernest Hilliard (Prince Josef Miguel); John Peters (Luque

Bernstorff); Carol Lombard (Millie Coudert); Harry Northrop (Ambassador D'Ray); James Ford (Heinrich); Alphonse Martel (Paul Coudert).

POWER (Pathé, 1928) 6,092'

Producer, Ralph Block; director, Howard Higgin; story-screenplay, Tay Garnett; assistant director, Robert Fellows; art director, Mitchel leisen; titles, John Krafft; camera, Peverell Marley; editor, Doane Harrison.

William Boyd (Husky); Alan Hale (Hanson); Jacqueline Logan (Lorraine LaRue); Jerry Drew (The Menace); Joan Bennett (A Dame); Carol Lombard (Another Dame); Pauline Curley (Third Dame).

SHOW FOLKS (Pathé, 1928) 6,581'

Producer, Ralph Block; director, Paul L. Stein; story, Philip Dunning; adaptation, Jack Jungmeyer; George Dromgold; art director, Mitchell Leisen; assistant director, Robert Fellows; song, Al Koppel, Billy Stone, and Charles Weinberg; camera, Peverell Marley; editor, Doane Harrison.

Eddie Quillan (Eddie); Lina Basquette (Rita); Carol Lombard (Cleo) Robert Armstrong (Owens); Bessie Barriscale (Kitty).

NED MC COBB'S DAUGHTER (Pathé, 1929) 71 M

Director, William J. Cowan; based on the play by Sidney Howard; adaptation, Beulah Marie Dix; assistant director, Ray Burns; art director, Mitchell Leisen; camera, David Abel.

Irene Rich (Carole); Theodore Roberts (Ned McCobb); Robert Armstrong (Babe Callahan); George Barraud (George Callahan); Edward Hearn (Butterworth); Carol Lombard (Jennie); Louis Natheaux (Kelly).

HIGH VOLTAGE (Pathé, 1929) 5,717'

Director, Howard Higgins; story, Elliott Clawson; dialogue, James Gleason; song, George Green and George Waggner; assistant director, Leigh Smith; camera, John Mescall; editor, Doane Harrison.

William Boyd (Bill The Boy); Owen Moore (Detective Dan Egan); Carol Lombard (Lily); Diane Ellis (The Kid); Billy Bevan (Gus, The Driver); Phillips Smalley (J. Milton Hendrickson, The Banker).

BIG NEWS (Pathé, 1929) 66 M.

Director, Gregory LaCava; based on the play *For Two Cents* by George S. Brooks; screenplay, Walter DeLeon, Jack Jungmeyer; dialogue, Frank Reicher; assistant director, Marty Santell; camera, Arthur Miller; editor, Doane Harrison.

Robert Armstrong (Steve Banks); Carol Lombard (Margaret Banks); Tom Kennedy (Sgt. Ryan); Warner Richmond (Phelps); Wade Boteler (O'Neill); Sam Hardy (Joe Reno); Louis Payne (Hensel); James Donlan (Deke); Cupid Ainsworth (Vera Wilson); Gertrude Sutton (Helen); Charles Sellon (Addison); Herbert Clark (Pells); George Hayes (Reporter); Lew Ayres (Copy Boy); Dick Cramer (Hood); Clarence H. Wilson (Coroner); Vernon Steele (A Reporter).

THE RACKETEER (RKO, 1929)

Associate producer, Ralph Block; director, Howard Higgins; story-adaptation, Paul Gangelin; dialog, A. A. Kline; camera, David Abel; editor, Doane Harrison.

Robert Armstrong (Mahlon Keane); Carol Lombard (Rhoda Philbrooke); Roland Drew (Tony Vaughan); Jeanette Loff (Millie Chapman); John Loder (Jack Oakhurst); Paul Hurst (Mehaffy); Kit Guard (Gus); Al Hill (Squid); Hedda Hopper (Karen Lee); Winter Hall (Sam Chapman); Winifred Harris (Margaret Chapman); Bobbie Dunn (The Rat); Bud Fine (Bernie Weber).

ARIZONA KID (FOX, 1930) 88 M.

Director, Alfred Santel; story, Ralph Block; screenplay, Block, Joseph Wright; dialogue, Block; camera, Glen MacWilliams; editor, Paul Weatherwax.

Warner Baxter (Arizona Kid); Mona Maris (Louta); Carol Lombard (Virginia Holt); Mrs. Jiminez (Pulga); Theodore Von Eltz (Nick Holt); Arthur Stone (Snakebite Pete); Walter P. Lewis (Sheriff Andrews); Jack Herrick (Hoboken Hooker); Wilfred Lucas (His Manager); Hank Mann (Bartender Bill); DeSacia Mooers (Molly); Larry McGrath (Homer Snook); Jim Gibson (Stage Driver).

As Carole Lombard:

SAFETY IN NUMBERS (PAR, 1930) 77½ M.

Director, Victor Schertzinger; story, George Marion, Jr., Percy Heath; screenplay, Marion Dix; choreographer, David Bennett; songs, George Marion, Jr. and Richard A. Whiting; camera, Henry Gerrard; editor, Robert Bassler.

Charles "Buddy" Rogers (William Butler Reynolds); Josephine Dunn (Maxine); Roscoe Karns (Bertram Shapiro); Carole Lombard (Pauline); Kathryn Crawford (Jacqueline); Francis McDonald (Phil Kempton); Richard Tucker (F. Carstair Reynolds); Raoul Paoli (Jules); Lawrence Grant (Commodore Brinker); Virginia Bruce (Alma McGregor); Louise Beavers (Messalina).

FAST AND LOOSE (PAR, 1930) 70 M.

Director, Fred Newmeyer; based on the play *The Best People* by David Gray, Avery Hopwood; screenplay, Doris Anderson, Jack Kirkland; dialogue, Preston Sturges; camera, William Steiner.

Miriam Hopkins (Marion Lenox); Carole Lombard (Alice O'Neil); Frank Morgan (Bronson Lenox); Charles Starrett (Henry Morgan); Henry Wadsworth (Bertie Lenox); Winifred Harris (Carrie Lenox); Herbert Yost (George Grafton); David Hutcheson (Lord Rockingham); Ilka Chase (Millie Montgomery); Hershel Mayall (Judge Summers).

IT PAYS TO ADVERTISE (PAR, 1931) 75 M.

Director, Frank Tuttle; based on the play by Roi Cooper Megrue, Walter Hackett; screenplay, Arthur Kober, Ethel Doherty; camera, A. J. Stout.

Skeets Gallagher (Ambrose Peale); Carole Lombard (Mary Grayon); Norman Foster (Rodney Martin); Eugene Pallette (Cyrus Martin); Judith Wood (Countess).

MAN OF THE WORLD (PAR, 1931) 71 M.

Director, Richard Wallace; story-screenplay, Herman J. Mankiewicz; camera, Victor Milner.

William Powell (Michael Trevor); Carole Lombard (Mary Kendall); Wynne Gibson (Irene Hoffa); Guy Kibbee (Harry Taylor); Lawrence Gray (Frank Reynolds); Tom Ricketts (Mr. Bradkin); Andre Cheron (Victor); George Chandler (Fred); Tom Costello (Spade Henderson); Maude Truax (Mrs. Jowitt).

LADIES' MAN (PAR, 1931) 75 M.

Director, Lothar Mendes; story, Rupert Hughes; screenplay, Herman J. Mankiewicz; camera, Victor Milner.

William Powell (Jamie Darricott); Kay Francis (Norma Page); Carole Lombard (Rachel Fendley); Gilbert Emery (Horace Fendley); Olive Tell (Mrs. Fendley); Martin Burton (Anthony Fendley); John Holland (Peyton Waldon); Frank Atkinson (Valet); Maude Turner Gordon (Therese Blanton); Hooper Atchley (Headwaiter); Clarence Wilson (Jeweler); Dick Cramer (Private Detective); Edward Hearn (Maitre D'); Lee Phelps (Desk Clerk); Frank O'Connor (News Clerk); Bill O'Brien (Elevator Starter); Lothar Mendes (Lobby Extra).

UP POPS THE DEVIL (PAR, 1931) 85 M.

Director, A. Edward Sutherland; based on the play be Albert Hackett and Francis Goodrich; screenplay Arthur Kober, Eve Unsell; camera, Karl Struss.

Skeets Gallagher (Benny Hatfield); Stuart Erwin (Stranger); Carole Lombard (Anne Merrick); Lilyan Tashman (Polly Griscom); Norman Foster (Steve Merrick); Edward J. Nugent (George Kent); Theodore Von Eltz (Gilbert Morrell); Joyce Compton (Luella May Carroll); Eulalie Jensen (Mrs. Kent); Harry Beresford (Mr. Platt); Effie Ellser (Mrs. Platt); Willie Best (Laundryman); Guy Oliver (Waldo); Kelly (Himself); Matty Roubert (Subscription Boy).

I TAKE THIS WOMAN (PAR, 1931) 72 M.

Director, Marion Gering; based on the novel *Lost Ecstasy* by Mary Roberts Rinehart; screenplay, Vincent Lawrence; assistant director, Slavko Vorkapich; camera, Victor Milner.

Gary Cooper (Tom McNair); Carole Lombard (Kay Dowling); Helen Ware (Aunt Bessie); Lester Vail (Herbert Forrest); Charles Trowbridge (Mr. Dowling); Clara Blandick (Sue Barnes); Gerald Fielding (Bill Wentworth); Albert Hart (Jake Mallory); Guy Oliver (Sid); Syd Saylor (Shorty); Mildred Van Dorn (Clara Hammell); Leslie Palmer (Phillips); Ara Haswell (Nora); Frank Darien (Station Agent); David Landau (Circus Boss); Lew Kelly (Foreman).

NO ONE MAN (PAR, 1932) 71 M.

Director, Lloyd Corrigan; story, Rupert Hughes; adaptation, Percy Heath; screenplay, Sidney Buchman, Agnes Leahy; camera, Charles Lang.

Carole Lombard (Penelope Newbold); Ricardo Cortez (Bill Hanaway); Paul Lukas (Dr. Karl Bemis); Juliette Compton (Sue Folsom); George Barbier (Alfred Newbold); Virginia Hammond (Mrs. Newbold); Frances Moffett (Delia); Irving Bacon (License Clerk); Arthur Pierson (Stanley McIlvaine); Jane Darwell (Patient).

SINNERS IN THE SUN (PAR, 1932) 70 M.

Director, Alexander Hall, based on the story *Beach-Comber* by Mildred Cramm; screenplay, Waldemar Young, Samuel Hoffenstein, camera, Ray June.

Carole Lombard (Doris Blake); Chester Morris (Jimmie Martin); Adrienne Ames (Claire Kinkaid); Alison Skipworth (Mrs. Blake); Walter Byron (Eric Nelson); Reginald Barlow (Mr. Blake); Zita Moulton (Florence Nelson); Cary Grant (Ridgeway); Luke Cosgrave (Grandfather Blake); Ida Lewis (Grandmother Blake); Russ Clark (Fred Blake); Frances Moffett (Mrs. Fred Blake); Pierre De Ramey (Louis); Veda Buckland (Emma); Rita LaRoy (Lil); Maude Turner Gordon (Wife).

VIRTUE (COL, 1932) 87 M.

Director, Eddie Buzzell; story, Ethel Hill; screenplay, Robert Riskin; camera, Joseph Walker.

Carole Lombard (Mae); Pat O'Brien (James); Mayo Methot (Lil); Jack LaRue (Toots); Shirley Bond (Gert).

NO MORE ORCHIDS (COL, 1932) 71 M.

Director, Walter Lang; story-screenplay, Gertrude Purcell; camera, Joe August.

Carole Lombard (Annie Holt); Lyle Talbot (Tony Gage); Walter Connolly (Bill Holt); Louise Closser Hale (Grandma Holt); Allen Vincent (Dick); Ruthelma Stevens (Rita); C. Aubrey Smith (Redric); Arthur Housman (Serge); William V. Mong (Burkehart); Charles Hill (Mailes Merriwell); Jameson Thomas (Prince Carlos); Ed LeSaint (Captain Of Ship); William Worthington (Cannon); Broderick O'Farrell (Benton-Butler); Belle Johnstone (Housekeeper); Harold Minjuir (Modiste); Sidney Bracy (Holmes).

NO MAN OF HER OWN (PAR, 1932) 70 M.

Director, Wesley Ruggles; story, Edmund Goulding, Benjamin Glazer; screenplay, Maurine Watkins, Milton H. Gropper; camera, Leo Tover.

Clark Gable (Jerry "Babe" Stewart); Carole Lombard (Connie Randall); Dorothy Mackaill (Kay Everly); Grant Mitchell (Charlie Vane); George Barbier (Mr. Randall); Elizabeth Patterson (Mrs. Randall); J. Farrell MacDonald (Detective Collins); Tommy Conlan (Randall); Walter Walker (Mr. Morton); Paul Ellis (Vargas); Lillian Harmer (Mattie); Frank McGlynn (Minister); Charley Grapewin (Newsstand Clerk); Clinton Rosemond (Porter); Oscar Smith (Porter); Wallis Clark (Thomas Laidlaw-Broker).

FROM HELL TO HEAVEN (PAR, 1933) 67 M.

Director, Erle Kenton; story, Lawrence Hazard; screenplay, Percy Heath, Sidney Buchman; songs, Sam Coslow and Arthur Johnston; Leo Robin and Ralph Rainger; camera, Henry Sharp.

Carole Lombard (Colly Tanner); Jack Oakie (Charlie); Adrienne Ames (Joan Burt); David Manners (Burt); Sidney Blackmer (Cuff Billings); Verna Hillie (Sonny Lockwood); James C. Eagles (Tommy Tucker); Shirley Grey (Winnie Lloyd); Bradley Page (Jack Ruby); Walter Walker (Pop Lockwood); Berton Churchill (Toledo Jones); Donald Kerr (Steve Wells); Nydia Westman (Sue Wells); Cecil Cunningham (Mrs. Chadman); Thomas Jackson (Lynch).

SUPERNATURAL (PAR, 1933) 64½ M.

Director, Victor Halperin; story, Garnett Weston; screenplay, Harvey Thew, Brian Marlow; camera, Arthur Martinelli.

Carole Lombard (Roma Courtney); Randolph Scott (Grant Wilson); Vivienne Osborne (Ruth Rogen); Alan Dinehart (Paul Bavian); H. B. Warner (Dr. Carl Houston); Beryl Mercer (Madame Gourjan); William Farnum (Nicky Hammond); Willard Robertson (Warden); George Burr MacAnnan (Max); Lyman Williams (John Courtney).

THE EAGLE AND THE HAWK (PAR, 1933) 72 M.

Director, Stuart Walker; story, John Monk Saunders; screenplay, Bogart Rogers, Seton Miller; camera, Harry Fishbeck.

Fredric March (Jerry Young); Cary Grant (Henry Crocker); Jack Oakie (Mike Richards); Carole Lombard (Beautiful Lady); Sir Guy Standing (Major Dunham); Forrester Harvey (Hogan); Kenneth Howell (John Stevens); Leyland Hodgson (Kinsford); Virginia Hammond (Lady Erskine); Crauford Kent (General); Douglas Scott (Tommy Erskine); Robert Manning (Voss); Adrienne D'Ambricourt (Fifi); Jacques Jou-Jerville (French General's Aide); Russell Scott (Flight Sergeant); Paul Cremonesi (French General); Yorke Sherwood (Taxi Driver); Lane Chandler, Dennis O'Keefe (Fliers); Olaf Hytten (Story-Telling Officer).

BRIEF MOMENT (COL, 1933) 71 M.

Director, David Burton; based on the play by S. N. Behrman; screenplay Brian Marlow; camera, Teddy Tetzlaff; editor, Gene Havlick.

Carole Lombard (Abby Fane); Gene Raymond (Rodney Deane); Monroe Owsley (Harold Sigrift); Donald Cook (Franklin Deane); Arthur Hohl (Steve Walsh); Reginald Mason (Mr. Deane); Jameson Thomas (Count Armand); Theresa Maxwell Conover (Mrs. Deane); Florence Britton (Kay Deane); Irene Ware (Joan); Herbert Evans (Alfred).

WHITE WOMAN (PAR, 1933) 68 M.

Director, Stuart Walker; story, Norman Reilly Raine, Frank Butler; story, Samuel Hoffenstein, Gladys Lehman, Jane Loring; camera, Harry Fischbeck.

Charles Laughton (Horace Prin); Carole Lombard (Judith Denning); Charles Bickford (Ballister); Kent Taylor (David Von Eltz); Percy Kilbride (Jakey); Charles B. Middleton (Fenton); James Bell (Hambley); Claude King (Chisholm).

BOLERO (PAR, 1934) 80 M.

Director, Wesley Ruggles; story, Carey Wilson, Kubec Glasmon, Ruth Ridenour; screenplay, Horace Jackson; camera, Leo Tover; editor, Hugh Bennett.

George Raft (Raoul DeBaere); Carole Lombard (Helen Hathaway); Sally Rand (Arnette); Frances Drake (Leona); William Frawley (Mike DeBaere); Raymond Milland (Lord Coray); Gloria Shea (Lucy); Gertrude Michael (Lady D'Argon); Del Henderson (Theatre Manager); Frank G. Dunn (Hotel Manager); Martha Bamattre (Belgian Landlady); Paul Panzer (Bailiff); Adolph Miller (German Beer Garden Manager); Anne Shaw (Young Matron); Phillips Smalley (Leona's Angel); John Irwin (Porter); Gregory Golubeff (Orchestra Leader).

WE'RE NOT DRESSING (PAR, 1934) 74 M.

Associate producer, Benjamin Glazer; director, Norman Taurog; based on the play *The Admirable Crichton*; adaptation, Glazer; screenplay, Horace Jackson, Francis Martin, George Marion, Jr; songs, Harry Revel and Mack Gordon; camera, Charles Lang; editor, Stuart Heisler.

Bing Crosby (Stephen Jones); Carole Lombard (Doris Worthington); George Burns (George); Gracie Allen (Gracie); Ethel Merman (Edith); Leon Errol (Hubert); Jay Henry (Prince Alexander Stofasi); Raymond Milland (Prince Michael Stofani); John Irwin (Old Sailor); Charles Morris (Captain); Ben. F. Hendricks, Ted Oliver (Ship's Officers); Ernie Adams (Sailor); Stanley Blystone (Doris' Officer).

TWENTIETH CENTURY (COL, 1934) 91 M.

Director, Howard Hawks; based on the play by Charles MacArthur, Ben Hecht Charles Bruce Milholland; screenplay, MacArthur, Hecht; camera, Joseph August; editor, Gene Havelick.

John Barrymore (Oscar Jaffe); Carole Lombard (Mildred Plotka/Lily Garland); Roscoe Karns (Owen O'Malley); Walter Connolly (Oliver Webb); Ralph Forbes (George Smith); Dale Fuller (Sadie); Etienne Girardot (Matthew J. Clark); Herman Bing, Lee Kohlmar (Bearded Men); James P. Burtis (Train Conductor); Billie Seward (Anita); Charles Lane (Max Jacobs); Mary Jo Mathews (Emmy Lou); Ed Gargan (Sheriff); Edgar Kennedy (McGonigle); Gigi Parrish (Schultz); Fred Kelsey (Detective On Train); Pat Flaherty (Flannigan); Ky Robinson; (Detective); Cliff Thompson (Lockwood); Nick Copeland (Treasurer); Sherry Hall (Reporter); Howard Hickman (Doctor Johnson); James Burke (Chicago Detective); George Reed (Uncle Remus); Clarence Geldert (Southern Colonel); Lillian West (Charwoman); Snowflake (Porter); Steve Gaylord Pendleton (Brother-In Play); King Mojave (McGonigle's Assistant); Eddy Chandler (Cameraman); Harry Semels (Artist); Lynton Brent (Train Secretary); Anita Brown (Stage Show Girl); Irene Thompson (Stage Actress).

NOW AND FOREVER (PAR, 1934) 82 M.

Producer, Louis D. Lighton; director, Henry Hathaway; based on the story "Honor Bright" by Jack Kirkland, Melville Baker; screenplay, Vincent Lawrence, Sylvia Thalberg; art director, Hans Dreier, Robert Usher; song, Larry Morey and Leigh Harline; camera, Harry Fischbeck; editor, Ellsworth Hoagland.

Gary Cooper (Jerry Day); Carole Lombard (Toni Carstairs); Shirley Temple (Penelope Day); Sir Guy Standing (Felix Evans); Charlotte Granville (Mrs. J. P. Crane); Gilbert Emery (George Higginson); Henry Kolker (Mr. Clark); Tetsu Komai (Mr. Ling); Jameson Thomas (Chris Carstairs); Harry Stubbs (Harry O'Neill); Egon Brecher (Doctor); Ynez Seabury (Extra); Buster Phelps (Boy With Skates); Rolfe Sedan (Hotel Manager); Richard Loo (Chinese Desk Clerk); Akim Tamiroff (French Jeweler).

LADY BY CHOICE (COL, 1934) 78 M.

Director, David Burton; story, Dwight Taylor; screenplay, Jo Swerling; camera, Ted Tetzlaff; editor, Viola Lawrence.

Carole Lombard ("Alabam"-Georgia Lee); May Robson (Patsy Patterson); Roger Pryor (John Mills); Walter Connolly (Judge Daly); Arthur Hohl (Charlie Kendall); Raymond Walburn (Front O'Malley); James Burke (Sgt. Brannigan); Mariska Aldrich (Lucretia); William Faversham (Malone); John Boyle (Walsh); Henry Kolker (David Opper); Lillian Harmer (Miss Kennedy); Abe Dinovitch (Louie); Fred "Snowflake" Toones (Mose); Charles Coleman (Butler); Hector V. Sarno (Florist); Harry C. Bradley (Court Clerk); Julius Tannen (Brooke); Christian J. Frank (Proprietor); Edith Conrad (Miss Kingsley's Assistant); Elizabeth Jones (Colored Woman); Irene Thompson (Chorus Girl); Harold Berquist (Bailiff); Adele Cutler Jerome (Dancing Teacher—Double For Carole Lombard); Gino Corrado (Head Waiter); Kit Guard, Jack Stone (Brawling Waiters); Charles King, William Irving, Cy Slokum, Billy Mann (Drunks); Lee Shumway, Allan Sears, Eddie Hearn (Detectives); Charles Sullivan, Jimmie Dundee, Harry Tenbrook (Sailors); Dennis O'Keefe (Dancing Extra); Eddie Foster (Radio Technician); Christine Signe (Maid).

THE GAY BRIDE (MGM, 1934) 80 M.

Director, Jack Conway; based on the story "Repeal" by Charles Francis Coe; adaptation, Bell and Sam Spewack; camera, Ray June; editor, Frank Sullivan.

Carole Lombard (Mary); Chester Morris (Office Boy); Zasu Pitts (Mirabel); Leo Carrillo (Mickey); Nat Pendleton (Magiz); Sam Hardy (Dingle); Walter Walker (McPherson); Joe Twerp (Lafcadio); Louis Nathoaux (Honk); Edward Le Saint (Justice of Peace); Frank Darien (Minister); Fred Malatesta (French Officer); William Von Brincken (German Official); Herbert Evans (British Official); Bobby Watson (Auto Salesman); Norman Ainsley (Waiter); Fred "Snowflake" Toones (Bootblack); Garry Owen, Ray Mayer, Fuzzy Knight (Cameramen); Clay Drew (Stage Doorman); Wedgwood Nowell (Stage Manager); Jack Baxley (Bum); Wilbur Mack (Banker); Lew Harvey (Gangster); Willie Fung (Chinaman); Mary Carr (Mrs. Bartlett); Gordon De-Main (Sergeant); Boothe Howard, Francis McDonald (Crooks).

RUMBA (PAR, 1935) 71 M.

Producer, William LeBaron; director, Marion Gering; idea, Guy Endore, Seena Owen; screenplay, Howard J. Green; songs, Ralph Rainger; Spanish lyrics, Francis B. de Valdes; additional dialogue, Harry Ruskin, Frank Partos; choreography, LeRoy Prinz; camera, Ted Tetzlaff.

George Raft (Joe Martin); Carole Lombard (Diana Harrison); Margo (Carmelita); Lynne Overman (Flash); Monroe Owsley (Hobart Fletcher); Iris Adrian (Goldie Allen); Gail Patrick (Patsy Fletcher); Samuel S. Hinds (Henry B. Harrison); Virginia Hammond (Mrs. Harrison); Jameson Thomas (Jack Solanger); Soledad Jimenez (Maria); Paul Porcasi (Carlos); Raymond McKee (Dance Director); Akim Tamiroff (Tony); Mack Gray (Assistant Dance Instructor); Dennis O'Keefe (Man In Diana's Party At Theatre); Eldred Tidbury (Watkins); Bruce Warren (Dean); Hugh Enfield (Bromley); Rafael Corio (Alfredo); Rafael Storm (Cashier); James Burke, James P. Burtis (Reporters); Dick Rush (Policeman); Bud Shaw (Ticket Taker); E.H. Calvert (Police Captain); Hooper Atchley (Doctor); Dick Alexander (Cop); Don Brodie, Charlie Sullivan, Jack Raymond (Gangsters); Frank Mills (Bouncer); Ann Sheridan (Dance Girl).

HANDS ACROSS THE TABLE (PAR, 1935) 81 M.

Producer, E. Lloyd Sheldon; director, Mitchell Leisen; story, Vina Delmar; screenplay, Norman Krasna, Vincent Lawrence, Herbert Fields; songs, Sam Coslow; Mitchell Parish, and Jean Delettre; Coslow and Frederick Hollander; camera, Ted Tetzloff; editor, William Shea.

Carole Lombard (Regi Allen); Fred MacMurray (Theodore Drew III); Ralph Bellamy (Allen Macklyn); Astrid Allwyn (Vivian Snowden); Ruth Donnelly (Laura); Marie Prevost (Nona); Bess Flowers (Diner); Marcelle Corday (Celeste-Maid); Harold Minjir (Couturier); Ferdinand Munier (Miles-Butler); Edward Gargan (Pinky Kelly); William Demarest (Matty); Joseph H. Tozer (Peter); Harold Miller (Barber Customer); Nell Craig (Saleslady); Jerry Mandy (Head Waiter); Phil Kramer (Waiter In Supper Club); Murray Alper (Cab Driver); Nelson McDowell (Man In Night Shirt); Sam Ash (Maitre D'Hotel); Edward Peil, Sr., Jerry Storm, Francis Sayles, Chauncey M. Drake, S. M. Young, Rafael Gavilan, Harry Williams, Sterling Campbell (Barbers); James Adamson (Porter); Fred "Snowflake" Toones (Porter); Peter Allen (Jewelry Clerk); Ira Reed (Florist Clerk); Pat Sweeney (Manicurist); Mary MacLaren (Chambermaid); Ira Reed, Dutch Hendrian (Taxi Drivers); John Huettner (Shoe Clerk).

LOVE BEFORE BREAKFAST (UNIV, 1936) 70 M.

Producer, Edmund Grainger; director, Walter Lang; suggested by the novel *Spinster Dinner* by Faith Baldwin; screenplay, Herbert Fields; camera, Ted Tetzlaff; editor, Maurice E. Wright.

Carole Lombard (Kay Colby); Preston Foster (Scott Miller); Cesar Romero (Bill Wadsworth); Janet Beecher (Mrs. Colby); Betty Lawford (Contessa Janie Campanella); Richard Carle (Brinkerhoff); Forrester Harvey (First Mate); Ed Burton (Jerry-Cabby); Sam Tong (Steward); Bob Thom (Chauffeur); Alphonse Martell, William Arnold (Waiters); Dennis O'Keefe, Robert Kent, Ralph Malone, Howard "Red" Christie, Ralph Brooks, David Tyrell, David Worth (College Boys); Earl Eby (Entertainer); Albert Richman (Proprietor); Pat Flaherty (Bouncer); Nick De Ruiz (Chef); Harry Tracy (Groom); Bert Roach (Fat Man); Joyce Compton (Mary Lee Jackson); Pushface Lombard (Junior); Charles Tannen, Bert Moorhouse, Jay Easton, Theodore von Eltz (Clerks); Edward Earle (Quartermaster); E. E. Clive (Captain); Jimmy Aye (Petty Officer); Lester Dorr, (Attendant); John King (Johnny); Nan Grey (Telephone Girl).

THE PRINCESS COMES ACROSS (PAR, 1936) 76 M.

Producer, Arthur Hornblow, Jr; director, William. K. Howard; based on the novel by Louis Lucien Rogger; adaptation, Philip MacDonald; screenplay, Walter DeLeon, Frances Martin, Frank Butler, Don Hartman; art director, Hans Dreier, Ernst Fegte; songs, Jack Schol and Phil Boutelje; George Marion, Jr, and Richard Whiting; Mack Gordon and Harry Revel; Leo Robin and Frederick Hollander; camera, Ted Tetzlaff;

Carole Lombard (Princess Olga); Fred MacMurray (Mantell); Douglass Dumbrille (Lorel); Alison Skipworth (Lady Gertrude Allwyn); William Frawley (Benton); Porter Hall (Darcy); George Barbier (Captain Nicholls); Lumsden Hare (Cragg); Siegfried Rumann (Steindorf); Mischa Auer (Morevitch); Tetsu Komai (Kawati); Bradley Page (Stranger); George Sorrell, Jacques Vanaire (Reporters); Gaston Glass (Photographer); Andre Cheron (Frenchman); Nenette Lafayette (Frenchwoman); Gladden James (Third Ship's Official); David Clyde (Assistant Purser); Tom Herbert (Cabin Steward); Larry Steers (Assistant Purser); Pat Flaherty (Officer); Paul Kruger (Assistant Purser); Dick Elliott (Ship's Surgeon); Henry Hayden (Master of Ceremonies); Milburn Stone (American Reporter); Edward Keane (Chief Purser); Creighton Hale (Officer).

MY MAN GODFREY (UNIV, 1936) 95 M.

Producer-director, Gregory LaCava; story, Eric Hatch; screenplay, Morrie Ryskind, Hatch, LaCava; camera, Ted Tetzlaff; editor, Ted Kent.

William Powell (Godfrey); Carole Lombard (Irene Bullock); Alice Brady (Angelica Bullock); Eugene Pallette (Alexander Bullock); Gail Patrick (Cornelia Bullock); Alan Mowbray (Tommy Gray); Jean Dixon (Molly); Mischa Auer (Carlo); Robert Light (George); Pat Flaherty (Mike); Robert Perry (Hobo) Selmer Jackson (Blake

—Guest); Grace Field, Kathryn Perry, Harley Wood, Elaine Cochrane, David Horsley, Philip Merrick (Socialities); Ernie Adams (Forgotten Man); Phyllis Crane (Party Guest); Eddie Fetherston (Process Server); Edward Gargan, James Flavin (Detectives); Art Singley (Chauffeur); Jane Wyman (Girl at Party); Bess Flowers (Guest); Chic Collins (Double for William Powell); Reginald Mason (Mayor).

SWING HIGH, SWING LOW (PAR, 1937) 97 M.

Producer, Arthur Hornblow, Jr.; director, Mitchel Leisen; based on the play *Burlesque* by George Manker Watters; screenplay, Virginia Van Upp, Oscar Hammerstein; art director, Hans Dreier, Ernst Fegte; music director, Boris Morros; songs, Ralph Rainger and Leo Robin; Sam Coslow and Al Siegal; Ralph Freed and Charles Kisco; camera, Ted Tetzlaff; editor, Eda Warren.

Carole Lombard (Maggie King); Fred MacMurray (Skid Johnson); Charles Butterworth (Harry); Jean Dixon (Ella); Dorothy Lamour (Anita Alvarez); Cecil Cunningham (Murphy); Harvey Stephens (Harvey Dexter); Charlie Arnt (Georgie); Franklin Pangborn (Henri); Anthony Quinn (The Don); Dennis O'Keefe (Purser); Charles Judels (Tony); Harry Semels (Chief of Police); Ricardo Mandia (Interpreter); Enrique DeRosas (Judge); Chris Pin Martin (Sleepy Servant), Charles Stevens (Panamanian at Cock Fight); Ralph Remley (Musselwhite); Oscar Rudolph (Elevator Boy); George Sorel (Manager); George W. Jimenez (Justice of Peace); Lee Bowman, Nick Lukats (Men in Nightclub); Lee Cooley (Radio Announcer); Richard Kipling (Army Surgeon); Esther Howard (Customer); Donald Kerr (Radio Technician); William Wright (Attendant); Spencer Chan (Cook).

NOTHING SACRED (UA, 1937) 75 M.

Producer, David O. Selznick; director, William A. Wellman; based on story by James H. Street; screenplay, Ben Hecht; music, Oscar Levant camera, W. Howard Greene; editor, Hal Kern.

Carole Lombard (Hazel Flagg); Fredric March (Wally Cook); Charles Winninger (Dr. Enoch Downer); Walter Connolly (Oliver Stone); Sig Rumann (Dr. Emile Egglehoffer); Frank Fay (Master Of Ceremonies); Maxie Rosenbloom (Max Levinsky); Margaret Hamilton (Drug Store Lady); Troy Brown (Ernest Walker); Olin Howland (Baggage Man); Hedda Hopper (Dowager); John Qualen (Swede Fireman); Art Lasky (Mug); Monty Woolley (Dr. Vunch); Hattie McDaniel (Mrs. Walker); Alex Schoenberg (Dr. Kerchinwisser); Alex Novinsky (Dr. Marachuffsky); Katherine Shelton (Downer's Nurse); Ernest Whitman, Everett Brown (Policemen); Ben Morgan, Hans Steinke (Wrestlers); George Chandler (Photographer); Nora Cecil (Schoolteacher); Claire Du Brey (Miss Rafferty—Nurse); A. W. Sweatt (Office Boy); Vera Lewis (Miss Sedgewick); Ann Doran (Telephone Girl); Jinx Falkenburg (Katinka); Bill Dunn, Lee Phelps (Electricians); Cyril Ring (Pilot); Mickey McMasters (Referee); Bobby Tracy (Announcer); Wimpy (The Dog)

TRUE CONFESSION (PAR, 1937) 85 M.

Producer, Albert Lewin; director, Wesley Ruggles; based on the play by Louis Verneuil, Georges Berr; screenplay, Claude Binyon; music director, Boris Morros; music, Frederick Hollander; songs, Hollander and Sam Coslow; art director, Hans Dreier, Robert Usher; camera, Ted Tetzlaff; editor, Paul Weatherwax.

Carole Lombard (Helen Bartlett); Fred MacMurray (Kenneth Barlett); John Barrymore (Charley); Una Merkel (Daisy McClure); Porter Hall (Prosecutor); Edgar Kennedy (Barney); Lynne Overman (Bartender); Fritz Feld (Krayler's Butler); Richard Carle (Judge); John T. Murray (Otto Krayler); Tom Dugan (Typewriter Man); Garry Owen (Tony Krauch); Toby Wing (Suzanne Baggart); Hattie McDaniel (Ella); Bernard Suss (Pedestrian); Pat West, Herbert Ashley, Dudley Clement, Walter Soderling, Jim Toney, Gertrude Simpson, Chester Clute, Irving White, George Ovey, Elmer Jerome, Peggy Melon, Jane Loofbourrow, George French, Anne Cornwall (Jurors); Frank Austin (Caretaker); Cora Shumway (Jail Matron); Arthur Lake (Attendant); Peggy Montgomery (Autograph Hunter); Irving Bacon (Coroner); Byron Foulger (Ballistic Expert); Sharon Lewis (Yvonne Bolero); Don Roberts (Court Attendant); Nick Copeland, Monte Vandergrift (Guards).

FOOLS FOR SCANDAL (WB, 1938) 81 M.

Producer-director, Mervyn LeRoy; story, Nancy Hamilton, James Shute, Rosemary Casey; screenplay, Herbert Fields, Joseph Fields; songs, Richard Rodgers and Lorenz Hartz; music director, Leo F. Forbstein; art director, Anton Grot; camera, Ted Tetzlaff; editor, William Holmes.

Carole Lombard (Kay Winters); Fernand Gravet (Rene); Ralph Bellamy (Phillip Chester); Allen Jenkins (Dewey Gibson); Marie Wilson (Myrtle); Isabel Jeans (Lady Malverton); Marcia Ralston (Jill); Ottola Nesmith (Agnes); Norma Varden (Cicely); Heather Thatcher (Sylvia Potter-Porter); Tempe Pigott (Bessie); Ara Gerald (Mrs. Bullit); Leyland Hodgson (Mr. Bullit); John Sutton (Bruce Devon); Jacques Lory (Papa Joli-Coeur); Jeni Le Gon (Specialty); Albert Petit, Andre Marsaudon (Gendarmes); Three Brown Sisters (Themselves); Elizabeth Dunne, Sarah Edwards (Tourists); Lionel Pape (Photographer); Michael Romanoff, Leon Lasky, Lotus Thompson, Hugh Huntley, Stephani Insull, Tina Smirnova (Party Guests); Rosella Towne (Diana); Elspeth Dudgeon (Cynthia); Lorraine Eddy MacLean (Valerie); Jean Benedict (Evelyn).

MADE FOR EACH OTHER (UA, 1939) 90 M.

Producer, David O. Selznick; director, John Cromwell; screenplay, Jo Swerling; art director, Lyle Wheeler; music director, Lou Forbes; production design, William Cameron Menzies; special effects, Jack Cosgrove; comera, Leon Shamroy; editor, Hal C. Kern, James E. Newcom.

Carole Lombard (Jane Mason); James Stewart (Johnny Mason); Charles Coburn (Judge Joseph Doolittle); Lucile Watson (Mrs. Mason); Harry Davenport (Dr. Healy); Ruth Weston (Eunice Doolittle); Donald Briggs (Carter); Eddie Quillan (Conway); Esther Dale (Annie—The Cook); Rene Orsell (Hilda); Louise Beavers (Lily—The Cook); Alma Kruger (Sister Agnes); Fred Fuller (Doolittle's Brother); Edwin Maxwell (Messerschmidt); Harry Depp (Hutch); Mickey Rentschler (Office Boy); Jackie Taylor (John, Jr.—Age One); Robert Emmett O'Connor (Elevator Starter); Milburn Stone (Sam); Bonnie Belle Barber (John, Jr.—Newly Born); Robert Strange, Perry Ivans, Gladden James (Doctors). Arthur Hoyt (Jury Foreman); Harlan Briggs (Judge); Betty Farrington (Hospital Cashier); Ruth Gillette (Blonde in Cafe); Ivan Simpson (Simon); Ward Bond (Jim Hatton); Jack Mulhall (Radio Operator); Russell Hopton (Collins); Olin Howland (Farmer): Fern Emmett (Farmer's Wife); Lane Chandler, Tom London (Rangers); Harry Worth (New York Hospital Chemist); Raymond Bailey (Salt Lake Hospital Chemist); J. M. Sullivan (John Hopkins' Chemist).

IN NAME ONLY (RKO, 1939) 94 M.

Producer, George Haight; director, John Cromwell; based on the novel "Memory Of Love" by Bessie Breuer; adaptation, Richard Sherman; camera, J. Roy Hunt; editor, William Hamilton.

Carole Lombard (Julie Eden); Cary Grant (Alec Walker); Kay Francis (Maida Walker); Charles Coburn (Mr. Walker); Helen Vinson (Suzanne); Katharine Alexander (Laura); Jonathan Hale (Dr. Gateson); Maurice Moscovich (Dr. Muller); Nella Walker (Mrs. Walker); Peggy Ann Garner (Ellen); Alan Baxter (Charley); Spencer Charters (Gardener); Harriet Mathews, Sandra Morgan, Harold Miller (Passengers on Boat); Doug Gordon (Steward); Tony Merlo (Waiter); Frank Puglia (Manager); Alex Pollard (Butler); Charles Coleman (Archie Duross); Florence Wix, Clive Morgan, Major Sam Harris, Kathryn Wilson, (Party Guests); Grady Sutton (Escort); Byron Foulger (Owen); Arthur Aylsworth (Farmer on Truck) Lloyd Ingraham (Elevator Operator); Robert Strange (Hotel Manager); Jack Chapin, Allan Wood (Bellhops); Edward Fligle (Night Clerk); John Laing (Chauffeur); Frank Mills (Bartender).

VIGIL IN THE NIGHT (RKO, 1940) 96 M.

Executive producer, Pandro S. Berman; producer-director, George Stevens; based on the novel by A. J. Cronin; screenplay, Fred Guiol, P. J. Wolfson, Rowland Leigh.

Carole Lombard (Anne Lee); Brian Aherne (Dr. Prescott); Anne Shirley (Lucy Lee); Julien Mitchell (Matthew Bowley); Robert Coote (Dr. Caley); Brenda Forbes (Nora); Rita Page (Glennie); Peter Cushing (Joe Shand); Ethel Griffies (Matron East); Doris Lloyd (Mrs. Bowley); Emily Fitzroy (Sister Gilson).

THEY KNEW WHAT THEY WANTED (RKO, 1940) 96 M.

Producer, Erich Pommer; director, Garson Kanin; based on the play by Sidney Howard; screenplay, Robert Ardrey; music, Alfred Newman; camera, Harry Stradling; editor, John Sturges.

Carole Lombard (Amy); Charles Laughton (Tony); William Gargan (Joe); Harry Carey (Doctor); Frank Fay (Father McKee); Joe Bernard (R.F.D.); Janet Fox (Mildred); Lee Tung-Foo (Ah Gee); Karl Malden(Red); Victor Kilian (Photographer); Effie Anderson (Nurse); Paul Lepere (Hired Hand); Marie Blake, Millicent Green, Grace Lenard, Patricia Oakley (Waitresses); Bobby Barber, Nestor Paiva (Pals at Table); Antonio Filauri (Customer); Joe Sully (Father of Family); Ricca Allen (Mrs. Thing); Tom Ewell (New Hired Hand); Pina Troupe (Themselves).

MR. AND MRS. SMITH (RKO, 1941) 95 M.

Producer, Harry E. Edington; director, Alfred Hitchcock; story-screenplay, Norman Krasna; art director, Van Nest Polglase; music, Edward Ward; special effects, Vernon L. Walker; camera, Harry Stradling; editor, William Hamilton.

Carole Lombard (Ann); Robert Montgomery (David); Gene Raymond (Jeff); Jack Carson (Chuck); Philip Merivale (Mr. Custer); Lucile Watson (Mrs. Custer); William Tracy (Sammy); Charles Halton (Mr. Deaver); Esther Dale (Mrs. Krausheimer); Emma Dunn (Martha); William Edmunds (Proprietor—Lucy's); Betty Compson (Gertie); Patricia Farr (Gloria); Pamela Blake (Lily); Frank Mills (Taxi Driver); Francis Compton (Mr. Flugle); Alec Craig (Thomas—Clerk); Jack Gardner (Elevator Boy); Ralph Sanford (Store Checker); Murray Alper (Harold—Driver); Georgia Carroll (Pretty Girl); Ralph Dunn (Cop); James Flavin (Escort); Jim Pierce (Doorman); Ronnie Rondell (Waiter Captain); Allen Wood, Ermie Alexander (Bellhops); Emory Parnell (Conway); Stan Taylor (Clerk).

TO BE OR NOT TO BE (UA, 1942) 98 M.

Producer-director, Ernst Lubitsch; story, Lubitsch, Melchior Lengyel; screenplay, Edwin Justus Mayer; art director, Vincent Korda; music director, Werner Heyman; camera, Rudolph Mate; editor, Dorothy Spencer.

Carole Lombard (Maria Tura); Jack Benny (Joseph Tura); Robert Stack (Lt. Stanislav Sobinski); Felix Bressart (Greenberg); Lionel Atwill (Kawitch) Stanley Ridges (Prof. Siletsky); Sig Rumann (Col. Ehrhardt); Tom Dugan (Bronski); Charles Halton (Dobosh—Producer); George Lynn (Actor—Adjutant); Henry Victor (Capt. Schultz); Maude Eburne (Anna—Maid); Armand Wright (Make-Up Man); Erno Verebes (Stage Manager); Halliwell Hobbes (Gen. Armstrong); Miles Mander (Maj. Cunningham); Leslie Dennison (Captain); Frank Reicher (Polish Official); Peter Caldwell (William Kunze); Wolfgang Zilzer (Man In Bookstore); Olaf Hytten (Polonius—In Warsaw); Charles Irwin, Leyland Hodgson (Reporters); Alec Craig, James Finlayson (Scottish Farmers); Edgar Licho (Prompter); Robert O. Davis (Gestapo Sergeant); Roland Varno (Pilot); Helmut Dantine, Otto Reichow (Co-Pilots); Maurice Murphy, Gene Rizzi, Paul Barrett, John Kellogg (R.A.F. Flyers), Sven-Hugo Bong (German Soldier).

With Kay Francis and William Powell in LADIES' MAN (Par '31)

With Norman Foster in IT PAYS TO AD-VERTISE (Par '31)

With Chester Morris in SINNERS IN THE SUN (Par '32)

Meredith Willson, Clark Gable, Charles Laughton, Reginald Owen (rear), Carole Lombard, Melvyn Douglas, Myrna Loy, Tyrone Power, and Ann Rutherford at an NBC radio broadcast, 1939.

In THE SWIM PRINCESS (Pathé '28)

With Edmund Lowe in MARRIAGE IN TRANSIT (Fox '25)

With Robert Armstrong in BIG NEWS (Pathé '29)

With Francis McDonald, Kathryn Crawford, Josephine Dunn, and Charles "Buddy" Rogers in SAFETY IN NUMBERS (Par '30)

With Gary Cooper in I TAKE THIS WOMAN (Par '31)

With William Powell and Guy Kibbee in MAN OF THE WORLD (Par '31)

With Clark Gable in NO MAN OF HER OWN (Par '32)

With Alan Dinehart in SUPERNATURAL (Par '33)

With Fredric March in THE EAGLE AND THE HAWK (Par '33)

In WHITE WOMAN (Par '33)

With George Raft in BOLERO (Par '34)

With Ray Milland, Bing Crosby, Leon Errol, and Ethel Merman in WE'RE NOT DRESSING (Par '34)

In TWENTIETH CENTURY (Col '34)

With Gary Cooper, Charlotte Granville, and Shirley Temple in NOW AND FOREVER (Par '34)

With Harry C. Bradley (behind post), May Robson, and Walter Connolly in LADY BY CHOICE (Col '34)

With Ralph Bellamy, Joseph R. Tozer, and Fred MacMurray in HANDS ACROSS THE TABLE (Par '35)

With William Powell in MY MAN GODFREY (Col '36)

With Fredric March in NOTHING SA-
CRED (UA '37)

With John Barrymore and Una Merkel in
TRUE CONFESSION (Par '37)

With Ralph Bellamy and Fernand Gravet
in FOOLS FOR SCANDAL (WB '38)

With Cary Grant in IN NAME ONLY (RKO
'39)

With Brian Aherne in VIGIL IN THE
NIGHT (RKO '40)

MARLENE DIETRICH

5'5"

106 pounds

Red-gold hair

Blue eyes

Capricorn

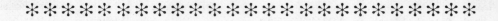

A RECENT film history—*Four Fabulous Faces* by Larry Carr (Arlington House, 1970)—pictorially traced the extraordinarily successful and long careers of four twentieth-century myths: Marlene Dietrich, Gloria Swanson, Greta Garbo, and Joan Crawford. Of this legendary grouping, Swanson was far more popular and vibrant than Marlene, Garbo more dramatically satisfying, and Crawford more humanly intriguing, but none of them matched her in combining physical allure with the understated ambiguity of the feminine mystique.

For too long it has been blithely assumed, and she herself wished it so believed, that Marlene's professional career would never have risen to its meteoric heights had she not come to Hollywood in 1930, after the huge success of her German-made *Der blaue Engel* (1930). Not so! By this point in her career, she had well utilized her striking Germanic beauty and the fortitude derived from her petty bourgeois breeding to achieve a steadily growing success as both a popular film player and a musical comedy stage personality. She was certainly well appreciated in pre-Hitler Berlin, and her screen reputation undoubtedly would have continued upward had she been willing to participate in the Nazi-controlled cultural movement in Europe during the 1930s and 1940s.

Once in America, perspicacious Marlene "allowed" herself to be transformed into a sleek American-style film star, but she retained much of the slick Continental allure that had initially appealed to the B. P. Schulberg-Paramount regime. With typical foresight, geared always to her enduring image, Marlene continued to submit to a complex tutelege-camaraderie relationship with Paramount film director Josef von Sternberg. Whether he or she piloted her film career through the early Hollywood years is still a source of controversy. What did result in her years at Paramount (1930–37) was a series of picaresque motion pictures all geared to explore and proliferate her beauty and legend.

There were few in the California movie colony of the 1930s, and even fewer in the worldwide cinema industry of today, who expended so much concentrated effort on perfecting a screen image. Marlene may have postured her way through role after role, providing few moments of human reality, but this was a side-effect of always portraying variations of Lola-Lola, the man-destroyer with a sympathetic heart for no person. Whereas other, less persevering performers would have chalked up defeat, Marlene refused to submit to the fate of being box-office poison in the 1937–38 period. She remolded her screen image and emerged as a more earthy love goddess in Universal's mock Western, *Destry Rides Again* (1939). The 38-year-old Marlene was now a boisterous screen heroine, equally at home as a saloon entertainer in the Old West or a big city clip-joint hostess, and surprisingly more popular (if less artistically enduring) than she had been in her prior screen vehicles as the aloof woman. Under her new guise, she was still the mankiller. Her tactics were more obvious and enthusiastic, but her world-weariness was now held in check behind a mask of lightheartedness and a volley of rousing cabaret songs.

In the 1940s Marlene garnered a positive reputation as a patriot with her three years of USO touring for the Allied troops during World War II, and she made the public aware of her intellectual appeal by hobnobbing with the international cultural set. She still attracted but usually ignored the high-toned social crowd, preferring her own intimate group of mind- and soul-stimulating types.

By the 1950s, Marlene, now a glamorous grandmother like Gloria Swanson, found her film career tapering off to brief guest-starring roles, usually to force feed chicness into lackluster pictures.

Marlene continued her professional activities in other media. She disliked the physical and cosmetic demands of television, but was heartily enthusiastic about radio and continued in that field long after most star names had abandoned the area. In 1953 she commenced the latest phase of her career to date as a superior mezzo-baritone chanteuse of the worldwide nightclub and stage circuit. It was 14 years of on-the-road trekking before she felt sufficiently prepared, in her own terms, to face the rigors of a Broadway appearance with her one-woman show. What has proven most amazing in her years as a singer is her enormous professionalism in judging not only lighting, makeup, and costuming, but the total ambiance of her performance, picking every nuance of emotion from the numbers she talked-sang and programming her synthetic emotions to highlight these facets.

Now in her seventies, Marlene has the background and audience reflex actions to carry her through more years of club appearances as an exquisitely garbed robot who is one of the greatest show people of all ages.

✳ ✳ ✳ ✳ ✳ ✳ ✳ ✳ ✳ ✳ ✳ ✳ ✳ ✳ ✳ ✳ ✳ ✳ ✳ ✳

Marlene (pronounced Marlain-ah) Dietrich was born Maria Magdalene Dietrich, December 27, 1901, in Schöneberg, Berlin (now part of West Berlin). She was the second daughter of Louis Erich Otto Dietrich, a lieutenant in the Royal Prussian Police, and Wilhelmina Elisabeth Josephine Felsing, the daughter of Conrad Felsing, head of the noted Berlin jewelry company.

Not too long after Marlene's birth, her father was reassigned to Weimar in Saxe-Weimar-Eisenach. The family still spent most of their time in Berlin. When Marlene was still a child, her father died. About 1914, the mother remarried, to Edouard von Losch, a member of the König grenadier regiment. He was stationed on the French front during most of World War I, and was transferred to the Russian front in 1918, where he was wounded in action and soon thereafter died.

Marlene and her older sister Elizabeth were brought up in the strict tradition of middle-class gentility: "My whole upbringing was aimed toward action. 'Don't contemplate yourself, act!' " The two girls were educated under the precise tutelege of a governess who taught them both English and French, and instilled in them a strong heritage of self-discipline. "My mother made acting difficult for me," Marlene would later reveal. "My whole upbringing was to mask my feelings—the last slap I had from mother was because of that. I was having dancing lessons, and had to dance with everyone in the room, including a young man I did not like. I made a long face. Mother saw it and slapped me as soon as we were alone. 'You must not show your feelings, it is bad manners,' she said."

Marlene was musically inclined as a child, and was given both piano and violin lessons. Her mother found the means to enroll Marlene in Berlin's Hochschule für Musik, the state academy of music. Marlene has recalled: "Actually, I wanted to be a concert violinist; I spent my whole youth working with that goal in mind. . . . I was always very persistent when I wanted to achieve a thing. At sixteen [sic] years of age, I used to practice six hours a day and was about to make my first public appearance in concert. And it would happen that at just that time I suffered a muscle damage, so that my arm couldn't be moved for a time. When I was finally well again, the Doctor forbade me to play any difficult pieces. This made a career as a concert violinist unthinkable and unbearable for me. I gave up completely."

Marlene then practically and swiftly transferred her enormous desire for a creative career to the motion pictures. She was a great fan of the popular screen actress Henny Porten, and managed by great persistence to gain an interview with her. She advised Marlene to continue with her theatrical ambitions.

Marlene determined to become part of Max Reinhardt's Deutsch Theaterschule, regardless of her theatrical inexperience or the school's extremely high standards. Her widowed mother consented to Marlene pursuing an acting career, but only if she avoided using the proud Von Losch name. Marlene agreed, and by combining her first two names (Marie and Magdalene) and taking her father's surname, arrived at Marlene Dietrich.

She obtained an interview with the great Reinhardt, who told her she was not experienced enough to study at the Deutsche Theaterschule. Thereafter, Marlene auditioned for a chorus position with Guido Thielscher's latest musical revue, which was embarking on a tour of outlying cities. Her shapely legs were enough to win her the job.

Marlene returned to Berlin after the tour in the spring of 1922. She again auditioned for the Deutsche Theaterschule and this time was accepted. Among her first acting assignments at the school were a bit in

Shakespeare's *The Taming of the Shrew* and the role of Hippolyta in *A Midsummer's Night Dream*. Her first break came when she was substituted for an ailing actress in *Der grosse Bariton* ("The Great Baritone") starring the well-known actor Albert Bassermann.

While appearing in this play, Marlene made her screen debut, as a housemaid in *Der kleine Napoleon,* a comedy with a distorted historical background. Produced in the fall of 1922, she was twelfth-billed in this 1923 release.

At the Theaterschule, Rudolf Sieber, a Sudeten Czech who was a production assistant of film director Joe May, selected Marlene to play a role in *Tragodie der Liebe* (1923), a UFA drama starring Emil Jannings. Reportedly, Marlene arrived at the studio dressed to the sophisticated hilt. Her garb was all wrong for her proposed role as a judge's mistress determined to attend the murder trial of wrestler Jannings, a homicide case which had scandalized all of Paris. Sieber took Marlene to the wardrobe department and reoutfitted her in a more appropriate costume. She reappeared for May's inspection, dressed in a feathered housecoat and sporting a monocle. In the final film, released in four parts, Marlene had a few showy scenes, especially in the courtroom where she sits enraptured, studying the goings-on with the benefit of opera glasses. Until *Der blaue Engel* (1930), the part of the floozie Lucie was her favorite screen role.

After the play *Der grosse Bariton* closed, Marlene had small roles in Wilhelm Dieterle's first feature *Der Mensch am Wege* (1923)—he would later direct her in *Kismet* (1944)—and an ingenue assignment in *Der Sprung ins Leben* (1924).

Marlene had been dating Rudolf Sieber since their initial meetings in 1923. His marriage proposal offered the potential security of family life, so Marlene accepted. They were wed on May 17, 1923, and she retired to supposedly joyful domesticity. Their daughter Maria was born December 12, 1924. It was at this time that Sieber filmed a short-subject home movie, *Die gluckliche Mutter* ("The Happy Mother"), which may have seen theatrical release in Germany in the late 1920s.

At her husband's insistence, Marlene reactivated her professional career in mid-1925. The first available job, now that her retirement had caused her to start almost from scratch again, was an extra bit in G. W. Pabst's *Die Freudlose Gasse* (1926) starring Greta Garbo. Marlene appears in the scene outside of the butcher's shop in the Depression-torn city, as part of the crowd of hungry food-seekers. The film was released in the United States in 1927 as *The Street of Sorrow.*

Marlene was eleventh-billed in the historical romance *Manon Lescaut,* shot in the fall of 1925 and released in February, 1926, in Berlin and later that year in the United States. By early 1926 she was appearing in Hans J. Rehfisch's stage comedy *Duell am Lido,* starring Fritz Kortner.

Back in the cinema, Hungarian director Alexander Korda cast Marlene in a small role in *Eine DuBarry von Heute* (1926), which starred his wife Maria Corda. It had American distribution in 1928.

Then Marlene appeared in the stage revue *Von Mund zu Mund* ("From Mouth to Mouth") starring Clare Waldoff. While in this musical show, Korda employed Marlene and John Loder as dress extras in the Marie Corda vehicle *Madame Wunscht Keine Kinder* (1926), released in America as *Madame Wants No Children* (1927). Marlene's husband Sieber was a production assistant on this film.

After three more small featured roles in films, Marlene had obtained a sufficient screen reputation to be able to be more selective. When UFA-based executive Victor Shutezsky offered Marlene a role in *Manner von der Ehe* ("Men Before Marriage"), starring Oskar Homolka, she refused, due to a salary dispute.

Marlene returned to the stage, accepting the role of the hip chorus girl Rubie in a version of Philip Dunning and George Abbott's American play *Broadway.* She had two song-dance numbers. When *Broadway* played Vienna, its star Willie Forst was engaged to make the movie *Café Electric.* At Forst's insistence, Marlene was given a role in this strong drama, which was released in Vienna in November, 1927. Marlene played the building contractor's daughter seduced by gigolo Forst. In her splashy role, she made a favorable impression on both critics and audiences. Already, she was being compared to Greta Garbo.

In 1927 Marlene made her first recording. It was entitled "Peter."

Next she was hired to appear at Max Reinhardt's Josefstädter Theatre in Carl Sternheim's *Die Schule von Uznack,* and simultaneously she filmed *Prinzessin Olala* (1928), a comedy directed by Robert Land. She attained noteworthy reception in Reinhardt's stage production *Es Lieght in der Luft* ("It's in the Air"), with music by Mischa Spoliansky, in which she sang the title song and a duet with the decidedly masculine Margo Lion, entitled "My Best Girl Friend." The latter number, with its blatantly lesbian connotation, caused quite a stir even in sophisticated Berlin.

By now, Marlene and her family were enjoying the tangible benefits of her increasing professional success, and they moved to a larger apartment, at 54 Kaiser Allee, Wilmersdorf, near where she had lived as a child. Here, as always, her daughter, nicknamed Heidike, was the focal point of the household.

Also for Robert Land, Marlene was featured as the Parisian divorcee in the sophisticated film comedy *Ich kusse ihre Hand, Madame* (1929), which headlined the very popular Harry Liedtke. Its sturdy reception in Germany did much to boost Marlene's screen image; in 1932 it was released in the United States as *I Kiss Your Hand, Madame,* distributed to cash in on the Dietrich craze here. By American standards, the film was too sentimentally unreal, and Marlene was labeled "coy."

After two additional features, Marlene was seen on the Berlin stage again in George Bernard Shaw's *Misalliance* and *Back to Methuselah.* For her intense performing in these productions, Marlene garnered critical raves and a large audience following.

Marlene's next feature film was *Gerfahren der Brautzeit* (1929), again with Willi Forst. She played the impoverished Evelyne, who is seduced by Baron Forst, but marries American Ernst Stahl-Machbaur. This romantic drama did better box-office business when reissued after the success of *Der blaue Engel.*

On stage Marlene starred in George Kaiser's revue *Zwei Krawatten* ("Two Neckties"), produced by Reinhardt and costarring Hans Albers. The show, with songs by Mischa Spoliansky, proved a hit, and Marlene, as the glamorous, wealthy American, had an opportunity to speak some English dialogue.

It was during the run of *Zwei Krawatten* in Berlin that Austrian-born director Josef von Sternberg, age 36, saw Marlene perform. Although under contract to Paramount he was on special assignment to UFA to film *Der blaue Engel* with Emil Jannings, who, until the advent of sound films, was a prestigious star of silent Paramount pictures. While Marlene in her post-

1950s nightclub act states that von Sternberg demanded that she sing a vulgar and a naughty song for her audition, the director claimed in his autobiography, *Fun in a Chinese Laundry:* "It is impossible that I ever asked anyone to be vulgar. As for my asking her to sing a 'naughty' song for the test, this too is not to be reconciled with what actually happened. As she could only sing what she knew, and that was very little, I sent her to the wardrobe to discard her street clothes and to change into something with spangles and she returned with a costume roomy enough to contain a hippopotamus. I pinned the dress to fit her somehow and asked her to sing something she knew in German and to follow it with an English song if possible." In the screen test, von Sternberg writes, "she came to life and responded to my instructions with an ease that I had never before encountered. She seemed pleased at the trouble I took with her, but she never saw the test, nor ever asked to see it. Her remarkable vitality had been channeled."

When Marlene was signed for the vamp role of Lola-Lola at von Sternberg's insistence (Jannings was not in favor of her and was greatly disturbed when she received special attention during the filming), she shed all associations with her past screen career. She had the remarkable ability, then as now, to will facts into what best suited her image and emotional needs. "She attached no value to it when I met her," recalled von Sternberg, "nor did she attach any value to anything else as far as I could ascertain, with the exception of her baby daughter, musical saw, and some recordings by a singer called Whispering Jack Smith. She was inclined to jeer at herself and at others, though she was extremely loyal to her friends. . . . She was frank and outspoken to a degree which might be termed tactless. Her personality was one of extreme sophistication and of an almost childish simplicity."

Der blaue Engel, based on the Heinrich Mann novel *Professor Unrath,* began production at UFA's Neubabelsberg Studios on the outskirts of Berlin on November 4, 1929, and continued through late-January, 1930. It premiered at the Gloria Palast Theatre, Berlin, on April 1, 1930, and proved an instantaneous success, offering one of the first major examples of fluid camerawork in the relatively new German sound film industry.

During production, Marlene had feared that the part of the crude, cruel Lola-Lola would taint her screen image. However, critics and audiences were enthralled by her characterization of the vixen cabaret singer. She proved to be the nemesis of the middle-aged professor played by Jannings, who sacrifices all his values in his misguided love of her. In the film, Jannings fluttered and sputtered, first in antagonism, then in rapture, and finally in abject submission as the troupe's buffoon. In contrast, Marlene remained imperturbably cool, shrugging off her husband's decline as easily as she did her coarse surrounding. Her plump appearance as the common temptress who used and discarded men like paper napkins was noteworthy for its understatement. Fleshing out her characterization as the low-class femme fatale were her renditions of the bawdy "I'm Naughty Little Lola" and the ironic "Falling in Love Again." One biting stanza of the latter song identified and established a screen image for Marlene that would endure through the next three decades: "Men clutter around me, like moths around a flame. If they get their wings burned, I am not to blame."

Marlene's performance in *Der blaue Engel* so exhilarated von Sternberg that he convinced B. P. Schulberg,* production head of Paramount's

*See Appendix.

West Coast studio, to hire Marlene. She was hesitant about leaving Germany for an unknown America, but the dramatic public reception to *Der blaue Engel* convinced her of the practicality of immediately accepting the offer. The Berlin critics were also enthusiastic about her: "Her ability to take over her scenes effortlessly, but with simple and total command is something we have until now never experienced."

When von Sternberg sailed back to America after completing *Der blaue Engel,* among his bon voyage presents was Marlene's gift of a copy of Benno Vigny's novel *Amy Jolly,* which dealt with the French Foreign Legion. He read the book and decided that if Marlene accepted Paramount's one-picture offer, this would be the basis for their next project together.

Leaving her husband and daughter behind, Marlene sailed for the United States on the *Bremen,* arriving in New York in mid-April, 1930, and after suitable press interviews traveled to the Coast. Although Adolph Zukor* was still president of the studio and Jesse L. Lasky* still first-vice-president, it was the 38-year-old Schulberg who had been instrumental in shaping the artistic course of the studio since his return there in 1926. With the departure that year of studio queen Gloria Swanson, and the incontestable fact that Polish import Pola Negri could not make the grade in America (for whatever reasons), Schulberg contractee Clara Bow, by natural selection, rose to assume the post as top drawing-card at the studio. In the last days of silent pictures, Nancy Carroll had shown great promise and would be a big Paramount asset till her career waned in the early 1930s. Sound films had ruined the further American cinema career of Emil Jannings who returned to Germany, and of Russian Olga Baclanova, who remained in the United States. However, Paramount had recently hired French boulevardier Maurice Chevalier and Hungarian actor Paul Lukas. More than European-oriented Universal Pictures under Carl Laemmle, Paramount was engaged in producing multilanguage versions of their pictures for foreign distribution. Thus there was a particularly congenial atmosphere at the studio for Continental talent like Marlene, and directors like von Sternberg, who had made a name for himself by helming a series of "realistic" dramas at Paramount: *The Last Command* (with Jannings); *Underworld* and *Drag-net* (both with George Bancroft and Evelyn Brent); and *Thunderbolt* (Bancroft and Fay Wray).

Perhaps the main driving force that persuaded Schulberg and Paramount to hire Marlene was the industry's obsessed search for another foreign exotic to duplicate the success of MGM's Greta Garbo. Throughout the 1930s, every film made by Marlene would be compared with those of her great predecessor on the Hollywood scene, Garbo.

Marlene's arrival in Hollywood was quieter than anticipated, because Paramount suddenly decided to await the opening of her first American-made feature before giving her the big publicity buildup. She was soon settled in an attractive Beverly Hills residence, complete with servants and a studio-provided Rolls Royce.

At the studio, von Sternberg began the transformation of the rather plump *hausfrau* into Marlene, the eternal female. Through a strict diet, massages, and cosmetic experiments, the legendary Marlene emerged with an Americanized figure, 36½–27½–38¼, topped by the immobile face with its slightly parted lips, hollow cheeks, exaggerated penciled eyebrows, and startling staring eyes unencumbered by obvious makeup. Capping it all was

*See Appendix.

her sleek blonde coiffure. It was not long before Marlene changed the standards of Hollywood and Western World beauty, with everyone jumping on the bandwagon in imitation.

Amy Jolly, retitled *Morocco,* premiered November 16, 1930, at the Rivoli Theatre. Its simplified plot set the standard for Marlene's future films under the von Sternberg banner. As Amy Jolly, a cabaret singer with a searing past, she arrives in Morocco aboard a tramp steamer. Aboard ship she has already refused the sophisticated proposal of wealthy Adolphe Menjou that he make life comfortable for her in the desert city. At a local cabaret where she is hired to sing, Marlene meets legionnaire Gary Cooper, the ungallant womanizer of his outfit. Her attraction to him is immediate, and is heightened when he rudely rejects her offer for a rendezvous—he is used to naming the time and the place. Later, they become lovers and he thinks of quitting the legion and taking her with him. But impulsively he changes his mind and she listlessly agrees to marry Menjou. However, before the marriage can take place, she learns that Cooper's legionnaire group has returned from a dangerous mission and he is thought dead. After much searching she locates him—of course, he is alive and well—and she discerns beneath his jaunty attitude that he cares for her deeply, though he is too set in his carefree ways to change his mode of life for her. The next morning, when the legionnaires embark for another encampment, she observes a group of women following the troops into the desert. Moments later, she yanks off her high-heeled shoes and silently tramps into the blowing sand to follow her man, irrationally content to be a camp follower for the man she loves, one of the legion of lost women.

The genius of *Morocco* lies in von Sternberg's ability to create the perfect romantic ambiance for this improbable love tale. With a variety of unique photographic effects, the lure of the desert is quickly established. The minimum of dialogue enhances the mystery of Marlene as femme fatale, constantly presented in an array of lush and sensuous camera angles. Von Sternberg did not want her sex appeal to depend on nudity, rather on the mystery of erotica. Her accented but perfect English added to her understated exoticism as she sang the ironic "What am I Bid for My Apples?" and "Give Me the Man." Her Amy Jolly fulfilled all the potential found in *Der blaue Engel.* With an economy of exposition she conveyed everything it was necessary to know about the world-weary sophisticate who on one hand could be blasé about kissing a woman full on the lips during her white-tie-and-black-tails club number and yet could be simplistically optimistic enough to follow her true love to an unknown future.

Gary Cooper was the top-billed star of *Morocco,* but it was Marlene (the ads billed her as "the woman all women want to see") who received the bulk of critical and audience attention. While Mordaunt Hall *(New York Times)* reported: "Her gamut of emotions here consists only of gazing intently, smiling and looking languid," it was more than enough for the public. Hollywood took heed of Marlene's tremendous screen impact and she was nominated for an Academy Award for her performance, but Marie Dressler won for *Min and Bill.*

It was generally assumed for a long time that von Sternberg was totally responsible for the camera angles, lighting, and shadows that accented Marlene's profile into classic prominence. Interviewed some 40 years after he was nominated for an Oscar for *Morocco,* cameraman Lee Garmes stated: "He [von Sternberg] left the lighting to me at all times. He was very particular about one thing only: sets. . . . Quite a lot of the picture was done in natural sunlight, rare at the time. The night scenes were shot at the Paramount ranch, and I did some of the best close-ups of Marlene Dietrich against a white wall there; it was artificially lit to simulate daylight. She still likes to have the north light to this day. She had a great mechanical mind, and knew the camera. She would always stop in the exact position that was right for her." Describing how he arrived at the lighting style used for Marlene, Garmes said: "Unfortunately I didn't have sufficient time to make tests of Marlene Dietrich; I had seen *The Blue Angel,* and based on that, I lit her with a sidelight, a half-tone, so that one half of her face was bright and the other half was in shadow. I looked at the first day's work and I thought, 'My God, I can't do this, it's exactly what Bill Daniels is doing with Garbo!' We couldn't, of course, have two Garbos! So, without saying anything to Jo, I changed to the north-light effect. He had no suggestions for changes, he went ahead and let me do what I wanted. The Dietrich face was my creation."

Paramount announced that Marlene would enact the hostess for the German-language edition of *Paramount on Parade* (1930), which seemingly did not take place; and she was also mentioned for *The Night Angel* (1931) which Nancy Carroll made. But Paramount did unleash a barrage of publicity about Marlene—it has been estimated that upwards of $3 million was eventually spent—claiming that the Teutonic wonder was the new successor to Greta Garbo on the screen and to the late Jeanne Eagels on the stage. As UFA had used the gimmick of posing Marlene as the incarnation of Thomas Gainsborough's "Blue Boy," so Paramount presented her as the modern "Mona Lisa" (via special effects) in a widely circulated photo layout.

Soon stories were circulating about "Svengali Joe" von Sternberg and his Trilby Marlene. She was rarely seen in public, except accompanied by von Sternberg, which led to rumors that off the set they were indulging in a torrid romance. (In 1932 von Sternberg's wife divorced the director and sued Marlene for $600,000, claiming alienation of affection and libel—Marlene contested the charge and proved her innocence.) On the set, von Sternberg ruled like a dictator, shooting and reshooting scene after scene in his determination to create perfect screen illusions to surround Marlene. She complied without noticeable complaint, and the crew dubbed the cooperative star the "pink angel."

Now that Marlene had established herself in America, Paramount released its English-language version of *Der blaue Engel* (shot simultaneously with the German edition). It opened at the Rialto Theatre on December 5, 1930. The harsh Germanic accents curtailed the American public's enthusiasm for *The Blue Angel,* and the studio would later reissue it in the original German version with English subtitles added. The *New York Times* reported that in *Der blaue Engel* Marlene was "much more the actress than she is in *Morocco.*" A pallid remake of *The Blue Angel*, starring Mai Britt, would be released in 1959 by Twentieth Century-Fox.

Marlene was sufficiently satisfied with the progress of her career to agree to continue with von Sternberg at Paramount. They both renewed their studio options at lucrative terms. (Reportedly, she would receive $125,-000 per film, von Sternberg was to be her director, and she would have control over all publicity about her—putting her at the top of the Paramount actress heap with one American-made film, giving her more favorable terms than top players Nancy Carroll, Ruth Chatterton, or Kay Francis had there.) Before beginning her next film, Marlene returned to Germany to visit with her husband and daughter. After directing Sylvia Sidney in *An American Tragedy* (1931), von Sternberg met her in Berlin with the script of *Dishonored* (1931) in hand, and they returned to California together.

Dishonored debuted March 5, 1931, at the Rialto Theatre, the same week as the opening of such other films as *The Easiest Way* (Constance Bennett), *Ten Cents A Dance* (Barbara Stanwyck), *Kiki* (Mary Pickford), and *Unfaithful* (Ruth Chatterton). *Dishonored* presented Marlene as an officer's widow turned streetwalker in World War I Vienna who is hired by the government as a spy. She is a recherché character to the hilt: "I am not afraid of life, although I am not afraid of death either." As agent X-27, she is successful in proving general Warner Oland a traitor aiding the Russians and he commits suicide. Now she must now track down Russian spy Victor McLaglen with whom Oland collaborated. She and McLaglen toy with each other in a cat-and-mouse game, with McLaglen trapping her at the Russian-Polish border where she has assumed the disguise of a peasant maid. She later escapes and when he follows her he is captured by the Austrians. Realizing she cares greatly for him, Marlene helps him to escape. For her efforts, she is sentenced to death as a traitor. She faces the firing squad, dressed in her preferred prostitute garb, and calmly applies her lipstick just before the guns are fired. Since she died in the line of duty, the final release title was certainly inappropriate.

Although McLaglen was far from the perfect leading man for Marlene (Cooper had refused the role, not wishing to work with von Sternberg again), *Dishonored* allowed her more latitude in which to maneuver as an actress and to create a variety of moods for her multifaceted characterization. As an intellectual-esthetic exercise, von Sternberg filled *Dishonored* with much interwoven symbolism. For instance, Marlene's ever-present black cat was used to reflect her changing moods. Richard Watts, Jr., *(New York Herald Tribune)* praised Marlene for "her almost lyrically ironic air of detachment." That Greta Garbo would appear in the similar *Mata Hari* (1932) to more convincing advantage, added to the studio-imposed competition for screen supremacy between the two film actresses. The temporary intrusion of Paramount's Tallulah Bankhead into the rivalry quickly ended when Bankhead retired in disgust from the screen in 1932 and returned to the stage. As time went on, Marlene would tire of the endless comparisons to Garbo, but she always spoke politely of the Swedish actress. Garbo, who was even more disinclined to chat with the press, is supposed to have once said, "But who is this Dietrich."

As soon as production concluded on *Dishonored,* Marlene returned to Berlin, which greatly upset von Sternberg, for he counted on her technical and intuitive sense to assist in the film's editing as she had done during *Der blaue Engel* and *Morocco.* When Marlene returned to Hollywood this time, she was accompanied by Sieber and Maria, who thereafter became a constant part of her entourage when in public. Meanwhile, Marlene's penchant for male attire (she wore pants, not slacks) had caught on in America and spread to Europe. Everywhere, women were following her example of wearing severely cut men's clothing and were adopting her cosmetic styles.

To quell the rumors that she was growing weary of her professional relationship with von Sternberg, Marlene advised the press: "Before I had my child, I stopped and looked at every child in the street, I was so crazy about all children. But now, when I have my own child, that is perfection. Why should I look at others; I feel that way about directors. I have the best —why should I look at others?"

When queried about her unusual marriage, Marlene offered the rationale: "When two people love one another, they should know how it is between them. I haven't a strong sense of possession towards a man. Maybe that's because I am not particularly feminine in my reactions. I never have been. Even when I was young I didn't want to attract boys—in fact, I very much wanted not to attract them. I had no beaux, no crushes, till I met my husband." With her husband and daughter completing her household, Marlene gave the perfect picture of domesticity in her select interviews. She would usually conclude the press meeting by offering the press samples of her cooking or some chosen recipe.

The first of Marlene's two 1932 releases, *Shanghai Express,* opened at the Rialto Theatre on February 17, 1932. It proved to be the most satisfying of Marlene's von Sternberg films and grossed over $3.7 million. It was helped enormously by Jules Furthman's tight script, which confined the bulk of the action to the steamy oriental express train as it travels from Peking to Shanghai during a period of internal unrest in China. Aboard are such diverse types as the infamous adventuress known as the "White Flower of China" (Marlene), a British Medical Corps officer (Clive Brook), a Western-educated Chinese girl with an uncertain past (Anna May Wong), a rebel leader disguised as an Eurasian merchant (Warner Oland), a gambling engineer (Eugene Pallette), a prissy boarding-house owner (Louise Closser Hale), a crippled dope smuggler (Gustav von Seyffertitz), a determined missionary (Lawrence Grant), and a dishonored former French officer (Emile Chautard); The film contains one of Marlene's best screen moments—high camp to some. She and Brook exchanged conversation outside her first-class compartment. Dressed all in black, and staring vacantly out the window, she informs her former lover: "Well, Doc, I've changed my name." He casually asks: "Married?" She, shaking her head in a slow, mocking voice. "No! It took more than one man to change my name to Shanghai Lily." She encased the impact of her statement with appropriately strong dramatic intensity. Thereafter, the Grand Hotel-like melodrama proceeds at a fast clip, with Marlene eventually agreeing to become Oland's mistress if the rebel leader will free Brook. She is spared the need for this sacrifice when Wong stabs Oland. She and Brook continue on to Shanghai and once there they plan their future together.

Garbed in an exotic yet stylish wardrobe created by Paramount's outstanding costume designer Travis Banton, Marlene reached the height of her von Sternberg apprenticeship in her most devastating screen role as a tramp. The *Times* of London observed: "Her acting finds its strength and impulses in her careful elimination of all emphasis, and the more seemingly careless and inconsequential her gestures the more surely do they reveal the particular shades and movements of her mind." The major weakness of *Shanghai Express* is the casting of overly sedate Brook as her tormented, stiff-upper-lip lover, his line readings constantly betraying the adult intention of the script. *Shanghai Express* would be remade as *Peking Express* (1951) with Corinne Calvet in Marlene's role.

With two such ego-possessed creatures as Marlene and von Sternberg, who both could manipulate fact and fancy into a suitable blend for any given moment, it is unlikely that the truth of their professional relationship will ever be fully known. Over the years both would refute their own and each other's statements about the other, depending on the particular status of their careers at the time. That Marlene endured for decades after concluding her working pact with von Sternberg and has outlived him gives her a decided edge in setting the record "straight." It was rumored at the time and was later reaffirmed in his glossy autobiography that von Sternberg wanted to terminate his association with Marlene by 1932. He is supposed to have said: "I have succeeded in the past three pictures, in keeping from the public the fact that Marlene Dietrich cannot act. I don't know if I can do it for this fourth picture." He reports in his book that the new studio creative head, Emanuel Cohen,* begged on his knees for von Sternberg to continue with Marlene and not wreak chaos on the new Paramount regime before it had even gotten started. Marlene was mentioned for roles in Ernest Hemingway's *A Farewell to Arms* (1932—which Helen Hayes did), *R.U.R.,* and a remake of *Blood and Sand.* Instead she starred in *Blonde Venus* (1932), based on an original story by von Sternberg, concocted posthaste as an alternative to the rash of inferior stories being submitted to him by Paramount for his protégée. This film attempted, unsuccessfully, to take the fashionable confession-sob genre and raise it to art, with Marlene the epitome of the noble wife and mother turned bad for the love of her husband and child. Paramount executives disapproved of the ending provided by von Sternberg for *Blonde Venus* and threatened to replace him on the project with director Richard Wallace. Marlene sided with von Sternberg and was put on suspension for a month. A compromise was reached and *Blonde Venus* proceeded into production.

The muddled plot line of *Blonde Venus* moved at a snail's pace and literally wandered all over the world. German café singer Marlene attracts Continental traveler Herbert Marshall, and he summarily marries her and brings her back to America, where he is a struggling research chemist. She gives birth to a son (Dickie Moore) and is a blissfully happy housewife, till she learns Marshall has contracted radium poisoning from his work and must go to Europe for a cure. She returns to her former singing profession to earn money, helped along by playboy Cary Grant who is more than intrigued with her, and who establishes her in a fancy apartment. The cured Marshall returns from Europe, discovers his wife's cozy situation, and demands custody of the child. She flees with her son, with Marshall's detectives always one step behind. After he finally obtains his son, she quickly reestablishes herself in show business and fast becomes the toast of Paris. Returning to New York, she visits Marshall, who by now realizes the truth. They reaffirm their love and look forward to a bright future with their son.

Blonde Venus premiered at the Paramount Theatre on September 23, 1932, and was generally disliked. "Too bad that the picture isn't as glamorous and interesting as Marlene herself" *(New York Herald Tribune)* was a typical critical reaction. Marlene had never looked lovelier, and her three song numbers provided an intriguing variation of costume and moods. In the famed Hot Voodoo interlude (clips of which appear in the compilation feature film *The Love Goddesses* (1965), Marlene sways onstage encased in a gorilla suit, which she slowly removes. She then dons a wild fuzzy blonde wig, and with spear and shield proceeds to move into her primitive-beat song; her other production ensembles find her in the sexually ambiguous white tuxedo, tie, and top hat, and finally she appears in a shimmering beaded gown carrying an oversized picture hat.

In *Blonde Venus,* von Sternberg extended Marlene's screen image to reflect her real-life absorption with her child: the mother love-sequences

*See Appendix.

are all idyllic if lachrymose, with Dickie Moore a less obnoxious child performer than was usually the case. Once again, it was the stodgy performance of the male lead, herein Herbert Marshall as the passive bluenose, which made the script's many weaknesses all the more apparent. In contrast, dapper Grant in his small role gave a boost to the banal proceedings. By late 1932 the degradation genre had been overworked, and viewers were not impressed as "From dive to dive, she [Marlene] becomes more picturesquely slattern." Even Garbo's ludicrous *Susan Lenox, Her Fall and Rise* (1931) offered more enduring moments of credible dramatics.

Marlene's husband Sieber had been given a position with Paramount's Joinville Studio operation in Europe in 1932, and after *Blonde Venus* Marlene went overseas to join him. There were rumors that Marlene might try the Broadway stage and appear in Ernst Lubitsch's* musical, with a score by Dmitri Tiomkin and dances by Albertina Rasch, but it was more likely a press agent's dream. Director von Sternberg meanwhile traipsed down to the West Indies, hopefully to film a storm in the making for the next Marlene project *The Hurricane,* a circus story scripted by Jules Furthman.

When Marlene returned to America in May, 1932, she was greeted by an anonymous threat to kidnap her daughter Maria. When this episode quieted down, the gossip columns lighted on Marlene's close friendship with Paramount star Maurice Chevalier.

When von Sternberg abandoned *The Hurricane* to work on *The Scarlet Empress* (1934), Paramount suggested that Marlene accept Rouben Mamoulian as director of *Song of Songs* (1933), a new reworking of Hermann Sudermann's *Lily Czepanek,* previously filmed with Elsie Ferguson and then with Pola Negri. Marlene initially objected, which brought her conflict with the studio to a head. She stormed out in June, 1932, claiming Paramount was trying to worm two pictures from her for the price of one. By January, 1933, the studio had begun legal suit for $200,000 damages, and imported Dorothea Wieck (German star of *Mädchen in Uniform*) as a threat to Dietrich, just as Britisher Sari Maritza had been signed for the same purposes in 1931. It was von Sternberg who persuaded Marlene to agree to the project, and once Fredric March was replaced by Brian Aherne —making his American film debut—filming began in February, 1933.

Song of Songs, pictorially and symbolically a resplendent feast, was a dud as cinema entertainment for the masses. Naive German peasant Marlene travels to Berlin to live with her aunt (Alison Skipworth). She is wooed by sculptor Aherne whom she poses for when not working in her aunt's bookshop. However, she marries the lecherous baron Lionel Atwill. She is transformed into a lady of class, but scampers away when Aherne reenters her tormented life. Aherne eventually locates her, now a shady lady employed as a songstress in a Berlin nightclub. At the fade-out he proposes marriage and she accepts.

The combination of Lionel Atwill's over-emphatic villain and Aherne's wavering esthete gave Marlene no viable support to help carry the artistically beautiful pageant. Critics noted Marlene's ability to handle a full-blown human characterization with decent credibility, even in ludicrous melodrama. As in *Blonde Venus,* she is first seen as a virginal country girl, who, although later corrupted by city ways, can still emerge regenerated by the man whom she loves. The *New York Times* observed: "She realizes the full impact of her climactic scenes by understating her acting."

*See Appendix.

Paramount's publicity for *Song of Songs* emphasized the erotic aspects of the story, particularly the nude statue of Marlene sculpted by Aherne (in the film she is only shown naked to the shoulder). Plaster of Paris replicas of the statue placed in theatre lobbies throughout the country did not noticeably boost audience attendance, although this Mamoulian pastiche did better business than *Blonde Venus*. Marlene's only full song in the film was Frederick Hollander's "Johnny," which she had previously recorded in German, and now sang in an English version. (She would later blithely state in her nightclub act that no English lyrics had ever been written for the tune.) Another number, "You Are My Song of Songs," was eliminated from the final release print. *Song of Songs* was banned in Germany as being immoral. More to the point was the fact that Marlene had shown no affection for the rising Nazi political faction. She and Douglas Fairbanks, Jr., would be heard in an adaption of *Song of Songs* on "Lux Radio Theatre" (December 20, 1937, CBS).

Marlene's strong position at Paramount dimmed in 1933 not only because of the poor showing of her last two films, but primarily because of the cyclonic arrival of Mae West on the lot in 1932. It was Mae West who would be credited with saving the studio from near-insolvency by the spectacular success of her pictures *She Done Him Wrong* and *I'm No Angel*. Marlene was still regarded by the studio regime as a valuable prestige property who was not to be unduly upset. Therefore, it allowed Marlene and von Sternberg to film *Her Regiment of Lovers,* based on an alleged diary of Catherine the Great. The film's later working title was *Catherine the Great,* but since Alexander Korda had completed his *Catherine the Great* (1934) in England, the Paramount version was again retitled to *The Scarlet Empress*. No one was quite prepared for the excesses that von Sternberg demanded on this $900,000 production. However, he must be credited with continually devising imaginative substitutes to flesh out the film, such as utilizing old footage from the Paramount vaults. Swiss sculptor Peter Ballbusch and German painter Richard Kollorz were imported to assist studio art director Hans Dreier in suggestively recreating the lavish majesty of imperial Russia with its Byzantine statuary, ikons, and set pieces strewn everywhere in camera range. The elaborate costuming was equally as expensive as the recreation of the eerie Peterhof Palace. All this work was to provide the background for Von Sternberg's elaborate tapestry of history. The director stated: "I intend it to be not necessarily an authentic work, but something beautiful to appeal to the eye and the senses" (clearly not the province of the mass audience).

With maddening relentlessness, *The Scarlet Empress* sacrifices every required element of an entertaining motion picture to focus on the stunning visual effects. The young German Princess Sophia Frederica (Marlene) is betrothed to a Russian prince, Grand Duke Peter (Sam Jaffe). The shy princess is overwhelmed at the palace by the decadent Empress Elizabeth (Louise Dresser) and horrified that the halfwit Peter is to be her groom. Disillusioned by the horrendous mismatch, she is soon transformed from a pathetically eager princess to a reckless court playgirl who revels in the palace's dissolute life. When the empress dies and the new emperor plots to murder her, Marlene, now an iron-willed autocrat, leads the army and peasants in a revolt. She is crowned Catherine, Empress of all Russia.

By the time *The Scarlet Empress* premiered on September 14, 1934, at the Paramount Theatre, the British-made *Catherine the Great* starring

Elisabeth Bergner, Douglas Fairbanks, Jr., and Flora Robson had already passed into release. Not only did it greatly lessen the box-office potential of *The Scarlet Empress,* but it also provided a high standard of satisfactory drama and performance that was most certainly not matched by the American picture. The *New York Times* lambasted von Sternberg for accomplishing "the improbable feat of smothering the enchanting Marlene Dietrich under his technique." "[She] has become a hapless sort of automaton" criticized the *New York Herald Tribune.* Those fragments of characterization which did survive the von Sternberg live recreation ensemble were negative attributes: as the royal Catherine, Marlene lacked the required imperial authority, although for a woman of 33 she offered a most convincing portrayal of an unsure 16-year-old in the early segments. Jaffe's mad Peter was a laughable Harpo Marx-ish caricature and Dresser was too American as the improvident Russian empress. John Lodge as Marlene's first Russian lover was appropriately dashing, and Marlene's own daughter Maria, in her screen debut, was pretty if ineffectual as the very young Sophia Frederica.

The Scarlet Empress had a short Broadway run, even with the added lure of the Fokine Ballet stage show to boost attendance. Nor were audiences around the country interested in this museum piece, where implausibility reaches new heights as Marlene, clad in her military dress uniform, gallops up the palace steps on her white charger. Leading the revolutionists onward, she looked more bewildered than imperturbable in this theatrical gesture.

While filming this debacle, Marlene confided to the press: "No, I am not like those actresses who have a story they have wanted all their lives to make. I have none. But then I am not an actress, no. Perhaps that is the secret." Once again Marlene lost out in the "competition" with Garbo. Although MGM's *Queen Christina* (1934) was not a box-office bonanza, it contained a good Garbo performance.

A projected picture, *Lorelei,* with script by John Dos Passos, and directed by von Sternberg, did not come about, so Marlene went abroad. When she returned, Emanuel Cohen had dropped to independent producer at the studio, and producer-director Ernst Lubitsch, no friend to the von Sternberg school of film-making, was in creative charge at Paramount. Nevertheless, Lubitsch agreed to the making of *Caprice Espagno,* based on Pierre Louys' *Le Femme et le Pantin* ("The Woman and the Puppet") (1935) which would conclude von Sternberg's Paramount contract. It had been previously filmed in 1920 with opera star Geraldine Farrar as the conscienceless Spanish temptress. Von Sternberg, who had conducted the music for *The Scarlet Empress,* announced that not only would he direct this production, but he would photograph it as well, assisted by Lucien Ballard.

The finished product was retitled by Lubitsch *The Devil Is a Woman* and premiered at the Paramount Theatre on May 3, 1935. For the average filmgoer it was a prodigious bore. Set in 1890s Seville, it cast Marlene as the devastating Concha Perez, who is about to ensnare political refugee Cesar Romero. He encounters an old army comrade. Lionel Atwill, who was once a respectable member of the military and is now a jobless wanderer. Atwill confides to the beguiled Romero his past passion for Marlene and how she had willfully drained him of money and vitality on several occasions. Romero will not heed the advice and the two engage in a pistol duel. Atwill is severely wounded. Marlene has packed to leave for Paris with Romero, but at the border changes her mind and returns to Atwill. The future is unknown but past patterns of behavior have been well charted.

The Devil Is a Woman, which cost approximately $800,000, was a financial failure. Audiences were no longer entranced by ever-lengthening variations of Marlene's scenic posing in the many faces and moods of love. Andrew Sennwald of the *New York Times* was one of the few intellectually stimulated by the film's "sly urbanity" and its "cruel and mocking assault upon the romantic sex motif." Others criticized Marlene for her "pouts and poses" and stated that "her lines are inane and the situations utterly silly."

The Devil Is a Woman gained some small notoriety when, in October, 1935, the Spanish government demanded worldwide withdrawal of the picture, claiming it "insults the Spanish armed forces," citing in particular that it showed Spanish soldiers drinking. (Not mentioned in the charge was the foolish characterization of Edward Everett Horton as the Spanish chief of police who would as soon shoot wrongdoers as arrest them.) On November 19, 1935, Paramount acceded to the Spanish request and withdrew *The Devil Is a Woman* from release. This picture was sufficient to end von Sternberg's Paramount career, demonstrating even to his studio champions that he was too esoteric and expensive for the stockholders' good. The fact that Joel McCrea had walked out of *The Devil Is a Woman* (Cesar Romero replaced him), and publicly announced that "All the spontaneity was being directed out of me," added further weight to the rumors that von Sternberg was in trouble. To top matters off the director had thrown out his trump card—Marlene's insistence that she would work only with him—when he announced during the production of *The Devil Is a Woman* "Fraulein Dietrich and I have progressed as far as possible together. My being with Dietrich any further will not help her or me. If we continued we would get into a pattern which would be harmful to both of us."

The Devil Is a Woman was always a personal favorite of both von Sternberg and Marlene. Her own print of the film was shown at the Museum of Modern Art's Marlene Dietrich retrospective in 1959. When the feature was revived at the New Yorker Theatre in 1961, she explained to the *New York Times:* "One of the modern elements of the film is its strong strain of ambiguity. In the end, the woman unexpectedly leaves the man she loves to return to the middle-aged officer she has ruined." To another interviewer, she said: "It is difficult to convey a glamorous image on the screen. I'd hate to see anyone else try the kind of thing we did in *The Devil Is a Woman.*" The story would be remade in Mexico as *The Devil Is a Woman* (1950) with Maria Felix, and in France as *La Femme et le Pantin* (1960) with Brigitte Bardot.

With von Sternberg officially through at Paramount—he did act as Marlene's consultant for a time—Gary Cooper agreed to appear opposite Marlene again in a contemporary romance yarn, *The Pearl Necklace* (retitled *Desire*), to be directed by Frank Borzage and produced under the personal supervision of Ernst Lubitsch. The latter was intrigued by the possibility of revealing a new Marlene as a living human being rather than the withdrawn femme fatale she had been in the fantasy world of von Sternberg's efforts. It was a remake of *Die Schönen Tage in Aranjuez* (1933) which had starred Brigette Helm, one of the actresses originally considered for the *Der blaue Engel* lead.

Desire premiered April 12, 1936, at the Paramount and was well received. The liberated Marlene appeared as a swank jewel thief who hides a stolen pearl necklace in Cooper's jacket pocket when passing through customs at the Spanish border. She exercises all her ingenuity and wiles to retrieve the expensive bauble, meanwhile becoming enamored of the

American engineer. When put to a choice, she renounces her confederates, returns the necklace, marries Cooper, and then departs for Detroit with him. Kate Cameron in her three-and-a-half star *New York Daily News* review reported: "[She] has come out of the trance she's been in for so long and acts once more like a flesh and blood heroine." Beautifully gowned by Travis Banton, Marlene crooned one Frederick Hollander-Leo Robin song, "Awake in a Dream," and beneath her elegant veneer revealed a latent ability to project wry humor and infectious charm. Marlene and Herbert Marshall were heard in *Desire* on "Lux Radio Theatre" (March 15, 1937).

Paramount, having exhausted the Marlene-Garbo feud, played up the supposed hostilities existing between Marlene and the equally illustrious studio luminary, Mae West. Marlene, who had never run into West on the soundstages or about town, paid a visit to the "blonde bombshell" on the set of *Klondike Annie.* Marlene reported: "She was very kind to me. And she's such a witty woman." Meanwhile, Marlene was seen socially with John Gilbert, age 40, former beau of Garbo, and still the husband of actress Virginia Bruce. That Marlene could be all things to all people, given the proper setting, was demonstrated by her dazzling appearance at Countess di Frasso's costume ball, dressed as Leda and the Swan. Earlier in 1935 she had equally amazed the public when photographs appeared of her and Claudette Colbert romping down a slide together at Carole Lombard's come-as-you-are-party held at the Venice Amusement Park. Both Paramount stars had arrived wearing masculine togs.

Paramount next cast Marlene as the chambermaid in *I Loved a Soldier,* a remake of Pola Negri's silent feature, *Hotel Imperial* (her one big American-made success). With Charles Boyer as her costar, and Henry Hathaway directing the John Van Druten screenplay, production got underway on January 3, 1936. Marlene feuded with producer Benjamin Glazer and he withdrew, leaving Lubitsch and Hathaway to film around Marlene's scenes while script changes to her satisfaction were being made. During this time, Lubitsch was replaced by William LeBaron* as head of Paramount production, and a further rift developed between star and front office. Marlene walked off the picture on February 11, 1936. At that point *I Loved a Soldier* had already cost $900,000. (Margaret Sullavan was borrowed from Universal to replace Marlene, but shortly after filming recommenced, she tripped over a lighting cable, breaking her left forearm. Paramount eventually shelved the project until 1939 when it reshot the screenplay as *Hotel Imperial,* starring Ray Milland and European import Isa Miranda, a look-a-like for Marlene.)

Marlene sailed for London in March, 1936, and when she returned the next month, ably negotiated a sturdy new Paramount contract. On her consent, she was loaned to David O. Selznick for *The Garden of Allah* (1936) when Garbo declined the role. Originally Selznick had contracted Merle Oberon for the lead in this remake of the Alice Terry silent feature, and he had to pay Oberon $25,000 in an out-of-court settlement. Marlene negotiated the then hefty salary of $200,000 for herself in this $2.2 million technicolor extravaganza.

Most everyone concerned with *The Garden of Allah* project, except Selznick, admitted it was hopelessly dated folderol, but he pushed ahead with location filming in the Mohave desert under Richard Boleslawski's direction. *The Garden of Allah* premiered at Radio City Music Hall on

*See Appendix.

November 19, 1936, and met with adverse reactions. The three-color photography was admired for its unobtrusive beauty (cameramen W. Howard Greene and Harold Rosson won Oscars) and the Max Steiner music score was endorsed. But the static scenario was termed "a pretty dull affair" (Variety). Marlene was a lustrous painted doll as the disenchanted Domini Enfielden who seeks peace of mind in the Algerian desert, and once there is spellbound by mysterious Boyer. They marry and on their desert honeymoon she learns his secret: he has broken Trappist vows, fleeing his monastery. She convinces him he must return to make amends with God. The ambiguously effete portrayal by French-accented Boyer, combined with Marlene's German-toned "sleep-walker," badly accentuated the sluggishness of the melodrama.

On June 2, 1936, Marlene was heard on "Lux Radio Theatre" in the initial broadcast (CBS) of The Legionnaire and the Lady, an adaptation of Morocco, with Clark Gable as her leading man.

When her past director Alexander Korda offered Marlene the unheard-of-sum of $450,000 plus expenses to star in an adaptation of James Hilton's Without Armour, Marlene sailed to England to appear opposite Robert Donat under Frenchman Jacques Feyder's direction. In Knight Without Armour (1937), Marlene was Countess Alexandra, widowed during the Bolshevik Revolution of 1917. She relies on British translator Robert Donat to aid her in escaping the Red purge. The episodic drama is filled with vignettes of prewar and postwar White and Red Russian life, but many thought it looked more like a Drury Lane musical. Marlene lacked the necessary exuberance of youth and interest, having "an air of unpardonable complacence at times as though she had just turned from a mirror" (New York Times). Others wondered if her enormous salary was merited by her taking "... two baths, revealing her beautiful legs, and shedding a hollow-cheeked glamour through 9,000 feet of British film" (Life magazine). Knight Without Armour, opening at the Radio City Music Hall on July 8, 1937, was not the box-office bonanza anticipated.

While in England, Marlene participated in London's swirling social life, most often accompanied by Douglas Fairbanks, Jr., and making the acquaintance of such celebrities as Noel Coward and Cecil Beaton. In Paris she hobnobbed with Erich Maria Remarque. During her London filming, Marlene was approached by representatives of Nazi Germany, who asked her to return to Germany to make films. She adamantly refused. When she returned to Los Angeles in March, 1937, she applied for her first papers towards American citizenship. Marlene announced: "I am working and living in America and my interests are here. I feel I should be a citizen of this great country." She became an American citizen on June 9, 1939.

Ernst Lubitsch, now an independent producer-director at Paramount, reunited with Marlene in Angel, which debuted November 3, 1937, at the Paramount Theatre. It offered Marlene as the modish neglected wife of British nobleman Herbert Marshall. On a Parisian lark, she visits her old friend Laura Hope Crews, madam of a swanky brothel. Marlene is mistaken as one of the girls by American Melvyn Douglas and she coyly goes along with the ruse. She later reencounters Douglas in London and must choose between him and her suddenly ardent husband. The famed Lubitsch touch faltered in Angel, and the film emerged too stagey and permeated with "the persistent odor of decay." The completely liberated screen Marlene received her full share of critical abuse: "The film comes to a full stop every time she raises or lowers the artificially elongated Dietrich eyelids—and she hoists them up and down at one-minute intervals like the strong man handling a 1,000-pound weight in a sideshow" *(New York Times)*. "[There] is scarcely a sequence in which one is not conscious that she is more aware of camera angles than the vitalizing of an intriguing character."

During production of *Angel,* Marlene and Lubitsch came to an impasse over the "direction," she insisting upon a wealth of studied close-ups of herself, he secretly adding footage of the other principals when she had left for the day. It was during this film that rumors leaked out that Marlene's famous masklike countenance was showing signs of age—there were wrinkles.

When Marlene turned up number 126 on the list of 1937 box-office attractions, the William LeBaron regime at Paramount paid her $200,000 not to appear in the scheduled *French Without Tears* (it was made in 1940 with Ellen Drew opposite Ray Milland) and tersely announced, "Marlene Dietrich will be permitted to work elsewhere." Another project, *Midnight,* which Paramount had planned for Marlene, would be made in 1939 with Claudette Colbert.

Although Marlene was considered washed up in Hollywood, she was able to negotiate one-picture commitments—at much lower salary fees—at Columbia and at Warner Brothers (she was to do a remake of *One Way Passage*). However, the studios and the star could not agree on a suitable project, and it was decided that her picture agreements for each company would be held for a later date.

Marlene embarked on a series of trans-Atlantic trips. During one of her London stays, she had a visit from Joachim von Ribbentrop, former German ambassador to the Court of St. James's, who brought a personal request from Adolph Hitler that Marlene return to her homeland to star in motion pictures. Marlene again declined. The projected *The Image* (1938) for French director Julien Duvivier never materialized.

On the advice of von Sternberg, Marlene agreed to return to Hollywood to star in a Western spoof for Universal, *Destry Rides Again* (1939). Her salary was a low $75,000 and she was a substitute for that studio's initial choice, Paramount's new star, Paulette Goddard. *Destry Rides Again* was released November 29, 1939, and revived Marlene's badly sagging film career. As *Der blaue Engel* had been the first turning point in her movie image, so *Destry Rides Again* was the second. She moved from ladies' pictures to he-man actioners with grace and ease. If she felt any discomfort or disdain for this strategic transformation, she kept her feelings to herself. *Variety* appraised Marlene's efforts: "Her work as the hardened, ever-scrapping ginmill entertainer serves pretty much as the teeterboard from which this picture flips itself from the level of the ordinary western into a class item." Quipped one reviewer ". . . [It took her] off her high horse and placed her in a horse opera."

Destry Rides Again was a rousing remake of Tom Mix's earlier straight Western *Destry,* and showcased Marlene as Frenchy, the premiere entertainer at Brian Donlevy's rough and tumble Long Chance saloon in the Western town of Bottle Neck. Whether chanting in her beer baritone "The Boys in the Back Room" to the crowds, brawling with enraged townswoman Una Merkel, or handing meek deputy James Stewart a mop and pail to clean up the town, Marlene was the rugged, independent soul. She revealed her heart of gold when she sacrificed her life to save Stewart from Donlevy's pistol shot. No longer was Marlene the untouchable woman—now she was an accessible broad with rouged cheeks and a zest for life that perked up in rugged masculine surroundings. Her scrap with Merkel was billed by Universal as "The Greatest Feminine Fist Fight Ever Filmed," and Marlene, anxious to prove her new image 100 percent, used no doubles for the stunt work, which required five hectic days before the scene was captured on film. Besides the memorable "Boys in the Back Room," Frederick Hollander and Frank Loesser composed the equally telling "You've Got that Look" and "Little Joe the Wrangler." *Destry Rides Again* would be remade as *Frenchy* (1950) with Shelley Winters, and in 1954 with Mari Blanchard, and also became a moderately successful Broadway musical.

In a beautiful legs contest dreamed up by some Hollywood press agents in 1939, Marlene's renowned gams placed fourth, with Virginia Gilmore, Ann Sheridan, and Linda Darnell in the three top spots.

When Marlene sailed for Europe in July, 1939, aboard the S. S. *Normandie,* the United States government attempted to seize her luggage, claiming she owed $142,000 in past taxes. The federal men finally settled for a box of Marlene's jewelry as collateral and Marlene the businesswoman later proved that, on the contrary, the tax bureau owed her a substantial refund.

With the box-office success of *Destry Rides Again,* Marlene was pacted by Universal for a series of features. *Seven Sinners,* once offered to Mae West, premiered at the Rivoli Theatre on November 17, 1940, and was a more than worthy follow-up. Marlene was Bijou Blanche, the infamous cabaret singer, ejected from countless South Seas islands for creating too much tropical unrest. She lands at Boni-Komba, and instantly takes a shine to stalwart naval officer John Wayne, but trouble is already brewing. (As one character says, "We don't need her around. The Navy already has plenty of destroyers.") While island-bound, she hires on as chanteuse at Billy Gilbert's Seven Sinners Cafe. Her competing admirers stage a tremendous free-for-all there, and she finds herself shipping out again. On board, she meets her old suitor Albert Dekker, a reformed drunkard who promises to be a lively traveling companion.

Marlene's varied and fantastic wardrobe for *Seven Sinners* was whipped up by costume designer Irene, bedecking Marlene with an amazing assortment of feathers, jewelry, and eye-catching unsubtle frocks. None were more enigmatically fascinating than her Navy ensign's uniform, complete with cap, worn while singing "The Man's in the Navy" (film clips of which appear in *Myra Breckinridge*). Her other memorable Frederick Hollander-Frank Loesser number was "I've Been in Love Before." Bosley Crowther *(New York Times)* aptly penned: "Her Bijou Blanche in *Seven Sinners* is a delightfully subtle spoof of all the Sadie Thompsons and Singapore Sals that have stirred the hot blood of cool customers south and east of Manila Bay. If Miss Dietrich and her comedies were just a little broader, Mae West would be in the shade." The picture would be remade as *South Seas Sinner,* with Shelley Winters again essaying one of Marlene's old roles.

In 1941 Marlene announced: "Of course I'm going to quit working. I want a chance really to see a bit of life before I die. . . . A film star's career must necessarily be brief. It can last only as long as one's youth lasts, and one's youth fades far quicker on the screen than on the stage. The public can be fooled on the stage, but never on the screen—and I'm going to quit while I'm still at the top."

Not heeding her own words, Marlene starred in *The Flame of New Orleans,* which opened at the Rivoli Theatre on April 25, 1941. It was a toss-up whether the film focused more on Marlene, a European adventuress who arrives in 1941 New Orleans seeking fresh wealth, or on the cinematic style of French refugee director Rene Clair, making his American film debut. The satiric tongue-in-cheek Clair touch abounded, but more as an intrusion than an overall asset. Some scenes were severely cut to please the censors. As the gold digger with an eye on banker Roland Young's fortune, Marlene sacrifices security for love and runs off with seaman Bruce Cabot. Marlene sang "Sweet as the Blush of May." *Variety* said: "Her attempts at coyness miss badly," but the feature was popular fare for escapist World War II audiences.

Warner Brothers then utilized Universal's hot mature property to costar with Edward G. Robinson (he received top billing) and George Raft in *Manpower* (Strand Theatre, July 4, 1941). There was much publicity during the filming, detailing Marlene's new on-the-set mirror unit which stood six feet high and contained such built-in equipment as a reclining chair, jewel box, makeup kit, and crystal vases. Marlene—so it was reported—relaxed on the set by entertaining the crew with doleful cowboy tunes played on her musical saw, a far cry from the aloof super star of the 1930s. *Manpower* was an assembly-line Warner Brothers triangular drama, with Marlene as clip joint hostess Fay Duval who marries admirer Robinson but really desires his power lineman pal Raft. When Robinson is accidentally killed in a fight with Raft, the path is clear for the two lovers to be together. Marlene blended well in this Raoul Walsh-directed actioner, singing two songs, "I'm in No Mood for Music Tonight" and "He Lied and I Listened." As the *New York Times* penned: "She does what she has to do well, but she's in to make trouble—and that's all." The "doing" consisted of looking sexy, playing at domesticity with Robinson, getting slapped around by the leads, crooning in her mock torchy style, and projecting her tough but vulnerable character to the hilt. For this film Marlene wore bangs, a hairdo that would be duplicated by Barbara Stanwyck in her later *Double Indemnity.* The star trio recreated *Manpower* on "Lux Radio Theatre" (March 16, 1942).

Columbia then starred Marlene in *The Lady Is Willing* (1942), hiring Paramount's Mitchell Leisen to direct her in this lightweight comedy, and that studio's Fred MacMurray as her vis-à-vis. She plays a scatterbrained musical comedy star with maternal instincts, who decides to raise an abandoned baby and allows herself to become infatuated with pedestrian pediatrician MacMurray. The finale was a piece of outrageous dramatics: Marlene, in her Irene-designed costume, attempts to get through her stage show production number "Strange Things" while awaiting word of the condition of the baby, who has undergone an emergency operation.

During production of *The Lady Is Willing,* Marlene fell on the set one day while carrying baby actor David James in her arms. She instinctively protected the infant in her fall, and severely sprained her ankle. Shooting continued, but to conceal Marlene's right leg being in a cast, she was always shown in full-length outfits (from gowns to slacks) and there was only one quick flash of her famed limbs, revealed in shadow. The feature passed muster, but the *New York Times* thought the comic incongruity of Marlene bouncing a baby on her knee was "a stagey exhibition in rather revolting taste."

Her second 1942 release was Universal's remake of *The Spoilers*, in which John Wayne and Randolph Scott vie for the affection of gin club owner Marlene in 1900 Nome, Alaska. The big moment in this fourth remake of Rex Beach's lusty novel was the climatic brawl between Wayne and Scott. Marlene was praised for outwesting Mae West as the most colorful gal of the gold rush days; she sashays about in low-cut gowns and silk net hose, and proves again that her legs "are not just a means of transportation." Universal would remake *The Spoilers* yet again in 1955 with Anne Baxter.

Marlene's most constant escort in Hollywood now was French actor Jean Gabin, age 39. He had escaped the German occupation and was now making films in America. Marlene's husband, Sieber, was employed by Universal's foreign department.

The trio of Marlene, John Wayne, and Randolph Scott was reunited in an update rehash of the plot of *The Spoilers,* entitled *Pittsburgh,* which was released in February, 1943. Marlene escapes her lowly origin as a Pennsylvania coal miner's daughter by becoming the mistress of a crooked fight promoter. She transfers her affections to coalminers Wayne and Scott, later marrying the up-and-coming steel executive Scott when Wayne goes highbrow and weds Louise Allbritton, daughter of a steel tycoon. Interweaved in this history of Pittsburgh's growth as a steel town is a pervading World War II patriotism. The fade-out finds Marlene, Wayne, and Scott locked arm in arm, with a plea to the audience to support Allied unity.

The routine *Pittsburgh* did far less business at theatres than had *The Spoilers,* and Marlene wisely concluded her barroom hostess period in Hollywood, in which as, Arthur Knight observed, "all her new employers could see was a sleazy, sexy hussy for strong men to fight over."

In March, 1943, Marlene volunteered her services to the United States Entertainment Organization (USO), and a few weeks later she landed in North Africa to begin what amounted to a three-year tour of liberated countries from Africa to the Aleutians. Her act consisted of comedy sketches, a mock strip, a telepathy routine, singing, and playing the musical saw, with her wardrobe ranging from a khaki fatigue outfit to evening gowns. Reportedly Marlene sold over $100,000-worth of her jewelry to finance her years of touring. With the same devoted abandon that had characterized her film and social career, Marlene now gave herself over to entertaining servicemen. She was particularly liked by the GIs for being democratic enough to hobnob with them on many occasions on the chow lines and at the hospitals, rather than mix exclusively with the officers for the VIP treatment usually accorded celebrities.

In between tours, Marlene made a guest appearance in Universal's all-star musical *Follow the Boys* (1944) as the turban-clad woman sawed in half by magician Orson Welles in Welles's Mercury Wonder Show sketch. In MGM's *Kismet* (1944) starring a static Ronald Colman, Marlene had the brief but showy role of Jamilla, dancing mistress of grand vizier Edward Arnold. With a $3 million plus budget, this version of the much-filmed Edward Knobloch play was directed at a slow pace by William Dieterle, but contained enough colorful spectacle to qualify as money-making escapist fare. Most noteworthy was Marlene's exotic interpretative dance "dressed, coiffed and enameled like a candy maker's masterpiece." Originally, Marlene was to wear pants of gold chain mail in this well-publicized production number. The mail continually broke, however, so her legs were painted in shimmering gold instead. The *New Yorker* noted: "She looks good and takes it easy." When televised, this World War II edition of *Kismet* is called *Oriental Dreams,* to avoid confusion with MGM's 1955 musical version starring Ann Blyth and Howard Keel, with Dolores Gray in Marlene's role.

On one visit back to the United States during the war, Marlene recorded several of her famous songs and other popular numbers in German versions for the Office of Political Warfare. Marlene later remarked: "I've often been dissatisfied with my work. But by recording these 'adapted' songs I believe I have done something really worthwhile."

Marlene received several Broadway offers, such as Oscar Wilde's *An Ideal Husband* to be produced by Alfred Fisher, and the musical version of W. Somerset Maugham's *Sadie Thompson*. However, she declined, stating: "Anyone who has played for soldiers audiences overseas is not going to be satisfied with any other kind of audience for a long time."

In March, 1945, Marlene was performing at the Stage Door Canteen in liberated Paris. In mid-1945, she journeyed to Berlin to visit her mother, who died November 6, 1945, of a heart attack at age 69, and to learn that her sister Elizabeth had survived internment in a Nazi concentration camp. Marlene had planned an additional Army hospital and camp tour, but a jaw infection prevented it.

Of her wartime efforts, Marlene has said: "It is the only important thing I've ever done."

Marlene agreed to star in French director Marcel Carne's film *Les Portes de la Nuit* (1946) in order to rebuild her depleted bank account. But she, and Jean Gabin who was to costar, disliked the script, and instead they appeared in *Martin Roumagnac* (1946), directed by George Lacombe. She portrayed a well-to-do widow in a French provincial town who is loved by builder Gabin. When he discovers she is a high-priced tart on the side, he kills her and is later murdered himself by one of her rejected suitors. Retitled *The Room Upstairs* and with 30 minutes of the sexy scenes excised, the French-language feature had spotty release in America in late 1948. Marlene was branded "uncommonly coy" in this "ponderous, hard-breathing drama."

She was scheduled to make other French films at the time, including one with Raimu (canceled because of his death), the role of death in Jean Cocteau's *Orphée* (eventually made in 1950), and *Dedée D'Anvers,* but none of these came to pass. When she returned to the United States in 1947, Marlene was awarded the Medal Of Freedom; it was presented to her by General Maxwell D. Taylor.

At a time when Hollywood was undergoing the post-World War II retrenchment of production, Marlene made her bid for a return to the American cinema. The combination of her past allure, her name continually in the news throughout her years of service camp touring, and the novelty of her making a Hollywood movie appearance after more than three years' absence, were sufficient to convince director Mitchell Leisen and Paramount that it was a safe bet to offer her the gypsy fortune-teller role in *Golden Earrings* (1947). Moreover, the top-billed role in the film was going to Ray Milland, whose recent Oscar-winning performance in *Lost Weekend,* would insure substantial audience interest in this project.

In *Golden Earrings.* Millard essayed the British intelligence officer who relies on wise gypsy Marlene to assist him in sneaking a poison gas formula out of Nazi Germany. The publicity ads announced: "The incomparable Marlene, as a wild and fabulous Gypsy coquette . . . kissing into submission a man who defied the startling challenge of her golden earrings!" Marlene devised her own makeup and costuming; dark brown body dye, a greasy black wig, dangling bracelets and golden earrings, and chewing garlic. That her famed legs were hidden beneath gypsy rags and her bewitching accent reduced to pidgin gypsy, even for the bits of gypsy songs she sang, were offset for many by her "competence as a comedienne." The picture's too wildly absurd premise prevented *Golden Earrings* from becoming top-notch box-office.

It was in *A Foreign Affair* (1948) that Marlene, age 47, reestablished herself as a respected box-office attraction. This Billy Wilder production top-cast another former Paramount studio player, Jean Arthur. Marlene was initially opposed to portraying Erika von Schuletow, the former mistress of a top-ranking Nazi officer, who earns her keep in post-World War II Berlin by singing at the Lorelei basement cabaret and engaging in the black market. (June Havoc tested for the role.) The part proved a personal triumph for Marlene. "For in Miss Dietrich's restless femininity, in her subtle suggestions of mocking scorn and in her daringly forward singing. . . . are centered not only the essence of the picture's romantic allure, but also its vagrant cynicism and its unmistakable point." *(New York Times).* Marlene as the nightclub tramp who croons such throaty Frederick Hollander tunes as "Black Market" and "Illusions," stole the limelight from Jean Arthur. The latter played a spinsterish busybody congresswoman who becomes enamored of American officer John Lund. As *Life* magazine observed: "Marlene Dietrich enjoys a triumphant return to the same sexy role that made her famous eighteen years ago in the German film *The Blue Angel*—the heartless siren who lures men to degradation and goes on singing."

The post-World War II Marlene charted no new courses in her screen appearances but craftily engaged in stabilizing her past movie fame by capitalizing on her ability to retain her looks and allure after nearly 20 years of Hollywood film exposure.

In 1948, Marlene's daughter Maria,* who had become an actress, gave birth to her first son by her second husband William Riva. Marlene rose to her new role admirably, and was soon labeled by the press as the world's most fabulous grandmother (Gloria Swanson had beaten Marlene to the punch and had been tagged the world's most glamorous grandmother). In May, 1950, when Maria had her second son, Marlene told reporters: "I'm getting a little weary of it. Naturally, I love my grandchildren. But why attach so much importance to my being a grandmother? Countless women have grandchildren—many of them, I am sure, much younger than I."

After a brief guest appearance in the filmed-in-New York *Jigsaw* (1949), a low-budget feature, Marlene was off the screen until 1950. Then Alfred Hitchcock invited her to England to "also star" in *Stage Fright* (1950) as the conniving musical comedy star Charlotte Inwood. Jane Wyman, who had just won an Oscar for *Johnny Belinda,* was top-billed as an acting student in London who wonders if boyfriend Richard Todd really murdered Marlene's husband. In her stunning Christian Dior gowns, and handling the acid dialogue adroitly, Marlene provided glamorous relief in this less than excellent Hitchcock whodunit. The reviewers said, "She sings [Cole Porter's "The Laziest Girl in Town"] and acts with equal nonchalance. . . . Looking more captivating than ever, she gives the show the sharp contrasts of levity and evil which Hitchcock is so fond of exploiting." When questioned about working with Marlene, Hitchcock made the terse statement: "Marlene Dietrich is a *professional*—a professional actress, a professional dress designer, a professional cameraman." The biting implications of his words

---

*She would become one of the most popular dramatic actresses of live television in the early 1950s, retiring from show business in 1957 after a summer tour of *Tea And Sympathy.* She now has four sons.

take on intriguing ramifications when one considers the clash of styles that existed between Marlene and Hitchcock: she with her preprogrammed performance and his requiring a completely malleable actor.

While in England filming *Stage Fright,* Marlene appeared at the Royal Film Performance, singing her famed "Lili Marlene" number. A year later Marlene returned to the British Denham Studios to costar in *No Highway in the Sky* (1951) opposite James Stewart. Once again she had a subordinate role, but she was paid for providing the touch of glamour. Bedecked in her Christian Dior-designed clothes, Marlene offered pleasant distractions from the somber drama. She plays a famed movie star who senses that fellow plane passenger Stewart may be right in his theories about the imminent structural disintegration of their aircraft. *No Highway in the Sky* premiered at the Roxy Theatre on September 21, 1951, and did much better business than had *Stage Fright.* Marlene was cited for being "delightfully adroit" "in a very sympathetic part." At one point in the dialogue, her cinema queen character Monica Teasdale wryly philosophizes about her movie career: "A few cans of celluloid on the junk-heap some day." Marlene and Stewart recreated their roles on "Lux Radio Theatre" (April 28, 1952).

In 1951 Marlene became a Chevalier of the French Legion of Honor for entertaining troops in Africa and France during the war. At the April, 1951, Academy Award show in Hollywood, Marlene made a well-calculated appearance, letting everyone know she was back in town. She arrived in a skin-tight Christian Dior black dress which had a slit large enough to expose her fabled legs as she promenaded across stage during her presentation chores. It was in this year that Marlene's little-seen husband Sieber retired from the film industry and purchased a chicken farm in the San Fernando Valley of California. He would later be quoted as saying, "She [Marlene] is away much of the time, but if you love someone you make sacrifices but you don't consider them sacrifices. She lives here with me for a few days each year and we are happy."

Marlene had been continuing with her radio appearances during the postwar years; for example, playing opposite Ray Milland in the "Theatre Guild Of The Air" version of *Grand Hotel* (March 24, 1948, ABC) and in the same series' *The Letter* (October 3, 1948) with Walter Pidgeon. In the fall of 1948 she was guest hostess of CBS radio's "G.E. Theatre," until Helen Hayes took over the assignment. In January, 1952, Marlene inaugurated a dramatic radio series, "Cafe Istanbul" (ABC), set in a Near Eastern cafe, with each program a complete episode. Marlene even wrote some of the scripts. *Variety* called it an "exotically upholstered soaper marked by top-flight production values." The second series of "Cafe Istanbul" commenced October 12, 1952, changing its locale to San Francisco. Said Marlene: "It's a hell of a job to do a dramatic show in half an hour. There just isn't time for singing because you have to worry about character and plot." She did warble a few bars of "La Vie en Rose" on occasion.

In 1952 her friend of many years, Ernest Hemingway (whom she dubbed "Papa"), observed: "If she had nothing more than her voice, she could break your heart with it. . . . I know that everytime I have seen Marlene Dietrich ever, it has done something to my heart and made me happy. If this makes her mysterious then it is a fine mystery. It is a mystery we have known about for a long time."

Marlene was more than happy when the opportunity arose for her to star in RKO's *Rancho Notorious* (1952). It was a shoestring production, but it presented the first feasible leading role offered her in a long time, and the chance to work with her long-time friend, German director Fritz Lang. However, Marlene and Lang were soon feuding on the set. He later accused her of not only trying to remold her role into a youthful siren, which was understandable, but of seeming to delight in pitting one actor against another. *Rancho Notorious* is as weird a film as the later *Johnny Guitar* (1954) starring Joan Crawford. It had the advantage of good technicolor, but its synthetic account of former saloon singer Marlene who harbors an assortment of outlaws on her horse ranch, was not well received. Marlene had little to do in this watered down *Destry Rides Again* (with the satire unfortunately removed). Her Ken Darby songs were undistinguished, and although her 36½–23–37 figure belied her 51 years, Marlene looked uncomfortably fragile trying to sustain her pose of a youngish wanton with a passion for gunman Mel Ferrer.

While making *Rancho Notorious,* Marlene received an honorary membership in the Makeup Artists and Hairdressers Union. The citation stated: "You know as much about the business as we do." On March 6, 1952, Marlene made her American stage debut in Chicago, while making a personal appearance tour for *Rancho Notorious,* singing a few numbers from her pictures. A projected follow-up, a 75-city stage tour produced by Paul Gregory, with a five-piece orchestra and a ten-voice male chorus, did not come about.

Marlene was on CBS radio's daytime show "Time for Love" in the spring of 1953, and was the much publicized ringmaster at the charity opening of Ringling Brothers–Barnum & Bailey Circus at Madison Square Garden.

On December 15, 1953, Marlene began a new career as a cabaret entertainer. As she demonstrated in the act, it was an entirely new beginning for her. In the early 1950s before television acquired her old feature films, Marlene's past cinema career was legendary, but to many her fame was second-hand, for they had never seen her in her movie heyday. With the facts of her pre-Hollywood life even more obscure at the time, she was safe in refashioning her biography as she saw fit, so she blithely dreamed up a cotton candy set of data to use as patter bridges between her song numbers, these were repeated by her and reporters so often that they almost came to be believed by everyone, including Marlene.

In her club act, Marlene employed the diseuse style, a method employed by speech singers whose sounds are speech but are considered song because they are spoken on key. Marlene premiered her act at the Hotel Sahara in Las Vegas at the top salary of $90,000 for three weeks. To insure that her initial appearance before the audience would be sensational, she commissioned Columbia Pictures' chief dress designer Jean Louis to create a $6,000 skin-tight black-net frock, lined with flesh-colored chiffon and sprinkled with sequins and rhinestones, with a transparent high-neck top disguised with a few rhinestones. Club patrons were flabbergasted by this dazzling vision of Marlene, which meant that from the start of each show she had won over her audience to her very theatrical presentation. She would sing her repertory of familiar songs (including "The Boys in the Back Room," "Falling in Love Again," "Lili Marlene," "The Laziest Girl in Town," etc.) and successfully wowed her audiences from the sophisticates on downward.

On June 21, 1954, she opened at London's Café de Paris, with her 40-minute song act introduced by Noel Coward. (It was recorded by Columbia Records, like many of her later club-touring engagements.) While Marlene would refine her orchestrations and periodically change her wardrobe and hairstyle, her act remained much the same; her precise knowledge of lighting, costuming, makeup, and projection afforded her complete control over her living legend as the eternal female.

During the 1950s Marlene played club engagements in Europe and South America, as well as making yearly returns to Las Vegas. Of these Nevada club dates Marlene said: "They spoil you. When they love you, it's forever. Of course, I do a different kind of show in Las Vegas. They want more emphasis on sex. In London, and the rest of Europe, I can sing French and German songs as well as English. There's more scope for me. But I enjoy nightclub work where it is."

Marlene had been contracted to appear in Columbia's *Pal Joey* (finally made in 1957) but she wanted Frank Sinatra to play opposite her, while studio mogul Harry Cohn was bent on substituting his new find Jack Lemmon. So Marlene withdrew and Rita Hayworth replaced her. She also bowed out of *Gigi* (1958) when her billing and salary terms were not met. She was one of the 44 stars to make a cameo appearance in Michael Todd's *Around the World in 80 Days* (1956). In the San Francisco sequence she played a dance hall queen, with seven short lines of dialogue. For the first time on the screen, she wore real tights. In her high-piled white blonde wig, her face looked particularly drawn, giving Marlene a most world-weary, worn appearance.

In late 1956 Marlene contracted to play opposite Vittorio de Sica in *The Monte Carlo Story* (1957), filmed in Italy. She accepted the mild technicolor comedy because De Sica was "the most romantic middle-aged man in the world." During production, she feuded with 16-year-old ingenue Natalie Trundy, supposedly ruffled because the girl referred to Marlene as a "cold fish." *The Monte Carlo Story* dribbled into showcase release on February 12, 1958, and was labeled "so out-dated [that] it creaks as much as a pair of dowager's corsets." Marlene did not photograph well and seemed very ill at ease, as if trying to rub away the rust from her screen love-making techniques.

She was much better received in Billy Wilder's film version of Agatha Christie's whodunit *Witness for the Prosecution* (Astor Theatre, February 6, 1958). In this taut courtroom melodrama she was second-billed as the German-born wife of Tyrone Power. He is on trial for the alleged murder of wealthy widow Norma Varden. Droll defense attorney Charles Laughton is hired to save Power's neck. To show off Marlene's gams, Wilder incorporated a specially written flashback sequence relating how Power had met songstress Marlene in a Berlin café during World War II, where she was singing "I May Never Go Home Again" and accompanying herself on the accordion. The scene, which ends with the customers brawling, cost $90,000 and gave a needed change of locale to the often claustrophobic Old Bailey setting.

Laughton and his wife Elsa Lanchester (the nurse) each received Oscar nominations for their roles in *Witness for the Prosecution*. Marlene was lauded for providing her first full-fleshed screen characterization in which her "frosty beauty is tellingly used." The *New York Herald Tribune* stated: "Miss Dietrich is a sultry siren, so inscrutable that even Laughton asks, 'What's the woman up to? What's her game?' Well might he ask. Whatever it is, she plays it with fire and finesse." There are reports that Marlene was responsible for assorted script revisions, and it has never been fully documented whether her footage as the cockney streetwalker was utilized or not in the final-release print. Marlene's hollow-cheeked face photographed particularly taut, making it subtle but obvious that she was utilizing cosmetic rejuvenators.

In Orson Welles's *Touch of Evil* (1958) Marlene had a guest star role as the dark-haired, cigar smoking Mexican madame who is the mistress of bulbous Texas law enforcer Welles. Her several scenes, shot in one night, were brittle and terse.

Marlene inaugurated a new radio series on October 4, 1958, for NBC radio's "Monitor." She was heard in 96 three to four minute tapes, answering letters sent to her and talking of life and love. As Marlene quipped: "You might say my radio show will be compassion versus the couch."

Marlene had refused for years to appear on television. Her detractors claimed it was for fear of the potentially unflattering close-ups. Marlene's rationale was: "I am a very busy woman and I could not put into television the terrific amount of work it requires. And what would television get me? Money? You can't keep it. Also, the risk of wearing out your welcome is too great. So if a performer is not an exhibitionist, and I am not, I see no reason to take on the burden of television." Plans for her hostessing an NBC television "Big Party" fell through, as did a TV special, a 60-minute "Dietrich in Paris" which Orson Welles was to helm. She was almost lured into changing her very definite mind by Revlon Cosmetics, who would have paid her $2 million for hostessing several television revue specials. However, an appropriate tax deferment plan could not be worked out to her satisfaction. Marlene finally made her television debut in Germany on October 6, 1962, when she was one of 15 stars in the talent array of a UNICEF charity show at Kongresse Halle. Her American video debut came in April, 1968, when she appeared on the televised "Tony Award Show" to accept a special award.

Marlene continued to wow customers in nightclub showcasing. She was more luxuriantly arrayed each time around, and benefited from the more modern musical arrangements of Burt Bacharach. She admitted she received high salaries, but reasoned: "Let's not fool anyone. It takes money to be glamorous nowadays. Glamor is what I sell in my act, and it costs plenty."

On April 7, 1959, the Museum of Modern Art kicked off a film tribute cycle to Marlene, with a special $12.50-per-ticket Evening with Marlene Dietrich. It was on this occasion that she voiced the perceptive statement: "Thank you [for the applause] and I don't ask whom you are applauding—the legend, the performer, or me. I, personally, liked the legend. Not that it was easy to live with, but I liked it. Maybe because I felt privileged to witness its creation at such close quarters. I never had any ambition to become a film star, but the fascination this creating process held for me gave me the élan to work and work very hard to please Mr. von Sternberg.

"The legend served me well, and I venture to say it served well all the other directors who took over after he decided I should go on alone. Even those who set out to debunk the legend and probe for better things behind the triple gauze curtain of Mr. von Sternberg's magic.

"It has been said that I was Trilby to his Svengali. I would rather say I was Eliza to his Henry Higgins."

Although she once said she would never be buried in Germany when she died, Marlene returned to her homeland for a multicity tour, opening her one-woman show at the Titania Palace Theatre in West Berlin on May 3, 1960. Along the way, there were some nasty minor incidents of anti-Marlene sentiment by the Germans, which left her hurt but resolute—she continued the tour despite an arm injury when she fell off the stage during her Wiesbaden engagement. Her Israeli appearances in June, 1960, proved more successful: the audiences even applauded her German language numbers. (In December, 1965, she was the first woman to receive the Medallion of Valor from the Israeli government.)

Marlene returned to the screen in Stanley Kramer's roadshow attraction *Judgment at Nuremberg* (1961). She was fourth-billed as Mme. Berthol, the world-weary widow of a Nazi general who is trying to survive with dignity in post-World War II Germany. Although her role was superfluous, her scenes with Spencer Tracy had a mellowness that greatly enhanced the picture, for she instilled her characterization with a "veiled arrogance tempered with sensitivity." Maximilian Schell as the defense counsel received an Oscar. The following year she narrated the Academy-Award winning *Black Fox* (1962), an incisive documentary on the repercussions of Adolph Hitler and the Third Reich. In the dismal *Paris When It Sizzles* (1964) starring Audrey Hepburn and William Holden, Marlene had a fleeting cameo. She is seen in a tailored white suit and wide-brimmed white hat, stepping from her limousine and quickly walking into the House of Dior. Plans for her to play Pirate Jenny in a Berlin-made film of *Three Penny Opera* never materialized.

The publication of *Marlene Dietrich's ABC* in July, 1962, was not her first literary effort. She had bylined "How to be Loved" for the January, 1954, issue of *Ladie's Home Journal* and wrote several advice-type pieces during the years that followed. The *ABC,* a short dictionary of observations, anecdotes, and advice, received respectable reviews and revealed Marlene as a woman with a most distinct point of view.

Throughout the 1960s Marlene continued touring her one-woman show, making a widely heralded 20-concert stay in Russia (1964) and an Australian appearance (1965). After appearing at Montreal's Expo '67 (June, 1967), Marlene finally made her much-postponed Broadway debut at the Lunt-Fontanne Theatre on October 9, 1967, accompanied by Burt Bacharach and a 26-piece orchestra. She wore her spectacular $30,000 Jean Louis-designed costume, with bugle beads lined with 14-carat gold, and dragging a white ermine wrap. Among her 22 song numbers was her new favorite, the antiwar "Where Have all the Flowers Gone?" As the *New York Times*'s Vincent Canby described it, "[she] is not so much a performer as a one-woman environment, assaulting the senses in all manner of means." After a successful 68-performance engagement, she returned the following fall to Broadway to almost equal success at the box office. A perfect, well-automated performer, she repeated each gesture, phrasing, and bow of her routine in the same precise manner every night, undisturbed by the human element involved in playing to a live audience. With her economical gestures, she was self-editing every movement on stage. That she had a hired entourage of young men to throw flowers at the end of each performance was all part of the well-calculated ambiance which was designed to showcase the enshrined Marlene.

Although Marlene claims she will not make any more movies, reports about Orson Welles's quietly made Hollywood feature *The Side of the Wind* list Marlene in a key role. The still uncompleted film deals with a crusty old director who returns to Hollywood after a long exile and confronts Beverly Hills hippiedom.

Now in her seventies, Marlene is still going "where they pay the most," touring the club circuits to good grosses, even if it is, as *Variety* penned, "the twilight of an incredible career." After a highly praised London charity stage appearance in September, 1971, Marlene repeated her one-woman show for sixteen SRO performances there in June, 1972. It has been rumored that Marlene might yet return to Broadway with her one-woman show. But it is reported that she demands a cover-all $17,000 weekly salary, which has yet to find a backer. She has recently negotiated to do filmed television commercials and has contracted with CBS-TV to star in a colorcast of her one-woman show to be taped in Hawaii. Marlene, the ever-shrewd businesswoman, engineered a reputed $225,000 salary for this 120-minute special. She is presently working on her memoirs, but is not willing to discuss the project.

DER KLEINE NAPOLEON (The Little Napoleon) (UFA, 1923) 2,713 meters

Director, Georg Jacoby; screenplay, Robert Liebmann, Georg Jacoby.

Egon Von Hagen (Napoleon Bonaparte); Paul Heidemann (Jerome Bonaparte); Harry Liedtke (Georg von Melsungen); Jacob Tiedtke (Jeremias von Katzenellenbogen); Antonia Dietrich (Charlotte); Loni Nest (Liselotte); Alice Hechy (Annemarie); Kurt Vespermann (Florian Wunderlich); Paul Biensfeld (Court Marshall Of The King); Kurt Fuss (Director of the Royal Ballet); Marquisette Bosky (The Prima Ballerina); Marlene Dietrich (Kathrin, Charlotte's Maid); Wilhelm Bendow (Jerome's Valet).

TRAGÖDIE DER LIEBE (Tragedy of Love) (UFA, 1923)

Part I—1,939 meters

Part II—1,790 meters

Part III—1,719 meters

Part IV—1,984 meters

Producer-director, Joe May; screenplay, Leo Birinski, Adolf Lantz; sets, Paul Leni; production assistant, Rudolf Sieber; synchronized music, Wilhelm Löwitt; camera, Sophus Wangoe, Karl Puth.

Emil Jannings (Ombrade, A Wrestler); Erika Glassner (Musette, His Mistress); Mia May (Countess Manon de Moreau); Kurt Vespermann (The Judge); Marlene Dietrich (Lucie, His Mistress); and: Ida Wust, Arnold Korff, Charlotte Ander, Curt Gotz, Rudolf Forster, Ferry Sikla, Loni Nest, Vladimir Gaidarow, Hermannn Vallentin, Hedwig Pauli-Winterstein, Paul Grätz, Eugen Rex, Hans Wassmann, Albert Patry.

DER MENSCH AM WEGE (Man by the Roadside) (Osmania, 1923) 1,657 meters

Director, Wilhelm Dieterle; based on the story by Leo Tolstoy; screenplay, Dieterle; decors, Hebert Richter-Luckian; camera, Willy Hameister, Willi Habentz.

Alexander Granach (Schuster); Wilhelm Dieterle (The Human Angel); and: Henirich George, Wilhelm Völker, Wilhelm Diegelmann, Dr. Max Pohl, Ernest Gronau, Ludwig Rex, Gerhard Bienert, Brockmann, Georg Hilbert, Fritz Kampers, Max Nemetz, Werner Pledath, Fritz Rasp, Rausch, Emilie Unda, Marlene Dietrich, Sophie Pagay, Liselotte Rolle, Bäck, Gerlach-Jacobi, Hegewald, Härling Herbst, Hermine Körner, Dolly Lorenz, Seeberg, Lotte Stein.

DER SPRUNG INS LEBEN (The Leap into Life) (UFA, 1924) 2,075 meters

Producer, Oskar Messter; director, Dr. Johannes Guter; screenplay, Franz Schultz; decors, Rudi Feldt; camera, Fritz Arno Wagner.

Xenia Desni (A Circus Acrobat); Walter Rilla (Her Partner); Paul Heidemann (A Young Scholar); Frida Richard (His Aunt); Kathe Haack (The Scholar's Associate); Leonhard Haskel (The Ringmaster); and: Olga Engl, Marlene Dietrich, Hans Brausewetter.

DIE FREUDLOSE GASSE (The Joyless Street) (Hirschal-Sofar, 1925) 3,738 meters

Director, Georg Wilhelm Pabst; based on the novel by Hugo Bettauer; screenplay, Willi Haas; assistant director, Marc Sorkin; decors, Hans Sohnle, Otto Erdmann; camera, Guido Seeber, Curt Oertel, Walter Robert Lach; editor, Anatol Litvak. U.S. *Street of Sorrow,* 127.

Jaro Furth (Councillor Josef Rumfort); Greta Garbo (Grete Rumfort); Loni Nest (Rosa Rumfort); Asta Nielsen (USA Lisa Kramm); Max Kohlhase, Silva Torf (Her Parents); Karl Ettlinger (Director General Rosenow); Ilka Gruning (His Wife); Countess Agnes Esterhazy (Regina Rosenow); Alexander Mursky (Dr. Leid, The Lawyer); Tamara (Lia Leid); Henry Stuart (Egon Stirner); Robert Garrison (Ganez); Einar Hanson (Lt. Davy, U.S.A.); Mario Cusmich (Col. Irving, U.S.A.); Valeska Gert (Mrs. Griefer); Countess Tolstoi (Miss Henriette); Mrs. Markstein (Mrs. Merkl); Werner Krauss (Josef Geiringer, The Butcher); Herta Von Walther (Else); Otto Reinwald (Her Husband); Grigory Chmara (A Waiter); Raskatoff (Trebitsch); Kraft Raschig (American Soldier); and: Marlene Dietrich (Young Woman on Breadline).

MANON LESCAUT (Universum-Film-Verleih, 1926) 2,645 meters

Director, Arthur Robison, based on the novel *L'Histoire de Manon Lescaut* by Abbé Prevost; screenplay, Hans Kyser, Robison; decors-costumes, Paul Leni; camera, Theodor Sparkuhl.

Lya De Putti (Manon Lescaut); Vladimir Gaidarov (Des Grieux); Eduard Rothauser (Marshall Des Grieux); Fritz Greiner (Marquis De Bli); Hubert Von Meyerinck (Son of De Bli); Fria Richard, Emilie Kurtz (Manon's Aunts); Lydia Potechina (Susanne); Theodor Loos (Tiberge); Siegfried Arno (Lescaut); Trude Hesterberg (Claire); Marlene Dietrich (Micheline); and: Karl Harbacher, Albert Paulig, Hans Junkermann.

EINE DU BARRY VON HEUTE (A Modern Du Barry) (UFA, 1926) 3,004 meters

Director, Alexander Korda; based on the story by Ludwig Biro; screenplay, Korda, Paul Reboux; decors, Otto Friedrich Werndorff; camera, Fritz Arno Wagner.

Maria Corda (Toinette, A Modern Du Barry); Alfred Abel (Sillon); Friedrich Kayssler (Cornelius Corbett); Julius Von Szöreghy (General Padilla); Jean Bradin (Sandro, King of Asturia); Hans Albers (Darius Kerbelian); Alfred Gerasch (Count Rabbatz); Alfred Paulig (Clairet); Hans Wassmann (Theatre Director); Karl Platen (Servant); Eugen Burg (Levasseur); Marlene Dietrich (A Coquette); Hilda Radnay (Juliette); Julia Serda (Aunt Julie); Hedwig Wangel (Rosalie); Lotte Lorring (Mannequin).

MADAME WÜNSCHT KEINE KINDER (Madame Wants No Children) (Deutsche Vereinsfilm, 1926), 2,166 meters

Producer, Karl Freund; associate producer, Karl Hartl, director, Alexander Korda; based on the novel *Madame ne veut pas d'enfants* by Clement Vautel; screenplay, Adolf Lantz, Bela Balzs; decors, Otto Friedrich; production assistant, Rudolf Sieber; camera, Theodor Sparkuhl, Robert Baberske.

Maria Corda (Elyane Parizot); Harry Liedtke (Paul Le Barroy); Maria Paudler (Louis Bonvin); Trude Hesterberg (Elyane's Mother); Dina Gralla (Lulu, Elyane's Sister); Hermann Vallentin (Paul's Uncle); Camilla Von Hollay (Louise's Maid); Olga Mannel (Louise's Cook); Ellen Muller (Elyane's Maid); and: Marlene Dietrich, John Loder.

KOPF HOCH, CHARLY! (Heads Up, Charly!) (UFA, 1926) 2,512 meters

Director, Dr. Willi Wolff; based on the novel by Ludwig Wolff; screenplay, Robert Liebmann, Dr. Willi Wolff; decors, Ernst Stern; camera, Axel Graatkjar.

Anton Pointner (Frank Ditmar); Ellen Richter (Charlotte "Charly" Ditmar); Michael Bohnen (John Jacob Bunjes); Max Gulsdorff (Harry Moshenheim); Margerie Quimby (Margie Quinn); George De Carlton (Rufus Quinn); Angelo Ferrari (Marquis D'Ormesson); Robert Scholz (Duke of Sanzedilla); Nikolai Malikoff (Prince Platonoff); Toni Tetzlaff (Frau Zangenberg); Marlene Dietrich (Edmée Marchand); Blandie Ebinger (Seamstress); and: Albert Paulig.

DER JUXBARON (The Imaginary Baron) (UFA, 1927) 2,179 meters

Director, Dr. Willi Wolff; based on the operetta by Prodes-Milo, Hermann Haller, Walter Kollo; screenplay, Robert Liebmann, Wolff; decors, Ernest Stern; camera, Axel Graatkjar.

Reinhold Schünzel (The Imaginary Baron); Henry Bender (Hugo Windisch); Julia Serda (Zerline Windisch); Marlene Dietrich (Sophie, Her Daughter); Teddy Bill (Hans Von Grabow); Colette Brettl (Hilda Von Grabow); Albert Paulig (Baron Von Kimmel); Trude Hesterberg (Fränze); Karl Harbacher (Sttoerwilhelm); Hermann Picha (Tramp); Firtz Kampers (Policeman); Karl Beckmann (Landlord).

SEIN GROSSTER BLUFF (His Greatest Bluff) (Sudfilm, 1927) 2,984 meters

Director, Henry Piel; screenplay, Henrik Galeen; decors, W. A. Heermann; assistant director, Edmund Heuberger; titles, Dr. Herbert Nossen; camera, Georg Muschner, Gotthardt Wolf, Zeiske-Leonard.

Harry Piel (Henry Devall/Harry Devall); Tony Tetzlaff (Madame Andersson); Lotte Lorring (Tilly, Her Daughter); Albert Pauling (Mimikry); Fritz Greiner (Hennessy); Charly Berger ("Count" Kiks); Boris Michailow (Sherry); Marlene Dietrich (Yvette); Paul Walker ("Goliath," a Dwarf); Kurt Gerron (Rajah Of Johore); Eugen Burg (Police Superintendent); Ossip Darmatow ("Count" Apollinaris); Vicky Werckmeister (Suzanne); Paul Moleska, Oswald Scheffel, Curt Bullerjahn, Charles Francois, Wolfgang Von Schwindt (Gangsters); and: Hans Breitensträter.

CAFE ELECTRIC (Wenn Ein Weib Den Weg Verliert) (Sascha Filmindustrie, 1927) 2,400 meters.

Executive producer, Karl Hartl; director, Gustav Ucicky; based on the play *Die Liebesbörse* by Felix Fischer; screenplay, Jacques Bachrach; decors, Artur Berger; camera, Hans Androschin.

Fritz Alberti (Göttlinger); Marlene Dietrich (Erni, His Daughter); Anny Coty (One of her Friends); Willi Forst (Ferdl); Nina Vanna (Hansi); Igo Sym (Max Stöger, an Architect); Felix Fischer (The Editor); Vera Salvotti (Paula); Wilhelm Völker (Dr. Lehner); Albert E. Kersten (Mr. Zerner); and: Dolly Davis.

PRINZESSIN OLALA (Princess Olala) (Deutsches Lichtspiel-Syndikat, 1928) 2,122 meters

Director, Robert Land; based on the operetta by Jean Gilbert, Rudolf Bernauer, Rudolf Schanzer; screenplay, Franz Schulz ,Land; decors, Robert Neppach; camera, Willi Goldberger, Fritz Brunn.

Hermann Böttcher (Prince); Walter Rilla (Prince Boris, His Son); Georg Alexander (Chamberlain); Carmen Boni (Princess Xenia); Ila Meery (Hedy, Her Friend); Marlene Dietrich (Chichotte de Gastoné); Hans Albers (René, Chichotte's Friend); Karl Götz (Old Cavalier); Julius Von Szoreghy (Strong Man); Lya Christy (Lady Jackson); Aribert Wascher (Police Superintendent); and: Alfred Abel.

ICH KUSSE IHRE HAND, MADAME (I Kiss Your Hand, Madame); (Deutsches LichtspielSyndikat, 1929) 2,020 meters

Director, Robert Land; story, Rolf E. Vanloo, Land; screenplay, Land; decors, Robert Neppach; song, Ralph Erwin and Fritz Rotter; camera, Fritz Brunn, Fred Zinnemann.

Harry Liedtke (Jacques); Marlene Dietrich (Laurence Gerard); Pierre De Guingang (Adolf Gerard, Her Ex-Husband); Karl Huszar-Puffy (Tallandier, Her Attorney).

DIE FRAU, NACH DER MAN SICH SEHNT (The Woman One Longs For) (Terra-Film, 1929) 2,360 meters

Director, Kurt Bernhardt; based on the novel by Max Brod; screenplay Ladislas Vadja; decors, Robert Neppach; music, Edward Kilenyi Walther Bransen; camera, Kurt Courant.

Marlene Dietrich (Stascha); Fritz Kortner (Dr. Karoff); Frida Richard (Mrs. Leblanc); Oskar Sima (Charles Leblanc); Uno Henning (Henry Leblanc); Bruno Ziener (Philipp, The Valet); Karl Ettlinger (Old Poitrier); Edith Edwards (Angela Poitrier, His Daughter).

DAS SCHIFF DER VERLORENEN MENSCHEN (The Ship of Lost Souls) (Orplid-Metro, 1929) 2,638 meters

Producer, Max Glass; director, Maurice Tourneur; based on the novel by Frenzos Kerzemen; screenplay, Tourneur; decors, Franz Schroedter; assistant director, Jacques Tourneur; camera, Nikolaus Farkas.

Fritz Kortner (Captain Fernando Vela); Marlene Dietrich (Miss Ethel, An Aviatrix); Gaston Modot (Morian, The Escaped Convict); Robin Irvin (T. W. Cheyne, A Young American Doctor); Boris De Fas (Sailor); Vladimir Sokoloff (Grischa, The Cook); Robert Garrison, Alfred Loretto, Fedor Chaliapin, Jr., Harry Grunwald (Crew); Max Maximilian (Second Mate).

GEFAHREN DER BRAUTZEIT (Dangers of the Engagement Period) (Hegewald-Film, 1929) 2,183 meters

Director, Fred Sauer; screenplay, Walter Wassermann, Walter Schlee; decors, Max Heilbronner; camera, Laszlo Schaffer.

Willi Forst (Baron Van Geldern); Marlene Dietrich (Evelyne); Lotte Lorring (Yvette); Elza Temary (Florence); Ernst Stahl-Nachbaur (McClure); Bruno Ziener (Miller); and Oskar Sima.

DER BLAUE ENGEL (The Blue Angel) (UFA, 1930) 99 M.

Producer, Erich Pommer; director, Josef von Sternberg; based on the novel *Professor Unrath* by Heinrich Mann; adaptation, Carl Zuchmayer, Karl Vollmoller; screenplay, Robert Liebmann; art director, Otto Hunte, Emil Hasler; music, Friedrich Hollander; camera, Gunther Rittau, Hans Schneeberger.

Emil Jannings (Professor Immanuel Rath); Marlene Dietrich (Lola-Lola, Fröhlich); Kurt Gerron (Kiepert, The Magician); Rosa Valetti (Guste, His Wife); Hans Albers (Mazeppa); Reinhold Bernt (The Clown); Eduard Von Winterstein (Director Of The School); Hans Roth (The Beadle); Rolf Muller (Angst); Rolant Varno (Lohmann); Karl Balhaus (Ertzum); Robert Klein-Lork (Goldstaub); Karl Huszar-Puffy (Publican); Wilhelm Diegelmann (Captain); Gerhard Bienert (Policeman); Isle Fürstenberg (Rath's Housekeeper).

MOROCCO (PAR, 1930) 90 M.

Director, Josef von Sternberg; based on the novel *Amy Jolly* by Benno Vigny; screenplay, Jules Furthman; art director, Hans Dreier, songs, Leo Robin and Karl Hajos; Millandy and Cremieux; camera, Lee Garmes; editor, Sam Winston.

Gary Cooper (Legionnaire Tom Brown); Marlene Dietrich (Amy Jolly); Adolphe Menjou (Lebessier); Ullrich Haupt (Adjutant Caesar); Juliette Compton (Anna Dolores); Francis McDonald (Corporal Barney Tatoche); Albert Conti (Colonel Quinnovieres); Eve Southern (Madame Caesar); Michael Visaroff (Barrative); Paul Porcasi (Lo Tinto); Theresa Harris (Camp Follower); Emile Chautard (Officer).

DISHONORED (PAR, 1931) 91 M.

Director-story, Josef von Sternberg; screenplay, Daniel H. Rubin; music, Karl Hajos; camera, Lee Garmes.

Marlene Dietrich (X-27); Victor McLaglen (Lt. Kranau); Lew Cody (Colonel Kovrin); Gustav Von Seyffertitz (Head Of The Secret Service); Warner Oland (General Von Hindau); Barry Norton (Young Lieutenant); Davison Clark (Court Officer); Wilfred Lucas (General Dymov); Bill Powell (Manager); George Irving (Contact At Cafe); Joseph Girard (Russian Officer); Ethan Laidlaw (Russian Corporal); William B. Davidson (Firing Squad Officer); Buddy Roosevelt (Russian Officer).

SHANGHAI EXPRESS (PAR, 1932) 80 M.

Director, Josef von Sternberg; based on the story by Harry Hervey; screenplay, Jules Furthman; art director, Hans Dreier; music, W. Franke Harling; camera, Lee Garmes.

Marlene Dietrich (Shanglai Lilly/Madeline); Clive Brook (Captain Donald Harvey); Anna May Wong (Hui Fei); Warner Oland (Henry Chang); Eugene Pallette (Sam Salt); Lawrence Grant (Reverend Carmichael); Louise Closser Hale (Mrs. Haggerty); Gustav Von Seyffertitz (Eric Baum); Emile Chautard (Major Lenard); James Leong (A Rebel); Claude King (Albright); Neshida Minoru (Chinese Spy); Willie Fung (Engineer); Leonard Carey (Minister); Forrestor Harvey (Ticket Agent); Miki Morita (Officer).

BLONDE VENUS (PAR, 1932) 80 M.

Director-story, Josef von Sternberg; screenplay, Jules Furthman, S. K. Lauren; art director, Wiard Ihnen; songs, Sam Coslow and Ralph Rainger; Leo Robin and Dick Whiting; music, Oscar Potoker; camera, Bert Glennon.

Marlene Dietrich (Helen Faraday); Herbert Marshall (Edward Faraday); Cary Grant (Nick Townsend); Dickie Moore (Johnny Faraday); Gene Morgan (Ben Smith); Rita La Roy ("Taxi Belle" Hooper); Robert Emmett O'Connor (Dan O'Connor); Sidney Toler (Detective Wilson); Francis Sayles (Charlie Blaine); Morgan Wallace (Dr. Pierce); Evelyn Preer (Iola); Robert Graves (La Farge); Lloyd Whitlock (Baltimore Manager); Cecil Cunningham (Norfolk Woman Manager); Emile Chautard (Chautard); James Kilgannon (Janitor); Sterling Holloway (Joe); Charles Morton (Bob); Ferdinand Schumann-Heink (Henry); Jerry Tucker (Otto); Harold Berquist (Big Fellow); Dewey Robinson (Greek Restaurant Owner); Clifford Dempsey (Night Court Judge): Bessie Lyle (Grace); Mildred Washington, Hattie McDaniel (Black Girls); Gertrude Short (Receptionist); Brady Kline (New Orleans Policeman).

SONG OF SONGS (PAR, 1933) 90 M.

Producer-director, Rouben Mamoulian; based on the novel *Das Hohe Lied* by Hermann Sudermann and the play by Edward Sheldon; music, Karl Hajos, Milen Rodern; songs, Franz Schubert; Friedrick Hollander and Edward Heyman; sculptures, S. C. Scarpitta; art director, Hans Dreier; music director, Nathaniel W. Finston; camera, Victor Milner.

Marlene Dietrich (Lily Czepanek); Brian Aherne (Waldow); Lionel Atwill (Baron Von Merzbach); Alison Skipworth (Frau Rasmussen); Hardie Albright (Walter Von Prell); Helen Freeman (Fraülein Von Schwartzfegger); Morgan Wallace ("Admirer"); Wilson Benge (Butler); Hans Schumm; Eric Wilton (Butler); and Richard Bennett, James Marcus.

THE SCARLET EMPRESS (PAR, 1934) 110 M.

Director, Josef von Sternberg; based on a diary of Catherine The Great; screenplay, Manuel Komroff; art director, Hans Dreier, Peter Ballbusch, Richard Kollorsz; music arrangers, W. Franke Harling, John M. Leipold, Milan Roder; special effects, Gordon Jennings; camera, Bert Glennon.

Marlene Dietrich (Sophia Frederica, Catherine II); John Lodge (Count Alexei);

Sam Jaffe (Grand Duke Peter); Louise Dresser (Empress Elizabeth); Maria Riva (Sophia As A Child); C. Aubrey Smith (Prince August); Ruthelma Stevens (Countess Elizabeth); Olive Tell (Princess Johanna); Gavin Gordon (Gregory Orloff); Jameson Thomas (Lt. Ostvyn); Hans Von Twardowski (Ivan Shuvolov); Davison Clark (Archimandrite Simeon Tevedovsky/Arch-Episcope); Erville Alderson (Chancellor Bestuchef); Marie Wells (Marie); Jane Darwell (Mlle. Cardell); Harry Woods (Doctor); Edward Van Sloan (Herr Wagner); Philip G. Sleeman (Count Lestocq); John B. Davidson (Marquis De La Chetardie); Gerald Fielding (Officer, Lt. Dmitri); James Burke (Guard); Belle Stoddard Johnstone, Nadine Beresford, Eunice Moore, Petra McAllister, Blanche Rose (Aunts); James Marcus (Innkeeper); Thomas C. Blythe, Clyde Davis (Narcissuses); Richard Alexander (Count Von Breummer); Jal Boyer, Bruce Warren, Eric Alden (Lackeys); George Davis (Jester); Agnes Steele, Barbara Sabichi, May Foster, Minnie Steele (Elizabeth's Ladies-In-Waiting); Katerine Sabichi, Julanne Johnson, Elinor Fair, Dina Smirnova, Anna Duncan, Patricia Patrick, Elaine St. Maur (Catherine's Ladies-In-Waiting).

THE DEVIL IS A WOMAN (PAR, 1935) 85 M.

Director-camera, Josef von Sternberg; based on the novel *La Femme et le Pantin* by Pierre Louys; screenplay, John Dos Passos, S. K. Winston; art director, Hans Dreier; songs, Leo Robin and Ralph Rainger; assistant camera, Lucien Ballard; editor, Sam Winston.

Marlene Dietrich (Concha Perez); Lionel Atwill (Don Pasqual); Cesar Romero (Antonio Galvan); Edward Everett Horton (Don Paquito); Alison Skipworth (Sonora Perez); Don Alvarado (Morenito); Morgan Wallace (Dr. Mendez); Tempe Pigott (Tuerta); Jill Bennett (Maria); Lawrence Grant (Conductor); Charles Sellon (Letter Writer); Luisa Espinal (Gypsy Dancer); Hank Mann (Foreman, Snowbound Train); Edwin Maxwell (Superintendant—Tobacco Factory); Donald Reed (Miquelito); Eddie Borden (Drunk in Carnival Cafe); Henry Roquemore (Duel Informant).

DESIRE (PAR, 1936) 89 M.

Producer, Ernst Lubitsch; director, Frank Borzage; based on the play by Hans Szekely, R. A. Stemmle; screenplay, Edwin Justus Mayer, Waldemar Young, Samuel Hoffenstein; art director, Hans Dreier, Robert Usher; music, Frederick Hollander; song, Hollander and Leo Robin; camera, Charles Lang.

Marlene Dietrich (Madeleine de Beaupre); Gary Cooper (Tom Bradley); John Halliday (Carlos Margoli); William Frawley (Mr. Gibson); Ernest Cossart (Aristide Duval); Akim Tamiroff (Police Official); Alan Mowbray (Dr. Edouard Pauquet); Zeffie Tilbury (Aunt Olga); Harry Depp (Clerk); Marc Lawrence (Valet); Henry Antrim (Chauffeur); Armand Kaliz, Gaston Glass; Albert Pollet (French Policeman); George Davis (Garage Man; Constant Franke (Border Official); Robert O'Connor (Customs Official); Stanley Andrews (Customs Inspector); Rafael Blanco (Haywagon Driver); Alden (Stephen) Chase (Hotel Clerk) Tony Merlo (Waiter); Anna Delinsky (Servant); Alice Feliz (Pepi); Enrique Acosta (Pedro); George MacQuarrie (Clerk With Gun); Isabel La Mal (Nurse); Oliver Eckhardt (Husband); Blanche Craig (Wife); Rollo Lloyd (Clerk In Mayor's Office); Alfonso Pedroza (Oxcart Driver).

THE GARDEN OF ALLAH (UA, 1936) 85 M.

Producer, David O. Selznick; director, Richard Boleslawski; based on the novel by Robert Hichens; screenplay, W. P. Lipscomb, Lynn Riggs; art director, Sturges Carne, Lyle Wheeler, Edward Boyle; assistant director, Eric Stacey; music, Max Steiner; producer's assistant, Willis Goldbeck; camera, W. Howard Greene; editor, Hal C. Kern, Anson Stevenson.

Marlene Dietrich (Domini Enfilden); Charles Boyer (Boris Androvsky); Basil Rathbone (Count Anteoni); C. Aubrey Smith (Father Roubier); Tilly Losch (Irena); Joseph Schildkraut (Batouch); John Carradine (Sand Diviner); Alan Marshal (De Trevignac); Lucile Watson (Mother Superior); Henry Brandon (Hadj); Helen Jerome Eddy (Nun); Nigel De Brulier (Lector); John Bryan (Brother Gregory); Charles Waldron (Abbe); Adrian Rosley (Mustapha); Ferdinand Gottschalk (Hotel Clerk); David Scott (Larby); Robert Frazer (Smain); Andrew McKenna (Mueddin); Bonita Granville, Marcia Mae Jones, Betty Jane Graham, Ann Gillis (Children At Convent); Marion Sayers, Betty Van Auken, Edna Harris, Frances Turnham (Oasis Girls); Leonid Kinsky (Voluble Arab); Louis Aldez (Blind Singer); Barry Downing (Little Boris); Jane Kerr (Ouled Nails Madam); Eric Alden (Anteoni's Lieutenant); Michael Mark (Coachman); Harlan Briggs, Irene Franklin (American Tourists); Louis Mercier, Marcel De La Brosse, Robert Stevenson (De Trevignac's Patrol).

KNIGHT WITHOUT ARMOUR (UA, 1937) 107 M.

Producer, Alexander Korda; director, Jacques Feyder; based on the novel *Without Armour* by James Hilton; adaptation, Frances Marion; screenplay, Lajos Biro, Arthur Wimperis; music, Miklos Rosza; music director, Muir Matheson; assistant director, Imlay Watts; settings, Lazare Meerson; special effects, Ned Mann; camera, Harry Stradling; editor, Francis Lyon.

Marlene Dietrich (Alexandra); Robert Donat (A. J. Fotheringill); Irene Vanburgh (Duchess); Herbert Lomas (Vladinoff); Austin Trevor (Colonel Adaxine); Basil Gill (Axelstein); David Tree (Maronin); John Clements (Poushkoff); Frederick Culley (Stanfield); Lawrence Hanray (Forrester); Dorice Fordred (Maid); Franklin Kelsey (Tomsky); Lawrence Kingston (Commissar); Hay Petrie (Station Master); Miles Malleson (Drunken Red Soldier); Lyn Harding (Bargeman); Raymond Huntley (White Officer); Peter Evan Thomas (General Andreyevitch).

ANGEL (PAR, 1937) 98 M.

Producer-director, Ernst Lubitsch; based on a play by Melchior Lengyel; adaptation, Guy Bolton, Russell Medcraft; screenplay, Samson Raphaelson; music, Frederick Hollander; song, Hollander and Leo Robin; assistant director, Joseph Lefert; art director, Hans Dreier, Robert Usher; special effects, Farciot Edouart; camera, Charles Lang; editor, William Shea.

Marlene Dietrich (Maria Barker); Herbert Marshall (Sir Frederick Barker); Melvyn Douglas (Anthony Halton); Edward Everett Horton (Graham); Ernest Cossart (Walton); Laura Hope Crews (Grand Duchess Anna Dmitrievna); Herbert Mundin (Greenwood); Ivan Lebedeff (Prince Vladimir Gregorovitch); Dennie Moore (Emma); Lionel Pape (Lord Davington); Phillis Coghlan (Maid, The Barker Home); Leonard Carey, Gerald Hamer (Footmen); Eric Wilton (English Chauffeur); Michael S. Visaroff (Russian Butler); Olaf Hytten (Photographer); Gwendolyn Logan (Woman With Maria); George Davis, Arthur Hurni (Taxi Drivers); Joseph Romantini (Headwaiter); Duci Kerekjarto (Prima Violinist); Suzanne Kaaren (Girl Who Gambles); Louise Carter (Flower Woman); Major Sam Harris (Extra at Club); James Finlayson (Footman); Gino Corrado (Assistant Hotel Manager); Herbert Evans (Lord's Butler).

DESTRY RIDES AGAIN (UNIV, 1939) 94 M.

Producer, Joe Pasternak; director, George Marshall; based on the novel by Max Brand; screenplay, Felix Jackson, Henry Meyers, Gertrude Purcell; assistant director, Vernon Keays; art director, Jack Otterson; music, Frank Skinner; music director, Charles Previn; songs, Frederick Hollander and Frank Loesser; camera, Hal Mohr; editor, Milton Carruth.

Marlene Dietrich (Frenchy); James Stewart (Tom Destry); Mischa Auer (Boris Callahan); Charles Winninger ("Wash" Dimsdale); Brian Donlevy (Kent); Allen Jenkins (Gyp Watson); Warren Hymer (Bugs Watson); Irene Hervey (Janice Tyndall); Una Merkel (Lily Belle Callahan); Tom Fadden, (Lem Claggett); Samuel S. Hinds (Judge Slade); Lillian Yarbo (Clara); Edmund MacDonald (Rockwell); Billy Gilbert (Loupgerou, The Bartender); Virginia Brissac (Sophie Claggart); Ann Todd (Claggett Girl); Dickie Jones (Eli Whitney Claggett); Jack Carson (Jack Tyndall); Carmen D'Antonio (Dancer); Joe King (Sheriff Keogh); Harry Cording (Rowdy); Minerva Urecal

(Mrs. DeWitt); Bob McKenzie (Doctor); Billy Bletcher (Pianist); Lloyd Ingraham (Turner, The Express Agent); Bill Cody, Jr. (Small Boy); Loren Brown, Harold DeGarro (Jugglers); Harry Tenbrook, Bud McClure (Stage Drivers); Alex Voloshin (Assistant Bartender); Chief John Big Tree (Indian); Bill Steele Gettinger, Dick Alexander (Cowboys).

SEVEN SINNERS (UNIV, 1940) 87 M.

Producer, Joe Pasternak; director, Tay Garnett; based on a story by Ladislaus Fodor, Lazlo Vadnay; screenplay, John Meehan, Harry Tugend; art director, Jack Otterson; music, Frank Skinner; music director, Charles Previn; songs, Frederick Hollander and Frank Loesser; camera, Rudolph Mate.

Marlene Dietrich (Bijou); John Wayne (Bruce); Broderick Crawford (Little Ned); Mischa Auer (Sasha); Albert Dekker (Dr. Martin); Billy Gilbert (Tony); Oscar Homolka (Antro); Anna Lee (Dorothy); Samuel S. Hinds (Governor); Reginald Denny (Captain Church); Vince Barnett (Bartender); Herbert Rawlinson (First Mate); James Craig (Ensign); William Bakewell (Ensign); Willie Fung (Shopkeeper); Richard Carle (District Officer); William Davidson (Police Chief); Russell Hicks (First Governor); Antonio Moreno (Rubio).

THE FLAME OF NEW ORLEANS (UNIV, 1941) 78 M.

Producer, Joe Pasternak; director, Rene Clair; screenplay, Norman Krasna; music, Frank Skinner; music director, Charles Previn; songs, Previn and Sam Lerner; art director, Jack Otterson, Martin Obzina, Russell A. Gausman; camera, Rudolph Mate; editor, Frank Gross.

Marlene Dietrich (Claire Ledeux); Bruce Cabot (Robert Latour); Roland Young (Charles Giraud); Mischa Auer (Zolotov); Andy Devine, Frank Jenks, Eddie Quillan (Sailors); Laura Hope Crews (Auntie); Franklin Pangborn (Bellows); Theresa Harris (Clementine); Clarence Muse (Samuel); Melville Cooper (Brother-In-Law); Anne Revere (Sister); Bob Evans (Williams); Emily Fitzroy, Virginia Sale, Dorothy Adams (Cousins); Anthony Marlowe (Opera Singer); Gus Schilling (Clerk); Bess Flowers, (Woman), Reed Hadley (Man); Shemp Howard (Waiter).

MANPOWER (WB, 1941) 105 M.

Executive producer, Hal B. Wallis; producer, Mark Hellinger; director, Raoul Walsh; screenplay, Richard Macaulay, Jerry Wald; art director, Max Parker; music, Adolph Deutsch; songs, Frederick Hollander and Frank Loesser; music director, Leo F. Forbstein; special effects, Byron Haskin, H. D. Koenekamp; camera, Ernest Haller; editor, Ralph Dawson.

Edward G. Robinson (Hank McHenry); Marlene Dietrich (Fay Duval); George Raft (Johnny Marshall); Alan Hale (Jumbo Wells); Frank McHugh (Omaha); Eve Arden (Dolly); Barton MacLane (Smiley Quinn); Walter Catlett (Sidney Whipple); Joyce Compton (Scarlet); Lucia Carroll (Flo); Ward Bond (Eddie Adams); Egon Brecher (Pop Duval); Cliff Clark (Cully); Joseph Crehan (Sweeney); Ben Weldon (Al Hurst); Carl Harbaugh (Noisy Nash); Barbara Land (Marilyn); Barbara Pepper (Polly); Dorothy Appleby (Wilma); Roland Drew, Eddie Fetherston, Charles Sherlock, Jeffrey Sayre, De Wolfe (William) Hopper, Al Herman (Men); Ralph Dunn (Man At Phone); Harry Strang (Foreman); Nat Carr (Whiter); Isabel Withers (Floor Nurse); Joan Winfield, Faye Emerson (Nurses); James Flavin (Orderly); Chester Clute (Clerk); Dorothy Vaughan (Mrs. Boyle); Billy Wayne (Taxi Driver); Nella Walker (Floorlady); Brenda Fowler (Saleslady); Joyce Bryant (Miss Brewster); Gayle Mellott Muriel Barr (Models); Joe Devlin (Bartender); Pat McKee (Bouncer); Georgia Caine (Head Nurse); Beal Wong (Chinese Singer); Harry Holman (Justice Of The Peace); Murray Alper, Charles Sullivan, Fred Graham, Elliott Sullivan, William Newell, Dick Wessel (Linemen); Eddy Chandler, Lee Phelps (Detectives).

THE LADY IS WILLING (COL, 1942) 92 M.

Producer-director, Mitchell Leisen; story, James Edward Grant; screenplay

Grant, Albert McCleery; art director, Lionel Banks, Rudolph Sternad; choreography, Douglas Dean, music director, Morris Stoloff; song, Jack King and Gordon Clifford; music, W. Frank Harling; camera, Ted Tetzlaff; editor, Eda Warren.

Marlene Dietrich (Elizabeth Madden); Fred MacMurray (Dr. Corey McBain); Aline MacMahon (Buddy); Stanley Ridges (Kenneth Hanline); Arline Judge (Frances); Roger Clark (Victor); Marietta Canty (Mary Lou); David James (Baby Corey); Ruth Ford (Myrtle); Sterling Holloway (Arthur Miggle); Harvey Stephens (Dr. Golding); Harry Shannon (Det. Sergeant Barnes); Elisabeth Risdon (Mrs. Cummings); Charles Lane (K. K. Miller); Murray Alper (Joe Quig); Kitty Kelly (Neelie Quig); Chester Clute (Income Tax Man); Robert Emmett Keane (Hotel Manager); Eddie Acuff (Murphy); Neil Hamilton (Charlie); Jimmy Conlin (Bum); Charles Halton (Dr. Jones); Helen Ainsworth (Interior Decorator); Myrtle Anderson (Maid).

THE SPOILERS (UNIV, 1942). 87 M.

Producer, Frank Lloyd; associate producer, Lee Marcus; director, Ray Enright; based on the novel by Rex Beach; screenplay, Lawrence Hazard, Tom Reed; art director, Jack Otterson, John B. Goodman; music, Hans J. Salter; music director, Charles Previn; costumes, Vera West; camera, Milton Krasner; editor, Clarence Kolster.

Marlene Dietrich (Cherry Mallotte); Randolph Scott (Alex McNamara); John Wayne (Roy Glennister); Margaret Lindsay (Helen Chester); Harry Carey (Dextry); Richard Barthelmess (Bronco Kid); George Cleveland (Banty); Samuel S. Hinds (Judge Stillman); Russell Simpson (Flapjack); William Farnum (Wheaton); Marietta Canty (Idabelle); Jack Norton (Mr. Skinner); Ray Bennett (Clark); Forrest Taylor (Bennett); Charles Halton (Struve); Bud Osborne (Marshall); Drew Demarest (Galloway); Robert W. Service (Poet); Charles McMurphy, Art Miles, William Haade (Deputies); Robert Homans (Sea Captain).

PITTSBURGH (UNIV, 1942). 90 M.

Producer, Charles K. Feldman; associate producer, Robert Fellows; director, Lewis Seiler; story, George Owen, Tom Reed; screenplay, Kenneth Gamet, Reed; additional dialogue, John Twist; art director, John B. Goodman; costumes, Vera West; music, Hans J. Salter; music director, Charles Previn; assistant director, Charles Gould; special effects, John P. Fulton; camera, Robert De Grasse; editor, Paul Landres.

Marlene Dietrich (Josie Winters); Randolph Scott (Cash Evans); John Wayne (Pittsburgh Markham); Frank Craven (Doc Powers); Louise Allbritton (Shannon Prentiss); Shemp Howard (Shorty); Thomas (Joe Malneck); Ludwig Stossel (Dr. Grazlich); Samuel S. Hinds (Morgan Prentiss); Paul Fix (Mine Operator); William Haade (Johnny); Douglas Fowley (Mort Brawley); Sammy Stein (Killer Kane); Harry Seymour (Theatre Manager); Nestor Paiva (Barney); Charles Coleman (Butler); Hobart Cavanaugh (Derelict); Virginia Sale (Mrs. Bercovici); Wade Boteler (Mine Superintendant); Mira McKinney (Tilda); Alphonse Martell (Carlos); Charles Sherlock (Chauffeur); Bess Flowers (Woman).

FOLLOW THE BOYS (UNIV, 1944) 122 M.

Producer, Charles K. Feldman; associate producer, Albert L. Rockett; director, Eddie Sutherland; screenplay, Lou Breslow, Gertrude Purcell; art director, John B. Goodman, Harold H. MacArthur; music director, Leigh Harline; songs, Sammy Cahn and Jule Styne; Kermit Goell and Walter Donaldson; Billy Austin and Louis Jordan; Dorothy Fields and Jimmy McHugh; Shelton Brooks; Inez James and Buddy Pepper; Phil Moore; Leo Robin, W. Franke Harling and Richard Whiting; Roy Turk and Fred Ahlert; Dick Charles and Larry Markes; assistant director, Howard Christie; choreography, George Hale; camera, David Abel; editor, Fred R. Reitshaus, Jr.

George Raft (Tony West); Vera Zorina (Gloria Vance); Grace McDonald (Kitty West); Charley Grapewin (Nick West); Charles Butterworth (Louis Fairweather); Ramsay Ames (Laura); Elizabeth Patterson (Annie); Regis Toomey (Dr. Henderson);

George Macready (Walter Bruce); Frank Jenks (Chic Doyle); Addison Richards (McDermott); Emmett Vogan (Harkness); Cyril Ring (Laughton); Theodore von Eltz (William Barrett); Martha O'Driscoll, Maxie Rosenbloom (Themselves); and: Jeanette MacDonald, Orson Welles' Mercury Wonder Show, Marlene Dietrich; Dinah Shore, Donald O.Connor, Peggy Ryan, W. C. Fields, The Andrew Sisters, Artur Rubinstein, Carmen Amaya and Her Company; Sophie Tucker, The Delta Rhythm Boys, Leonard Gautier's The Bricklayer Dog Act, Ted Lewis And His Band, Freddie Slach And His Orchestra, Charlie Spivak And His Orchestra, Louis Jordan and His Orchestra (Guest Stars); in the Hollywood Victory Committee scene: Louise Allbritton, Evelyn Ankers, Louise Beavers, Noah Beery, Jr., Nigel Bruce, Turhan Bey, Lon Chaney, Jr., Alan Curtis, Peter Coe, Andy Devine, Thomas Gomez, Samuel S. Hinds, Clarence Muse, Gale Sondergaard.

KISMET (MGM, 1944) 100 M.

Producer, Everett Riskin; director, William Dieterle; based on the play by Edward Knobloch; screenplay, John Meehan; art director, Cedric Gibbons, Daniel B. Cathcart; assistant director, Marvin Stuart; music, Herbert Stothart; special effects, A. Arnold Gillespie, Warren Newcombe; camera, Charles Rosher; editor, Ben Lewis.

Ronald Colman (Hafiz); Marlene Dietrich (Jamilla); James Craig (Caliph); Edward Arnold (Mansur, The Grand Vizier); Hugh Herbert (Feisal); Joy Ann Page (Marsinah); Florence Bates (Karsha); Harry Davenport (Agha); Hobart Cavanaugh (Moolah); Robert Warwick (Alfife); Beatrice and Evelyne Kraft (Court Dancers); Barry Macollum (Amu); Victor Killian (Jehan); Charles Middleton (Miser); Harry Humphrey (Gardener); Nestor Paiva (Police Captain); Eve Whitney (Cafe Girl); Cy Kendall (Herald); Minerva Urecal (Retainer); Dan Seymour (Fat Turk); Dale Van Sickel (Assassin); Pedro DeCordoba (Meuzin).

MARTIN ROUMAGANAC (The Room Upstairs) (Alicna, 1946) 115 M.

Producer, Marc Le Pelletier; director, Georges Lacombe; based on the novel by Pierre-Rene Wolf; screenplay, Pierre Very; art director, George Wakhevitch; camera, Roger Hubert.

Marlene Dietrich (Blanche Ferrand); Jean Gabin (Martin Roumagnac); Margo Lion (Martin's Sister); Marcel Herrand (Consul); Jean D'Yd (Blanche' Uncle); Daniel Gelin (Lover); Jean Darcante (Lawyer); Henri Poupon (Gargame); Marcel Andre (Judge); Paulot (Perez); Charles Lemontier (Bonnemain); and: Michel Ardan, Paul Faivre, Marcelle Geniat, Lucien Nat.

GOLDEN EARRINGS (PAR, 1947) 95 M.

Producer, Harry Tugend; director, Mitchell Leisen; based on the novel by Yolanda Foldes; screenplay, Abraham Polonsky, Frank Butler, Helen Deutsch; art director, Hans Dreier, John Meehan; assistant director, Johnny Coonan, music, Victor Young; song, Victor Young, Jay Livingston and Ray Evans; choreography, Billy Daniels; orchestration, Leo Shuken, Sidney Cutler; special effects, Gordon Jennings; process camera, Farciot Edouart; camera, Daniel L. Fapp; editor, Alma Macrorie.

Ray Milland (Col. Ralph Denistoun); Marlene Dietrich (Lydia); Murvyn Vye (Zoltan); Bruce Lester (Byrd); Dennis Hoey (Hoff); Quentin Reynolds (Himself); Reinhold Schunzel ((Professor Korsigk); Ivan Triesault (Major Reimann); Hermine Sterler (Greta Korsigk); Eric Feldary (Zweig); Gisela Werbiserk (Dowager); Larry Simms (Page Boy); Hans von Morhart (S.S. Trooper); Mme. Louise Colombet (Flower Woman); Robert Val, Gordon Arnold (Gypsy Boys); Martha Bamattrê (Wise Old Woman); Antonia Morales (Gypsy Dancer); Jack Wilson (Hitler Youth Leader).

A FOREIGN AFFAIR (PAR, 1948) 116 M.

Producer, Charles Brackett; director, Billy Wilder; story, David Shaw; adaptation, Robert Harari; screenplay, Brackett, Wilder, and Richard L. Breen; music-songs, Frederick Hollander; art director, Hans Dreier, Walter Tyler; assistant director, C. C.

Coleman, Jr.; special effects, Gordon Jennings; process camera, Farciot Edouart, Dewey Wrigley; camera, Charles B. Lang, Jr.; editor, Doane Harrison.

Jean Arthur (Phoebe Frost); Marlene Dietrich (Erika von Schuotow); John Lund (Captain John Pringle); Millard Mitchell (Col. Rufus J. Plummer); Peter von Zerneck (Hans Otto Birgel); Stanley Prager (Mike); Bill Murphy (Joe); Gordon Jones, Freddie Steele (M.P.s) Raymond Bond (Pennecott); Boyd Davis (Giffin); Robert Malcolm (Kraus); Bobby Watson (Adolph Hitler In Film Clip); Charles Meredith (Yandell); Michael Raffetto (Salvatore); James Larmore (Lt. Hornby); Damian O'Flynn (Lt. Colonel); Frank Fenton (Major); William Neff (Lt. Lee Thompson); Harland Tucker (General McAndrew); George Carleton (General Finney).

JIGSAW (UA, 1949) 70 M.

Producer, Edward J. Danziger, Harry Lee Danziger; director, Fletcher Markle; story, John Roeburt; screenplay, Markle, Vincent McConnor; music, Robert Stringer; assistant director, Sal J. Scoppa, Jr; special effects, William L. Nemeth; camera, Don Malkames; editor, Robert Matthews.

Franchot Tone (Howard Malloy); Jean Wallace (Barbara Whitfield); Myron McCormick (Charles Riggs); Marc Lawrence (Angelo Agostini); Winifrid Lenihan (Mrs. Hartley); Betty Harper (Caroline Riggs); Hedley Rainnie (Sigmund Kosterich); Walter Vaughn (D. A. Walker); George Breen (Knuckles); Robert Gist (Tommy Quigley); Hester Sondergaard (Mrs. Borge); Luella Gear (Pet Shop Owner); Alexander Campbell (Pemberton); Robert Noe (Waldron); Alexander Lockwood (Nichols); Ken Smith (Wylie); Alan Macateer (Museum Guard); Manuel Aparicio (Warehouse Guard); Brainard Duffield (Butler); Marlene Dietrich, Fletcher Markle (Nightclub Patrons); Henry Fonda (Nightclub Waiter); John Garfield (Street Loiterer); Marsha Hunt (Secretary-Receptionist); Leonard Lyons (Columnist); Burgess Meredith (Bartender).

STAGE FRIGHT (WB, 1950) 110 M.

Producer-director, Alfred Hitchcock; based on the stories "Outrun the Constable" and "Man Running" by Selwyn Jepson; adaptation, Alma Reville; screenplay, Whitfield Cook; additional dialogue, James Bridie; music, Leighton Lucas; music director, Louis Levy; song, Cole Porter; camera, Wilkie Cooper; editor, Edward Jarvis.

Jane Wyman (Eve Gill); Marlene Dietrich (Charlotte Inwood); Michael Wilding (Smith); Richard Todd (Jonathan Cooper); Alistair Sim (Commodore Gill); Kay Walsh (Nellie); Dame Sybil Thorndike (Mrs. Gill); Miles Malleson (Bibulous Gentleman); Hector MacGregor (Freddie); Joyce Grenfell (Shooting Gallery Attendant); Andre Morell (Inspector Byard); Patricia Hitchcock (Chubby); Alfred Hitchcock (Passerby); and: Cyril Chamberlain, Helen Goss, Everly Gregg, Irene Handl, Arthur Howard.

NO HIGHWAY (NO HIGHWAY IN THE SKY) (20th, 1951) 98 M.

Producer, Louis D. Lighton; director, Henry Koster; based on the novel by Nevil Shute; screenplay, R. C. Sherriff, Oscar Millard, Alec Coppel; assistant director, Bluey Hill; art director, C. P. Norman; camera, George Perinal; editor, Manuel Del Campo.

James Stewart (Mr. Honey); Marlene Dietrich (Monica Teasdale); Glynis Johns (Marjorie Corder); Jack Hawkins (Dennis Scott); Ronald Squire (Sir John); Janette Scott (Elspeth Honey); Niall McGinnis (Captain Samuelson); Elizabeth Allan (Shirley Scott); Kenneth More (Dobson); David Hutcheson (Penworthy); Ben Williams (Guard); Maurice Denham (Major Pease); Wilfrid Hyde White (Fisher); Hector MacGregor, Basil Appleby (Engineers); Michael Kingsley (Navigator); Peter Murray (Radio Operator); Dora Bryan (Rosie).

RANCHO NOTORIOUS (RKO, 1952) 89 M.

Producer, Howard Welsch; director, Fritz Lang; based on the story by Sylvia

Richards; screenplay, Daniel Taradash; production designer, Wiard Ihnen; music, Emil Newman; assistant director, Emmett Emerson; songs, Ken Darby; production supervisor,Ben Hersh; camera, Hal Mohr; editor, Otto Ludwig.

Marlene Dietrich (Altar Keane); Arthur Kennedy (Vern Haskell); Mel Ferrer (Frenchy Fairmont); Lloyd Gough (Kinch); Gloria Henry (Beth); William Frawley (Baldy Gunder); Lisa Ferraday (Maxine); John Raven (Chuck-A-Luck Dealer); Jack Elam (Gary); George Reeves (Wilson); Frank Ferguson (Preacher); Francis McDonald (Harbin); Dan Seymour (Comanche Paul);John Kellogg (Factor); Rodric Redwing (Rio); Stuart Randall (Starr); Roger Anderson (Red); Charles Gonzales (Hevia); Felipe Turich (Sanchez); Jose Dominguez (Gonzales); Stan Jolley (Deputy Warren); John Doucette (Whitey); Charlita (Mexican Girl In Bar); Ralph Sanford (Politician); Lane Chandler (Sheriff Hardy); Fuzzy Knight (Barber); Fred Graham (Ace Maguire); Dick Wessel (Deputy); Dick Eliott (Story teller); William Haade (Sheriff Bullock).

AROUND THE WORLD IN 80 DAYS (UA, 1956) 168 M.

Producer, Michael Todd; associate producer, William Cameron Menzies; director, Michael Anderson; based on the novel by Jules Verne; screenplay, S. J. Perelman, John Farrow, James Poe; choreography, Paul Godkin, music, Victor Young; art director, Ken Adam; James W. Sullivan; camera, Lionel Lindon; editor, Gene Ruggiero, Paul Weatherwax.

David Niven (Phileas Fogg); Cantinflas (Passepartout); Robert Newton (Mr. Fix); Shirley MacLaine (Princess Aouda); Charles Boyer (Monsieur Gasse); Joe E. Brown (Station Master); Martine Carol (Tourist); John Carradine (Col. Proctor Stamp); Charles Coburn (Clerk); Ronald Colman (Official Of Railway); Melville Cooper (Steward); Noel Coward (Mesketh-Baggott); Finlay Currie (Whist Partner); Reginald Denny (Police Chief); Andy Devine (First Mate); Marlene Dietrich (Dance Hall Hostess); Luis Miguel Dominguin (Bullfighter); Fernandel (Coachman); Sir John Gielgud (Fost); Hermione Gingold (Sportin' Lady); José Greco (Dancer); Sir Cedric Hardwicke (Sir Francis Gromarty); Trevor Howard (Fallentin); Glynis Johns (Companion); Buster Keaton (Conductor); Evelyn Keyes (Flirt); Beatrice Lillie (Revivalist); Peter Lorre (Steward); Edmund Lowe (Engineer); Victor McLaglen (Helmsman); Colonel Tim McCoy (Commander); A. E. Mathew (Club Member); Mike Mazurki (Character); John Mills (Cabby); Alan Mowbray (Consul); Robert Morley (Ralph); Edward R. Murrow (Narrator); Jack Oakie (Captain); George Raft (Bouncer); Gilbert Roland (Achmed Abdullah); Cesar Romero (Henchman); Basil Sydney, Ronald Squire (Members); Harcourt Williams (Hinshaw); Ava Gardner (Spectator); Red Skelton (Drunk); Frank Sinatra (Piano Player).

THE MONTE CARLO STORY (UA, 1957) 99 M.

Producer, Marcello Girosi; director, Samuel A. Taylor; story, Girosi, Dino Risi; screenplay, Taylor; art director, Gastone Medin; assistant director, Luisa Alessandri, Roberto Montemurro, Maria Russo; songs, Michael Emer; camera, Giuseppe Rotunno.

Marlene Dietrich (Marquise Maria de Crevecoeur); Vittorio De Sica (Count Dino della Fiaba); Arthur O'Connell (Mr. Hinkley); Natalie Trundy (Jane Hinkley); Jane Rose (Mrs. Freeman); Clelia Matania (Sophia); Alberto Rabagliati (Albert); Mischa Auer (Hector); Renato Rascel (Duval) Carlo Rizzo (Henri); Truman Smith (Mr. Freeman); Mimo Billi (Roland); Marco Tulli (Francoise); Guido Martufi (Paul); Jean Combal (Hotel Managing Director); Vera Garretto (Caroline); Yannick Geffroy (Gabriel); Betty Philippsen (Zizi); Frank Colson (Walter); Serge Fligers (Harry); Frank Elliott (Mr. Ewing); Betty Carter (Mrs. Ewing); Gerlaine Fournier (German Lady); Simonemarie Rose (Lady In Magenta); Clara Beck (American Oil Heiress).

WITNESS FOR THE PROSECUTION (UA, 1958) 116 M.

Producer, Arthur Hornblow, Jr.; director, Billy Wilder; based on the play by Agatha Christie; adaptation, Larry Marcus; screenplay, Wilder, Harry Kurnitz; assistant director, Emmett Emerson; art director, Alexandre Trauner; music, Matty Malneck; song, Ralph Arthur Roberts and Jack Brooks; music conductor, Ernest Gold; camera, Russell Harlan; editor, Daniel Mandell.

Tyrone Power (Leonard Vole); Marlene Dietrich (Christine Vole); Charles Laughton (Sir Wilfrid Robarts); Elsa Lanchester (Miss Plimsoll); John Williams (Brogan-Moore); Henry Daniell (Mayhew); Ian Wolfe (Carter); Una O'Connor (Janet MacKenzie); Torin Thatcher (Mr. Meyers); Francis Compton (Judge); Norma Varden (Mrs. French); Philip Tonge (Inspector Hearne); Ruta Lee (Diana); Molly Roden (Miss McHugh); Ottola Nesmith (Miss Johnson); Marjorie Eaton (Miss O'Brien); J. Pat O'Malley (Shorts Salesman).

TOUCH OF EVIL (UNIV, 1958) 93 M.

Producer, Alfred Zugsmith; director, Orson Welles; director, additional scenes, Harry Keller; based on the novel *Badge of Evil* by Whit Masterson; screenplay, Orson Welles; assistant director, Phil Bowles, Terry Nelson; art director, Alexander Golitzen, Robert Clatworthy; music, Henri Mancini; camera, Russell Metty; editor, Virgil W.Vogel, Aaron Stell.

Charlton Heston (Ramon Miguel Vargas); Janet Leigh (Susan Vargas); Orson Welles (Hank Quinlan); Joseph Calleia (Pete Menzies); Akim Tamiroff ("Uncle" Joe Grandi); Joanna Moore (Marcia Linnekar); Ray Collins (Adair); Dennis Weaver (Night Man); Valentin De Vargas (Pancho); Mort Mills (Schwartz); Victor Milan (Manuelo Sanchez); Lalo Rios (Risto); Michael Sargent ("Pretty Boy"); and: Joseph Cotten, Marlene Dietrich, Zsa Zsa Gabor, Mercedes McCambridge (Guest Stars).

JUDGMENT AT NUREMBERG (UA, 1961) 178 M.

Producer, Stanley Kramer; associate producer, Philip Langner; director, Kramer; screenplay, Abby Mann; assistant director, Ivan Volkman; art director, Rudolph Sternad; music, Ernest Gold; camera, Ernest Laszlo; editor, Fred Knudtson.

Spencer Tracy (Judge Dan Haywood); Burt Lancaster (Ernst Janning); Richard Widmark (Colonel Tod Lawson) Marlene Dietrich (Mme. Bertholt); Maximilian Schell (Hans Rolfe); Judy Garland (Irene Hoffman); Montgomery Clift (Rudolf Peterson); William Shatner (Captain Byers); Edward Binns (Senator Burkette); Kenneth MacKenna (Judge Kenneth Norris) Werner Klemperer (Emil Hahn); Alan Baxter (General Merrin); Torben Meyer (Werner Lammpe); Ray Teal (Judge Curtiss Ives); Martin Brandt (Friedrich Hofstetter); Virginia Christine (Mrs. Halbestadt); Ben Wright (Halbestadt); Joseph Bernard (Major Abe Radnitz) John Wengraf (Dr. Wieck); Karl Swenson (Dr. Geuter); Howard Caine (Wallner); Otto Waldis (Pohl); Olga Fabian (Mrs. Lindnow) Bernard Kates (Perkins); Sheilia Bromley (Mrs. Ives); Jana Taylor (Else Scheffler); Paul Busch (Schmidt). Joseph Crehan (Spectator).

BLACK FOX (MGM, 1962) 89 M.

Executive producer, Jack Le Vien; producer-director-screenplay, Louis Clyde Stoumen; animation supervisor, Al Stahl; production supervisor, Richard Kaplan; music, Ezra Laderman; editor, Kenn Collins, Mark Wortreich.

Marlene Dietrich (Narrator).

PARIS WHEN IT SIZZLES (PAR, 1964) 110 M.

Producer, Richard Quine, George Axelrod; director, Quine; story, Julien Duvivier, Henri Jeanson; screenplay, Axelrod; assistant director, Paul Feyder; music, Nelson Riddle; set director, Jean D'Eauboune; camera, Charles Lang, Jr.; editor, Archie Marshek.

William Holden (Richard Benson); Audrey Hepburn (Gabrielle Simpson); Gregoire Alsan (Police Inspector); Noel Coward (Alexander Mayerheimer); Raymond Bussieres (Gangster): Christian Duvallex (Maitre D'Hotel); Tony Curtis, Marlene Dietrich, Mel Ferrer (Guest Appearances); Fred Astaire, Frank Sinatra (Voices Of).

h Joan Crawford, about 1934–35

In THE FLAME OF NEW ORLEANS (Univ '41)

h Orson Welles in FOLLOW THE
YS (Univ '44)

On the set of WITNESS FOR THE PROSE-
CUTION (UA '57) with director Billy
Wilder

In DIE FRAU, NACH DER MAN SICH SEHNT (Terra '29)

With Victor McLaglen in DISHONORED (Par '31)

With Gary Cooper in DESIRE (Par '36)

With Gary Cooper in MOROCCO (Par '30)

With Charles Boyer, Basil Rathbone, and C. Aubrey Smith in GARDEN OF ALLAH (UA '36)

With Cary Grant in BLONDE VENUS (Par '32)

With Charles Boyer in the unfinished Paramount picture, I LOVED A SOLDIER, 1937

With Robert Donat in KNIGHT WITHOUT ARMOUR (UA '37)

With Brian Donlevy and James Stewart in DESTRY RIDES AGAIN (Univ '39)

With John Wayne in SEVEN SINNERS (Univ '40)

With George Raft, Beal Wong, Edward G. Robinson, and Frank McHugh in MAN-POWER (WB '41)

With John Wayne and Randolph Scott in THE SPOILERS (Univ '42)

With Ronald Colman in KISMET (MGM '44)

With Jean Arthur in A FOREIGN AFFAIR (Par '48)

With Richard Todd in STAGE FRIGHT (WB '50)

With Glynis Johns and James Stewart in NO HIGHWAY IN THE SKY (20th '51)

With Cantinflas, David Niven, and Frank Sinatra in AROUND THE WORLD IN 80 DAYS (UA '56)

In PARIS WHEN IT SIZZLES (Par '64)

MIRIAM HOPKINS

5'3"

105 pounds

Silver blonde hair

Blue Eyes

Libra

✳✳✳✳✳✳✳✳✳✳✳✳✳✳✳✳✳✳✳✳✳✳

MIRIAM HOPKINS today has retained little of the lustrous film reputation she acquired in the 1930s. Then she was regarded as one of the screen's most versatile dramatic luminaries, who seemed equally at ease whether portraying a cockney music hall floozie in *Dr. Jekyll And Mr. Hyde* or a lovelorn school teacher in *These Three*. She did her best cinema work in a trio of sophisticated Ernst Lubitsch Paramount features *The Smiling Lieutenant, Trouble in Paradise,* and *Design for Living;* in each of these, as an effervescent belle, she employed her chic surface emotions and abundance of theatrical gestures with effective results.

Miriam joined Paramount in 1930, after ten years on Broadway as a successful ingenue, essaying variations of the cuddly coquette with blonde curls and displaying her Southern charm. During her five years at the studio she made 13 features, including the then daring screen version of *Sanctuary,* called *The Story of Temple Drake*.

Her best performance seems to have been her success in dazzling studio executives and film critics alike into believing that she was a multifaceted star with just the right amount of delicate femininity. In fact she was anything but these things, being rather big boned and bovine in build. In the mid-1930s she signed with Samuel Goldwyn as his replacement for the unsuccessful import, Anna Sten. In the late 1930s she convinced Jack Warner that she was just right for Warner Brothers. There, pitted against strong dramatic stars, she met her match in Bette Davis, who outclassed her in both *The Old Maid* and *Old Acquaintances.*

By the 1940s Miriam's tenure as a screen star had ended. She had aged rather badly. She spent the next two decades alternating between Broadway assignments (her most successful were replacement roles in *The Skin of Our Teeth* and *Look Homeward Angel*) and sporadically appearing in featured roles in classy A-films. Only occasionally did she make a foray into television, but her performances were too strident to be effective.

Miriam Hopkins was born Ellen Miriam Hopkins on Gordon Street in Savannah, Georgia, on October 18, 1902, the daughter of Homer A. and Ellen D. (Cutler) Hopkins. Her father was an insurance salesman. Little is known about Miriam's childhood—she has always been most secretive on this subject—except that she spent most of her formative years living with her maternal grandmother in nearby Bainbridge. As a child she sang in the boys' choir at St. John's Episcopal Church there. (When Miriam was a star in the 1930s, Mr. Hopkins was discovered residing in a small Oklahoma town. He admitted that he had not been in touch with his famous daughter for over two decades.)

When Miriam was 14, she and her mother went north, while two other sisters remained behind. Miriam was sent to Goddard Seminary in Barre, Vermont, to complete her secondary education. While there she won a $2 gold piece in an oratory competition ("Perhaps that really started the idea in my subconscious mind of going on the stage," Miriam later recalled). At Syracuse University, where her uncle was a geology professor, Miriam was very active in the drama society, although she was fonder of art classes and ballet dancing. She nearly lost her role in the graduation play when she broke her ankle, but she managed to go on.

After college, Miriam moved to Manhattan, determined someday to become premiere danseuse in a ballet company. She settled for a chorus job in the *Music Box Revue* (Music Box Theatre, September 22, 1921). In this Irving Berlin show, she was paid $40 a week for performing in a water lily ballet and other numbers. She later auditioned for a South American tour with a ballet company, but shortly before the group was to leave, she broke her ankle again, and was out of work.

For the next two years, Miriam played the vaudeville circuit, often acting in a skit devised by performer May Tully. In *Little Jessie James,* a musical farce about a naive Kansas girl in New York which premiered on Broadway on August 15, 1923, Miriam was Juliet. Next to Miriam on the dance line was Claire Booth, future playwright and celebrity. One reviewer noted that Miriam "sang pleasantly and danced gracefully."

Her theatrical lowpoint in 1924 was being fired from *The Two Mrs. Smiths,* a stage skit being performed in Staten Island. She then joined the cast of *High Tide,* which tried out and closed in Washington, D.C., in December, 1924.

Miriam's first substantial stage success came in *Puppets* (Selwyn Theatre, March 9, 1925). She had replaced another promising stage ingenue, Claudette Colbert, in the lead role of Angela Smith, a Southerner who marries the director (C. Henry Gordon) of a marionette theatre. When Gordon marches off to war and is presumed killed in action, she weds Fredric March. Gordon returns and trauma commences. The *New York Times* reported: "Miriam Hopkins carried her role of Angela into no little sweetness, too much for some in the audience and not enough for others perhaps." The drama lasted 57 performances.

Next she was fired from Channing Pollock's *The Enemy* (1925) because the author regarded her as unsuitable to play the mother of a six-year-old. Fay Bainter was substituted. In October, 1925, Miriam opened on Broadway in the romantic *Lovely Lady* and was termed a "pretty and intense little chit." She left that show to accept the lead in *The Matinee Girl,* but withdrew from the cast during its December, 1925, tryout engagement in Wilkes-Barre, Pennsylvania.

By now Miriam was in the leading rank of Broadway ingenues, and her name constantly appeared in the news. On May 11, 1926, she married actor Brandon Peters. He was 24 years old and it was his first marriage. (As they were both active stage performers, the couple usually found themselves working in different cities. From 1928 to 1931 he appeared on the Australian stage. Miriam and he were divorced in June, 1931.)

Miriam won the lead in Anita Loos's gold-digging comedy *Gentlemen Prefer Blondes* (1926), but the authoress decided she was not wide-eyed enough and replaced her with June Walker. Miriam then took the featured role of Sondra Finchley in a dramatization of Theodore Dreiser's *An American Tragedy* (Longacre Theatre, October 11, 1926) which ran for 216 performances. Although it was a prestigious assignment for Miriam, best reviews went to stars Morgam Farley and Katharine Wilson. The *New York Herald Tribune* observed that Miriam's performance as the society girl "was a truly admirable one." (When Paramount filmed *An American Tragedy* [1931] as a vehicle for Sylvia Sidney, Frances Dee played Miriam's stage role.)

In *The Garden of Eden,* which opened in September, 1927, Miriam caused quite a stir as Toni Lebrun, a chaste Parisian cabaret girl who succumbs to rich Douglass Montgomery. The big wedding-night scene required Miriam to remove her outer garments in full view of the audience. It created no little sensation. The *New York Times*'s Brooks Atkinson wrote: "There is a delightful freshness about her personality. But certainly her present part treats her shabbily; she is not quite brazen enough to pull off its dramatic excesses." The show folded after 23 performances. Tallulah Bankhead—a professional rival of Miriam's over the next two decades—starred in this play to more noteworthy success in London.

In the fall of 1927 Miriam played in *The Home Towner* and *Give and Take* in Chicago. She was Elsa McCoy in *Excess Baggage* (Ritz Theatre, December 26, 1927). This play, which had a run of 216 performances, was another inside look at theatre life à la *Burlesque* and *Broadway.* As the bride of struggling vaudeville performer Eddie Kane, Miriam had to choose between a tempting cinema contract and a quieter life as a devoted wife. The *New York Times* acknowledged that she "was always beautiful and her acting at all times showed finesse."

After portraying a Long Island flapper who becomes pregnant in *Flight* (Longacre Theatre, February 18, 1929), Miriam had a more substantial role in the Theatre Guild's *The Camel Through the Needle's Eye,* which premiered in April, 1929. She was tenement girl Susi Pesta in love with Claude Rains's son. The *New York Times* commented: "Though lacking a little in variety, she gives, on the whole, an understanding, easy performance." Helen Westley as Miriam's shrewish mother netted the best reviews.

On September 23, 1929, Miriam made her London stage debut in *The Bachelor Father,* starring C. Aubrey Smith. The British newspaper *The Era* noted: "She is pretty, fluffy-haired, with a direct style and attack that won all our hearts." She withdrew from the London success to return to America to costar with Ernest Truex in *Ritzy* (Longacre Theatre, February 10, 1930), dealing with a married couple who quarrel bitterly once they obtain wealth. It was short-lived.

Miriam was Kalonika in the distinguished production of Aristophanes' *Lysistrata,* which played Broadway in June, 1930, featuring Fay Bainter, Sydney Greenstreet, Ernest Truex, and Albert Dekker. Norman Bel Geddes directed and designed the elaborate production.

After this, Miriam, then 28 years old, accepted a Paramount term contract. The studio's production head, B. P. Schulberg,* had been raiding Broadway to recruit many of its leading players to bolster his star roster. Other actresses who accepted Paramount's offer were Claudette Colbert (age 25) and Sylvia Sidney (age 20). It was a wise move for Miriam. Although she had been consistently employed in the theatre throughout the 1920s, she never had a truly outstanding vehicle that might have elevated her to the ranks of a top legitimate star like Helen Hayes or Eva Le Galienne.

Miriam went to Hollywood for her screen debut in *Fast and Loose* (1930) a remake of the studio's 1925 romantic drama. She then boarded the train back to New York to appear in *His Majesty's Car* (Ethel Barrymore Theatre, October 23, 1930). She played a lowly typist who pretended to be a king's mistress. This artificial comedy folded after 12 performances.

Fast and Loose opened at the Paramount Theatre on November 30, 1930. It was not a fortuitous cinema debut vehicle for Miriam. She appeared as the wealthy daughter of indulgent Frank Morgan and becomes enamored of auto mechanic Charles Starrett. Despite the Preston Sturges script, the film had a most conventional plot line. Miriam presented anything but star material with her unpetite frame frocked in unbecoming garb and her hair a frizzy mess. Even her diction was over-enunciated in a most stagey manner. *Variety* reported: "This stage artiste plays tick-tack-toe with the camera, sometimes winning, sometimes losing, but the merit of her performance will be universally obvious." Seen to much better advantage in *Fast and Loose* was another Paramount contractee, Carole Lombard.

After more moviemaking Miriam returned to New York (she spent seven months of her first film contract year in Manhattan) to portray Mimi in Arthur Schnitzler's *Anatol* (Lyceum Theatre, January 16, 1931). With Joseph Schildkraut in the title role, she was the operatic hussy in this episodic romancer. The critics found her "vastly amusing, gorging shamelessly at the table, flying into a passion, tearing angrily around the room," and so forth.

Her second feature film was an entirely different story. It was the prestigious Ernst Lubitsch production *The Smiling Lieutenant* (1931), a meticulous example of high sophistication in the then popular light operetta genre. It was filmed at the studio's Astoria, Long Island, facilities. On a weekly salary of $1,500, Miriam was third-billed to stars Maurice Chevalier and Claudette Colbert. Austrian lieutenant Chevalier has a twinkle in his eye for all pretty women, but is accidentally compromised into marrying frumpish Princess Miriam. His former playmate, beer garden singer and violinist Colbert, arrives by royal order to advise dowdy Miriam on the art of dress, coiffure, and wit. Typical of the musical dialogue was a talk-sing number which had enraptured Miriam saying: "He's gracious. Not audacious, And Romance wakens at his touch. I like him. Oh, I like him. I like him so much." *The Smiling Lieutenant* was a popular success with Miriam's presence and assistance fully acknowledged. It gave her a big boost in the cinema community. She, Colbert, and Chevalier repeated their assignment in the French version of *The Smiling Lieutenant*.

In the turgid *Twenty-Four Hours* (1931), which packed a lot of plot into 66 minutes, Miriam was a cabaret singer (with two songs) having an affair with Clive Brook. When she is murdered by gangster Regis Toomey, Brook is suspected. Neither Miriam nor the picture's star Kay Francis received

*See Appendix.

much astute direction from Marion Gering. Nevertheless, Miriam's theatrically forceful personality exerted itself and the critics allowed that she "shines." Like her rival, Tallulah Bankhead, who was also making pictures for Paramount now, Miriam's dynamic presence could carry her in almost any mediocre vehicle. Miriam would succeed in the movie medium because of her energetic perseverance, while the more glamorous and resourceful actress Bankhead would fail for lack of interest in her film career and for being too extravagantly exotic for the common moviegoer's taste.

Having divorced Brandon Peters in mid-1931, Miriam soon thereafter wed playwright-scenarist Austin Parker, age 39. He was part of the intellectual set with which Miriam associated in Hollywood (although she could just as easily be the most Southern belle on the nightclub circuit.) She and Parker were divorced in 1932. When he died on March 20, 1938, Miriam, then remarried, was quoted as saying at the funeral home: "If you had known him the way we knew him you would realize he merely wanted his close friends to come and sit around, just as you would in a living room, and talk about what a swell guy he was and that is what we are doing."

Miriam's most productive year on the screen proved to be 1932. In *Dr. Jekyll and Mr. Hyde* (1932), she had the opportunity to show her mettle as a guttersnipe in a classy setting. She originally wanted to play the gentle ingenue (assigned to Rose Hobart), but director Rouben Mamoulian convinced her otherwise. With Fredric March in the Oscar-winning dual role, Miriam was Ivy Pearson, the music hall singer whom Jekyll rescues from molesters in the street. Mamoulian's carefully directed photoplay sharply contrasts Jekyll's relationship with Miriam and demure Hobart along with hideous Hyde's attraction to the two opposing women. For a change, Miriam displayed some sexual allure. On the street she pulls up her skirt to show Jekyll, "Look, where he kicked me." Later, at the dance hall, she sings the raucous "Champagne Ivy," evoking a believable sensuality. When the agonized Jekyll turns into the deranged Hyde, Miriam becomes a victim of his twisted jealousy. Her murder by strangulation is delicately masked from audience view behind a conveniently placed screen. The very tasteful *Dr. Jekyll and Mr. Hyde* was an audience pleaser and Miriam received her critical dues ("does splendidly" announced the *New York Times*).

As a result of this performance, Miriam became a top-ranking Paramount attraction, but she had already been cast in three lesser productions. *Two Kinds of Women* (1932), based on Robert Sherwood's play *This Is New York,* had Miriam, the daughter of a senator from Sioux Falls, eager to see glittering Manhattan. Once there, chance brings her and Phillips Holmes together. When his wife commits suicide, they choose to leave hurly-burly New York. She was acknowledged for giving a "clever portrayal" in this programmer.

Dancers in the Dark (1932) was mostly a Jack Oakie vehicle. He played against type as a grasping band leader with a yen for taxi dancer Miriam. When her saxophone-playing beau, William Collier, Jr., trots off to Pittsburgh, Oakie makes a play for her. Gangster George Raft, who hangs around the club to hear his favorite tune, "St. Louis Blues," is on the lam for a killing and shocks the club habitues back to their senses. Raft and European import Lyda Roberti attracted most audience interest. Miriam appeared ill at ease in her characterization.

John Cromwell directed the bizarre *The World and the Flesh* (1932), which attempted to recreate the troublesome days of 1917 Russia during which a group of aristocrats flee the revolutionists. Miriam was second-billed as ballerina Maria Yaskaya. Bolshevik sailor leader George Bancroft craves her, and she sleeps with the gruff brute in order to save her White Russian friends from the firing squad. A beauty-and-the-beast love affair develops, as the exiles are pushed back and forth between White and Red Russian forces. Had the production values been more expansive, and Miriam and Bancroft more subtle in their acting styles, *The World and the Flesh* might have been convincing melodrama.

Miriam displayed an unrevealed trait of domesticity when she surprisingly adopted a baby boy, Michael, from the Evanston Cradle Society in Chicago on May 4, 1932. Thereafter, he, a governess, and a pet dog were constantly in tow wherever Miriam went. She purchased a Santa Monica Canyon abode which once had been occupied by Greta Garbo.

Her last 1932 release proved to be one of her best pictures, the chic *Trouble in Paradise.* It placed her squarely in a brilliant artificial setting of drawing room comedy, where her theatrical mannerisms seemed far more natural and acceptable. Produced and directed by Ernst Lubitsch, the film featured Miriam and Herbert Marshall as two in-love society swindlers who launch a campaign to dupe millionairess perfumer Kay Francis (her company's motto is: "It doesn't matter what you say, it doesn't matter how you look—it's how you smell"). Marshall becomes her secretary and Miriam is hired as a typist. When Marshall becomes infatuated with the alluring Francis, Miriam seeks revenge by plotting her own private money-stealing. The finale finds worldly Francis acknowledging money cannot buy or retain everything, and Miriam and the regretful Marshall departing with their combined haul and a new sense of love. Miriam remains to him, "My little shoplifter, my sweet little pickpocket, my darling." Mordaunt Hall *(New York Times)* stated: "Miss Hopkins makes Lily a very interesting person, who steals as another girl might sing. Lily even steals her way out of the last scene in the film."

By the end of 1932 Paramount had undergone an executive changeover —B. P. Schulberg became an independent producer at the studio, and Emanuel Cohen* was the new chief executive under president Adolph Zukor. The studio—and the public—had by now sorted out its female star roster of talking films. Clara Bow, the moneymaker of the late 1920s, was off the lot; dramatic ingenue Evelyn Brent had faded into free-lancing; and the once very popular Nancy Carroll was floundering in *Wayward* (1932), overshadowed by George Raft in *Undercover Man* (1932), and by 1933 would have left Paramount for good. Ruth Chatterton and Kay Francis, who had graced a succession of Paramount programmers and lesser A-films would be snapped up by Warner Brothers in a talent raid (along with William Powell) and Jean Arthur would drift off the lot and appear to better advantage at Columbia. Tallulah Bankhead concluded her Paramount contract with *Faithless* (1932) and would not make another film for 11 years. New contractees like Frances Dee would play second leads, but never garner stardom for themselves. Dee at least netted Paramount player Joel McCrea as a husband in 1933.

Thus of the actresses who joined Paramount in 1930, Miriam would in 1932 rank alongside of Claudette Colbert, Sylvia Sidney, Carole Lombard, and studio love-goddess Marlene Dietrich. Her sparkling performance in *Trouble in Paradise* substantiated her promising performance in *Dr. Jekyll and Mr. Hyde,* suggesting that she could provide the studio with the strong

*See Appendix.

dramatic type it required to balance its spectrum of players. Although the studio categorized its players on one hand, it still considered many of them interchangeable. Thus when Miriam dropped out of *The Sign of the Cross* (1932) due to production overlap, Colbert assumed the role, just as Colbert had been assigned to replace Clara Bow in *Manslaughter* (1930). When Miriam refused to make *No Men of Her Own* (1932) ("I couldn't play a wriggly flapper. I'm not that, you know," said Miriam), Carole Lombard was cast in the movie opposite Clark Gable. At one point, Miriam was slated for *Song of Songs* (1933), but Marlene Dietrich eventually appeared in the Rouben Mamoulian-directed picture.

With the arrival of Mae West at Paramount for *Night after Night* (1932), the studio unknowingly ushered in a wave of moral freedom on screen that would reach its peak in West's *She Done Him Wrong* (1933) and *I'm No Angel* (1933). As part of the same (un)conscious daring which acceded to George Raft's request that Mae be hired for *Night after Night*—her saucy way with a sexual innuendo on the stage was undisputed—Paramount acquired the screen rights to William Faulkner's controversial, earthy novel *Sanctuary*. It was restructured and retitled *The Story of Temple Drake* (1933). Miriam appears in it as the neurotic Southern flapper to the manor born, who finds herself deposited one rainy night in the hideout of an inbred gang of bootleggers. When lead hood Jack LaRue takes a fancy to her, he murders the half-wit thug who champions her virtue, and seduces the distraught victim. She emerges from her room the next morning in a state of post-rape trauma. Rather than return home, she accompanies LaRue to the big city and takes up residence in a bordello. There is a strong suggestion that she is more than fascinated by her descent into disgrace. She eventually appears at the murder trial and admits her shocking new past on the witness stand.

In *The Story of Temple Drake*, Miriam overindulged her penchant for unreal theatrics. Her emotions ran the gamut from gaiety, discomfort, fear, and shock (she is most unconvincing in the long car ride as she remains stiffly posed in a state of upset) to acceptance and moral regeneration. However, audiences of the day found her style perfectly acceptable, particularly when the moral censorship issues aroused by this film made it a "hot" picture that had to be seen for its titillation value alone. In fact, Richard Watts, Jr. *(New York Herald Tribune)* was moved to write: "[Hers] is a completely and genuinely brilliant performance, which is so honest and penetrating in its frank character dissection that it must certainly be the finest piece of acting provided by an American screen actress all season." The Academy Award voters obviously did not agree. Miriam was not even nominated for best actress of the year.

The gamey subject—despite the whitewashed presentation—of *The Story of Temple Drake* caused tremendous consternation among film censor boards throughout America, and many sequences were chopped down or eliminated from the release print—the important rape sequence had been filmed by director Stephen Robes in near-darkness, with the glow of LaRue's cigarette as the "main" source of light. This feature, with the Paramount screenings of Mae West, was largely responsible for the revised production code in late 1933 and for the formation of the National Legion of Decency. *Sanctuary* would provide the basis for James Hadley Chase's sex-gangster novel *No Orchids for Miss Blandish,* which would be filmed in England in 1948 and remade in America in 1971 as *The Grissom Gang,* with Kim Darby in Miriam's role. Another version of *Sanctuary*—also a distortion of the Faulkner original—would be made by Twentieth Century-Fox in 1961 with Lee Remick.

On loanout to MGM for *Stranger's Return* (1933), Miriam undertook the more sedate part of a girl who returns to the Iowa farm of her grandfather (Lionel Barrymore), and becomes attracted to neighbor Franchot Tone. He is married to Irene Hervey and eventually returns East, Miriam, however, stays to supervise the farm after Barrymore dies. Beulah Bondi was the tight-lipped spinster stepdaughter and Stuart Erwin essayed the whiskey-drinking farm hand. Miriam "has never been more effective" claimed the *New York Times* and others. While directing the film, King Vidor became "infatuated with the soft Southern talk of this Georgia queen," and they had a brief romance.

Her third 1933 release, *Design for Living,* was also her third performance for Ernst Lubitsch. The new movie production code necessitated drastic alterations in this witty Noel Coward play about a worldly woman who simultaneously loves two gentlemen (who are best friends). The essence of Ben Hecht's screenplay was that he removed all of Coward's charming dialogue and substituted a puffed-up account of farcical puppets. Thus, commercial artist Miriam's arrangement with promising playwright Fredric March and budding painter Gary Cooper becomes a gentleman's agreement, ruling out sex. Their three-corner bedroom banter is about promising potentialities, not about rich realities. *Design for Living* was given a grand send-off by Paramount at its Criterion Theatre premiere (November 23, 1933) with a reserved-seat engagement. But Depression-weary audiences were not enchanted by its superficial joviality and the film proved a financial disappointment. Richard Watts, Jr. *(New York Herald Tribune)* even complained: "She [Miriam] fails to bring to the part the air of sparkling grandeur that Miss [Lynn] Fontanne introduced to the [stage] part." Years later, when an interviewer asked Miriam what she recalled of this film, she responded: "I remember one train scene in which I wore one of those hats that clung to the head and came down over one eye. I remember telling myself 'Oh goodie, now I'll look like Dietrich.' "

Miriam had a bout of illness while filming *Design for Living,* and the studio substituted Carole Lombard opposite George Raft in *Bolero* (1934). For Miriam, working with Lubitsch was always a rewarding experience: "He has the qualities of exactness, sureness and authority. He knows just what he wants and gets it, not by screaming or ranting, but with a Billiken-like grin."

She then returned to Broadway to star in Owen Davis's pre-Civil War drama *Jezebel* (Ethel Barrymore Theatre, December 19, 1933), replacing ailing Tallulah Bankhead. Miriam was fiery Julie Kendrick who weaves her flirtatious spell over New Orleans mankind. Cora Witherspoon, Owen Davis, Jr., and Joseph Cotten were others in the sumptuously mounted production. Burns Mantle *(New York Daily News)* reported: "Tallulah [Bankhead], I suspect, would have been better for it. Miss Hopkins, while the better actress, is still a trifle too normal, too conventionally the mistress of the feminine arts of the actress, to suggest that touch of hereditary eccentricity the author is at pains to indicate. . . . But always last night there was the weight of the part she could neither quite throw off nor illuminate with those character flashes demanded."

Jezebel collapsed after 32 performances. Four years later it would be filmed with Bette Davis, who won an Oscar in the part. Miriam remained in New York to appear in a condensed skit version of *The Affairs of Anatol,* which played the Paramount Theatre for a week and then toured the metropolitan cinema circuit. Tallulah Bankhead, not to be outdone by her rival, quickly whipped up a scene from *The Affairs of Anatol,* which was broadcast on Rudy Vallee's radio hour.

While in New York, Miriam was the subject of many newspaper interviews. She told one journalist her rationale for returning to the stage: "How can a motion picture reflect real life when it is made by people who are living artificial lives? The only thing to do is to get a better perspective. I believe that any star will make better pictures if she will take six months of each year away from Hollywood. That's what I intended to do."

About fame and kin: "I don't like to have children named after me, and I don't like to name children after anyone else. My sister wanted to name her new little baby girl Miriam. I told her please not to. I'll send her to college anyway."

In Paramount's *All of Me* (1934) Miriam was the student sweetheart of college professor Fredric March. He wants to leave the academic scene for an engineering project at Boulder Dam. Rich, spoiled Miriam refuses his matrimonial offer. Instead she returns to the big city and becomes involved with hoodlum George Raft and his sweetheart Helen Mack. Later on, to escape the law, Raft and Mack jump from a window ledge to their death. This harrowing episode shocks Miriam into realizing March's worth, and she rushes off to join him. The *Times* of London commented: "She is one of the few actresses who do not forget that the characters they play are supposed, in theory at any rate to have respectable minds, as well as overdeveloped hearts."

She Loves Me Not (1934) offered the unlikely teaming of Miriam with Paramount's resident crooner, Bing Crosby. She is fugitive showgirl Curly Flagg. Because she was the witness to a murder, both the police and gangsters are in hot pursuit of her. Miriam takes refuge at Princeton University and is hidden by obliging collegian Crosby and his pals. Several sequences thereafter reveal her sporting male garb and hairstyle while she masquerades as an Ivy Leaguer. The subterfuge inevitably stalls Crosby's romance with dean Henry Stephenson's daughter, Kitty Carlisle. *She Loves Me Not* was not brilliant burlesque, and the story wanders from Philadelphia to Princeton to New York and back to the campus. *Variety* criticized: "No amount of synthetic coyness can overcome the obvious physical shortcomings in a role that calls for a night club kidlet in her early teens, and not an actress who has played mature, sophisticated dramatic parts." The movie did have the following distinctions: it sported the popular song "Love in Bloom"; Crosby for the first time on the screen refused to have his ears pinned back with tape; and it was Miriam's last picture under her Paramount contract. The story was remade as *True to the Army* in 1942 with Judy Canova and in 1955 as *How to Be Very Very Popular* with Betty Grable and Sheree North.

Miriam was doubtlessly irked that under the new regime at Paramount, Mae West and Marlene Dietrich were the queen bees, with Claudette Colbert and Carole Lombard in second position as studio favorites. She had worked hard to create the illusion on and off screen of being the uncrowned dramatic queen of Hollywood. Her ploys worked well with the press, especially the fan magazines. One movie tabloid of the time described her as follows: "Miriam is one of the most intelligent women in Hollywood. But maybe you haven't heard that she is probably the most unconventional woman in the movie colony. She doesn't advertise the fact—as those who have the reputation for unconventionality are prone to do. She doesn't cut strange didoes in public, bite her escorts' ears, wear freakish attire, or try to shock her interviewers with brutally blunt statements planned well in advance. Her unconventionality isn't physical; it's mental. That mind of hers is working every minute and it doesn't travel in a rut!"

Miriam's status was equally high with the producers, and she had bids from several companies in 1934 to sign long-term contracts. With all her stage charm she captivated iconoclastic producer Samuel Goldwyn and accepted his lucrative offer in March, 1934. To celebrate her financial triumph, Miriam purchased a five-bedroom duplex apartment at 13 Sutton Place, New York City. It was a subtle way of advising her new studio boss that neither he nor Hollywood was the end-all to her existence. Goldwyn took the hint, and none too kindly.

On loanout to RKO along with Joel McCrea, Miriam starred in *The Richest Girl in the World,* which opened at Radio City Music Hall on September 20, 1934. This film demonstrated that Miriam was generally up to the demands of semiscrewball comedy-pathos and thusly, opened up a new genre of silver screen roles for her. The film's premise had her swapping social positions with her secretary (Fay Wray) to determine if McCrea loved her for her inner qualities. He at first is turned by Wray's supposed wealth, but after Miriam has suffered an appropriate time, he realizes he loves her. The critics complimented Miriam for making "the heroine a real and genuinely likable person." RKO remade the picture as *Bride by Mistake* (1944) with Laraine Day.

Perhaps the highpoint of Miriam's movie tenure was her selection to portray the central character of William Thackeray's *Vanity Fair.* RKO's *Becky Sharp* was to be the first technicolor feature film made in Hollywood. Filming began under the direction of Lowell Sherman on December 4, 1934. Three weeks later he died of pneumonia and Rouben Mamoulian was substituted. He started over from scratch. Like most cinema translations of complex classic novels, the screenplay was rather simplistic. Conniving Becky (Miriam) graduates from Miss Pinkerton's exclusive school in early nineteenth century England and commences her career of maneuvering others to make her own way in the world. Through her classmate Frances Dee, she finds a home and an entree into society. Via assorted husbands— Alan Mowbray, Cedric Hardwicke—she climbs the social ladder, only to end up with Dee's bumbling brother, Nigel Bruce. The episodic drawing-room drama demanded extravagant overplaying and Miriam gladly pulled out all stops in the posturing portrayal.

Becky Sharp premiered at Radio City Music Hall on June 13, 1935, and the *New York Times* termed it "probably the most significant event of the 1935 cinema." That newspaper's reviewer reported: "Miriam Hopkins is an indifferently successful Becky, who shares some excellent scenes with many others in which she is strident and even nerve-racking." Howard Barnes *(New York Herald Tribune)* said: "In the big sequences she is superbly assured but too frequently she overacts as though afraid her radiant appearance in many hues will make one miss a gesture or an intonation." Mamoulian was more effective in his creative direction of the innovative technicolor to reflect the changing moods. His masterly handling of the ballroom scene in which Lord Wellington's officers are informed that Waterloo will be fought on the morrow is all the more memorable when contrasted to the inept dynamics of the identical scene in the much more lavish *Waterloo* (1971). *Becky Sharp* was not the financial success anticipated.

Miriam remained in costume to star in the panoramic *Barbary Coast*

(1935). Samuel Goldwyn had first announced his new discovery Anna Sten for the flashy role, then slated Miriam for the part, then mentioned that Gloria Swanson might make this her comeback assignment, and finally returned the project to Miriam. She is the Easterner who comes to the wild San Francisco of the mid-nineteenth century, via Cape Horn, to find that her beau has been shot on the day of her arrival. At a loss for a livelihood, she accepts a hostessing job in Edward G. Robinson's crooked gambling house, where she becomes the infamous Swan. She has almost resigned herself to a life of opulence and self-contempt when she meets idealistic prospector Joel McCrea. Eventually they are united and Robinson is disposed of by the local vigilantes. Miriam won good notices as the "gracefully soiled heroine" who proved more than a match for the machinations of Robinson, his chief henchman Brian Donlevy, and the rowdy saloon crowd. The *New York Post* said: "Hers is the only sanely written part in the picture, and her performance is a steadying point against the footlight savagery of Edward G. Robinson and the troubadour excesses of Joel McCrea."

Her third 1935 release, *Splendor,* again teamed her with Joel McCrea, in a contemporary woman's story written especially for the screen by Rachel Crowthers. Its bathos was typical of the day. McCrea, the scion of a once wealthy Fifth Avenue family, rejects an advantageous marriage to wed poor girl Miriam. She encourages his literary ambitions, but they cannot make ends meet. She takes up with McCrea's wealthy cousin Paul Cavanagh in order to obtain financial assistance. Because of her new liaison, the marriage is shattered and she becomes a salesgirl. McCrea becomes a hardworking newspaper reporter. Eventually they start all over again. *Variety* noticed: "Miss Hopkins is not altogether at ease as the sweet young thing in the first few scenes, but as she finds herself placed in the family she gets the most possible out of her assignment without seeming to fight for it."

Navy Born, a 1935 Goldwyn project to be written by Mildred Cram and set in Hawaii, never developed, nor in 1936 did *Maximilian of Mexico* which was to unite Miriam, Gary Cooper, and Merle Oberon on the screen.

The peak of Miriam's Goldwyn years occurred with *These Three* (1936), a screen alteration of Lillian Hellman's controversial stage play *The Children's Hour,* for which Goldwyn paid $125,000. To pacify the Hays Office, not only the lesbian subject matter of the original had to be deleted, but the title had to be changed as well. What evolved was a normal love triangle: private-school teachers Miriam and Merle Oberon desire doctor Joel McCrea. He and Oberon are engaged, while Miriam loves him in silence. A vicious student (Bonita Granville) spreads a nasty rumor that Miriam is having an affair with McCrea and everyone's placid existence is shattered. After the repercussions are sorted out, McCrea and Oberon go off together. Best reviews went to Granville as the bullying liar, Marcia Mae Jones as her terrified accomplice, and Catherine Doucet as Miriam's self-centered aunt. Miriam was cited for her "directness, honesty and admirable reticence." It was the first of four features Miriam would appear in for director William Wyler.

In mid-1936, Miriam embarked with her entourage for a vacation in England. While there, she was engaged by Alexander Korda to star in *Men Are Not Gods* (1937). This arch comedy cast Miriam as the secretary to a nasty theatre critic. She is persuaded by stage actress Gertrude Lawrence to alter her boss's newspaper review of *Othello,* which stars Lawrence and her actor husband Sebastian Shaw. Miriam impulsively does so and Shaw emerges an overnight star; he and Miriam flirt, but she graciously disappears when Lawrence announces she is pregnant. The feature's major distinction was that ten years before *A Double Life* it used the gimmick of recreating *Othello* before and beyond the footlights.

The Woman I Love (1937) was a cliched triangular love story set in World War I France. Pilot Louis Hayward adores Miriam, but she is married to his friend and superior officer Paul Muni. Hayward is eventually shot down in combat. When Muni later falls desperately ill, Miriam repents, and their marriage is saved. The aerial dog fights were the film's top attraction. The *New York Times*'s Frank Nugent found: "Miss Hopkins moves in a tragic haze and does not bring Mme Maury through at all." A week before this costume drama opened at Radio City Music Hall (April 15, 1937), Miriam and Hayward recreated their roles on Campbell Soup's radio program.

One productive, if personal, result of *The Woman I Love* was that Miriam and her director Anatole Litvak fell in love. The 35-year-old Russian-born film director had built quite a cinema reputation in Germany and later in France with *Coeur de Lilacs* (1932) and *Mayerling* (1936). *The Woman I Love* was his first American-made film. On September 4, 1937, he and Miriam eloped to Yuma, Arizona. They honeymooned at the seaside community of Coronado, California.

Woman Chases Man (1937) was the zenith of the Miriam-Joel McCrea screen teaming, and a daffy bit of sheer nonsense. The entertaining end result belied the difficulty Goldwyn had in producing the project: scenarists Bella and Sam Spewack and director William Wellman exited from the film in a tizzy, and other creative help had to be summoned. Scheming architect Miriam encounters bankrupt promoter Charles Winninger. He has a wealthy son (McCrea) who refuses to loan his squandering dad any more cash. Sugar-coated Miriam and wily Winninger plot to wheedle McCrea into giving them $100,000 to finance a promising real estate development. The last 20 minutes of the slapdash comedy are set in a sprawling magnolia tree outside of McCrea's bedroom window. Miriam has climbed out onto a limb and is meowing away, determined to break down McCrea's stubborn nature. The film proved a commercial success when premiered at Radio City Music Hall on June 10, 1937. Tough-to-please Howard Barnes (*New York Herald Tribune*) said: "Miss Hopkins breezes through the complications of the plot with uplifted face and a pleasant muting of the romance."

Although Samuel Goldwyn had further screen plans for Miriam (he had purchased *Honeymoon in Reno,* a Virginia Kellogg comedy, as a vehicle for her), she had the itch to return to the live theatre. She signed on for the Theatre Guild's production of S. N. Behrman's comedy *Wine of Choice,* with Britisher Leslie Banks as a New Mexico senator, Alexander Woollcott as a pugnacious reporter, and Miriam as the girl. Upset by the daily revisions of the project, Miriam left the ill-fated show in Pittsburgh in January, 1938. She was replaced by Claudia Morgan. It closed shortly after its New York opening.

Her last feature made during her Goldwyn period, *Wise Girl,* was released by RKO in January, 1938. It was another entry in the oversaturated market of screwball comedies, with everyone still trying to top Carole Lombard's performances in *Twentieth Century, My Man Godfrey,* and *Nothing Sacred.* Wealthy Miriam is intent upon luring her two orphaned nieces away from the influence of Greenwich Village artist Ray Milland (the girls' uncle). She moves into the Bohemian setting, claiming she is an out-of-work actress. Before long Miriam has fallen under Milland's spell. In required fashion she must renounce her vapid society playmates as overstuffed puppets and demonstrate that she is mortal. Her two best moments are modeling a negligee in a 14th Street store window, and a scene at a prize fight where an overenthusiastic Miriam lands a knockout punch on a seatmate because her favorite boxer, Guinn Williams, is losing the bout. *Wise Girl* did not make out well financially, and it brought to an end the second phase of Miriam's screen career. The *New York Times* wrote: "Miss Hopkins, with her almost Red Indian immobility of countenance, is less abandoned, less careful of her exquisite make-up and coiffure, than the malleable-featured, frankly string-haired Lombard, but Miriam has her moments."

Miriam soon proved that at age 36 she was still a powerhouse figure on the Hollywood scene. Her husband Anatole Litvak was now directing major features at Warner Brothers, and there had been some talk in 1937 of starring Miriam in *Tovarich* (first announced for Kay Francis, then given to Claudette Colbert) and in a project entitled *Episode* with Ian Hunter and Charles Winninger. In addition, she and Kay Francis were to costar in *The Sisters* (1938), but Miriam balked at cobilling even with her pal. Litvak directed the film with Bette Davis top-lined.

Like everyone else in Hollywood, Miriam was a contender for the prize role of Scarlett O'Hara in *Gone with the Wind*. The Women's Club of Atlanta, Georgia, embarked on a volatile campaign to convince producer David O. Selznick that Southern-born Miriam was the ideal choice for the film. He was not swayed, and British Vivien Leigh, 11 years her junior, won out.

Miriam signed a two-picture contract with Warner Brothers in September, 1938. Under Jack B. Warner's aegis, the studio had the reputation of knowing how to handle strong-willed actresses, as reigning Warners' star Bette Davis could well attest. But Miriam was a tough customer. She informed the press that her new contract gave her complete script approval: "You can blame me entirely if you don't like any of my pictures now. Because I'm not going to do anything I don't like. So it will be my responsibility." It is a testimony to Miriam's personal magnetism that she maneuvered such a favorable agreement. Even though Samuel Goldwyn had restored some of the luster to a screen career damaged by Paramount's constant miscasting, Miriam was now 36 years old. Her recent films had revealed that not even the best cameraman could disguise her fading blonde looks and make her still seem the ingenue—a quality still considered de rigeur for all but the top stars like Greta Garbo.

Miriam was scheduled to appear in *We Are Not Alone,* a James Hilton story, but that was canceled. She accepted second billing to Bette Davis in *The Old Maid* (1939), based on the Edith Wharton novel and the Zoe Akins prize-winning play. The elaborately filmed drama is set near Philadelphia in Civil War days. Miriam jilts irresponsible George Brent and marries successful but stodgy Jerome Cowan. On her wedding day, Brent arrives home and her younger cousin (Davis), who has always loved him, consoles the soldier. Brent is later killed at Vicksburg and Davis has his child. After the war, she opens an orphans' home so she can raise her child without suspicion. When Miriam uncovers the truth, she insists Davis call off her marriage to Cowan's brother, James Stephenson. After 15 years pass, it evolves that Miriam has "adopted" Tina (Jane Bryan) as her own. The widowed, matronly Miriam and old maid Davis vie for Bryan's affection, all the time detesting one another but drawn together by blood ties, memories, and loneliness. Miriam convinces Davis not to reveal the truth to Bryan on the eve of the girl's wedding. Davis agrees. Her only reward is to receive the last farewell kiss from her daughter as the bride embarks on her honeymoon. Miriam and Davis are now alone with each other, resigned to their bleak future together. As the charming but malicious Delia Lovell, Miriam made a strong screen impact. Kate Cameron in her four-star *New York Daily News* review observed: "The surprise of the picture is that Miriam Hopkins, who hasn't been doing very much on the screen lately, shines with a brilliance that is equal to Miss Davis's own." But *The Old Maid* was geared as a Davis vehicle, and most of the attention was directed to her sympathetic role.

Throughout the leisurely filming of *The Old Maid*, gossip columnists delighted in reporting the feuding and scene stealing indulged in by these two headstrong stars. At one point Davis kiddingly advised the press: "Hoppy and I are going to get a couple of pairs of boxing gloves and pose for a picture glowering at each other like a couple of fighters in their corners. It's the only answer I can make to all the nonsense about how we can't get along." Davis was not quite so frivolous about the matter in her 1962 autobiography: "Miriam is a perfectly charming woman socially. . . . Working with her is another story. . . . Miriam used, and I must give her credit, knew every trick in the book. I became fascinated watching them appear one by one. . . . When she was supposed to be listening to me, her eyes would wander off into some world in which she was the sweetest of them all. Her restless little spirit was impatiently awaiting her next line, her golden curls quivering with expectancy. . . . Miriam was her own worst enemy. I usually had better things to do than waste my energies on invective and cat fights."

On her part, Miriam ever so sweetly explained to journalists about her alleged temperamental reputation: "One reason may be that I've worked in so many pictures with other women—it makes a good story when women have feuds on their pictures. That was how it started on *The Old Maid* . . . somebody thought it would be good publicity for Bette Davis and me to have a feud. Bette's a good friend of mine, and she called a halt to that. I've worked with Kay Francis and we're friends, with Merle Oberon and we're friends, and with Claudette Colbert, and we're friends." (Years later, Veronica Lake in her autobiography would quote Miriam as having said about Davis: "She's evil, evil.")

On October 11, 1939, Miriam and Litvak were divorced—perhaps one of the reasons she lost out to Davis for the prize role of the school teacher in *All This and Heaven Too,* which was directed by Litvak. Plans to unite Miriam and Davis again in a story about the Bronte sisters did not jell.

Soon after Miriam agreed to replace Olivia de Havilland in the Errol Flynn Western, *Virginia City* (1940), a poor follow-up to the studio's successful *Dodge City*. Miriam was presented as Julia Hayne, a daughter of the South aiding its cause in the Civil War. As a spy, she travels westward with Yankee Flynn. Her assignment is to assist rebel colonel Randolph Scott in obtaining a $5 million gold shipment badly needed to replenish the South's bankroll. Signing on a dancehall girl, Miriam finds time to entertain the customers by singing "Rally Round the Flag, Boys" and performing an abortive can-can, sporting black sequin shorts and silk tights. It was one of the more ludicrous moments in this not-so-super-Western (which also boasted Humphrey Bogart as a most unconvincing Mexican-accented villain). Miriam's few scenes with Flynn and Scott were stilted, and not always mercifully brief.

When the movie premiered in Virginia City, Nevada, on March 16, 1940, Warner Brothers sent a bevy of star(let)s to give sparkle to the proceedings. Neither Miriam nor Flynn showed up. *Virginia City* made money, but the critics roasted the rather conventional film in general and Miriam in particular: "[she] just stands around most of the time looking harried" *(New York Herald Tribune)*; "Miss Hopkins recites her stilted lines by rote" *(New York Times)*. Most agreed that "her antiseptic performance was not enhanced by the black and white photography, which showed the bloom of youth had well passed."

Once again, word spread about Miriam's temperamental behavior on the set. Neither Flynn nor director Michael Curtiz had wanted Miriam in the film. She later recalled: "The director was Michael Curtiz, a complete madman—mad and adorable. For twelve weeks he yelled at me and I yelled back at him. We're exactly alike."

Her other 1940 release, *Lady with Red Hair,* filmed in black and white, had potentials that went sadly unrealized. Miriam portrayed the fiery actress Mrs. Leslie Carter in this fictional account of 15 years in her life from 1889 onward. Interspersed with scenes from stage triumphs was the story of the actress's losing fight to regain custody of her son from her divorced husband. Miriam was bedecked in a red wig and wore attractive period costumes, and there was a good supporting cast: Claude Rains as theatre impresario David Belasco, Laura Hope Crews as Miriam's mother, and Helen Westley as the proprietor of a theatrical boarding house. Beyond the conventional soap opera treatment of Mrs. Carter's life, *Lady with Red Hair* made the fatal error of suggesting in scene after scene that an ability to throw extended tantrums was tantamount to theatrical greatness. The film slipped into the Palace Theatre (December 5, 1940) on a double-bill with a Kay Kyser programmer.

Said reviewer James Agate about Miriam's performance, "I don't feel she is a sufficiently good actress to impersonate one who was, in Mr. Shaw's words, 'a melodramatic actress of no mean powers.' " The director of *Lady with Red Hair* stated that Miriam had been "terribly difficult to work with" and the *Harvard Lampoon* voted her the "least desirable companion on a desert island."

On radio Miriam had a wide range of opportunities to perform in roles given to others on the screen: *She Got the Job* (October 31, 1937), *They Knew What They Wanted* (July 2, 1938—"an uncannily realistic portrayal"), *Tovarich* (May 15, 1939—"Many lines were delivered by Miriam Hopkins in the grand manner when they should have been read with quiet firmness"), and *Jezebel* (February 14, 1940).

Miriam rejected Warner's *Law of the Tropics* (1941) because she felt herself "too old" to star opposite studio contractee Jeffrey Lynn. (Constance Bennett, three years Miriam's junior, accepted the vacated role in this loose remake of *Oil for the Lamps of China.)*

Unhappy in Hollywood, Miriam again returned to the East and the stage. She created a mild rhubarb in July, 1940, when she failed to appear in a production of *The Guardsman* at Harrison, Maine. Veteran Italian-born leading man Tullio Carminatti had walked out as her leading man when Miriam insulted Mussolini. No suitable replacement could be found in time and Miriam was fined $1,000 by Actors Equity Association. Then she accepted the lead in Tennessee Williams's drama *Battle of Angels,* which had its pre-Broadway tryout at the Wilbur Theatre in Boston on December 10, 1940. Miriam was a silent partner in the Theatre Guild production.

Wesley Addy and Edith King were featured in this mishmash which combined "Freud, a psychiatrist's nightmare and a not too refined *Tobacco Road.*" Set in the Mississippi delta, Miriam was Myra Torrance, the earthy wife of a crippled shopkeeper. She has an affair with a passing stud. The critics disliked the play, although Miriam was cited as "often shocking, but always gripping." The Boston board of censors were outraged by the drama's morality and started an investigation. Miriam's remarks to the press did not endear her to the local citizenry: "The dirt is something in the mind of some of the people who have seen it. They read messages into it according to their own suppressed feelings." During one performance, the climactic fire on stage went out of control and the audience, in a near panic, had to be hastily evacuated. *Battle of Angels* closed in January, 1941, for repairs. It re-emerged off-Broadway 15 years later as *Orpheus Descending* and was filmed as *The Fugitive Kind* with Anna Magnani in Miriam's role.

There was talk of Miriam starring in *The Man Who Broke His Heart* at Paramount in 1941 (dealing with the 1910 San Francisco waterfront) and Miriam was announced for the lead in *Bad Lands of Dakota* (1941) but withdrew and was replaced by Ann Rutherford in this Universal Western. A projected *Nellie Bly* also came to naught. Strangely, Miriam agreed to replace Ilona Massey in United Artists' *A Gentleman After Dark,* released April 16, 1942. It was a dated melodrama produced on a too modest budget. She played vindictive Flo Mellon, who had turned in her gem thief husband (Brian Donlevy) for the police reward. Donlevy's boyhood friend Preston Foster, now a detective, adopts Miriam and Donlevy's daughter. Eighteen years pass, and fun-loving Miriam is currently blackmailing her own child. Donlevy escapes from prison, gives Miriam her comeuppance, and virtue triumphs. Miriam may have given the part "lurid authority," but the numerous close-ups were unflattering, and the long shots revealed that she had gained weight.

On short notice, Miriam contracted to replace her old rival Tallulah Bankhead in *The Skin of Our Teeth* on Broadway. For playing Sabina, she received $1,250 a week. Miriam debuted May 31, 1943. George Freedley *(New York Morning Telegraph)* penned: "Miss Hopkins is unquestionably indebted to her fellow southerner for many of her inflections and most of her readings. She plays vivaciously, attractively, knowingly and with even more consciousness of the audience than the role requires. Hers is a better than adequate performance." When asked if she would star in the road company, she advised: "Not the road, never. Life's too short. I have nothing against the road cities. But I simply can't bear the road, because I get lonely going from the theater to those hotels every night. Of course if it were my own company and I had a big piece of the show, like Hepburn did with *The Philadelphia Story,* I don't suppose I'd then mind trouping all the way to Denver and back."

Before signing on for *The Skin of Our Teeth,* Miriam had made *Old Acquaintance* (1943) which reunited her with Bette Davis at Warner Brothers. Davis had tried to persuade ex-MGM star Norma Shearer to take the assignment, but that star did not care for a role that required her to play the mother of a grown daughter. Again Miriam was the bitch, with Davis the top-cast heroine. As Davis later said: "We were always old somehow; everything but old friends." The script calls for Miriam and Davis to be schoolgirl chums. Davis develops into a serious authoress, while flustery, explosive Miriam settles for marriage to John Loder. After Davis comes for a visit, jealous Miriam sets about writing fatuous sexy novels that prove popular.

She no longer has time for her husband or daughter. Loder leaves Miriam, and proposes marriage to Davis, but she nobly rejects him. Years later, during World War II, Davis is being escorted by Naval officer Gig Young, ten years her junior. Army major Loder arrives on the scene to admit he is about to be remarried and informs Miriam that he once loved Davis. Davis discovers that Miriam's daughter (Dolores Moran) and Young are in love, so she gracefully accepts the inevitable. In the teary ending, Miriam and Davis are left sitting on a sofa, staring at the fire, and drinking a toast to their facing middle age together.

The sentimental *Old Acquaintance* was enormously popular. One highlight of the 110-minute picture had Davis giving Miriam a mighty wallop across the face to stop one of the belle's endless tantrums. As Davis later described the scene: "It was rather like a prizefight ring. . . . We rehearsed this scene for hours . . . but [eventually] stand still she did—and take the slap she did. To be sure, her eyes filled with tears of self-pity—but the camera couldn't see it. It was on her back!"

The critics were mixed about Miriam's performance as the vixenish Millie Drake: ". . . a vibrant and shrill exhibition of a shrew, but she does it with such determined malice that you wonder she can even endure herself" (Bosley Crowther, *New York Times*). "Miss Hopkins is right on the edge of burlesque in her characterization" (Howard Barnes, *New York Herald Tribune*). Miriam and Alexis Smith would star in the "Lux Radio Theatre" adaptation of *Old Acquaintance* on May 29, 1944. This film ended the third phase of Miriam's Hollywood career: it was the last time she would have a (co) starring role in a grade-A picture.

Miriam opened on Broadway in Samson Raphaelson's *The Perfect Marriage* at the Ethel Barrymore, Theatre on October 26, 1944. Victor Jory played her husband in this talky study of the "felicities of marriage and the hazards of divorce." It straggled on for 92 performances. *Variety* summed up: "Both are real troupers but have done better in other parts." When later filmed, *The Perfect Marriage* would team Loretta Young and David Niven.

On October 23, 1945, Miriam married reporter Raymond B. Brock, and shortly thereafter went into rehearsal for *St. Lazare's Pharmacy*. This unintentional comedy set in 1900s Quebec was adapted by Eddie Dowley and featured Herbert Berghof. In a flashback, an elderly pharmacist details the facts surrounding his wife's indiscretions. It played Montreal and Chicago in late 1945 and early 1946, never reaching Broadway. *Variety* reported that Miriam: "over-acts flagrantly. Her opening lines are done with fine restraint, but she soon flounders to a weak beg-off."

Miriam played the stock-theatre circuit in *Laura* (1946) with Otto Kruger and Tom Neal. She was back on Broadway in James Parrish's *Message for Margaret* (Plymouth Theatre, April 16, 1947), along with Mady Christians and Roger Pryor. As the selfish, exasperating mistress of a recently deceased publisher, Miriam "[did] little more than walk through a part, which is perhaps the best way to have handled the assignment" (*New York Herald Tribune*). It died after five performances and Miriam returned to stock in *There's Always Juliet* (1947).

Director William Wyler requested Miriam for the supporting role of Aunt Lavinia Penneman in *The Heiress*, a filming of Henry James's *Washington Square*. The film opened at Radio City Music Hall on October 6, 1949. Olivia de Havilland received an Oscar for her restrained portrayal of the repressed spinster daughter of tyrant Dr. Ralph Richardson, who finally rejects her mercenary suitor Montgomery Clift. Paramount spared no expense in recreating the turn-of-the-century settings and costumes. Miriam was termed "delightful" and "fine" as the flibbertigibbet widow of a parson ("When I think of the meals I set before the Reverend Penniman . . .") who bestows unbridled affection on her forlorn niece De Havilland. That same summer Miriam toured in stock with *The Heiress*— this time playing the lead role of Catherine Sloper.

Miriam's next Hollywood assignment was in Paramount's artificial comedy *The Mating Season* (1951), which nominally starred Gene Tierney and John Lund. The real gem of the feature was Thelma Ritter as Lund's mother, the owner of a hamburger stand, who pays an unexpected visit to her son and his new bride, the aristocratic Tierney. She is mistaken for a domestic and plays along with the the gambit. Everything functions smoothly until Miriam, Tierney's social butterfly mother, arrives on the scene, dripping in magnolia scent and heavy accent. Miriam milked the featured part for all it was worth—and then some. *Time* magazine approved of her "expert playing of a bitchy lady of quality."

Miriam and Raymond Brock were divorced in 1951.

In Twentieth Century-Fox's pedestrian remake of Bret Harte's *Outcasts of Poker Flat* (1952), Miriam was third-billed as the world-weary Duchess, caught up with the group of pariahs snowbound in the mountain cabin. Her small part required her to be mostly a spectator to the interaction within the log shelter.

More noteworthy, but equally small, was her part in William Wyler's screen version of Theodore Dreiser's *Sister Carrie* (1952). This elaborate period drama about a naive girl (Jennifer Jones) making her way in Chicago and New York of the early 1900s, found Miriam as the shrewish wife of bar-restaurant owner Laurence Olivier. Miriam's role had been fleshed out from the novel, providing her with some opportunities to delineate vicious Julie Hurstwood, who would rather destroy her husband than part with any bit of his wealth. Miriam garnered good reviews. "She puts across the only idea of the moral rigidity of the age" (*New York Times*); "A bow is due Miriam Hopkins for her portrayal of the irritable Mrs. Hurstwood" (*New Yorker*); "Miriam Hopkins is almost too convincing as Hurstwood's venomous wife" (*Saturday Review*). Another former Paramount star, Nancy Carroll, had tested for Miriam's role.

Miriam toured with *Hay Fever* and also appeared in *A Night at Mme. Tussaud's* with Peter Lorre in the summer of 1952, and the following year she both acted in and directed a version of *Hay Fever*. Miriam bubbled: "You should have seen me jumping back and forth over the footlights. At one rehearsal I missed two of my own cues because I was in the audience giving directions."

She made no little stir when she pontificated to one reporter in the early 1950s: "Women over thirty-five have had it!" She went on to explain, "Does she still have the wherewithal to attract as many men as she'd like to surround herself with?" No one made mention that Miriam was now approaching 50 years old.

On August 5, 1954, her father, then age 82, died in Kankakee, Illinois. He had retired 15 years before as an insurance salesman. Besides Miriam, he was survived by his two other daughters, Mrs. Katherine Cox and Mrs. Ruby Welch. Miriam had no public statement to make about his death.

Miriam was scheduled to appear on Broadway in early 1957 in *Catch a Falling Star*, but instead took a version of *Old Maid* on summer tour. She made one of her infrequent television appearances on "Climax" (May 30,

1957) in *The Disappearance of Amanda Hale*, enacting a famous actress beset by strange events on a Broadway opening night. Lloyd Bridges and Carolyn Jones were featured in the 60-minute drama.

To date, the last highlight of Miriam's stage career occurred in June, 1958, when she replaced Jo Van Fleet in the Broadway production of *Look Homeward Angel*. In the demanding role of Eliza Brant, she proved superlative. "She has chosen her own design. Her Eliza Brant is more indigenously Southern. She is also more cheerful and lighter on her feet. But these beguiling personal characteristics dim the significance of the part" (Brooks Atkinson, *New York Times*). "A brilliant portrayal, one of the ablest of her career, and nothing stands in the way of her force and skill" (Richard Watts, Jr., *New York Post*).

Miriam was again in popular demand for interviews. Re her stage return: "Everybody seems to remember me. Isn't that lovely?" On her old feature films being televised: "You watch a new television play that you've done and you worry about everything from the way you acted a scene to the angle at which you held your chin. But watching an old, old movie, you find a horrible hairdo or a dreadful dress something to laugh at. It's all very impersonal."

Regarding the various media: "TV is the toughest medium because there's more strain, but the theatre requires the most work. Movies are the easiest. You can sip coffee between takes." About her future: "I prefer looking toward the future. I have no scrap-books, clippings or old photos to drag out and bore people with. People aren't interested in hearing about your past."

Miriam went on tour with *Look Homeward Angel* through much of 1959. She was seen also on "Twilight Zone" (December 16, 1960, CBS).

Under the more liberal morality of the 1960s, William Wyler fashioned a movie remake of *The Children's Hour* (1962) and summoned Miriam to portray Mrs. Lily Mortar, the selfish actress aunt of Shirley MacLaine (who inherited Miriam's role from *These Three*). This time around the lesbian theme was reinstated, but in such a bland, insensitive manner that the result was a prodigious bore. Fay Bainter was brought out of semi-retirement to emote as the grandmother of Karen Balkin, the snit who spreads rumors that she saw private-school teachers MacLaine and Audrey Hepburn kissing. Miriam was very dowdy in her few unsubtle scenes and was accused of "artificial laboring" in which she "conducts every scene as if it were a fanfare."

When Miriam arrived on the West Coast to film *The Children's Hour*, reporter Bob Thomas inquired if she noticed any changes in Hollywood. "Honestly, I wouldn't know. If you mean whether the movie crowd still gambles at the Clover Club and goes to the Trocadero, the answer is no. But I never went for that, anyway. I did some when I was married to Anatole Litvak—he's the Russian director, you know—because he likes the night life."

Thomas also queried Miriam about her reputed temperament: "Me temperamental? I never was. Proof of that is that I made four pictures with Willie Wyler, who is a very demanding director. I made two with Rouben Mamoulian, who is the same. Two [sic] with Ernst Lubitsch, such a dear man." (A popular story then circulating in Hollywood said that Wyler had learned to cope with the overly loquacious Miriam by always placing her on the side of his deaf ear.

Throughout the 1960s Miriam resided in Manhattan, subletting her fabulous Sutton Place abode to assorted notables, and living in a smaller but equally well appointed East Side apartment. She was seen in a television episode of "The Outer Limits" (January 20, 1964, NBC) about the same time she dropped out of an off-Broadway double-bill drama *Riverside Drive*. Sylvia Sidney replaced her in the short-lived production.

Then Miriam was persuaded to "star" as Mrs. Maude Brown in a German-made sexploitation version of *Fanny Hill* (1965). This quickie bed-sheet tale of lascivious eighteenth-century England was directed by Russ Myers. Miriam minced about in seeming bewilderment as the proprietress of a bustling brothel, mouthing such tasteless lines as: "It isn't much, but we call it a house." The movie smirked its way through satisfactory box-office returns, but highbrows were aghast that the once-stately Miriam should have been caught standing "serenely amidst this alien corn."

In the expensively mounted *The Chase* (1966), which boasted a Lillian Hellman screenplay and a cast that included Marlon Brando, Robert Redford, Jane Fonda, and James Fox, Miriam was seventh-billed as Mrs. Reeves. She is the distraught mother of escaped convict Redford. When he returns to his Texas town, she attempts to bribe sheriff Brando into letting her son go. *The Chase* was panned by the critics and ignored by most filmgoers. Miriam projected a bundle of energy in her small role as the deluded Southern mama, with overblown results. Along with E. G. Marshall and Janice Rule, Miriam was accused of "chewing up all the scenery in sight with enormous zest and relish." Hollis Alpert (*Saturday Review*) apologized: "Well, best to avert one's embarrassed eyes from the screen, when she's on."

It was not until 1968 that Miriam returned to Hollywood to appear in an episode of the teleseries "The Flying Nun," playing Sister Adelaide, an early star of the talkies. She insisted to the press that this was not another comeback—like Mae West she had never been away—and that being financially solvent, she only worked when she wanted to.

In late 1969 Miriam was contracted by Congdon Films to costar with Gale Sondergaard, John Garfield, Jr., and Minta Durfee Arbuckle in *Comeback*, a suspense thriller. She portrayed an aging film star, now an alcoholic, who exists in the glorious past. The film has yet to be distributed.

Miriam currently resides in Manhattan, occassionally attending a Broadway opening or a movie premiere. She recently came to a private screening of two of her early 1930s features. The contrast between the actress on the screen and the star in person is tremendous—she is now considerably heavier, and her hair is bleached; but the strong Southern drawl remains. Watching the films, she precisely recalls events that took place nearly 40 years ago as if they were yesterday.

Although a grandmother and past 70, Miriam still abides by her decision: "I will never retire. Put that down and underline it. The world is too nice—and so have been all the breaks."

FAST AND LOOSE (PAR, 1930) 70 M.

Director, Fred Newmeyer; based on the play *The Best People* by David Gray, Avery Hopwood; screenplay, Doris Anderson, Jack Kirkland; dialogue, Preston Sturges; camera, William Steiner.

Miriam Hopkins (Marion Lenox); Carol Lombard (Alice O'Neil); Frank Morgan (Bronson Lenox); Charles Starrett (Henry Morgan); Henry Wadsworth (Bertie Lenox); Winifred Harris (Carrie Lenox); Herbert Yost (George Grafton); David Hutcheson (Lord Rickingham); Ilka Chase (Millie Montgomery); Herschell Magall (Judge Summers).

THE SMILING LIEUTENANT (PAR, 1931) 102 M.

Director, Ernst Lubitsch; based on the novel *Nux der Prinzgemahl* by Hans Muller and the operetta *A Waltz Dream* by Leopold Jacobson, Felix Dormann, Oscar Strauss; adaptation-screenplay, Ernest Vadja, Samson Raphaelson, Lubitsch; songs, Strauss, Clifford Grey; art director, Hans Dreir; camera George Folsey.

Maurice Chevalier (Niki) Claudette Colbert (Franzi); Miriam Hopkins (Princess Anna); George Barbier (King Adolf); Charles Ruggles (Max); Hugh O'Connell (Orderly); Robert Strange (Adjutant Col. Rockoff); Janet Reade (Lily) Lon MacSunday (Emperor); Elizabeth Patterson (Baroness von Schwedel); Harry Bradley (Count von Halden); Werner Saxtorph (Josef); Karl Stall (Master Of Ceremonies); Granville Bates (Bill Collector); Maude Allen (Woman); Charles Wagenheim (Arresting Officer).

(The French version, LE LIEUTENANT SOURIANT, (PAR, 1931) also starred Chevalier, Colbert, and Miriam Hopkins.)

TWENTY FOUR HOURS (PAR, 1931) 66 M.

Director, Marion Gering; story, Louis Bromfield, William C. Lengel; Lew Levenson; screenplay, Louis Wertzenkorn; camera, Ernest Haller.

Clive Brooks (Jim Towner); Kay Francis (Fanny Towner); Miriam Hopkins (Rosie Dugan); Regis Toomey (Tony Breezzi); George Barbier (Hector Champion); Adrienne Ames (Ruby Wintringham); Charlotte Granville (Sairna Jerrold); Minor Watson (David Melbourn); Lucille LaVerne (Mrs. Dacklehorse); Wade Boteler (Pat Healy); Robert Kortman (Dave the Slapper); Malcolm Waite (Murphy); Thomas Jackson (Police Commissioner).

TWO KINDS OF WOMEN (PAR 1932) 75 M.

Director, William C. deMille; based on the play *This Is New York* by Robert E. Sherwood; screenplay, Benjamin Glazer; camera, Karl Struss.

Miriam Hopkins (Emma Krull); Phillips Holmes (Joseph Gresham, Jr.); Wynne Gibson (Phyllis Adrian); Stuart Erwin (Hauser) Irving Pichel (Senator Krull); Stanley Fields (Glassman); James Crane (*Joyce*); Vivienne Osborne (Helen); Josephine Dunn (Clarissa Smith); Larry Steers (Menchard); Adrienne Ames (Jean); Claire Dodd (Shiela); Terrance Ray (Babe Sevito); June Nash (Mrs. Brown); Kent Taylor (Milt Flusser); Edwin Maxwell (Police Dept. Commissioner); Lindsay McHarris (Radio Announcer).

DR. JEKYLL AND MR. HYDE (PAR, 1932) 90 M.

Producer-director, Rouben Mamoulian; based on the novel by Robert Louis Stevenson; screenplay, Samuel Hoffenstein, Percy Heath; assistant director, Bob Lee; art director, Hans Dreier; camera, Karl Struss; editor, William Shea.

Fredric March (Dr. Henry Jekyll/Mr. Hyde); Miriam Hopkins (Ivy Pearson); Rose Hobart (Muriel Carew); Holmes Herbert (Dr. Lanyon); Edgar Norton (Poole); Halliwell Hobbes (Brig.-Gen. Carew); Arnold Lucy (Utterson); Tempe Pigott (Mrs. Hawkins); Colonel McDonnell (Hobson); Eric Wilton (Briggs); Douglas Walton (Student); John Rogers (Waiter); Murdock MacQuarrie (Doctor); Major Sam Harris (Dance Extra).

DANCERS IN THE DARK (PAR, 1932) 74 M.

Director, David Burton; based on the play *Jazz King* by James Ashmore Creelman; adaptation, Brian Marlow, Howard Emmett Rogers; screenplay, Herman J. Mankiewicz; camera, Karl Struss.

Miriam Hopkins (Gloria Bishop); Jack Oakie (Duke Taylor); William Collier, Jr. (Floyd Stevens); Eugene Pallette (Gus); Lyda Roberti (Fanny Zabowolski); George Raft (Louie Brooks); Maurice Black (Max); Frances Moffett (Ruby); DeWitt Jennings (Sgt. McGroody); Alberta Vaughn (Marie); Walter Hiers (Ollie); Paul Fix (Benny); Paul Gibbons, Steve Grajeda, Alberto Maten, Eduardo Aguilar (Eduardo Duran's Orchestra); Kent Taylor (Saxophone Player); James Bradbury, Jr. (Happy —Trombonist); William Halligan (Terry—Trumpet Player); Fred Warren (Al—Pianist); All Hill (Smitty—Bouncer); Mary Gordon (Cleaning Lady); George Bickel (Spiegel).

THE WORLD AND THE FLESH (PAR, 1932) 74 M.

Director, John Cromwell; based on the play by Philipp Zeska, Ernst Spitz; screenplay, Oliver H. P. Garrett; camera, Karl Struss.

George Bancroft (Kylenko); Miriam Hokpins (Maria Yaskaya); Alan Mowbray (Dimitri); George E. Stone (Rutchkin); Emmett Corrigan (General Spiro); Mitchell Lewis (Sukhanov); Oscar Apfel (Banker); Harry Cording (Ivanovitch); Max Wagner (Vorobiov); Reginald Barlow (Markov); Ferike Boros (Sasha—Maria's Maid); Francis McDonald, Michael Mark, Henry Victor, Bob Kortman (Reds); Lucien Prival (Cossack).

TROUBLE IN PARADISE (PAR, 1932) 83M.

Producer-director, Ernst Lubitsch; based on the play *The Honest Finder* by Laszlo Aladar; screenplay, Grover Jones, Samson Raphaelson; songs W. Franke Harling and Leo Robin; art director, Hans Dreier; camera, Victor Milner.

Miriam Hopkins (Lily Vautier); Kay Francis (Mariette Colet); Herbert Marshall (Gaston Monescu); Charlie Ruggles (The Major); Edward Everett Horton (Francois Filiba); C. Aubrey Smith (Adolph Giron); Robert Greig (Jacques—The Butler); George Humbert (Waiter); Rolfe Sedan (Purse Salesman); Luis Alberni (Annoyed Opera Fan); Leonid Kinsky (Radical); Hooper Atchley (Insurance Agent); Nella Walker (Mme. Bouchet); Perry Ivins (Radio Commentator); Tyler Brooke (Singer); Larry Steers (Guest Extra).

THE STORY OF TEMPLE DRAKE (PAR, 1933) 70 M.

Director, Stephen Roberts; based on the novel *Sanctuary* by William Faulkner; screenplay, Oliver H. P. Garrett; camera, Karl Struss.

Miriam Hopkins (Temple Drake); Jack LaRue (Trigger); William Gargan (Stephen Benbow); William Collier, Jr. (Toddy Gowan); Irving Pichel (Lee Goodwin); Sir Guy Standing (Judge Drake); Elizabeth Patterson (Aunt Jennie); Florence Eldridge (Ruby Lemar); James Eagles (Tommy); Harlan E. Knight (Pap); James Mason (Van); Jobyna Howland (Miss Reba); Henry Hall (Judge); John Carradine (Courtroom Extra); Frank Darien (Gas Station Proprietor); Clarence Sherwood (Lunch Wagon Proprietor); Oscar Apfel (District Attorney); Kent Taylor, Clem Beauchamps (Jellybeans).

STRANGER'S RETURN (MGM, 1933) 88 M.

Director, King Vidor; based on the novel by Phil Stong; screenplay, Brown Holmes, Stong; camera, William Daniels; editor, Ben Lewis.

Lionel Barrymore (Crandpa Storr); Miriam Hopkins (Louise Storr); Franchot Tone (Guy Crane); Stuart Erwin (Simon); Irene Hervey (Nettie); Beulah Bondi (Beatrice); Grant Mitchell (Allan Redfield); Ted Alexander (Widdie); Aileen Carlyle (Thelma Redfield).

DESIGN FOR LIVING (PAR, 1933) 88 M.

Director, Ernst Lubitsch; based on the play by Noel Coward; adaptation-screenplay, Ben Hecht; art director, Hans Dreier; music, Nathaniel Finston; camera, Victor Milner; editor, Francis Marsh.

Fredric March (Tom Chambers); Gary Cooper (George Curtis); Miriam Hopkins (Gilda Farrell); Edward Everett Horton (Max Plunkett); Franklin Pangborn (Mr. Douglas); Isabel Jewell (Lisping Stenographer); Harry Dunkinson (Mr. Egelbauer); Helena Phillips (Mrs. Egelbauer); James Donlin (Best Man); Vernon Steele (First Manager); Thomas Braidon (Second Manager); Jane Darwell (George's Housekeeper); Armand Kaliz (Mr. Burton); Adrienne d'Ambricourt (Proprietress of Cafe); Wyndham Standing (Max's Butler); Emile Chautard (Conductor); Nora Cecil (Tom's English Secretary); Olaf Hytten (Englishman at Train); Mary Gordon (Theatre Chambermaid); Lionel Belmore (Laughing Theatre Patron); Rolfe Sedan (Bed Salesman); Charles K. French (Extra at Theatre).

ALL OF ME (PAR, 1934) 70 M.

Producer, Louis Lighton; director, James Flood; based on the play *Chrysalis* by Rose Porter; screenplay, Sidney Buchman, Thomas Mitchell; dialog director, Mitchell; camera, Victor Milner; editor, Otho Lovering.

Fredric March (Don Ellis); Miriam Hopkins (Lydia Darrow); George Raft (Honey Rogers); Helen Mack (Eve Haron); Nella Walker (Mrs. Darrow); William Collier, Jr. (Jerry Helman); Gilbert Emery (Dean); Blanche Frederici (Miss Haskell); Kitty Kelly (Lorraine); Guy Usher (District Attorney); John Marston (Nat Davis); Edgar Kennedy (Guard).

SHE LOVES ME NOT (PAR, 1934) 85 M.

Producer, Benjamin Glazer; director, Elliott Nugent; based on the novel by Edward Hope and the play by Howard Lindsay; screenplay, Glazer; songs, Mack Gordon and Harry Revel; Ralph Rainger and Leo Robin; camera, Charles Lang; editor, Hugh Bennett.

Bing Crosby (Paul Lanton); Miriam Hopkins (Curly Flagg); Kitty Carlisle (Midge Mercer); Edward Nugent (Buzz Jones); Henry Stephenson (Dean Mercer); Warren Hymer (Mugg Schnitzel); Lynne Overman (Gus McNeal); Judith Allen (Frances Arbuthnot); George Barbier (J. Teorval Jones); Henry Kolker (Charles M. Lawton); Maude Turner Gordon (Mrs. Arbuthnot); Margaret Armstrong (Martha); Ralf Harolde (J.B.); Matt McHugh (Andy); Franklin Ardell (Arkle); Vince Barnett (Baldy O'-Mara.

THE RICHEST GIRL IN THE WORLD (RKO, 1934) 76 M.

Producer, Pandro S. Berman; director, William A. Seiter; story-adaptation, Norman Krasna; music director, Max Steiner; camera, Nick Musuraca; editor, George Crone.

Miriam Hokins (Dorothy Hunter); Joel McCrea (Tony Travis); Fay Wray (Sylvia Vernon); Henry Stephenson (Jonathan Connors); Reginald Denny (Philip Vernon); Beryl Mercer (Marie—The Maid); George Meeker (Donald); Wade Boteler (Orsatti); Herbert Bunston (Cavendish); Burr McIntosh (David Preston); Edgar Norton (Butler);

Fred Howard (Haley); William Gould (Executive); Selmer Jackson (Dr. Harvey); Olaf Hytten (Valet); Dale Van Sickel (Dance Extra).

BECKY SHARP (RKO, 1935) 83 M.

Producer, Kenneth Macgowan; director, Rouben Mamoulian; based on the play by Landon Mitchell adapted from the novel *Vanity Fair* by William Makepeace Thackeray; screenplay, Francis Edward Faragoh; production designer, Robert Edmond Jones; music, Roy Webb; assistant director, Argyle Nelson; camera, Ray Rennahan; editor, Archie Marshek.

Miriam Hopkins (Becky Sharp); Frances Dee (Amelia Sedley); Sir Cedric Hardwicke (Marquis of Steyne); Billie Burke (Lady Bareacres); Alison Skipworth (Julia Crawley); Nigel Bruce (Joseph Sedley); Alan Mowbray (Captain Randon Crawley); Colin Tapley (Captain William Dobbin); G. P. Huntley, Jr. (George Osborne); William Stack (Pitt Crawley); George Hassell (Sir Pitt Crawley); William Faversham (Duke of Wellington); Charles Richman (General Tufto); Doris Lloyd (Duchess of Richmond); Leonard Mudie (Lloyd Tarquin); Bunny Beatty (Lady Blanche); Charles Coleman (Bowles); May Beatty (Briggs); Finis Barton (Miss Flowery); Olaf Hytten (Prince Regent); Pauline Garon (Fifine); James "Hambone" Robinson (Page); Elspeth Dudgeon (Miss Pinkerton); Tempe Pigott (Charwoman); Ottola Nesmith (Lady Jane Crawley); Margaret Dee (Young Girl); Pat Ryan Nixon (Ballroom Dancer); Pat Somerset, Creighton Hale (Officers).

BARBARY COAST (UA, 1935) 97 M.

Producer, Samuel Goldwyn; director, Howard Hawks; story and screenplay, Ben Hecht, Charles MacArthur; camera, Ray June; editor, Edward Curtis.

Miriam Hopkins (Mary Rutledge "Swan"); Edward G. Robinson (Louis Chamalis); Joel McCrea (Jim Carmichael); Walter Brennan (Old Atrocity); Frank Craven (Col. Marcus Aurelius Cobb); Brian Donlevy (Kunckles Jacoby); Otto Hoffman (Peebles); Rollo Lloyd (Wigham); Donald Meek (Sawbuck McTavish); Roger Gray (Sandy Ferguson); Clyde Cooke (Oakie); Harry Carey (Jed Slocum); J. M. Kerrigan (Judge Harper); Matt McHugh (Broncho); Wong Chung (Ah Wing); Russ Powell (Sheriff); Fredrik Vogeding (Ship's Captain); Cyril Thornton (Steward); Clarence Wertz (Drunk); Harry Semels (Lookout); David Niven (Sailor Thrown Out of Saloon); Ben Hall (Printer); Kit Guard (Kibitzer); Herman Bing (Fish Peddler); Harry Holman (Mayor); Ethel Wales (Mayor's Wife); Captain Anderson, Edward Peil, Sr., Sidney D'Albrook (Vigilantes); Jim Thorpe (Indian); Tom London (Ringsider With Girl); Harry Depp (Jeweler).

SPLENDOR (UA, 1935) 77 M.

Producer, Samuel Goldwyn; director, Elliott Nugent; story-screenplay, Rachel Crowthers; assistant director, Hugh Boswell; music director, Alfred Newman; art director, Richard Day; camera, Gregg Toland; editor, Margaret Clancey

Miriam Hopkins (Phyllis); Joel McCrea (Brighton); Helen Westley (Mrs. Lorrimore); Katharine Alexander (Martha); David Niven (Clancey); Ruth Weston (Edith); Paul Cavanagh (Deering); Billie Burke (Clarissa); Ivan F. Simpson (Fletcher); Arthur Treacher (Captain Ballinger); Torben Meyer (Von Hoffstatter); Reginald Sheffield (Billy Grimes); William R. "Billy" Arnold (Jake); Maidel Turner (Mrs. Hicks); Clarence H. Wilson (Process Server); Violet Axelle (Brighton Maid); Eddie Craven (Elevator Man); Lois January (Lena Limering); Cosmo Kyrle Bellow, Connie Howard (Guests At Dinner); Betty Blair (Fitter); Clinton Lyle (Chauffeur); Jeanie Roberts (Gertie).

THESE THREE (UA, 1936) 93 M.

Producer, Samuel Goldwyn; director, William Wyler; based on the play *The Children's Hour* by Lillian Hellman; screenplay, Hellman; assistant director, Walter Mayo; music, Alfred Newman; camera, Gregg Toland; editor, Danny Mandell.

Miriam Hopkins (Martha Dobie); Merle Oberon (Karen Wright); Joel McCrea (Dr. Joseph Cardin); Catherine Doucet (Mrs. Mortar); Alma Kruger (Mrs. Tilford); Bonita Granville (Mary Tilford); Marcia Mae Jones (Rosalie); Carmencita Johnson (Evelyn); Mary Ann Durkin (Lois); Margaret Hamilton (Agatha); Mary Louise Cooper (Helen Burton); Walter Brennan (Taxi Driver).

MEN ARE NOT GODS (UA, 1937) 82 M.

Producer, Alexander Korda; director adaptation , Walter Reisch; camera, Charles Rosher; editor, Henry Cornelius; screenplay, G. B. Stern, Iris Wright.

Miriam Hopkins (Ann Williams); Gertude Lawrence (Barbara); Sebastian Shaw (Edmund Davey); Rex Harrison (Tommy); A. E. Matthews (Skeates); Val Gielgud (Producer); Laura Smithson (Katherine); Lawrence Grossmith (Stanley); Sybil Grove (Painter); Winifred Willard (Mrs. Williams); Wally Patch (Gallery Attendant); James Harcourt (Porter); Noel Howlett (Cashier); Rosamund Greenwood (Piano Player); Paddy Morgan (Kelly); Nicholas Nadyin (Iago); Michael Hogarth (Cassio).

THE WOMAN I LOVE (RKO, 1937) 85 M.

Producer, Albert Lewis; director, Anatole Litvak; based on the novel *L'Equipage* by Joseph Kessel and the French film *L'Equipage*; screenplay, Mary Borden; music, Arthur Honneger, Maurice Thiriet; music director, Roy Webb; art director, Van Nest Polglase; special effects, Vernon Walker; camera, Charles Rosher; editor, Henri Rust.

Paul Muni (Lt. Claude Maury); Miriam Hopkins (Mme. Helene Maury); Louis Hayward (Lt. Jean Herbillion); Colin Clive (Capt. Thelis); Minor Watson (Deschamps); Elizabeth Risdon (Mme. Herbillion); Paul Guilfoyle (Berthier); Wally Albright (Georges); Mady Christians (Florence); Alec Craig (Doctor); Owen Davis, Jr. (Mezziores); Sterling Holloway (Duprez); Vince Barnett (Mathieu); Adrian Morris (Marbot); Donald Barry (Michel); Joe Twerp (Narbonne); William Stelling (Pianist).

WOMAN CHASES MAN (UA, 1937) 71 M.

Producer, Samuel Goldwyn; associate producer, George Height; Franklyn Fenton; screenplay, Joseph Anthony, Mauel Seff, David Hertz; music director Alfred Newman; art director, Richard Day; camera, Gregg Toland; editor, Daniel Mandell.

Miriam Hopkins (Virginia Travis); Joel McCrea (Kenneth Nolan); Charles Winninger (B. J. Nolan); Erik Rhodes (Henri Saffron); Ella Logan (Judy); Leona Maricle (Tennyson); Broderick Crawford (Hunk); Charles Halton (Mr. Judd); William Jaffrey (Doctor); George Chandler (Taxi Driver); Alan Bridge, Monte Vandegrift, Jack Baxley, Walter Soderling (Process Servers); Al K. Hall, Dick Cramer (Men in Subway).

WISE GIRL (RKO, 1938) 70 M.

Producer, Edward Kaufman; director, Leigh Jason; story, Allan Scott, Charles Norman; adaptation, Scott; assistant director, Kenneth Holmes; camera, Peverell Marley; editor, Jack Hively.

Miriam Hopkins (Susan Fletcher); Ray Milland (John O'Halloran); Walter Abel (Karl); Henry Stephenson (Mr. Fletcher); Alec Craig (Dermont O'Neil); Guinn Williams (Mike); Betty Philson (Joan); Marianna Strelby (Katie); Margaret Dumont (Mrs. Bell-Rivington); Jean de Briac (George); Ivan Lebedeff (Prince Michael); Rafael Storm (Prince Ivan); Gregory Gaye (Prince Leopold); Richard Lane, Tom Kennedy (Detectives); James Finlayson (Jailer).

THE OLD MAID (WB, 1939) 95 M.

Executive producer, Hal Wallis, associate producer, Henry Blanke; director, Edmund Goulding, based on the novel by Edith Wharton and the play by Zoe Akins; art director, Robert Haas; music, Max Steiner; camera, Tony Gaudio; editor, George Amy.

Bette Davis (Charlotte Lovell); Miriam Hopkins (Delia Lovell); George Brent (Clem Spender); Jane Bryan (Tina); Donald Crisp (Dr. Lanskell); Louise Fazenda (Dora); James Stephenson (Jim Ralston); Jerome Cowan (Joe Ralston); William Lundigan (Lanning Halsey); Cecilia Loftus (Henrietta Lovell); Rand Brooks (Jim); Janet Shaw (Dee Ralston); Marlene Burnett (Tina—As A Child); DeWolf (William) Hopper (John Ward); Frederick Burton (Mr. Halsey); Doris Lloyd (Aristocratic Maid).

VIRGINIA CITY (WB, 1940) 121 M.

Executive producer, Hal B. Wallis; associate producer, Robert Fellows; director, Michael Curtiz; screenplay, Robert Buckner; art director, Ted Smith; assistant director, Sherry Shourds; music, Max Steiner; special effects, Byron Haskin, H. F. Koenekamp; camera; Sol Polito; editor, George Amy.

Errol Flynn (Kerry Bradford); Miriam Hopkins (Julia Haynes); Randolph Scott (Vance Irby); Humphrey Bogart (John Murrell); Frank McHugh (Mr. Upjohn) Alan Hale (Olaf Swenson); Guinn Williams ("Marblehead"); John Litel (Marshal); Moroni Olsen (Dr. Cameron); Russell Hicks (Armistead); Douglass Dumbrille (Major Drewery); Dickie Jones (Cobby); Monte Montague (Stage Driver); Frank Wilcox (Officer) George Regas (Half-Breed); Russell Simpson (Gaylor); Thurston Hall (General Meade); Charles Middleton (Jefferson Davis); Victor Kilian (Abraham Lincoln); Charles Trowbridge (Seddon); Howard Hickman (General Page); Charles Halton (Ralston); Roy Gordon (Major-General Taylor); Ward Bond (Sgt. Sam McDaniel (Sam); Bud Osborne (Stage Driver); Lane Chandler (Soldier Clerk); Trevor Bardette (Fanatic); Spencer Charters, George Guhl (Bartenders); Ed Parker, DeWolfe Hopper (Lieutenants); Paul Fix (Murrell's Henchman); Walter Miller, Reed Howes (Sergeants); George Reeves (Telegrapher)

LADY WITH RED HAIR (WB, 1940) 78 M.

Executive producer, Jack L. Warner; associate producer, Edmund Grainger; director, Kurt Bernhardt; based on the memoirs of Mrs. Leslie Carter; story, N. Brewster Morse, Norbert Faulkner; screenplay, Charles Kenyon, Milton Krims; camera, Arthur Edison; editor, James Gibbon.

Miriam Hopkins (Mrs. Leslie Carter); Claude Rains (David Belasco); Richard Ainley (Lou Payne); John Litel (Charles Bryant); Laura Hope Crews (Mrs. Dudley); Helen Westley (Mrs. Frazier); Mona Barrie (Mrs. Brooks); Victor Jory (Mr. Clifton); Fritz Leiber (Mr. Poster); Cecil Kellaway (Mr. Russell (Dudley Carter); Florence Shirley (Daisy Dawn); Halliwell Hobbes (Judge); Selmer Jackson (Henry De Mille); William Davidson (Stock Company Manager); Doris Lloyd (Teacher); Thomas Jackson (Mr. Harper); Alexis Smith (Girl); William Hopper (Attendant); Creighton Hale (Reporter); Maurice Cass (Scenic Artist); Russell Hicks (Man); Cyril Ring (Playwright); Huntley Gordon (Actor).

A GENTLEMAN AFTER DARK (UA, 1942) 74 M.

Producer, Edward Small; director, Edwin L. Martin; Richard Washburn Child; screenplay, Patterson McNutt, George Bruce; camera, Milton Krasner; editor, Arthur Roberts.

Brian Donlevy (Harry Melton); Miriam Hopkins (Flo Melton); Preston Foster (Lt. Tommy Gaynor); Harold Huber (Stubby); Philip Reed (Eddie Smith); Gloria Holden (Miss Clark); Douglass Dumbrille (Enzo Calibra); Sharon Douglas (Diana Melton Gaynor); Bill Henry (Paul Rutherford); Ralph Morgan (Morrison); Jack Mulhall (Desk Clerk); William Haade (Relief Cop); William Ruhl (Detective); Edgar Dearing (Joe); David Clarke (Bell Boy).

OLD ACQUAINTANCE (WB, 1943) 110 M.

Producer, Henry Blanke; director, Vincent Sherman; based on the play by John Van Druten; screenplay, Van Druten, Leonore Coffee; art director, John Hughes; music, Franz Waxman; camera, Sol Polito; editor, Terry Morse.

Bette Davis (Kitty); Miriam Hopkins (Millie); Gig Young (Budd Kendall); John Loder (Preston Drake); Dolores Moran (Deirdre); Philip Reed (Lucian Grant); Roscoe Karns (Charlie Archer); Anne Revere (Belle Carter); Leona Maricle (Julia Brondbank); Esther Dale (Harriett); George Lessey (Dean); Joseph Crehan (Editor); James Conlin (Photographer); Marjorie Hoshelle (Margaret Kemp); Tommye Adams, Kathleen O'Malley, Timmy Sabor, Frances Ward, Virginia Patton, Lucille LaMarr, Harriett Olsen, Dorothy Schoemer (College Girls); Francine Rufo (Dierdre—As A Child); Ann Codee (Mademoiselle); Creighton Hale (Stage Manager); Pierre Watkin (Mr. Winter); Frank Darien (Stage Doorman); Philip Van Zandt (Clerk); Charles Jordan (Bootlegger); Herbert Rawlinson (Chairman); Gordon Clark (Usher) Ann Doran (Saleslady); Frank Mayo, Jack Mower, Major Sam Harris (Army officers); Charles Sullivan (Taxi Driver).

THE HEIRESS (PAR, 1949) 115 M.

Producer-director, William Wyler; based on the play *The Heiress* by Ruth and Augustus Goetz, suggested by the novel *Washington Square* by Henry James; screenplay, the Goetzes; art director, John Meehan; music, Aaron Copland; song, Ray Evans and Jay Livingston; camera, Leo Tover; editor, William Hornbeck.

Olivia de Havilland (Catherine Sloper); Montgomery Clift (Morris Townsend); Ralph Richardson (Austin Sloper); Miriam Hopkins (Lavinia Penniman); Vanessa Brown (Maria); Mona Freeman (Marian Almond); Ray Collins (Jefferson Almond); Betty Linley (Mrs. Montgomery); Selena Royle (Elizabeth Almond); Paul Lees (Arthur Townsend); Harry Antrim (Mr. Abeel); Russ Conway (Quintus); David Thursby (Geier).

THE MATING SEASON (PAR, 1951) 101 M.

Producer, Charles Brackett, director, Mitchell Leisen; screenplay, Brackett, Walter Reisch, Richard Breen; music, Joseph J. Lilley; art director, Hal Pereira, Roland Anderson; camera, Charles B. Lang, Jr.; editor, Frank Bracht.

Gene Tierney (Maggie Carleton); John Lund (Val McNulty); Miriam Hopkins (Fran Carleton); Thelma Ritter (Ellen McNulty); Jan Sterling (Betsy); Larry Keating (Mr. Kalinger, Sr.); James Lorimer (George C. Kalinger, Jr.); Gladys Hurlbut (Mrs. Conger); Cora Witherspoon (Mrs. Williamson); Malcolm Keen (Mr. Williamson); Ellen Corby (Annie); Billie Bird (Mugsy); Samuel Colt (Colonel Conger); Grayce Hampton (Mrs. Fahnstock); Stapleton Kent (Dr. Chorley); Jean Ruth, Laura Elliot (Bridesmaids); Charles Dayton (Best Man At Wedding); Bob Kortman (Janitor); Jean Acker, Sally Rawlinson, Tex Brodux, Bob Rich (Party Guests); Franklyn Farnum, Richard Neill, Sam Ash, Jack Richardson (Board of Directors); Beulah Christian, Kathryn Wilson, Beulah Parkington, Margaret B. Farrel (Board Of Directors' Wives); Beth Hartman (Receptionist); Mary Young (Spinster); Gordon Arnold, John Bryant (Ushers At Wedding); Bess Flowers (Friend At Wedding).

OUTCASTS OF POKER FLAT (20th, 1952) 80 M.

Producer, Julian Blaustein; director, Joseph M. Newman; based on the story by Bret Harte; screenplay, Edmund H. North; Hugo Friedhofer; camera, Joseph LaShelle; editor, William Reynolds.

Anne Baxter (Cal); Dale Robertson (John Oakhurst); Miriam Hopkins (Duchess); Cameron Mitchell (Ryker); Craig Hill (Tom Dakin); Barbara Bates (Piney); Billy Lynn (Jake); Dick Rich (Drunk); John Ridgely (Bill Akeley); Harry T. Shannon (Bearded Miner); Harry Harvey, Sr. (George Larabee); Lee Phelps, Kit Carson (Men); Jack Byron (Miner); Tom Greenway, Harry Carter (Townsmen); Bob Adler, Russ Conway (Vigilante); Frosty Royce, Joe P. Smith (Possemen); Albert Schmidt, Joe Haworth (Gunmen).

CARRIE (Paramount, 1952) 118 M.

Producer-director, William Wyler; based on the novel *Sister Carrie* by Theodore Dreiser; screenplay, Ruth and Augustus Goetz; art director, Hal Pereira, Roland Anderson; camera, Victor Milner; editor, Robert Swank.

Laurence Oliver (George Hurstwood); Jennifer Jones (Carrie Meeber); Miriam Hopkins (Julia Hurstwood); Eddie Albert (Charles Drouett); Basil Ruysdael (Fitzgerald); Ray Teal (Allen); Barry Kelley (Slawson); Sara Berner (Mrs. Oransky); William Reynolds (George Hurstwood, Jr.); Harry Hayden (O'Brien); Walter Baldwin (Carrie's Father); Dorothy Adams (Carrie's Mother); Royal Dano (Captain); James Flavin (Mike—Bartender); Harlan Briggs (Joe Brant); Melinda Plowman (Little Girl); Margaret Field (Servant Girl); Jasper D. Weldon (Porter); Irene Winston (Anna); Charles Halton (Factory Foreman); Leon Tyler (Connell); George Melford. Al Ferguson (Patrons At Slawson's); John Alvin (Stage Manager); Don Beddoe (Goodman); Judith Adams (Bride); Julius Tannen (John); Snub Pollard (Man); Franklyn Farnum, Stuart Holmes (Restuarant Patrons); Kit Guard (Bum); Frances Morris (Maid).

THE CHILDREN'S HOUR (UA, 1962) 107 M.

Producer-director, William Wyler; associate producer, Robert Wyer; based on the play by Lillian Hellman; adaptation, Hellman; screenplay, John Michael Hayes; assistant director, Robert E. Relyea, Jerome M. Siegel; music, Alex North; art director, Fernando Carrere; camera, Franz F. Planer, editor, Robert Swink.

Audrey Hepburn (Karen Wright); Shirley MacLaine (Martha Dobie); James Garner (Dr. Joe Cardin); Miriam Hopkins (Mrs. Lily Mortar); Fay Bainter (Mrs. Amelia Tilford); Karen Balkin (Mary Tilford); Veronica Cartwright (Rosalie); Jered Barclay (Grocery Boy).

FANNY HILL (Pan World, 1965) 104 M.

Producer, Albert Zugsmith; director, Russ Meyer; based on the novel by John Cleland; screenplay, Robert Heel; assistant director, Elfie Tillack; music, Erwin Halletz; camera, Heinz Hilscher; editor, Alfred Arp.

Miriam Hopkins (Miss Maude Brown); Letitia Roman (Fanny Hill); Walter Giller (Hemingway); Alex D'Arcy (Admiral); Helmut Weiss (Mr. Dinklespieler); Chris Howland (Mr. Norbert); Ulli Lommel (charles); Cara Garnett (Phoebe); Karen Evans (Martha); Syra Marty (Hortense); Albert Zugsmith (Grand Duke); Christiane Schmidtmer (Fiona); Heidi Hansen (Fenella); Erica Ericson (Emily); Patricia Houstoun (Amanda); Marshall Raynor (Johnny); Hilda Sessack (Mrs. Snow); Billy Frick (Percival); Jurgen Nesbach (James); Herbert Knippenberg (Mudge); Susanne Hsiac (Lotus Blossom); Renate Hutte (Niece); Ellen Velero (Girl).

THE CHASE (COL., 1966) 138 M.

Producer, Sam Spiegel; director, Arthur Penn; based on the novel and play by Horton Foote; screenplay, Lillian Hellman; assistant director, Russell Saunders; music, John Barry; camera, Joseph LaShelle; editor, Gene Milford.

Marlon Brando (Calder); Jane Fonda (Anna); Robert Redford (Bubber); E. G. Marshall (Val Rogers); Angie Dickinson (Ruby Calder); Janice Rule (Emily Stewart); Miriam Hopkins (Mrs. Reeves); Martha Hyer (Mary Fuller); Richard Bradford (Damon Fuller); Robert Duvall (Edwin Stewart); James Fox (Jason "Jake" Rogers); Diana Hyland (Elizabeth Rogers); Henry Hull (Briggs); Jocelyn Brando (Mrs. Briggs); Katherine Walsh (Verna Dee); Lori Martin (Cutie); Marc Seaton (Paul); Paul Williams (Seymour); Clifton James (Lem); Malcolm Atterbury (Mr. Reeves); Nydia Westman (Mrs. Henderson); Joel Fluellen (Lester Johnson); Steve Ihnat (Archie); Maurice Manson (Moore); Bruce Cabot (Sol); Steve Whittaker (Slim); Pamela Curran (Mrs. Sifftifieus); Ken Renard (Sam); Eduardo Cianelli.

COMEBACK (Congdon, unreleased)

Executive producer, J. Talmadge Congdon; Producer-director-screenplay, Donald Wolfe.

Miriam Hopkins, Gale Sondergaard, John Garfield, Jr., Minta Durfee Arbuckle, Joe Besser, Virginia Wing, Katina Garner, Morris Reese, Bud Douglass, Eddie Baker.

In THE CAMEL THROUGH THE NEEDLE'S EYE (1929)

With Franchot Tone in STRANGER'S RE-TURN (MGM '33)

Miriam Hopkins in 1937

With studio head Jack L. Warner at th Cafe Marcel, Hollywood, about 1939

In FAST AND LOOSE (Par '30)

With Maurice Chevalier in THE SMILING
LIEUTENANT (Par '31)

With Phillips Holmes in TWO KINDS OF
WOMEN (Par '32)

In DR. JEKYLL AND MR. HYDE (Par '32)

With Claire Dodd, Jack Oakie, and Walter
Hiers in DANCERS IN THE DARK (Par '32)

With George Bancroft in THE WORLD
AND THE FLESH (Par '32)

With Kay Francis and Herbert Marshall in
TROUBLE IN PARADISE (Par '32)

With William Gargan in THE STORY OF
TEMPLE DRAKE (Par '33)

With Gary Cooper in DESIGN FOR LIVING
(Par '33)

With George Raft in ALL OF ME (Par '3

With Alan Mowbray in BECKY SHARP
RKO '35)

With Merle Oberon in THESE THREE (UA
'36)

With Ella Logan, Broderick Crawford, and
Charles Winninger in WOMAN CHASES
MAN (UA '37)

With Joel McCrea in WOMAN CHASES
MAN (UA '37)

With Bette Davis and Cecilia Loftus in
THE OLD MAID (WB '39)

With Randolph Scott in VIRGINIA CITY
(WB '40)

With Bette Davis in OLD ACQUAINT-
ANCE (WB '43)

With Ralph Richardson, Montgomery
Clift, and Olivia de Havilland in THE HEIR-
ESS (Par '49)

With Marlon Brando in THE CHASE
'66)

With Gene Tierney in THE MATING SEA-
SON (Par '51)

SYLVIA SIDNEY

5'4"

104 pounds

Dark brown hair

Blue green eyes

Leo

✳✳✳✳✳✳✳✳✳✳✳✳✳✳✳✳✳✳✳✳✳✳✳

FEW AMERICAN film stars have been so bound by the ethos of their time as Sylvia Sidney, one of the five reigning queens at Paramount in the early 1930s. From her first major feature film appearance in *City Streets* (1931), she was categorized as a highly emotional actress best showcased in deeply dramatic roles in which she represented the prime buffer against society's ills. It little mattered then—and few remember now—that during her screen career she essayed such divergent types as a Japanese geisha girl, a New Mexican Indian, a Eurasian, and a Ruritanian princess. That she could blend her acting style with such self-effacing ease in tandem with diverse costars like Spencer Tracy, Cary Grant, Henry Fonda, Gary Cooper, and George Raft, is a prime reason why Sylvia was constantly overlooked in the Academy Awards sweepstakes. No matter how complex the dynamics of her characterizations, her emoting seemed so natural that it could not possibly be hard work.

In the mid-1920s, when Sylvia began appearing on Broadway, she earned a healthy reputation as an astute performer dedicated to her craft. More so than contemporary stage ingenues Claudette Colbert and Miriam Hopkins, who also joined Paramount in 1929–30, Sylvia remained a stage actress sojourning in Hollywood. Her unconventionally quiet beauty was not typical of silver-screen pulchritude. She had to win her movie fame through earnest portrayals of woebegone working girls snarled in society's web, as in *An American Tragedy* and *Street Scene*. Most of her five years at Paramount were controlled not by her choice or by fate, but by her mentor, B. P. Schulberg, for a time creative head of the studio.

Sylvia broke away from Paramount in 1935, trusting producer Walter Wanger to help her break the screen stereotype and work up to glamorous stardom. Unfortunately, she found herself assigned to more social-comment drama. Several of these films were outstanding: *Fury, You Only Live Once,* and *Dead End.* Needless to say, so was Sylvia.

In 1938, at age 28, Sylvia deserted Hollywood for the New York stage with unspectacular results. She turned in a succession of highly polished performances in a wide range of rehashed successes in stock and on the road.

By the time she engineered her delayed comeback in Hollywood in the 1940s, World War II had altered the country's social milieu. Inexorably associated in everyone's mind with the Depression, she was considered old hat. She had not aged well, and without the support of the kind of revamped publicity campaign that only a large studio could afford, she was unable to reestablish herself in the film industry.

Throughout the next three decades she devoted herself industriously to appearing in a wide range of stage productions—once again, mostly on tour —and to essaying mature emotional roles on television. She was rarely seen in Broadway productions—usually only in secondary roles, as in *Enter Laughing,* or in replacement assignments such as *Barefoot in the Park.*

These days she seems content to ignore the past and future, and devotes much of her time to perfecting her talent for needlepoint and to breeding her favorite pug dogs.

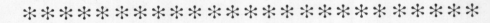

Sylvia Sidney was born Sophie Kosow in New York City, August 8, 1910, the daughter of Russian-born Victor Kosow and Rumanian Rebecca (Saperstein) Kosow. Shortly thereafter, her parents divorced. When her mother married Dr. Sigmund Sidney, a dental surgeon, he legally adopted Sylvia. (Years later, after Sylvia had attained stardom, Kosow reappeared on the scene, hoping to be reinstated as her legal father; Sylvia chose to remain her stepfather's adopted daughter.)

As a child, Sylvia stammered and was very nervous. Her parents encouraged the shy, introspective youngster to be more outgoing, and even enrolled her for elocution lessons at the age of ten. She detested the lessons, but when she announced her decision that she wanted a stage career, her parents fostered her theatrical ambitions. "They were happy to get me out of the house," Sylvia later recalled.

While attending Washington Irving High School, 15-year-old Sylvia enrolled in the Theatre Guild's school for acting, after having been rejected by the American Academy of Dramatic Arts. Winthrop Ames of the faculty selected Sylvia for the title role in *Prunella*, the school's graduation play. The graduation plays were always presented as a special matinee performance at a Broadway theatre. The *New York Times*, reviewing the June 15, 1926, graduation play, which was performed at the Garrick Theatre, found that "Sylvia Sidney in the title role had very definitely the qualities of charm and wistfulness, and endowed her *Prunella* with them in the proper proportions."

Sylvia later reflected: "I suppose fifteen is a rather early age to decide what you want to be. But I wanted so much to go on the stage. From my first consciousness of life, almost, I loved the theatre. I wasn't stage struck in the sense that most youngsters are ... rather I felt somehow that in the theatre one has a medium for the expression of beauty combining all other expressions of beauty, we know as art, and that I would never be truly happy until I became identified with it."

Next, James Gleason and Ernest Truex hired Sylvia for a role in *The Challenge of Youth* (Poli Theatre, Washington, D.C., October 11, 1926). She played Desire Adams in this shocking story of the mores of the younger generation in a small New England town. *Variety* noted: "But for a blur at times in her enunciation, [she] promises something worthwhile." Sylvia collapsed on stage during the second night's performance. The attending physician diagnosed her ailment as a ruptured appendix. The determined Sylvia said nonsense to an immediate operation, and went on with the show. The play folded in Washington after the second week. The "ruptured appendix" turned out to have been no more than a torn ligament.

Sylvia made definite progress in her stage career when she replaced Dorothy Stickney as Anita in Blanche Yurka's production of *The Squall* in January, 1927. Her first leading role on Broadway was in *Crime* (Ettinge Theatre, February 22, 1927) by Samuel Shipman and John B. Hymer. Other "unknowns" in the cast were Kay Francis, Chester Morris, Douglass Montgomery, and Kay Johnson. One critic thought Sylvia as Annabelle Porter "looks and perfoms like a composite of Katherine Cornell, Helen Menken and a frightened deer." Most shared the opinion of Percy Hammond *(New York Herald Tribune)*: "[her] skillful ingenuousness makes Mr. [James] Rennie's last act sacrifice a little less incredible." The show ran 186 performances.

While in *Crime*, Sylvia made her motion picture debut. First National was filming a Broadway rags-to-riches tale, *Broadway Nights* (May, 1927).

The studio starred Lois Wilson in the film and photographed some on-location scenes of stage personalities, including Sylvia. Other guest performers were Georgette Duval, June Collier, and Henry Sherwood. Another newcomer from the stage who made her initial screen appearance in *Broadway Nights* was Barbara Stanwyck, who had the role of a fan dancer.

Sylvia's next role was Mary Norton in *Mirrors* (Forrest Theatre, January 18, 1928). In this inside look at wanton life among Westchester's flaming youth, Sylvia was "winning" and had "her moments" as a 16-year-old observer on the scene. The play closed after 13 performances.

In *The Breaks* (Klaw Theatre, April 16, 1928), a melodrama set in a small Texas town, Sylvia was the hired girl. This J. C. and Elliot Nugent play lasted for eight showings.

With no other Broadway roles forthcoming, Sylvia accepted a 14-week engagement at the Elitch Gardens Theatre, Denver, Colorado, as leading lady. Fredric March, Florence Eldredge, and Isobel Elsom were part of the stock company that season.

While there, Sylvia was spotted by Hollywood talents scouts, then desperately searching for stage actors for the new talking films because of their ability to enunciate clearly. She was contracted by Fox Pictures, and went from Denver to Hollywood. The studio assigned her to its third sound feature film, *Thru Different Eyes* (1929), a melodrama starring Warner Baxter, Mary Duncan, Edmund Lowe, and Earle Fox. The gimmick of this courtroom tale was the retelling of the homicide from the viewpoint of both the prosecution and the defense. The denouement was left to Sylvia. As Valerie Briand, she screams out in hysteria when Lowe is found guilty of artist Baxter's murder. She rushes forward to tell the judge and jury (and movie audience), through a third flashback, how the killing really happened. The feature was released April 7, 1929, publicized as an "all dialogue murder trial novelty."

Like many stage performers before and after her, Sylvia found it terribly difficult to adjust to the disconcerting procedures of film-making. She was artistically dissatisfied with her overblown role, which was so quickly forgotten by almost everyone concerned that two years later she could again be publicized as making her film debut. Contract or not, she hated the Hollywood system, and when the last retakes were finished, she returned to Manhattan. According to a 1931 *Modern Screen* magazine interview, one of her leading men in *Thru Different Eyes* attempted to make a pass, which she quickly rebuffed. Said the self-assured Sylvia: "That is the only unpleasant experience I've ever had in all my job hunting and theatrical work. I doubt that any girl out in the world has had less."

Meanwhile, back on Broadway Sylvia appeared as Rosalie in *Gods of the Lightning* (Little Theatre, October 24, 1928). This Maxwell Anderson drama was based on the controversial Sacco-Vanzetti trial and presented Sylvia in one of her first clearly defined social-victim roles. She was both the sweetheart of Charles Bickford, one of the condemned men, and the daughter of the man actually guilty of the payroll robbery-murder. She garnered fine reviews: "I enjoyed the theatrical way in which they ended it; with Miss Sidney hearing the news of her lover's execution and employing all the difficult pyrotechnics of hysteria as the curtain fell. She sent us homeward bubbling with pity and agitation" (Percy Hammond, *New York Herald Tribune*). "She acts this searing episode with an unadorned poignancy that recapitulates and compresses all the emotion of *Gods of Lightning* into one living moment" (Brooks Atkinson, *New York Times*). Roaring Twenties audiences were not impressed by this sociological study and it closed after 22 performances.

Sylvia then joined George Cukor's stock company in Rochester, New York, playing several weeks of repertory. Bette Davis had worked briefly with the same group a few seasons before.

After this, Sylvia returned to Broadway in *Nice Women* (Longacre Theatre, June 10, 1929) with Robert Warwick and Verree Teasdale. As Elizabeth Gerard, Sylvia was one of two sisters whose contrasting attitudes toward life formed the play's central theme. When the play closed in 64 performances, Sylvia joined *Cross Roads* (Morosco Theatre, November 11, 1929), a study of contemporary college life. Franchot Tone was also in this soon-to-close Martin Flavin play. Of her performance, the *New York Times* said: "[she] forms the part of Patricia into a coherent image of sensitive, earnest young womanhood, by all odds the finest work she has done."

Sylvia next appeared in the tearjerker *Many-a-Slip* (Little Theatre, February 3, 1930). Douglass Montgomery, Dorothy Sands, Elisha Cook, Jr., and Maude Eburne filled out the cast. As Patsy Coster, Sylvia essayed the Boston debutante who pretends to be pregnant in order to trick her Greenwich Village lover into marrying her. The reviews reflected Sylvia's growing reputation as Broadway's leading young exponent of the ill-used girl: "Miss Sidney has her usual quota of sobbing to do, and is made to appear thoroughly miserable throughout the play"; "[she] finds her handkerchief indispensable to her tears."

Unlike the other stage ingenues of the day, Sylvia was not a livewire in her social life. Her name rarely appeared in the gossip columns of the period, save to mention that she was considering yet another play role. Though not yet 21, she was already a thoroughgoing, seasoned professional.

It was *Bad Girl* (Hudson Theatre, October 2, 1930) which brought about her Hollywood return. Costarred with Paul Kelly and Charlotte Wynters, Sylvia was Dot, the Bronx girl with a boorish husband. Each of them suspects the other of resenting their newborn baby. Sylvia received her customary fine notices. "Miss Sidney gives a moving performance as Dot—brave, sincere, pliable" *(New York Times).*

One night, B. P. Schulberg,* managing director of Paramount's West Coast studio, attended a performance of *Bad Girl* and the next morning—at the suggestion of his wife Adeline Jaffel—sent Sylvia a telegram requesting her to meet with him at the Paramount Pictures Building on Broadway that day. "I went," Sylvia recalls, "because I thought it stupid from a business point of view not to go. Stage and motion picture interests were growing closer all the time. Schulberg was hardly a man to offend. But honestly, I hoped he wouldn't make me a movie offer that I couldn't afford to refuse. I had loathed Hollywood and I didn't want to go back.

"That is, I didn't want to go back when I started out. After I'd talked to Mr. Schulberg for a little while I wasn't so sure. He knew about my previous fiasco. He talked of the many things Paramount had planned for the future. He explained to me how talkies had been perfected.

"He also spoke of the different books and plays and how he felt they should be interpreted on the screen. Before he had finished I found myself ambitious to have some small part in all these plans.

"He brought up the subject of a contract finally and I was delighted. I've never changed my mind so completely in all my life."

*See Appendix.

Actually aside from the lucrative contract which made her stage salary ridiculous in comparison, there were two prime reasons for Sylvia's Hollywood turnabout in Paramount's favor. First was Schulberg's dangling of the prize Roberta Alden role in the planned filming of *An American Tragedy*. There had been much publicity when Paramount commissioned the Russian director Sergei Eisenstein to supervise a screen version of the Theodore Dreiser novel. Now that Paramount and Eisenstein had terminated their agreement, director Josef von Sternberg was being ballyhooed to direct the potentially distinguished production. The other factor that convinced Sylvia was the 39-year-old married executive, Schulberg. Sylvia and Schulberg developed an immediate attraction for one another, and were soon engaged in one of Hollywood's better-known love affairs.

Schulberg returned to the Coast, and Sylvia followed in December, 1930, after completing her engagement in *Bad Girl*.

Paramount was sorely in need of a new crop of players to populate its production schedule. Of the featured actresses who had appeared in the studio's all-star revue, *Paramount on Parade* (April, 1930), all would disappear from the lot within the next few years: Jean Arthur, Clara Bow, Evelyn Brent, Mary Brian, Virginia Bruce, Nancy Carroll, Ruth Chatterton, Kay Francis, Mitzi Green, Helen Kane, Mitzi Mayfair, Zelma O'Neal, Joan Peers, Lillian Roth, and Fay Wray (as well as operetta star Jeanette MacDonald). By late 1930 Schulberg had recruited Claudette Colbert, Miriam Hopkins, and Sylvia from Broadway. From Pathé Pictures he gained Carole Lombard, and from the German cinema he obtained Marlene Dietrich. These five would form Paramount's nucleus of actress stars for the first half of the 1930s. Stage luminary Tallulah Bankhead would leave both Paramount and the cinema in 1932, disgusted by the flabby scenarios in which she had to perform, and disheartened that her appeal was too special for the general public. As she was departing, Mae West arrived, to establish her own special category of stardom at the studio. Never touted sufficiently but equally important to the rash of underworld and upper-crust society pictures that Paramount favored at the time, were such featured performers as Natalie Moorhead, Lilyan Tashman, and Wynne Gibson. This trio of tough broads sparkled many a film with their stark sophisticate and shilling bar or gangster's moll characterizations.

The casting of Sylvia in her first Paramount release came about accidentally. Because of a too-well-publicized scandal and poor health, the studio had removed the former "It" girl Clara Bow from the lead of *City Streets* (1931), a refashioning of her successful silent picture *Ladies of the Mob* (1928). The still quite popular Nancy Carroll was filming at Paramount's Long Island studio and had voiced her lack of interest in this gangster melodrama. Sylvia recalls: "Rouben Mamoulian [the film's director] had known me in New York and he told them 'There's a girl right here on the lot who would be perfect for it.' So I made *City Streets* first. But Mamoulian always said Clara Bow would have been wonderful in it!"

City Streets opened at the Paramount Theatre on April 17, 1931, with Sylvia second-billed as Nan and Gary Cooper starred as The Kid. She and the film were unqualified hits. Sylvia played the daughter of gangland underling Guy Kibbee. Implicated in a murder he has committed, she is sent to jail. Meanwhile, the once carefree Cooper becomes a prime force in the beer gang run by Paul Lukas. When Sylvia is freed, she returns to Cooper, but offers herself to Lukas because he threatens to eliminate The Kid. Lukas is later shot by his ex-mistress Wynne Gibson. In the finale, Cooper pretends to take Sylvia for a one-way car ride. Once rid of the accompanying hoods, they escape to freedom.

In his first Hollywood-made film, director Mamoulian indulged his penchant for symbolism (cats and eagles abound) and innovations (overlapping sound). Being decorous by nature, he fashioned the screenplay to avoid violence. He later said: "You know, there are ten killings in this film, and you don't actually *see* one of them."

Mamoulian's technical originality did much to showcase Sylvia's performance. She is first seen in a memorable opening close-up with one eye inexplicably closed. Then the camera pans back to reveal her at a sideshow shooting booth. Later in the film comes the scene of Cooper visiting Sylvia in jail. It has often been imitated to lesser effect. The two lovers are separated by the mesh grillwork, straining to touch, but only able to brush their lips together in a brief kiss. When Sylvia is returned to her cell, she relives scenes from her past, with Cooper's voice and her own thoughts echoing on the soundtrack—then a startling new cinematic technique.

Variety summed up the excellent critical reaction to Sylvia: "Picture is lifted from mediocrity through the intelligent acting and appeal of Sylvia Sidney. This legit girl makes her first screen appearance here as co-star with Gary Cooper. From a histrionic standpoint she's the whole works, and that's not detracting from the others who perform ably. She is not so well known inland, but Cooper and other names in the cast compensate. She won't be unknown long."

In retrospect it seems logical that the large-eyed, soulful, wronged-girl image Sylvia had created for herself on the stage should have transferred itself to her screen work. Yet at the time it was not Paramount's immediate intention. With her unconventional beauty and deep-seated seriousness, she obviously could not be the successor to vivacious cutie Clara Bow. However, her stage experience attested to the fact that she had a versatile if somewhat limited scope, and, if publicized in enough glamorous poses, she might create her own brand of screen elegance. Such elegance might be different from but just as appealing as that offered by such divergent types as Kay Francis, Claudette Colbert, and Miriam Hopkins. Ironically, the studio would rarely exploit her shapely 34–24–34 figure.

With *The American Tragedy* project still not ready, Sylvia was rushed into *Confessions of a Co-Ed* (1931), touted as the first authentic college drama. It was anything but that, being such sloppy soap opera that no one would take screen credit for the scripting effort. In the picture, Sylvia loves Phillips Holmes, but marries classmate Norman Foster, not revealing that she is pregnant by Holmes. Later Holmes reappears for the inevitable confrontation. The postgraduate cast looked as out of place on the Stanford University campus as they did in the slushy drawing-room scenes in the later part of the film. Yet Mordaunt Hall *(New York Times)* admitted: "Claudia Dell and Sylvia Sidney give a fairly good account of themselves in their roles."

Sylvia finally appeared in *An American Tragedy*, released August 5, 1931. Director Josef von Sternberg—in between directing Marlene Dietrich films—had an affinity for the Theodore Dreiser work and relied largely on the writer's own words for the film's dialogue. The 95-minute film starred Phillips Holmes as Clyde Griffiths, confused and contorted by his poverty upbringing and the typical American greed for material wealth and physical beauty. Sylvia was an earnest Roberta Alden, the farm girl turned factory worker whose pregnancy stands in Clyde's way to marrying wealthy

Frances Dee. As in the George Stevens remake, *A Place in the Sun,* with Shelley Winters in the part, the lovelorn girl is drowned, leading to Clyde's capture, trial, and execution. (Yet Sylvia was given a more sympathetic presentation than Winters in the later version, which was truer to Dreiser's concepts.) The *New York Times* called Sylvia "earnest" and *Variety* said: "On the sympathetic end, Sylvia Sidney will capture the major reaction as the trusting Roberta, which she mainly accomplishes by means of a wistful smile."

The meticulously but inexpensively produced *An American Tragedy* was not successful with the Depression-weary public and was written off as an artistic failure. Had Warners Brothers handled the project, it would have been a gutsy, fast-clipped presentation that retained the "sociological elements" instead of eliminating them as von Sternberg did. Dreiser, who had approved the Eisenstein scenario (which before it was through cost Adolph Zukor's regime $500,000 in "dormant investment"), sued Paramount to prevent distribution of the von Sternberg version. He lost his case. Omitted from Dreiser's diatribe was Sylvia. He approved of her thoughtful performance.

Also released in 1931 was a two-reel Vitaphone sound short that Sylvia had made while appearing in *Many-a-Slip* (1930) on Broadway. *Five Minutes from the Station,* written by Elaine Stearn Carrington, had as a cast Sylvia, Lynne Overman, and Burton Churchill. The playlet concerned an earnest employee who brings his boss home for dinner, hoping to obtain a better job, only to find that the employer has his eye on his worker's wife.

With her growing reputation as a fine actress, Samuel Goldwyn borrowed Sylvia for his filming of Elmer Rice's Pulitzer Prize-winning play *Street Scene* (1931). Paramount's Nancy Carroll had originally been announced for the role of Rose Moran, whose adulterous mother is shot by her father. The action of the film centers on the slum street outside the tenement where Sylvia lives, and the reactions of various neighborhood people to the killing on this hot summer night. The exceptionally fine cast included Beulah Bondi and Estelle Taylor, and overrode the stagey direction of King Vidor. Said Richard Watts, Jr. *(New York Herald Tribune)* "[Sylvia] grows more expert in the ways of the cinema with each production, [and] is honestly moving and entirely simple and credible as the girl of the story, providing one of the most satisfying characterizations of the year." *Variety* analyzed the kernel of Sylvia's screen appeal which would brand her in the stereotype of a slum waif oppressed by a cruel world: "[she] gives an even, persuasive performance in a role for which she is particularly fitted, typifying as she somehow does here, the tragedy of budding girlhood cramped by sordid surroundings. Even her lack of formal beauty intensifies the pathos of the character." Being top-billed, Sylvia came East to the premiere at the Rivoli Theatre (August 26, 1931). One on-the-scene observer penned: "She was so nervous that she could not talk. She kissed her hands as the sign of her appreciation of the applause."

With five releases, 1932 proved to be Sylvia's busiest year on the screen, as it was for Claudette Colbert (six films) and Miriam Hopkins (five pictures). Carole Lombard made five features in 1932, but 1934, with six releases, was her most productive year. Marlene Dietrich appeared in two 1932 motion pictures. But the workhorse nature of the Paramount stars pales in comparison to Warner Brothers, where leading players like Joan Blondell were churning out ten features in 1932.

By now, Sylvia's Hollywood image had solidified, despite her protests to the contrary. She was the princess of murky tragedy. No one could register the slaps of a cruel world quite so well as Sylvia, with her tears due to society's injustices to poor but honest girls like herself. Combined with her quivering lips and trembling husky voice, she was the epitome of the Depression heroine. An unlikely prototype for glamorous Paramount Pictures, one might say, but so was her relationship with B. P. Schulberg, who was already estranged from his wife and was considered a most definite part of Sylvia's life. She had acquired a lush Beverly Hills mansion as well as a Malibu beach house.

In *Ladies of the Big House* (1932), Sylvia and Gene Raymond are a married couple framed on a murder charge by her gangster ex-boyfriend. They are sent to prison, where Sylvia suffers unstoically but dramatically, proving she could outdo Barbara Stanwyck and others in the genre.

In the remake of *The Miracle Man* (1932), Sylvia was Helen Smith, one of a gang of crooks who are redeemed by a faith healer they have found and exploited. In the Betty Compson role, reviewers thought Sylvia "all right."

With a fanfare of publicity—since she rarely had a screen wardrobe worthy of discussion—it was announced that Sylvia had shorn her waist-length dark tresses to play the chic, if unhappy, debutante in *Merrily We Go to Hell.* (1932). Costarred with Fredric March, she was the heiress who marries a drunken reporter-turned-playwright. He has a fling with an actress. Sylvia's baby is stillborn, and eventually she and March reconcile. The plot bears a striking similarity to Columbia's *Platinum Blonde,* starring Jean Harlow.

Sylvia was among the many Paramount players who appeared in quickie cameo appearances in *Make Me a Star* (1932), featuring Stuart Erwin as a would-be movie actor in this loose remake of *Merton of the Movies.*

Sylvia once told a fan magazine writer: "With a face like mine, of slightly Oriental cast, I always dreamed of playing an Oriental character." Her wish was fulfilled in *Madame Butterfly* (1932), an updated version of the vintage David Belasco play. She was Cho-Cho-San, the Japanese geisha girl in love with American Navy lieutenant Cary Grant. She commits suicide when he cavalierly passes her by for an Occidental beauty. Most thought the film a "heavy-handed bore," but as the almond-eyed Oriental, Sylvia's performance rated more than satisfactory. Richard Watts, Jr. *(New York Herald Tribune)* called her "honest, sympathetic and genuinely touching" but noted: "[she] seems to have occasional trouble with her accent, in a manner which caused her to drop from the pidgin English of a Nipponese girl to a sort of broken French and then to a bit of Swedish—wherein she says 'Ay tank I go.'" *Madame Butterfly* was unimaginatively managed by the Polish director Marion Gering, who had directed Sylvia on Broadway in *Bad Girl* and would helm five of her Hollywood features with uniformly unnoteworthy results.

Sylvia began 1933 with *Pick-Up.* As Mary Richards, she operates a badger game in which a victim dies. She and hubby William Harrigan are convicted of the crime, and she is nicknamed Baby Face Mary by a police reporter. The film traces her postprison tribulations and her romance with cab driver George Raft. This uneven programmer was quickly dismissed, but critics wrote that Sylvia played with "her customary sanity." It was her third feature for director Gering. Sylvia later recalled: "They thought Gering who had directed the *Bad Girl* play, could 'handle' me. I was supposed to need 'handling' then because I was inclined to be impatient with some of the trimmings surrounding stardom. I liked my independence and wanted to live my own life and not be at the mercy of fan magazines, columnists and studio press agents. I was discontented with the shoddiness of many of my movies. And the small talk of Hollywood social life bored me. After I finished a movie I wanted to get back to New York where I could feel stimulated."

Once in a while, Sylvia performed in live dramatics on the Coast, as when she appeared at the Pasadena Community Playhouse in *Liliom* (February 28, 1933).

Once again with Gering directing, Sylvia appeared in another Theodore Dreiser chronicle, *Jennie Gerhardt.* This turgid story traced the assorted calamities befalling Sylvia (Jennie) from 1904 to 1933. She is betrayed by Senator Edward Arnold and her illegitimate baby is born after his death. She then becomes a servant in wealthy Donald Cook's home; they fall in love but he eventually weds widow Mary Astor. The black and white production was handsome if ineffective, but was marred by choppy, trite dialogue and a lack of suspense. Howard Barnes *(New York Herald Tribune)* noted: "In the motion picture's drawn out and uninteresting conclusion, when she gives up her lover and follows his career vicariously, she is quite unsuccessful in overcoming the deficiencies of the material." Nevertheless, Sylvia did receive a congratulatory telegram from Dreiser: "Yours is a beautiful interpretation of Jennie Gerhardt. My compliments and thanks."

Sylvia and her mentor Schulberg hoped to produce yet another Dreiser work, *Sister Carrie,* but since Schulberg, in a power play at Paramount, had been "demoted" to the status of independent producer, and Emanuel Cohen* was in charge of production, there was no enthusiasm for the project.

Paramount substituted Frances Farmer in the Miriam Hopkins-Fredric March-George Raft *All of Me* (1934) so that Sylvia could take the lead opposite Maurice Chevalier in *The Way to Love* (1934). Sylvia was dissatisfied with both her role and the film. On August 1, 1933, she withdrew from the production, claiming she was still suffering from the effects of a glandular throat operation. The studio counterclaimed that this was "professional anarchy" and gossip columnists suggested that it was merely another example of Sylvia's mounting professional temperament. Sylvia took the first available train East—accompanied by Schulberg—and her scenes in *The Way to Love* were reshot with Ann Dvorak. Sylvia complained to the press that the studio physicians treated her "like a nobody, although I am a somebody." She was unavailable for *Reunion,* a project to be lensed in October, 1933, in which she was supposed to portray a woman spy, with Herbert Marshall as her male lead.

But the studio-star differences were patched up, and Sylvia returned to the Coast to star in three 1934 releases. When the planned filming of *R.U.R.* (from the play by Karel Capek) was dropped, she and Fredric March were stuck into the potboiler *Good Dame* (1934), another hard-luck tale. Sylvia plays Lillie Taylor, a chorus girl stranded in a small town in the Midwest and obliged against her will to accept the aid of cardsharp, con man March. March badly hammed up his performance with a wide sprinkling of "deses," "dems," and "doze" which did not suffice for a characterization of an uncultured tough guy. But Sylvia, according to *Variety,* "Holds straight to character." She has a gem of a closing scene in the courtroom where she and March are on trial for his petty larceny and assault and battery. In open

*See Appendix.

court he finally admits that he loves her, and in a rare moment of exuberance Sylvia wonderingly inquires whether he feels the same heart-skipping love throb that she does. He affirms that he does, and the judge marries them instead of sentencing them to terms in jail.

Thirty Day Princess (1934) was unusual in that Sylvia had a rare opportunity to essay both a screen comedy and a dual role. Princess Catterina (Sylvia) comes to New York to seal a loan for her country but contracts the mumps. Actress Nancy Lane (Sylvia) is hired to impersonate her. Cary Grant plays a newspaper publisher who at first is opposed to banker Edward Arnold granting the large foreign loan. The *Los Angeles Times* pointed out; "wistful Miss Sidney, playing both Nancy and the Princess, makes the contrast really count only in the somewhat difficult scene wherein both occupy the screen at once. While the difference between the two is chiefly one of enunciation, Miss Sidney also manages to speak in tones of unlike pitch."

Though scheduled for them in 1934, Sylvia did not do *Cosmetic* (based on a play by Stephen Bekeffi), or *One Way Ticket,* or *Limehouse Blues* that year, but she did appear in the Schulberg-produced *Behold My Wife* (1934). Sylvia had the offbeat role of a New Mexico Indian maiden whom wealthy Gene Raymond weds and brings back to New York to show up his snobbish family. At best the feature contained no more than some silly melodrama. Philip K. Scheuer *(Los Angeles Times)* said: "As for Miss Sidney, the gibberish she sometimes speaks does little to make her seem like an Indian. She is more convincing later on, playing the lady. This tendency toward unintelligible noises, by the way, appears to have been inherited from an earlier role, that is *Thirty Day Princess.* It isn't very good . . . But because it manages to escape the formula of Miss Sidney's previous vehicles (i.e., a series of misled close-ups), the picture must surely be reckoned a departure and a most welcome one, at that."

In September, 1934, columnists were quick to report that Sylvia and Schulberg had reconciled after a short rift. But then, in a sudden bit of openness to the press, Schulberg announced at a news conference on October 25, 1934, that his social relationship with Sylvia "is definitely at an end." This was seemingly confirmed a month later when he was reconciled with his wife Adeline, who had been separated from him since February, 1932. She had become a talent agent in the meantime.

In the film adaptation of Samson Raphaelson's play *Accent on Youth* (1935), Sylvia was top-billed as Linda Brown, the young secretary who becomes infatuated with her middle-aged playwright-employer, Herbert Marshall. Phillip Reed was Marshall's younger, athletic rival for Sylvia's affection, Director Wesley Ruggles altered the carefree abandon of the original for a more wistful semiserious charm. Some critics noted Sylvia's "furrowed brow and fretful expression in several scenes," but others were in accord with Richard Watts, Jr. *(New York Herald Tribune)* who said: "[she] is admirable as the amorous secretary, playing the part with humor, forthrightness and conviction." However, neither studio executives nor the public could forget the put-upon working girl image that had surrounded Sylvia's screen image for so long. With Claudette Colbert and Carole Lombard on hand at Paramount to essay the glamorous and comedy roles, the studio felt that there was no need to remold Sylvia's public identification into a new category. Paramount would later rework the story line of *Accent on Youth* for *Mr. Music* and *But Not for Me.* Sylvia would appear in a touring version of the play in the early 1940s with her second husband, Luther Adler.

Sylvia was scheduled to appear in *That's What Girls Are Made Of* in 1935, with studio newcomer Fred MacMurray, but producer Schulberg and Paramount severed their ties, and he accepted a post at Columbia Pictures as an independent producer-executive. Sylvia's studio contract, which had always been negotiated by and with Schulberg, expired in 1935, and both parties failed to agree on a renewal. Sylvia was greatly impressed by the independent ventures produced by Walter Wanger, and early that year she signed a four-year contract with him. Among the grandiose projects proposed by the Sylvia-Wanger team, with her as star, were: *Ivanhoe* (in which she was to portray Rebecca, costarring with Gary Cooper and Madeleine Carroll), the title role in *Tess of The D'Urbervilles, Wuthering Heights* (opposite Charles Boyer), and *Arabian Nights.* Had any of these elegant features been made with Sylvia, the future of her screen career might have been entirely different.

Meanwhile, Sylvia continued her transcountry traveling, returning to New York whenever possible. She later reflected about Hollywood: "I never knew much about it and I never lived there much. I was a world's champion commuter. . . . I never adjusted. If I made a movie, they called me a stage actress. If I was in a play they called me that movie actress."

Her first picture under the Wanger contract was *Mary Burns, Fugitive,* produced at Paramount. Wanger succumbed to the easy inevitability of allowing Sylvia to star in yet another tearjerker as society's perpetual victim. She plays an honest coffee-shop owner, in love with gangster Alan Baxter and ignorant of his criminal deeds. Through circumstantial evidence, she is arrested by the police and sentenced to a long prison term. The law permits her to escape, trusting she will lead them to her desperado boyfriend. While at liberty she meets convalescing explorer Melvyn Douglas, with whom she discovers reciprocal love. Baxter is captured after much pursuit, and is shot during the police roundup, leaving Sylvia and Douglas to look ahead to a brighter future. Rose Pelswick *(New York Evening Journal)* aptly described the career trap Paramount, and now Wanger, had thrust Sylvia into: "No one on the screen has a gloomier time of it than Sylvia Sidney. Each of her film roles is fashioned so that she appears as a pathetic little figure buffeted about by circumstances beyond her control. It's only occasionally that she's allowed a fleeting smile, for the by now standardized Sidney formula demands that, once before the cameras, the wistful brunette go about with a melancholy quaver in her appealing voice and never, never be let off anything until the very end when the hero promises to make her life happier in the future." The *New York Times* criticized Sylvia for being "too abject in her whining helplessness."

Rumors that Sylvia and Random House president Bennett Cerf, aged 37, were seriously dating, were confirmed when the couple married in Phoenix, Arizona, October 1, 1935. But the marriage was short-lived; the couple separated after three months, and were divorced after eight. Cerf later quipped: "One should never legalize a hot romance."

Wanger returned Sylvia to Paramount to play the lead in the studio's remake of *Trail of the Lonesome Pine* (1936), noteworthy for being the first feature to be shot outdoors with the new technicolor process. Sylvia was June Tolliver, the fiery hillbilly girl who leaves her rural surroundings to obtain an education, but reverts to her savage, intense self when her younger brother Henry Fonda is killed in a family feud. Fred MacMurray was the citified influence, and Beulah Bondi appeared as Sylvia's peace-loving mother. This atmospheric film, the third production of the John Fox,

Jr., novel, directed by Henry Hathaway, premiered at the Paramount Theatre on February 19, 1936, and did fine business, although reviewers had many reservations about it. Richard Watts, Jr. *(New York Herald Tribune)* wrote: "In fact, I was rather disappointed in Miss Sidney, as I was in the photoplay. It seemed to me that her hysterical screams were the sort of tricky emotional outbursts that pass for good acting only among the less judicious."

Next MGM borrowed Sylvia to play opposite Spencer Tracy in Fritz Lang's first American-made movie, *Fury* (1936). No one at the time had high hopes for this overly somber study of mob violence, least of all the studio or the director. But the screen chemistry was right, and the final results proved highly effective. Tracy plays an ordinary guy on his way to meet his schoolteacher fiancée, Sylvia. Stopping off in a small town where a kidnapping has occurred, he is suspected of the crime and arrested. The citizens become aroused, form a lynch mob, and burn down the jail. Tracy is thought dead, but he has escaped. With the help of his brothers he obtains prints of newsreel footage shot at the mob scene and initiates a murder trial against these overzealous townsfolk. At the trial, his brothers and Sylvia beg him to reveal himself, since the mob was not actually guilty of murder. Tracy eventually does speak up in court, making an impassioned plea about the dangers of mob rule. The studio insisted that the camera show Sylvia and Tracy kissing at the closeout, a concession to Hollywoodian demands for a happy ending. It took some of the bite out of Tracy's tour de force final speech. While critics duly noted that top-billed Sylvia was "appealingly tragic," "rises to the proper heights in the dramatic testimony," and "played with great depth of feeling," the film unequivocally was Tracy's dramatic vehicle.

Hoping to break her casting mold, Sylvia accepted an offer to star in Alfred Hitchcock's *The Woman Alone* (1937). Stopping off in New York on her way to England for the filming, Sylvia told the press about her collaborating efforts on a play *Susanna Shakespeare,* which would deal with the daughter of the famed playwright. She frankly admitted that she had once had a temperamental nature: "I used to fight. Yes, it's true. I even used to throw telephone books and anything else I could get to at the time. Everything which didn't go smoothy annoyed me terribly. And I flew off the handle, and got myself greatly disliked. But now—well, now I keep my mouth shut, and my hands busy with knitting needles. I give in on all minor issues, and get my way about the important big things." Sylvia had nothing to say about her romantic life, but later that year (December, 1936) Schulberg told the press: "If you ask her if we're getting married, she'd deny it, and so would I but I guess we will get married soon. In a couple of months I'm getting a divorce." (They never did wed.)

The Woman Alone was based on Joseph Conrad's *The Secret Agent.* It was a brooding mystery yarn in which Oscar Homolka plays a dastardly saboteur who attempts to destroy London's main avenues of existence. He maintains a front as the owner of a small cinema and lives in the theater with his young wife Sylvia and her little brother. Detective John Loder initiates a rapport with Sylvia, hoping to uncover Homolka's machinations. When Homolka gives her brother a package containing a bomb to carry across town and it explodes, killing the child, Sylvia seeks revenge on her spouse. In a much-appreciated dramatic sequence at the dinner table, Sylvia is suddenly drawn by the carving knife in front of her. The audience becomes aware that she is going to murder her husband just as Homolka grasps the same realization. As she drives the knife into his stomach, she utters a short cry of agony, astounded by what she has done. Because the theatre is blown up in an explosion, Sylvia's crime is not discovered and she and Loder go off together.

This Hitchcock thriller opened at the Roxy Theatre on February 27, 1937, receiving better than average notices. Sylvia was given her due praise, but as *Variety* pointed out: "She has only one really gripping scene, and merely walks through the majority of the episodes. Photographer never flatters her and the costume department apparently dished her whatever was handy. In addition, the sole opportunity, via the romance with the youthful detective, is so haphazardly developed that it proves incidental to the central theme."

The film is not one of Hitchcock's favorites, nor is it one of the public's, and it is rarely shown on television. When interviewed by Francois Truffaut for *Hitchcock* (1966), the director discoursed on Sylvia's performance, which he found "Not entirely [satisfactory]." He added: "I must admit that I found it rather difficult to get any shading into Sylvia Sidney's face, yet on the other hand she had nice understatement."

Walter Wanger reunited Sylvia with Henry Fonda and director Fritz Lang in the memorable study of social injustice, *You Only Live Once* (1937). In this grim story, Fonda, a petty crook with three previous convictions, is framed on a robbery-murder charge and sent to prison. Unable to bear up, he breaks out, killing his priest friend Pat O'Brien, who had come to tell him that he has been pardoned. With his wife Sylvia, Fonda tries to escape to Canada. The hunted couple are shot in a road blockade near the border, but they manage to cross over the line, where they die in each other's arms. (Reportedly, an alternative happy ending was filmed but not utilized.)

You Only Live Once captured all the protest of innocent people so hounded by circumstances and desperation that eventually they become the antisocial animals they were branded long before. Lang effectively caught the poetic contrast between the idyllic courting and honeymoon scenes between Sylvia and Fonda; the irony of the innocent Fonda becoming a murderer; the necessity of the fleeing couple to leave their newborn baby behind, the inhumanity of people they meet along the way, and their final peace in death. Sylvia received plaudits from all the critics. Howard Barnes *(New York Herald Tribune)* was full of praise: "Miss Sidney plays the heroine with splendid understanding and emotional depth. The portrait is stamped with tragedy almost from the first, but it is human and always in character. Her stout-hearted secretary, who gradually loses her faith in justice, gives the needed note of poignancy to a stark chronicle." The film was considered too grim by the public and did not fare well in release. Many at the time noted similarities between the movie's "heroes" and the real life Bonnie and Clyde. In subsequent years, *You Only Live Once* has gained considerable repute as an unheralded little masterpiece, and it has enjoyed constant revival on television and in college cinema courses. When *Bonnie and Clyde* (1967) appeared, contemporary critics harked back to *You Only Live Once* for comparison and source, adding additional interest to this stark 1937 drama.

Sylvia's other release of the year was Samuel Goldwyn's prestigious version of Sidney Kingsley's realistic drama *Dead End,* which had been a rousing Broadway success. Director William Wyler intended lensing the drama on New York's East Side, but producer Goldwyn insisted that a back-lot set be utilized. It was no coincidence that Sylvia, who had starred for

Goldwyn in *Street Scene* (1931), should have been selected for the role of Drina, for it was the epitome of the screen type she had been enacting for years. She was top-billed as the hard-working sister of tenement kid Billy Halop. Her earnest efforts to elevate herself in the world coincide with her love for out-of-work architect Joel McCrea. The latter in turn is infatuated with gangster mistress Wendy Barrie. As the "tenement blossom," Sylvia looked younger and softer than usual, pulling out all stops in her intense performance. The drama premiered at the Rivoli Theatre on August 24, 1937, and Sylvia was cited for demonstrating "splendid power and restraint" and for being "tender, moving and tragic." Once again, her too-good-to-be-true role was overshadowed by a group of newcomers from the Broadway stage, the Dead End Kids, making their cinema debut. They, along with Humphrey Bogart as the crude killer Baby Face Martin and Marjorie Main as his bitter, law-abiding mother, stole the limelight. This production marked the highpoint in Hollywood of the sociological message film; in this instance, the message being that tenements breed gangsters in a recurring vicious cycle and society does nothing to solve the problem. Sylvia, with her archetypical performances in these 1930s message films, was considered part and parcel of the genre. When the genre passed, as it soon did, she would be considered passé.

Feeling overly constrained by her Hollywood assignments, it did not take much to lure Sylvia back to the Broadway stage. The Theatre Guild asked her to star in Ben Hecht's new wish-fulfillment message drama, *To Quinto and Back.* An exuberant Sylvia informed the New York press: "This time the homecoming is doubly exciting because after an absence of seven years from the stage, I'm returning to my first love. . . . Seven years is a long time—long enough to forget the lessons learned in the theatre and the differences between motion picture and stage technique. But I am excited about my part, because it's unlike anything I've ever done in pictures."

To Quinto and Back concerned writer Leslie Banks, who deserts his wife to run off to Ecuador with Sylvia, who mistakenly believes he will obtain a divorce and marry her. They hold endless discussions on the current state of affairs; thereafter he leaves her and is killed in an abortive Communist revolution. The play debuted at the 52nd Street Theatre on October 6, 1937, and died after 46 performances. Besides lambasting author and director Philip Moeller, critics took Sylvia to task. Burns Mantle *(New York Daily News)* observed: "Sylvia Sidney is a talented young woman within her sphere, but when she tries to take on emotional stature she has little to work with except a frown and a suggestion of hurt pride. I can't believe she could be one to inspire a moody idealist of the Hecht breed."

Shortly afterwards, on August 3, 1938, while on vacation in London, Sylvia married actor Luther Adler, age 38. He was a member of a well-known theatrical family which included his sister Stella Adler and his brother Jay Adler.

Sylvia was reteamed with George Raft and Fritz Lang for *You and Me* (1938), a melodramatic object lesson filmed at Paramount. This moralistic tale has department-store-owner Harry Carey employing ex-convicts, one of whom is Raft. In a weak moment, Raft recruits other parolee coworkers to help rob the premises. In the midst of the robbery, ex-con salesgirl Sylvia, Raft's sweetie and soon-to-be-wife, talks them out of their plan, with a blackboard mathematical lecture proving that crime cannot pay. A tacked-on comedy finish has Raft visiting Sylvia in the maternity ward. Using his upbeat conventional finish and Kurt Weill songs, Lang attempted to soften his preaching, but *You and Me* was a commercial flop.

After Walter Wanger sold his *Wuthering Heights* project to Samuel Goldwyn, who did not, however, purchase the services of Sylvia and Charles Boyer as costars, Wanger offered Sylvia the role of the casbah girl in *Algiers* (1938). Sylvia thought the part was too stereotyped and refused. She bought up her remaining contract from Wanger, and left Hollywood for New York to star in Irwin Shaw's *The Gentle People* (Belasco Theatre, January 5, 1939). Others in the cast of this Group Theatre production were Sam Jaffe, Franchot Tone, Elia Kazan, Lee J. Cobb, and Martin Ritt. The social drama was a modest success and ran 141 performances. John Anderson *(New York Journal American)* said: "Miss Sidney does by far the best piece of work that she has done on the stage since she first went off to Hollywood, and does it more surely and with sharper definition."

Sylvia decided to settle in the East so she could be closer to her husband Adler and to work in the theatre. She and Adler bought a 120-acre farm in Flemington, New Jersey.

Despite her decision to avoid moviemaking, especially movies calling upon her to repeat her stereotyped poor-girl role, Sylvia was intrigued by the social import of the Federal Theatre Project *One-Third Of A Nation* which had played in New York in 1938. She starred in the movie version filmed in New York, which opened at the Rivoli Theatre on February 10, 1939. Sylvia was a shopgirl who persuades a wealthy landlord to tear down his slum properties and put up good buildings. Leif Erikson played her radical boyfriend, and Sidney Lumet was her crippled young brother, who is killed in a tenement fire. This over-earnest, hackneyed drama made little impression on a public more concerned with World War II and eager to find exciting escapist entertainment.

Jody, Sylvia's first—and only—child, was born October 22, 1939, at Woman's Hospital in Manhattan. Years later Sylvia would admit: "Prima donnas in anything are bad. . . . Having a child was a great leveling agent. Those babies couldn't care less that their parents were famous."

While in New York, Sylvia accepted a guest-starring role as a movie actress in the radio soap opera "Pretty Kitty Kelly" (CBS). It was a strange choice of acting work for one who had such high artistic standards in her career.

Sylvia returned to California to costar with Humphrey Bogart in *The Wagons Roll at Night* (1941), a remake of *Kid Galahad*. In the revised Bette Davis role (changed from a singer to a carnival fortune teller in Bogart's circus), Sylvia had a distinctly secondary assignment. She is smitten with Bogart, but makes a pass at lion-tamer Eddie Albert, who in turn yens for Bogart's sweet young sister Joan Leslie. Bogart is killed by a berserk lion, and Sylvia is left with her crystal ball and cards. This actioner was quickly passed over by the critics, who did mention, however, that Sylvia had "lost much of her volatile and melodramatic temperament" and that she was "properly sultry and self-sacrificial." With her overlong false eyelashes, fluttering eyes, drawn face, and nervous hand gestures, Sylvia demonstrated all too clearly that her ingenue days in the cinema were over. She was 31 at the time.

Returning again to Manhattan, Sylvia embarked on a lengthy run of summer and winter stock engagements, sometimes on the unprestigious subway circuit among the borough playhouses in New York City. Among her vehicles were *Angel Street* (1941), *Margin For Error* (1942), *Pygmalion*

(1942), *Jane Eyre* (1943), and *We Will Never Die* (Madison Square Garden, 1943).

When James Cagney cast Sylvia as the lovely Eurasian, Iris Hilliard, in his production *Blood on the Sun* (1945), there was much talk of Sylvia making her movie comeback. This fast-paced adventure picture was set in 1929 Japan, with newspaper editor Cagney learning about the Tanaka plan for Oriental world conquest. Sylvia was the half-Chinese siren whom Cagney enlists to assist him in smuggling the valuable plan out of the country. She never looked more exotic than as the bewitching Chinese-American spy, and wisely hired Michael Woulfe, her protégé dress designer from New York, to clothe her. *Variety* reported: "Miss Sidney, back after a too-long hiatus from Hollywood, is gowned gorgeously and photographs ditto."

While *Blood on the Sun* was not a dynamic enough film to engender much renewal of audience interest in Sylvia, it did lead to other screen assignments. She returned to Paramount to costar in *The Searching Wind* (1946), based on Lillian Hellman's indictment of bewildered spectators who allowed World War II to develop and continue unchecked. William Dieterle directed the Hal Wallis production. Sylvia was second-billed as Cassie Bowman, the newspaperwoman who loves diplomat Robert Young. The film, while tracing the growing power and aftermath of Hitler and Mussolini, follows careers and love life of Sylvia and Young. She encounters Young again after World War II, when he is considering leaving his socialite wife Ann Richards. However, the combination of Sylvia's decision not to interfere and the disillusionment of Young's veteran son (Douglas Dick) combine to cause Young to remain with his wife and try to shape a better future. Bosley Crowther *(New York Times)* wrote: "Sylvia Sidney is romantically appealing as the writing lady who has political x-ray eyes, but the plainness with which the role is written makes her seem quite improbable." An intellectualized propaganda drama, *The Searching Wind* was not well received by a public too anxious to return to civilian life and forget the moral questions of World War II.

In 1946 Sylvia divorced Luther Adler; the two remained good professional friends, often turning to each other for professional advice, and appearing together in the same stage productions. In 1947 Sylvia married publicist Carlton W. Alsop.

For producer Benedict Bogeaus, Sylvia was reteamed with George Raft in the quickie *Mr. Ace,* released by United Artists in 1947. As a rich, spoiled congresswoman out to win the gubernatorial nomination, she is backed by gangster Raft on a new independent reform ticket. In the midst of her unscrupulous campaigning, she is hit by religion and gets a change of heart. This shallow, unstimulating political drama did not grab much audience interest and quickly passed from sight. The *New York Times* thought Sylvia "warm and sincere" as the well-dressed predatory female.

As if to officially mark her descent from screen stardom, Sylvia starred in a low-budget remake of *Love from a Stranger* (1947), which had been filmed in England a decade before with Ann Harding and Basil Rathbone. In this perennial costume thriller, John Hodiak appeared as the mysterious gentleman whom Sylvia learns is an insane murderer only after she marries him. Ann Richards was her patient friend, John Howard played the suitor, and Isobel Elsom was her eccentric aunt. *Variety* cited Sylvia for her "direct and spirited performance," but there was no hiding the inadequacies of Hodiak in the pivotal role, or the fact that the clichéd premise had not been dressed in a sufficiently new guise. In the early days of television,

Love From a Stranger was one of the most frequently shown feature films: because it had been relatively unsuccessful in its theatrical release, Eagle Lion quickly sold it to the new video medium.

Sylvia returned to stage work, touring with John Loder in *O Mistress Mine* (Alfred Lunt had been taken ill after the Broadway run and his wife Lynn Fontanne refused to tour without him); *Kind Lady, Pygmalion, Anne of the 1000 Days, Bell, Book and Candle, Joan of Lorraine, The Constant Wife,* and in 1950 *The Innocents.* In late 1951 Sylvia assumed the lead role in the British thriller *Black Chiffon* for a brief post-Broadway run after the play had a moderately successful Broadway run with Flora Robson starring.

On March 22, 1951, Sylvia filed for divorce from Alsop in Los Angeles, claiming extreme cruelty. She then returned to the screen in a small featured role in yet another remake of Victor Hugo's *Les Miserables* (1952), this time starring Michael Rennie as Jean Valjean. Sylvia was fifth-billed as the tragic Fantime, having only a few scenes in this melodramatic version. The Twentieth Century-Fox feature premiered at the Rivoli Theatre on August 14, 1952, to middling reviews. Sylvia received token acknowledgment for her cameo part.

Sylvia, now 42, was candid enough to tell the press: "Women who try to hide their age just call attention to it. Why lie about it? I don't feel any younger . . . I don't look any younger. Somebody finds out about your real age eventually. It's easier to be frank about it . . . I've enjoyed every age in my life. I've never wanted to go back."

In the summer of 1952, Sylvia starred on the tent circuit in Joseph Kramm's *The Gypsies Wore High Hats,* which did not make Broadway. The drama was set in the Hungarian section of New York City in the early 1900s. *Variety* recorded: "Miss Sidney's flair for weepy, emotional acting also is given a field day. Serving throughout the play as an arbiter between the husband and the exasperated Nina, her big scene occurs when she explains to her dubious daughter the essentially generous quality of her husband's character. She brings warmth and dignity to the role."

In December of 1952, Sylvia replaced Betty Field in *The Four Poster,* which was enjoying a long Broadway run.

Throughout the 1950s, Sylvia lent her distinctive acting style to a number of television dramas. One of her most notable performances as the personification of the neurotic stage mother (her video stereotype) was on the "Philco TV Playhouse" production of *Catch My Boy on Sunday* (February 12, 1954, NBC). Said *Variety* of this Paddy Chayefsky drama directed by Arthur Penn: "To no one's surprise, Sylvia Sidney as the troubled wife and mastermind of her little genius, socked over in the overwrought, emotional role, giving it the underplaying where it was most needed, but sticking so fast to the unsympathetic rigging as to bring it the very sympathy that Chayefsky intended since it would not be difficult for even the 'contented' housewife to find here a personal identification." Chayefsky remarked that Sylvia had given "the most perfect performance of any of my characters." It got so that whenever a television script required a troubled, dish-pan-hand, mother role, Sylvia was summoned to play it. She had a change of pace portraying the tough corporation executive in *A Leaf out of the Book* on "Climax" (February 3, 1955, CBS), but was back to a role as a strong mother in *The Helen Morgan Story* on "Playhouse 90" (May 18, 1957), with Polly Bergen starred. Sylvia was brought back to Hollywood to appear in Twentieth Century-Fox's *Violent Saturday* (1955), a study of individuals involved in a bank robbery in Brandenville, a small Arizona town. She was seventh-billed in this Cinemascope drama directed by Richard Fleischer, as Elsie, the frumpish kleptomaniac librarian. Victor Mature starred as the mining executive, with Stephen McNally, J. Carrol Naish, and Lee Marvin as the three hoods come to town. According to Bosley Crowther *(New York Times),* "Lost and forgotten in the scramble of the writers and director to include all these people in the happenings is Sylvia Sidney, who plays the lady librarian. She is fortunately given a fast brush. The last expression we see on her baffled visage as much as says: 'What the heck is going on?' "

The following year, Sylvia's last theatrical film to date, *Behind the High Walls* (1956), was released by Universal. This pedestrian prison melodrama featured her as the crippled wife of corrupt warden Tom Tully. It passed from theatrical release to television with little notice. Since then, assorted Hollywoodites have tried to find a proper vehicle to return Sylvia to the screen. The late Jerry Wald (who died in 1962) planned to star Sylvia in *High Heels.* In addition, such disparate types as Ross Hunter and Rock Hudson have mentioned to the press their fondness for Sylvia's acting abilities and a desire to feature her in one of their productions.

Sylvia was next on Broadway in *A Very Special Baby* (Playhouse Theatre, November 14, 1956). She dropped out of *Protective Custody,* another stage project, to star in the Robert Alan Aurthur drama. When Ezio Pinza died, director Martin Ritt hired Luther Adler to portray the egotistical father whose daughter (!) Sylvia sacrifices her youth for him. She is determined to help her middle-aged brother (Jack Warden) make his break to a life of independence. The critics commented that Sylvia "goes about her chores with becoming attention to what the role suggests" and that her performance was "tense with nerves and frustration." The overwrought drama folded after five performances.

Having toured with Miriam Hopkins in *The Old Maid* (1957), Sylvia returned to Broadway to play an atypical glamorous-comedy role in the City Center's revival of *Auntie Mame,* which opened its limited Manhattan engagement on August 12, 1958. Her edition had been touring by bus and truck since April of that year. Richard Watts, Jr. *(New York Herald Tribune)* reported: "Since Sylvia Sidney is less tall than Rosalind Russell and has an appealing manner as an actress, *Auntie Mame* in her hands takes on a curious suggestion of wistfulness. One is afraid those big people surrounding the little lady are going to start bullying her. . . . The insane frenzy that Miss Russell put into her desperate struggle with rebellious telephone cords and recalcitrant sales slips has lost some of its wild hilarity and becomes almost a little touching as Miss Sidney battles her inanimate enemies. The play's newest star has her own way of managing a role." More than one columnist noted that tempers had flashed between producer and star during the tour.

On NBC's "Special For Women" shows, Sylvia starred in *Change of Life* (April 13, 1961), a show dealing with menopause. She was in the news on November 29, 1961, when she sued NBC Television Network for $350,000 in Los Angeles superior court, claiming libel per se. The network had televised a video trailer commercial for an upcoming Bobby Darin variety show. It ran as follows:

"Are you Bobby Darin?"

"Yes."

"Are you the Bobby Darin that has Sylvia Sidney and her all-mother harmonica band on Tuesday in color?"

The case was settled out of court.

Sylvia played in *The Glass Menagerie* (1962) at Ann Arbor and toured in *The Matchmaker* (1962) for the New York State Council Of Arts.

In the two-part "The Defenders" television episode entitled *The Madman* (October 20, 1962, October 27, 1962, CBS), Sylvia portrayed the distraught mother of confessed murderer Don Gordon. She won an Emmy nomination for her performance, but lost out to veteran actress Glenda Farrell, who had appeared to outstanding notices on a "Ben Casey" television episode.

Next Sylvia accepted a nominal starring role in Carl Reiner's *Enter Laughing* (Henry Miller Theatre, March 14, 1963). She was Mrs. Kalowitz, the caricature Jewish mother of stagestruck Alan Arkin in this episodic spoof. The comedy ran for 419 performances, but Sylvia left it on October 12, 1963, replaced by Mae Questra. In the later film version, Shelley Winters inherited Sylvia's part.

When Miriam Hopkins withdrew from the off-Broadway production *Riverside Drive* (Theatre De Lys, February 4, 1964) Sylvia took over. The two one-act plays costarred Donald Woods. In the first drama, Sylvia, as the uncultured widow of a not so successful literary agent, attempted to take over the business. In the other, she was part of a highly successful husband-wife acting team who have lost communication with the realities of the world. Sylvia received excellent notices for her virtuoso acting, but the show closed after 15 performances.

Later in 1964, Sylvia toured in *The Silver Cord* and *The Pleasure of His Company*, again displaying her versatility on the stage.

In 1965 she joined the National Repertory Theatre for a ten-city expedition which started in Greensboro, North Carolina, in October that year, and concluded in New York in April, 1956. Sylvia played a crony of Eva Le Gallienne in *The Madwoman of Chaillot*, Mrs. Malaprop in *The Rivals,* and the chief of the chorus in *The Trojan Women.*

When asked how she went about her stagecraft, Sylvia told the press: "I believe in reducing a part to basic emotions—and they haven't changed since drama began, and they won't. . . . If you start worrying about style in a play you create a lot of confusion you don't have to have. Once you've got emotions analyzed, the playwright's lines almost automatically take care of particular style."

About her career: "What's the use of talking about a favorite role if you can't get it. . . . The role you're doing ought to be your favorite. If you don't like a part it's probably because you've a feeling of inadequacy about it."

Of Hollywood: "Hollywood! It's like an old chair—if it's useful, keep it; if not, give it to Goodwill."

Sylvia headed the touring company of Neil Simon's *Barefoot in the Park,* playing 23 cities from October to December, 1966, and succeeding Ilka Chase in the Broadway edition on April 4, 1967.

Recently, Sylvia has spent most of her time breeding pug dogs and devoting more effort to her needlepoint craftwork. In 1968, her chatty *Sylvia Sidney Needlepoint Book* was published to outstanding reviews. In her book, Sylvia says: "My hands have always been full—with play scripts, pugs, or canvases, and generally all three at once. Actually needlepoint was just a logical step in the progression of knitting, sewing, embroidering, and the like with which I have been engaged since I can remember."

Sylvia had a guest-starring role on Fred MacMurray's "My Three Sons" (April 19, 1969, ABC), portraying a tyrannical English teacher. After a two-year hiatus, she returned to California in the summer of 1971 to appear in the telefeature *Do Not Fold, Spindle Or Mutilate* (November 9, 1971), an "ABC Movie of the Week" co-starring Helen Hayes, Myrna Loy, Mildred Natwick, and Vince Edwards. The chiller dealt with four old biddies who have a penchant for practical jokes, until their love of a good laugh (they join a computer dating service, using an imaginary composite girl) gets them hooked up with a psychotic. While Hayes and Natwick played it all very broadly, both Sylvia and Loy were too self-conscious to be the eccentric women intended. While on the coast, Sylvia also guested on ABC's "Movie Game."

Her last video assignment to date was in a Bayer aspirin commercial, seemingly designed to destroy any illusion that Sylvia was ever a noted screen star. The tele-ad showed her seated in a living room busily at work on her needlepoint. Then the bespectacled Sylvia confided to the audience that when an arthritis attack threatened to stop her needlepoint activity, she would reach for a Bayer. The precise diction that had always been a trademark of the silver screen Sylvia was no longer evident.

These days, Sylvia seems content to quietly reside in Roxbury, Connecticut. She recently opened a needlecraft boutique in nearby Washington, Connecticut. Not one to hold onto the past, a number of years ago, she threw away all her scrapbooks and professional mementos. Sylvia lives only for the present, a fruitful but unglamorous existence far removed from most emeritus movie stars. Her son Jody, still unmarried, has made a name for himself in scientific photography and has an executive position with the telephone company. Sylvia says that being a movie star never meant much to her, but "being an actress did."

Feature Film Appearances

BROADWAY NIGHTS (FN, 1927) 6,765'

Director, Joseph Boyle; story, Norman Houston, adaptation, Forrest Halsey; camera, Ernest Haller.

Lois Wilson (Fannie Fanchette); Sam Hardy (Johnny Fay); Louis John Bartel (Baron); Philip Strange (Bronson); Barbara Stanwyck (Dancer); Bunny Weldon (Night Club Producer); Sylvia Sidney (Herself); and: Henry Sherwood, Georgette Duval, June Collyer.

THRU DIFFERENT EYES (FOX, 1929) 5,166'

Producer-director, John Blystone; based on the play by Milton Gropper, Edna Sherry; dialogue, Tom Barry, Gropper; assistant director, Jasper Blystone; song, William Kernell and Dave Stamper; sound, Edmund H. Hansen; camera, Ernest Palmer, Al Brick; editor, Louis Loeffler.

Mary Duncan (Viola); Edmund Lowe (Harvey Manning); Warner Baxter (Jack Winfield); Natalie Moorhead (Frances Thornton); Earle Foxe (Howard Thornton); Donald Gallaher (Spencer); Florence Lake (Myrtle); Sylvia Sidney (Valerie Briand); Purnell Pratt (Marston, District Attorney); Dolores Johnson (Anna); Selmer Jackson (King, Defense Attorney); Nigel de Brulier (Maynard); Lola Salvi (Maid); Stepin Fetchit (Janitor); DeWitt Jennings (Paducah); Arthur Stone (Crane); George Lamont (Traynor); Natalie Warfield (Aline Craig); Jack Jordan, Marian Spitzer, Stan Blystone, Stuart Erwin (Reporters); and Frank Brownlee.

CITY STREETS (PAR, 1931) 84 M.

Director, Rouben Mamoulian; story, Dashiell Hammett; adaptation, Max Marcin; screenplay, Marcin, Oliver H. P. Garrett; music, Sidney Cutner; camera, Lee Garmes; editor, William Shea.

Gary Cooper (The Kid); Sylvia Sidney (Nan); Paul Lukas (Big Fella Maskal); Guy Kibbee (Pop Cooley); William (Stage) Boyd (McCoy); Wynne Gibson (Agnes); Betty Sinclair (Pansy); Stanley Fields (Blackie); Terry Carroll (Esther March); Edward Le Saint (Shooting Gallery Patron); Robert Homans (Inspector); Willard Robertson (Detective); Hal Price (Shooting Gallery Patron); Ethan Laidlaw (Killer at Prison); George Regas (Machine Gunner); Bob Kortman (Servant); Leo Willis (Henchman); Bill Elliott (Dance Extra); Allan Cavan (Cop); Bert Hanlon (Baldy); Matty Kemp (Man Stabbed With Fork); Norman Foster (Extra on Midway).

CONFESSIONS OF A CO-ED (PAR, 1931) 77 M.

Director, Dudley Murphy, David Burton; art director, Hans Dreier; camera, Lee Garmes.

Phillips Holmes (Dan); Sylvia Sidney (Patricia); Norman Foster (Hal); Claudia Dell (Peggy); Florence Britton (Adelaide); Martha Sleeper (Lucille); Dorothy Libaire (Mildred); Marguerite Warner (Sally); George Irving (President); Winter Hall (Dean Winslow); Eulalie Jensen (Dean Marbridge); Bruce Coleman (Mark); Bing Crosby (Band Vocalist Bing).

AN AMERICAN TRAGEDY (PAR, 1931) 95 M.

Director, Josef von Sternberg; based on the novel by Theodore Dreiser; adaptation, von Sternberg, Samuel Hoffenstein; screenplay, von Sternberg; art director, Hans Dreier; camera, Lee Garmes.

Phillips Holmes (Clyde Griffiths); Sylvia Sidney (Roberta Alden); Frances Dee (Sondra Finchley); Irving Pichel (Orville Mason); Frederick Burton (Samuel

Griffiths); Claire McDowell (Mrs. Samuel Griffiths); Wallace Middleton (Gilbert Griffiths); Vivian Winsten (Myra Griffiths); Emmett Corrigan (Belknap); Lucille La-Verne (Mrs. Asa Griffiths); Charles B, Middleton (Jephson); Albert Hart (Titus Alden); Fanny Midgley (Mrs. Alden); Arline Judge (Bella Griffiths); Arnold Korff (Judge); Russell Powell (Coroner Fred Heit); Richard Cramer (Deputy Sheriff Kraus); Evelyn Pierce (Bertine Cranston); Elizabeth Forrester (Jill Trumbull); Imboden Parrish (Earl Newcomb); George Irving (Finchely); Claire Dodd (Grace Warren).

STREET SCENE (UA, 1931) 80 M.

Producer, Samuel Goldwyn, director, King Vidor, based on the play by Elmer Rice; screenplay, Rice; camera, George Barnes; editor, Hugh Bennet.

Sylvia Sidney (Rose Maurrant); William Collier, Jr. (Sam Kaplan); Max Mantor (Abe Kaplan); David Landau (Frank Maurrant); Estelle Taylor (Anna Maurrant); Russell Hopton (Steve Sankey); Louis Natheaux (Henry Easter); Greta Grandstedt (Mae Jones); Beulah Bondi (Emma Jones); T. H. Manning (George Jones); Matthew McHugh (Vincent Jones); Adele Watson (Olga Olsen); John M. Qualen (Karl Olsen); Anna Kostant (Shirley Kaplan); Nora Cecil (Alice Simpson); Lambert Rogers (Willie Maurrant); Allan Fox (Dick McGann); George Humbert (Filippo Fiorentino); Eleanor Wesselhoeft (Greta Fiorentino); Virginia Davis (Mary Hildebrand); Helen Lovett (Laura Hildebrand); Kenneth Selling (Charles Hildebrand); Conway Washburne (Dan Buchanan); Howard Russell (Dr. John Wilson); Richard Powell (Officer Harry Murphy); Walter James (Marshall James Henry); Harry Wallace (Fred Cullen); and: Monti Carter, Jane Mercer, Margaret Robertson, Walter Miller.

LADIES OF THE BIG HOUSE (PAR, 1931) 77 M.

Director, Marion Gering; story, Ernest Booth; screenplay, Louis Weitzenkorn; camera, David Abel.

Sylvia Sidney (Kathleen Storm); Gene Raymond (Standish McNeil); Wynne Gibson (Susie Thompson); Rockcliffe Fellowes (Martin Doremus); Earle Foxe (Kid Athens); Frank Sheridan (Warden Hecker); Purnell Pratt (John Hartman); Edna Bennett (Countess); Esther Howard (Clara Newman);Fritzi Ridgeway (Reno Maggie); Ruth Lyons (Gertie); Louise Beavers (Ivory);Miriam Goldina (Mexican Woman); Hilda Vaughn (Millie); Jane Darwell (Mrs. Turner); Mary Foy (Mrs. Lowry); Noel Francis (Thelma); Theodor von Eltz (Frazer); Evelyn Preer (Black Woman).

THE MIRACLE MAN (PAR, 1932) 85 M.

Director, Norman McLeod; based on the play by Frank L. Packard, Robert H. Davis, George M. Cohan; screenplay, Waldemar Young, Samuel Hoffenstein; camera, David Abel.

Sylvia Sidney (Helen Smith); Chester Morris (John Madison); Irving Pichel (Henry Holmes); John Wray (The Frog); Robert Coogan (Bobbie); Hobart Bosworth (Patriarch); Boris Karloff (Nikko); Ned A. Sparks (Harry Evans); Lloyd Hughes (Thornton); Virginia Bruce (Margaret Thornton); Florence McKinney (Betty); Frank Darien (Hiram Higgins); Lew Kelly (Parker).

MERRILY WE GO TO HELL (PAR, 1932) 78 M.

Director, Dorothy Arzner; based on the novel *I Jerry Take Thee, Joan* by Cleo Lucas; screenplay, Edwin Justis Mayer; camera, David Abel.

Sylvia Sidney (Joan Prentiss); Fredric March (Jerry Corbett); Adrienne Allen (Claire Hempstead); Richard Gallagher (Buck); Florence Britton (Charlcie); Esther Howard (Vi); George Irving (Mr. Prentice); Kent Taylor (Gregory Boleslavsky); Charles Coleman (Damery); Leonard Carey (Butler); Milla Davenport (Housekeeper); Robert Greig (Baritone); Rev. Neal Dodd (Minister); Mildred Bond (June); Cary Grant (Charlie Baxter "De Brion"); Gordon Westcott, Jay Eaton, Pat Somerset (Friends); Theresa Harris (Powder Room Attendant); LeRoy Mason (Guest);

Dennis O'Keefe (Usher); Tom Ricketts (Guest at Wedding); Edwin Maxwell (Jake Symonds); Bill Elliott (Dance Extra); Ernie S. Adams (Reporter).

MAKE ME A STAR (PAR, 1932) 68 M.

Director, William Beaudine; based on the novel *Merton of the Movies* by Harry Leon Wilson and the play by George S. Kaufman, Moss Hart; adaptation, Sam Wintz, Walter De Leon, Arthur Kober; camera, Allen Siegler; editor, Leroy Stone.

Stuart Erwin (Merton Gill); Joan Blondell ("Flips" Montague); Zasu Pitts (Mrs. Scudder); Ben Turpin (Ben); Charles Sellon (Mr. Gashwiler); Florence Roberts (Mrs. Gashwiler); Helen Jerome Eddy (Tessie Kearns); Arthur Hoyt (Hardy Powell); Dink Templeton (Buck Benson); Ruth Donnelly (The Countess); Sam Hardy (Jeff Baird); Oscar Apfel (Henshaw); Frank Mills (Chuck Collins); Polly Walters (Doris Randall); Victor Potel, Bobby Vernon, Snub Pollard, Billy Bletcher, Bud Jamison, Nick Thompson (Fellow Actors); Tallulah Bankhead, Clive Brook, Maurice Chevalier, Claudette Colbert, Gary Cooper, Phillips Holmes, Fredric March, Jack Oakie, Charlie Ruggles, Sylvia Sidney (Themselves).

MADAME BUTTERFLY (PAR, 1932) 86 M.

Director, Marion Gering; based on the play by John Luther Long, David Belasco; screenplay, Josephine Lovett, Joseph M. March; camera, David Abel.

Sylvia Sidney (Cho-Cho San); Cary Grant (Lt. B. F. Pinkerton); Charlie Ruggles (Lt. Barton); Sandor Kallay (Goro); Irving Pichel (Yomadori); Helen Jerome Eddy (Cho-Cho's mother); Edmund Breese (Cho-Cho's Grandfather); Judith Vosselli (Madame Goro); Louise Carter (Suzuki); Dorothy Libaire (Peach Blossom); Sheila Terry (Mrs. Pinkerton); Wallis Clark (Commander Anderson); Berton Churchill (American Consul); Philip Horomato (Trouble).

PICK-UP (PAR, 1933) 76 M.

Director, Marion Gering; story, Vina Delmar; screenplay, S. K. Lauren, Agnes Brand Leahy; camera, David Abel.

Sylvia Sidney (Mary Richards); George Raft (Harry Glynn); William Harrigan (Jim Richards); Lilian Bond (Muriel Stevens); Clarence Wilson (Sam Foster); George Meeker (Artie Logan); Louise Beavers (Magnolia); Florence Dudley (Freda); Eddie Clayton (Don); Dorothy Layton (Peggy); Alice Adair (Sally); Robert McWade (Jerome Turner).

JENNIE GERHARDT (PAR, 1933) 85 M.

Producer, B. P. Schulberg; director, Marion Gering; based on the novel by Theodore Dreiser; adaptation, Josephine Lovett, Joseph M. March, S. K. Lauren, Frank Portos; camera, Leon Shamroy.

Sylvia Sidney (Jennie Gerhardt); Donald Cook (Lester Kane); Mary Astor (Letty Pace); Edward Arnold (Senator Brander); H. B. Warner (William Gerhardt); Theodor von Eltz (Robert Kane); Dorothy Libaire (Louise Kane); Gilda Storm (Vesta—Age 17); Greta Meyer (Ada); David O'Brien (Bass Gerhardt); David Durand (Willie Gerhardt); Betsy Ann Hisle (Veronica Gerhardt); Morgan Wallace (O'Brien); Ernest Wood (Will Whitney); Frank Reicher (Old Weaver); Gene Morgan (Hotel Clerk); Rose Coghlan (Old Weaver's Granddaughter); Jane Darwell (Boarding House Keeper); Lillian Harmer (Midwife).

GOOD DAME (PAR, 1934) 72 M.

Director, Marion Gering; story, William K. Lipman; screenplay, Lipman, Vincent Lawrence, Frank Partos, Sam Hellman; camera, Leom Shamroy; editor, Jane Loring.

Sylvia Sidney (Lillie Taylor); Fredric March (Mace Townsley); Jack LaRue (Blush Brown); Noel Francis (Puff Warner); Russell Hopton ("Spats" Edwards); Bradley Page (Regan); Guy Usher (Fallon); Kathleen Burke (Zandra); Joseph J. Franz (Scanion); Miami Alverez (Cora); Walter Brennan (Elmer Spicer); John Marston (Judge Goddard); James Crane (Mr. Hill); William Farnum (Judge Flynn); Patricia Farley (Emily); Florence Dudley (Stella); Jill Bennett (Rose); Erin LaBissoniere (Mac); Ernest S. Adams (Night Clerk); Kenneth McDonald (Assistant Supt. to Hill); Cecil Weston (Mrs. Hill); James Burke (Cop); Jack Baxley (Barker For Dame Show); Edward Gargan (Man in Hotel Room).

THIRTY DAY PRINCESS (PAR, 1934) 74 M.

Producer, B. P. Schulberg; director, Marion Gering; based on the novel by Clarence Budington Kelland; adaptation, Sam Hellman, Edwin Justus Mayer; screenplay, Preston Sturges, Frank Partos; camera, Leon Shamroy.

Sylvia Sidney (Nancy Lane/Princess Catterina); Cary Grant (Porter Madison III); Edward Arnold (Richard Gresham); Henry Stephenson (King Anotol); Vincent Barnett (Count Nicholeus); Edgar Norton (Baron); Ray Walker (Mr. Kirk); Lucien Littlefield (Parker); Robert McWade (Managing Editor); George Baxter (Spottswood); Marguerite Namara (Lady-in-Waiting); Eleanor Wesselhoeft (Mrs. Schmidt); Frederic Sullivan (Doctor at Gresham's); Robert E. Homans, William Augustin (Detectives); Ed Dearing (Policeman at Mrs. Schmidt's); Bruce Warren (Spottswood's Friend); William Arnold (City Editor); Dick Rush (Sergeant of Police); J. Merrill Holmes (Radio Man at Boat); Thomas Monk (Gresham's Butler).

BEHOLD MY WIFE (PAR, 1934) 79 M.

Producer, B. P. Schulberg; director, Mitchell Leisen; based on the novel *The Translation of a Savage* by Sir Gilbert Parker; adaptation, William R. Lipman, Oliver La Farge; screenplay, Vincent Lawrence, Grover Jones; camera, Leon Shamroy.

Sylvia Sidney (Tonita Storm Cloud); Gene Raymond (Michael Carter); Juliette Compton (Diana Carter-Curson); Laura Hope Crews (Mrs. Carter); H. B. Warner (Hubert Carter); Monroe Owsley (Bob Prentice); Kenneth Thomson (Jim Curson); Ann Sheridan (Mary White); Charlotte Granville (Mrs. Sykes); Dean Jagger (Pete); Charles B. Middleton (Juan Storm Cloud); Eric Blore (Benson—Butler); Ralph Remley (Jenkins); Cecil Weston (Gibson); Dewey Robinson (Detective Bryan); Charles G. Wilson (Police Captain); Edward Gargan (Detective Connolly); Olin Howland (Mattingly); Gregory Whitespear (Medicine Man); Jim Thorpe (Indian Chief); Otto Hoffman (Minister); Evelyn Selbie (Neighbor Woman); Raymond Turner (Porter); Ferdinand Munier (Arthur); Nella Walker (Mrs. Copperwaithe); Countess Rina De Liguero (Countess Slavotski); Virginia Hammond (Mrs. Lawson); Fuzzy Knight (News Photographer); Jack Mulhall, Martin Malone, Neal Burns (Reporters at Train); Phillips Smalley (Society Man); Mabel Forrest (Society Dowager); Matt McHugh (Chunky); Gwenllian Gill (Miss Copperwaithe); Joseph Sawyer (Michael's Chauffeur); Joan Standing (Miss Smith); Kate Price (Mrs. MacGregor—Cook).

ACCENT ON YOUTH (PAR, 1935) 77 M.

Producer, Douglas MacLean; director, Wesley Ruggles; based on the play by Samson Raphaelson; screenplay, Herbert Fields, Claude Binyon; camera, Leon Shamroy; editor, Otho Lovering.

Sylvia Sidney (Linda Brown); Herbert Marshall (Steven Gaye); Phillip Reed (Dickie Reynolds); Astrid Allwyn (Genevieve Lang); Holmes Herbert (Frank Galloway); Catherine Doucet (Eleanor Darling); Ernest Cossart (Flogdell); Donald Meek (Orville); Lon Chaney, Jr., Dick Foran (Friends); Florence Roberts (Mrs. Beuham); Laura Treadwell (Mrs. Galloway); Elsie Clark (Janet); Albert Taylor (Cashier).

MARY BURNS, FUGITIVE (PAR, 1935) 84 M.

Producer, Walter Wanger; director, William K. Howard; story, Gene Towne, Graham Baker; screenplay, Towne, Baker, Louis Stevens; camera, Leon Shamroy; editor, Pete Fritsch.

Sylvia Sidney (Mary Burns); Melvyn Douglas (Barton Powell); Alan Baxter ("Babe" Wilson); Pert Kelton (Goldie Gordon); Wallace Ford (Harper); Brian Donlevy (Spike); Esther Dale (Kate); Frank Sully (Steve); Boothe Howard (Red Martin); Norman Willis (Joe); Frances Gregg (Matron); Charles Waldron (District Attorney); William Ingersoll (Judge); Rita Stanwood Warner (Nurse Agnes); Grace Hayle (Nurse Jennie); Daniel Haynes (Jeremiah); Joe Twerp (Willie); James Mack (Farmer); William Pawley (Mike); Isabel Carlisle (Woman Tourist); Henry Hall (Man Tourist); Dorothy Vaughn (Irish Matron); Esther Howard (Landlady); Morgan Wallace (Managing Editor); Phil Tead (Reporter); Ann Doran (Newspaper Girl); Fuzzy Knight (Dance Hall Attendant); Max Wagner (Sailor); Gertrude Walker, Treva Lawler (Hostesses); Charles Wilson (G-Man In Dance Hall); Ivan Miller, Kernan Cripps (G-Man); George Chandler (Cashier); Sammy Finn (Dapper Mobster); Richard Pawley (Slim Fergus); Bert Hanlon (Hymie); Cora Sue Collins (Littel Girl); Tom Ford (Orderly); Patricia Royale (Scullery Maid); Walter Downing (Farmer); Earl Ebbe (Photographer).

TRAIL OF THE LONESOME PINE (PAR, 1936) 102 M.

Producer, Walter Wanger; director, Henry Hathaway; based on the novel by John Fox, Jr.; screenplay, Grover Jones, Harvey Thew, Horace McCoy; songs, Paul Francis Webster and Louis Alter; camera, Howard Green; editor, Robert Bischoff.

Sylvia Sidney (June Tolliver); Henry Fonda (Dave); Fred MacMurray (Jack Hale); Fred Stone (Judd Tolliver); Nigel Bruce (Mr. Thurber); Beulah Bondi (Melissa); Robert Barrat (Buck Palin); Spanky McFarland (Buddy); Fuzzy Knight (Tater); Otto Fries (Corsey); Samuel Hinds (Sheriff); Alan Baxter (A Tolliver); Fern Emmett (Lena); Richard Carle (Ezra); Henry Brandon (Wade Falin); Philip Barker (Meed Falin); Bob Kortman (Gorley Falin); Charlotte Wynters (Jack Hale's Sister); Frank Rice (Zeke); Hilda Vaughn (Captown Teacher); Charles Middleton (Blacksmith); Russ Powell (Storekeeper); Irving Bacon (Mail Man); John Larkin (Ebony); Clara Blandick (Landlady); Frank McGlynn, Sr. (Preacher); Lowell Drew (Bartender); Lee Phelps (Taylor); Jack Curtis (Store Clerk); Betty Farrington (Louisville Teacher); Jim Burke (Leader); John Beck, Fred Burns, Jim Welch, Hank Bell, Bud Geary, Ed LeSaint (Tolliver Clan); Bill McCormick, Jim Corey (Falin Clan); Margaret Armstrong, Ricca Allen (Tollivers); Norman Willis (Old Dave—Prologue); George Ernest (Dave—Age 10); Powell Clayton (Dave—Age 5); Tuffy (The Dog).

FURY (MGM, 1936) 90 M.

Producer, Joseph L. Mankiewicz; director, Fritz Lang; story, Norman Krasna; screenplay, Bartlett Cormack, Lang; assistant director, Horace Hough; art director, Cedric Gibbons, William A. Horning, Edwin B. Willis; music, Franz Waxman; camera, Joseph Ruttenberg; editor, Frank Sullivan.

Spencer Tracy (Joe Wheeler); Sylvia Sidney (Catherine Grant); Walter Abel (District Attorney); Edward Ellis (Sheriff); Walter Brennan (Buggs Mayers); Bruce Cabot (Bubbles Dawson); George Walcott (Tom); Frank Albertson (Charlie); Arthur Stone (Durkin); Morgan Wallace (Fred Garrett); George Chandler (Milt); Roger Gray (Stranger); Edwin Maxwell (Vickary); Howard C. Hickman (Governor); Jonathan Hale (Defense Attorney); Leila Bennett (Edna Hooper); Esther Dale (Mrs. Whipple); Helen Flint (Fanchette); Edward Le Saint (Doctor); Everett Sullivan (New Deputy); Ben Hall (Goofy); Janet Young (Prim Woman); Jane Corcoran (Praying Woman); Murdock MacQuarrie, Frank Mills, Edwin J. Brady, James Quinn, Al Herman (Dawson's Friends); George Offerman, Jr. (Defendant); Mira McKinney (Hysterical Woman); Dutch Hendrian (Miner); Ray Brown (Farmer); Nora Cecil (Albert's Mother); Guy Usher (Assistant Defense Attorney); Frederick Burton (Judge Hopkins); Tom Mahoney (Bailiff); Tommy Tomlinson (Reporter); Sherry Hall (Court Clerk); Jack Daley (Factory Foreman); Duke York (Taxi Driver); Charles Coleman (Innkeeper); Esther Muir (Girl In Nightclub); Raymond Hatton (Hector); Clara Blandick (Judge's Wife); Herbert Ashley (Oscar); Harry Hayden (Lock-Up Keeper); Si Jenks (Hillbilly); Ward Bond (Objector) Arthur Hoyt (Grouch); Carl Stockdale (Hardware

Man); Clarence Kolb (Burgermeister); Minerva Urecal (Fanny); Edna Mae Harris (Black Woman); Sam Hayes (Announcer).

A WOMAN ALONE/SABOTAGE (Gaumont British, 1937,) 77 M.

Producer, Michael Balcon, Ivor Montagu; director, Alfred Hitchcock; based on the play by Campbell Dixon, adapted from the novel *The Secret Agent* by Joseph Conrad; adaptation, Alma Reville; screenplay, Charles Bennett; dialogue, Ian Hay, Jesse Lasky, Jr.; music, Louis Levy; camera, Bernard Knowles; editor, Charles Frend.

Sylvia Sidney (Mrs. Verloc); Oscar Homolka (Karl Anton Verloc); Desmond Tester (Stevie); John Loder (Sgt. Ted Spencer); Joyce Barbour (Renee); Matthew Boulton (Superintendent Talbot); S. J. Warrington (Hollingshead); William Dewhurst (Professor); Austin Trevor (Vladimir); Charles Hawtrey (Studious Boy); Torin Thatcher (Yunct); Peter Bull (Michaelis); Aubrey Mather (Contact) and: Pamela Bevan, Sara Allgood, Martita Hunt, Clara Greet, Sam Wilkinson.

YOU ONLY LIVE ONCE (UA, 1937) 85 M

Producer, Walter Wanger; director, Fritz Lang; story, Gene Towne; screenplay, Graham Baker; art director, Alexander Toluboff; music, Alfred Newman; camera, Leon Shamroy; editor, Daniel Mandell.

Henry Fonda (Eddie Taylor); Sylvia Sidney (Joan Graham); Barton MacLane (Stephen Whitney); Jean Dixon (Bonnie Graham); William Gargan (Father Dolan); Jerome Cowan (Dr. Hill); Charles "Chic" Sale (Ethan); Margaret Hamilton (Hester); Warren Hymer (Muggsy); John Wray (Warden); Jonathan Hale (District Attorney); Ward Bond (Guard); Wade Boteler (Policeman); Henry Taylor (Kozderonas); Jean Stoddard (Stenographer); Ben Hall (Messenger).

DEAD END (UA, 1937) 93 M.

Producer, Samuel Goldwyn; associate producer, Merritt Hulburd; director William Wyler; based on the play by Sidney Kingsley; screenplay, Lillian Hellman; art director, Richard Day; music director, Alfred Newman; assistant director, Eddie Bernoudy; camera, Gregg Toland; editor, Daniel Mandell.

Sylvia Sidney (Drina); Joel McCrea (Dave); Humphrey Bogart (Baby Face Martin); Wendy Barrie (Kay); Claire Trevor (Francie); Allen Jenkins (Hunk); Marjorie Main (Mrs. Martin); Billy Halop (Tommy); Huntz Hall (Dippy); Bobby Jordan (Angel); Leo Gorcey (Spit); Gabriel Dell (T.B.); Bernard Punsley (Milty); Charles Peck (Philip Griswold); Minor Watson (Mr. Griswold); James Burke (Mulligan); Ward Bond (Doorman); Elizabeth Risdon (Mrs. Connell); Esther Dale (Mrs. Fenner); George Humbert (Pascagli); Marcelle Corday (Governess); Jerry Cooper (Milty's Brother); Kath Ann Lujan (Milty's Sister); Bud Geary (Kay's Chauffeur); Gertrude Valerie (Old Lady); Tom Ricketts (Old Man); Esther Howard (Woman With Coarse Voice); Micky Martin, Wesley Girard (Tough Boys); Mona Monet (Nurse); Don Barry (Interne); Earl Askam (Griswold Chauffeur); Frank Shields, Lucile Brown (Well-Dressed Couple).

YOU AND ME (PAR, 1938) 90 M.

Producer-director, Fritz Lang; story, Norman Krasna; screenplay, Virginia Van Upp; art director, Hans Dreier, Ernst Fegte; songs, Kurt Weill and Sam Coslow; Ralph Freed and Frederick Hollander; camera, Charles Lang, Jr.; editor, Paul Weatherwax.

Sylvia Sidney (Helen); George Raft (Joe Dennis); Harry Carey (Mr. Morris); Barton MacLane (Mickey); Warren Hymer (Gimpy); Roscoe Karns (Cuffy); Robert Cummings (Jim); George E. Stone (Patsy); Adrian Morris (Knucks); Roger Gray (Bath House); Cecil Cunningham (Mrs. Morris); Vera Gordon (Mrs. Levine); Egon Brecher (Mr. Levine); Willard Robertson (Dayton); Guinn Williams (Taxi); Bernardene Hayes (Nellie); Joyce Compton (Curly Blonde); Carol Paige (Torch Singer); Harlan Briggs (McTavish); William B. Davidson (N. G. Martin); Oscar G. Hendrian (Lucky); Edward J. Pawley (Dutch); Joe Gray (Red); Jack Pennick, Kit Guard (Gansters); Paul Newlan

(Bouncer); Hal K. Dawson (Information Clerk); Herta Lynd (Swedish Waitress); Matt McHugh (Newcomer); Jimmie Dundee (Bus Driver); Jack Mulhall, Sam Ash (Floorwalkers); Julia Faye (Secretary); Arthur Hoyt (Mr. Klein); Max Barwyn (German Waiter); Harry Tenbrook (Bartender); Ernie Adams (Nick—Waiter); James McNamara (Big Shot); Gwen Kenyon (Hat Check Girl); Ellen Drew (Cashier); Sheila Darcy (Perfume Clerk); Ruth Rogers (Salesgirl); Fern Emmett (Mother); Cheryl Walker, Dorothy Dayton, Carol Parker, Juanita Quigley (Girls); Jane Dewey, Joyce Mathews (Clerks).

ONE THIRD OF A NATION (PAR, 1939) 79 M.

Producer-director, Dudley Murphy; based on the play by Arthur Arent; screenplay, Murphy, Oliver H. P. Garrett; camera, William Miller; editor, Duncan Mansfield.

Sylvia Sidney (Mary Rogers); Leif Erikson (Peter Cortlant); Myron McCormick (Sam Moon); Hiram Sherman (Donald Hinchley); Sidney Lumet (Joey Rogers); Muriel Hutchison (Ethel Cortlant); Percy Waram (Arthur Mather); Otto Hulitt (Assistant District Attorney); Horace Sinclair (Butler); Iris Adrian (Myrtle); Charles Dingle (Mr. Rogers); Edmonia Nolley (Mrs. Rogers); Hugh Cameron (Mr. Cassidy); Julia Fassett (Mrs. Cassidy); Baruch Lumet (Mr. Rosen); Byron Russell (Inspector Castle); Robert George (Building Inspector); Wayne Nunn (Inspector Waller); Max Hirsch (Mr. Cohen); Miriam Goldina (Mrs. Cohen); Bea Hendricks (Min).

THE WAGONS ROLL AT NIGHT (WB, 1941) 83 M.

Producer, Harlan Thompson; director, Ray Enright; story, Frank Wallack; screenplay, Fred Niblo, Jr., Barry Trivers; assistant director, Jesse Hibbs; art director, Hugh Reticker; music, Heniz Roemheld; camera, Sid Hickox; special effects, Byron Haskins, H. F. Koenekamp; editor, Frederick Richard.

Humphrey Bogart (Nick Coster); Sylvia Sidney (Flo Lorraine); Eddie Albert (Matt Varney); Joan Leslie (Mary Coster); Sig Rumann (Hoffman The Great); Cliff Clark (Doc); Frank Wilcox (Tex); John Ridgely (Arch); Charles Foy (Snapper); Clara Blandick (Mrs. Williams); Aldrich Bowker (Mr. Williams); Garry Owen (Gus); Jack Mower (Bundy); Frank Mayo (Wally); Tom Wilson, Al Herman, George Riley, Cliff Saum (Barkers); Eddie Acuff (Man); George Guhl (Deputy Sheriff); Jimmy Fox (Customer); Grace Hayle (Mrs. Grebnick); Beverly Quintanilla and Barbara Quintanilla (Baby); Richard Elliott (Mr. Paddleford); John Dilson (Minister); Ted Oliver (Sheriff); Fay Helm (Wife); Anthony Nace (Husband); Freddy Walburn, Buster Phelps, Bradley Hall, Tom Braunger, Robert Winkler, Harry Harvey, Jr., George Ovey (Boys).

BLOOD ON THE SUN (UA, 1945) 98 M.

Producer, William Cagney; director, Frank Lloyd; based on a story by Garrett Fort; screenplay, Lester Cole; technical adviser, Alice Barlow; production designer, Wiard B. Ihnen; music, Miklos Rosza; assistant director, Harvey Dwight; camera, Theodor Sparkuhl; editor, Truman Wood, Walter Hanneman.

James Cagney (Nick Condon); Sylvia Sidney (Iris Hilliard); Wallace Ford (Ollie Miller); Rosemary De Camp (Edith Miller); Robert Armstrong (Colonel Tojo); John Emery (Premier Tanaka); Leonard Strong (Hijikata); Frank Puglia (Prince Tatsug); John Halloran (Captain Oshima); Hugh Ho (Kajioka); Philip Ahn (Commander Yamamoto); Joseph Kim (Hayoshi); Marvin Miller (Chief Yamada); Rhys Williams (Joseph Casell); Porter Hall (Arthur Bickett); James Bell (Charley Sprague); Grace Lem (Amah); Oy Chan (Chinese Servant); George Paris (Hotel Manager); Hugh Beaumont (Johnny Clarke); Gregory Gay, Arthur Loft, Emmett Vogan, Charlie Wayne (Correspondents).

THE SEARCHING WIND (PAR, 1946) 108 M.

Producer, Hal Wallis; director, William Dieterle; based on the play by Lillian Hellman; screenplay, Hellman; art director, Hans Dreier, Franz Bachelin; music, Victor Young; camera, Lee Garmes; editor, Warren Low.

Robert Young (Alex Hazen); Sylvia Sidney (Cassie Bowman); Ann Richards (Emily Hazen); Douglas Dick (Sam); Dudley Digges (Moses); Albert Basserman (Count Von Stammer); Dan Seymour (Torrone); Marietta Canty (Sophronia); Charles D. Brown (Carter); Don Castle (David); William Trenk (Ponette); Mickey Kuhn (Sam —As A Boy); Ann Carter (Sarah); Dave Willock (Male Attendant—Hospital); Fred Gierman (Eppler); Henry Rowland (Captain Heyderbreck); Arthur Loft (Dr. Crocker); Frank Ferguson (Embassy Attendant); John Mylong (Hotel Manager); Eva Heyde (Woman Customer); Daniel De Jonghe, Adolph Freeman (Jewish Waiters); Albert Ferris (German Officer); Al Winters, Hans Hoebus (German Agents); Eugene Borden, Maurice Marsac (French Reporters); Reginald Sheffield (Prissy Little Man); Harry Semels (Waiter—In Madrid); Elmer Serrano (Spanish Major); Jack Mulhall, Frank Arnold (Reporters); Louis Lowy (French Bartender).

MR. ACE (UA, 1946) 84 M.

Producer, Benedict Bogeaus; director, Edwin L. Marin; story-screenplay, Fred Finklehoffe; music, Heinz Roemheld; song, Sid Silvers and Finklehoffe; camera, Karl Struss; editor, James Smith.

George Raft (Eddie Ace); Sylvia Sidney (Margaret Wyndham Chase); Stanley Ridges (Toomey); Sara Haden (Alma); Jerome Cowan (Peter Craig); Sid Silvers (Pencil); Alan Edwards (Chase); Roman Bohnen (Professor Adams).

LOVE FROM A STRANGER (Eagle Lion, 1947) 97 M.

Producer, James J. Geller; director, Richard Whorf; based on the play by Frank Vosper and the story by Agatha Christie; screenplay, Philip MacDonald; art director, Perry Smith; music, Irving Friedman; camera, Tony Gaudio; editor, Fred Allen.

John Hodiak (Manuel Cortez); Sylvia Sidney (Cecily Harrington); Ann Richards (Mavia); John Howard (Nigel Lawrence); Isobel Elsom (Auntie Loo-Loo); Frederic Worlock (Inspector Hobday); Ernest Cossart (Billings); Philip Tonge (Dr. Gribble); Anita Sharp-Bolster (Ethel—Maid); Billy Bevan (Cab Driver); John Goldsworthy (Clerk); David Cavendish; Keith Hitchcock (Policemen); Phyllis Barry (Waitress); Gerald Rogers (Postman); Colin Campbell (Bank Teller); Bob Corey (Cab Driver); Eugene Eberle (Bellboy); Charles Coleman (Hotel Doorman); Nolan Leary (Man In Bar); Donald Kerry, Abe Dinovitch (Men).

LES MISERABLES (20th, 1952) 105 M.

Producer, Fred Kohlmar; director, Lewis Milestone; based on the novel by Victor Hugo; screenplay, Richard Murphy; music, Alex North; art director, Lyle Wheeler, J. Russell Spencer; camera, Joseph LaShelle; editor, Hugh Fowler.

Michael Rennie (Jean Valjean); Debra Paget (Cosette); Robert Newton (Javert); Edmund Gwenn (Bishop); Sylvia Sidney (Fantine); Cameron Mitchell (Marius); Elsa Lanchester (Madame Magloire); James Robertson Justice (Robert); Joseph Wiseman (Genflou); Rhys Williams (Brevet); Florence Bates (Madame Bonnett); Merry Anders (Cicley); John Rogers (Bonnet); Charles Keane (Corporal); John Dierkes (Bosum); John Costello (Cochespaille); Norma Varden (Madame Courbet); William Cottrell (Dupuy); Queenie Leonard (Valjean's Maid); Bobby Hyatt (Garroche); Sanders Clark (Lieutenant); Sean McClory (Bamtasbois); John O'Malley (Worker); Leslie Denison (Mounted Policeman); Alex Frazer (Silversmith); June Hillman (Mother Superior); Jack Raine (Captain); John Sherman (Town Corporal); Dayton Lummis (Defense); Lester Matthews (Mentou, Sr.); Jimmie Moss (Mentou's Grandson); Ian Wolfe (Presiding Judge); Victor Wood (Prosecutor); Robert Adler (Valjean's Coachman); Victor Romito (Man); Olaf Hytten, Frank Baker (Judges); Charlotte Austin (Student); Michael Granger, Jerry Miley, Jack Baston (Policemen); Mary Forbes, Moyna MacGill (Nuns); Tudor Owen, Leonard Carey, William Dalzell (Citizens); Charles Fitzsimons (Noel—Student); Roger Anderson (Revolutionary).

VIOLENT SATURDAY (20th, 1955) 90 M.

Producer, Buddy Adler; director, Richard Fleischer; based on the novel by William L. Heath; screenplay, Sydney Boehm; music, Hugo Friedhofer; art director, Lyle Wheeler, George W. Davis; camera, Charles G. Clarke; editor, Louis Loeffler.

Victor Mature (Shelley Martin); Richard Egan (Boyd Fairchild); Stephen McNally (Harper); Virginia Leith (Linda); Tommy Noonan (Harry Reeves); Lee Marvin (Dill); Margaret Hayes (Emily); J. Carroll Naish (Chapman); Sylvia Sidney (Elsie); Ernest Borgnine (Stadt); Dorothy Patrick (Helen); Billy Chapin (Steve Martin); Brad Dexter (Gil Clayton); Donald Gamble (Bobby); Raymond Greenleaf (Mr. Fairchild); Richey Murray (Georgie); Robert Adler (Stan); Harry Carter (Bart); Ann Morrison (Mrs. Stadt); Kevin Corcoran (David Stadt); Donna Corcoran (Anna Stadt); Noreen Corcoran (Mary Stadt); Boyd "Red" Morgan (Slick); Florence Ravenel (Miss Shirley); Dorothy Phillips (Bank Customer); Virginia Carroll (Marion—Secretary); Ralph Dumke (Sidney); Robert Osterloh (Roy—Bartender); Harry Seymour (Conductor); Helen Mayon (Mrs. Pilkas); John Alderson (Amish Farmer); Esther Somers (Amish Woman On Train); Jeri Weil, Pat Weil (Amish Children).

BEHIND THE HIGH WALL (UNIV, 1956) 85 M.

Producer, Stanley Rubin; director, Abner Biberman; story, Wallace Sullivan, Richard K. Polimer; screenplay, Harold Jack Bloom; music, Joseph Gershenson; art director, Alexander Golitzen, Robert E. Smith; camera, Maury Gertsman; editor, Ted J. Kent.

Tom Tully (Frank Carmichael); Sylvia Sidney (Hilda Carmichael); Betty Lynn (Anne MacGregor); John Gavin (Johnny Hutchins); John Larch (William Kiley); Barney Phillips (Tom Reynolds); Don Beddoe (Todd MacGregor); Ed Kemmer (Charlie Rains); John Beradino (Carl Burkhardt); Raymond Barnes (George Miller); Robert Forrest (Al Loomis); Nicky Blair (Roy Burkhardt); Frances Osborne (Mrs. Loomis); David Garcia (Morgan); Glen Kramer, Phil Harvey, Harry Raven (Inmates); Peter Leeds, Jim Hyland (Detectives); William Forrest (Corby); Paul Keast (Jim Hardy); Herbert C. Lytton (Professor Reese); Amzie Strickland (Mrs. Maynarr); Will J. White (Yard Officer); Jack Mather (Captain); Ewing Mitchell (Judge); Hal Taggart (Bailiff); George Mather (Reporter); John Logan (First Gun Guard); Edward Rickard (Priest); Thomas Murray, Bill Boyett (Policemen); Floyd Simmons, Bing Russell, Dale Van Sickel, George Barrows, Roy Darmour (Guards).

With Leo Bulgakov in GODS OF THE LIGHTNING (1928)

In 1932

At the age of 22

With Miriam Hopkins on the Paramount lot, about 1933

Arriving in New York with her second husband, Luther Adler, September 1, 1938

With John Locer in ANNE OF THE THOUSAND DAYS (1950)

In *Barefoot in the Park* (1966)

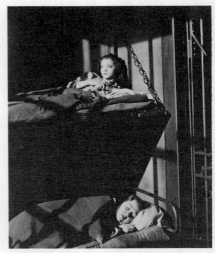
In CITY STREETS (Par '31)

In AN AMERICAN TRAGEDY (Par '31)

With Gene Raymond in LADIES OF THE BIG HOUSE (Par '32)

With Chester Morris in THE MIRACLE MAN (Par '32)

With Cary Grant in MADAME BUTTERFLY (Par '32)

With Fredric March in GOOD DAME (Par '34)

With Gene Raymond in BEHOLD MY WIFE (Par '34)

With Phillip Reed and Dick Foran in AC-CENT ON YOUTH (Par '35)

With Henry Fonda in TRAIL OF THE LONESOME PINE (Par '36)

With Spencer Tracy in FURY (MGM '36)

With Henry Fonda in YOU ONLY LIVE ONCE (UA '37)

With Joel McCrea in DEAD END (UA '37)

With Humphrey Bogart, Joan Leslie, and Eddie Albert in THE WAGONS ROLL AT NIGHT (WB '41)

With James Cagney in BLOOD ON THE SUN (UA '45)

With Ann Richards and Robert Young in THE SEARCHING WIND (Par '46)

With John Hodiak in LOVE FROM A STRANGER (Eagle Lion '47)

With Tom Tully in BEHIND THE HIGH WALL (Univ '56)

MAE WEST

5'4"
126 pounds
Blonde hair
Violet eyes
Leo

****

Now IN her eighth decade as a performer, Mae West has been variously described as everything from an outrageous female impersonator to the ultimate screen sex goddess, with an assortment of conglomerate images in between. Her projection of the liberated tough female is such a unique blend of vitality, irreverence, and sincerity that no one has ever been able to duplicate it. Mae brought to the screen a frank approach to the battle of the sexes, and proved that a woman with a sharp mind, a lingering eye, a slumbering slouch, and "what takes her time" can successfully snare any male challenger. That Mae snared what seems to be perpetual fame with her first three Paramount features in 1932–33—she has only made eleven features to date—attests to her powerful impact as a performer.

Mae had been a vaudeville performer, playwright, and stage actress for over 30 years before she finally made her screen debut in Paramount's *Night after Night* (1932) as a featured player. Her success in this George Raft vehicle hastily promoted the studio to star her in her own films. Her two best were an adaptation of *Diamond Lil* as *She Done Him Wrong* (1933) and *I'm No Angel* (1933), in both of which she captured moviegoers' imaginations with her double entendre quips, leering looks, and hip-swinging strut. Even the fact that she was more than 40 years of age and possessed an exaggerated hour-glass figure did not hinder Mae's acceptance with the usually conventional minded audiences.

Mae soon became the queen bee of Paramount, earning an enormous salary as performer and an additional $100,000 per film for preparing the screenplay. In the mid-1930s she was the prime star attraction of Hollywood and such a beloved freak success that every VIP who came to town demanded an audience with her, and hopefully was influenced by some of her crude forthrightness.

From 1936 onward, Mae's box-office draw began slipping. She had seemingly exhausted the variations on her good-woman-gone-wrong theme; also, the revised film production code had inhibited her rowdy humor. After leaving Paramount in 1938, Mae had a brief resurgence of her movie career when teamed with the equally iconoclastic W. C. Fields in Universal's mock Western *My Little Chickadee* (1940), in which each performer parodied the other's unique style with marvelously amusing results. It was a catchy teaming of the screen's two greatest enthusiasts of word play and innuendo.

Throughout the 1940s Mae appeared on Broadway and on the road with *Catherine Was Great* and in revivals of *Diamond Lil*, adding no new glories to her illustrious career but keeping her legend intact. Her last major invasion of the entertainment media was her nightclub act in the 1950s which again turned the tables on the male-female relationship. She was the insouciant star with a chorus of loin-clothed musclemen, giving the agog audience something new for their money and demonstrating that Mae still had va-voom.

Just as radio had quickly tampered with her original approach to life in the late 1930s, so it was a generally sedate Mae who made occasional television appearances in the late 1950s and early 1960s, mainly to let her fans know she was alive, well, and as full of leering bedroom talk as ever.

It was not until 1970 that Mae, now 78, returned to the screen in the abysmal *Myra Breckinridge*. She and the nostalgic film clips inserted in the vulgar production were the picture's only saving graces. Some observers called Mae a well-preserved mummy and just a shadow of her past self, a travesty mouthing old concepts and lines; but she had the enormous egolove to make her role come off with a minimum of embarrassing concessions to her advanced age.

Nasal-singing, man-baiting Mae continued to be a subject of controversy and interest long after most of her competitors have retired or died. Her individuality and love of self remain unchallenged. The chief siren of the screen is still winning new admirers, no mean accomplishment in today's helter-skelter world where bizarre individuality has become almost commonplace. Newcomers to the Mae West camp may not be taken aback by her once-daring approach to life and men, but her unique way with a line of dialogue and her ability to case a sucker with an all-absorbing glance continue unabated to amaze and titillate. And perhaps most alluring about Mae is that everything she has accomplished in the professional world, she owes to her own abilities and showmanship. No publicity agent or Svengalian director hatched this blonde exotic . . . she is 100 percent herself . . . first and seemingly last of her kind.

✳ ✳

Mae West was born August 17, 1892, in the Bushwick section of Brook-lyn, New York, the first child of John Patrick West, an Irish prizefighter known as Battling Jack, and Matilda Delker Doelger, a German-born im-migrant who had been a corset and fashion model before marriage, and who was related to the Doelger Breweries family of New York. The family would soon also include a younger sister, Beverly (born 1897), and a brother, Jack (born 1898).

Mae's childhood was not plush, but her middle-class parents were able to provide her with a good deal of the nice extras in life. She was more drawn to her well-bred mother than her raucous father whom she resented: "Father made a living for us—but Mama added the color and style." Her mother would later recall that at even an early age Mae was "a child that has to be humored and can't be forced or ordered. She resents even an unfavorable tone of voice."

Mae began lessons at "Professor" Watts's Dancing School in Brooklyn at the age of seven. She so impressed her instructor with her natural per-forming talents and her mature bearing, that he soon featured her in one of his weekly Sunday night programs at Brooklyn's Fulton Street Royal Theatre. For her debut she sang "Movin' Day" and performed a tap dance. She won the gold medal first prize, and was so encouraged that she entered other amateur contests in the metropolitan area, and grabbed other top prizes.

From the start, Mae was never one for formal education, and she was overjoyed when performer Hal Clarendon persuaded her parents to allow her to join his stock company, promising to look after her academic training while the troupe was on the road. This so-called formal education ended when she was 13. Mae's salary rose from $18 to $25 to $30 a week during the next four years, as she played the juvenile leads in such standards as *East Lynne, Ten Nights in a Bar Room, Mrs. Wiggs of the Cabbage Patch, The Fatal Wedding,* and *Little Nell the Marchioness.* When there was no suit-able role for her in a production, Mae would be called upon to entertain in front of footlights during the intermissions. She found this solo format more suitable to her talents and more satisfying to her burgeoning ego.

After Mae left the Clarendon company, she set her sights on having a vaudeville act. She worked as a strongwoman in a Coney Island acrobatic act, and about this time began dating vaudevillian Joe Schenck, who gra-ciously helped his girl to refine her vocal talents.

By 1911 Mae was playing the lesser Eastern vaudeville circuit as Huck-leberry Finn's girlfriend in a skit with performer William Hogan. Also on the same bill was jazz singer Frank Wallace. He convinced Mae to join him in a song and dance act, and together they played New Jersey, Pennsyl-vania, and the Midwest. Mae married Wallace on August 11, 1911, in Mil-waukee, Wisconsin. Wallace was 21 and Mae was 19 years old. A few months later she became disenchanted with him, broke up their act, and separated from him. They were not divorced till many years later, during which time the marriage was kept a closely guarded secret. As Mae said about Wallace: "Sure I was married once. I got talked into it. I wasn't really in love with the man, but it kept me from marrying other men. I always had a chain of men around me. I'd fall for one, then another'd come along and then I'd see another one that was kinda interestin' . . . I guess you could say there's always safety in numbers."

Mae returned to her solo act on the circuit. One Sunday she performed her new routine at the weekly showcase night at the Columbia Theatre,

Manhattan. Florenz Ziegfeld's office offered her a spot in his latest rooftop revue, but she had her heart set on his *Follies* and rejected the lesser bid. She did agree to join Ned Wayburn's revue *A La Broadway* (Follies Bergere Theatre, September 22, 1911). Her two featured spots were "They Are Irish" a song she rewrote to her own specifications, and the production number "The Philadelphia Drag." Mae stopped the show with her enthusiastic performance and garnered her first important reviews. "Miss Mae West . . . seems to be a sort of female George M. Cohan with an amusingly impudent manner and an individual way of making her points" (*New York World*). "A girl named Mae West, hitherto unknown, pleased by her grotesquerie and a snappy way of singing and dancing." Unfortunately, the show only lasted eight performances—its producer (Jesse L. Lasky*) and one of the cowriters, William LeBaron,* would later be Paramount executives during Mae's regime at the studio.

Mae had better luck with the Shuberts' production of *Vera Violetta* (Winter Garden Theatre, November 20, 1911), which rang up 112 performances. Al Jolson and Gaby Deslys were the stars, but Mae as Mlle Angelique got a healthy share of critical plaudits.

Next she joined with the Gerard Brothers in a song and dance act which played the Northeastern vaudeville circuit. Mae encountered her first censorship problems in New Haven, where her song and shimmy routine pleased the Yale students and sailors but upset morality-minded citizens. A New Haven newspaper reported: "Her Wriggles Cost Mae West Her Job. . . . that enchanting, seductive, sin-promising wiggle. She shook in a devastating slow motion that has conquered New York. She sang in a wonderful champagne-laden voice!"

After she split with the Gerard Brothers, Mae revamped the act into an attention-getting solo turn, opening her bill with the number "I've Got a Style All My Own." According to Mae: "My basic style I never changed; never have changed. I couldn't if I wanted to. I am captive of myself. It or I created a Mae West and neither of us could let the other go, or want to."

Back on Broadway Mae appeared in *A Winsome Widow* (Moulin Rouge Theatre, April 1, 1912), a free adaptation of *A Trip to Chinatown*, in which she was La Petite Daffy. Leon Errol was also in the show, which ran a healthy 172 performances. The following year (July, 1913) she appeared in the farce *Such Is Life* in San Francisco, playing Maria Tamburri. She then commenced a tour for the United Booking Office circuit, billed as Vaudeville's Youngest Headliner. Her biggest competition was Eva Tanguay, who, Mae graciously admitted, "was the greatest song-seller vaudeville ever had."

Mae opened in Arthur Hammerstein's *Sometime* (Shubert Theatre, October 4, 1918), as Mayme Dean, a fun-loving tramp from Hoboken, New Jersey. Ed Wynn was costarred in this musical comedy about the loves and adventures of a theatrical company. Mae sang Rudolf Friml's "Any Kind of a Man." The *New York Evening World* noted: "This audacious young lady was tough but funny." During one matinee performance, Mae gave her fellow performers an unexpected bonus by adding a new dance. Since it proved to be a show-stopper, she kept it in the act—it was her adaptation of the "shimmy-shawobble," which she had seen performed by black couples in a Chicago South Side café. Thus Mae—all contenders aside—introduced the shimmy to an agog Broadway. *Sometime* continued for 283 per-

*See Appendix.

formances and then went on a road tour. Mae decided against repeating her assignment, wanting to try something new after so many months of *Sometime*.

After touring with her *Demi-Tasse Revue* in vaudeville, Mae joined the revue *The Mimic World of 1921* (Century Promenade Roof Theatre, August 15, 1921) with Cliff Edwards, El Brendel, and dancer Miriam Miller. Among other numbers, Mae did imitations of Alla Nazimova and a French vamp and played a male impersonator. She also performed in a skit burlesquing *The Shimmy Trial*. Critics cited *The Mimic World* as the best girly show in town.

It was during the run of *The Mimic World* that heavyweight boxing champ Jack Dempsey suggested Mae make a screen test at Pathé Studios' uptown New York facilities for an upcoming film *Daredevil Jack* in which he was to star. Although the test was successful, the deal was quashed by Mae's attorney-manager-former lover James A. Timony because it required Mae and Dempsey to undertake a too-strenuous vaudeville promotional tour. The project was regretfully dropped.

Mae revamped her act in *The Mimic World* into a vaudeville turn, with Harry Richman as her accompanist and assistant. She did her French number, a torch song, assorted imitations, and, by popular demand, her famed shimmy. When she played the Palace Theatre in 1922, her turn included the skit "You Don't Have to be Beautiful to be a Vamp." *Zit's Vaudeville* review read: "Stepping right out with her running boots on, Mae West, one of the prettiest entries that ever appeared on the Palace track, went to the front the moment the barrier went up." At the time, Mae was holding out for $750 a week from the Albee circuit, whose managers only wanted to pay her $500. She and Richman transferred their act to the *Ginger Box Revue* at the Greenwich Village Theatre in 1923. However, Mae preferred the wider exposure of vaudeville and returned to that medium, while Richman went on to club work and his own fame.

After a spell, Mae had a yearning to return to Broadway and see her name in big lights. Unable to find a suitable stage vehicle to showcase her talents, she followed her mother's suggestion and set about writing her own play. Mae would later say: "If I hadn't started writing plays back when I did, I think I could have gone the other way and wasted my whole mentality and life on sex. I don't ever remember not feeling sexy. I used to get tired of feeling that way. I used to exercise, thinking that would stop it."

Mae's self-written play *Sex* tried out in New Haven. Word of mouth stirred up curiosity among the sailors stationed there and they soon were attending the performances in droves, turning the project into an out-of-town success. (Years later—after Mae was an established institution—the most faithful of her fans and advocates would be homosexuals, a group not noted until very recently for supporting any talent on the unsure way to fame.) *Sex* made its splashy bow in Manhattan at Daly's 63rd Street Theatre on April 26, 1926. Mae coproduced the venture with C. V. Morgenstern. She used the pseudonym of Jane Mast for her author's credit, but soon everyone in the know was aware who the playwright really was. Despite newspaper refusal to advertise the show's risqué title, *Sex* was an immediate hit— particularly with the serviceman crowd, who relished the comedy drama about Margie LaMont (Mae) employed in a Montreal brothel. The script went from the "undeniably adroit to the unbelievably inept," with Mae's performance described as a "slouching, whisky tenor manner."

Although Mae found the show's director Edward Elsner uncongenial to her temperament and acting style, the veteran showman, by not interfering, allowed Mae to expand her stage character as a larger-than-life reflection of her own unique personality. At one point he advised her: "You have a definite *sexual* quality, gay and unrepressed. It even mocks you personally. . . . Don't lose it. You don't have to act it, or try to be that way. You are just *it*."

Sex would have lasted well beyond its 375 performances, but New York City underwent a vice suppression campaign, and Mae, Timony, and her production were brought to trial. Mae was fined $500 and sentenced to ten days in jail at Blackwell's Island. Her sentence, which made terrific headlines and garnered Mae incredible publicity, was reduced to eight days for good behavior. Mae vivdly recalls: "I didn't have to go to jail, but I knew they'd treat me like a society prisoner. . . . The warden was very nice . . . he used to take me out driving every night. . . . He had a nice mother, too . . . a very good cook . . . and a lot of my fans were there." While incarcerated, Mae wrote an article for *Liberty* magazine (for which she was paid $1,000) and mapped out future play projects for herself.

While in *Sex*, Mae had written *The Drag*, concerning homosexuality. The play was extremely advanced for its time, especially in its serious rather than exploitive nature. Under Edward Elsner's direction, *The Drag* —Mae was not in the cast—opened a pre-Broadway engagement in Paterson, New Jersey, in early 1927. Dramatics aside, the big Drag-ball scene was enough to insure the play's success. Mae grossed a $30,000 profit, post-production recoupment. The play never made Broadway because New York City officials persuaded Mae and Timony that the controversial play would cause a holocaust there.

Mae next penned *The Wicked Age* (Daly 63rd Street Theatre, November 4, 1927), a raunchy study of bathing beauty contest exploitation in which she starred as Evelyn "Babe" Caron. Marjorie Main played her mother. By now, every opening of a new play by Mae West was a wild social event that drew participants from adventurous blue bloods down to rowdy lowlifes. One opening-night reviewer reported that the occasion "needs the talent of a police reporter far more than a recorder of theatrical events." Mae sang "You Can Neck 'Em" and "My Baby's Kisses," and gave a good demonstration of her by now standard strutting walk and jaunty manner. "One could never tell where art began and actually left off," said another reviewer. Mae shuttered the show after 19 performances, despite the lush advance sale of tickets, because she was dissatisfied with her costar and disgusted with the Actors Equity Association's refusal to allow her to fire him. The union squabble had drained all the pleasure from this project, and Mae was financially and professionally strong enough to indulge any whim that entered her fast-moving mind.

Mae claims it was the night porter at her Manhattan hotel who provided the basis for her next opus, *Diamond Lil*. He had reminisced to Mae about his turn-of-the-century, Bowery sweetheart who had all the men chasing her, and wore an abundance of diamonds supplied by grateful admirers. During the tryout engagement at Teller's Shubert Theatre, Brooklyn, the show broke all box-office records, and that during Holy Week! *Diamond Lil*'s sensational Broadway opening occurred at the Royale Theatre on April 9, 1928. The cast included Jack La Rue, Helen Vincent, Raffaella Ottiano, and Mae's sister Beverly (playing Sally, the young innocent), and the play was set in the 1890s. Mae starred as the Bowery jezebel lovely involved in the shady goings-on at the Suicide Hare saloon on the edge of Chinatown. She sang her now classic "Frankie and Johnny" ballad. For a change the critics were not just titillated by her script ("vulgar without being brazen") and performance, but extolled her virtues as a stage luminary who, according to one, was "more admired by her public than is Jane Cowl, Lynne Fontanne, Helen Hayes or Eva Le Gallienne." Said another: "So regal is Miss West's manner, so assured is her artistry, so devastating are her charms in the eyes of all red-blooded men, so blonde, so beautiful, so buxom is she that she makes Miss Ethel Barrymore look like the late lamented [female impersonator] Mr. Bert Savoy." Percy Hammond (*New York Herald Tribune*) noted: "She walks with a cunning strut and she talks in a quiet monotone, never disturbing her humorous lips with the noise of elocution." Said Mae in her own telegraphic style: "With *Diamond Lil* I had it made." About the character Diamond Lil, she would say: "I'm her and she's me and we're each other." Mae would later turn the property into a novel, as well as the scenario for *She Done Him Wrong* (1933).

During her *Diamond Lil* triumph (it ran 328 performances), Mae wrote and opened *Pleasure Man* (Biltmore Theatre, October 1, 1928), dealing with a slick vaudeville headliner who used all the girls. Moral-toned blue bloods alerted the police, who were unexpected guests at the opening-night performance, raiding the show between the second and third acts. Mae was hauled into court for having written a lewd play (the *New York Sun* had decried: "No play in our time has had less excuse for such a sickening excess of filth"—another described it as "perversion used to give diversion"). Mae eventually won the court case but decided not to reopen *Pleasure Man.* "The edge was off the show. We had refunded all advance sale money, and when the trial was over, I said 'It would be like putting on a revival to open again.' "

Mae went on a successful tour with *Diamond Lil.* It was greeted with enthusiasm throughout the country. She was back in New York in 1929 to be with her critically ill mother, who died later that year.

Having revived *Sex* in Chicago (Garrick Theatre, August, 1930), Mae followed J. J. Shubert's suggestion and dramatized her recently published novel *The Constant Sinner* (Royale Theatre, September 14, 1931). She played Babe Gordon, a wicked lady of pleasure who is involved with pugs, racketeers, and Harlem nightlife. Despite bad reviews—"Her bag of acting tricks becomes familiar before the long evening has run its course" (*New York Times*), "That she is an atrocious playwright and appears in her own dramas is her only failing as an actress" (*New York Herald Tribune*)—the show lasted 64 performance. Not all bad during those shaky Depression days, such a run attested to her great public following.

It was during the playing of *The Constant Sinner* that Paramount offered Mae a chance to make her screen debut. According to cinema historian Gene Ringgold, her previous movie test with Jack Dempsey had been pirated and shown in some New York City theatres, and there are unconfirmed reports that she had even made two sound musical shorts.

The Paramount bid contained no provision for Mae to "assist" with the screenplay, which bothered her greatly, but Timony convinced her that $50,000 for ten weeks of work in *Night After Night,* an adaptation of a Louis Bromfield story, was worth the concession. She left by train for the Coast and arrived in Hollywood in June, 1932. As she put it: "I'm not a little girl from a little town makin' good in a big town. I'm a big girl from a big town makin' good in a little town."

Mae waited six weeks to see a copy of the screenplay for this George

Raft vehicle. It was one of his first starring roles at Paramount. He had known Mae during her Broadway days when he was the collector for one of her underworld backers, and he personally requested that Mae be offered a role in this production. When she discovered that her fourth-billed part as Maude Triplett was a relatively small affair, she advised the Paramount regime and producer William LeBaron that she would refund the $30,000 she had already received if they canceled the contract. LeBaron soothed Mae with the counter suggestion that she rewrite her part. Everything went fine until she arrived on the set and clashed with director Archie Mayo over her interpretation of the role. Her fast-cracking undulating style was in direct contrast to the laconic, icy mood provided by Raft. Even more to the point, *Night After Night* was supposed to focus on the ex-hoofer and not on Mae, the cinema newcomer. Mayo summoned LeBaron and studio creative head Emanuel Cohen* to referee but they sided with Mae.

Night After Night dealt with successful ex-boxer Raft who acquires a snazzy Manhattan speakeasy. He employs matronly Alison Skipworth to acquaint him with the refinements of life, largely because he has become infatuated with Park Avenue blue blood Constance Cummings, who appears unescorted at the club night after night, talking to no one. It develops that the mansion used to be hers, before the Depression ruined her family. Raft arranges for Skipworth to join him and Cummings for dinner to soothe over any rough spots in his tableside manner, only to find that his old flame Mae has reappeared and parlayed the dinner into a social foursome. With wisecracking Mae on the scene, Raft worries lest Cummings suspect his gentility. At the same time, Raft must contend with his ex-mistress Wynne Gibson. Being jealous of Cummings, she threatens to shoot Raft, but he coolly dissuades her, which impresses the unthawable Cummings. In a dramatic gesture to prove himself a gentlemen, Raft sells the club to gangsters, but when Cummings later walks out of his life, he reneges on the deal. Just as the hoods start wrecking the joint in revenge, Cummings reappears to proclaim her love, and the jubilant Raft is happy to let the club go.

Night After Night premiered October 30, 1932, at the Paramount Theatre. Advance screenings had indicated that Mae was the film's sensation, not Raft, and its release conclusively proved the point. Richard Watts, Jr. *(New York Herald Tribune)* described it: "On the screen, though, she brings some of that quality of rowdiness which the increasingly effete cinema needs and in *Night After Night* she is in an engagingly gutter fashion a delight."

Mae never saw *Night After Night,* afraid her enthusiasm would not match that of her admirers. As George Raft would exclaim: "She stole everything but the camera." Mae's scenes were few, but exceedingly memorable. Besides her famous retort to the hatcheck girl who asks about her lovely diamonds: "Goodness had nothing to do with it, dearie" (followed by her hip-swaying walk up the club's lobby steps), Mae had some bright moments teaching Skipworth how to drink, and managing to give Raft the obvious and comprehensive once-over in her own inimitable style.

Mae had planned to return to New York following *Night After Night,* possibly to reopen *The Constant Sinner.* Paramount's Cohen was not about to let this potential gold mine go, however, and he offered her a lucrative —in excess of $100,000—contract to make another film for the studio. He finally consented that the vehicle could be a film version of *Diamond Lil,*

*See Appendix.

which she then sold to Paramount for $25,000. There was further conflict between Mae and the studio but finally she won her way and was allowed to retain the Gay Nineties gaslight setting. Retitled *Ruby Red* to appease the Hays Office and then changed to *She Done Him Wrong,* the film went into production on November 21, 1932, and was completed in an amazingly short 18 days of shooting at a cost of $200,000. Mae, who had also devised the scenario, suggested that the leading players, including studio newcomer Cary Grant (whom she had selected to play Captain Cummings, "The Hawk"), rehearse for a week before filming. Director Lowell Sherman, a former stage and film actor, willingly complied with Mae's request.

 She Done Him Wrong premiered at the Paramount Theatre on February 9, 1933, and outdid everyone's expectations. It earned $2 million domestic grosses alone within three months! Despite the whitewashing demanded by the screen censors, Mae managed to bring alive the bawdy Bowery of the Gay Nineties and to make its clothing styles a hit on both sides of the Atlantic. Once again she was Lady Lou, "one of the finest women who ever walked the streets," who knows full well that "when women go wrong, men go right after them." Mae is the headlined singer in gruff Noah Beery, Sr.'s tony saloon, where a painting of her is prominently displayed over the bar ("Yeah, I gotta admit that is a flash, but I do wish Gus hadn't hung it up over the free lunch"), but she is unaware that the bar is a cover for Beery's lucrative white slave trade and counterfeiting racket. Everyone is hot for Mae, including a fashionable gigolo played by Gilbert Roland and crook David Landau. But it is Grant, who runs a Salvation Army mission next door, who attracts Mae's undivided attention. When he comes to plead with her to tone down the raucous activity at the saloon, he apologizes: "I'm sorry to be taking your time." To which she leers: "What do you think my time is for?" Later, after appraising his virtues from top to bottom, she drawls. "You can be had," and bids him, "Why don't you come up sometime, see me? . . . Come up. I'll tell your fortune."

 When waif Rochelle Hudson is brought to the saloon and Beery plans to ship her abroad, Mae finally realizes the score. In an argument with Beery's cohort, Russian Rita (Rafaella Ottiano), Mae accidentally stabs her, then covers over the traces of her act and maneuvers herself out of the clutches of ex-lover Owen Moore, who has escaped from jail just to get even with her. Still later, Grant, revealing his identity as undercover investigator for the police, arrests Beery for counterfeiting and reluctantly takes Mae into protective custody. As Grant approaches her with handcuffs, Mae asks: "Are those absolutely necessary? You know, I wasn't born with them."

> *Grant:* "No. A lot of men would have been safer if you had."
> *Mae:* "I don't know. Hands ain't everything."

Grant escorts Mae to jail in a private cab, and on the way, presents her with a single diamond ring.

> *Mae:* "Dark and handsome."
> *Grant:* "You bad girl."
> *Mae:* "You'll find out."

Fade out.

 Mae's songs in *She Done Him Wrong* included "Frankie and Johnnie," "A Guy What Takes Takes His Time," and "Easy Rider." They set a new standard in screen vocalizing. Her style, a blend of black spiritual and honky-tonk, had its own sensuous manner and got its message across to even the least sophisticated. Mae's buxom hourglass figure (37½–29½–37½) did not go unnoticed by the camera or the audience. The flattering camera-work of Charles Lang accentuated the oversized hips and breasts, bringing the overly full figure back into national popularity.

The bawdiness was all there in *She Done Him Wrong,* taking the vibrant risqué out of the merely suggestive and splashing it blatantly across the screen. Richard Watts, Jr. *(New York Herald Tribune)* summed it up: "It is one of the grandest things about Miss West's robust comedy that she is so frankly and heroically proud of her roughness that never is anything leering or underhanded about it." *Variety* reported: "Miss West in picture hats, strait-jacket gowns and with so much jewelry she looks like a Knickerbocker ice plant. . . . gets across each jibe and point with a delivery that will soon be imitated. . . . her handling of lovers, past, present and prospective comprises the whole picture."

She Done Him Wrong is listed as one of the key factors in the restructuring, of the production code of the motion picture industry for moral strictness, and the formation of the Episcopal Committee on Motion Pictures, which became the long-lived National Legion of Decency. Austria banned *She Done Him Wrong,* after one showing in Vienna. In February, 1938, Mae would be sued by writer Mark Linden, who claimed he had coauthored the screenplay. The case was dismissed. Frankie Baker of New Orleans also unsuccessfully sued Mae, stating that the "Frankie and Johnny" ballad was based on events of her own life. Although it was probably true, Baker never received a penny from the popular song, and died almost broke in 1952 at the age of 75.

That Mae, at age 41, was able to become a major motion picture star, is an astounding phenomenon, rarely duplicated in American cinema history. Fannie Ward of silent screen fame aside, there was the specialty superstar Marie Dressler, who at age 57 made a screen comeback in MGM's *The Callahan and the Murphys* (1927), going on to win an Oscar for *Min and Bill* (1931), and becoming the nation's number-one box-office attraction that year, only to die of cancer in 1934. Next in line was Ruth Chatterton, who at age 35 came from the stage to make an impressive showing in Paramount's silent film *Sins of the Fathers* (1928) opposite Emil Jannings, and went on in sound films to become a prime Paramount star of romantic melodramas, before she was wooed away by Warner Brothers in 1932.

Mae's arrival at Paramount for *Night After Night* gave no real indication of what would happen. Granted, she had a sizable Broadway reputation as a successful performer and her name usually meant a guarantee of attention-getting publicity. But in Hollywood there was an abundance of celebrity performers. Then too, as written, her role in *Night After Night* could have been played by such tough-dame veterans as Wynne Gibson, Natalie Moorhead, or even the more elegant Lilyan Tashman. But what Mae did with her revamped *Night After Night* role, and more especially with her role in *She Done Him Wrong,* was to turn Hollywood screen standards topsy-turvy all by herself. Her precedent-shattering characterizations (or caricatures) gave an astounding new twist to the old concept that it was a man's world and the only way a woman could enter the enviable domain was by looks and wiles. She made her femme fatale a self-sufficient bad girl who did not sneak into the realm of masculine dominance by the back door . . . but charged in through the front entrance and made sure everyone was well aware of her arrival and knew immediately the full scope of her intentions. When she saw a man who caught her fancy, she would attack the challenge with all her reserves of energy. Giving him an exaggerated once-over, she would strut up to her victim and demand her due. There was never any ambiguity as to who was initiating the seduction, who was the weaker and who was the sucker in the combat. It was Mae's world and whatever she wanted she got.

With her statuesque figure, Mae long before had learned that she had to rely on the suggested promise of her sexuality, rather than flaunt her gams or reveal her breasts with a plunging neckline. Wisely she encased herself in long gowns and period trappings, projecting by her very strong confidence, that she possessed more potential for sexual satisfaction that anything on two legs. Her cockiness carried over the bluff reality. Almost from the start of every one of her films, plays, and nightclub engagements, it was quickly established that while Mae might be gently chiding her full-bodied figure and her rough-diamond breeding, it was not in the viewer's domain to join in the jesting, but rather to take her as seriously as possible for the full appreciation of her satire: That audiences from the 1920s onward accepted her in their own manner, did not hurt the success of her act. Rather, their amused tolerance of her vulgarity of manner and her outsize figure enhanced her audience appeal and box-office draw. She manuevered and said everything women had been feeling for generations but never dared admit, let alone demonstrate for the males in the audience, it was a rare novelty to have their own cavalier standards of masculine prerogative thrown back into their faces by such an audacious dish of unusual femininity.

Mae's appearance on the Paramount scene was more fortuitous than anyone could image. With the decline of Clara Bow's box-office magnetism in 1930, and Nancy Carroll's faltering marquee attractiveness after 1931, the studio was in rare need of a highly marketable commodity to refill its badly drained resources. When B. P. Schulberg* was tossed out of the post of creative head at Paramount in early 1932, and Emanuel Cohen* elevated in his stead, the studio had a good crop of proven players including Claudette Colbert, Gary Cooper, Marlene Dietrich, W. C. Fields, Miriam Hopkins, Carole Lombard, Paul Lukas, Herbert Marshall, Fredric March, Jack Oakie, George Raft, and Sylvia Sidney. Ruth Chatteron, Kay Francis and William Powell would be grabbed by Warner Brothers that year when their options were allowed to lapse. Nevertheless, there was no one to dynamically lead the studio out of the red, not even the hot German import Dietrich, whose features were costing an increasingly large sum and earning considerably less at the box office. Thus, when the company latched onto Mae, they had found a trendsetter, who if given her easily satisfied demands, could turn out a finished product with a minimum of problems or unexpected costs.

Mae's rise to Hollywood stardom had repercussions far beyond the confines of Paramount. Once established after *She Done Him Wrong,* all the old-fashioned ways were tossed for a loop, such as the handling of star buildups, advertising campaigns, and the presentation on screen of the new personality.

Paramount announced in the spring of 1933 that Mae's next film would be *Barnum's Million Dollar Beauty,* based on the career of Louise Montague, with a screenplay by Mae. However, in the meantime, her friend,

*See Appendix.

writer-publisher Lowell Brentano, had written a scenario *The Lady and The Lions,* derived from a casual remark Mae once made that she had always wanted to be a lion-tamer. Brentano's script appealed to Mae, who was then in New York making personal appearances. She took it back to California, and rewrote it to her screen specifications. Directed by Wesley Ruggles and completed at a cost of $225,000, *I'm No Angel* premiered at the Paramount Theatre on October 13, 1933. So popular was Mae now that in its first week there, some 180,000 people saw the feature, breaking the theatre's records. It grossed $2.85 million in domestic release, provoking *Variety* to declare her "the biggest conversation provoker, free space grabber and all-around boxoffice bet in the country. She's as hot an issue as Hitler."

I'm No Angel, produced before the production code went into effect, was the most freewheeling of all Mae's screen vehicles, and the most satisfying of the lot. As free-and-easy Tira, a midway dancer in Big Bill Barton's Wonder Show, a low-class carnival playing the Midwest circuit, she is the casual lover of pickpocket Ralf Harolde. Her motto is, "Take all you can get and give as little as possible." When she attempts to demonstrate this in her town hotel room, her intended victim remarks: "I've been places and seen things." Mae shoots back: "I've been things and seen places." Suddenly, Harolde jealously breaks into the room and slugs Mae's date. Leaving him for dead, Mae and Harolde return to the carnival. When the police arrive and arrest Harolde and her, Mae borrows money from the show's owner, Edward Arnold, to hire New York attorney Gregory Ratoff to handle her pending trial. To obtain the loan from Arnold, she agrees to star in his new big show, which will feature her taming the lions and putting her head in the mouth of one of the beasts. The act plays Madison Square Garden and is a smashing success, making Mae the toast of the town, with all the society swells courting her.

Mae recalls in her autobiography, *Goodness Had Nothing to Do With It,* how she convinced the Paramount bigwigs to allow her to attempt the dangerous stunt of entering the lions' cage alone (there were men with shotguns posted around the cage in case of mishap). She entered the cage in her outfit of white silk tights, gold braided military jacket, plumed cap, and ermine service cape. "The lions snarled. Their immense paws reached out toward me. I stepped back and cracked my whip again.

"Then the huge, glorious beasts began their act, leaping from stool to stoop, rearing rampant, climbing a ladder and jumping to the ground to follow one another in a line that circled about me as I kept cracking my whip, acting out my dream role.

"Excitement began to take hold of me. . . . I could see nothing, hear nothing, feel nothing but an overpowering sense of increasing mastery that mounted higher and higher until it gratified every atom of the obsession that had driven me."

The act is a whopping success, and Tira (Mae) moves from tent to penthouse. Bluenose Kent Taylor courts her, ignoring the rebukes of his fiancée (Gertrude Michael). Mae advises him: "I like sophisticated men to take me out."

Taylor: "I'm not really sophisticated."
Mae: "You're not really out yet, either."

Later Michael confronts Mae and demands that she stops seeing Taylor. She exclaims: "You haven't a streak of decency in you." Mae replies: "I don't show my good points to strangers." When Michael slams out of the apartment, bored Mae sashays back into her living room and orders her maid: "Beulah, peel me a grape." (This bon mot was inspired by Mae's pet African monkey Boogie, who had a proclivity for peeling grapes before eating them.)

Taylor's cousin Cary Grant is eventually persuaded to call on Mae at her apartment to politely request that she stop seeing Taylor. He leaves, conquered by her common charms, with victorious Mae mumbling to him: "You'll hear from me." As time passes, a romance develops between Mae and the unwilling Grant, and she advises him: "When I'm good, I'm very good. But, when I'm bad, I'm better."

Meanwhile, Arnold, hoping to keep Mae with his profitable show, uses jailbird Harolde to convince Grant that Mae is playing him for a sucker. Mae sues Grant for breach of promise to marry, and this leads to the classic courtroom scene. She disqualifies the assorted witnesses by conducting her own cross-examination and putting their character into question. Grant sees the light of day, and he and Mae are reunited. As she is triumphantly parading out of the courtroom, a reporter asks: "Why did you admit to knowing so many men?" Mae flips back: "It's not the men in my life, but the life in my men."

In the course of the 88-minute feature, Mae sings "They Call Me Sister Honky Tonk" (at the carnival show), "No One Loves Me Like That Dallas Man" (to her hotel room victim), "I Found a New Way to Go to Town" (to her three maids), "I Want You" (to Grant), and "I'm No Angel" (over the end titles).

When *I'm No Angel* had its Los Angeles opening at Grauman's Chinese Theatre, Mae commented: "It's rather nice to be in a place where they take your footprints instead of your fingerprints." About the obvious absence of stars at the gala: "Maybe they figure seeing this picture would come under the heading of homework." When asked to describe her role in the picture: "She's the kind of girl who climbed the ladder of success, wrong by wrong."

Richard Watts, Jr. (*New York Herald Tribune*) analyzed Mae and *I'm No Angel*: "She does go in for audience sympathy and a sentimental rather than a rowdy, happy ending, with the result that her new vehicle is pretty moderate stuff in comparison to the frank handsome roughness of her first pictures.... She is important, not as an actress, but as an amiably outspoken personage.... Any attempt, no matter how sly, to sentimentalize her a bit is certain to be dangerous."

By the end of 1933, Mae ranked eighth as a box-office attraction, and she renegotiated her Paramount contract to $300,000 per film, plus another $100,000 for her screenplays. Her father (who would become a chiropractor), brother, and sister had moved to Hollywood.

I'm No Angel proved to be the zenith of Mae's screen career. It made her the top attraction at Paramount and one of the most controversial personalities on the screen. The success of *She Done Him Wrong* and *I'm No Angel* is credited with saving Paramount from bankruptcy at a time when it was contemplating selling out its facilities to MGM and converting its 1,700 theatres into office buildings.

Shortly after the success of *I'm No Angel*, Mae posed as the Statue of Liberty for *Vanity Fair* magazine (George Jean Nathan decided "She looks more like 'the Statue of Libido' "). British writer Hugh Walpole observed: "Only Charlie Chaplin and Mae West in Hollywood dare to directly attack with their mockery the fraying morals and manners of a dreary world."

Paramount was all atwitter about the new code's reaction to future Mae vehicles, fearing it would remove all the zest from her screen personality and reduce her to the commonplace. Her next feature *Belle of the Nineties,* directed by Leo McCarey, underwent a spate of title changes which vaguely reflected the trepidations the Paramount authorities had about the censorial reaction to Mae's next picture: from *That St. Louis Woman* to *It Ain't No Sin* to *It Isn't Any Sin* to *Belle of New Orleans* to *Belle of St. Louis,* and then to the final choice.

George Raft had been signed to costar with Mae in this period comedy which was intended to revive the flavor of *Diamond Lil.* When the final script had to be revamped to appease the censors, and the male lead role reduced in scope, Raft bowed out and Roger Pryor was gamely substituted. The cleaned-up scenario (originally Mae was to have been a musical comedy star who is acquitted of her lover's murder and becomes the sensation of St. Louis) had Mae as a St. Louis entertainer, knocking the customers cold with her tableau shows. She is displayed as an American rose, a butterfly, a bat, and so forth, and then as the Statue of Liberty, with a crooner singing "My American Beauty." Mae is romantically tied to boxer Pryor, the pride of the Middle West, but when his manager frames Mae so that his prize property will concentrate on fighting again, Mae travels to New Orleans, where she is hired by John Miljan to sing in his Sensation House saloon. Miljan asks her: "You were born in St. Louis. What part?" Mae answers: "Why . . . all of me." Miljan soon discards his mistress Katherine DeMille in favor of the voluptuous Mae. She had earlier told him, "A man in the house is worth two in the street." He now extolls her virtues: "I must have your golden hair, fascinating eyes, alluring smile, your lovely arms, your form divine . . ." Mae says: "Wait a minute! Wait a minute. Is this a proposal or are you taking an inventory?" But Mae comprehends Miljan's duplicity: "That guy's no good. His mother should have thrown him out and kept the stork." Not to rely on just one beau, she accepts the streams of gifts and diamonds offered by local figure Johnny Mack Brown, her theory being: "It's better to be looked over than overlooked."

Later Miljan hires Pryor to compete in a boxing event he is staging, but first tricks him into robbing Mae of her diamonds. Mae gets her revenge during the big match. Miljan has bet heavily on Pryor to win, but Mae drugs his water bottle, thus allowing Brown to collect huge winnings on Pryor's opponent in the ring. In the finale confrontation, Pryor kills Miljan, and he and Mae are reconciled. Later, when Pryor is cleared of the murder charge, they are married.

Belle of the Nineties charged into the Paramount Theatre on September 21, 1934. It had cost far more than her previous films—estimates range at close to $1 million—because in this personal showcase, Mae insisted on such lush additions as hiring the expensive Duke Ellington and his orchestra to backstop her renditions of "Memphis Blues," "Troubled Waters," and "My Old Flame," as well as expansive costuming and an enlarged number of full sets. When first released, *Belle of the Nineties* suffered a loss of continuity from initial censorship cuts, and when distributed in various states, local morality boards demanded further snipping. Mae's reasoned response to the situation was: "I've never believed in going haywire on stage or screen. Obviously no medium of mass entertainment can be allowed to throw all restraint out the window. Strict censorship, however, has a reverse effect. It creates resentment on the part of the public. They feel that their freedom of choice is being dictated. They don't want their morals legislated by other than criminal law. The professional reformers, the organized pressure groups, the easily impressed do-gooders, can look upon the enormous obscenity that is war and do very little that is effective."

Despite the cuts, *Belle of the Nineties* had enough nifties and fine musical numbers to rack up good grosses, but there were those who bemoaned it as "...lacking in flavor, comedy richness and shrewdness of plot manipulation" *(New York Herald Tribune)*.

Unlike most Hollywood celebrities, Mae remained essentially a private person. Her usual escort when she went to sporting events or when she made one of her infrequent forays to a movie premiere—usually her own films—was James A. Timony. When one fan magazine in 1935 uncovered her alleged marriage to Frank Wallace, she denied it. Later she would even squelch persistent rumors that her sister Beverly had been her understudy when on Broadway. (Cinema historian Gene Ringgold records that a noted female impersonator once stated he had been Mae's standby during the run of one of her plays.)

Mae had tempting offers to transfer her film services to MGM, RKO, and Warner Brothers, but she remained loyal to producer William LeBaron and stayed at Paramount, where she knew everything would be as close to her desires as could be expected. It was for LeBaron's independent production unit, Major Pictures, that Mae agreed to star in *How Am I Doin'?*, which went before the cameras on December 18, 1934, with a two-month shooting schedule, and was released as *Goin' to Town* (Paramount Theatre, May 10, 1935).

As saloon entertainer Cleo Borden, Mae is the highlight of a Western town. Fred Kohler rides into town and proclaims his interest in marrying her: "With you I'm dynamite." "Yeah," says Mae, "An' I'm your match." She recklessly proposes that they toss the dice in an all or nothing bet. He wins, which means he has to marry Mae and deed all his property to her. But he is killed before the wedding and Mae finds herself the contented owner of vast oil well holdings.

She soon takes a shine to British geological engineer Paul Cavanagh who is making surveys on her ranch, but he overtly snubs her. "This is the first time I ever came in contact with a woman like you." Mae replies: "If I can help it, it won't be the last." When he leaves for Buenos Aires, she decides to follow him and impress him by becoming part of the social swim. Once there, she soon increases her financial stake by winning the big horse race, but earns the enmity of snippy social leader Marjorie Gateson. Mae is advised that if she wants to jump into the world of swells on a permanent basis, she should marry a blue blood. So she agrees to marry impoverished dandy Monroe Owsley.

The honeymoon couple set up residence in Southampton, Long Island, but Mae is disturbed to find herself stymied in her further social ambitions by Gateson and her swank social circle. Therefore, she decides to throw a big bash and show the local bigwigs that she means business. The party is a huge success, but during the evening Owsley is killed by the former gigolo lover of Gateson, who had been imported and hired to discover Mae's unsavory reputation. Once the murder is solved, Mae is free to marry Cavanagh, who has just inherited a peerage.

Goin' to Town started off as a Western, with Mae wearing breeches in some scenes, although for the remainder of the crashing-society plot she was encased in assorted evening gown-styled glad rags. Mae sang "Love Is

Love," "He's a Bad Man," "Now I'm a Lady," and the film's most distinctive number, the "My Heart at Thy Sweet Voice" from *Samson and Delilah.* (Re Delilah she says: "I have a lot of respect for that dame. There's one lady barber that made good.") The spoofing operatic number, not played entirely for laughs, proved Mae had an effective singing voice.

Another facet of *Goin' to Town* was the attempt to feminize her in a more conventional way, from her costume in the bar in which she wears a ribbon in her hair and manages to stay ladylike as she moves among the rough-and-tumble customers, to her stay in Buenos Aires, where she seems much more vulnerable than usual among the high-toned social set.

Goin' to Town was the first feature to play five weeks at Manhattan's Paramount Theatre. It was not Mae's direct attack on hypocritical social mores, or her less than spectacular musical numbers, that attracted the crowds, but the overabundance of wisecracks and double entendres which skirted by the Hays Office and hit the public full face. Nevertheless, her screen impact was beginning to wear a bit thin with the critics (as it later would with the public): "No amount of epigrammatic hypoing can offset the silly story" *(Variety),* "There are times when Miss West fairly outdoes herself as a rather vulgar retailer of indelicate wisecracks" *(New York Herald Tribune).*

Mae was at her financial peak in 1935, earning $480,833. With only one release she was eleventh on the tally of moneymaking stars, no mean feat. (She had grossed $229,840 in 1933 and $344,160 in 1934. She was considered top royalty at the studio and was the prime mecca of visiting VIPs, who did not consider a trip to Hollywood complete without an audience with Mae on the Paramount lot. Among the notables who paid their respects to her at the Marathon Street facilities were the Sultan and Sultana of Johore, Elliott Roosevelt, Lady Furness and Mrs. Reginald Vanderbilt, Gayelord Hauser, and Noel Coward. Viscount and Lady Byng invited Mae to join them at the Jubilee celebration of George V in London. Mae sent a wire of regret: "Sorry, George—too busy."

Mae returned to period settings in *Klondike Annie* (1936), derived from a play *Frisco Kate* she had been preparing as a stage vehicle a year before she went to Hollywood. About the same time, she received an unsolicited story from Marian Morgan and George B. Dowell which contained a few similarities to her own project. Mae insisted that the reluctant studio purchase the new work as well, although it had little material that would be used. Mae's reasoning to Paramount executives was: "You better learn to respect writers."

Klondike Annie premiered at the Paramount Theatre on March 11, 1936, using the advertising catchphrase: "She Made the Frozen North . . . Red Hot!" A quite plump Mae was Frisco Doll, the pearl of lotus flower possessed by Oriental Harold Huber. She describes her plight in the café song "(I'm an) Occidental Woman (In an Oriental Mood for Love)." When Huber becomes overbearingly jealous, Mae and he scrape, and she accidentally kills him. She slips aboard a ship bound for the Klondike; it is captained by Victor McLaglen, who is soon besmitten with her and says: "I can always tell a lady when I see one." "Yeah?" replies Mae. "What do you tell 'em?" As they travel northward, he become more impressed and polite with Mae. He says: "If there's anything you want, just yell for it." She queries: "Do you have to yell for it?" When another passenger, Helen Jerome Eddy, a Salvation Army missionary, dies, Mae adopts her identity as a disguise to avoid the police. Arriving in the Klondike, she speedily sets about putting the Ten Commandments on a paying basis, by making the mission a thriving institution once again.

Mae the sermonizer has her own special brand of preachment. She has been deeply moved by the letter missionary lady Eddy sent on from Vancouver. After singing a version of "Little Bar Butterfly" to the agog congregation, she explains her mission: "You people have been on the wrong track an' I'm going to steer you right. You'll never get anywhere, 'cause you don't know how to wrassle the Devil. Tying a knot in his tail won't throw him on his back. Ya got to grab him by the horns. Ya got to know him, know his tricks. I know him. And how! I know him."

It is not long before Mae's strong-arm methods have cleared up the mission's $876 debt, set the dance hall girls into cooperating with the mission on Sunday nights, and made the townfolk fervent attendees at the weekly meetings. After singing popularized hymms and offering her sermon, Mae has the collection plates passed among the people, her ushers all men with only one arm.

Despite her religious calling, Mae still finds men attractive, and invites handsome Mountie Phillip Reed to "park his dog sled." By the wrap-up, she has done her assorted good deeds, and is heading back to the States aboard McLaglen's ship, prepared to make amends for her wrongs. She now has a man she really wants. ("You ain't exactly an oil painting; but you fascinate me.") Mae's brief career as a soul-saver has taught her: "Anytime you take religion for a joke the laugh's on you."

Despite the rather gentle nature of Mae's spoof, directed by Raoul Walsh, many—William Randolph Hearst and his newspaper chain in particular—took offense at Mae portraying a religious person, and demanded prompt congressional action. None was forthcoming. As had been expected, censorship problems with *Klondike Annie* required Mae and Paramount to tame down some of the sequences, to the detriment of the film's original spicier intent. The critics were no longer partial to Mae's now familiar brand of humor: "There is no place anywhere for the stupid substitute that Miss West is now trying to pass as comedy *(New York Times),* "Vulgar without being funny and rowdy without being gay" *(New York Herald Tribune).* Others noted that her songs lacked the bite of those in her previous movies. With the exception of Sam Coslow's "My Medicine Man," they were written by Gene Austin, who accompanied Mae at the organ for several selections, including such tunes as "Cheer Up, Little Sister" and "It's Better to Give Than to Receive."

During Ernst Lubitsch's* regime as production head of Paramount from late 1934 to early 1936, he and Mae never saw eye to eye. He publicly admitted: "Mae West has proved beyond a doubt that she is one of the greatest international stars in Hollywood. But she is not a director's star. Her personality is quite powerful enough to fill out any picture, and there is no room left for directorial technique. Her films are vehicles built around her, and I, personally, cannot make a good picture unless I am dealing with someone more pliable." On a more personal level, Lubitsch snidely advised Mae: "In every story there must be parts for two players, like *Romeo and Juliet."* The indignant star replied: "That was Shakespeare's technique, but it ain't mine." Thus for Mae: "Paramount didn't seem like home to me any longer."

Mae remained on the Paramount lot because former production head

*See Appendix.

and now independent producer Emanuel Cohen had purchased the Gladys George stage success *Personal Appearance.* With some rewriting Mae thought it might do nicely for her next picture. (MGM had wanted the property for Jean Harlow, and Gladys George had been signed on at Paramount as a result of her Broadway performance in the show.)

Retitled *Go West, Young Man,* it opened at the Paramount Theatre on November 18, 1936. Temperamental movie star Mavis Arden (Mae) of Superfine Pictures is making a lengthy personal appearance tour for her new film, *Drifting Lady.* Since her movie contract bars marriage for five years, and because her policy has always been "a thrill a day keeps the chill away," studio publicity director Warren William is along to keep her romantically disentangled. After a stopover in Washington, D.C., where she reencounters her old beau Lyle Talbot, a congressional candidate, Mae's car breaks down in the Pennsylvania countryside. She is forced to stay at Alice Brady's boarding house while automobile repairs are made. She is greatly admired by members of the household, although aunt Elizabeth Patterson remarks: "In my time, women with hair like that didn't come out in the light." Mae takes a shine to Randolph Scott ("I can't tell ya the number of men I've helped to realize themselves") and soon plans to take him back to Hollywood with her, ostensibly to sponsor his new sound-recording device. But William persuades Mae not to separate him from his rural sweetheart, Margaret Perry. At this juncture, Talbot catches up with the group, and has William arrested for allegedly kidnapping Mae. William confesses he loves Mae, and she secures his release.

With the aid of softly focused camera work, Mae, in contemporary garb, came across in a much less harsh manner, particularly in her haystack seduction scenes with Scott. Mae sang "On a Typical Tropical Night," "I Was Saying to the Moon," and "Go West, Young Man," but her snappiest moments were in the satirical thank you speech to the Washington, D.C., movie audience who have just seen a showing of *Drifting Lady.* Sweeping out to stage-center with all the majesty of Gloria Swanson, she grandly informs them that she is "just a simple country girl doomed to live in an Eye-talian villa" and explains the "dullness and simplicity of my life there." As she extravagantly throws kisses to her fans, she bids the crowd, "Tell all of your friends I said good night." It was as nice a take-off on Swanson as one could wish. Later, Mae's scenario provides stagestruck maid Isabel Jewell with an audition scene a la Marlene Dietrich. Mae was scoring all her points against the love goddesses of the day. Mae's other sparkling sequence is an impromptu interview with the press, who catch up with her at a rendezvous with Talbot. The reporters inquire: "Have you any particular platform." She quips: "The one I act on." She then launches into a doubletalking diatribe demanding the government endow matrimony on the same basis as hospitals.

The critics all too fondly remembered Gladys George's stage performance, and did not take kindly to the cleaned-up *Go West, Young Man.* "[S]he never makes the central character sufficiently credible to be laughed at" *(New York Herald Tribune).* "The mannerisms are beginning to be tedious" *(New York Post).* Despite the presence of her famed lip-parting sneer, her luxurious moans and groans, her eye rolling and hip waving, it was now just a rehash of before. Having bland Randolph Scott as her potential love interest gave no boost of virility to the proceedings.

Mae went back to club work for a time, appearing successfully in New York, Miami, and Chicago. When she returned to Paramount in late 1937, she hoped to convince Emanuel Cohen to film a story about Catherine the Great. But Cohen and Paramount all too well remembered the debacle of Dietrich's *The Scarlet Empress,* and quickly tallying the probably extravagant costs against the possible profit, vetoed the suggestion. Morever, Cohen had already invested a great deal in the preproduction costs of a new Gay Nineties musical, particularly an elaborate set of Rector's Restaurant in turn-of-the-century New York. Neither Cohen nor Mae—once she heard it —were impressed by the available script, and after listening to Sam Coslow play the film's songs for her, she dictated a new story line, which emerged as *Every Day's a Holiday* (1938).

In this film Mae is Peaches O'Day, a high-pressure confidence girl who sells the Brooklyn Bridge to any willing sucker. Says one admirer: "You've broken every law but the law of gravity." Mae replies: "That's an idea. I'll go to work on it." Her motto is "Keep a diary and someday it'll keep you," and with her circle of suitors, it soons proves to pay off in spades. She traps blustery Manhattan reform leader Charles Winninger for a shakedown, but he eludes her clutches. Under threat of arrest, she hastily departs for Boston by boat. When she returns, it is as the black-wigged Mademoiselle Fifi, a French music hall singer. New York chief of detectives Edmund Lowe eventually discovers her alias, but by then, he and Mae are in love. She assists him in battling corrupt politician Lloyd Nolan ("He's so crooked he uses a corkscrew for a ruler") in the mayoral election, and Lowe wins.

This time around, Mae was virtually the only doll in the cast, which included a fine roster of comedians, such as acerbic butler Charles Butterworth and the addled play producer Walter Catlett.

As background for some of Mae's songs ("Flutter By, Little Butterfly," "Every Day's a Holiday," "Along the Broadway Trail," "Jubilee," and "Mademoiselle Fifi") there was Louis Armstrong and his band. Mae had learned, early on, that a fine musical accompaniment would showcase her singing style to good advantage, and was adamant in forcing the studio to hire top-notch bands, such as Count Basie, and, in this case, the high priced group of Louis Armstrong.

With the deletion of two lines, "I wouldn't lift my veil for that guy" and "I wouldn't let him touch me with a ten-foot pole," the Hays Office issued *Every Day's a Holiday* an "A" certificate, which permitted children to attend Mae's film for the first time.

Just before the Hollywood preview (December 18, 1937) of *Every Day's a Holiday,* Mae made her highly-touted radio "debut" on the Edgar Bergen-Charlie McCarthy Sunday night show on NBC. Actually Mae had first been heard on radio prior to the release of *She Done Him Wrong,* guesting on Rudy Vallee's show along with Fred Astaire, Claude Rains, and Weber and Fields, for which she had been paid $1,050. Mae was getting all sorts of radio offers from 1933 onward, ranging from $6,000 to $7,000 per broadcast, but she rejected them all. On this particular Bergen-McCarthy show, she and Don Ameche appeared in a "Garden Of Eden" skit written by Arch Oboler. The bit of dialogue which caused national indignation was Mae's interpretive reading of "Would you, honey, like to try this apple sometime?" Church groups united in outraged condemnation of Mae, screaming about the audacity of her gall to defile the Lord's Day as well, and threatening to boycott any furthur radio program on which Mae might appear. The networks caved in to such threats, and Mae became persona non grata on the medium for 12 years! For a long time it was forbidden for anyone to even mention her name on the airwaves.

Variety predicted that December (1937): "Miss West's public relations are somewhat entangled by criticisms of a national broadcast. Such protests are likely to have a commercial influence." *Every Day's a Holiday* met with public indifference when it had its delayed release (Paramount Theatre, January 26, 1938), and the Benny Goodman stage show received better reviews than the film, the latter termed "witless, humorless, tiresome." Others razzed the feature for being "clean and dull . . . she is far from persuasive as a pickpocket and con woman turned square." The feature made money, but the lush profits of her earlier efforts were obviously a thing of the past. Mae was among those branded as box-office poison by Harry Brandt and a group of independent theatre owners in a trade-paper advertisement in 1938, and this onerous label frightened off potential producers of Mae vehicles.

Ironically, Mae in person was still a tremendous draw. To spark the West Coast opening of *Every Day's a Holiday,* Mae put together a 46-minute stage act which included a male sextet in tails, and it proved quite popular. When the revue reached New York in April, 1938, it appeared at the Loew's State Theatre where Mae received $5,000 a week plus a percentage for her performances.

Mae left Paramount at just about the same time Marlene Dietrich departed, and like Dietrich she considered the possibility of a stage return to reconsolidate her waning popularity. She thought of doing a musical *Up the Ladder,* based on a French comedy she was revamping, but she abandoned this, as she would thoughts of a musical version of *Lysistrata.* She continued playing the club and stage-show circuit with her act, and coauthored a play, *Clean Beds,* in which she did not appear. The weak comedy never made it to Broadway.

Meanwhile, Mae retained hopes of producing a film about Catherine the Great, and to this end she incorporated Mae West Empire Pictures Corp., with San Francisco financier Louis Lurie as a partner. But with the advent of World War II, the European film distribution market dwindled and potential backers were dubious of the practicality of investing in Mae's epic spoof, which she insisted should be filmed in expensive technicolor. Plans for her to costar with Clark Gable in *New Orleans* at MGM came to naught. B. G. DeSylva* had picked *Gentleman's Choice* as a screen vehicle for Mae, but part of the deal required Mae to tour with a stage version first. She declined and Ethel Merman was substituted in the revamped film, which was retitled *DuBarry Was a Lady.*

In the late summer of 1939, Mae followed Marlene Dietrich's example and signed with Universal. She was to costar with W. C. Fields in a comedy Western. Each would receive a salary plus a percentage of the profits. Mae would not admit it then or now, but the Universal project was a distinct comedown for the former movie queen.

Universal had concocted an original screenplay *The Jaywalkers,* which left both Mae and Fields unmoved, so she whipped up her own story, *The Lady and the Bandit,* and it won the approval of the bulbous-nosed comedian. Mae's contract provided that Fields had to abstain from drinking on the set and during shooting, and save for one day of imbibing, he obliged. The completed feature, following Mae's story line, evolved as *My Little Chickadee* and premiered at the Roxy Theatre on March 15, 1940. Mae received top-performer billing, but was disturbed to note that Fields was

*See Appendix.

listed as coauthor, for having contributed his impromptu routine to the story.

As Flower Belle Lee, the shady beauty of a small Western town of the 1880s, Mae is hauled into court for having consorted with a masked bandit, about which she later recalled: "I was in a tight spot but managed to wriggle out of it." The judge inquires: "Are you trying to show contempt for the court? Mae answers: "No, I'm doing my best to hide it." She is forced to leave town, and on the train she meets Fields, a snake oil salesman, who politely inquires: "I wonder what kind of woman you are?" Mae: "Sorry, I can't give out samples." Thinking Fields well-to-do, she agrees to a hasty marriage which will provide her with needed respectability. Their marriage ceremony is as fraudulent as Fields's satchelful of greenbacks, which was a prime ingredient in inducing Mae to wed him in the first place. Once in Greasewood City, Mae successfully avoids consummating the marriage while wavering between her ardent suitors, the masked bandit Joseph Calleia and newspaper editor Dick Foran. Later, she graciously saves Fields, duped into becoming the town's sheriff, from being lynched as the supposed bandit. At the finale, each exits parodying the other's trademark catchphrase. He tells her: "Come on up and see me some time." She thanks him: "My little chickadee."

Mae sang "Willie of the Valley" in this film, and has her best moment in the schoolroom, where as a substitute teacher she lectures her agog pupils on the art of mathematics: "I learned early that two and two are four, and five will get you ten if you know how to work it." Having reduced to a slimmer 120 pounds, Mae looked more shapely than previously, but her age (48) was definitely showing to disadvantage.

Although *My Little Chickadee* became a minor screen classic, it is not Mae at her best. Under A. Edward Sutherland's indulgent direction the Western burlesque smacks too much of tackiness, a flimsy plot, poor production values, and a generally unnoteworthy supporting cast. As the *London Times* admonished: "[It] moves in a series of fits and starts. . . . [it] obstinately refuses to gather momentum." The *New York Times* said: "It's one thing to burlesque sex and quite another to be burlesqued by it." That Mae and Fields had only a few scenes together bothered quite a number of patrons, who expected a joyous session of interaction between the two iconoclasts.

Despite the general success of *My Little Chickadee*, Mae was unhappy about the film and particularly disliked her experience working with Fields. To this day when asked if "she misses Fields" she adamantly replies: "No!" Universal offered Mae a three-picture contract, but she did not care for the projects they had in mind: *Seven Sinners* or *Sin Town* (Marlene Dietrich did the first, and Constance Bennett made the latter). Nothing came of an inspiration to team her with John Barrymore in a tale by Myron Fagan about a woman private detective who encounters a former Romeo, Warner Brothers talked of remaking *The Great Divide* and Columbia considered having Mae produce her own films, if she provided 75 percent of the financing.

Through the years, Mae had been having her problems with onetime husband Frank Wallace, who had married Rae Blakely in 1916 and divorced her in 1935. At one time he did a song and dance act, billing himself as Mae West's husband. In 1937 he made demands on Mae for an accounting of his half of her $3-million-plus inventory under the California joint property law, claiming his second marriage was invalid. Then, in August, 1940, he filed a $105,000 damage suit, charging that manager James A. Timony and Mae had lived together and that they both had threatened to ruin Wallace's show business career if he ever revealed that he had been married to Mae. This suit was dismissed. In September, 1941, he filed another suit in San Bernardino, California, accusing Mae of adultery with assorted undesirables such as Bugsie Siegel, and requesting $1,000 monthly separation payments. Mae replied with a cross-claim asking for a divorce. She was granted her interlocutory decree in July, 1942.

In 1942 the British RAF tagged their newly structured life jackets "Mae Wests." Much pleased, Mae remarked, "I've been in Who's Who and I know what's what, but it's the first time I ever made the dictionary."

In 1943, former actor and now director Gregory Ratoff induced Mae to star in a film version of the stage musical *Tropicana* at Columbia. The revamped script proved so weak that Mae wanted to renege, but Ratoff begged her to remain. She rewrote some of her scenes. *The Heat's On* opened at Loew's State Theatre on November 25, 1943, and was a turkey. As Mae later admitted: "That was one picture I should never have made. It was the biggest mistake of my film career and I prefer to forget it."

As Fay Lawrence, Mae is the tempestuous star of producer William Gaxton's forthcoming musical *Indiscretion*, in which her big number is "Stranger in Town," sung to a chorus of attentive males. When the show folds, Mae signs with Gaxton's rival Alan Dinehart for the lead in a new revue, *Tropicana*, Gaxton obtains financial backing from Victor Moore to acquire *Tropicana* so he can manage Mae again. Moore has agreed, planning to force Gaxton to hire his niece Mary Roche for a part in the show, ignoring the threats of his morality minded sister Almira Sessions that she will close down the whole shebang with her awesome League of Purity. After Gaxton acquires the revue, Mae threatens to walk out, then changes her mind. Hailed as a big success, the show is highlighted by her finale number, "Hello Mi Amigo."

The Heat's On was a minor mishmash lightened by the guest star performances of Xavier Cugat and his orchestra, vocalist Linda Romany, and pianist Hazel Scott. The occasional intrusion of the plot seemed a poor afterthought. Mae's only glowing screen moment in this film was her courtship scene with Moore, who arrives at her suite decked out in his new toupee. When it slips down over his eyes, Mae delicately remarks: "Ohh. Don't look now, honey, Your hair's skiddin'." Many of her other scenes were excised, telescoped, and botched. Obviously Columbia studio mogul Harry Cohn couldn't have cared much about the project or the well-being of Mae as star. The *New York Herald Tribune* decided: "The Mae West manner which was so popular only a few years ago seems as outdated as the style of the costumes she wears."

From this point onward in her career, Mae embarked, knowingly or otherwise, on an extended program of reconsolidating her fame and adding longevity to her legend. She could not outdo her earlier movie and stage successes merely prove to new audiences what talents she had to offer. At age 51, preservation of her image was of chief importance to Mae, whose ego demanded that she remain firmly and fully in the limelight. She lived at the Ravenswood Apartments (one of the first luxury apartment buildings on North Rossmore, near Beverly Hills) and wisely invested in real estate with highly remunerative results.

Mae was only too happy to accept J. J. Shubert's offer that Mike Todd produce and stage her *Catherine Was Great* as a lavish theatrical vehicle with a prologue and 11 scenes. It debuted on August 2, 1944, at the Shubert

Theatre to critical ennui and audience enthusiasm. Customers paid top musical-comedy show prices for a production that had only one song: Mae, outfitted in a black wig and peasant costume doing "Strong, Solid and Sensational." The lengthy show was filled with typical Westian dialogue—"Come up to the royal suite later tonight—and we'll talk Turkey"—and it concluded with her famous curtain speech: "I'm glad you like my Catherine. I like her too. She ruled thirty million people and had three thousand lovers. I do the best I can in two hours."

After 191 performances of *Catherine Was Great* and a subsequent road tour, Mae was back in Hollywood in late 1945, rehearsing a new play, *Come On Up—Ring Twice*, a bedroom farce which she adapted to her style. She was an FBI agent posing as a nightclub thrush involved with Nazis. During her stay in Washington, D. C., an accommodating French cook floats several balloons out her hotel window, inviting the recipients to come on up and keep the incommunicado Mae occupied. Mae toured the country with the comedy, but was considered too lightweight for Broadway. *Variety* called it: "Claptrap farce, overladen with cheap cracks and vulgar asides, and presented in honky-tonky fashion."

Mae took *Diamond Lil* to England in late 1947. After playing the provinces, it opened at London's Prince of Wales Theatre (January 24, 1948). Audience demand was so huge that Mae did two performances a night of *Diamond Lil* for eight months. Back in the United States, she toured again with the show before making a return bow on Broadway (Coronet Theatre, February 12, 1949) with Steve Cochran and Richard Coogan as her leading men. It met with nostalgic popular approval, although some critics now snickered: "Mae West, the most gifted female impersonator since Julian Eltinge" (*New York Daily News*). Mae played *Diamond Lil* throughout America over the next four years, making further forays on Broadway with this production.

On January 5, 1949, Mae gave her first American radio performance in 12 years on Perry Como's "Chesterfield Supper Club." In October, 1950, she was being touted for a disc jockey spot on WOR radio, New York. The job never materialized, for station censors were concerned about the potential scope of the impromptu remarks she might voice.

In 1952 Mae toured again with *Come On Up*, and in 1952 she announced she would make her television debut in a filmed half-hour video series, "Great Romances of History," playing such characters as Cleopatra, Priscilla Mullen, and Camille. William LeBaron was to be coproducer, with Paul Sloane handling the adaptions. Unfortunately, it never came about. Instead, Mae made her Las Vegas debut in July, 1954, at the Sahara Hotel. Her act was staged by choreographer Charles O'Curran, former husband of Betty Hutton. Mae's arrival was no less sensational than Marlene Dietrich's debut at the gambling capital the year before. Although Dietrich revealed a great range of untapped audience appeal, Mae was just doing what she always did fine and dandy. To her chorus of eight loin-clothed musclemen, Mae sang "I Like to Do All Day What I Do All Night," performed a repertory of songs from her films, and sashayed through a self-mocking skit about her private life. *Time* magazine said: "Mae's troupe proved invigorating even for jaded Las Vegas. . . .Never breathless except when stirred by her own emotions."

When columnist Hedda Hopper asked the 60-year-old star how she kept so vital, Mae replied: "I'm the baby-doll type. I don't do much—but exercise. Walk five miles every day. . .Some reporter libeled me; said I walked with two dogs. I walk with men, dearie. . . .Sometimes when I'm not working. I put on eight pounds, but I take it off with diet—eat nothing but steaks. But my public never liked me too thin."

Mae then took her new club act on the road, breaking all records when she played New York's Latin Quarter in October, 1954, with film players Anthony Dexter and Louise Beavers as part of her act. She told reporters who wanted the secret of her spectacular stage appearance (in a form-fitting black net gown with sequins): "Good to the last drop? It's not the men you see me out with—it's the men you don't see me out with." Mae received $12,500 a week from the Latin Quarter, which included payment for her staff. She toured for two more years, playing the Latin Quarter again in April, 1956. During the 1956 tour, she had a well-touted rhubarb with Jayne Mansfield, both fighting over Mickey Hargitay then part of Mae's act.

Mae played the summer circuit again in 1956 with *Come on Up—Ring Twice*. Audiences were still intrigued, and chuckled just as loud at such cracks as "A man in the house is worth two on the street." Mae was now an institution to be revered, and everyone was happy enough to have the chance of seeing this living legend in person.

In 1957 Mae was one of the many celebrities who sued *Confidential* magazine for libel. The publication's headlined story had read: "Mae West's Open Door Policy" and claimed that in the mid–1930s, former-boxer Chalky Wright, a Mexican black, had been more than a chauffeur in her household. Mae replied: "My, my. Those charges are certainly ridiculous."

Deciding it was time both to make her television debut and to liven up the annual Academy Award telecast, Mae appeared on the March 26, 1958, edition (NBC) singing "Baby, It's Cold Outside" to Rock Hudson. She was dressed in a bespangled black gown with a white fur hood, and her sizzling rendition was a literal show-stopper. Mae next turned up on the "Dean Martin Show" (May 3, 1959, ABC), dueting with Martin and joking with guest Bob Hope. Harriet Van Horne (*New York World Telegram*) reported: "To the rising generation, the sight of Mae West, advancing into the camera 'mid a thicket of red plumes and gold lace, must have been fairly astonishing."

Mae had taped a segment of "Person to Person" (October 16, 1959, CBS) with Charles Collingwood, but at the last moment, the network canceled the interview. Mae shrugged: "I don't know what it could be. . . .It was nothing but good clean fun." She lampooned this bit of television censure when she guested on the "Red Skelton Show" (March 1, 1960, CBS). About working with this comedian, she explained: "Red is a slapstick comedian and I have to work a little rougher than I like to in that kind of situation. I don't like to exaggerate my type. I like to keep a regalness, a little insinuation."

It was not until March 22, 1964, that Mae again appeared on television, and this time was on NBC's "Mr. Ed (The Talking Horse)", of all shows. She enjoyed the outing as much as viewers did and she returned the following season to do the segment "Mae Goes West," playing a saloon-keeper. During the summer of 1967, Mae, wearing a miniskirt, filmed an expensive color video test, preparatory for a"Hollywood Palace" (ABC) guesting, but her material was considered too far out for this family-type variety program. In 1969 Mae reportedly prepared a television special, "A Night with Mae West," produced by Robert Wise and with Cary Grant as guest star. If actually taped, it has never been publicly telecast. Plans in mid–1970 for Mae to make a Singer Company video special were suddenly scrubbed when the sponsor concluded that Mae was not the proper image for its sewing machine products.

Meanwhile, on September 28, 1959, Mae's autobiography, *Goodness Had Nothing to Do with It*, was published. It was dedicated to her mother. She had written 550 pages of text, but cut it in half: "Because if you took 550 pages to bed you'd have to wrestle it instead of reading it. They did cut an awful lot of men out. . . .Sometimes it seems I've known so many men the FBI ought to come to me first to compare fingerprints." The well-documented volume received favorable reviews. Mae updated it in 1970 to include her *Myra Breckinridge* experiences.

In 1961, Mae's official fan club, begun in 1945 with 75 people, had more than 3,000 members. About this time, Mae made public the fact that a recent medical examination had revealed her to have a double thyroid, which, she claimed, was responsible for her lifelong pursuit of men. In an assortment of court suits and appeals, she contested the right of buxom blonde singer Marie Lind in San Francisco to use the professional name of Diamond Lil. Mae lost a 1960 decision but would win a later suit in 1964.

After more successful nightclub appearances, Mae took a new play, *Sextet*, on the road in 1961. Mae adapted Frances Hope's sex romp to her own specifications. It dealt with a London-based celebrity about to embark on her sixth stab at marriage. The comedy played Chicago, Detroit, Warren and Columbus, Ohio, and Miami, but Mae decided: "I don't want to spend the time and energy needed to bring it to Broadway." Among her male leads on the tour were Jack LaRue and Alan Marshal, the latter dying of a heart attack on the road.

Mae had produced some single recordings over the years, which had been combined into a Decca souvenir album, and in 1955 she recorded an LP of songs utilized in her club act; this LP would be reissued in 1970 as *The Fabulous Mae West*. In 1963, for Plaza Records, she cut the single "Am I Too Young," a dialogue between Mae and a teenager, with Mae informing the 18-year-old: "If we can make it across the state line without getting arrested, it's a deal." The reverse side contained "He's Bad, But He's Good For Me." The single "Peel Me a Grape" appeared later, and in 1966, the unstoppable Mae made two LP albums for Tower Records. *Way Out West* contained, among other numbers, Bob Dylan's "If You Gotta Go" and the Beatles' "Day Tripper." Mae learned to play the electric guitar to accompany herself on this album. About the LP's contemporary songs, Mae reasoned: "The kids have the right idea. They grew up hearing the same old thing—no wonder they want something new." In the LP *Wild Christmas* Mae gave her inimitable interpretation of assorted Christmas standards, as well as adding a few new holiday numbers like "Santa Baby" in which she requests the gift-giver to "put a sable under the tree for me." Mae recorded *The Naked Ape* in 1969, but this LP has yet to be released. She was slated to record Mother Goose stories for Fox Records in 1970, but the project was abandoned.

Over the years, there have been numerous announcements of film projects to star Mae in her screen return. There was *Goodness, Me!* in the early 1950s, a comedy drama to be produced in London by J. Arthur Rank. When Marlene Dietrich abandoned Columbia's *Pal Joey* project in the mid–1950s, Mae was considered, but she declined and Rita Hayworth assumed the role, RKO wanted her for *The First Traveling Saleslady* (1956). There was talk of her doing a new movie about the Klondike in 1958. She refused the role of a dance-hall hostess in *Four for Texas* (1963), decided not to play Elvis Presley's mother in *Roustabout* (1964), and balked at *The Art of Love* (1965), because producer Ross Hunter would not permit her to rewrite and expand her role. Ethel Merman was substituted for her in that picture. Frederico Fellini paged Mae for *Guiletta* (1965), and in 1968 claimed that she, Michael J. Pollard, Danny Kaye, Anna Magnani, Groucho Marx, and Jimmy Durante would all appear in *Satryicon* (1970), but none of these stars did. Mae had refused his offer, claiming the trip to Rome might be too much for her. In October, 1968, it was announced Mae would appear in a film adaptation of *Sextet* for Warner Brothers-7 Arts, with a possible cast of Cary Grant, Rock Hudson, David Niven, and Sheldon Leonard. With a changeover of studio regimes, the film was dropped from the production lineup, to be later reactivated and then dropped again in 1970.

Finally, in August, 1969, Mae was signed at $350,000 for the film version of Gore Vidal's *Myra Breckinridge*, with billing above Raquel Welch who was portraying the title role. Amidst the squabbles between producer Robert Fryer and director Michael Sarne, Mae coolly announced, "The script didn't grab me." She proceeded to rewrite her dialogue as Leticia Van Allen, Hollywood's most lascivious talent agent (men clients only). Mae insisted: "It's a return, not a comeback. I've never really been away, just busy." About her dialogue: "I'll supply the humor. I just hope it doesn't bring on the censors like before. But if this doesn't stir them up, I don't know what will." After rewriting her part, Mae admitted the new morality's effect on her choice of dialogue: "I already knew all the words, but this was the first time I could use them. . . .Still, I don't use any four-letter words. I don't think I need them." She told another interviewer: "Oh, I'm never dirty, dear. I'm interestin' without bein' vulgar. I have—*taste*. I *kid* sex. I was born with sophistication and sex appeal, but I'm never vulgar. Maybe it's breedin'— I come from a good family, descended from Alfred the Great. In the script, I have a line, 'I've got the judge by the . . . .' but I never say the word, just make the motions [cupping her hands] . . .I don't like obscenity and I don't have to do it at any time. They thought I might be willing for *Myra*, because it's in vogue now, but I won't. I just—suggest."

Reportedly there were clashes between Mae and Welch during production of *Myra Breckinridge* ("That other woman" Mae called her). Mae obliquely admitted: "Today, you have sex symbols without sex personalities." Mae did admit that when Raquel attempted to invade her priority of color schemes for costuming, Mae and her pal, designer Reggie Allen, outfoxed the newcomer on more than one occasion.

After a tremendous buildup, with most of the attention centered on Mae's cinema return after 27 years, *Myra Breckinridge*, an X-rated film, premiered at the Criterion Theatre on June 24, 1970. The $3-million-plus production met with unanimous pans from the critics, and the few moments of audience delight mostly were culled from Mae's scenes. The production had gone way over budget, requiring Fox to shut down the picture and slap together a hasty ending. To bridge the episodic story line, a large dose of clips from old Fox features (and one Universal Pictures sequence of Marlene Dietrich) were spliced into the film to add satirical parallels. These nostalgic moments were the highlight of the feature. Mae's screen role suffered most from the restructured final script, which reduced her part to a short cameo, and deleted some of her more outrageous moment. She makes her entrance when the picture is already several reels into the story, sashaying into her Beverly Hills talent agency, and advising the lineup of male applicants: "Okay boys, take out your resumes." Later on, when an overenthusiastic Italian actor arrives with a letter of introduction from Fellini and proceeds to smother Mae with polite kisses from fingertip to shoulder, she inquires: "Did Fellini send you to meet me or eat me?"

Mae made a special trip to Manhattan, her first in more than a decade, to meet the press and to greet her fans at the opening. She proved to be the most sought-after celebrity New York had welcomed in many a year. Accompanied by Paul Novak, an alumnus of her muscleman chorus line of the 1950s, she met with reporters at her hotel suite, and on the night of June 23, 1970, attended the preopening premiere of *Myra Breckinridge* at the Criterion Theatre. Strategically arriving after the miffed Raquel Welch, Mae was met by a mob of fans lining the width of Broadway. After waving to her fans inside the theatre, she sat through part of the film, and then went to the special party arranged for her after the screening. So intense was the division between the Mae and Welch camps, that two separate receptions had to be held that evening.

Mae's public was glad to see her back on the technicolor screen, but the critics were less enthusiastic. She was cited as "everybody's favorite raunchy old lady," the "septuagenarian sensualist," and the "mummified robot." Howard Thompson of the *New York Times* reported: "[she] has finally been done wrong by getting short shrift. . . .she sweeps in regally, sumptuously gowned and coiffed, and intoning a few amusing lines. Most of them you'll never hear on the late show—or the early one, for that matter." Mae originally had two singing production numbers in the film, but in the release version they received short shrift. "You Gotta Taste All the Fruit" and "Hard to Handle" would be released by Fox Records as a single 45 RPM. Some of Mae's free-flowing dialogue was still considered too offensive for today's filmgoing audiences, thus a few of her filmed sequences were eliminated. In one planned-for scene, she visits a hospital. A Vietnam veteran complains that his artificial arm and leg both screw off, to which Mae replies: "Well, come up and see me sometime and I'll show ya how to *screw* your *heads* off." In the much publicized but deleted orgy interlude, Mae arrives at the situs to find a Bacchanalian party in progress. Her voiced reaction is: "Ummm, guess this is what they mean by lettin' it all hang out."

To cap her stay in New York, the studio arranged for a grand press reception on June 24, 1970, in the Royal Box Room of the Americana Hotel. With a pink-lit throne as a backdrop, Mae, wearing hot pink slacks, loose fitting top, and a sweater on her shoulders, hip-wiggled onto the platform, and shot out answers to the round of questions fired at her. She stated that she would never have played the title role, and that after seeing the film, she wondered how"any actress with any kind of a following could have." Mae was satisfied with her part in the film, "But I wish there were more of it," she said. On Women's Lib: "I'm all for it." On Gay Lib: "It looks like the gay boys are takin' over." On celebrity-follower Rex Reed's screen debut as Myron Breckinridge: "No comment." Mae was eager to announce that she was now negotiating for George Cukor to direct her in a color remake of *Diamond Lil* and that she would also make *Sextet*, as well as do a television special. As a final thought to the admiring throng, she stated that no matter what foreigners can do with sex movies in Europe, "we can make them dirtier here."

Myra Breckinridge opened to initial good grosses throughout the country but quickly died at the box office once curiosity seekers had spread the word about its bomb status. It was generally conceded that without Mae's appearance the feature would have been more of a total commercial disaster.

During the rest of 1970, there were on-again-off-again reports about

Mae's pending film projects, but by 1971 it seemed likely that the interest of all bidders had been conclusively dampened by the poor showing of *Myra Breckinridge*.

Mae returned to her quiet life in California, alternating between her Hollywood apartment and her 22-room beach house in Santa Monica. Mae's brother died in 1967 and her sister Beverly has lived the past years at Mae's ranch in the San Fernando Valley. Mae still lives alone, and her private life remains as much of a mystery as always. She rarely reads, and only on occasion goes out to dine or to see a movie, usually accompanied by her good friends George Cukor or Robert Wise. Much of her daily life is concerned with the "care and feeding of Mae West." She once stated: "My secret is positive thinking and no drinking." She continually exercises, and is occasionally seen taking a stroll along the beach, accompanied by her companion Paul Novak.

Mae has very definite views about the newest of the enduring mediums, television. "TV should be censored! You can't have those awful new sex movies on TV. It's repulsive. You can get sick to your stomach watching them. Sex has to have the greatest love behind it to mean anything. Today, sex is like nothing! It has no more value—it's a bunch of animals out there!" About the potential sex appeal of women on television today, Mae stated: "If they are sexy, they are not allowed to show it. That is assuming, of course, that they had it and could show it. Personally, I think it's something they just haven't got."

Mae is the first to admit that she is her own greatest fan in watching her old movies on television: "Honey, every one of my pictures was a gem. . . .There'll never be another star like me."

Whatever the topic of conversation with Mae, whether her preoccupations with spiritualism and healthy living, or whatever, she is bound to say: "I hold records all over the world. That's my ego, breaking records." And, to date, she has incontestibly proven that statement, spurred on because: "I've always lived for myself. I've had nothing else to think of about but myself. . . .All my life I've worried only about myself. Some people live for other people and a lotta women put men up there. I've gotta be up there."

NIGHT AFTER NIGHT (PAR, 1932) 70 M.

Director, Archie Mayo; based on the novel *Single Night* by Louis Bromfield; screenplay, Vincent Laurence; camera, Ernest Heller.

George Raft (Joe Anton); Constance Cummings (Jerry Healy); Wynne Gibson (Iris Dawn); Mae West (Maude Triplett); Alison Skipworth (Mrs. Mabel Jellyman); Roscoe Karns (Leo); Al Hill (Blainey); Louis Calhern (Dick Bolton); Harry Wallace (Jerky); Dink Templeton (Patsy); Bradley Page (Frankie Guard); Marty Martyn (Malloy).

SHE DONE HIM WRONG (PAR, 1933) 66 M.

Producer, William LeBaron; director, Lowell Sherman, based on the play *Diamond Lil* by Mae West; screenplay, Harry Thew, John Bright; songs, Ralph Rainger; art director. Bob Usher; choreographer, Harold Hecht; assistant director, James Dugan; camera, Charles Lang; editor, Alexander Hall.

Mae West (Lady Lou); Cary Grant (Captain Cummings/'The Hawk'); Owen Moore (Chick Clark); Gilbert Roland (Serge Stanioff); Noah Beery, Sr. (Gus Jordan); David Landau (Dan Flynn); Rafaela Ottiana (Russian Rita); Dewey Robinson (Spider Kane); Rochelle Hudson (Sally); Tammany Young (Connors); Fuzzy Knight (Ragtime Kelly); Grace LaRue (Frances); Robert E. Homans (Doheney); Louise Beavers (Pearl); Wade Boteler (Pal); Aggie Herring (Mrs. Flaerty); Tom Kennedy (Big Billy); James C. Eagles (Pete); Tom McGuire (Mike); Al Hill, Arthur Houseman (Bar Flies); Mary Gordon (Cleaning Lady); Michael Mark (Janitor); Mike Donlin (Tout); Harry Wallace (Steak McGarry); Lee Kohlmar (Jacobson); Frank Moran (Framed Convict); Henie Conklin (Street Cleaner); Jack Carr (Patron); Ernie Adams (Man in Audience).

I'M NO ANGEL (PAR, 1933) 87 M.

Producer, William LeBaron; director, Wesley Ruggles; story, Lowell Brentano; continuity, Harlan Thompson; screenplay, Mae West; songs, Harvey Brooks, Gladys du Boise, and Ben Ellison; camera, Leo Tover; editor, Otho Lovering.

Mae West (Tira); Cary Grant (Jack Clayton); Gregory Ratoff (Benny Pinkowitz); Ralf Harolde (Slick Wiley); Edward Arnold (Big Bill Barton); Kent Taylor (Kirt Lawrence); Gertrude Michael (Alicia Hatton); Russell Hopton (Flea Madigan, The Barker); Dorothy Peterson (Thelma); Libby Taylor, Hattie McDaniel (Maids); Gertrude Howard (Beulah); Irving Pichel (Bob, The Attorney); Nigel de Brulier (Rajah); Tom London (Spectator); William B. Davidson (Ernest Brown, The Chump); Monte Collins, Ray Cooke (Sailors); George Bruggeman (Omnes); Walter Walker (Judge); Morrie Cohan (Chauffeur); Edward Hearn (Courtroom Spectator); Dennis O'Keefe (Reporter).

BELLE OF THE NINETIES (PAR, 1934) 75 M.

Producer, William LeBaron; director, Leo McCarey; story-screenplay, Mae West; songs, Arthur Johnston and Sam Coslow; art director, Hans Dreier, Bernard Herzbrun; camera, Karl Struss; editor, LeRoy Stone.

Mae West (Ruby Carter); Roger Pryor (Tiger Kid); John Mack Brown (Brook Claybourne); Katherine DeMille (Molly Brant); John Miljan (Ace Lamont); James Donlan (Kirby); Stuart Holmes (Dirk); Harry Woods (Slade); Tom Herbert (Gilbert); Edward Gargan (Stogie); Libby Taylor (Jasmine); Frederick Burton (Colonel Claybourne); Augusta Anderson (Mrs. Claybourne); Benny Baker (Blackie); Morrie Cohan (Butch); Warren Hymer (St. Louis Fighter); Wade Boteler (Editor); George Walsh (Man); Eddie Borden, Fuzzy Knight, Tyler Brooke (Comedians); Duke Ellington and Orchestra (Themselves); Kay Deslys (Beef Trust Chorus Girl); Sam McDaniel (Revivalist); Mike Mazurki (Extra).

GOIN' TO TOWN (PAR, 1935) 74 M.

Producer, William LeBaron; director, Alexander Hall; story, Marbo Morgan, George Dowell; screenplay, Mae West; songs, Sammy Fain and Irving Kahal; camera, Karl Struss; editor, LeRoy Stone.

Mae West (Cleo Borden) Paul Cavanagh (Edward Carrington); Ivan Lebedeff (Ivan Veladov); Tito Coral (Taho); Marjorie Gateson (Mrs. Grace Brittony); Fred Kohler, Sr. (Buck Gonzales); Monroe Owsley (Fletcher Colton); Gilbert Emery (Winslow); Luis Alberni (Signor Vitola); Lucio Villegas (Senor Ricardo Lopez); Mona Rico (Dolores Lopez); Paul Harvey (Donovan); Adrienne d'Ambricourt (Annette); Grant Withers (Young Fellow); Wade Boteler (Foreman Of Ranch); Stanley Andrews (Engineer); Rafael Storm (Senor Alvarez); Vladimar Bykoff (Lt. Mendoza); Andres De Segurola (President Racing Association); Bert Roach, Irving Bacon (Buck's Cowboys); Pearl Eaton (Girl); Francis Ford (Sheriff); Jack Pennick (Dancing Cowboy); Robert Dudley (Deputy); Albert Conti (Head Steward); Frank Mundin (Mrs. Brittony's Jockey); Harold Entwistle (Colton's Butler); Stanely Price (Attendant); Frank McGlynn (Judge); Leonid Kinskey (Interior Decorator); Virginia Hammond (Miss Plunkett); Laura Treadwell, Nell Craig (Society Women); Morgan Wallace (J. Henry Brash); Cyril Ring (Stage Manager); James Pierce, Tom London, Sid Saylor (Buck's Cowboys); Tom Ricketts (Indian Seller); Tom Monk (English Butler); Paulette Paquet, Mirra Rayo (French Maids); Henry Roquemore (Match King); Ted Oliver, Charles McMurphy (Policemen); Franco Corsaro (Italian Officer).

KLONDIKE ANNIE (PAR, 1936) 80 M.

Producer, William LeBaron; director, Raoul Walsh; story Mae West, Marion Morgan, George B. Dowell, Frank Mitchell Dazey; songs, Sam Coslow and Gene Austin; camera, George Clemer, editor, Stuart Heisler.

Mae West (The Frisco Doll); Victor McLaglen (Bull Brackett); Phillip Reed (Jack Forrest); Helen Jerome Eddy (Annie Alden); Harry Beresford (Brother Bowser); Harold Huber (Chan Lo); Conway Tearle (Vance Palmer); Lucile Webster Gleason (Big Tess); Esther Howard (Fanny Radler); Soo Yong (Fah Wong); Ted Oliver (Grigsby); John Rogers (Buddie); Tetsu Komai (Lan Fang); James Burke (Bartender); George Walsh (Quartermaster); Chester Gan (Ship's Cook); Jack Daley (Second Mate); Jack Wallace (Third Mate); D'Arcy Corrigan, Arthur Turner Foster, Nell Craig, Nella Walker (Missionaries); Philip Ahn (Wing); Mrs. Wong Wing (Ah Toy); Guy D. Ennery (Alvaredos); Maidel Turner (Lydia Bowley); Huntly Gordon (Clinton Reynolds); Paul Kruger; Edwin Brady, John Lester Johnson (Sailors); Jack Mulhall (Officer); Gene Austin (Organist); Russ Hall (Candy); Otto Heimel (Cocoa); Gladys Gale, Edna Bennett, Pearl Eaton, Kathleen Key, Ilean Hume, Marie Wells (Dance Hall Girls); Mrs. Chan Lee (Blind Woman); Dick Allen (Miner); Jackson Snyder (Little Boy).

GO WEST, YOUNG MAN (PAR, 1936) 82 M.

Producer, Emanuel R. Cohen; director, Henry Hathaway; based on the play *Personal Appearance* by Lawrence Riley; adaptation, Mae West; songs, Arthur Johnson and John Burke; music director, George Stoll; camera, Karl Struss; editor, Ray Curtiss.

Mae West (Mavis Arden); Warren William (Morgan); Randolph Scott (Bud); Lyle Talbot (Butch Harrigan); Alice Brady (Mrs. Struthers); Isabel Jewell (Gladys); Elizabeth Patterson (Aunt Kate); Margaret Perry (Joyce); Etienne Girardot (Professor Rigby); Maynard Holmes (Clyde); Alice Ardell (French Maid); Nicodemus (Himself); Jack LaRue (Rico); G. P. Huntley, Jr. (Embassy Officer); Robert Baikoff (Officer); Xavier Cugat and his Orchestra (Themselves)

EVERY DAY'S A HOLIDAY (PAR, 1938) 80 M.

Producer, Emanuel Cohen; director, A. Edward Sutherland; story-screenplay, Mae West; art director, Wiard Ihnen; music director, George Stoll; choreography, LeRoy Prinz; songs, Stanley Adams and Hoagy Carmichael; Sam Coslow; Barry Trivers and Coslow; assistant director, Earl Rettig; special effects, Gordon Jennings; camera, Karl Struss; editor, Ray Curtiss.

Mae West (Peaches O'Day/Mlle. Fifi); Edmund Lowe (Captain McCarey), Charles Butterworth (Graves); Charles Winninger (Van Reighle Van Pelton Van Doon); Walter Catlett (Nifty Baily); Lloyd Nolan (Honest John Quade); George Rector (Himself); Herman Bing (Fritz Krauftmeyer); Roger Imhof (Trigger Mike); Chester Conklin (Cabby); Lucien Prival (Danny The Dip); Adrian Morris (Assistant Police Commissioner); Francis McDonald, John Indrisano (Henchmen).

MY LITTLE CHICKADEE (UNIV, 1940) 83 M

Producer, Lester Cowan; director, Edward Cline; screenplay, Mae West, W. C. Fields; art director, Jack Otterson; music, Frank Skinner; song, Ben Oakland, Milton Drake; camera, Joseph Valentine; editor, Ed Curtiss.

W. C. Fields (Cuthbert J. Twillie); Mae West (Flower Belle Lee); Joseph Calleia (Jeff Badger/Masked Bandit); Dick Foran (Wayne Carter); Margaret Hamilton (Mrs. Gideon); George Moran (Clarence); Si Jenks (Old Man); James Conlin (Bartender); Gene Austin (Himself); Russell Hall (Candy); Otto Heimel (Coco); Eddie Butler, Bing Conley (Henchmen); Fuzzy Knight (Cousin Zeb); Anne Nagel (Miss Foster); Ruth Donnelly (Aunt Lou); Willard Robertson (Uncle John); Donald Meek (Budge); William B. Davidson (Sheriff); Addison Richards (Judge); Otto Hoffman (Printer); Jackie Searle, Billy Benedict, Délmar Watson, George Billings, Ben Hall, Buster Slaven, Danny Jackson, Charles Hart (Boys); Mark Anthony (Townsman); Lane Chandler (Porter). Lita Chevret (Indian Squaw); Chester Gan (Chinaman); George Melford (Sheriff); Slim Gaut (Bow-Legged Man).

THE HEAT'S ON (COL, 1943) 80 M.

Associate producer, Milton Carter; director, Gregory Ratoff; screenplay, Fitzroy Davis, George S. George, Fred Schiller; art director, Lionel Banks; music director, Yasha Bunchuk; music, John Leopold; songs, Henry Meyers, Edward Eliscu and Jay Gorney; Leo Huntley, John Blackburn and Fabian Andre; Edmund L. Gruber; camera, Franz F. Planer; editor, Otto Meyer.

Mae West (Fay Lawrence); Victor Moore (Hubert Bainbridge); William Gaxton (Tony Ferris); Lester Allen (Mouse Beller); Mary Roche (Janey Bainbridge); Almira Sessions (Hannah Bainbridge): Hazel Scott (Herself); Alan Dinehart (Forrest Stanton); Lloyd Bridges (Andy Walker); Sam Ash (Frank); Lina Romay (Lina); Xavier Cugat and his Orchestra (Themselves).

MYRA BRECKINRIDGE (20th, 1970) 95 M.

Producer, Robert Fryer; director, Michael Sarne; based on the novel by Gore Vidal; screenplay, Sarne, David Giler; music director, Lionel Newman; songs, John Phillips; choreography, Ralph Beaumont; art director, Jack Martin Smith, Fred Harpman; assistant director, Dick Glassman; camera, Richard Moore; editor Danford B. Greene.

Mae West (Leticia Van Allen); John Huston (Buck Loner); Raquel Welch (Myra Breckinridge); Rex Reed (Myron Breckinridge); Farrah Fawcett (Mary Ann); Roger C. Carmel (Dr. Montag); Roger Herron (Rusty); George Furth (Charlie Flager, Jr.); Calvin Lockhart (Irving Amadeus); Jim Backus (Doctor); John Carradine (Surgeon); Andy Devine (Coyote Bill); Grady Sutton (Kid Barlow); Robert Lieb (Charlie Flager, Sr.); Skip Ward (Chance); Kathleen Freeman (Bobby Dean Loner); B. S. Pully (Tex); Buck Kartalian (Jeff); Monty Landis (Vince); Tom Selleck (Stud); Peter Ireland (Student); Nelson Sardelli (Mario); Genevieve Waite (Dental Patient); William Hopper (Judge).

In vaudeville, 1912

With Welfare Island Prison warden Harry Schleth, 1927

With George Raft in NIGHT AFTER NIGHT (Par '32)

With Cary Grant in SHE DONE HIM WRONG (Par '33)

Mrs. Harry Woods, Marilee Woods, the Sultana of Johore, the Sultan, Cary Grant, Mrs. Anna Lumsden, sister of the Sultana; (back row) detective A. Butler, Captain A. Abdullah, and Harry Woods with Mae West on the Paramount backlot, 1934

With Randolph Scott in GO WEST, YOUNG MAN (Par '36)

With Charlie McCarthy on radio, 1937

In *Catherine Was Great* (1944)

Advertisement for THE HEAT'S ON (Col '43)

As *Diamond Lil* (1949)

At home, 1959

In MYRA BRECKINRIDGE (20th '70)

With Cary Grant and Noah Beery in SHE
DONE HIM WRONG (Par '33)

With Noah Beery, Robert Homans, an
Rafaela Ottiano in SHE DONE HIM
WRONG

With Nat Pendleton and Harry Schultz in
'M NO ANGEL (Par '33)

With Gregory Ratoff in I'M NO ANGEL

With John Miljan in BELLE OF THE NINE-
TIES (Par '34)

With Johnny Mack Brown in BELLE OF
THE NINETIES

With Ivan Lebedeff, John Indrisano (rear),
nd Marjorie Gateson in GOIN' TO TOWN
Par '35)

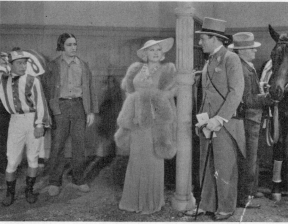

With Joe Frye, Tito Coral, and Paul Cavanagh in GOIN' TO TOWN

With Helene Jerome Eddy in KLONDIKE ANNIE (Par '36)

With Victor McLaglen in KLONDIKE AN-NIE

With Warren William in GO WEST, YOUNG MAN (Par '37)

With Randolph Scott in GO WEST, YOUNG MAN

With Walter Catlett, Charles Winninger, and Charles Butterworth in EVERY DAY'S A HOLIDAY (Par '38)

In EVERY DAY'S A HOLIDAY

With W. C. Fields in MY LITTLE CHICK-
ADEE (Univ '40)

With Margaret Hamilton in MY LITTLE
CHICKADEE

In THE HEAT'S ON (Col '43)

With John Huston in MYRA BRECKIN-
RIDGE (20th '70)

With Victor Moore in THE HEAT'S ON

DOROTHY LAMOUR

5′5″
117 pounds
Blue-gray eyes
Black hair
Sagittarius

CALL HER Ulah, Marama, Tura, Dea, Mima, Aloma, Tama, or Lona. Sarong-clad Dorothy Lamour played them all in Paramount's assorted jungle movies of the 1930 and 1940s. Dorothy was at her finest as a tableau motion picture star, one whose screen magic resided primarily in an ability to strike effective still-life poses: wistfully singing of love in the moonlight, officiating at a native festival, or clutching her latest screen lover in a passionate embrace. She proved far more exotic and more enduring than Universal's Maria Montez or Yvonne DeCarlo—and Dorothy could sing.

For 12 years (1936–47) Dorothy remained moviedom's prime South Seas maiden. As such, she and faithful sarong outfit became American institutions. During World War II, GIs ranked her with Betty Grable, Jane Russell, Lana Turner, and Rita Hayworth as one of their favorite pinup girls.

Dorothy periodically forced her film producers to allow her to go legitimate and contemporary, but the screen results were usually far from satisfactory. She proved far more effective in the kidding offshoots of her tropical vehicles: the ultrapopular "Road To" series, costarring Paramount's top-moneymaking male performers, Bing Crosby and Bob Hope. It was no mean feat to play cutesy while Crosby and Hope sallied wisecracks and slapstick routines back and forth. As the series developed, Dorothy's skills as a comedienne sharpened. She soon learned to put over her song numbers in mocking tones which gave them added zest. Before long, she was more than holding her naive own against the rambunctious boys.

Dorothy was dropped by Paramount in the 1947 economy wave and her professional career foundered badly. No longer an enticing ingenue, she was not versatile enough as an actress to successfully carry even the modest dramatic features assigned her elsewhere. Her last decent comeback role was in *Road to Bali* (1953).

Since then Dorothy has alternated between domesticity and nightclub tours. In the 1960s she promulgated a nostalgic aura about her golden Hollywood years. As the prime exponent of the Dorothy Lamour legend, she has expanded her multimedia show business career into the 1970s with better than average results.

Dorothy Lamour was born Mary Leta Dorothy Stanton on December 10, 1914, in New Orleans, of French-Irish-Spanish ancestry. Her mother* later remarried, and Dorothy adopted her stepfather's surname of Lambour.

She was a stagestruck youngster almost from the start. At the age of four, she was performing on a soap box, singing patriotic songs and selling thrift stamps. The following year, she wandered into a neighborhood theatre, sang a song, and won a basket of groceries (which a local thug stole from her on her way home). After attending the Beauregard Grammar School, Dorothy went to the John McDonough High School, planning to become a teacher. However, when she was 14, unstable family finances necessitated her quitting school and finding work. She took a six-month course at Spencer Business College and then secured a position as private secretary to a local manufacturer of brass faucets.

Already a strikingly attractive teenager—until the age of 15, she had blonde hair—Dorothy entered assorted beauty contests. She was urged on by her good friend Dorothy Dell, who would have a short film career of her own before being killed in a car crash. Upon winning the Miss New Orleans title, Dorothy decided to use the prize money to foster a show business career. After a short tour with an amateur stock company (Dell was part of the group), Dorothy moved to Chicago, accompanied by her mother. At least now she was closer to the entertainment scene. She found employment at the Marshall Field department store, earning $17 a week for selling toys, checking stock, and running an elevator.

One evening, her friend Dorothy Gulman, who handled public relations for the Morrison Hotel, entered Dorothy in the hotel's celebrity-night talent show. In a burst of inspiration—or so the story goes—Dorothy wrapped herself in a borrowed one-and-a-half yards of silks and sang "Stars Fell on Alabama." Herbie Kaye, the orchestra leader, heard Dorothy's rendition and signed her as his group's vocalist.

It was while she was touring with Kaye over the next year that her last name was altered to Lamour. According to legend, a Dallas sign-painter accidentally streamlined the spelling, and the new name—French for "love"—stuck. On May 10, 1935, Dorothy, age 21, and Kaye, 26, eloped. They were married in Waukegan, Illinois.

When Kaye and Dorothy moved on to New York, he approached his Yale classmate Rudy Vallee, then riding the peak of his crooner-orchestra leader success. Vallee obligingly introduced Dorothy to host Sherman Billingsley, who hired her at $150 a week to be the songstress for his Stork Club. Dorothy later recalled her nightclub debut: "At El Morocco it was no, but I got a job at the Stork Club, and on my opening night, everything went fine. They were still applauding when I went to sit down at a ringside table where my coat was spread over the back of my chair. As I sat down I pulled it over my shoulders. Some man thought I was going to get up, so he pulled the chair out from under me. I fell, and from the floor where I was sitting I could see the spotlights which had never left me, shining on my fingers, which were desperately clutching the tabletop."

After her Stork Club engagement, Dorothy became part of a stage act with two pianists, Julius Monk and Joe Lilly (the latter would become a top music director at Paramount). Soon Dorothy joined NBC radio's "The

*Mrs. Lambour would move to Hollywood, during Dorothy's screen heyday and was one of the original members of Motion Picture Mothers. She died on February 12, 1972, in Hollywood after a long illness. She was then 79 years old.

Dreamer of Songs" weekly show. Increasingly popular as a club vocalist and recording artist, she was asked by Vitaphone to appear in their two-reel musical short *The Stars Can't Be Wrong* (1936), which also featured Emerson's Mountaineers, O'Connell and Blair, Dale Winthrop, Hal Thompson, George Pembroke, and the Smart Set Singers.

When the NBC radio show switched its broadcasting to the West Coast, Dorothy went along. She was spotted by several studio executives and finally Paramount asked her to screen test and then to sign a term contract. She agreed. Her husband Kaye continued touring with his orchestra, particularly in the Midwest where he had a large following.

Paramount had been having difficulty in casting the exotic lead for a minor tropical-romance story, *The Jungle Princess*. Studio executives finally decided on Dorothy when makeup tests revealed that she looked sufficiently sultry. The simple plot had British hunter Ray Milland being injured on a tropical island. He is rescued by innocent native girl Dorothy and her pets: the tiger Kimau and the chimpanzee Bogo. With plenty of idle time on his hands, he instructs the naive sarong-clad beauty in English and in the process discovers that he loves her. Meanwhile, Akim Tamiroff has stirred up the local natives against Dorothy and her patient, hollering that Dorothy is a voodoo girl. At the last perilous moment, the chimp Bogo comes to the rescue. Milland then chooses Dorothy over his not-so-polite English fiancee, Molly Lamont.

It was surely accidental that song interludes became an integral part of Paramount's jungle capers. Dorothy remembers: "My first sarong was blue. I asked for it because that's my lucky color. We made the picture on some hard-to-reach mountain crags in California. While we were there they remembered I could sing, so they wrote 'Moonlight and Shadows' and sent the guy on a donkey with it through the passes."

Paramount had budgeted *The Jungle Princess* as a black and white programmer and saw no reason to change its mind after the picture's completion. But trade screenings and exhibitor reaction told them differently. *Variety* enthused: "She lands powerfully in spite of the highly improbable story which makes her a female Tarzan and calls upon her to play a rather difficult role. Many much more seasoned actresses could not have come through on the assignment so impressively." The studio quickly altered its sales campaign and gave the movie a bigger build-up. It was still not highly enough regarded as a potential money-maker to unspool at the flagship theatre, the Paramount, so it opened at the nearby Rialto Theatre on December 24, 1936. Wanda Hale in her two and one-half star *New York Daily News* review evaluated Dorothy as "a gal we'll put our money on for the best musical find of the season."

In one lucky stab, Dorothy had found a safe niche in filmdom. Her sultry beauty—accentuated by dark body makeup—caught the public's fancy. They were intrigued by her languid singing (herein both in "native" dialect and English), made all the more impressive by shapely figure and long, flowing hair silhouetted against the lush settings. That her acting was as primitive as her screen character's ancestry, seemed to bother only a few.

Paramount immediately placed Dorothy among its promising new faces in trade advertisements: other female competitors in this category were: Olympe Bradna, Frances Farmer, Mary Carlisle, Marsha Hunt, Eleanor Whitney, Irene Dale, Priscilla Lawson, Helen Burgess, June Martel, Frances Dee, and Ida Lupino.

The first of Dorothy's five 1937 releases was *Swing High, Swing Low,* a reworking of the stage success *Burlesque*. Trumpeter Fred MacMurray meets and weds nightclub singer Carole Lombard in Panama. When more lucrative jobs bring him to New York, he forgets her and soon succumbs to alcohol. Lombard divorces him, but later returns to help him redeem himself. Dorothy was fifth-billed as Anita Alvarez, a high-living dancer who comes between MacMurray and Lombard. Dorothy sang "Panamania," which proved to be one of her most popular songs. The *New York Daily Mirror* found Dorothy, as the seductive heavy, "just as effective in civilized settings."

Due to a busy filmmaking schedule, Dorothy had been off the radio for nearly a year. She returned to the airwaves in May, 1937, as vocalist on the "Chase and Sanborn Sunday Night Show" (NBC) starring W. C. Fields and Edgar Bergen and Charlie McCarthy.

Last Train from Madrid (1937) was a decidedly inferior mixture of *Grand Hotel* and *Shanghai Express*. The B-melodrama had the distinction of being the first American feature to deal with the Spanish Civil War, but in typical Hollywood fashion, its script took no sides. Paramount contract players were strewn helter-skelter into the potpourri: Lew Ayres functioned as the flip American reporter, Gilbert Roland as the heavyish hero; Anthony Quinn as a military escort, Karen Morley as the baroness who shoots villainous Lee Bowman, Robert Cummings as the pacifist army deserter, Helen Mack as a tough broad who is shot, and nominal star Dorothy as Roland's mysterious sweetheart. While Dorothy was a "looker" here, some reviewers thought she "ought to stick to the radio."

Studio production chief William LeBaron* was still maneuvering to guide Paramount back onto the path of more popular filmfare after the year (1935–36) of higher cultural product under Ernst Lubitsch's supervision. Thus Dorothy, like most of Paramount's new contractees, was flipped indiscriminately back and forth between prestigious and run-of-the-mill pictures. In so doing, Paramount took longer than need be to discover whether its new player had box-office potential in any particular direction.

High, Wide and Handsome (1937) was a $1.9 million saga of Pennsylvania oil well pioneering in the 1850s, directed in elaborate style by Rouben Mamoulian, with a fine score by Oscar Hammerstein II and Jerome Kern. The film has Randolph Scott as hero. He leads his men in laying oil pipelines themselves in order to prevent corrupt railroad president Alan Hale from monopolizing the industry. But the film was Irene Dunne's vehicle. She sashayed through it as the gentle but firm circus performer who weds Scott, only to leave him—for a traumatic spell—when he seemingly prefer business to her company. For added flavor in the brew, Paramount cast Elizabeth Patterson as Scott's perky grandmother, Akim Tamiroff as a foreigner gambler, Ben Blue as a confused hired hand, and Charles Bickford as the roughneck thug. Dorothy was third-billed as Molly, a honky-tonk torch singer who is Hale's flashy mistress. She adequately rendered "The Things I Want," but it paled in comparison to Dunne's vocalizing of such better songs such as "Folks Who Live on the Hill." Howard Barnes *(New York Herald Tribune)* decided: "Dorothy Lamour is rather ill at ease in the shadowy part of a shanty boat singer that might better have been scrapped."

Independent producer Samuel Goldwyn was perspicacious enough to realize Dorothy's true box-office potential. He traded the services of Joel McCrea to Paramount for their *Union Pacific* in return for borrowing Doro-

*See Appendix.

thy, whom he placed in his $2 million South Pacific idyll *The Hurricane,* directed by John Ford. Set on the Samoan island of Manukura, Dorothy appeared as Marama, daughter of the native chief, who weds Polynesian sailor Jon Hall. He is constantly in trouble with the British authorities, whose laws are sternly enforced by island governor Raymond Massey. Others involved in the plot were: C. Aubrey Smith, a kindly old priest, local doctor Thomas Mitchell, Mary Astor, Massey's spirited wife, and prison warden John Carradine. When the devastating storm rips the island apart, Hall appears in time to save his wife and child by lashing them to a boat's mast. For rescuing Astor, Massey pardons Hall, who then paddles off into the sunset with Dorothy and their child.

The Hurricane only required Dorothy to pose prettily, sing "The Moon of Manakoora," and smile wistfully at handsome male lead Hall (said to be a relative of *The Hurricane*'s coauthor James Hall). Special effects director James Basevi, who created the earthquake in *San Francisco* and the fire in *In Old Chicago,* supervised the creation of the spectacular $400,000 hurricane. The roadshow picture debuted at the Astor Theatre on November 9, 1937, and was a popular success. Dorothy's reviewers focused almost exclusively on her physical attributes. Nevertheless, this prestigious production made her well known to both the industry and the filmgoing public.

Her final release of the year was *Thrill of a Lifetime* (1937). A contrived musical outing set in a summer resort camp, it featured the unblended talents of Betty Grable, Judy Canova, Eleanor Whitney, Johnny Downs, and the Yacht Club Boys. Dorothy was plunked into the story line merely to sing the title tune. Wearing a slinky coat ensemble, she suddenly appears in front of a satin backdrop, accompanied by a 20-piece orchestra. Carped Howard Barnes of the *New York Herald Tribune* (who would lead the critical disenchantment with Dorothy's screen magic): "It might be rude to give my exact impression of her act."

Plans to feature Dorothy in *Artists and Models* (1937) and Cecil B. DeMille's *The Buccaneer* (1938) did not materialize, but she did join the studio's newest vaudeville extravaganza, *The Big Broadcast of 1938.* This musical was notable for W. C. Field's dual role, Bob Hope in his feature film debut, the appearance of opera star Kirsten Flagstad, Martha Raye's slapstick shenanigans, and the dueting of Hope and Shirley Ross in the Oscar-winning song "Thanks for the Memory." As sedate Miss Wyndham, Dorothy held panting fiance Hope at bay while inciting the romantic temperature of seaman-inventor Leif Erikson. On the cross-Atlantic jaunt, she offered a most dispirited "You Took the Words Right Out of My Heart." Confined to contemporary attire and coiffure, even her physical appeal was greatly diminished.

Paramount then followed Goldwyn's lead and reteamed Dorothy with Ray Milland in the technicolor *Her Jungle Love* (1938). As Tura, the sarong-clad child of nature, she finds British aviator Milland when his plane crashes on her Malayan isle. Lynne Overman capered as Milland's copilot, Jiggs the chimpanzee and Meewa the lion cub cavorted, Dorothy Howe added complications as Milland's erstwhile fiancee, and J. Carrol Naish was the native villain who hoped to feed the white men to the crocodiles; a timely earthquake prevented the sacrificing. Surrounded by multihued tropical foliage, Dorothy warbled "Coffee and Kisses," "Jungle Love," and "Lovelight in the Starlight." The *New York Herald Tribune*'s Howard Barnes complained: "She never fails to make even more preposterous the preposterous happenings of the film." Dorothy disagreed: "Believe me, it's harder to say 'What is Kiss, Kiss?' and make it sound good, than to play a big dramatic scene." Audiences were responding to Dorothy's screen magic in a big way, and Paramount increased her salary to $1,000 a week.

Dorothy was again paired with Ray Milland in *Tropic Holiday* (1938), set in Rosita, Mexico. Milland was a scriptwriter seeking local color for inspiration, Dorothy was a love-hungry senorita, Martha Raye was Milland's bumptious secretary, and hayseed Bob Burns was Martha's American beau. Dorothy was heavy-lidded and fetching in her south-of-the-border wardrobe, but the singing honors went to authentic Mexican performer Elvia Rios. One reviewer quipped: "From the way Dorothy Lamour sings of love you may be sure that Lamour is not her right name. It is likely she was born Legume."

Spawn of the North (1938) was two years in preparation. Originally Carole Lombard had been scheduled for the lead, but by the time director Henry Hathaway had completed outdoor location shooting, she had taken ill, so Dorothy was hastily substituted. Set in the 1890s far north, the vigorous action film focused on the salmon-canning industry, with American fishermen combatting Russian poachers. John Barrymore played the local newspaper editor, whose college-bred daughter, Louise Platt, hankers for Henry Fonda, owner of a cannery. Fonda's boyhood chum, George Raft, is an inventive conniver, who later gives up his life to save Fonda. Dorothy was third-billed as Nicky Duval, a French Canadian fishing camp gal in love with Raft. Attractively attired in sweaters, and spouting good dialogue, Dorothy inspired Frank S. Nugent of the *New York Times* to write: "It may not be a good performance; but at least she is trying and that's more than we can say about her previous screen efforts." Dorothy and Raft recreated their roles from *Spawn of the North* on "Lux Radio Theatre" (September 12, 1938). When Paramount remade the story as *Alaska Seas* (1954), Jan Sterling had Dorothy's part.

By 1938, Dorothy's marriage was more than shaky. She thought having a baby might patch everything up, and informed the studio: "I want a baby of my own and I want it before I am twenty-five." Dorothy suggested that she would take a year off the screen. Her horrified employers countered that it might be wiser if she adopted a child. As a valuable part of the studio's star lineup, she was now being paid $1,500 for each six days of work.

St. Louis Blues (1939) was a minor-league *Show Boat* in which top-billed Dorothy portrayed a Broadway musical comedy star who leaves New York to avoid playing yet another sarong role. She encounters showboat skipper Lloyd Nolan (George Raft had refused the part) who befriends her and plans to star her in his new revue. Competing carnival-owner William Frawley learns that Dorothy has violated her stage contract and almost prevents the big show from going on. Dorothy had stiff competition in the singing department in *St. Louis Blues:* Tito Guizar and black vocalist Maxine Sullivan sparkled. Dorothy's singing of "Junior," "Blue Nightfall," "I Go for That," and "Let's Dream in the Moonlight" led the *New York Post*'s Archer Winsten to pen: "Her lugubrious delivery retains her top ranking among the 'Let's Cry' thrushes." One wag tagged the minimusical "Sarong With the Wind."

On April 21, 1939, Dorothy's husband Herbie Kaye filed suit for divorce in Chicago on the grounds of desertion. Dorothy confessed it was " . . . the worst thing that ever happened to me. . . . We agreed we couldn't stay married as things are. We arranged it all over the telephone. We're still more than friends."

Then Martin Starr, a WMCA (New York) radio commentator and former talent agent, filed—and later dropped—a $35,000 law suit against Dorothy, claiming that in 1934 he had been her manager and press agent and was responsible for her show business build-up. In the same year, Alfred C. Evans of NBC radio's music department sued Dorothy for $6,000 for vocal lessons—the claim was settled out of court. In mid-year, when socialite Alma Alderman sued performer Ruth Etting for alienating Mr. Alderman's affections, she offhandedly mentioned in her testimony that contrary to gossip, actresses Dorothy Lamour and Dorothy Page were "nice girls" and wouldn't have kissed and led on her husband.

Man About Town (1939), a Jack Benny musical-comedy vehicle, was to feature Betty Grable opposite the comedian. However, when she became ill, Dorothy was substituted. The flimsy tale found producer Benny in London with his new show and dating Binnie Barnes to get girlfriend Dorothy appropriately jealous. Dorothy harmonized "That Sentimental Sandwich" with Phil Harris, and solo sang "Enchantment." Grable recovered in time to do a special song for *Man About Town.* Her energetic "Fidgity Joe" nearly stole the limelight.

Dorothy went Eurasian and dramatic in *Disputed Passage* (1939) a fitful adaptation of Lloyd Douglas's spiritual novel. John Howard was cast as the ethereal doctor student of clinic surgeon Akim Tamiroff. Dorothy appeared as Audrey Hilton, who had been raised by Chinese foster parents. When Howard's infatuation for her threatens to disrupt his studies, Tamiroff convinces Dorothy that it would be best for her to leave. She returns to China. Howard later turns up there, and is seriously injured in a bombing raid. Tamiroff arrives to operate and Dorothy reappears to offer Howard the faith necessary for recovery. This tepid drama went nowhere at the box office. Frank S. Nugent *(New York Times)* noted: "She strikes a note as false as a cracked Chinese gong."

On loanout to Twentieth Century-Fox Dorothy costarred with Tyrone Power in the gangster melodrama *Johnny Apollo* (1940), directed by Henry Hathaway. Power, the college-bred son of crooked stockbroker Edward Arnold, turns dishonest when his father is sent to prison for embezzlement. He becomes the right-hand man of racketeer Lloyd Nolan and finds better friendships among the sinners than he had among more saintly society. Power and Arnold are later reunited in jail, where the father is almost killed trying to prevent his son from making a break. Dorothy was presented as Lucky Dubarry, Nolan's uneducated moll who develops a yen for Power. As the nightclub thrush, she warbles: "This Is the Beginning of the End" and "Dancing for Nickels and Dimes." As R. R. Crisler observed in the *New York Times:* "The only slow moments arrive when Dorothy Lamour sings sad songs in a get-up which demi-mondaines discarded back in the seventies." As if anticipating the adverse critical reaction, Dorothy stated: "Some day I hope the critics will say of me, not only that I wear a sarong becomingly, but also that I give a good performance. I've never had any real theatrical training you know." No one mentioned that even her mink coat wardrobe did not hide her extra poundage. Dorothy appeared with Burgess Meredith and Edward Arnold in the "Lux Radio Theatre" dramatization of *Johnny Apollo* on February 17, 1941.

In *Typhoon* (1940), the cinema's first lady of the sarong was Dea, a castaway on an island off Dutch Guiana since childhood. The scenario had Robert Preston shanghaied by Lynne Overman to help search for black pearls. When the crew mutinies, the duo are left on Dorothy's isle. The natives are stirred up by J. Carrol Naish, who plots to destroy the visiting white men. But a typhoon occurs lensed in widescreen magnascope, killing the evil ones and saving the good people. *Typhoon* was filmed in technicolor on Catalina Island with the lagoon sequences lensed at Baldwin Lake. Dorothy sported an abbreviated sarong and a lavalava, and palled around with Koko the chimpanzee. Her only song was "Palms of Paradise."

To promote *Typhoon,* Dorothy made a personal appearance tour; she played the New York Paramount Theatre in February, 1940. *Variety* reported: "For her Paramount [stage] debut, Miss Lamour is garbed most of the time in a sarong and gold necklace. Her underpinnings are covered by a skirt matching the sarong when she first delivers a couple of torchy numbers of current release. A quick trip to the wings and she returns for a medley of numbers from her pictures. That's the extent of her routine. Everything is sold with a maximum of sound and insinuating s.a. The latter even applies to her bow-taking. In returning for the ceremony, she wears a flimsy armless cape which she keeps clutching as it slides off one shoulder and then the other."

Then came what proved to be the most fortuitous screen teaming of her career. Paramount had dusted off an old tropical drama and had it revamped as a comedy turn for Fred MacMurray and Jack Oakie. When they turned out to be unavailable, Bing Crosby and Bob Hope were substituted; Dorothy seemed a natural choice for the girl on the jungle isle. Crosby is the scion of a shipping family, but he would rather loaf and more particularly avoid marrying fiancée Judith Barrett. He ships out with pal Hope and they land on Kaigoon. The boys save Dorothy from a tough dancing partner and she comes to live in their hut, quickly teaching them "right from sarong." Dorothy agrees that Crosby should return home and marry, so she reluctantly accepts Hope's marriage proposal. But events intervene, and she and Crosby are reunited.

Road to Singapore (1940) proved a hefty box-office success. Its winning quality was its self-kidding, leisurely approach, combined with slapstick, wisecracks, songs, and the plush beauty of Dorothy in luxuriant settings. For the public, the combination of Crosby's crooning, Hope's extravagant doubletakes and snappy dialogue, and Dorothy's presence in a sarong, was more than enough. With Crosby, Dorothy sang "Too Romantic" and by herself she lulled "The Moon and the Willow." Howard Barnes *(New York Herald Tribune)* snapped: "She achieves something of a performing tour-de-force by utterly failing to take advantage of either main narrative or the by-play." Dorothy would later admit: "After the first 'Road' film, I never studied dialogue. Never. I'd wait to get on the set to see what they were planning. I was the happiest and highest paid straight woman in the business."

Moon over Burma (1940) was hardly the vehicle for Dorothy to appear in when she decided to go legitimate and prove her forte as a straight performer. She had her long tresses shorn and kept a drama coach on the set with her all through the filming. A mediocre jungle-triangle romancer resulted. Robert Preston and Preston Foster operate a teak lumber camp for blind owner Albert Basserman. Foster tumbles for American entertainer Dorothy who is stranded in Rangoon. A log jam and a forest fire ensue before the conventional wrap-up. The trivial script had Dorothy going through such inanities as turning to a group of natives who are tuning up their instruments: "Put that all together and it sounds just like a song I know." (Then she sings "Moon over Burma.") Snappy Doris Nolan, as Basserman's daughter, quips about the not-so-ritzy Dorothy: "I knew the jungle was full of rare flowers, but what bush did she grow on." Without the necessary finesse, Dorothy mumbles back: "Flatbush!"

On loanout again to Twentieth Century-Fox, Dorothy costarred with Henry Fonda in *Chad Hanna* (1940), a technicolor saga of circus life in 1841 upstate New York. Dorothy was Albany Yates, the bareback rider whom Fonda adores. When she exits Guy Kibbee's circus for a better job, Fonda marries her replacement, Linda Darnell. Later, Fonda spats with Darnell and has a rendezvous with Dorothy. Wrapped up in an old comforter she nearly seduces the naive man, but virtue triumphs. She sends him away, saying she can tell by his embrace that he really loves his wife. *Chad Hanna*, which opened at the Roxy Theatre on December 25, 1940, was not the huge moneymaker anticipated. Robert W. Dana *(New York Herald Tribune)* noted: "Miss Lamour does about her best job yet."

Dorothy began 1941 with a follow-up "Road" series entry, *Road to Zanzibar*. In this one she was Donna Latour, stranded in Africa with her show business partner Una Merkel. They latch onto ex-carnival performers Crosby and Hope, baiting them to get help for the trek back to civilization. For a change, Dorothy had no sarong; instead she wears a tattered dress, and in one scene, a leaf outfit. Her highlight in this jungle spoof was the satirical "You're Dangerous," which begins with her and Crosby discussing soupy romantic song numbers. As they paddle along in their canoe, they parody the amorous formula. By now the "Road" films were filled with asides to the audience, assorted in-jokes, and frantic slapstick. Archer Winsten *(New York Post)* commented: "In their [Crosby's and Hope's] reflected glory, Dorothy Lamour, ceasing her feverish efforts to be An Actress, begins to shine in a new light. She seems more natural, and therefore half again as tolerable."

By now Dorothy was Paramount's most ever-present asset and worth all of her $5,000 a week. In the cheesecake sweepstakes at the studio, she outranked the very shapely Paulette Goddard, and overshadowed such newer contractees as Ellen Drew. Dorothy played straight lady to Bob Hope in *Caught in the Draft* (1941). She was the colonel's daughter whom movie star Hope desires, but cannot win until he demonstrates his patriotism and manliness by enlisting in the Army and becoming a certified hero. The obvious slapstick service comedy proved that Dorothy had progressed as a farceur and could hold her own in a moderate way. She sang "Love As I Am."

The technicolor *Aloma of the South Seas* (1941) reunited her with Jon Hall. Samuel Goldwyn had hoped to reteam them himself in *Tahiti*. The *New York Sun*'s tolerant reviewer said it all: "Lamour's back in her sarong and all's right with the world. . . . Dottie's back in the islands, dishing out the poi, drinking whatever it is that the islanders drink during feasts and weddings, flashing in and out of pellucid pools and fleeing the blood-red lava of dat old debbil Fire Mountain which goes into full eruption on Dottie's wedding day." For the compulsory musical interlude, Dorothy did "The White Blossoms of Tah-Ni." The film followed the conventions of the genre by alternating close-ups of Dorothy's languid beauty with shots of Hall's well-muscled torso. For war-weary audiences, *Aloma of the South Seas* was a winning ticket, even if it did have a most disappointing volcanic explosion finale.

The Fleet's In (1942) was a remake of the 1928 Clara Bow picture and *Lady Be Careful* (1936). The plot's premise established woman-shy gob

William Holden being photographed kissing dance-hall chanteuse Dorothy in a publicity pose. The admiral's coy daughter, Barbara Britton, demands that Holden persuade Kellogg's swingland temptress to grace a party she is giving. Holden's shipmates take bets on the outcome: the film eventually ends with Holden and Dorothy linked romantically. Although Dorothy was top-starred, *The Fleet's In* served more as a buildup for Betty Hutton, a Broadway discovery of Paramount's new chieftain, B. G. DeSylva.* Hutton, in tandem with countrified comedy lead Eddie Bracken, proved to be the film's big drawing attraction. Ironically, Howard Barnes *(New York Herald Tribune)* conceded: "It finds Miss Lamour giving just about her best performance to date, if that's possible." The film was loosely remade as the Dean Martin-Jerry Lewis vehicle *Sailor Beware* (1951).

Beyond the Blue Horizon (1942) showcased Dorothy as Tama, who had been deserted on a tropical island when her socialite parents were killed by a rampaging elephant during a hunting expedition. Dorothy matures with a domesticated chimpanzee and a swimming tiger as her only companions. Eventually she is rescued and is brought back to San Francisco to claim her inheritance. When her authenticity is disputed, she leads a safari back to the Malayan island. Her heart is easily won by circus tree-swinger Richard Denning, although the boobery of publicist Jack Haley and the scoffing of Patricia Morison interfere. The ending has her faithful tiger killing the mad elephant in a death lunge over a cliff. Dorothy vocalized "Pagan Lullaby" and "A Full Moon and an Empty Heart." Her unfavorite Manhattan newspaper critic sallied: "Some one forgot to tell her that this show was a burlesque. She makes a safari to her ill-fated birthplace as though such a characterization required solid dramatics."

Road to Morocco (1942) enhanced Dorothy's strong position in the Paramount star firmament, without adding any new facets to her screen personality. This time she was Princess Shalmar, royalty in an Arab kingdom. When Crosby and Hope are stranded in Morocco, the former eagerly sells the latter for a few dollars. Dorothy purchases Hope to be her husband, because the prophets have predicted that her first marriage will be a short one. Naturally, Crosby arrives at the palace and promptly wins Dorothy's interest. In this exceedingly popular lampoon of the desert epics, the tone was set by a talking camel, who says early on, "This is the screwiest picture I've ever been in." Dorothy sang the catchy tune "Constantly."

Her final screen contribution for 1942 was a guest appearance in *Star Spangled Rhythm.* In "A Sweater, a Sarong, and a Peekaboo Bang," Paulette Goddard, Dorothy, and Veronica Lake were required to spoof their screen trademarks.

On loanout to Samuel Goldwyn, Dorothy and Bob Hope appeared in the lumbering *They Got Me Covered,* which premiered at Radio City Music Hall on March 4, 1943. Hope was a Pulitzer Prize-winning foreign correspondent who is fired by his news agency for incompetence. He returns to Washington, hoping to regain his job and to freeload on Dorothy, the agency's star secretary and his girlfriend. He soon involves her in mild mayhem as he inadvertently breaks up a spy ring headquarters in the city. Dorothy looked more bewildered than bewitching, had no numbers to sing, and was outshone by Lenore Aubert as a modern Mata Hari. Even the usually generous *Variety* panned Dorothy, "whose flat delivery of her comparatively numerous lines makes Hope have to work twice as hard to sell his gags."

*See Appendix.

Since her 1939 divorce, Dorothy had been dating attorney Gregory Bautzer, among others. But in 1942 she met Captain William Ross Howard III of Baltimore, Maryland, who was stationed at a military base near Los Angeles. The couple were married on April 7, 1943, in a double-ring ceremony in Beverly Hills, with 250 guests attending. They celebrated their honeymoon in San Bernardino, since Howard had to report for duty the next day. Dorothy would later reminisce: "When I married, I thought I'd want to retire. I've had my career, if you want to call it that. I thought I was entitled to settle down. I had everything—I have everything. Nobody could be luckier or happier than I am. But instead of sitting back, I got serious about my acting for the first time. I can't explain it. I wanted to start all over again on a different basis. Maybe to prove something to somebody."

The technicolor costume musical *Dixie* (1943) purported to be the biography of Dan Emmett, composer of the title tune and many others. It is set in pre-Civil War New Orleans. Bing Crosby, as Emmett, has wed his hometown sweetheart, Marjorie Reynolds. To prove his worth to her dour father, Crosby sets out to become a success. Working on a riverboat, he is flushed by cardsharp Billy De Wolfe who later teams with Crosby to form a new-style minstrel act. At Raymond Walburn's theatrical boarding house, Crosby is smitten with Walburn's daughter Dorothy. However, once he has produced his innovating revue she convinces him to return to the now crippled Reynolds. Dorothy sets her sights on De Wolfe. Dressed in overflowing crinolines and spouting a syrupy Southern accent, Dorothy was easily lost in the shuffle. Her only singing was in the ensemble finale number, "Dixie." Dorothy and Crosby performed their *Dixie* roles on "Lux Radio Theatre," December 20, 1943.

Her third 1943 release, *Riding High,* was the shoddy Christmas entry at the Paramount Theatre. She is Ann Castle, an ex-burlesque queen who returns home to Arizona when her show folds. Father Victor Moore has bungled his silver mine deal, and even mining engineer Dick Powell has difficulty selling sufficient stock to re-finance the operation. Dorothy hires on as entertainer at Cass Daley's dude ranch to earn her keep. Eventually the stock is subscribed, the silver vein pans out, and Powell charms Dorothy. To pep up the drab color musical, Dorothy pranced through several scens in a scant squaw's outfit shaking her body for all it was worth. But it was the energetic gymnastics of Cass Daley and Gil Lamb, and the fumbling comedy style of Moore which lightened the heavy going.

Dorothy was an eager volunteer during World War II to assist the Allied cause. She made numerous war bond tours, raising a tremendous amount of money during these sales, and she received more than 22,000 fan letters a week, mostly from servicemen overseas. The troops of various divisions named her "sweetheart of the fox hole," "paratrooper pet," "glider girl," "queen bee of the South Pacific Island," and so forth. At one juncture in a bond tour, there was much public furor when it was thought Dorothy had entered a busy industrial plant during working hours. Dorothy was careful to explain to the press that she fully realized such a distraction could cost the war effort at least 1,000 man-working-hours per appearance, and that she would never be so thoughtless or unpatriotic.

By April 1, 1944, Dorothy was headlining NBC radio's "Palmolive Party" on Saturday evenings, with Barry Wood and Patsy Kelly supporting the bill.

And the Angels Sing (1944) again teamed old guard Dorothy with the new studio regime's Betty Hutton—and for good measure, newcomers Mimi

Chandler and maturing studio ingenue Diana Lynn. They were the singing sister act who become intertwined in the life of cagey bandleader Fred MacMurray. He has fleeced the girls of $190 and they pursue him to the Brooklyn club where his band is now playing. Each sister mistakenly believes her talents lie in other fields, but their father Raymond Walburn, fate, and love convince them otherwise. Dorothy pretended to play the accordion in the sister act, but really performed a hot jive dance with Frank Faylen, introduced the ballad "It Should Happen to You," and as the nominal star won MacMurray. However, it was the frenzied vocalizing of Hutton to "And His Rocking Horse Ran Away" and "Bluebirds in My Belfry" which garnered the most public attention.

Rainbow Island (1944) was an out and out technicolor spoof of the waning sarong cycle. Dorothy is Lona, a white girl brought up on the Pacific island by her doctor father. Merchant marines Barry Sullivan, Eddie Bracken, and Gil Lamb make a forced landing there while escaping from the Japanese. Only because Bracken resembles a native god are the whites spared from sacrificial death. There is the usual quota of lush vegetation, painted rocks, sapphire blue pools, ill-tempered natives, and bountiful feasts. Only one of the four songs, "Beloved," was sung by Dorothy. Howard Barnes *(New York Herald Tribune)* noted that she "never fails to act as though she were appearing on a Hollywood set."

After touring in the charity-raising Hollywood Victory Caravan in 1945 with Betty Hutton, Diana Lynn, Barbara Stanwyck, and others, Dorothy returned to the screen in John Steinbeck's *A Medal for Benny* (1945). It revolved around a small town hypocritically honoring one of its war dead —the late hero had been run out of town. Dorothy was Benny's fiancee, who transfers her affection to stay-at-home Arturo De Cordova. J. Carrol Naish as Benny's father received the best critical notices. When the political factions in the town attempt to use him as a pawn, he objects and tries to convince everyone of the brotherhood of man. Said 31-year-old Dorothy about her cinematic change of pace: "The sarong and I can sever diplomatic relations any old time as far as I'm concerned. Ten years is a long time to be in pictures. But ten years in a sarong is too long, Personally I've had enough."

In the studio's all-star *Duffy's Tavern* (1945), Dorothy, minus her sarong, was on hand long enough to join Betty Hutton, Diana Lynn, Bing Crosby, and Arturo De Cordova in a satire on "Swinging on a Star."

Masquerade in Mexico (1945), a padded remake of *Midnight,* found stranded entertainer Dorothy being hired by Mexican banker Patric Knowles to entice matador Arturo De Cordova away from Knowles's straying wife Ann Dvorak. To accomplish her task, Dorothy pretends to be a Spanish countess. Her song routines were cloying and the vulgar attempt at Latin splendor sabotaged any potential charm. Mikhail Rasumny had an amusing bit as a music-loving taxi driver.

With the end of the war, Dorothy's husband returned to California and found employment in the advertising field. They adopted a son, Ridgely, in late 1945.

Road to Utopia (1946) was completed in May, 1944, but was not released until March, 1946, due to the backlog of product churned out during the lucrative war period. When her father is murdered, Dorothy heads to the Klondike, hoping to locate the gold mine which he had discovered. Meanwhile, con men Bing Crosby and Bob Hope find the map and arrive in the far north. After much losing and regaining of the map, Hope makes off with

Dorothy and the riches, leaving Crosby behind on an ice floe to face the villains. Years later, Crosby visits the elderly married Dorothy and Hope. In the movie's comedy capper, their son appears—he is the spitting image of Crosby. Narrated by Robert Benchley and filled with dancing bears and talking fishes, the musical was another top grosser. Of Dorothy's two songs, "Would You?" outshone "Personality." *Newsweek* remarked: "Art lovers may be critical because the plot of 'Utopia' requires Miss Lamour to dress for subzero weather." But Dorothy does don a sarong for a brief scene, while wearing a muff to keep her hands warm.

In 1947, her last year at Paramount, Dorothy had four major releases, although all in a costarring capacity. Paired with Bob Hope again in *My Favorite Brunette* (1947), Dorothy plays an affluent heroine seeking help to locate her kidnapped uncle. She enters Alan Ladd's private detective agency and mistakes baby photographer Hope for a gumshoe. She convinces him to take the case. She holds the map—at least for a time—which tells the whereabouts of valuable mineral deposits. International crooks Charles Dingle, Peter Lorre, and Lon Chaney, Jr. scramble to get there first. Hope is later arrested on a murder charge, and just a few moments before he is to go to the electric chair (Bing Crosby is the executioner), Dorothy obtains a pardon from the governor. Dorothy sang "Beside You," took her pratfall gracefully, and as Bosley Crowther complimented in the *New York Times,* "does very nicely." Dorothy and Hope repeated their *My Favorite Brunette* roles on radio's "Screen Guild Players" (October 13, 1947, CBS).

Variety Girl (1947) Paramount's third and final 1940s all-star revue, had Dorothy and Alan Ladd featured in a production number "Tallahassee." Their scene opens in an airplane where tough guy Ladd, at pistol point, orders the pilots to land. Then he backs into the passenger cabin and breaks into song with stewardess Dorothy. Despite his mild singing talent, Ladd appeared relatively at ease. In contrast, Dorothy projected total nervousness, as if perplexed as to what her song partner might do next.

Wild Harvest (1947) again teamed Dorothy in support of Alan Ladd (they had even done a "Lux Radio Theatre" episode together, appearing in *Coney Island* on April 17, 1944). Here she was the sizzling prairie siren, married to Robert Preston but in love with sterling Alan Ladd. Tay Garnett's heavy-handed account of violent tempers on the Western plains did no one's career any good. Otis L. Guernsey, Jr. *(New York Herald Tribune)* panned it: "Not since Theda Bara has there been anything like the slinky siren scenes involving Dorothy Lamour as a bucolic Circe." James Agee in *Time* magazine observed: "Director [Tay Garnett] shows what a good movie this might have been. His harvesters' dance is a fine, forlorn scene, and he stages quite a hair-raising wheat fire and a particularly violent chase. But he seems to have realized that nothing could be done with the tense Lamour-Ladd relationship except to treat it as slightly ridiculous."

Road to Rio (1947) redeemed Dorothy with her public, who preferred her in nonserious situations in which she would treat her love goddess position with tongue in cheek. As Lucia Maria de Andrade, she is on her way to Brazil with her evil aunt, Gale Sondergaard, who has hypnotized the girl into consenting to a marriage of convenience. Crosby and Hope are down-at-the-heels musicians who stowaway on the ship. Other passengers on the liner are the Andrews Sisters, who join Crosby for the delightful "You Don't Have to Know the Language." By the completion of this travelogue spoof, Dorothy has shed her aunt and become quite attached to Crosby. She sings "Experience."

Beginning July 6, 1947, Dorothy hosted the NBC radio musical show "Front and Center," which was an Army recruiting program. Al Jolson had turned down the 13-week assignment, thinking it unpatriotic to accept money for such a task.

In the mid-1940s Dorothy had candidly told an interviewer: "My hips are too big, my feet aren't very pretty and my shoulder blades stick out." By 1947 she was past 33. The postwar film recession had set in, and Paramount studio bosses Henry Ginsberg and Y. Frank Freeman agreed that many of the company's expensive stars could be axed. Of the still remaining 1940s stalwarts, only Paulette Goddard and Betty Hutton were kept under contract; Dorothy, Veronica Lake, Joan Caulfield, and others were let go. A new, less expensive crop of talent had arrived at the Marathon Street lot, including Wanda Hendrix, Lizabeth Scott, and Kristine Miller.

Dorothy drifted into free-lance work, trading on her past big marquee name to carry her through a succession of mediocre roles in generally minor films. Despte her limited acting range, she was now required to carry a picture on her own, something she was not up to and which the public would not buy.

For producer-actor Burgess Meredith and his wife Paulette Goddard, Dorothy appeared in the multi-episode failure *On Our Merry Way,* which opened at the Warner Theatre on February 3, 1948. In the second vignette, she essayed an aspiring starlet and Victor Moore portrayed a silent film era hasbeen. Dorothy sang the satirical "The Queen of the Hollywood Islands." The low-budget production quickly passed into obscurity, although it was a perennial late show offering for a long stretch.

Lulu Belle was one of Columbia's economy releases of June, 1948. In adapting the 1926 Broadway play for the screen, the lead character was changed from a grasping prostitute to an ambitious chanteuse. Set in the 1900s, the sordid tale is related through a flashback. It traces the career of Natchez-bred Dorothy, who marries attorney George Montgomery, dallies with prize fighter Gregg McClure, flirts with his manager Albert Dekker, and then scoots off to New York with millionaire Otto Kruger and becomes a stage star. Later she is shot; the rest is a tepid whodunit. The teaser ads for *Lulu Belle* proclaimed: "There was something about the way she looked at a man that rang bells." The Memphis Board of Censors banned the film, terming Dorothy's performance as "catering to the lowest impulses of audiences." Neither this potential publicity attracter nor her five songs drew much audience reaction. Her histrionics found few supporters.

Her other 1948 release was more dismal. *The Girl from Manhattan* cast her as a New York model returning home to find that uncle Ernest Truex has mortgaged his boarding house to the hilt. Dorothy soon becomes involved with preacher George Montgomery and Bishop Charles Laughton. The end product had few redeeming entertainment qualities.

Manhandled crept into the Paramount Theatre on May 25, 1949. It had been packaged by the programmer unit of her old studio. As secretary to bogus psychiatrist Harold Vermilyea, Dorothy becomes implicated in the murder of patient Alan Napier's wife, Irene Hervey. Her involvement is furthered by her connections with boarding house neighbor and louse Dan Duryea. It takes obnoxious insurance investigator Art Smith and some plot contriving to solve the crime and end the film. Boyfriend Duryea knocks her out cold twice in the story and later attempts to dump her off a roof. Undergoing these perils did nothing to bolster her declining box-office standing.

The Lucky Stiff opened one day after *Manhandled.* It found Dorothy as club singer Anna Marie St. Claire who has supposedly been executed for murdering her employer. In reality this was attorney Brian Donlevy's gambit to smoke out the suspects in the homicide case. Marjorie Rambeau as a fussy old client and Claire Trevor as Donlevy's long-suffering secretary took the few acting honors. Dorothy sang "Loveliness" but was branded "limp" by the critics. For some unknown reason, Jack Benny produced this United Artists venture.

Slightly French (1949) was an above-average black and white remake of *Let's Fall in Love* (1934), which had featured Ann Sothern. Here Dorothy appeared as Mary O'Leary, an Irish cooch dancer at a carnival whom film director Don Ameche transforms into an exotic French import named Rochelle Olivia. Willard Parker as the harassed producer and Janis Carter as Ameche's sister rounded out the sparse proceedings. Dorothy sang "Night," "I Want to Learn About Love," and "Let's Fall in Love." She wore no sarong, but did don a bathing suit. In the "Fifi from the Folies Bergere" numbers, Dorothy demonstrated the can-can. Reviewers were gracious enough to admit her French accent had "a certain technical conviction."

On October 20, 1949, Dorothy gave birth to a son, Richard. She and her family moved back to Baltimore, her husband's hometown. Dorothy, now the content housewife, announced: "Now that I have two boys I can do my own *Road* pictures at home. That house, believe me, is as crazy as a *Road* picture with the two kids yelling at once."

Occasionally, Dorothy would be lured away from domesticity. She played the London Palladium Theatre in May, 1950, and then appeared at the Empire Theatre in Glasgow before returning home. The British and Scots received her performances enthusiastically.

As a favor to Bing Crosby, Dorothy made a brief guest appearance in his starring vehicle *Here Comes the Groom* (1951). In an airplane sequence, she, Louis Armstrong, Cass Dailey, and Phil Harris join Crosby in singing "Misto Christofo Columbo."

In April, 1951, Dorothy won $84,945.80 in a lawsuit against producer Benedict Bogeaus for failure to pay her salary in 1948 for *Lulu Belle* and *The Girl from Manhattan*.

Then Cecil B. DeMille cast Dorothy as Phyllis, the aerialist in his *The Greatest Show on Earth* (1952). She had the flashy but unimportant role of the performer who swings from a wire with a bit in her teeth. On the ground she offers bits of advice and encouragement to fellow-performer Betty Hutton. This circus extravaganza premiered at Radio City Music Hall on January 10, 1952. Dorothy was fetching in tights and assorted multihued show outfits, but most of the attention went to the spectacle of the big top itself. While Dorothy was on location with the film at Sarasota Springs, Florida, her son Ridgely contacted polio. She received much publicity and a great deal of fan sympathy. She carried on in the movie and her son recovered.

Dorothy was considered a must when Bing Crosby and Bob Hope made their sixth "Road" feature, *Road to Bali* (1952). It was the series' first in color. Dorothy was still shapely as Balinese Princess Lalah of Scottish descent. Her dastardly half-brother Murvyn Vye hires Crosby and Hope to dive for a pearl treasure horde at the ocean's bottom which belonged to her people. As of old, Crosby and Hope vied for Dorothy's love interest. And there were edgy headhunting natives, shipwrecks, and erupting volcanos. Nonhuman performers included an amorous gorilla and the giant squid guarding the treasure. There are cameo appearances by Dean Martin, Jerry Lewis, Bob Crosby, and Jane Russell, and a film clip of Humphrey Bogart dragging along the *African Queen.* At the finish Crosby wins both Dorothy and Russell. Dorothy sings "Moon Flowers." About donning a sarong for the first time in five years, Dorothy confessed: "It felt so good after all those years that I'm wearing seven different ones in the picture. Can't buck a trademark, can I?" Bosley Crowther *(New York Times)* observed: "Mr. Crosby, Mr. Hope and Miss Lamour may have looked lovelier, but never better in their happy excursions down the *Roads."*

Throughout the 1950s Dorothy made guest appearances on television, including: the "Colgate Comedy Hour" (NBC) with Eddie Cantor in 1952; a most sentimental subject on "This Is Your Life" (NBC) in 1956; *The Mink Doll* episode on "Damon Runyon Theatre" (ABC) in 1957; and the "Arthur Murray House Party" (NBC) in the 1960 two-part tribute to Bob Hope, on which she and Jayne Mansfield gave Hope "The Greatest Lover of Them All" award.

She made the rounds of nightclubs, from Miami (1956) to New Orleans (1957) to New York (1958). She toured for 7,000 miles in the pre-Broadway tryout of a dismal comedy *Roger the Sixth* with Robert Alda. On July 13, 1958, she made her Broadway stage debut when she replaced Abbe Lane in the faltering Tony Randall musical comedy *Oh! Captain.* The show dragged on only another week. On May 9, 1958, she returned to the Palladium in London with a 40-minute act culled from her movie musical numbers. She donned a sarong which pleased the gallery and her routine was rated "fine" by *Variety.*

Dorothy has been frequently quoted about her past cinema glories. "Sometimes when I see one of my old picture—me, the Sarong Girl—I say to myself, 'Golly, Dottie, just look at you. Weren't you something!" About screen beauty: "Glamour is just sex that got civilized. A pretty girl tastefully posed in a scant costume, is even a sort of cultural achievement."

Having been on the road with her nightclub act in 1961, Dorothy played New York's Latin Quarter late that year. Leonard Harris *(New York World-Telegram)* wrote: "Though the sarong was missing, Miss Lamour didn't disappoint her audience on other reminiscences. She pulled memories out of her hat like rabbits. . . . Her voice is not strong, but it's just right for her unaffected delivery." Dorothy also managed to find time to serve on the board of directors of the American Guild of Variety Artists, to organize Dorothy Lamour, Inc. to market beauty products, and to pen *Road to Beauty.*

Dorothy was always quick to volunteer that she regarded herself as still in the swim of the moviemaking world: "I've had plenty of scripts sent to me from Italy, from England, and from here. But you should see what they want me to play. I always made pictures that the whole family could see. I'm not going to turn my back on that. Even though I haven't made a picture for nine years, the public is amazingly loyal."

Bing Crosby and Bob Hope, whose film careers were badly sagging, announced in 1961 that they would make a new "Road" picture. Speculation ran high whether Dorothy would be back with the duo. Offered a small cameo role and told the female lead would be played by British actress Joan Collins, Dorothy balked. Since backing for the independent venture depended on delivering Dorothy as part of the package, her part was enlarged —although not substantially. *The Road to Hong Kong* (1962) was filmed in London, and Dorothy drew most of the publicity. "People sort of expect me in *The Road to Hong Kong.* More than anything, I owe it to my public. They've really been lovely to me." The thin slapstick farce had Hope and

Crosby involved with international intrigue and the launching of a space rocket. Dorothy came on late in the film, at a point where the boys rush into a nightclub. They relate their plight to her. She asks: "Is that the plot of the picture so far?" They nod. Dorothy says: "I'd better hide you." "From the killers?" ask the boys. "No, the critics," she replies. Then she launches into "Warmer Than a Whisper." Dorothy's presence proved a boon to the light-weight entry. *Time* magazine wrote: "For auld lang zing, Dorothy Lamour puts in an appearance, boldly slinking around in a sarong and looking half her age."

Dorothy made no bones about being peeved at her teammates for short-shrifting her. After filming a television special with Bob Hope to plug the new movie, she barked to the press: "My role in the TV trailer is bigger than the one I've got in the picture. Imagine—me doing four lines and one small number in a *Road* picture! Those jerks—Bing and Bob—I don't know, but I still love them."

In John Ford's minor color adventure yarn *Donovan's Reef* (1963), Dorothy took sixth billing as Fleur, a "kind of Mae Westian saloon performer" in northern Hawaii. She remains on the sidelines while John Wayne and Lee Marvin battle it out. Elizabeth Allen wins Wayne, and Dorothy, wearing a muumuu, sings "Silent Night," is tossed into a pool, and eventually lands Marvin. A. H. Weiler *(New York Times)* pointed out: "Miss Lamour's contribution is slight, but she obviously appreciates the free-and-easy spirit of the whole wacky affair."

In 1963 Dorothy performed in a three-month stock tour of *DuBarry Was a Lady* with Jack Goode, and participated as part of the Baltimore Civic Center Commission.

Dorothy next turned up in the low-budgeted teenage musical film *Pajama Party* (1965), playing a saleswoman in a dress store. Between the mild shenanigans and vocalizing of Martian Tommy Kirk and heroine Annette Funicello, and the lowbrow comedy of Elsa Lanchester and Buster Keaton, Dorothy warbled a brief song and pranced a few steps. She claimed she accepted the innocuous role just to let people in the industry know she was still available.

Dorothy was in the news in June, 1966, when she entertained troops at the United States Naval base at Guantanamo Bay, at the request of her son Ridgely. Purred Dorothy: "I've heard of mothers entertaining their sons' friends, but this is ridiculous." On November 26, 1966, she was nostalgically reunited with Bing Crosby on "The Hollywood Palace" (ABC).

With the success of *Hello, Dolly!* on Broadway, road companies vied for suitable singing stars to head the various tours. Dorothy replaced Carol Channing for one week in March, 1967, in Louisville, Kentucky, and then went on tour with the musical, traveling 23,000 miles through 34 states to 114 cities. In Las Vegas at the Riviera Hotel, she and Ginger Rogers each did one of the two evening shows. Dorothy reveled in her newfound popularity: "It's the same at every performance. You become one with the audience. A real love feast both ways."

In May, 1968, Dorothy told columnist Earl Wilson: "I cry [watching my old films on television] because of the money they're making—none of which I get." That year, she and her husband left Baltimore and moved back to Hollywood, purchasing a home near that of Bob Hope. She appeared on a Bob Hope-Bing Crosby video special.

In 1969 Dorothy turned up in dramatic guest shots on "I Spy" (ABC) and "The Name of the Game" (NBC), and performed songs and dances on "Jimmie Durante Presents the Lennon Sisters" (ABC). In a 1971 episode of "Marcus Welby, M.D." (ABC) she played a matronly mother.

Dorothy's last feature to date is a cameo appearance in *The Phynx* (1970), a pseudonostalgic fizzle that has had scant theatrical release.

Dorothy found a most compatible nightclub costar in Hawaiian entertainer Don Ho, and they appeared at the Now Grove club in Los Angeles in November, 1970, and elsewhere. Said the obviously proud Dorothy: "Kids today know who Dottie Lamour is. I'm no Elizabeth Taylor, but they know me and my name." At a charity rally at the Houston Astrodome that year, one of her sarongs sold for $50,000 and Dorothy's singing won a standing ovation from the 46,000 attendees. (Another of her sarongs is now in the Smithsonian Institution's collection.)

In March, 1971, Dorothy top-cast a revival of Cole Porter's musical *Anything Goes* at San Diego's Off Broadway Theatre. It costarred Stanley Holloway. The *Los Angeles Times* reported: "Miss Lamour, still an eyeful, is singing like always . . . [and] is a pro all the way, playing Reno Sweeney, the Texas Guinan-type singer with her troupe of Fallen Angels. She . . . never misses a gesture or fails to point up an ancient line, even if it's terrible."

Dorothy is frequently asked about the new movie morality: "I'm no prude. I know you have to come up a little bit modern. But all this filth and homosexuality and sex and nudity today are ruining any hope of our young people having the beautiful life. The kids don't know how badly they want the old-type pictures like today's *Airport* so they can take their girl friends to movies again."

Looking back on her career, Dorothy has stated: "One small thing. I wouldn't be so easy with the front office. I'd demand they give me something to act in, even if I laid a bomb."

THE JUNGLE PRINCESS (PAR, 1936) 85 M.

Producer, E. Lloyd Sheldon; director, William Thiele; story, Max Marcin; screenplay, Cyril Hume, Gerald Geraghty, Gouverneur Morris; music director, Boris Morros; songs, Frederick Hollander, Leo Robin; camera, Harry Fischbeck; editor, Ellsworth Hoagland.

Dorothy Lamour (Ulah); Ray Milland (Christopher Powell); Akim Tamiroff (Karen Neg); Lynne Overman (Frank); Molly Lamout (Ava); Mala (Melan); Hugh Buckler (Colonel Neville Lane); Sally Martin (Ulah—As a Child); Roberta Law (Lin); Kimau (Tiger); Bogo (Chimpanzee); Erville Alderson (Priest); Bernard Siegel (Ulah's Grandfather); Richa:d Terry (Maley Hunter); Nick Shaid (Headman Of Tribe); Dan Crimmins (Head Tribesman); John George, Bhogwan Singh, Eddie Sturgis, James P. Spencer, Al Kikume, Kim Maki, Mickey Phillips, Inez Gomez, Mural Sharada, Emilia Diaz, Ray Roubert (Natives).

SWING HIGH, SWING LOW (PAR, 1937) 97 M.

Producer, Arthur Hornblow, Jr.; director, Mitchell Leisen; based on the play *Burlesque* by George Manker Watters; screenplay, Virginia Van Upp, Oscar Hammerstein II; art director, Hans Dreier, Ernst Fegte; music director, Boris Morros; songs, Ralph Rainger and Leo Robin; Sam Coslow and Al Siegal; Ralph Freed and Charles Kisco; camera, Ted Tetzlaff; editor, Eda Warren.

Carole Lombard (Maggie King); Fred MacMurray (Skid Johnson); Charles Butterworth (Harry); Jean Dixon (Ella); Dorothy Lamour (Anita Alvarez); Cecil Cunningham (Murphy); Harvey Stephens (Harvey Dexter); Charlie Arnt (Georgie); Franklin Pangborn (Henri); Anthony Quinn (The Don); Dennis O'Keefe (Purser); Charles Judels (Tony); Harry Semels (Chief Of Police); Ricardo Mandia (Interpreter); Enrique DeRosas (Judge); Chris Pin Martin (Sleepy Servant); Charles Stevens (Panamanian At Cock Fight); Ralph Remley (Musselwhite); Oscar Rudolph (Elevator Boy); George Sorel (Manager); George W. Jimenez (Justice Of Peace); Lee Bowman, Nick Lukats (Men in Night Club); Lee Cooley (Radio Announcer); Richard Kipling (Army Surgeon); Esther Howard (Customer); Donald Kerr (Radio Technician); William Wright (Attendant); Spencer Chan (Cook).

LAST TRAIN FROM MADRID (PAR, 1937) 85 M.

Producer, George M. Arthur; associate producer, Hugh Bennett; director, James Hogan; story, Paul H. Fox, Elsie Fox; screenplay, Louis Stevens, Robert Wyler; music director, Boris Morros; camera, Harry Fischbeck; editor, Everett Douglass.

Dorothy Lamour (Carmelita Castillo); Lew Ayres (Bill Dexter); Gilbert Roland (Eduardo de Soto); Karen Morley (Helene Rafitte); Lionel Atwill (Colonel Vigo); Helen Mack (Lola); Robert Cummings (Juan); Olympe Bradna (Maria Ronda); Anthony Quinn (Captain Ricardo Alvarez); Lee Bowman (Michael Balk); Jack Perrin, Harry Semels (Guards); Frank Leyva (Chauffeur); George Lloyd (Intelligence Officer); Louise Carter (Rosa Delgado); Hooper Atchley (Martin); Francis McDonald (Mora); Stanley Fields (Avila); Sam Appel (Warden); Stanley Price (Clerk); Henry Brandon (Radio Announcer); Maurice Cass (Waiter); Harry Worth (Gomez); Bess Flowers (Saleswoman); Evelyn Brent (Woman); Tiny Newland (Turnkey); Charles Middleton (Warden); Harry Woods (Government Man).

HIGH, WIDE AND HANDSOME (PAR, 1937) 110 M.

Producer, Arthur Hornblow, Jr.; director, Rouben Mamoulian; original screenplay-lyrics, Oscar Hammerstein II; additional dialogue, George O'Neill; music, Jerome Kerne; music director, Boris Morros; choreography, LeRoy Prinz; camera, Victor Milner; special effects, Gordon Jennings; editor, Archie Marshek.

Irene Dunne (Sally Watterson); Randolph Scott (Peter Cortlandt); Dorothy La-
mour (Molly Fuller); Elizabeth Patterson (Grandma Cortlandt); Raymond Walburn
(Doc Watterson); Charles Bickford (Red Scanlon); Akim Tamiroff (Joe Varese); Ben
Blue (Zeke); William Frawley (Mac); Alan Hale (Walt Brennan); Irving Pichel (Mr.
Stark); Stanley Andrews (Lem Moulton); James Burke (Stackpole); Roger Imhof (Pop
Bowers); Lucien Littlefield (Mr. Lippincott); Purnell Pratt (Colonel Blake); Edward
Gargan (Foreman); Helen Lowell (Mrs. Lippincott); Jack Clifford (Wash Miller); Rus-
sell Hopton (John Thompson—Civil Engineer); Ivan Miller (Marble); Raymond
Brown (P. T. Barnum); Constance Bergen (Singer); Tommy Bupp (Boy); Billy Bletcher
(Shorty); Paul Kruger (Man); Claire McDowell (Seamstress); Fred Warren (Piano
Player); Rolfe Sedan (Photographer); Marjorie Cameron (Blonde Singer); John T.
Murray (Mr. Green); Sherry Hall (Piano Player); Edward Keane (Jones); Pat West
(Razorback); John Maurice Sullivan (Old Gentleman); Ernest Wood (Hotel Clerk);
Lew Kelly (Carpenter); Dell Henderson (Bank President); John Marshall (Teller);
Philip Morris (Teamster); Harry Semels (Bartender); Frank Sully (Gabby Johnson).

THE HURRICANE (UA, 1937) 110 M.

Producer, Samuel Goldwyn; associate producer, Merritt Hulburd; director, John
Ford; co-director, Stuart Heisler; based on the novel by Charles Nordhoff, James
Norman Hall; adaptation, Dudley Nichols, Oliver H. P. Garrett; music, Alfred New-
man; song, Frank Loesser and Newman; art director, Richard Day, Alexander Go-
litzen; assistant director, Wingate Smith; special effects, James Basevi; camera, Bert
Glennon; editor, Lloyd Nosler.

Dorothy Lamour (Marama); Jon Hall (Terang); Mary Astor (Madame De Laage);
C. Aubrey Smith (Father Paul); Thomas Mitchell (Dr. Kersaint); Raymond Massey
(Governor De Laage); John Carradine (Warden); Jerome Cowan (Captain Nagle); Al
Kikume (Chief Mehevi); Kuulei De Cleag (Tita); Layne Tom, Jr. (Mako); Mamo Clark
(Hitia); Movita Castenada (Aral); Mary Shaw (Marunga); Spencer Charters (Judge);
Roger Drake (Captain OF Guards); Inez Courtney (Girl on Ship); Flora Hayes (Mama
Rua); Pauline Steele (Mata); Francis Kaai (Tavi); Reri (Himself); Paul Stader (Stunt-
man).

THRILL OF A LIFETIME (PAR, 1937) 72 M.

Producer, Fanchon; director, George Archainbaud; story, Seena Owen, Grant Gar-
rett; screenplay, Owen, Garrett, Paul Gerard Smith; art director, Hans Dreier, Franz
Bachelin; choreography, LeRoy Prinz; songs; Frederick Hollander and Sam Coslow;
Yacht Club Boys; music director, Boris Morros; camera, William C. Mellor; editor,
Doane Harrison.

Yacht Club Boys (Themselves); Judy Canova (Judy); Ben Blue (Skipper); Eleanore
Whitney (Betty Jane); Johnny Downs (Stanley); Betty Grable (Gwen); Leif Erikson
(Howdy Nelson); Larry Crabbe (Don); The Fanchonettes, Dorothy Lamour (Speciali-
ties); Zeke Canova, Anne Canova (Themselves); Tommy Wonder (Billy); Franklin
Pangborn (Mr. Williams); June Shafer (Receptionist); Howard M. Mitchell (Business
Man); Si Jenks (Messenger Boy).

THE BIG BROADCAST OF 1938 (PAR, 1938) 97 M.

Producer, Harlan Thompson; director, Mitchell Leisen; story, Frederick Hazlitt
Brennan; adaptation, Howard Lindsay, Russell Crouse; screenplay, Walter DeLeon,
Francis Martin, Ken Englund; choreography, LeRoy Prinz; cartoon sequence, Leon
Schlesinger; music director, Boris Morros; songs, Leo Robin and Ralph Rainger; Tito
Guizar; Jack Rock; special effects, Gordon Jennings; camera, Harry Fischbeck; editor,
Eda Warren, Chandler House.

W. C. Fields (T. Frothingill Bellows and S. B. Bellows); Martha Raye (Martha
Bellows); Dorothy Lamour (Dorothy Wyndham); Shirley Ross (Cleo Fielding); Lynne
Overman (Scoop McPhail); Bob Hope (Buzz Fielding); Leif Erikson (Bob Hayes);
Grace Bradley (Grace Fielding); Rufe Davis (Turnkey); Tito Guizar (Himself); Lionel

Pape (Lord Droopy); Virginia Vale (Joan Fielding); Russell Hicks (Captain Stafford); Leonid Kinskey (Ivan); Patricia Wilder (Honey Chile); Shep Field And His Rippling Rhythm Orchestra, Kirsten Flagstad, Wilfred Pelletier (Themselves); Archie Twitchel, James Craig (Stewards); Richard Denning, Michael Brooke, Jack Hubbard, Bill Roberts, Clive Morgan, John Huettner, Bruce Wyndham, Kenneth Swartz (Officers); Rex Moore, Bernard Punsley, Don Marton (Caddies); James Conlin (Reporter); Irving Bacon (Prisoner—Harmonica Player); Wally Maher (Court Clerk); Muriel Barr (Showgirl); Mary MacLaren, Florence Wix, Carol Holloway, Gertrude Astor, Nell Craig, Ethel Clayton, Gloria Williams (Women); Ray Hanford (Pilot); Jerry Fletcher, Robert Allen (Gas Station Attendants); Bud Geary (Helmsman).

HER JUNGLE LOVE (PAR, 1938) 81 M.

Producer, George M. Arthur; director, George Archainbaud; story, Gerald Geraghty, Kurt Siodmak; screenplay, Joseph M. March, Lillie Hayward, Eddie Welch; songs, Leo Robin and Ralph Rainger; Ralph Freed and Frederick Hollander; camera, Ray Rennahan; editor, Hugh Bennett.

Dorothy Lamour (Tura); Ray Milland (Bob Mitchell); Lynne Overman (Jimmy Wallace); J. Carrol Naish (Kuasa); Virginia Vale (Eleanor Martin); Jonathan Hale (J. C. Martin); Archie Twitchell (Roy Atkins); Edward Earle (Captain Avery); Jiggs (Gaga, The Chimpanzee); Meewa (Lion Cub); Sonny Chorre, Tony Urchel (Guards); Richard Denning, Phillip Warren (Pilots).

TROPIC HOLIDAY (PAR, 1938) 78 M.

Producer, Arthur Hornblow, Jr.; director, Theodore Reed; story, Don Hartman, Frank Butler; screenplay, Hartman, Butler, John C. Moffett, Duke Atteberry; songs; Ned Washington and Augustin Lara; Leo Robin and Ralph Rainger; camera, Ted Tetzlaff; editor, Archie Marshek.

Dorothy Lamour (Manuela); Bob Burns (Breck Jones); Martha Raye (Midge MIller); Ray Milland (Ken Warren); Binnie Barnes (Marilyn Joyce); Tito Guizar (Ramon); Pepito (Chico); Chris Pin Martin (Pancho); Elvira Rios (Rosa); Michael Visaroff (Felipe); Bobbie Moya (Repito); Roberto Soto (Roberto); Frank Puglia (Co-Pilot); Jesus Topete (Pedro); Fortunio Bonanova (Barrera); Dominguez Bros. San Cristobal Marimba Band (Themselves).

SPAWN OF THE NORTH (PAR, 1938) 110 M.

Producer, Albert Lewin; director, Henry Hathaway; story, Barrett Willoughby; screenplay, Talbot Jennings, Jules Furthman; camera, Charles Lang; editor, Ellsworth Hoagland.

George Raft (Tyler Dawson); Henry Fonda (Jim Kimmerlee); Dorothy Lamour (Nicky Duval); Akim Tamiroff (Red Skain); John Barrymore (Windy); Louise Platt (Diane); Lynne Overman (Jackson); Fuzzy Knight (Lefty Jones); Vladimir Sokoloff (Dimitri); Duncan Renaldo (Ivan); John Wray (Dr. Sparks); Michio Ito (Indian Dancer); Stanley Andrews (Partridge); Richard Ung (Tom); Slicker (Himself); Alex Woloshin (Gregory); Archie Twitchell, Lee Shumway, Wade Boteler, Galan Galt, Arthur Aylesworth, Rollo Lloyd, (Fishermen); Guy Usher (Grant); Henry Brandon (Davis); Egon Brecher (Erickson); Robert Middlemass (Davis); Adia Kuznetzoff (Vashia); Eddie Marr, Frank Puglia, Leonid Snegoff (Red's Gang); Edmund Elton (Minister).

ST. LOUIS BLUES (PAR, 1939) 92 M.

Producer, Jeff Lazarus; director, Raoul Walsh; story, Eleanore Griffin, William Rankin; adaptation, Frederick Hazlitt Brennan; screenplay, John C. Moffitt, Malcolm Stuart Boylan; choreography, LeRoy Prinz; songs, Frank Loesser and Burton Lane; Loesser and Matty Malneck; Walsh and Malneck; Leo Robin, Sam Coslow, Hoagy Carmichael; camera, Theodor Sparkuhl.

Dorothy Lamour (Norma Malone); Lloyd Nolan (Dave Guerney); Tito Guizar (Rafael San Ramos); Jerome Cowan (Ivan DeBrett); Jessie Ralph (Aunt Tibbie); William Frawley (Major Martingale); Mary Parker (Punkins); Maxine Sullivan (Ida); Cliff Nazarro (Shorty); Victor Kilian (Sheriff Burdick); Walter Soderling (Mr. Hovey); The King's Men (Deck Hand Quartette); Virginia Howell (Mrs. Hovey); Matty Malneck and his Orchestra (Themselves); Spencer Charters, Emmett Vogan (Judges); Joseph Crehan (Simpson); Billy Arnold (Hotel Clerk); George Guhl (Turnkey); Archie Twitchell (Cameraman); Florence Dudley (Secretary); Gene Morgan (Publicity Man); Emory Parnell (Police Officer White); Ernie Adams, Eddie Borden, Edward Hearn, Carl Harbaugh (Actors); Clarence Harvey (Old Man); Sterling Holloway (Boatman); Nora Cecil (Storekeeper); Wade Boteler (Police Lt.); Lane Chandler (Man in Audience); James Burtis (Sailor in Boiler Room).

MAN ABOUT TOWN (PAR, 1939) 85 M.

Producer, Arthur Hornblow, Jr.; director, Mark Sandrich; story, Morrie Ryskind; Alan Scott, Zion Myers; screenplay, Ryskind; art director, Hans Dreier, Robert Usher; music director, Victor Young; songs, Frank Loesser and Frederick Hollander; Loesser and Matty Malneck; Leo Robin and Ralph Rainger; camera, Ted Tetzlaff; editor, LeRoy Stone.

Jack Benny (Bob Temple); Dorothy Lamour (Diana Wilson); Edward Arnold (Sir John Arlington); Binnie Barnes (Lady Arlington); Phil Harris (Ted Nash); Eddie Anderson (Rochester); Monty Woolley (Monsieur Dubois); Isabel Jeans (Mme. Dubois); Betty Grable (Susan); E. E. Clive (Hotchkiss); Leonard Mudie (Gibson); Herbert Evans (Englishman); Clifford Severn (English Bellboy); Cyril Thornton (Walter); Kay Linaker (Receptionist).

DISPUTED PASSAGE (PAR, 1939) 87 M.

Producer, Harlan Thompson; director, Frank Borzage, based on the novel by Lloyd C. Douglas; screenplay, Anthony Veiller, Sheridan Gibney; art director, Hans Dreier, Roland Anderson; music, Frederick Hollander and John Leopold; camera, William C. Mellor; editor, James Smith.

Dorothy Lamour (Audrey Hilton); Akim Tamiroff (Dr. "Tubby" Forster); John Howard (John Wesley Beaven); Judith Barrett (Winifred Bane); William Collier, Sr. (Dr. William Cunningham); Victor Varconi (Dr. LaFerriere); Gordon Jones (Bill Anderson); Keye Luke (Andrew Abbott); Elisabeth Risdon (Mrs. Cunningham); Gaylord Pendleton (Lawrence Carpenter); Billy Cook (Johnny Merkle); William Pawley (Mr. Merkle); Renie Riano (Landlady); Z. T. Nyi (Chinese Ambassador); Philson Ahn (Kai); Dr. E. Y. Chung (Dr. Ling); Philip Ahn (Dr. Fung); Lee Ya-Ching (Aviatrix); Roger Gray (Gibson); Jack Chapin (Terrence Shane); Dave Alison (Interne); Mary Skalek (Dirty Nurse); Alma Eidnea (Scrub Nurse); Paul M. MacWilliams (Doctor); Charles Trowbridge (Dean); Dorothy Adams, Joleen King, Henrietta Kaye, Hortense Arbogast, Edith Cagnon, Patsy Mace, Fay McKenzie, Gloria Williams (Nurses); Jimmy F. Hogan (Messenger Boy); Kitty McHugh (Telephone Operator); James B. Carson (Hotel Clerk); Paul England (Britisher); Richard Denning (Student).

JOHNNY APOLLO (20th, 1940) 93 M.

Producer, Darryl F. Zanuck; associate producer, Harry Joe Brown; director, Henry Hathaway; story, Samuel G. Engel, Hal Long; screenplay, Philip Dunne, Rowland Brown; songs, Frank Loesser and Lionel Newman; Loesser and Alfred Newman; Mack Gordon; camera, Arthur Miller; editor, Robert Bischoff.

Tyrone Power (Bob Cain); Dorothy Lamour ("Lucky" Dubarry); Edward Arnold (Robert Cain, Sr.); Lloyd Nolan (Nickey Dwyer); Charles Grapewin (Judge Emmett F. Brennan); Lionel Atwill (Jim McLaughlin); Marc Lawrence (Bates); Jonathan Hale (Dr. Brown); Russell Hicks (District Attorney); Fuzzy Knight (Cellmate); Charles Lane (Assistant District Attorney); Selmer Jackson (Warden); Charles Trowbridge (Judge); George Irving (Mr. Ives); Eddie Marr, Anthony Caruso (Henchmen); Harry

Rosenthal (Piano Player); William Pawley (Paul); Eric Wilton (Butler); Stanley Andrews (Welfare Secretary); Wally Allbright (Office Boy); Charles Williams (Photographer); Bess Flowers (Secretary); Milburn Stone, Phil Toad, Charles Tannen (Reporters); Tom Dugan (Prisoner); Jim Pierce, Walter Miller, William Haade, Louis Jean Heydt, Stanley Blystone, James Flavin, Don Rowan, James Blain (Guards); Robert Shaw (Clerk); Edward Gargan, Charles D. Brown (Detectives); Emmett Vogan (Guard-Announcer).

TYPHOON (PAR, 1940) 70 M.

Producer, Anthony Veiller; director, Louis King; story, Steve Fisher; screenplay, Allen Rivkin; art director, Hans Dreier, John Goodman; music, Frederick Hollander; song, Hollander and Frank Loesser; camera, William Mellor; special effects, Gordon Jennings; editor, Alma Macrorie.

Dorothy Lamour (Dea); Robert Preston (Johnny Potter); Lynne Overman (Skipper Joe); J. Carrol Naish (Mekaike); Chief Thundercloud (Kehi); Frank Reicher (Doctor); John Rogers (Barkeep); Paul Harvey (Dea's Father); Norma Nelson (Dea—As A Child); Jack Carson (The Mate); Al Kikume (Cook); Angelo Cruz, Paul Singh (Kehi's Bodyguards).

ROAD TO SINGAPORE (PAR, 1940) 84 M.

Producer, Harlan Thompson; director, Victor Schertzinger; story, Harry Hervey; screenplay, Don Hartman, Frank Butler; art director, Hans Dreier, Robert Odell; music director, Victor Young; choreography, LeRoy Prinz; songs, Johnny Burke and Jimmy Monaco; Burke and Schertzinger; camera, William C. Mellor; editor, Paul Weatherwax.

Bing Crosby (Josh Mallon); Dorothy Lamour (Mima); Bob Hope (Ace Lannigan); Charles Coburn (Joshua Mallon IV); Judith Barrett (Gloria Wycott); Anthony Quinn (Caesar); Jerry Colonna (Achilles Bombanassa); Johnny Arthur (Timothy Willow); Pierre Watkin (Morgan Wycott); Steve Gaylord Pendleton (Gordon Wycott); Miles Mander (Sire Malcolm Drake); Pedro Regas (Zato); Greta Grandstadt (Babe); Edward Gargan (Bill); Don Brodie (Fred); John Kelly (Sailor); Kitty Kelly (Sailor's Wife); Roger Gray (Father); Harry C. Bradley (Secretary); Richard Keene (Cameraman); Gloria Franklin (Ninky Poo); Monte Blue (High Priest); Cyril Ring (Ship's Officer); Helen Lynd (Society Girl).

MOON OVER BURMA (PAR, 1940) 76 M.

Director, Louis King; story, Wilson Collison; screenplay, Frank Wead, W. P. Lipscomb, Harry Clork; songs, Frank Loesser and Harry Revel; Loesser and Frederick Hollander; camera, William Mellor; editor, Stuart Gilmore.

Dorothy Lamour (Arla Dean); Robert Preston (Chuck Lane); Preston Foster (Bill Gordon); Doris Nolan (Cynthia Harmon); Albert Bassermann (Basil Renner); Frederick Worlock (Stephen Harmon); Addison Richards (Art Bryan); Harry Allen (Sunshine); Frank Lackteen (Khran); Stanley Price (Khuda); Hans Schumm (Baumgarten); Paul Porcasi (Storekeeper); Henry Roquemore (Jovial Plantation Owner); Catherine Wallace (Plantation Owner's Wife); Ella Neal (Girl on Rangoon Street); Ralph Sencuya (Native Waiter); Nick Shaid, Ram Singh, Maro Cortez (Natives).

CHAD HANNA (20th, 1940) 86 M.

Producer, Darryl F. Zanuck; associate producer, Nunnally Johnson; director, Henry King; based on the novel *Red Wheels Rolling* by Walter D. Edmonds; screenplay, Johnson; art director, Richard Day; music, David Buttolph; camera, Ernest Palmer, Ray Rennahan; editor, Barbara McLean.

Henry Fonda (Chad Hanna); Dorothy Lamour (Albany Yates/Lady Lillian); Linda Darnell (Caroline); Guy Kibbee (Huguenine); Jane Darwell (Mrs. Huguenine); John Carradine (Bisbee); Ted North (Fred); Roscoe Ates (Ike Wayfish); Ben Carter

(Bell Boy); Frank Thomas (Burke); Olin Howland (Cisco Tridd); Frank Conlan (Mr. Proudfoot); Edward Conrad (Fiero); Edward McWade (Elias); Edward Mundy (Joe Duddy); George Davis (Pete Bostock); Paul Burns (Budlong); Sarah Padden (Mrs. Tridd); Elizabeth Abbott (Mrs. Pamplon); Leonard St. Leo (Mr. Pamplon); Tully Marshall (Mr. Mott); Almira Sessions (Mrs. Mott); Virginia Brissac (Landlady); Si Jenks (Farmer); Victor Kilian (Potato Man); Louis Mason (Constable); Charles Middleton (Sheriff); Rondo Hatton (Canvasman); Nelson McDowell (Man); Clarence Muse (Black Man); Maxine Tucker (Servant Girl); Jim Pierce, Dick Rich, Herbert Ashley, Paul Sutton (Men).

ROAD TO ZANZIBAR (PAR, 1941) 92 M.

Producer, Paul Jones; director, Victor Schertzinger; based on the story "Find Colonel Fawcett" by Don Hartman, Sy Bartlett; screenplay, Frank Butler, Hartman; songs, Johnny Burke and Jimmy Van Heusen; camera, Ted Tezlaff; editor, Alma Macrorie.

Bing Crosby (Chuck Reardon); Bob Hope (Fearless [Hubert] Frazier); Dorothy Lamour (Donna Latour); Una Merkel (Julia Quimby); Eric Blore (Charles Kimble); Iris Adrian (French Soubrette in Cafe); Lionel Royce (Monsieur Leben); Buck Woods (Taonga); Leigh Whipper (Scarface); Ernest Whitman (Whiteface); Noble Johnson (Chief); Leo Gorcey (Boy); Joan Marsh (Dimples); Luis Alberni (Proprietor—Native Booth); Robert Middlemass (Police Inspector); Norma Varden (Clara Kimble); Paul Porcasi (Turk At Slave Mart); Ethel Loreen Greer (Fat Lady); Georges Renavent (Saunders); Jules Strongbow (Solomon); Priscilla White, LaVerne Vess (Curzon Sisters—Iron Jaw Act); Harry C. Johnson, Harry C. Johnson, Jr. (Acrobats); Alan Bridge (Policeman); Henry Roquemore (Proprietor in Cafe); James B. Carson (Waiter); Eddy Conrad (Barber); Charlie Gemora (Gorilla); Ken Carpenter (Commentator); Richard Keene (Clerk).

CAUGHT IN THE DRAFT (PAR, 1941) 82 M.

Producer, B. G. DeSylva; director, David Butler; story-screenplay, Harry Tugend; art director, Hans Dreier, Haldane Douglas; music, Victor Young; song, Frank Loesser and Louis Alter; camera, Karl Struss; editor, Irene Morra.

Bob Hope (Don Gilbert); Dorothy Lamour (Tony Fairbanks); Lynne Overman (Steve); Eddie Bracken (Bert); Clarence Kolb (Col. Peter Fairbanks); Paul Hurst (Sgt. Burns); Ferike Boros (Yetta); Phyllis Ruth (Margie); Irving Bacon (Cogswell); Arthur Loft (Director); Edgar Dearing (Recruiting Sgt.); Murray Alper (Makeup Man); Dave Willock (Colonel's Orderly); Rita Owin (Cleaning Nurse); Frances Morris (Stretcher Nurse); Ella Neal, Eleanor Stewart, Earlene Heath, Gloria Williams, Marie Blake (Nurses); Terry Ray, Ed Peil, Jr. (Patients); Jimmy Dodd (Indignant Patient); Archie Twitchell (Stretcher Patient); Jack Chapin, Victor Cutler (Rookies); Jack Luden Jerry Jerome, Frank Mitchell (Captains); Ray Flynn (Lt. Colonel); David Oliver (Cameraman); Frank O'Connor (Major); Frank Marlowe (Twitchell); Heinie Conklin (Sign Hanger); Phyllis Kennedy (Susan); Arch Macnair (Toothless Man); Weldon Heyburn (Sgt. at Examining Depot); George McKay (Quartermaster Sgt.); Andrew Tombes (Justice of the Peace); Len Henry (Corporal).

ALOMA OF THE SOUTH SEAS (PAR, 1941) 77 M.

Associate producer, Monte Bell; director, Alfred Santell; story, Seena Owen, Kurt Siodmack; screenplay, Frank Butler, Owen, Lillie Hayward; music director, Andrea Setaro; art director, Hans Dreier, William Perira; song, Frank Loesser and Frederick Hollander; camera, Karl Struss; special effects, Gordon Jennings; editor, Arthur Schmidt.

Dorothy Lamour (Aloma); Jon Hall (Tanoa); Lynne Overman (Corky); Philip Reed (Revo); Katherine deMille (Kari); Fritz Leiber (High Priest); Dona Drake (Nea); Esther Dale (Tarusa; Pedro de Cordoba (Ramita); John Barclay (Ilkali); Norma Jean Nelson (Aloma—As a Child); Evelyn Del Rio (Nea—As a Child); Scotty Beckett

(Tanoa—As a Child); Billy Roy (Revo—As a Child); Noble Johnson (Moukali); Ella Neal, Dena Coaker, Emily LaRue, Patsy Mace, Dorothy Short, Paula Terry, Carmella Cansino, Esther Estrella (Aloma's Handmaidens); John Bagni (Native); Nina Campana (Toots); Charlene Wyatt, Janet Dempsey (Girls).

THE FLEET'S IN (PAR, 1942) 93 M.

Associate producer, Paul Jones; director, Victor Schertzinger; story, Monte Brice, J. Walter Ruben; screenplay, Walter De Leon, Sid Silvers; songs, Johnny Mercer and Schertzinger; Joseph J. Lilley; Frank Loesser and Schertzinger; camera, William Mellor; editor, Paul Weatherwax.

Dorothy Lamour (The Countess); William Holden (Casey Kirby); Eddie Bracken (Barney Waters); Betty Hutton (Bessie Dale); Cass Daley (Cissie); Gil Lamb (Spike); Leif Erickson (Jake); Betty Jane Rhodes (Diane Golden); Lorraine and Rognan (Dance Team); Jack Norton (Kellogg); Jimmy Dorsey and his Band (Themselves); Barbara Britton (Eileen Wright); Robert Warwick (Admiral Wright); Roy Atwell (Arthur Sidney); Dave Willock, Rod Cameron (Sailors); Harry Barris (Pee Wee); Hal Dawson (Diane's Manager); Charlie Williams (Photographer); Lyle Latell (Drunk); Oscar Smith (Valet); Stanley Andrews (Commander); Chester Clute (Minister).

BEYOND THE BLUE HORIZON (PAR, 1942) 76 M.

Associate producer, Monta Bell; director, Alfred Santell; story, E. Lloyd Sheldon, Jack DeWitt; screenplay, Frank Butler; art director, Hans Dreier, Earl Hedrick; songs, Frank Loesser and Jule Styne; Mort Greene and Harry Revel; camera, Charles Boyle; editor, Doane Harrison.

Dorothy Lamour (Tama); Richard Denning (Jackra); Jack Haley (Squidge); Patricia Morison (Sylvia); Walter Abel (Thornton); Helen Gilbert (Carol); Elizabeth Patterson (Mrs. Daly); Edward Fielding (Judge Chase); Gerald Oliver Smith (Chadwick); Frank Reicher (Sneath); Abner Biberman (La'oa); Charles Stevens (Panao); Charles Cane (Broderick—Chauffeur); Bill Telaak (Willys—Footman); Warren Ashe (Alvin Chase); Ann Doran (Margaret Chase); Ann Todd (Tama—As a Child); Inez Palange (Native Nurse); King Kong (Squat Native); Joe Bautista, E. Baucin, Bobby Barber, Tom Plank, Ralph Soneuya, Rito Punay (Members of La'oa's Gang); Dagmar Oakland, King Mojave, Gale Ronn, Kenneth Gibson, Mary Dunbar, Mildred Mernie, David Newell, Monya Andre, Keith Richards, William Cabanne (Guests at Chase's Residence); Barbara Britton (Pamela); Laurie Douglas, Ella Neal (Girls at Circus); Frances Gifford (Charlotte); Eleanor Stewart (Diana); Carlie Taylor, Russell Huestis, Eric Alden, Bert Moorhouse (Photographers); John Holland (Herrick).

ROAD TO MOROCCO (PAR, 1942) 83 M.

Associate producer, Paul Jones; director, David Butler; screenplay, Frank Butler; Don Hartman; music director, Victor Young; songs, Johnny Burke and James Van Heusen; art director, Hans Dreier, Robert Usher; camera, William Mellor; editor, Irene Morra.

Bing Crosby (Jeff Peters); Bob Hope (Turkey Jackson); Dorothy Lamour (Princess Shalmar); Anthony Quinn (Mulley Kasim); Dona Drake (Mihirmah); Mikhail Rasumny (Ahmed Fey); Vladimir Sokoloff (Hyder Khan); George Givot (Neb Jolla); Andrew Tombes (Oso Bucco); Leon Belasco (Yusef); Monte Blue, Jamiel Hanson (Aides to Mullay Kasim); Louise LaPlanche, Theo de Voe, Brooke Evans, Suzanne Ridgway, Patsy Mace, Yvonne de Carlo, Poppy Wilde (Handmaidens); George Lloyd, Sammy Stein (Guards); Ralph Penney (Arabian Waiter); Dan Seymour (Arabian Buyer); Pete G. Katchenaro (Philippine Announcer); Brandon Hurst (English Announcer); Richard Loo (Chinese Announcer); Leo Mostovoy (Russian Announcer); Vic Groves, Joe Jewett (Knife Dancers); Michael Mark (Arab Pottery Vendor); Nestor Paiva (Arab Sausage Vendor); Stanley Price (Idiot); Rita Christiani (Specialty Dancer); Robert Barron (Gigantic Bearded Arab); Cy Kendall (Proprietor—Fruit Stand); Sara Berner (Voice for Lady Camel); Kent Rogers (Voice for Man Camel);

Edward Emerson (Bystander); Sylvia Opert (Dancer); Blue Washington (Nubian Slave); Harry Cording, Dick Botiller (Warriors).

STAR SPANGLED RHYTHM (PAR, 1942) 99 M.

Associate producer, Joseph Sistrom; director, George Marshall; screenplay, Harry Tugend; music, Robert Emmett Dolan; songs, Johnny Mercer and Harold Arlen; art director, Hans Dreier, Ernst Fegte; camera, Leo Tover, Theodor Sparkuhl; editor, Arthur Schmidt.

Betty Hutton (Polly Judson); Eddie Bracken (Jimmy Webster); Victor Moore (Pop Webster); Anne Revere (Sarah); Walter Abel (Frisbee); Cass Daley (Mimi); Macdonald Carey (Louie the Lug); Gil Lamb (Hi-Pockets); William Haade (Duffy); Bob Hope (Master of Ceremonies); Marion Martin, William Bendix, Dorothy Lamour, Paulette Goddard, Veronica Lake, Arthur Treacher, Walter Catlett, Sterling Holloway, Vera Zorina, Frank Faylen, Fred MacMurray, Franchot Tone, Ray Milland, Lynne Overman, Susan Hayward, Ernest Truex, Mary Martin, Dick Powell, Golden Gate Quartette, Walter Dare Wahl and Co., Cecil B. DeMille, Preston Sturges, Ralph Murphy, Alan Ladd, Gary Crosby, Jack Hope, Katherine Dunham, Rochester, Marjorie Reynolds, Betty Rhodes, Dona Drake, Bing Crosby, Jimmy Lydon, Ellen Drew, Charles Smith, Frances Gifford, Susanna Foster, Robert Preston (Themselves); Woody Strode (Rochester's Motorcycle Chauffeur); Dorothy Granger (Officer); Barbara Pepper, Jean Phillips, Lynda Grey (Girls); Eddie Dew, Rod Cameron (Petty Officers); Keith Richards (Officer); Irving Bacon (New Hampshire Farmer—Old Glory Number); Virginia Brissac (Lady From Iowa—Old Glory Number); Matt McHugh (Man From Brooklyn—Old Glory Number); Peter Potter (Georgia Boy—Old Glory Number); Tom Dugan (Hitler); Richard Loo (Hirohito); Paul Porcasi (Mussolini).

THEY GOT ME COVERED (RKO, 1943) 95 M.

Producer, Samuel Goldwyn; director, David Butler; story, Leonard Q. Ross, Leonard Spigelgass; screenplay, Harry Kurnitz; music, Leigh Harline; music director, C. Bakaleinikoff; camera, Rudolph Mate; special effects, Ray Binger; editor, Daniel Mandell.

Bob Hope (Robert Kittredge); Dorothy Lamour (Christina Hill); Lenore Aubert (Mrs. Vanescu); Otto Preminger (Fauscheim); Eduardo Ciannelli (Baldanacco); Marion Martin (Gloria); Donald Meek (Little Old Man); Phyllis Ruth (Sally); Philip Ahn (Nichimuro); Donald MacBride (Mason); Mary Treen (Helen); Bettye Avery (Mildred); Margaret Hayes (Lucille); Mary Bryne (Laura); William Yetter (Holtz); Henry Guttman (Faber); Florence Bates (Gypsy Woman); Walter Catlett (Hotel Manager); John Abbott (Vanescu); Frank Sully (Red); Wolfgang Zilzer (Cross); Nino Pipitone (Testori); George Chandler (Smith); Stanley Clements (Office Boy); Don Brodie (Joe McGuirk); Arnold Stand (Drug Store Boy); Etta McDaniel (Georgia); Hugh Prosser (Captain); Donald Kerr (Stage Manager); Doris Day (Beautiful Girl In Sheet); Gil Perkins (Nazi); Lane Chandler, Dick Keene (Reporters); Edward Gargan (Cop).

DIXIE (PAR, 1943) 89 M.

Associate producer, Paul Jones; director, A. Edward Sutherland; story, William Rankin; screenplay, Karl Tunberg, Darrell Ware; songs, Johnny Burke and James Van Heusen; music director, Robert Emmett Dolan; choreography, Seymour Felix; art director, William Flannery; camera, William C. Mellor; special effects, Gordon Jennings.

Bing Crosby (Dan Emmett); Dorothy Lamour (Millie Cook); Marjorie Reynolds (Jean Mason); Billy DeWolfe (Mr. Bones); Lynne Overman (Mr. Whitlock); Eddie Foy, Jr. (Mr. Felham); Raymond Walburn (Mr. Cook); Grant Mitchell (Mr. Mason); Louis Dardon (Minstrel Dancer); Clara Blandick (Mrs. Mason); Tom Hurbert (Homer); Olin Howlin (Mr. Devereaux); Robert Warwick (Mr. La Plant); Stanley Andrews (Mr. Masters); Norma Varden (Mrs. La Plant); Hope Landin (Mrs. Masters); James Burke

(River Boat Captain); Jimmy Conlin, George Anderson (Publishers); Wilbur Mack (Publisher's Assistant); Henry Roquemore (Man in Audience); Sam Flint (Southern Colonel); Brandon Hurst (Dignified Man in Audience); Harry Barris (Drummer); Dell Henderson (Stage Manager); Fortunio Bonanova (Waiter In Restaurant); Willie Best (Steward); Jack Perrin (Fireman); John "Skins" Miller, Donald Kerr, Fred Santley, Warren Jackson, Jimmy Ray, Hal Rand, Charles Mayon, Allen Ray, Jerry James, Jimmy Clemons (Minstrel Show).

RIDING HIGH (PAR, 1943) 88 M.

Associate producer, Fred Kohlmar; director, George Marshall, based on the play *Ready Money* by James Montgomery; screenplay, Walter DeLeon, Arthur Phillips, Art Arthur; choreography, Danny Dare; songs, Ralph Rainger and Leo Robin; Johnny Mercer and Harold Arlen; Joseph J. Lilley; music director, Victor Young; art director, Hans Dreier, Ernst Fegte; camera, Karl Struss, Harry Hallenberger; process camera, Farciot Edouart; editor, LeRoy Stone.

Dorothy Lamour (Ann Castle); Dick Powell (Steve Baird); Victor Moore (Mortimer J. Slocum); Gil Lamb (Bob "Foggy" Day); Cass Daley (Tess Connors); Bill Goodwin (Chuck Stuart); Rod Cameron (Sam Welch); Glenn Langan (Jack Holbrook); Milt Britton and his Band (Themselves); George Carleton (Dad Castle); Andrew Tombes (P. D. Smith); Douglas Fowley (Brown); Tim Ryan (Jones) Pierre Watkin (Masters); James Burke (Pete Brown); Roscoe Karns (Shorty); Patricia Mace (Jean Holbrook); Gwen Kenyon (Ginger); Lorraine Miller (Blanche); Stanley Andrews (Reynolds); Wade Boteler (Mailman); Fred A. Kelsey (Honest John Kelsey); Russell Simpson (Frenchy McQuire); Matt McHugh (Murphy); Tom Kennedy (Wilson); Cy Landry (Specialty Dancer); Stanley Price (Train Conductor); Dwight Butcher, Lane Chandler, William Edwards (Cowboys); Bruce Cameron (Head of Cameron Troupe); Leonard St. Leo, Ray Spiker, Walter Pietila, Bonnadene Wolfe, Flash Gordon, Paul Unger, Ramon Schaller, Richard Gottlieb (Members of Cameron Troupe); Charles Soldani (Indian Chief); John Heistand (Commentator); Napoleon Whiting (Red Cap); Hal K. Dawson (Master of Ceremonies).

AND THE ANGELS SING (PAR, 1944) 96 M.

Associate producer, E. D. Leshin; director, Claude Binyon; screenplay, Melvin Frank, Norman Panama; art director, Hans Dreier, Hal Pereira; music director, Victor Young; choreography, Danny Dare; songs, Johnny Burke and James Van Heusen; camera, Karl Struss; editor, Eda Warren.

Dorothy Lamour (Nancy Angel); Fred MacMurray (Happy Morgan); Betty Hutton (Bobby Angel); Diana Lynn (Josie Angel); Mimi Chandler (Patti Angel); Raymond Walburn (Pop Angel); Eddie Foy, Jr. (Fuzzy Johnson); Frank Albertson (Oliver); Mikhail Rasumny (Schultz); Frank Faylen (Holman); George McKay (House Man); Harry Barris (Saxy); Donal Kerr (Mickey); Perc Launders (Miller); Tom Kennedy (Potatoes); Erville Alderson (Mr. Littlefield); Edgar Dearing (Man); Tim Ryan (Stage Door Man); Jimmy Conlin (Messenger); Leon Belasco (Waiter At "Polanaise Cafe"); Douglas Fowley (N.Y. Cafe Manager); Siefgried Arno (Mr. Green); William Davidson (Theatrical Agent); Otto Reichow (Polish Groom); Hillary Brooke (Polish Bride); Julie Gibson (Cigarette Girl); Arthur Loft (Stage Manager); Matt McHugh (Doorman At "33 Club"); Libby Taylor (Attendant in Powder Room); Drake Thorton (Page Boy); Buster Phelps (Spud); Jack Norton (Drunk); Buddy Gorman (Messenger); Roland Dupree (Boy); Louise La Planche (Ticket Taker).

RAINBOW ISLAND (PAR, 1944) 98 M.

Associate producer, I. D. Leshin; director, Ralph Murphy; story, Seena Owen; screenplay, Walter DeLeon, Arthur Phillips; art director, Hans Dreier, Haldane Douglas; music, Roy Webb; choreography, Danny Dare; songs, Ted Koehler and Burton Lane; special effects, Gordon Jennings; camera, Karl Struss; process camera, Farciot Edouart.

Dorothy Lamour (Lona); Eddie Bracken (Toby Smith); Gil Lamb (Pete Jenkins); Barry Sullivan (Ken Masters); Forrest Orr (Doctor Curtis); Anne Revere (Queen Okalana); Reed Hadley (High Priest Kahuna); Marc Lawrence (Alcoa); Adia Kuznetzoff (Executioner); Olga San Juan (Miki); Elena Verdugo (Moana); George Urchell (Executioner's Helper); Aggie Auld, Renee DuPuis, Irish Lancaster, Lena Belle, Virginia Lucas, Audrey Young, Louise LaPlanche (Native Girls); Theodore "Pete" Rand, Satini Pualioa, Alex Montoya, Alex McSweyn, Rudy Masson, Baudelio Alva, Rod Redwing, Robert St. Angelo (Queen's Guard); Yvonne De Carlo, Noel Neill (Lona's Companions); Stanley Price (Tonto); Hopkins Twins (Specialty Swimmers); Dan Seymour (Fat Native Man); George T. Lee, Leon Lontoc, Jimmie Lano (Jap Pilots); Luis Alberni (Jerry); Eddie Acuff (Sailor).

A MEDAL FOR BENNY (PAR, 1945) 77 M.

Associate producer, Paul Jones; director, Irving Pichel; story, John Steinbeck, Jack Wagner; screenplay, Frank Butler; art director, Hans Dreier, Hal Pereira; music, Victor Young; camera, Lionel Lindon; special effects, Gordon Jennings; editor, Arthur Schmidt.

Dorothy Lamour (Lolita Sierra); Arturo de Cordova (Joe Morales); J. Carrol Naish (Charley Martin); Mikhail Rasumny (Raphael Catalina); Fernando Alvarado (Chito Sierra); Charles Dingle (Zach Mibbe); Frank McHugh (Edgar Lovekin); Rosita Moreno (Toodles Castro); Grant Mitchell (Mayor of Pantera); Douglass Dumbrille (General); Nestor Paiva (Frank Alviso); Eva Puig (Mrs. Catalina); Pepito Perez (Pamfilo Chaves); Minerva Urecal (Mrs. Chavez); Frank Reicher (Father Bly); Robert Homans (Chief of Police); Edward Fielding (Governor); Max Wagner (Jake); Isabelita Castro (Luz); Oliver Blake, Victor Potel, Harry Hayden (Pepsters); Jack Gardner (Cameraman); Eddy Chandler (Bank Guard); Tom Fadden (Eddie Krinch); Alice Fleming (Dowager); Jack Gardner (Red); Chico Sandoval (Paisano); Maxine Fife (Telephone Operator); Jimmie Dundee (Cop).

DUFFY'S TAVERN (PAR, 1945) 97 M.

Associate producer, Danny Dare; director, Hal Walker; screenplay, Melvin Frank, Norman Panama; art director, Hans Dreier, William Flannery; choreography Billy Daniels; music director, Robert Emmett Dolan; songs, Johnny Burke and James Van Heusen; Ben Raleigh and Bernie Wayne; camera, Lionel Lindon; special effects, Gordon Jennings; process camera, Farciot Edouart; editor, Arthur Schmidt.

Bing Crosby, Betty Hutton, Paulette Goddard, Alan Ladd, Dorothy Lamour, Eddie Bracken, Brian Donlevy, Sonny Tufts, Veronica Lake, Arturo De Cordova, Cass Daley, Diana Lynn, Gary Crosby, Phillip Crosby, Dennis Crosby, Lin Crosby, William Bendix, Maurice Rocco, James Brown, Joan Caulfield, Gail Russell, Helen Walker, Jean Heather (Themselves); Barry Fitzgerald (Bing Crosby's Father); Victor Moore (Michael O'Malley); Barry Sullivan (Danny Murphy); Marjorie Reynolds (Peggy O'Malley); Ed Gardner (Archie); Charles Cantor (Finnegan); Eddie Green (Eddie—The Waiter); Ann Thomas (Miss Duffy); Howard Da Silva (Heavy); Billy De Wolfe (Doctor); Walter Abel (Director); Charles Quigley (Ronald); Olga San Juan (Gloria); Robert Watson (Masseur); Frank Faylen (Customer); Matt McHugh (Man Following Miss Duffy); Emmett Vogan (Make-Up Man); Cyril Ring (Gaffer); Noel Neill (School Kid).

MASQUERADE IN MEXICO (PAR, 1945) 96 M.

Producer, Karl Tunberg; director, Mitchell Leisen; story, Edwin Justus Mayer; Franz Spencer; screenplay, Tunberg; music director, Victor Young choreography, Billy Daniels; songs, Bob Russell, Eddie Lisbona and Maria T. Lara, Ben Raleigh; and Bernie Wayne; art director, Hans Dreier, Roland Anderson; special effects, Gordon Jennings; camera, Lionel Lindon; editor, Alma Macrorie.

Dorothy Lamour (Angel O'Reilly); Arturo de Cordova (Manolo Segovia); Patric Knowles (Thomas Grant); Ann Dvorak (Helen Grant); George Rigaud (Boris Cassall); Natalie Schafer (Irene Denny); Mikhail Rasumny (Paolo); Billy Daniels (Rico Fenway); Guadalajaro Trio (Themselves); Martin Garralaga (Jose); Lester Luther (Felipe Diaz); Dina Smirnova (Friedo Diaz); Enrique Valadez, Rita Lupino (Specialty Dancers); Mimi Doyle (Stewardess); Lucille Porcett (Woman At Airport); Al Haskell, Leo Murtin, Art Felix, Ray Beltram (Taxi Driver); Eddie Laughton, William Newell, James Flavin, Charles A. Hughes (F.B.I. Men); Robert Middlemass, George Anderson, Perc Launders (Customs Officials); Don Avalier (Headwaiter); Frank Faylen (Brooklyn); Pepito Perez (Angel's Chauffeur); Frank Leyva (Newspaperman); Mae Bush, Julia Faye, Ernest Hilliard, Miriam Franklin, Stan Johnson, Roberta Jonay, Jean Acker, John Marlowe, Gordon Arnold, Allen Pinson, Charles Teske (Guests); Ted Rand, Guy Zanette (Servants).

ROAD TO UTOPIA (PAR, 1945) 89 M.

Producer, Paul Jones; director, Hal Walker; screenplay, Norman Panama, Melvin Frank; music, Leigh Harline; music director, Robert Emmett Dolan; choreography, Danny Dare; songs, Johnny Burke and James Van Heusen; art director, Hans Dreier, Roland Anderson; animation, Jerry Fairbanks; camera, Lionel Lindon; process camera, Farciot Edouart; editor, Stuart Gilmore.

Bing Crosby (Duke Johnson/Junior Hooton); Bob Hope (Chester Hooton); Dorothy Lamour (Sal Van Hoyden); Hillary Brooke (Kate); Douglass Dumbrille (Ace Larson); Jack LaRue (LeBec); Robert Barrat (Sperry); Nestor Paiva (McGurk); Robert Benchley (Narrator); Will Wright (Mr. Latimer); Jimmy Dundee (Ringleader of Henchmen); Jim Thorpe (Passenger); William Benedict (Newsboy); Art Foster (Husky Sailor); Arthur Loft (Purser); Stanley Andrews (Official At Boat); Alan Bridge (Captain on Boat); Lee Shumway, Al Ferguson (Policemen); Romaine Callender (Top Hat); George Anderson (Townsman); Edgar Dearing, Charles Wilson (Official Cops); Brandon Hurst, Don Gallaher, Bud Harrisons (Men at Zambini's); Edward Emerson (Master of Ceremonies); Ronnie Rondell (Hotel Manager); Allen Pomeroy, Jack Stoney (Henchmen); Frank Moran, Bobby Barber, Pat West (Bartenders); Larry Daniels (Ring Leader); Ferdinand Munier (Santa Claus); Ethan Laidlaw (Saloon Extra); Jimmy Lono (Eskimo); Charles Gemora (Bear); Paul Newlan (Tough Ship's Purser).

MY FAVORITE BRUNETTE (PAR, 1947) 88 M.

Producer, Daniel Dare; director, Elliott Nugent; screenplay, Edmund Beloin, Jack Rose; art director, Hans Dreier, Earl Hedrick; song, Jay Livingston and Ray Evans; music director, Robert Emmett Dolan; assistant director, Mel Epstein; special effects, Gordon Jennings; camera, Lionel Lindon; editor, Ellsworth, Hoagland.

Bob Hope (Ronnie Jackson); Dorothy Lamour (Carlotta Montay); Peter Lorre (Kismet); Lon Chaney (Willie): John Hoyt (Dr. Lundau); Charles Dingle (Major Simon Montague); Reginald Denny (James Colling); Frank Puglia (Baron Montay); Ann Doran (Miss Rogers); Willard Robertson (Prison Warden); Jack LaRue (Tony); Charles Arnt (Crawford); Garry Owen, Richard Keane (Reporters); Tony Caruso ("Raft" Character); Matt McHugh ("Cagney"); George Lloyd (Prison Guard—Sgt.); Jack Clifford (Prison Guard—Captain); Ray Teal, Al Hill (State Troopers); Boyd Davis (Mr. Dawsen); Clarence Muse (Man in Condemned Row); Helena Evans (Mabel); Roland Soo Hoo (Baby Fong); Jean Wong (Mrs. Fong); Charley Cooley (Waiter); John Westley (Doctor); Ted Rand (Waiter Captain); Tom Dillon (Policeman); Harland Tucker (Room Clerk); Reginald Simpson (Asst. Manager); James Flavin (Mac—Detective); Jim Pierce, Budd Fine (Detectives); John Tyrrell (Bell Captain); Joe Recht (Newsboy); Bing Crosby (Executioner); Alan Ladd (Himself).

VARIETY GIRL (PAR, 1947) 83 M.

Producer, Daniel Dare; director, George Marshall; screenplay, Edmund Hartman, Frank Tashlin, Robert Welch, Monte Brice; music, Joseph J. Lilley; songs Johnny Burke and James Van Heusen; Frank Loesser; Allan Roberts and Doris Fisher; choreography, Billy Daniels, Bernard Pearce; assistant director, George Templeton; art director, Hans Dreier, Robert Clatworthy; special Puppetoon sequence,

Thornton Hoe, William Cottrell; special effects, Gordon Jennings; camera, Lionel Lindon, Stuart Thompson; editor, LeRoy Stone.

Mary Hatcher (Catherine Brown); Olga San Juan (Amber LaVonne); DeForest Kelley (Bob Kirby); William Demarest (Barker); Frank Faylen (Stage Manager) Frank Ferguson (J. R. O'Connell); Russell Hicks, Crane Whitley, Charles Coleman, Hal K. Dawson, Eddie Fetherston (Men at Steambath); Catherine Craig (Secretary); Bing Crosby, Bob Hope, Gary Cooper, Ray Milland, Alan Ladd, Barbara Stanwyck, Paulette Goddard, Dorothy Lamour, Veronica Lake, Sonny Tufts, Joan Caulfield, William Holden, Lizabeth Scott, Burt Lancaster, Gail Russell, Diana Lynn, Sterling Hayden, Robert Preston, John Lund, William Bendix, Barry Fitzgerald, Cass Daley, Howard Da Silva, Billy De Wolfe, Macdonald Carey, Arleen Whelan, Patric Knowles, Mona Freeman, Cecil Kellaway, Johnny Coy, Virginia Field, Richard Webb, Stanley Clements, Cecil B. DeMille, Mitchell Leisen, Frank Butler, George Marshall, Roger Dann, Pearl Bailey, The Mulcay's, Spike Jones and his City Slickers, George Reeves, Wanda Hendrix, Sally Rawlinson (Themselves); Ann Doran (Hairdresser); Jack Norton (Brown Derby Busboy); Eric Alden (Make-Up Man); Frank May (Director).

WILD HARVEST (PAR, 1947) 92 M.

Producer, Robert Fellows; director, Tay Garnett; story, Houston Branch; screenplay, John Monks, Jr.; music, Hugo Friedhofer; art director, Hans Dreier, Haldane Douglas; camera, John F. Seitz; editor, George Tomasine.

Alan Ladd (Joe Madigan); Dorothy Lamour (Fay Rankin); Robert Preston (Jim Davis); Lloyd Nolan (Kink); Dick Erdman (Mark Lewis); Allen Jenkins (Higgins); Will Wright (Mike Alperson); Griff Barnett (Hankin); Anthony Caruso (Pete); Walter Sande (Long); Frank Sully (Nick); Gaylord Pendleton (Swanson); Caren Marsh (Natalie); William Meader (Drury); Bob Kortman (Sam); Frances Morris (Mrs. Swanson); Chet Root, Tex Swan, Gordon Carveth, Pat Lane (Madigan Crew); Harry Wilson, Mike Lally, Danny Stewart, Frank Moran, Frank Hagney, Constantine Romanoff (Alperson Crew); Ian Wolfe (Martin); Eddy C. Waller (Mr. Hatfield); Edgar Dearing (Man); Al Ferguson, Bill Wallace (Husky Farmers); Vernon Dent (Farmer); Gloria Williams (Girl); Al Murphy (Bartender).

ROAD TO RIO (PAR, 1947) 100 M.

Producer, Daniel Dare; director, Norman Z. McLeod; story-screenplay, Edmund Beloin, Jack Rose; songs, Johnny Burke, Jimmy Van Heusen; music director, Robert Emmett Dolan; choreography, Bernard Pearce, Billy Daniels; art director, Hans Dreier, Earl Hedrick; assistant director, Oscar Rudolph; special effects, Gordon Jennings, Paul Lerpal; camera, Ernest Laszlo; editor, Ellsworth Hoagland.

Bing Crosby (Scat Sweeney); Bob Hope (Hot Lips Barton); Dorothy Lamour (Lucia Maria De Andrade); Gale Sondergaard (Catherine Vail); Frank Faylen (Trigger); Joseph Vitale (Tony); Frank Puglia (Rodrigues); Nestor Paiva (Cardoso); Robert Barrat (Johnson); Jerry Colonna (Cavalry Captain); Wiere Brothers (Musicians); Andrews Sisters, Carioca Boys, Stone-Barton Puppeteers (Themselves); George Meeker (Sherman Malley); Stanley Andrews (Captain Harmon); Harry Woods (Ship's Purser); Tor Johnson (Samson); Donald Kerr (Steward); Stanley Blystone (Assistant Purser); George Sorel (Prefeito); John "Skins" Miller (Dancer); Alan Bridge (Ship's Officer); Arthur Q. Bryan (Mr. Stanton); Babe London (Woman); Gino Corrado (Barber); George Chandler (Valet); Paul Newlan, George Lloyd (Butchers); Fred Zendar (Stevedore); Ralph Gomez, Duke York, Frank Hagney (Roustabouts); Ralph Dunn (Foreman); Pepito Perez (Dignified Gentleman); Ray Teal (Buck); Brandon Hurst (Barker); Barbara Pratt (Airline Hostess); Tad Van Brunt (Pilot); Patsy O'Bryne (Charwoman.)

ON OUR MERRY WAY (UA, 1948) 107 M.

Producer, Benedict Bogeaus, Burgess Meredith; director, King Vidor, Leslie Fenton; story, Arch Oboler; screenplay, Laurence Stalling; art director Ernst Fegte, Duncan Cramer; music director, David Chudnow, Skitch Henderson; camera, Joseph Biroc, Gordon Avil, John Seitz, Edward Cronjager; editor, James Smith.

Burgess Meredith (Oliver Pease); Paulette Goddard (Martha Pease); Fred MacMurray (Al); Hugh Herbert (Elisha Hobbs); James Stewart (Slim); Dorothy Lamour (Gloria Manners); Victor Moore (Ashton Carrington); Ellene Janssen (Peggy Thorndyke); Henry Fonda (Lank); William Demarest (Floyd); Dorothy Ford (Lola); Charles D. Brown (Editor); Betty Caldwell (Cynthia); David Whorf (Sniffles Dugan); Frank Moran (Bookie); Tom Fadden (Deputy Sheriff); Chester Clute (Bank Teller); Carl Switser (Zoot); Nana Bryant (Housekeeper); John Qualen (Mr. Atwood); Walter Baldwin (Livery Stable Man); Lucien Prival (Jackson); Paul A. Burns (Boss—Want Ad Dept.); Almira Sessions (Mrs. Cotton).

LULU BELLE (COL, 1948) 87 M.

Producer, Benedict Bogeaus; associate producer, Arthur M. Landau; director, Leslie Fenton; based on the play by Charles MacArthur and Edward Shelton; screenplay, Everett Freeman; art director, Duncan Cramer; songs, Edgar DeLange and Henry Russell; Russell; Russell and John Lehman; George Mitchell and James Dempsey; Lester Lee and Allan Roberts; camera, Ernest Laszlo.

Dorothy Lamour (Lulu Belle); George Montgomery (George Davis); Albert Dekker (Mark Brady); Otto Kruger (Harry Randolph); Glenda Farrell (Molly Benson); Greg McClure (Butch Cooper); Charlotte Wynters (Mrs. Randolph); Addison Richards (Commissioner Dixon); William Haade (Duke Weaver); Clancy Cooper (Bartender); George Lewis (Captain Ralph); Ben Erway (Doctor); John Indrisano, Bud Wiser (Brady's Bodyguards).

THE GIRL FROM MANHATTAN (UA, 1948) 81 M.

Producer, Benedict Bogeaus; director, Alfred E. Green; story-screenplay, Howard Estabrook; art director, Jerome Pycha; music director, David Chudnow; camera, Ernest Laszlo; editor, James E. Smith.

Dorothy Lamour (Carol Maynard); George Montgomery (Rev. Tom Walker); Charles Laughton (The Bishop); Ernest Truex (Homer Purdy); Hugh Herbert (Aaron Goss); Constance Collier (Mrs. Brooke); William Frawley (Mr. Bernouti); Sara Allgood (Mrs. Beeler); Frank Orth (Oscar Newsome); Howard Freeman (Sam Griffin); Raymond Largay (Wilbur J. Birth); George Chandler (Monty); Selmer Jackson (Dr. Moseby); Adeline de Walt Reynolds (Old Woman); Maurice Cass (Mr. Merkel); Eddy Waller (Jim Allison); Everett Glass (Committee Man); Marie Blake (Committee Woman).

MANHANDLED (PAR, 1949) 97 M.

Producer, William H. Pine, William C. Thomas; director, Lewis R. Foster; based on the novel *The Man Who Stole a Dream* by L. S. Goldsmith; screenplay Loster, Whitman Chambers; art director, Lewis H. Creber; music director, David Chudnow; camera, Ernest Laszlo; editor, Howard Smith.

Dorothy Lamour (Merl Kramer); Dan Duryea (Karl Benson); Sterling Hayden (Joe Cooper); Irene Hervey (Mrs. Alton Bennet); Philip Reed (Guy Bayard); Harold Vermilyea (Dr. Redman); Alan Napier (Mr. Alton Bennet); Art Smith (Det. Sgt. Dawson); Irving Bacon (Sgt. Fayle).

THE LUCKY STIFF (UA, 1949) 99 M.

Producer, Jack Benny; director, Lewis R. Foster; story, Craig Rice; screenplay, Foster; art director, Lewis H. Creber; music director, David Chudnow; camera, Ernest Laszlo; editor, Howard Smith.

Dorothy Lamour (Anna Marie St. Claire); Brian Donlevy (John J. Malone); Claire Trevor (Marguerite Seeton); Irene Hervey (Mrs. Childers); Marjorie Rambeau (Hattie Hatfield); Robert Armstrong (Von Flanagan); Billy Vine (Joe Di Angelo); Warner

Anderson (Eddie Britt); Virginia Patton (Millie Dale); Richard Gaines (District Attorney Logan); Joe Sawyer (Tony); Larry Blake (Louie Perez); Bob Hopkins (Mac Dougal); Sidney Miller (Bernstein); Charles Meredith (Mr. Childers); Jimmy Ames (Rico Di Angelo).

SLIGHTLY FRENCH (COL, 1949) 81 M.

Producer, Irving Starr; director, Douglas Sirk; story, Herbert Fields; screenplay, Karen DeWolf; music director, M. W. Stoloff; songs, Allan Roberts and Lester Lee; Ted Koehler and Harold Arlen; camera, Charles Lawton; editor, Al Clark.

Dorothy Lamour (Mary O'Leary); Don Ameche (John Gayle); Janis Carter (Louisa Gayle); Willard Parker (Douglas Hyde); Adele Jergens (Yvonne LaTour); Jeanne Manet (Nicolette); Frank Ferguson (Marty Freeman); Myron Healey (Stevens); Leonard Carey (Wilson); Earle Hodgins (Barker); William Bishop (Voice Of J.B.—Producer); Patricia Barry (Hilda); Jimmy Lloyd, Michael Towne (Assistants); Fred Sears (Cameraman); Frank Mayo (Soundman); Fred Howard, Robert B. Williams (Newsmen); Charels Jordan (Studio Policeman); Hal K. Dawson (Director); Carol Hughes (Secretary); Frank Wilcox (Starr—Playwright); Will Stanton (Cockney Barker); Al Hill (Brazilian Barker); Pierre Watkin (Publicity Man).

HERE COMES THE GROOM (PAR, 1951) 113 M.

Producer-director, Frank Capra; story, Robert Riskin, Liam O'Brien; screenplay, Virginia Van Upp, O'Brien, Myles Connolly; songs, Jay Livingston and Ray Evans; Johnny Mercer; Hoagy Carmichael; camera, George Barnes; editor, Ellsworth Hoagland.

Bing Crosby (Pete); Jane Wyman (Emmadel Jones); Alexis Smith (Winifred Stanley); Franchot Tone (Wilbur Stanley); James Barton (Pa Jones); Robert Keith (George Degnan); Jacques Gencel (Bobby); Beverly Washburn (Suzi); Connie Girst (Ma Jones); Alan Reed (Mr. Godfrey); Minna Gombel (Mrs. Godfrey); Howard Freeman (Governor); Maidel Turner (Aunt Abby); H. B. Warner (Uncle Elihu); Nicholas Joy (Uncle Prentiss); Ian Wolfe (Uncle Adam); Ellen Corby (Mrs. McGonigle); James Burke (Policeman); Irving Bacon (Baines); Ted Thorpe (Mr. Paul Pippitt); Art Baker (Radio Announcer); Anna Maria Alberghetti (Theresa); Laura Elliot (Maid); Dorothy Lamour, Frank Fontaine, Louis Armstrong, Phil Harris, Cass Daley (Themselves); Chris Appel (Marcel); Odette Myrtil (Grey Lady); Michele Lange (French Matron); Charles Lane (Burchard—FBI); Adeline de Walt Reynolds (Aunt Amy); Connie Conrad (Seamstress); Andre Charlot (French Doctor); Bess Flowers (Woman Guest); Franklyn Farnum (Man); Carl D. Switzer (Messenger); John "Skins" Miller (Guest); Walter McGrail (Newsreel Director); Julia Faye, Almira Sessions (Women).

THE GREATEST SHOW ON EARTH (PAR, 1952) 153 M.

Producer, Cecil B. DeMille; associate producer, Henry Wilcoxon; director, DeMille; story, Frederic M. Frank, Theodore St. John, Frank Cavett; screenplay, Frank, Barre Lyndon, St. John; art director, Hal Pereira, Walter Tyler; music, Victor Young; songs, Ned Washington and Young; John Murray Anderson and Henry Sullivan; Ray Goetz and John Ringling North; camera, George Barnes, J. Peverell Marley; Wallace Kelby; editor, Anne Bauchens.

Betty Hutton (Holly); Cornel Wilde (Sebastian); Charlton Heston (Brad); Dorothy Lamour (Phyllis); Gloria Grahame (Angel); James Stewart (Buttons); Henry Wilcoxon (Detective); Emmett Kelly (Himself); Lyle Bettger (Klaus); John Ridgely (Jack Steelman); Lawrence Tierney (Henderson); John Kellogg (Harry); Frank Wilcox (Circus Doctor); Bob Carson (Ringmaster); Lillian Albertson (Buttons' Mother); Julia Faye (Birdie); John Ringling North (Himself); Tuffy Genders (Tuffy); John Parrish (Jack Lawson); Keith Richards (Keith); Adele Cook Johnson (Mable); Brad Johnson (Reporter); Lydia Clarke (Circus Girl); John Merton (Chuck); Lane Chandler (Dave); Bradford Hatton (Osborne); Herbert Lytton (Foreman); Norman Field (Truesdale);

Everett Glass (Board Member); Lee Aaker (Boy); Ethan Laidlaw (Hank); Bing Crosby, Bob Hope, Mona Freeman, Nancy Gates, Clarence Nash, Bess Flowers (Spectators); William Boyd (Hopalong Cassidy); Edmond O'Brien (Circus Midway Barker); Lou Jacobs, Felix Adler, Liberty Horses, The Flying Concellos, Paul Jung, The Maxellos (Circus Acts).

ROAD TO BALI (PAR, 1952) 91 M.

Producer, Harry Tugend; director, Hal Walker; story, Frank Butler, Tugend; screenplay, Butler, Hal Cantor, William Morrow; art director, Hal Pereira, Joseph McMillan Johnson; music director, Joseph L. Lilley; songs, Johnny Burke and James Van Heusen; choreography, Charles O'Curran; orchestra arranger, Van Cleve; camera, George Barnes; editor, Archie Marshek.

Bob Hope (Harold Gridley); Bing Crosby (George Cochran); Dorothy Lamour (Lalah); Murvyn Vye (Ken Arok); Peter Coe (Gung); Ralph Moody (Bhoma Da); Leon Askin (Ramayana); Jane Russell, Dean Martin, Jerry Lewis, Bob Crosby (Themselves); Jack Claus (Specialty Dancer); Bernie Gozier (Bo Kassar); Herman Cantor (Priest); Pat Dane, Sue Casey, Patti McKaye, Judith London, Leslie Charles, Jean Corbett, Betty Onge (Handmaidens); Bunny Lewbel (Lalah—At Age Seven); Jan Kayne (Verna); Carolyn Jones (Eunice); Richard Keene (Conductor); Roy Gordon (Eunice's Father); Harry Cording (Verna's Father); Donald Lawton (Employment Agency Clerk); Michael Ansara (Guard); Charles Mauu, Al Kikume, Satini Puailoa, Kuka L. Tuitama (Warriors).

THE ROAD TO HONG KONG (UA, 1962) 91 M.

Producer, Melvin Frank; director, Norman Panama; screenplay, Panama, Frank; art director, Sydney Cain, Bill Hutchinson; music, Robert Farnon; songs, Sammy Cahn and Jimmy Van Heusen; choreography, Jack Baker, Sheila Meyers; assistant director, Bluey Hill; camera, Jack Hildyard; editor, Alan Obiston, John Smith.

Bing Crosby (Harry Turner); Bob Hope (Chester Babcock); Joan Collins (Diane); Dorothy Lamour (Herself); Robert Morley (The Leader); Walter Gotell (Dr. Zorbb); Roger Delgardo (Jhinnah); Felix Aylmer (Grand Lama); Peter Madden (Lama); Alan Gifford, Robert Ayres, Robin Hughes (American Officials); Julian Sherrier (Doctor); Bill Nagy (Agent); Guy Standeven (Photographer); John McCarthy (Messenger); Simon Levy (Servant); Mei Ling (Chinese Girl); Katya Douglas (Receptionist); Harry Baird, Irving Allen (Nubians); Peter Sellers, Frank Sinatra, Dean Martin, David Niven, Zsa Zsa Gabor, Dave King, Jerry Colonna (Guest Stars); and: Jacqueline Jones, Victor Brooks, Roy Patrick, John Dearth, David Randall, Michael Wynne.

DONOVAN'S REEF (PAR, 1963) 104 M.

Producer-director, John Ford; story, Edmund Beloin; screenplay, Frank Nugent, James Edward Grant; music, Cyril Mockridge; assistant director, Wingate Smith; art director, Hal Pereira, Eddie Imagzu; special effects, Paul K. Lerpae; camera, William Clothier; editor, Otho Lovering.

John Wayne (Guns); Lee Marvin (Gilhooley); Elizabeth Allen (Amelia); Jack Warden (Dr. Dedham); Cesar Romero (The Governor); Dick Foran (Sean O'Brien); Dorothy Lamour (Fleur); Marcel Dalio (Father Cluzeot); Mike Mazurki (Sgt. Menkowicz); Jacqueline Malouf (Lelani); Cherylene Lee (Sally); Tim Stafford (Luki); Edgar Buchanan (Francis X. O'Brien); Jon Fong (Mister Eu); Yvonne Peattie (Sister Matthew); Ralph Volkie (James); Frank Baker (Capt. Martin); June Y. Kim, Midori (Servants); Ron Nyman (Naval Officer); Carmen Estrabeau (Sister Gabrielle); Pat Wayne (Aussie Officer); Chuck Roberson (Festus); Mae Marsh, Sara Taft, Carl M. Leviness, Fred Jones, Scott Seaton, Major Sam Harris (Members of the Family); Duke Green (Mate); King Lockwood (Lawyer).

PAJAMA PARTY (American International, 1965) 82 M.

Producer, James H. Nicholson, Samuel Z. Arkoff; co-producer, Anthony Carias; director, Don Weiss screenplay, Louis M. Heyward; assistant director, Clark Paylow; music, Les Baxter; camera, Floyd Crosby; editor, Fred Feitshans, Eve Newman.

Tommy Kirk (Go-Go); Annette Funicello (Connie); Elsa Lanchester (Aunt Wendy); Harvey Lembeck (Eric Von Zipper); Jesse White (J. Sinister Hulk); Jody McCrea (Big Lunk); Ben Lessy (Fleegle); Doona Doen (Vikki); Susan Hart (Jilda); Bobbi Shaw (Helga); Cheryl Sweeten (Francine); Luree Holmes (Perfume Girl); Candy Johnson (Candy); Buster Keaton (Chief Rotten Eagle); Dorothy Lamour (Head Saleslady); Renie Riano (Maid); Joi Holmes (Toyless Model); Nooney Ricket 4 (Themselves); Andy Romano, Linda Rogers, Allen Fife, Alberta Nelson, Bob Harvey, Jerry Brutsche (Rat Pack).

THE PHYNX (WB, 1970) 81 M.

Producer, Bob Booker, George Foster; director, Lee H. Katzin; story, Booker, Foster; screenplay, Stan Cornyn; songs, Mike Stoller and Jerry Leiber; music supervisor, Sonny Burke; production designer, Stan Jollye; camera, Michael Hugo; editor, Dann Cahn.

Patty Andrews, Busby Berkeley, Xavier Cugat, Fritz Feld, John Hart, Ruby Keeler, Joe Louis, Marilyn Maxwell, Maureen O'Sullivan, Harold "Odd Job" Sakata, Ed Sullivan, Rona Barrett, James Brown, Cass Daley, Leo Gorcey, Louis Hayward, Patsy Kelly, Guy Lombardo, Butterfly McQueen, Richard Pryor, Colonel Harland Sanders, Rudy Vallee, Johnny Weissmuller, Edgar Bergen, Dick Clark, Andy Devine, Huntz Hall, George Jessel, Dorothy Lamour, Trini Lopez, Pat O'Brien, Jay Silverheels, (Themselves); A. Michael Miller, Ray Chippeway, Dennis Larder, Lonny Stevens (The Phynx); Joan Blondell (Ruby); Martha Raye (Foxy); Lou Antonio (Corrigan); Mike Kellin (Bogey); Michael Ansara (Colonel Rostinov); George Tobias (Markevitch); Clint Walker (Sgt. Walker); Sally Anne Struthers (World's No 1 Fan); Ultra Violet (Felice); Larry Hankin (Philbaby); Teddy Eccles (Wee Johnny Wilson); Pat McCormick (Father O'Hoolihan); Joseph Gazal (Yakov); Bob Williams (Number One); Barbara Noonan (Bogey's Secretary); Rich Little (Voice in the Box); Sue Bernard (London Belly); Sherry Miles (Copenhagen Belly); Ann Morell (Italian Belly); Motha (Motha).

Dorothy Lamour, queen of jungle films, 1937

With her first husband Herbie Kaye, Edgar Bergen, and Martha Raye at the Ambassador Hotel, Hollywood, 1938

With Wayne Morris in *The Mink Doll* on "Damon Runyon Theatre" (ABC-TV, 1957)

With Fred MacMurray and Jean Dixon in SWING HIGH, SWING LOW (Par '37)

With Ray Milland in THE JUNGLE PRINCESS (Par '36)

With Jon Hall in THE HURRICANE (UA '37)

In HER JUNGLE LOVE (Par '38)

With Lloyd Nolan in ST. LOUIS BLUES (Par '39)

With George Raft in SPAWN OF THE NORTH (Par '38)

With Tyrone Power in JOHNNY APOLLO (20th '40)

With Jack Benny, Isabel Jeans, and Binnie Barnes in MAN ABOUT TOWN (Par '39)

With Robert Preston in TYPHOON (Par '40)

With Henry Fonda in CHAD HANNA (20th '40)

With Jimmy Dorsey, Helen O'Connell, and Bob Eberle in THE FLEET'S IN (Par '42)

In RIDING HIGH (Par '43)

With Bing Crosby, Bob Hope, and Dona Drake in ROAD TO MOROCCO (Par '42)

With Frank Faylen in AND THE ANGELS SING (Par '44)

With J. Carroll Naish in A MEDAL FOR BENNY (Par '45)

With Bob Hope in MY FAVORITE BRUNETTE (Par '47)

With Bing Crosby in ROAD TO RIO (Par '47)

With Alan Ladd, Robert Preston, and Allen Jenkins in WILD HARVEST (Par '47)

With Victor Moore in ON OUR MERRY WAY (UA '48)

In THE GREATEST SHOW ON EARTH (Par '52)

With Bing Crosby and Bob Hope in ROAD TO BALI (Par '52)

With Bob Hope in THE ROAD TO HONG KONG (UA '62)

With John Wayne, Elizabeth Allen, Jack Warden, Lee Marvin, Cherylene Lee, Cesar Romero, and Tim Stafford in DONOVAN'S REEF (Par '63)

With Buster Keaton and Bobbi Shaw in BEACH PARTY (American International '65)

PAULETTE GODDARD

5'4"
110 pounds
Dark brown hair
Blue Eyes
Gemini

PAULETTE GODDARD, a keen individualist with striking good looks, progressed from Ziegfeld chorus girl to cinema leading lady with amazing agility and success. She is best remembered for a saucy insouciance on screen which highlighted her flair as a light comedienne and as a decorative addition to costume dramas. Off screen she employed her wit and looks to dazzle and marry an assortment of twentieth-century culturists, ranging from Charles Chaplin to Burgess Meredith to Erich Maria Remarque, proving that cinema fame could be parlayed nicely into social prominence and financial security.

Paulette's initial years in Hollywood (1929–32) as a walk-on, Goldwyn chorus girl, and Hal Roach cheesecake contractee, afforded little indication of her future glory. Under Chaplin's tutelage she refined her acting techniques and personality to make a successful movie reentry as the gamin leading lady of *Modern Times*.

Once signed by Paramount in 1939, Paulette demonstrated that she was a unique asset to the studio. She was not as classy as Claudette Colbert, but she had more verve and pliability than superstar Barbara Stanwyck, and these qualities made her performances, whether Bob Hope comedies or Cecil B. DeMille historical extravaganzas, extremely enjoyable. Because Paulette was extraordinarily vivacious and versatile, she was more capable of carrying the box-office burden of a major picture than fellow Paramount luminary Dorothy Lamour. In the expensive historical pastiche *Kitty,* she projected the feline gutter waif so pertly that she easily overshadowed the major asset of period costumes and sets.

When Paulette slipped away from Paramount in 1949 at age 38, she elected to salvage her diminishing status as a movie star by performing in low-budget pictures for six more years. These minor pictures highlighted all too clearly that she was not capable of essaying valid dramatics, and that in middle age she could no longer pass for an ingenue, even in sappy cheap actioners. She left the screen in the mid-1950s to dabble in television and summer stock, but her major emphasis in these years was on escalating her social status and bank account. In these latter two areas, she succeeded with notable success.

Today Paulette is a celebrated member of the international social set. She has not acquired the aristocratic aura of her contemporary, Merle Oberon, but she has a special dash of her own that sparkles as much as her famous diamonds.

* *

Paulette Goddard (née Pauline Marion Goddard Levee) was born June 3, 1911, in Whitestone Landings, Long Island, New York. Her parents, Joseph Russell Levee and Alta (Goddard) Levee, separated when Paulette was quite young. To avoid further legal hassling with her husband, Mrs. Levee and her daughter moved from city to city, and for a time lived in Canada. When they returned to New York, they resided in the suburb of Great Neck.

Because of her transient youth, Paulette had a very sketchy formal education. She attended Mt. St. Dominic Academy in New Jersey for a short while. Later, after one year of high school, she quit to become her mother's breadwinner. She had already become a seasoned model, first in children's clothing at Sak's Fifth Avenue, and later as a $50-a-week Hattie Carnegie mannequin.

With her hair dyed blonde and already a confirmed flapper, Paulette decided it might be fun to try show business. Her mother agreed and coached her effectively. Then, through family friends, she wangled an introduction to elite stage producer Florenz Ziegfeld. He was sufficiently impressed by her striking figure (34–23–35) to hire her for his new summer revue *No Foolin',* which debuted at the Globe Theatre in Manhattan on June 24, 1926. The musical show featured James Barton, Greta Nissen, and Ray Dooley, with Paulette as a saucy chorus member. *No Foolin'* ran for 108 performances.

Even at an early age Paulette was shrewd enough to know the value of publicity. She organized a chorus girls' committee to picket and sue Ziegfeld for his alleged preference of brunettes to blondes. The gimmick received appropriate newspaper coverage.

Also for Ziegfeld, Paulette appeared in the chorus of *Rio Rita,* a lush musical starring zany comedians Bert Wheeler and Robert Woolsey. It premiered at the Ziegfeld Theatre on February 2, 1927, and proved a substantial hit. Paulette was tagged the "perfect sitter" by fellow chorus members because in one sketch she rested demurely on a prop moon—scantily clothed—while a crooner vocalized. Within three weeks of the opening, Paulette left the cast to assume the lead role in Archie Selwyn's Broadway-bound comedy *The Unconquerable Male.* The play opened and closed in Atlantic City within three days. In later years Paulette would conveniently overlook these fledgling Broadway outings.

On one of the pre-Broadway jaunts of the Ziegfeld revues, Paulette had met playboy Edward James, a wealthy lumber executive from Ashville, North Carolina. Later in 1927 they were married and moved to Ashville. However, his blue blood background and her nightlife razzmatazz orientation did not blend. By early 1929 Paulette had obtained a Reno, Nevada, divorce and a healthy $100,000 cash settlement. She took a European trip and then visited an Arizona dude ranch. Being so near California, resourceful Paulette decided to crash the movies. Her initial foray proved fruitless, and she returned to the dude ranch. After recovering from a subsequent automobile accident, she reappeared in Hollywood, this time behind the wheel of her $19,000 Duesenberg roadster, determined to launch a new frontal attack on the cinema industry.

One of her first movie assignments was a brief walk-on in *Berth Marks* (1929), a Laurel and Hardy sound short subject, produced by Hal Roach for MGM release. Within a year Paulette had graduated to walk-ons in feature productions, landing quickie extra work in Paramount's *The Girl Habit* (1931) starring Charlie Ruggles, and Warner Brothers' *The Mouthpiece* (1932) with Warren William. Then Paulette became part of the beauty herd hired by producer Samuel Goldwyn to decorate his rash of movie musicals. In *The Kid from Spain* (1932), the still blonde, bobbed-haired Paulette can be spotted in a chorus ensemble. Betty Grable was another would-be movie star in the Busby Berkeley-directed girlie line. According to legend, Goldwyn fired rambunctious Paulette on four different occasions. Finally, Paulette took the hint, and accepted a stock contract at Hal Roach's comedy factory, then producing at the MGM lot. She was hired as just another bit of glorified cheesecake to decorate Roach's two-reel comedies.

When Paulette was completing the stock resumé form for Roach's publicity department, she wrote in the blank for the subject's age: "Oscar Wilde and Goddard say that 'Any woman who tells her age tells anything.'"

Paulette has recalled about these days when she was one of the town's madcaps: "Life was very easy as a blonde. I didn't have to think, I didn't have to talk. All I had to do was waltz around."

At the busy Roach studio, Paulette appeared in such quickly churned out items as *Young Ironsides* and *Girl Grief,* both 1932 shorts with comedian Charlie Chase. She was featured in a slew of bathing suit publicity poses, and her shapely legs were utilized in close-up shots in other Roach film shorts.

About her Roach sojourn Paulette recollects: "I think everybody at the studio thought I had a boy friend who owned a garage because I used to go to work every morning in such big cars. Actually, you see, I was financially independent, and my passion was automobiles. I had three of them, all shiny and expensive." Paulette was not above ostentatious display to prove that, at least off screen, she merited more attention than she was getting in front of the cameras.

In late 1932, at one of producer Joseph Schenck's perpetual yachting parties, Paulette, age 21, met Charlie Chaplin, then 43 years old. The millionaire screen comic had already been divorced twice, had two sons, and was renowned for his passionate short-term love affairs. His latest feature, the all-silent *City Lights,* had premiered the year before, and he was then creating a new project and a fresh leading lady. Paulette and he became fast friends when he wisely advised her not to invest $50,000 of her savings in a phony film company.

The duo soon became inseparable, and the great comedy star let it be known that he found Paulette "absolutely unique." Chaplin exercised his feudal rights as a reigning Hollywood Monarch by purchasing Paulette's contract from Roach and announcing that his new protégée would costar with him in his new film. Under the maestro's tutelage, Paulette allowed her hair to regain its normal dark brown color and to grow longer. She took drama lessons from Samuel Kayzer (and later from Constance Collier) and embarked on an intensive program to develop all aspects of her acting abilities. She was the (un)official hostess at all social gatherings held at Chaplin's plush home. Whenever the delicate question of the couple's marital status arose, they refused to make any public comment.

Shooting of the $1.5 million *Modern Times* commenced in early October, 1934, and continued for a lengthy ten months. Chaplin did not finish tinkering with it until early 1936, but finally it premiered at the Rivoli Theatre on February 5, 1936. Once again Chaplin had bucked the establishment by making his new feature a basically silent movie—save for Chaplin's own talking debut on screen in a garbled talk song.

Chaplin played an insignificant factory worker who goes berserk because of the monotony of his assembly-line job and life. After a spell in the hospital and jail, he is freed and encounters waterfront gamin Paulette, who has been pilfering food for her two sisters and unemployed father. The tramp and Paulette escape arrest, and they make their home in a deserted Hooverville shack. He is hired as a night watchman for a huge department store, but is jailed after he innocently becomes involved in a store robbery. To support herself, Paulette becomes a cabaret dancer, and when Chaplin is freed he is hired at the cabaret as a singing waiter. But a juvenile-court officer patrolling the slum café spots the under-age Paulette, and she and Chaplin have to scram. At the final fade-out, Charlie and Paulette are trudging down a road which stretches over the horizon. Walking shoulder to shoulder, they are weary but unbeaten.

It was a difficult role in which to be "introduced" to the filmgoing public. It required more than just an engaging screen presence to make pure pantomime acceptable to movie audiences used to sound films. Paulette demonstrated that she responded to painstaking direction well and could perform the typically over-rehearsed Chaplin scene with delightful spontaneity. *Variety* said: "Paulette Goddard, a winsome waif attired almost throughout in short ragged dress and bare legs above the knees, is naturally introduced. She registers handily." Frank S. Nugent (*New York Times*) endorsed her as "a winsome waif and a fitting recipient of the great Charlot's championship." Chaplin's black and white production proved moderately successful in initial box-office release. It provided artistic substantiation for Paulette's overnight rank as a top Hollywood personality.

In the past, Chaplin's leading ladies and/or actress wives had not been able to sustain their screen careers after their initial film appearance with the great comic. Hollywood skeptically awaited Paulette's fate.

In March, 1936, Paulette, her mother, and Chaplin embarked on a world cruise. The couple vaguely suggested to the press that they were engaged; later rumors circulated that they married in Singapore. It is most likely that they were wed in mid-1935 on Chaplin's yacht anchored off Catalina Island.

When the trio returned to Hollywood, Chaplin began meticulous preparations for a new project to star Paulette. At one point he was adapting *Regency* from the D. L. Murphy novel, and then he switched his attentions to an original screenplay entitled *White Russian,* to costar Paulette and perhaps Gary Cooper. (This latter project would be filmed three decades later as *A Countess from Hong Kong* with Sophia Loren.) Plans to remake his *A Woman of Paris* were also on his agenda for Paulette at one time.

Meanwhile, Paulette contented herself with becoming deeply involved in the social swim of the movie colony, seemingly unmindful of her dormant screen career. Everyone noted how well she got along with Chaplin's two sons—Charles, Jr., and Sydney—and even with the star's most tempestuous ex-wife, Lita Grey Chaplin. Paulette found time in 1936 to have a discreet romance with 38-year-old song composer George Gershwin. The musician begged Paulette to leave Chaplin and marry him. She refused. Cynics said her decision was based on her knowledge of Gershwin's extremely poor health (he would die July 11, 1937) and the fact that Chaplin's bank account and industry status far outweighed what Gershwin could offer her.

When 1937 came and went with Chaplin still not ready to shoot a new film, Paulette decided—and her mentor-husband acquiesced—that she should accept a contract offer from producer David O. Selznick. At the time she was receiving $2,500 a week under her Chaplin contract.

Probably the most coveted acting role in Hollywood in 1938 (and forever after) was Scarlett O'Hara in the upcoming Selznick film *Gone with the Wind* (1939). Every female in Hollywood—with the possible exception of Anna May Wong and Lassie—had tested or been mentioned for the role. When Selznick hired Paulette, it was believed that this indicated she was now a top contender for the role. Selznick would not affirm or deny the rumor.

Now Paulette felt called upon to explain her recent silence to reporters: "The reason I have not given any interviews is because I have done nothing to be interviewed about. Now that I am back at work in pictures I am willing to discuss subjects of interest concerning motion pictures. . . . As for being a mystery woman, I see no basis for it. In fact, I deny it. Probably the big reasons for giving me the unwarranted title is that I spend my time with people whom I know very well." She later added: "I am not temperamental. I just know what I want—and if I don't have it, I try to get it."

Selznick cast Paulette in *The Young in Heart,* which opened at Radio City Music Hall on November 3, 1938. She was third-billed to Janet Gaynor and Douglas Fairbanks, Jr., in this charming comedy of an old lady (Minnie Dupree) who transforms a family of ne'er-do-wells into decent folk. Paulette was a poor secretary fond of ex-crook Fairbanks who was employed in her office. Miss Dupree clearly stole the limelight, but *Variety* said that Paulette was "an eye filler and possessed an exciting screen personality." Her speaking voice was found to be quite pleasant.

A few weeks later *Dramatic School* (1938) premiered. Paulette made this one on loanout to MGM, supporting Luise Rainer in this sappy melo-dramatic account of Parisian theatre students. Gale Sondergaard was a stern teacher and Lana Turner appeared as another National Theatre Dramatic School pupil. Paulette ambled through as the working girl who arranged parties for the students to meet eligible men about town. Paulette's social rank in the movie colony demanded the courtesy of respectable reviews. *New York Daily News* critic Kate Cameron, in her three-star review, decided: "[she] handles the role of a sophisticated, sharp-tongued student admirably."

Paulette was announced to make her dramatic stage "debut" in a stock version of *Accent on Youth* at the Cape Playhouse, Dennis, Massachusetts, in the summer of 1938, but her film schedule prevented it.

Meanwhile, the contest for the leading female role in *Gone with the Wind* continued. As the fall, 1938, shooting date for the color epic approached, Selznick still had not decided upon a final choice. An MGM press release—which was later retracted—announced that Paulette had been signed for the part. But Paulette lost out. Some said it was because of Paulette and Chaplin's ambiguous marital status: Selznick did not wish to brook the potential moral indignation of filmgoers. Others agreed that Selznick was no longer hot on Paulette's acting potential. Paulette's version is that at a garden party she and Chaplin gave for Selznick after production of *Gone with the Wind* began, one of the guests was British actress Vivien Leigh. Selznick spotted her, was entranced, and soon thereafter signed her for the lead part, for which she garnered an Oscar. Paulette accepted the turn of events with amazing good grace.

Next Paulette was loaned out to MGM for their female-star-studded *The Women* (1939), based on the Clare Boothe Broadway success. She was fifth-billed to Norma Shearer, Joan Crawford, Rosalind Russell, and Mary Boland. As Miriam Aarons, the predatory chorus girl and home-wrecker, she eventually has the opportunity to pay off an old score with vicious Russell, in one of the screen's most unusual action sequences. Paulette's Miriam is not content with spewing forth assorted barbs, but lets loose with a swift kick to Russell's backside. Soon the two gals are hair-pulling and tossing around the ground where Russell manages to give Paulette a healthy bite on the leg. Although not up to the sting of the Broadway version, *The Women* had its own brand of sophistication and polish, and its cast received universal plaudits. Paulette surprised not a few by standing her ground so ably with such a top-ranking cast. MGM would produce an indifferent musical remake, *The Opposite Sex,* in 1956.

The combination of Paulette's enviable social position in Hollywood's hierarchy and her growing box-office popularity, inspired Paramount to offer her an attractive seven-year contract, with options that would soon bring her $5,000 a week in salary. Selznick had lost interest in Paulette and readily agreed to selling her contract to Paramount.

Paramount was in the market for bright personalities to decorate their plethora of mindless college musicals and pseudosophisticated comedies. Perky ingenues Ann Sheridan and Ida Lupino had already left the stable for Warner Brothers; Mary Carlisle, Frances Farmer, Gail Patrick, Marsha Hunt, and Shirley Ross, among others, were not providing the necessary marquee lure, or would soon move on to other studios, as did starlet Betty Grable after 1939. By 1938 Marlene Dietrich, Mae West, Sylvia Sidney, and Carole Lombard all would have exited, leaving a big breach to be filled. Signing Paulette proved to be one of the wisest decisions of the William LeBaron* regime at Paramount since hiring Dorothy Lamour a few years earlier.

One of Paulette's first assignments at Paramount was to appear on the "Lux Radio Theatre" dramatization of *Front Page Woman* (January 16, 1939), costarring with Fred MacMurray. It was her initial opportunity to work under the direction of Cecil B. DeMille, producer and overall supervisor of the radio show.

The studio first cast Paulette opposite funnyman Bob Hope in their remake of Universal's hoary silent melodrama, *The Cat and the Canary* (1939). The script was revamped to play it purely for laughs, allowing the snappy Hope to finally realize his screen potential. Paulette was Annabelle, one of the potential heirs to a large fortune, who comes to the spooky old mansion. She must survive the night in order to collect her sizable inheritance. There are an appropriate number of red herrings, including the malevolent housekeeper Gale Sondergaard, and an escaped lunatic who crawls about on all fours, thinking he is a cat. With sliding panel doors, mysterious shadows, the murders of assorted frightened relatives, it is ineffectual, timid Hope who tries to corral the murderer and save lovely Paulette. She made a properly vulnerable and beautiful heroine. Frank S. Nugent (*New York Times*) conceded: "Paulette Goddard's screams would part a traffic snarl in Times Square."

Paulette was mentioned for the role of Frenchy in Universal's *Destry Rides Again,* but Marlene Dietrich won the lead. (Paulette did play the role on radio in 1941.) A projected Selznick motion picture *The Titanic* to feature Paulette was also canceled.

Meanwhile, Chaplin has been preparing a new screenplay about a case of mistaken identity between a Hitler-like dictator and a meek barber in wartorn Europe. It was called *The Great Dictator* (1940). The idea for his

*See Appendix.

first all-talking feature came from British producer Sir Alexander Korda. Paulette agreed to appear as Hannah, the Jewish ghetto washerwoman, a symbol of downtrodden humanity in the chaos of war. In the Berlinlike slum, she has a fleeting romance with Chaplin, the Jewish soldier veteran of World War I, who suffers from amnesia and has become a barber there. When he speaks out of turn and is sent to a concentration camp, she flees to Austria and new hope. The barber escapes from confinement and crosses the border to a neighboring country, where he is mistaken as Hynkel, dictator of Tomania. For further laughs, there is Jack Oakie as Napoli, and Henry Daniell and Billy Gilbert as the dictator's sinister but inept aides.

The Great Dictator began filming on September 9, 1939, and continued through March, 1940, at a cost of over $2 million. It premiered on October 15, 1940, at the Astor and Capitol theatres. Pacifist America was not ready for an ultraserious film from its former comedy idol, and the movie met with a great deal of box-office resistance. Audiences found it overlong and repetitious, and were taken aback by the propaganda finale in which Chaplin as the dictator directs an impassioned plea for peace. Among others, Eileen Creelman *(New York Sun)* was critical: "She [Paulette], and the star too, could do with a professional director and makeup man. Miss Goddard adds nothing but a pretty face to the film."

Paulette was also experiencing difficulties on the personal front. The September 2, 1938, issue of *Collier's* magazine contained a rather revealing biographical article on Paulette entitled "The Perils of Paulette," by Kyle Crichton. It factualized many aspects of her obscure past that she had chosen to ignore. Paulette, in typical fashion, shrugged it off; but her father Joseph Levee brought a libel suit against *Collier's* in 1940 for $150,000, claiming he had lost his $150-a-week position as a film salesman due to the story's derogatory nature. Then, on May 8, 1940, Levee sued Paulette for $600 monthly personal support (he was then receiving $300 monthly from her), claiming he should not "be required to lower his previous standard of living merely because Miss Goddard was unwilling to provide him with the means." Paulette twice refused to appear in court; on one occasion claiming to the press that Levee was not her relative. The matter was eventually settled out of court.

Then, just before the premiere of *The Great Dictator,* Paulette was the victim of a smear campaign. One evening she was dining at Ciro's Hollywood restaurant with director Anatole Litvak, former husband of Miriam Hopkins. One of the shoulder straps of Paulette's evening gown slipped off. Litvak gallantly lifted the tablecloth and Paulette slid under the table to repair the damage. The maitre d' quickly encased the table with screens. Rumors immediately circulated about town that Paulette and Litvak had indulged in fornication under the table. Within a few days, Paramount and United Artists (the distributors of *The Great Dictator*) received a flood of phone calls, nearly all of them demanding that they not release any more films starring Paulette because of her scandalous behavior. Peculiarly, most of the calls consisted of the same speech, word for word. The studios quickly agreed that the calls were the result of an anti-Chaplin political faction and ignored the demands. (*Confidential* magazine, in its November, 1953, issue would rake up the story. Surprisingly for this publication, it too agreed that Paulette was not guilty of having committed an immoral act in public, proving that it would have been almost physically impossible under the circumstances.)

The disappointing public reaction to *The Great Dictator* hastened the marital split between Paulette and Chaplin. At the film's premiere, she was introduced to British writer H. G. Wells, then almost 80 years old. Infatuated by his intellect and prestige, she managed to show up in the same cities as he did during his subsequent American tour. Thereafter, she was romantically linked with Washington, D.C., political advisor Harry Hopkins.

Paramount took due note of the hefty financial returns on *The Cat and the Canary* and reteamed Paulette with Bob Hope in a zany followup, *The Ghost Breakers* (1940). It was another horror-film comedy spoof, featuring Paulette as Mary Carter, a nightclub entertainer who inherits a supposedly haunted castle on an island near Cuba. She arrives there to claim her property, accompanied by cowardly radio commentor Hope, who is on the lam for a murder he did not commit. Once more Paulette plays straight lady to Hope's wisecracking character. She dishes out such lines as: "Cold chills are running down my back." He replies, "They must be running over from mine." At appropriate intervals, Paulette looks frightened and screams at the mysterious shadows and lurching figures. The script made few demands on Paulette's histrionic abilities, still requiring her to frequently change her outfits in front of the camera in order to reveal her decorous lingerie. Paulette seemed more at ease in front of the camera, especially when parading in a $100,000 fur coat of platina fox skins. The critics decided that while she "hasn't a great to do, [she] looks very beautiful doing it." (The studio would remake the film in 1953 as *Scared Stiff,* a Dean Martin and Jerry Lewis vehicle, with Lizabeth Scott in a truncated version of Paulette's role.)

Paulette's growing reputation as a screen beauty and a classy chassis in a sweater was further consolidated in 1940 when Jefferson Machamer and a jury of fellow artists voted her as having the most beautiful body in the world. She was now receiving $85,000 per film at Paramount. She told reporters: "I have to work to be busy, to learn something new. It isn't that I have any goals. I haven't. But I've lots of energy and I'm lucky that I can put it to work in something I enjoy."

Each time a new Cecil B. DeMille extravaganza was announced for production, Hollywood actors vied with each another and exerted all sorts of pressures to obtain a role in the prestigious film. In addition to the prestige, lengthy production schedule would mean a hefty salary. Paulette, based on the same lot with the great producer-director, was no exception. When word of *North West Mounted Police* (1940) reached her, she set her sights on the potentially intriguing part of Louvette Corbeau, the half-breed daughter of a criminal. Many leading Hollywood personalities were considered for the rather small role, including ex-Paramount leading lady Marlene Dietrich. With ingenuity, utter perseverence and gall, Paulette convinced DeMille she was the proper choice.

Set in western Canada in 1885, *North West Mounted Police* dealt with the Indians and half-breeds who revolted against the British. Texas Ranger Gary Cooper rides into Canada on the trail of murderer George Bancroft who is leading the revolt. He finds himself in competition with Mountie Preston Foster to bring Bancroft to justice and win the affection of English-born nurse Madeleine Carroll. Bancroft's untamed daughter Paulette is romanced by Mountie Robert Preston, and through him she causes a group of Mounties to be ambushed by the warring Indians. Justice eventually triumphs, with Cooper retrieving his man and returning to Texas, while Carroll and Foster plan to marry.

DeMille's initial technicolor feature opened at the Paramount Theatre on November 6, 1940, and proved enormously successful. In its first four weeks at the theatre, it grossed $214,000. Paulette, loping around the obvious sound-stage outdoor sets with abandon in nutbrown makeup and squaw clothing, was termed by the *New York Times* as "the typical half breed charmer, only more so." Forced to mouth such cutsie catch phrases as "sonamagum" and other pidgin English, she established no new histrionic highs. Nevertheless, contemporary audiences found her evil Métis wildcat characterization alluring. It set the tone for her future screen career, in which she would alternate between costumers and smart modern-day comedies. She, Cooper, Foster, *et al.* repeated their *North West Mounted Police* roles on "Lux Radio Theatre," April 13, 1942.

In December, 1940, Paulette renegotiated her Paramount contract, which now paid her $5,000 a week and allowed her to make one outside film a year. She was announced as costar with Ray Milland in *The Lady Eve* (1941), but Barbara Stanwyck and Henry Fonda were finally assigned to the Preston Sturges comedy.

Paulette's first 1941 release was *Second Chorus,* playing opposite Fred Astaire and Burgess Meredith. The thin story had Astaire and Meredith as trumpeters who have remained in college for years in order to take advantage of lucrative collegiate band bookings. They discover Paulette and hire her as their manager. The trio eventually arrive in New York, planning to join up with Artie Shaw's swing band, but they meet with failure. Eventually Astaire convinces Shaw to use his composition at a Carnegie Hall concert and it proves the hit of the evening. Paulette performed one dance number with Astaire, "I Ain't Hep to That Step, But I'll Dig It." Following in the sparkling footsteps of past Astaire screen partner Ginger Rogers, Paulette was decorative and bright, but not up to the fast company. The *New York Times* chided that she was "a feeble partner" for the master hoofer, and many moviegoers found this intimate musical a rather shoddy affair. She later admitted: "I'll never try dancing on the screen again. I was determined that the dance would be good. Imagine me dancing with Astaire. And I guess it was all right. We did it just once, one Saturday morning for the cameras. Just one take. I'm glad it was all right, for I couldn't have done it again. I couldn't possibly ever have done it once again."

Yet in her next film, *Pot o' Gold* (1941), made on loanout to United Artists, Paulette sang and danced a little with costar James Stewart. As a maid in irascible Charles Winninger's home, she is charmed by his nephew Stewart. The two lovers dream up a radio giveaway show in order to find employment for Horace Heidt's band, out-of-work musicians living at the boarding house run by Paulette's mother. Featured in the lightweight story was an extended dream sequence, a fantasy of Paulette in the sixteenth century. *Variety* appraised: "Miss Goddard flashes an ingenue smile, rolls her eyes and sings at the microphone. She is also variously photographed registering vexation, determination and romance."

Her third 1941 release teamed her again with box-office bonanza Bob Hope in *Nothing but the Truth*. She was the niece of investment broker Edward Arnold who entrusts naive Hope with $10,000 which he is supposed to double on the market. Hope becomes involved in a wager that he will tell only the truth for two days, which nearly wrecks his romance with Paulette and almost loses his clients' investments. Anything with Hope in those World War II days made money, but it was not one of the comedian's wittier vehicles. Paulette had little opportunity to contribute much to the hilarity of the movie. It was the last time she would appear opposite Hope—save for the studio's omnibus all-star musicals. By now, Dorothy Lamour had demonstrated in the "Road" pictures that she was the more appropriate vis-à-vis for Hope, being more languid and defenseless than the brisk, self-sufficient Paulette.

Hold Back the Dawn (1941) was an exceedingly popular melodrama, directed by Mitchell Leisen, Paramount's top styler under the new B. G. DeSylva* regime at the studio. This Charles Brackett-Billy Wilder screenplay starred Charles Boyer as a European-born gigolo attempting to cross from Mexico into the United States. Paulette was Anita Dixon, his gold-digging former dance partner who makes her living off rich tourist suckers. It is glib Paulette who advises Boyer to marry an American to solve his immigration problems, thus setting into motion his romance and wedding to repressed schoolteacher Olivia De Havilland. *Hold Back the Dawn* had the gimmick of being told in flashback by Boyer, who has come to Paramount Pictures to sell director Mr. Saxon (Mitchell Leisen) the rights to film his life story. Paulette held her own in the showy, brief role of a "lively vixen." Paulette, Boyer, and Susan Hayward appeared in the "Lux Radio Theatre" version of *Hold Back the Dawn* on November 10, 1941.

Always one to take advantage of attempting a showy role, Paulette accepted the lead in the radio rendition of *The Gorgeous Hussy* (December 29, 1941, NBC) on "Cavalcade of America."

Paulette's charms were analyzed in 1941 by playwright William Saroyan, whose impressions of ultrafeminine women appeared in a national magazine that year: "What she has is an inner twinkle, and it goes around in a strictly non-sorrowing frame, all of it is attractively tough, challenging, mischievous, coquettish, wicked and absolutely innocent. It's probably less sex appeal than fun appeal, which in some cases are the same thing, and in all cases should be."

Paulette replaced sometime Paramount star Madeleine Carroll in *The Lady Has Plans*, (1942), an uneasy mixture of spy melodrama and romantic comedy. She played a news reporter assigned to assist broadcaster Ray Milland in Lisbon. Nazi agents there, headed by Albert Dekker, mistake her for a lady spy who has secret Allied plans drawn on her back. Before the wrap-up, which unites her with Milland, the couple have been chased in and out of a Lisbon hotel lobby and dungeon, and have proven that Margaret Hayes is the actual spy. *New York Times* critic Bosley Crowther said, "[Paulette] lends herself to it with generous but sometimes ponderous grace." The Paramount Theatre stage show featuring Ina Ray Hutton and Jack Haley received much better notices.

Paulette returned to the luxuriant DeMille fold and costume drama in *Reap the Wild Wind* (1942). Katharine Hepburn had been offered the lead female role first. In this technicolor sea yarn, Paulette's family have long made their living rescuing crews and cargoes of ships caught on the rocks on their voyages from Charleston, South Carolina, to the Caribbean. But their business is severely curtailed by ruthless Raymond Massey, whose boats manage to reach the scene of the wrecks first, since they are instigating most of the calamities anyway. Paulette rescues Captain John Wayne from drowning when his ship goes down and promptly takes a strong fancy to him. When she seeks backing against Massey from lawyer Ray Milland, he becomes an instant rival for her love. Later Wayne and Milland dive to the ocean bottom to obtain evidence against Massey, and Wayne is called

*See Appendix.

upon to sacrifice himself to save Milland from the clutches of a giant sea squid. Finally, Massey is shot by his brother Robert Preston for having caused a shipwreck which claimed the life of stowaway Susan Hayward, Paulette's cousin and Preston's great love.

Despite the wartime restrictions on materials, DeMille turned out a lavish spectacle, replete with expansive ballroom scenes, storms at sea, and oversized special effects. Paulette and Hayward—the latter in a much abbreviated role—had the opportunity to cavort unchallenged as Southern belles, complete with drippy accents, coquettish grace, and splendid frilly clothes and bonnets. (Both actresses had been contenders for the Scarlett O'Hara role in *Gone with the Wind;* it would remain for Hayward to make her mark after she left Paramount and joined Walter Wanger's banner; she became a top performer at Twentieth Century-Fox in the early 1950s.)

In June, 1942, Paulette obtained a Mexican divorce from Chaplin. According to the *New York Times,* the event was so secret that the same jurist who entered the decree had been ordered to remove it from the records. Paulette reputedly received a $1 million settlement.

The Forest Rangers, a mild technicolor action yarn, was released on October 21, 1942. Paulette and Susan Hayward again were rivals, this time in competition for the attention of district ranger Fred MacMurray. Hayward owns and operates a prosperous lumbermill. She desires MacMurray but he regards her as just one of the boys. He, in turn, is entranced with society gal Paulette and marries her. Hayward attempts to break up the union. After quelling a forest blaze in which Paulette rescues Hayward, MacMurray and Paulette patch up their troubles. Paulette was more decorative than effective, although she had a good bit in a slapstick logrolling scene. The star trio made the most of a bundling sequence in which both gals share a blanket in the forest with bemused MacMurray. (Originally, Madeleine Carroll, Sterling Hayden, and Patricia Morison had been slated for this less-than-exciting cinema excursion.)

As one of the studio's 16 top stars, Paulette graced Paramount's revue *Star Spangled Rhythm* (1942). She joined Dorothy Lamour and Veronica Lake in the satirical "A Sweater, a Sarong and a Peekaboo Bang" song number. Of the star trio, Paulette was the least typed by her special screen gimmick (i.e., as a pinup girl), and she could manage nicely in a varied assortment of roles.

Paulette was paired again with Ray Milland in *The Crystal Ball* (1943) when Ginger Rogers and Charles Boyer proved unavailable. She was chipper Toni Gerard, a Texas girl stranded in the big city after losing a beauty contest. She is befriended by a shyster crystal-ball-gazer Gladys George, and while substituting for her, encounters attorney Milland. After much conniving, she weans Milland away from grasping widow Virginia Field. Paulette was pleasantly aggressive in this B-film, which director Elliot Nugent attempted to whip up into a grade A-concoction. It was one of the several Paramount concoctions sold to United Artists for theatrical release in 1943.

In *So Proudly We Hail* (1943) Paulette found herself in tough competition for the limelight. She was second-billed to veteran studio star Claudette Colbert in this patriotic account of combat nurses at Bataan and Corregidor during World War II. As Jean O'Doul, Paulette was a flip nurse who refuses to be deglamorized despite the hardships of rugged battlefront duty. When her morale does crack, she pulls a sheer black nightgown out of her pack, and her good cheer immediately returns. Sonny Tufts was cast as her love interest. Most of the acting laurels went to Colbert as the stiff-lipped nurse leader, and to Veronica Lake as the nurse who turns herself into a human bomb to help her comrades escape the Japs. Alton Cook, writing in the *New York World-Telegram,* pointed out: "The surprise of the group is Miss Goddard, until now not much more than a fluttery pretty-pretty but this time an actress of vigor and zest for life."

Veronica Lake would later record in her autobiography that Paulette and Colbert maintained a steady feud during the filming of *So Proudly We Hail.* Reporters had asked Paulette which of her costars she preferred, and she answered "Veronica, I think. After all we are closer in age." Colbert fumed, Goddard smirked, and the picture was completed. The star trio later recreated their roles on "Lux Radio Theatre" (November 1, 1943).

Paulette was among those who tested for the prize role of Maria in Ernest Hemingway's *For Whom the Bell Tolls* (1943), but she lost out to studio newcomer Vera Zorina, who was later replaced by Ingrid Bergman.

To do her share in the war effort, Paulette made some war bond tours; there was a mild rhubarb when they were cut short by her filming schedule.

She returned to her special forte of wisecracking romantic comedy in *Standing Room Only* (1944), Paramount's study of hotel-room and maid shortage in wartime Washington, D.C. As Fred MacMurray's practical secretary, she accompanies him to the capital to arrange the conversion of his Indiana toy factory into a munitions factory. When they cannot find living accommodations, resourceful Paulette hires her boss and herself out as a servant couple to wealthy Roland Young and his blustery war-worker wife Anne Revere. Paulette is given ample opportunity to prove her worth in the kitchen and to match wits for MacMurray's attention against Edward Arnold's daughter, Hillary Brooke. The film was well-paced fun, but not on a par with *The More the Merrier* and *The Doughgirls* which dealt with the same topic. Irene Thirer of the *New York Post* rated Paulette and MacMurray as "elegantly teamed and do just fine." Paulette and MacMurray repeated their roles on "Lux Radio Theatre," October 30, 1944.

Since appearing in *Second Chorus* with Burgess Meredith, Paulette had been frequently dating him. She was impressed by his healthy reputation as a noted stage actor and more than competent film performer. The couple were married May 21, 1944. He was then 35, and twice divorced. At the time, Paulette informed gossip columnist Louella Parsons: "I feel this is right. We are congenial—we have so much in common. We like to laugh, to study together, and Burgess takes great pride in my career as an actress."

I Loved a Soldier (1944) was essentially a starring vehicle for Paulette, with mild box-office support being supplied by Sonny Tufts. This overladen drama had Paulette a welder in a San Francisco defense plant who is introduced to soldier Sonny Tufts at a USO dance. After initial resistance, self-possessed Paulette gives in to his charm, but she hesitates about becoming his wartime bride. She changes her opinion after observing the plight of spinster Beulah Bondi, and of her own roomate Ann Doran, whose Army husband is shipped home blinded. Barry Fitzgerald as a moustached trolley car operator and Mary Treen as Paulette's man-hungry cohort provided amusing characterizations. The *New York Times* reported that when Paulette "has to register emotion . . . she is simply bewildered."

Paulette's only 1945 release was a token appearance in the all-star *Duffy's Tavern.* In a short blackout skit, Brian Donlevy and Sonny Tufts portray rivals for her affection.

Paulette and her new husband Meredith were heard together on the "Theatre Guild on the Air" (ABC) in *At Mrs. Beams,* October 28, 1945.

The highpoint of Paulette's screen popularity occurred with *Kitty* (1946). Paramount had lost out in the sweepstakes to purchase Kathleen Windsor's racy historical tome *Forever Amber* and was determined to beat Twentieth Century-Fox to the box-office punch with a similar vehicle—which it did. Using Rosamund Marshall's novel about a dirty young street waif in eighteenth-century London as a basis, the studio whipped together an expensively mounted picture, directed by Mitchell Leisen, who also designed the well-appointed costumes. Paramount demonstrated its faith in Paulette's ability to carry such an expensive production by casting her in the flashy leading role.

The film traces Paulette's rise from the gutter, which begins when she attempts to snatch the buckles from painter Thomas Gainsborough's shoes. He impulsively decides to paint her portrait rather than prosecute her. The picture gives her the first boost into the city's social world. But it is impoverished fop Ray Milland who changes her life the most. He has an immediate attraction for the heroine and performs a Pygmalion-like conversion of his find, aided by his drunken titled aunt, Constance Collier. When Milland is tossed into debtors' prison, Paulette marries unsavory Dennis Hoey to pay for her lover's release. Hoey is later killed, and Milland engineers her wedding to elderly duke Reginald Owen. She gives birth to Hoey's child, with the addled Owen not knowing the difference. Eventually, Paulette wins her true love Milland and a position of nobility. Other period types she meets along the way are Sara Allgood, a female Fagin, likable aristocrat Patric Knowles, and the bewildered butler Eric Blore.

Although the heavily brocaded technicolor *Kitty* was completed by mid-1945, its premiere was delayed until March 31, 1946, at the Rivoli Theatre. *Kitty* was a financial success, earning $3.5 million in domestic gross rentals. Paulette was well received as the light-haired hussy, although her cockney accent (and later high-toned diction) were not always convincing. Said the critics: "Paulette Goddard has worked up blazing temperament to go with her ravishing beauty in the title role" (*New York World Telegram*). "If she is less fetching as a late eighteenth century duchess, it is because the script runs thin on humor and drama. In any case, she gives the work the correct touch of wry romanticism."

Much less enthusiastically received was *The Diary of a Chambermaid* (1946), the initial coproducing venture of Paulette and Burgess Meredith, released by United Artists. This morbid study of an opportunist serving-girl in nineteenth-century France was erratically directed by Frenchman Jean Renoir. Paulette played a blonde vixen in the household of martinet Judith Anderson and her doddering husband Reginald Owen. Hurd Hatfield was their neurotic son, Francis Lederer the sadistic major domo, and Meredith appeared as the retired army captain residing next door. In the clash of personalities, Lederer murders Meredith, beats up Hatfield, and absconds with Anderson's family silver. Paulette remains behind to marry Hatfield. "Miss Goddard is equal to all the requirements of her assignment," stated the *New York Herald Tribune*. Others thought it her finest screen performance, and a match for the later, more brooding remake of the Octave Mirbeau novel which starred Jeanne Moreau and was directed by Luis Buñuel.

In late 1946 Paulette signed a new seven-year contract with Paramount, which still allowed for one outside picture per year. The secure star commented, "We're both stuck." Paulette had come through the World War II years in rare form. Initially a light comedienne, she proved adept as a wholesomely sexy diversion in large-scale actioners, and, when pushed, could handle dramatic assignments more than competently. With Colbert gone, Paulette and Dorothy Lamour were the studio's top female attractions; singing sensation Betty Hutton was in her own private category.

Paulette did not appear in the scheduled *The Sin Field* about a baseball player and a ballerina, but she did make the old hat *Suddenly It's Spring* (1947), which found her and MacMurray performing robotlike under Mitchell Leisen's surprisingly uninspired direction. She was the WAC captain who arrives home only to learn that her law-partner husband MacMurray wants a divorce because he is infatuated with Arleen Whelan. With Macdonald Carey as a man on the prowl for Paulette, the film is filled with embarrassing leers, double-takes, and triple talk. Sensing the thinness of the dialogue, the visuals were given more than their due—for example, Paulette decked out in a diaphanous negligee. The critics panned this "motheaten bundle of horse feathers in which Paulette Goddard and Fred MacMurray are rudely stuffed" and blamed the stars for not behaving "with any genuine comic grace." Coming at the tail end of the wartime entertainment boom, the picture squeaked by at the box office. Television had not quite yet made moviegoers the discriminating viewers of years to come.

In Paramount's *Variety Girl* (1947), Paulette's contribution was purely cheesecake. She takes a luxuriant bubble bath in a tub mounted on a dais.

Her third and final outing with Cecil B. DeMille was in the $4.5 million technicolor spectacle *Unconquered,* which premiered at the Rivoli Theatre on October 10, 1947. As Abby Hale, the comely mid-eighteenth century English convict girl, she has been sentenced to deportation to the American colonies. Captain Gary Cooper, Virginia militiaman, prevents Paulette from being auctioned off into slavery, arousing the wrath of villainous fur trader Howard Da Silva. Before the climax, Cooper has overcome Da Silva and his cohorts, who are selling firearms to the warring Indians, and has saved Fort Pitt from savage massacre. Paulette underwent an athletic workout: an unceremonious bath in a barrel, torture at the stake, a spill from a canoe into the rapids, and so forth.

The critics thought *Unconquered* a "flaccid epic," engineered as a "celebration of Gary Cooper's virility, Paulette Goddard's femininity, and the American Frontier Spirit." Bosley Crowther (*New York Times*) queried: "Isn't the chance of watching Gary Cooper, in a colonial costume and tricorner hat, acting the gallant frontiersman sufficient for anyone? If it isn't there's Paulette Goddard as the red-headed, flashing-eyed slave, exhibited in numerous situations, from a bathtub to an Indian torture stake." Other reviewers recorded that Paulette smiled and winked more alluringly herein, took her bath well, and become hysterical only once—when tied to an Indian torture stake.

Despite DeMille's penchant for utilizing unconvincing soundstage sets for even the more elemental outdoor sequences, the crude plotting (the Indians not being able to spot Paulette and Cooper scarcely camouflaged behind a handy branch), and the hammy acting of Boris Karloff (as the Chief of the Senecas) and others, audiences relished *Unconquered.* Few minded the liberties taken with American history, and the picture grossed a tidy sum in initial release and subsequent reissues.

So that Meredith could learn the ways of business, Paulette and he, in December, 1947, opened an antique shop, High Tor Associates, near Suffern, New York.

Since Paramount had nothing at hand for their once prime glamour star, Paulette heeded the offer of British producer Sir Alexander Korda to make a film in London. A *Carmen* project was much discussed and then dropped. Paulette was then convinced to star in a filmization of Oscar Wilde's *An Ideal Husband* (1948). She flew to London in style, bringing an entourage that included her personal Swedish hairdresser. The presence of her own hair styler on the set caused a furor with the local unions and a two-day strike ensued. The delayed production finally got underway and when finished was released by Twentieth Century-Fox in the United States. Paulette was miscast as Mrs. Cheveley, the blackmailer of an upstanding member of Parliament. In the stylized setting of 1890s upper-class British society, she was out of key, despite her Cecil Beaton gowns and a good old American try. Bosley Crowther (*New York Times*) wagged: "[she] plays it as though she were the girl who lived next to the firehouse." *An Ideal Husband,* like Fox's own *The Fan* (based on Oscar Wilde's *Lady Windemere's Fan),* did little business in the shrinking cinema of the late 1940s.

Out of misguided loyalty, Paulette appeared in her husband's coproduction venture *On Our Merry Way* (1948), a dismal multiepisode yarn for United Artists. As the prodding wife of reporter Meredith, she urges him to dig up some human interest stories. The film died at the box office.

Her next film *Hazard* (1948), was a well-intentioned but misfired comedy drama of compulsive gambler Paulette running out on a wager. She had agreed to marry the winner. Private detective Macdonald Carey chases her across the country. Weakly reminiscent of *It Happened One Night,* it was "a good bit this side of inspired" (*New York Times*). Most of Paramount's inventiveness for this B-picture went into its advertising slogan: "The new-fangled, kiss-angled, star-spangled" picture.

As art and as entertainment, *Bride of Vengeance* (1949) proved to be the nadir of Paulette's Paramount tenure. It was such a turkey that the studio held up its release for well over a year, not knowing how to slip the lemon quietly onto the market. In concept, director Mitchell Leisen had an interesting idea. The film was to be a tapestry of Renaissance skullduggery, focusing on the reign of terror under the nefarious Borgia clan. But from the start the project went badly. Ray Milland later said the picture portended so badly that it was the first feature he rejected in all his years at Paramount. There were no saving graces beyond the Leisen-inspired costuming and settings, and not even color to highlight the scenery. Paulette photographed badly and acted worse as the wicked but naive Lucretia, vying with her corrupt brother (a bearded, sneering Macdonald Carey) and pushed into a loveless marriage with John Lund. The *New York Times* reported: "Miss Goddard plays Lucretia as a grande-dame right out of a wardrobe room, with the suavity and voluptuousness of a model in a display of lingerie. And her speaking of such speeches as 'Cesare! You used an assassin to murder the boy who loved me and then used me to murder the man I—!' (she swoons) is grievous to hear." Needless to say, this mess about medieval evil promptly died at the box office, and finished off the careers of most of those involved, at least as far as Paramount was concerned. All except Paulette, who was indeed no longer potent box office, but still retained a sharp talent for dazzling studio executives into believing in her screen worth.

Meanwhile, Paulette and Meredith had been drifting further apart as wife and husband. It was rumored that she had absorbed all the cultural tidbits he had to offer, and that he could no longer abide or afford her penchant for expensive material furnishings. They were divorced on June

6, 1949, in Cuernevaca, Mexico. He soon thereafter remarried. In 1953 he filed a legal action for an accounting of $400,000 in joint property they had maintained in California. She promptly countersued to determine if their Mexican divorce was really valid (he was then married to his fourth wife, Kaja Sundsten, an exotic dancer). As Paulette later phrased her matrimonial preferences: "Actors are for Dr. Menninger. The ideal man is one who has $8 million and no complexes. To such a man I could give security."

Paulette should have been awarded a special astuteness prize for the Paramount contract she wangled in mid 1949. Despite her string of four box-office failures, her advanced age of 38, and the rapidly declining theatrical film market, she did what her contemporary luminaries (Dorothy Lamour, Joan Caulfield, et al.) could not achieve—she maintained an aura of success and box-office value. To commence the following year, the new contract provided for her to perform in one film a year for Paramount for the next ten years! She was to have script approval and 60 days notice before the start of production, and would receive a salary during filming commensurate with her past $5,000 a week. Paulette informed the press that her new contract "is so set up that any mistakes will be on my own head."

She accepted the lead in Columbia Pictures' filmization of the mid-1940s controversial stage drama *Anna Lucasta* (1949). Susan Hayward had been the original choice for the title role of the whore, but Paulette was available and agreed to a salary of $175,000 plus a percentage of the profits. The undaring screenplay was adapted from the original version of *Anna Lucasta,* dealing with a bizarre family of farmers of Polish extraction in rural Pennsylvania. On off-Broadway the concept had been changed to a black household.

In her Anna Christie-like role, Paulette played the daughter cast out by her drunken, incest-driven father (Oscar Homolka). She goes to the big city where she becomes a waitress. Later she is prodded to return home by her father, who wants her as bait to catch wealthy, college-educated farmer William Bishop. Her relationship with Bishop is marred by her guilt about her immoral past, and by his learning of her reputation. Broderick Crawford played her callous, brutal brother, with Mary Wickes as the snippy, selfish sister. *Variety* pointed out: "[Paulette's] physical accoutrements do not measure up to the lush requirements of the part. Her Anna is a game attempt in that direction but the lack of corporeal apparatus keeps the sparks from flying." *Cue* magazine was more to the point: "Most of the time, she slouches through her role like the party of the second part in a nightclub Apache dance—all sin, scintillation and sex." At one point, it was announced Paulette would appear in a stage version of *Anna Lucasta* in Paris. It would remain for an all-black film version of *Anna Lucasta* (1958), starring Eartha Kitt, to restore vitality to the drama.

Paulette continued with her radio dramatic assignments. Among these were the "Theatre Guild on the Air" version of *The Passing of The Third Floor Back* (December 25, 1949) with Cedric Hardwicke; and the same series' *The Trial of Mary Dugan* (May 14, 1950) with Pat O'Brien.

Paulette had appeared with Dublin's Abbey Theatre back in 1947 for a month, playing in *Winterset* with her husband Meredith, but it was not until the summer of 1950 that Paulette finally made her American legitimate theatre debut. She appeared at the Cape Playhouse in Dennis, Massachusetts, in Bernard Shaw's *Caesar and Cleopatra.* While working in this stock production, she informed Boston theatre critic Elliot Norton: "I've wanted to do this—to act on the stage, to be in this play—for a long time. I want to learn. . . . Certainly I didn't do this for money, or for self aggrandizement. I am on vacation now between pictures."

At Paramount, neither she nor the studio could come to any agreement on a suitable project. She had definitely passed her box-office peak, and the new forces on the lot preferred other alternatives than risking a major picture on the diminished strength of Paulette's name. Producer Hal B. Wallis* had his own private stable of players, from Lizabeth Scott to Polly Bergen to Corinne Calvet, and he could also negotiate short-term agreements with such free-lancing stars as Joan Fontaine, Eleanor Parker, and Barbara Stanwyck. Under contract to Paramount there were still Diana Lynn, Mona Freeman, and Wanda Hendrix, newcomer Rhonda Fleming, and the everpresent Nancy Olsen.

Paulette was slated to do *Beyond the Sunset* with William Holden at Paramount in 1950, but instead turned up in a shot-in-Mexico quickie, *The Torch.* This low-breed costumer concerned the capture of a Mexican town by revolutionary Pedro Armendariz and the various townsmen who defy him or curry his favor. Paulette was flirtatious Maria Dolores, the daughter of a wealthy aristocrat. The *New York Times* carped: "Her whole manner is cheap and coarse and throws the character of a lady of breeding completely off-key." The low-budget feature quickly disappeared in a minimal circuit release.

Paulette was off screen for the next two years. Romantically, she was linked with diet-expert Gayelord Hauser. Then she met novelist Erich Maria Remarque, age 53. (He had previously been a close friend of Marlene Dietrich.) They became a steady couple on the social scene. She received much publicity as Queen of the Costume Ball (April 21, 1951) of the Art Students' League, held at the Waldorf Astoria in New York. At age 40, she still maintained a sleek figure.

Announced for *Hurricane Williams* at Paramount in 1952 (it became *Hurricane Smith* and starred Yvonne DeCarlo), she appeared in the low-budget *Babes in Bagdad,* an United Artists release of 1952. A murky color spoof, it presented Paulette and Gypsy Rose Lee as harem beauties who acquire a streak of independence. The sloppily made movie was shot in Spain, and Paulette owned 25 percent of the production. It came and went quickly on the grind circuit.

In *Vice Squad* (1953) she accepted second billing to police captain Edward G. Robinson. Paulette sashayed through her role as Mona, head of an "escort" bureau, whose girls provide the police with leads in a homicide case.

She told reporter Vernon Scott that year (1953): "Actors and actresses who say they never go to see their own pictures are talking through their hats. . . . You don't have to be a Freud to know that the most fascinating person in the world—actors or anybody—is yourself. I also take in my own pictures to see what I do wrong and what I do right. There's always room for improvement. And anyhow, I enjoy it. . . . And when I sit in the theatre by myself I don't kid myself. I make all kinds of mental notes and follow them through."

By now Paulette was being tagged—in a friendly manner—"Hollywood's greatest non-actress" and "the best bad girl in Hollywood." A standing gag had it that Paulette could not take a walk around the block without coming back with a gift. She would never accept flowers ("I take

*See Appendix.

nothing perishable") and enjoyed "treating furs as if they were rags." When asked how she acquired a necklace of 50 diamonds, she quipped: "I got it by getting engaged so often. . . . I never give anything back."

One of the most typical and revealing anecdotes about Paulette concerns Jim Thompson, president of Tahi Silk Company of Bangkok. They were dining together one evening and she admired his silk suit. "I'll give it to you," he said, and promptly removed it and did so. Said Paulette: "What was so touching about it was that this happened in my home, not his. Thompson said good night at three A.M. and walked out the door—in his shorts."

Paulette's other two 1953 releases were also programmers. *Paris Models* was a tedious multi-vignette yarn tracing the history of an $890 gown ("Nude at Midnight") as it passed from owner to owner. Paulette's episode had her as a secretary with designs on her boss. She purchases a copy of the gown to entice her employer, only to have his wife show up in the same outfit. *Variety* thought her "competent."

Sins of Jezebel (1953) attempted to cash in on the then current biblical cycle. In wide-screen and color, it was a pretentiously moral-toned drama about the evils committed by Phoenician princess Paulette. While making this film—which cost $100,000 and was lensed in three days—Paulette admitted: "I used to say I'd rather have a short part with long eyelashes, than a long part with short eyelashes. But I'm not that outspoken any more." About this weak double-bill fare, the *Hollywood Reporter* charged: "Her rages too often emerge as weak petulance."

Charge of the Lancers (1954) did nothing for Paulette's declining screen reputation. It was a stock romantic actioner about the Crimean War. She was a gypsy intrigued with Frenchman Jean-Pierre Aumont. Her next film, *The Unholy Four* (1954), based on George Sanders's book *Strangers at Home,* was made cheaply in England. She was the lackluster wife of William Sylvester in this routine whodunit. When he is slugged on the head during a fishing trip, he suffers a three-year lapse of memory. The night he reappears, one of his three partners who had accompanied him on that fateful excursion is killed. The *New York Times* warned that if Paulette made many more plodding films like this one, she might "find herself collecting the pieces of a career."

Paulette's most noteworthy work of the year was an interview with columnist Art Buchwald in Paris. She informed him: "I'm a very nervous shopper. I can't stand people with me. . . . I always buy myself some dresses at Christmas time. You know it's always been considered very lucky in France to have a Christian Dior dress on Christmas eve."

Her father Joseph Levee died on September 2, 1954, in Denver, Colorado. He had been a Warner Brothers district sales aide there. He left an $89,910 estate, with a token $1 bequeathed to Paulette. She refused to accept it.

There was talk of Paulette starring in a television series, "White Collar Girl," to be written by Anita Loos, but it never materialized. She popped up in such video dramatic offerings as a new version of *The Women* (February 8, 1955, NBC), costarring with Ruth Hussey, Mary Astor, and Shelley Winters. She played Sylvia, the role Rosalind Russell had essayed in the 1939 film. Jack Gould (*New York Times*) reported: "She seemed more the impish tease than a frightened female." She appeared in six episodes of the syndicated "Errol Flynn Theatre" (1956–57), and also took on roles in such anthology series as "Ford Theatre," "Joseph Cotten Theatre," "Climax," and in 1959, two segments of ABC's "Adventures in Paradise." About working in this medium, she informed the *New York Daily News:* "I love doing TV. It's such a breakneck pace you know. It's kiss and go with your leading man. You meet them in the morning and go right into a clinch. The filming is over before you get to know their last names. As for live TV, it's like a premiere on Broadway that closes after the opening night."

Before embarking on a stage tour of *Waltz of the Toreadors* with Melvyn Douglas in September, 1957 (having turned down several Broadway offers), Paulette told the press: "I keep getting offers for my life story but I'm too busy living it, I'll wait until I'm 80. My mother is a little worried about my philosophy of life. 'What will you do when you're lonely at 70?' she asks me. That's when I'll get the education she could not afford to give me." She quit the show in Detroit in January, 1958, because of her impending marriage to Remarque.

The couple ended several years of speculation by finally getting married. On February 25, 1958, they had a civil ceremony in Branford, Connecticut. It was his second marriage. Uniquely, they maintained separate apartments in Manhattan at 320 East 57th Street—he on the fourteenth floor and she on the fifteenth. Explained Paulette: "We're planning to keep both apartments. When people work as hard as we do and keep different hours it is better to have separate apartments."

After a two-week stage appearance in *Laura* with Reginald Gardiner in 1959, Paulette's public activities were largely confined to luxurious living at Remarque's villa in Locarno, Switzerland, and to the European social swim. She told Sheila Graham in early 1960: "I was quite poor to begin with. But I think a background of poverty is good; you can always go back to living on $20 a week. You feel like a bandit when you take the good things in life. But these mean less to me now, perhaps because I have a great deal." She confided to Leonard Lyons: "Business deals are beyond me. They frighten me. I've made it a rule never to sign my name to any paper more than once a year. It saves me a great deal of money and litigation. I have another rule —I never give anything back."

In the 1960s, when many former cinema queens were making movie comebacks in horror films, Paulette refused all such offers. She commented at the time: "I'm always slightly embarrassed to meet other actresses of my vintage. We have so little in common. They're all so dedicated, I find—so desperate."

It was under less than happy circumstances that Paulette finally returned to the screen in the Italian-made *Time of Indifference* (1966), her last movie to date. It was a pompous adaptation of Albert Moravia's first novel, filmed in the neorealistic style. Paulette postured ineffectively as the impoverished countess widow Mariagrazi, who is blind to the fact that her lover Rod Steiger is romancing her daughter (Claudia Cardinale) on the side. Even making allowances for the synchronized English sound track, Paulette came across "chirpy and fighty." The camera closeups were very unflattering to her 55-year-old face.

When questioned by Leonard Lyons in 1968 as to how she spent her time, Paulette stated: "We spend the winters in Rome for Erich's health and my pleasure." Remarque died on September 25, 1970, of a heart attack; he was buried on a hilltop near their Swiss home. Paulette spent the succeeding months negotiating the sale of his last novel.

Paulette was among the regal celebrities who turned up at the Living Legends Ball held at the Four Seasons restaurant in New York in January,

1971. The still shapely Paulette (she practices yoga) posed for pictures with another cinema queen, Joan Crawford. In 1972 Paulette came out of professional retirement in *The Snoop Sisters,* an NBC telefeature with Helen Hayes, Mildred Natwick, and Art Carney. She played the role of a movie star who is murdered.

Recently, Paulette told a national magazine: "You live in the present and you eliminate things that don't matter. You don't carry the burden of the past. I'm not impressed by the past very much. The past bores me, to tell you the truth; it really bores me. I don't remember many movies and certainly not my own.

"I lived in Hollywood long enough to learn to play tennis and become a star, but I never felt it was my home, I was never looking for a home, as a matter of fact. I collect Egyptian cats—I have a collection larger than the Metropolitan Museum's—but I don't like to collect anything I can't pack.

"I never really counted on how it was all going to turn out. I bounce back. A year is like a weekend now, just like a moment, and as you get older it gets worse. But I never have missed anything and if I wanted to work more I could—don't you think so?"

THE GIRL HABIT (PAR, 1931) 77 M.

Director, Edward Cline; story, A. E. Thomas, Clayton Hamilton; screenplay, Owen Davis, Gertrude Purcell; camera, Larry Williams; editor, Barney Rogan.

Charlie Ruggles (Charlie Floyd); Tamara Geva (Sonya Maloney); Sue Conroy (Lucy Ledyard); Margaret Dumont (Blanche Ledyard); Allen Jenkins (Tony Maloney); Donald Meek (Jonesy); Douglas Gilmore (Huntley Palmer); Jerome Daley (Warden Henery); Betty Garde (Hattie Henery); Ed Gargan (Detective); Murray Alper (Hood); Jean Ackerman, Paulette Goddard, Erica Newman, Norma Taylor (Lingerie Salesgirls).

THE MOUTHPIECE (WB, 1932) 90 M.

Director, James Flood, Elliott Nugent, based on the play by Frank J. Collins; screenplay, Earl Baldwin; camera, Barney McGill; editor, George Amy.

Warren William (Vincent Day); Sidney Fox (Celia); Aline MacMahon (Miss Hickey); William Janney (John); John Wray (Barton); Polly Walters (Gladys); Ralph Ince (J.B.); Mae Madison (Elaine); Noel Francis (Miss Da Vere); Morgan Wallace (Smith); Guy Kibbee (Bartender); J. Carrol Naish (Tony); Walter Walker (Forbes); Jack LaRue (Garland); Stanley Fields (Pondapolis); Murray Kinnell (Jarvis); Emerson Treacy (Wilson); Paulette Goddard (Girl).

THE KID FROM SPAIN (UA, 1932) 90 M.

Producer, Samuel Goldwyn; director, Leo McCarey; based on a story by William Anthony McGuire; Bert Kalmar, Harry Ruby; screenplay, McGuire, Kalmar, Ruby; choreography, Busby Berkeley; songs, Kalmar and Ruby; camera, Gregg Toland; editor, Stuart Heisler.

Eddie Cantor (Eddie Williams); Lyda Roberti (Rosalie); Robert Young (Ricardo); Ruth Hall (Anita Gomez); John Miljan (Pancho); Noah Beery (Alonzo Gomez); J. Carrol Naish (Pedro); Robert Emmett O'Connor (Detective Crawford); Stanley Fields (Jose); Paul Porcasi (Gonzales); Julian Rivero (Dalmores); Theressa Maxwell Conover (Martha Oliver); Walter Walker (Dean); Ben Hendrick, Jr. (Red); Sidney Franklin (Himself); Paulette Goddard, Betty Grable (Girls).

MODERN TIMES (UA, 1936) 87 M.

Producer-director-screenplay, Charles Chaplin; assistant director, Carter de Haven, Henry Bergman; music, Chaplin; music director, Alfred Newman; camera, R. H. Totheroh, Ira Morgan.

Charles Chaplin (A Tramp); Paulette Goddard (A Gamin); Henry Bergman (Cafe Proprietor); Chester Conklin (Mechanic); Stanley Sandford (Big Bill); Hank Mann, Louis Matheaux (Assembly Workers—Burglars); Allen Garcia (President of the Steel Company); Murdock MacQuarrie (J. Widdecombe Biddle); Wilfred Lucas (Juvenile Officer); Richard Alexander (Tramps's Cell-Mate); Heinie Conklin, James C. Morton (Assembly Workers); Lloyd Ingraham (Diner); Mira McKinney (Minister's Wife); Walter James (Assembly Line Foreman); Sammy Stein (Turbine Operator); Stanley Blystone (Gamin's Father); Gloria De Haven (Gamin's Sister); Fred Malatesta (Waiter); Ted Oliver (Biddle's Assistant); Edward LeSaint (Sheriff Conlon); Frank Hagney (Shipbuilder); Chuck Hamilton, Harry Wilson, Bobby Barber (Workers); and: Juana Sutton, Edward Kimball, John Rand, Dr. Cecil Reynolds.

THE YOUNG IN HEART (UA, 1938) 90 M.

Producer, David O. Selznick; director, Richard Wallace; based on the play, *The Gay Banditti* by I. A. R. Wylie; screenplay, Paul Osborn, Charles Bennett; art director,

Lyle Wheeler; music, Franz Waxman; special effects, Jack Cosgrove; camera, Leon Shamroy; editor, Hal C. Kern.

Janet Gaynor (George-Ann); Roland Young (Sahib); Billie Burke (Marmy); Douglas Fairbanks, Jr. (Richard); Richard Carlson (Duncan McCrea); Minnie Dupree (Miss Fortune); Paulette Goddard (Leslie); Henry Stephenson (Amstruther); Eily Maylon (Sarah); Tom Ricketts (Andrew); Irvin S. Cobb (Mr. Jennings); Margaret Early (Adela Jennings); Lucile Watson (Mrs. Jennings); Ian McLaren (Doctor); Billie Bevan (Kennel Man); Walter Kingsford (Prefect); George Sorel, George Renevant (Detectives); Lionel Pape (Customer).

DRAMATIC SCHOOL (MGM, 1938) 78 M.

Producer, Mervyn LeRoy; director, Robert B. Sinclair; based on the play *School of Drama* by Hans Szekely, Zoltan Egyed; screenplay, Ernst Vadja, Mary McCall, Jr; art director, Cedric Gibbons; camera, William Daniels; editor, Frederick Y. Smith.

Luise Rainer (Louise); Paulette Goddard (Nana); Alan Marshal (Andre D'Abbencourt); Lana Turner (Mado); Anthony Allan (John Hubbard) (Fleury); Henry Stephenson (Pasquel, Sr.); Genevieve Tobin (Gina Bertier); Gale Sondergaard (Madame Charlot); Melville Cooper (Boulin); Erik Rhodes (Georges Mounier); Virginia Grey (Simone); Ann Rutherford (Yvonne); Hans Conried (Ramy); Rand Brook (Pasquel, Jr.); Jean Chatburn (Mimi); Marie Blake (Annette); Cecilia C. Callejo (La Brasiliana); Margaret Dumont (Pantomimic Teacher); Frank Puglia (Alphonse); Dorothy Granger (Fat Girl).

THE WOMEN (MGM, 1939) 132 M.

Producer, Hunt Stromberg; director, George Cukor, based on the play by Clare Boothe; screenplay, Anita Loos, Jane Murfin; art director, Cedric Gibbons; music, Edward Ward, David Snell; song, Chet Forrest, Bob Wright, and Ed Ward; camera, Oliver T. Marsh; Joseph Ruttenberg; editor, Robert J. Kerns.

Norma Shearer (Mary Haines); Joan Crawford (Crystal Allen); Rosalind Russell (Sylvia Fowler); Mary Boland (Countess Delave); Paulette Goddard (Miriam Aarons); Joan Fontaine (Peggy Day); Lucile Watson (Mrs. Moorehead); Phyllis Povah (Edith Potter); Florence Nash (Nancy Blake); Virginia Weidler (Little Mary); Ruth Hussey (Miss Watts); Muriel Hutchison (Jane); Margaret Dumont (Mrs. Wagstaff); Dennie Moore (Olga); Mary Cecil (Maggie); Marjorie Main (Lucy); Esther Dale (Ingrid); Hedda Hopper (Dolly Dupuyster); Mildred Shay (Helene—French Maid); Priscilla Lawson, Estelle Etterre (Hairdressers); Ann Morris (Exercise Instructress); Mary Beth Hughes (Miss Trimmerback); Marjorie Wood (Sadie—Old Maid in Powder Room); Virginia Grey (Pat); Cora Witherspoon (Mrs. Van Adams); Theresa Harris (Olive); Vera Vague, Virginia Howell (Receptionists); Mariska Aldrich (Singing Teacher); Judith Allen (Model); Aileen Pringle (Saleslady).

THE CAT AND THE CANARY (PAR, 1939) 72 M.

Producer, Arthur Hornblow, Jr.; director, Elliott Nugent; based on the play by John Willard; screenplay, Walter DeLeon; Lynn Starling; art director, Hans Dreier, Robert Usher; music, Dr. Ernst Toch; camera, Charles Lang; editor, Archie Marshek.

Bob Hope (Wally Campbell); Paulette Goddard (Joyce Norman); John Beal (Fred Blythe); Douglass Montgomery (Charlie Wilder); Gale Sondergaard (Miss Lu); Elizabeth Patterson (Aunt Susan); Nydia Westman (Cicily); George Zucco (Lawyer Crosby); John Wray (Henricks); George Regas, Chief Thundercloud (Indian Guides); Milton Kibbee, (Photographer); Charles Lane, Frank Melton (Reporters).

THE GHOST BREAKERS (PAR, 1940) 82 M.

Producer, Arthur Hornblow, Jr; director, George Marshall; story, Paul Dickey, Charles Goddard; screenplay, Walter De Leon; art director, Hans Dreier, camera, Charles Lang; editor, Ellsworth Hoagland.

Bob Hope (Larry Lawrence); Paulette Goddard (Mary Carter); Richard Carlson (Geoff Montgomery); Paul Lukas (Parada); Willie Best (Alex); Pedro De Cordoba (Havez); Virginia Brissac (Mother Zombie); Noble Johnson (The Zombie); Anthony Quinn (Ramon/Francisco Maderos); Tom Dugan (Raspy Kelly); Paul Fix (Frenchy Duval); Lloyd Corrigan (Martin); Emmett Vogan (Announcer); Grace Hayle (Screaming Woman); Herbert Elliott (Lt. Murray); James Blaine (Police Sgt.); Jack Hatfield (Elevator Boy); David Durand (Bellhop); James Flavin (Hotel Porter); Leonard Sues (Newsboy); Jack Edwards (Ship Bellboy); Max Wagner (Ship Porter); Paul Newlan (Baggage Man); Francisco Maran (Headwaiter); Jack Norton (Drunk); Blanca Vischer (Dolores); Douglas Kennedy, Robert Ryan (Internes); Kay Stewart (Telephone Girl).

THE GREAT DICTATOR (UA, 1940) 129 M.

Producer-director-screenplay, Charles Chaplin; art director, J. Russell Spencer; music director, Meredith Willson; assistant director, Dan James, Wheeler Dryden, Bob Meltzer; camera, Karl Struss, Roland Totheroh; editor, Willard Nico.

Charles Chaplin (Hynkel/A Jewish Barber); Paulette Goddard (Hannah); Jack Oakie (Napaloni—Dictator of Bacteria); Reginald Gardiner (Schultz); Henry Daniell (Garbitsch); Billy Gilbert (Herring); Maurice Moscovich (Mr. Jaeckel); Emma Dunn (Mrs. Jaeckel); Grace Hayle (Madame Napaloni); Carter de Haven, (Bacterian Ambassador); Bernard Gorcey (Mr. Mann); Paul Weigel (Mr. Agar); and: Chester Conklin, Hank Mann, Esther Michelson, Florence Wright, Eddie Gribbon, Robert O. Davis, Eddie Dunn, Nita Pike, Peter Lynn.

NORTH WEST MOUNTED POLICE (PAR, 1940) 125 M.

Executive producer, William LeBaron, producer, Cecil B. DeMille; associate producer, William H. Pine; director, DeMille; screenplay, Alan LeMay, Jesse Lasky, Jr., C. Gardner Sullivan; music, Victor Young; camera, Victor Milner, W. Howard Green; editor, Anne Bauchens.

Gary Cooper (Dusty Rivers); Madeleine Carroll (April Logan); Paulette Goddard (Louvette Corbeau); Preston Foster (Sgt. Jim Brett); Robert Preston (Ronnie Logan); George Bancroft (Jacques Corbeau); Lynne Overman (Tod McDuff); Akim Tamiroff (Dan Duroc); Walter Hampden (Big Bear); Lon Chaney, Jr. (Shorty); Montagu Love (Inspector Cabot); Francis McDonald (Louis Riel); George E. Stone (Johnny Pelang); Willard Robertson (Supt. Harrington); Regis Toomey (Constable Jerry Moore); Richard Denning (Constable Thornton); Douglas Kennedy (Constable Carter); Robert Ryan (Constable Dumont); James Seay (Constable Fenton); Lane Chandler (Constable Fyffe); Ralph Byrd (Constable Ackroyd); Eric Alden (Constable Kent); Wallace Reid, Jr. (Constable Rankin); Bud Geary (Constable Herrick); Evan Thomas (Captain Gower); Jack Pennick (Sgt. Field); Rod Cameron (Corp. Underhill); Davison Clark (Surgeon Roberts); Jack Chopin (Bugler); Chief Thundercloud (Wandering Spirit); Harry Burns (The Crow); Lou Merrill (Lesur); Clara Blandick (Mrs. Burns); Ynez Seabury (Mrs. Shorty); Eva Puig (Ekawo); Julia Faye (Wapiskau); Norma Nelson (Niska); Phillip Terry (Constable Judson); Jack Luden (Constable Douglas); John Hart (Constable Norman); Kermit Maynard (Constable Adams); Emory Parnell (George Higgins); James Flavin (Mountie); Anthony Caruso (Half-Breed—Riel's Hdqtrs); Nestor Paiva (Half-Breed); Jim Pierce (Corporal); Ray Mala, Monte Blue, Chief Yowlachie, Chief Thunderbird (Indians).

SECOND CHORUS (PAR, 1941) 84 M.

Producer, Boris Morros; associate producer, Robert Stillman; director, H. C. Potter; story, Frank Cavett; screenplay, Elaine Ryan, Ian McClellan Hunter; assistant director, Edward Montague; songs, Johnny Mercer and Hal Borne; Mercer and Bernie Hanighen; Artie Shaw; Mercer and Shaw; camera, Theodor Sparkuhl.

Fred Astaire (Danny O'Neill); Paulette Goddard (Ellen Miller); Burgess Meredith (Hank Taylor); Charles Butterworth (Mr. Chisholm); Artie Shaw and His Band

(Themselves); Frank Melton (Stu); Jimmy Conlon (Mr. Dunn); Adia Kuznetzoff (Boris); Michael Visaroff (Sergai); Joseph Marievsky (Ivan); Don Brodie (Hotel Clerk); Billy Benedict (Ticket Taker); Ben Hall (Western Union Boy).

POT O'GOLD (UA, 1941) 86 M.

Producer, James Roosevelt; director, George Marshall; story, Monte Brice, Andrew Benninson, Harry Tugend; screenplay, Walter De Leon; music director, Lou Forbes; choreography, Larry Ceballos; songs, Mack David and Vee Lawnhurst; Hy Heath and Fred Rose; Dave Franklin; Eorbes and Henry Sullivan; set designer, Hans Peters; assistant director, William Tummel; camera, Hal Mohr; editor, Lloyd Nosler.

James Stewart (Jimmy); Paulette Goddard (Molly); Horace Heidt (Himself); Charles Winninger (C. J. Haskell); Mary Gordon (Mom); Frank Melton (Jasper); Jed Prouty (Louderman); Dick Hogan (Willie); James Burke (Lt. Grady); Charlie Arnt (Parks); Dona Wood (Molly's Sister); Larry Cotton (Larry); Henry Roquemore (Samson); William Gould (Chalmers); Aldrich Bowker (Judge Murray); Mary Ruth (Mary Simmons); Beverly Andre (Alice); Jay Ward (Boy Friend); James Flavin (Bud Connolly); Master Stan Worth (Tommy); Edgar Dearing (McGinty); Nestor Paiva (Guide); Purnell Pratt (Thompson).

NOTHING BUT THE TRUTH (PAR, 1941) 90 M.

Producer, Arthur Hornblow, Jr.; director, Elliott Nugent; story, James Montgomery, Frederick S. Isham; screenplay, Don Hartman, Ken Englund; art director, Hans Dreier, Robert Usher; camera, Charles Lang; editor, Alma Macrorie.

Bob Hope (Steve Bennett); Paulette Goddard (Gwen Saunders); Edward Arnold (T. T. Ralston); Leif Erickson (Van); Willie Best (Samuel); Glenn Anders (Dick Donnelly); Grant Mitchell (Mr. Bishop); Catharine Doucet (Mrs. Van Dusen); Rose Hobart (Mrs. Donnelly); Clarence Kolb (Mr. Van Dusen); Leon Belasco (Dr. Zarak); Mary Forbes (Mrs. Ralston); Helene Millard (Miss Turner); William Wright (Mr. Prichard); Oscar Smith (Shoe Shine Boy); Wilson Benge (Fredericks); Jack Chapin, Rod Cameron (Sailors); Dick Chandlee (Office Boy); Catherine Craig (Receptionist); Edward McWade (Elderly Clerk); Keith Richards (Boy); James Blane (Doorman); Jack Egan (Elevator Starter); Jim Farley (Watchman); Victor Potel (Pedestrian); Lee Shumway (Cop); Eleanor Counts (Maid); Buck Woods (Porter); Billy Dawson (Newsboy).

HOLD BACK THE DAWN (PAR, 1941) 115 M.

Producer, Arthur Hornblow; director, Mitchell Leisen; story, Ketti Frings; screenplay, Charles Brackett, Billy Wilder; art director, Hans Dreier, Robert Usher; song, Frank Loesser, Jimmy Berg, Fred Spielman, and Fred Jacobson; camera, Leo Tover; editor, Doane Harrison.

Charles Boyer (Georges Iscovescu); Olivia de Havilland (Emmy Brown); Paulette Goddard (Anita Dixon); Victor Francen (Van Den Luecken); Walter Abel (Inspector Hammock); Curt Bois (Bonbois); Rosemary DeCamp (Berta Kurz); Eric Feldary (Josef Kurz); Nestor Paiva (Flores); Eva Puig (Lupita); Michaeline Cheirel (Christine); Madeleine LeBeau (Anni); Billy Lee (Tony); Mikhail Rasumny (Mechanic); Mitchell Leisen (Mr. Saxon); Brian Donlevy, Richard Webb (Actors); Veronica Lake (Actress); Sonny Boy Williams (Sam); Edward Fielding (American Consul); Don Douglas (Joe); Gertrude Astor (Young Woman at Climax Bar); Carlos Villarias (Mexican Judge); Arthur Loft (Hollander Planter); Charles Arnt (Mr. MacAdams); Ella Neal (Bride); Ray Mala (Young Mexican Bridegroom); June Wilkins (Miss Vivienne Worthington); Leon Belasco (Mr. Spitzer); Chester Clute (Man at Climax Bar).

THE LADY HAS PLANS (PAR, 1942) 77 M.

Associate producer, Fred Kohlmar; director, Sidney Lanfield; story, Leo Birinski; screenplay, Harry Tugend; camera, Charles Lang; editor, William Shea.

Ray Milland (Kenneth Harper); Paulette Goddard (Sidney Royce); Roland Young (Ronald Dean); Albert Dekker (Baron Von Kemp); Margaret Hayes (Rita Lenox);

Cecil Kellaway (Peter Milen); Addison Richards (Paul Baker); Edward Norris (Frank Richards); Charles Arnt (Pooly); Hans Schumm, Hans von Morhart (Germans); Genia Nikola (German Maid); Gerald Mohr (Joe Scalsi); Lionel Royce (Guard); Thomas W. Ross (Abner Spencer); Arthur Loft (Mr. Weston); Paul Phillips, Warren Ashe (G-Men); Lee Shumway (Cop); Terry Ray (Taxi Driver); Mel Ruick (Announcer); Keith Richards, George Dobbs (Hotel Clerks); Yola d'Avril (Hotel Maid); Richard Webb (Hotel Information Clerk); Nestor Paiva (Portuguese Porter); Sigurd Tor (German Guard).

REAP THE WILD WIND (PAR, 1942) 123 M.

Producer, Cecil B, DeMille; associate producer, William Pine; director, DeMille; story, Thelma Strabel; screenplay, Alan LeMay, Charles Bennett, Jesse Lasky, Jr.; music, Victor Young; art director, Hans Dreier, Roland Anderson, process camera, Farciot Edouart; special effects, Gordon Jennings; camera, Victor Milner; editor Anna Bauchens.

Ray Milland (Stephen Tolliver); John Wayne (Captain Jack Stuart); Paulette Goddard (Loxi Claiborne); Raymond Massey (King Cutler); Robert Preston (Dan Cutler); Lynne Overman (Captain Phillip Philpott); Susan Hayward (Drusilla Alston); Charles Bickford (Mate of the "Tyfib"); Walter Hampden (Commodore Devereaux); Louise Beavers (Maum Maria); Martha O'Driscoll (Ivy Devereaux); Elisabeth Risdon (Mrs. Claiborne); Hedda Hopper (Aung Henrietta); Victor Kilian (Widgeon); Oscar Polk (Salt Meat); Janet Beacher (Mrs. Mottram); Ben Carter (Chinkapin); Wee Willie (The Lamb); Lane Chandler (Sam); Davison Clark (Judge Marvin); Frank M. Thomas (Dr. Jepson); Keith Richards (Captain Carruthers); J. Farrell Macdonald (Port Captain); Victor Varconi (Lubbock); Harry Woods (Mace); Raymond Hatton (Master Shipwright); Milburn Stone (Lt. Farragut); Barbara Britton, Julia Faye (Charleston Ladies); Constantine Romanoff (Pete—Sponge Boat); Nestor Paiva (Man with Suspenders); James Flavin (Father Of Girl); Frank Lackteen, Alan Bridge, Al Ferguson, (Cutler Men in Barrel Room); Dick Alexander (Stoker Boss); Byron Foulger (Devereaux Courier); Dorothy Sebastian (Woman in Ballroom); Jack Luden (Southern Gentleman at Tea); Monte Blue (Office at tea); Dale Van Sickel (Member of Falcon Crew); Leo Sulky, Cap Anderson, Sam Appel, Harry Dean, Billy Elmer (Jurymen).

THE FOREST RANGERS (PAR, 1942) 87 M.

Associate Producer, Robert Sisk; director, George Marshall; story, Thelma Strabel; screenplay, Harold Shumate; art director, Hans Dreier, Earl Hedrick; songs, Frank Loesser and Frederick Hollander; Joseph J. Lilley; camera, Charles Lang; editor, Paul Weatherwax.

Fred MacMurray (Don Stuart); Paulette Goddard (Celia Huston); Susan Hayward (Tana Mason); Lynne Overman (Jammer Jones); Albert Dekker (Twig Dawson); Eugene Pallette (Mr. Huston); Regis Toomey (Frank Hatfield); Rod Cameron (Jim Lawrence); Clem Bevans (Terry McCabe); James Brown (George Tracy); Kenneth Griffith, Keith Richards, William Cabanne (Rangers); Jimmy Conlin (Mr. Hansen); Arthur Loft (John Arnold); Chester Clute (Judge); George Chandler, Tim Ryan, Lee Phelps, Edwin J. Brady (Keystone Cops); Sarah Edwards (Mrs. Hansen); Harry Woods, Robert Homans, (Lumbermen); Wade Boteler (Sheriff); Robert Kent, Jack Mulhall (Lookouts); Byron Foulger (Collector); Howard Mitchell (Doctor); Ethan Laidlaw, Karl Vess, Bob Kortman, Al Thompson, George Bruggeman, Harry Templeton (Lumberjacks).

STAR SPANGLED RHYTHM (PAR, 1942) 99 M.

Associate producer, Joseph Sistrom; director, George Marshall; screenplay, Harry Tugend; music, Robert Emmett Dolan; art director, Hans Dreier, Ernest Fegte; songs, Johnny Mercer and Harold Arlen; camera, Leo Tover; Theodor Sparkuhl; editor, Paul Weatherwax.

Betty Hutton (Polly Judson); Eddie Bracken (Jimmy Webster); Victor Moore (Pop Webster); Anne Revere (Sarah); Walter Abel (Frisbee); Cass Daley (Mimi); Macdonald Carey (Louie the Lug); Gil Lamb (Hi-Pockets); William Haade (Duffy); Bob Hope (Master of Ceremonies); Marion Martin, William Bendix, Dorothy Lamour, Paulette Goddard, Veronica Lake, Arthur Treacher, Walter Catlett, Sterling Holloway, Vera Zorina, Frank Faylen, Fred MacMurray, Franchot Tone, Ray Milland, Lynne Overman, Susan Hayward, Ernest Truex, Mary Martin, Dick Powell, Golden Gate Quartette, Walter Dare Wahl and Co., Cecil B. DeMille, Preston Sturges, Ralph Murphy, Alan Ladd, Gary Crosby, Jack Hope, Katherine Dunham, Rochester, Marjorie Reynolds, Betty Rhodes, Dona Drake, Bing Crosby, Jimmy Lydon, Ellen Drew, Charles Smith, Frances Gifford, Susanna Foster, Robert Preston (Themselves); Tom Dugan (Hitler); Richard Loo (Hirohito); Paul Porcasi (Mussolini); Dorothy Granger (Officer); Woody Strode (Rochester's Motorcycle Chauffeur); Barbara Pepper, Jean Phillips, Lynda Grey (Girls); Eddie Dew, Rod Cameron (Petty Officers); Keith Richards (Officer); Irving Bacon (New Hampshire Farmer—Old Glory Number); Virginia Brissac (Lady from Iowa—Old Glory Number); Matt McHugh (Man from Brooklyn—Old Glory Number); Peter Potter (Georgia Boy—Old Glory Number).

THE CRYSTAL BALL (UA, 1943) 81 M.

Producer, Richard Blumenthal; director, Elliott Nugent; story, Steven Vas; adaptation, Virginia Van Upp; music, Victor Young; art director, Hans Dreier, Roland Anderson; camera, Leo Tover; editor, Doane Harrison.

Ray Milland (Brad Cavanaugh); Paulette Goddard (Toni Gerard); Gladys George (Madame Zenobia); Virginia Field (Jo Ainsley); Cecil Kellaway (Pop Tibbets); William Bendix (Biff Carter); Mary Field (Foster); Frank Conlan (Dusty); Ernest Truex (Mr. Martin); Mabel Paige (Lady with Pekinese); Regina Wallace (Mrs. Smythe); Peter Jamieson (Brad Cavanaugh's Secretary); Donald Douglas (Mr. Bowman); Nestor Paiva (Stukov); Sig Arno (Waiter at Stukov's); Hillary Brooke (Friend of Jo Ainsley's); Tom Dugan (Plumber); Iris Adrian (Mrs. Martin); Babe London, June Evans (Tandem Riders); Reginald Sheffield (Dad in Shooting Gallery); Maude Eburne ("Apple Annie" Character); Yvonne DeCarlo, Maxine Ardell (Secretaries).

SO PROUDLY WE HAIL (PAR, 1943) 126 M.

Producer-director, Mark Sandrich; screenplay, Allan Scott; art director, Hans Dreier, Earl Hedrick; music, Miklos Rozsa; song, Edward Heyman and Rozsa; special effects, Gordon Jennings, Farciot Edouart; camera, Charles Lang; editor, Ellsworth Hoagland.

Claudette Colbert (Lt. Janet Davidson); Paulette Goddard (Lt. Jean O'Doul); Veronica Lake (Lt. Olivia D'Arcy); George Reeves (Lt. John Summers); Barbara Britton (Lt. Rosemary Larson); Walter Abel (Chaplain); Sonny Tufts (Kansas); Mary Servoss (Capt. "Ma" McGregor); Ted Hecht (Dr. Jose Hardin); John Litel (Dr. Harrison); Dr. Hugh Ho Chang (Ling Chee); Mary Treen (Lt. Sadie Schwartz); Kitty Kelly (Lt. Ethel Armstrong); Helen Lynd (Lt. Elsie Bollenbacker); Lorna Gray (Lt. Toni Bacelli); Dorothy Adams (Lt. Irma Emerson); Ann Doran (Lt. Betty Paterson); Jean Willes (Lt. Carol Johnson); Lynn Walker (Lt. Fay Leonard); Joan Tours (Lt. Margaret Stevenson); Jan Wiley (Lt. Lynne Hopkins); James Bell (Colonel White); Dick Hogan (Flight Lt. Archie McGregor); Bill Goodwin (Capt. O'Rourke); James Flavin (Capt. O'Brien); Byron Foulger (Mr. Larson); Elsa Janssen (Mrs. Larson); Richard Crane (Georgie Larson); Boyd Davis (Col. Mason); Will Wright (Col. Clark); William Forrest (Major—San Francisco Dock); Isabel Cooper, Amparo Antenercrut, Linda Brent (Filipino Nurses); James Millican (Young Ensign); Damian O'Flynn (Young Doctor); Victor Kilian, Jr. (Corp); Julia Faye, Hazel Keener, Frances Morris, Mimi Doyle, (Nurses); Edward Earle, Byron Shores (Doctors); Harry Strong (Major Arthur); Edward Dew (Capt. Lawrence); Yvonne DeCarlo (Girl); Hugh Prosser (Captain); Charles Lester (Soldier).

STANDING ROOM ONLY (PAR, 1944) 83 M.

Associate producer, Paul Jones; director, Sidney Lanfield; story, Al Martin; screenplay, Darrel Ware, Karl Tunberg; music, Robert Emmett Dolan; art director, Hans Dreier, Earl Hedrick; camera, Charles Lang; editor, William Shea.

Paulette Goddard (Jane Rogers); Fred MacMurray (Lee Stevens); Edward Arnold (T. J. Todd); Roland Young (Ira Cromwell); Hillary Brooke (Alice Todd); Porter Hall (Hugo Farenhall); Clarence Kolb (Glen Ritchie); Anne Revere (Major Cromwell); Isabel Randolph (Mrs. Ritchie); Veda Ann Borg (Peggy Fuller); Marie McDonald (Opal); Josephine Whittell (Miss Becker); Sig Arno (Waiter); Boyd Davis (Admiral); Roy Gordon (Commander); Herbert Heyes (Colonel); Eddie Dunn, Arthur Loft (Foremen); Yvonne DeCarlo, Noel Neill (Secretaries); Gayne Whitman (Voice Over Dictograph); Frank Faylen (Cab Driver); Ethel May Halls, Georgia Backus, Grayce Hampton, Rita Gould, Forbes Murray, Edwin Stanley (Guests at Richie Home).

I LOVE A SOLDIER (PAR, 1944) 106 M.

Producer-director, Mark Sandrich; screenplay, Allan Scott; music, Robert Emmett Dolan; art director, Hans Dreier, Earl Hedrick; process camera, Farciot Edouart; camera, Charles Lang; editor, Ellsworth Hoagland.

Paulette Goddard (Eve Morgan); Sonny Tufts (Dan Kilgore); Beulah Bondi (Etta Lane); Walter Sande (Stiff Banks); Mary Treen (Cissy Grant); Ann Doran (Jenny); Marie McDonald (Gracie); James Bell (Williams); Barry Fitzgerald (Murphy); Frank Albertson (Little Soldier); Almira Sessions (Mrs. Munn); James Millican (Georgie); Eddie Hall (Freddie Rogers); Bobby Barber (Attendant—Fun House); Frank Moran (Hammer Machine Opr.); Hugh Beaumont (John); Charles Quigley (Soldier); Larry Steers (Minister); Jimmie Dundee, Eddie Dunn (Passengers); Barbara Pepper, Terry Adams (Blondes).

DUFFY'S TAVERN (PAR, 1945) 97 M.

Associate producer, Danny Dare; director, Hal Walker; screenplay, Melvin Frank, Norman Panama; music director, Robert Emmett Dolan; choreography, Billy Daniels; songs, Johnny Burke and Jimmy Van Heusen; Ben Raleigh and Bernie Wayne; process camera, Farciot Edouart; special effects, Gordon Jennings; camera, Lionel Lindon; editor, Arthur Schmidt.

Bing Crosby, Betty Hutton, Paulette Goddard, Alan Ladd, Dorothy Lamour, Eddie Bracken, Brian Donlevy, Sonny Tufts, Veronica Lake, Arturo De Cordova, Cass Daley, Diana Lynn, Gary Crosby, Phillip Crosby, Dennis Crosby, Lin Crosby, William Bendix, Maurice Rocco, James Brown, Joan Caulfield, Gail Russell, Helen Walker, Jean Heather (Themselves); Barry Fitzgerald (Bing Crosby's Father); Victor Moore (Michael O'Malley); Marjorie Reynolds (Peggy O'Malley); Barry Sullivan (Danny Murphy); Ed Gardner (Archie); Charles Cantor (Finnegan); Eddie Green (Eddie—The Waiter); Ann Thomas (Miss Duffy); Howard Da Silva (Heavy); Billy De Wolfe (Doctor); Walter Abel (Director); Charles Quigley (Ronald); Olga San Juan (Gloria); Robert Watson (Masseur) Frank Faylen (Customer); Matt McHugh (Man Following Miss Duffy); Emmett Vogan (Make-Up Man); Cyril Ring (Gaffer); Noel Neill (School Kid).

KITTY (PAR, 1946) 103 M.

Producer, Karl Tunberg; director, Mitchell Leisen; based on the novel by Rosamund Marshall; screenplay, Darrell Ware, Tunberg; music, Victor Young; art director, Hans Dreier, Walter Tyler; choreography, Billy Daniels; settings-costumes, Rene Pene DuBois; special effects, Farciot Edouart, Gordon Jennings; camera, Daniel L. Fapp; editor, Alma Macrorie.

Paulette Goddard (Kitty); Ray Milland (Sir Hugh Marcy); Patric Knowles (Brett Hardwood, Earl of Carstairs); Reginald Owen (Duke of Malmunster); Cecil Kellaway (Thomas Gainsborough); Constance Collier (Lady Susan Dewitt); Dennis Hoey (Jonathan Selby); Sara Allgood (Old Meg); Eric Blore (Dobson); Gordon Richards (Sir Joshua Reynolds); Michael Dyne (The Prince of Wales); Edgar Norton (Earl of Campton); Patricia Cameron (Elaine Carlisle); Mary Gordon (Nancy); Anita Bolster (Mullens); Heather Wilde (Lil); Charles Coleman (Major Domo); Mae Clarke (Molly); Ann

Codee (Madame Aurelie); Douglas Walton (Philip); Alec Craig (McNab); Edward Cooper (Sir Herbert Harbord); Anne Curson (Duchess of Gloucester); Tempe Pigott (Woman in Window); John Rice (Cockney Cart Driver); Doris Lloyd (Woman Fish Hawker); Sybil Burton (Magic Lantern Woman); Snub Pollard (Hugh's Rental Coachman); Ruth St. Denis (Duchess); Mary McLeod (Mrs. Sheridan); Dodo Bernard (Taffy Tarts Peddler); Gibson Gowland (Prison Guard); Cyril Delevanti ("All Hot" Hawker); Byron Poindexter (Col. St. Leger).

THE DIARY OF A CHAMBERMAID (UA, 1946) 86 M.

Producer, Benedict Bogeaus, Burgess Meredith; director, Jean Renoir; based on the novel by Octave Mirbeau, and the play by Andre Heuse, Andre de Lorde, Thielly Nores; screenplay, Meredith; production designer, Eugene Laurie; assistant director, Joseph Depew; special effects, Lee Zavitz; camera, Lucien Andriot; editor, James Smith.

Paulette Goddard (Celestine); Burgess Meredith (Captain Mauger); Hurd Hatfield (Georges); Francis Lederer (Joseph); Judith Anderson (Madame Lanlaire); Florence Bates (Rose); Irene Ryan (Louise); Almira Sessions (Marianne); Reginald Owen (Captain Lanlaire).

SUDDENLY IT'S SPRING (PAR, 1947) 87 M.

Producer, Claude Binyon; director, Mitchell Leisen; story, Binyon; screenplay, Binyon, P. J. Wolfson; music, Victor Young; camera, Daniel L. Fapp; editor, Alma Macrorie.

Paulette Goddard (Mary Morely); Fred MacMurray (Peter Morely); Macdonald Carey (Jack Lindsay); Arleen Whelan (Gloria Fay); Lillian Fontaine (Mary's Mother); Frank Faylen (Harold Michaels); Victoria Horne (Lt. Billings); Frances Robinson (Captain Rogers); Georgia Backus (Major Cheever); Jean Ruth (WAC Corp. Michaels); Roberta Jonay (WAC Sgt.); Willie Best (Porter on Train); Griff Barnett (Conductor on Train); Isabel Randolph (Dowager in Elevator); Beulah Parkington, Ella Ethridge, Helen Dickson, Jack Davidson (People in Elevator); Richard Brandon (Captain Jergens); Francis Morris (Red Cross Worker): William Hall (M.P.—Phone Booth); Eddie Johnson, Eddie Coke (Photographers); James Milligan, Len Hendry (M.P.s); John Kellogg (Newsreel Man); Paul Oman (Violinist); James Dundee (Violinist); Pat McVey, Perc Launders, George Lynn (Reporters); Chester Clute (Workman); Crane Whitley, Stanley Blystone (Hotel Detectives).

VARIETY GIRL (PAR, 1947) 83 M.

Producer, Daniel Dare; director, George Marshall; screenplay, Edmund Hartman, Frank Tashlin, Robert Welch, Monte Brice; music, Joseph J. Lilley; songs, Johnny Burke and James Van Heusen; Frank Loesser; Allan Roberts and Doris Fisher; choreography, Billy Daniels, Bernard Pearce; assistant director, George Templeton; art director, Hans Dreier, Robert Clatworthy; special effects, Gordon Jennings; camera, Lionel Linden, Stuart Thompson; editor, LeRoy Stone.

Mary Hatcher (Catherine Brown); Olga San Juan (Amber LaVonne); DeForest Kelley (Bob Kirby); William Demarest (Barker); Frank Faylen (Stage Manager); Frank Ferguson (J.R. O'Connell); Russell Hicks, Crane Whitley, Charles Coleman Hal K. Dawson, Eddie Fetherston (Men at Steambath); Catherine Craig (Secretary); Bing Crosby, Bob Hope, Gary Cooper, Ray Milland, Alan Ladd, Barbara Stanwyck, Paulette Goddard, Dorothy Lamour, Veronica Lake, Sonny Tufts, Joan Caulfield, William Holden, Lizabeth Scott, Burt Lancaster, Gail Russell, Diana Lynn, Sterling Hayden, Robert Preston, John Lund, William Bendix, Barry Fitzgerald, Cass Daley, Howard Da Silva, Billy De Wolfe, Macdonald Carey, Arleen Whelan, Patric Knowles, Mona Freeman, Cecil Kellaway, Johnny Coy, Virginia Field, Richard Webb, Stanley Clements, Cecil B. DeMille, Mitchell Leisen, Frank Butler, George Marshall, Roger Dann, Pearl Bailey, The Mulcay's, Spike Jones City Slickers, George Reeves, Wanda

Hendrix, Sally Rawlinson (Themselves); Ann Doran (Hairdresser); Jack Norton (Brown Derby Busboy); Eric Alden (Make Up Man); Frank Mayo (Director).

UNCONQUERED (PAR, 1947) 135 M.

Producer-director, Cecil B. DeMille; based on the novel by Neil H. Swanson; screenplay, Charles Bennett, Fredric M. Frank, Jesse Lasky, Jr.; music, Victor Young; assistant director, Edward Slaven; dialogue director, Robert Foulk; choreography, Jack Crosby; special effects, Gordon Jennings, Paul Perpae, Devereux Jennings, Farciot Edouart; camera, Ray Rennahan; editor, Anna Bauchens.

Gary Cooper (Captain Christopher Holden); Paulette Goddard (Abby Hale); Howard Da Silva (Martin Gath); Boris Karloff (Guyasuta—Chief of the Senecas); Cecil Kellaway (Jeremy Love); Ward Bond (John Fraser); Katherine DeMille (Hannah); Henry Wilcoxon (Captain Steele); Sir C. Aubrey Smith (Lord Chief Justice); Victor Varconi (Captain Simson Ecuyer); Virginia Grey (Diana); Porter Hall (Leach); Mike Mazurki (Dave Bone); Richard Gaines (Col. George Washington); Virginia Campbell (Mrs. John Fraser); Gavin Muir (Lt. Fergus McKenzie); Alan Napier (Sir William Johnson); Nan Sunderland (Mrs. Pruitt); Marc Lawrence (Sioto—Medicine Man); Jane Nigh (Evelyn); Robert Warwick (Pontiac—Chief of the Ottawas); Lloyd Bridges (Lt. Hutchins); Oliver Thorndike (Lt. Baillie); Rus Conklin (Wamaultee); John Mylong (Col. Henry Bouquet); Raymond Hatton (Venango Scout); Julia Faye (Widow Swivens); Paul E. Burns (Dan McCoy); Clarence Muse (Jason); Jeff York (Wide Shouldered Youth); Dick Alexander (Slave); Syd Saylor (Spieler for Dr. Diablo); Si Jenks (Farmer); Bob Kortman (Frontiersman); Edgar Deering, Hugh Prosser, Ray Teal (Soldiers—Gilded Beaver); Chief Thundercloud (Chief Killbuck); Noble Johnson (Big Ottowa Indian); John Merton (Corporal); Buddy Roosevelt (Guard); John Miljan (Prosecutor); Jay Silverheels (Indian); Lex Barker (Royal American Officer); Jack Pennick (Joe Lovat); Byron Foulger (Townsman); Denver Dixon (Citizen).

AN IDEAL HUSBAND (20th, 1948) 96 M.

Producer-director, Alexander Korda; based on the play by Oscar Wilde; screenplay, Lajos Bir; art director, Joseph Bate; music, Dr. Hubert Clifford; camera, Georges Perinal; editor, Oswald Haffenrichter.

Paulette Goddard (Mrs. Cheveley); Michael Wilding (Lord Goring); Diana Wynyard (Lady Chiltern); Glynis Johns (Mabel Chiltern); Constance Collier (Lady Markby); Sir Aubrey Smith (Lord Caversham); Hugh Williams (Sir Robert Chiltern); Harriette Johns (Lady Baseldon); Christine Norden (Mrs. Marchmont); Michael Anthony (Vicomte de Nanjac); Allan Jeayes (Phipps).

ON OUR MERRY WAY (UA, 1948) 107 M.

Producer, Benedict Bogeaus, Burgess Meredith, director, King Vidor, Leslie Fenton; story Arch Oboler; screenplay, Laurence Stallings; art director, Ernst Fegte, Duncan Cramer; music director, David Chudnow, Skitch Henderson; camera, Joseph Biroc, Gordon Avil, John Seitz, Edward Cronjager; editor, James Smith.

Burgess Meredith (Oliver Pease); Paulette Goddard (Martha Pease); Fred MacMurray (Al); Hugh Herbert (Elisha Hobbs); James Stewart (Slim); Dorothy Lamour (Gloria Manners); Victor Moore (Ashton Carrington); Elene Janssen (Peggy Thorndyke); Henry Ford (Lank); William Demarest (Floyd); Dorothy Ford (Lola); Charles D. Brown (Editor); Betty Caldwell (Cynthia); David Whorf (Sniffles Dugan); Frank Moran (Bookie); Tom Fadden (Deputy Sheriff); Walter Baldwin (Livery Stable Man); Tom Fadden (Sheriff's Deputy); Paul A. Burns (Boss—Want Ad Dept.); Lucien Prival (Jackson); Almira Sessions (Mrs. Cotton); Nan Bryant (Housekeeper).

HAZARD (PAR, 1948) 95 M.

Producer, Mel Epstein; director, George Marshall; story, Roy Chanslor; screenplay, Arthur Sheekman, Chanslor; art director, Hans Dreier, Robert Clatworthy; music, Frank Skinner; camera, Daniel L. Fapp; editor, Arthur Schmidt; song, Ray Evans, Jay Livingston, and Troy Sanders.

Paulette Goddard (Ellen Crane); Macdonald Carey (J. D. Storm); Fred Clark (Lonnie Burns); Stanley Clements (Joe—Bellhop); Maxie Rosenbloom (Truck Driver); James Millican (Houseman); Percy Helton (Beady); Charles McGraw (Chick); Frank Faylen (Oscar); Mary Adams (Matron); Walter Baldwin (Superintendent); Isabel Randolph (Woman in Hotel); Taylor Holmes (Mr. Meeler); Jimmy Conlin (Mr. Tilson); Ann Doran (Nurse); Howard Mitchell, Frank Henry, Ralph Montgomery, Dudley James, Sam Ash (Poker Players); Ed Randolph, Ralf Harolde, Ralph Peters (Taxi Drivers); Babe London, Betty Danko (Matrons); Jack Searl (Public Defender); Charles B. Williams (Little Man); Earle Hodgins (Doctor); Benson Fong (Chinese House Boy); Frank Fenton (Sheriff); Phillip Barnes (Dealer); George Douglas (Better).

BRIDE OF VENGEANCE (PAR, 1949) 92 M.

Producer, Richard Maibaum; director, Mitchell Leisen; story, Michael Hogan; screenplay, Cyril Hume, Hogan; additional dialogue, Clemence Dane; art director, Hans Dreier, Roland Anderson; music, Hugo Friedhofer; camera, Daniel L. Fapp; editor, Alma Macrorie.

Paulette Goddard (Lucretia Borgia); John Lund (Alfonso D'Este); Macdonald Carey (Cesare Borgia); Albert Dekker (Vanetti); John Sutton (Bisceglie); Raymond Burr (Michelotto); Charles Dayton (Bastino); Donald Randolph (Tiziano); Rose Hobart (Eleanora); Nicholas Joy (Chamberlain); Fritz Leiber (Filippo); Billy Gilbert (Beppo); William Farnum (Peruzzi); Kate Drain Lawson (Gemma); Anthony Caruso (Captain of the Guard); Douglas Spencer (False Physician); Dean White (Sentry); Nestor Pavia (The Mayor); Frank Puglia (Bolfi); Ian Wolfe, Robert Greig, Don Beddoe (Councillors); Franklyn Farnum (Special Prisoner); Richard Webb (Prisoner); Jimmie Dundee, George Robotham (Assassins); Hugh Murray (Surgeon); Clayton Moore (Long Bowman); Robert Kellard, James Anderson, Len Hendry, Robert Bice, Kirk Alyn (Guards); Gil Warren, Henry Cordon (Scouts); John Bleifer, Gordon Nelson, Victor Desny (Doctors); Morgan Farley (Treasurer).

ANNA LUCASTA (COL, 1949) 86 M.

Producer, Philip Yordan; director, Irving Rapper; based on the play by Philip Yordan; screenplay, Yordan, Arthur Laurents; art director, George Brooks; music director, Morris Stoloff; camera, Sol Polito; editor, Charles Nelson.

Paulette Goddard (Anna Lucasta); William Bishop (Rudolf Strobel); Oscar Homolka (Joe Lucasta); John Ireland (Danny Johnson); Broderick Crawford (Frank); Will Geer (Noah); Gale Page (Katie); Mary Wickes (Stella); Whit Bissell (Stanley); Lisa Golm (Theresa); James Brown (Buster); Dennie Moore (Blanche); Anthony Caruso (Eddie); Grayce Hampton (Queenie); Babe London (Woman in Bar); Joe McTurk (Man in Bar); Paul E. Burns, Olin Howlin (Station Masters); Jean Andren (Woman on Street); Harry Cheshire (Minister); William Cabanne (Young Man); Joseph Ploski (Man); Esther Dale (Mrs. Pulaski).

THE TORCH (Eagle Lion, 1950) 83 M.

Producer, Bert Granet; director, Emilio Fernandez; screenplay, Inigo de Martino Noriega, Fernandez; music, Antonio Diaz Conde; camera, Gabriel Figueroa; editor, Charles K. Kimball.

Paulette Goddard (Maria Dolores); Pedro Armendarez (Jose Juan Reyes); Gilbert Roland (Father Sierra); Walter Reed (Dr. Robert Stanley); Julio Villareal (Don Carlos Penafiel); Carlos Musquez (Fidel Bernal); Margarito Luna (Captain Bocanegra); Jose A. Torvay (Captain Quinones); Garcia Pana (Don Apolinio); Antonio Kaneen (Adeli).

BABES IN BAGDAD (UA, 1952) 79 M.

Producer, Edward J. Danziger, Harry Lee Danziger; director, Edgar G. Ulmer; screenplay, Felix Feist, Joe Anson; additional dialogoue, Reuben Levy, John Roeburt; assistant director, Leon Lenoir; music, J. Leoz; camera, Jack Cox; editor, Edith Lenny.

Paulette Goddard (Kyra); Gypsy Rose Lee (Zohara); Richard Ney (Ezar); John Boles (Hassan); Thomas Gallagher (Sharkhar); Sebastian Cabot (Sinbad); Macdonald Parke (Caliph); Natalie Benesh (Zalika); Hugh Dempster (Omar); Peter Bathurst (Officer); Christopher Lee (Slave Dealer).

VICE SQUAD (UA, 1953)

Producer, Jules V. Levey, Arthur Gardner; director, Arnold Laven; based on the novel *Harness Bull* by Leslie T. White; screenplay, Lawrence Roman; music, Herschel Burke Gilbert; art director, Carroll Clark; camera, Joseph F. Biroc; editor, Arthur H. Nadel.

Edward G. Robinson (Capt. Barnaby); Paulette Goddard (Mona); K. T. Stevens (Ginny); Porter Hall (Jack Hartrampf); Adam Williams (Marty Kusalich); Edward Binns (Al Barkis); Jay Adler (Frankie); Joan Vohs (Vickie); Lee Van Cleef (Pete); Dan Riss (Lt. Imlay); Mary Ellen Kay (Carol).

PARIS MODEL (COL, 1953) 81 M.

Producer, Albert Zugsmith; director, Alfred E. Green; story-screenplay, Robert Smith; music, Albert Glasser; art director, William Glasgow; camera, William Bradford; editor, W. Donan Hayes.

Eva Gabor (Gogo Montaine); Tom Conway (Maharajah of Kim-Kepore); Laurette Luez (Lisa); Aram Katcher (Louis—Jean Vacheron); Bibs Borman (Berta Courtallez); Marilyn Maxwell (Marion Parmelee); Cecil Kellaway (Patrick J. Sullivan); Florence Bates (Mrs. Nora Sullivan); Robert Bice (Jack Parmelee); Byron Foulger (Ernest Boggs); Paulette Goddard (Betty Barnes); Leif Erickson (Edgar Blevins); Gloria Christian (Cora Blevins); Barbara Lawrence (Marta Jensen); Robert Hutton (Charlie Johnson); El Brendel (Papa Jensen); Prince Michael Romanoff (Himself).

SINS OF JEZEBEL (Lippert, 1953) 74 M.

Producer, Sigmund Neufeld; director, Reginald LeBorg; screenplay, Richard Landau; music, Bert Shefter; art director, F. Paul Sylos; camera, Gilbert Warrenton; editor, Carl Pierson.

Paulette Goddard (Jezebel); George Nader (Jehu); John Hoyt (Elijah); Eduard Franz (Ahab); John Shelton (Loram); Marcia Dean (Deborah); Joe Besser (Yonkel—Chariot Man); Ludwig Donath (Naboth); Carmen D'Antonio (Dancer).

CHARGE OF THE LANCERS (COL, 1954) 73 M.

Producer, Sam Katzman; director, William Castle; story-screenplay, Robert E. Kent; assistant director, Irving Moore; music director, Ross Di Maggio; art director, Paul Palmentola; camera, Henry Freulich; editor, Henry Bautista.

Paulette Goddard (Tanya); Jean Pierre Aumont (Captain Eric Evoir); Richard Stapley (Major Bruce Lindsay); Karin Booth (Maria Sand); Charles Irwin (Tom Daugherty); Ben Astar (General Inderman); Lester Matthews (General Stanhope); Ivan Triesault (Dr. Manus).

THE UNHOLY FOUR (Lippert, 1954)

Producer, Michael Carreras; director, Terence Fisher; based on the novel by George Sanders; screenplay, Carreras; assistant director, Jack Causey; music, Ivor Slaney; camera, James Harvey; editor, Bill Lenney.

Paulette Goddard (Angie); William Sylvester (Philip Vickers); Patrick Holt (Job Crandall); Paul Carpenter (Bill Saul); Alvys Mahen (Joan Merrill); Russell Napier (Inspector Treherne); David King Wood (Sessions); Pat Owens (Blonde); Kay Callard (Jenny); Jeremy Hawk (Sgt. Johnson); Jack Taylor (Brownie); Kim Mills (Roddy).

TIME OF INDIFFERENCE (GLI INDIFFERENTI) (Italian) (Continental, 1966)

Producer, Franco Cristaldi; director Francesco Marselli; based on the novel by Alberto Moravia; adaptation, Suso Cecchi D'Amico; screenplay, Marselli; music, Giovanni Fusco; camera, Gianni Di Venanzo.

Rod Steiger (Leo); Claudia Cardinale (Carla); Shelley Winters (Lisa); Paulette Goddard (Mariagrazia); Tomas Milian (Michele).

Sailing to Europe, about 1929

With Charles Chaplin at Del Monte, California, June, 1936

With Charles Chaplin in MODERN TIMES (UA '36)

Erik Rhodes, Louis Adlon, Alan Marshal, Hans Conried, and Luise Rainer in DRAMATIC SCHOOL (MGM '38)

n THE CAT AND THE CANARY (Par '39)

With Paul Weigel, Chester Conklin, Charles Chaplin, Bernard Gorcey, Maurice Moscovich, and Reginald Gardiner in THE GREAT DICTATOR (UA '40)

With Fred Astaire in SECOND CHORUS (Par '41)

With Charles Boyer in HOLD BACK THE DAWN (Par '41)

With Leif Erikson, Edward Arnold, Bob Hope, and Glenn Anders in NOTHING BUT THE TRUTH (Par '41)

With John Wayne in REAP THE WILD WIND (Par '42)

With Clem Bevans, Fred MacMurray, Rod Cameron and Susan Hayward in THE FOREST RANGERS (Par '42)

With Fred MacMurray and Edward Arnold in STANDING ROOM ONLY (Par '44)

In KITTY (Par '46)

With Gary Cooper in THE UNCON-QUERED (Par '47)

With Burgess Meredith in ON OUR MERRY WAY (UA '48)

With William Cabanne and Oscar Ho-molka in ANNA LUCASTA (Col '49)

With Gypsy Rose Lee in BABES IN BAG-AD (UA '53)

With Shelley Winters, Rod Steiger, and Claudia Cardinale in TIME OF INDIFFER-ENCE (Continental '66)

VERONICA LAKE

5'2"
92 pounds
Ash blonde hair
Blue-gray eyes
Scorpio

POSSIBLY NO candidate for the pantheon of cinema love goddesses was admitted on such a gimmicky whim as Veronica Lake, whose sulky but beauteous face was characteristically half-obscured by tossed locks of her blonde hair. Of her 28 movies to date, only six films made in the mid-1940s are satisfactory. Her initial cinema popularity was extended by a fortuitous teaming with stone-faced Alan Ladd, he of the sloppy fedora and trench-coat. They created a new brand of screen lovers: calculating, conscienceless, self-possessed individuals. Their love scenes together were the epitome of restrained ego-feeding, filled with non-sequitur conversation, wisps of cigarette smoke, and bristling icy stares.

In her best pictures, Veronica slunk about magnificently in sequinned, square-shouldered gowns. The essence of hauteur, she proved the perfect screen bitch: a lithe, provocative figure, topped by luscious blonde hair partially revealing a lean face with slightly sunken cheeks, big cold eyes . . . and the surprise of her husky, mature voice.

As a zombie sex siren, Veronica was tops in her category. But when the script required her to step down from the pedestal and mix democratically with the hoi polloi, she fumbled disastrously, revealing her gross inadequacies as an actress.

After World War II, Veronica and her peekaboo hairdo became as obsolete as ration coupons. Paramount had phased out its line of fantasy-realistic movies in the postwar return to cultural naivete. The few tough-broad parts that came along went to superstar Barbara Stanwyck or to second stringer Lizabeth Scott. Veronica's comeback attempts on the stage and on television only slowed the decline. Her downhill course was not atypical, but her no-nonsense reaction to the loss of looks, fame, and fortune proved noteworthy. Periodically, she would be rescued from oblivion by an enterprising journalist ferreting out her latest plight. In 1968 she lay bare her sordid years in the ghost-written autobiography *Veronica,* once again revealing that she was no mere Hollywood concoction, but a game girl who was undaunted by alcoholism and poverty.

✳✳✳✳✳✳✳✳✳✳✳✳✳✳✳✳✳✳✳✳✳

Veronica Lake was born Constance Ockleman in Brooklyn, New York, on November 14, 1919, the daughter of Harry and Constance Charlotta (Trimble) Ockleman. Her father, of German-Danish extraction, was a seaman working on tankers in the Brooklyn waterfront yards of the Sun Oil Company.

Veronica's preschool years were spent in Florida, then the family moved back to Brooklyn. She remembers being a rugged tomboy and the "toughest broad on the block." At the age of eight she made her acting debut in a grade school production of *Poor Little Rich Girl,* sporting her long blonde corkscrew curls and singing two songs.

In February, 1932, her father was killed in an explosion on a ship in Philadelphia, and the following year her mother married Anthony Keane, a staff artist with the *New York Herald Tribune.* Veronica adopted her stepfather's surname.

Because of Mr. Keane's recurrent illness, the family moved around quite a bit. For a spell they lived in Montreal, where Veronica attended the Roman Catholic Villa Maria School. (Later publicity releases from Paramount would glamorize her background by including an enrollment at Montreal's McGill University in a premedical course.) Summers were spent at Saranac Lake, New York, where Mr. Keane was undergoing a tuberculosis cure.

Afterwards, the family returned to Miami, Florida. Veronica completed her education at Miami High School. On a lark, she entered the Miss Miami beauty contest, and won third place. One of the judges, Broadway celebrity and womanizer Harry Richman, thought Veronica a real knockout who ought to try her luck in Hollywood. (This notion deeply impressed Veronica's mother.) In the subsequent Miss Florida contest, Veronica won the top prize, but she was disqualified when it was discovered that she was underage.

In the summer of 1938, Veronica, her stepfather, her mother, and her cousin Helen Nelson drove to California, ostensibly for her stepfather's health. They rented a small bungalow on Oakhurst Drive in Beverly Hills, and settled down. As Veronica later recollected: "Adapting to the new situation really didn't prove as trying an experience as it might have been. Change had been a fairly constant part of my life."

Mrs. Keane promptly enrolled Veronica at the Bliss Hayden School of Acting in Hollywood. Says Veronica: "I began lessons convinced I would not become a movie star. Or, to soften my vehemence, quite sure it could not happen until I was at least fifty years old." Among her workshop productions at Bliss Hayden was *She Made Her Bed,* which included future screen actor Richard Webb in the cast.

One of Veronica's acquaintances at Bliss Hayden was Gwen Horn, a seasoned movie extra. When Gwen was told to report to RKO Studios for a casting call for *Sorority House* (1930), she dragged Veronica along for company. Veronica found herself hired as an extra for this programmer about the tribulations of college freshmen. Studio ingenue Anne Shirley played the groceryman's daughter who hoped to be accepted by the snobbish sorority; James Ellison was the handsome football hero. Veronica found director John Farrow—husband of actress Maureen O'Sullivan—very thoughtful and a resourceful craftsman. At the end of production, she gifted him with a St. Christopher's medal. (He later told her that it saved his life during combat action in World War II.) In short order, Veronica was cast in another RKO collegiate yarn, *All Women Have Secrets* (1939), concerning the more melodramatic subject of student marriage. Both minor efforts opened in May, 1939, to lukewarm receptions. Veronica had no illusions about her histrionic abilities in those days: "I was so lousy that you could put all the talent I had into your left eye and still not suffer from impaired vision. I was that bad."

Then Veronica appeared as the child bride of rubber-legged comedian Leon Errol in *The Wrong Room,* a RKO comedy short released in September, 1939. Her dramatics in this skit comedy consisted of innumerable fainting pratfalls.

Quickly falling into the gypsy routine of a movie extra, Veronica next found employment at Twentieth Century-Fox in a Jones Family (Jed Prouty-Spring Byington) series entry, *As Young as You Feel.* Another cinema fledgling in this B-film was Joan Leslie.

Back at RKO, Veronica was cast yet again as another student in Eddie Cantor's first dramatic feature, *Forty Little Mothers* (1940), a pallid remake of the charming French film success *Le Mioche.* Cantor is the meek professor who becomes the unwilling guardian of Baby Quintanilla and finds it is near impossible to both care for the infant and maintain his academic standards under strict headmistress Judith Anderson. For a change, Veronica was given a characterization in this assignment, as a hoydenish schoolgirl who delights in playing pranks and jousting about as a tomboy. Cantor objected to the "sheepdog" look caused by Veronica's fine blonde hair constantly falling over one eye. Director Busby Berkeley decided her accidental hair style was effectively distinctive, and decreed that it should remain so. But the fuss was for naught. *Forty Little Mothers* unreeled at the Capitol Theatre on April 18, 1940, to general disinterest. Veronica's trademark hairdo caused no stir.

By now Veronica had become acclimated to the busy Hollywood scene. She was well aware of her physical assets. ("I had a full figure at sixteen, with surprisingly full breasts, a fact that many people assume was never the case with me.") She made it her business to be seen around town at the various studios. One day she was spotted by MGM junior executive Freddie Wilcox, who suggested that she make a screen test. The results were dismal.

Later on, Veronica managed to be signed on by the aristocratic William Morris Agency, where agent Johnny Hyde (the future Svengali for Marilyn Monroe) took a slight interest in her budding career.

When Paramount producer Arthur Hornblow, Jr., was preparing the groundwork for his expensive *I Wanted Wings*—a tribute to the nation's aviators—William Morris convinced him to test their client Veronica for the role of Sally Vaughn, a slinky nightclub chanteuse. The test scene required her to be tipsy while sitting in a nightclub. Veronica recalled: "My hair kept falling over one eye and I kept brushing it back. I thought I had ruined my chances for the role. . . . But Hornblow was jubilant about that eye-hiding trick. An experienced showman, he knew that the hair style was something people would talk about. He had a big picture and lots of talk would bring customers to see it."

Since Ray Milland, William Holden, Wayne Morris, and the aerial photography were to be the real stars of *I Wanted Wings*, Hornblow felt justified in taking a chance on newcomer Veronica—she was signed for the film. The energetic producer insisted that she change her name; she was soon dubbed Veronica Lake.

Meanwhile, she had met MGM art director John Detlie, age 33, and they were already a steady duo when she left for location filming in Texas for

I Wanted Wings in August, 1940. Veronica had personality clashes with costar Constance Moore, but generally found the real acting experience exhilarating. Part-way through production, Paramount brought staff director Mitchell Leisen in as the film's new director to insure that this government-sponsored project would be a whopping commercial success. It was the first large-budgeted American aviation picture inspired by World War II.

In November, 1940, Veronica and Detlie were married.

I Wanted Wings had its big Broadway opening at the Astor Theatre on March 26, 1941. The two-a-day roadshow production was given a terrific sendoff by the Army brass. Except for Paul Mantz's fine stunt-flying sequences, the film was pretty standard fare, filled with overzealous patriotism and clichéd situations. Through flashbacks it traces the fate of three enrollees in the Army Air Corps: socialite Ray Milland, football star Wayne Morris, and garage mechanic William Holden. Brian Donlevy was brought in as the tough Air Corps instructor. Before the prolonged fade-out, Morris dies in a plane crash, Holden is discharged from the service, and Milland is promoted to bomber commander. Veronica was sixth-billed as a husky-voiced honey-blonde cabaret singer (her song "Born to Love" was dubbed by Martha Mears, who would do her "singing" in films thereafter) who proves a nemesis to the three male leads. Thanks to Paramount's enterprising publicity department, which had saturated the country with fetching poses of Veronica, the critics and the public were aware that the studio had a shapely newcomer spliced into this mammoth service tribute.

No one was quite prepared for the reaction to Veronica in the film itself . . . it was a stereotyped unsympathetic role. "She displays more acting ability than one expects in one so young and sleek looking, thus arousing anticipation for her future appearances" (Archer Winsten, *New York Post*). "Miss Lake is supposed to be a *femme fatale*, and to that end it was arranged that her truly splendid bosom be unconfined and draped only ever so slightly—in a manner to make the current crop of sweater girls, by comparison, a bunch of prigs" (Cecilia Ager, *P.M.*). "Veronica Lake is a newcomer, an exotic young blonde with fantastic hairdo and makeup" (Eileen Creelman, *New York Sun*). A few critics such as Howard Barnes (*New York Herald Tribune*) bothered to remark on her acting: "Miss Lake is of scant aid in building up a substance of genuine, dramatic honesty in the offering. She has a startling hair-do, with overlong blonde tresses that she occasionally strings out as though she were about to use her head as a violin, but she has almost no histrionic persuasion."

Largely due to Veronica's emoting as the hussy in *I Wanted Wings*, the Legion of Decency placed the film on its B ("objectionable in part") list. Veronica, Holden, and Milland recreated their roles for "Lux Radio Theatre" (CBS) on March 30, 1942.

I Wanted Wings proved a huge financial bonanza, and Veronica became a household name. Most discussion centered on her unique hairdo, which overnight revolutionized the beauty industry. According to an article in *Life* magazine, Veronica had about 150,000 hairs, each measuring about 0.0024 in cross section, with the locks 17 inches in front, 24 inches in back, and falling about 8 inches below her shoulders. Her hair was washed each morning before appearing in front of the cameras, twice in Nulava shampoo and once in Maro oil, and then it was rinsed in vinegar. Comedians had a field day with the topical, novel hairdo. "Veronica Lake wears her hair over one eye because it's a glass eye" (Bob Hope). "I opened up my mop closet the other day and I thought Veronica Lake fell out" (Groucho Marx). Women everywhere went crazy trying to duplicate her peekaboo coiffure. Said Veronica: "I certainly would have preferred to have made my mark in Hollywood's shortest hair style. Everything would have been easier." The more discerning *Harvard Lampoon* voted Veronica the worst new actress of 1941.

Veronica was quite anxious to make another film, but Paramount wanted to find just the right project. She had been promoted from $75 a week to $150 after completing *I Wanted Wings*, and with the reception of that movie, Paramount renegotiated her contract again.

Kitti Frings's *Blonde Venus* and *China Pass* were considered for Veronica, but neither project materialized. Then ace studio writer-director Preston Sturges decided Veronica would be just fine for his new satirical comedy *Sullivan's Travels* (1942), and he persuaded the front-office executives to assign her to the production. Shooting was to start in May, 1941, and Veronica was already pregnant. She denied the baby rumor and won the part.

Sullivan's Travels starred Joel McCrea as a noted Hollywood director of comedies who plans a serious feature, *Brother, Where Art Thou?* The studio scoffs, but he insists, and sets out on a hobo tour of the United States to rediscover life's honest values. He picks up unsuccessful movie extra Veronica as a tag-along companion, and this wry comedy traces their cross-country misadventures. Later in the story McCrea finds himself part of a chain gang. One evening, in the midst of all the misery, the prisoners are shown some movies. During a funny Walt Disney cartoon, McCrea perceives the true joy of laughter. Thereafter, when he is freed, he contentedly returns to making movie audiences chuckle.

During production of *Sullivan's Travels*, Veronica found it difficult to produce a natural performance in front of the camera. Sturges advised the novice: "Don't ever walk on my set knowing anything about your lines or scenes." Veronica added: "I didn't for the rest of the film and for most of the films I worked in after *Sullivan's Travels*. The word got around I was better without advance preparation and most directors accepted that and worked with it."

Sturges was vocal in his enthusiasm about the blonde star(let): "She's one of the little people. Like Mary Pickford, Douglas Fairbanks, and Freddie Bartholomew when he started, who take hold immediately with their audiences. She's nothing much in real life—a quiet, rather timid little thing. But the screen transforms her, electrifies her, and brings her to life. I think, she's the biggest bet in the business."

Veronica gave birth to daughter Elaine on August 21, 1941.

Before *Sullivan's Travels* premiered, Paramount released *Hold Back the Dawn* (1941). In the story within the story, Veronica appears on a Paramount sound stage when gigolo Charles Boyer comes to sell director Mitchell Leisen his life story. She is shown preparing to perform the telephone scene with Richard Webb from *I Wanted Wings*. This brief sequence had been lensed during production of that aviation picture.

Sullivan's Travels opened at the Paramount Theatre on January 28, 1942. Veronica, second-billed as "the girl," received a good critical reception. Howard Barnes (*New York Herald Tribune*) penned; "Even Veronica Lake is not bad in *Sullivan's Travels*." Kate Cameron in her three-star *New York Daily News* review extolled: "[she] fulfills the promise she gave in *I Wanted Wings* by giving a first-rate performance." *Newsweek* observed:

"Now Sturges swaddles her principal asset in a hobo's outfit, stuffs her hair under a disreputable cap and reveals for the first time that the lady has two profiles and decided possibilities as an actress." It is ironic that Veronica's finest screen performance required her to be outfitted in a manner so alien to her conventional movie image. But she was still projecting the gutsy self-sufficiency that so typified her screen personality. Veronica recreated her *Sullivan's Travels* role opposite Ralph Bellamy on "Lux Radio Theatre" on November 9, 1942.

In an inspired piece of accidental casting, Paramount paired Veronica opposite Alan Ladd in *This Gun for Hire*, based on Grahame Greene's rugged novel *A Gun for Sale*. Ladd, then 29 years old, had been milling around Hollywood for a decade, mostly playing extra roles, and had only recently graduated to featured parts. Only 5 feet, 4 inches tall, it had been difficult to cast him opposite many taller leading ladies on the lot.

This Gun for Hire was transplanted to a contemporary California setting. Its revamped story now focused on industrialist Tully Marshall and nightclub owner Laird Cregar who are conspiring in a fifth-columnist plot to sell poison gas to Japan. Conscienceless killer Ladd arrives on the scene, trailing the people who double-crossed him. He becomes enmeshed in the Axis plot and forces singer-dancer Veronica (her two songs were dubbed) to be his accomplice. She has already maneuvered a post in Cregar's night spot (Where she archly sings "I've Got You") to help United States government agents uncover the enemy scheme. Robert Preston appears as the Los Angeles policeman in love with tough-as-nails Veronica. After Ladd is gunned down and the caper is at last solved, Preston wins Veronica.

This adventure yarn opened May 13, 1942, at the Criterion Theatre, clicking well with audiences who immediately dug the icy magnetism projected by Veronica and rugged pretty boy Ladd. For viewers bored with syrupy romances, Veronica and Ladd offered a more realistic, if equally farfetched, change of pace. The cool way each star appraised the other, their mutual disdain and their apathy about life in general, their terse bits of biting conversation, combined to make them rebel idols. No one seemed to mind that close-ups of the handsome blonde duo resembled an opthalmologic nightmare: Ladd with his sleepy eyes half-closed, and Veronica with only one eye clear for vision.

Variety commented about Ladd's death scene in Veronica's lap: "Better men have died with their heads in less pleasant places." *Life* said: "Veronica, the paradox, can cool the fevered brow of a sick man with one stroke and with another stroke produce a fever in a well man." Leo Mishkin (*The Morning Telegraph*) offered: "And you will probably be surprised to learn that in addition to being something to look at, she is also emerging as a very fine actress, which is something entirely different." *This Gun for Hire* was unofficially remade as James Cagney's *Short Cut to Hell* (1956).

Veronica was now earning $350 a week, not very much for someone with her attention-getting personality and obvious box-office draw. Unable to manufacture any off-screen romance between Veronica and Ladd (she was still married, he would marry former actress Sue Carol in 1942; and besides both Paramount players were too self-willed and taciturn to participate in any prefabricated coupling that would require them to become part of the hectic nightlife of Hollywood in World War II), the studio quickly reteamed their new hot love duo in a well-paced remake of Dashiell Hammett's *The Glass Key* (1942) with stocky Brian Donlevy in the lead role of the tough political boss.

Ladd was his cool assistant and Veronica portrayed Janet Henry, the vacillating, chic daughter of gubernatorial candidate Moroni Olsen. Joseph Calleia was the head of a gambling syndicate, with rugged William Bendix as the sadistic mauler. As Veronica later remembered: "Alan and I attacked the project with all the enthusiasm of time clock employees, a pretty cocky approach for two people without acting credentials and only the instant star system to thank for our success."

Regarding *The Glass Key*, the *New York Times* commented that the come-hither girl has "little more than a sullen voice and a head of yellow hair." More reflective of the public's adulation of curvaceous Veronica was James Corby's review in the *Brooklyn Daily Eagle*: "What makes Veronica Lake such a good actress is the equipment she can bring to bear on a task in hand. Even without her voice and without her sense of timing in speech and action, and without her ability to cast a spell over her audience by her sheer modernity, Miss Lake would undoubtedly pass for a good actress just by making her appearance in a scene. A girl with her surplus of charms is bound to get herself across anyway—but Veronica Lake is a fine actress as well." Overenthusiastic? Perhaps.

I Married a Witch (1942) was made at Paramount for United Artists release by French director Rene Clair. It was an ultra light-toned romp about two Salem witches (Veronica and her father Cecil Kellaway) burned at the stake by the Puritans. The victims put a curse on their denouncer and his descendants. Through the centuries, Veronica continually pops up in reincarnated forms. In the present day, she haunts gubernatorial candidate Fredric March, and falls in love with him, thus losing her bewitching powers. She outmaneuvers his predatory fiancée Susan Hayward, and marries the slightly baffled politician. They have three children—one of them with her peekaboo hair style. Veronica appeared at her ethereal best in this comedy, fully exploiting her mocking eyes, soft drawl, and frozen-smile lips. Throughout the scenarios she was scantily clad. One taxi sequence featured her wearing nothing but a fur coat, which she then tossed out the window with disdain as a parting gesture. This film proved to be the artistic highpoint of her career. The critics were ecstatic: "The strange and beautiful illusion that Veronica Lake is completely unreal is being quite charmingly nourished in Rene Clair's new film *I Married a Witch*. You recall that Miss Lake was first manifest on the screen as an ambulating hank of hair, from behind which emerged dulcet noises and a calorific glow" (Bosley Crowther, *New York Times*). "If you have been of the faction wondering what constitutes the allure of Veronica Lake, this picture may solve your dilemma. You never saw a more hexy display from any witch."

Veronica, already noted for being hot-tempered on the set, found working with March a chore. ("He treated me like dirt under his talented feet. Of all actors to end up under the covers with. That happened in one scene and Mr. March is lucky he didn't get my knee in his groin.") She still harbored a grudge 29 years later when she gleefully proceeded to pull March apart on a series of television talk shows.

For Paramount's star-clustered musical revue *Star Spangled Rhythm* (1942), Veronica appeared in the gimmicky (and deliberately self-revelatory) song number, "A Sweater, a Sarong, and a Peekaboo Bang," in which she, Paulette Goddard, and Dorothy Lamour were required to lampoon their screen trademarks. After a few choruses, Arthur Treacher, Walter Catlett, and Sterling Holloway were used to parody the parody. Martha Mears dubbed Veronica's vocals in this film.

Veronica was one of the many stars who participated in war bond rallies when not picture-making. Before embarking on a national bond tour in October, 1942, she resided for a few months in Seattle, Washington, where her husband was stationed with the Army. In the course of the tour, Veronica was a guest speaker at a Boston charity drive. Arriving late in the evening, she proceeded to berate the assembled crowd for not fully respecting her dignity as a star and remaining to listen to her speech with full politeness—this gained her no new friends with the press or public.

The War Production Board requested that Veronica refrain from wearing her hair long for the duration of the war, since so many female workers at war plants were getting their tresses caught in the machinery. Veronica patriotically sought to comply as often as Paramount would allow. (Ironically, it was not until Ella Raines in 1943, Lauren Bacall in 1944, and Lizabeth Scott in 1946 made their screen debuts, that other movie actresses blatantly copied Veronica's languid hair style.)

Veronica was one of the trio of Paramount female stars top-cast in *So Proudly We Hail* (1943), a flag-waving tribute to the brave nurses stationed on the battle lines of the Bataan Peninsula during World War II. Claudette Colbert was the pivotal figure; Paulette Goddard portrayed the wise-cracking glamor-puss nurse; and Veronica was prim Olivia D'Arcy, the Jap-hating healer (her fiancée had been blown to bits at Pearl Harbor). With her famous hair severely parted in the middle and tightly rolled up on her neck, Veronica properly used her stock icy rigidity to convey an emotionally distraught person. When her fellow nurses are cut off from retreat on a patch of Corregidor by marauding Japanese soldiers, Veronica calmly places a live grenade down her shirt front, and slowly walks into the enemy's midst —wearing a most pathetically wry smile. For many film fans this stark sequence is the dramatic highlight of Veronica's movie career to date.

So Proudly We Hail opened at Radio City Music Hall and exceeded its ambitious expectations. Newcomer Sonny Tufts as Goddard's vis-à-vis garnered much public attention, but he did not overshadow Veronica's histrionic impact. The *New York World Telegram* said: "Miss Lake brings a biting savagery to her girl." Lee Mortimer (*New York Daily Mirror*): "Playing the kind of role scoffers said she couldn't, the blond bombshell foresakes sex for tragedy in her all too few appearances before the camera in this film. Veronica not only gives the finest performance of her youthful career, but steps out in front as one of the Hollywood greats."

Veronica, Colbert, Goddard, and Tufts recreated their roles from *So Proudly We Hail* on the "Lux Radio Theatre" on November 1, 1943.

While completing the shooting of her next feature, *The Hour Before the Dawn* (1944), Veronica tripped on a lighting cable, and as a result she gave premature birth to a son, William Anthony Detlie, on July 8, 1943. A week later the baby died of uremic poisoning. In those days the press was quick to print any act of rebellion or uncooperation manifested by Veronica. At one point, Veronica confided to columnist Louella Parsons (she had just been linked socially with a married man): "I think now I have worked out everything and Paramount knows I am no longer an unreliable harum-scarum girl. Seventeen [*sic*] is only a child. A girl that age needs sympathy and understanding, not censure, scolding and bitter criticism." In December, 1943, Veronica and John Detlie were divorced. He claimed she was an unfit wife and mother, because of her moviemaking and war bond touring, which kept her away from home.

Her only 1944 release was *The Hour Before the Dawn* loosely adapted from Somerset Maugham's chauvinistic study of England under wartime tension. The cavalier filmization cast Veronica as Dora Druckmann, an Austrian refugee (and Nazi sympathizer) staying in England near a secret military airport. To remain there, she must marry placid Britisher Franchot Tone. He is a scholarly pacifist who loves to farm. However, when he learns that his wife is helping the planned Axis invasion of England, he throws off all calmness, strangles her, and then enlists in the service. Veronica was clearly out of her element as the sneering, leering, snickering enemy agent. Her accent was excessively phony, and her motives were always too obvious. There definitely was no screen chemistry between her and serene Tone. Dorothy Masters in her two and one-half star *New York Daily News* review summed it up: "Veronica Lake is not at her best as an enemy agent, particularly when the role occasions only one glimpse of her in flowing locks and revealing nightdress." Another evaluator decided: "The picture sinks with her into the realm of painfully obvious melodrama."

Meanwhile, Veronica was now at the peak of her movie popularity. She was earning $4,500 a week ($500 shy of the top figure Paramount paid its stars) and was a free agent in the busy social scene of war-rich Hollywood. But, as she later explained: "There's no doubt I was a bit of a misfit in the Hollywood of the forties. The race for glamour left me far behind. I didn't really want to keep up. I wanted my stardom without the usual trimmings. Because of this, I was branded a rebel at the very least. But I don't regret that for a minute. My appetite was my own and I simply wouldn't have it any other way. . . . I did become Hollywood queen of the kitchen party, my own brand of party, and I reigned in this capacity all during 1944, my footloose and fancy-free year." Among those she dated at the time were producer William Dozier, ship tycoon Aristotle Onassis, and the Egyptian filmmaking brothers, the Hakims.

Veronica was still being asked about her famous hairdo: "I prefer my hair tied back. . . . I can talk about that hair as though it is on some other person. Veronica Lake on the screen doesn't seem to me, Constance Keane, to be myself. I even want to reach up on the screen and yank that hair back from the girl's eye. . . . it isn't going to keep a girl on the screen simply because she has her hair over one eye."

About performing on the silver screen: "I am a motion picture actress because it pays and darn well too. I never had an urge to be an actress, never wanted to get on the stage. It happened, and only because my mother wanted me to act. But like it?"

As to her histrionic abilities: "No, I don't think I am outstanding; in fact, I don't even believe it is necessary to being a star. The audience doesn't want that, they don't want the best of acting on the screen. What they want is a personality, something new, something different, and a trademark helps."

Late in 1944, Henry Ginsberg succeeded ailing B. G. DeSylva as head of production at Paramount. During the period of executive changeover, the lot stagnated. No one quite knew what to do with Veronica: many executives echoed the sentiments of Russell Taylor: "Poor Veronica Lake: she was never so exciting once her hair had been reduced to normal proportions." Everyone was sure she was not the sweet ingenue type (like upcoming Joan Caulfield, Marjorie Reynolds, Diana Lynn, Gail Russell, Jean Heather, or Barbara Britton), and that she did not belong in the nostril-twitching dramatic set (like Susan Hayward, Hillary Brooke, and past contractee Ellen Drew), or among the pulchritudinous exotics (like Dorothy Lamour and

Paulette Goddard). So Paramount left Veronica at loose ends for much of 1944. Then, with typical movieland abandon, they tossed her into a series of mediocre musical comedies that not even studio blonde bombshell Betty Hutton could have salvaged. To make this batch of films even more deadly for Veronica's box-office image, she was cast opposite shy hayseed Eddie Bracken, who was on the decline because of oversaturation of his bumbling, stuttering screen characterizations.

While filming *Bring on the Girls* (1945), Veronica met knockabout Hungarian film director Andre de Toth, then age 44. After a whirlwind, dragout courtship, they were married December 16, 1944. He adopted her daughter Elaine.

Bring on the Girls was a tepid technicolor musical in which multimillionaire Eddie Bracken joins the Navy, hoping to meet a girl who will marry him for himself, not his money. Veronica, a lively gold-digging cigarette girl at a swank Miami resort, sets her sights on him. Marjorie Reynolds—who did most of the film's singing—settles for Bracken's gob pal Sonny Tufts. Alan Mowbray bumbles around as the funny butler, and Spike Jones and his City Slickers are on hand to make noise and tomfoolery. As a stick figure in the midst of total silliness, svelte Veronica had only to give the sex-hungry men her pouty come-hither look—from both eyes this time, and to mouth an occasional bit of insipid dialogue.

Out of this World (1945) was another waste of Veronica's presence. She had the secondary part of secretary to a New York entertainment-booking executive who inadvertently helps turn telegram boy Eddie Bracken into a bobby-soxer sensation, à la Frank Sinatra (the gimmick here was having Bing Crosby dub Bracken's vocalizing, a trick later used to better effect in the Bowery Boys' picture *Blue Busters* [1950]). As the smooth meanie, Veronica vies for Bracken's devotion with wide-eyed Diana Lynn, leader of an all girl's band. Because Lynn was the promising new studio ingenue, the script allowed her to win the roly-poly comedian.

Veronica did requisite box-office duty in *Duffy's Tavern* (1945). In an amusing blackout sketch, she and Alan Ladd are rehearsing a murder mystery radio script. Addled Victor Moore is convinced the tense situation is for real.

Hold That Blonde (1945) was more of a bore than her preceding releases. Its flat premise established Eddie Bracken as a timid well-to-do gentleman (with Willie Best as his eye-popping, Adam's apple gulping manservant) afflicted with kleptomania. His psychiatrist suggests that a romance might well cure his disease. With rare idiocy, Bracken latches onto Veronica, an innocent member of a jewel robbery gang out to steal the Romanoff necklace. On the road to love and cure, he endeavors to prevent her from participating. During the endless 76 minutes, there are chases up and down hotel corridors and window ledges, outings in disguise, and a variety of mishandled, stale slapstick. Howard Barnes of the *New York Herald Tribune* objected: "Veronica Lake postures as the walking cure for the unwilting and unwilling pickpocket. . . . Her performance is notable for its lack of conviction or variety of make-believe."

Veronica gave birth to a son, Anthony Michael De Toth III, on October 26, 1945.

Miss Susie Slagle's finally had its release on February 6, 1946 (it had been filmed in 1944). In this whimsical melodrama set in 1910 Baltimore, Veronica was Nan Rogers, the student nurse in love with medical interne Pat Phelan. When he dies of diphtheria, and life loses all meaning for her, boarding house marm Lillian Gish suggests she might carry on in his place as a medical missionary. The period atmosphere of the sets, the penetrating nostalgic flavor provided by Gish as the loving den mother of the immature Johns Hopkins Medical School students, and the wholesomeness of the romance between lumbering student Sonny Tufts and china-doll chambermaid Joan Caulfield, created a plausible backdrop for Veronica's solemn role. It was lensed at a time (mid-1944) when Paramount still had Veronica's best interests at heart; before other contract star (lets) would appear on the lot in the postwar changeover. Veronica's characterization was custombuilt to allow her to logically perform in her favorite key of projection—self-contained, emotional sterility. Bosley Crowther (*New York Times*) complimented her "respectably modest performance" and *Variety* approved of her "subdued playing."

Veronica's stormy marital life was much in the news in 1946. One night in mid-February, she and De Toth (they were known as Ronnie and Bandi) were in Manhattan at the Stork Club. As they were leaving, Seward Hewitt, a 20-year-old fan, reached out to touch Veronica's famed hair; De Toth spun around, slugging the youth four or five times and the resultant hassle made headlines. In May, 1946, they purchased a 23½-acre farm in the San Fernando Valley for $300,000 (mostly her money). On September 10, 1946, her stepfather died, a loss which affected her greatly.

The Blue Dahlia, Veronica's second 1946 release, proved to be the last highpoint of her fading Paramount contract. Reteamed with Ladd (he now commanded top billing), it benefited from a smooth screenplay by ace detective-story writer Raymond Chandler. Ladd was a discharged Navy flier who discovers that his wife has been unfaithful. When she is murdered, he is implicated and must find the culprit. On a rainy drive to Malibu, he meets the loose Veronica, the separated wife of club-owner Howard Da Silva. Others entangled in the caper are William Bendix, a shell-shocked veteran pal of Ladd's; police captain Tom Powers; cool gangster Howard Freeman; and mealy-mouthed house detective Will Wright. The scenes between Veronica and Ladd were their best ever: to the point, emotionless, and high-charged with magnetic self-sufficiency. The combination of two handsome, blonde-haired individuals, each with frosted eyes, deadpan face, and brittle soul, helped to make the movie a winner. Bosley Crowther (*New York Times*) perceived: "[Veronica's] contribution is essentially that of playing a girl slightly starved for a good man's honest affection, to which she manifests an eagerness to respond. And it is indeed remarkable how obvious she makes this look without doing very much." James Agee writing in *The Nation* (June 8, 1946) commended Veronica and Ladd because "they and the sets and moods they move through all seem to me convincing and entertaining in a dry, nervous electric way." A few critics made comparisons between the Veronica-Ladd screen team and the new joint efforts of Lauren Bacall and Humphrey Bogart; giving the latter duo the benefit of classier hedonistic self-conceit and lip-snarling.

On loanout to United Artists, Veronica starred in the Western *Ramrod* (1947) directed by her husband De Toth. Set in 1870, Veronica inherits a cattle ranch when chief crook Preston Foster runs her fiancé out of town. She bucks the odds and makes a go of the spread, hiring on Joel McCrea as her ramrod (boss of the cattle outfit). To awaken McCrea to Foster's corrupt power, she instigates a self-damaging stampede and blames it on Foster. This leads to the death of sheriff Donald Crisp and pal Don DeFore, and the inevitable showdown between McCrea and Foster. McCrea is the obvious victor, and when he discerns Veronica's deceit, he rejects her and returns to the waiting arms of seamstress Arleen Whelan. Despite the novelty of a female lead in a sagebrush tale, it remained a fitfully sluggish Western. The *New York Times* allowed that its star made "a fairly convincing predatory baggage."

At Paramount, Veronica made a brief celebrity-star appearance in *Variety Girl* (1947), the studio's personality-laden hodgepodge musical.

Her last year at Paramount, 1948, witnessed the release of three mediocre double-bill attractions, each one more decrepit than the previous effort.

Saigon slipped into the Paramount Theatre on March 31, 1948. The screen magic that once existed between Veronica and Alan Ladd had diminished greatly. It is set in postwar Indo-China. Ladd and two other veteran airmen are seeking adventure. They come across a black marketeer who will pay them $10,000 for a plane ride to steal $500,000 out of the territory. Veronica is the enigmatic adventuress—puffing cigarettes and looking lissome, deadpan, and somnambulistic—who arrives in Saigon from Shanghai; she is obviously up to no good; but later repents of her sins. This weak programmer helped no one's career. About filming this miniadventure drama, Veronica later recalled: "By this time working with Alan was like carrying on a conversation with an old friend. There were no surprises between us and no friction. We continued our aloof but friendly relationship and it was smooth sailing all the way."

Next, Veronica was coupled with another soon-to-be-exiled Paramount star, Joan Caulfield, in *The Sainted Sisters* (1948). She and Caulfield were two 1900s confidence girls, on the lam from New York, who find themselves bunked down in a small Maine town near the Canadian border. The town's benevolent protector Barry Fitzgerald soon relieves the spunky misses of their $25,000 (to be distributed to the poor) and effects their moral redemption. The *New York Herald Tribune*'s Howard Barnes wrote: "Miss Lake is properly predatory as the lass who loses her ill-gotten wealth and almost gets it back with interest in the climax." Even in the best slapstick moments, the two blondes seemed woefully out of place in this period comedy, filled with overblown rural jokes and horseplay. In her autobiography Veronica describes the tension she created on the set with Caulfield: "I played it so cool. And professionally bitchy. Everyone would come down to see the rushes and walk away shaking their heads at the scenes in which Joan and I appeared together. Everytime Joan gave lines, I'd just stand there and stare at her. I was good at that, so good that people in the business began talking about my ability to steal scenes without doing anything. And no one appreciated it more than Joan Caulfield. There were times she'd leave the screening room in a rage."

Isn't It Romantic? (1948), a tedious period musical (with no charming resemblance to *Meet Me in St. Louis, Summer Holiday,* or *Centennial Summer,* tossed together several contract players. It did not even have the good grace to sport redeeming technicolor. Veronica, Mona Freeman, and Mary Hatcher—(the later two, promising studio starlets)—were the daughters of Civil War veteran Roland Culver. They all live in a cozy house in quaint rural Indiana. Veronica is romanced by slicker Patric Knowles, a peddler of fake oil stock. Billy DeWolfe is her disappointed suitor, who obtains vicarious enjoyment from presenting a pell-mell satire on silent movie serials. And Richard Webb conducts a proper courtship with teenager Hatcher. The highpoint of this constricted musical is the Fourth of July picnic. Pearl Bailey as the sharp-tongued family maid offered the movie's only alive performance. She sings such numbers as "I Shoulda Quit When I Was Ahead." New York critics rated the movie a "perfect entertainment vacuum" and duly noted Veronica's "inanimate presence."

On October 16, 1948, Veronica gave birth to daughter Diana. Just at this time, Veronica's mother sued her for $500-a-month support and a $17,416 lump-sum settlement. She claimed that her famous daughter had neglected her and was not abiding by the 1943 agreement whereby the movie actress consented to pay her parents $200 a week. Veronica's reaction to the mess was: "I feel awful that a mother and daughter should have that sort of relationship. But I don't want to live my life under a threat." The case was settled out of court.

After her dismal last year at Paramount, Veronica was unceremoniously dumped on the job market, an unwanted commodity in short-memoried Hollywood. Veronica later discovered that husband De Toth had been intercepting job offers sent to her and turning them down on his own, deciding they were not suitable for his wife. When De Toth directed a Linda Darnell-Richard Widmark starrer at Twentieth Century-Fox, Veronica was handed the secondary female role. *Slattery's Hurricane* (1949) was a study of storm-spotters for the U.S. Weather Bureau in Florida. Veronica essayed the pathetic secretary in love with callous Widmark. He is a cad pilot who falls for Darnell, the wife of Navy aviator John Russell. Gary Merrill appeared as the forthright commander. The special effects department received the best notices for the creation of the realistic storm sequences. *Slattery's Hurricane* premiered on a Navy plane on August 11, 1949, with its airborne audience viewing the film a day before it opened at the Roxy Theatre. The *New York Times* gratuitously noted: "Veronica Lake is pleasing, too, as the other girl."

With no decent film roles forthcoming, Veronica in 1950 flew to New York to pawn some jewelry and to guest star as the hostess on "Your Show of Shows" (November 18, 1950, NBC). She and comedian Sid Caesar performed the skit "We Love Life." To earn a few more dollars to pay for the upkeep of her California ranch, Veronica starred as a witch in *Beware This Woman*, an episode of "Lights Out" (December 4, 1950, NBC).

Desperate for money and a chance to resume her dormant screen career, Veronica was easily persuaded to accept the lead in a cheaply made costume film, *Stronghold,* shot in Mexico. Set in the 1850s, it cast Veronica as a wealthy silver mineowner. On her return to Taxco from the United States, she is kidnapped by bandit leader Arturo De Cordova, who needs money to support his revolt against Emperor Maximilian. Veronica is quickly won over to De Cordova and the cause of the peons. Zachary Scott grumbles around the plot as the mine overseer who eventually blows up the dam to flood the mine. Made in English and Spanish versions, *Stronghold* finally saw release in 1952 on the double-bill kiddie market in America. *Variety* charitably noted: "Miss Lake does the best she can." Veronica more accurately observed: "It was a dog but the pay was decent." At least an amusing anecdote came out of her trip to Mexico: "I went to the bull fights [in Mexico City] and sat in the President's box. I was all done up in a beautifully tailored red suit with gold hat and gold shoes. And the Mexicans started shouting 'Veronica! Veronica!' So naturally I got up and took bows. I didn't know that they were shouting for the matador to execute a turn called a 'Veronica.' "

By April 16, 1951, Veronica and De Toth were forced to declare voluntary bankruptcy, with their $120,000 home to be sold at auction. (There were no bidders.) She and De Toth separated in June, 1951, and their divorce became final on June 2, 1952.

Veronica rejected offers to star in assorted low-class films, reasoning: "I really didn't want to go back through the grind of playing sexy sirens in grade-B thrillers all for the silk purses of the studio management." Instead, Veronica left Hollywood, putting her three children in the custody of a governess.

After some more guesting on television variety shows such as Milton Berle's program, Veronica made her legitimate stage debut. She costarred with Carl Betz in *The Voice of the Turtle* in theatre-in-the-round in Atlanta, Georgia. Then she toured the Eastern summer theatre circuit with this play and *The Curtain Rises*. She defended this professional comedown: "I loved every minute of it. Gone was the plush facade of Hollywood. Replacing it was honesty, raw and meaningful vitality that shone bright in the murky memories of California and its film factory."

She hastily accepted a road tour of *Peter Pan.* This version of the J. M. Barrie play, with music and lyrics by Leonard Bernstein, had been performed on Broadway in 1950 with Jean Arthur. The new edition was directed by Frank Corsaro and costarred Lawrence Tibbett. It opened at the Lyric Theatre in Baltimore on October 10, 1951. According to *Variety,* Veronica gave "a boyish quality and engaging matter-of-fact reading to the whimsical lead character that projects to the entire audience, young and old." Audiences were amazed to discover that Veronica's trademark hairstyle was gone, replaced by a short pixie haircut. There were many rumors about the star's temperament during the shortened tour.

In the next few years, Veronica appeared in stock versions of *The Gramercy Ghost, Remains to Be Seen, Cat on a Hot Tin Roof,* and *I Am a Camera,* always receiving better than adequate reviews. She starred in a Broadway-bound romantic comedy *Masquerade* which wobbled into Philadelphia on April 16, 1953, after a warm-up engagement in Springfield, Massachusetts. The play was set in present-day Rome, and Veronica was a street gamin involved with Charles Korvin. In *Variety*'s assessment, she was "unable to extract much sense from the role of the virtuous waif." The show folded in Philadelphia.

Periodically, Veronica would be asked if she missed her moviemaking life. Her 1955 reply was: "I'm not mad at Hollywood or show business and I'm not complaining. I should and I do appreciate the good fortune I found. Certainly the people I worked with, more often than not, were wonderful to me. I simply lost my personal identity and wanted to get it back." About New York living: "Since I've lived there as a resident, I've found myself being something more real than a movie star. Everyone else when they have a job start work at one hour and finish at another, but every Miss Glamour Puss is expected to work at it twenty-four hours a day and no one can exist like that."

On August 28, 1955, Veronica, 36, married Joe McCarthy, 32, a music publisher, in Traverse City, Michigan, where she was appearing in *State of the Union.* During a run of *The Little Hut* in Detroit in October, 1955, Veronica collapsed on stage from exhaustion and had to cancel the remainder of the ten-month tour.

By March, 1959, Veronica's marriage to McCarthy had disintegrated. Their only moments of marital compatibility were when they went on drunken toots. She served him with separation papers, charging him with assault (she later withdrew this charge), and he countersued for separation. She demanded temporary alimony of $13,000 a year, but she eventually accepted $65 a week from him. That spring she made a television guest appearance on Eddie Cantor's syndicated anthology series in the comedy episode *A Hunting We Will Go*, costarring with Craig Stevens.

Then followed three years of professional inactivity in which she existed in minimum comfort. Difficulties with her teenaged son Michael and assorted physical accidents compounded her problems. Her unfortunate circumstances were dragged forth for public consumption in the June 11, 1961, issue of the *National Enquirer*. The tabloid newspaper carried a front page story "How Did It Happen?" reacquainting everyone with her story and asking, "Whatever happened to Veronica Lake?"

The press had a field day from March 21, 1962, when Veronica was discovered living at the less-than-ritzy Martha Washington Hotel on Manhattan's East 29th Street (paying $7 a day rent) and working as a barmaid in the Colonnade Room cocktail lounge there. She was registered in the hotel as Connie De Toth. Battered but unflinching, Veronica flippantly told the press: "I just fell into this job. What brought me here? I happen to live here and I like people. But then, how do you explain me to anybody? My duties? It's not a case of duties. Just people. I play it by ear. I thoroughly enjoy it here. I really do." She would later add: "You play all kinds of parts, but this wasn't a long run [at the hotel]. It was just a fill in."

Fans sent Veronica money, but she proudly returned it.

She then met merchant seaman Andy Elickson, with whom she fell in love. Their romance continued through the next four years, until his death in 1966. About him she would say: "Unlike my other marriages, there was no competition between us to see who could be the wealthier or the more famous. All my husbands were in show business, and as a result, there was professional jealousy and frustration all the time. The fact that I was better known than they were, wounded their egos, and this didn't help one bit. It was an impossible situation. But with Andy none of this existed. One of the tragedies of my life is that he died of a terrible illness before we could get married."

Veronica was heard in a guest spot on NBC's "Monitor 62" (May 12, 1962). In August, 1962, Veronica went to Buenos Aires with actor-manager Ronald House for television appearances in connection with her old features. She then accepted the offer of WJZ-TV in Baltimore to hostess the station's Saturday evening movie show. She proved quite popular in the post, and continued with the assignment off and on through the subsequent years. In December, 1962, the attorney general's department of New York State named Veronica an innocent dupe in a bogus real-estate scheme (State Wide Restaurants). Her name had been used to obtain front money for the operation.

The press hounded Veronica for her opinions on any subject, now that the 43-year-old blonde (tinged red) was hot news for their curiosity-seeking readers. About her movie career: "I was never geared for Hollywood. I value my privacy too much and I don't like to get dressed up very often. I like to slop around in blue jeans or slacks. . . . [I left Hollywood] on a sort of a sabbatical but as time went on, it became too frightening to go back." She admitted she regarded herself as "still a child, but with firmness and a sense of direction."

About media work: "I prefer live audiences. They're the greatest teachers of timing, subtlety. Many things which you can't learn from a camera.

. . . you must feel each audience and figure out how to entertain it, and seek its recognition and respect."

Veronica was next in the news when she replaced Paula Wayne in the off-Broadway production of the musical *Best Foot Forward*. As Gale Joy, she was the fading movie queen who romps with the Winsocki High School hellions. Said the jubilant Veronica: "I'm really playing a burlesque of myself, of Veronica Lake. But I don't mind because I like to clown and how else can you explain clowning?" About her opening night on August 29, 1963, at Stage 73: "I was scared silly. But it was great. Damn, it's great to be back. I think in this show, people will be able to see what I can do."

The critics were respectful of Veronica's kidding portrayal, and the columnists predicted a nice comeback in store for the nostalgic champ of the 1940s. Nothing developed.

By this time, Veronica was a grandmother of two, but she rarely saw her children. "We never had much in common, but now that they're married we have even less to do with each other. My son and I am particularly remote. He was always something of a problem to me and one which I never managed to lick. The last time we met I told him I loved him but I didn't like him. We have never seen each other since."

On April 13, 1965, Veronica was photographed paying a $25 fine in Galveston, Texas, for being drunk in public. She had been arrested beating at the door of St. Mary's Cathedral. She explained that she had gone to Galveston to look up old friends but could not locate them. Later in the evening she decided she needed to confer with a priest, but the church was locked up.

This bit of notoriety was sufficient to interest the Gallery Restaurant Playhouse in Miami in hiring Veronica at $1,250 a week to star in *Goodbye Charlie*. When she arrived in Miami in late May—her first return to Florida in ten years—the press were on hand to greet her. One reporter described the scene: "Her hair was knotted on top of her head in a dark blonde tangle. Flesh-colored band-aids were taped to several fingers. The only makeup on her face was a touch of lipstick and her complexion looked pasty in the bright sunlight."

The show opened on June 4. The *Miami Herald* noted: "The talent and personal magnetism of one-time movie great Veronica Lake have not run dry." Veronica eventually had to sue the producer for $2,849 in uncollected salary.

She settled in Miami, soon becoming a prize celebrity in the city's homosexual bar circles. In August, 1967, she appeared in *Goodbye Charlie* at the Priscilla Beach Theatre in Plymouth, Massachusetts.

During this time, she starred in two ultra-low-budget horror films. *Footsteps in the Snow* was lensed in Canada and dealt with "dope traffic and ski bums and other goodies." It has not yet had any United States theatrical release. The other quickie film was *Flesh Feast*, photographed in Miami. This creature feature cast Veronica as the austere Dr. Elaine Frederick, recently released from a Florida mental institution. She has uncovered a youth restoration process, using preconditioned flesh-eating maggots. She establishes a laboratory in a Miami Beach mansion, with a front operation of renting rooms to student nurses. The head of a worldwide revolutionary group arrives for treatment, causing a rash of stolen bodies from hospital morgues and the murder of those nurses who stumble onto the secret laboratory. *Flesh Feast* was unleashed theatrically in late-1970 and made a satisfactory return in the action-market cinemas. (Veronica once mentioned that an outtake from this film, in which she flubbed her lines and suddenly swore "Shit on a bicycle," is exceedingly popular in black-market circles.)

After an appearance (October 28, 1967) at Boston's John Hancock Auditorium for a dramatic reading of *The World of Carl Sandburg*, Veronica remained a private citizen for the next two years, living in Miami and in Freeport, Bahamas. She wrote her autobiography *Veronica*, ghosted by Donald Bain, and it was published in England early in 1969. To promote the tome, the publishers brought her to London. Once there, stage producers signed her to a $1,250-a-week agreement to star in the play *Madame Chairman*.

She was Lady Louise Peverell, a seemingly scatter-brained American widow who takes over her English husband's business interests and proves she was really the dynamo behind him. Veronica admitted about the show: "It's a nice, pleasant little play. No deep message, just good entertainment." About her stage hairstyle: "I will wear a wig, but not a long one. That other style was all right for a girl in her 20s. But I'm 46 now and it would be cheating the public."

Much interviewed by the British press during rehearsals, Veronica was described as a frank, hard-working professional, who drank a bit much, but was up to the rigorous part. During tryouts, she suffered a back injury. Characteristically she announced: "My back may be killing me, but at least I won't die of boredom." By July, 1969, the production was in trouble in Southsea. Veronica exclaimed: "But if this goddammed play is going to make it in the West End, I want it to come in with dignity! I've got to pull this company together. I've put so much of my own money into this show I feel like an angel. I'm rewriting the script every day and paying a stenographer out of my own pocket to type the changes so these kids will have time to learn their new lines. You don't know how many times I've wanted to walk out on this show, but I couldn't jeopardize the jobs of ten other actors. But this goddammed company is the most mismanaged I've ever seen." The show soon folded. Not too long afterwards, another former cinema great, Betty Grable, suffered a similar fate with the musical *Belle Starr,* which managed to hobble to the West End, only to shutter soon thereafter.

Veronica remained in England and costarred with ex-television Western hero Ty Hardin in *A Streetcar Named Desire.* The show played at the New Theatre, ten miles outside of London, for three weeks in September, with Veronica receiving $240 a week. The Reuters stage critic wrote: "[She] gained confidence as the evening progressed and showed the heroine's final mental breakdown movingly."

Veronica then settled in Ipswich, a port city on England's eastern coast. "I find England so relaxing after the turmoil of living in America. And I plan to make my life here." To another reporter she confessed: "Now I'll admit I have an acid tongue and a very fluent manner of expression. . . . Here, people seem to be more on my own personal wave length and take my remarks in the spirit they're intended."

Re her professional talents: "I think I've developed into an actress because I've worked darn hard at it and I've learned a great deal from a lot of gifted people. And if I have nothing else to show for my life, apart from a scrapbook full of faded cuttings, I have the knowledge that my early days in Hollywood weren't in vain."

Veronica's autobiography was published in the United States in March, 1971. The *New York Times* likened it to "a workable scenario for a fable about the silver screen as life-guide and treasure map." She came to New York amidst much fanfare to promote the highly exploitable book (the most candid study since Mary Astor's diary, one ad claimed). Her appearances on the various television and radio talk shows were candid, to say the least, with no slight of the past left unaired. She came across as a tough broad who saw life realistically, and rather enjoyed her new post as a nostalgic martyr. Her face reflects her less than pristine past ("I earned this face"), her figure is stouter, and her husky voice still tosses out expletives at will. When questioned whether alcohol had greatly affected her life: "To each his own. At least I'm not a mainliner and it's more fun getting high without a needle. At least you can get over booze."

She prefers to be known as a former sex-zombie rather than sex-symbol. "That really names me properly. I was laughing at everybody in all of my portraits. I never took that stuff seriously. I will have one of the cleanest obits of any actress. I never did cheesecake like Ann Sheridan or Betty Grable. I just used my hair."

About women's liberation, Veronica is quite vocal: "Don't try to make me anything but feminine! I don't need a movement. . . . if you are one [a woman], you don't need to prove it."

On being a mother: "I wasn't a bad mother, nor was I a storybook mother. As a result, the children and I have an excellent relationship because there's no lie between us. We just lead different lives. I am not going to hang on to my blood, nor am I going to allow them to hang on to me. I know what was done to me by my mother and I'm not going to do that."

Veronica made a well-annotated return to Hollywood in June, 1971, to ballyhoo her book. About her old hunting grounds, she says: "If I had stayed in Hollywood I would have ended up like Alan Ladd and Gail Russell—dead and buried by now. That rat race killed them and I knew it eventually would kill me so I had to get out. I was never psychologically meant to be a picture star. I never took it seriously. I couldn't 'live' being a 'movie star' and I couldn't 'camp' it and I hated being something that I wasn't.

"I could take the people of Hollywood today, if I lived here, but not back then. You know everybody thinks I ran out on Hollywood because my career was going downhill but I left to save my life. I never cared about the career."

About the changes in Hollywood: "Yes, most of my friends are dead. Places where orchard groves used to be are now lit up like Christmas tree areas. I can't wait to leave here again just remembering how uncomfortable I was. I fully intend to see the year 2000."

Of her past movies: "*Sullivan's Travels* and *I Married a Witch* are my favorites, although everyone expects me to say *So Proudly We Hail!* Frankly, some of them were good commercial products but an awful lot of them were yecchhh."

Re remarriage and her future: "I'd like to [remarry], but after three unsuccessful tries, I'm a bit frightened to risk it. I'm tough, but I'm also sensitive and there comes a time when the hurt gets too much to bear.

"So, instead, I shall continue to work at my career. The world owes me nothing, but I owe it a great deal and before I get much older I intend to deliver the goods."

As: Constance Keane

ALL WOMEN HAVE SECRETS (PAR, 1939) 59 M.

Producer, Edward T. Lowe; director, Kurt Neumann; story, Dale Eunson; adaptation, Agnes Christine Johnson; song, Ned Washington and Victor Young; camera, Theodor Sparkuhl; editor, Arthur Schmidt.

Jean Cagney (Kay); Joseph Allen (John); Virginia Dale (Jennifer); Peter Hayes (Slats); Betty Moran (Susie); John Arledge (Joe); Lawrence Grossmith (Professor Hewitt); Una O'Connor (Mary); George Meeker (Doc). Constance Keane, Fay McKensie (Students).

SORORITY HOUSE (RKO, 1939) 64 M.

Producer, Robert Sisk; director, John Farrow; story, Mary Coyle Chase; adaptation, Dalton Trumbo; music director, Roy Webb; camera, Nicholas Musurca; editor, Harry Marker.

Anne Shirley (Alice); James Ellison (Bill); Barbara Read (Dotty); Pamela Blake (Merle); J. M. Kerrigan (Lew Fisher); Helen Wood (Mme. President); Doris Jordan (Neva Simpson); June Storey (Norma Hancock); Elisabeth Risdon (Mrs. Scott); Margaret Armstrong (Mrs. Dawson); Selmer Jackson (Mr. Grant); Chill Wills (Mr. Johnson); Constance Keane (Sorority Girl).

YOUNG AS YOU FEEL (20th, 1940) 59 M.

Associate producer, John Stone; director, Malcolm St. Clair; story, Lewis Beach; screenplay, Joseph Hoffman, Stanley Rauh; camera, Charles Clarke; editor, H. Reynolds.

Jed Prouty (Jones); Spring Byington (Mrs. Jones); Joan Valerie (Bonnie); Russell Gleason (Herbert Thompson); Kenneth Howell (Jack); George Ernest (Roger); June Carlson (Lucy); Florence Roberts (Granny); William Mahan (Bobby); Helen Ericson (Sandra); George Givot (Boris Mousilvitch); Marvin Stephens (Tommy McGuire); Harlan Briggs (Dr. Kinsley); Harry Shannon (Gillespie); Jack Carson (Norcross); Guy Repp (Baron Gonzales de Corbana); Brodelet Esther (Polly Marshall); Gladys Blake (Mrs. Blake); Irma Wilson (Brenda Walters); John Sheehan (Fire Chief); Lee Shumway (New York Policeman); John H. Elliott (Ambulance Doctor); Bruce Warren (Norcross Representative); Joan Leslie, Constance Keane (Girls); Billy Lechner (Boy).

FORTY LITTLE MOTHERS (MGM, 1940) 88 M.

Producer, Harry Rapf; director, Busby Berkeley, based on the play *Monsieur Petiot* by Jean Grulton; screenplay, Dorothy Yost, Ernest Pagono; songs, Charles Tobias, Nat Simon; camera, Charles Lawton; editor, Ben Lewis.

Eddie Cantor (Gilbert J. Thompson); Judith Anderson (Madame Granville); Rita Johnson (Marian Edwards); Bonita Granville (Doris); Ralph Morgan (Judge Joseph M. Williams); Diana Lewis (Marcia); Nydia Westman (Mlle. Cliche); Margaret Early (Eleanor); Martha O'Driscoll (Janette); Charlotte Munier (Lois); Louise Seidel (Betty); Baby Quintanilla ("Chum"); Constance Keane (Classmate).

As: Veronica Lake

I WANTED WINGS (PAR, 1941) 131 M.

Producer, Arthur Hornblow, Jr.; director, Mitchell Leisen; based on the book by Lt. B. Lay, Jr.; adaptation, Eleanor Griffin, Frank Wead; screenplay, Richard Maibaum, Lay, Sid Herzig; assistant director, Arthur Jacobson; art director, Hans Dreier,

Robert Usher; song, Ned Washington and Victor Young; camera, Leo Tover; editor, Hugh Bennett.

Ray Milland (Jeff Young); William Holden (Al Ludlow); Wayne Morris (Tom Cassidy); Brian Donlevy (Capt. Mercer); Constance Moore (Carolyn Bartlett); Veronica Lake (Sally Vaughn); Harry Davenport ("Sandbags" Riley); Phil Brown (Jimmy Masters); Edward Fielding (President Of The Court); Willard Robertson (Judge Advocate); Richard Lane (Flight Commander); Addison Richards (Flight Surgeon); Hobart Cavanaugh (Mickey); Douglas Aylesworth (Lt. Hopkins); John Trent (Lt. Ronson); Archie Twitchell (Lt. Clankton); Richard Webb (Cadet Captain); John Hiestand (Radio Announcer); Lane Chandler (Ranger); Harlan Warde (Montgomery —Co-Pilot); Jack Chapin, Charles Drake, Alan Hale, Jr., Renny McEvoy (Cadets); Lane Allen (Corporal—Mechanic); Ed. Peil, Sr., Frank O'Connor (Detectives); George Turner, Hal Brezeale (Privates); Hedda Hopper (Mrs. Young); Herbert Rawlinson (Mr. Young); John Sylvester (Flight Dispatcher); Jack Luden, Anthony Nace (Captains at Court Martial); Lee Shumway (Policeman in Car); Rod Cameron (Voice— Loud Speaker) Edward Peil, Jr. (Lt.); Lester Dorr (Evaluating Officer); James Farley (Fire Chief); Charles D. Waldron (Commanding Officer); Gladden M. James (Surgeon).

HOLD BACK THE DAWN (PAR, 1941) 115 M.

Producer, Arthur Hornblow, Jr.; director, Mitchell Leisen; story, Ketti Frings; screenplay, Charles Brackett, Billy Wilder; art director, Hans Dreier, Robert Usher; song, Frank Loesser, Jimmy Berg, Fred Spielman, and Fred Jacobson; camera, Leo Tover; editor, Doane Harrison.

Charles Boyer (Georges Iscovescu); Olivia De Havilland (Emmy Brown); Paulette Goddard (Anita Dixon); Victor Francen (Van Den Luecken); Walter Abel (Inspector Hammock); Curt Bois (Bonbois); Rosemary DeCamp (Berta Kurz); Eric Feldary (Josef Kurz); Nestor Paiva (Flores); Eva Puig (Lupita); Micheline Cheirel (Christine); Madeleine LeBeau (Anni); Billy Lee (Tony); Mikhail Rasumny (Mechanic); Mitchell Leisen (Mr. Saxon); Brian Donlevy, Richard Webb (Actors); Veronica Lake (Actress); Sonny Boy Williams (Sam); Edward Fielding (American Consul); Don Douglas (Joe); Gertrude Astor (Young Woman at Climax Bar); Carlos Villarias (Mexican Judge); Arthur Loft (Hollander, Planter); Charles Arnt (Mr. MacAdams); Ella Neal (Bride); Ray Mala (Young Mexican Bridegroom); June Wilkins (Miss Vivienne Worthington); Leon Belasco (Mr. Spitzer); Chester Clute (Man at Climax Bar).

SULLIVAN'S TRAVELS (PAR, 1942) 90 M.

Producer, Paul Jones; director-story-screenplay, Preston Sturges; camera, John Seitz, Farciot Edouart; editor, Stuart Gilmore.

Joel McCrea (John L. Sullivan); Veronica Lake (The Girl); Robert Warwick (Mr. Lebrand); William Demarest (Mr. Jones); Franklin Pangborn (Mr. Casalais); Porter Hall (Mr. Hadrian); Byron Foulger (Mr. Valdelle); Margaret Hayes (Secretary); Robert Greig (Sullivan's Butler); Eric Blore (Sullivan's Valet); Torben Meyer (The Doctor); Victor Potel (Cameraman); Richard Webb (Radio Man); Charles Moore (Chef); Almira Sessions (Ursula); Esther Howard (Miz Zeffie); Frank Moran (Tough Chauffeur); George Renavent (Old Tramp); Harry Rosenthal (The Trombenick); Alan Bridge (The Mister); Jimmy Conlin (Trusty); Jan Buckingham (Mrs. Sullivan); Robert Winkler (Bud); Chick Collins (Capital); Jimmie Dundee (Labor); Harry Hayden (Mr. Carson); Willard Robertson (Judge); Pat West (Counterman—Roadside Lunch Wagon); J. Farrell Macdonald (Desk Sergeant); Edward Hearn (Cop—Beverly Hills Station); Arthur Hoyt (Preacher); Paul Newlan (Truck Driver); Roscoe Ates (Counterman—Owl Wagon); Robert Dudley (One-Legged Bum); Monte Blue (Cop in Slums); Harry Tyler (R.R. Information Clerk); Dewey Robinson (Sheriff); Madame Sul-te-wan (Harmonica Player); Jess Lee Brooks (Black Preacher); Harry Seymour (Entertainer in Air-Raid Shelter); Chester Conklin (Old Bum); Frank Mills (Drunk in Theatre); Edgar Dearing (Cop—Mud Gag); Emory Parnell (Man at R.R. Shack); Julius Tannen (Public Defender).

THIS GUN FOR HIRE (PAR, 1942) 80 M.

Producer, Richard M. Blumenthal; director, Frank Tuttle; based on the novel by Graham Greene; screenplay, Albert Maltz, W. R. Burnett; art director, Hans Dreier; songs, Frank Loesser and Jacques Press; camera, John Seitz; editor, Archie Marshek.

Veronica Lake (Ellen Graham); Robert Preston (Michael Crane); Laird Cregar (Willard Gates); Alan Ladd (Philip Raven); Tully Marshall (Alvin Brewster); Mikhail Rasumny (Slukey); Marc Lawrence (Tommy); Pamela Blake (Annie); Harry Shannon (Finnerty); Frank Ferguson (Albert Baker); Bernadine Hayes (Baker's Secretary); James Farley (Night Watchman); Virita Campbell (Cripple Girl); Roger Imhof (Senator Burnett); Victor Kilian (Brewster's Secretary); Olin Howland (Fletcher); Emmett Vogan (Charlie); Chester Clute (Mr. Stewart); Charles Arnt (Will Gates); Virginia Farmer (Woman in Shop); Clem Bevans (Old Timer); Harry Hayden (Restaurant Manager); Tim Ryan (Guard); Yvonne De Carlo (Show Girl); Ed Stanley (Police Captain); Eddy Chandler (Foreman); Phil Tead (Machinist); Charles R. Moore (Dining Car Waiter); Pat O'Malley (Conductor); Katherine Booth (Waitress); Sarah Padden (Mrs. Mason); Louise La Planche (Dancer); Richard Webb (Young Man); Frances Morris (Receptionist); Cyril Ring (Waiter); Lora Lee (Girl in Car); William Cabanne (Laundry Truck Driver).

THE GLASS KEY (PAR, 1942) 85 M.

Producer, Fred Kohlmar; director, Stuart Heisler; based on the novel by Dashiell Hammett; screenplay, Jonathan Latimer; art director, Hans Dreier, Haldane Douglas; music, Victor Young; camera, Theodor Sparkuhl; editor, Archie Marshek.

Brian Donlevy (Paul Madvig); Veronica Lake (Janet Henry); Alan Ladd (Ed Beaumont); Bonita Granville (Opal Madvig); Richard Denning (Taylor Henry); Joseph Calleia (Nick Varna); William Bendix (Jeff); Frances Gifford (Nurse); Donald MacBride (Farr); Margaret Hayes (Eloise Matthews); Moroni Olsen (Ralph Henry); Eddie Marr (Rusty); Arthur Loft (Clyde Matthews); George Meader (Claude Tuttle); Pat O'Malley, Ed Peil, Sr., James Millican (Politicians); Edmund Cobb, Jack Luden, Joe McGuinn, Jack Gardner, Frank Bruno (Reporters); John W. DeNoria (Groggins); Jack Mulhall (Lynch); Al Hill (Bum); Dane Clark (Henry Sloss); George Turner (Doctor); Tom Dugan (Jeep); William Benedict (Sturdy); Lillian Randolph (Entertainer—Basement Club); Tom Fadden (Waiter); Charles Sullivan (Taxi Driver).

I MARRIED A WITCH (UA, 1942) 82 M.

Producer-director, Rene Clair; based on the novel *The Passionate Witch* by Thorne Smith, Norman Matson; adaptation, Robert Pirosh; Marc Connelly; art director, Hans Dreier, Ernst Fegte; music director, Roy Webb; special effects, Gordon Jennings; camera, Ted Tetzlaff; editor, Eda Warren.

Fredric March (Wallace Wooley); Veronica Lake (Jennifer); Robert Benchley (Dr. Dudley White); Susan Hayward (Estelle Masterson); Cecil Kellaway (Daniel); Elizabeth Patterson (Margaret); Robert Warwick (J. R. Masterson); Eily Malyon (Tabitha Wooley); Robert Creig (Town Crier); Viola Moore (Martha); Mary Field (Nancy Wooley); Nora Cecil (Harriet); Emory Parnell (Allen); Helen St. Rayner (Vocalist); Aldrich Bowker (Justice of the Peace); Emma Dunn (His Wife); Harry Tyler, Ralph Peters (Prisoners); Charles Moore (Rufus) Ann Carter (Jennifer, Jr.—the Daughter); George Guhl (Fred); Wade Boteler (Policeman); Eddy Chandler (Motorcycle Cop) Jack Luden (Ambulance Driver); Monte Blue (Doorman); Lee Shumway (Fireman); Billy Beva (Puritan Vendor); Marie Blake (Puritan); Reed Hadley (Young Man); Florence Gill (Woman Playing Chess).

STAR SPANGLED RHYTHM (PAR, 1942) 99 M.

Associate producer, Joseph Sistrom; director, George Marshall; screenplay, Harry Tugend; music, Robert Emmett Dolan; art director, Hans Dreier, Ernest Fegte; songs, Johnny Mercer and Harold Arlen; camera, Leo Tover, Theodor Sparkuhl; editor, Paul Weatherwax.

Betty Hutton (Polly Judson); Eddie Bracken (Jimmy Webster); Victor Moore (Pop Webster); Anne Revere (Sarah); Walter Abel (Frisbee); Cass Daley (Mimi); Macdonald Carey (Louie the Lug); Gil Lamb (Hi-Pockets); William Haade (Duffy); Bob Hope (Master of Ceremonies); Marion Martin, William Bendix, Dorothy Lamour, Paulette Goddard, Veronica Lake, Arthur Treacher, Walter Catlett, Sterling Holloway, Vera Zorina, Frank Faylen, Fred MacMurray, Franchot Tone, Ray Milland, Lynne Overman, Susan Hayward, Ernest Truex, Mary Martin, Dick Powell, Golden Gate Quartette, Walter Dare Wahl and Co., Cecil B. DeMille, Preston Sturges, Ralph Murphy, Alan Ladd, Gary Crosby, Jack Hope, Katherine Dunham, Rochester, Marjorie Reynolds, Betty Rhodes, Dona Drake, Bing Crosby, Jimmy Lydon, Ellen Drew, Charles Smith, Frances Gifford, Susanna Foster, Robert Preston (Themselves); Woody Strode (Rochester's Motorcycle Chauffeur); Dorothy Granger (Officer); Barbara Pepper, Jean Phillips, Lynda Grey (Girls); Eddie Dew, Rod Cameron (Petty Offiers); Keith Richards (Officer); Irving Bacon (New Hampshire Farmer—Old Glory Number); Virginia Brissac (Lady From Iowa—Old Glory Number); Matt McHugh (Man From Brooklyn—Old Glory Number); Peter Potter (Georgia Boy—Old Glory Number); Paul Porcasi (Mussolini); Richard Loo (Hirohito); Tom Dugan (Hitler).

SO PROUDLY WE HAIL (PAR, 1943) 126 M.

Producer-director, Mark Sandrich; screenplay, Allan Scott; art director, Hans Dreier, Earl Hedrick; music, Miklos Rozsa; song, Edward Heyman and Rozsa; special effects, Gordon Jennings, Farciot Edouart; camera, Charles Lang, editor, Ellsworth Hoagland.

Claudette Colbert (Lt. Janet Davidson); Paulette Goddard (Lt. Jean O'Doul); Veronica Lake (Lt. Olivia D'Arcy); George Reeves (Lt. John Summers); Barbara Britton (Lt. Rosemary Larson); Walter Abel (Chaplain); Sonny Tufts (Kansas); Mary Servoss (Capt. "Ma" McGregor); Ted Hecht (Dr. Jose Hardin); John Litel (Dr. Harrison); Dr. Hugh Ho Chang (Ling Chee); Mary Treen (Lt. Sadie Schwartz); Kitty Kelly (Lt. Ethel Armstrong); Helen Lynd (Lt. Elsie Bollenbacker); Lorna Gray, later Adrian Booth (Lt. Toni Bacelli); Dorothy Adams (Lt. Irma Emerson); Ann Doran (Lt. Betty Paterson); Jean Willes (Lt. Carol Johnson); Lynn Walker (Lt. Fay Leonard); Joan Tours (Lt. Margaret Stevenson); Jan Wiley (Lt. Lynne Hopkins); James Bell (Colonel White); Dick Hogan (Flight Lt. Archie McGregor); Bill Goodwin (Capt. O'Rourke); James Flavin (Capt. O'Brien); Byron Foulger (Mr. Larson); Elsa Janssen (Mrs. Larson); Richard Crane (Georgie Larson); Boyd Davis (Col. Mason); Will Wright (Col. Clark); William Forrest (Major—San Francisco Dock); Isabel Cooper, Amparo Antenercrut, Linda Brent (Filipino Nurses); James Millican (Young Ensign); Damian O'Flynn (Young Doctor); Victor Kilian, Jr. (Corp.); Julia Faye, Hazel Keener, Frances Morris, Mimi Doyle (Nurses); Edward Earle, Byron Shores (Doctors); Harry Strang (Major Arthur); Edward Dew (Capt. Lawrence); Yvonne DeCarlo (Girl); Hugh Prosser (Captain); Charles Lester (Soldier).

THE HOUR BEFORE THE DAWN (PAR, 1944) 75 M.

Associate producer, William Dozier; director, Frank Tuttle; based on the novel by W. Somerset Maugham; adaptation, Lester Samuels; screenplay, Michael Hogan; art director, Hans Dreier, Earl Hedrick; music, Miklos Rozsa; special effects, Gordon Jennings; camera, John F. Seitz; editor, Stuart Gilmore.

Franchot Tone (Jim Hetherton); Veronica Lake (Dora Bruckmann); John Sutton (Roger Hetherton); Binnie Barnes (May Hetherton); Henry Stephenson (General Hetherton); Phillip Merivale (Sir Leslie Buchannan); Nils Asther (Kurt van der Breughel); Edmond Breon (Freddy Merritt); David Leland (Tommy Hetherton); Aminta Dyne (Hertha Parkins); Morton Lowry (Jackson) Ivan Simpson (Magistrate); Donald Stuart (Farmer Searle); Harry Allen (Mr. Saunders); Mary Gordon (Annie); Ernest Severn (Willie); Raymond Severn (Jim as a Boy); Leslie Denison (Captain Atterley); Harry Cording (Sam); Hilda Plowright (Mrs. Merritt); Viola Moore (Maid); David Clyde (Farmer); Tempe Pigott (Mrs. Saunders); Marjean Neville (Evie); Marie deBecker (Amelia); Thomas Louden (Wilmington); Deidre Gale (Emma); Nigel Morton (Observer Pilot); Otto Reichow, Charles H. Faber (German Pilots).

BRING ON THE GIRLS (PAR, 1945) 92 M.

Associate producer, Fred Kohlmar; director, Sidney Lanfield; story, Pierre Wolff; screenplay, Karl Tunberg, Darrell Ware; music director, Robert Emmett Dolan; songs, Jimmy McHugh and Harold Adamson; choreography, Danny Dare; art director, Hans Dreier, John Meehan; camera, Karl Struss; editor, William Shea.

Veronica Lake (Teddy Collins); Sonny Tufts (Phil North); Eddie Bracken (J. Newport Bates); Marjorie Reynolds (Sue Thomas); Grant Mitchell (Uncle Ralph); Johnny Coy (Benny Lowe); Peter Whitney (Swede); Alan Mowbray (August); Porter Hall (Dr. Efrington); Thurston Hall (Rutledge); Lloyd Corrigan (Beaster); Sig Arno (Joseph); Joan Woodbury (Gloria); Andrew Tombes (Dr. Spender); Frank Faylen, Huntz Hall, William Moss (Sailors); Norma Varden (Aunt Martha); Golden Gate Quartette, Spike Jones and his Orchestra (Themselves); Marietta Cantry (Ida); Dorothea Kent (Myrtle); Stan Johnson (Petty Officer); Jimmie Dundee (Chief—Master At Arms); Walter Baldwin (Henry); Veda Ann Borg (Girl at Bar With Phil); Noel Neill (Cigarette Girl); Jimmy Conlin (Justice of the Peace); George Turner (Marine); Louise LaPlanche (Girl); Yvonne DeCarlo (Hat Check Girl); Alec Craig (Stage Doorman); Barry Watkins (Rube—Comedy Skit); Kay Linaker (Commander's Wife); Frank Hagney (Flunky); Harry Hays Morgan (Waiter).

OUT OF THIS WORLD (PAR, 1945) 96 M.

Associate producer, Sam Coslow; director, Hal Walker; story, Elizabeth Meehan, Coslow; screenplay, Walter DeLeon, Arthur Phillips; music director, Victor Young; art director, Hans Dreier, Haldane Douglas; choreography, Sammy Lee; songs, Johnny Mercer and Harold Arlen; Eddie Cherkose, Felix Bernard, and Coslow; Coslow; Ben Raleigh and Bernie Wayne; camera, Stuart Thompson; editor, Stuart Gilmore.

Eddie Bracken (Herbie Fenton); Veronica Lake (Dorothy Dodge); Diana Lynn (Betty Miller); Cass Daley (Fanny, The Drummer); Parkyakarkus (Gus Palukas); Donald MacBride (J. C. Crawford); Florence Bates (Harriet Pringle); Gary Crosby, Phillip Crosby, Dennis Crosby, Lindsay Crosby (Children in Audience); Olga San Juan, Nancy Porter, Audrey Young, Carol Deere (Glamourette Quartette); Carmen Cavallaro, Ted Fiorito, Henry King, Ray Noble, Joe Reichman (Themselves); Don Wilson (Radio Announcer/M.C.); Mabel Paige (Mrs. Robbins); Charles Smith (Charlie Briggs); Irving Bacon (Irving Krunk); Toni LaRue (Marimba Player); Mary Elliott (Arlen—Trumpet Player); Carmella Bergstrom (Margy—Trombone Player); Betty Walker (Guitar Player); Virginia Morris, June Harris (Trumpet Players); Laura Gruver, Marguerite Campbell (Violin Players); Inez Palange (Mrs. Palukas); Esther Dale (Abbie Pringle); Charles B. Williams (Joe Welch); Gloria Saunders (Vicky Kelly); Lorraine Krueger (Maizie); Milton Kibbee (Bald Headed Man); Davison Clark (Pullman Conductor); Nell Craig (Woman); Virginia Sale (Spinster); Charles R. Moore (Porter); Norman Nesbitt (Announcer); The Voice of Bing Crosby; Selmer Jackson (Doctor); Sammee Tong (Chinese Announcer); Michael Visaroff (Russian Announcer).

DUFFY'S TAVERN (PAR, 1945) 97 M.

Associate producer, Danny Dare; director, Hal Walker; screenplay, Melvin Frank, Norman Panama; music director, Robert Emmett Dolan; choreography, Billy Daniels; songs, Johnny Burke and Jimmy Van Heusen; Ben Raleigh and Bernie Wayne; process camera, Farciot Edouart; special effects, Gordon Jennings; camera, Lionel Lindon; editor, Arthur Schmidt.

Bing Crosby, Betty Hutton, Paulette Goddard, Alan Ladd, Dorothy Lamour, Eddie Bracken, Brian Donlevy, Sonny Tufts, Veronica Lake, Arturo De Cordova, Cass Daley, Diana Lynn, Gary Crosby, Phillip Crosby, Dennis Crosby, Lindsay Crosby, William

Bendix, Maurice Rocco, James Brown, Joan Caulfield, Gail Russell, Helen Walker, Jean Heather (Themselves); Barry Fitzgerald (Bing Crosby's Father); Victor Moore (Michael O'Malley) Marjorie Reynolds (Peggy O'Malley); Barry Sullivan (Danny Murphy); Ed Gardner (Archie); Charles Cantor (Finnegan); Eddie Green (Eddie-The Waiter); Ann Thomas (Miss Duffy); Howard Da Silva (Heavy); Billy De Wolfe (Doctor); Walter Abel (Director); Charles Quigley (Ronald); Olga San Juan (Gloria); Robert Watson (Masseur); Frank Faylen (Customer); Matt McHugh (Man Following Miss Duffy); Emmett Vogan (Make-Up Man); Cyril Ring (Gaffer); Noel Neill (School Kid).

HOLD THAT BLONDE (PAR, 1945) 76 M.

Producer, Paul Jones; director, George Marshall; based on the play by Paul Armstrong; screenplay, Walter DeLeon, Earl Baldwin; E. Edwin Moran; art director, Hans Dreier, Walter Tyler; special effects, Gordon Jennings; process camera, Farciot Edouart; music, Werner Heymann; camera, Daniel L. Fapp; editor, LeRoy Stone.

Eddie Bracken (Ogden Spencer Trulow III); Veronica Lake (Sally Martin); Albert Dekker (Inspector Callahan); Frank Fenton (Mr. Phillips); George Zucco (Pavel Sorasky); Donald MacBride (Mr. Kratz); Lewis L. Russell (Mr. Henry Carteret); Norma Varden (Mrs. Henry Carteret); Ralph Peters (Mr. Reddy); Robert Watson (Edwards, A. Butler); Lyle Latell (Tony); Edmund MacDonald (Victor); Willie Best (Willie Shelley); Jack Norton (A Drunk); Lee Shumway (Dectective); William Frambes (Elevator Boy); James Flavin (Laundry Truck Driver); Jody Gilbert (Matron); Crane Whitley (Newspaper Reporter); Boyd Davis (Mr. Sedgemore); Mira McKinney (Mrs. Sedgemore); Olaf Hytten (Charles); Grayce Hampton (Mrs. Case); Ralph Dunn (Radio Cop); Shimen Ruskin (Russian Waiter); Kenneth Hunter (Mr. Van Gelder); Mary Currier (Mrs. Van Gelder); Jim Toney (Kent); Kernan Cripps (Murphy).

MISS SUSIE SLAGLE'S (PAR, 1946) 88 M.

Associate producer, John Houseman; director, John Berry; based on the novel by Augusta Tucker; adaptation, Anne Froelick, Adrian Scott; screenplay, Anne Froelick, Hugo Butler; additional dialogue, Theodore Strauss; art director, Hans Dreier, Earl Hedrick, music, Daniele Amfitheatrof; song, Ben Raleigh and Bennie Wayne; camera, Charles Lang, Jr.; process camera, Farciot Edouart; editor, Archie Marshek.

Veronica Lake (Nan Rogers); Sonny Tufts (Pug Prentiss); Joan Caulfield (Margarette Howe); Ray Collins (Dr. Elijah Howe); Billy De Wolfe (Ben Mead); Bill Edwards (Elijah Howe, Jr.); Pat Phelan (Elbert Riggs); Lillian Gish (Miss Susie Slagle); Roman Bohnen (Dean Wingate); Morris Carnovsky (Dr. Fletcher); Renny McEvoy (Clayton Abernathy); Lloyd Bridges (Silas Holmes); Michael Sage (Irving Asrom); E. J. Ballantine (Dr. Metz); Theodore Newton (Dr. Boyd); J. Lewis Johnson (Hizer); Ludwig Stossel (Otto); Charles E. Arnt (Mr. Johnson); Isabel Randolph (Mrs. Howe); Kathleen Howard (Miss Wingate); Frederick Burton (Dr. Bowen); Chester Morrison (Paul); William Meader, Albert Ruiz, Stan Johnson Jerry James, Harold Bernardi (Students); Cyril Ring (Instrumental Man); Pierre Watkin (Superintendent); Alan Bridge (Taxi Driver); Byron Poindexter (Orderly); Milton Kibbee (Lttle Man); Mary Herriot (Gwen); William Challee (Interne); Connie Thompkin (Alice).

THE BLUE DAHLIA (PAR, 1946) 96 M.

Producer, George Marshall; associate producer, John Houseman; director, Marshall; screenplay, Raymond Chandler; art director, Hans Dreier, Walter Tyler; music, Victor Young; process camera, Farciot Edouart; camera, Lionel Lindon; editor, Arthur Schmidt.

Alan Ladd (Johnny Morrison); Veronica Lake (Joyce Harwood); William Bendix (Buzz Wanchek); Howard Da Silva (Eddie Harwood); Doris Dowling (Hel Morrison); Tom Powers (Captain Hendrickson); Hugh Beaumont (George Copeland); Howard Freeman (Corelli); Don Costello (Leo); Will Wright ('Dad' Newell); Frank Faylen (The Man); Walter Sande (Heathe); Vera Marshe (Blonde); Mae Busch (Jenny The Maid); Harry Hayden (Assistant Hotel Manager); Harry Barris (Bellhop); Paul Gustine (Doorman); Roberta Jonay (Girl Hotel Clerk); Milton Kibbee (Night Hotel Clerk); Anthony Caruso (Marine Corporal); Matt McHugh (Bartender); Arthur Loft ("The Wolf"); Ernie Adams (Man in Coveralls); Jack Clifford (Plainclothes Dick); George Sorel (Paul—Captain of Waiters); Douglas Carter (Bus Driver); Jimmy Dundee (Driver of Gangster Car); Dick Elliott (Motor Court Operator); Noel Neill, Mavis Murray (Hat Check Girls); Franklin Parker (Police Stenographer).

RAMROD (UA, 1947) 94 M.

Producer, Harry Sherman; assistant producer, Gene Strong; director, Andre De Toth; based on a story by Luke Short; screenplay, Jack Moffitt, Graham Baker, Cecile Kramer; music, Adolph Deutsch; assistant director, Harold Godsoe; camera, Russell Harlan, Harry Pedmond, Jr.; editor, Sherman A. Rose.

Veronica Lake (Connie Dickason); Joel McCrea (Dave Nash); Ian McDonald (Walt Shipley); Charlie Ruggles (Ben Dickason); Preston Foster (Frank Ivey); Arleen Whelan (Rose); Lloyd Bridges (Red Cates); Donald Crisp (Sheriff Jim Crew); Rose Higgins (Annie); Chick York (Dr. Parks); Sarah Padden (Mrs. Parks); Trevor Bardette (Bailey); Don DeFore (Bill Schell); Nestor Paiva (Curley); Cliff Parkinson (Tom Peebles); John Powers (Pokey); Ward Wood (Link Thomas); Hal Taliaferro (Jess Moore); Wally Cassell (Virg Lee); Ray Teal (Burma); Jeff Corey (Bice).

VARIETY GIRL (PAR, 1947) 83 M.

Producer, Daniel Dare; director, George Marshall; screenplay, Edmund Hartman, Frank Tashlin, Robert Welch, Monte Brice; music, Joseph J. Lilley; songs, Johnny Burke and James Van Heusen; Frank Loesser; Allan Roberts and Doris Fisher; choreography, Billy Daniels, Bernard Pearce; assistant director, George Templeton; art director, Hans Dreier, Robert Clatworthy; special puppetoon sequence, Thornton Hoe, William Cottrell; special effects, Gordon Jennings; camera, Lionel Lindon, Stuart Thompson; editor, LeRoy Stone.

Mary Hatcher (Catherine Brown); Olga San Juan (Amber LaVonne); De Forest Kelley (Bob Kirby); William Demarest (Barker); Frank Faylen (Stage Manager); Frank Ferguson (J. R. O'Connell); Russell Hicks, Crane Whitley, Charles Coleman, Hal K. Dawson, Eddie Fetherston (Men at Steambath); Catherine Craig (Secretary); Bing Crosby, Bob Hope, Gary Cooper, Ray Milland, Alan Ladd, Barbara Stanwyck, Paulette Goddard, Dorothy Lamour, Veronica Lake, Sonny Tufts, Joan Caulfield, William Holden, Lizabeth Scott, Burt Lancaster, Gail Russell, Diana Lynn, Sterling Hayden, Robert Preston, John Lund, William, Bendix, Barry Fitzgerald, Cass Daley, Howard Da Silva, Billy De Wolfe, Macdonald Carey, Arleen Whelan, Patric Knowles, Mona Freeman, Cecil Kellaway, Johnny Coy, Virginia Field, Richard Webb, Stanley Clements, Cecil B. DeMille, Mitchell Leisen, Frank Butler, George Marshall, Roger Dann, Pearl Bailey, The Mulcay's, Spike Jones and his City Slickers, George Reeves, Wanda Hendrix, Sally Hawlinson (Themselves); Ann Doran (Hairdresser); Jack Norton (Brown Derby Busboy); Eric Alden (Make-Up Man); Frank Mayo (Director).

SAIGON (PAR, 1948) 93 M.

Producer, P. J. Wolfson; director, Leslie Fenton; story, Julian Zimet; screenplay; Wolfson, Arthur Sheekman; art director, Hans Dreier, Henry Bumstead; music, Robert Emmett Dolan; camera, J. F. Seitz; editor, William Shea.

Alan Ladd (Major Larry Briggs); Veronica Lake (Susan Cleaver); Douglas Dick (Captain Mike Perry); Wally Cassell (Sgt. Pete Rocco); Luther Adler (Lt. Keon); Morris Carnovsky (Alex Maris); Mikhail Rasumny (Clerk); Luis Van Rooten (Simon); Eugene Borden (Boat Captain); Griff Barnett (Surgeon); Frances Chung (Chinese Nurse); Betty Bryant (Singer—Waterfront Cafe); Dorothy Eveleigh (Portuguese Woman); Harry Wilson (Stevedore); William Yip (Cafe Proprietor); Allen Douglas (American Soldier); Kenny O'Morrison (Air Corps Lt.); Leo Abbey (Sinister Driver); Charles Stevens (Driver of Susan's Car); Tommy Lee (Ox Cart Driver); Moy Ming (Proprietor—Tea House); Oie Chan (Flower Vendor); Kanza Omar (Russian Entertainer); Philip Ahn (Boss Merchant); Harold G. Fong (Bartender); Andre Charlot (Priest); Jack Chefe (Hotel Clerk); Jimmie Dundee (Stunt Man); George Sorel (Travel Agent).

THE SAINTED SISTERS (PAR, 1948) 89 M.

Producer, Richard Maibaum; director, William D. Russell; story, Elisa Black, Alden Nash; screenplay, Harry Clark; art director, Hans Dreier, Henry Bumstead; music, Van Cleave; camera, Lionel Lindon; editor, Everett Douglas.

Veronica Lake (Letty Stanton); Joan Caulfield (Jane Stanton); Barry Fitzgerald (Robbie McCleary); William Demarest (Vern Tewilliger); George Reeves (Sam Stoaks); Beulah Bondi (Hester Rivercomb); Chill Wills (Will Twitchell); Darryl Hickman (Jud Tewilliger); Jimmy Hunt (David Frisbee); Kathryn Card (Martha Tewilliger); Ray Walker (Abel Rivercomb); Harold Vermilyea (Laderer); Clancy Cooper (Cal Frisbee); Dorothy Adams (Widow Davitt); Hank Worden (Taub Beasley); Don Barclay (Dr. Benton); Edwin Fowler (Rev. Hallrack); Dick Elliott (Mil Freeman); Eddie Parks (Clem Willis); Rudolf Erickson, Sidney D'Albrook, Perc Launders, Douglas Spencer, Max Wagner, Jack Woody, Jimmie Dundee (Townsmen); June Smaney, Maria Tavares (Townswomen); Eula Guy (Emmy Lou); Beulah Hubbard (Mrs. Prentiss); Frances Sanford (Mrs. Grigsby); Gigi Perreau (Beasley Girl); Alex Gerry (District Attorney); Hal Rand (Asst. District Attorney); David McMahon (Policeman); Richard Bond (Detective).

ISN'T IT ROMANTIC? (PAR, 1948) 87 M.

Producer, Daniel Dare; director, Norman Z. McLeod; story, Jeannette C. Nolan; screenplay, Theodore Strauss, Joseph Mischel, Richard L. Breen; art director, Hans Dreier, Robert Clatworthy; music director, Joseph J. Lilley; songs, Ray Evans and Jay Livingston; camera, Lionel Lindon; editor, LeRoy Stone.

Veronica Lake (Candy); Mona Freeman (Susie); Mary Hatcher (Rose); Billy De Wolfe (Horace Frazier); Roland Culver (Major Euclid Cameron); Patric Knowles (Richard Brannon); Richard Webb (Benjamin Logan); Kathryn Givney (Clarisse Thayer); Larry Olsen (Hannibal); Pearl Bailey (Addie); Charles Evans (Judge Thomas Logan); Jeff York (Burly Gent); Eddie Johnson (Jerry—Piano Player); Johnny Garrett (Jasper); Dick Keene (Mr. Hagerty); Olin Howlin (Hotel Clerk); Bill Meader (Assistant Clerk); Perle Kincaid, Julia Otho, Mattie Kennedy, Mabel Hart, Sally Hale, Ethel Getty, Ivanetta Gardner, Rose DeHaven, Mabel Butterworth (Corinthian Circle Members); Syd Saylor (Bartender); Hal Bartlett (Carter Dixon); Chester Conklin, Snub Pollard, Duke York, Bobby Barber (Men); Sarah Edwards (Bird-Like Woman).

SLATTERY'S HURRICANE (20th, 1949) 83 M.

Producer, William Perlberg; director, Andre De Toth; based on a book by Herman Wouk; screenplay, Wouk, Richard Murphy; music director, Lionel Newman; art director, Lyle Wheeler; special effects, Fred Sersen, Ray Kellogg, Albert Hogsettt; camera, Charles G. Clarke, editor, Robert Simpson.

Richard Widmark (Will Slattery); Linda Darnell (Aggie Hobson); Veronica Lake (Dolores Greaves); John Russell (Lt. F. J. Hobson); Gary Merrill (Commander Kramer); Walter Kingsford (Milne); Raymond Greenleaf (Admiral William F. Ollenby); Stanley Waxman (Frank); Joseph De Santis (Gregory); Norman Leavitt (Waiter); Kenny Williams (M.C.); Morris Ankrum (Doctor); Amelita Ward (Marie, B-Girl); William Hawes (Dispatcher); Lee MacGregor (Navigator); John Davidson (Maitre D'); Don Hicks (Tower Operator); Frank Richards (Bartender); Ted Jordan (Radarman); David Wolfe (Dr. Ross); Grandon Rhodes (Meteorologist); John Wald (Newscaster); Gene Reynolds, Harry Lauter (Control Tower Operators).

STRONGHOLD (Lippert, 1952) 72 M.

Director, Steve Sekeley; screenplay, Wells Root; music director, Antonio Diaz Conde; camera, Stanley Cortez; editor, Charles L. Kimball.

Veronica Lake (Mary Stevens); Zachary Scott (Don Miguel Navarro); Arturo De Cordova (Don Pedro Alvarez) and: Rita Lacedo, Alfonso Bedoya, Yadin Jiminez, Fanny Schiller, Gilberto Gonzalez, Carlos Muzquiz, Frederick A. Mack, Rock Galbin, Gustavo Rojo, Irene Ajay, Felipe de Albe.

FOOTSTEPS IN THE SNOW (Evergreen, 1966) 90 M.

Director, Martin Green; screenplay, Dan Daniels, Green.

With: Veronica Lake, Peter Kastner, Meredith McRae, Ovila Legare.

FLESH FEAST (Viking International, 1970) 72 M.

Producer, V. L. Grinter; director, Brad F. Grinter; story-screenplay, Thomas Casey; special effects, Doug Hobart; camera, Casey.

Veronica Lake (Dr. Elaine Frederick); Phil Philbin (Ed Casey); Heather Hughes (Kristine); and: Martha Mischon, Uanka Mann, Dian Wilhite, Chris Martell.

With SULLIVAN'S TRAVELS director Preston Sturges

Demonstrating the dangers of wearing long hair while working with factory machinery

With good friend Andy Elickson

Advertisement for DUFFY'S TAVERN (Par '45)

Today

Baby Quintanilla, Eddie Cantor, Diana Lewis, Veronica Lake, Bonita Granville, Margaret Early, and Louise Seidel in FORTY LITTLE MOTHERS (MGM '40)

With Joel McCrea in SULLIVAN'S TRAVELS

With Alan Ladd in THIS GUN FOR HIRE (Par '42)

With Alan Ladd in THE GLASS KEY (Par '42)

With Dorothy Lamour, Paulette Goddard, Lynne Overman, Albert Dekker, Alan Ladd, Bing Crosby, and Victor Moore in STAR SPANGLED RHYTHM (Par '42)

With Claudette Colbert in SO PROUDLY WE HAIL (Par '43)

With Franchot Tone in THE HOUR BEFORE THE DAWN (Par '44)

With Grant Mitchell, Eddie Bracken, and Norma Varden in BRING ON THE GIRLS (Par '45)

With Diana Lynn and Cass Daley in OUT OF THIS WORLD (Par '45)

With Howard da Silva in DUFFY'S TAVERN (Par '45)

With Bill Edwards in MISS SUSIE SLAGLE'S (Par '46)

With Howard da Silva in THE BLUE DAHLIA (Par '46)

With Billy De Wolfe in ISN'T IT ROMAN-TIC? (Par '48)

With Douglas Dick, Wally Cassell, and Alan Ladd in SAIGON (Par '48)

With John Russell, Linda Darnell, and Richard Widmark in SLATTERY'S HURRI-CANE (20th '49)

DIANA LYNN

5'6½"

115 pounds

Brownish-blonde hair

Blue eyes

Libra

✳✳✳✳✳✳✳✳✳✳✳✳✳✳✳✳✳✳✳✳✳✳✳

DIANA LYNN's screen reputation rests on her distinctive performance in three Paramount features of the mid-1940s. In two of these comedies *(The Major and the Minor, The Miracle of Morgan's Creek),* she essayed with expertise the bratty teenager whose exasperating mannerisms disguised an amazingly adult perception. In the nostalgic *Our Hearts Were Young and Gay,* she moved gracefully into the role of a young adult whose physical maturity belied her irrepressible impishness.

A child prodigy with the promise of a career as a concert pianist, Diana accidentally drifted into motion pictures as part of the background of a 1939 feature concerning music school pupils. Two years later she gave up her career at the piano for one in acting with notable success. At post-1945 Paramount, Diana suffered from the dual problem of being superseded by contemporary Mona Freeman as the brat in residence, yet being too typecast as the rambunctious young thing to be given much opportunity to expand her acting range in other films.

Diana's forte at Paramount had been her unique ability to breathe validity into a stereotype, a quality not found in the performances of the maturing Shirley Temple, Jane Withers, Virginia Weidler, or the later teenaged Margaret O'Brien. Yet after Diana left Paramount in 1938 to freelance, she allowed herself to fit too easily into the mold of the sweet young ingenue and became mired in roles of unending sameness. Her sporadic screen appearances as a tough girl did nothing to jar her wholesome image as the pixie with the deep-modulated voice. Eventually Diana transformed her energies to television, where she proved to be one of the medium's leading dramatic actresses. But fame and fortune in the video field in the 1950s was nothing comparable to screen prominence. Like her sparkling stage performances, most of her early television work was done live, leaving only reviews of her accomplishments as her legacy.

Today too many cinema enthusiasts mistakenly recall Diana as a forerunner of the Tab Hunter malted milk set, forgetting her contributions to the craft of acting.

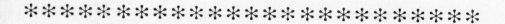

Diana Lynn was born Dolores Loehr on October 7, 1926, in Los Angeles, California, the daughter of Louis William Loehr and Eartha (Ihes) Loehr. Her father was an oil supply superintendent. Her mother was a music teacher. They lived in a comfortable colonial house in Beverly Hills in rather affluent surroundings.

Mrs. Loehr was a fine pianist and, almost from the beginning she was determined that her precocious child should become a concert pianist. Diana would recall her comprehensive training course: "Mother would turn on three radios full blast and I would have to memorize a Bach prelude against that noise. I learned concentration." There were always two pianos at home, so mother and daughter could play duets together.

Diana attended Miss Grace's Private School in Los Angeles. By the age of 11, she was a prominent member of the Los Angeles Junior Symphony Orchestra, and soon would say, "I was slow getting started. I did nothing to further my career until I was eight. I call the years prior to that my lost years. I was foundering. I had not found myself."

When Diana was 13, she trooped along with a violinist girlfriend who was auditioning for Samuel Goldwyn's film *They Shall Have Music* (1939). The executives were so impressed with Diana's accompaniment on the piano that they hired her for a background role in the movie.

They Shall Have Music, Goldwyn's bid to bring culture to the movies, presented Jascha Heifetz in his cinema debut. The concocted entertainment had Walter Brennan and his daughter Andrea Leeds running a music school that is mainly populated with ragamuffin slum children. When financial problems threaten the school's existence, Heifetz is persuaded to present a concert to raise funds. Diana was among the "students" performing the classical ensemble numbers. Joel McCrea was tossed in as Leeds's romantic interest, and youngster Gene Reynolds was the focal point as the child prodigy. The overproduced musical drama bowed at the Rivoli Theatre on July 25, 1939. The public was not enthusiastic about the ersatz concertizing.

Diana considered her film debut a lark and returned to her piano career, making occasional concert tours away from Los Angeles. Then in 1941 Paramount began casting its youth and classical music feature, *The Hard Boiled Canary.* Diana was auditioned and contracted to appear with other teenaged prodigy musicians in this tale about the National Music Camp at Interlocken, Michigan. The not-so-ingenious plot cast Paramount singing starlet Susanna Foster (age 16) as a reform school girl and junior burlesque singer who is offered a scholarship to the music camp by its liberal owner, William Collier, Sr. At first ignored by the other serious-minded pupils, she soon wins their confidence with an ingratiating performance of Marlene Dietrich imitations. Boyish Allan Jones as Collier's son takes a shine to Foster. Paramount executives were so enthused about the completed musical that they withdrew the picture from its planned release, retitled it *There's Magic in Music,* and afforded the property a substantial publicity send-off. *There's Magic in Music* premiered at Loew's Criterion on June 8, 1941. Diana, tenth-billed as herself (Dolly Loehr), was noted in passing as one of the "young musical geniuses." Originally Diana had been scheduled to play a few piano bits in the film, but during production she was given some lines of dialogue, and then was asked on the spur of the moment if she could learn the Grieg Piano Concerto in time to play in the film. Diana said yes; her mother was not so sure. A week later Diana played the difficult piece for the picture. The earnest picture did modest box-office business.

By now, Diana was intrigued with filmmaking and the possibilities of a motion picture career. "Acting was my own decision, a kind of rebellion," Diana once explained. "I loathe playing [piano] for people and I always have." She later amplified by stating: "I was so young when I started; I was used and exploited, and I didn't have the courage or the brains—to say no to the use of whatever talents I had."

Diana readily agreed to a Paramount term contract when it was offered in 1941 and she joined the studio's repertory players. At 15 she was the youngest contract starlet on the lot. She was placed in the Paramount High School of Education (from which she graduated) and studied acting with William Russell and other studio drama coaches. To appease her mother, she continued with her intensive piano lessons while in the fledgling stages of her acting career.

She was at an awkward stage: too old to play the preteen roles that had introduced Virginia Wiedler to the screen, and not physically mature enough to play adult assignments as Linda Darnell did at Twentieth Century-Fox when she was only 15. For her debut as a screen actress, Paramount cast her in Billy Wilder's charming comedy *The Major and the Minor* (1942). Ginger Rogers starred as a New York working gal who poses as a child to obtain a half-fare train ticket back to Iowa. Aboard, she is taken in hand by muddled Army major Ray Milland, who much against his will has been posted to a boys' military academy. Rogers is later forced to continue with the masquerade at the school in order to substantiate Milland's cover story. His fiancée Rita Johnson had discovered him and the supposed girl child together in the same sleeping compartment.

Once at the academy, director-scripter Wilder's satirical penchant is more fully revealed. The young cadets there prove more wolfish to the "adolescent" Rogers than the adult variety had been in Manhattan. Johnson's precocious younger sister Diana immediately penetrates Rogers's ruse. Only because Diana cannot abide her fatuous sister ("she's a stinker"), does she willingly aid Rogers in her deception. Wilder clearly perceived that adolescents usually do less playacting than adults in the game of life, and therefore have the capacity to interact more naturally and to observe more astutely than their older counterparts.

Diana was fifth-billed in *The Major and the Minor* under her new screen name—Diana Lynn—and she carried off her potentially irritating assignment as a "wise kid" with polish and expert timing. *Variety* summed it up: "Miss Lynn has a wealth of screen personality and assurance that tabs her as a good future bet."

Just as MGM did with its "Andy Hardy" series, Paramount utilized its ongoing "Henry Aldrich" series as a testing ground for new contractees. Diana was added to the series as Phyllis Michael, the faithful sweetheart of high school perennial Henry Aldrich (Jimmy Lydon in *Henry Aldrich Gets Glamour* (1943). A good deal of this episode is localed in Hollywood because Henry wins the "Date with Hilary" contest and journeys to the cinema city to meet sarong star Hilary Dane (Frances Gifford). Such a change of scenery allowed for a sketchy look-see at Paramount's studio facilities and a gentle kidding of Paramount's own moneymaker, Dorothy Lamour. As a result of his Hollywood Trip, unsophisticated Henry is mistakenly hailed as a wolf and becomes the hearthrob of the school. Seductive coed Gail Russell appears on the scene and poor Diana must wait patiently until Henry comes to his senses. *Henry Aldrich Gets Glamour* opened as the companion piece to Warner Brothers' *Edge of Darkness* at the Brooklyn Fox on April 30, 1943. Russell, in her screen debut, was radiant if stilted, and at 19 years of age was already too mature for the adolescent nonsense of the Henry Aldrich mystique. She and Diana would appear in four films together, each depicting contrasting elements of wholesome, maturing womanhood, ideals precious to audiences of the time.

Along with "Henry Aldrich" series regulars Jimmy Lydon, John Litel, Olive Blakeney, Charles Smith, Diana and Martha O'Driscoll (the vagrant second-string leading lady of the 1940s), appeared in the short subject *The Aldrich Family Gets in the Scrap* (1943), dramatizing the importance of scrap metal in wartime.

Diana was utilized in four Paramount releases in 1944. In *The Miracle of Morgan's Creek* (1944), producer-director-scripter Preston Sturges typecast Diana as the know-it-all younger sister of rambunctious Betty Hutton. Their befuddled dad is small-town policeman William Demarest, more indignant Keystone Kop than anything else. One night, Hutton gets drunk, marries, and is impregnated, but she cannot remember who the lucky soldier was. It is prematurely wise Diana, a perceptive 14-year-old, who suggests that her volcanic older sister marry bumbling 4-F suitor Eddie Bracken. After much misadventure the couple eventually marry, only to learn that their wedding was illegal. But Hutton gives birth to sextuplets (all boys) and governor Brian Donlevy, proclaiming it a patriotic miracle, legalizes the marriage and labels Bracken a hero. Done in the Sturges style, the film has much physical slapstick slapped between the wry observations of 1940s Middle American culture.

Diana again collected outstanding notices in *The Miracle of Morgan's Creek* for her fully developed characterization of bratty but practical Emmy Kockenlocker, a superior gal with no use for stodgy American institutions and an ability to snap out crackling remarks on life. Archer Winsten (*New York Post*) lauded her as "simply wonderful," adding that "she is at once unique and the essence of all girls who have ever been fourteen and self-confident." Her performances herein and in the previous *The Major and the Minor,* both minor classics, contain her most memorable screen assignments, revealing her sharp talent in portraying the know-it-all girl-woman. She was almost 18 when she essayed the Emmy Kockenlocker part, but still made it ring true and not just a broad caricature.

And the Angels Sing (1944), joined Diana with Dorothy Lamour, Betty Hutton, and newcomer Mimi Chandler as the four singing Angel sisters. When Hutton is tricked into gifting the team's hard-earned cash to rascally band leader Fred MacMurray, the foursome troop after him to his Brooklyn Copacabana nightclub engagement. Like her small-town sisters, Diana is positive her creative forte lies in other areas, in her case musical composition. The girls are given no guidance by their ineffectual father Raymond Walburn, who only dreams of owning a farm. The sisters eventually realize that singing is their god-given gift and stick with it. Lamour—as the top-billed star—wins MacMurray's affection.

Diana held her own, against the dominating personality of Hutton and the glamour of Lamour. She seemed most at ease when playing the piano as part of the act, although her freewheeling scampering in the song-and-dance numbers was perfectly in accord with the other players. (That her voice was dubbed for the vocal spots was forgivable; unlike Hutton on the clarinet, Lamour on the guitar, and Chandler with the accordion, Diana could really tap the piano keyboard.) It was unfortunate that in long shots it was often difficult to distinguish Diana from Chandler. Since neither girl was afforded any depth of characterization by the screenplay, a little more physical individuality would have benefited both their performances. Most critics politely cited Diana for doing nicely with the "acid comedy" material handed her, but James Agee (*The Nation*) perceptively noted: "I am especially sorry to watch the exciting potentialities of Diana Lynn turning, more and more, into mere narcissistic chilly cuteness."

Interspersed with major productions, Paramount placed Diana in programmers such as *Henry Aldrich Plays Cupid* (1944) which did nothing to advance her screen career, since they merely gave her exposure in one-dimensional characterizations similar to those she had essayed before. In this film she was again Phyllis Michael, Henry's wide-eyed, frizzy-haired sweetheart. This time around, Henry must graduate with honors in order to obtain a legacy. To soften the heart of the principal, who, Henry is convinced, is responsible for his low grades, Henry acts as matchmaker and enrolls him in a matrimonial agency. Diana's acting chores were quite secondary, merely jumping in and out of the action as a pert Miss Fix-it. More showy was Vera Vague as one of the women attracted to the principal.

For her final 1944 release, Diana had a splashy role in *Our Hearts Were Young and Gay*, a well-conceived piece of nostalgia that received first-class production values. Diana had read the book by Cornelia Otis Skinner and Emily Kimbrough, and fell in love with the part of Emily. Gail Russell would write in a by-lined article in the *Saturday Evening Post* (May 27, 1950): "Diana Lynn practically pushed me into the role of Cornelia Otis Skinner . . . she decided that I must play Cornelia." (It proved to be Russell's favorite film.) Thus Diana and Russell got to portray the two upper-class flappers making their debut transatlantic crossing the S.S. *Dalmania* in 1923. Honest but naive, the duo make every conceivable *faux pas* in their efforts to be chic women of the world. Diana played the more practical and inventive of the two, as the giddy heroines find themselves in one madcap scrape after another, climaxed by their escapade atop Notre Dame Cathedral in Paris. James Brown and Bill Edwards were their two wholesome American beaux, with Charlie Ruggles and Dorothy Gish offering warm performances as Russell's indulgent but concerned parents. At the time, Diana and Russell were lauded for their infectious, winsome portrayals. Since the maddeningly dumb stunts the girls pulled were based largely on actual events, few complained that their antics were labored farce. Viewed today, the pacing is extremely leisurely and the clichéd comedy so filled with telegraphed punches that one has to stretch one's imagination to capture the film's elusive charm.

About her postadolescent years, Diana remembers: "It was like a convent [the studio], extremely difficult to strike a balance. I didn't date till I was sixteen. Nice boys were afraid of young movie stars." In these years, she decided against becoming a full-time pianist: "I gave up playing professionally because I couldn't be as good as I should be. It requires long hours of practice, tremendous physical strength. There are few good women concert pianists; they tend to sentimentalize the music as a substitute for power and precision. But someday I'll go back to the piano—when I'm too old to act."

Diana was given third billing in the mild musical *Out of this World* (1945), which focused on Western Union messenger Eddie Bracken who discovers he can become a sensational crooner (since he has a voice like Bing Crosby's—Crosby dubbed the singing). Diana was ambitious but sweet Betty Miller, the head of an all-girl orchestra who naively overcommercializes her singing discovery. Veronica Lake sauntered through the film as the nominal menace, and Cass Daley overenergized as the gymnastic drummer in Diana's band. It was a thankless part for Diana. "[She] tries her best to be convincing as well as comely" (*New York Herald Tribune*).

In Paramount's star-clustered *Duffy's Tavern* (1945), Diana joined Betty Hutton, Dorothy Lamour, Arturo De Cordova, and others in the satirical rendition of "Swinging on a Star." Shown to better advantage were Gail Russell, junior star Helen Walker, and promising ingenue Jean Heather, who accompanied Bing Crosby in another segment of the "Swinging on a Star" number. Diana was also among the Paramount stars in the studio's short subject *Hollywood Victory Caravan* (1945), detailing how the performers were providing talent shows to entertain the servicemen.

The *Motion Picture Herald* belatedly named Diana one of its stars of tomorrow for 1945. Other actresses selected that year were Jeanne Crain, Peggy Ann Garner, and Marilyn Maxwell.

Paramount could not resist making a sequel to *Our Hearts Were Young And Gay*—the follow-up was titled *Our Hearts Were Growing Up* (1946). Diana was again second-billed to Gail Russell. This film was a bit of hokum that suffered from being an entirely fictitious, more burlesque than sentimental, version of the Roaring Twenties. Carefree Diana and Russell are attending a big Princeton football weekend and end up with bootleggers Brian Donlevy and William Demarest as their most unwilling escorts. Even the added comedy relief of Billy DeWolfe and Mikhail Rasumny as hungry Greenwich Village artists did not aid the claptrap shenanigans. At the post-World War II box office, where more film reality was increasingly welcomed, this feature did not fare too well. The *New York Times* criticized the two feminine leads for their "super-saccharinity."

Diana's other 1946 release was the comedy dud *The Bride Wore Boots*. Barbara Stanwyck was the predatory, equestrian, Southern bride of historian Robert Cummings (her cold, determined look should have been enough to forewarn frivolous Cummings). Diana had now graduated to adult roles. In this film she was the gooey neighbor with bedroom eyes for Stanwyck's mate. Unfortunately, Diana proved more superfluous then seductive as a magnolia-scented vamp. The supporting cast of Peggy Wood, Robert Benchley, and Willie Best were commended by reviewers for their attempts to salvage this labored screwball comedy, which many critics were sure was "designed to discourage film-going."

Diana was loaned to David O. Selznick in the late summer of 1946 for the upcoming *Little Women* to be directed by Mervyn LeRoy. Diana was to be Amy, the role Joan Bennett had portrayed in the memorable 1933 RKO version. According to Selznick scholar Rudy Behlmer, the confirmed cast for the project included the following performers: Jennifer Jones (Jo), Diana (Amy), Bambi Linn (Beth), Rhonda Fleming (Meg), John Dall (Laurie, Anne Revere (Marmee), Charles Coburn (Laurie's Grandfather), Philip Friend (Brooke), Constance Collier (Aunt March), and Elizabeth Patterson (Hannah). Technicolor wardrobe and set tests were made through September, 1946, when Selznick finally decided to sell the property to MGM due to the postwar retrenchment within the industry. In the 1949 MGM release, Elizabeth Taylor inherited Diana's role.

In January, 1947, Diana made a national tour to plug Paramount's product and herself. It at least provided her with an opportunity to perform in front of a live audience. *Variety* caught her act at the Chicago Theatre, Chicago: "[She] has much more than the average Hollywood performer to offer on stage dates. Gal knows how to play piano and sticks to just that.

Starts out with 'Lover,' then swings into 'Clair de Lune' and ends with a Gershwin melody. She is simply dressed in a blue satin hoop gown and makes nifty appearance. Gets solid response."

Easy Come, Easy Go (1947) was a frivolous production-line comedy at best. Contract blarney star Barry Fitzgerald operates a cheap Third Avenue, New York, boarding house, but the old sot prefers the race track and the lure of the $2 bets. When returning Seabee Sonny Tufts asks to marry Fitzgerald's daughter (Diana), the old duffer fights against the plan because it will rob him of an efficient housekeeper and loving child. Besides, the house may be sold for unpaid taxes and he needs Diana's moral support and practical help. Rounding out the simulated Irish flavor were Frank McHugh, Allen Jenkins, John Litel, Arthur Shields, George Cleveland, and the famed 1940 film prototype Irish- or Scotsman, Rhys Williams, as the local priest.

In Paramount's *Variety Girl* (1947), Diana joined Dorothy Lamour, Barry Fitzgerald, and Gary Cooper in a barbershop-quartette-style chorus of the production number "Harmony."

For some time it had been apparent Diana was in a rut at Paramount. The studio had the services of Mona Freeman—the same age as Diana—who had succeeded her as the studio's brat-in-residence, proving her box-office worth in *Our Hearts Were Growing Up* and, especially, *Dear Ruth* (1947), in which she played the obnoxious younger sister. Diana had begged the front office for the lead in *Dear Ruth,* but lost out to more elegant Joan Caulfield. As Diana described it, it was time to look elsewhere. She had reached her plateau at Paramount, never earning the $5,000 a week salary commanded by top studio personalities. Diana remembers: "My awkward age didn't arrive 'til I was eighteen. By that time, however, everyone at Paramount regarded me as their kid sister. When I became eighteen, the boys up front still thought of me as that pink-cheeked youngster they'd known so long. They considered me too young for ingenue roles, too young for glamour roles and too young for romance.... From eighteen until well past nineteen, I didn't do anything. Everyone thought I was old hat—and it eventually got me scared. So I gave up some of my dates and decided to concentrate on business. I studied diction, voice, dancing and piano. Finally, I struck out as a free-lance actress."

In 1948 Diana appeared in Eagle Lion's low-budget melodrama *Ruthless,* which told, in flashback style, the chronicle of scoundrel financier Zachary Scott. Diana was presented in dual roles as the 1920s and the later 1940s girlfriends of Louis Hayward, who both times is weaned away by his alleged friend Scott. Running an overlong 104 minutes, this programmer did boast an intriguing cast: Sydney Greenstreet as an ousted magnate, Lucille Bremer as his unstable wife, and Martha Vickers as a woman with connections. *Variety* kindly appraised Diana as "wistful and appealing."

Texas, Brooklyn and Heaven (1948) from United Artists was unmitigated corn served in pedestrian wrappings. The shoddy plot presented clean-living Texan Guy Madison enamored of Brooklyn-based Diana, and she just loves horses. A few moments of comedy relief were provided by bartender James Dunn and pickpocket Florence Bates, but the end results were "flat and dull."

In RKO's *Every Girl Should Be Married* (1949), Diana was relegated to playing third fiddle to Cary Grant and newcomer Betsy Drake. She had a distinctly supporting role as the sidekick (the first of several such parts to come) of relentless Drake, who has set her heart on marrying pediatrician

Grant, and maps out a meticulous plan of attack. Franchot Tone went through the motions as Drake's department-store boss, utilized as a foil in the marriage-baiting proceedings. Diana injected breeziness to the degree in her relatively few scenes, but she was excess baggage to the plot.

When she was 21, Diana exerted some personal independence by purchasing her own home—albeit on property adjoining the one she had bought for her parents (Diana had banked much of her Paramount salary and the proceeds from such tie-in merchandising as dolls, using some cash to invest in real estate). On December 18, 1948, she married architect John C. Lindsay, age 30, at the Healy Chapel at the University of Southern California.

Hal B. Wallis* added a strange twist to Diana's Paramount tenure when he signed her to a three-picture contract in late 1948. Both parties must have agreed that Diana's established screen image was no longer marketable, but in only one of the trio of Wallis pictures in the next two years did Diana have an opportunity to play contra-type.

Diana was almost totally wasted as Marie Wilson's patient roommate in *My Friend Irma* (1949). Based on the popular radio series about two scatterbrained Manhattan secretaries, the ultra-clean slapstick comedy provided the screen debut for Dean Martin and Jerry Lewis, the latest additions to Wallis's stable of contract players. John Lund, unconvincing in a Damon Runyonesque role, was moronic Irma's boyfriend, who graciously lends her walk-up apartment to Martin and Lewis. Juice counterman Martin, who aspires to be a singer, develops a crush on Diana, and gold-digging Diana reciprocates, promptly forgetting about her well-heeled boss (Don DeFore). Sadly, Wilson as Irma received short shrift in this movie adaptation of the world's dumbest blonde. Everything in the picture happens around her, but little to her. She is spotted on occasions being very predictably stupid—for example, walking into an open manhole. *My Friend Irma* proved a substantial moneymaker; it launched Martin and Lewis as potential top stars and led producer Wallis away from drama to the more youth-oriented comedy-musical screen genre. In *My Friend Irma,* Diana was judged "able" (*Variety*) and filled with "well-affected flounce" (*New York Times*)—in short, a polite way of stating that she functioned well as a living mannequin. This was her only 1949 release.

Paid In Full (1950), a middle-class soap opera, demonstrated Diana's burgeoning dramatic abilities, which had yet to solidify into a consistent performance. The offbeat casting had her as the vixen younger sister of unusually noble Lizabeth Scott, with smiling Robert Cummings as the advertising executive both girls desire. Diana woos Cummings away from self-sacrificing Scott and marries him. Later they divorce, and she retains custody of their child, who is killed by Scott in a subsequent accident. Repentant Scott then weds Cummings and allows herself to become pregnant, knowing full well that a hereditary disease makes childbirth fatal to her. She is determined to "replace" the dead infant and does so. A. Weiler (*New York Times*) criticized that Diana's performance "contains more declamation than emotion." (But she did get to jangle off several bars of music at the keyboard, as, in the best Zachary Scott manner, she connives to manipulate Cummings' life.) The contrived scenario was largely to blame for the invalid performances of both actresses, and having Cummings as the leading man was no asset. Because this tearjerker broke no box-office records, both Diana

*See Appendix.

and Scott were returned to screen type, a sad creative mistake that damaged the potential of both actresses' future screen standing.

So Diana was unceremoniously shoved into *My Friend Irma Goes West* (1950), concocted to exploit the hot box-office draw of comedians Dean Martin and Jerry Lewis. This time around, there was no haggling about making Marie Wilson's dizzy Irma character a secondary figure in the sight-gag high jinks; the camera was firmly focused on Lewis's maneuvers as he capered about with Pierre the chimp, the pet of curvacious Corinne Calvet (another Wallis contractee). The story was pegged on the group heading west because it seems likely that Martin may have latched on to a movie contract. On the cross-country train trip, Calvet gives potential celebrity Martin a ferocious rush. Diana was just comely set dressing functionally used to narrate the trek to glittery Hollywood. It was her last feature at Paramount for four years.

In Columbia's modestly satisfying *Rogues of Sherwood Forest* (1950), Diana inherited the role of Lady Marianne that had proved so helpful to Olivia DeHavilland in *The Adventures of Robin Hood.* If John Derek was less than dynamic as the son of the forest outlaw, George Macready more than made up for it as the villainous Prince John.

Peggy (1950) was the first of three features Diana would make for Universal, cast into their mold of the comely ingenue á la Julie Adams and Peggy Dow. The film was built around the annual tournament of Roses in Pasadena and its Rose Queen contest. Diana and Barbara Lawrence, the daughters of retired professor Charles Coburn, both enter the pageant contest, with Diana being disqualified because she is secretly married to Ohio State football star Rock Hudson. Adding an aura of expertise to the technicolor tale were Charlotte Greenwood as the man-hunting neighbor of Coburn, Charles Drake as her clean-cut son fond of the two girls, Jerome Cowan as a no-nonsense contest judge, Ellen Corby as an ever-helpful librarian, and Connie Gilchrist as a dynamic nurse. The *New York Times* labeled Diana "elfin and natural," meaning that she blended nicely into this transparent mixture of prefabricated romance and stock footage of the Rose Bowl parade.

Having found such green pastures with its animal pictures, the "Francis the Talking Mule" film series and *Harvey* (the invisible rabbit), Universal branched out with *Bedtime for Bonzo* (1951). This film situated Ronald Reagan as a determined college psychology professor out to verify that environment and human conditioning, not heredity, mold a person's character. What better subject for the experiment could there be than a frisky baby chimpanzee? Diana was tossed into the comedy as a farmgirl hired as housekeeper to bachelor Reagan. She soon demonstrates that her homespun goodness is more alluring than the wily charms of his fiancée Lucille Barkley. Also supporting the chimp were Walter Slezak as a jovial but dubious professor and Jesse White as a harassed district attorney. Aimed at juvenile audiences, the script explored all possible ways of demonstrating that Bonzo was more human than a baby and allowed the jungle creature full rein with such runaway props as a bouncing vacuum cleaner. Diana was described as "earnest" in her undemanding assignment. The following year Universal released a sequel, *Bonzo Goes to College*—Diana and Reagan were missing from the lineup.

The People Against O'Hara (1951) brought Diana from the ridiculous to the sluggish. This middleweight MGM courtroom drama starred Spencer Tracy as a drunken ex-criminal attorney whose comeback case proves disastrous for his innocent client James Arness. Tracy thereafter stalks the real culprit on his own, finally nailing him at the expense of his own life. With Pat O'Brien as the homicide cop, John Hodiak as the district attorney, Eduardo Ciannelli as the racket boss, and William Campbell as a repulsive perjurer, Diana gave a straightforward performance as Tracy's long-suffering daughter. Once again Diana had the bad luck to be caught in an unimportant major picture that did not command the big sell MGM could still offer one of its prime products. Morever as a free-lance player of an unshowy nature, Diana did not warrant a large publicity boost from her producer employers. She had a middle-rung position in the Hollywood star-status system, and everyone seemed to be content to leave it as such.

Since the late 1940s, Diana had been preparing herself for more challenging acting assignments than Hollywood features could or would offer her. She studied stage techniques for six months with Sanford Meisner in Los Angeles, and then with Benno Schneider for three years. At the La Jolla Playhouse she appeared in *Dear Ruth, The Voice of the Turtle,* and *Ring Around the Moon.* Her better than competent acting notices still left Hollywood producers unconvinced of her burgeoning talent, and her change from the sweet brat of *The Major and the Minor.* On December 26, 1951, she made her New York stage debut in Ibsen's *The Wild Duck* at the City Center Theatre, costarred with such theatre veterans as Maurice Evans, Mildred Dunnock, and Kent Smith. George Freedley (*New York Morning Telegraph*) reported: "Only Diana Lynn escapes the general blight, possibly because even [director] Max Faber cannot smother the poetry inherent in Hedvig. In fact, she is extraordinarily satisfactory."

Diana had been accepting any strong dramatic assignment offered her on radio. She made her debut on the prestigious "Theatre Guild of the Air" (ABC) on December 11, 1949, in Elmer Rice's *Street Scene,* which costarred Shirley Booth, Karl Malden, and Richard Conte. Later she appeared in the same series' *Casanova Brown* (October 7, 1951) and *The Silver Whistle* (April 6, 1952) opposite James Stewart.

From 1950 onward, Diana energetically devoted herself to becoming a vital part of television, taking full advantage of the expanding medium's tremendous need for experienced, versatile actresses. In the early 1950s, Alan Young, Ken Murray, and Ed Wynn frequently had Diana as a guest on their programs. Along with Maria Riva and Mary Sinclair, she was soon much in demand and rose to star status in the new medium. (The pay scale was not up to Hollywood's—Riva and Sinclair at their peak earned approximately $20,000 per year—but the exposure and experience were desirable.) Diana was considered for the lead in the domestic comedy teleseries "My Favorite Husband" (1953), but once again she lost out to Joan Caulfield, also now free-lancing because Paramount had dropped her contract. Diana was among the actresses featured on the May 5, 1952, cover of *Life* magazine in its survey article on "TV's Leading Ladies."

In 1952 Diana was still adept enough at the piano to record two LP albums for Capitol Records; one strictly classical, the other devoted to more popular material. She was signed for a Las Vegas engagement which would have highlighted her keyboard virtuosity, but she backed out of the agreement out of fear of facing an audience in this capacity.

Diana's only 1952 film release had her in the innocuous technicolor musical *Meet Me at the Fair,* teaming her with song and dance man Dan Dailey. Set in 1904, it revolved around medicine man Dailey who takes a shine to orphan boy Chet Allen, which leads the plot to orphan reforms and the ouster of ward-heeling politicos. Diana was mildly effective as the prim settlement worker who jilts her crooked district attorney fiancé Hugh O'Brien when spieler Dailey starts courting and humanizing her. Assisting with the ten middling song numbers was black comic "Scat Man" Crothers, who played Dailey's sideshow helper. The movie was not splashy like Dailey's Twentieth Century-Fox vehicles with Betty Grable. Nor was it sincere enough to qualify in the same league with the impromptu infectiousness of Universal's Donald O'Connor-Peggy Ryan-Gloria Jean musicals of an earlier time.

Between her busy television guesting—and at that time most of the major shows were televised from New York—Diana replaced Dawn Addams in Andrew Rosenthal's play *Horses in Midstream,* which debuted on Broadway on April 2, 1953. It was a quiet sex comedy about novelist Cedric Hardwicke living on the isle of Elba with his common-law wife, Lili Darvas. Diana had the thankless role of his "pert and dimpled" granddaughter. The *New York Journal American* carped: "Her voice still stands in need of training and more theatrical experience." But this was a minority opinion. Most critics agreed with the *New York Times,* which wrote of her "delightful presence and radiant personality." The show lasted a meager four performances. Despite the artistic failure of *Horses in Midstream*, Diana told columnist Ward Moorhouse: "I'm glad, so glad that I did this play. I've been creeping up on Broadway for two years and nobody threw anything at me at the Royale. Maybe I can now start to call myself a New York actress."

Next Diana accepted the lead role of Patty O'Neill in the once-upon-a-time risqué comedy *The Moon Is Blue,* which commenced its West Coast tour at the La Jolla Playhouse in the spring of 1953. She remained with the show when it opened in London at the Duke of York Theatre (July 7, 1953), joined by Robert Lansing and Biff McGuire as her vis-à-vis. Diana received critical acclaim from the British press for her effervescent heroine who decides that a pick-up date whom she meets at the top of the Empire State Building might make a permanent bedmate. John Barber (*London Express*) extolled: "I invite you to go only for Diana Lynn; you will see young brains at work. You will come out just a bit in love." The *London Times* confirmed: "[The] play takes its life from Miss Lynn, whose display of innocence is so delightfully free from pertness or complacency."

Diana later told reporters: "I've learned more working in the theatre and I've now done my seventh play. Coming direct from pictures to the stage I had to learn it all the hard way. On the coast, *The Moon Is Blue* frightened me at first, but I played it for fifteen weeks and I was always finding out something new about it and the girl, I suppose you play into a part and only by playing it do you really know it. . . . I'm probably a girl who has to do everything the hard way."

Plunder of the Sun (1953) began Diana's professional association with producer Robert Fellows, head of the (John) Wayne-Fellows production unit at Warner Brothers. Set and filmed mostly in Mexico, it related the search for buried treasure near Oaxaco and the Zapoltecan ruins. Glenn Ford, as the passive American insurance adjuster, is sucked into this smuggling and murder caper revolving around stolen Aztec documents and doublecross blackmailing. Sean McClory played a cheerful villain, with Francis L. Sullivan as the obese heavy. Diana was cast extremely against type as the man-chasing lush who receives adult treatment from the harassed Ford. *Plunder of the Sun* utilized a flashback technique which effectively killed any potential suspense. *Cue* magazine, among others, found Diana ineffective: "And baby-faced Diana Lynn's attempts to play a femme fatale and a self-styled vamp are school girlish." The film opened to unimpressive results at the Paramount Theatre on August 26, 1953.

The following year, Diana costarred in the offbeat allegory *Track of the Cat*, directed by William A. Wellman. It dealt with eight people on a snow-bound cattle ranch in the northern California of the 1890s. There was Pa (Philip Tonge); Ma (Beulah Bondi), a Bible-loving, hypocritical martinet, son Curt (Robert Mitchum), a boastful, violent bully, son Arthur (William Hopper), quiet, sane, and middle-aged, son Harold (Tab Hunter), the youngest son and very unsure of himself, daughter Grace (Teresa Wright), a 40-year-old spinster, Joe Sam (Carl Switzer), an ancient Piute Indian, and Gwen (Diana), Hunter's visiting fiancée. In the course of the somber story, a huge mountain lion terrorizes the group, Hopper is killed by the beast, Mitchum falls to his death over a precipice, and weak Hunter is left to eventually kill the cat and become the ranch's head man. Although filmed in color and widescreen, Wellman used multihues very sparingly and only to heighten the symbolism: beside the blue sky, the green trees on Mt. Rainier, the red and black mackinaw worn by Mitchum, and Diana's yellow blouse (i.e., a ray of hope), everything was lensed in dreary tones of black and white. *Track of the Cat* was an interesting experiment, but too lachrymose as screen entertainment. It did nothing to boost Diana's stagnant screen career. At age 26, she needed a juicy role in a major production to revitalize her box-office appeal.

On June 5, 1954, Diana and John Lindsay were divorced. He claimed she was an emotional "idiot" and detrimental to his architectural career. She received only a $1,700 property settlement from him.

Diana appeared in the lead role of *Sabrina Fair* which opened its West Coast tour at the La Jolla Playhouse in mid-1954. Good as she was in the part Margaret Sullavan had originated on Broadway, Paramount cast its British import Audrey Hepburn in the film version.

Diana's last productive year in the cinema was 1955. *An Annapolis Story* emerged as a harmless patriotic look at the regimen of the Naval Academy. Trainee brothers John Derek and Kevin McCarthy both vie for charming Diana's affection. The elder, played by McCarthy, eventually gains her devotion after he is rescued by Derek when he is shot down in action over Korean waters. The color footage of Academy routine, action on an aircraft carrier, and combat duty at the Korean war front bolstered the standard triangular love tale. The *New York Times* correctly noticed: "Seldom have so many wholesome, scrubbed-looking young people thronged any picture." Since *An Annapolis Story* was released by minor-league Allied Artists, its lower-class playdate was less than conducive to changing the downward trend of Diana's film career.

In an odd bit of casting, Diana was featured in Paramount's slapdash remake of *The Major and the Minor,* which was converted into *You're Never Too Young,* a comedy vehicle for stars Dean Martin and Jerry Lewis. In the revamped plotting, Lewis had the Ginger Rogers role, masquerading as a little child, this time on the lam from pursuing jewel thief Raymond Burr. Diana inherited Ray Milland's part as a teacher at a fashionable girls' school who shelters the apparent adolescent Lewis. Martin was the fellow school instructor who hankers after Diana. The once subtle double entendres of *The Major and the Minor* became crudely blatant in this remake (e.g., Diana about to take a shower, and discovering Lewis hiding in the stall). Bosley Crowther (*New York Times*) branded Diana "pert, pedestrian and dull."

The Kentuckian (1955) was an unrobust Western suffering from Burt Lancaster in the dual capacity of star and director (his debut in this latter capacity). He showcased himself as an 1820s buckskin-clad Kentuckian who is sure that life on the wild Texas frontier will be less confining than it is in the already civilized Midwest. Diana had the subordinate assignment of a local schoolteacher who attempts to civilize him, but it is Diana Foster as the indentured servant Lancaster purchases (with the money he intended to get himself and son Donald MacDonald to Texas) who captures Lancaster's heart. Walter Matthau essayed a one-dimensional saloonkeeper villain, and John McIntire was the leading-citizen brother of uncivilized Lancaster. Diana seemed as ill at ease singing "Possum in the Gumtree" with Lancaster *et al.* as she did in her other few scenes of saccharine femininity.

Diana received some unexpected publicity during the filming of *The Kentuckian* in Owensboro, Kentucky. While she was signing autographs one day, an 18-year-old fan handcuffed himself to her. Lancaster's bit of color Americana proved to be Diana's last feature film for 14 years.

Television audiences continued to see a great deal of Diana in 1955. Contrasting with her starkly brave performance in *The Final Hours of Joan of Arc* (CBS) on "You Are There" was her valid characterization of Terry Randall on *Stage Door,* televised April 6, 1955, on CBS. This 60-minute live drama, adapted by Gore Vidal, was performed by Rhonda Fleming, Victor Moore, Peggy Ann Garner, Elsa Lanchester, Dennis Morgan, and others. J. P. Shanley (*New York Times*) observed: "Miss Lynn did not break the spell. She was convincing and admirable in her portrayal of the uncompromising Terry." Diana fared well with critics who recalled Margaret Sullavan's performance on Broadway and Katharine Hepburn's in the 1937 film version.

In 1956 Diana was a lively *Princess O'Rourke* on "Lux Video Theatre" (NBC), filled in on the "Loretta Young Show" (NBC, in the episode *Mount of Decision*), and was a frequent guest star on CBS's "Playhouse 90" in such dramas as Rod Serling's *Forbidden Area.*

On December 7, 1956, Diana, age 30, married Mortimer W. Hall, then president of Los Angeles radio station KLAC. His mother, Dorothy Schiff, was publisher of the *New York Post,* and in 1968, Mortimer and his family moved to New York, where he assumed an executive position on the newspaper. He and Diana would have a town house in Manhattan's East '80s and a weekend home on Oyster Bay, Long Island.

During 1957 the versatile Diana top-cast, among other video offerings, *A Sound of Different Drummers* on "Playhouse 90" (October 3, 1957). In this *Farenheit 451*-like drama by Robert Alan Aurthur, her co-star was Sterling Hayden. Jack Gould (*New York Times*), a hard critic to please, found that she "had extremely effective moments as the girl who believed in the reality of idealism." As a pleasant change of pace, Diana headed a cast (which included Don Ameche, Joan Bennett, Carol Lynley, and David Wayne) in a musical version of the stage comedy *Junior Miss* (December 20, 1957, CBS). Diana and Wayne dueted the Dorothy Fields-Burton Crane tune "I'll Buy It."

On July 6, 1958, Diana gave birth to her first child, Matthew.

A penetrating *TV Guide* profile of Diana, "TV's Timid Wildcat," in the August 22, 1959 issue, quoted an anonymous close friend as saying: "Diana is complex. People meeting her for the first time often do not want to try to crack that shell of hers again. But thrown in with her, you come to love her. She's human and fun. She calls her husband 'chum.' She bums rides on the back of Steve McQueen's motorcycle. And at work she buckles down like a man. She's a real old-fashioned honest-to-goodness, blood-sweating work-horse of a performer." A director associate was reported as stating: "In character, Diana either can't scream above a whisper or is murmuring 'I love you' at the top of her lungs."

By now Diana was quite perspicacious about herself: "I was a scared kid in this business. I had no training. All I had was a kind of desperate honest quality." About her present professional life: "I am forever shifting from one point of view to the other. The one point of view is that you have to keep working no matter what happens—it's good for your muscles. And the other is that I've got a very good life for myself here just being Mrs. Mortimer W. Hall."

Diana continued with her myriad of video assignments, including *A Marriage of Strangers* ("Playhouse 90," May 14, 1959), which teamed her with Red Buttons and Joan Blondell in a somber tale of unhappy homelife. Perhaps Diana's best remembered television performance was in *The Philadelphia Story* (December 7, 1959, NBC). As Tracy Lord, the spoiled heiress, she recreated Katharine Hepburn's stage and film role. The 90-minute adaptation of Philip Barry's comedy boasted a versatile cast, including Christopher Plummer, Gig Young, Ruth Roman, Mary Astor, and Don DeFore. *Variety* was more academic than reflective of public opinion when it reported: "It was a tough assignment for Miss Lynn. She was too letter perfect and was certainly obedient to all the prescribed rules. But that indefinable touch that particularly today is so necessary to hoist a *Philadelphia Story* from its outdated style and shallow profundities, just wasn't there."

On April 26, 1960, Diana gave birth to daughter Dorothy, and on July 2, 1962 to another daughter, Mary.

She returned to Broadway on January 21, 1963, to replace Inger Stevens (who had replaced Barbara Bel Geddes) in the long-lasting comedy *Mary, Mary*. As a celebrity in residence, Diana was often quoted by the New York press during this period. She told one journalist: "My public image was 'the kind of girl you bring home to mother.' . . . I'd be a dreadful bore if there were no sign of inner maturity."

Re motherhood versus a stage career: "I see no barrier between family and career. I had my children in the past five years and think I can achieve the proper separation. I don't burden my husband with every detail of stagecraft. I try to be instinctive about raising my children; I try to hear what they are not saying. It's working out. They're nice; they're happy; they've got manners."

On her future: "I'm no longer ruled by the ambition to be a movie star or get my picture in *Photoplay*. I've had those things. What I want to develop now is the use of myself; the use of my head, my limbs, my powers. Being an actress is like being an athlete; it requires enormous amounts of energy. You can't be half there. You never know whether you'll pass this way again. Besides, anybody who finds a job he loves is lucky."

On self-importance: "If I'm with my husband at a party and someone calls me Miss Lynn, I feel downright immoral. People who call me Miss Lynn run the risk of having their heads handed to them."

After leaving *Mary, Mary* in June, 1963 (she was replaced by Patricia

Smith), Diana returned to the West Coast where she studied acting with Curt Conway and appeared on television dramas, although with less frequency. On August 6, 1964, she gave birth to her fourth child, a daughter. Although less active in the entertainment world, she became increasingly prominent on the social scene. Among her many Hollywood-based friends was playwright Mart Crowley, who wrote much of the play *The Boys in the Band,* working in the seclusion of Diana's library.

For Universal studios Diana appeared in a crime story telefeature *The Protectors* in early 1969, filmed entirely on location in Denver, Colorado. Originally supposed to premier on television, the feature was theatrically released the next year under a new title *Company of Killers.* Diana had fourth billing (beneath Van Johnson, Ray Milland, and Susan Oliver) as the wife of business executive Milland. He refers to her indolent nature: "She thinks a new fur coat and a trip to Europe will keep her young and keep me." Obviously, it did not, because devious Milland is having an affair with his secretary, and hires a paid killer (John Saxon) from Fritz Weaver's Murder, Inc. to eliminate a business competitor (Robert Middleton). Diana had only three brief scenes, mostly seen in reaction shots to the dialogue spoken by Milland. The color cameras were most unflattering to her, revealing that her facial features had thickened and her grayish blonde hair only accentuated her middle-aged status. *Company of Killers* played the bottom half of double bills in the few market areas where it was released.

In March, 1970, Diana showed up in the news in quite a diverse field from acting. She was announced as the director of GO (Travel) Agency, headquartered at Bonwit Teller's Department Store in Manhattan. The now shrewd businesswoman announced to the press: "I'm no dilettante and I'm not playing games. I intend to give the business the attention necessary to make it work. . . . When it comes to catering to the specific needs of a client, I think I qualify. . . . I can gauge the type of client who would climb the walls in a Hilton hotel as opposed to one who would love it."

Like fellow-actress Betsy Palmer, who became the public relations agent for Manhattan's old guard Hotel Plaza, Diana carried her methodical habits into the business world, extending her talents in other directions. Dissatisfied with being known merely as a former leading ingenue of motion pictures, radio, television, and the stage, and as a onetime child prodigy pianist, she had become a successful business woman.

Then, on December 18, 1971, Diana died at Mount Sinai Hospital, nine days after suffering a stroke. The public, which still remembered her as the screen ingenue of the early 1940s, was more amazed to learn that she had reached the age of 45, than by the realization that she was dead.

Ironically, Diana was planning a return to the world of theatrical films after an absence of 16 years. She was to have a leading role in the forthcoming picturization of Joan Didion's best selling novel *Play It As It Lays.* She was replaced by Tammy Grimes.

Diana was survived by her husband Mortimer Hall, now treasurer of the *New York Post,* and their four children. A memorial service was held December 20, 1971, at the All Saints Episcopal Church in Beverly Hills, with the funeral service taking place two days later at the Episcopal Church of the Heavenly Rest, also in Beverly Hills.

A strange bit of cinema history, that both Diana and Gail Russell should be outlived by the much older Emily Kimbrough and Cornelia Otis Skinner, whom they played so successfully in both *Our Hearts Were Young and Gay* and *Our Hearts Were Growing Up.*

As: *Dolly Loehr*

THEY SHALL HAVE MUSIC (UA, 1939) 105 M.

Producer, Samuel Goldwyn; director, Archie Mayo; story, Irmgard Von Cube; screenplay, John Howard Lawson; music director, Alfred Newman; camera, Gregg Toland; editor, Sherman Todd.

Jascha Heifetz (Himself); Andrea Leeds (Ann Lawson); Joel McCrea (Peter); Gene Reynolds (Frankie); Walter Brennan (Professor Lawson); Porter Hall (Flower); Terry Kilburn (Limey); Walter Tetley (Rocks); Chuck Stubbs (Fever); Tommy Kelly (Willie); Jacqueline Nash (Betty); Alfred Newman (Musical Director); Mary Ruth (Lizzie); John St. Polis (Davis); Alexander Schonberg (Menken); Marjorie Main (Mrs. Miller); Arthur Hohl (Mr. Miller); Paul Harvey (Hotel Manager); Dolly Loehr (Pianist); Peter Meremblum California Junior Symphony Orchestra.

THERE'S MAGIC IN MUSIC (PAR, 1941) 80 M.

Producer-director, Andrew L. Stone; screenplay, Stone, Robert Lively; art director, Hans Dreier, Earl Hedrick; music supervision, Phil Boutelje; camera, Theodor Sparkuhl; editor, James Smith.

Allan Jones (Michael Maddy); Susanna Foster (Toodles LaVerne); Margaret Lindsay (Sylvia Worth); Lynne Overman (George Thomas); Grace Bradley (Madie Duvalie); William Collier, Sr. (Dr. Joseph E. Maddy); Heimo Haitto, William Chapman, Dolly Loehr, Ira Petina, Richard Bonelli, Richard Hageman, Tandy MacKenzie, Baby Mary Ruth (Themselves); Fay Helm (Miss Wilson); Esther Dale (Miss Clark); Fred Hoose (Mr. Stevens); Ottola Nesmith (Mrs. Stevens); Bertram Marburgh (Mr. Myers); Ruth Robinson (Mrs. Myers); Hobart Cavanaugh (Announcer); Ruth Rogers (Receptionist); Bert Roach (Cop); Charles Bimbo (Bum); Emmett Vogan (Stokes); Russ Coller (Elevator Boy); Astrid Allwyn, Rosella Towne, Jean Porter, Elena Verdugo, Adele Horner (Girls).

As: *Diana Lynn*

THE MAJOR AND THE MINOR (PAR, 1942) 100 M.

Producer, Arthur Hornblow, Jr.; director, Billy Wilder; suggested by the play "Connie Goes Home" by Edward Childs Carpenter, and the story "Sunny Goes Home" by Fannie Kilbourne; screenplay, Charles Brackett, Wilder; art directors, Hans Dreier, Roland Anderson; music, Robert Emmett Dolan; assistant director, C. C. Coleman, Jr.; camera, Leo Tover; editor, Doane Harrison.

Ginger Rogers (Susan Applegate); Ray Milland (Major Kirby); Rita Johnson (Pamela Hill); Robert Benchley (Mr. Osborne); Diana Lynn (Lucy Hill); Edward Fielding (Colonel Hill); Frankie Thomas, Jr. (Cadet Osborne); Raymond Roe (Cadet Wigton); Charles Smith (Cadet Korner); Larry Nunn (Cadet Babcock); Billy Dawson (Cadet Miller); Lola Rogers (Mrs. Applegate); Aldrich Bowker (Reverend Doyle); Boyd Irwin (Major Griscom); Byron Shores (Captain Durand); Richard Fiske (Will Duffy); Norma Varden (Mrs. Osborne); Gretl Sherk (Mrs. Shackleford); Stanley Desmond (Shumaker); Dell Henderson (Doorman); Ed Peil, Sr. (Station Master); Ken Lundy (Elevator Boy); Marie Blake (Bertha); Billy Ray (Cadet Summerville); Will Wright, William Newell (Ticket Agents); Tom Dugan (Dead Beat); Tom McGuire (News Vendor); George Anderson (Man With Esquire); Stanley Andrews, Emory Parnell (Conductors); Guy Wilkerson (Farmer—Truck Driver); Milt Kibbee (Station Agent); Archie Twitchell (Sergeant); Alice Keating (Nurse); Ralph Gilliam, Dick Chandlee, Buster Nichols, Kenneth Grant, Bradley Hail, Bill O'Kelly (Cadets).

HENRY ALDRICH GETS GLAMOUR (PAR, 1943) 72 M.

Producer, Walter MacEwen; associate producer, Jules Schermer; director, Hugh Bennett; story, Aleen Leslie; screenplay, Edwin Blum, Leslie; art director, Hans Dreier, Earl Hedrick; music, Robert Emmett Dolan; camera, Daniel Fapp; editor, Arthur Schmidt.

Jimmy Lydon (Henry Aldrich); Charles Smith (Dizzy Stevens); John Litel (Mr. Aldrich); Olive Blakeney (Mrs. Aldrich); Diana Lynn (Phyllis Michael); Frances Gifford (Hilary Dane); Gail Russell (Virginia Lowry); Vaughan Glaser (Mr. Bradley); Anne Rooney (Evelyn); William Blees (Irwin Barrett); Janet Beecher (Mrs. Lowry); Bill Goodwin (Steve); Betty Farrington (Miss Goodhue); Lucien Littlefield (Mr. Quid); Harry Hayden (Mr. Jennifer); Walter Fenner (Mr. Vance); Harry Bradley (Mr. Japes); Ann O'Neal (Mrs. Ikeley); Joe Brown, Jr. (George); Shirley Mills (Hortense); Patti Brilhante (Ida); Marilynn Harris (Gwendolyn); Johnny Arthur (Hotchkiss); Isabel Randolph (Mrs. Stacey); Billy Wayne (Albert—Waiter); Arthur Loft (Jackson); Dick Elliott (McCluskey); Nell Craig (Teddy's Mother); Dick Chandlee, Dick Baron (Droops); Buddy Messinger (Soda Clerk); Walter "Spec" O'Donnell (Bell Boy); Keith Richards (Assistant Director); Syd Saylor (Bus Driver); Oscar Smith (Boot Black); Beverly Pratt (Girl).

THE MIRACLE OF MORGAN'S CREEK (PAR, 1944) 99 M.

Director-screenplay, Preston Sturges; art director, Hans Dreier, Ernst Fegte; music, Leo Shuken; Charles Bradshaw; camera, John Seitz; editor, Stuart Gilmore.

Eddie Bracken (Norval Jones); Betty Hutton (Trudy Kockenlocker); Diana Lynn (Emmy Kockenlocker); William Demarest (Officer Kockenlocker); Porter Hall (Justice of the Peace); Emory Parnell (Mr. Tuerck); Alan Bridge (Mr. Johnson); Julius Tannen (Mr. Rafferty); Victor Potel (Newspaper Editor); Brian Donlevy (McGinty); Akim Tamiroff (The Boss); Almira Sessions (Wife of Justice of Peace); Esther Howard (Sally); J. Farrell Macdonald (Sheriff); Frank Moran (First M.P.); Georgia Caine (Mrs. Johnson); Connie Tompkins (Cecilia); Torben Meyer (Doctor); George Melford (U.S. Marshal); Jimmy Conlin (The Mayor); Harry Rosenthal (Mr. Schwartz); Chester Conklin (Pete); Hal Craig, Roger Creed (State Police); Keith Richards, Kenneth Gibson (Secret Service Men); Byron Foulger, Arthur Loft (McGinty's Secretaries); Jack Norton (Man Opening Champagne); Joe Devlin (Mussolini); Bobby Watson (Hitler).

AND THE ANGELS SING (PAR, 1944) 96 M.

Associate producer, E. D. Leshin; director, Claude Binyon; screenplay, Melvin Frank, Norman Panama; art director, Hans Dreier, Hal Pereira; music director, Victor Young; choreography, Danny Dare; songs, Johnny Burke and Jimmy Van Heusen; camera, Karl Struss; editor, Eda Warren.

Dorothy Lamour (Nancy Angel); Fred MacMurray (Happy Morgan); Betty Hutton (Bobby Angel); Diana Lynn (Josie Angel); Mimi Chandler (Patti Angel); Raymond Walburn (Pop Angel); Eddie Foy, Jr. (Fuzzy Johnson); Frank Albertson (Oliver); Mikhail Rasumny (Schultz); Frank Faylen (Holman); George McKay (House Man); Harry Barris (Saxy); Donald Kerr (Mickey); Perc Launders (Miller); Tom Kennedy (Potatoes); Erville Alderson (Mr. Littlefield); Edgar Dearing (Man); Tim Ryan (Stage Door Man); Jimmy Conlin (Messenger); Leon Belasco (Waiter at "Polonaise Cafe"); Douglas Fowley (N.Y. Cafe Manager); Siegfried Arno (Mr. Green); William Davidson (Theatrical Agent); Otto Reichow (Polish Groom); Hillary Brooke (Polish Bride); Julie Gibson (Cigarette Girl); Arthur Loft (Stage Manager); Matt McHugh (Doorman at "33 Club"); Libby Taylor (Attendant in Powder Room); Drake Thorton (Page Boy); Buster Phelps (Spud); Jack Norton (Drunk); Buddy Gorman (Messenger); Roland Dupree (Boy); Louise La Planche (Ticket Taker).

HENRY ALDRICH PLAYS CUPID (PAR, 1944) 65 M.

Associate producer, Michael Kraike; director, Hugh Bennett; story, Aleen Leslie; screenplay, Muriel Roy Bolton, Val Burton; music director, Irvin Talbot; art director, Hans Dreier, Franz Bachelin; camera, Daniel Fapp; editor, Everett Douglas.

Jimmy Lydon (Henry Aldrich); Diana Lynn (Phyllis Michael); Charles Smith (Dizzy); John Litel (Mr. Aldrich); Olive Blakeney (Mrs. Aldrich); Vaughan Glaser (Mr. Bradley); Paul Harvey (Senator Caldicott); Vera Vague (Blue Eyes); Arthur Loft (Clancy); Walter Fenner (Stewart); Barbara Pepper (Wild Rose); Richard Elliott (Matthews); Harry Hayden (Anderson); Mikhail Rasumny (Konrad); Luis Alberni (Tony); Sarah Edwards (Mrs. Bradley); Harry Bradley, Gladden James, Betty Farrington (Teachers); Shirley Coates (Western Union Girl); Maude Eburne (Homely Woman); Ronnie Rondell (Reporter); Oscar Smith (Porter); George Anderson (Mr. Benton); Nell Craig (Miss Lewis); Sue Moore (Mrs. Olson); Armand "Curley" Wright (Guiseppe); Bobby Barber (Waiter); Mary Field (Anxious); Ferris Taylor (Mayor).

OUR HEARTS WERE YOUNG AND GAY (PAR, 1944) 81 M.

Associate producer, Sheridan Gibney; director, Lewis Allen; based on the book by Cornelia Otis Skinner, Emily Kimbrough; screenplay, Gibney; art director, Hans Dreier, Earl Hedrick; music, Werner Heymann; song, Kermit Goell and Ted Grouya; special effects, Gordon Jennings; process camera, Farciot Edouart; camera, Theodor Sparkuhl; editor, Paul Weatherwax.

Gail Russell (Cornelia Otis Skinner); Diana Lynn (Emily Kimbrough); Charlie Ruggles (Mr. Otis Skinner); Dorothy Gish (Mrs. Skinner); Beulah Bondi (Miss Abigail Horn); James Brown (Avery Moore); Bill Edwards (Tom Newhall); Jean Heather (Frances Smithers [Smitty]); Alma Kruger (Mrs. Lamberton); Helen Freeman (Mrs. Smithers); Joy Harington, Valentine Perkins (English Girls); Georges Renavent (Monsieur Darnet); Roland Varno (Pierre Cambouille); Holmes Herbert (Captain); Reginald Sheffield (Purser); Edmond Breon (Cockney Guide); Nina Koshetz (Herself); Noel Neill, Maxine Fife, Carmelle Bergstrom (Girls); Will Stanton (Cockney Room Steward); Olaf Hytten (Deck Steward); Roland Dupree (Boy at Dance); Nell Craig (Mother of Little Girl); Maurice Marsac (Headwaiter); Ronnie Rondell (Waiter); Will Thunis, Alphonse Martell (Guards); Ottola Nesmith (Fur Shop Owner); Evan Thomas (Bus Driver); Eugene Borden (Coachman); Marie McDonald (Blonde); Queenie Leonard (Maid); Frank Elliott (Doctor); Betty Farrington (Woman).

OUT OF THIS WORLD (PAR, 1945) 96 M.

Associate producer, Sam Coslow; director, Hal Walker; story, Elizabeth Meehan, Coslow; screenplay, Walter DeLeon; Arthur Phillips; art director, Hans Dreier, Haldane Douglas; music director, Victor Young; choreography, Sammy Lee; songs, Johnny Mercer and Harold Arlen; Eddie Cherkose, Felix Bernard and Coslow; Coslow; Ben Raleigh and Bernie Wayne; camera, Stuart Thompson; editor, Stuart Gilmore.

Eddie Bracken (Herbie Fenton); Veronica Lake (Dorothy Dodge); Diana Lynn (Betty Miller); Cass Daley (Fanny, The Drummer); Parkyakarkus (Gus Palukas); Donald MacBride (J. C. Crawford); Florence Bates (Harriet Pringle); Gary Crosby, Phillip Crosby, Dennis Crosby, Lindsay Crosby (Children in Audience); Olga San Juan, Nancy Porter, Audrey Young, Carol Deere (Glamourette Quartette); Carmen Cavallaro, Ted Fiorito, Henry King, Ray Noble, Joe Reichman (Themselves); Don Wilson (Radio Announcer/M.C.); Mabel Paige (Mrs. Robbins); Charles Smith (Charlie Briggs); Irving Bacon (Irving Krunk); Toni LaRue (Marimba Player); Mary Elliott (Arlen—Trumpet Player); Carmelle Bergstrom (Margy—Trombone Player); Betty Walker (Guitar Player); Virginia Morris, June Harris (Trumpet Players); Laura Gruver, Marguerite Campbell (Violin Players); Inez Palange (Mrs. Palukas); Esther Dale (Abbie Pringle); Charles B. William (Joe Welch); Gloria Saunders (Vicky Kelly); Lorraine Krueger (Maizie); Milton Kibbee (Bald-Headed Man); Davison Clark (Pullman Conductor); Nell Craig (Woman); Virginia Sale (Spinster); Charles R. Moore (Porter); Norman Nesbitt (Announcer); Jamiel Hasson (Arabian Chief—Announcer); Michael Visaroff (Russian Announcer); Jimmie Lono (Eskimo Announcer); Sammee Tong (Chinese Announcer); Lal Chand Mehra (Hindu Announcer); Leon Belasco (Himself); Selmer Jackson (Doctor); The Voice of Bing Crosby.

DUFFY'S TAVERN (PAR, 1945) 97 M.

Associate producer, Danny Dare; director, Hal Walker; screenplay, Melvin Frank, Norman Panama; art director, Hans Dreier, William Flannery; choreography; Billy Daniels; music director, Robert Emmett Dolan; songs, Johnny Burke and James Van Heusen; Ben Raleigh and Bernie Wayne; camera, Lionel Lindon; special effects, Gordon Jennings; process camera, Farciot Edouart; editor, Arthur Schmidt.

Bing Crosby, Betty Hutton, Paulette Goddard, Alan Ladd, Dorothy Lamour, Eddie Bracken, Brian Donlevy, Sonny Tufts, Veronica Lake, Arturo De Cordova, Cass Daley, Diana Lynn, Gary Grosby, Phillip Crosby, Dennis Crosby, Lin Crosby, William Bendix, Maurice Rocco, James Brown, Joan Caulfield, Gail Russell, Helen Walker, Jean Heather (Themselves); Barry Fitzgerald (Bing Crosby's Father); Victor Moore (Michael O'Malley); Marjorie Reynolds (Peggy O'Malley); Ed Gardner (Archie); Barry Sullivan (Danny Murphy); Charles Cantor (Finnegan); Eddie Green (Eddie—The Waiter); Ann Thomas (Miss Duffy); Howard Da Silva (Heavy); Billy De Wolfe (Doctor); Walter Abel (Director); Charles Quigley (Ronald); Olga San Juan (Gloria); Robert Watson (Masseur); Frank Faylen (Customer); Matt McHugh (Man Following Miss Duffy); Emmett Vogan (Make-Up Man); Cyril Ring (Gaffer); Noel Neill (School Kid).

OUR HEARTS WERE GROWING UP (PAR, 1946) 83 M.

Producer, Daniel Dare; director, William D. Russell; story, Frank Waldman; screenplay, Norman Panama, Melvin Frank; music, Victor Young; art director Hans Dreier, Haldane Douglas; process camera, Farciot Edouart; camera, Stuart Thompson; editor, Doane Harrison.

Gail Russell (Cornelia Otis Skinner); Diana Lynn (Emily Kimbrough); Brian Donlevy (Tony Minnetti); James Brown (Avery Moore); Bill Edwards (Dr. Tom Newhall); William Demarest (Peanuts Schultz); Billy De Wolfe (Roland Du Frere); Sharon Douglas (Suzanne Carter); Mary Hatcher ("Dibs" Downing); Sara Haden (Miss Dill); Mikhail Rasumny (Bubchanko); Isabel Randolph (Mrs. Southworth); Frank Faylen (Federal Agent); Virginia Farmer (Miss Thatcher); Ann Doran (Monica Lonsdale); Douglas Walton (Terence Marlowe); Charles Williams, Matt McHugh (Taxi Driver); Nell Craig (Teacher); Garry Owen (Bellboy); Byron Barr (Roger); Eddie Carnegie (Clerk In Newstand); Roland Dupree, Charles Saggau (Freshmen); John Indrisano (Maxie); Cy Ring (Hotel Desk Clerk); Mona Freeman (Girl); Gladys Gale (Mrs. Appley); Al Hill (Louie); Guy Zanette (Barney); Sam Finn, Benny Burt, Theodore Rand, Sam Bazley (Gangsters); Arthur Loft (Desk Sergeant); James Millican (Stage Manager); Pierre Watkin (Producer); John "Skins" Miller (Cab Driver); Carol Deere, Maggie Mahoney, Ada Ruth Butcher, Gwen Martin, Dorothy Jean Reisner, Mary Kay Jones, Patricia Murphy (Lowell Schoolgirls).

THE BRIDE WORE BOOTS (PAR, 1946) 85 M.

Producer, Seton I. Miller; director, Irving Pichel; based on a play by Harry Segall and a story by Dwight Mitchell Wiley; screenplay, Wiley; art director, Hans Dreier, John Meehan; music Frederick Hollander; special effects, Gordon Jennings; camera, Stuart Thompson; editor, Ellsworth Hoagland.

Barbara Stanwyck (Sally Warren); Robert Cummings (Jeff Warren); Diana Lynn (Mary Lou Medford); Patric Knowles (Lance Gale); Peggy Wood (Grace Apley); Robert Benchley (Tod Warren); Willie Best (Joe); Natalie Wood (Carol Warren); Gregory Muradian (Johnnie Warren); Mary Young (Janet Doughton); Frank Orth (Judge); Charles D. Brown (Wells); Richard Gaines (Jeff's Attorney); Myrtle D. Anderson (Florence); Alice Keating, Eula Guy, Gertrude Hoffman, Janet Clark, Ida Moore (Club Women); Steve Darrell (Spectator); James Millican (Kerwin Haynes); George Anderson, Forbes Murray, George Melford (Judges); Mae Busch (Woman); Harry Hayden (Clergman); Walter Baldwin (Postman); Milton Kibbee (Hotel Manager); Catherine Craig (Mrs. Medford); Minerva Urecal (Lady).

EASY COME, EASY GO (PAR, 1947) 77 M.

Producer, Kenneth Macgowan; director, John Farrow; based on the "Third Avenue Stories" by John McNulty; screenplay, Francis Edward Faragah, McNulty; Anne Froelick; art director, Hans Dreier, Haldane Douglas; music, Roy Webb; song, Ray Evans and Jay Livingston; special effects, Farciot Edouart; camera, Daniel L. Fapp; editor, Thomas Scott.

Barry Fitzgerald (Martin L. Donovan); Diana Lynn (Connie Donovan); Sonny Tufts (Kevin O'Connor); Dick Foran (Dale Whipple); Frank McHugh (Carey); Allen Jenkins (Nick); John Litel (Tom Clancy); Arthur Shields (Mike Donovan); Frank Faylen (Boss); James Burke (Harry Weston); George Cleveland (Gilligan); Ida Moore (Angela Orange); Rhys Williams (Priest); Oscar Rudolph (Bookie); Lou Lubin (Tailor); Olin Howlin (Gas Man); Tom Fadden (Sanitation Man); Howard Freeman (Magistrate); Hobart Cavanaugh (Auto Repair Shop Mgr.); Byron Foulger (Sports Good Shop Owner); Rex Lease (Gambler); Chester Clute (Waiter); Crane Whitley (Prosecutor); Matt McHugh (Worker); Perc Launders (Bartender); Charles Sullivan (Cabbie); Stanley Price, Pat McVey (Gamblers); Stanley Andrews (Detective); James Flavin (Plainclothes Man); Polly Bailey (Housewife); Harry Hayden (Bank Teller); James Davies, James Cornell (Neighborhood Men).

VARIETY GIRL (PAR, 1947) 83 M.

Producer, Daniel Dare; director, George Marshall; screenplay, Edmund Hartman, Frank Tashlin; Robert Welch, Monte Brice; music, Joseph J. Lilley; songs, Johnny Burke and James Van Heusen; Frank Loesser; Allan Roberts and Doris Fisher; choreography, Billy Daniels, Bernard Pearce; assistant director, George Templeton; art director, Hans Dreier, Robert Clatworthy; special Puppetoon sequence, Thornton Hoe, William Cottrell; special effects, Gordon Jennings; camera, Lionel Lindon, Stuart Thompson; editor, LeRoy Stone.

Mary Hatcher (Catherine Brown); Olga San Juan (Amber LaVonne); DeForest Kelley (Bob Kirby); William Demarest (Barker); Frank Faylen (Stage Manager); Frank Ferguson (J. R. O'Connell); Russell Hicks, Crane Whitley, Charles Coleman, Hal K. Dawson, Eddie Fetherston (Men at Steambath); Catherine Craig (Secretary); Bing Crosby, Bob Hope, Gary Cooper, Ray Milland, Alan Ladd, Barbara Stanwyck, Paulette Goddard, Dorothy Lamour, Veronica Lake, Sonny Tufts, Joan Caulfield, William Holden, Lizabeth Scott, Burt Lancaster, Gail Russell, Diana Lynn, Sterling Hayden, Robert Preston, John Lund, William Bendix, Barry Fitzgerald, Cass Daley, Howard Da Silva, Billy DeWolfe, Macdonald Carey, Arleen Whelan, Patric Knowles, Mona Freeman, Cecil Kellaway, Johnny Coy, Virginia Field, Richard Webb, Stanley Clements, Cecil B. DeMille, Mitchell Leisen, Frank Butler, George Marshall, Roger Dann, Pearl Bailey, The Mulcays, Spike Jones and his City Slickers, George Reeves, Wanda Hendrix, Sally Rawlinson (Themselves); Ann Doran (Hairdresser); Jack Norton (Brown Derby Busboy); Eric Alden (Make-Up Man); Frank Mayo (Director).

RUTHLESS (Eagle Lion, 1948) 104 M.

Producer, Arthur S. Lyons; director, Edgar G. Ulmer; based on the novel *Prelude to Night* by Dayton Stoddert; screenplay, S. K. Lauren, Gordon Kahn; music, Werner Janssen; camera, Bert Glennon; editor, Francis D. Lyon.

Zachary Scott (Horace Vendig); Louis Hayward (Vic Lambdin); Diana Lynn (Martha Burnside/Mallory Flagg); Martha Vickers (Susan Dunne); Sydney Greenstreet (Buck Mansfield); Lucille Bremer (Christa Mansfield); Edith Barrett (Mrs. Burnside); Dennis Hoey (Mr. Burnside); Raymond Burr (Pete Vendig); Joyce Arling (Kate Vendig); Charles Evans (Bruce McDonald); Bob Anderson (Horace—As A Child); Arthur Stone (Vic—As A Child); Anne Carter (Martha—As A Child); Edna Holland (Libby Sims); Fred Worlock (J. Norton Sims); John Good (Bradford Duane); Claire Carleton (Bella).

TEXAS, BROOKLYN AND HEAVEN (UA, 1948) 76 M.

Producer, Robert S. Golden; associate producer, Lewis J. Rachmil; director, William Castle; story, Barry Benefield; screenplay, Lewis Meltzer; art director, Jerome Pycha, Jr.; music director, Emil Newman; camera, William Mellor; editor, James Newcom.

Guy Madison (Eddie Tayloe); Diana Lynn (Perry Dunklin); James Dunn (Mike); Lionel Stander (The Bellhop); Florence Bates (Mandy); Michael Chekhov (Gaboolian); Margaret Hamilton (Ruby Cheever); Moyna Magill (Pearl Cheever); Irene Ryan (Opal Cheever); Colin Campbell (MacWirther); Clem Bevans (Captain Bjorn); Roscoe Karns (Carmody); William Frawley (The Agent); Alvin Hammer (Bernie); Erskine Sanford (Dr. Danson); John Gallaudet (McGonical); James Burke (Policeman); Guy Wilkerson (Thibault); Audie Murphy (Copy Boy); Tom Dugan (Bartender); Jesse White (Customer); Frank Scannell (Barker); Dewey Robinson (Sergeant); Ralph Peters (Cop on Phone); Herb Vigran (Man in Subway); Jody Gilbert (Lady); Mary Treen (Wife); Charles Williams (Reporter).

EVERY GIRL SHOULD BE MARRIED (RKO, 1948) 85 M.

Executive producer, Dore Schary; producer-director Don Hartman; story, Eleanor Harris; screenplay, Hartman, Stephen Morehouse Avery; music director, C. Bakaleinikoff; art director, Albert S. D'Agostino, Carroll Clark; camera, George S. Diskant; editor, Harry Marker.

Cary Grant (Dr. Madison Brown); Franchot Tone (Roger Sanford); Diana Lynn (Julie Howard); Betsy Drake (Anabel Sims); Alan Mowbray (Mr. Spitzer); Elizabeth Risdon (Mary Nolan); Richard Gaines (Sam McNutt); Harry Hayden (Gogarty); Chick Chandler (Soda Clerk); Leon Belasco (Violinist); Fred Easler (Pierre); Anna Q. Nilsson (Saleslady); Charmienne Harker (Miss King); Marjorie Walker, Alvina Tomin, Rosalie Coughenour, Joan Lybrook (Models); Louise Franklin (Elevator Girl); Dan Foster (Cigar Store Clerk); Lois Hall, Pat Hall (Girls); Carol Hughes (Girl at Counter); Claire DuBrey (Mrs. Willoughby); Anne Nagel (Woman); James Griffith (Insurance Salesman); Selmer Jackson (Clergyman).

MY FRIEND IRMA (PAR, 1949) 103 M.

Executive producer, Hal. B. Wallis; producer, Cy Howard; director George Marshall; based on the radio show by Howard; screenplay, Howard, Parke Levy; music, Roy Webb; songs, Jay Livingston and Ray Evans; art director, Hans Dreier, Henry Bumstead; camera, Leo Tover; editor, LeRoy Stone.

John Lund (Al); Diana Lynn (Jane Stacy); Don DeFore (Richard Rhinelander; Marie Wilson (Irma Peterson); Dean Martin (Steve Baird); Jerry Lewis (Seymour); Hans Conried (Professor Kropotkin); Kathryn Givney (Mrs. Rhinelander); Percy Helton (Mr. Clyde); Erno Verebes (Mr. Chang); Gloria Gordon (Mr. O'Reilly); Maggie Mahoney (Alice); Charles Coleman (Butler); Douglas Spencer (Interior Decorator); Ken Niles (Announcer); Francis Pierlot (Income Tax Man); Chief Yowlachie (Indian); Jimmie Dundee (Wallpaper Man); Tony Merrill (Newspaper Man); Jack Mulhall (Photographer); Nick Cravat (Mushie); Leonard B. Ingoldest (Orchestra Leader).

PAID IN FULL (PAR, 1950) 98 M.

Producer, Hal B. Wallis; director, William Dieterle; based on a story by Dr. Frederic M. Loomis; screenplay, Robert Blees, Charles Schnee; art director, Hans Dreier, Earl Hedrick; music, Walter Lang, Victor Young; camera, Leo Tover; editor, Warren Low.

Robert Cummings (Bill Prentice); Lizabeth Scott (Jane Langley); Diana Lynn (Nancy Langley); Eve Arden (Tommy Thompson); Ray Collins (Dr. Fredericks); Frank McHugh (Ben); Stanley Ridges (Dr. Winston); Louis Jean Heydt (Dr. Carter); John Bromfield (Dr. Clark); Kristine Miller (Miss Williams); Laura Elliot (Tina); Ida Moore (Dorothy); James Nolan (Charlie Malloy); Geraldine Wall (Miss Ames); Rolland Morris (Bunny Howard); Jane Novak (Mrs. Fredericks); Carole Mathews (Model); Carol Channing (Mrs. Peters); Dorothy Adams (Emily Burroughs); Arlene Jenkins, Christine Cooper (Secretaries); Byron Barr (Man at Bar); Marie Blake (Tired Woman); Jimmie Dundee (Truck Driver); Gladys Blake (Talkative Woman); Douglas Spencer (Crib Man); Dewey Robinson (Diaper Man); Charles Bradstreet (Marc Hickman); Harry Cheshire (Minister).

MY FRIEND IRMA GOES WEST (PAR, 1950) 91 M.

Producer, Hal B. Wallis; associate producer, Cy Howard; director, Hal Walker; based on characters created by Howard; screenplay, Howard, Parke Levy; music, Leigh Harline; songs, Jay Livingston and Ray Evans; art director, Hans Dreier, Henry Bumstead; camera, Lee Garmes; editor, Warren Low.

John Lund (Al); Marie Wilson (Irma Peterson); Diana Lynn(Jane Stacey); Dean Martin (Steve Baird); Jerry Lewis (Seymour); Corinne Calvet (Yvonne Yvonne); Lloyd Corrigan (Sharpie); Donald Porter (Mr. Brent); Harold Huber (Pete); Joseph Vitale (Slim); Charles Evans (Mr. C. Y. Sanford); Kenneth Tobey (Pilot); James Flavin (Sheriff); David Clark (Deputy Sheriff) Wendell Niles (M.C.); George Humbert (Chef); Roy Gordon (Jensen); Link Clayton (Henry); Mike Mahoney (Cigarette Gag Man); Bob Johnson (Red Cap); Al Ferguson (News Vendor); Napoleon Whiting (Waiter); Paul Lees (Unemployment Clerk); Stan Johnson, Charles Dayton (Reporters); Jasper D. Weldon, Ivan H. Browning (Reporters); Julia Montoya, Rose Higgins (Indian Women); Maxie Thrower (Bartender); Chief Yowlachie (Indian Chief); Joe Hecht (Vendors); Gil Herman, Gregg Palmer (Attendants); Jimmie Dundee (Deputy).

ROGUES OF SHERWOOD FOREST (COL, 1950) 79 M.

Producer, Fred M. Packard; director, Gordon Douglas; story, Ralph Bettinson; screenplay, George Bruce; art director, Harold MacArthur; music director, Morris Stoloff; camera, Charles Lawton, Jr; editor, Gene Havlick.

John Derek (Robin, Earl of Huntington); Diana Lynn (Lady Marianne); George Macready (King John); Alan Hale (Little John); Paul Cavanagh (Sir Giles); Lowell Gilmore (Count of Flanders); Billy House (Friar Tuck); Lester Matthews (Alan-A-Dale); William Bevan (Will Scarlett); Wilton Graff (Baron Fitzwalter); Donald Randolph (Archbishop Stephen Langton); John Dehner (Sir Baldric); Gavin Muir (Baron Alfred); Tim Huntley (Baron Chandos); Paul Collins (Arthur); Campbell Copelin, James Logan (Officers); Valentine Perkins (Milk Maid); Gilliam Blake (Lady in Waiting); Pat Aherne (Trooper); Olaf Hytten (Charcoal Burner); Symona Boniface (Charcoal Burner's Wife); Paul Bradley (Court Official); Matthew Boulton (Abbot); Nelson Leigh (Merton); Colin Keith Johnson (Munster); Byron Poindexter (Man).

PEGGY (UNIV, 1950) 76 M.

Producer, Ralph Dietrich; director, Frederick de Cordova; story, Leon Ware; screenplay, George W. George, George F. Slavin; art director, Bernard Herzbrun, Richard H. Fiedel; music director, Joseph Gershenson; camera, Russell Metty; editor, Ralph Dawson.

Diana Lynn (Peggy Brookfield); Charles Coburn (Professor Brookfield); Charlotte Greenwood (Mrs. Emelia Fielding); Barbara Lawrence (Susan Brookfield); Charles Drake (Tom Fielding); Rock Hudson (Johnny Higgins); Connie Gilchrist (Miss Zim); Griff Barnett (Dr. Wilcox); Charles Trowbridge (Dean Stockwell); James Todd (Mr. Gardiner); Jerome Cowan (Mr. Collins); Ellen Corby (Mrs. Privet); Peter Brucco (Mr. Winters); Donna Martell (Contestant); Ann Pearce (Pretty Girl); James Best (Frank); Jack Gargan (Chauffeur); Olan Soule (Simmons); Marjorie Bennett (Flossie); Jack Kelly (Lex); Bill Kennedy, Michael Cisney (Reporters); Tim Graham (Dr. Stanton); Wheaton Chambers (Gateman); Jim Congdon (Football Player on Train); Bill Waker (Porter); Smoki Whitfield, Dudley Dickerson (Red Caps); Floyd Taylor (Newsboy); Jim Hayes, Bill Cassady (Football Players in Dormitory); Donald Kerr (Taxi Driver); Paul Power, Art Howard (Judges); John Wald (Announcer); David Alison, Joe Recht, John McKee (Photographers).

BEDTIME FOR BONZO (UNIV, 1951) 83 M.

Producer, Michel Kraike; director, Frederick de Cordova; story, Raphael David Blau; Ted Berkman; screenplay, Val Burton, Lou Breslow; art director, Bernard Herzbrun, Eric Orbom; music, Frank Skinner; camera, Carl Guthrie; editor, Ted J. Kent.

Ronald Reagan (Professor Peter Boyd); Diana Lynn (Jane); Walter Slezak (Professor Hans Neumann); Jesse White (Babcock); Lucille Barkley (Valerie Tillinghast); Herbert Heyes (Dean Tillinghast); Herbert Vigran (Lt. Daggett); Leslye Banning, Midge Ware, Ginger Anderson (Coeds); Bridget Carr (Girl in Auto); Ed Gargan (Policeman); Ed Clark (Fosdick); Joel Friedkin (Mr. DeWitt); Brad Browne (Chief of Police); Harry Tyler (Knucksy); Elizabeth Flournoy (Miss Swithen); Tommy Bond, Brad Johnson, Larry Crane, Bill Mauch, Larry Carr, Steve Wayne, Chip Perrin (Students); Ann Tyrrell, Irmgard Dawson (Telephone Operators); Larry Williams, Philo McCullough, Jack Gargan (Faculty Members).

THE PEOPLE AGAINST O'HARA (MGM, 1951) 101 M.

Producer, William H. Wright; director, John Sturges; story, Eleazar Lipsky; screenplay, John Monks, Jr.; art director, Cedric Gibbons, James Basevi; music, Carmen Dragon; camera, John Alton; editor, Gene Ruggiero.

Spencer Tracy (James Curtayne); Pat O'Brien (Vincent Ricks); Diana Lynn (Ginny Curtayne); John Hodiak (Louis Barra); Eduardo Ciannelli ("Knuckles" Lanzetta); James Arness (Johnny O'Hara); Yvette Duguay (Mrs. Lanzetta); Jay C. Flippen (Sven Norson); William Campbell (Frank Korvac); Richard Anderson (Jeff Chapman); Henry O'Neill (Judge Keating); Arthur Shields (Mr. O'Hara); Louise Lorimer (Mrs. O'Hara); Ann Doran (Betty Clark); Emile Meyer (Capt. Tom Mulvaney); Regis Toomey (Fred Colton); Katharine Warren (Mrs. Sheffield); Paul Bryar (Detective Howie Pendleton); Peter Mamakos (James Korvac); Perdita Chandler (Gloria Adler); Frank Ferguson (Al); Don Dillaway (Monty); Anthony Hughes (George); Lee Phelps (Emmett Kimbaugh); Lawrence Tolan (Vincent Korvan); Jack Lee (Court Clerk); Tony Barr ("Little Wolfie"); Frankie Hyers (Bartender); Michael Dugan (Detective); Jim Toney (Officer Abrams); Mae Clarke (Receptionist); Dan Foster (Assistant District Attorney); Lou Lubin (Eddie); Jack Kruschen (Uniformed Detective); Jeff Richards (Ambulance Driver); Charles Bronson (Angelo Korvac); Bill Fletcher (Pete Korvac); Richard Bartlett (Tony Korvac); William Self (Technician); Brooks Benedict, Sammy Finn (Gamblers); William Shallert (Interne); Celia Lovsky (Mrs. Korvac).

MEET ME AT THE FAIR (UNIV, 1953) 87 M.

Producer, Albert J. Cohen; director, Douglas Sirk; based on the novel *The Great Companions* by Gene Markey; adaptation, Martin Berkeley; screenplay, Irving Wallace; choreography, Kenny Williams; songs, Stan Freberg; Kenny Williams and Marvin Wright; F. E. Miller and Scat Man Crowthers; Frederick Herbert and Milton Rosen; camera, Maury Gertsman; editor, Russell Schoengarth.

Dan Dailey (Doc Tilbee); Diana Lynn (Zerelda Wing); "Scat Man" Crothers (Enoch); Chet Allen (Tad); Hugh O'Brian (Chilton Corr); Rhys Williams (Pete McCoy); Carole Mathews (Clara); Russell Simpson (Sheriff Evans); Thomas E. Jackson (Billy Gray); George Chandler (Leach); Paul Gordan (Cyclist); Johnson And Diehl (Juggling Act); Black Brothers (Acrobatic Comedy Act); George L. Spaulding (State Governor); Virginia Brissac (Mrs. Spooner); John Maxwell (Mr. Spooner); Edna Holland (Miss Burghey); George Riley (M.C.); Iron Eyes Cody (Indian Chief); Donald Kerr (Stage Manager); Franklyn Farnum, Harte Wayne, Roger Moore (Wall Street Tycoons); Dante Dipaolo (Specialty Dancer); Robert Shafto (Disraeli); George Arglen (Howie); Jon Gardner (Ed); Sam Pierce (Party Stooge); Max Wagner (Iceman); Jack Gargan (D.A.'s Secretary); Brick Sullivan (Policeman).

PLUNDER OF THE SUN (WB, 1953) 81 M.

Producer, Robert Fellows; director, John Farrow; based on the novel by David Dodge; screenplay, Jonathan Latimer; music, Antonio D. Conde; song, E. Fabregat; art director, Al Ybarra; assistant director, Andrew V. McLaglen; camera, Jack Draper; editor, Harry Marker.

Glenn Ford (Al Colby); Diana Lynn (Julie Barnes); Patricia Medinia (Anna Luz); Francis L. Sullivan (Thomas Berrien); Sean McClory (Jefferson); Eduardo Noriega (Raul Carnejo); Julio Villareal (Ubaldo Navarro); Charles Rooner (Capt. Bergman); Douglass Dumbrille (Carter).

TRACK OF THE CAT (WB, 1954) 102 M.

Producer, Robert Fellows; director, William A. Wellman; based on the novel by Walter Van Tilburg Clark; screenplay, A. I. Bezzerides; assistant director, Andrew V. McLaglen; art director, Al Ybarra; music, Roy Webb; camera, William H. Clothier; editor, Fred MacDowell.

Robert Mitchum (Curt); Teresa Wright (Grace); Diana Lynn (Gwen); Tab Hunter (Harold); Beulah Bondi (Ma Bridges); Philip Tonge (Pa Bridges); William Hopper (Arthur); Carl Switzer (Joe Sam).

AN ANNAPOLIS STORY (AA, 1955) 81 M.

Producer, Walter Mirisch; director, Don Siegel; story, Dan Ullman; screenplay, Ullman; Geoffrey Homes; music, Marlan Skiles; songs, Joseph W. Crowley and Skiles; technical advisor, Com. Marcus L. Lowe, Jr., U.S.N.; camera, Sam Leavitt; editor, William Austin.

John Derek (Tony Scott); Kevin McCarthy (Jim Scott); Diana Lynn (Peggy Lord); Pat Conway (Tim Dooley); Alvy Moore (Willie Warren); L. Q. Jones (Watson); John Kirby (Macklin); Fran Bennett (Connie); Barbara Brown (Mrs. Scott); Lt. Robert Boniol (Lt. Preston); Don Kennedy (McClaren); George Eldredge (Capt. Lord); Betty Lou Gerson (Mrs. Lord); Robert Osterloh (AGC Austin); Don Haggerty (Lt. Prentiss); Christian Drake (1st Classman); Richard Travis (Comdr. Wilson); James Anderson (Instructor); Robert Pike (Professor); Dabbs Greer (Professor); Don Keefer (Air Officer); John Doucette (Boxing Coach); John Lehman (Storekeepter); John Ayres (Superintendant); Sam Peckinpah (Pilot); Tom Harmon (Announcer); William Schallert (Tony's Instructor); Richard Carlson (Introductory Narration).

YOU'RE NEVER TOO YOUNG (PAR, 1955) 102 M.

Producer, Paul Jones; director, Norman Taurog; story, Edward Childs Carpenter, Fannie Kilbourne; screenplay, Sidney Sheldon; art directors, Hal Periera, Earl Hedrick; music, Walter Scharf; camera, Daniel L. Fapp; editor, Archie Marshek.

Jerry Lewis (Wilbur Hoolick); Dean Martin (Bob Miles); Diana Lynn (Nancy Collins); Nina Foch (Gretchen Brendan); Raymond Burr (Noonan); Mitzi McCall (Skeets); Veda Ann Borg (Mrs. Noonan); Margery Maude (Mrs. Ella Brendan); Romo Vincent (Ticket Agent); Nancy Kulp (Marty's Mother); Milton Frome (Lt. O'Malley); Donna Percy (Girl); Emory Parnell (Conductor); James Burke (Pullman Conductor); Tommy Ivo (Marty); Whitey Haupt (Mike Brendan); Mickey Finn (Sergeant Brown); Peggy Moffitt (Agnes); Johnstone White, Richard Simmons (Professors); Louise Lorimer, Isabel Randolph (Faculty Members); Robert Carson (Tailor); Hans Conried (Francois); Stanley Blystone (Passenger); Bobby Barber (News Boy); Donna Jo Gribble, Irene Walpole, Gloria Penny Moore (School Girls); Bob Morgan (Texan).

THE KENTUCKIAN (UA, 1955) 104 M.

Producer, Harold Hecht; director, Burt Lancaster; based on the novel *The Gabriel Horn* by Felix Holt; screenplay, A. B. Guthrie, Jr.; music, Bernard Herrmahn; songs, Irving Gordon; assistant director, Richard Mayberry; camera; Ernest Laszlo; editor, William B. Murphy.

Burt Lancaster (Big Eli); Dianne Foster (Hannah); Diana Lynn (Susie); John McIntire (Zack); Una Merkel (Sophie); Walter Matthau (Bodine); John Carradine (Fletcher); Donald MacDonald (Little Eli); John Litel (Babson); Rhys Williams (Constable); Edward Norris (Gambler); Lee Erikson (Luke); Clem Bevans (Pilot); Lisa Ferraday (Woman Gambler); Douglas Spencer, Paul Wexler (Fromes Brothers).

COMPANY OF KILLERS (UNIV, 1970) 90 M.

Producer, E. Jack Neuman, Jerry Thorpe; associate producer, Lloyd Richards; director, Thorpe; screenplay, Neuman; music, Richard Hazard; camera, Jack Marta; art direction, Alexander Golitzen, Joseph Alves; editor, John Elias; assistant director, Paul Cameron.

Van Johnson (Sam Cahil); Ray Milland (Georges DeSalles); John Saxon (Dave Poohler); Clu Gulager (Frank Quinn); Brian Kelly (Nick Andros); Fritz Weaver (John Shankalien); Susan Oliver (Thelma Dwyer); Diana Lynn (Edwina DeSalles); Robert Middleton (Owen Brady); Terry Carter (Max Jaffie); Anna Capri (Maryjane Smythe); Anthony James (Jimmy Konic); Marian Collier (Sylvia Xavier); Nate Esformes (Peterson); Mercer Harris (Luke); Joyce Jameson (Marnie); Gerald Hiken (Chick); Vince Howard (Dale Christian); Larry Thor (Clarington); Donna Michelle (Gloria); Jeanne Bal (Patricia Cahill).

At the age of 15

In the costume test for LITTLE WOMEN (Selznick-International '46)

In 1951

With Ginger Rogers in THE MAJOR AND THE MINOR (Par '42)

With William Demarest in THE MIRACLE OF MORGAN'S CREEK (Par '44)

With Betty Hutton, Dorothy Lamour, Mimi Chandler, and Fred MacMurray in AND THE ANGELS SING (Par '44)

With Nell Craig, Eddie Bracken and Cass Daley in OUT OF THIS WORLD (Par '45)

With Marie Wilson in MY FRIEND IRMA

With Jerry Lewis, Marie Wilson, and Dean Martin in MY FRIEND IRMA GOES WEST (Par '50)

In PEGGY (Univ '50)

In PLUNDER OF THE SUN (WB '53)

BETTY HUTTON

5'4"
112 pounds
Hazel eyes
Blonde hair
Pisces

BETTY HUTTON, a charter member of the fraternity of entertainment greats, has slipped into undeserved obscurity, not because her vast talents seem pedestrian by today's standards, but because the bulk of her musical feature films have dated badly and she has left no legacy of readily available recordings from her prime years of vocalizing. Throughout the 1940s in motion pictures and the 1950s on the stage and in nightclubs, Betty closely rivaled Judy Garland in critical endorsement and enormous fan adoration. Like Garland, she required strong outside guidance to channel her multiple talents constructively, and like the late "Over the Rainbow" girl she never received that professional control from business associates or her assorted spouses. Unlike Judy, however, she never ceased to grow as a consummate performer, and this makes her present professional inactivity a sad waste.

A big band vocalist and Broadway player in the late 1930s, Betty joined Paramount Pictures in 1941 and immediately made a terrific screen impact. She soon inherited Jean Harlow's "blonde bombshell" title, but for entirely different physical reasons. Betty was never a sex symbol, not even as the sweet little girl next door. She was too rambunctious and exuberant in her display of singing and dancing to elicit waves of even brotherly protection from filmgoers. Betty could belt out a humorous ballad, turn cartwheels, and then spin into a jitterbug dance. A second later, with a broad grin on her face, she would be yelling for more. If anything, audiences required protection from Betty's superselling of herself.

In her later musical biography movies, Betty revealed a growing ability to handle dramatic and light comedy assignments. She might have created a new film career for herself in the 1950s had she not turned her back on Hollywood. However, despite her silver screen success (none of her features ever lost money!) she had other, more human needs. Hungry for live audience adoration, she decided to concentrate on stage appearances. She was a wow, at both the Palace Theatre and the London Palladium, and she strengthened her status in the entertainment world with several highly successful nightclub engagements.

But then she was increasingly beset with personal problems, triggered by her failure to make the same tremendous impact on television that she had in every other media. Her shell of confidence crumbled and she mistakenly cried on the public's shoulder once too often in her several retirement bids and hasty comebacks. As the years passed she found less and less suitable work. Being a stubborn and expensive perfectionist restricted her value on video guest-spot assignments, and even on the comedown level of summer-stock touring shows.

Today, Betty lives in unwanted retirement on the West Coast, refusing communication with even those who love her the most—her fans. She is still waiting for that big chance to come and whisk her back to the top of the entertainment heap.

✳ ✳

Betty Hutton was born Betty June Thornburg on February 26, 1921, in Battle Creek, Michigan, the younger daughter of Percy and Mabel Lum Thornburg. Her older sister Marion had been born on March 10, 1920, in Little Rock, Arkansas.*

In 1923, Mr. Thornburg, a railroad brakeman, left his family for parts unknown. Mrs. Thornburg moved her family to Detroit, where she worked in an auto assembly plant. Then she decided it might be more lucrative to open a small speakeasy and cash in on the Prohibition lunacy. Betty would recall about her colorful childhood: "Mom didn't do anything real bad. How is a woman supposed to make her living with two kids when her husband deserted her? Mom just ran a job on a small scale. We'd operate until the cops got wise. Then they'd move in and close us down, and we'd move somewhere else. Marion and I would entertain the customers by dancing and singing. We really lived that way until we were twelve and fourteen years old. . . . Things were really tough. At one time we were down to one can of beans." (Sometimes Mrs. Thornburg had to rely on the generosity of local church charities to feed her daughters.)

About Betty's formative years, her mother once detailed: "Betty was jealous of her sister right from the start. She was always in my lap, always after affection. She would stand on her head, do cartwheels, yell or do anything to attract attention away from her quieter sister. . . . Marion was always good and helpful. But that Betty! If it wasn't one thing, it was another!"

At age five, Betty was caught in a neighborhood melee and was thrown off the end of a pier. She earned a slight scar on her left cheek for this episode, a memento which deepened her inborn inferiority complex.

When she was nine years old, rambunctious Betty made her first public appearance. She belted out a rendition of "Son of the Nile" at a school celebration. Two years later she did an impersonation of Mae West in another school production. At age 13, she won a job as vocalist with a summer resort band in Michigan and by the next year she was the songstress with a band of high school boys. When she was 15, ambitious Betty scraped together $200 and journeyed to New York to break into show business. She was advised by all concerned to go home, which she did.

Discussing her adolescent years in 1943, Betty recalled: "Mother is the reason I'm a success. She never beefed. We really lived in a tenement. Marion was a soda jerk in a downtown Walgreen's Drug Store in Detroit for $15 a week, and Mother took me around to places singing. We went to beer gardens, anywhere they'd listen to me. That's why I have no desire to go back to Detroit. I have no friends there—I had none when I was there. I was working all the time. We'd go around and I'd sing for pennies, nickels and dimes. We'd go around and collect it with a hat and sometimes we'd go out with several dollars. When I was ten or eleven, I also cooked and kept house for a German family, for $5 a week.

*Marion was at first partnered with Betty in a singing act with Vincent Lopez's band. She had the more subdued vocal style of the two sisters, utilizing the more typical cotton-candy tone favored during the big band era. In September, 1938, she joined the Glenn Miller band and gained national recognition as his lead female vocalist. She became a major radio star when Miller moved into that medium. In the 1940s she fell under her sister's shadow and found it difficult to develop a film career in her own right. Her appearances in such musicals as *Orchestra Wives* (1942) and *Crazy House* (1944) and comedies such as *In Society* (1944) and *Love Happy* (1950) were unremarkable. Like Betty, she was much-married.

"I planned ahead. I was always telling Mother that someday we would have all we need. It sounded like a dream then.

"I was just going into my senior year in high school. I was way ahead of the other kids just because I was in such a hurry to get out. I had been double promoted three times. One night Marion's boyfriend took me to the Continental Nightclub in Detroit and the m.c. asked me to get up and sing a song.

"[Vincent] Lopez happened to be there and signed me on the spot for $65 a week."

Meanwhile, in 1937, Betty's father committed suicide. He bequeathed $100 to each of his daughters; he had not seen either of them in years.

When touring with the popular Vincent Lopez band, Betty was billed as Betty Darling (she had previously used the professional name of Betty Jane Boyer). Lopez's musicians did not appreciate the iconoclastic, loud, explosive singing style of their new vocalist. More than once they almost convinced the sedate Lopez to fire his find. One evening, when Betty knew the job axe might fall at any moment, she cut loose with a rousing version of "The Dipsy Doodle," outdoing herself with vocal and physical gymnastics. Compared to the subdued style of most band vocalists, Betty came on like a tornado and took the audience, Lopez, and his band by storm. Thereafter, with her new approach to singing down pat, there was no further talk of dismissing her. Under her contract with Lopez, the band leader received 20 percent of all her earnings from whatever media.

Although later she would have cause to regret this restrictive agreement, Betty freely admitted that Lopez "took me outta the beer halls, and taught me table manners and how to keep my voice down in a restaurant —I used to scream all the time. He told me what to wear, too."

During a Boston engagement of the Lopez group in the summer of 1938, rising band leader Glenn Miller caught a performance, and was greatly impressed by Betty and her sister Marion (then also singing with the group). Miller decided to hire the more demure Marion as his band vocalist, reasoning that she would present fewer problems than the vociferous Betty.

In the fall of 1938, Lopez settled down to a New York engagement at Billy Rose's Casa Manana Club with Betty continuing on as the lead vocalist. *Variety* described her caterwauling performance: "Miss Hutton is a petite and somewhat unusual type who puts great poundage into her singing, screwing her face up into poses at times that are very different and effective. She has a manner of working and diving into her work hard that finally gets under the skin, even if vocally she's far from the doors of the Met. Miss Hutton employs slightly wild, rowdy techniques that really sells her, 'A-Tisket' and 'Old Man Mose' are right up her alley."

At this time it was reported that Betty had signed a term contract with Twentieth Century-Fox, but it never materialized. During 1939 she appeared in several movie musical short subjects filmed in New York. These included: *One for the Book* (Vitaphone, 1939) with Hal Sherman; *Public Jitterbug # 1* (Vitaphone, 1939) with Chaz Chase, Hal LeRoy, and Emerson's Sextette; *Vincent Lopez and Orchestra* (Vitaphone, 1939); and the more elaborate one-reel musical filler *Three Kings and a Queen* (Paramount, 1939).

Also in 1939, Betty joined Lopez's group on a vaudeville circuit tour which played the East Coast and Midwestern cities. With her rollicking style, she was soon billed as America's Number One Jitterbug. It was an inaccurate tag that was to haunt her professionally for decades. Explained

Betty: "It was just an unfortunate label that was pasted on. I just was a screwball. I sang crazy songs. I did just whatever came to my mind. They didn't know what to call me, so they called me a jitterbug. I don't dance. A jitterbug has to dance."

One trade paper, reviewing Betty in vaudeville, described her as "A bouncing, bawling femme, dressed to look like an exaggerated woolly-headed doll. The younger set love her bouncing renditions; the oldsters soon tired of her wearing presentation." Betty worked her turn for all it was worth, mugging, clowning, and jumping about the stage, pulling the musicians or anyone nearby into her act. She well deserved the titles of "bombastic blonde" and "roughhouse smasheroo." She was then earning $175 a week.

Betty was also Lopez's swing vocalist for his Wednesday and Thursday late-evening WABC radio show. Working with the enterprising band leader gave Betty a prime introduction to audiences of all media within a short space of time.

Betty then decided to strike out on her own. Without an audition, she was hired at $100 a week for the musical revue *Two for the Show*, which debuted at the Booth Theatre on February 8, 1940. This successor to the previous season's *One for the Money* also had sketches and lyrics by Nancy Hamilton. Its cast of relative newcomers included Eve Arden, Alfred Drake, Richard Haydn, Tommy Wonder, and Keenan Wynn. With sketches directed by Joshua Logan and the overall production supervised by John Murray Anderson, the show proved reasonably diverting to pre-World War II audiences.

Brooks Atkinson of the *New York Times* reported that Betty "dances like a mad sprite and sings breathlessly as though she enjoyed it." Other critics termed her "the blonde bombshell," "riotous," "zippy," "dynamic," and "full of pep and personality." Her socked-across numbers were: "Calypso Joe," "Little Miss Muffett," with Wynn portraying the spider, and "A House With a Red Barn." A few reviewers cautioned: "It will pay her directors, and Miss Hutton, not to overdo her appearances. The physical strain is considerable and an over-stimulated vanity too, is bad for talented youngsters." The show ran for 129 performances. During its stay, she moonlighted, singing in the late show at the La Martinique café.

Betty begrudgingly paid Lopez his 20 percent fee throughout the run of *Two for the Show*. Then she refused to pay the band leader further sums. He sued. Betty consulted attorney Abe L. Berman, who handled the matter out of court.

More importantly to Betty's career, Berman suggested Betty to producer B. G. DeSylva* for a part in his forthcoming Broadway musical *Panama Hattie*. Betty was signed on—without an audition—at $500 a week, to support Ethel Merman, James Dunn, Rags Ragland, and Arthur Treacher in this Cole Porter songfest. *Panama Hattie* unveiled on October 30, 1940, at the 46th Street Theatre to rousing acclaim. Its raucous plot had vamp Phyllis Brooks trying to woo away nightclub performer Merman's beau (Dunn). Intermingled with the main story was a sillier plot line about the blowing up of the Panama Canal. Betty was Florrie, a dizzy Canal Zone soubrette; she backstopped Merman's bravura performance with such tunes as "Fresh as a Daisy," "They Ain't Doin' Right By Our Nell," and "All I Gotta Get Is My Man." Critical acclaim was focused on Merman—in her first solo star-

*See Appendix.

ring vehicle—and an non-obnoxious eight year old Joan Carrol. Betty was given her enthusiastic due by the reporters, although some cynical critics suggested she "should be given one number, if that, in the course of the evening and then be permitted to work off her surplus energies elsewhere." June Allyson was Betty's understudy in the show, and got to go on when Betty had the measles. Members of the chorus included Lucille Bremer, Janis Carter, and Vera-Ellen.

Panama Hattie ran for 501 performances. Betty was enthusiastic about her role in the show. "It is a very great thrill to memorize lines. Up to now all I have done is run on stage, sing a song, like this—brrrump—and then run off again. You have nothing to carry when you do this. You simply have to be funny for the few minutes you are on the stage, and then when you run off you don't have to carry anything."

Next, *Panama Hattie* producer B. G. DeSylva hired Betty for a featured role in Paramount's upcoming musical movie *The Fleet's In* (1942). She was to be paid $1,000 a week for three months' work.

When DeSylva took over the production reins at Paramount in late 1941, he ushered in a new era of wholesomeness at the studio. Successful stars remained (Claudette Colbert, Dorothy Lamour, Paulette Goddard), but gone were the ultrasophisticated days of Marlene Dietrich, Joseph von Sternberg, and Ernst Lubitsch. Rowdy sex queen Mae West had been pastureized, and the antic music humor of Judy Canova and Martha Raye had been dissipated and discarded. Betty Grable's option at the studio had lapsed, and after a stretch on Broadway in DeSylva's *DuBarry Was a Lady* she returned to Twentieth Century-Fox before DeSylva could grab her contract. The studio's biggest assets were Bob Hope and Bing Crosby.

DeSylva accurately saw that World War II was tightening Middle America's taste to a broad base of conservatism which reflected all the fantasies of virtuous small-town life. Since contract musical players Mary Martin and Susanna Foster were not drawing impressive reactions from the public, DeSylva thought Betty might be just the ticket—he was right.

The Fleet's In (1942) starred Paramount's sarong princess Dorothy Lamour as the uppity hostess of a San Francisco nightclub. Meek sailor William Holden is mistaken as a killer-diller with the girls. His ship pals bet whether or not he can kiss shapely but aloof Lamour. He eventually does, and wins her too. The familiar plot had been the basis of Clara Bow's *The Fleet's In* (1928) and *Lady Be Careful* (1936). Betty was Lamour's boisterous roommate, who establishes her own romance with roly-poly gob Eddie Bracken. (His mother's-little-boy hayseed image would be overworked throughout the early 1940s, with Paramount force-feeding him on a moviegoing public which did not have the gumption to fight back and declare that he was not representative of American malehood. The rare exception of virile sexuality among the studio's then current roster of male stars was Alan Ladd—the rest were as bland as could be: Fred MacMurray, Joel McCrea, Ray Milland, William Holden, Brian Donlevy, Sonny Tufts, and Robert Preston.)

With Bracken, Betty had the attention-getting number: "Arthur Murray Taught Me Dancing in a Hurry," and the solo song "Build a Better Mousetrap." Her impact as the male-hungry hoyden in *The Fleet's In* is best summed up by *PM:* "[Her] facial grimaces, body twists and man-pummelling gymnastics take wonderfully to the screen. But the surrealist insanity she gives off with no effort is repeated—with more effort—by Lorraine and Rogman and by Cass Daley, which is too much time to spend in a madhouse." (Daley, a more homely and bumpkinish version of Betty, made her Paramount debut in *The Fleet's In*. Clearly of the Judy Canova tradition, she made a mild impact in the early 1940s musicals, and like MGM's classier Virginia O'Brien, would largely disappear from the cinema scene before the end of the decade.)

Betty proved a more than satisfactory focal point in the multistar musical *Star Spangled Rhythm*, which premiered at the Paramount Theatre on December 30, 1942. She was second-billed as Polly Judson, the irrepressible telephone operator at Paramount Pictures in love with gob Eddie Bracken. Bracken and his sailor friends pay a surprise visit to the studio, expecting to receive a VIP tour from Bracken's pop Victor Moore, who always passed himself off as the studio boss and not the gate watchman. Betty enthusiastically agrees to assist woebegone Moore in playing through the deception. While escorting the servicemen around the lot, she banters with an unstudied naturalness with the company's top personalities. Her exuberant naiveté made the contrived plot work satisfactorily. Her solo number was "I'm Doing It for Defense." About this potpourri of entertainment, the *New York Herald Tribune* stated: "It takes an honest-to-goodness vaudeville turn, assisted by Betty Hutton, to give the show authenticity." It is obvious that director George Marshall had difficulty containing Betty's pyrotechnic talent within prescribed camera shots, and he finally advised the lensmen to follow her random movements as best they could.

The *Motion Picture Herald*'s Fame Poll named Betty a star of tomorrow in 1942. When not filming at the studio, Betty was acting as comedy foil songstress on Bob Hope's weekly radio program.

Already volatile Betty was becoming renowned for her overly romantic notions of personal relationships. After her stint at a huge war bond rally at Madison Square Garden, she announced: "I think you folks will be glad to know that I've just become engaged to a local boy, Charles Martin." It was news to him. She had been dating makeup director Perc Westmore. In 1942 he went overseas for Army duty and the couple announced their engagement. After he returned to the States to recuperate from a battle wound, the pending marriage was canceled.

Happy Go Lucky (1943) was primarily a technicolor musical vehicle to utilize the services of tepid Mary Martin and Dick Powell. To pep up the action, Betty was cast opposite Eddie Bracken—yet again—and a non-singing Rudy Vallee. Martin was an ex-cigarette girl who jaunts to a Caribbean isle to pursue rich playboy Vallee. Once-wealthy Powell, now a singing beachcomber, assists Martin in nabbing the recalcitrant Vallee. They soon discover each other. Betty was rung in as a jive singer out to catch up with her runaway boyfriend Bracken; she does—and how. Betty's big number was "Murder, He Says," relating her beau's reactions when she kisses him. Every once in a while, Betty and Bracken would be handed a bit of witty repartee and she proved she could deliver a line knowingly. More often, she and Bracken would engage in slightly risqué but harmless interchanges bordering on the burlesque. For example, a running gag had her complaining that she has been wearing sweaters for months and still has no eligible male in sight. Smiling Bracken retorts: "You know you only get out of a sweater what you put into it." *Variety* described Betty in *Happy Go Lucky* as "the bouncing bundle of energetic jive who is ripening into a more than passable comic under the Paramount studio tutelage."

Let's Face It (1943), based on the Cole Porter Broadway musical that had starred Danny Kaye, gave Betty her opportunity to play opposite the studio's top banana, Bob Hope, on whose radio show she often appeared. As Winnie Potter, she directs a health farm for overweight women. Her fiancé Hope is stationed at nearby Camp Arthur. He is devoted enough to Betty to smuggle in candy to the fat women at the resort so they will have to stay there longer, but he can never raise enough money or stay out of trouble long enough for them to be married. Three middle-aged wives (Eve Arden, Zasu Pitts, and Phyllis Povah) want to wreak vengeance on their gallivanting husbands. Hope and two cronies are hired as weekend escorts for the female trio. The expected complications ensue with everyone's girlfriend and wife appearing at the wrong moment. It concludes with Hope tricking a Nazi sub into grounding off Long Island Sound and becoming a hero. For the first time on the screen, Paramount gave Betty the semi-glamour treatment. But she was still capable of engaging in a jujitsu bout with Hope and knocking his teeth caps off, and shouting out the ironic but frenetic "Let's Not Talk About Love." She and Hope proved an "okay romantic team" and the production-numberless musical cleaned up at the box office. Even hard-to-please Howard Barnes (*New York Herald Tribune*) admitted: "The chances are that she will become an actress one of these days, for she has vitality and a good sense of comic timing." Hope quipped about his effervescent costar: "If they put a propeller on Hutton and sent her over Germany, the war would be over by Christmas."

As part of her contribution to the war effort, Betty joined Fred Astaire, Lucille Ball, James Cagney, Greer Garson, Judy Garland, Jose Iturbi, Harpo Marx, William Powell, Mickey Rooney, and others in a two-week train tour in 1943. Two years later she would be among those appearing in Paramount's short subject *Hollywood Victory Caravan*.

Then Betty was taken in hand by Paramount's resident director genius, Preston Sturges, whose satirical comedies bolstered the studio's production schedule throughout the early 1940s. He cast her as the female lead of his *The Miracle of Morgan's Creek* (1944), which became the comedy movie hit of the year. Betty plays daffy Trudy Kockenlocker, who gets drunk one night and wakes up the next morning vaguely recalling she has married someone called Private Ratzkywatzsky—she thinks. After discovering she is pregnant, Betty agrees to the wise advice of her precocious younger sister Diana Lynn, who suggests she nab unwanted 4-F suitor Eddie Bracken as her spouse. Betty confides all to birdbrain bank clerk Bracken and he good-naturedly agrees to wed her. He even muffs that. The walloping climax has Betty giving birth to male sextuplets (the miracle), with governor Brian Donlevy declaring the marriage valid and Bracken a military hero.

The Miracle of Morgan's Creek was the first film in which Betty did not sing. She was as energetic as ever, but for once her personality was subdued to the characterization. Alton Cook (*New York World Telegram*) congratulated her: "Betty Hutton who has been just a bumptious hoyden, becomes a sweet and amusing little comedienne." Others aiding the mirthful movie were Keystone Cop-like William Demarest as the sisters' policeman dad, justice of the peace Porter Hall, and political boss Akim Tamiroff. Sturges had high praise for Betty: "She's a full-fledged actress with every talent the noun implies. She plays in musicals because the public, which can practically do nothing well, is willing to concede its entertainers only one talent." Betty always thought this film could have been the turning point of her career for the better. She would have liked to work with Sturges again, but he never used his Paramount leading ladies (Claudette Colbert,

Barbara Stanwyck, Betty Field, Ella Raines, Ellen Drew, Veronica Lake) more than once.

And the Angels Sing coasted into the Paramount Theatre on July 12, 1944. The musical costarred Betty with Dorothy Lamour, Diana Lynn, and newcomer Mimi Chandler. Fred MacMurray was delegated to play opposite the singing-sister quartette as a conniving bandleader. The concocted premise had Lamour really wanting to paint, Lynn hoping to be a classical composer, and Chandler planning to be an actress; only Betty enjoyed vocalizing. Guileless Betty is hoodwinked out of the group's $190 by MacMurray, who promptly uses the money to take his band back to Brooklyn for a club date. The girls pursue him, and Lamour finally acknowledges that she loves the sappy musician. Betty managed to steal the show with her rousing rendition of "His Rocking Horse Ran Away" and "Bluebird in My Belfry," both of which became trademark numbers. Raymond Walburn chortled through as the girls' father. Archer Winsten (*New York Post*) explained: "Miss Hutton, it is perfectly clear, is the closest possible human approximation of a buzz bomb. Whether singing, dancing, or making love to a helpless male, her preliminary whizzing assault is followed by an incomparable explosion." Despite the rather blatant crudeness and formula pandering of *And the Angels Sing*, James Agee could write in *The Nation:* "But Betty Hutton is almost beyond good and evil, so far as I am concerned."

Betty's Paramount contract now provided that she be paid $5,000 a week, placing her in the top stable of studio stars.

Despite her heavy filmmaking load, Betty found time and energy to return to vaudeville in the summer of 1944. She expressed her professional drive: "If I could just come across to every audience, if I could just look at them out there and tell them 'There's nothing I wouldn't do for you.' " When her six-a-day act was caught in Boston at the RKO Theatre in August, 1944, *Variety* reported that Betty "knocks herself out at each show" and that her rendition of the ballad "It Had to Be You" "gives her the chance to do smooth sentiment, and she pours it out in a husky black velvet to wow."

In a telling interview with *Boston Post* critic Elliot Norton, Betty confided: "For years, I haven't had time to think about getting married. I had dates and I had fun. But I wanted a career first. Now I have it. Now I'm a star. Now I can look around. But the funny thing about it is this. When you get to this point you suddenly realize that you are making so much money that there are only about ten men in the world that are making that much. Then you have to worry about that." (At the time, she was dating the recently divorced director, Mervyn LeRoy.)

In 1944 B. G. DeSylva considered the possibility of teaming Betty with her sister Marion in a musical *My Sister and I,* but the project was shelved when DeSylva became ill and then left his executive post at Paramount later that year.

For her third 1944 release, *Here Come the Waves,* Betty was teamed with Paramount's resident crooner, Bing Crosby. He had the dubious distinction of competing with two Bettys in this overzealous patriotic salute. She portrayed identical twins (one blonde, the other brunette) who have joined the WAVES. Casual Crosby is harassed and romanced into assisting with the WAVE recruiting show by the dignified Betty; and sleepy-eyed Sonny Tufts is awakened by the jive-baby Betty. Her musical highlight was "There's a Fella Waitin' in Poughkeepsie." Another comedy number, "My Mamma Thinks I'm a Star," was deleted from the release print. Bosley Crowther (*New York Times*) penned: "Regarding Miss Hutton's dual performance, it should not be mistaken for high art, but it certainly can be commended as very vigorous virtuosity."

After completing *Here Come the Waves,* Betty embarked on an eight-week USO tour of the South Pacific. Her troupe entertained in Honolulu, Johnson Island, Saipan, Tinian, Guam, Antawarak, Nemur, Tarawa, the Gilbert Islands, the Marianas, Roi, and Majuro.

The studio finally succumbed to Betty's wishes to go dramatic by allowing her to "emote" in the fictionalized musical biography, *Incendiary Blonde* (1945), the life of 1920s nightclub personality Texas Guinan. (Republic Pictures had planned a biography film of Guinan, *Hello Sucker,* in 1941, but it never got beyond the scripting stage. In the late 1960s, Martha Raye appeared in a pre-Broadway fizzle, a musical life of Guinan called *Hello Sucker.*)

Incendiary Blonde, which began production in 1943 but was shelved to push out more topical product, was a lushly told account of Guinan's mercurial rise in the show business world before and during the Roaring Twenties, culminating in her untimely death. It was filled with crazy capers which blurred the facts, but Betty gave a marathon performance. She belted forth many of the period songs and emoted in earnest. She even had an acrobatic workout with the Maxellos. The critics approved of her "well-rounded performance" and agreed that she "knocks herself out in the picture, but to considerable effect." Barry Fitzgerald was her hammy father, a wild dreamer of fantastic financial schemes, and Arturo De Cordova essayed the Wild West operator/gangster who became her lover. If *Incendiary Blonde* had been filmed by Warner Brothers it would have been gutsier; if by MGM it would have been more splendiferous; if by Twentieth Century-Fox it would have been gaudier; and if by Universal it would have been produced on a lower budget and aimed at even a more pedestrian ("democratic," in those days) level. As it evolved, it was typical Paramount, middle-of-the-road film fare; wavering unsteadily between pure fantasy and polite realism. The sets never seemed real, the costumes were always too spanking new, and the cinematic staging was usually too conventional; but everything was undertaken on a most professional, lavish level. Paramount product tended to satisfy the pseudosophisticated notions World War II audiences had as to what constituted a good movie, and as a result *Incendiary Blonde* proved a big moneymaker.

For *Duffy's Tavern* (1945), a lesser World War II all-star musical hodgepodge, Betty performed "The Hard Way," a number sung to psychiatrist Billy De Wolfe, explaining why she cannot make up her mind about the men in her life. With Dorothy Lamour, Diana Lynn, Arturo De Cordova, and others, Betty joined in a satirical rendition of "Swinging on a Star."

On September 2, 1945, Betty was married at the Drake Hotel in Chicago to camera manufacturer Ted Briskin, age 28. It was typical of the girl who never became part of the swank Hollywood social set to marry someone from outside the profession.

After B. G. DeSylva retired as production chief at Paramount, he prepared several independent ventures for the studio. The modestly mounted *The Stork Club* (1945), shot in 47 days, was his initial project, and it starred his favorite singing actress, Betty. This Cinderella tale presented Betty as a hat-check girl who saves millionaire Barry Fitzgerald from drowning. He is ever so grateful and makes Betty his protégée. Her boyfriend, bandleader Don DeFore, misunderstands the May-December platonic relationship. All resolves nicely in this living commercial for the Manhattan night spot.

Presumably it boosted the club's business as much as the Betty Grable vehicle *Billy Rose's Diamond Horseshoe* (1945) did for that competing personality haven. Howard Barnes *(New York Herald Tribune)* was inspired to tribute Betty as "the most vigorous worker in the Paramount vineyard . . . who practically blows her top in making 'Stork Club' an inviting entertainment." Her tom-boisterous musical highlight was "Doctor, Lawyer, Indian Chief"; she also had a more relaxed duet with Andy Russell, "If I Had a Dozen Hearts," and the solo "I'm a Square in the Social Circle." Robert Benchley worked in a few acidy remarks as Fitzgerald's deadpan attorney, with Bill Goodwin as Sherman Billingsley, host of the club. Spiffy Iris Adrian was Betty's wisecracking cloakroom pal. This pretty package of fluff burst into the Paramount Theatre on December 19, 1945, and grossed $3.2 million in its national release.

Cross My Heart (1946) was an indifferent remake of Carole Lombard's zany *True Confession* (1937). The preposterous premise had wacky Betty confessing to a murder she did not commit in order to spotlight the career of her attorney beau Sonny Tufts. Others handcuffed to the dumb tale were Rhys Williams as the infernal prosecuting attorney, Alan Bridge as a brow-beating detective, Ruth Donnelly as Betty's atypical mother, and Michael Chekhov as an eccentric Russian actor fond of making the murders in *Hamlet* more realistic. Spliced into the plot were vacant stretches in which Betty was able to sing "That Little Dream Got Nowhere," "How Do You Do It," and "Love Is the Darndest Thing." The programmer won no laurels for anyone concerned.

Betty gave birth to her first child, Candy, on November 23, 1946. Because of her pregnancy, she had to forgo a guest spot in the studio's *Variety Girl* (1947). So that her presence would not be missed, Dorothy Lamour did an imitation of Betty in a barbershop quartette number in *Variety Girl,* teamed with Barry Fitzgerald, Diana Lynn, and Gary Cooper.

As a wise follow-up to *Incendiary Blonde,* Paramount produced an expensively mounted *The Perils of Pauline* (1947). Betty recreated the purported life of great silent serial queen Pearl White. The biocomedy traced her rise from sweatshop worker to dumb member of a lowly theatrical troupe and then to leading exponent of risk-taking filmmaking in action-packed cliffhangers. The backdrop of the 1910s and 1920s allowed for broad burlesques of the unsubtle style of the old serial movies. Such authentic veterans of the early cinema as William Farnum, Paul Panzer, Snub Pollard, and Chester Conklin created a degree of verisimilitude that was not entirely undone by the more contemporary gagging of Billy De Wolfe (Shakespearian ham), William Demarest (silent film director), Constance Collier (old trouper), and John Lund (arrogant stage actor and Betty's fiancé). To ring in pathos with the yoks, the scenario called for Betty's (near) demise at the finale. She suffers a crippling fall while performing on the Paris stage, with the implication that she will not live long. Within the leisurely paced 98 minutes, several songs were introduced: "Poppa Don't Preach to Me," "I Wish I Didn't Love You So," "Rumble, Rumble," "Poor Pauline," and so on.

Time magazine, analyzing *The Perils of Pauline,* commented: "Betty Hutton has a capacity for pathos which is rather crudely exploited in this film, and a capacity for comedy which is exploited just as crudely, but oftener and more successfully, several of her missteps as a stage neophyte are good for laughs." Others found that her "ebullient, energetic, athletic manner" perfectly matched Pearl White's "original dynamic style of acting." The film was a big financial success and spurred the studio onward to develop more musical biography films for her.

Betty gave birth to her second daughter, Lindsay, on April 14, 1948. Her pregnancy had cost her the starring role in Warner Brothers' *Romance on The High Seas* (1948)—Doris Day was substituted. When Betty returned to the screen, it was in the badly conceived *Dream Girl* (1948). Paramount had paid $200,000 for the rights to Elmer Rice's stage success, which had starred his wife Betty Field, an on-again, off-again Paramount player. The studio then proceeded to undermine the point of the fantasy-drama by converting the lead character, Georgina Allerton, into the petulant daughter of a millionaire. Thus, the daydreaming visions she undergoes seem to be no more than the peevish wishings of a pampered miss: e.g., breaking up her sister's marriage to a bounder, running off to Mexico with a cad, living on a ranch with her sister's nemesis, and experiencing an operatic triumph as Madame Butterfly. Tedious Macdonald Carey was Betty's confused newspaper reporter boyfriend. The public stayed away from *Dream Girl* in droves and the critics roasted the film in general and Betty in particular. "Betty Hutton is a dud as the poor little millionaire's daughter who goes wandering in cuckooland" *(New York Times)*. "She still should have known better than to employ a disagreeable accent and a perpetual pout." *(New York Herald Tribune)*. Even Betty later admitted: "I loused that movie up because I didn't understand the girl I was playing. But a 'Kitty Foyle,' that kind of everyday girl, I could understand."

Part of the sting of this box-office failure was removed when Betty went to London to appear at the Palladium Theatre, for $17,500 a week. This late-1948 stage appearance was a tremendous personal success for her.

Paramount posthaste tossed Betty into more typical fare, *Red, Hot and Blue* (1949), which shared only the same title in common with the 1936 Cole Porter musical comedy. For a change, Betty had a virile, if laconic, leading man in Victor Mature—he would essay Samson in Cecil B. DeMille's *Samson and Delilah* that same year. In this film, he was the dedicated, no-nonsense young director who seeks to mold aspiring actress Betty and a stock troupe into a good performing company. Betty is put on the spot when a gangster, turned theatrical backer, is killed in her apartment. She is caught between battling cops and hoods, each wanting to learn who did it. Others in this Runyonesque musical pandemonium were June Havoc as Betty's more stable roommate and composer Frank Loesser as a dumb piano-loving racketeer. Betty's best moment was the song "That's Loyalty"; other tunes included "I Wake Up," a burlesque on Shakespeare entitled "Hamlet," and the ballad "Now That I Need You." *Cue* described Betty's dynamo performance thusly: "Betty Hutton, whose leaping, screaming, windmill style of song-and-dance delivery brings up images of a pogo stick in petticoats, is back again at her old stand." Betty recreated her *Red, Hot and Blue* role on the "Lux Radio Theatre" (February 6, 1950), with John Lund as her vis-à-vis.

In 1949, B. G. DeSylva had intended starring Betty in the movie version of the story of Theda Bara, but Betty rejected the script concept, despite her devotion to the producer. "Buddy had faith in me. What's more, he gave me faith in myself. Then he died. It was depression for me. . . . [If he had lived,] I would have become a great dramatic actress, because he was heading me toward that way, then he had a very bad heart attack." Later on, Betty would be announced by Paramount for film biographies of Clara Bow, Mabel Norman, and Sophie Tucker—projects which never came to be.

Betty and her husband Ted Briskin separated in January, 1950, and were divorced in April of that year. Betty explained: "I wanted that marriage to work more than anything in the world. Hell, I'd have cooked dinner for him every night." Later that year, she was dating actor Robert Sterling. When that romance terminated, she announced: "I'm not in a position to get too serious, and we were seeing each other, y'know, every five minutes."

Ever since the opening of Irving Berlin's musical *Annie Get Your Gun* on Broadway (May 16, 1946, 1,147 performances) Betty had been maniacal to win the lead in the projected movie version. Judy Canova was another hot contender for the part, but it was decided she was not pretty enough to portray Annie Oakley. When MGM purchased the screen rights to the smash play as a screen vehicle for their Judy Garland, Betty was disconsolate. In a May, 1950, *Esquire* article—"How to be Unhappy on $300,000 a Year"—Betty was quoted as saying: "It's the biggest disappointment I've known. It's been my whole life and right now I know it isn't worth that. I thought a really big picture success would be the greatest thing in the world. But it's rat race. No matter how good you are in one film the next has got to be better. You've got to keep topping yourself or you're dead." The article tabulated that since 1936 Betty had earned $1.5 million, but had not managed to save much of it. Said Betty: "Talent is my social security. When I run out of talent I'll be dead."

When Judy Garland was taken ill during the initial filming of *Annie Get Your Gun,* hasty contractual manipulations transpired so that Betty could be borrowed for the role. By the time shooting got underway again, director Busby Berkeley had been replaced by Charles Walters and then by George Sidney, and the later Frank Morgan by Louis Calhern, and costar Howard Keel had recovered from the broken leg caused by a horse falling on him. As part of the deal, Betty was optioned to make another film at MGM besides this musical; it never developed. Work on Paramount's own *Let's Dance,* pairing Betty with Fred Astaire, was wrapped up quickly so that the MGM production could proceed.

MGM's $2 million plus *Annie Get Your Gun* debuted at Loew's State Theatre on May 17, 1950, and proved a blockbuster hit. The technicolor tune show remained essentially the same woolly yarn of crack-shot tomboy Annie Oakley who joins Buffalo Bill's Wild West show and falls madly in love with champion sharpshooter Howard Keel. Within the film's expansive 107 minutes, director Sidney captured the raucous gaudiness of turn-of-the-century outdoor circus life, and the elemental verve of Betty's courtship and competition with Keel. Eight tunes were cut from the original score. Betty warbled "You Can't Get a Man With a Gun," "Doin' What Comes Naturally," "I'm an Indian Too," and "I've Got the Sun in the Morning," and dueted with Keel "Anything You Can Do," and "They Say It's Wonderful." The rousing "There's No Business Like Show Business" summed up the story's insistence on the glory of the entertainment life. In buckskin regalia and with her trusty rifle at her side, Betty carried the musical through its stodgy transitional moments and kept the audience's attention riveted on the score and the scenic splendor. Her ability to "keep the action vivid and vaguely plausible" won her the critics' appreciation. The *New York Daily News* proclaimed her "a joy to behold," but denatured Annie's uncouth, stubborn personality, and that Betty "fails to make as funny as Miss Merman did the running gag of freezing in slack-jawed adoration whenever Frank Butler gives her the eye." Keel did not think much of Betty, finding her "too self-centered" and too concerned with her own performance rather than with the film as a whole. MGM was impressed enough by Betty's sensational work to offer to buy her Paramount contract, but the latter studio adamantly refused. Betty was at her peak (on the cover of *Time* magazine, *Photoplay's* most popular actress of the year, etc.) and they did not intend losing her.

Betty continued making radio appearances in 1950. She was heard in *Daisy Mayne* (January 20, 1950), and in *Page Miss Glory* (May 21, 1950) with Ronald Reagan; both for the prestigious "Theatre Guild on the Air" (ABC).

Let's Dance (1950) was released in the trail of *Annie Get Your Gun,* with Betty top-billed over dancing star Fred Astaire. The paltry premise cast her and Astaire as World War II entertainers. When her flyer husband perishes in the war, she returns to Boston to care for her small child. Five years later, she makes a show business comeback and finds that Astaire is now a member of the business world. He rejoins the act and they slip into love. The villainess of the piece is puritanical mother-in-law Lucile Watson, who is seeking to gain custody of the child. Roland Young and Melville Cooper offer comedy relief as the crusty Watson attorneys; and Barton Mac-Lane is the nightclub owner. Betty's soloed "Why Fight the Feeling," "Can't Stop Talking About Him," and "Tunnel of Love." She and Astaire performed the lively "Oh Them Dudes" together. Geared more to Betty's talents than to those of Astaire, *Let's Dance* was a moderate theatrical success. Otis L. Guernsey, Jr. *(New York Herald Tribune)* pointed out: "A good partner in the production numbers, Miss Hutton might or might not complement him [Astaire] successfully in a better setting, her hoarse comedy is not an exact fit with the Astaire subtleties."

Astaire would later comment: "Working with Betty Hutton keeps anybody moving. She's so talented and conscientious that if you don't watch yourself you feel you're standing still and letting her do all the work."

Betty signed an RCA Victor recording contract in 1950. Her first single for them was "I Can't Stop Thinking About You" from *Let's Dance.*

At Paramount, Betty continued to ride high. Despite the inroads of television into the motion picture industry, she was still big box office. While other dramatic and glamour stars were dropped from the studio roster, Paramount retained its top musical comedy performer under contract—technicolor musicals were still a big drawing factor in luring blasé audiences away from their video boxes, as Warner Brothers found with Doris Day musicals and Twentieth Century-Fox experienced with its Betty Grable, June Haver, and Mitzi Gaynor tune pictures.

Like B. G. DeSylva, Cecil B. De Mille sensed greater talent in Betty than her screen roles had provided. In 1950 he signed her for the prestigious lead female role in his colossal circus tribute *The Greatest Show on Earth* (1952). The fact that she could perform on a trapeze as well as sing was a key factor in her copping the prize plum when Hedy Lamarr rejected the part. Betty spent much of 1951 working on this 151-minute production, which marched into Radio City Music Hall on January 10, 1952. As Holly, the expert trapeze artist in love with circus boss Charlton Heston, Betty proved an engaging focal point. Whether vying with Cornel Wilde in daring high-bar stunts for number-one trapeze spot, or urging Heston to forsake a few circus responsibilities and remember her, she was an unyielding bundle of energy. When the machinations of lion trainer Lyle Bettger cause the circus train to derail, it is Betty's guiding spirit which pulls the circus troupe together to carry on the show.

The Greatest Show on Earth was vintage De Mille, basic in plot, sophomoric and crude in histrionics, but always a massive bundle of crowd-pleasing entertainment. Betty was complimented by most critics for making her sequences on the swinging bars so authentic. (The Ringling Brothers, Barnum and Bailey Circus elected her to its Hall of Fame.) The big-top movie has grossed over $14 million to date.

Having prepared a new stage act while touring for the USO in Korea in 1951, Betty made her debut at New York's Palace Theatre on April 12, 1952. Judy Garland had dynamically brought the two-a-day show policy back to the Palace on her enormously successful October, 1951–February, 1952 engagement there, and Betty was considered the only follow-up headliner in America capable of attracting the necessary large audience. She opened with a $40,000 advance sale and wowed the town. The *New York Times* noted: "If she stops bouncing for sixty seconds in the entire fifty minutes, it isn't clear to the naked eye." Supporting acts on the bill included the Skylarks, Herb Shriner, and Borrah Minnevitch's Harmonica Rascals. Her four-week stay was a complete sellout.

As a result of the arduous Palace Theatre stint, Betty lost her voice, and it was discovered that she had a growth on her vocal cords. Betty was operated on, then went into rehearsal for her new Paramount musical *Somebody Loves Me* (1952), but she lost her voice again. This time she was forced to consult a voice instructor and retrain her projecting style.

While filming *Somebody Loves Me,* Betty made a cameo appearance in the Dean Martin-Jerry Lewis comedy *Sailor Beware* (1952) filming on an adjacent sound stage. She is seen in a frantic dockside farewell scene, giving a crushing goodbye to the sailors.

Somebody Loves Me, opening at the Roxy Theatre on September 24, 1952, proved to be Betty's last Paramount picture to date. It was loosely based on the careers of vaudeville headliners Blossom Seeley and Benny Fields (Ralph Meeker). The technicolor movie starts in 1906 on San Francisco's Barbary Coast, and traces the chanteuse's career through her World War I volunteer work and the inevitable Broadway successes. Weaved into the multiple stage and club song interludes is an account of resentful performer Meeker marrying Betty and his temporary departure. Adele Jergens portrays a haughty theatre performer, Sid Tomack and Henry Slate are Betty's initial stage partners, and even Jack Benny is drawn into the plot in a cameo spot. Among the 20 tunes Betty sings are: "On Stage," "Jealous," "Rose Room," "Teasin' Rag," and "Way Down Yonder in New Orleans." Betty was applauded for "always finding the right twist of mannerism or personality to fit the number" and since she is "less the jitterbug in the physical merchandising of the numbers, putting them over with show-wise touches that make credible use of her physical attributes. She handles the Seely characterization authoritatively to keep attention high." She performed her role again on "Lux Radio Theatre" (April 27, 1953) with Gene Barry in the Ralph Meeker assignment. RCA issued a soundtrack LP album of the film.

Betty married Charles O'Curran (the choreographer of *Somebody Loves Me*) on March 18, 1952, in Las Vegas. When Betty informed Paramount that her new husband was to direct her next film (*Topsy and Eva,* the life of the Duncan Sisters), the studio balked. On July 10, 1952, she walked out on her contract, which was not due to expire till the end of that year. Paramount subsequently hired the volatile and shapely popular songstress Rosemary Clooney to perform in its declining number of musical entertainments.

Betty returned to the Palladium Theatre in London for a three-week engagement, commencing September 20, 1952. She sang many numbers from *Somebody Loves Me,* and closed her act with a highly expert stanza on the trapeze bars. The *Variety* reviewer said: "Whether doing a Charleston or singing about New Orleans, she is a hip performer with a bubbling personality that projects throughout the theater. . . . This was show biz at its best." She took her packaged show to suburban English theatres and to Glasgow before returning to the United States. Before she left England, J. Arthur Rank offered her a role in the color feature *Matthew the Matador,* to costar Norman Wisdom and to be lensed in Spain. Negotiations were never completed.

After various nightclub appearances in America, Betty made a return engagement at the Palace Theatre in New York, opening October 14, 1953. There was a $50,000 advance sale after only 13 days' notice of her forthcoming appearance, substantiating that she still retained an adoring following. O'Curran staged her half of the bill; others in the show were the Skylarks and comedian Dick Shawn. The critics were enraptured anew by her Trojan performance, which included firing two six-shooters, and singing a lengthy medley of all her motion-picture hit songs. Despite her bombastic stage turn, Betty informed the press: "Now I don't have to come on like gang busters, because I'm sick with fright. I know the $4.80 group has to relax with you first. Fortunately this is where I came from, so I can do it till the right picture is ready. There's no room for a good picture. It's gotta be great."

Betty had been a long-standing holdout from the television medium. As a perfectionist who took her time about achieving the desired results, she refused to jump into any quickie production in order to cash in on her reputation. After all, the new medium was the last chance for her to enter a phase of show business with a clean slate: to be a working major star and not just a former movie great dabbling in the video scene. In 1954, she finally succumbed to the blandishments of wunderkind producer Max Liebman and the lavish terms offered by NBC network. Her initial vehicle was to be *Satin and Spurs,* a 90-minute spectacular musical to be televised in color. The production was budgeted at $300,000 and Betty's salary was $50,-000. Ray Evans and Jay Livingston wrote the songs and her husband Charles O'Curran was in charge of the choreography.

Satin and Spurs concerned lively rodeo queen Cindy, performing her routine at Madison Square Garden. A handsome feature photographer from a national magazine turns up to do the big inside story on her career. They naturally become enamored. Guy Raymond, Kevin McCarthy, Neva Patterson, and Genevieve filled out the cast. The songs included: "Whoop-Diddy-Ay-I've Had Enough," "Little Rock Roll," and others. Capitol Records (Betty's new record-company employer) issued a soundtrack album ahead of time.

The highly touted *Satin and Spurs* was telecast on September 12, 1954, and laid one of the biggest bombs in the history of entertainment. Any fortuitous resemblance between the telemusical and *Annie Get Your Gun* was purely accidental. John Crosby *(New York Herald Tribune)* reported: "Miss Hutton shook like a bowl of jelly through about five song numbers. . . . Whenever things started running down—and they started running down all the time—Miss Hutton sprang up and started shaking like a bowl of jelly. . . . Miss Hutton seemed to be trying to disprove the idea that girls are girls —and she did pretty well at it."

The spectacular flop of *Satin and Spurs* devastated the supersensitive Betty, and initiated a long series of show business failures. Four days before the telecast she had fired her husband from the show. Her initial enthusiasm for the medium and for director Liebman soured overnight with the bad reviews. She called Liebman a "cuckoo" and was bitter that she had received all the blame for the colossal turkey. She decided not to consider doing any other specials in a medium which she felt was only suitable for "young people." For days after the telecast she would not go out in public, for fear of being pointed at by disappointed fans.

Betty eventually returned to nightclub work in October, 1954. At the conclusion of her successful Desert Inn, Las Vegas, engagement on November 9, 1954, she weepingly told the audience: "This is the end. I'm giving up show business" to devote more time to the "kids and knitting." The public was genuinely moved at her tearful exit.

On February 21, 1955, she divorced O'Curran (he married Patti Page). For a brief time she was engaged to screen writer Norman Krasna. On March 8, 1955, she wed Alan W. Livingston, a Capitol Records executive. (He had two children by a previous marriage.) To add to her troubles, Betty suffered a miscarriage in August, 1955.

Betty suddenly reappeared on television as star of an hour special (October 26, 1955, NBC), clowning and singing away. Her guests were Jimmy Durante and Bob Hope. The *New York Times* reported: "She sang, shouted, wrinkled her nose, scurried, threw a man over her shoulder, helped carry a ladder and became winded.... The unpleasant fact is, however, that Miss Hutton fought a futile battle from the start. She worked much too hard and it showed."

She was still hoping to launch a splashy movie return, possibly on an independent production basis with the Sophie Tucker story. The unlikely vehicle that returned her to the screen was *Spring Reunion* (1957) a low-keyed sentimental drama based on a 1954 teleplay. Originally Judy Garland had been slated for the United Artists release. Betty accepted $100,000 plus 25 percent of the net take for performing in the picture. Much publicity was spewed forth to the effect that an entirely new Betty was returning to movies; no longer a temperamental, demanding, stubborn superstar. Shortly after preproduction work began, actress Florence Halop was fired from the cast and Jean Hagen substituted. It was rumored that Betty regarded Halop (of "Meet Millie" TV fame) as too much of a look-alike. Nevertheless, Betty told columnist Joe Hyams: "No more shouting and yelling. When I came on screen [in the past], people used to smile and say 'Here we go again.' It was a question of who could endure the most, me or the audience. And when I came into the room, people expected me to swing from the chandelier."

After wrapping up production on *Spring Reunion,* Betty was guest star on the "Dinah Shore Chevy Show" (October 2, 1956, NBC), releasing "boundless fury." *Variety* gasped: "No performer ever tried to do so much in one show, both qualitatively long and short.... What laughs she dredged [in the nonsinging comedy spots] stemmed from her physical efforts and the plaudits for her frantic agitation in enveloping such a broad scope of seemingly tireless caricature." She then packaged a musical revue which tried out at the Sombrero Playhouse, Phoenix, in December, 1956. The best segments of the show had her saluting the blues, backed up by the Cheerleader song group. The revue played the Sahara Hotel for four weeks, with Betty receiving a $25,000 weekly paycheck.

Spring Reunion ironically opened at the site of her past live triumphs, the Palace Theatre, on May 5, 1957. The slight plot featured Betty as a graduate of Carson High, class of 1941. She now is working in her father's real estate office and lives at home. At the fifteenth class reunion, she is attracted to drifter Dana Andrews, but is afraid of marriage. Eventually they go off to San Francisco together. Jean Hagen was winning as the bored housewife classmate who flirts with married man Gordon Jones. James Gleason appeared as the philosophical lighthouse-keeper who advises Betty and Andrews on life when their boat capsizes near his station. Betty sang one song "That Old Feeling." A. Weiler (*New York Times*) observed: "Miss Hutton is a restrained heroine unlike the ebullient songstress she has portrayed on the screen in the past. She only projects the dramatic poignancy inherent in the role, in a climactic speech stating her desperate desire for marriage and a home of her own." The lukewarm reception given *Spring Reunion* greatly diminished Betty's box-office worth. New film offers were now few and far between.

At one point Betty was considered for the lead in John Golden's short-lived Broadway musical *Seventh Heaven*. She was the star attraction at the much-delayed opening of Lou Walters's Café de Paris club in Manhattan in May, 1958. The newspapers termed her a "superb showwoman." That same year, Betty joined the Lutheran Church. She explained that reading *The Power of Positive Thinking* by Dr. Norman Vincent Peale had led to the decision: "Joining the Church has been the most outstanding thing that's happened to me lately. My family is now together and we're all very happy. . . . I owed it to my daughters to find a religion for them. I've always been a religious person, but I never really belonged to a church."

Betty remained leery of television: "I'm a perfectionist. If a show can't be done as well as possible I'd rather skip it. I've been on TV only five times in my life [on March 22, 1958, and April 27, 1958, she had made two more appearances on the "Dinah Shore Chevy Show"]. I'm afraid of it unless I'm in charge of what I'm going to do."

Again in mid-1958, Betty retired from show business because "I had never given myself the chance to be a housewife." A few months later, she again reactivated her career because: "I still had pride enough in myself as a performer not to simply drop out of the business, leaving people asking 'Say whatever became of Betty Hutton anyhow?' "

Betty responded to CBS TV's tempting offer to star in "The Betty Hutton Show," originally tagged "Goldie." Betty played a talkative manicurist who becomes recipient of a large legacy and the custody of three children (Gigi Perreau, Richard Miles, Dennis Joel) when a rich Wall Street customer dies. Betty was bubbly about the show's prospects: "It's so cotton pickin' funny you'll just die when you see it." Unfortunately, the series proved deadly video fare from its debut October 1, 1959, onward. Betty's irrepressible style was hampered by a leaden script and "tedious attention to unnecessary detail." The show was canceled in the spring of 1960. Betty announced: "No matter what you heard, it was MY decision and nobody else's to end the series. I couldn't stand by while a bunch of rank amateurs from the advertising agency representing the sponsor tried to ruin the show." She explained that she had tackled the rigors of a weekly shooting schedule because club and theatre work did not completely satisfy her professional needs: "When the band cuts out, and the curtain comes down, I can't bear it. It's that feeling of being left alone behind the curtain that gets me. I want to shout: 'Don't bring it down! Please don't bring it down!' " The series has never been rerun. It would have given part-owner Betty a nice income.

In 1959 Warner Brothers Records issue a new Betty Hutton LP album recorded live at the Saints and Sinners Ball. It received little promotion and quickly disappeared from sight, another example of the bad planning currently hounding Betty's professional career.

While fulfilling an engagement at Manhattan's Basin Street East club in September, 1960, Betty made a rare guest appearance on Jack Paar's talk show (NBC) to plug her nightclub act. As part of her stint on the program, she mockingly lit into Paar, calling him a "square," and so forth. Later on the telecast the indignant Paar compared Betty to Mickey Rooney, whom he had accused of being drunk on an earlier show. A wild feud between Betty and Paar flew up, and was grist for the gossip columns for weeks thereafter.

Betty divorced Livingston, then an NBC-TV executive, on October 21, 1960. They had previously been separated and reconciled twice. Each charged the other with mental cruelty; he noted that she earned $150,000 a year and did not need a man around the house. On December 24, 1960, Betty and trumpeter Peter Candoli, age 37, were married in Las Vegas at the Lutheran Reformation Church. She had known the musician for the past 12 years. He had a daughter Tara by a prior marriage.

Reporters still found Betty newsworthy. When asked how she became a star, Betty candidly admitted: "I shoved and clawed my way up." Asked whether she was now content: "I knew when I was very young that I was going to be a star and have enough money so that I'd be able to blot out all those bitter years. I made the money, but I didn't blot the memory and I guess I never will."

Betty's constant companion on all her tours had been her mother (the latter once explained: "Any one else would drive Betty crazy"). The mother died January 1, 1962, in a fire in her Hollywood home.

Betty starred in a summer tour of *Gypsy* in 1962. Leading man Vincent Beck withdrew from the cast because of artistic differences with her. The Actors Equity Association fined Betty $1,000 for being uncooperative. Her reply: "Summer stock is amateur night in Dixie." She had to relinquish a projected package of *Calamity Jane* later that summer because she was pregnant. Ginger Rogers substituted. Betty gave birth to daughter Carolyn in late 1962.

In the summer of 1963, Betty made her fifth comeback, headlining a packaged tour of *Annie Get Your Gun*. She was still using the press as a psychoanalytical substitute: "I'm just too much of a perfectionist. I'm not satisfied with pleasing myself. Most of the time I think I'm awful." Her husband viewed the situation differently: "All she needs is someone to keep telling her how good she is. Someone she believes in."

When Carol Burnett temporarily left the faltering Jule Styne musical *Fade Out, Fade In* due to bad health, Betty assumed the role on Broadway for one week in July, 1964. Her box-office power had noticeably shrunk, even taking into account the weak vehicle at hand, her hasty takeover, summertime, and the then current World's Fair in Flushing, New York. Betty next performed in a run of *Gentlemen Prefer Blondes* in Chicago. She had once been considered for the lead in the original Broadway version.

Betty popped up on the television Western series "Gunsmoke" (CBS) on the May 1, 1965, episode, playing a prim Bostonian whose husband had been murdered; she becomes a saloon singer and to avenge her spouse's death by killing Marshall James Arness. Betty also had a brief cameo role on a "Burke's Law" (ABC) tele-episode that same year.

Betty was still complaining about her past glories: "That's all I was—a personality. A great nothing dying to be loved. I don't have to tell you how I feel. I'll kill myself, I'll bleed to have applause. I thought I was some kind of nut until I met Al Jolson who told me that applause was the only thing that mattered in his life, too."

Betty and her husband Candoli obtained a Mexican divorce in September, 1966, but later patched up their marriage. She later confided to Earl Wilson: "My husband and I don't spend the night together. He goes home at night to his own pad. Pete likes to write music at night and he can't stand the baby making noise. And I can't stand the scrambling for the bathroom in the morning. Besides I like the whole bed to myself. Pete and I weren't getting along for a while. We tried this to make it work and it has. He comes to breakfast. I see him as much as any wife sees her husband except at night." (They would finally divorce in November, 1971; he wed performer Edie Adams in 1972.)

Betty was signed to star in two of A. C. Lyles's low-budget Paramount Westerns in 1967. Lyles thought it a good nostalgic gimmick to team Betty with her *Annie Get Your Gun* screen partner, Howard Keel. Shortly after starting work on *Red Tomahawk* (1967), Betty was fired and replaced by another former Paramount star, Joan Caulfield. Keel explained the substitution: "We usually had a 10-day shooting schedule and I remember a day on which we filmed 40 pages of dialogue. Betty wasn't used to working that fast and was unable to complete scenes in one or two takes. If they hadn't dropped her the picture would have gone way over budget." Caulfield also assumed the female lead in *Buckskin* (1968), the other quickie intended for Betty.

On June 9, 1967, Betty declared bankruptcy, listing debts of $150,000.

In the following years, Betty's name occasionally appeared in the press, usually in reference to another projected comeback: "I've got the zest to go again. I'm still a frenzy of movement like they used to say. I want everybody to know I'm not as old as Methuselah." But even to ride in the Hollywood Santa Claus Lane Parade (November 24, 1971)—her first public appearance in seven years—was an emotional hassle for Betty.

In a recent nostalgia issue of a national magazine, Betty was one of the featured attractions. She was quoted as saying: "I'm so blue. I'm so mixed-up and blue. I just can't take any more setbacks.

"It's been a nightmare. I lost my mother, my two older girls walked away from me. I had a very bad marriage, and my career stopped, except for summer stock at some cockamamie places I never would have been booked into before. And once you accept one of those, zoom! down the tube. It's a fast downward trend. . . .

"I don't know the 'in' crowd in Hollywood anymore, the people who run the industry. They're making peculiar, bizarre, nutty stories. I don't even have many friends anymore because I backed away from them; when things went wrong for me I didn't want them to have any part of my trouble. . . .

"I think things are going to go right for me again. I'm not old. I'm old enough, but I photograph young, thank God, and I still have a public. I still get fan mail. . . .

"I don't know where it's all going to lead. I have no idea where I'm going. I would just like to be happy."

THE FLEET'S IN (PAR, 1942) 93 M.

Associate producer, Paul Jones; director, Victor Schertzinger; story, Monte Brice, J. Walter Ruben; screenplay, Walter De Leon; Sid Silvers; songs, Johnny Mercer and Schertzinger; Joseph J. Lilley; Frank Loesser and Schertzinger; camera, William Mellor; editor, Paul Weatherwax.

Dorothy Lamour (The Countess); William Holden (Casey Kirby); Eddie Bracken (Barney Waters); Betty Hutton (Bessie Dale); Cass Daley (Cissie); Gil Lamb (Spike); Leif Erickson (Jake); Betty Jane Rhodes (Diane Golden);Lorraine and Rognan (Dance Team); Jack Norton (Kellogg); Jimmy Dorsey and his Band (Themselves); Barbara Britton (Eileen Wright); Robert Warwick (Admiral Wright); Roy Atwell (Arthur Sidney); Dave Willock, Rod Cameron (Sailors); Harry Barris (Pee Wee); Hal Dawson (Diana's Manager); Charlie Williams (Photographer); Lyle Latell (Drunk); Oscar Smith (Valet); Stanley Andrews (Commander); Chester Clute (Minister).

STAR SPANGLED RHYTHM (PAR, 1942) 99 M.

Associate producer, Joseph Sistrom; director, George Marshall; screenplay, Harry Tugend; music, Robert Emmett Dolan; songs, Johnny Mercer and Harold Arlen; art director, Hans Dreier, Ernst Fegte; camera, Leo Tover, Theodor Sparkuhl; editor, Arthur Schmidt.

Betty Hutton (Polly Judson); Eddie Bracken (Jimmy Webster); Victor Moore (Pop Webster); Anne Revere (Sarah); Walter Abel (Frisbee); Cass Daley (Mimi); Macdonald Carey (Louie the Lug); Gil Lamb (Hi-Pockets); William Haade (Duffy); Bob Hope (Master of Ceremonies); Marion Martin, William Bendix, Dorothy Lamour, Paulette Goddard, Veronica Lake, Arthur Treacher, Walter Catlett, Sterling Holloway, Vera Zorina, Frank Faylen, Fred MacMurray, Franchot Tone, Ray Milland, Lynne Overman, Susan Hayward, Ernest Truex, Mary Martin, Dick Powell, Golden Gate Quartette, Walter Dare Wahl and Co., Cecil B. DeMille, Preston Sturges, Ralph Murphy, Alan Ladd, Gary Crosby, Jack Hope, Katharine Dunham, Rochester, Marjorie Reynolds, Betty Rhodes, Dona Drake, Bing Crosby, Jimmy Lydon, Ellen Drew, Charles Smith, Frances Gifford, Susanna Foster, Robert Preston (Themselves); Tom Dugan (Hitler); Richard Loo (Hirohito); Paul Porcasi (Mussolini); Dorothy Granger (Officer); Woody Strode (Rochester's Motorcycle Chauffeur); Barbara Pepper, Jean Phillips, Lynda Grey (Girls); Eddie Dew, Rod Cameron (Petty Officers); Keith Richards (Officer); Irving Bacon (New Hampshire Farmer—Old Glory Number);Virginia Brissac (Lady from Iowa—Old Glory Number); Matt McHugh (Man from Brooklyn—Old Glory Number); Peter Potter (Georgia Boy—Old Glory Number).

HAPPY GO LUCKY (PAR, 1943) 81 M.

Associate producer, Harold Wilson; director, Curtis Bernhardt; story, Michael Uris; adaptation, John Jacoby; screenplay, Walter DeLeon, Melvin Frank, Norman Panama; music director, Robert Emmett Dolan; choreography, Paul Oscard; art director, Hans Dreier, Raoul Rene DuBois; songs, Frank Loesser and Jimmy McHugh; camera, Karl Struss, Wilfred Cline; editor, Ellsworth Hoagland.

Mary Martin (Marjory Stuart); Dick Powell (Pete Hamilton); Betty Hutton (Bubbles Hennessy); Eddie Bracken (Wally Case); Rudy Vallee (Alfred Monroe); Mabel Paige (Mrs. Smith); Eric Blore (Mr. Vespers); Clem Bevans (Mr. Smith); Rita Christiani (Specialty Dancer); Sir Lancelot (Singer); Ben Carter (Joe Brown); Lillian Randolph (Tessie); Paul McVey (Assistant Manager); Frederick Clarke (Doorman); William B. Davidson (Husband); Almira Sessions (Overstuffed Matronly Woman); Tom Dugan (Meek Little Man); Sarah Edwards (Spinster); Hillary Brooke (Young Society Girl); Napoleon Simpson (Tessie's Husband); Leyland Hodgson (Reporter in Lobby); Irving Bacon, Arthur Loft (Reporters); Donald Kerr (Photographer); Gene Cole (Dancer); Olaf Hytten (Jeweler); Kay Linaker (Suzanne); Jean Fenwick (Agnes);

Harry Barris (Master of Ceremonies); Edgar Norton (Captain of Waiters); Charles R. Moore (Pandro); Lyle Latell (Man in Kissing Routine).

LET'S FACE IT (PAR, 1943) 76 M.

Producer, Fred Kohlmar; director, Sidney Lanfield; based on the musical play by Dorothy and Herbert Fields, Cole Porter; and the play *Cradle Snatchers* by Norma Mitchell, Russell G. Medcraft; songs, Porter; Sammy Cahn and Jule Styne; camera, Lionel Lindon; editor, Paul Weatherwax; art director, Hans Dreier, Earl Hedrick; music director, Robert Emmett Dolan.

Bob Hope (Jerry Walker); Betty Hutton (Winnie Potter); Dona Drake (Muriel); Cully Richards (Frankie Burns); Eve Arden (Maggie Watson); Zasu Pitts (Cornelia Figeson); Marjorie Weaver (Jean Blanchard); Raymond Walburn (Julian Watson); Phyllis Povah (Nancy Collister); Joe Sawyer (Sgt. Wiggins); Dave Willock (Barney Hilliard); Nicco and Tanya (Dance Team); Andrew Tombes (Judge Henry Pigeon); Grace Hayle (Mrs. Wigglesworth); Evelyn Dockson (Mrs. Taylor); Kay Linaker (Canteen Hostess); Frederic Nay (Walsh); George Meader (Justice of the Peace); Joyce Compton (Wiggin's Girl); Florence Shirley (Woman in Sun Shell Cafe); Barbara Pepper (Daisy); Robin Raymond (Mimi); Phyllis Ruth (Lulu); Lionel Royce (Submarine Commander); Emory Parnell (Colonel); Andria Moreland, Brooke Evans (Milk-Maids); Don Kerr (Specialty Dancer); Edward Dew (Sergeant); Eddie Dunn (Cop); Elinor Troy (Elinor); Eleanor Prentiss (Woman In Court); Cyril Ring (Head-Waiter); William B. Davidson (Man in Boat); Yvonne DeCarlo, Noel Neill, Julie Gibson, Jayne Hazard (Girls).

THE MIRACLE OF MORGAN'S CREEK (PAR, 1944) 99 M.

Director-screenplay, Preston Sturges; art director, Hans Dreier, Ernst Fegte; music, Leo Shuken, Charles Bradshaw; camera John Seitz; editor, Stuart Gilmore.

Eddie Bracken (Norval Jones); Betty Hutton (Trudy Kockenlocker); Diana Lynn (Emmy Kockenlocker); William Demarest (Officer Kockenlocker); Porter Hall (Justice of the Peace); Emory Parnell (Mr. Tuerck); Alan Bridge (Mr. Johnson); Julius Tannen (Mr. Rafferty); Victor Potel (Newspaper Editor); Brian Donlevy (McGinty); Akim Tamiroff (The Boss); Almira Sessions (Wife of Justice of the Peace); Esther Howard (Sally); J. Farrell Macdonald (Sheriff); Frank Moran (First M.P.); Georgia Caine (Mrs. Johnson); Connie Tompkins (Cecilia); Torben Meyer (Doctor); George Melford (U.S. Marshal); Jimmy Conlin (Mayor); Harry Rosenthal (Mr. Schwartz); Chester Conklin (Pete); Hal Craig, Roger Creed (State Police); Keith Richards, Kenneth Gibson (Secret Service Men); Byron Foulger, Arthur Loft (McGinty's Secretaries); Jack Norton (Man Opening Champagne); Joe Devlin (Mussolini); Bobby Watson (Hilter).

HERE COME THE WAVES (PAR, 1944) 99 M.

Producer-director, Mark Sandrich; screenplay, Allen Scott, Ken Englund, Zion Myers; songs, Harold Arlen and Johnny Mercer; music director, Robert Emmett Dolan; art director, Hans Dreier, Roland Anderson; process camera, Farciot Edouart; special effects, Gordon Jennings, Paul Lerpae; camera, Charles Lang; editor, Ellsworth Hoagland.

Bing Crosby (Johnny Cabot); Betty Hutton (Susie Allison/Rosemary Allison); Sonny Tufts (Windy); Ann Doran (Ruth); Gwen Crawford (Tex); Noel Neill (Dorothy); Catherine Craig (Lt. Townsend); Marjorie Henshaw (Isabel); Harry Barris (Band Leader); Mae Clarke (Ensign Kirk); Minor Watson (High Ranking Officer); Roberta Jonay, Guy Zanett (Specialty Dancers); Louise LaPlanche (Girl Photographer); Mona Freeman, Carlotta Jelm (Painting Girls); Jack Norton (Waiter—Cabana Club); Jimmie Dundee (Chief Petty Officer); James Flavin (Shore Patrolman); Babe London (Girl Window Washer); Oscar O'Shea (Commodore); Cyril Ring (Lt. Colonel); Frances Morris (Wave); Yvonne De Carlo (Girl); Jerry James (Sailor).

INCENDIARY BLONDE (PAR, 1945) 113 M.

Producer, Joseph Sistrom; director, George Marshall; screenplay, Claude Binyon, Frank Butler; music, Robert Emmett Dolan; choreography, Danny Dare; songs, Maurice Abrahams and Lewis F. Muir; Eddie Leonard; Lew Brown and Albert Von Tilzer; Howard Johnson, Joseph McCarthy and Jimmy Monaco; William Jerome and Monaco; Shelton Brooks; Gus Kahn and Isham Jones; Henry Tucker and George Cooper; camera, Ray Rennahan; editor, Archie Marshek.

Betty Hutton (Texas Guinan); Arturo De Cordova (Bill Kilgannon); Charlie Ruggles (Cherokee Jim); Albert Dekker (Cadden); Barry Fitzgerald (Mike Guinan); Mary Phillips (Bessie Guinan); Bill Goodwin (Tim Callahan); Eduardo Ciannelli (Nick, The Greek); The Maxellos (Themselves); Maurice Rocco (Himself); Ted Mapes (Waco Smith); Charles C. Wilson (Mr. Ballinger); Ann Carter (Pearl Guinan—Age 7); Carlotta Jelm (Pearl Guinan—Age 17); Maxine Fife (Pearl Guinan—Age 21); George Nokes (Tommy Guinan—Age 5); Eddie Nichols (Tommy—Age 15); Billy Lechner (Tommy—Age 19); Robert Winkler (Billie Guinan); Patricia Prest (Texas Guinan—Age 9); Billy Curtis (Baby Joe); Edmund MacDonald (Charley Rinaldo); Don Costello (Gus Rinaldo); Erville Alderson, Fred Kelsey, Francis Ford (Ranch Owners); Pat West (Bartender); Matt McHugh (O'Keefe); Russell Simpson (Jenkins); Arthur Loft (McKee); Andrew Tombes (Hadley); Pierre Watkin (Otto Hammel); James Millican (Hector); Edwin Stanley (Mr. Zweigler); Dewey Robinson (Proprietor of Speakeasy); Etta McDaniel (Maid); Frank Faylen (Hotel Clerk); Harry Hayden (Horace Biggs) Jimmie Dundee (Cadden's Bodyguard); Jack Luden (Man); Ruth Roman (Woman); Emmett Vogan (Doctor).

DUFFY'S TAVERN (PAR, 1945) 97 M.

Associate producer, Danny Dare; director, Hal Walker; screenplay, Melvin Frank, Norman Panama; art director, Hans Dreier, William Flannery; choreography, Billy Daniels; music director, Robert Emmett Dolan; songs, Johnny Burke and James Van Heusen; Ben Raleigh and Bernie Wayne; camera, Lionel Lindon; special effects, Gordon Jennings; process camera, Farciot Edouart; editor, Arthur Schmidt.

Bing Crosby, Betty Hutton, Paulette Goddard, Alan Ladd, Dorothy Lamour, Eddie Bracken, Brian Donlevy, Sonny Tufts, Veronica Lake, Arturo De Cordova, Cass Daley, Diana Lynn, Gary Crosby, Phillip Crosby, Dennis Crosby, Lin Crosby, William Bendix, Maurice Rocco, James Brown, Joan Caulfield, Gail Russell, Helen Walker, Jean Heather (Themselves); Barry Fitzgerald (Bing Crosby's Father); Victor Moore (Michael O'Malley); Barry Sullivan (Danny Murphy); Marjorie Reynolds (Peggy O'Malley); Ed Gardner (Archie); Charles Cantor (Finnegan); Eddie Green (Eddie—The Waiter); Ann Thomas (Miss Duffy); Howard Da Silva (Heavy); Billy De Wolfe (Doctor); Walter Abel (Director); Charles Quigley (Ronald); Olga San Juan (Gloria); Robert Watson (Masseur); Frank Faylen (Customer); Matt McHugh (Man Following Miss Duffy); Emmett Vogan (Make-Up Man); Cyril Ring (Gaffer); Noel Neill (School Kid).

THE STORK CLUB (PAR, 1945) 98 M.

Producer, B. G. DeSylva; associate producer, Harold Wilson; director, Hal Walker; screenplay, DeSylva, John McGowan; music director, Robert Emmett Dolan; songs, Paul Francis Webster and Hoagy Carmichael; Ray Evans and Jay Livingston; Paul Francis Webster and Harry Revel; Sammy Cahn and Jule Styne; art director, Hans Dreier, Earl Hendrick; camera, Charles Lang, Jr.; editor, Gladys Carley.

Betty Hutton (Judy Peabody); Barry Fitzgerald (Jerry B. Bates); Don DeFore (Danny Wilton); Robert Benchley (Tom Curtis); Bill Goodwin (Sherman Billingsley); Iris Adrian (Gwen); Mikhail Rasumny (Coretti); Mary Young (Mrs. Edith Bates); Andy Russell (Jim); Perc Launders (Tom—Band Member); Mary Currier (Hazel Billingsley); Noel Neill (Jacqueline Billingsley); Gloria Donovan (Barbara Billingsley); Mae Busch (Vera); Pierre Watkin (Hotel Manager); Charles Coleman (Bates' Butler); Dorothy Garrett (Cashier); Cosmo Sardo (Rocco—Stork Club Waiter); Grady Sutton (Peter—Salesman); Audrey Young (Jenny—Check Girl); Roberta Jonay (Molly—

Check Girl); Anthony Caruso (Joe—Fisherman); Jimmy Dundee (Fred—Fisherman); Darrell Huntley (Fred—Fisherman); Franklyn Farnum (Diner); Sam Ash (Ringsider); Reed Howes (Patron).

CROSS MY HEART (PAR, 1946) 85 M.

Producer, Harry Tugend; director, John Berry; based on the play by Louis Verneiul, George Berr; screenplay, Tugend, Claude Binyon; additional dialogue, Charles Schnee; music arrangement, Joseph J. Lilley; music, Robert Emmett Dolan; songs, Johnny Burke and James Van Heusen; camera, Charles Lang, Jr., Stuart Thompson; editor, Ellsworth Hoagland.

Betty Hutton (Peggy Harper); Sonny Tufts (Oliver Clarke); Rhys Williams (Prosecutor); Ruth Donnelly (Eve Harper); Alan Bridge (Detective Flynn); Howard Freeman (Wallace Brent); Iris Adrian (Miss Baggart); Lewis L. Russell (Judge); Michael Chekhov (Peter); Milton Kibbee, Nolan Leary, Shimen Ruskin, John Kelly, Ethyl Mae Halls, Chester Morrison, Besse Wade, Mae Busch, Wilbur Mack, William Meader (Jurors); Ida Moore (Little Lady Juror); Jimmy Conlin (Jury Foreman); Lou Lubin (Tony Krouch); Tom Dugan, Tom Fadden (Truck Drivers); Almira Sessions (Old Hag); Dorothy Vaughan (Matron); Larry Thompson (Mr. Dennis—Assistant Prosecutor); Arthur Loft (Deputy); Walter Baldwin (Coroner); Syd Saylor, Frank Ferguson, Harry Harvey (Reporters); Frank Faylen (Fingerprint Expert); Jody Gilbert (Miss Stewart); Kathleen Howard (Mrs. Klute); Bobby Larson (Newsboy).

THE PERILS OF PAULINE (PAR, 1947) 98 M.

Producer, Sol C. Siegel; director, George Marshall; story, J. P. Wolfson music score, Robert Emmett Dolan; art director, Hans Dreier, Roland Anderson; songs, Frank Loesser; Raymond Walker and Charles McCarron; camera, Ray Rennahan; editor, Arthur Schmidt.

Betty Hutton (Pearl White); John Lund (Michael Farrington); Billy De Wolfe (Timmy); William Demarest (Chuck McManus); Constance Collier (Julia Gibbs); Frank Faylen (Joe Gurt); William Farnum (Hero—Western Saloon Set); Paul Panzer (Gent—Interior Drawing Room); Snub Pollard (Propman—Western Saloon); Creighton Hale (Marcelled Leading Man); Chester Conklin, James Finlayson, Hank Mann (Chef Comics); Bert Roach (Bartender—Western Saloon); Francis McDonald (Heavy —Western Saloon); Heinie Conklin (Studio Cop); Franklyn Farnum (Friar John); Eric Alden (Officer); Ethel Clayton (Lady Montague); (Juliet); Harry Hayden (Stage Manager); Julia Faye (Nurse); Chester Clute ("Willie" Millick); Myrtle Anderson (Maid); Frank Ferguson (Theatre Owner); Rex Lease, Stanley Blystone, Sidney D'Albrook (Reporters); John "Skins" Miller (Cameraman—Drawing Room Set); Bess Flowers, Paula Ray (Reporters); Tom Dugan (Balloonist); Eugene Borden (French Doctor); Byron Poindexter (Man); Raymond de Ravenne (Call Boy); Jack Shea (Workman).

DREAM GIRL (PAR, 1947) 85 M.

Producer, P. J. Wolfson; director, Mitchell Leisen; based on the play by Elmer Rice; screenplay, Arthur Sheekman; art director, Hans Dreier, John Meehan; music, Victor Young; camera, Daniel L. Fapp; editor, Alma Macrorie.

Betty Hutton (Georgina Allerton); Macdonald Carey (Clark Redfield); Patric Knowles (Jim Lucas); Virginia Field (Miriam Allerton Lucas); Walter Abel (George Allerton); Peggy Wood (Lucy Allerton); Lowell Gilmore (George Hand); Zamah Cunningham (Mme. Kimmeloff); Frank Puglia (Antonio); Selmer Jackson (Judge "Jed" Allerton); Georgia Backus (Edna); Charles Meredith (Charles); Dorothy Christy (Mollie Hand); Antonio Morales (Lovelita); John Dehner (Radio Announcer); Tad Van Brunt (Dramatic Student); Catherine Price (Aunt); Gordon Arnold, George Peters, Robert Rich, John S. Roberts (Ushers); Mary MacLaren (Judge Allerton's Wife); Bess Flowers (Social Secretary); Frederic Nay (Assistant Florist); Gino Corrado (Chef);

Jerry James (Best Man); Ida Moore (A Woman); John Butler (Shabby Little Man); Al Kikume (South Sea Island Policeman); Noble Johnson (Bartender).

RED, HOT AND BLUE (PAR, 1949) 84 M.

Producer, Robert Fellows; director, John Farrow; story, Charles Lederer; screenplay, Hagar Wilde, Farrow; art director, Hans Dreier, Franz Bachelin; music director, Van Cleve; songs, Frank Loesser; camera, Daniel L. Fapp; editor, Eda Warren.

Betty Hutton (Eleanor Collier); Victor Mature (Denny James); William Demarest (Charlie Baxter); June Havoc (Sandra); Jane Nigh (No-No); Frank Loesser (Hair-Do Lempke); William Talman (Bunny Harris); Art Smith (Laddie Corwin); Raymond Walburn (Mr. Creek); Onslow Stevens (Captain Allen); Joseph Vitale (Carr); Barry Kelley (Lt. Gorham); Robert Watson (Barney Stratum); Jack Kruschen (Steve); Percy Helton (Stage Manager); Philip Van Zandt (Head Waiter); Don Shelton (Hamlet); Herschel Daugherty (Laertes) Dorothy Abbott (The Queen); Julia Faye (The Housekeeper); James Davies, Douglas Spencer, Noel Neill, Paul Lees, James Cornell, Joey Ray (Members of Theatre Group); Julie Adams (Starlet); Lestor Dorr (Drug Store Manager); Billy Daniels, Rita Lupino (Dance Team); Harland Tucker (Saunders); Bess Flowers (Woman); Tim Ryan (Stranger); Roscoe Behan (Bartender—Perrina Club); Cy Ring (Photographer); Lee Phelps (Policeman); Jimmie Dundee (Gangster); Al Ferguson, Billy Engle, Ed Peil, Sr., Douglas Carter (Piano Tuners); Robert Kellard (Police Switchboard Operator); Marie Thomas, Jacqueline Park (Showgirls).

ANNIE GET YOUR GUN (MGM, 1950) 107 M.

Producer, Arthur Freed; director, George Sidney; based on the play by Dorothy and Herbert Fields and Irving Berlin; screenplay, Sidney Sheldon; choreography, Robert Alton; music director, Adolphe Deutsch; songs, Berlin; art director, Cedric Gibbons, Paul Groesse; camera, Charles Rosher; editor, James E. Newcom.

Betty Hutton (Annie Oakley); Howard Keel (Frank Butler); Louis Calhern (Buffalo Bill); J. Carrol Naish (Sitting Bull); Edward Arnold (Pawnee Bill); Keenan Wynn (Charlie Davenport); Benay Venuta (Dolly Tate); Clinton Sundberg (Foster Wilson); James H. Harrison (Mac); Bradley Mora (Little Jake); Diane Dick (Nellie); Susan Odin (Jessie); Eleanor Brown (Minnie); Chief Yowlachie (Little Horse); W. P. Wilkerson, Shooting Star, Charles Mauu, Riley Sunrise, Tom Humphreys, John War Eagle (Indian Braves); Edith Mills, Dorothy Skyeagle (Squaws); Sue Casey, Mary Ellen Gleason, Mary Jane French, Meredith Leeds, Helen Kimball, Dorinda Clifton, Mariette Elliott, Judy Landon (Cowgirls); Jack Trent, Michael Dugan, Carl Sepulveds, Warren Macgregor, Carol Henry, Archie Butler, Fred Gilman (Cowboys); Tony Taylor (Little Boy); Ed Kilroy (Guest); Wiliam Tannen (Barker); Evelyn Beresford (Queen Victoria); Andre Charlot (President Loubet of France); Nino Pipitone (King Victor Emanuel); John Mylong (Kaiser Wilhelm II); Al Rhein, Charles Regan (Barkers); Elizabeth Flournoy (Helen); Nolan Leary, Budd Fine (Immigration Officers); John Hamilton (Ship Captain); Marjorie Wood (Constance); Mae Clarke Langdon (Mrs. Adams); Lee Tung Foo (Waiter).

LET'S DANCE (PAR, 1950) 111 M.

Producer, Robert Fellows; director, Norman Z. McLeod; based on the story "Little Boy Blue" by Maurice Zolotow; screenplay, Allan Scott; additional dialogue; Dane Lussier; songs, Frank Loesser; music director, Robert Emmett Dolan; art director, Hans Dreier, Roland Anderson; camera, George Barnes; editor, Ellsworth Hoagland.

Betty Hutton (Kitty McNeil); Fred Astaire (Donald Elwood); Roland Young (Mr. Edmund Pohlwhistle); Ruth Warrick (Carola Everett); Lucile Watson (Serena Everett); Gregory Moffett (Richard Everett); Barton MacLane (Larry Channock); Shepperd Strudwick (Timothy Bryant); Melville Cooper (Mr. Charles Wagstaffe); Harold Huber (Marcel); George Zucco (Judge); Peggy Badley (Bubbles Malone); Virginia Toland (Elsie); Sayre Dearing (Process Server); Ida Moore (Mrs. McGuire); Nana Bryant (Mrs. Bryant); Boyd Davis (Butler); Bobby Barber (Bartender); Herbert Virgan

(Chili Parlor Owner); Rolfe Sedan (Jewelry Clerk); Ralph Peters (Cab Driver); Paul A. Pierce (Square Dance Caller); Eric Alden (Captain); Milton Delugg (Himself); Harry Woods (Police Lt.); Chester Conklin (Watchman); Major Sam Harris, Bess Flowers, Marion Gray (Guests); Peggy O'Neill (Woman).

THE GREATEST SHOW ON EARTH (PAR, 1952) 153 M.

Producer, Cecil B. DeMille; associate producer, Henry Wilcoxon; director, De-Mille; story, Frederic M. Frank; Theodore St. John, Frank Cavett; screenplay, Frank, Barre Lyndon, St. John; art director, Hal Pereira, Walter Tyler; music, Victor Young; songs, Ned Washington and Young; John Murray Anderson and Henry Sullivan; Ray Goetz and John Ringling North; camera, George Barnes, J. Peverell Marley, Wallace Kelley; editor, Anne Bauchens.

Betty Hutton (Holly); Cornel Wilde (Sebastian); Charlton Heston (Brad); Dorothy Lamour (Phyllis); Gloria Grahame (Angel); James Stewart (Buttons); Henry Wil-coxon (Detective); Emmett Kelly (Himself); Lyle Bettger (Klaus); John Ridgely (Jack Steelman); Lawrence Tierney (Henderson); John Kellogg (Harry); Frank Wilcox (Cir-cus Doctor); Bob Carson (Ringmaster); Lillian Albertson (Buttons' Mother); Julia Faye (Birdie); John Ringling North (Himself) Tuffy Genders (Tuffy); John Parrish (Jack Lawson); Keith Richards (Keith); Adele Cook Johnson (Mabel); Brad Johnson (Reporter); Lydia Clarke (Circus Girl); John Merton (Chuck); Lane Chandler (Dave); Bradford Hatton (Osborne); Herbert Lytton (Foreman); Norman Field (Truesdale); Everett Glass (Board Member); Lee Aaker (Boy); Ethan Laidlaw (Hank); Bing Crosby, Bob Hope, Mona Freeman, Nancy Gates, Clarence Nash, Bess Flowers (Spectators); William Boyd (Hopalong Cassidy); Edmond O'Brien (Circus Midway Barker); Lou Jacobs, Felix Adler, Liberty Horses, The Flying Concellos, Paul Jung, The Maxellos (Circus Acts).

SAILOR BEWARE (PAR, 1952) 108 M.

Producer, Hal B. Wallis; director, Hal Walker; based on the play by Kenyon Nicholson; screenplay, James Allardice, Martin Rackin; art director, Hal Pereiera, Henry Bumstead; music director, Joseph J. Lilley; songs, Mack David and Jerry Liv-ingston; camera, Daniel L. Fapp; editor, Warren Low.

Dean Martin (Al Crowthers); Jerry Lewis (Melvin Jones); Corinne Calvet (Guest Star); Marion Marshall (Hilda Jones); Robert Strauss (Lardoski); Leif Erickson (Com-mander Lane); Don Wilson (Mr. Chubby); Vincent Edwards (Mac); Dan Barton ('Bama); Mike Mahoney ('Tiger); Mary Treen (Ginger); Betty Hutton (Betty); Dick Stabile (Band Leader); Donald MacBride (Chief Bos'n Mate); Louis Jean Heydt (Na-val Doctor); Elaine Stewart (Lt. Saunders); Danny Arnold (Turk); Drew Cahill (Bull); James Flavin (Petty Officer); Dan Willis, James Dean (Sailors); Irene Martin, Mary Murphy (Pretty Girls); Darr Smith (Jeff Spencer); Bobby and Eddie Mayo (Them-selves); Eddie Simms (Killer Jackson); Marshall Reed, John V. Close (Hospital Corps-man); Jimmie Dundee (Bartender); Larry McGrath (Referee); The Marimba Merry Makers (Themselves).

SOMEBODY LOVES ME (PAR, 1952) 97 M.

Producer, William Perlberg; director-screenplay, Irving Breecher; music direc-tor, Emil Newman; songs, Jay Livingston and Ray Evans; choreography, Charles O'Curran; art director, Hal Pereira, Earl Hedrick; camera, George Barnes; editor, Frank Bracht.

Betty Hutton (Blossom Seeley); Ralph Meeker (Benny Fields); Robert Keith (Sam Doyle); Adele Jergens (Nola Beach); Billie Bird (Essie); Henry Slate (Forrest); Sid Tomack (Lake); Ludwig Stossel (Mr. Grauman); Sydney Mason (Mike Fritzol); Vir-ginia Hall (Jean); Bea Allen, Les Clark (Specialty Dancers); Howard Joslin, Jimmie Dundee (Dealers); George Chandler (Stage Hand); Lester Dorr, Franklyn Farnum (Waiters); Herbert Vigran (Booker); Kenneth R. MacDonald, Milton Parsons (Doc-tors); Charles O'Curran (French Soldier); Nick Adams (Western Union Boy); Jack

Benny (Himself); James Cross (M.C.); Richard H. Gordon, Charles Quirk (Men in Audience).

SPRING REUNION (UA, 1957)

Producer, Jerry Bresler; director, Robert Pirosh; based on a story by Robert Alan Aurthur; screenplay, Pirosh, Elick Moll; music, Herbert Spencer, Earle Ugen; song, Johnny Mercer and Harry Warren; choreography, Sylvia Lewis; assistant director, John Burch; camera, Harold Lipsteen.

Dana Andrews (Fred Davis); Betty Hutton (Maggie Brewster); Jean Hagen (Barna Forrest); Sara Berner (Paula Kratz); Robert Simon (Harry Brewster); Laura LaPlante (May Brester); Gordon Jones (Jack Frazer); James Gleason (Mr. Collyer); Irene Ryan (Miss Stapleton); Richard Shannon (Nick); Ken Curtis (Al); Herbert Anderson (Edward); Richard Benedict (Jim); Vivi Janiss (Grace); Florence Sundstrom (Mary); Shirley Mitchell (Receptionist); Richard Deacon (Sidney); Mimi Doyle (Alice); Sid Tomach (Caterer); George Chandler (Zimmie); Dorothy Neumann (Roseanne); Barbara Drew (Verna); Don Haggerty (Pete); Leon Tyler (Teenager in Car).

With daughters Lindsay and Candy in
Palm Springs, March, 1954

Her show business "farewell" at the Desert Inn in Las Vegas, October, 1954

With her third husband, Alan W. Livingston, and Desert Inn hotel-owner Wilbur
Clark on her wedding day, March 8, 1955

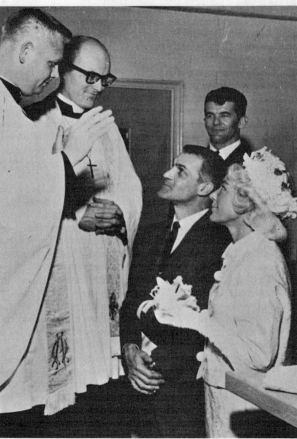

At home, 1969

Being married to Peter Candoli by Rev.
Richard I. Sowers and pastor George Atwood, with best man Jerry Finch in attendance

In THE FLEET'S IN (Par '42)

With Dick Powell, Eddie Bracken, and Mary Martin in HAPPY GO LUCKY (Par '43)

With Bob Hope, Zasu Pitts, Phyllis Povah, Cully Richards, Eve Arden, Joe Sawyer, and Joyce Compton in LET'S FACE IT (Par '43)

With Bob Hope in STAR SPANGLED RHYTHM (Par '42)

With Torben Meyer, Diana Lynn, Julius Tannen, Alan Bridge, Nora Cecil, William Demarest, Victor Potel (standing), and Eddie Bracken, Georgia Caine, and George Melford (seated) in THE MIRACLE OF MORGAN'S CREEK (Par '44)

With Bing Crosby and Sonny Tufts in
HERE COMES THE WAVES (Par '44)

With John Deauville, singing "What Do
You Want to Make Those Eyes at Me For"
in INCENDIARY BLONDE (Par '45)

With Victor Moore, Marjorie Reynolds,
James Flavin, Ed Gardner, and Jack Perrin
in DUFFY'S TAVERN (Par '45)

In THE STORK CLUB (Par '45)

With Barry Fitzgerald and Iris Adrian in
THE STORK CLUB (Par '45)

With Iris Adrian and Sonny Tufts in
CROSS MY HEART (Par '46)

With Constance Collier and John Lund in
THE PERILS OF PAULINE (Par '47)

With Fred Astaire in "Tunnel of Love"
number from LET'S DANCE (Par '50)

With Cornel Wilde in THE GREATEST
SHOW ON EARTH (Par '52)

In SOMEBODY LOVES ME (Par '52)

JOAN CAULFIELD

5'5"
110 pounds
Blue eyes
Blonde hair
Gemini

✳✳✳✳✳✳✳✳✳✳✳✳✳✳✳✳✳✳✳✳✳✳✳✳✳✳

DEMURE JOAN CAULFIELD most fully represented all the star qualities that Paramount Pictures desired in the 1940s. She exuded a beauty as delicate as Dresden china, and her good breeding and womanly deference were character traits lacking in most of the studio's other female players. To a lesser degree than aristocratic Britisher Madeleine Carroll, who was frequently starred by Paramount during the same period, Joan could tellingly exhibit refined femininity and sophisticated charm. It would remain for the more dramatic Grace Kelly in the 1950s to supersede Joan in the category of high tone and cool screen beauty.

Paramount had difficulty in properly casting Joan. She was too cultivated in manner to be the girl next door like MGM's June Allyson or Warner Brothers' Joan Leslie and Joyce Reynolds. Nor was Joan fiery enough to carry dramatic assignments like Twentieth Century-Fox's Gene Tierney or Anne Baxter. She definitely was not the adolescent devilish type like Paramount's own Diana Lynn and Mona Freeman.

During her seven years at Paramount (1944–49), Joan appeared in 11 feature films; only two are memorable for her performances, *Dear Ruth* and its less successful sequel *Dear Wife*. Her other screen assignments cast her as a lively bit of set dressing who proved particularly unsuitable for strong histrionics or skilled singing and dancing.

Dear Ruth allowed Joan to exhibit her winning portrayal of the naive, warm girl-woman. She had previously played this type successfully on Broadway as the young star of *Kiss and Tell* and would later essay a more mature version of the type in the 1953 teleseries "My Favorite Husband." In this genre, she ably displayed her special flair for breezy light comedy, relying on sweetness rather than sexiness for audience appeal. That she made it all seem so easy, allowed people to dismiss Joan from consideration as a vital part of the 1940s crop of cinema stars.

Joan Caulfield (née Beatrice Joan Caulfield) was born June 1, 1922, in Orange, New Jersey, the second of three girls (the eldest: Mary; the youngest, Bell). Her father, Henry R. Caulfield, was comptroller for a Manhattan-based aircraft company.

Joan was educated at private schools; first at the nearby Miss Bean's School for Girls, and, after the family moved to New York City, at the Lincoln School of Teachers College. By the time she entered Columbia University in the fall of 1940, Joan had already decided on a modeling career. Her forays into dramatics with the Morningside Players, an Upper West Side Manhattan theatrical group, netted her poor notices.

Joan would later recall about her college days: "What energy we have when we're young! I was a demon fifteen years ago. I modeled night and day all the time I was going to Columbia. I was majoring in English which meant hours of reading. I also joined the Morningside Players. When I wasn't holed up in the library I was learning lines or tearing around to photographers' studios . . . or visiting the orthodontist. I lived way up on Riverside Drive. All the photographers in those days were on Lexington Avenue. I studied on buses and subways. I don't know when I slept. But I was never tired."

With her natural aristocratic good looks, Joan soon became a client of the Harry Conover Modeling Agency and received top fashion photography assignments. For the May 11, 1942, cover of *Life* magazine, she posed for a layout entitled "Fluffy Ruffles." It showed her peeping demurely from under a most fussy hat.

According to one account, prolific Broadway producer-director George Abbott spotted Joan's *Life* photograph and requested her to audition for one of his upcoming stage musicals, *Beat the Band,* which was to star Jack Whiting and Jerry Lester. Another version has it that Joan blithely walked into Abbott's production office and naively inquired: "Are you looking for talent?"

In any case, Joan was assigned the role of Veronica, a blonde dumb Dora who spends most of her few scenes in *Beat the Band* being chased by men, and parading in the then risqué attire of black bra and black filmy panties. Joan's parents were not quite prepared for her undecorous bow into professional show business. Joan remembers: "My mother all but fainted [when seeing the play]. Then she practically fainted again when I started my lines. They were decidedly off-color and believe me I was pretty corn-fed myself. I didn't even know what some of them meant. I was so dumb, in fact, that the stage manager gave me a large key to keep for him and said it was the key to the curtain, and I believed him."

Beat the Band, dealing with a bandleader, an affectionate heiress on the lam from the Caribbean, and a talent-casting agent, opened at the 46th Street Theatre on Broadway on October 14, 1942. The critics were unenthused by the book or the songs by Johnny Green and George Marion, Jr. Susan Miller as the vivacious rich girl garnered most of the good notices. The *Newark Evening News* did report: "A most attractive member of the cast is Joan Caulfield as the much pursued Veronica, who has some amusing scenes with Lester and sundry other susceptibles. Miss Caulfield hails from the Oranges and is decidedly winsome." The musical lasted 64 performances.

George Abbott was sufficiently impressed with Joan's potential light-comedy skills to offer her the lead in F. Hugh Herbert's *Kiss and Tell,* which debuted at the Biltmore Theatre on March 19, 1943. Set in a small American town near an Army camp, the comedy concerned 15-year-old Corliss Archer, who connives to hide her brother's marriage to her best friend, while keeping her own assorted beaux at bay. Jessie Royce Landis and

Robert Keith played Joan's parents, Richard Widmark was her brother, and Frances Bavier appeared as the maid. Critics and audiences alike were captivated by the play's wholesome charm and Joan immediately joined the ranks of Broadway's favored ingenues. Lewis Nichols *(New York Times)* praised her for giving "a most exact portrait of the combination of childishness and dignity which forms that happy season of age." Other notices hailed her as "natural and endearing," "excellent," "attractive and winning," "well-poised, pretty," and "utterly delectable." In *Variety*'s annual New York Drama Critics' poll for 1943, Joan was selected the year's most promising new actress. She was also gaining popularity as a GI favorite. The 716th Battalion of the Second Service Command named her "Lady of the Battalion."

After romping through 480 performances of *Kiss and Tell,* Joan left the comedy in early 1944. There had been much publicity when Joan's younger sister Bell, then age 17, was signed in mid-1943 as Joan's understudy. *Kiss and Tell* ran for 962 performances; it was turned into two Shirley Temple features and inspired both a radio and a television series.

Like early 1940s ingenues Gene Tierney and Anne Baxter, Joan also insisted she would not be lured away from the stage by Hollywood. She refused a film contract offered her by Samuel Goldwyn, but in early 1944 she succumbed to a lucrative bid from Paramount. She told the press: "I guess I'll just have to fall back on the old feminine prerogative—the right of a woman to change her mind." Her studio contract, which escalated to four figures, gave her a yearly option to work six months on Broadway.

Joan was exactly the type of ingenue Paramount head B. G. DeSylva* was seeking: well-bred, radiant, and charming. Like that studio's Diana Lynn and Warner Brothers' Joan Leslie and Joyce Reynolds, Joan represented the ideal woman of the 1940s. Her sexual appeal never burst into overtness and she seemed the type of female happy to be a woman in a man's world.

Upon arriving in Hollywood, Joan was given a starring role in *Miss Susie Slagle's* which would not be released until 1946. Her mother had accompanied Joan to the Coast. The 22-year-old leading lady explained: "I'm quite a lonely type of person and I have to have someone about that knows me." In December, 1944, Joan took a highly publicized vacation trip to New York. Journalists plied her with the usual queries. Joan cooed: "Everyone has been very kind to me, and I wouldn't criticize anything out there [Hollywood] because it would be ungrateful. But, after all, I am myself, and the life isn't my kind of fun. I was never too much of a party girl."

Joan returned to Hollywood to share top billing in two Paramount musicals, *Duffy's Tavern* (1945) and *Blue Skies* (1946). This placed her in the unique position of having made three feature films in a star capacity, without having any of them yet released for public judgment.

Duffy's Tavern, which premiered at the Paramount Theatre on September 15, 1945, gave filmgoers their first brief glimpse of the much-heralded Joan. In this all-star production, Joan had a quick walk-on bit. Much more prominently displayed were starlet Marjorie Reynolds as addled Victor Moore's daughter and Jean Heather, Helen Walker, and Gail Russell, a trio of Paramount newcomers who performed a musical number with Bing Crosby.

Since she was linked socially with Bing Crosby, it was no surprise when Joan drew the female lead in Mark Sandrich's *Blue Skies.* Shortly after production began on this $3 million technicolor songfest, Sandrich died, and the new producer started from scratch, dropping Joan from the produc-

*See Appendix.

tion, among other changes. Then he was replaced by Sol Siegel and director Stuart Heisler, who were persuaded to reinstate Joan. Fred Astaire was coaxed out of retirement to make this his "final" film. It reunited the successful combination of Crosby-Astaire-Irving Berlin from *Holiday Inn.*

Eschewing a Hollywood-style musical-biography tribute to Irving Berlin, *Blue Skies* settled for a mundane story line allowing for a host of songs. Disk-jockey Astaire recounts the history of several tunes being spun over the air, recalling personal events from 1919 to date which are tied to the songs. He relates how he and fellow song-and-dance man Crosby each loved chorine Joan, how Crosby and Joan married, why she later divorced him when he became an itinerant nightclub owner, and how she now runs a flower shop. By the fade-out, the ex-marrieds are reunited and everyone is friends again.

The highlight of *Blue Skies* was Astaire's masterful dancing to "Puttin' on the Ritz" on a multileveled set with eight miniature versions of himself on screen as a dancing chorus. While Crosby crooned "You Keep Coming Back Like a Song" to Joan, it was really starlet Olga San Juan who did all the female thrushing. Especially good was her energetic rendition of "I'll See You in C–U–B–A." Billy De Wolfe was sandwiched into the musical numbers with vaudeville gags and his standby routine—a female impersonation of housewife Mrs. Mergotroyd. With 20 songs, 47 sets, and luscious costuming, the production went on to earn $5.7 million in net domestic rentals. Bosley Crowther *(New York Times)* noted: "[Joan] is most lovely and passive as the girl who stands none too seriously or firmly between Crosby and Astaire." Most of the soggy moments in this nostalgic musical were the love scenes between Crosby and Joan. While she was one of the most beautiful of Astaire's "dancing" partners, her time-stepping with him was unmemorable to say the most.

Miss Susie Slagle's was finally released on February 7, 1946, proving to be a pleasant if inconsequential medical soap opera, set in 1910 Baltimore. Lillian Gish was the boarding house marm whose roomers were would-be doctors studying at Johns Hopkins Medical School. Joan was cast as the brash maid at Slagle's—her father had roomed there—who hoped to marry shy plodder Dr. Sonny Tufts. Much of their screen moments together were devoted to her encouraging him in his studies and helping him to overcome an abnormal fear of dealing with death, heightened by a classmate's demise during an epidemic. In direct contrast to Joan was Paramount's super-icy star Veronica Lake, this time essaying a heartbroken nurse whose boyfriend doctor has died. To add comedy relief, Billy DeWolfe popped into focus now and again. *Newsweek* reported that Joan "cinches her Hollywood debut with a nice combination of charm and ability."

When filming *Miss Susie Slagle's* in 1944, fledgling actress Joan told the press: "Mr. [John] Berry [the director] is young, only twenty-six and full of plans. For all I know, he may be using a new technique in picture making. He is out of the theatre, used to be with Orson Welles, and he rehearsed us before the shooting, just as he would if we were doing a play. It made the Hollywood axiom—you're only as good as the script and your direction—seem so true."

Joan's third 1946 release was *Monsieur Beaucaire,* a comedy romp very slightly derived from Booth Tarkington's novel, and even more remote from the silent Rudolph Valentino feature. The scenario was adjusted to Bob Hope's visual and verbal talents: herein, he is a bumbling barber at King Louis XV's court, who is sent to Spain to masquerade as a court dandy and help prevent war between France and Spain. Joan is a former scullery maid anxious to make the royal scene, Hillary Brooke appears as the infamous Madame Pompadour, with Constance Collier as the Queen, Marjorie Reynolds as the Spanish Infanta, and Joseph Schildkraut as the slick villain. The gracious settings and period costumes helped suspend disbelief, and allowed the burlesque to work well. Bosley Crowther (*New York Times*) wrote: "As a chambermaid in the palace for whom Mr. Hope has a passionate yen, Joan Caulfield is delightfully nimble and gives reasonable justification for same."

Joan had been scheduled to appear in *The Well Groomed Bride* (1946), but her role went to a new contractee, Wanda Hendrix. By the fall of 1946, Joan had become a definite part of the Hollywood colony, and she gave up any thoughts of returning to the stage—her contract was altered accordingly. For the press, she analyzed: "I came from Broadway and I guess they figured that if I could play a leading role there I must be good. Also I happen to be darn lucky that I photograph well in Technicolor." She admitted that her idols were Joan Fontaine on the screen and Margaret Sullavan on the stage.

Largely due to the success of *Blue Skies,* Joan was number ten in *Variety*'s list of 1946's top-grossing film stars. Bing Crosby was in first position.

The peak of Joan's cinema career came with *Dear Ruth,* which premiered at the Paramount Theatre on June 10, 1947. The movie was based on Norman Krasna's 1944 Broadway success which ran for 683 performances, starring Virginia Gilmore—an almost Twentieth Century-Fox star. The plot gimmick had the younger daughter of a Queens, New York, judge corresponding with an Army lieutenant based overseas. As bait, she sends her older sister's photograph. The soldier comes to visit the Kew Gardens family on leave, planning to marry his supposed pen-pal. Before the older sister decides she loves him, she passes through all the required game-playing every nice girl did in 1940s plays and movies.

Paramount assembled an amazingly congenial cast to act out the cockeyed love affair: Edward Arnold as the harassed judge, Mary Philips as the matronly wife, Joan as the sweet but strong-willed older daughter, and Paramount fledgling Mona Freeman as the hellion younger sister. William Holden breezed through as the apple-pie wholesome serviceman and Billy DeWolfe portrayed Joan's ineffectual banker fiancé. The *New York Herald Tribune* accorded that Joan "is a vision of loveliness (as well as a good actress) in the title role." If anything, *Dear Ruth* cemented the stereotyped role of the healthy young miss that would haunt Joan for the remainder of her acting career. Joan, Holden, De Wolfe, Arnold, and Freeman recreated their *Dear Ruth* roles on "Lux Radio Theatre" on April 26, 1948, December 5, 1949, and February 19, 1951.

The second of Joan's four 1947 releases was *Welcome Stranger,* a low-keyed piece of blarney put together to reteam the popular stars of *Going My Way,* Bing Crosby and Barry Fitzgerald. Fitzgerald essayed the aging physician of Fallsbridge, Maine, with Crosby the wandering doctor who substitutes while Fitzgerald takes a vacation. The townsfolk, especially conniving rich man Charles Hingle, do not cotton to Crosby's city ways. It is only when Crosby performs an emergency operation on Fitzgerald for a ruptured appendix—aided by schoolteacher Joan—that the local inhabitants recognize his competence and good intentions. Adding needed flavor to the film were Percy Kilbride as the taxi driver, Elizabeth Patterson as the housekeeper, and Robert Shayne as the petulant pharmacist. The *New York Times* cited Joan for being "lovely and competent." Audiences adored this work of celluloid corn which allowed Joan to be no more than lovely set dressing.

On loanout to Warner Brothers, Joan had top billing over Claude Rains in *The Unsuspected* (1947), a road-company version of *Laura.* Rains portrayed a radio crime-program writer who brings about the real thing in his own bizarre household. Joan, as his wealthy (and innocuous) ward, is supposedly dead at the film's opening. Her reappearance starts a weird chain of events which culminate in hero Michael North almost being murdered. The movie opened with a brisk flow of excitement and quickly dropped to a slow whirl of clichés. Perking up the story were Audrey Totter as a sultry lady, Hurd Hatfield as a ne'er-do-well, and Constance Bennett as a wise-cracking production secretary. The *New Yorker* termed *The Unsuspected* a "seedy mystery film" and the *New York Times* (Bosley Crowther) accused the entire cast of being "as patly artificial as the plot."

Less than two weeks later, *Variety Girl* opened at the Paramount Theatre (October 15, 1947). Joan was among the studio stars parading forth in this tribute to the Variety Club of America. Mary Hatcher (a discovery from the Broadway cast of *Oklahoma!*) and Olga San Juan were the leads in this episodic musical. Joan was spotted in a song-and-dance sketch with Ray Milland, William Holden, and Cass Daley. Not being a showy performer, her efforts were lost in the shuffle.

During 1947 there was talk that Billy Wilder would remake *An American Tragedy* with Joan as one of its leads.

Instead, *The Sainted Sisters* (1948) again costarred Joan with Veronica Lake and Barry Fitzgerald. It proved to be Miss Lake's swan song at the studio, and some of her ire is noticeable in her scene-stealing from Joan. Set in the early 1900s, Joan and Veronica are sisters fleeing from New York, where they have fleeced a gullible millionaire of $25,000. They land in Grove Falls, Maine (population 453), a town bordering on Canada. The duo take shelter in Fitzgerald's home and before long he has reformed them, distributed their ill-gotten gains to the needy, and helped them find local beaux and respectability. One wag described the mild slapstick affair as "buggies, bustle and Barry Fitzgerald." For humor, much was made of such props as the kitchen stove, surreys, layers of petticoats, and nightshirts. The two blonde actresses sported period bathing attire in one sequence. Next in honors to Fitzgerald's coy characterization came the workmanship of Beulah Bondi as the town's rich shrew, and William Demarest's performance as the cagey sheriff. Howard Barnes *(New York Herald Tribune)* acknowledged that Joan and Veronica were: "comely and remarkably authentic in bustle get-ups."

Larceny, opening at the Winter Garden Theatre on September 13, 1948, was made on loanout to Universal. It was a dreary production based on the unpleasant theme of con man John Payne fleecing naive war-widow Joan for large sums of money to supposedly construct a memorial to her dead service-hero husband. Located in a small California town, the unrealistic drama's few live moments came when Shelley Winters appeared on the screen. She was the moll of gang brain Dan Duryea, but she yearns for Payne. Her blowsy vulgarity is only quieted by a bullet in the melee that takes place when Payne turns himself and the others over to the police—he has been reformed by love for pure Joan. The *New York Times* summed up: "Joan Caulfield plays the languid widow to the point of weariness." Joan and Payne repeated their *Larceny* characterization on "Lux Radio Theatre," October 11, 1948.

In the summer of 1948, Joan and Payne toured in John Van Druten's *The Voice of the Turtle.*

Joan's last film under her Paramount contract was *Dear Wife,* (1950) a sequel to *Dear Ruth.* Released on February 1, 1950, it proved popular but not up to its predecessor. In this continuation, Joan and William Holden have married, and by some trickery, he and Judge Edward Arnold are running for the same seat in the state senate. Even more so now, Mona Freeman is the meddling bobby-soxer, running both her parents' and her sister's households. Much of the quiet humor derives from a nonrational look at the early months of married unbliss, the housing shortage, and the romantic complications created when political worker Arleen Whelan enters the scene. Billy De Wolfe trooped in to display his battery of expected sight gags. The *New York Times* admitted: "The nature of Miss Caulfield's role as Ruth doesn't call for spectacular histrionic displays, but there is quiet competence in her acting." By the time *Dear Brat,* the third in the series, was released in 1951, Mona Freeman was the focal point, and Joan was not in the film.

A combination of the recession in the post-World War II film business and Joan's own growing unhappiness with her roles, led to her Paramount contract not being renewed in 1949. As she later told writer Erskine Johnson: "I didn't go Hollywood on the outside with flashy cars, upstairs maids and mink covered bathroom fixtures. I went Hollywood on the inside—and that's worst of all. . . . I played a character only in one picture—my first. From then on I was this movie star named Joan Caulfield. I tried to avoid being natural. I lowered my voice. I copied the mannerisms of other stars. I struck poses. I received bad advice—from dramatic coaches, from agents and from studio executives. I stopped being a human being. I blame myself and I blame Hollywood's star system."

For one who hoped to break away from gooey one-dimensional heroine roles, Joan did not have much luck free-lancing. For Columbia Pictures she costarred with Robert Cummings in the nondescript technicolor foolishness *The Petty Girl* (1950). Cummings essayed the renowned calendar and magazine artist who becomes intrigued with staid college professor Joan, urging her to pose for some of his serious art work. First he chases after her to Braymore College, then she scampers after him to New York, where she gets drunk and finds herself scampering through a third-rate burlesque show. *The Petty Girl* was heavily larded hokum that barely passed muster at the box office. One of the film's few inspired moments occurred near the beginning: Joan did a reverse strip tease, with the camera tracking her as she dresses and sings "Fancy Free."

Joan and producer Frank Ross had been dating since 1949. The 46-year-old producer was then married to sometime-Paramount-star Jean Arthur. Columnists suggested Joan was more capable of giving Ross encouragement for his long-delayed film project *The Robe,* which he had been planning since 1944. In turn, Ross became Joan's artistic mentor. On April 29, 1950, having received his divorce from Arthur, he and Joan were married.

With Ross producing and directing, Joan starred in *The Lady Says No,* a minor comedy which opened on January 6, 1952, as the bottom half of a double bill with Bette Davis's *Another Man's Poison.* Joan was featured as the writer of a best-selling novel warning women against men. David Niven was seen as the dapper national magazine photographer who comes to Monterey, California, to prepare a feature story on her. The critics roasted the film and audiences ignored it. Since the production was all in the family, Joan agreed to make a public appearance tour to ballyhoo the movie. *Variety* caught her act in the Fifth Avenue Theatre of Seattle, Washington, on January 23, 1952: "[She] makes a nice appearance on the stage; is obviously sincere and is a looker, but her material doesn't help any." Part of her routine was a skit in which she impersonated Judy Holliday as Billie Dawn (of *Born Yesterday*) in a radio interview with Katharine Hepburn.

With no noteworthy film offers coming her way, Joan took to the summer-stock circuit, and in the next few years she appeared in *Claudia* and *Dream Girl.* She became more vocal regarding her stereotyped wholesome image: "I've had that label for years and I'm thoroughly sick of it. I'm not wholesome at all. I detest homey things like cooking and bedmaking and Peter Pan collars. I like to wear slacks and play golf. I'll never be a homebody." In another press session, she complained: "They had me going through an entire picture with what amounted to a blank expression on my face. Real pretty and no character."

Joan began accepting dramatic roles on assorted television anthologies such as "Ford Theatre." Recalled Joan: "Other actors started complimenting my work and when they did I knew I had erased all bad memories of Joan Caulfield, the big movie star. I had become an actress—and a person —again."

Then Joan starred in a live television series, "My Favorite Husband," which premiered from CBS-TV's Hollywood studio on September 19, 1953. (Lucille Ball and Richard Denning had top-lined the popular radio version, based on Isabelle Scott Rovich's book *Mr. and Mrs. Cugat,* from 1948–51.) As Joan enthusiastically described the 30-minute family show: "I play a sort of whacky dumb-smart wife in the series and this opportunity to play comedy is something I've waited for for a long time. From the scripts I have seen so far, I'd say I'll have ample opportunity to make up for lost time in this department." Barry Nelson played her clean-cut husband, George Cooper.

The reviews for the show were enthusiastic and won Joan a legion of upper-middle-class housewife fans—she was the demure prototype of what they had always sought to be. *Variety* championed: "Major credit for the show's brisk and breezy pace belongs to Joan Caulfield (Liz) and Barry Nelson (George). Miss Caulfield is an ideal young frau—a looker with a sense of comedy timing that's surefire delight."

Joan stayed with "My Favorite Husband" through October 3, 1954, when the series switched to film and Vanessa Brown assumed the lead role. At the time Joan claimed that she preferrred the spontaneity of live television and that it made her performances better. "Of course you have that fear that you'll forget your lines, but you can't let fear or panic take over, that's all. If we were filming the show there'd be the other problem of boredom. This way we have the excitement of an opening night every Saturday night. And it takes nerve to stand there for the camera and do a delayed double-take! I found that out! It takes nerve to do a comedy show!"

Later Joan would admit about "My Favorite Husband": "That was the one time my so-called acumen wasn't working for me. If I had only filmed those shows, they would be still showing—and the residuals would be pouring in."

Meanwhile, her husband Ross had at last produced *The Robe* (1953), which grossed $17.5 million for Twentieth Century-Fox in net domestic rentals. Fox allowed Ross carte blanche at the studio and he chose to produce a remake of *The Rains Came,* entitled *The Rains of Ranchipur* (1955). In this version of the Louis Bromfield novel of mixed races and emotions in twentieth-century India, Lana Turner was the selfish wife of loafing lord Michael Rennie. She has a yen for noble Indian doctor Richard Burton, but waspish Indian dowager Eugenie Leontovich snafus the romance. Fred MacMurray was the American architect turned to drink, and Joan played chipper Fern, the missionary's daughter from Iowa who finds MacMurray an ideal subject for reformation. (Brenda Joyce had her role in the original.) The overblown dramatics were barely saved by the novelty of Cinemascope and color, and by a clever reuse of the earthquake-flood footage from the original sepia version. As *Variety* tactfully commented: "Joan Caulfield is cute in a part that seems to have been written for a younger girl." There was some sharp talk about Joan's high salary for the film being a result of her marital status rather than her box-office drawing power.

Commenting to columnist Joe Hyams in 1955 on her screen image, Joan confessed: "I guess I'm just not the film femme fatale type. I giggle too much. I have freckles and a turned-up nose and I walk like an athlete. As

George Abbott once said, I look better on a tennis court than in a bedroom. Of course, I can raise a shoulder and wet my lower lip, but when I do, I look like I'm imitating someone."

Joan returned to guest-starring on assorted television series, including *The Bankmouse* on "Playhouse of Stars" (July 24, 1956, CBS), *Apples on the Lilac Tree* on "Screen Directors Playhouse" (July 25, 1956, ABC), *Only Yesterday* on "Lux Video Theatre" (September 27, 1956, NBC), and *House of Glass* on "Ford Theatre" (September 11, 1957). Joan was among the several celebrity stars trooped in as subjects on "This Is Your Life" (NBC) by host Ralph Edwards during the 1956–57 season. As Joan explained to celebrity-interviewer Faye Emerson: "I believe I'm geared to television. It moves fast, and that's what I like. There is no bickering and fighting and most of all, no temperament. There just isn't time to put up with temperamental people in television. So it is pleasant work, although often pretty hectic."

Once again Joan joined forces with her husband Ross to produce, on a 100 percent ownership basis, the "Sally" television series, which debuted September 15, 1957, on NBC. Joan was salesgirl Sally who becomes the zany traveling companion of wealthy matron Marion Lorne. Ironically, this series was filmed, and at her old studio—Paramount.

Variety's review of the series ran: " 'Sally' as a starter often showed itself as a slickly handled and well mounted though innocuous situationer with dual assets. The preemer was inclined to reach a bit for its laughs, with some of the setups designedly telegraphic. . . . The laugh track was an irritant at times."

Pitted against "Bachelor Father" (CBS) in the same time slot, "Sally" did not fare well in the rating game. Joan was quick to advise the press that December (1957): "If people don't like 'Sally,' they just don't have taste. I'm a tough audience. I've done some shows that make me cringe. But some of the 'Sally' shows have made me real proud."

The series struggled through March, 1958, but was never able to buck the competition. In later episodes, the format was altered to cut down on Joan's story-line traveling, and Gale Gordon and Artie Johnson were added to the cast of regulars.

In March, 1959, Joan sued Ross for divorce, only to learn in June that she was pregnant. On November 7, 1959, she gave birth to her first child, Caulfield. She had had four previous miscarriages. Her divorce decree became final on April 5, 1960. The divorce settlement required Ross to pay her $847 a month for ten years. Joan said at the time: "That's what broke up my marriage in the first place. Frank and I both worked on 'Sally' and were just too much with it. We took out all our frustrations on one another. It was a horrible experience for us."

One of Joan's last major television appearance was on "G.E. Theatre" (March 22, 1959, CBS) in the episode *The Lady's Choice.* In this tale set in the 1880s, she played a girl going to the untamed West to marry. Don DeFore and William Bishop were costarred. Joan's forays into the business world were unremarkable; in the late 1950s she was vice president of the North Star Company of Nevada, an oil-interest combine.

Joan made the headlines in early 1960 when she was in an automobile accident. Journalists at the time quizzed her regarding the status of her career and life in general: "Few people realize what a handicap it is to be well, what people call a beautiful woman. I'm glad, of course, that I don't look like an unmade bed, but too often I'm just taken at face value. And there aren't many men who believe a beautiful woman can have any brains."

Following a national road tour in Frank Vosper's melodrama *Love from a Stranger* in 1960, Joan married dentist Dr. Robert Peterson, age 42, on November 24, 1960. She gave birth to son John on March 22, 1962.

During the summer of 1962, she appeared in a stock version of the comedy *Cactus Flower.*

Joan made her first feature film in eight years at MGM in 1963. *Cattle King* emerged as a sluggish, all-too-typical Western. It laboriously dealt with the National Trail Act, which threatened to open much of the grazing land in 1880s Nevada to open-rangers. Joan was Sharleen, whose neighbor is idealistic rancher Robert Taylor. William Windom, as Joan's alcoholic brother who joins with badman Robert Middleman against Taylor, had the best role. The *New York Post* remarked "Mercifully for her [Joan], she's shot long before the picture's end." The low-budget Western opened on showcase in the New York area on July 31, 1963, to spotty box-office business. The camera close-ups all too realistically revealed Joan's 41 years.

In yet another attempt to return to Broadway, Joan joined the cast of the Harold Prince produced-directed comedy fluff *She Didn't Say Yes,* which made the summer-theatre circuit in 1963. The Lonnie Coleman play co-starred Peggy Cass, William Redfield, and Joan Hackett. As with most such New York-bound ventures that begin in a burst of heightened publicty and grandiose aims, it quietly disappeared after the last playhouse engagement that summer, and a disappointed Joan returned to California. It was yet another reversal in her once-promising show business career.

By 1965 Joan was vice-president of Lustre Shine Co., Inc. and spoke of reviving the "My Favorite Husband" television series. On June 9, 1966, she was divorced from Peterson, claiming: "A very fine dentist who doesn't care much about working. As a matter of fact, I'm still trying to get an appointment to get my own teeth fixed."

Joan was among the several former film stars hired by producer A. C. Lyles for his string of ultra low-budget Westerns churned out at Paramount —in about ten days apiece—to feed the declining supporting-bill program. She replaced Betty Hutton in *Red Tomahawk,* which opened on the circuits in 1967. It was a mild little color effort which relied more on stock footage than central casting for its contingents of warring Indians. Joan was Dakota Lil in love with Army captain Howard Keel. *Variety* observed: "She is only slightly tarnished and then, it's blamed on the Indians." The following year, Joan costarred in *Buckskin* (1968) as Nora Johnson, a former schoolteacher now a weary saloon tart in the town of Gloryhole, Montana, controlled by villain Wendell Corey. Barry Sullivan and ex-Corey henchman John Russell persist in saving the town. *Variety* reported: "Joan Caulfield can do nothing but try to get through it." Both films revealed that her porcelain beauty looks had not weathered well.

These two quickie Western features are Joan's last pictures to date. Her most recent binge of non-show business publicity occurred in 1969 when she sued and won against a Los Angeles investment broker who had bought her Beverly Hills home and thrown out all of her memorabilia. Included in the discard, said Joan, was a wartime letter from the then Prince Philip of England saying she had a most "slappable bottom."

Like many other former film stars, Joan continually makes forays back to the theatre, especially summer stock, where her name still retains nostalgic drawing power. In June, 1971, Joan commenced a six-week run at the Showboat Dinner Theatre near St. Petersburg, Florida, starring in Neil Simon's *Plaza Suite.* Reported one local critic: "Miss Caulfield uses the setting, the furniture and the space as an actress who knows how to make the most of what's given her." From all indications, Joan has at last and perhaps too late matured as an actress, and she is now capable of displaying the depths of emotion so sorely missing from her Paramount and subsequent films.

DUFFY'S TAVERN (PAR, 1945) 97 M.

Associate producer, Danny Dare; director, Hal Walker; screenplay, Melvin Frank, Norman Panama; music director, Robert Emmett Dolan; art director, Hans Dreier, William Flannery; songs, Johnny Burke and Jimmy Van Heusen; Ben Raleigh and Bernie Wayne; choreography, Billy Daniels; special effects, Gordon Jennings; process camera, Farciot Edouart; camera, Lionel Lindon; editor, Arthur Schmidt.

Bing Crosby, Betty Hutton, Paulette Goddard, Alan Ladd, Dorothy Lamour, Eddie Bracken, Brian Donlevy, Sonny Tufts, Veronica Lake, Arturo De Cordova, Cass Daley, Diana Lynn, Gary Crosby, Phillip Crosby, Dennis Crosby, Lin Crosby, William Bendix, Maurice Rocco, James Brown, Joan Caulfield, Gail Russell, Helen Walker, Jean Heather (Themselves); Marjorie Reynolds (Peggy O'Malley); Barry Fitzgerald (Bing Crosby's Father); Victor Moore (Michael O'Malley); Barry Sullivan (Danny Murphy); Ed Gardner (Archie); Charles Cantor (Finnegan); Eddie Green (Eddie—The Waiter); Ann Thomas (Miss Duffy); Howard Da Silva (Heavy); Billy De Wolfe (Doctor); Walter Abel (Director); Charles Quigley (Ronald); Olga San Juan (Gloria); Robert Watson (Masseur); Frank Faylen (Customer); Matt McHugh (Man Following Miss Duffy); Emmett Vogan (Make-Up Man); Cyril Ring (Gaffer); Noel Neill (School Kid).

BLUE SKIES (PAR, 1946) 104 M.

Producer, Sol C. Siegel; director, Stuart Heisler; based on an idea by Irving Berlin; adaptation, Allan Scott; screenplay, Arthur Sheekman; music director, Robert Emmett Dolan; songs, Irving Berlin; choreography, Hermes Pan; special effects, Gordon Jennings, Paul K. Lepal, Farciot Edouart; camera, Charles Lang, Jr., William Snyder; editor, LeRoy Stone.

Bing Crosby (Johnny Adams); Fred Astaire (Jed Potter); Joan Caulfield (Mary O'Hara); Billy De Wolfe (Tony); Olga San Juan (Nita Nova); Robert Benchley (Business Man); Frank Faylen (Mack); Victoria Horne (Martha—Nurse); Karolyn Grimes (Mary Elizabeth); Roy Gordon (Charles Dillingham); Jack Norton (Drunk); Jimmy Conlin (Valet); Len Hendry (Electrician); John M. Sullivan (Sugar Daddy); Charles La Torre (Mr. Rakopolis); Joan Woodbury (Flo); John Kelly (Tough Guy); Roberta Jonay (Hat Check Girl); Frances Morris (Nurse); John "Skins" Miller (Ed); Roxanne Collins, Paula Ray, Larry Steers, Major Sam Harris (Guests); John Gallaudet (Stage Manager); Neal Dodd (Minister); Peggy McIntyre (Mary Elizabeth); Michael Brandon (Charlie—Stage Manager); Will Wright (Dan —Stage Manager); Albert Ruiz, Joel Friend (Specialty Dance); Vicki Jasmund, Norma Grieger, Joanne Lybrook, Louise Saraydar (Girls in Quartette); Barbara Slater (Myrtle); Carol Andrews (Dolly).

MISS SUSIE SLAGLE'S (PAR, 1946) 88 M.

Producer, John Houseman; director, John Berry; based on the novel by Augusta Tucker; adaptation, Anne Froelich, Adrian Scott; additional dialogue, Theodore Strauss; screenplay, Froelich, Scott; music, Daniele Amfitheatrof; technical advisor, Dr. Benjamin Sacks; camera, Charles Lang, Jr., editor, Archie Marshek.

Veronica Lake (Nan Rogers); Sonny Tufts (Pug Prentiss); Joan Caulfield (Margarette Howe); Ray Collins (Dr. Elijah Howe); Billy De Wolfe (Ben Mead); Bill Edwards (Elijah Howe, Jr.); Pat Phelan (Elbert Riggs); Lillian Gish (Miss Susie Slagle); Roman Bohnen (Dean Wingate); Morris Carnovsky (Dr. Fletcher); Renny McEvoy (Clayton Abernathy); Lloyd Bridges (Silas Holmes); Michael Sage (Irving Asron); E. J. Ballantine (Dr. Metz); Theodore Newton (Dr. Boyd); J. Lewis Johnson (Hizer); Ludwig Stossel (Otto); Charles E. Arnt (Mr. Johnson); Isabel Randolph (Mrs. Howe); Kathleen Howard (Miss Wingate); Frederick Burton (Dr. Bowen); Chester Morrison (Paul); William Mender, Albert Ruiz, Stan Johnson, Jerry James, Harold Topf Bernardi (Students); Cyril Ring (Instrument Man); Pierre Watkin (Superintendent); Alan Bridge (Taxi Driver); Byron Poindexter (Orderly); Milton Kibbee (Little Man); Connie Thompkins (Alice); Mary Herriot (Gwen); William Challee (Interne).

MONSIEUR BEAUCAIRE (PAR, 1946) 93 M.

Producer, Paul Jones; director, George Marshall; based on the novel by Booth Tarkington; screenplay, Melvin Frank, Norman Panama; art director, Hans Dreier, Earl Hedrick; music director, Robert Emmett Dolan; songs, Jay Livingston and Ray Evans; choreography, Billy Daniels, Josephine Earl; special effects, Gordon Jennings; camera, Lionel Linden; editor, Arthur Schmidt.

Bob Hope (Monsieur Beaucaire); Joan Caulfield (Mimi); Patric Knowles (Duc de Chandre); Marjorie Reynolds (Princes Maria of Spain); Cecil Kellaway (Count D'Armand); Joseph Schildkraut (Don Francisco); Reginald Owen (King Louis XV of France); Constance Collier (The Queen); Hillary Brooke (Madame Pompadour); Fortunio Bonanova (Don Carlos); Douglass Dumbrille (George Washington); Mary Nash (The Duenna); Leonid Kinskey (Rene); Howard Freeman (King Philip of Spain); Dorothy Vernon (Servant); Jack Mulhall, Philip Van Zandt (Guards); Eric Alden (Swordsman); Helen Freeman (Queen of Spain); Alan Hale, Jr., Hugh Prosser, John Maxwell (Couriers); Lane Chandler (Officer); George Sorel (Duke); Anthony Caruso (Masked Horseman); Jean DeFriac (Minister of Finance); Jean Del Val (Minister of War); John Mylong (Minister Of State); Nino Pipitone (Lackey); Lynne Lyons (Signora Gonzales); Mona Maris (Marquisa); Charles Coleman (Major Domo); Brandon Hurst (Marquis); Buddy Roosevelt, Manuel Paris (Spanish Guards); Catherine Craig (Duchess); Noreen Nash (Baroness); Nina Borget (Wife); Robert "Buddy" Shaw (Husband); Sherry Hall (Sentry); Tony Paton (Waiter).

DEAR RUTH (PAR, 1947) 95 M.

Producer, Paul Jones; director, William D. Russell; based on the play by Norman Krasna; screenplay, Arthur Sheekman; art director, Hans Dreier, Earl Hedrick; music, Robert Emmett Dolan; camera, Ernest Laszlo; editor, Archie Marshek.

Joan Caulfield (Ruth Wilkins); William Holden (Lt. William Seacroft); Edward Arnold (Judge Harry Wilkins); Mary Philips (Edith Wilkins); Mona Freeman (Miriam Wilkins); Billy De Wolfe (Albert Kummer); Virginia Welles (Martha Seacroft); Marietta Canty (Dora—The Maid); Kenny O'Morrison (Sgt. Chuck Vincent); Irving Bacon (Delivery Man); Isabel Randolph (Mrs. Teaker).

WELCOME STRANGER (PAR, 1947) 106 M.

Producer, Sol C. Siegel; director, Elliott Nugent; story, Frank Butler; adaptation, Arthur Sheekman, N. Richard Nash; screenplay, Sheekman; art director, Hans Dreier, Franz Bachelin; songs, Johnny Burke and James Van Heusen; camera, Lionel Lindon; editor, Everett Douglas.

Bing Crosby (Jim Pearson); Joan Caulfield (Trudy Mason); Barry Fitzgerald (Dr. Joseph McRory); Wanda Hendrix (Emily); Frank Faylen (Bill Waters); Elizabeth Patterson (Mrs. Gilley); Robert Shayne (Roy Chesley); Larry Young (Dr. Ronnie Jenks); Percy Kilbride (Nat Dorkas); Charles Dingle (C. J. Chesley); Don Beddoe (Mort Elker); Thurston Hall (Congressman Beeker); Lillian Bronson (Miss Lennek); Mary Field (Secretary); Paul Stanton (Mr. Daniels); Pat McVey (Ed Chanock); Milton Kibbee (Ben, The Bus Driver); Charles Middleton (Farmer Pinkett); Clarence Muse (Steward); Clarence Nordstrom (Man); Elliott Nugent (Dr. White); Julia Faye (Woman); Gertrude Hoffman (Miss Wendy); John "Skins" Miller (Citizen); Frank Ferguson (Mr. Crane); Ethel Wales (Mrs. Sims).

THE UNSUSPECTED (WB, 1947) 103 M.

Producer, Charles Hoffman; associate producer, George Amy; director, Michael Curtiz; story, Charlotte Armstrong; adaptation, Bess Meredyth; screenplay, Ranald

MacDougall; music, Franz Waxman; art director, Anton Grot; camera, Woody Bredell; editor, Frederick Richards.

Joan Caulfield (Matilda Frazier); Claude Rains (Victor Grandison); Audrey Totter (Althea Keane); Constance Bennett (Jane Maynihan); Hurd Hatfield (Oliver Keane); Michael North (Steven Frances Howard); Fred Clark (Richard Donovan); Harry Lewis (Max); Jack Lambert (Mr. Press); Ray Walker (Donovan's Assistant); Nana Bryant (Mrs. White); Walter Baldwin (Justice of the Peace).

VARIETY GIRL (PAR, 1947) 83 M.

Producer, Daniel Dare; director, George Marshall; screenplay, Edmund Hartman, Frank Tashlin, Robert Welch, Monte Brice; music, Joseph J. Lilley; songs, Johnny Burke and James Van Heusen; Frank Loesser; Allan Roberts and Doris Fisher; choreography, Billy Daniels, Bernard Pearce; assistant director, George Templeton; art director, Hans Dreier, Robert Clatworthy; special puppetoon sequence, Thornton Hoe, William Cottrell; special effects, Gordon Jennings; camera, Lionel Lindon, Stuart Thompson; editor, LeRoy Stone.

Mary Hatcher (Catherine Brown); Olga San Juan (Amber LaVonne); DeForest Kelley (Bob Kirby); William Demarest (Barker); Frank Faylen (Stage Manager); Frank Ferguson (J. R. O'Connell); Russell Hicks, Crane Whitley, Charles Coleman, Hal K. Dawson, Eddie Fetherston (Men at Steambath); Catherine Craig (Secretary); Bing Crosby, Bob Hope, Gary Cooper, Ray Milland, Alan Ladd, Barbara Stanwyck, Paulette Goddard, Dorothy Lamour, Veronica Lake, Sonny Tufts, Joan Caulfield, William Holden, Lizabeth Scott, Burt Lancaster, Gail Russell, Diana Lynn, Sterling Hayden, Robert Preston, John Lund, William Bendix, Barry Fitzgerald, Cass Daley, Howard Da Silva, Billy De Wolfe, Macdonald Carey, Arleen Whelan, Patric Knowles, Mona Freeman, Cecil Kellaway, Johnny Coy, Virginia Field, Richard Webb, Stanley Clements, Cecil B. DeMille, Mitchell Leisen, Frank Butler, George Marshall, Roger Dann, Pearl Bailey, The Mulcay's, Spike Jones and his City Slickers, George Reeves, Wanda Hendrix, Sally Rawlinson (Themselves); Ann Doran (Hairdresser); Jack Norton (Brown Derby Busboy); Eric Alden (Make-Up Man); Frank Mayo (Director).

THE SAINTED SISTERS (PAR, 1948) 89 M.

Producer, Richard Maibaum; director, William D. Russell; based on the play by Elisa Black and Alden Nash; adaptation, Mindret Lord; screenplay, Harry Clark, N. Richard Nash; art director, Hans Dreier, Henry Bumstead; music, Van Cleave; camera, Lionel Lindon; editor, Everett Douglass.

Veronica Lake (Letty Stanton); Joan Caulfield (Jane Stanton); Barry Fitzgerald (Robbie McCleary); William Demarest (Vern Tewilliger); George Reeves (Sam Stoaks); Beulah Bondi (Hester Rivercomb); Chill Wills (Will Twitchell); Darryl Hickman (Jud Tewilliger); Jimmy Hunt (David Frisbee); Kathryn Card (Martha Tewilliger); Ray Walker (Abel Rivercomb); Harold Vermilyea (Laderer); Clancy Cooper (Cal Frisbee); Dorothy Adams (Widow Davitt); Hank Worden (Taub Beasley); Don Barclay (Dr. Benton); Edwin Fowler (Reverend Hallrack); Dick Elliott (Milt Freeman); Eddie Parks (Clem Willis); Rudolf Erickson, Sidney D'Albrook, Perc Launders, Douglas Spencer, Max Wagner, Jack Woody, Jimmie Dundee (Townsmen); June Smaney, Maria Tavares (Townswomen); Eula Guy (Emmy Lou); Beulah Hubbard (Mrs. Prentiss); Frances Sandford (Mrs. Girgsby); Gigi Perreau (Beasley Girl); Alex Gerry (District Atorney); Hal Rand (Asst. District Attorney); David McMahon (Policeman); Richard Bond (Detective).

LARCENY (UNIV, 1948) 89 M.

Producer, Aaron Rosenberg; director, George Sherman; based on the novel *The Velvet Fleece* by Lois Ely, John Fleming; screenplay, Herbert F. Margolis, Louis Markein, William Bowers; art director, Bernard Herzbrun, Richard Reidel; music, Leith Stevens; camera, Irving Glassberg; editor, Frank Gross.

John Payne (Rick Maxon); Joan Caulfield (Deborah Owens Clark); Dan Duryea

(Silky Randall); Shelley Winters (Tory); Dorothy Hart (Madeline); Richard Rober (Max); Dan O'Herlihy (Duke); Nicholas Joy (Walter Vanderline); Percy Helton (Charlie Jordan); Walter Greaza (Mr. Owens); Patricia Alphin (Waitress); Harry Antrim (Mr. McNulty); Russ Conway (Detective); Paul Brinegar (Mechanic); Don Wilson (Master of Ceremonies); Barbara Challis (Maid); Grandon Rhodes (Harry Carson); Ruth Lee (Patricia Carson); Gene Evans (Horace); Bill Walker (Butler); Sam Edwards (Y.A.A. President); Don Garner (College Boy); Pat Walker (Peggy); Jack Chefe (Bald Headed Waiter); John Carpenter (Man Bidder); Jasper Weldon (Porter); Oliver Hartwell (Black Porter); Bob E. Perry (Bartender); Alex Davidoff (Waiter), Donald Dewar (Boy).

DEAR WIFE (PAR, 1950) 87 M.

Producer, Richard Maibaum; director, Richard Haydn; a sequel to Norman Krasna's play *Dear Ruth;* screenplay, Arthur Sheekman, N. Richard Nash; art director, Hans Dreier, Earl Hedrick; camera, Stuart Thompson; editor, Archie Marshek.

William Holden (Bill Seacroft); Joan Caulfield (Ruth Seacroft); Billy De Wolfe (Albert Kummer); Mona Freeman (Miriam Wilkins); Edward Arnold (Judge Wilkins); Arleen Whelan (Tommy Murphy); Mary Philips (Mrs. Wilkins); Harry Von Zell (Jeff Cooper); Raymond Roe (Ziggy); Elisabeth Fraser (Kate Collins); Bill Murphy (Dan Collins); Mary Field (Mrs. Bixby); Irving Bacon (Mike Man); Gordon Jones (Taxi Cab Driver); Marietta Canty (Dora); Don Beddoe (Metcalfe); Richard Haydn (Early Riser); William J. Cartledge (Western Union Boy); Franklyn Farnum, Edward Biby (Campaign Men); Roger Davis (Committee Chairman); Len Hendry (Bank Teller); Tom Dugan (Painter); Bess Flowers (Mrs. Grindle); Paul E. Burns (Mr. Grindle); Harland Tucker (Mr. Burroughs); Patty Lou Arden (Clara); Ida Moore (Blowsy Woman).

THE PETTY GIRL (COL, 1950) 88 M.

Producer, Nat Perrin; director, Henry Levin; story, Mary McCarthy; screenplay, Perrin; songs, Harold Arlen and Johnny Mercer; art director, Walter Holscher; camera, William Snyder; editor, Al Clark.

Robert Cummings (George Petty); Joan Caulfield (Victoria Braymore); Elsa Lanchester (Dr. Crutcher); Melville Cooper (Beardsley); Audrey Long (Connie); Mary Wickes (Professor Whitman); Frank Orth (Moody); John Ridgely (Patrolman); Raymond Largay (B. J. Manton); Ian Wolfe (President Webb); Frank Jenks (Jaye); Tim Ryan (Durkee); Mabel Paige (Mrs. Hibach) Kathleen Howard (Professor Langton); Edward Clark (Professor Ramsey); Douglas Wood (Professor Stratton); Everett Glass (Professor Haughton); Sarah Edwards (Professor Morrison); Movita Castaneda (Carmelita); Lyn Thomas (Patti McKenzie); Dorothy Vaughn (Maid); Richard Avonde (M. C./Orchestra Leader); Ray Teal, Pat Flaherty (Policemen); Earle Hodgins (Boatman); Henry Hall (Faculty Member); Russell Hicks (Tycoon); Herbert Heywood (Doorman); Shirley Ballard (January—Petty Girl); Jetsy Parker (February); Barbara Freking (March); Shirley Whitney (April); Claire Dennis (May); Betsy Crofts (June); Joan Larkin (July); Lucille LaMarr (August); Eileen Howe (September); Carol Rush (October); Eloise Farmer (November); Dorothy Abbott (December); Tippi Hedren (Ice Box); Lois Hall (Coca Cola); Mona Knox (Mazola).

THE LADY SAYS NO (UA, 1951) 80 M.

Producer, Frank Ross, John Stettman, Jr.; director, Ross; story-screenplay, Robert Russell; art director, Perry Ferguson; music director, Emil Newman; camera, James Wong Howe; editor, George Amy.

Joan Caulfield (Dorinda); David Niven (Bill); James Robertson Justice (Uncle Matt); Lenore Lonergan (Goldie); Frances Bavier (Aunt Alice); Peggy Maley (Midge); Henry Jones (Potsy); Jeff York (Goose); George Davis (Bartender); Robert Williams (General); Mary Laurence (Mary).

THE RAINS OF RANCHIPUR (20, 1955) 104 M.

Producer, Frank Ross; director, Jean Negulesco; based on the novel by Louis Bromfield; screenplay, Merle Miller; art director, Lyle R. Wheeler, Addison Hehr; music, Hugo Friedhofer; special effects, Ray Kellogg; assistant director, Eli Dunn; camera, Milton Krasner; editor, Dorothy Spencer.

Lana Turner (Lady Edwina Esketh); Richard Burton (Dr. Safti); Fred MacMurray (Tom Ransone); Joan Caulfield (Fern); Michael Rennie (Lord Esketh); Eugenie Leontovich (Maharani); Gladys Hurlbut (Mrs. Simon); Madge Kennedy (Mrs. Smilley); Carlo Rizzo (Mr. Adoani); Beatrice Kraft (Oriental Dancer); King Calder (Mr. Smiley); Argentina Brunetti (Mrs. Adoani); John Banner (Ranchid); Ivis Goulding (Louise); Ram Singh (Major Domo); Lou Krugman (Courier); Rama Bai (Lachmaania); Naji Babbay (Wagonlit Porter); Jugat Bhatia (Head Hunter); Phyllis Johannes (Nurse Gupta); George Brand (Mr. Simon); Elizabeth Prudhomme (Nurse Patel).

CATTLE KING (MGM, 1963) 88 M.

Producer, Nat Holt; director, Tay Garnett; screenplay, Thomas Thompson; assistant director, Henry E. Brill; art director, Walter P. Holscher; music, Paul Sawtell, Bert Shafter; camera, William Snyder; editor, George White.

Robert Taylor (Sam Brassfield); Joan Caulfield (Sharleen); Robert Loggia (Johnny Quatro); Robert Middleton (Clay Mathews); Larry Gates (President Chester A. Arthur); Malcolm Atterbury (Clevenger); William Windom (Harry Travers); Virginia Christine (Ruth Winters); Ray Teal (Ed Winters); Richard Devon (Vince Bodine); Robert Ivers (Webb Carter); Maggie Pierce (June Carter); Woodrow Parfrey (Stafford); Richard Tretter (Hobie); John Mitchum (Tex).

RED TOMAHAWK (PAR, 1967) 82 M.

Producer, A. C. Lyles; director, R. G. Springsteen; based on a novel by Steve Fisher; screenplay, Fisher; music, Jimmie Haskell; art director, Hal Pereira, Al Roelofs; camera, W. Wallace Kelley; editor, John F. Schreyer.

Howard Keel (Capt. Tom York); Joan Caulfield (Dakota Lil); Broderick Crawford (Columbus Smith); Scott Brady (Ep Wyatt); Wendell Corey (Elkins); Richard Arlen (Telegraph); Tom Drake (Bill Kane); Tracey Olson (Sal); Ben Cooper (Lt. Drake); Donald Barry (Bly); Reg Parton, Roy Jenson (Prospectors); Gerald Jann (Wu Sing); Dan White (Ned Crone); Henry Wills (Samuels); Saul Gorss (Townsman).

BUCKSKIN (PAR, 1968) 97 M.

Producer, A. C. Lyles; director, Michael Moore; screenplay, Michael Fisher; art director, Al Roelofs; music, Jimmie Haskell; assistant director, Joseph Kenney; camera, W. Wallace Kelley; editor, Jack Wheller.

Barry Sullivan (Chaddock); Wendell Corey (Rep Marlowe); Joan Caulfield (Nora Johnson); Lon Chaney (Sheriff Tangley); John Russell (Patch); Barbara Hale (Sarah Cody); Bill Williams (Frank Cody); Gerald Michenaud (Akii); Barton MacLane (Doc Raymond); Aki Aleong (Sung Li); Michael Larrain (Jimmy Cody); Leo Gordon (Travis); George Chandler (Storekeeper Perkins); Richard Arlen (Townsman); Craig Littler (Browdie); James X. Mitchell (Baker); Emile Meyer (Corbin); Robert Riordan (Telegrapher); LeRoy Johnson (Bartender); Manuela Thiess (Moni).

Joan Caulfield at the age of 25

In "Sally" (NBC-TV, 1957)

With producer-director Harold Prince, playwright Lonnie Coleman, and coplayers Joan Hackett, William Redfield, and Peggy Cass preparing for *She Didn't Say Yes* (1963)

With Sonny Tufts in MISS SUSIE SLAGLE'S (Par '46)

With Bing Crosby and Fred Astaire in BLUE SKIES (Par '46)

With Bob Hope in MONSIEUR BEAUCAIRE (Par '46)

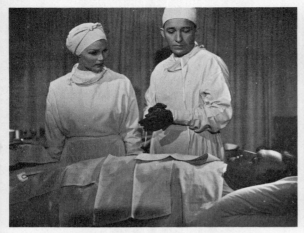

With Bing Crosby and Barry Fitzgerald in
WELCOME STRANGER (Par '47)

With Barbara Stanwyck in VARIETY
GIRL (Par '47)

With William Holden, Edward Arnold, and
Mary Philips in DEAR WIFE (Par '50)

In THE PETTY GIRL (Col '50)

With Robert Taylor and William Windom
in CATTLE KING (MGM '63)

With Fred MacMurray in THE RAINS OF
RANCHIPUR (20th '55)

LIZABETH SCOTT

5'6"

115 pounds

Tawny blonde hair

Hazel eyes

Libra

✳✳✳✳✳✳✳✳✳✳✳✳✳✳✳✳✳✳✳✳✳✳

LIZABETH SCOTT, disclaimed by members of the film intelligentsia in the late-1940s as a second-rate Lauren Bacall, has in the past few years been gaining a belated reputation as a superior actress, thanks to television showings of her features. Her unmannered projection of the now archaic tough girl is direct and vibrant, elevating it from the confines of its times.

Unlike her predecessors at Paramount, Lizabeth Scott was not contracted to the studio but to the company's leading independent producer, Hal B. Wallis, who, like David O. Selznick before him, made a lucrative business of loaning his contractees to other producers with substantial profit for himself. This breakdown of the omnipotent studio's star system worked to Lizabeth's strong disadvantage. Paramount was disinclined to promote a free-lance player who was so tenuous a part of its set-up. Compounding her plight was her rebellious individuality. She had little use for the conventional homage usually paid to the establishment in the film industry, and rarely kowtowed to the ranking institutions, gossip columnists Louella Parsons and Hedda Hopper.

With rare exceptions, Lizabeth was stereotyped on the screen as the corrupt chanteuse who had no desire or will to change her sinister ways, and was doomed to find a worthwhile good guy to love her only when it was too late and she had already passed the point of redemption. She worked best in tandem with such strong screen personalities as Burt Lancaster, Kirk Douglas, and Charlton Heston.

By the mid-1950s, Lizabeth's screen career had tapered off altogether, ended not so much by an exposé of her personal life in *Confidential* magazine as by poor professional management, which allowed the dissipation of her screen image by constant repetition of the same role to continually lesser advantage. Only recently has Lizabeth shown an inclination to become active again in show business, after having rejected many television and screen offers over the years because they failed to meet her high financial and artistic standards.

Lizabeth Scott was born Emma Matzo in the industrialized mining town of Scranton, Pennsylvania, on September 29, 1922, one of six children. Her father, John, was English-born, and her mother was of Russian descent. Looking back from the comfortable side of the fence, Lizabeth can now suggest, as she did to *Film Fan Monthly* interviewer Don Stanke, in one of her few public interviews in recent years: "Mother wanted me to be a complete human being and I was given all kinds of lessons toward being a well-rounded person"* (which, according to the Lizabeth of 1971, included six years of piano lessons and two years of voice, along with elocution training). Lizabeth also told Stanke: "As a child I had so many ambitions. I once wanted to be a nun because of an aunt who had gone into a convent. When I told this to mother, she said, 'No, that's out of the question." Lizabeth also had notions of entering such professions as journalism, opera, and industry.

After graduating from Central High School, Lizabeth auditioned for and won a summer job with May Desmond's stock company at Lake Ariel, New York. She had always been intrigued by the magic of the theatre and motion pictures, and decided to turn her entertainment joys into a way of life for herself. Lizabeth spent six months at most at Scranton's Marywood College, a Catholic institution. "I never wanted to finish college because of the feeling I had had—even at age 14—that life was very short and there were so many more important aspects of life to be explored."

Lizabeth then moved to Manhattan, convinced she had the ability to become a professional actress. She studied at the Alvienne School of Dramatics for 18 months, and to support herself became a fashion model. During this period she resided at the Ferguson Residence for Girls. "Alvienne was very good, with excellent teachers," Lizabeth told Stanke. "We did a different play each week. Sometimes I had the lead and at other times I had a small role. It was a terrific experience."

Of these days, Lizabeth recalls: "There was one period of five months in New York when I was always hungry. My folks wanted me to come home and cut my allowance to $12 a week. Out of that I paid $6.25 for my room. From what was left I ate, though sometimes I would have to buy stockings, or something, out of my eating money. I lived on sandwiches. I made hundreds of calls on producers and agents, but couldn't get a job."

Lizabeth did land a chorus girl's role in the touring version of Olsen and Johnson's enormously successful madcap stage revue *Hellzapoppin.* The road company featured Billy House and Eddie Garr as the masters of mayhem, with Ann Pennington in the lead support position. The tour opened November 3, 1940, at the Shubert Theatre in New Haven. Lizabeth has said, "It was really *Hellzapoppin* all the time. For a year and half we traveled from coast to coast. During one stretch we made sixty-four one-night stands in succession. It got so we weren't conscious of what town we were playing in. Just sixty-four days of daze. We were congenial and jolly, except when were dead for lack of sleep. But in such close intimacy, there was no privacy. Misunderstandings were magnified, under the pressure, into quarrels. My dream then, my joy now, is to be alone—to lock my apartment door and not even answer the phone."

*When Lizabeth first arrived in Hollywood she was less circumspect about her childhood and told reporters: "As a child, my mother used to tell me to keep my emotions subdued, to be 'a lady.' Instead of which I was a noisy, screaming little brat, definite about everything."

In the early fall of 1942, Lizabeth was performing with the 52nd Street Stock Company Theatre, playing the lead role in *Rain,* the dramatization of Somerset Maugham's "Sadie Thompson." She was billed as Elizabeth Scott. During its run, she was signed for a bit part, as a drum majorette, in Thornton Wilder's *The Skin of Our Teeth* (Plymouth Theatre, November 18, 1942). More importantly, the producers of the Pulitzer Prize play engaged her also to understudy the drama's star, Tallulah Bankhead (twice Lizabeth's age) in the role of Sabina, the Lilith-like maid in this chronicle of man's survival through the ages. Others in the strong cast included Fredric March, Florence Eldridge, Montgomery Clift, and Florence Reed. Lizabeth later reminisced with some wryness: "For seven months, I waited for the Long Island train to break down or for Tallulah to get a cold. But the train ran and she remained robustly healthy. Finally I felt desperate, that I was just losing time, so I quit and went back to fashion modeling and drama study." Later, when Gladys George had taken over for Miriam Hopkins who had replaced Bankhead, Lizabeth was rushed in to substitute for one performance. During her stay with *The Skin of Our Teeth,* Lizabeth remembers that Bankhead only spoke to her directly one time. That occurred when ex-Paramount star Hopkins was signed as Tallulah's replacement. Bankhead told her understudy, "You could play the role as well as her."

(Years later, when *All About Eve* (1950) emerged as a top-notch film, rumors circulated among Broadway observers that the basis for the backstage story had been derived from the relationship of Lizabeth and Bankhead during *The Skin of Our Teeth* run. *Eve* authoress Orr claims that the concept evolved from a bad experience actress Elizabeth Bergner had once had with a young performer during the run of a show.)

The following year was far from affluent or noteworthy for Lizabeth, although she picked up several modeling assignments from *Harper's Bazaar* at $25 and appeared in at least one *Esquire* full-page personality photo. On September 22, 1943, when she was at the Stork Club celebrating her birthday, Lizabeth, as she now tells the story, ran into Irving Hoffman, leg man for columnist Walter Winchell. He and Scott had met previously and he had taken an interest in her career. He suggested she meet a friend of his from Hollywood, producer Hal B. Wallis.* The movie man was impressed by her striking features and suggested a screen test. Later, through agent Charles Feldman, he had her come to Hollywood. But says Lizabeth now: "I wanted to be a great stage actress. I never once thought of movies. But it was off season on Broadway—January or February—and since I wasn't able to find a job there, I thought it might be a good experience to come to Hollywood and find out what it was all about."

Lizabeth did not have an overwhelming reception when she reached the Coast. Instead, she lolled around the Beverly Hills Hotel for two months, receiving a pay check every week from Feldman's office, but with no work forthcoming. When she threatened to return to New York, a test was immediately arranged at Warner Brothers. She received a script the night before the filming and only had a few hours' sleep before reporting to the sound stage. Of this test Lizabeth now reflects: "The privilege of being a screen actor is having the opportunity of seeing yourself as others see you. Believe me, it is very traumatic. When I saw myself, I thought, 'Get a train ticket and leave.' "

*See Appendix.

Jack L. Warner, head executive at Warner, was equally unimpressed: "She'll never be a star, only a second leading lady." His dismissal was a roundabout way of stating that Warner Brothers was already fully committed to propelling the career of sultry new contract-star Lauren Bacall, whom Lizabeth resembled both in her husky voice and her projection of a tough style. Then too, with her over-the-eye hairdo, Lizabeth had a superficial look-alike quality to peekaboo luminary Veronica Lake, then ensconced at Paramount.

Feldman persuaded Lizabeth to remain in Hollywood and audition for Universal. The same script-arriving-the-night-before-testing procedure ensued and the studio rejected Lizabeth's services. So back to New York and modeling. Lizabeth took little heed of Wallis's statements that he had liked her Warners' test and that when the situation was "right" he would be in touch.

In August, 1944, Feldman telegraphed Lizabeth that Wallis wanted to sign her to a contract, now that he had planned his departure from Warner Brothers and was joining Paramount as a gilt-edged independent executive producer with carte blanche powers on the lot. Lizabeth was the first player he signed, pacting her to a seven-year contract. She arrived in Hollywood in November, 1944, one of the many newcomers hired on to replenish the acting rosters of the still lucrative film factories.

At the time, Paramount was undergoing a transition following the end of the B. G. DeSylva* regime, which had seen the fostering of such wholesome types as Betty Hutton, Eddie Bracken, Diana Lynn, and Joan Caulfield. With postwar realism values already abounding, the studio's new executives relied on Wallis and others to instill a vigor so long lacking from their screen product. Wallis would soon hire Kirk Douglas, Burt Lancaster, Kristine Miller, and Wendell Corey for his stock company, relying on such veteran stars as gutsy Barbara Stanwyck to add box-office lure to his packaged productions.

Lizabeth's professional status at Paramount was tenuous from the start and never received the definition necessary to launch her as a potential major star. Initially the studio's publicity department capitalized on Lizabeth's similarity to rival Hollywood actress Bacall and tagged her "The Threat"—following in the footsteps of Marie "The Body" McDonald, Lauren "The Voice" Bacall, and Anita "The Look" Colby.

Part of "The Threat" title referred to Lizabeth's tough dame veneer (acquired in her uneasy childhood), which made her an obvious contender for roles which once would have gone automatically to home-lot queen Veronica Lake, then still riding the post-peak of her screen popularity. Since their hair styles and cool demeanors made them superficially the same type, Wallis assumed that Lizabeth might provide a tidy income on loanout to Paramount as replacement for the recalcitrant Lake or to other studios as a substitute for Bacall.

The disadvantage of being so close in bearing to Lake was that it had never been studio policy to establish two top-level personalities in the same mold. Since Paramount handled all the promotion, publicity, and distribution for Wallis, it was not about to sacrifice Lake's unique marquee value for a contractee of an independent producer, a player whom it could not call upon at will to work in this or that production as the studio head saw fit. Thus Paramount never really claimed Lizabeth as one of its own.

*See Appendix.

Once Paramount had played out plugging Lizabeth as "The Threat," it soon embarked on the usual hackneyed ballyhoo treatment accorded any mindless new actress in Hollywood. The studio did not, or could not, realize that Lizabeth was a strong individualist who had her own variation of the tough dame appeal. On the way to success, she had acquired a most distinctive patina. As she explained to the press at the time: "Everything that has happened to me during the past six years, the bad as well as the good, has prepared me for my present opportunity. . . . Now I can see that the experience [the struggling New York years] was a privilege. It gave me qualities —confidence, appreciation, tolerance. What most impressed me was the feeling that every human being had something holy within him, I hope I never forget that." Lizabeth personified women's liberation 20 years before it became fashionable.

Wallis groomed Lizabeth for several months with screen wardrobe and makeup tests before assigning her to her first feature—the slick soap opera *You Came Along* (1945), which boasted Ayn Rand as coscreenwriter and had a nine-week shooting schedule.

Second-billed as Ivy Hotchkiss, Lizabeth was pitched in the advertisements as; "Here's to Lizabeth Scott. Beautiful . . . blonde . . . aloof . . . alluring." And she had three acceptable leading men to bounce off her range of dramatic expression in this prefabricated bit of love, bravery, and patriotism. She was the treasury department official assigned to take three GIs (Bob Cummings, Don DeFore, and Charles Drake) on a war bond tour. She and Cummings fall in love and marry, only to have their bliss cut short by his death from leukemia. With restraint, she milked the potentially soapy role for all its romantic, schmaltzy worth, but the critics were slow to cotton to her: "Slim, husky-voiced Miss Scott is reminiscent of three other actresses. She drawls like Dorothy McGuire, has the slow sultry 'look' of Lauren Bacall and sometimes catches the sparkle of Katharine Hepburn" *(Life).* "Perhaps Miss Scott might have jammed the romantic passages with power, irrespective of the staging" *(New York Herald Tribune).* The picture premiered at the Paramount Theatre on July 4, 1945, with a special later showing in Lizabeth's hometown of Scranton, Pennsylvania. It made a respectable financial showing.

Lizabeth was often seen with her mentor-boss Wallis on the social scene, but she had no widely publicized romances, real or manufactured, in her initial months in Hollywood. She told the press: "What time have I for such? Launching a career is a serious business and a full time job. It doesn't permit the luxury of a romance. Love never should be regarded lightly. It takes a lot of thought and effort to make a happy marriage. Of course, I hope for that someday, but right now I want no such interference. That will come in its proper time and place."

Of her impressions of Hollywood, Lizabeth told Myrtle Gebhart of the *Boston Sunday Post* in January, 1946: "I'm tired of that smart New York set who blast Hollywood calling it an intellectual void. Plenty of silly things are done here, but Hollywood isn't so very screwball. They do fine things in the theatre and splendid things out here, too. Baddies crop up on both coasts. I dislike it when critics sell Hollywood short."

Her only 1946 release was the brooding *Strange Love of Martha Ivers,* directed by Lewis Milestone. It proved to be the most prestigious and best-produced film of her entire screen career. Ostensibly a vehicle of twisted emotions and theatrics for Barbara Stanwyck, Lizabeth was third-slotted as Toni Marachek. She is a girl on parole who strays to the country town run by wealthy Stanwyck and her drunken, warped district-attorney husband Kirk Douglas. Lizabeth is harbored by easy-going Van Heflin, Stanwyck's childhood love. All her scenes were played in low key, creating a subtle portrayal of an emotionally bruised woman: self-sufficient, but not over-bearing or bitter. In her confrontations with Stanwyck over who will get Heflin, Lizabeth came off best, being far less mannered than the high-powered superstar. She not only won Heflin in the soggy script, but attracted most of the audience interest, especially in the scene in which she models a pair of walking shorts. The *New York Times* carped: "[She] has some pretty silly-sounding lines, and her performance generally lacks convic-tion." However, the *Hollywood Reporter* evaluated—if a little overen-thusiastically; "Lizabeth Scott justifies her quick ascent to stardom with another of her strangely haunting portrayals. . . . Her sultry approach to the character gives it vitality and life. Miss Scott has all it takes to write her own ticket in Hollywood."

The *Motion Picture Herald* named Lizabeth star of tomorrow for 1946, along with such others as Jackie "Butch" Jenkins, Zachary Scott, and Don DeFore. It was a minor indication that her emoting as the staunch girl alone in life was gaining her a distinctive reputation in the Hollywood commu-nity, different from the tawdry self-sufficient dames being played by Mar-tha Vickers, Audrey Totter, and others.

For her next assignment, Wallis loaned Lizabeth to Columbia Pictures, at a healthy profit for his outfit, to team her in the modestly budgeted *Dead Reckoning* (1947) with Humphrey Bogart. Having been compared to Bo-gart's screenmate and real-life wife so often, Lizabeth now had the oppor-tunity to prove how she stacked up against her rival. As Coral Chandler, the cool nightclub singer, she quickly becomes attached to Bogart. He has been tearing apart Gulf City, Florida, to discover who killed his service buddy William Prince. Before the finale, the script has Lizabeth, as Prince's fian-cée, more interested in club-owner Morris Carnovsky's wealth and attention than concerned about a little murder. Like Mary Astor in *The Maltese Fal-con*, Lizabeth had a pleasing scene with Bogart in which she begs the moral tough guy to give her a break for the sake of love. Having been worked over too often by the club's bodyguards, Bogart knows her score, and reluctantly turns Lizabeth over to the police, with the electric chair looming in her future. Despite Lizabeth's singing abilities, Columbia dubbed in her voice in the torchy club-room number "Either It's Love or It Isn't."

Dead Reckoning did nicely at the box office, and left few filmgoers feeling cheated for having seen Bogart paired with Lizabeth. But the critics were still not convinced. "Miss Scott plays her role as though she was trying to do a take-off on a long-haired blues singer, and this seems to be about equally the fault of performance and of the synthetic quality of her pseudo-sophisticated comments on life and love as set down in the script" *(New York Herald Tribune)*. Quipped the *New Yorker* magazine: "Miss Scott not only resembles Miss Bacall closely but can flare her nostrils even more vigorously."

Desert Fury (1947) was Lizabeth's first technicolor film. She played Paula Haller, whose mother, Mary Astor, runs Chuckawalla's whore house and controls the cops and politicians. Lizabeth's role called for her to be sophisticated (she had been to some of the best finishing schools in the East), temperamental, and petulant. John Hodiak, a gambler on the run, stops in the desert town, accompanied by his gunman, Wendell Corey. Local police deputy Burt Lancaster desires Lizabeth but must wait patiently to marry her until her infatuation with murderer Hodiak is ended by the latter's violent death. With such high-powered personalities, the movie was charged with nervous energy which unfortunately never channeled into satisfactory entertainment. Lizabeth was obviously ill at ease with the badly-defined characterization, and Lewis Allen's direction was too passive to give her much assist. *Variety* could only muster up praise that she "is a wonderful clotheshorse for the far-west outdoor costumes provided by Edith Head." Even the regional critics were unpleased by Lizabeth's performance: "As the nitwit heroine, [she] is no better than she has been in previous pictures. She has a too-ready smile which she switches on and off like an electric sign and nothing more to offer than a set of innocuous mannerisms" *(Baltimore Sun)*.

Lizabeth rounded off 1947 with a token appearance in the all-star Paramount vaudeville feature *Variety Girl.* It was the only film in which Lizabeth would appear with the studio's major stars, including her nemesis Veronica Lake. Lizabeth made a self-conscious appearance in the circus production-number segment. Cowboy Burt Lancaster is to shoot a cigarette out of Lizabeth's mouth. Dressed in riding togs, she smiles wanly, and there is a cloud of smoke. Then Lancaster is shown placing a sign on the wall: "Girl Wanted." H. B. Darrach of *Time* magazine described her performance in *Variety Girl* as "a Milton Caniff version of the Mona Lisa."

In a publicity release of the time, Lizabeth was said to have stated: "When you say ambition to me—that's when you get me started! My greatest ambition is to be the whoppingest best actress in Hollywood. You can't blame a girl for trying! I don't want to be classed as a 'personality.' Something to stare at. I want to have my talents respected, not only by the public but by myself. So I'm working madly to perfect myself." About poise: "I don't believe in hiding emotions. Never did. Control them, yes, now that I'm older. But pretending not to feel what I'm feeling is out of the question." (These offbeat qualities would not endear her to the gossip queen bees of Hollywood, Louella Parsons and Hedda Hopper, who expected and demanded abject subjugation from everyone, especially starlets.)

On loanout to United Artists, Lizabeth costarred with Dick Powell in the neat suspenser *Pitfall* (1948). It was directed by Veronica Lake's then-husband Andre De Toth. The tightly knit plot presented Powell as a claims adjuster for an insurance company—à la *Double Indemnity*—overly bored with his sweet wife Jane Wyatt and his humdrum family life. He is easy prey for grasping model Lizabeth, whom he chances upon when repossessing gifts given her by an absconded boyfriend, now in jail. Another former beau, grisly private detective Raymond Burr, attempts to make something dirty of the time Lizabeth and Powell spend together. Before long, Powell is tossed into jail for having killed Lizabeth's paroled boyfriend and for his calm shooting of the pestering Burr. Powell is later released for justifiable homicide and meekly returns to his loving family, giving a happy ending to everyone but Lizabeth. The *New York Times* approved of Lizabeth's crisp performance, finding her "provocative, and acting better than she has ever done before. A nice performance, to be sure." Lizabeth, Powell, Burr, and Wyatt recreated their roles from *Pitfall* for the "Lux Radio Theatre" (November 8, 1948).

Her other 1948 release was with the Wallis stock company in the Paramount release *I Walk Alone.* She was second-billed to Burt Lancaster, and appeared as Kay Lawrence, a pliant nightclub singer, employed by café-owner Kirk Douglas in the post-Prohibition period. Lancaster is an ex-rum runner who has been double-crossed by Douglas and spent 14 years in jail. Although rehabilitated in prison, his crushing experiences outside soon make him bitter. Wendell Corey rounded out the cast as Douglas's wan, spent mobster henchman. Lizabeth "sang" "Don't Call It Love," going through all the mannerisms that had become associated with her club-siren roles: moist eyes, clutching a chiffon handkerchief in one hand, holding onto the microphone with a determined desperation, keeping her tight-jawed face immobile in its ambiguous feminity. Howard Barnes *(New York Herald Tribune)* penned: "Miss Scott is an actress of promise, but she still evidences more promise than accomplishment at the Paramount. While she croons and plays the piano pleasantly, her amorous predicament is less than believable." Paramount's advertising catchphrase almost gave away the whole story line: "He fell for the oldest trick in the world. If you want to pump a guy—send a dame." The stars of *I Walk Alone* were heard in the "Lux Radio Theatre" version, May 24, 1948.

For a shoddy cheapie entry, *Too Late for Tears* (1949), directed by Byron Haskin for United Artists release, crammed a plethora of mayhem into its 99 minutes. Lizabeth was a female bluebeard par excellence, and had the feature been released in today's highly individualistic promotional temper, it might have been a much bigger commercial hit. Lizabeth and husband number-two Arthur Kennedy (she drove her first mate Don DeFore to suicide) receive $60,000 in cash as a result of a case of mistaken identity. Blackmailer Dan Duryea (in one of his more fully realized characterizations) convinces her to murder Kennedy. Once done with Kennedy, she sets about poisoning sniveling Duryea. Having fled to Mexico she is cornered by the police; she falls to her death from a tenth-story window. Critical reaction about Lizabeth's work was again divided. Otis L. Guernsey, Jr. *(New York Herald Tribune)* said: "As a femme fatale she is uninteresting and her performance has quantity of expression without quality." A. Weiler of the *New York Times* decided: "Lizabeth Scott is a taut, seductive, husky voiced schemer who is fascinatingly convincing in a completely unsympathetic role."

Her other 1949 film, *Easy Living,* was also made on loanout, this time for RKO. Lizabeth was given third billing to that studio's Victor Mature and Lucille Ball in this less-than-pleasant study of human nature. Mature is seen as a pro-football player for the New York Chiefs. Though suffering from a heart defect, he continues playing in an effort to hold onto his straying, ambitious wife, Lizabeth. Ball, the team's secretary, is in love with Mature. When Mature finally accepts a coaching post at a small college, he has to literally slap his spoiled wife back to her senses. This pedestrian black-and-white feature opened at the Criterion Theatre on October 12, 1949, and drew no particular audience enthusiasm. *Cue* labeled Lizabeth "utterly inadequate to her role" and the *New York Times* smirked: "Even Lizabeth Scott, as the wife, turns her lip chewing to advantage."

Lizabeth had given up a Broadway role in the projected *Uncle Sugar* when she accepted her Hollywood contract, and she was anxious now to test her mettle on the stage again. In July, 1949, she came east during a break between films to appear in the title role of *Anna Lucasta* at the McCarter Theatre, Princeton, New Jersey. Another Paramount star, Paulette Goddard, would appear in Columbia's adaptation of the dramatization, released later that year.

Although Lizabeth's social life still remained a mystery, she was not averse to discussing her theories on romance and other subjects with a few journalists. A widely quoted remark of nonconformist Lizabeth was: "I believe in sex—completely and absolutely."

Lizabeth continued with her radio-broadcast guesting, appearing on the "Lux Radio Theatre" in *Perfect Marriage* (April 12, 1948) with Ray Milland, *Saigon* (September 15, 1949) with John Lund, and *California* (January 30, 1950) with Ray Milland and Raymond Burr.

Lizabeth had proved she was a permanent fixture in fickle Hollywood, but she had not succeeded in making many inroads in her home studio. Wallis, already involved in the highly profitable exploitation of his new contractees Dean Martin and Jerry Lewis, parceled Lizabeth out in a two-picture agreement with RKO, which paid him $100,000 for her services. Lizabeth only received her far smaller salary under the original Wallis contract.

RKO in 1950 was struggling to survive in the diminishing theatrical film market, and under the aegis of board chairman Howard Hughes it was not faring too well. Stars Jane Russell and Robert Mitchum were its chief box-office attractions, and like Columbia, RKO would employ once-famous stars like Claudette Colbert and Irene Dunne at bargain rates for standardized features. Therefore, like Paramount, RKO was neither inclined nor in any position to exploit Lizabeth's potential with a fresh publicity campaign. Instead, they photographed her in unimaginative poses, usually in sports attire, and described her for the fan magazines as the "svelte, tawny blonde, [with an] angular Vogue-like figure." When queried by the press about her quiet social life, Lizabeth replied: "I'm in love with a wonderful life; a life of living alone. Peace, quiet, solitude—they're all mine."

In 1950 Lizabeth was seen exclusively in Paramount releases. In *Paid in Full* (1950), she again took second billing to Robert Cummings in a turgid tale of selfishness and selflessness. An overdramatized account of two sisters of opposite natures, this film provided Lizabeth with her first good-girl role in some time. Unfortunately, she looked surprisingly wan, which adversely tinged her performance with a seeming neuroticism, and thus spoiled her desired new screen image. Maturing Paramount ingenue Diana Lynn portrayed her irresponsible young sister, who maliciously steals away and marries advertising executive Cummings. When self-sacrificing Lizabeth inadvertently causes the death of the couple's baby, she vows to make amends. The opportunity comes when, after Lynn divorces Cummings, Lizabeth and he wed. A congenital malfunction makes having babies fatal for her, but Lizabeth insists upon giving birth to Cummings's child so that she can replace the lost infant. This time around, the critics were more enthusiastic about Lizabeth. "[She] adds another portrait to her gallery of ill-used heroines. And while her assignment is far from plausible, her portrayal is warm and restrained" *(New York Times)*. "Miss Scott turns in a capital performance as the unselfish sister" *(Variety)*. But Paramount failed to give this feature a properly gimmicky sales campaign—like Columbia's tearjerker *No Sad Songs for Me,* which was pushed as the "brave picture of the year." Besides, a growling Lizabeth as the wronged bad girl was always more exciting to view than her mechanical portrayal of a demure heroine. The picture finally showed up on New York television in March, 1972, advertised as a campy soap opera, which it unfortunately was.

Her other 1950 release, *Dark City,* opened at the Paramount Theatre on October 17, 1950, and teamed her with Charlton Heston, making his feature film debut as the bruised romantic turned into a cynical gambler. After he and his associates take Don DeFore in a sharp card game, the latter hangs himself. DeFore's crazed brother Mike Mazurki stalks the gamblers, seeking revenge. Lizabeth once again essayed a nightclub thrush; this time she craved Heston. She "sang" "If I Didn't Have You," and paraded her by now standardized repertoire of interaction within the confines of the club, on the stage floor, at the gaming table, and in the assorted tête-à-têtes with the film's principals. There were sufficient close-up shots to remind viewers of Lizabeth's icy beauty—dark eyebrows, luminous large eyes, moist wet lips, and the de rigueur, cooly inexpressive face. Viveca Lindfors was wasted in a smallish part as DeFore's widow and Dean Jagger popped into the story line as a stereotyped persistent police captain. The action progressed from Los Agneles to Las Vegas, with Lizabeth and Heston reunited by the fade-out. Otis L. Guernsey, Jr. *(New York Herald Tribune)* summed up Lizabeth's stock assignment: "[Her] role consists of singing significant songs at the hero from a night-club platform and reproaching him with the fact that he does not love her enough."

During the summer session at the University of Southern California, Lizabeth audited courses in philosophy and political science, demonstrating that there was greater depth to her than fan magazine write-ups had led the public to believe.

Lizabeth had a change of screen profession in RKO's *The Company She Keeps* (1951). Tastefully directed by John Cromwell, this film was better than it should have been, considering the modest budget and the severe limitations of the contrived scenario. Lizabeth played Joan, a Los Angeles probation officer (on the right side of the law for a change!) who is dedicated beyond the call of duty in converting parolee Jane Greer to the path of righteousness. Lizabeth almost loses her boyfriend Dennis O'Keefe to the ungrateful Greer. Nevertheless, she remains steadfast in assisting Greer at every turn, nobly saving the rule-breaking con from a return to jail for abetting another misguided parolee. Lizabeth played most of her scenes wearing her stock-in-trade trench coat and over-the-shoulder handbag. Both Lizabeth and Greer worked hard to be convincing in their counter-casting. As Bosley Crowther *(New York Times)* noted, Elizabeth was "the least of its [the film's] sheer absurdities."

The second of her three releases in 1951—her busiest year on the screen—was Columbia's *Two of a Kind.* This film demonstrated that Lizabeth was a Hollywood talent who should have made it big on the silver screen. She is the broad who picks up Edmund O'Brien in an amusement arcade and solicits his assistance in a confidence scheme she and attorney Alexander Knox have planned. He is to pose as the long lost son of an elderly couple, putting him in position to claim a $10 million inheritance. The son had one distinguishing physical characteristic—the tip of one finger was missing. Lizabeth and O'Brien park outside a hospital, and Lizabeth crushes his finger in the car door so that it has to be removed. Later she is quick to shed the homicide-prone Knox for the more pliable O'Brien, while maneuvering to prevent the couple's nosy niece, Terry Moore, from uncovering their plot. At the finale, when Knox has perished, O'Brien philosophizes about Lizabeth: "[She's] like me. She's got a lot of larceny in her soul, but she's no killer." This was a perfect summation of Lizabeth's inviting screen image. The *New York Times* cracked about Lizabeth in *Two of a Kind:* "She emotes as though she was continually savoring the ["smarty alecky dialogue"]."

Lizabeth performed box-office duty for RKO by costarring with Robert Mitchum in *The Racket* (1951), a somber black-and-white study of corruption in a big city. Mitchum is the honest police captain who will not accept bribes from politician Ray Collins and must come to grips with the racketeers headed by tough Robert Ryan. This time around, Lizabeth is Irene, a scared nightclub songstress in love with reporter Robert Hutton. The bulk of the action centers around the Mitchum-Ryan flip talk and assorted racketeer versus police brutalities; Lizabeth had little to do, beyond looking stunning in her gowns, offering her wan smile, and in her song number, mouthing the words to the dubbed rendition of "A Lovely Way to Spend an Evening." When Lizabeth informs about Ryan's sordid doings, she suffers one of the classic abuses of filmdom. In the police station, Ryan spins around and spits at Lizabeth: "Why, you cheap little clip joint canary!" The *Hollywood Reporter* was one of the few trade journals to think she "carries off her role with warm conviction."

In late 1951 Lizabeth confided to the press: "The crux of being an actress comes between pictures. In six years I've made thirteen pictures and that's not half enough to suit me. Sometimes I don't think I can last between films."

Paramount finally decided to cast Lizabeth opposite Alan Ladd in *Red Mountain* (1951). By this time Ladd was physically past his prime and was facing a box-office slump in his career. The lumbering Western, under William Dieterle's faltering direction, was no plum for Lizabeth. She had a secondary, passive assignment, as the Yankee-loving woman of Reb gold-miner Arthur Kennedy. Ladd meandered through the film as a Confederate captain who is slow to realize that renegade leader John Quantrill (John Ireland) is a self-serving phony. With Lizabeth trailing about in her long skirts and looking abject most of the time, it was no wonder the *Chicago Daily Tribune* opined: "[She] performs with all the animation of a chunk of cement."

During 1952 Lizabeth was frequently a guest on Dean Martin and Jerry Lewis's radio show, a result of her all-inclusive contract with Martin and Lewis's producer-mentor, Wallis. She also performed in some radio dramatic stints, such as an adaptation of *The Red Hand,* opposite James and Jeanne Cagney.

Wallis evidently could not or was not trying to obtain prime loanout assignments for his once-prized property. Lizabeth traveled to England to appear with Paul Henried in *Stolen Face* (1952), a low-budget effort exploiting once-prime cinema names. The only acting challenge it offered was a dual role. She was a concert pianist who has a short romance with plastic surgeon Henried. When she leaves him to return to her Army lover, Henried recompenses himself by remolding the face of a female crook patient into a likeness of Lizabeth, and then weds the unreformed girl. Lizabeth the pianist reappears, and when her double is disposed of in an accidental train fall, the true lovers are free to marry. In reviewing the programmer, *Variety* noted that Lizabeth was "capable enough in both [roles], considering the heavy-handed, slow direction by Terence Fisher."

By 1953 Lizabeth's screen career was languishing badly. Wallis was too preoccupied with moneymakers Martin and Lewis, and had a batch of newer contractees coming and going: Polly Bergen, Corinne Calvet, and, soon, Shirley MacLaine. In the placid 1950s, tough dames were out of style. Veronica Lake had left Hollywood in 1951, Lauren Bacall was no longer hot box-office, and the new crop of ingenues were generally sweet young things who could be interchanged without much notice by audiences.

Lizabeth was still decorously answering the most persistent press question: Why wasn't she a flamboyant part of the social set? In April, 1953, she told United Press reporter Venon Scott: "I'm really not a recluse, you know. Is there anything wrong with a gal just because she doesn't show up at every premiere and party in Hollywood?

"Don't worry, if I enjoyed the party circuit and premieres, I'd go to 'em. And I don't object to people who do. It's just that the rat race isn't for me.

"When I'm working on a picture, I don't mind working overtime to get my lines down pat. But that's strictly business. It's different when I have to work overtime on publicity to promote Liz Scott.

"I do a lot of reading and I have a growing art collection that I'm awfully proud of. People say you can't live a normal life in Hollywood but they're wrong. I'm having a wonderful time doing just what I want."

Wallis cast Lizabeth in *Scared Stiff* (1953), a financially successful remake of *The Ghosts Breakers*. The diluted new version was built around the talents of Dean Martin and Jerry Lewis. Cavalierly employing Lizabeth in flabby comedy-heroine part, Wallis wangled the services of Carmen Miranda, the Brazilian bombshell, who returned to the screen in an equally pointless role as a Latin American club performer. In her straight-man role as Mary Carroll, Lizabeth inherits an allegedly haunted castle on a remote Caribbean island. Cabaret singer Martin and his crony Lewis come to Lizabeth's aid in unraveling the mystery: the villain hopes to prevent her from discovering the vein of gold under the castle. Even cameo appearances by Bing Crosby and Bob Hope and Lewis's wild imitation of Miranda did not spark this juvenile hair-raiser.

Either very loyal to Wallis or able to discern something in her role that escaped viewers, Lizabeth kindly explained about her screen-comedy debut in *Scared Stiff*: "It was a panic. Those two characters [Martin and Lewis] are like perpetual motion. I'd like to do another picture with them, but with a couple of months' notice so I could go 'into training.'" Next to *You Came Along, Scared Stiff* is her favorite film; she reasons that it shows a different facet of her screen personality.

Of her years as Wallis's free-lancing round-robin contract player, Lizabeth admitted: "I guess that isn't exactly conformist either. But it is fun."

Bad for Each Other, opening December 24, 1953, at the Palace Theatre, reunited Lizabeth with Charlton Heston in a heavy-handed drama released by Columbia. An Army doctor returning to his coal-mining hometown after service in the Korean War, he must choose whether to minister to the miners or to cater to a swank Pittsburgh clientele. Under the tempting influence of Lizabeth, a wealthy mineowner's divorcee daughter, he selects the latter. When they marry, she steers her wealthy friends to her husband for medical attention. But a mine explosion cuts loose, and Heston undergoes a catharsis, renounces Lizabeth, and turns to loyal nurse Dianne Foster. *Variety* correctly estimated: "The picture hardly helps the careers of Miss Scott, Heston or director Irving Rapper."

Lizabeth's only 1954 release was RKO's *Silver Lode,* a hasty imitation of *High Noon.* Set in old Nevada, all the action takes place on a July Fourth holiday. Lizabeth is set to marry respectable rancher John Payne, but their wedding is delayed by the arrival of Dan Duryea who rides into town posing as a U.S. Marshal. He is seeking revenge for his brother, who was killed fairly by Payne during a card game. As the town's richest woman, Lizabeth was given little to do, beyond repeatedly pleading for the life of her future husband. It is Dolores Moran as the saloon entertainer, also in love with Payne, who helps prove Duryea is a fraud. The quickie Western opened quietly at the Palace Theatre on July 23, 1954. Those who bothered to review the film perked up at the volley of gunfire that concluded the picture. Because Samuel Fuller directed *Silver Lode,* the color sagebrush tale has acquired a mild reputation of its own.

Suddenly—at least for most of naive America—Lizabeth's name was smeared by a front-page story in the September 25, 1954, issue of *Confidential.* The exposé write-up nearly ended Lizabeth's professional career. The banner headline read: "The vice cops expected to find a few big name customers when they grabbed the date books of a trio of Hollywood jezebels. But even their cast iron nerves got a jolt when they got to the S's."

The magazine's reportage was tied into the arrest of Sandra Ann Betts (age 23), Joyce Hicks (age 20), and a 17-year-old girl arrested in a Los Angeles vice raid. The article editorialized: "Liz was a strange girl even for Hollywood and from the moment she arrived in the cinema city. She never married, never even gets close to the altar. With the exception of a long-time affair with a noted Hollywood producer, her life was startlingly free of the hectic, on-and-off romance rumors, which are run-of-the-mill to movie beauties. . . .

"Liz, according to the grapevine buzz, was taking up almost exclusively with Hollywood's weird society of baritone babes. She was seldom seen in the well-known after-dark spots, but those who did catch a glimpse of 'Scotty' as she calls herself, reported spotting her from time to time in off-color joints that were favorite hangouts for movieland's twilight set. . . .

". . . but Liz herself raised Hollywood eyebrows with an interview she gave columnist Sidney Skolsky. She confided that she always wore male colognes, slept in men's pajamas and positively hated frilly, feminine dresses.

". . . In recent years, Scotty's almost non-existent screen career has allowed her to roam farther afield and—on one jaunt to Europe—she headed straight for Paris' Left Bank where she took up with Frede, that city's most notorious Lesbian queen and the operator of a night club devoted exclusively to entertaining deviates like herself."

And so on. The article concluded: "Insiders began putting together the pieces of the puzzle that was Lizabeth Scott and it didn't take them long to get the answer. They know that shocking fact that one of the screen's top glamour girls is listed in the little black books kept by Hollywood prostitutes."

On July 25, 1955, Lizabeth's attorney Jerry Giesler instituted a $2.5 million suit against *Confidential,* stating that his client had been portrayed in a "vicious, slanderous and indecent" manner. For whatever reason, further developments regarding the suit failed to materialize in any newspaper, and only the pungent aftermath of the scandal itself remained.

Had Lizabeth ignored the dirt, as did former Paramount star Marlene Dietrich, who received the same sort of story in *Confidential,* the storm might have blown over and been forgotten soon. However, the exposé rocked Hollywood and became known throughout the country, wherever *Confidential* was sold.

Lizabeth went to England in November, 1955, happy to have the opportunity to work in a low-budget British quickie *The Weapon,* not distributed in the United States until 1957. In this taut melodrama, she is the mother of a boy who accidentally shoots a friend with a gun found in the remains of a destroyed London building. The gun is actually the only clue to a decade-old unsolved murder case, which brings Inspector Herbert Marshall and CID officer Steve Cochran into the case. This more than adequate entry could only obtain modest distribution in America, although *Variety* stated that the "acting is top-rate."

To complete her Hal Wallis contract, Lizabeth made *Loving You* (1957), playing second fiddle to gyrating rock 'n' roll star Elvis Presley. She played Glenda Markle, a hard-boiled publicist who discovers orphaned-boy Presley and turns the hillbilly singer into a national sensation. She is aided by cynical bandleader Wendell Corey, her former spouse who still moons for her. The wide-screen color musical opened on showcase release on July 17, 1957, making the expected bundle of money for Wallis, Paramount, and Presley. The *Hollywood Reporter* observed: "Corey and Miss Scott are handicapped by speaking their lines in the teeth of a hurricane, but they are responsible for a large amount of the friendliness and charm that the picture generates." Like Barbara Stanwyck, who would later work out her Wallis contract in a Presley vehicle, Lizabeth was superfluous background.

In late 1957, with no other film roles forthcoming, Lizabeth indulged her interest in a vocalizing career and signed on to record an LP album entitled *Lizabeth Sings,* which included such numbers as "So Nice to Have a Man Around" and "Deep Dark Secret." As she explained: "I got the notion I wanted to do some singing some three years ago, but my studio wasn't too excited about the idea. Then a year or so ago, I just made up my mind I was going to take singing lessons and this is what's come of it. After all, the worst that could happen is that people won't play my records." The album was bought by curiosity collectors to such a sufficient degree that RCA Victor signed Lizabeth to a three-year recording contract. Lizabeth confided to the press: "Now I want to make more and more albums, take on singing appearances in television and in nightclubs. My acting? Oh, I'm not doing away with that. I don't intend to sing to the exclusion of acting. Singing is just part of my career. One thing helps the others, if you know what I mean."

Lizabeth dabbled late in her career in television dramatic roles. She was co-starred with Richard Conte and Richard Eyer in *Overnight Haul* (May 12, 1956, CBS) on "The Twentieth Century-Fox Hour," the drama being a compressed remake of that studio's earlier feature, *Thieves' Highway.* In some overseas countries, the 56-minute television segment was shown as a theatrical feature. The following year, Lizabeth began making frequent appearances on video musical programs, such as the Patti Page show, usually in the guise of guest vocalist.

Two years passed before Lizabeth returned to television, guest-starring on *The Amazon* episode of "Adventures in Paradise" (March 21, 1960, ABC). She is a yachting expert who hires series' star Gardner McKay and his boat, the *Tiki.* Explaining her absence from television, Lizabeth said: "There's no point putting your heart and soul into a part when you know in advance it isn't worth the trouble. I'm not speaking as a dedicated actress. Enthusiasm and hard work are requisites for any job a person undertakes. I'd rather starve than perform in a picture or TV show just for money. I tried working for just money once and it made me almost physically ill." In the syndicated 1960 teleseries, "The Third Man," Lizabeth guest-starred in an episode directed by Paul Henried—the segment had been specially written for actress Marie Windsor who proved unavailable at the last moment.

Throughout the 1960s Lizabeth would occasionally be spotted at a Hollywood premiere, but she remained absent from the television scene except for a few appearances on Hollywood-taped video game shows. Reportedly, her demands were so stringent that film and television casting directors soon stopped asking her to consider possible parts.

In the late 1960s, Lizabeth's name appeared in a lawsuit filed by the sister of the late oilman William Lafayette Dugger, Jr., of San Antonio, Lizabeth, described in his will as "my fiancée," had been named for a substantial inheritance. As a result of the court proceedings (affirmed in May, 1971) she was removed as a beneficiary.

Lizabeth currently resides in the residential section of Hollywood Boulevard, in the same apartment that she maintained during her active film-making years. She says that her wise investments made for her by her business manager make work unnecessary. Reporters have constantly requested interviews with Lizabeth, many of them making it clear that they admire her screen work and hope to create new interest in her among producers. She usually declines, merely stating that since she is not quite ready to make a comeback, articles on her would be pointless.

Lizabeth did an about-face in 1971 when she made her television talk-show debut on Mike Douglas's program (April 12, 1971, CBS). She had come to New York to see the musical *Applause!* Rumors circulated that she was being considered for a road-company tour of the show, which starred her old rival Lauren Bacall. Lizabeth later admitted: "I am fascinated with the idea of doing a Broadway musical. That would be idyllic. The spirit moves me again. I don't want to go to Australia or anywhere else—I want to go back to Broadway. That is my aim right now." Nothing developed re a show.

Lizabeth accepted her first assignment in a decade. She flew to Malta to appear opposite Michael Caine in United Artists' *Pulp,* a theatrical film of international intrigue. Lizabeth plays what is described as an aristocratic nymphomaniac.

But for Lizabeth, who still takes regular singing lessons and continually audits college courses in psychology, philosophy and other subjects, the essence of her present existence is not show business. "My personal life— my development as a human being—is the most important thing." She would like to be known as an activist: "Let's be *for* things. There are too many who are against things."

YOU CAME ALONG (Par, 1945) 103 M.

Producer, Hal Wallis; director, John Farrow; story, Robert Smith; screenplay, Smith, Ayn Rand; art director, Hans Dreier, Hal Peirera; music, Victor Young; technical advisor, Col. C. A. Shoop; process camera, Farciot Edouart; camera, Daniel L. Fapp; editor, Eda Warren.

Robert Cummings (Bob Collins); Lizabeth Scott (Ivy Hotchkiss); Don DeFore (Shakespeare); Charles Drake (Handsome); Julie Bishop (Joyce Heath); Kim Hunter (Frances Hotchkiss); Rhys Williams (Col. Stubbs); Franklin Pangborn (Hotel Clerk); Minor Watson (Uncle Jack).

THE STRANGE LOVE OF MARTHA IVERS (Par, 1946) 116 M.

Producer, Hal B. Wallis; director, Lewis Milestone; story, Jack Patrick; screenplay, Robert Rossen; art director, Hans Dreier, John Meehan; music, Miklos Rozsa; process camera, Farciot Edouart; camera, Victor Milner; editor, Archie Marshek.

Barbara Stanwyck (Martha Ivers); Van Heflin (Sam Masterson); Lizabeth Scott (Toni Marachek); Kirk Douglas (Walter O'Neil); Judith Anderson (Mrs. Ivers); Roman Bohnen (Mr. O'Neil); Darryl Hickman (Sam Masterson—As a Boy); Janis Wilson (Martha Ivers—As a Girl); Ann Doran (Secretary); Frank Orth (Hotel Clerk); James Flavin (Detective); Mickey Kuhn (Walter O'Neil—As a Boy); Charles D. Brown (Special Investigator).

DEAD RECKONING (COL, 1947) 100 M.

Producer, Sidney Biddell; director, John Cromwell; story, Gerald Adams, Biddell; adaptation, Allen Rivkin; screenplay, Oliver H. P. Garrett, Steve Fisher; assistant director, Seymour Friedman; art director, Stephen Goosson, Rudolph Sternad; music, Marlin Skiles; song, Allan Roberts and Doris Fisher; music director, Morris Stoloff; camera, Leo Tover, editor.

Humphrey Bogart (Rip Murdock); Lizabeth Scott (Coral Chandler); Morris Carnovsky (Martinelli); Charles Cane (Lt. Kincaid); William Prince (Johnny Drake); Marvin Miller (Krause); Wallace Ford (McGee); James Bell (Father Logan); George Chandler (Louis Ord); William Forrest (Lt. Col Simpson); Ruby Dandridge (Hyacinth).

DESERT FURY (PAR, 1947) 95 M.

Producer, Hal B. Wallis; director, Lewis Allen; story, Ramona Stewart; screenplay, Robert Rossen; music, Miklos Rozsa; art director, Perry Ferguson; camera, Charles Lang, Edward Cronjager; editor, Warren Low.

Lizabeth Scott (Paula Haller); John Hodiak (Eddie Bendix); Burt Lancaster (Tom Hanson); Mary Astor (Fritzi Haller); Kristine Miller (Claire Lindquist); Wendell Corey (Johnny Ryan); William Harrigan (Judge Berle Lindquist); James Flavin (Sheriff Pat. Johnson); Jane Novak (Mrs. Lindquist).

VARIETY GIRL (PAR, 1947) 83 M.

Producer, Daniel Dare; director, George Marshall; screenplay, Edmund Hartman, Frank Tashlin, Robert Welch, Monte Brice; music, Joseph J. Lilley; songs, Johnny Burke and James Van Heusen; Frank Loesser; Allan Roberts and Doris Fisher; choreography, Billy Daniels, Bernard Pearce; assistant director, George Templeton; art director, Hans Dreier, Robert Clatworthy; special Puppetoon sequence, Thornton Hoe, William Cottrell; special effects, Gordon Jennings; camera, Lionel Lindon, Stuart Thompson; editor, LeRoy Stone.

Mary Hatcher (Catherine Brown); Olga San Juan (Amber La Vonne); De Forest Kelley (Bob Kirby); Bing Crosby, Bob Hope, Gary Cooper, Ray Milland, Alan Ladd, Barbara Stanwyck, Paulette Goddard, Dorothy Lamour, Veronica Lake, Sonny Tufts, Joan Caulfield, William Holden, Lizabeth Scott, Burt Lancaster, Gail Russell, Diana Lynn, Sterling Hayden, Robert Preston, John Lund, William Bendix, Barry Fitzgerald, Cass Daley, Howard da Silva, Billy De Wolfe, Macdonald Carey, Arleen Whelan, Patric Knowles, Cecil Kellaway, Johnny Coy, Virginia Field, Richard Webb, Stanley Clements, Cecil B. DeMille, Mitchell Leisen, Frank Butler, George Marshall, Roger Dann, Pearl Bailey, The Mulcays, Spike Jones and his City Slickers, Mary Edwards, Virginia Welles, Wanda Hendrix, George Reeves, Sally Rawlinson (Themselves); Russell Hicks, Crane Whitley, Charles Coleman, Hal K. Dawson, Eddie Fetherston (Men at Steambath); Catherine Craig (Secretary); Frank Ferguson (J. R. O'Connell); Jack Norton (Busboy—Brown Derby); Ann Doran (Hairdresser); Eric Alden (Makeup Man); Frank Mayo (Director); Ralph Dunn (Cop); William Demarest (Barker); Frank Faylen (Stage Manager).

PITFALL (UA, 1948) 85 M.

Producer, Samuel Bischoff; director, Andre De Toth; based on the novel *The Pitfall* by Jay Dratler; music director, Louis Forbes; art director, Arthur Lonergan; assistant director, Joseph Depew; camera, Harry Wild; editor, Walter Thompson.

Dick Powell (John Forbes); Lizabeth Scott (Mona Stevens); Jane Wyatt (Sue Forbes); Raymond Burr (MacDonald); John Litel (District Attorney); Byron Barr (Bill Smiley); Jimmy Hunt (Tommy Forbes); Ann Doran (Maggie); Selmer Jackson (Ed Brawley); Margaret Wells (Terry); Dick Wessel (Desk Sergeant).

I WALK ALONE (PAR, 1948) 97 M.

Producer, Hal B. Wallis; director, Byron Haskin; based on the play *Beggars Are Coming to Town* by Theodore Reeves; adaptation, Robert Smiler, John Bright; screenplay, Charles Schnee; music, Victor Young; song, Ned Washington and Allie Wrubel; camera, Leo Tover; editor, Arthur Schmidt.

Burt Lancaster (Frankie Madison); Lizabeth Scott (Kay Lawrence); Kirk Douglas (Noll Turner); Wendell Corey (Dave); Kristine Miller (Mrs. Richardson); George Riguad (Maurice); Marc Lawrence (Nick Palestro); Mike Mazurki (Dan); Mickey Knox (Skinner); Roger Neury (Felix).

TOO LATE FOR TEARS (US, 1949) 99 M.

Producer, Hunt Stromberg; director, Byron Haskin; based on the serialized story by Roy Huggins; screenplay, Huggins; music, Dale Bietts; music director, Morton Scott; art director, James Sullivan; camera, William Mellor; editor, Harry Killer.

Lizabeth Scott (Jane Palmer); Don DeFore (Dan Blake); Dan Duryea (Danny Fuller); Arthur Kennedy (Alan Palmer); Kristine Miller (Kathy Palmer); Barry Kelly (Lt. Breach).

EASY LIVING (RKO, 1949) 77 M.

Producer, Robert Sparks; director, Jacques Tourneur; based on the story "Education of the Heart" by Irwin Shaw; screenplay, Charles Schnee; music, Roy Webb; camera, Harry J. Wild; editor, Frederic Knudtson.

Victor Mature (Pete Wilson); Lucille Ball (Anne); Lizabeth Scott (Liza Wilson); Sonny Tufts (Tim McCarr); Lloyd Nolan (Lenahan); Paul Stewart (Argus); Jack Paar (Scoop Spooner); Jeff Donnell (Penny McCarr); Art Baker (Howard Vollmer); Gordon Jones (Bill Holloran); Don Beddoe (Jaegar); Dick Erdman (Buddy Morgan); William "Bill" Phillips (Ozzie); Charles Lang (Whitey); Kenny Washington (Benny); Julia Dean (Mrs. Belle Ryan); Everett Glass (Virgil Ryan); James Backus (Dr. Franklin); Robert Ellis (Urchin); Steven Flagg (Gilbert Vollmer); Alex Sharp (Don); Russ Thorson (Hunk Edwards); June Bright (Bill Duane); Eddie Kotal (Curley); Audrey Young (Singer); Los Angeles Rams (Themselves).

PAID IN FULL (PAR, 1950) 98 M.

Producer, Hal B. Wallis; director, William Dieterle; based on a story by Dr. Frederic M. Loomis; screenplay, Robert Blees, Charles Schnee; art director, Hans Dreier, Earl Hedrick; music, Walter Lang, Victor Young; camera, Leo Tover; editor, Warren Low.

Robert Cummings (Bill Prentice); Lizabeth Scott (Jane Langley); Diana Lynn (Nancy Langley); Eve Arden (Tommy Thompson); Ray Collins (Dr. Fredericks); Frank McHugh (Ben); Stanley Ridges (Dr. Winston); Louis Jean Heydt (Dr. Carter); Kristine Miller (Miss Williams); Laura Elliot (Tina); Ida Moore (Dorothy); James Nolan (Charlie Malloy); Geraldine Wall (Miss Ames); Rolland Morris (Bunny Howard); Jane Novak (Mrs. Fredericks); Carole Mathews (Model); Carol Channing (Mrs. Peters); Dorothy Adams (Emily Burroughs); Arlene Jenkins, Christine Cooper (Secretaries); Byron Barr (Man at Bar); Laura Elliot (Bridesmaid); Marie Blake (Tired Woman); Jimmie Dundee (Truck Driver); Gladys Blake (Talkative Woman); Douglas Spencer (Crib Man); Dewey Robinson (Diaper Man); Charles Bradstreet (Marc Hickman); Harry Cheshire (Minister).

DARK CITY (PAR, 1950) 97 M.

Producer, Hal B. Wallis; director, William Dieterle; based on the story "No Escape" by Larry Marcus; adaptation, Ketti Frings; screenplay, John Meredyth Lucas, Marcus; song, Harold Spina, Jack Elliott; music, Franz Waxman; art director, Franz Bachelin; camera, Victor Milner; editor, Warren Low.

Charlton Heston (Danny Haley); Lizabeth Scott (Fran); Viveca Lindfors (Victoria Winant); Dean Jagger (Captain Garvey); Don De Fore (Arthur Winant); Jack Webb (Augie); Ed Begley (Barney); Henry Morgan (Soldier); Walter Sande (Swede); Mark Keuning (Billy Winant); Mike Mazurki (Sidney Winant).

THE COMPANY SHE KEEPS (RKO, 1951) 82 M.

Producer, John Houseman; director, John Cromwell; story-screenplay, Ketti Frings; music, Leigh Harline; camera, Nicholas Musuraca; editor, Robert Swink.

Lizabeth Scott (Joan); Jane Greer (Diane); Dennis O'Keefe (Larry); Fay Baker (Tilly); John Hoyt (Judge Kendall); James Bell (Mr. Nelley); Don Beddoe (Jamieson); Bert Freed (Smitty); Irene Tedrow (Mrs. Seeley); Marjorie Wood (Mrs. Haley); Marjorie Crossland (Mrs. Griggs); Virginia Farmer (Mrs. Harris).

TWO OF A KIND (COL, 1951) 75 M.

Producer, William Dozier; director, Henry Levin; story, James Edward Grant; screenplay, Lawrence Kimble, James Grunn; music, George Duning; camera, Burnett Guffey; editor, Charles Nelson.

Edmond O'Brien (Lefty Farrell); Lizabeth Scott (Brandy Kirby); Terry Moore (Kathy McIntyre); Alexander Knox (Vincent Mailer); Griff Barnett (William McIntyre); Robert Anderson (Todd); Virginia Brissac (Maida McIntyre).

THE RACKET (RKO, 1951) 89 M.

Producer, Edmund Grainger; director, John Cromwell; based on the play by Bartlett Cormack; screenplay, William Wister Haines, W. R. Burnett; art director, Albert S. D'Agostino, Jack Okey; music director, Mischa Bakaleinikoff; camera, George E. Diskant; editor, Sherman Todd.

Robert Mitchum (Thomas McQuigg); Lizabeth Scott (Irene Hayes); Robert Ryan (Nick Scanlon); Robert Hutton (Dave Ames); Brett King (Joe Scanlon); William Talman (Johnson); Les Tremayne (Harry Craig); Walter Sande (Delaney); Iris Adrian (Sadie); Walter Baldwin (Sullivan); William Conrad (Sgt. Turck); Joyce MacKenzie (Mary McQuigg); Virginia Huston (Lucy Johnson); Don Porter (Connolly); Max Wagner (Durko).

RED MOUNTAIN (PAR, 1951) 84 M.

Producer, Hal B. Wallis; director, William Dieterle; story, George F. Slavin, George W. George; screenplay, John Meredyth Lucas, Slavin, George; music, Franz Waxman; camera, Charles B. Lang, Jr.; editor, Warren Low.

Alan Ladd (Capt. Brett Sherwood); Lizabeth Scott (Chris); Arthur Kennedy (Lane Waldron); John Ireland (Quantrell); Jeff Corey (Skee); James Bell (Dr. Terry); Bert Freed (Randall); Walter Sande (Benjie); Neville Brand (Dixon); Carlteon Young (Morgan); Whit Bissell (Miles).

STOLEN FACE (Lippert, 1952) 71 M.

Producer, Anthony Hinds; director, Terence Fisher; screenplay, Richard Landau, Martin Berkeley; camera, Walter Harvey; editor, Maurice Rootes.

Paul Henried (Dr. Phillip Ritter); Lizabeth Scott (Alice Brent and Lilly [B]); Andre Morell (David); Mary MacKenzie (Lilly [A]); John Wood (Dr. Jack Wilson); Susan Stephen (Betty); Arnold Redley (Dr. Russell); Everley Gregg (Lady Harringay); Cyril Smith (Alf); Janey Burnell (Maggie); Grace Gavin (Nurse); Terence O'Reagan (Pete Snipe); Diana Beaumont (May); Alexis France (Mrs. Emmett); John Bull (Charles Emmett); Dorothy Bramhall (Miss Simpson); Ambrosene Philpotts (Miss Patten); Richard Wattis (Wentworth); Russell Napier (Cutler).

SCARED STIFF (PAR, 1953) 108 M.

Producer, Hal Wallis; director, Goerge Marshall; based on the play *The Ghost Breakers* by Paul Dickey, Charles W. Goddard; screenplay, Herbert Baker, Walter De Leon, additional dialogue, Ed Simmons, Norman Lear; music, Leith Stevens; choreography, Billy Daniels; art director, Hal Pereira, Franz Bachelin; songs, Mack David, Jerry Livingston; camera, Ernest Laszlo; editor, Warren Low.

Dean Martin (Larry Todd); Jerry Lewis (Myron Myron Mertz); Lizabeth Scott (Mary Carroll); Carmen Miranda (Carmelita Castina); George Dolenz (Mr. Cortega); Dorothy Malone (Rosie); William Ching (Tony Warren); Paul Marion (Carriso Twins); Jack Lambert (Zombie); Tom Powers (Police Lieutenant); Tony Barr (Trigger); Leonard Strong (Shorty); Henry Brandon (Pierre); Hugh Sanders (Cop on Pier); Frank Fontaine (Drunk); Bob Hope, Bing Crosby (Themselves).

BAD FOR EACH OTHER (COL, 1954) 83 M.

Director, Irving Rapper; story, Horace McCoy; screenplay, Irving Wallace, McCoy; music director, Mischa Bakaleinikoff; camera, Frank Planer; editor, Al Clark.

Charlton Heston (Dr. Tom Owen); Lizabeth Scott (Helen Curtis); Dianne Foster (Joan Lasher); Mildred Dunnock (Mrs. Mary Owen); Arthur Franz (Dr. Jim Crowley); Ray Collins (Dan Reasonover); Marjorie Rambeau (Mrs. Roger Nelson); Lester Matthews (Dr. Homer Gleeson); Rhys Williams (Doc Scobee); Lydia Clarke (Rita Thornburg); Cris Alcaide (Pete Olzoneski); Robert Keys (Joe Marzano); Frank Tully (Tippy Kashko); Ann Robinson (Lucille Grellett); Dorothy Green (Ada Nicoletti).

SILVER LODE (RKO, 1954) 81 M.

Executive producer, Leon Chooluck; producer, Benedict Bogeaus; director, Allan Dwan; screenplay, Karen De Wolfe; art director, Van Nest Polgase; music, Louis Forbes; camera, John Alton; editor, James Leicester.

John Payne (Dan Ballard); Dan Duryea (Ned McCarthy); Lizabeth Scott (Rose Evans); Dolores Moran (Dolly); Emile Meyer (Sheriff Wooley); Harry Carey, Jr. (Johnson); Morris Ankrum (Zachary Evans); John Hudson (Michael "Mitch" Evans); Robert Warwick (Judge Cranston); Stuart Whitman (Wickers); Alan Hale, Jr. (Kirk); Frank Sully (Paul Herbert); Paul Birch (Rev. Field); Florence Auer (Mrs. Elmwood); Roy Gordon (Dr. Elmwood); Edgar Barrier (Taylor); Al Hill (Townsman); Al Haskel (Deputy); William Haade, Frank Ellis, Stan Jolley (Searchers); Barbara Wooddell,

Sheila Bromley (Townswomen); Lane Chandler (Man at Fire); Joe Devlin (Walt Little); Burt Mustin (Spectator); John Dierkes (Blacksmith); Byron Foulger (Prescott, banker); Gene Roth (Townsman); Ralph Sanford (Joe, bartender); Myron Healey (Rider).

THE WEAPON (REP, 1957) 77 M.

Producer, Hal E. Chester; director, Val Guest; story, Chester, Fred Freiberger; screenplay, Freiberger; art director, John Stoll; music, James Stevens; camera, Reg Wyer; editor, Peter Rolfe Johnson.

Steve Cochran (Mark); Lizabeth Scott (Elsa); Herbert Marshall (Mackenzie); Nicole Maurey (Vivienne); Jon Whiteley (Erik); George Cole (Joshua); Laurence Naismith (Jamison); Stanley Maxted (Colonel); Denis Shaw (Groggins); Fred Johnson (Fitzsimmons).

LOVING YOU (PAR, 1957) 101 M.

Producer, Hal B. Wallis; associate producer, Paul Nathan; director, Hal Kanter; based on the story "A Call from Mitch Miller" by Margaret Agnes Thompson; screenplay, Herbert Baker, Kanter; art director, Hal Pereira, Albert Nozaki; music, Walter Scharf; special effects, John P. Fulton; camera, Charles Lang, Jr; editor, Howard Smith.

Elvis Presley (Deke Rivers); Lizabeth Scott (Glenda Markle); Wendell Corey (Walker "Tex" Warner); Dolores Hart (Susan Jessup); James Gleason (Carl Meade); Paul Smith (Skeeter); Ken Becker (Wayne); Jana Lund (Daisy); Ralph Dumke (Tallman); The Jordanaires (Themselves); Yvonne Lime (Sally); Skip Young (Teddy); Vernon Rich (Harry Taylor); David Cameron (Castle); Grace Hayle (Mrs. Gunderson); Dick Ryan (Mack); Steve Pendleton (O'Shea); Sydney Chatton (Grew); Jack Latham (TV Announcer); William Forrest (Mr. Jessup); Irene Tedrow (Mrs. Jessup); Hal K. Dawson (Lieutenant); Madge Blake (Woman); Joe Forte (Editor); Almira Sessions (Woman); Beach Dickerson (Glenn); Gail Lund (Candy); Harry Cheshire (Mayor); Gladys Presley (Extra in Audience).

PULP (UA, 1973)

Producer, Michael Klinger; director-screenplay, Mike Hodges.

Michael Caine; Lizabeth Scott; Mickey Rooney, Lionel Stander; Nadia Cassini; Dennis Price.

At the age of 22

Advertisement for DEAD RECKONING (Col '47)

About 1952

In 1957

With Robert Cummings, Charles Drake, and Don DeFore in YOU CAME ALONG (Par '45)

With Kirk Douglas and Charles D. Brown in THE STRANGE LOVE OF MARTHA IVERS (Par '46)

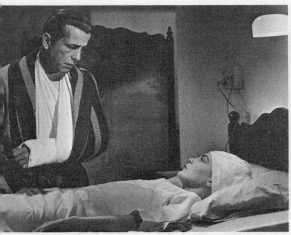

With Humphrey Bogart in DEAD RECKONING (Col '47)

With Eve Arden in PAID IN FULL (Par '50)

With Robert Cummings and Salvador Baguez (right) in PAID IN FULL (Par '50)

With Jane Greer in THE COMPANY SHE
KEEPS (RKO '51)

With Alan Ladd and Arthur Kennedy in
RED MOUNTAIN (Par '52)

In BAD FOR EACH OTHER (Col '53)

With Dolores Hart, Elvis Presley, and
Wendell Corey in LOVING YOU (Par '57)

SHIRLEY MACLAINE

5′6½″
118 pounds
Reddish-brown hair
Blue eyes
Taurus

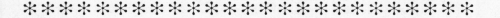

SHIRLEY MACLAINE emerged in the mid-1950s as one of the last major stars to be created under the old and dying Hollywood studio system, as well as one of the first dynamic personalities to arrive on the scene in a long time. From the start, Shirley was different from the usual star(let)—at the time she was branded kooky, now she is termed an individualist—demanding to retain her identity as a person first and to be promoted as a cinema celebrity second. Early in her movie career, Shirley found her perfect screen role, that of the good-hearted slob in *Some Came Running* (1958), which netted her an Oscar nomination. This role revealed her as a natural, instinctive actress who created no barriers between her characterization and the viewer's interpretation.

Hal B. Wallis selected Shirley for screen grooming after watching her understudy take-over performance in the Broadway musical *Pajama Game* (1954). He was immediately impressed by her gaminlike qualities, and so was director Alfred Hitchcock, who borrowed Shirley to make her screen debut in the black comedy *The Trouble With Harry* (1955).

Just as stars before her had fought with their studios, so Shirley feuded with her contract-employer Wallis, champing under contract terms which allowed him to loan her out on any type of inferior assignment, and, as her star status rose, to make fabulous sums doing this while she received a pittance. Nowadays, with every would-be actor or actress a self-incorporated business, this brand of exploitation cannot occur.

As Shirley rose to superstar status, 1960s style, her feature films became fewer and farther in between, and each new picture became more and more an overweight extravaganza which proved too much for her oversized but definitely limited talents. Just as it seemed that her descent from the box-office heights was a sign that her career was over (only 26 pictures in 15 years), she branched out in new directions with startling success, proving that the new breed of Hollywood star did not have to rely only on movie popularity for success. Shirley's completely self-written autobiography, *Don't Fall off the Mountain,* appeared in 1970 and met with outstanding reactions from all quarters. This joyous text demonstrated that Shirley had blossomed even further as a thinking person with an original mind during her years as a cinema luminary.

Few people had high expectations for Shirley's 1970 contract for a British-produced television series, which also provided that she could star in an indefinite number of low-budget features. The first of these theatrical film ventures, *Desperate Characters* (1971) discloses a new, mature Shirley, who has gained sufficient scope as a dramatic actress to overcome her earlier, stereotyped screen image. Now nearing 40, she has reversed the trend of past studio-manufactured screen stars by illustrating that it is possible to gain a new and respectable, if not spectacular, screen career if one is an expansive and ever-growing human spirit.

Shirley MacLaine Beatty (pronounced Bay-tee) was born April 24, 1934, in Richmond, Virginia, the first child of Ira O. and Kathlyn (MacLean) Beatty. Her father, of Irish descent, had been a musician and bandleader before settling down in Richmond in the real estate business. Mrs. Beatty was of Scottish origin; a former teacher of dramatics at Maryland College, she performed in little-theatre productions and directed group-theatre activities in Richmond.

As Shirley would later detail: "I was born into a cliché-loving, middle-class Virginia family. . . . Conformity was the rule of behavior in our neighborhood. We were all Baptists." Shirley found it difficult to conform to her father's ultraconservative, dour nature, or to accept her mother's soft-pedaled optimism. She later reflected: "Thank goodness, when I was three, a companion in adjustment and rebellion entered my life" (i.e., her brother Warren, born: March 30, 1937).

To help strengthen her weak ankles, Shirley was entered in ballet classes at the age of two and a half. Enthralled by the discipline and the possibility of expressing herself creatively, she continued with dance training for 15 years. Dance training and acting in her mother's theatricals were her only concessions to childhood femininity. Around her neighborhood the freckle-faced, red-topped Shirley was known as the "powerhouse" because of her expert batting average on the sandlot baseball team, not to mention her offering a clobbering finale to any fights in which brother Warren found himself.

When the Beatty family moved to Arlington, Virginia, Shirley began lessons at the Washington School of the Ballet, headed by Lisa Gardiner and Mary Day. By the time she was 12 years old, Shirley was performing with the group in ballets presented by the National Symphony Orchestra at Constitution Hall in Washington. As the tallest person in the class, she was usually assigned the male roles.

At Washington-Lee High School, Shirley participated in a few variety shows. On one occasion her father rebuked her for making a fool of herself performing "I Can't Say No" from *Oklahoma!* at the entertainment assembly program. Shirley states in her autobiography: "It was then that I determined to make the most of whatever equipment I had been born with, and part of that equipment was to dare. But mostly I didn't want to be a disappointment to myself."

When she was 16, Shirley broke her ankle during a performance of the *Cinderella* ballet and was laid up for four months. It was at this time that she convinced her mother to let her try her luck in New York. Once there, she obtained chorus work in the City Center Theatre's revival of *Oklahoma!* At the end of the run, the entire cast was invited to the Berlin Arts Festival. Shirley refused, deciding to return home and complete high school.

Two years later, Shirley was ready to launch another attack on New York and Broadway. She remembers: "I don't think either of us [she and Warren] ever seriously considered that we *wouldn't* be able to make something of ourselves. We *had* to; it was the only way we'd have any respect for ourselves. We *wanted* to live up to whatever our potentials might be. . . . Warren and I had a precise blueprint of how *not* to be."

With money she had saved from babysitting, Shirley arrived back in New York City in June, 1952. She took a sub-sublet apartment on 116th Street and Broadway, just south of Harlem (it was a fifth-floor walkup, renting at $64 a month). She won a chorus post in the Lambertsville, New Jersey, Music Circus for the summer. That fall she obtained a dance job in the traveling industrial show for Servel Ice Box. As Queen of the Swans, her routine was to perform segments of *Swan Lake* around a refrigerator. During this tour she dropped Beatty from her professional name.

Back in Manhattan, Shirley made the rounds of casting offices. After three assaults on the Richard Rodgers-Oscar Hammerstein II production office, she was auditioned and hired for the chorus line of *Me and Juliet* (Majestic Theatre, May 28, 1953). This middling musical, starring Isabel Bigley, Bill Hayes, and Joan McCracken, ran 358 performances. While in the dance line, Shirley met William T. (Steve) Parker. He was then 32 years of age. A former actor and off-Broadway director, he was hoping to angle himself into the producing phase of show business. He had spent many of his formative years in Japan, and had served in World War II in the Army. When he was discharged as a captain at age 22, he decided he would someday return to Japan to live. Shirley recalls: "So intense was our involvement, we forgot to get married until 1954."

After *Me and Juliet,* Shirley accepted another chorus position in the Hal Prince-Richard Griffith musical *Pajama Game* (St. James Theatre, May 13, 1954). This musical comedy of labor relations and love was an instantaneous hit. It starred Janis Paige, John Raitt, Eddie Foy, Jr., and the show's overnight sensation, Carol Haney. For $75 a week, Shirley danced in the chorus and was understudy to Haney. On the fourth day after the opening, Haney broke her ankle, and the unrehearsed Shirley was told to go on in the role of the seductive Gladys. (Ironically, Shirley had brought her resignation notice to the theatre that day, determined not to be an unseen fixture in yet another long-running production.) Because Shirley had not been coached to tackle the total role, John Raitt was forced to sing her first act song "Hernando's Hideaway." Act Two opened with the much-admired dance "Steam Heat," performed by the Gladys character and two male dancers. As the nervous Shirley knew she would, she dropped her twirling derby hat. Her muttered "Shit" was overheard by most of the startled audience. At the curtain calls, the same audience that had booed when the management announced Haney's illness, applauded loudly for Shirley. "They cheered and threw kisses. I felt as though a giant caress had enveloped me. . . . When you're trained as a ballet dancer you are trained to be part of a team. You devote your talent to being a link that makes up the chain. . . . I was [now] out in front of the chain and I felt lonely, and yet at the same time I felt so much that I belonged. . . . I belonged to myself and from then on I would have to devote all of me to developing that self the best way I knew how. . . . Talent was nothing but sweat."

Shirley and her boyfriend Steve Parker made a habit of sending *Pajama Game* tickets to any likely actors' agents and film producers in New York, hoping some prominent industryite would view her live audition, and speed up the progress of her career.

One night Paramount's independent executive producer, Hal B. Wallis,* came to see *Pajama Game.* After the show he went backstage and offered Shirley an eight-year film contract if her screen test proved successful. She tested in New York ("I had a hole in my tights") and after canvassing the situation—no other movie offers were pending—she accepted the producer's terms on June 21, 1954. Wallis informed Shirley that he would bring her to Hollywood when she was needed. Meanwhile, she remained in *Pajama Game,* substituting for Haney on several occasions.

*See Appendix.

In early September, 1954, Alfred Hitchcock was in the audience of *Pajama Game* and witnessed Shirley's latest substitution for Haney. At a conference with the famed director, Shirley admitted she had had no previous stage or television roles and probably was unequipped for the proposed lead-female part in the pending *The Trouble With Harry* (1955). Rotund Hitchcock replied: "All this simply means that I shall have fewer bad knots to untie. You're hired."

Shirley was told to report to Vermont in three days for location shooting. Hitchcock negotiated a loanout agreement with Wallis for Shirley's screen services (made simple because Hitchcock was then based at Paramount). On September 17, 1954, the day before Shirley left New York City for Vermont, she and Parker were married at the Marble Collegiate Church, with Dr. Norman Vincent Peale officiating at the ceremony.

The Trouble With Harry was filmed largely on location near Barre, Vermont, with the remaining sound stage work completed at Paramount's Hollywood studio. Under Hitchcock's puppetmasterlike direction, Shirley felt restrained, but she survived the ordeal of her initiation into picture-making.

The Trouble With Harry premiered in Barre, Vermont, on October 3, 1955, with later bookings throughout the country. The offbeat black comedy received excellent critical notices, but failed to stir would-be filmgoers. It jovially dealt with the subject of murder. Three shots are heard in the countryside of a small Vermont town one day. Upon investigation, the body of Harry Rogers is found. Several local people who had no love for the deceased, fear they may be guilty: retired sea captain Edmund Gwenn, abstract painter John Forsythe, old maid Mildred Natwick, and Harry's charmingly natural wife Shirley. For most of the film, everyone is scooting madly about trying to dispose of the troublesome corpse that does not seem to want to stay buried. At the wrap-up it is discovered that Harry died of natural causes. The much-relieved Shirley and Forsythe discover they are in love.

Shirley won good notices for her screen debut. Bosley Crowther *(New York Times)* said: "And there's an especially disarming screwball blandness about the manner of Miss MacLaine." The *Christian Science Monitor* approved: "[she] shows a flair for comedy in an apparently guileless straight faced style that is thoroughly her own." *Variety* pointed out: "Miss MacLaine impressed despite the handicap of some high school, amateur mannerisms, which manage to get by here but will need correction for the future."

The Trouble With Harry was a financial dud in the United States, although it did well in its European art-house release. Shirley had her own evaluation of the film: "Privately, I didn't see anything funny about dragging a corpse around for five reels—but we did terrific in Europe, though not so great over here. We were especially big in the Orient where, obviously, it is considered hilarious to deal with death."

On her arrival in Hollywood, Shirley's worst anticipations were realized. Wallis had a most secure berth at Paramount with his independent production unit. In the last decade he had carefully nurtured a lucrative business of signing up new talent for showcasing in his Paramount-released features. If they proved popular, so much the better. They could be loaned out to other producers at a sizable profit. So far his batting average had proven extraordinarily high. Lizabeth Scott joined his player stable in 1944–45; later there were Kirk Douglas, Burt Lancaster, Wendell Corey, and the relative failure of the crop, Kristine Miller. In 1948 Wallis astutely signed the comedy team of Dean Martin and Jerry Lewis to a long-term contract. Once launced into motion pictures with *My Friend Irma* (1949), the duo proved a financial bonanza to all concerned. Wallis was always contracting new ingenue talent to display in the Martin and Lewis features. The newcomer only had to look comely and demonstrate a potential screen personality. Before Shirley's arrival on the Wallis scene, there had been Corinne Calvet, Polly Bergen, Pat Crowley, and Marion Marshall. In the mid-1955s, after Martin and Lewis split their act, Wallis latched onto rock country-singer Elvis Presley, who made several pictures under the Wallis banner. In these productions and others, Wallis promoted the careers of Joan O'Brien and Joan Blackman, but they would never catch the public's fancy. Shirley arrived just at the time when Wallis required a new female star to juggle into his busy production schedule.

Neither Wallis nor Paramount were sure how to handle Shirley—the same problem that had befallen Lizabeth Scott a decade before. With her red pixie hairdo, fey looks, and full-fleshed appearance, Shirley was not a typical example of promising screen beauty in an era when the wholesome Natalie Wood look was in vogue. Nor did Shirley dress or think like the usual cinema starlet.

Wallis and Paramount embarked on a crash program to transform her into a synthetic silver screen personality, which upset Shirley no end. "There was no time for reflection. There was only time to mold and produce an engaging, attractive commodity and show up. . . . Slowly, slowly, I was slipping away from myself." In contrast, the fan magazines immediately dubbed Shirley the kooky young star(let) from Broadway who lived in a one-room shack in Malibu. This was not the real Shirley, but a categorization of her as a freak specimen in the shaken world of 1950s Hollywood.

Wallis was not about to waste time pruning Shirley's unusual qualities without obtaining some value for his effort. He employed the reluctant Shirley as set dressing in the Dean Martin-Jerry Lewis vehicle *Artists and Models* (1955). She and Dorothy Malone were Greenwich Village neighbors of comic-strip artists Martin and Lewis. Martin derives most of the inspiration for his gruesome comic-book creations from the wild nightmare ravings of Lewis. Cooperative Shirley agrees to pose for nutty Lewis as the weird Bat Lady, a special strip project Lewis is drawing. When even the unsubtlest advances fail to lure him into a marriage proposal, Shirley becomes basic and sits on the frenetic Lewis until he is agreeable. Bosley Crowther *(New York Times)* noted the waste of Shirley's talents: "Miss MacLaine has the makings of a lively comedienne, as she shows in one comic dance with Jerry and in a couple of passing scenes. But the script does not give her material, . . . Maybe next time, Hal Wallis, the film's producer, will let Miss MacLaine and Jerry go it together without Dean or anyone to get in their way." The wide-screen color feature was a profitable venture like the previous Martin and Lewis forays.

In 1955 Shirley's husband returned to Japan to prepare theatrical productions over there and make a professional reputation for himself. This began a series of lengthy geographic separations that were to give Hollywood gossip reporters much to hint at in their columns.

When Betty Grable had to withdraw from a "Shower of Stars" (CBS) television special in 1955, Shirley was rushed in as a substitute, and soon she was getting video guest spots with Bob Hope, Pat Boone, Dinah Shore, and others.

Meanwhile, on the Malibu beach one day in 1955, Shirley encountered entrepreneur Michael Todd. He was immediately taken by her gaminlike qualities and soon after proposed that she play the lead in his upcoming movie *Around the World in 80 Days* (1956). Largely because the filming would include on-location shooting in Japan, Shirley accepted the part. She was reunited with her husband in Tokyo by Christmas, 1955. In between location filming, she began to learn something about the Japanese culture that he found so attractive.

The wheeling and dealing that preceded, accompanied, and followed the lensing of *Around the World in 80 Days* is an amazing chapter in the story of a bluffing impresario producer snowballing a shoestring budget into a colossal motion picture. With his gift of persuasion, Todd wangled guest cameo appearances from 44 international stars, ranging from Marlene Dietrich to Beatrice Lillie, hoping to bolster what even he knew to be an uninspired story.

When Shirley returned to Hollywood in March, 1956, she was pregnant and unable to accept any pending film projects. After amending her Hal Wallis contract,* she sat at home, unbolstered by the pervading rumors that *Around the World* was a bomb and that she was a jinx. On September 1, 1956, she gave birth to Stephanie Sachiko (Sachie). Parker flew from Japan to California to see his new child. He helped Shirley move to more appropriate quarters and then returned to Japan.

Around the World in 80 Days charged onto Broadway on October 17, 1956, at the Rivoli Theatre. The two-a-day roadshow production, filmed in the Todd-A-O wide-screen process, was disliked by the critics, but it attracted a huge audience which accepted the gaudy star-filled travelogue as sufficient entertainment. It played 102 weeks on Broadway in its original engagement, and grossed $21.75 million in its first release spread.

As Shirley anticipated, the major role of the Indian princess Aouda (which had her outfitted in dark wig, dark contact lenses, and appropriately disfiguring skin darkeners and veils) did nothing positive for her career. Director Michael Anderson had mistakenly permitted Shirley to portray the pivotal role straight; in comparison to the tongue-in-cheek approach of stars David Niven, Cantinflas, and Robert Newton, this made Shirley's honest but uninspired emoting appear ludicrously out of place. It was well known in the film community that at the last minute producer Todd had caused Shirley's screen voice to be redubbed, deciding her accent was not sufficiently cultured to match the characterization.

With her nondescript reviews, Shirley faced a job impasse with no offers forthcoming. Shirley recalls: "[Even] Wallis was making pictures with people he *didn't have* under contract."

She then accepted a costarring part in the West Coast touring version of Terence Rattigan's *The Sleeping Prince,* teamed with Hermione Gingold and Francis Lederer. Shirley inherited Barbara Bel Geddes's Broadway role of the American chorus girl loose in Edwardian London and courted by a Ruritanian prince. (When it was transferred to the screen as *The Prince and the Showgirl,* Marilyn Monroe would play the lead.) The comedy debuted November 28, 1956, at the Huntington Hartford Theatre to excellent re-

*Under Shirley's revised Hal Wallis contract (March, 1956), she received $6,000 per picture during the first period (encompassing two films), $7,500 in the second, $10,000 in the third, $15,000 in the fourth, and $20,000 per film in the fifth. Wallis would exercise his third option on Shirley's contract on February 24, 1959.

views but poor business. *Variety* reported: "The show is a triumph for Miss MacLaine, and stamps her as a bright comedy talent combining perception and variation to create a character that lives and sparkles." She also reveals an appealing gamin personality. The tour ended in San Francisco 13 weeks later.

Hal Wallis attended a performance of *The Sleeping Prince* in San Francisco and was struck anew by Shirley's acting potential. After the run of the play, he immediately cast her in two Paramount productions to be shot on the home-lot in 1957, and loaned her to MGM (at a fancy profit) for three features to be lensed at Culver City.

Now busily working again in pictures, Shirley was again good copy for the press. She told one journalist: "If and when I'm a star, I don't want to be a fad. I want to be somebody who will last."

Not particularly satisfied with the varied but inappropriate film roles provided her by Wallis, Shirley exercised the contractual provision that allowed her to make numerous television appearances. There she could be herself: capering, dancing, and singing. Shirley appeared most frequently on the "Dinah Shore Chevy Show" (NBC), often as guest hostess; for example, on the December 8, 1957, segment which headlined Nanette Fabray and Rowan and Martin, and the January 5, 1958, edition, which costarred Tom Ewell, Anna Marie Alberghetti, and John Raitt. Early in 1958, Shirley signed a three-year $500,000 NBC agreement (a great deal of the profit went to Wallis) which called for 15 forthcoming appearances.

About her media work, Shirley explained: "I love dancing on television and acting before movie cameras but I prefer working on the stage. There's nothing like appearing before a live audience. You can sense how you're doing and if your efforts are appreciated you know it right away and it gives you a warm feeling."

Meanwhile, MGM's *The Sheepman* arrived at the Capitol Theatre on May 7, 1958, without fanfare. It was a low-key Western, filmed in cinemascope and color, with placid Glenn Ford top-billed in yet another of his somnambulistic characterizations. Filled with self-mockery of the genre, *The Sheepman* dealt with cattlemen—headed by villain Leslie Nielsen—combatting sheepmen—led by virtuous Ford in the 1890s West. Shirley appeared as the tomboy fiancée of Nielsen, who soon decides she prefers honest Ford. Adding appropriate flavor were Mickey Shaughnessy as Nielsen's fumbling henchman and Edgar Buchanan as a cracker-barrel philosopher. Shirley as Dell Payton was allowed to be her casual, loose-limbed self (even dressed in her ladylike best, she still wore work boots). Usually Shirley's Dell was garbed in jeans and work shirt and a sloppy felt hat—quite the opposite of the typical gingham-clad Western movie heroine. Her perky nature even forced Ford to come alive at times. The *New York Herald Tribune* said: "Her hair delicately crimson in Metrocolor, [she] flits with an insouciant air, as the rancher's daughter. Miss MacLaine's charm is as much as anything else responsible for the film's genial irresistibility. She has an abrupt and cackling laugh that springs alive from her throat and a little girl's forthrightness that fits the role like a wedding dress." That segment of the once-great filmgoing audience which still attended movie theatres, were oversatiated by television Western fare, and *The Sheepman*, like Columbia's even more impressive *Cowboy* (1958) (also with Glenn Ford starring), failed to arouse sufficient box-office interest. Later MGM changed the title of *The Sheepman* to *Stranger With a Gun*, but this did not noticeably improve audience attendance. At least *The Sheepman* restored Shirley's stock with the intelligentsia, demonstrating that she possessed a distinctive screen personality, full of moxie.

Shirley's next release was *The Matchmaker* (1958), starring Paramount's Broadway-star import, Shirley Booth, who outdid herself in re-creating Ruth Gordon's stage role of the matronly miss from Yonkers who decides it is time to remarry. Flitting about the 1880s period sets (overblown in vistavision) were blustering Paul Ford as Booth's prospective groom; naive store clerks Anthony Perkins and Robert Morse, and demure milliner Shirley—who has a crush on angular Perkins. With its stylized dialogue and many asides to the audience, director Joseph Anthony created a rather faithful version of Thornton Wilder's play; but it was distinctly unstimulating cinema. Shirley was properly sweet and confused, but had too little opportunity to be her extroverted, relaxed self. Four years later, *The Matchmaker* would appear as the Broadway musical hit *Hello, Dolly!*

Shirley's third 1958 picture was the Hal Wallis production of *Hot Spell*, featuring Shirley Booth as a Louisiana mother whose family is falling apart at the seams. Husband Anthony Quinn is a sensual creature, distraught by his wife's posturing and her perpetual dreaming of past glories. He eventually runs off to Florida with his 19-year-old mistress and is killed in a car crash. Shirley was third-billed as physically maturing daughter Virginia, whose mind is still confused by the adult world. Acting hastily and rashly on her mother's romantic advice, she loses her beau, Warren Stevens. What might have been an incisive bit of screen drama was hampered by the film's too sentimental approach and diffuse point of view: i.e., whether to feel sorry for the incapable Booth or for her frustrated, steaming husband Quinn. *Films in Review* stated: "The only thing worth noting [in *Hot Spell*] . . . is the change in appearance, and acting style of Shirley MacLaine. A change from what she was in *The Trouble With Harry* that is, I'm delighted to say, for the better."

Paramount had intended teaming Shirley with its Italian contract-star Sophia Loren in 1958, but nothing materialized.

Then came the big break which transformed Shirley into a major motion picture star; the role of Ginny Moorhead in *Some Came Running* (1959). Frank Sinatra and Dean Martin had been cast by MGM to star in this adaptation of the James Jones novel. According to Sinatra, "one night when we [he and director Vincente Minnelli] were watching the Dinah Shore show we saw our Ginny dancing toward us, wearing a tight black leotard and belting out a song out in an off-key voice best described as a clamor. It was Shirley MacLaine, but the cuteness, the strength, the humor—everything we wanted in Ginny—was wrapped up in that one package. Shirley was signed the next day." (Actually, there was much conflict between contract boss Hal Wallis, who offered to accept half of MGM's offer of $75,000 since he would be getting $24,400 of the sum, and Shirley's powerful agent, Music Corporation of America, which demanded the full amount MGM had offered. Knowing it was a powerhouse role, Shirley convinced her agent to go along with Wallis.)

Some Came Running was a case of a movie being much better than its rambling book original. Sinatra was the ex-serviceman–novelist–drifter returning to his Southern hometown of Parkman to visit with his wealthy brother Arthur Kennedy. He arrives on the Chicago bus, accompanied by Ginny ("even she knows she's a pig"), a whore he had picked up the night before. She has mistaken his drunken sentimentality for genuine affection and willingly comes along for the ride. He brushes her off, but she is determined to stay anyway in case he should change his mind. Kennedy proves to be a hypocritical Middle American, carrying on an affair with his secretary Nancy Gates, while complaining about his daughter's loose behavior. His aristocratic wife, Leora Dana, will have nothing to do with Sinatra until her learned neighbors, Professor Larry Gates and his schoolteacher daughter Martha Hyer, express interest in the novelist brother-in-law. Soon Sinatra is enamored of the antiseptic Hyer, although he is morally lax enough to keep Shirley around for quick good times. Even his newly acquired gambling pal, Dean Martin, berates Sinatra about Shirley, and he is flabbergasted when Sinatra marries her. The staccato finale has Shirley's ex-lover returning to Parkman determined to gun down Sinatra. In the amusement park chase, Shirley instinctively steps in front of Sinatra to shield him from the gun shots, and is herself killed.

Some Came Running premiered at Radio City Music Hall on January 22, 1959, and was a commercial success grossing $4.3 million in net domestic rentals. As the "docile and affectionate tramp," Shirley's role contained all the essential elements of her best film stereotype: the good-natured slob. From the second she steps off the bus in her too-short, too-tight skirt, Shirley captured audience attention. Perhaps her finest moment of total submersion in the role occurred shortly thereafter. Straddling a stool in the bar and grill and gobbling a hamburger, and, with her mouth stuffed, yelling to her gambler ex-lover: "Will ya take your paws off me!" She is entirely believable as the dumb broad drawn to a superior person (she informs Sinatra: "I love you, but I don't understand you. What's the matta with that?"). The uncultured Shirley works in the local bra factory and thinks it is perfectly legitimate to autograph copies of Sinatra's newly published magazine story for her fellow workers: "I hope you like it, Love Ginny." When Shirley confronts the sophisticated Hyer in the college classroom, the opposing aspects of womanhood are shown in excellent contrast. Slumped like a little schoolgirl in a student's chair, she pathetically inquires: "I gotta know, are you gonna marry him?" That Shirley's Ginny character is a vulgar creature is seen in the Terre Haute Club scenes in which she drunkenly slobbers around the floor and screams out a few choruses of "After You're Gone."

The critics were avid in their praise of Shirley in *Some Came Running*. "She plays it with wonderful abandon." "With her performance, Miss MacLaine moves into the front row of film actresses. She isn't conventionally pretty. Her hair looks like it was combed with an eggbeater. But it doesn't make any difference, because she elicits such empathy and humor that when she offers herself to Sinatra, she seems eminently worth taking."

Shirley received her first Academy Award nomination for best actress for *Some Came Running,* but lost out to Susan Hayward who won for *I Want to Live.*

According to Shirley, it was while the cast of *Some Came Running* was on location in Madison, Indiana, that her relationship with the famous "clan" ("ratpack") began. Shirley recalls: "For some reason I was the only woman allowed in their [Sinatra and Martin's] house. I spent a lot of time there. . . . All they did was play gin, but they were more fun to be around than anyone I had met in the business. . . . Eventually the clan expanded to include Sammy Davis, Jr., Peter Lawford, Joey Bishop, and a few others. . . . They taught me comedy routines, cinema comedy techniques, and, most important, how to cheat at gin." About her costar's performance: "I wish Frank had worked harder; Dean was marvelous."

Her next film, *Ask Any Girl* (1959), was based on a very popular novel that was equally successful on the screen. It was revamped by MGM as a tailor-made vehicle for Shirley, although David Niven was top-billed. She portrayed Meg Wheeler, the naive, virtuous country girl who arrives in New York to make good. Because each new employer is more lecherous than the last, she is constantly losing her job. Finally she lands a post in natty Niven's motivation research agency. To bring his playboy brother Gig Young to his senses, Niven makes Shirley the ideal composite of all the ingredients Young seeks in womanhood. Inevitably attracted to stuffy Niven, Shirley wins him despite his aloofness. The episodic story line was filled with enough double entendres and modest slapstick to push the obvious plot right along. Reviewers delighted in discovering Shirley, the new comedy star. *Time* magazine raved about her vigorous performance: "Shirley Mac-Laine is an extraordinarily funny girl. She has the face of an idealized Raggedy Ann, the body of a chorus girl, the dead-eyed, wag-jawed delivery of a ventriloquist's dummy, and she probably possesses beauty, talent and mass appeal in greater degree than any cinema comedienne since Carole Lombard."

At the International Film Festival in Berlin, *Ask Any Girl* won the Silver Bear Prize.

In Hal Wallis's production of *Career* (1959), Shirley enacted a harsh variation of her good-natured tramp: this time she was the drink- and sex-starved daughter of wealthy stage producer Robert Middleton. What had been a sensitive off-Broadway play in the mid-1950s became an oversized, crude screen study in clichés. Via flashbacks, *Career* purported to chronicle the life of struggling actor Anthony Franciosa through the rough years up until he acquires stage stardom. Along the way, he drops his conventional hometown wife Joan Blackman, discards opportunist director pal Dean Martin, uses his loyal agent Carolyn Jones, and reviles pushy drunk Shirley. The movie concludes on Franciosa's triumphant Broadway opening night, with patient Jones inquiring backstage: "Was it worth it?" Too many critics recalled too fondly the tour-de-force performance of Norma Crane in the stage version, and Shirley suffered in comparison, being blamed for turning "a mentally sick woman into one of a fun-loving gamin who merely gets cuter with every drink." Bosley Crowther *(New York Times)* snapped: "Shirley MacLaine is as soggy as a dishrag as a semi-professional dipsomaniac."

By now Shirley was top news as reflective of a new breed of screen star, along with Paul Newman. Each represented a disparate type bred within the decaying studio star system. Both had such dynamic personalities that they easily pushed aside other contenders for top audience interest. *Time* magazine analyzed in its June 22, 1959, issue: "The surprise is not that Shirley has moved to the top, but that she has been able to do it on her own terms . . . without studio supervised romances, even without a swimming pool. It could have happened only in the new Hollywood, which has found that kookiness can be more appealing than yesterday's gilded glamour." More conventional Hedda Hopper interpreted: "Shirley MacLaine is farther from looking and acting like a movie star than anyone I've ever met. When she made her first picture, Hollywood called her a pixie; they've wound up tagging her a kook, with no insult intended. It's just a way of cataloging a girl who's liked and admired but not understood."

Shirley had her own notions on screen beauty: "I think it's necessary for people like Kim Novak and Marilyn Monroe to be as glamorous as the parts they play, but frankly I wouldn't know how. I've never been blessed or cursed with beauty."

Although Shirley visited her husband Parker in Japan whenever possible (their daughter Sachie spent much time there learning about Oriental culture), rumors of a marital split persisted. Shirley informed Sheilah Graham in 1960: "When I look back, sure, it's been difficult. But it's nearly over. Steve's such a sweetheart. From now on, I'll do only one picture a year. I'll just be with him. We've been parted more than we've been together in our six years of marriage. He's been doing what I love to do best—travel."

Shirley's disenchantment with mogul producer Wallis was becoming more vocal, but was still polite: "We've had our fights. We've had some dillies. But we're friends. However, I don't want to put my name to anything again, not even a grocery check, without some expert advice."

When Frank Sinatra and his undisciplined clan made the Las Vegas robbery caper *Ocean's Eleven* (1960) for Warner Brothers, Shirley performed an unbilled cameo as a motel drunk.

Then Shirley costarred in *Can-Can* (1960), her first movie musical, made for Twentieth Century-Fox with Frank Sinatra top-cast. Originally Fox's Marilyn Monroe had been announced for the role; when she dropped out, Sinatra requested Shirley. In a by-lined article in the February 21, 1960, issue of *This Week* magazine, Sinatra gushed: "I admit I'm prejudiced about that girl. Shirley is one of the liveliest, funniest, most loyal friends anyone could have. But the real reason I'm doing this typewriter bit is that I firmly believe she is the best comedienne in this crazy business." Such unsolicited praise from the powerful Sinatra did much to enhance Shirley's stock in the topsy-turvy Hollywood of the 1960s, when the independent producer was the best game in town and everyone was madly trying to package film properties with hot performers to intrigue financial institutions into bank-rolling their motion pictures.

The studio spared no expense ($6 million) in making the Cole Porter 1953 stage musical into a lavish screen production in Todd-A-O and color. It blithely transformed a saucy but intimate tale into a vulgar potpourri of nonsense. Shirley was Simone Pistache, the 1890s Montmarte bistro-owner who may go to jail for performing the risqué can-can dance in her club. Playboy lawyer Sinatra is on hand to wangle a favorable decision from investigating Gallic judges Maurice Chevalier and Louis Jourdan.

Can-Can gained much preopening publicity when visiting Russian premier Nikita Khrushchev and his wife visited the set of the film at Fox. They were openly shocked by the obvious sexuality of the can-can production number. Khrushchev pontificated: "The face of mankind is prettier than its backside." Shirley's public reply was: "Our dance is not nearly as risqué as the can-can was originally." Nevertheless, the public was intrigued to see what the rhubarb was all about. It was the beginning of the age of permissiveness and the smallest titillation seemed overwhelming in those days.

Can-Can premiered on a reserved-seat basis at the Rivoli Theatre on March 9, 1960. Dismissed by all levels of critics, and enjoyed by much of the public, it grossed $4.2 million in domestic net rentals. Shirley's performance as the svelte French club-owner was severely criticized as reeking of a cheap Brooklyn chorus girl. Dancer Juliet Prowse, who had been dating Sinatra at the time, won plaudits for her nifty leg work which made Shirley's obvious toe-tapping look that much more amateurish. Bosley Crowther *(New York Times)* decried: "The best—or, let's say, the least annoying—of these is a fast apache thing in which four rather violent young fellows play beanbag with Shirley MacLaine. She being suited to that purpose and not very nimble on her feet, the sport in this energetic number is in the zest with which they keep her in the air."

In the highly touted, seductive "Adam and Eve" ballet number, Shirley sported a small bandage on one leg, detracting from any possible sense of natural beauty. Her "singing" of such well-known tunes as "Come With Me" and "Let's Fall in Love" could best be classified as uncouth shouting.

Fortunately, Shirley was able to restore much of her previous cinema esteem by her Oscar-nominated performance in Billy Wilder's *The Apartment* (1960). Cast as Fran Kubelik, the elevator operator having an affair with middle-aged executive Fred MacMurray, she takes a shine to go-getting Jack Lemmon. He is a lowly clerk in the same massive insurance corporation as MacMurray, and seeks a foothold on the corporate ladder by lending out his bachelor pad to higher-ups requiring a local rendezvous site. When MacMurray uses Lemmon's apartment for a night with Shirley, and callously informs her their relationship is terminated, she attempts suicide. Her plight awakens Lemmon to his heel status and he lambastes MacMurray—turning in his status key to the executive washroom.

Everyone seemed to enthuse about Shirley's depiction of daffy, lovelorn Fran: "Miss MacLaine has never been more appealing, more enticing, more forlorn, more a girl you would like to help no matter what the hazards, a girl for whom you would risk job, future, past, happy home, what-have-you" *(New York Post).* "[Her] neurotically debonair elevator girl is as subtle a piece of work as she has turned in so far" *(New York Herald Tribune).* "Again in pixie hairdo, [she] is a prize that's consistent with the fight being waged for her affection. Her ability to play it broad where it should be broad, subtle where it must be subtle, enables the actress to effect reality and yet do much more. Rather than a single human being, Miss MacLaine symbolizes the universal prey, of convincing conniving men within the glass walls of commerce" *(Variety).*

The Apartment was Shirley's biggest personal success to date in the cinema; the wry comedy grossed $9.3 million in domestic net rentals. Shirley was named best actress of 1960 at the Venice Film Festival. She lost out in the Oscar race to Elizabeth Taylor, who ostensibly won for *Butterfield 8,* although her victory was more due to a sympathy vote because of her near-fatal illness.

Plans for Shirley to costar in the Dino De Laurentis-Paramount production of *Five Branded Women* (1960) in Rome were dropped, and Vera Miles substituted.

Shirley was back to the carrot-top pixie stereotype in *All in a Night's Work* (1961), made for Hal Wallis at Paramount. This ribbon-candy farce established Shirley as a determined virgin from Florida who innocently finds herself half-clad in a publisher's Palm Beach hotel room when he dies. The late tycoon's nephew Dean Martin assumes she was his coy mistress; he attempts to buy her off, but instead romances her. In the process, Shirley loses her boyfriend Dr. Cliff Robertson, and decides preying wolf Martin might be just dandy if somewhat civilized. Charles Ruggles provided a brief touch of wryness as Robertson's observant father. *All in a Night's Work* was popular film fare, but hardly justified the solid effort of Shirley and Martin to instill a semblance of originality into the comedy. *Cue* commented about Shirley's clutsy kook assignment: "Playing drunk or sober, [she] is one of the best little comediennes on stage or screen."

For MGM Shirley appeared in the mawkish melodrama *Two Loves* (1961), based on Sylvia Ashton-Warner's highly regarded novel *Spinster.*

The offbeat casting featured Shirley as the warm plain-Jane schoolteacher from Pennsylvania employed in the hinterlands of New Zealand. While warm in her dealings with her pupils, she is most frigid romantically. Her entanglement with irrational fellow-teacher Laurence Harvey concludes with his violent end in a motorcycle crackup. She is nagged out of her feeling of guilt by senior school inspector Jack Hawkins. Shirley was more miscast than effective in this well-photographed trivia, in which the novel's basic racial issue was all but stifled.

Plans to star Shirley in the photoplay of *Roman Candle,* a prior Broadway entry, petered out when proper financial packaging could not be arranged at United Artists in 1961.

Director William Wyler made a determined effort to better his first attempt when he remade *The Children's Hour* (1962). The 1936 version, *These Three,* had given in to the demands of the movie production code and altered the lesbian-suicide motifs of the Broadway original to a normal heterosexual love triangle. The new edition demonstrated how badly dated the subject matter had become in the promiscuous 1960s. Compounding the drabness of the screenplay and direction was the casting of Audrey Hepburn—an occasional Paramount star of the 1950s—and Shirley as the New England private-school teachers who are haunted by Shirley's unspoken love for Hepburn. When one of the students spreads a vicious rumor that Shirley has been kissing Hepburn, chaos breaks loose. Hepburn almost loses her fiancée, doctor James Garner. At the finish, Shirley cannot stand the burden of guilt and hangs herself. Fay Bainter offered a restrained performance as the lying student's grandmother, while former Paramount star Miriam Hopkins, who had played Shirley's role in *These Three,* was stridently ineffective as the selfish aunt. Bosley Crowther of the *New York Times* noted: "[Shirley] inclines to be too kittenish in some scenes and to do too much vocal handwringing toward the end."

Years later, Shirley admitted about *The Children's Hour:* "I should have fought more with Billy Wyler to investigate the lesbian relationship. John Michael Hayes wrote a brilliant script from Lillian's play. In one scene, I baked a chocolate cake [for Audrey Hepburn], cut it like a work of art, placed the doilies just so. Every nuance was the act of a lover. There were several scenes like that, but Wyler was afraid, so they were cut from the script the day before we started shooting. And I'd built the concept of my character on precisely those scenes."

Shirley had long wanted to have her husband Steve Parker produce one of her films, and *My Geisha* (1962), filmed in Japan for Paramount release, presented the perfect opportunity. The old-fashioned hokum was done in bright colors and wide screen. Cinema luminary Shirley demands the lead in husband Yves Montand's new movie *Madame Butterfly,* and masquerades as a geisha girl to win the role. The silly premise wasted a good cast: genial producer Edward G. Robinson, vain leading man Robert Cummings, and bon vivant director Montand. *Variety* said: "[Shirley] gives her customary spirited portrayal in the title role, yet skillfully submerges her unpredictably gregarious personality into that of the dainty, tranquil Geisha for the bulk of the proceedings." Shirley received wide publicity for her on-the-spot researching of the role when she spent two weeks training in Tokyo's Caburenjo geisha training school. No Westerner had ever been allowed into the institution before.

With *Two for the Seesaw* (1962), Shirley entered the rarified ranks of the superstars. A 1960 studio package deal involving $13 million eventually encompassed Shirley, who replaced Elizabeth Taylor in *Two for the Seesaw* and *Irma la Douce* (1963) and two other undetermined projects. Along with Taylor, Paul Newman, John Wayne, Gregory Peck, Doris Day, and Elvis Presley, Shirley had become of the few names supposedly able to carry any sort of motion picture to financial success.

The screen *Two for the Seesaw* was a bowdlerlization of the sensitive Broadway drama that had starred Henry Fonda and Anne Bancroft. Gregory Peck had been the first choice for the male lead. Robert Mitchum, cast against type, was not believable as the agonized Nebraska lawyer who seeks comfort from the spunky Bronx girl Shirley. Filmed on location in New York, the two-character drama was opened up by Robert Wise's direction, but it still remained an unresolved talkfest with a tagged-on sentimental ending. Shirley, black wig, dumpy clothes, and all, was out of her element as the ulcer-ridden Gittel Mosca. Said one critic: "Too much of what on stage was so surprisingly right has disappeared because Miss MacLaine doesn't have the Bronx accent and frame of mind in which this work can thrive. It is like switching a salt water creature to a fresh water tank."

Throughout her film career, Shirley has revealed continually that movie-making is not her prime concern in life. She joined with Marlon Brando and others in protesting the execution of condemned killer Caryl Chessman, and she campaigned for John F. Kennedy in the 1962 Presidential election as she had for Adlai Stevenson previously.

For some time Shirley had been waging a running battle with producer Hal Wallis. Her original five-year contract had undergone many extensions because of suspensions and the complexities of her loanouts. Wallis demanded that she accept the lead in the upcoming film comedy *Wives and Lovers* (1963). Shirley refused (Janet Leigh accepted the part) and decided to bring the matter to a head by suing Wallis in court for violation of the California labor code. Shirley explained: "My best pictures had been made on loan-out. . . . They used to collect $500,000 for lending me out and hand me $6,000. The one thing I like doing most is traveling. I couldn't afford to travel on the subway when I was under contract." She was particularly irritated "at being a piece of meat" in the Wallis contract-player stable. Two days before the trial, the case was settled out of court, with Shirley paying her ex-employer $150,000 to be released from her old contract. She reasoned that under the circumstances, and due to all the pressure groups involved, she would not win even if the court decided in her favor. Her settlement was considered a draw by Hollywood observers.

Because of the pending Wallis hassle, MGM withdrew its offer for Shirley to headline its big screen musical *The Unsinkable Molly Brown* (1964) and Debbie Reynolds was given the showcase role.

During the days of her war with Wallis, Shirley earned the enmity of veteran gossip columnist Mike Connolly of the *Hollywood Reporter*. When she rejected the *Wives and Lovers* role, he wrote in his column that she was "throwing 400 people out of work at Christmas time." Then, in the June 10, 1963, issue of that trade paper, he headlined an article, "Shirley MacLaine told Hal Wallis, Okay You Win," which was far from accurate. Shirley was so enraged that she went to his office accompanied by her secretary Loretta Lee, and smacked Connolly across the face a few times. The incident received wide media coverage. Shirley's official statement read: "Mr. Connolly is employed in a profession which is obligated to deal with truths and facts. In my opinion he is an irresponsible and inaccurate representative of that profession. He has been repeatedly inaccurate in reporting on my life and career. As a result I have seen fit to express myself. It's the first time I ever slugged a powderpuff."

Shirley's pal, President John F. Kennedy, wired her: "Dear Shirley—Congratulations on your fight—stop—now if you had real guts you'd slug Wallace—governor not Hal. JFK."

Irma la Douce (1963) reunited Shirley with Jack Lemmon and director Billy Wilder. Charles Laughton had been set for the role of Moustache, but he was then in the terminal stages of cancer, and was replaced by Lou Jacobi. Following the lead of another recent stage musical turned into a dramatic movie, *Fanny,* Wilder removed all the songs from *Irma la Douce* and transformed it into a stylized comedy of manners in which the subject of prostitution was presented and then romantically ignored. The 1954 Broadway version had been an essentially all-male show, but Wilder added a wide assortment of femmes to the story line.

Despite playing the title role, Shirley took second billing to Lemmon. He was the carefree *mec* (pimp) who inherits prostitute Shirley as his prize employee. Before long, Lemmon is enchanted with his Irma, the best whore on the Parisian block, and he devises a plan to spend one night a week with her by masquerading as a bucktoothed Englishman. To earn the money to pay for the evening, he works in the fish markets while Irma is asleep. Their sustaining mutual love provides the movie with an upbeat ending.

The public enthusiastically accepted *Irma la Douce* (it grossed $12.1 million in domestic net rentals), but reviewers noted that the cinema version had reduced the plot to a one-joke story stretched to 147 minutes. The atmosphere of the Les Halles settings was praised even by native Frenchmen, and surprisingly few objected to ultra-Americans Shirley and Lemmon essaying such typical French types. Shirley, clad in her hooker's wardrobe of a tight short dress, green stockings, exaggerated makeup, and swinging pocketbook, gave her characterization a crude joie de vivre and a sense of befuddled integrity. *Time* magazine carped: "Miss MacLaine is nice, but too wise to be innocent, which Irma must be to make her seamy story funny and convincing." On the other hand, Bosley Crowther *(New York Times)* thought: "[She] has a wondrously casual and candid air that sweeps indignation before it and leaves one sweetly enamored of her. Though the film is less hers than Mr. Lemmon's, she is cheerful, impudent and droll."

Film Daily named Shirley best actress of 1963 for *Irma la Douce.* She received another Oscar nomination, but lost to Patricia Neal, who won for *Hud.* However, Shirley did win a Golden Globes award from the Foreign Press Association for the film. At the televised acceptance ceremony, she proceeded to inform video viewers how she had researched the role in the whores' alleys of Les Halles, and that it seemed so much fun, she had considered giving up acting.

Shirley later mentioned in a discussion of screen nudity that as a Christmas present for the crew of *Irma,* "I took all my clothes off in the bathtub [scene]. Why not? Why should I keep it for myself?"

About working with Wilder: "With him as director, you hold back a bit knowing it's wise to be a puppet since he knows exactly what's right. I'm a little afraid of him."

Among Shirley's other 1963 acts of distinction were placing her handprints at Grauman's Chinese Theatre, and accepting the Woman of the Year Award from Harvard's Hasty Pudding Club.

In 1964 Shirley felt called upon to answer the persistent claims that she and her now successful movie-star brother Warren Beatty were feuding: "Warren and I are friends, contrary to all those stupid reports. We may not see each other for a year, but then we're closer, I'll bet, than most family people. Our paths separated when I was about fifteen. I must say, he's lived an awful lot for my little brother."

Shirley also felt obligated to explain her relationship with the clan: "Nobody understands about the friendship I have with Frank [Sinatra] and Dean [Martin] either. We enjoy kidding around. But sometimes a month will go by without us seeing each other. We're not a tightly knit group, the so-called 'clan.' We just like and accept each other and don't ask questions. Maybe they don't understand about my marriage either, but nobody says anything." (To keep in touch with her husband and child in Japan, Shirley was spending $200,000 a year on traveling, and about $6,000 on phone calls.)

By 1964 Shirley was earning $800,000 in salary per film, often in addition to a deferred percentage of the profit. She was now number six at the box office (according to the *Motion Picture Herald*) with Doris Day, Jack Lemmon, Rock Hudson, John Wayne, and Cary Grant in the first five slots. Shirley told the press about the dangers of becoming a packaged commodity: "I'm not knocking the star system, the image buildup. It made me. But you have to fight to preserve your individuality. Not that it's any easier here [New York City]. It's just as tough at Sardi's. That sneering attitude toward Hollywood sickens me, and I sneered a bit at first." About her night-life activity: "I'm no social butterfly hanging around Chasen's [in Hollywood]. I finish work and head for home in the San Fernando Valley."

What a Way to Go! (1964) was a lumbering satire devoted to the proposition that affluence in America is inescapable. Shirley played Louisa, the mother-ridden girl who only wants to lead the simple life on a farm, but each man she marries turns ultrasuccessful and dies thereafter, leaving her even wealthier. The lushly filmed production is told in a series of flashbacks as Shirley confides her woes to psychiatrist Bob Cummings. Each segment had the unsuccessful gimmick of being directed by J. Lee Thompson in a parody of film styles, from new wave to pseudo-Busby Berkeley, and so on.

Proving that Shirley had indeed reached a pinnacle of superstardom, Twentieth Century-Fox provided her with a bevy of top leading men: Paul Newman, Robert Mitchum, Gene Kelly, Dick Van Dyke, Bob Cummings, and Dean Martin. For the first time on screen, Shirley's role demanded that she be elegantly attired. She modeled 72 Edith Head-designed outfits in *What a Way to Go!* and wore $3.5 million of jewelry. In the assorted segments, her hair color changed from brunette to blonde to redhead to pink-head. At best, her wardrobe was "gaudy and tasteless."

What a Way to Go! had a special premiere at the Better Living Pavilion at the New York World's Fair (with stars, celebrities, and the press riding to Flushing Meadows on a special subway train) the day before it opened at the Criterion Theatre on May 13, 1964. The movie ("over-opulent, over-loaded; it totters") was heavily panned and did not produce the expected box-office revenue.The *New York Times* rated: "As for Miss MacLaine and her performance, they are both not quite up to snuff. She herself seems peculiarly sallow, and her performance is showy but dull."

The artistic lowpoint of Shirley's career was *John Goldfarb, Please Come Home* (1965). Produced by husband Steve Parker and directed by J. Lee Thompson, it was completed in early 1964. Its unlikely premise cast Shirley as a drab, businesslike magazine photographer who agrees to be smuggled into the harem of King Fawz to garner the big scoop. Meanwhile,

Jewish-American former football player Richard Crenna, now a military aviator, accidentally lands his U-2 jet plane in Fawzia. King Peter Ustinov will only release him and prevent an international incident if Crenna coaches the Fawzian football team and leads them to victory against Notre Dame. To insure a win over visiting Notre Dame, the King tosses a big harem banquet, satiating the football players with drink and women. By the wrap-up of this tasteless melee, Shirley and Crenna are enamored of one another.

In 1964, Twentieth Century-Fox was suffering from the debacle of *Cleopatra* and needed product in the theatres to earn some quick revenue. *John Goldfarb* was scheduled for a Christmas, 1964, release, but the University of Notre Dame won a court injunction preventing Fox from distributing the film, on the legal grounds that the studio's film had "knowingly and illegally misappropriated, diluted and commercially exploited for their private profit the names, symbols, football team, high prestige, reputation and goodwill" of the University. After a tremendous amount of fuss, counterclaims, appeals and publicity, Fox was allowed to release *John Goldfarb* on March 24, 1965. Had it not been for Notre Dame's action—which backfired on the University—the witless $4 million production would have died at the box office. Its flat political satire of the U.S. State Department, the humorless slapstick of Ustinov riding around the palace in a souped-up golf cart, the vulgar double entendres and burlesque-type harem jokes, were enough to finish this color feature. Shirley won plaudits for her unappealing one-dimensional vamp role, garbed in scanty harem dress and pasty white makeup, in which "she dares expose a knobby frame in the company of a bevy of females who put her painfully in the shade."

Shirley was scheduled to appear in a Hollywood version of the stage musical *Bloomer Girl* in 1965 for Twentieth Century-Fox, directed by George Cukor; Katharine Hepburn was to be a possible costar. For assorted reasons, the studio canceled the production and as a substitute offered Shirley the *Big Country, Big Man* project which she rejected. She sued Fox for $750,000 for negation of the agreement—the court decision in her favor was upheld in the subsequent 1970 appeal. In 1965 Columbia offered Shirley a $1 million contract to star in *Casino Royale* (1967), but she turned down the James Bond spoof.

In the plushly mounted *The Yellow Rolls Royce* (1965), Shirley was but one of many stars. She was third-billed in the European-lensed MGM feature. The multiepisode plot traced the ownership of a specially built Phantom II Rolls-Royce automobile first purchased by British Foreign Office big shot Rex Harrison. Segment number two, set in the 1930s, finds the car brought to Italy by gangster George C. Scott for his dumb moll Shirley. Scott returns to America to supervise a gangland war, leaving henchman Art Carney to chaperone the brassy fiancée. Before long, she is having clandestine meetings with street photographer Alain Delon. Like the rest of the overproduced soap opera, this episode suffered from heartless grandeur. With gum-chewing Shirley twirling her beads and muttering such lines as "So it leans" (upon seeing the Tower of Pisa), and Delon at his wide-eyed, bright-teeth best, their byplay was more conventional than memorable. The *New York Times* observed: "Miss MacLaine is simply brash and occasionally sad."

The Yellow Rolls Royce premiered at Radio City Music Hall on May 13, 1965, and became a healthy money-earner. With such international star bait as Shirley, Delon, Rex Harrison, Jeanne Moreau, Ingrid Bergman, and

Omar Sharif, it was almost impossible for it not to attract a huge movie-going audience.

When Shirley told the press in 1965 that she was writing her autobiography, to be entitled *It's Better With Your Shoes Off*, she was met with incredulity by the trade.

In the meantime, Shirley next teamed up with the then highly popular Michael Caine—she was still big enough box office herself to rate first billing—in Universal's *Gambit* (1966), a deftly constructed robbery caper á la *Topkapi*. The film's initial gimmick becomes apparent one-half hour into the narrative. Con artist Caine reveals that what has transpired is merely the idealized version of his intricate plan to rob Middle East potentate Herbert Lom of a priceless family bust. Caine locates Eurasian Shirley in a Hong Kong girlie joint and hires her for the heist because she closely resembles Lom's late wife and the heirloom statue. The remainder of *Gambit* traces the bumbling reality of the actual burglary step by step as it reaches its backfiring finish. The finale is compounded by five or more anticlimaxes. One of the biggest novelties of *Gambit* was watching a stone-faced, speechless Shirley parading through the initial dream sequence, garbed in "some dreamy attire" by Jean Louis. The *New York World Journal Tribune*'s Judith Crist was impressed by Shirley's unusual performance: "Let me give you advance notice too of Miss MacLaine who had been getting louder and louder and more and more frantic by the film. This time out, courtesy, we suspect, of director Ronald Neame, Miss MacLaine is the Shirley we fell for way back, a deft and subtle comedienne and a thoroughly charming and warmly appealing young woman."

Just as *John Goldfarb, Please Come Home* had been a misguided artistic fiasco for Shirley, *Woman Times Seven* (1967) would push her into the realm of financial failure—an unforgivable sin in the commercially shaky cinema world of the mid-1960s. Apparently no one had profited from the error of *What a Way to Go!*, in which Shirley's talents were stretched beyond her versatility in an ultraflat story line. Embassy Pictures' *Woman Times Seven* purported to showcase Shirley's multifaceted acting abilities in seven ministries of adultery. Neither Shirley nor the scenario was up to the tough challenge. Directed on location in Europe by Vittorio De Sica, the blackout episodes included: "Funeral Possession" (a wayward widow at her husband's funeral); "Amateur Night" (an enraged wife soliciting on the streets in revenge); "Two Against One" (a seemingly prudish girl is not); "Super Simone" (a wife vainly attempts to divert her overengrossed writer husband); "At the Opera" (the outrageous repercussions of wealthy women battling over a supposedly exclusive original dress); "Suicides" (two feckless individuals balking at their death pact); and "Snow" (a would-be suitor is really a private detective hired by the jealous husband). The most sincere and biting episode of the lot was "Snow," in which Shirley, with fashionable friend Anita Ekberg, treks about winterized Paris, while mysterious Michael Caine silently follows her. The crisp photography and the bittersweet music created by Riz Ortolani nicely backstop the irony of the situation and the vanity of the flattered Shirley. *Time* magazine argued about *Woman Times Seven:* "Despite help from the makeup and wardrobe departments, she seldom departs from her customary screen self and all seven women suffer from an unflattering family resemblance." Whatever the role demanded, it seemed Shirley remained "the brassy strumpet with a heart of gold." It was the real beginning of the toppling of Shirley MacLaine, superstar.

With her very relaxed filming schedule in the mid-1960s, Shirley embarked on several self-educatory trips about the globe. "To make even a stab at understanding what I learned and saw as I traveled, I had to reject nearly everything that had conditioned my moral ethics growing up in America." The fall of 1967 found Shirley spending six weeks in India, devoted to the studying of the principles of Yoga; then she departed for a trek through the American South, speaking out for the cause of civil rights; next a safari into the dangerous Masai country of East Africa, a visit to Moscow which almost did not end, and later still a climb into the Himalayan kingdom of Bhutan where she narrowly avoided becoming a victim of a local revolution. Everywhere she went, Shirley became involved in humanitarian causes, ranging from mixed-blood orphans in Vietnam and Korea to anti-war protesters in America. As she explained to columnist Sheilah Graham: "If you're blessed with the capacity of earning large sums of money with its attached reservoirs of power, it's a huge responsibility. I'm not knocking it: it's a goal. But I want to be hungry sometimes. I want to be thirsty. I want the struggle, I want the pain, I want the rain so I can enjoy the sunshine. Utopia is the most preposterous place. It's the fight to get there, not the end that brings happiness."

Due to corporate changeovers in the vastly streamlined Paramount Pictures, a small but showy link in the conglomerate holdings of Gulf and Western Industries (as of October 19, 1966), the studio, virtually just a releasing company and renter of sound stages now, held back the distribution of *The Bliss of Mrs. Blossom* (1968) for well over one and a half years. The picture was sneaked out onto the showcase circuit in December, 1968, with a held-over lemon, *Danger: Diabolik.* The British-made feature, produced by globe-trotting Josef Shaftel, did not deserve its cast-off fate. An original, if curious, comedy, it found Shirley the restless wife of brassiere manufacturer Richard Attenborough. When mechanic James Booth is sent to repair her sewing machine, she is attracted to him and installs him in the ménage—in a secret upstairs room—to be her daytime playmate. At night she conscientiously devotes herself completely to her eccentric spouse. Andrew Sarris *(Village Voice)* billed *The Bliss of Mrs. Blossom* "The sleeper of the year." At times, the obvious playing out of the farce was heavyhanded, but Shirley gave a valid performance, relying on her past winning qualities as she romped through the comedy. Needless to say, its negligible distribution kept the picture a hidden minor gem.

Recurring rumors that Shirley was now washed up in movies were countered when producer Ross Hunter cast her in the title role of *Sweet Charity,* (1969), which he announced, would be a grand retelling of the 1966 Broadway success, itself based on the Italian film *Notti di Cabiria* (1957). The big-budgeted Universal film was considered daring in an age when lavish movie musicals like *Chitty Chitty Bang Bang* and *Camelot* had been huge commercial disappointments. In an unusual reaction to production conflict, Hunter withdrew from the project, because, it was claimed, director Bob Fosse (whose wife Gwen Verdon had starred in the stage version) refused to whitewash the game story line to the degree Hunter demanded. As Charity Hope Valentine, a cheap Broadway dancehall girl, Shirley essayed the epitome of the heart-on-her-shoulder dumb broad, forever seeking happiness. Jilted by her gigolo, she has a brief encounter with Italian screen star Ricardo Montalban, and then lapses into a tender but inconclusive romance with introverted John McMartin. At the climax, her heart is again bent, but still not broken. She wistfully hopes for true love and the rewards of marriage. That her past experiences have taught her nothing in judging the character of men makes her plight all the more understandable and sad.

The $20 million *Sweet Charity* opened its reserved-seat engagement at the Rivoli Theatre on April 1, 1969, and met with box-office resistance from the start. The public was not buying musical comedy, and overinflating a once intimate musical into a garish, large-scale production running for 149 minutes was a sure token of failure. Shirley was featured in 237 of the 275 scenes, so the burden of carrying the film was dumped squarely on her shoulders. That she had somewhat improved her singing style since *Can-Can* was evident in her handling of "If My Friends Could See Me Now," "I'm a Brass Band" (expanded into a prolonged Wall Street parade), and "Where Am I Going?" Arthur Knight *(Saturday Review)* reported: "A lot of the style, a lot of the exhilaration have gone out of her dancing; and one often gets the impression that choreographer Fosse assigned to her the simpler steps, then cut away to others for the more intricate maneuvers." Vincent Canby *(New York Times)* carped: "Miss MacLaine occasionally assumes the cock-eyed waif pose, but in a four-walled Hall of Records, it suggests someone with a bone problem, not an attitude toward life."

When *Sweet Charity* flopped on its initial roadshow engagements, Universal yanked the bomb into a conventional grind engagement, but even the reduced admission prices did not draw the needed number of viewers. When the musical was eventually sent onto the showcase theatre circuit, Universal adopted an entirely new advertising campaign, pushing the film's limited sex angles to the hilt. Even after these saturation playdates, it seemed dubious that *Sweet Charity* would ever recoup its negative cost. At this stage, superstar Shirley was officially listed on the skids, and was no longer considered reliable box-office material.

Recently, Shirley admitted about *Sweet Charity:* "It was splashy and slick, one of the best visual musicals, like *West Side Story,* but I should have fought harder to make Charity a straight-out hooker. Her hung-up vulnerabilty would have been much more devastating if you'd seen her tough side, seen her doing anything for money. A lot of authenticity was lost."

After completing *Sweet Charity,* Shirley stayed off the screen for more than a year to complete her autobiography. She took time to attend the 1968 Democratic National Convention as a delegate, and to make occasional trips to Japan. Re her marriage: "I don't consider my marriage strange. It's all right for me. I happen to believe that constant attendance isn't necessary for love. I don't feel abandoned or estranged at not seeing the person I love."

Shirley returned to the screen in 1969 in *Two Mules for Sister Sara,* a very offbeat Western directed with élan by action-expert Don Siegel for Universal. Elizabeth Taylor had once been announced for the lead. Because of executive power struggles at the studio, *Two Mules for Sister Sara* became a luckless pawn of the opposing regimes. It was sluffed into secondary theatrical distribution in 1970 and received little studio-supplied promotion. In all the advertisements, former Italian Western star Clint Eastwood was top-billed as the marquee bait, with Shirley reduced to subordinate billing. The Budd Boetticher story of mid-nineteenth-century Mexico concerned a prostitute who is raising money for the Mexican army and fleeing from the French forces. Disguised as a nun, she is saved from rape by American mercenary Eastwood. He is on a mission for the Juaristas to gain control of the French garrison at Chihuahua and plans to capture its store of gold. The two opposite types are continually "saving each other's bacon" as they set about accomplishing Eastwood's mission. As the seasoned whore who inventively rises to all challenges, Shirley was most effective. That she projected herself as an awkward nun, was well within the context of her role, and provided an intriguing contrast to the laconic performance of he-man Eastwood (considered the foremost box-office attraction in the world).

Solely from word of mouth and positive reviews, *Two Mules for Sister Sara* earned $5,048,812 in domestic net rentals during 1970, much to Universal's surprise. *Time*, in reviewing the feature, included a capsule report on Shirley's career "[She] has considerable range and some charm [in *Two Mules For Sister Sara*], both of which have been pretty well blunted by the monotonous consistency of her roles. Things do not bode well for the future either. Next year she will be making a television series for the 1971–72 season, which is like going from confinement to prison."

Shirley's completely self-written autobiography, *Don't Fall Off the Mountain* (the title derived from a telegram her husband had once sent her), was published in the fall of 1970 and proved a surprise best-seller, of more general appeal than the revealing and well written *My Story* by Mary Astor (1959), the best show business autobiography to this time. Shirley had shelved the book several times over the previous five years, feeling most uncomfortable about the quality of the manuscript. In her book Shirley contends: "I search not only my own values but my own perceptions or the question why I'm curious at all." Only a small amount of the tome focuses on her show business career. The *New York Times* acclaimed the book: "Miss MacLaine has not employed and does not need a ghost. She writes with grace and wit . . . There are hilarious scenes, which have a way of turning into something serious. But what really distinguishes *Don't Fall Off the Mountain* is Miss MacLaine's capacity and willingness to feel her way into 'other realities'——those of a Masai warrior, for instance, or a middle-aged Japanese male she reaches." Celebrity follower Rex Reed wrote of Shirley's book: "If Garbo would speak, I'm sure she would admire this clown-faced scarecrow, because she's one of the few legitimate individualists of this era."

Shirley proved a most effective late-evening television talk show guest in October, 1970, when she was plugging her literary effort. Harriet Van Horne *(New York Post)* analyzed: "She is not concerned with her 'image.' Her curiosity may be morbid, but masochism rampant and the rationale for her life-style self-deluding and immature, she goes her own way."

Shirley by then had already accepted a lucrative offer from British television impresario Sir Lew Grade (of ATV-ITC) to star in a television series, "Shirley's World." The series made its video debut on September 15, 1972, on ABC-TV and proved a fizzle. She portrays Shirley Logan, a globe-trotting magazine photographer and journalist, with John Gregson as her London editor. *Variety* analyzed: "[Producer] Sheldon Leonard has placed a heavy burden on Miss MacLaine's able shoulders. As a femme version of Hildy Johnson in this Blighty update of the old *Front Page,* she's going to have to be a lot less liberated than the booze-swilling newshounds in the Hecht-MacArthur original. . . . Unless Miss MacLaine's personal life becomes more interesting in the series 'World' is going to look repetitive." After the Nielsen television ratings were in for the first two installments—Shirley placed third in the network sweepstakes—drastic steps were taken to revitalize the anemic show. Leonard was dropped and a new producer brought in to handle the remaining episodes under Shirley's 24-segment commitment for the 1971–72 season. The problem was the same as with *Woman Times Seven* and *What a Way to Go!*: it appears that Shirley's on-camera personality is just not incisive and versatile enough to sustain constant exposure in the same story frame of reference. The program was yanked off television after the January 9, 1972, episode. Following the show's cancellation, there were many trade paper items referring to Shirley receiving her just comeuppance for having seized complete control of her series and deciding that her light adventure show required a "message." By this time, British producer Grade had already latched onto a hotter television commodity, Julie Andrews, who made a similar video series-feature film contract with Grade, but, at an even higher gate.

As part of the $12 million package deal with Sir Lew Grade, Shirley was to be bankrolled by Grade's organization to make several under $3 million feature films. Shirley told *Variety*'s reporter her rationale for venturing into television: "What I want to do is to stimulate the movie market by appearing on television. The market has shifted so fast and so tremendously that we're going to have to go after them and bring them back into the theatre. To do this, you have to take into account the personalities involved."

The first of these theatrical features was *Desperate Characters,* which premiered at the Festival Theater on September 22, 1971. Produced-written-directed by Frank D. Gilroy at a cost of $300,000, and filmed in and around Manhattan in late 1970, it focuses on 48 hours in the life of a Brooklyn couple—Shirley, an occasional book translator, and her attorney husband (Kenneth Mars)—whose marriage is undergoing intense pressure as they find themselves forced to cope with a world which they have attempted to shut out of their lives. *Variety* said: "A major asset is an upper case performance as the wife by Shirley MacLaine, one of the best in an always interesting career, and one in which she displays a new and most attractive sureness and maturity." Rex Reed enthused about Shirley's "metamorphosis," and the *New York Daily News* glowingly reported: "[She] is finally allowed to build her forces into the portrait of a woman composed of blood and guts and human dignity, instead of disposable celluloid." Because of its respectable Manhattan art-house success, Paramount acquired the film for U.S. and Canadian distribution. Contrary to the critics, this author found Shirley to have gone off the deep edge of pseudo-artiness, laboring to make an inconsequential script seem important, using such by-now hackneyed methods as extended pauses between lines of dialogue, supposedly meaningful eye-searching, and vociferous sighing and shrugging.

But for most, it is films like *Desperate Characters* that will partially restore Shirley's battered celebrity image. At the 1971 Berlin Film Festival, Shirley was corecipient of the Silver Bear Award for best actress (the other winner was Simone Signoret in *The Cat*). Paramount was sufficiently impressed by the track record of *Desperate Characters* to acquire it for distribution.

In the more expensive ($1.3 million) *The Possession of Joel Delaney,* filmed in New York in early 1971, and later also picked up by Paramount for mid-1972 release, Shirley portrays a divorcee with two children, an arch member of the East Side set who spends most of her limited income on fashionable clothes. The film is in the psychological suspense-thriller genre, dealing with Spiritism, a form of witchcraft. Despite her haute couture role, Shirley admitted on the set: "I get all dressed up and in 20 minutes I'm falling apart. It takes great concentration to stay well ordered. I get interested in what's going on around me and lose focus on myself." During production, producer Martin Poll left the project because of artistic differences with Shirley. Yet Shirley could later tell the press: "We did it all together. . . . I'm very much enamoured with the new way of making films. I don't want to go back to the old way of working on sets. This is much more stimulating—and three million dollars cheaper." As with *Desperate Characters*, Shirley took a deferment percentage deal, rather than a straight salary.

In the near future, Shirley plans to direct one of her own screenplays, dealing with the subject of "the growth of a woman's consciousness." She believe it is time "I should do something I'm familiar with. . . . If I fail, it will at least be my mistake."

She is also half-way through writing another nonfiction book: utilizing a stream-of-consciousness style, it is filled with "reminiscing of the cobblestones of [her] youth," and will hopefully analyze "the don't-rock-the-boat psychology of the middle class and [her] transition into radicalism."

Despite her busy schedule, Shirley insists on maintaining her intense participation in politics and current events. On June 14, 1971, she was the first woman in its 137-year history to speak before the National Democratic Club, addressing the group at its New York headquarters and devoting her talk largely to the subject of planned parenthood and birth control. On December 8, 1971, she delivered a speech to members of the senior graduating class at Yale University in New Haven.

Shirley, approaching 40 years of age, is still hopscotching around the world for work and pleasure. "My home is inside my own head." No longer does she look or act like the pixie goof-off of the 1950s and 1960s who, as she described it, was "the kind of person who gets down on her hands and knees to push a peanut with her nose, with a daisy on her behind." The stunning new Shirley, now wearing her hair long, has developed a flair for dress and an interest in smart fashions. She is more intrigued with the world of politics than the entertainment industry: "What I'm most interested in these days is manipulating the system. And today the communications are more important than the politics. They have become the new politics. And maybe the communicators are the new politicians. . . . I will unabashedly use my celebrity to try to influence people. I think this a proper use of power."

Her marriage to Steve Parker remains the geographical separation it has been for the last 16 or more years. Her daughter Sachie is completing her education at a Swiss school. Socially, Shirley has been linked with television newscaster Sander Vanocur, her frequent escort at public functions.

Shirley defends her venture into television: "There are 450 million people out there, and there is nothing more exciting than reaching an audience like that. What a challenge! I've never been involved with such an intricate risk before."

Of her two dozen or so feature films, Shirley once admitted: "I'm embarrassed that I didn't care enough, that I didn't put up a fight. I was too interested in myself as a woman. I rested too much on my talent." More recently she decided: "I know that I'll never be a really fine actress, not compared to what I *could* be. I suppose I could be good if I really devoted myself to the craft, if I could be that self-centered. But I can't do it. I'm too distracted by life. I'm a personality who can act well, and I have a hard time figuring out who I am. It's kind of good to know that I have made the transition into being over 35. When you have mileage on your soul, you have to let it show—which is dangerous for an actress, since we're all so youth-oriented these days. . . . But finally, the various currents have all come together and I feel more of myself a woman than as a performer."

As Shirley has summed herself up: "I'm my own best invention. I try to keep from going bananas myself. One has to start with oneself. There's no other way to hack it."

THE TROUBLE WITH HARRY (PAR, 1955) 99 M.

Producer-director, Alfred Hitchcock; based on the novel by John Trevor Story; screenplay, John Michael Hayes; music, Bernard Herrmann; song, Mack David and Raymond Scott; art director, Hal Pereira, John Goodman; camera, special effects, John P. Fulton; camera, Robert Burks; editor, Alma Macrorie.

Edmund Gwenn (Captain Albert Wiles); John Forsythe (Sam Marlowe); Shirley MacLaine (Jennifer Rogers); Mildred Natwick (Miss Gravely); Jerry Mathers (Tony Rogers); Mildred Dunnock (Mrs. Wiggs); Royal Dano (Alfred Wiggs); Parker Fennelly (Millionaire); Barry Macollum (Tramp); Dwight Marfield (Dr. Greenbow); Leslie Woolf (Art Critic); Philip Truex (Harry Worp); Ernest Curt Bach (Chauffeur).

ARTISTS AND MODELS (PAR, 1955) 109 M.

Producer, Hal B. Wallis; associate producer, Paul Nathan; director, Frank Tashlin; based on the story "Rock-A-Bye Baby" by Michael Davidson, Norman Lessine; adaptation, Don McGuire; screenplay, Tashlin, Hal Kanter, Herbert Baker; art director, Hal Pereira, Tambi Larsen; music director, Walter Scharf; songs, Harry Warren and Jack Brooks; camera, Daniel L. Fapp; editor, Warren Low.

Dean Martin (Rick Todd); Jerry Lewis (Eugene Fullstack); Shirley MacLaine (Bessie Sparrowbush); Dorothy Malone (Abigail Parker); Eddie Mayehoff (Mr. Murdock); Eva Gabor (Sonia); Anita Ekberg (Anita); George Winslow (Richard Stilton); Jack Elam (Ivan); Herbert Rudley (Secret Service Chief); Richard Shannon, Richard Webb (Secret Service Agents); Alan Lee (Otto); Kathleen Freeman (Mrs. Muldoon); Art Baker (Himself); Emory Parnell (Kelly); Carleton Young (Col. Drury); Nick Castle (Specialty Dancer).

AROUND THE WORLD IN 80 DAYS (UA, 1956) 168 M.

Producer, Michael Todd; associate producer, William Cameron Menzies; director, Michael Anderson; based on the novel by Jules Verne, screenplay, S. J. Perelman, James Poe, John Farrow; choreography, Paul Godkin; music, Victor Young; art director, Ken Adam, James W. Sullivan; camera, Lionel Lindon; editor, Gene Ruggiero, Paul Weatherwax.

David Niven (Phileas Fogg); Cantinflas (Passepartout); Robert Newton (Mr. Fix); Shirley MacLaine (Aouda); Charles Boyer (Monsieur Gasse); Joe E. Brown (Stationmaster); Martine Carol (Tourist); John Carradine (Col. Proctor Stamp); Charles Coburn (Clerk); Ronald Colman (Official Of Railway); Melville Cooper (Steward); Noel Coward (Hesketh-Baggott); Finlay Currie (Whist Partner); Reginald Denny (Police Chief); Andy Devine (First Mate); Marlene Dietrich (Hostess); Luis Miguel Dominguin (Bullfighter); Fernandel (Coachman); Sir John Gielgud (Foster); Hermione Gingold (Lady); Jose Greco (Dancer); Sir Cedric Hardwicke (Sir Francis Gromarty); Trevor Howard (Fallentin); Glynis Johns (Companion); Buster Keaton (Conductor); Evelyn Keyes (Flirt); Beatrice Lillie (Revivalist); Peter Lorre (Steward); Edmund Lowe (Engineer); Victor McLaglen (Helmsman); Colonel Tim McCoy (Commander); A. E. Mathews (Club Member); Mike Mazurki (Character); John Mills (Cabby); Alan Mowbray (Consul); Robert Morley (Ralph); Edward R. Murrow (Narrator); Jack Oakie (Captain); George Raft (Bouncer); Gilbert Roland (Achmed Abdullah); Cesar Romero (Henchman); Basil Sydney, Ronald Squire (Members); Harcourt Williams (Hinshaw); Ava Gardner (Spectator); Red Skelton (Drunk); Frank Sinatra (Pianist); Dick Wessell (Train Fireman); Case MacGregor (Engineer).

THE SHEEPMAN (MGM, 1958) 85 M.

Producer, Edmund Grainger; director, George Marshall; based on a story by James Edward Grant; adaptation, William Roberts; screenplay, William Bowers,

Grant; art director, William A. Horning, Malcolm Brown; music, Jeff Alexander; assistant director, Al Jennings; camera, Robert Bronner, editor, Ralph E. Winters.

Glenn Ford (Jason Sweet); Shirley MacLaine (Dell Payton); Leslie Nielsen (Johnny Bledsoe /alias Col. Stephen Bedford); Mickey Shaughnessy (Jumbo McCall); Edgar Buchanan (Milt Masters); Willis Bouchey (Mr. Payton); Pernell Roberts (Choctaw); Slim Pickens (Marshall); Buzz Henry (Red); Pedro Gonzales Gonzales (Angelo).

THE MATCHMAKER (PAR, 1958) 101 M.

Producer, Don Hartman; director, Joseph Anthony; based on the play by Thornton Wilder; screenplay, John Michael Hayes; art director, Hal Pereira, Roland Anderson; music, Adolph Deutsch; camera, Charles Lang; editor, Howard Smith.

Shirley Booth (Dolly Levi); Anthony Perkins (Cornelius); Shirley MacLaine (Irene Molloy); Paul Ford (Horace Vandergelder); Robert Morse (Barnaby Tucker); Perry Wilson (Minnie Fay); Wallace Ford (Malachi Stack); Russell Collins (Joe Scanlon); Rex Evans (August); Gavin Gordon (Rudolph); Torben Meyer (Maitre D').

HOT SPELL (PAR, 1958) 86 M.

Producer, Hal B. Wallis; associate producer, Paul Nathan; director, Daniel Mann; based on the play *Next of Kin* by Lonnie Coleman; screenplay, James Poe; assistant director, Michael D. Moore; art director, Hal Pereira, Tambi Larsen; music, Alex North; special effects, John P. Fulton; camera, Loyal Griggs; editor, Warren Low.

Shirley Booth (Alma Duval); Anthony Quinn (Jack Duval); Shirley MacLaine (Virginia Duval); Earl Holliman (Buddy Duval); Eileen Heckart (Fan); Clint Kimbrough (Billy Duval); Warren Stevens (Wyatt); Jody Lawrence (Dora May); Harlan Warde (Harry); Valerie Allen (Ruby); Irene Tedrow (Essie Mae); Anthony Jochim (Preacher); Elsie Weller (Librarian).

SOME CAME RUNNING (MGM, 1958) 127 M.

Producer, Sol C. Siegel; director, Vincente Minnelli; based on the novel by James Jones; screenplay, John Patrick, Arthur Sheekman; art directors, William A. Horning, Urie McCleary; music, Elmer Bernstein; camera, William H. Daniels; editor, Adrienne Fazan.

Frank Sinatra (Dave Hirsh); Dean Martin (Bama Dillert); Shirley MacLaine (Ginny Moorhead); Martha Hyer (Gwen French); Arthur Kennedy (Frank Hirsh); Nancy Gates (Edith Barclay); Leora Dana (Agnes Hirsh); Betty Lou Keim (Dawn Hirsh); Larry Gates (Prof. Robert Haven French); Steven Peck (Raymond Lanchak); Connie Gilchrist (Jane Barclay); Ned Wever (Smitty); Carmen Phillips (Rosalie); John Brennan (Wally Dennis); William Schallert (Al); Roy Engel (Sheriff); Marion Ross (Sister Mary Joseph); Denny Miller (Dewey Cole); Chuck Courtney (Hotel Clerk); Paul Jones (George Huff); Geraldine Wall (Mrs. Stevens); Janelle Richards (Virginia Stevens); George Brengel (Ned Deacon); George Cisar (Hubie Nelson); Donald Kerr (Dr. Henderson); Frank Mitchell (Waiter); Don Haggerty (Ted Harperspoon); Jan Arvan (Club Manager); Len Lesser (Dealer); Ric Roman (Joe); George E. Stone (Slim); Anthony Jochim (Judge Baskin).

ASK ANY GIRL (MGM, 1959) 98 M.

Producer, Joe Pasternak; director, Charles Walters; based on the novel by Winifred Wolfe; screenplay, George Wells; assistant director, Al Jennings; music, Jeff Alexander; song, Jimmy McHugh and Dorothy Fields; art director, William A. Horning, Urie McCleary; camera, Robert Ronner; editor, John McSweeney, Jr.

David Niven (Miles Doughton); Shirley MacLaine (Meg Wheeler); Gig Young (Evan Doughton); Rod Taylor (Ross Taford); Jim Backus (Mr. Maxwell); Claire Kelly (Lisa); Elisabeth Fraser (Jeannie Boyden); Dody Heath (Terri Richards); Read Morgan (Bert); Carmen Phillips (Refined Young Lady).

CAREER (PAR, 1959) 105 M.

Producer, Hal B. Wallis; associate producer, Paul Nathan; director, Joseph Anthony; based on the play by Anthony; screenplay, James Lee; music, Franz Waxman; song, Sammy Cahn and James Van Heusen; assistant director, Michael Moore; art director, Hal Pereira, Walter Tyler; special effects, John P. Fulton; process camera, Farciot Edouart; camera, Joseph LaShelle; editor, Warren Low.

Dean Martin (Maury Novak); Anthony Franciosa (Sam Lawson); Shirley MacLaine (Sharon Kensington); Carolyn Jones (Shirley Drake); Joan Blackman (Barbara); Robert Middleton (Robert Kensington); Donna Douglas (Marjorie Burke); Jerry Paris (Allan Burke).

OCEAN'S 11 (WB, 1960) 127 M.

Producer-director, Lewis Milestone; associate producer, Henry W. Sanicola; Milton Ebbins; story, George Clayton Johnson, Jack Golden Russell; screenplay, Harry Brown, Charles Lederer; assistant director, Ray Gosnell, Jr.; music, Nelson Riddle; art director, Nicolai Remisoff; songs, Sammy Cahn and James Van Heusen; camera, William H. Daniels; editor, Philip W. Anderson.

Frank Sinatra (Danny Ocean); Dean Martin (Sam Harmon); Sammy Davis, Jr. (Josh Howard); Peter Lawford (Jimmy Foster); Angie Dickinson (Beatrice Ocean); Richard Conte (Anthony Bergdorf); Cesar Romero (Duke Santos); Patrice Wymore (Adele Ekstrom); Joey Bishop (Mush O'Conners); Akim Tamiroff (Spyros Acebos); Henry Silva (Roger Corneal); Ilka Chase (Mrs. Restes); Buddy Lester (Vincent Massler); Richard Benedict (Curly Steffens); Jean Willes (Mrs. Bergdorf); Norman Fell (Peter Rheimer); Clem Harvey (Louis Jackson); Hank Henry (Mr. Kelly); Charles Meredith (Mr. Cohen); Anne Neyland (Delores); Joan Staley (Helen); George E. Stone (Proprietor); Marjorie Bennett (Customer); Louis Quinn (De Wolfe); Laura Cornell (Sugarface); John Indrisano (Texan); Shiva (Snake Dancer); Steve Pendleton (Major Taylor); Ronnie Dapo (Timmy); Carmen Phillips (Hungry Girl); Paul Bryar (Police Officer); Red Skelton (Client); John Craven (Cashier); Lew Gallo (Jealous Young Man); John Holland (Man); Shirley MacLaine (Drunk Girl); Barbara Sterling (Girl); Murray Alper (Deputy); Tom Middleton (TV Newscaster); Hoot Gibson (Roadblock Deputy); Sparky Kaye (Riviera Manager); Forrest Lederer (Sands Manager); George Raft (Jack Strager); Rummy Bishop (Castleman); Gregory Gay (Freeman); Don "Red" Barry (McCoy); William Justine (Parelli).

CAN-CAN (20th, 1960) 131 M.

Producer, Jack Cummings; associate producer, Saul Chapin; director, Walter Lang; based on the play by Abe Burrows and Cole Porter; screenplay, Dorothy Kingsley, Charles Lederer; music, Nelson Riddle; songs, Porter; art director, Lyle Wheeler, Jack Martin Smith; choreography, Hermes Pan; camera, William H. Daniels; editor, Robert Simpson.

Frank Sinatra (Francois Durnais); Shirley MacLaine (Simone Pistache); Maurice Chevalier (Paul Barriere); Louis Jourdan (Philippe Forrestier); Juliet Prowse (Claudine); Marcel Dalio (Andre—Headwaiter); Leon Belasco (Arturo—Orchestra Leader); Jean Del Val (Judge Merceaux); John A. Neris (Photographer); Eugene Borden (Chevrolet); Jonathan Kidd (Recorder); Marc Wilder (Adam); Peter Coe (Policeman Dupont); Marcel de la Broesse (Plainclothesman); Renee Godfrey, Lili Valenty (Dowagers); Charles Carmen (Knife Thrower); Carole Bryan (Gigi); Barbara Carter (Camille); Jane Earl (Renee); Ruth Earl (Julie); Laura Fraser (Germaine); Vera Lee (Gabrielle); Lisa Mitchell (Fifi); Wanda Shannon (Maxine); Wilda Taylor (Lili); Darlene Tittle (Gisele); Ambrogio Malerba (Apache Dancer); Alphonse Martell (Butler); Genevieve Aumont (Secretary); Edward Le Veque (Judge); Maurice Marsac, Nestor Paiva (Bailiffs).

THE APARTMENT (UA, 1960) 125 M.

Producer-director, Billy Wilder; associate producer, Doane Harrison, I. A. L. Diamond; screenplay, Wilder, Diamond; assistant director, Hal Polaire; art director, Alexander Trauner; music, Adolph Deutsch; songs, Deutsch, Charles Williams; camera, Joseph LaShelle; editor, Daniel Mandell.

Jack Lemmon (C. C. "Bud" Baxter); Shirley MacLaine (Fran Kubelik); Fred MacMurray (Jeff D. Sheldrake); Ray Walston (Joe Dobisch); David Lewis (Al Kirkeby); Jack Kruschen (Dr. Dreyfuss); Joan Shawlee (Sylvia); Edie Adams (Miss Olsen); Hope Holiday (Margie MacDougall); Johnny Seven (Karl Matuschka); Naomi Stevens (Mrs. Dreyfuss); Frances Weintraub Lax (Mrs. Lieberman); Joyce Jameson (The Blonde); Willard Waterman (Mr. Vanderhof); David White (Mr. Eichelberger); Benny Burt (Bartender); Hal Smith (Santa Claus); Dorothy Abbott (Office Worker).

ALL IN A NIGHT'S WORK (PAR, 1961) 94 M.

Producer, Hal B. Wallis; director, Joseph Anthony; based on a story by Margit Veszi and a play by Owen Elford; screenplay, Edmund Beloin, Maurice Richlin, Sidney Sheldon; art director, Hal Pereira, Walter Tyler; music, Andre Previn; assistant director, Daniel J. McCauley; camera, Joseph LaShelle; editor, Howard Smith.

Dean Martin (Tony Ryder); Shirley MacLaine (Katie Robbins); Cliff Robertson (Warren Kingsley, Jr.); Charles Ruggles (Warren Kingsley, Sr.); Norma Crane (Marge Coombs); Jack Weston (Lasker); Gale Gordon (Oliver Dunning); Jerome Cowan (Sam Weaver); Mabel Albertson (Mrs. Kingsley, Sr.); Mary Treen (Miss Schuster); Charles Evans (Col. Ryder); Gertrude Astor (Customer); John Hudson (Harry Lane); Ralph Dumke (Baker); Roy Gordon (Albright); Ian Wolfe (O'Hara); Rex Evans (Carter).

TWO LOVES (MGM, 1961) 100 M.

Producer, Julian Blaustein; director, Charles Walters; based on the novel *Spinster* by Sylvia Ashton-Warner; screenplay, Ben Maddow; art director, George W. Favis, Urie McCleary; music, Bronslaw Kaper; assistant director, William Shanks; special effects, Robert R. Hoag, Lee LeBlanc; camera, Joseph Ruttenberg; editor, Frederic Stunkamp.

Shirley MacLaine (Anna); Laurence Harvey (Paul); Jack Hawkins (Abercrombie); Nobu McCarthy (Whareparita); Ronald Long (Headmaster Reardon); Norah Howard (Mrs. Cutter); Juano Hernandez (Rauhuia); Edmund Vargas (Matawhero); Neil Woodward (Mark Cutter); Lisa Sitjar (Hinewaka); Alan Roberts (Seven).

THE CHILDREN'S HOUR (UA, 1962) 109 M.

Producer, William Wyler; associate producer, Robert Wyler; director, William Wyler; based on the play by Lillian Hellman; adaptation, Hellman; screenplay, John Michael Hayes; art director, Fernando Carere; assistant director, Robert E. Relyea; music, Alex North; camera, Franz F. Planer; editor, Robert Swink.

Audrey Hepburn (Karen Wright); Shirley MacLaine (Martha Dobie); James Garner (Dr. Joe Cardin); Miriam Hopkins (Mrs. Lily Mortar); Fay Bainter (Mrs. Amelia Tilford); Karen Balkin (Mary Tilford); Veronica Cartwright (Rosalie).

MY GEISHA (PAR, 1962) 119 M.

Producer, Steve Parker; director, Jack Cardiff; screenplay, Norman Krasna; music, Franz Waxman; song, Waxman and Hal David; assistant director, Harry Kratz; art director, Hal Pereira, Arthur Lonegan, Makoto Kikuchi; camera, Shunichuo Nakao; editor, Archie Marshek.

Shirley MacLaine (Lucy Dell/Yoko Mori); Yves Montand (Paul Robaix); Edward G. Robinson (Sam Lewis); Bob Cummings (Bob Moore); Yoko Tani (Kazumi Ito); Tatsuo Saito (Kenichi Takata); Alex Gerry (Leonard Lewis); Nobuo Chiba (Shig); Ichiro Hayakawa (Hisako Amatsu); George Furness (George).

TWO FOR THE SEESAW (UA, 1962) 119 M.

Producer, Walter Mirisch; director, Robert Wise; based on the play by William Gibson; screenplay, Isobel Lennart; music, Andre Previn; assistant director, Jerome M. Siegel; camera, Ted McCord; editor, Stuart Gilmore.

Robert Mitchum (Jerry Ryan); Shirley MacLaine (Gittel Mosca); Edmond Ryan (Taubman); Elisabeth Fraser (Sophie); Eddie Firestone (Oscar); Billy Gray (Mr. Jacoby).

IRMA LA DOUCE (UA, 1963) 147 M.

Producer, Billy Wilder; associate producer, I. A. L. Diamond, Doane Harrison; director, Wilder; based on the play by Alexandre Breffort; screenplay, Wilder, Diamond; assistant director, Hal Polaire; art director, Alexander Trauner; music, Andre Previn (score for original stage play by Marguerite Monnot); special effects, Milton Rice; camera, Joseph LaShelle; editor, Daniel Mandell.

Jack Lemmon (Nestor); Shirley MacLaine (Irma la Douce); Lou Jacobi (Moustache); Bruce Yarnell (Hippolyte); Herschel Bernardi (Lefevre); Hope Holiday (Lolita); Joan Shawlee (Amazon Annie); Grace Lee Whitney (Kiki the Cossack); Tura Satana (Suzette Wong); Harriet Young (Mimi the Maumau); Paul Dubov (Andre); Howard McNear (Concierge); Cliff Osmond (Police Sgt.); Diki Lerner (Fojo); Herb Jones (Casablanca Charlie); Ruth and Jane Earl (Zebra Twins); Lou Krugman, John Alvin (Customers); James Brown (Texas Customer); Bill Bixby (Tattooed Sailor); Susan Woods (Poule With Balcony); Sheryl Deauville (Carmen); Billy Beck (Officer Dupont); Jack Sahakian (Jack); Don Diamond (Man with Samples); Edgar Barrier (General Lafayette); Richard Peel (Englishman); Joe Palma (Prison Guard).

WHAT A WAY TO GO! (20th, 1964) 111 M.

Producer, Arthur P. Jacobs; director, J. Lee Thompson; based on a story by Gwen Davis; screenplay, Betty Comden, Adolph Green; art director, Jack Martin Smith, Ted Haworth; music, Nelson Riddle; songs, Comden, Green, and Jule Styne; choreography, Gene Kelly; assistant director, Fred R. Simpson; camera, Leon Shamroy; editor, Marjorie Fowler.

Shirley MacLaine (Louisa); Paul Newman (Larry Flint); Robert Mitchum (Rod Anderson); Dean Martin (Leonard Crawley); Gene Kelly (Jerry Benson); Bob Cummings (Dr. Steffanson); Dick Van Dyke (Edgar Hopper); Reginald Gardiner (Painter); Margaret Dumont (Mrs. Foster); Lou Nova (Trentino); Fifi D'Orsay (Baroness); Maurice Marsac (Rene); Wally Vernon (Agent); Jane Wald (Polly); Lenny Kent (Hollywood Lawyer).

JOHN GOLDFARB, PLEASE COME HOME (20th, 1964)

Producer, Steve Parker; director, J. Lee Thompson; story-screenplay, William Peter Blatty; music, Johnny Williams; assistant director, John Flynn; choreography, Paul Godkin; camera, Leon Shamroy; editor, William B. Murphy.

Shirley MacLaine (Jenny Ericson); Peter Ustinov (King Fawz); Richard Crenna (John Goldfarb); Scott Brady (Sakalakis); Jim Backus (Miles Whitepaper); Jerome Cowan (Mr. Brinkley); Charles Lane (Editor—Strife Magazine); Wilfrid Hyde-White (Guz); Harry Morgan (Deems Sarajevo); David Lewis (Subtile Cronkite); Fred Clark (Heinous Overreach); Telly Savalas (Harem Recruiter); Richard Deacon (Maginot); Angela Douglas (Mandy); Leon Askin (Samir); Pat Adiarte (Prince Ammud); Richard Wilson (Frobish); Milton Frome (Air Force General); Jerome Orbach (Pinkerton);

Jackie Coogan (Father Ryan); Nai Bonet, Sultana (Specialty Dancers); Barbara Bouchet (Astrid Porche); Anne Morrell (Floating Harem Girl); Irene Tsu, Shelby Grant, Eve Bruce, Gari Hardy, Jayne Wald (Harem Girls); Linda Foster (Girl).

THE YELLOW ROLLS ROYCE (MGM, 1965) 122 M.

Producer, Anatole de Grunwald; associate producer, Roy Parkinson; director, Anthony Asquith; screenplay, Terence Rattigan; assistant director, Kip Gowans; art director, Elliott E. Scott, William Kellner; music, Riz Ortolani; camera, Jack Hildyard; editor, Frank Clarke.

Rex Harrison (Marquess of Frinton); Jeanne Moreau (Marchioness of Frinton); Edmund Purdom (John Fane); Moira Lister (Lady St. Simeon); Roland Culver (Norwood); Michael Hordern (Harmsworth); Lance Percival (His Assistant); Harold Scott (Taylor); Gregoire Aslan (Albanian Ambassador); Isa Miranda (Duchesse d'Angouleme); Jacques Brunius (Duc d'Angouleme); Richard Pearson (Chauffeur); Shirley MacLaine (Mae Jenkins); George C. Scott (Paolo Maltese); Alain Delon (Stefano); Art Carney (Joey); Riccardo Garrone (Bomba); Ingrid Bergman (Mrs. Gerda Millett); Omar Sharif (Davich); Joyce Grenfell (Miss Hortense Astor); Wally Cox (Ferguson); Guy Deghy (Mayor); Carlo Groccolo (Chauffeur); Martin Miller (Waiter); Andrea Malandrinos (Hotel Manager); and: Richard Vernon, Reginald Beckwith, Tom Gill, Dermot Kelly.

GAMBIT (UNIV, 1966) 107 M.

Producer, Leo L. Fuchs; director, Ronald Neame; based on a novel by Sidney Carroll; screenplay, Jack Davies, Alvin Sargent; assistant director, Joseph Kenny; music, Maurice Jarre; camera, Clifford Stone; editor, Alma Macrorie.

Shirley MacLaine (Nicole); Michael Caine (Harry); Herbert Lom (Shahbandar); Roger C. Carmel (Ram); Arnold Moss (Abdul); John Abbott (Emile); Richard Angarola (Colonel Salim); Maurice Marsac (Hotel Clerk).

WOMAN TIMES SEVEN (Embassy, 1967) 100 M.

Executive producer, Joseph E. Levine; producer, Arthur Cohn; director, Vittorio De Sica; screenplay, Cesare Zavattini; assistant director, Marc Monnet; art director, Bernard Evein; music, Riz Ortolani; camera, Christian Matras; editor, Teddy Darvas, Victoria Mercanton.

Shirley MacLaine (Paulette/Maria Teresa/Linda/Edith/Eve/Marie/Jeanne); Peter Sellers (Jean); Elspeth March (Annette); Rossano Brazzi (Giorgio); Catherine Samie (Jeannine); Judith Magre (Bitter Thirty); Laurence Badie (Prostitute); Vittorio Gassman (Cenci); Clinton Greyn (MacCormick); Lex Barker (Rik); Elsa Martinelli (Pretty Woman); Robert Morley (Dr. Xavier); Adrienne Corri (Mme. Lisiere); Patrick Wymark (Henri); Alan Arkin (Fred); Michael Caine (Young Man); Anita Ekberg (Claudie); Philippe Noiret (Victor).

THE BLISS OF MRS. BLOSSOM (PAR, 1968) 93 M.

Producer, Josef Shaftel; director, Joseph McGrath; based on the play by Alec Coppel; story, Shaftel; screenplay, Coppel, Denis Norden; art director, George Lack, Bill Alexander; music, Riz Ortolani; songs, Ortolani, Norman Newell, and Geoffrey Stephens; assistant director, David Besgrove; camera, Geoffrey Unsworth; editor, Ralph Sheldon.

Shirley MacLaine (Harriet Blossom); Richard Attenborough (Robert Blossom); James Booth (Ambrose Tuttle); Freddie Jones (Det. Sgt. Dylan); William Rushton (Dylan's Assistant); Bob Monkhouse (Dr. Taylor); Patricia Routledge (Miss Reece); John Bluthal (Judge); Harry Towb (Docrot); Barry Humphries (Art Dealer); and: Clive Dunn, Julian Chagrin, Sandra Caron, Sheila Staefel, Frank Thornton, John Cleese, Geraldine Sherman.

SWEET CHARITY (Universal, 1969) 149 M.

Producer, Robert Arthur; director Bob Fosse; based on the play by Neil Simon, Cy Coleman, Dorothy Fields, adapted from the screenplay *Notti di Cabiria* by Federico Fellini, Tullio, Pinelli, Ennio Flaiano; art director, Alexander Golitzen, George C. Webb; music, Coleman; music director, Joseph Gershenson; songs, Coleman and Fields; assistant director, Douglas Green; camera, Robert Surtees; editor, Stuart Gilmore.

Shirley MacLaine (Charity Hope Valentine); Sammy Davis, Jr. (Big Daddy); Ricardo Montalban (Vittorio Vitale); John McMartin (Oscar); Chita Rivera (Nickie); Paul Kelly (Helene); Stubby Kaye (Herman); Barbara Bouchet (Ursula); Alan Hewitt (Nicholsby); Dante D'Paulo (Charlie); John Wheeler (Rhythm of Life Dancer); John Craig (Man in Fandango Ballroom); Dee Carroll (Woman on Tandem); Tom Hatten (Man on Tandem); Sharon Harvey, Charlie Brewer (People on Bridge); Richard Angarola (Maitre D' at Cinematheque); Henry Beckman, Jeff Burton (Cops); Ceil Cabot (Married Woman); Alfred Dennis (Waiter at Chili Hacienda); David Gold (Panhandler); Nolan Leary (Manfred); Buddy Lewis (Appliance Salesman); Diki Lerner (Man with Dog on Bridge); Alma Platt (Lady with Hat on Bridge); Maudie Prickett (Nurse on Bridge); Robert Terry (Doorman at East Fifties); Roger Till (Greeter at Pompeii Club); Buddy Hart, Bill Harrison (Baseball Players); Suzanne Charny (Lead Frog Dancer).

TWO MULES FOR SISTER SARA (UNIV, 1970) 116 M.

Producer, Martin Rackin, Carroll Case; director, Don Siegel; story, Budd Boetticher; screenplay, Albert Maltz; assistant director, Joe Cavalier; second unit director, Cavalier, Rene Cardona; art director, Jose Rodriguez Granada; music, Ennio Morricone; camera, Gabriel Figueroa; special effects, Frank Brendel, Leon Ortega; editor, Robert F. Shugrue, Juan Jose Marino.

Shirley MacLaine (Sara); Clint Eastwood (Hogan); Manolo Fabregas (Col. Beltran); Alberto Morin (General LeClaire); Armando Silvestre, John Kelly, Enrique Lucero (Americans); David Estuardo (Juan); Ada Carrasco (Juan's Mother); Poncho Cordoba (Juan's Father); Jose Chavez (Horacio).

DESPERATE CHARACTERS (PAR, 1971) 87 M.

Producer, Frank D. Gilroy; co-producer, Paul Leaf; director, Gilroy; based on the novel by Paula Fox; screenplay, Gilroy; assistant director, Norman Cohen, Francois Moullin; music, Lee Konitz, Jim Hall, Ron Carter; camera, Urs Furrer; editor, Robert Q. Lovett.

Shirley MacLaine (Sophie); Kenneth Mars (Otto); Gerald O'Loughlin (Charlie); Sada Thompson (Claire); Jack Somack (Leon); Chris Gampel (Mike); Mary Ellen Hokanson (Flo); Robert Bauer (Young Man); Carol Kane (Young Girl); Michael Higgins (Francis Early); Michael McAloney (Racounteur); Wallace Rooney (Man on Subway); Rose Gregorio (Ruth); Elena Karam (Saleslady); Nick Smith (Caller); Robert Delbert (Hospital Attendant); Shanueille Ryder (Woman Doctor); Gonzaleo Ford (Nurse); Patrick McVey (Mr. Haynes); L. J. Davis (Tom).

THE POSSESSION OF JOEL DELANEY (PAR, 1972) 105 M.

Director, Waris Hussein; based on the novel by Ramona Stewart; screenplay, Matt Robinson, Grimes Grire; music, Joe Raposo; camera, Arthur J. Ornitz; editor, John Victor Smith.

Shirley MacLaine (Norah); Perry King (Joel Delaney); Barbara Trentham (Sherry); Robert Burr (Ted); Edmundo Rivera Alvarez (Don Pedro); Lisa Kohane (Carrie Benson); David Elliott (Peter Benson); Miriam Colon (Veronica); Lovelady Powell (Erika); and: Teodorino Bello, Michael Hordern, Earl Hyman, Renee Semes.

In 1958

Shirley MacLaine with her husband Steve Parker, 1955

In TWO LOVES (MGM '61)

The Many Men Of MacLaine

Actress Shirley MacLaine shares her affections among seven different leading men in Joseph E. Levine's "Woman Times Seven," Embassy Pictures' new color comedy opening .... at the .... Theatre. Under the astute directorial helm of Vittorio De Sica, Shirley is courted, cajoled and caressed by such cosmopolitan cinema idols as Michael Caine, Peter Sellers, Alan Arkin, Rossano Brazzi, Vittorio Gassman, Lex Barker and Patrick Wymark. And not a Frenchman in the crowd! Anita Ekberg and Elsa Martinelli add distaff support to Miss MacLaine.

MICHAEL CAINE

PETER SELLERS

ALAN ARKIN

ROSSANO BRAZZI

VITTORIO GASSMAN

LEX BARKER

PATRICK WYMARK

Copyright © 1967, Embassy Pictures Corp. Permission granted for Newspaper and Magazine reproduction. (Made in U.S.A.)

WTS-PUB-5

Joseph E. Levine presents
WOMAN TIMES SEVEN   IN COLOR
An Arthur Cohn Production — An Embassy Pictures release

Advertisement for WOMAN TIMES SEVEN (Embassy '67)

In 1971

With Dean Martin and Jerry Lewis in ARTISTS AND MODELS (Par '55)

With Glenn Ford in THE SHEEPMAN (MGM '58)

With Robert Newton, Cantinflas, and David Niven in AROUND THE WORLD IN 80 DAYS (UA '56)

With Shirley Booth in HOT SPELL (Par '58)

With Elisabeth Fraser, Dody Heath, Carol Byron, Norman French, and Claire Kelly in ASK ANY GIRL (MGM '59)

With Marc Wilder (as Adam) in CAN-CAN (20th '60)

With Jack Lemmon and Edie Adams in THE APARTMENT (UA '60)

With Dean Martin and Cliff Robertson in ALL IN A NIGHT'S WORK (Par '61)

With Laurence Harvey in TWO LOVES (MGM '61)

With Robert Mitchum in TWO FOR THE SEESAW (UA '62)

With Jack Lemmon, Hope Holiday, and
Lou Jacobi in IRMA LA DOUCE (UA '63)

In WOMAN TIMES SEVEN (Embassy '67

With Paul Newman and Fifi D'Orsay in
WHAT A WAY TO GO! (20th '64)

With Clint Eastwood in TWO MULES FOR
SISTER SARA (Univ '70)

With James Booth in THE BLISS OF MRS.
BLOSSOM (Par '68)

APPENDIX

EMANUEL COHEN was born in Hartford, Connecticut, on August 5, 1892. After attending Townsend Harris High School, he went to the College of the City of New York, from which he graduated in 1912. For the next two years he was a writer on politics and economics for various New York publications.

In 1914 Emanuel joined the expanding Pathé News organization as an associate editor, and the next year he became editor of Pathé's film newsreel service. He remained with the company for the next decade, also functioning as head of the Pathé Review and the studio's short-subject program.

Paramount hired Emanuel in 1926 to supervise its news and short feature program, which thrived under his control. In late 1932 he was in Europe forming the company's new Continental-news weekly division when he was requested to return to Hollywood and assume the post of vice-president in charge of all production for Paramount; he also became a member of the board of directors of Paramount Publix Corporation. George J. Schaefer was hired as sales manager, succeeding Sidney R. Kent who had gone over to Fox Films. At the time Emanuel assumed control, Paramount Pictures had a $6 million deficit and the theatre division had a $12 million loss. Under his regime the studio returned to a profit-making basis.

By early 1935, studio politics had swung the balance of power and Emanuel was replaced as operating chief by film director Ernst Lubitsch. But Emanuel retained his Paramount association by forming Major Pictures, which not only produced some of the Mae West vehicles, for instance *Go West, Young Man,* but turned out such other movies as *Mind Your Own Business, Outcast,* and *Dr. Rhythm,* all released by Paramount. (Major's Bing Crosby musical *Pennies from Heaven* was distributed by Columbia in 1937.) In 1938, culminating a four-year feud between Paramount-topper Adolph Zukor and Emanuel, Paramount terminated its contract with Major Pictures.

During World War II, Emanuel was on active duty at Governor's Island as an Army major. He never again regained a foothold in the motion picture industry. Deceased—Date unknown.

CECIL B(LOUT). DeMILLE was born August 12, 1881, at Ashfield, Massachusetts, the younger of the two sons of Henry Churchill De Mille and Mathilda Beatrice (Samuel) DeMille. The father taught English at Columbia University, preached sermons, and wrote four plays in collaboration with David Belasco. The mother not only ran a girls' school after her husband's death (1893), but later formed her own theatrical agency as well as writing several plays and stories. Having attended the Pennsylvania Military College, Cecil enrolled at the Academy of Dramatic Arts in New York City in the fall of 1898 and in February, 1900, made his Broadway stage debut in a small role in *Hearts Are Trumps*. In 1902 he wed actress Constance Adams. She later gave birth to a daughter Cecelia, and they would adopt three other children: John, Richard, and Katherine, the latter becoming a featured actress at Paramount and elsewhere in the mid-1930s.

Besides serving as general manager for his mother's theatrical company, Cecil wrote several plays with his brother William, who had already become recognized as an important force in the American drama. He himself would later be a film director and screenwriter.

Among Cecil's show business acquaintances was Jesse L. Lasky, a vaudeville musician with whom he collaborated on several operettas, including *California*. In 1913 Cecil and Lasky joined with glove-seller Samuel Goldfish (later Goldwyn) and attorney Arthur Friend in forming the Jesse L. Lasky Feature Play Company. With Cecil as director-general, it was decided to film Edwin Milton Royle's successful play *The Squaw Man* (1914) out west, with the new film company establishing its headquarters on Selma Avenue in Hollywood. *The Squaw Man,* which he codirected with Oscar C. Apfel, was the first of 70 features Cecil would helm during his long cinema career.

In 1916 the Famous Players-Lasky firm was merged into the parent Paramount corporation, and DeMille remained with the company until 1925, producing and directing such features as *The Trail of the Lonesome Pine* (1916), *Joan the Woman* (1917), *Male and Female* (1919), *The Affairs of Anatol* (1921), and *The Ten Commandments* (1923). In the meantime, he had formed his own Cecil B. DeMille Productions, Inc., in 1921.

To gain more artistic freedom, Cecil moved over to the Producers' Distributing Corporation (which merged with Pathé Exchange, Inc.) in 1925 and remained with it through 1929, when he joined MGM for three unfruitful years: *Dynamite* (1929), *Madame Satan* (1930), and *The Squaw Man* (1931).

By 1932 Cecil had returned with honor to the reorganized Paramount Pictures and he remained with the Marathon Street studio for the remainder of his career, which included such features as *The Sign of the Cross* (1932), *Cleopatra* (1934), *The Plainsman* (1937), *Union Pacific* (1939), *Reap the Wild Wind* (1942), *Unconquered* (1947), *Samson and Delilah* (1949), *The Greatest Show on Earth* (1952), and *The Ten Commandments* (1956).

Besides his film producing-directing activities, Cecil was very deeply involved in radio production (at a $100,000 yearly salary), most notably heading the slick "Lux Radio Theatre" until 1944, when he refused to pay the $1 membership levy demanded by the American Federation of Radio Artists to oppose a California ballot proposal to abolish the closed shop system. DeMille's refusal forced him out of the radio medium, and in retaliation he established the DeMille Foundation for Political Freedom to champion anti-closed-shop work laws.

During his filmmaking years, Cecil, who on occasion took guest acting assignments in films (Star Spangled Rhythm, Sunset Boulevard), was credited with having fostered the screen careers of such luminaries as Mildred Harris, Geraldine Farrar, Monte Blue, Theodore Roberts, Elliot Dexter, Raymond Hatton, Wallace Reid, and most notably Gloria Swanson. Rightly or not, he soon became identified in the filmgoing public's mind as the chief purveyor of daring society sex dramas (with the trademark bathtub scenes) and oversized biblical spectacles, genres which earned Paramount enormous sums over the years in original release and on subsequent reissues.

At the time of his death (January 21, 1959) he was preparing a large survey history of the Boy Scouts, entitled Be Prepared. That same year The Autobiography of Cecil B. DeMille was published posthumously by Prentice-Hall. Deliberately sketchy in many areas of his career, it remains the definite study of "Hollywood's greatest primitive artist."

B. G. (BUDDY) DE SYLVA (real name: George Gard) was born January 27, 1895, in New York City. The De Sylvas moved to Los Angeles when the boy was two. He attended the grade and high school at the University of Southern California and matriculated at the University, but soon quit to work full time in a dance band, playing the ukulele and serving as vocalist. With his song-writing abilities, he soon became a popular supplier of tunes for such Broadway figures as Al Jolson, and had his songs showcased in The Ziegfeld Follies and George White's Scandals. In 1919 he collaborated with George Gershwin on La La Lucette, launching him on a career as a Broadway musical comedy writer. By the time he was in his mid-twenties, De Sylva was earning $30,000 a year from his show business activities.

In 1926 he formed the music publishing firm of De Sylva, (Ray) Henderson, and (Lew) Brown. (The company would later be sold to Warner Brothers for $4 million, and the professional careers of the three composer-founders would be the basis for a fictionalized musical biography, The Best Things in Life Are Free, produced by Twentieth Century-Fox in 1956.) Meanwhile, De Sylva continued to be an active participant on the Broadway scene, collaborating on such musicals as Three Cheers, Good News, Hold Everything, and Take a Chance.

The song-writing trio was brought to Hollywood by Fox Films in 1929 to produce-script-compose songs for Sunny Side Up, which starred Janet Gaynor and Charles Farrell. Although the three partners split up the following year, De Sylva remained with Fox to produce Just Imagine (1930), and during the next seven years he functioned as (associate) producer on such Shirley Temple vehicles as The Little Colonel, The Littlest Rebel, Captain January, The Poor Little Rich Girl, and Stowaway. Sometimes, he would function as coscenarist, as with Bottoms Up in 1934.

De Sylva left Fox to free-lance on producing and script-writing assignment at MGM, Universal, and RKO, but by 1939 he had returned to Broadway where he packaged a trio of highly successful stage musicals: *DuBarry Was a Lady, Louisiana Purchase,* and *Panama Hattie.*

He then returned to Hollywood and joined Paramount where he produced the box-office winner *Caught in the Draft* (1941) a Bob Hope-Dorothy Lamour vehicle. Its popularity consolidated De Sylva's position at the studio and when William LeBaron resigned as executive in charge of production, De Sylva was given the post in February, 1941. He remained in charge until September, 1944, when poor health forced him to resign. During his regime, the studio made a sharp swing away from the sophisticated, Continental-style product that had typified the 1930s Paramount film, into the area of wholesome Americana. Among the stars De Sylva discovered and/or fostered were Betty Hutton, Alan Ladd, Diana Lynn, Eddie Bracken, Sonny Tufts, Arturo De Cordova, William Bendix, and Gail Russell.

By 1945 De Sylva had organized his own production company, which put together *The Stork Club,* a musical film with Betty Hutton. Later, De Sylva would become chairman of the board of Capitol Records.

De Sylva died July 11, 1950, in Hollywood, of a heart attack. He was survived by his wife Marie Wallace (they had wed in 1925, but separated in 1944) and an illegitimate son, born to a former Ziegfeld showgirl who was later De Sylva's secretary.

Many of his more than 500 songs have remained standards, including "April Showers, "Sonny Boy," "Avalon," and "You're the Cream in My Coffee."

JESSE L. LASKY was born in San Francisco on September 13, 1880, the son of an impoverished shoe-salesman and the grandson of a German immigrant who had come to America in 1848. Jesse grew up in San Francisco where he attended school, and later became a professional cornet player with a touring medicine show. After a brief stint as a worker on a San Francisco newspaper, he became one of the first men from the West Coast to go to Alaska at the time of the earliest gold rush and one of the first hundred to reach Nome. On his return from the north country, he was joined by his sister Blanche in a cornet duo act, touring America and Europe. At one point, he headed the Royal Hawaiian Band of Honolulu, and later he presented a number of musical acts in association with Henry R. Harris. In 1908 he wed Bessie Gains, the daughter of a Russian immigrant in Boston, and later that year she gave birth to a son, Jesse, Jr. The boy would become a screenwriter.

In 1912 Jesse lost nearly $100,000 in an attempt to establish the plush Folies Bergeres restaurant in Manhattan. The following year he joined with his brother-in-law Samuel Goldfish (later Goldwyn), Cecil B. DeMille, and lawyer Arthur Friend in founding the Jesse L. Lasky Feature Play Company; in January, 1914, the group sent its director-general DeMille to the West to film the firm's first feature, *The Squaw Man* (1914), starring Dustin Farnum. With the success of this Western, the company went on to picturize several of David Belasco's famous dramas, including *The Rose of the Rancho, The Girl of the Golden West, The Warrens of Virginia* and *The Woman.* Among the film stars appearing under the Lasky banner were Geraldine Farrar, Edith Tallaferro, Victor Moore, Ina Claire, Fannie Walker, Laura Hope Crews, and Carlyle Blackwell.

After the Lasky company combined with Adolph Zukor's Famous Players Film Company on July 19, 1916, to become Famous Players-Lasky, Jesse was made first vice-president of the new corporation. From then until June, 1932, he served as first vice-president in charge of all production for the studio's Hollywood and Long Island operations. When the organization, which had now become Paramount Publix Corporation, went into receivership in mid-1932, Lasky lost most of his fortune ($12 million) and was forced out of the studio, a virtual bankrupt.

In September, 1932, Jesse organized Jesse L. Lasky Productions, releasing his product through Fox Film Company, including such features as *Zoo in Budapest, Berkeley Square, As Husbands Go, The White Parade, Springtime for Henry,* and *The Gay Deception.* With Mary Pickford, Jesse formed Pickford-Lasky Productions, Inc. in October, 1935, releasing through United Artists such pictures as *One Rainy Afternoon* and *The Gay Desperado.* In 1937 he joined RKO as a producer and remained there through 1940. During this period he produced the popular radio program "Gateway to Hollywood." Next he allied with Warner Brothers as a producer, supervising such prestigious films as *Sergeant York, The Adventures of Mark Twain,* and *Rhapsody in Blue.* In the late 1940s he was connected for a time with MGM.

Jesse coauthored his autobiography *I Blow My Own Horn* (1957), a lively if close-mouthed account of his movie years. That same year he returned to Paramount to prepare a long-envisioned film project *The Big Brass Band,* which was to be made in association with Cecil B. DeMille and Samuel Goldwyn. The latter, who had been estranged from Jesse for some time, agreed to insure financing for the new movie, since Lasky was heavily in debt to the Bureau of Internal Revenue. However, the picture was never produced because Jesse died on January 13, 1958, at the age of 77.

WILLIAM LE BARON was born February 16, 1883, in Elgin, Illinois. He attended the University of Chicago and then New York University. By 1918 he was managing editor of *Collier's* magazine, and had written such plays as *The Very Idea, Apple Blossoms, The Love Letter, Her Regiment,* and *Moonlight.*

His first entry into motion pictures was in 1919 when he was hired as a scripter for Cosmopolitan Productions in New York. He remained there for five years, eventually directing some of the company's films. In 1924 he joined Famous Players' Long Island Studios as an associate producer and continued in this post through 1927, when he left to join Film Booking Offices (FBO, the forerunner of RKO Pictures) as vice-president. In 1929 he was made vice-president in charge of production for RKO Radio, where he personally produced such features as *Rio Rita, Street Girl, Cimarron, Beau Geste, When Knighthood Was in Flower,* and *Humoresque,* as well as authoring the screenplay for *Lovin' the Ladies.*

William returned to Paramount in 1932 as an associate producer, supervising such films as *Terror Abroad, College Humor, Rumba, Here Comes Cookie,* Mae West's *She Done Him Wrong, I'm No Angel, Goin' to Town, Belle of the Nineties,* and W. C. Field's *The Old Fashioned Way* and *The Man on the Flying Trapeze.* After Ernst Lubitsch's short reign as Paramount chief in 1935, William succeeded him as "studio czar," a post he retained through 1941. During this time he coscripted *Baby Face Harrigan* (MGM, 1935), and produced the Bing Crosby musical *Rhythm on the River* (Paramount, 1940).

In 1941 he moved over to Twentieth Century-Fox as an independent producer and supervised such musical features as *Kiss the Boys Goodbye, Weekend in Havana, Song of the Island, Iceland, Springtime in the Rockies, Pin Up Girl,* and the low-budget comedy *Don Juan Quilligan.* After leaving Fox, he produced United Artists' *Carnegie Hall* (1947).

In the 1950s William was announced as coproducer on several pending television series projects, one for Mae West, but none of them materialized. He died February 9, 1958, at the age of 75.

ERNST LUBITSCH was born January 28, 1892, in Berlin, the only child of Sophie and Anna Lubitsch. The father was a tailor who owned a successful men's clothing shop in a fashionable part of the German capital. Ernst attended the Sophien-Gymnasium, where he took an interest in acting. At the age of 16, he left school to become a bookkeeper in his father's store and to study acting with Victor Arnold, a stage comedian. Three years later Arnold induced the noted Max Reinhardt to enroll Ernst in his school workshop, and the youth remained there for two years, dividing his time between small roles on stage and screen.

It was in 1918 that he directed the movies *Carmen* (U.S. title: *Gypsy Blood*) and *Madame Du Barry* (U.S. title *Passion*), both starring Pola Negri. After directing several other features, he was brought to Hollywood in 1923 to supervise Mary Pickford's *Rosita* for United Artists. The following years, during which he made *The Marriage Circle, Three Women, Forbidden Paradise,* and *The Student Prince,* solidified his reputation as the prime director of sophisticated comedy spiced with adult sexual innuendos. He joined Paramount in 1928 to helm *The Patriot* with Emil Jannings, and remained with the studio to handle several important sound musicals, including *Love Parade, Monte Carlo* and *The Smiling Lieutenant,* and then returned to his forte of soufflé comedies filled with the "Lubitsch touch" with *Trouble in Paradise, Design for Living,* and an episode of *If I Had a Million.*

In early 1935 Ernst followed Emanuel Cohen as general production manager of Paramount, a post which proved unfelicitous for all parties concerned. During his brief tenure he personally supervised the making of Marlene Dietrich's *Desire,* directed by Frank Borzage. By the following year he was back to producing-directing (*Angel* [1937] with Dietrich) and in 1938 he made his final Paramount picture, *Bluebeard's Eighth Wife* with Claudette Colbert.

At MGM he made Garbo laugh in *Ninotchka* (1939) and helmed the sentimental *The Shop Around the Corner* (1940) with Margaret Sullavan. After the mild *That Uncertain Feeling* (United Artists, 1941), he produced-directed-scripted Carole Lombard's last movie *To Be or Not to Be,* a black comedy that was not appreciated in its time. At the beginning of 1943 he signed a producer-director agreement with Twentieth Century-Fox, where he prepared *Heaven Can Wait* (1943), started *A Royal Scandal* (1945) but became ill and was replaced by Otto Preminger on this Tallulah Bankhead film, and completed *Cluny Brown* (1946), a faltering comedy of manners with Jennifer Jones and Charles Boyer. After eight days of filming on *That*

Lady in Ermine (1948) he was stricken with his sixth heart attack, and Otto Preminger completed the unpoignant historical satire. Ernst died November 30, 1947.

The most relevant study of Ernst Lubitsch's filmmaking career was authored by Herman G. Weinberg; it is entitled *The Lubitsch Touch* (1968).

B(ENJAMIN). P(ERCIVAL). SCHULBERG was born January 19, 1892, in Bridgeport, Connecticut. After attending the City College of New York for a spell, he obtained a reporting job on the *New York Mail* in April, 1909. Two years later, he left to become associate editor of *Film Reports,* a magazine organized in the interest of independent producers and exhibitors.

In 1912 he accepted the dual post of publicity director and scenario writer with Rex Pictures Corporation in New York, and later that year was asked to join Adolph Zukor's Famous Players Company in the same capacities. He was reponsible for the publicity campaign to launch the firm's imported feature-length film, *Queen Elizabeth.* When Famous Players combined with Jesse L. Lasky Feature Play Company in 1915, Schulberg retained his double post.

After World War I, Schulberg left Paramount to form his own motion picture production company, which released its low-budget movies through United Artists. For a time he shared studio space with his past associate, Louis B. Mayer, in Hollywood. Three years later Schulberg rejoined Paramount in the newly devised capacity of associate producer, bringing with him such contract players as Clara Bow, Donald Keith, Gilbert Roland, and Alyce Miller. Later he became production head of Paramount's West Coast studio, a post he retained through June, 1932. During this period he wielded enormous power within the organization, and was responsible for the studio's Broadway talent raid in 1929–30, which brought to Paramount such new screen talent as Claudette Colbert, Fredric March, Miriam Hopkins, Sylvia Sidney, Phillips Holmes, and, from Europe, Marlene Dietrich.

After he was ousted as virtual studio chief and replaced by Emanuel Cohen, Schulberg continued his Paramount association for an additional three years by releasing his B. P. Schulberg Productions through the company, including such Sylvia Sidney vehicles as *Jennie Gerhardt, Thirty Day Princess, Good Dame,* and *Behold My Wife.*

In April, 1935, he joined Columbia Pictures in a production executive capacity, producing such features as *Crime and Punishment* (1935) and *And So They Were Married* (1936). In 1937 he distributed his personal productions through Paramount, including *John Meade's Women* and *Blossoms on Broadway.*

He relinquished all connection with Paramount as of July, 1937, and next was employed by David O. Selznick's Selznick-International. Nothing creative materialized from this relationship, and in 1940, he returned to Columbia, turning out such films as *He Stayed for Breakfast* (1940), *Bedtime Story* (1941), and *Adventures of Martin Eden* (1942). In February, 1943, he left Columbia.

Schulberg's last industry post was as advertising director of the ill-fated Enterprises Studios which flopped in 1946. Thereafter, he could not obtain any industry position, having antagonized too many people who were now influential on the Hollywood scene. Despite a big trade ad campaign in

October, 1949, announcing to the film world that he was capable, experienced, and wanted work, nothing developed.

He died February 26, 1957, in Key Biscayne, Florida, survived by his second wife, former screen actress Helen McHale Keebler, a daughter, and two sons (one of whom, Budd, became a well-known screenwriter and novelist).

HAL B. WALLIS was born in Chicago in 1894. He first entered the film industry in 1922 by obtaining a managerial position in a Los Angeles movie theatre, and then a few years later joined the publicity department of Warner Brothers. He left after a year to join Principal Pictures Corporation, but after seven months returned to Warner Brothers and the exploitation field, working on such films as *The Jazz Singer.*

By 1931 he had become a producer at the studio, supervising such productions as *Dawn Patrol, Little Caesar,* and *Five Star Final.* Under Warner production chief Darryl F. Zanuck, Hal became an executive producer. When Zanuck left the organization in 1933 to form Twentieth Century Productions, Hal succeeded him. In 1938 and 1943 he received the Irving Thalberg Memorial Award for outstanding producership.

In 1944 Hal joined with Joseph Hazen to form Wallis-Hazen Productions, which was based at Paramount Pictures. He personally produced such films as *You Came Along, Sorry Wrong Number, Rope of Sand, My Friend Irma, Come Back Little Sheba, Gunfight at the OK Corral, G.I. Blues, Becket, Roustabout, The Sons of Katie Elder, Barefoot in the Park,* and *True Grit,* among others. By 1971 Hal had moved his production unit to Universal Studios, where he supervised *Mary, Queen of Scots* and others.

Once wed to the late film comedienne Louise Fazenda, Hal is currently married to actress Martha Hyer.

ADOLPH ZUKOR was born in Riese, Hungary, on January 7, 1873, the son of Jacob and Hannah Zukor. The father was an impoverished storekeeper and farmer; he died a year after Adolph's birth. The son lived with an uncle and was apprenticed as a clerk until he emigrated to the United States in 1889. His first job was as a fur store sweeper in New York City. In 1892 he went to Chicago where he became a successful fur merchant before returning to Manhattan in 1901. In the meantime he had married, and had become the father of a son Eugene in 1897 (he would be a film producer).

With fellow furrier Marcus Loew, Adolph enterd the penny arcade business in 1903, which led to the formation of the Marcus Loew Enterprises, for which organization Adolph was treasurer. He left this outfit in 1912 to inaugurate Engadine Corporation, a company created to exhibit the imported feature film *Queen Elizabeth* (1912) starring Sarah Bernhardt. The same year he formed Famous Players Film Company, relying heavily on the services of stage producer Daniel Frohman to provide famous players in famous plays for the screen. Not long afterward he signed screen ingenue Mary Pickford for productions in Hollywood, which guaranteed an enormous market for the studio's block-booked product. In 1916 Zukor instigated the merger of Famous Players with the Jesse L. Lasky Feature Play Company. In the resulting new corporation, Famous Players-Lasky, Adolph was president, Lasky vice-president, Sam Goldwyn chairman, and Cecil B. De-Mille director-general. At this juncture, he deemed it wise to again merge, this time absorbing Paramount Pictures Corporation (which had been founded by W. W. Hodkinson in 1914 and had been distributing the Famous Players product, as well as the films of Lasky and others).

Having a combined producing-distributing corporation, it was not long before Adolph began building his own theatres, which led to the formation of the Publix Theatre Corporation in 1926. The studio changd its name to Paramount Famous-Lasky Corporation in 1927, and three years later became the Paramount Publix Corporation.

During Paramount's near-bankruptcy period in the Depression years of the early 1930s, there were several attempts to oust Adolph from his post as corporate president. In 1935, after the studio was reorganized as Paramount Pictures, Inc. he was replaced as president by film exhibitor Barney Balaban (died 1971) and became chairman of the board, operating from New York (which had been his headquarters since the late 1910s). After a brief stay at the Marathon Street studio in 1937, he returned to the East Coast, continuing to operate as a figurehead but powerfully influential board chairman. Now nearing 100 years old, he remains board chairman emeritus of Paramount, which on October 19, 1966, merged with Gulf and Western Industries, with Gulf and Western as the surviving corporation and Paramount as a subsidiary with its own management.

Adolph's autobiography *The Public Is Never Wrong,* written with Dale Kramer in 1953, is factual to a point but less than candid.

JAMES ROBERT PARISH, New York-based free lance writer, was born near Boston on April 21, 1944. He attended the University of Pennsylvania and graduated as a Phi Beta Kappa with a degree in English. A graduate of the University of Pennsylvania Law School, he is a member of the New York Bar. As president of Entertainment Copyright Research Co., Inc., he headed a major researching facility for the film and television industries. Later he was a film interviewer-reviewer for *Motion Picture Daily* and *Variety*. He has been responsible for such reference volumes as *The American Movies Reference Book: The Sound Era,* and *The Emmy Awards: A Pictorial History*. He is the author of *The Fox Girls, The Great Movies Series, The Slapstick Queens,* and co-author of *The Cinema of Edward G. Robinson*.

* * * *

T. ALLAN TAYLOR, the godson of the late Margaret Mitchell, was born in Greenwich Village, attended Wesleyan University, and is currently the production manager at Engineering Index, Inc. He was manuscript editor on *The Fox Girls, Good Dames* and *Screen Scoundrels*. Mr. Taylor is also a commentator on classical music for various record journals.

* * * *

Since the age of five, thirty-two year-old Brooklynite JOHN ROBERT COCCHI has been viewing and collating data on motion pictures and is now regarded as one of the most energetic film researchers in the United States. He is the New York editor of *Boxoffice* magazine. He was research associate on *The American Movies Reference Book, The Fox Girls, The Cinema of Edward G. Robinson* and many other volumes, and has written cinema history articles for such journals as *Film Fan Monthly* and *Screen Facts*.

* * * *

New York-born FLORENCE SOLOMON attended Hunter College and then joined Ligon Johnson's copyright research office. Later she was appointed director for research at Entertainment Copyright Research Co., Inc and is currently a reference supervisor at A.S.C.A.P.'s Index Division. Miss Solomon has collaborated on such works as *The American Movies Reference*

Book: *The Sound Era, TV Movies, The Great Movies Series,* and *Movie Monster Makers* and *The Six Shooters.* She is the niece of the noted sculptor, the late Sir Jacob Epstein.

* * * *

GENE ANDREWSKI of Oklahoma City attended the University of Oklahoma. For five years he was an editor of the Manhattan-based *Paris Review.* In the early 1960s he produced the Off-Broadway edition of Sandy Wilson's *Valmouth* and co-produced *Anything Goes,* both of which pre-dated the current nostalgia craze. He is the inventor of the board game *Movie Moguls.* Mr. Andrewski's extensive photo archives have been utilized to illustrate many recent volumes on the cinema.